March 18–21, 2018
Stockholm, Sweden

Association for Computing Machinery

Advancing Computing as a Science & Profession

TEI'18

Proceedings of the Twelfth International Conference on Tangible, Embedded, and Embodied Interaction

Sponsored by:

ACM SIGCHI

Supported by:

RI.SE, KTH, & Panafold

Association for
Computing Machinery

Advancing Computing as a Science & Profession

The Association for Computing Machinery
2 Penn Plaza, Suite 701
New York, New York 10121-0701

ISBN: 978-1-4503-5568-1 (Digital)

ISBN: 978-1-4503-5878-1 (Print)

Additional copies may be ordered prepaid from:

ACM Order Department
PO Box 30777
New York, NY 10087-0777, USA

Phone: 1-800-342-6626 (USA and Canada)
+1-212-626-0500 (Global)
Fax: +1-212-944-1318
E-mail: acmhelp@acm.org
Hours of Operation: 8:30 am – 4:30 pm ET

Foreword

Welcome to ACM TEI'18, the 12th International Conference on Tangible, Embedded and Embodied Interactions, hosted at KTH, Royal Institute of Technology, in Stockholm, Sweden, from the 18th to the 21st of March 2018. This is TEI's first visit to Scandinavia!

The TEI conference series is dedicated to issues of human-computer interaction, novel tools and technologies, interactive art, and user experience. This year's conference focuses on the concepts of physical and material interaction through the lens of Post-Digital Design. The digital has become mundane, inseparable from our everyday experiences. In post-digital design we see a turn to vintage materials and craftsmanship, but also to real world circumstances of human bodies on a global scale. Old media and natural materials have regained interest for interaction designers, and traditional practices are being cherished in new ways as part of digital experiences. Designing for the post-digital does not mean blindly embracing nostalgia or turning away from technology – it means embracing a process of design that equalizes the status of digital, analogue, electronic, mechanical and tactile, and that brings focus to form, meaning and function, rather than technicalities.

The intimate size of this single-track conference provides a unique forum for exchanging ideas and presenting innovative work through talks, interactive exhibits, demos, hands-on studios, posters, art installations and performances. TEI'18 hosts a four-day program, starting on Sunday March 18th with the Graduate Student Consortium and a series of Studios that engage participants in the concrete making of novel interfaces and interactions. The main program starts with an opening keynote on Monday March 19th, followed by a series of talks on shape changing materials, followed by a hands-on session showcasing Work in Progress demonstrations as well as exemplars from full papers accepted to the proceedings.

The Tuesday starts with the remainder of the demonstrations and the Student Design Challenge, this year with a theme of common place, mundane technologies from the future. Paper presentations on technology for children, and Virtual and Augmented reality precede a second session of demos from full paper submissions. The evening of the second day finds the conference in Kulturhuset, Stadsteatern, one of the largest cultural institutions in Northern Europe, for a curated exhibition of art installations and live performances exploring the post-digital. A total of 25 works will be presented over the evening, which is also open to the public. On Wednesday, March 21st, sessions present talks on evaluation and community, followed by a closing panel session.

This year we received 130 submissions to the Papers track. A total of 37 papers were selected after a double-blind peer review process of at least three reviewers and a meta-reviewer, resulting in an acceptance rate of 28%.

For the Work-in-Progress track we received 70 submissions, which were subjected to a double blind peer review process of two reviewers each. This resulted in 32 accepted submissions, making for an acceptance rate of 45%.

For the Arts track, we received 77 submissions, subject to a three person curation committee who performed the selection based on the artistic merits of the work and their engagement with issues relevant to the field of tangible and embedded interactive art. 24 submissions were accepted (plus one more submitted as a full paper and subject to the double-blind reviewing process above) for an acceptance rate of 31%.

Of course, organizing this conference could not have been possible without the energy and commitment of many, many people. We would like to thank everyone who contributed to TEI'18: the authors for submitting their quality work to the conference, all the organizing committee chairs for managing their part of the conference, the program committee and external reviewers for safeguarding the quality of the conference, the local organizing committee, the sponsors, supporters and partners, and the TEI steering committee.

Ylva Fernaeus
TEI'18 General Chair
Royal Institute of Technology, Sweden

Donald McMillan
TEI'18 General Chair
Stockholm University, Sweden

Martin Jonsson
TEI'18 General Chair
Södertörn University, Sweden

Audrey Girouard
TEI'18 Program Chair
Carleton University, Canada

Jakob Tholander
TEI'18 Program Chair
Stockholm University, Sweden

Table of Contents

TEI 2018 Conference Organization xii

TEI 2018 Sponsor & Supporters xv

Paper Session 1: Shapechanging & Moving Interfaces
Session Chair: Tanja Döring *(University of Bremen)*

- **Working with an Autonomous Interface: Exploring the Output Space of an Interactive Desktop Lamp** 1
  Diana Nowacka *(University College London)*, Katrin Wolf *(Hamburg University of Applied Sciences)*,
  Enrico Costanza *(University College London)*, David Kirk *(Northumbria Univeristy)*
- **Morphology Extension Kit: A Modular Robotic Platform for Physically Reconfigurable Wearables** 11
  Sang-won Leigh, Timothy Denton *(Massachusetts Institute of Technology)*,
  Kush Parekh *(Rhode Island School of Design)*,
  William Peebles, Magnus Johnson, Pattie Maes *(Massachusetts Institute of Technology)*
- **TwistBlocks: Pluggable and Twistable Modular TUI for Armature Interaction in 3D Design** 19
  Meng Wang, Kehua Lei, Zhichun Li, Haipeng Mi, Yingqing Xu *(Tsinghua University)*
- **Digitally Enchanted Wear: A Novel Approach in the Field of Dresses as Dynamic Digital Displays** 27
  Rebecca Kleinberger *(Massachusetts Institute of Technology)*, Alisha Panjwani *(SEEDS Studio Labs)*

WIP 1

- **The Cuebe: Facilitating Playful Early Intervention for the Visually Impaired** 35
  Peter Fikar, Florian Güldenpfennig, Roman Ganhör *(TU Wien)*
- **Soft-bodied Fidget Toys: A Materials Exploration** 42
  Peter Cottrell, April Grow, Katherine Isbister *(University of California, Santa Cruz)*
- **NewsThings: Exploring Interdisciplinary IoT News Media Opportunities via User-Centred Design** 49
  John Mills, Mark Lochrie *(University of Central Lancashire)*, Tom Metcalfe *(Thomas Buchanan)*,
  Peter Bennett *(University of Bristol)*
- **Mechamagnets: Tactile Mechanisms with Embedded Magnets** 57
  Clement Zheng, Ellen Yi-Luen Do *(University of Colorado Boulder)*
- **The Evolving Design of Tangibles for Graph Algorithmic Thinking** 65
  Andrea Bonani, Vincenzo Del Fatto, Rosella Gennari *(Free University of Bozen-Bolzano)*
- **The Artistic Potential of Tactile Vision Interfaces: A First Look** 73
  Antal Ruhl, Michel van Dartel *(Avans University of Applied Sciences)*, Alwin de Rooij *(Tilburg University)*
- **Embodied Interactions with E-Textiles and the Internet of Sounds for Performing Arts** 80
  Sophie Skach, Anna Xambó, Luca Turchet, Ariane Stolfi, Rebecca Stewart,
  Mathieu Barthet *(Queen Mary University of London)*
- **Designing a Smart Reading Environment with and for Children** 88
  Pedro Ribeiro, Anna Michel, Ido Iurgel, Christian Ressel *(Rhine-Waal University of Applied Sciences)*,
  Cristina Sylla *(University of Minho)*, Wolfgang Müller *(University of Education Weingarten)*
- **Kniwwelino: A Lightweight and WiFi Enabled Prototyping Platform for Children** 94
  Valérie Maquil, Christian Moll, Lou Schwartz,
  Johannes Hermen *(Luxembourg Institute of Science and Technology (LIST))*

- **CRISPEE: A Tangible Gene Editing Platform for Early Childhood** ... 101
  Clarissa Verish *(Wellesley College)*, Amanda Strawhacker, Marina Bers *(Tufts University)*, Orit Shaer *(Wellesley College)*,
- **Exploring Around-Device Tangible Interactions for Mobile Devices with a Magnetic Ring** ... 108
  Victor Cheung, Audrey Girouard *(Carleton University)*
- **Investigation of Touch Interfaces Using Multilayered *Urushi Circuit*** ... 115
  Koshi Ikegawa, Shuhei Aoyama, Shogo Tsuchikiri, Takuto Nakamura, Yuki Hashimoto, Buntarou Shizuki *(University of Tsukuba)*
- **Tangible Interaction in the Dentist Office** ... 123
  Frode Guribye *(University of Bergen)*, Tor Gjøæter *(Bryggen Research)*
- **Paper Circuitry and Projection Mapping: An Interactive Textbook Approach to Veterinary Education** ... 131
  Margaret Cook, Jinsil Hwaryoung Seo, Michelle Pine, Annie Sungkajun *(Texas A&M University)*
- **Touch Connection: A Vibrotactile, Textile Prototype** ... 136
  Lucie Hernandez *(Falmouth University)*
- **Designing an Expandable Illuminated Ring to Build an Actuated Ring Chart** ... 140
  Maxime Daniel, Guillaume Rivière, Nadine Couture *(ESTIA, Estia-Recherche & University Bordeaux, CNRS, LaBRI)*

Paper Session 2: Shapechanging Textiles & Interactive Materials

Session Chair: Ian Oakley *(Ulsan National Institute of Science and Technology)*

- **HäirIÖ–: Human Hair as Interactive Material** ... 148
  Christine Dierk, Sarah Sterman, Molly Jane Pearce Nicholas, Eric Paulos *(University of California, Berkeley)*
- **Integrating Textile Materials with Electronic Making: Creating New Tools and Practices** ... 158
  Irene Posch, Geraldine Fitzpatrick *(TU Wien)*
- **ShapeTex: Implementing Shape-Changing Structures in Fabric for Wearable Actuation** ... 166
  Jiachun Du, Panos Markopoulos, Qi Wang, Marina Toeters *(Eindhoven University of Technology)*, Ting Gong *(Ting Gong Studio)*
- **Beyond LED Status Lights - Design Requirements of Privacy Notices for Body-worn Cameras** ... 177
  Marion Koelle *(University of Oldenburg)*, Katrin Wolf *(Hamburg University of Applied Sciences)*, Susanne Boll *(University of Oldenburg)*

Demo Session 1: Textile, Light, and Shape Changing Interfaces

- **zPatch: Hybrid Resistive/Capacitive eTextile Input** ... 188
  Paul Strohmeier, Jarrod Knibbe, Sebastian Boring, Kasper Hornbæk *(University of Copenhagen)*
- **COLORISE: Shape- and Color-Changing Pixels with Inflatable Elastomers and Interactions** ... 199
  Juri Fujii, Takuya Matsunobu, Yasuaki Kakehi *(Keio University)*
- **Plux: Exploring Light Settings through Hybrid Control** ... 205
  Tom van Rooij, Saskia Bakker *(Eindhoven University of Technology)*
- **Screenprinting and TEI: Supporting Engagement with STEAM through DIY Fabrication of Smart Materials** ... 211
  Stacey Kuznetsov, Piyum Fernando, Emily Ritter, Cassandra Barrett, Jennifer Weiler, Marissa Rohr *(Arizona State University)*
- **W.O.U.S.: Widgets of Unusual Size** ... 221
  Zann Anderson, Michael Jones, Kevin Seppi *(Brigham Young University)*
- **Tailor-made Accessible Computers: An Interactive Toolkit for Iterative Co-Design** ... 231
  Florian Güldenpfennig *(Vienna University of Technology (TU Wien))*

WIP 2

- **Augmented Metacognition: Exploring Pupil Dilation Sonification to Elicit Metacognitive Awareness** 237
  Alwin de Rooij, Hanna Schraffenberger, Mathijs Bontje *(Tilburg University)*
- **Designing Bimanual Tangible Interaction for Stroke Survivors** 245
  Mikko Kytö, David McGookin, Wilfried Bock *(Aalto University)*,
  Héctor A. Caltenco, Charlotte Magnusson *(Lund University)*
- **MacroScope: First-Person Perspective in Physical Scale Models** 253
  Dorothé Smit, Thomas Grah, Martin Murer, Vincent van Rheden, Manfred Tscheligi *(University of Salzburg)*
- **SENSE-SEAT: Challenging Disruptions in Shared Workspaces through a Sensor-Based Seat** 260
  Nils Ehrenberg *(Madeira-ITI)*,
  José Luís Silva *(Madeira-ITI & Instituto Universitário de Lisboa (ISCTE-IUL), & ISTAR-IUL)*,
  Pedro Campos *(Universidade da Madeira & Madeira-ITI)*
- **EMS Painter: Co-creating Visual Art using Electrical Muscle Stimulation** 266
  Ashley Colley, Aki Leinonen, Meri-Tuulia Forsman, Jonna Häkkilä *(University of Lapland)*
- **Mobile, Exercise-agnostic, Sensor-based Serious Games for Physical Rehabilitation at Home** 271
  Ana Vasconcelos, Francisco Nunes, Alberto Carvalho, Catarina Correia *(Fraunhofer Portugal AICOS)*
- **Feeling Virtual Worlds: An Exploration into Coupling Virtual and Kinaesthetic Experiences** 279
  Joey Campbell *(University of Bristol)*, Trevor Hogan *(Cork Institute of Technology)*,
  Mike Fraser *(University of Bristol)*
- **Your Body of Water: A Display that Visualizes Aesthetic Heart Rate Data from a 3D Camera** 286
  Lee Jones *(Carleton University)*, Paula Gardner *(McMaster University)*, Nick Puckett *(OCAD University)*
- **Charged Utopia VR: Exploring Embodied Sense-making in the Virtual Space** 292
  Rosa van der Veen *(RISE Interactive & Eindhoven University of Technology)*, Jeroen Peeters *(RISE Interactive)*,
  Ambra Trotto *(RISE Interactive & Umeå School of Architecture)*
- **Designing the Interaction with the Internet of Tangible Things: A Card Set** 299
  Leonardo Angelini, Elena Mugellini *(University of Applied Sciences and Arts Western Switzerland)*,
  Nadine Couture *(ESTIA LaBRI)*,
  Omar Abou Khaled *(University of Applied Sciences and Arts Western Switzerland)*
- **Sew-Flow: A Craft Interpretation of a Digital Game** 307
  Kinneret Itzhak *(Shenkar College)*, Kamila Kantek *(SWPS University)*,
  Dafna Levi, Shachar Geiger, Shoval Nir, Michal Rinott *(Shenkar College)*
- **Full Body Interaction beyond Fun: Engaging Museum Visitors in Human-Data Interaction** 313
  Swati Mishra, Francesco Cafaro *(Indiana University-Purdue University Indianapolis)*
- **Prototyping and Simulating Complex Systems with Paper Craft and Augmented Reality: An Initial Investigation** 320
  Seokbin Kang, Leyla Norooz, Virginia Byrne, Tamara Clegg, Jon E. Froehlich *(University of Washington)*
- **Flyables: Exploring 3D Interaction Spaces for Levitating Tangibles** 329
  Pascal Knierim, Thomas Kosch *(LMU Munich)*, Alexander Achberger *(University of Stuttgart)*,
  Markus Funk *(TU Darmstadt)*
- **TUIst: A Collaborative and Computationally Enhanced Game Board** 337
  Trisha Garcia, Shannon Brown, Siona Dev *(Wellesley College)*
- **Crimson Wave: Shedding Light on Menstrual Health** 343
  Margaret Flemings, Shanzay Kazmi, Rachel Pak, Orit Shaer *(Wellesley College)*

Paper Session 3: Toys, Talk, & Play

Session Chair: Jörn Hurtienne *(University of Würzburg)*

- **Smart Toys Design Opportunities for Measuring Children's Fine Motor Skills Development** 349
  Svetlana Mironcika, Antoine de Schipper, Annette Brons, Huub Toussaint, Ben Kröse, Ben Schouten *(Amsterdam University of Applied Sciences)*
- **ClassBeacons: Designing Distributed Visualization of Teachers' Physical Proximity in the Classroom** 357
  Pengcheng An, Saskia Bakker *(Eindhoven University of Technology)*, Sara Ordanovski *(Utrecht University)*, Ruurd Taconis, Berry Eggen *(Eindhoven University of Technology)*
- **Evolving Tangibles for Children's Social Learning through Conversations: Beyond TurnTalk** 368
  Rosella Gennari, Alessandra Melonio, Mehdi Rizvi *(Free University of Bozen-Bolzano)*
- **Come and Play: Interactive Theatre for Early Years** 376
  Roma Patel, Holger Schnädelbach, Boriana Koleva *(University of Nottingham)*

Paper Session 4: Sensing in Virtual & Augmented Reality

Session Chair: Stacey Kuznetsov *(Arizona State University)*

- **Sensory VR: Smelling, Touching, and Eating Virtual Reality** 386
  Daniel Harley *(York University)*, Alexander Verni, Mackenzie Willis, Ashley Ng, Lucas Bozzo, Ali Mazalek *(Ryerson University)*
- **"You Better Eat to Survive": Exploring Cooperative Eating in Virtual Reality Games** 398
  Peter Arnold, Rohit Ashok Khot, Florian 'Floyd' Mueller *(RMIT University)*
- **Situated Game Level Editing in Augmented Reality** 409
  Gary Ng, Joon Gi Shin *(Korea Advanced Institute of Science and Technology)*, Alexander Plopski, Christian Sandor *(Nara Institute of Science and Technology)*, Daniel Saakes *(Korea Advanced Institute of Science and Technology)*
- **Ani-Bot: A Modular Robotics System Supporting Creation, Tweaking, and Usage with Mixed-Reality Interactions** 419
  Yuanzhi Cao, Zhuangying Xu, Terrell Glenn, Ke Huo, Karthik Ramani *(Purdue University)*

Demo Session 2: Kids, Arts, Music, Theatre & Augmented Reality

- **Tquencer: A Tangible Musical Sequencer Using Overlays** 429
  Martin Kaltenbrunner, Jens Vetter *(University of Art and Design)*
- **Real-time Recognition of Guitar Performance Using Two Sensor Groups for Interactive Lesson** 435
  Yejin Shin, Jemin Hwang, Jeonghyeok Park, Soonuk Seol *(Korea University of Technology and Education)*
- **Loominary: Crafting Tangible Artifacts from Player Narrative** 443
  Anne Sullivan *(University of Central Florida)*, Joshua McCoy *(University of California, Davis)*, Sarah Hendricks, Brittany Williams *(American University)*
- **Interactive and Open-Ended Sensory Toys: Designing with Therapists and Children for Tangible and Visual Interaction** 451
  Florian Güldenpfennig, Peter Fikar, Roman Ganhör *(TU Wien)*
- **MOD: A Portable Instrument for Mixing Analog and Digital Drawing for Live Cinema** 460
  Ali Momeni *(Carnegie Mellon University)*, Daniel McNamara *(CalArts)*
- **SWAY – Designing for Balance and Posture Awareness** 470
  Simon Asplund *(Royal Institute of Technology - KTH)*, Martin Jonsson *(Södertörn University)*
- **Hard and Soft Tangibles: Mixing Multi-touch and Tangible Interaction in Scientific Poster Scenarios** 476
  Alexandre G. de Siqueira, Brygg Ullmer *(Clemson University & Louisiana State University)*, Mark Delarosa *(Solano Community College & Louisiana State University)*, Chris Branton *(Drury University & Louisiana State University)*, Miriam K. Konkel *(Clemson University)*

Arts Session: TEI Arts

- **Opto-Phono-Kinesia (OPK): Designing Motion-Based Interaction for Expert Performers** 487
  Steve Gibson *(Northumbria University)*
- **PainByte: Chronic Pain and BioMedical Engineering through the Lens of Classical Ballet & Virtual Reality** 493
  Genevieve Smith-Nunes *(ReadySaltedCode)*, Alex Shaw *(GlastonBridge Software)*, Camilla Neale *(Worcester University)*
- **The Cloakroom: Documentary Narratives in Embodied Installation** 498
  Ella Dagan *(University of California, Santa Cruz)*,
- **Nettle: An Exploration of Communication Interface Design for Older Adults** 506
  Audrey M. Fox *(Parsons School of Design)*
- **The Shared Individual** 511
  Asreen Rostami *(Stockholm University)*, Emma Bexell, Stefan Stanisic *(Bombina Bombast)*
- **Au Clair de la Lune on Gramophone – For Édouard-Léon Scott and László Moholy-Nagy – (1860 / 1923 / 2015)** 517
  Kazuhiro Jo *(Kyushu University & YCAM)*
- ***Objektivisering:* Text Physicalization and Self-introspective Post-digital Objecthood** 521
  Marinos Koutsomichalis *(Norwegian University of Science and Technology)*
- **DeepWear: A Case Study of Collaborative Design between Human and Artificial Intelligence** 529
  Natsumi Kato, Hiroyuki Osone, Daitetsu Sato, Naoya Muramatsu, Yoichi Ochiai *(University of Tsukuba)*
- **Op 1254: Music for Neutrons, Networks and Solenoids using a Restored Organ in a Nuclear Reactor** 537
  Leif Handberg, Ludvig Elblaus *(KTH Royal Institute of Technology)*, Chris Chafe, Elliot Kermit Canfield-Dafilou *(Stanford University)*
- **Embodisuit: A Wearable Platform for Embodied Knowledge** 542
  Sophia Brueckner *(University of Michigan)*, Rachel Freire *(Rachel Freire Studio)*
- **The Bronze Key: Performing Data Encryption** 549
  Susan Kozel *(Malmö University)*, Ruth Gibson *(Gibson/Martelli & Coventry University)*, Bruno Martelli *(Gibson/Martelli)*
- **Tracking, Animating, and 3D Printing Elements of the Fine Arts Freehand Drawing Process** 555
  Piyum Fernando, Jennifer Weiler, Stacey Kuznetsov, Pavan Turaga *(Arizona State University)*
- **The Screaming Sun: Choreographing Synesthesia** 562
  Mithru Vigneshwara *(New York University)*
- **Twinkle: A Flying Lighting Companion for Urban Safety** 567
  Honghao Deng, Jiabao Li, Allen Sayegh *(Harvard University)*, Sebastian Birolini *(University of Bergamo)*, Stefano Andreani *(Harvard University)*
- **Synesthetic Experience in S T R A T I C** 574
  Vygandas "Vegas" Šimbelis, Anders Lundström *(KTH - Royal Institute of Technology)*
- **Thou and I: Exploring Expressive Digital Interaction with Interactive Characteristic Wigs** 581
  Young Suk Lee *(Indiana University)*
- **Beacon: Exploring Physicality in Digital Performance** 586
  Anna Weisling *(Georgia Institute of Technology)*, Anna Xambó *(Queen Mary University of London)*
- **Marching Cubes Made Tangible** 592
  Jesse Colin Jackson *(University of California, Irvine)*
- **SKIN – Embodied Navigation through WiFi Traffic using Vibro-Tactile Feedback** 598
  Bas van den Boogaard, Louise Ørsted Jensen, Stefan Engelbrecht Nielsen, Vibeke Thorhauge Stephensen, Karina Lindegaard Aae Jensen, Markus Löchtefeld *(Aalborg University)*

- **I Want To: Multi-media Installation for Understanding Our Desire** 605
  Laewoo Kang *(Cornell University)*
- **Rewilding Wearables: Sympoeitic Interfaces for Empathic Experience of Other-than-human Entities** 611
  Patricia Flanagan *(University of New South Wales)*, Raune Frankjaer *(Aarhus University)*
- **Code{strata} Sonifying Software Complexity** 617
  Denez Thomas *(University of Rennes 2)*, Nicolas Harrand *(INRIA)*,
  Benoit Baudry *(KTH - Royal Institute of Technology)*, Bruno Bossis *(University Rennes 2)*
- **Let's *F*ake News'** 622
  Léon McCarthy *(University of Limerick)*

Paper Session 5: Evaluating Tangible Interactions

Session Chair: Michael Rinott *(Shenkar – Engineering. Design. Art)*

- **Evaluating Learning with Tangible and Virtual Representations of Archaeological Artifacts** 626
  Christina Pollalis, Elizabeth Joanna Minor, Lauren Westendorf, Whitney Fahnbulleh,
  Isabella Virgilio *(Wellesley College)*, Andrew L. Kun *(University of New Hampshire)*,
  Orit Shaer *(Wellesley College)*
- **The Impact of Tangible Props on Gaming Performance and Experience in Gestural Interaction** 638
  Daniel Reinhardt, Jörn Hurtienne *(Julius-Maximilians-Universität Würzburg)*
- **Multimodal Effects of Color and Haptics on Intuitive Interaction with Tangible User Interfaces** 647
  Diana Löffler, Robert Tscharn, Jörn Hurtienne *(University of Würzburg)*
- **Being in the Sky: Framing Tangible and Embodied Interaction for Future Airliner Cockpits** 656
  Catherine Letondal, Jean-Luc Vinot *(University of Toulouse - ENAC)*,
  Sylvain Pauchet *(University of Toulouse - ENAC & Astrolab)*, Caroline Boussiron *(Ingenuity i/o)*,
  Stéphanie Rey *(University of Toulouse & Berger-Levrault)*, Valentin Becquet *(University of Toulouse)*,
  Claire Lavenir *(Intactile Design)*

Paper Session 6: Theory, Communities & Frameworks

Session Chair: Jelle Saldien *(Ghent University)*

- **Cohousing IoT: Design Prototyping for Community Life** 667
  Tom Jenkins *(Georgia Institute of Technology)*
- **Through the Glance Mug: A Familiar Artefact to Support Opportunistic Search in Meetings** 674
  Ahmet Börütecene, İdil Bostan, Ekin Akyürek, Alpay Sabuncuoğlu, İlker Temuzkuşu, Çağlar Genç,
  Tilbe Göksun, Oğuzhan Özcan *(Koç University)*
- **Focus Framework: Tracking Prototypes' Back-Talk** 684
  Markus Lorenz Schilling *(Simon Fraser University)*,
  Ron Wakkary *(Eindhoven University of Technology & Simon Fraser University)*,
  William Odom *(Simon Fraser University)*
- **Understanding Transformations through Design: Can Resilience Thinking Help?** 694
  Rosa van der Veen *(RISE Interactive Umeå & Eindhoven University of Technology)*,
  Viola Hakkerainen *(Stockholm Resilience Centre)*, Jeroen Peeters *(RISE Interactive)*,
  Ambra Trotto *(RISE Interactive & Umeå School of Architecture)*

GSC

- **Exploring the Potential of Data Physicalization for STEM Learning** 703
  Sarah Hayes *(Cork Institute of Technology)*
- **Designing for Instructed Physical Training** 706
  Laia Turmo Vidal *(Uppsala University)*

- **Understanding and Designing Embodied Experiences Through Mid-air Tactile Stimulation** 709
  Dario Pittera *(University of Sussex)*
- **The Interactive Carpet - Smart Textile Interface for Children on Autism Spectrum Disorder** 712
  Yulia Zhiglova *(Tallinn University)*
- **Choreographic Computational Composites: Investigating Small-Size Shape-Change Architecture through Performative Arts** 715
  Alice Rzezonka *(University of Wuppertal)*
- **Creating and Staging Interactive Costumes** 718
  Michaela Honauer *(Bauhaus-Universität Weimar, HCI Group)*
- **Unfolding an Industrial Design Approach to Physical Computing** 721
  Clement Zheng *(University of Colorado Boulder)*

Studios

- **Sociomateriality: Infrastructuring and Appropriation of Artifacts** 724
  Tom Jenkins *(Georgia Institute of Technology)*,
  Karey Helms, Vasiliki Tsaknaki, Ludvig Elblaus *(Royal Institute of Technology)*,
  Nicolai Brodersen Hansen *(Eindhoven University of Technology)*
- **Designing eTextiles for the Body: Shape, Volume & Motion** 728
  Rachel Freire *(Rachel Freire Studio)*, Paul Strohmeier *(University of Copenhagen)*,
  Cedric Honnet *(Universite Paris Sorbonne - UPMC)*, Jarrod Knibbe *(University of Copenhagen)*,
  Sophia Brueckner *(University of Michigan)*
- **Deformable Controllers: Fabrication and Design to Promote Novel Hand Gestural Interaction Mechanisms** 732
  Victor Cheung, Alexander Keith Eady, Audrey Girouard *(Carleton University)*
- **Kinetic Body Extensions for Social Interactions** 736
  Kate Hartman *(OCAD University)*, Boris Kourtoukov *(Oslo School of Architecture and Design)*,
  Erin Lewis *(University of Borås)*
- **Internet of Tangibles: Exploring the Interaction-Attention Continuum** 740
  Leonardo Angelini, Elena Mugellini, Omar
  Abou Khaled *(University of Applied Sciences and Arts Western Switzerland)*, Nadine Couture *(ESTIA LaBRI)*,
  Elise van den Hoven *(University of Technology Sydney & Eindhoven University of Technology)*,
  Saskia Bakker *(Eindhoven University of Technology)*
- **Tracking Well-Being – Design Explorations through Object Theatre** 744
  Andreas A. Heiberg Skouby, Merja Ryöppy, Robb Mitchell *(University of Southern Denmark)*

Author Index 748

TEI 2018 Conference Organization

General Chairs: Ylva Fernaeus (*KTH Royal Institute of Technology, Sweden*)
Donald McMillan (*Stockholm University, Sweden*)
Martin Jonsson (*Södertörn University, Sweden*)

Program Co-Chairs: Audrey Girouard (*Carleton University, Canada*)
Jakob Tholander (*Stockholm University, Sweden*)

Studios Chairs: Martin Murer (*University of Salzburg, Austria*)
Vasiliki Tsaknaki (*KTH Royal Institute of Technology, Sweden*)

Publication Chair: Jarmo Laaksolahti *(KTH Royal Institute of Technology, Sweden)*

Arts and Performance Chairs: Robyn Taylor (*Newcastle University, UK*)
Asreen Rostami (*Stockholm University, Sweden*)
Vygandas "Vegas" Šimbelis (*KTH Royal Institute of Technology, Sweden*)

Work In Progress Chairs: Katrin Wolf (*Hamburg University of Applied Science, Germany*)
Preben Hansen (*Stockholm University, Sweden*)
Sven Mayer (*University of Stuttgart, Germany*)

Graduate Student Consortium Chairs: Ellen Yi-Luen Do (*University of Colorado Boulder, USA*) & *National University of Singapore, Singapore*)
Stephen Brewster (*University of Glasgow, UK*)
Ian Oakley (*Ulsan National Institute of Science and Technology, South Korea*)

Accessibility Co-Chairs: Sylvaine Tuncer (*Stockholm University, Sweden*)
Rob Comber (*KTH Royal Institute of Technology, Sweden*)

Demo Co-Chairs: Mattias Jacobsson (*RISE Research Institutes of Sweden, Sweden*)
Robin Palmblad (*KTH Royal Institute of Technology, Sweden*)

Local Co-Chairs: Roberto Bresin (*KTH Royal Institute of Technology, Sweden*)
Cristian Bogdan (*KTH Royal Institute of Technology, Sweden*)

Web Chair: Karey Helms (*KTH Royal Institute of Technology, Sweden*)

Social Media Chair: Airi Lampinen (*Stockholm University, Sweden*)

Sponsorship Chair: Maria Holm (*RISE Research Institutes of Sweden, Sweden*)

Student Design Challenge Chairs: Kjetil Falkenberg Hansen (*KTH Royal Institute of Technology, Sweden*)
Kiel Long (*Northumbria University, UK*)

Student Volunteer Chairs: Sophie Landwehr Sydow (*Södertörn University, Sweden*)
Marie Louise Juul Søndergaard (*Aarhus University, Denmark*)

Steering Committee: Albrecht Schmidt (*Universität Stuttgart, Germany)*
Ali Mazalek (*Georgia Tech, USA & Ryerson University, Canada)*
Alissa Antle (*Simon Fraser University, Canada)*
Andreas Butz (*LMU, Germany)*
Audrey Girouard (*Carleton University, Canada)*
Bart Hengeveld (*Eindhoven University of Technology, the Netherlands)*
Brygg Ullmer (*Louisiana State University, USA)*
Caroline Hummels (*Eindhoven University of Technology, the Netherlands)*
Elise van den Hoven (*University of Technology Sydney, Australia & TU/e, the Netherlands)*
Ellen Yi-Luen Do (*University of Colorado Boulder*, USA & *National University of Singapore*, *Singapore*)
Eva Hornecker (*Bauhaus-Universität Weimar, Germany)*
Hiroshi Ishii (*MIT Media Lab, USA)*
Lian Loke (*University of Sydney, Australia)*
Martin Kaltenbrunner (*UFG, Austria)*
Nicolas Villar (*Microsoft Research, UK)*
Orit Shaer (*Wellesley College, USA*)
Rob Jacob (*Tufts University, USA)*
Ron Wakkary (*Simon Fraser University, Canada)*
Saskia Bakker (*Eindhoven University of Technology, the Netherlands)*
Sergi Jorda, (*UPF, Spain)*
Wendy Ju (*Stanford University, USA)*
Ylva Fernaeus (*KTH, Sweden)*

Program Committee: Ali Mazalek (*Ryerson University, Canada*)
Andrea Bianchi (*KAIST, Korea*)
Andrew Kun (*University of New Hampshire, USA*)
Andrew Smith (*CSIR Meraka Institute, South Africa*)
Andy Wilson (*Microsoft Research, USA*)
Bart Hengeveld (*Technische Universiteit Eindhoven, Netherlands*)
Beat Signer (*Vrije Universiteit Brussel, Belgium*)
Chiara Rossitto (*Stockholm University, Sweden*)
Daniel Saakes (*KAIST, Korea*)
Dzmitry Aliakseyeu (*Philips Research Europe, Netherlands*)
Ehud Sharlin (*University of Calgary, Canada*)
Enrico Rukzio (*University of Ulm, Germany*)
George Khut (*UNSW Art and Design, Australia*)
Ian Oakley (*Ulsan National Institute of Science and Technology, South Korea*)
Jelle Saldien (*Ghent University, Belgium*)
Jelle van Dijk (*University Twente, the Netherlands*)
Jörn Hurtienne (*University of Würzburg, Germany*)
Juan David Hincapie-Ramos (*University of Manitoba, Canada*)
Kris Luyten (*Hasselt University, Belgium*)
Lian Loke (*University of Sydney, Australia*)
Liwei Chan (*National Chiao Tung University, Taiwan*)
Luc Geurts (*KU Leuven, Belgium*)
Manfred Lau (*Lancaster University, United Kingdom*)
Manfred Tscheligi (*ICT&S Center, Austria*)
Martin Murer (*University of Salzburg, Austria*)
Michal Rinott (*Shenkar – Engineering. Design. Art, Israel*)
Mike Fraser (*University of Bristol, United Kingdom*)
Mike Horn (*Northwestern University, USA*)
Rohit Ashok Khot (*RMIT University, Australia*)
Rong-Hao Liang (*Eindhoven University of Technology, the Netherlands*)
Saskia Bakker (*Eindhoven University of Technology, the Netherlands*)
Stacey Kuznetsov (*Arizona State University, USA*)
Tanja Döring (*University of Bremen, Germany*)
Trevor Hogan (*Cork Institute of Technology, Ireland*)
Valérie Maquil (*Luxembourg Institute of Science and Technology, Luxembourg*)
Vero Vanden Abeele (*KU Leuven, Belgium*)
Victor Cheung (*Carleton University, Canada*)
Yuta Sugiura (*Keio University, Japan*)

Additional reviewers: See the TEI 2018 web: https://tei.acm.org/2018/people/

TEI 2018 Sponsor & Supporters

Sponsor

Supporters

Working with an Autonomous Interface: Exploring the Output Space of an Interactive Desktop Lamp

Diana Nowacka
University College London, UK
d.nowacka@ucl.ac.uk

Katrin Wolf
Hamburg University of Applied Sciences, Germany
katrin.wolf@haw-hamburg.de

Enrico Costanza
University College London, UK
e.costanza@ucl.ac.uk

David Kirk
Northumbria University
Newcastle upon Tyne, UK
david.kirk@northumbria.ac.uk

ABSTRACT
Increasing sophistication and ubiquity of digital devices is creating potential for the development of new kinds of actuated interfaces. In this paper, we explore the design space around movement as a form of gestural communication for information output, in simple actuated desktop devices. We were curious as to how people might envision interacting with autonomous technology in the office. Accordingly, we focused our attentions on one prevalent desktop object, an interactive lamp, with three actuated joints, which allowed us to explore the interaction space of such devices. We invited 13 participants to design and enact movements with the lamp to communicate 20 simple messages. We explored a subset of these generated gestures, using the lamp as a personal cueing device in an office setting with 14 new participants. We present our qualitative findings from both studies that let users imagine the usage of an interactive desktop lamp through actuation.

Author Keywords
Actuated Interfaces; Interactive Desktop Lamp; Autonomous Technology; Qualitative Evaluation.

INTRODUCTION
The decreasing costs of embedded sensors, processors and actuators enable the design of actuated artefacts for everyday use. Interactive objects are merging with our environments [36] and interfaces can now be 'brought to life' through such technology [24]. This phenomenon of ubiquitous computing has proved to be useful in many different application areas, such as domestic, health and office spaces [2, 3]. Commercial products, such as small personal robots (jibo.com), just started to occupy this space and are in great demand. In this paper, we seek to understand how users perceive and interact with everyday objects that 'come to life' through actuators.

TEI '18, March 18–21, 2018, Stockholm, Sweden

ACM ISBN 978-1-4503-5568-1/18/03...$15.00
https://doi.org/10.1145/3173225.3173227

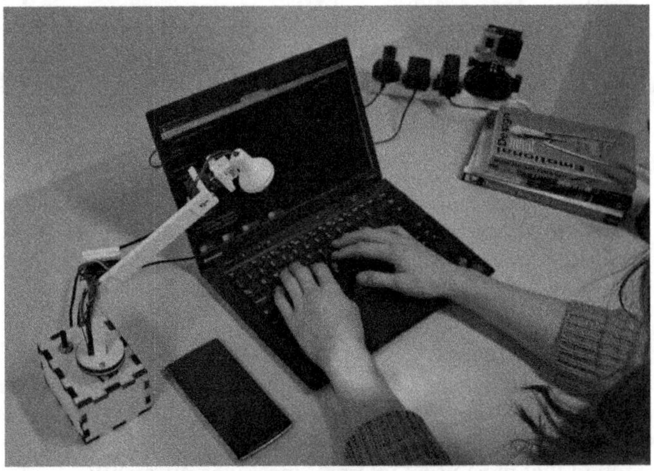

Figure 1. The actuated desktop lamp.

There is an underlying similarity in interaction when we compare devices producing actuation (e.g. light, sound, movement). Research has shown that - consciously [8] but also unconsciously [28] - people react socially towards these interfaces. Interface design is also commonly used to create an illusion of systems being alive and having a personality [13, 26]. To explore these areas, we developed an interactive desk lamp for the office (pictured in Fig. 1). Our interest lies in the limits and edges of intelligence and autonomy in interaction design. Within this inquiry, we are particularly aiming at creating a tangible autonomous interface [25], a device which is less complex than a robot, but a tangible user interface that exhibits autonomous behaviours. But how do people actually feel about such interfaces in an everyday setting? Which consequences does this have for designing technology?

We envision a scenario where the lamp could be a personal device, reacting to input provided through a digital calendar or also through physiologically monitoring the user. In this paper, through exploratorily imagining a scenario in the office with participants, we want to research how to design an autonomous desktop lamp as a notification device. Our key interest lies in understanding the space between humans and autonomous interfaces.

We report on two studies that are built around a smart desktop lamp, functioning as an autonomous interface to support office work. In the first study, we let participants actively explore how an interactive lamp might display a range of messages related to a work scenario through enacting various motions with a passive lamp. The ideas collected in the first study helped to design potential interactions for an interactive desktop lamp for the office desk. But how acceptable and usable would our generated design be in real life? In the second study, we tested a subset of the generated movements with a new set of participants in a semi-realistic, exploratory office setting. We invited the participants to sit at a desk and work for 30 minutes. In a Wizard-of-Oz setup, the lamp provided output to the participants. We then followed up with a semi-structured interview to investigate the functionality and practicability of the lamp. We focused on social reactions to technology to qualitatively understand how users would like such a lamp to function and how they would feel about interacting with it.

RELATED WORK

Research previously explored technological augmentation of desks to support the user with daily tasks [4, 33]. Here, we want to focus on actuated objects and interactive desktop lamps and how these influenced our work.

Actuated Objects

Product Movement is a design field focusing on using actuation to deliver information to the user. Jung et al. [19] created an abstract robotic torso, which can move and rotate. They found that most users interpret messages differently, as plain movement might not be distinct enough to communicate something that all people can agree on. Context is needed to make messages more explicit and movement should be seen as an additional modality that can be used along with other outputs. Building on their work, they further evaluated three actuated prototypes [18] in the shape of everyday objects (shaking water bottle, moving assignment box, rotating recycle bin). Although some movements were confusing, the devices quickly caught attention. They observed that people treated the devices as life-like and showed affection and empathy, speculating that in the future humans may build relationships with such technology. However, they also mentioned that some movements were frightening or annoying. *Breakaway* [16] is a small paper strip on the desktop that slouches when the user is sitting for too long, to foster behaviour change. An initial study with one participant over two weeks revealed that *Breakaway* indeed motivated movement and was not intrusive.

These prototypes serve as great examples to show the feasibility of actuated products to communicate through movement. However, such design needs to be carefully balanced between the actual movement, the context, and the purpose of the device. Otherwise, abstract actuation might not bring any benefit and lead to confusion or annoyance. We were interested in how people would react to an actuated desk lamp and which emotions people would convey towards such a device. Especially, we wanted to find a suitable design for the context of a work environment and how to avoid annoying movements.

Camy [30] is a dog-shaped web camera covered in fabric (used as an electronic assistant), which can move next to the screen and also has a digital counterpart on the screen. The authors explored how animal analogies (especially to pets) could be used in ubicomp product design. The study indicated that the users personified *Camy* and associated a character with it. The authors conclude that due to its social presence, *Camy* might achieve a higher acceptability as a product, as users at times seemed more forgiving towards certain otherwise distracting functions. Research on the perception of insect behaviour identified new design opportunities for notification cues, leveraging knowledge from lifelong experience and building on associations with living beings [23, 22]. However, interfaces with zoomorphic appearance are, at the moment, still challenging to implement and far from being able to behave like the model they resemble. Therefore it is advisable to not evoke expectations through visual resemblances (e.g. make an interface look like an animal) that may be broken and lead to disappointment [7, 5]. To avoid these pitfalls, we lay high importance on functional and plain appearance and focus on machine-like technology. Therefore we chose a lamp.

In related work on actuated interfaces, may it be helium balloons [24], quadcopters [20], kitchen bowls with morse output [35], bespoke radio devices [10]; researchers always seem to report the same two phenomena: people perceive these actuated devices as animals or even pets and participants tend to perceive them as social beings. Remarkably, the devices only have the actuation in common, visually their designs are diverse. What is it about the design of these interfaces that makes people react in that way? Conventional autonomous technologies in the office environment, like Clippy, proved to be distracting and annoying and were not well received [37]. Research also showed that reminder technology needs to show a degree of 'politeness' to be acceptable [6]. Hence, we are asking: How could we leverage the fact that people react socially towards actuated technology to create autonomous devices that are acceptable? Ultimately, we are interested in aspects that make autonomous technology suitable at work. Against this background of work, we wanted to research how the lamp could establish itself as an embodied, social desktop companion and therefore enable a more enjoyable interaction.

Interactive Desktop Lamps

DeVito et al. [9] created an actuated desk lamp and used a user-centred approach to design hand gestures for different control tasks, such as switching the light on or off and shining at a certain object. A more playful prototype is *disco lamp* [21], which tracks a hand to provide light at that area and also dances to music. The most sophisticated robotic lamp was presented by Hoffman [14]. In a workspace setting, users directed a lamp's head and therefore guided the light with their hands as well as changed the light's colour. Participants were impressed with the robot's performance and collaboration worked well. Some even stated a feeling of inferiority when making mistakes, while the prototype solved its tasks. These studies focus on gestures for the user and their interaction to control the light. Our aim was to understand the possible movements for more expressive output of an actuated lamp. *Gertie* [12] is a desk lamp with five degrees of freedom (DOF). In an online survey, four different emotions (fear, joy, sadness, surprise) that the lamp was intended to convey were evaluated. Participants reliably identified joy and sadness, but not fear and surprise, which oftentimes were confused with surprise and disgust. Whereas this work focused on the display of emotions, we are exploring how a lamp could display various cues to support the user with their tasks in the office and how this opens up an interaction space.

In summary, more research is needed in autonomous desktop interfaces to understand which kind of interactive object behaviours users would accept and want. We aim to do this using a lamp as an exemplary object in a user-centred approach. Instead of focusing on user's gestures, we explore to which extent it is possible to communicate certain messages through movements in the context of a working environment and how these movements affect a user's perception of a device.

In the following we describe the first study, consisting of the gesture collection, its evaluation and findings. Following on that, we describe the second study, a follow-up, exploring the designed movements in a semi-realistic setting.

STUDY ONE - GESTURE COLLECTION

Prototype

The appearance of the lamp is aimed to look like a regular lamp. As already mentioned, we want to avoid deception and possibly frustration with the device. Various designs and different degrees of freedom were explored. In the end, we decided on two actuators as this does not make the device overly complex and allows for a fair amount of output movements. Therefore, the lamp consists of two segments; the cone as the top (holding the LED), which can rotate, and the middle joint, which can bend forwards and backwards (see Fig. 2). To not bias the participants, we did not give the lamp a name.

Setup

We recruited 13 participants, aged 22-53 (6 females and 7 males, mean age 30). The setup of our first experiment was an office room with a desk (audio and video recorded). We

Figure 2. The lamp prototype for the first study with a potentiometer to control the light intensity.

created a realistic setting by cluttering the desk with various objects; laptop, books, a mobile phone, some pens and a water bottle. Although this still presents a lab setup as the participants were not sitting at their own desks, such a setup surely does not represent an unusual configuration as it resembles a modern hot-desking situation in various workspaces [15].

Procedure

To discover possible lamp movements, we chose the approach of user-defined lamp actions (which is quite common for other technologies such as surface computing [38]). We asked our participants to use the lamp like a puppet and let the lamp display messages to a person at the desk (in this case themselves). We gave 20 tasks to the participants (in random order, each task was printed on a card) and they could change the lamp's pose, position, and light intensity. They were invited to talk along and explain their thoughts and ideas. To explore a wide range of possible task types, we chose specific tasks (e.g. new email arrived) as well as more ambiguous and open ones (e.g. catch user's attention). The tasks consisted of drawing the attention of the user to something (e.g. a person / something on the desk / outside the room), notifying the user of incoming messages or events coming up (from a calendar, mobile phone, email client, to go for lunch), changing the user's behaviour (drink water, motivate the user to stand up, calm them down because their heartbeat is too fast) and two social messages: say hello and goodbye. The sessions lasted 15-45 mins.

Analysis and Findings

For analysis, we looked at the lamp output that users created, but also carefully observed any behaviour and comments that were made towards the lamp. We transcribed all comments that point at an envisioned usage or subtle utterances that describe the relationship the users might form or imagine with such a device. Using these snippets, we conducted a thematic analysis. There are two elements to our findings. First, we describe the physical movements, which our participants generated. Second, we report on people's expectations of how the lamp should behave that we retrieved from their statements.

Generated Lamp Movements

Essentially, there were two different ways in which the participants manipulated the lamp to communicate with the user. They either let the lamp *point* at something / someone / somewhere by directing the top to orient towards the desired target; or changed the *posture* of the lamp to resemble a (human) posture, movement or gesture (leaning back to relax, bend over to sleep, wave to greet). Each participant stated that it is difficult to create a unique movement for each task. Therefore, to convey a certain message, participants tried to place the lamp in a certain context related to the message.

Overall, for more than half of the tasks (12 out of 20), the majority of the participants found it easiest for the lamp to point at something. Especially for catching attention or draw attention to something, participants used the lamp to point (70%). To remind the user of something, the participants again mostly pointed to the object of interest (66%) and flashed the light (45%). These reminder tasks were similar to the tasks attracting the attention, as for the participants they followed a similar agenda: find the object of interest and direct the user's attention towards it. For the behaviour change tasks (engage in physical activity, calm down), most participants saw the lamp as a physical role model, mimicking what a human should be doing, e.g. getting up or breath slowly. To remind the participant to drink water, all 13 participants pointed to the water bottle. Typical responses for the 'social' tasks were to point or 'look' at the user's face and then change the posture (58%) by e.g. waving as 'hello' or 'bye'.

We also observed a number of unusual interactions. One participant let the lamp nudge it's mouth (to indicate it's time for lunch), another his wrist to get attention or knock against the wall (to point to another room). One person placed the lamp between himself and his laptop for the case that the lamp urgently needs to attract attention. Participants also mentioned that the light could blink in a certain pattern (e.g. morse) and therefore encode more information (although they acknowledged that they would not understand it).

Behavioural Expectations and Guidelines

It was interesting to us how diversely each participant imagined the lamp to function. Each person had their own interpretation to start with, their own way of approaching the device. Some saw it as a companion, others as a mirror of oneself, a teacher or parent (a device that dictates its use), others just as a light. We compiled the following recommendations from the participant's feedback: *The lamp needs to be polite* - unsurprisingly the lamp should act in a way that is appropriate in an office. Although its movements are highly mechanical, the device should still 'behave' like a polite human. Some form of eye-contact could be a means of respectfully checking in with the user and initiating contact. *The lamp needs to be aware* - the lamp should be able to recognise when a cue has been detected by the user and stop giving hints. It should also be aware about a task being urgent and demand the user to act as this would make the lamp useful and help to not miss out on important tasks. Furthermore, it would be helpful if the lamp knows about its environment, the things that are laying around, the room it is located in. *The lamp needs to change over time* - the longer the interaction, the more a user gets used to the lamp's cues. Therefore, with time, shortcuts can be made. After having interacted with the lamp for longer, the lamp can decrease the magnitude of its movements. It may only need to make small movements which the user would be able to understand because they got familiar with the lamp's movements. *The lamp needs to be customisable* - different people need different cues. It should be possible to adjust the messages (and their frequency) or add new functions.

STUDY TWO - GESTURE EXPLORATION

Prototype

During the first study, the users frequently turned the lamp around. Therefore the lamp was slightly altered for the second study and one additional motor was added to the bottom (see Fig. 1), which allows the lamp to rotate around its centre (approx. 200 deg). The second lamp comprises an Arduino Yun board, its movements and light are controlled remotely through a python program via Wifi. The prototype's hardware and software are open-source [1].

To make robots appear more life-like, roboticists explored principles of animation to create more natural forms of movement [34, 29]. Decades ago, animators established a set of practices which enhance cartoon character's motions to realistically convey their emotions and attitudes [32, 27]. For our prototype, we aimed at a more simple and functional design and therefore we designed the movement in a mechanistic way without applying the animator's guidelines. The lamp initiates its movement and it stays at the same speed until the movement stops. We do this to explore human responses to machine-like interfaces, which don't aim to copy human movement but are expressive in their own, technical way.

Setup

We chose to run a follow-up study in a semi-realistic office setting with 14 new participants and a study setup similar to the first study. Again, we set up a desk in a small meeting room with a laptop, books, a glass of water and pens and placed the desk lamp on it (see Fig. 1). We were curious about the appropriateness of the prompts and how people would react to a little desktop device. Participants were aged 23-39 years, 7 females and 7 males took part with a mean age of 30.

We based our selection of the prompts, which the lamp would display during the study, on the participants' statements about the most useful and/or desired cues: (1) Say Hi, (2) a text message arrived, (3) an email arrived, (4) drink some water, (5) look outside the room, (6) say bye. To create these cues, we looked at the corresponding, proposed movements from the first study. We made sketches of the proposed gestures and identified the most common occurrences as the movements for our study. Based on the majority, when more than half of the participants performed the same gesture, we adapted this choreography for the according cue. For (2), (3), (4), (5) this meant that the lamp would move from the default position (see Fig. 1) and point at the phone, laptop, glass of water, door and flash three times. For 'saying hi' the lamp waved the upper part up and down for a few seconds. For 'goodbye' the lamp also waved and then folded down.

Based on key issues identified by the participants in the first study, we made two further design decisions. To be *aware*, the lamp registers a message as 'received' or noticed by the user, when the user makes eye contact. If the user does not react, the lamp repeats the cue after 10 seconds. As identified in study one, the lamp could get annoying quite quickly. Therefore, to be *polite*, the lamp only repeats a cue up to three times.

Procedure

In the first study, 'gaze', so the lamp pointing at a user's face, was often identified as more polite, 'friendly' and engaging. We wanted to explore how 'gaze' impacts on interaction and if people prefer it to rather functional behaviour. Therefore, for the second study, we split the session in half. Each session lasted about 30 minutes in total and consisted of two conditions. The prompts were presented twice to the participants, in counterbalanced order. In the first 15 minutes, the lamp would provide the cue directly, in the other half the cue was preceded by 'gaze'. This means the lamp established 'eye-contact' by turning the top part (containing the LED) and therefore facing the participant for a few seconds (with the LED turned off) before displaying a cue.

We created a protocol to make sure the lamp shows the same behaviour for each participant, leaving no room for ambiguity for the experimenter. We used Wizard-of-Oz, the conductor of the study hid in the back of the next room in a way that she could look through the glass door, see the participant, and remotely trigger the movements without being seen. Every 3-4 minutes the lamp would provide a cue to the user. A random email or text message was sent to the participant before the lamp would point towards one of these devices. To resemble a more typical hot-desking situation, we asked our participants to bring their laptop, phone and something to read. While the participant read and signed the consent form, we placed their laptop and phone next to the lamp on the desk in the room. Then the participants were asked to go into the room. As soon as the participant sat down by the desk, the first cue ('Say hello') was given. To explore how easily understandable the movements are, we didn't tell the participants the movement's meanings. We merely mentioned that this study evaluates autonomous technologies, and we told them that they should go into the room, sit down and work or read.

Data Collection

The sessions were audio and video recorded. Right after the study, we conducted a semi-structured interview lasting 20-30 minutes. The interview explored the understanding of the lamp's functioning, preferences, acceptability of its behaviour and participant's general perception of such a device. In the interview, we also explicitly asked the participants if they noticed a difference between the two different conditions and about their interpretation of each gesture. This involved replaying the cues during the interview. We further questioned whether the lamp was perceived as a social actor. Participants were also asked to clarify or reflect on specific behaviours which were noticed by the experimenter during the study.

Analysis and Findings

Our interests lied in how people make sense of the lamp's actions and how this can be seen in their behaviour. Furthermore, we wanted to understand how the design of the lamp leads people to react in certain ways and if these situations can be seen as opportunities for design. The data was analysed in two ways. First, we conducted a thematic analysis on the interview data and identified four overarching themes (presented below). Second, we picked up unusual, surprising or accidental situations from the video data. We analysed people's reactions, facial expressions and behaviours through performing an interaction analysis [17], which are marked as **Vignettes** below. We placed the vignettes within the themes. To develop a broader understanding of the potential of autonomous office technology, we unpacked these specific behaviours that occurred during the study. That is, to understand how people perceive and react to certain actions of our prototype and how a social situation with technology is constructed.

A lamp as a thinking entity

During the study a number of participants stated that they were wondering what the lamp might be 'thinking'. One participant explained that the lamp came across like an intentional entity:

"I thought it was looking off into the distance, and I was like 'what is it looking at'? It looked past the screen so my impression was that it was just looking by itself, at stuff that it was interested in." (P14)

It is fascinating that in the study this participant tried to figure out what drives the lamp, and he does it by trying to understand the lamp's 'thought process'. Almost as if the lamp would be a living being with thoughts. Consequently, he is worried about his actions on the desk and how this might be perceived by the lamp, e.g. picking up his phone. He continued reflecting:

"You do get the sense it's looking at stuff, I know that doesn't really make a lot of sense, well I guess it does, but you're just making that up, it's not looking, it's doing the opposite, it's projecting." (P14)

This all happens despite the fact that the participant knows that the lamp is only a piece of technology, a desktop lamp, and he is realising that he is making analogies that are a bit odd, such as interpreting the shining as looking. Still, the lamp seems alive. Other participants felt similar and when talking about the lamp, it sounded like they were talking about a person:

"Yes it seemed that it was observing what I was doing. It really seemed that it has a life on its own. Like an assistant remind you of things that you forget when you are drawn too much into what you're doing." (P5)

"It's a bit alive, I didn't interact with it, it interacted with me. We do understand each other though, but I'll have to teach it, if it would live with me. The movements, it has its own style. But the actions. I don't know if I would be creative enough [to customise it], it would need to be crowdsourced like 'oh other people teached their lamp to do this trick' or suddenly my lamp started doing things it has seen other people do." (P4)

For this participant it would be important to have a 'library of actions' to choose from so he can make more use of the lamp. In his descriptions it seems like he is referring to a living being, a pet or something similar, that can 'see' and 'learn'. In some cases, interpreting too much into the use of such words, i.e. describing object actions using terms, which would only be used for humans or animals, is problematic as it might just be a lingual artifact. We refer to tables having legs without actually anthropomorphising them and thinking of them as being alive. In such dissections, we have to be careful and aware of this fact. Our participants are however making explicit comments about the lamp 'thinking' and 'caring', which strongly indicates that this artefact can be dismissed in our case. They directly refer to the lamp as a conscious entity.

Vignette: The pet lamp

The lamp indicated that a new email arrived. P13 didn't react to the cue at first, but chose to stroke the top of the lamp after it returned to the default position (Fig.3(a)). In the interview she explains her action:

Figure 3. Four snapshots of interesting situations that emerged during the study, left to right, (a)-(d).

"It looked at me and it felt like it was acting like it was a pet. It was just moving [...] and I thought it needed some reassurance that I was aware of it, that it knows I am aware of it doing something. I have a pet, that might be why, my cat does that. [...] I am used to having something that moves around, he sometimes even goes on my keyboard. Because the lamp was here it reminded me of that, because the cat would poke its head out at the same spot. I liked it!"

Although our prototype shows no visual resemblance to a cat, the participant felt reminded of her experiences with her pet at home and therefore reacted the same way she does at home to show approval and compliancy. This situation illustrates how the lamps mechanical behaviour triggers some association with routine domestic behaviours.

A lamp that cares

People felt sympathy towards the lamp and interpreted it as good willing, as if it would actually care for them. The perceptions went far beyond the intended functions:

"It kind of made me feel like I had a little companion and like I should be sat here working rather than checking facebook and things, so I went on twitter, but very quickly, because there was this little thing that was kind of trying to make me more productive." (P8)

We received quotes that demonstrated that some people felt the lamp would motivate them to work, keep up a schedule and live more balanced. Others thought that it acts like an aid and it wants them to live healthier: *"Seemed benevolent, good willing, it was suggesting that I stayed healthy, [...] I think I made a new friend." (P4)*

One participant was not sure about the lamp's intention and the thought came up that it only wanted to distract him:

"It was weird, sometimes I just thought 'oh, it sort of cares about me, it tries to help me by pointing at my phone and stuff', but then other times it was just felt like it was just trying to distract, [...] at times I ended up to me like 'what was I doing again? Can't remember. So he's troubled that one!" (P14)

The actions of the lamp, e.g. pointing at water or the phone were interpreted as support but at times as a distraction as well. Pointing to things in this scenario meant caring for the user and their health or inviting to act or respond. The lamp observing the user and its purpose to keep the user up to date was interpreted as a friendly aid. Ambiguity in the lamp's purpose helped the people to make their own interpretation of the lamp's behaviour. This shows that purposeful autonomous technology is perceived as positive, friendly assistance.

Vignette: The persuasive lamp

In the middle of the second session, the lamp pointed at the water. P4 didn't show any reaction, he ignored the cue and kept typing. The researcher couldn't observe a reaction so ten seconds later she repeated the cue. After the second prompt, the participant followed the lamp's suggestion and took a sip of water (Fig. 3(b)).

"I was just finishing off some code and it flashed at the water and I was like 'yeah, good idea, but I'm gonna ignore you, because I am doing code, maybe next time'. But then it did it again immediately, so I said, 'fine, ok, I'll have a drink'. Then it didn't prompt me a third time so I guess that was me responding to it and it responding to me by stopping."

This situation nicely illustrates the lamp succeeding at persuading the user to do something.

A lamp that fosters a relationship

In general, the responses towards the lamp were positive. When analysing the video, we noticed that the first reaction of most participants, when they sat down and saw the lamp greet them for the first time, was to smile or even laugh. People perceived the lamp as a "little desk companion" (P3, P4, P8, P13), that supports them in everyday tasks. They saw it as their friend (P3), assistant (P5), co-worker (P12): *"I felt like the chemistry was right between us."* (P14) Participants also noticed that they were acting socially towards the lamp: *"I think we kind of teamed up after a while, I also noticed that I was kind of moving a little bit closer to the lamp." (P11)*

The participant continues to explain how her perception changed during the course of the study:

"I perceived it after a while as, you know, it's my team partner in this room and we are working together on something somehow. So even when it pointed out 'ok take a drink', I was like 'oh thank you'. [...], so actually now it's partner in crime." (P11)

This quote indicated that the user, in the short period of the study, engaged in some kind of relationship with the lamp, almost feeling closeness and togetherness. Earlier comments already indicated how participants saw the lamp as a kind of friendly and well-intentioned assistant.

"It is a nice company to working I think when you're alone, when you're kind of in an isolated mode of working, it's quite cheerful. The gestures they are quite unusual for me, I don't have anything like this in my home or so." (P13)

Vignette: The greeting lamp

The situation depicted in (d) occurred at the start of the session with P9. As soon as he sat down, the lamp faced the participant (gaze mode) and then performed the movement 'Say hello'. He was struck by the this movement and felt then compelled to wave directly to the lamp. Afterwards, he remembered this moment in the interview:

"It seemed like it had a vivid character to it. Little bit playful I think, how it's started, I don't know if I did it or not but I tempted to wave to say hello. It's not like it's a cold device, it felt like it had some warmth and it's colourful as well. The first time the motors suddenly kicked in made me jump though."

The participant's first reaction to the greeting is to greet back. He explains that the lamp made a friendly impression on him and therefore he reacted in that way. This shows how autonomous technology can make a friendly first impression and quickly initiate social reactions.

A lamp that is misunderstood

Three participants had trouble understanding the lamp's purpose at all and its behaviour was not apparent to them. They struggled to understand the movement and the functionality in a meaningful way: *"I: Did it seem like it had an intention? P12: No it didn't, not to me, but that may well be because I didn't make the connection between the different things."*

This shows that throwing the participants in at the deep end doesn't work for everyone and some people couldn't make sense of the lamp without an explanation.

To our surprise, 10 out of our 14 participants preferred the version with the lamp not facing them before providing prompts. Eye contact demands immediate response, which seems unnecessary for autonomous desktop technology. Participants stated that it would be distracting. Although participants in our first study identified eye contact between the lamp and the user as something that could help to bond, in practice it is rather irritating and disruptive. However, the four participants that did choose the gaze explained that it felt personal and nice to them. However, these participants also acknowledged that 'gaze' would make the lamp less functional for that reason: *"I don't really think that the facing you is necessary but it would add a bit of personality or something." (P10)*

"When it points into the face I thought it was more cute, like I feel like I can just look at it, smile, and look back, it didn't feel like it was asking me to do anything. It felt like it was just checking I was there, like a pet." (P7)

Vignette: The reprimanding lamp

For participant 12, due to a transmission error, a delay of about 10 seconds occurred before the first cue. The participant sat down and examined the lamp. She wanted to turn the light up and touched the rotor, when the lamp started its movement to 'Say hello'. She immediately went backwards and said "sorry" out loud. Then she looked at the lamp, waiting for a reaction to her apology (c). In the interview she recollected the event:

"I wondered if I could make it brighter, so I touched the control there and it span round and did it, whatever it does, so I was like "oh" better not touch that again. I: Did the lamp seem alive to you? P12: Not really, well that's funny cause I did say sorry to it so that kind of implies that I was treating it as a sentient being. [...] I could tell it was doing something, I just didn't know what that something meant." (P12)

The 'reaction' of the lamp to her trying to change the light was interpreted as reprimanding and the lamp not allowing her to do it. This situation illustrates how the participant showed a spontaneous social reaction to the lamp despite the disaccord.

Summary

Overall, our participants behaved socially towards the lamp and this happened because they felt they interacted with an intentional character. They saw a purpose in the lamp's actions. The presence of the lamp made them feel observed and therefore more aware of their own actions. Despite its mechanical appearance and movement, the participants perceived the lamp as a cute little assistant that helped them with their tasks.

An interesting finding was that the difference in behaviour - so the difference between session one and session two, which was the additional gaze - was not so apparent to the participants. When being asked if they noticed a difference between the two sessions, only four participants noted that the gaze of the lamp was different in each session. Four more recollected the difference after they have been told about it. This confirms related work stating that relative small changes in autonomous behaviour (for short interactions) are hard to notice for users [24]. Interestingly, the participants preference towards not using gaze turned out to be oppositional to the recommendation from the first study. Although having a 'gaze' helped the participant to understand where the lamp was pointing towards, making eye-contact through gaze was not wanted and felt weird to the majority of participants.

Comparing our findings to literature, it is striking to notice that from our study we find that conveying simple messages is less ambiguous than conveying emotions (reported on in related work). From 84 gestures that were shown to participants, only 24 gestures were not identified correctly. This is due to 10 participants not understanding the cue for 'email arrived', as pointing at the computer was too ambiguous. Furthermore, another pattern that emerged was that participants either understood most of the cues or hardly any. This again underlines the need for customisation.

DISCUSSION

Understanding the broader social consequences of machine autonomy has been identified as a key challenge [13]. To address this, we studied an application scenario in an exploratory way. Our aim is to push the scope for technology innovation in this space. Our contributions further include the following design implications derived from our observations, with the description of what worked well and what didn't.

The situations presented above make visible why and how participants might treat (mechanical) technology as a social actor. Each behaviour describes the people's perception of the lamp but also how they expected to treat the lamp and react to it. This analysis presents a snapshot of situations around autonomous objects giving us deeper insights into human-machine interaction. The vignettes show how participants resolve uncertain situations and otherwise unknown interaction with machines. In throwing our participants into these uncharted situations and leaving them to themselves to figure out the situation and the meaning of the setup, we were able to capture a number of fascinating occurrences and illustrate the richness of social interactions expressed towards mechanical, autonomous technology.

Generally, participants can imagine such a lamp on their desktop, which however requires careful design. Our first study revealed that there are mainly two different ways users imagine desktop devices to convey messages, either by pointing at something or by mimicking basic human postures and movements. We found that users attached great importance to customisation, as the same movement evoked different feelings in users, and therefore movement needs personal adjustment. Unlike most traditional computers and devices that have the same output convention for each user, interactive objects with pro-active behaviour should act with respect to the preferences of the user. In the second study, we showed that it is possible to create a functional and plain looking interface that lets people get emotionally attached and even makes them feel cared for. We explain this by the fact that they saw a purpose in the lamp's actions, which was to assist and support them in their daily tasks. Leaving the purpose of the device open and letting the participants discover it for themselves, while still giving the lamp a function [11], proved successful in our case. We want to close this paper with a discussion on implications for autonomous interface design.

Is anthropomorphism unavoidable?

Our second study showed that an actuated device might be much more acceptable than we thought. When we put our lamp on a desk next to a person working, most participants felt positive about it. As already discussed, previous literature proved that bio-metaphoric resemblances carry pitfalls. However, resort to human or animal like appearance and behaviour can help in understanding cues. For autonomous interfaces this happens quite naturally and is hard to avoid [24]. Therefore, it needs to be carefully balanced. For example, our lamp was interpreted as having an 'eye' to point at things, being able to 'wave an arm' like a human or 'bow' to rest. To communicate different messages, the lamp was treated as a proxy to imitate human behaviour, like 'dancing' or 'sleeping'. Using these 'anthropomorphic affordances' [31] proved successful for communication between the autonomous interface and the user. There is a fine line between borrowing social metaphors which are pleasant, e.g. using gaze to point versus using gaze to make eye contact, which may feel unpleasant.

Social behaviour and norms of technology

In the end, it turned out that the lamp, although being mechanical and its movements functional, was perceived as a social actor and led to rich social behaviour in users. This confirms the literature, an interface doesn't need to resemble animals or other living entities to seem alive and evoke social reactions. The effect that people can't help but treat actuated interfaces, even highly mechanical ones, as social actors has an important implication. Even functional technology needs to contain some knowledge about social norms and retain an awareness of social behaviour (e.g. respect personal space, acknowledge requests with some form of response). This knowledge would make interacting with the lamp pleasant and make sense to the user. People have a socialised understanding of the world, which also extends to autonomous technology. In other words, as soon as we design autonomous behaviour into an interface, we also need to provide a socialised understanding, as there will always be a social response from people.

Transmitting social signals

A great amount of work is put into lamps following a user's face[1]. Interestingly, our study revealed that users might not accept 'mechanical eye-contact' and prefer a more salient and subtle style, which nevertheless seems friendly and inviting. Our participants stated that in a practical setting, not relying on eye contact made it easier to use or ignore the lamp if they want to. Eye contact is a strong social means of communication that doesn't seem to work with mechanical interfaces. It makes the interaction weird as people are not able to understand why the device is 'looking' at them. This is grounded in the fact that human eyes are much more expressive, allowing for more explicit signals, which is not the case with the lamp's top. Because the lamp is constrained, the only sensible output for it is to use its gaze to point, which did work well in the study. Users could confirm to the lamp that they received a cue by simply looking at the device, and this seemed to work well as participants reported this as a convenient way to interact. There were a few more downsides when people interpreted the lamp's actions in a social way. The 'gaze' of the lamp was felt as a form of monitoring, the repeated cues were seen as insisting and not letting the user alone. When the lamp stopped moving, it was seen as 'dead'. We however suspect that careful design could circumvent these, by for example adding slow 'breathing' gestures to keep the lamp alive [39].

CONCLUSION

In this paper, we presented our findings from a study that lets users imagine the usage of an interactive desktop lamp in short encounters to explore first impressions, perceptions and how people start to get familiar with autonomous devices. We discussed the participants' outputs, presented ways in which an interactive lamp can communicate, and explored these in a semi-realistic setting. We closed with insights and design implications for interactive lamps. Users' expectations of smart objects around them that are proactively behaving were gathered, and we showed that a quasi-social behaviour, politeness, and a learning curve in understanding each other are desirable. Interestingly, the finding from the first study, that gaze would make the lamp more interesting, turned out not to be suitable when tested. We further found that people have socialised understandings of mechanical movement and therefore interactive technology needs to include knowledge about social norms. With this work, we aim to open up design spaces, and inspire and generate new ideas for actuated interfaces.

ACKNOWLEDGEMENTS

This work is partly supported by the Engineering and Physical Sciences Research Council, EP/N014243/1. The research data on which this paper is based is provided in this paper. Ethical approval has been granted by Newcastle University, Ref:10196/2016.

[1]Pinokio (ben-dror.com/pinokio), Anados (anodos.co.jp/ral), Junior (trieuvyluu.nl/living-lamps)

REFERENCES

1. Accessed: 2017-12-08. *An Actuated Desktop Lamp - Instructable.* http://www.instructables.com/member/DianaN.
2. Greenfield Adam. 2006. Everyware: The Dawning Age of Ubiquitous Computing. (2006).
3. Patrick Bader, Valentin Schwind, Norman Pohl, Niels Henze, Katrin Wolf, Stefan Schneegass, and Albrecht Schmidt. 2015. Self-Actuated Displays for Vertical Surfaces. In *Human-Computer Interaction–INTERACT 2015*. Springer, 282–299.
4. Gilles Bailly, Sidharth Sahdev, Sylvain Malacria, and Thomas Pietrzak. 2016. LivingDesktop: Augmenting Desktop Workstation with Actuated Devices. In *Proceedings of the 2016 CHI Conference on Human Factors in Computing Systems*. ACM, 5298–5310.
5. Christoph Bartneck, E Croft, and D Kulic. 2008. Measuring the anthropomorphism, animacy, likeability, perceived intelligence and perceived safety of robots. In *Metrics for HRI Workshop, Technical Report*, Vol. 471. Citeseer, 37–44.
6. Timothy Bickmore, Daniel Mauer, Francisco Crespo, and Thomas Brown. 2007. Persuasion, task interruption and health regimen adherence. In *International Conference on Persuasive Technology*. Springer, 1–11.
7. Cynthia Breazeal. 2002. *Designing Sociable Robots*. MIT Press, Cambridge, MA, USA.
8. K. Dautenhahn. 2002. Design spaces and niche spaces of believable social robots. In *Proc. 11th IEEE International Workshop on Robot and Human Interactive Communication*. 192–197.
9. Matthew P DeVito and Karthik Ramani. 2014. Talking to TAD: Animating an Everyday Object for Use in Augmented Workspaces. In *ASME 2014 International Design Engineering Technical Conferences and Computers and Information in Engineering Conference*. American Society of Mechanical Engineers, V01BT02A025–V01BT02A025.
10. William Gaver, Mike Michael, Tobie Kerridge, Alex Wilkie, Andy Boucher, Liliana Ovalle, and Matthew Plummer-Fernandez. 2015. Energy Babble: Mixing Environmentally-Oriented Internet Content to Engage Community Groups. In *Proceedings of the 33rd Annual ACM Conference on Human Factors in Computing Systems (CHI '15)*. ACM, New York, NY, USA, 1115–1124.
11. William W. Gaver, Jacob Beaver, and Steve Benford. 2003. Ambiguity As a Resource for Design. In *Proc. of CHI '03*. ACM, 233–240.
12. Fabian Gerlinghaus, Brennand Pierce, Torsten Metzler, Iestyn Jowers, Kristina Shea, and Gordon Cheng. 2012. Design and emotional expressiveness of Gertie (An open hardware robotic desk lamp). In *RO-MAN, 2012 IEEE*. IEEE, 1129–1134.
13. John Helmes, Alex S Taylor, Xiang Cao, Kristina Höök, Peter Schmitt, and Nicolas Villar. 2011. Rudiments 1, 2 & 3: design speculations on autonomy. In *Proceedings of the fifth international conference on Tangible, embedded, and embodied interaction*. ACM, 145–152.
14. Guy Hoffman and Wendy Ju. 2014. Designing Robots With Movement in Mind. *Journal of Human-Robot Interaction* 3, 1 (2014), 89–122.
15. Heather Höpfl and Alison Hirst. 2011. Settlers, vagrants and mutual indifference: unintended consequences of hot-desking. *Journal of Organizational Change Management* 24, 6 (2011), 767–788.
16. Nassim Jafarinaimi, Jodi Forlizzi, Amy Hurst, and John Zimmerman. 2005. Breakaway: An Ambient Display Designed to Change Human Behavior. In *Ext. Abstracts CHI'05*. ACM, 1945–1948.
17. Brigitte Jordan and Austin Henderson. 1995. Interaction analysis: Foundations and practice. *The journal of the learning sciences* 4, 1 (1995), 39–103.
18. Jinyung Jung, Seok-Hyung Bae, and Myung-Suk Kim. 2013a. Three Case Studies of UX with Moving Products. In *Proceedings of the 2013 ACM International Joint Conference on Pervasive and Ubiquitous Computing (UbiComp '13)*. ACM, New York, NY, USA, 509–518.
19. Jinyung Jung, Seok-Hyung Bae, Joon Hyub Lee, and Myung-Suk Kim. 2013b. Make It Move: A Movement Design Method of Simple Standing Products Based on Systematic Mapping of Torso Movements & Product Messages. In *Proceedings of the SIGCHI Conference on Human Factors in Computing Systems (CHI '13)*. ACM, New York, NY, USA, 1279–1288.
20. Hyun Young Kim, Bomyeong Kim, and Jinwoo Kim. 2016. The Naughty Drone: A Qualitative Research on Drone as Companion Device. In *Proceedings of the 10th International Conference on Ubiquitous Information Management and Communication*. ACM, 91.
21. Hung-Sheng Lin, Yi-Tung Shen, Tzu-Han Lin, and Pei-Chun Lin. 2014. Disco lamp: An interactive robot lamp. In *Automation Science and Engineering (CASE), 2014 IEEE International Conference on*. IEEE, 1214–1219.
22. Diana Löffler, Alexandra Kaul, and Jörn Hurtienne. 2017. Expected Behavior and Desired Appearance of Insect-Like Desk Companions. In *Proceedings of the Eleventh International Conference on Tangible, Embedded, and Embodied Interaction (TEI '17)*. ACM, New York, NY, USA, 289–297.
23. Diana Löffler, Takashi Toriizuka, Yuki Sakakibara, Philipp Schaper, and Jörn Hurtienne. 2015. Examining the design space of insect inspired notifications. In *Proceedings of the 2015 ACM International Joint Conference on Pervasive and Ubiquitous Computing and Proceedings of the 2015 ACM International Symposium on Wearable Computers*. ACM, 145–148.

24. Diana Nowacka, Nils Y Hammerla, Chris Elsden, Thomas Plötz, and David Kirk. 2015. Diri-the actuated helium balloon: a study of autonomous behaviour in interfaces. In *Proceedings of the 2015 ACM International Joint Conference on Pervasive and Ubiquitous Computing*. ACM, 349–360.
25. Diana Nowacka and David Kirk. 2014. Tangible autonomous interfaces (TAIs): Exploring autonomous behaviours in tuis. In *Proc. of TEI '14*. ACM, 1–8.
26. Ivan Poupyrev, Tatsushi Nashida, and Makoto Okabe. 2007. Actuation and Tangible User Interfaces: The Vaucanson Duck, Robots, and Shape Displays. In *Proceedings of the 1st International Conference on Tangible and Embedded Interaction (TEI '07)*. ACM, New York, NY, USA, 205–212.
27. David A Price. 2009. *The Pixar touch: The making of a company*. Vintage.
28. Byron Reeves and Clifford Nass. 1996. *The Media Equation: How People Treat Computers, Television, and New Media Like Real People and Places*. Cambridge University Press.
29. Tiago Ribeiro and Ana Paiva. 2012. The illusion of robotic life: principles and practices of animation for robots. In *Proceedings of the seventh annual ACM/IEEE international conference on Human-Robot Interaction*. ACM, 383–390.
30. Yea-Kyung Row and Tek-Jin Nam. 2014. CAMY: Applying a Pet Dog Analogy to Everyday Ubicomp Products. In *Proceedings of the 2014 ACM International Joint Conference on Pervasive and Ubiquitous Computing (UbiComp '14)*. ACM, New York, NY, USA, 63–74.
31. Michael Schmitz. 2011. Concepts for life-like interactive objects. In *Proc. of TEI 2011*. ACM, 157–164.
32. F Thomas and O Johnson. 1981. Disney the Illusion of Life. (1981).
33. Brygg Ullmer and Hiroshi Ishii. 1997. The metaDESK: models and prototypes for tangible user interfaces. In *Proceedings of the 10th annual ACM symposium on User interface software and technology*. ACM, 223–232.
34. AJN Van Breemen. 2004. Bringing robots to life: Applying principles of animation to robots. In *Proceedings of Shapping Human-Robot Interaction workshop held at CHI 2004*. Citeseer, 143–144.
35. Ron Wakkary, Doenja Oogjes, Sabrina Hauser, Henry Lin, Cheng Cao, Leo Ma, and Tijs Duel. 2017. Morse Things: A Design Inquiry into the Gap Between Things and Us. In *Proceedings of the 2017 Conference on Designing Interactive Systems (DIS '17)*. ACM, New York, NY, USA, 503–514.
36. Mark Weiser and John Seely Brown. 1997. The coming age of calm technology. In *Beyond calculation*. Springer, 75–85.
37. Brian Whitworth and Hokyoung Ryu. 2008. A comparison of human and computer information processing. *Encyclopedia of Multimedia Technology and Networking, Second Edition* (2008).
38. Jacob O Wobbrock, Meredith Ringel Morris, and Andrew D Wilson. 2009. User-defined gestures for surface computing. In *Proceedings of the SIGCHI Conference on Human Factors in Computing Systems*. ACM, 1083–1092.
39. Oren Zuckerman and Guy Hoffman. 2015. Empathy Objects: Robotic Devices as Conversation Companions. In *Proceedings of the Ninth International Conference on Tangible, Embedded, and Embodied Interaction*. ACM, 593–598.

Morphology Extension Kit: A Modular Robotic Platform for Physically Reconfigurable Wearables

Sang-won Leigh[1] Timothy Denton[1] Kush Parekh[2] William Peebles[1] Magnus Johnson[1] Pattie Maes[1]
[1]MIT Media Lab, Cambridge, MA USA
[2]Rhode Island School of Design, Providence, RI, USA
sangwon@media.mit.edu twdenton@mit.edu kparekh@risd.edu {wpeebles, magnetron}@mit.edu pattie@media.mit.edu

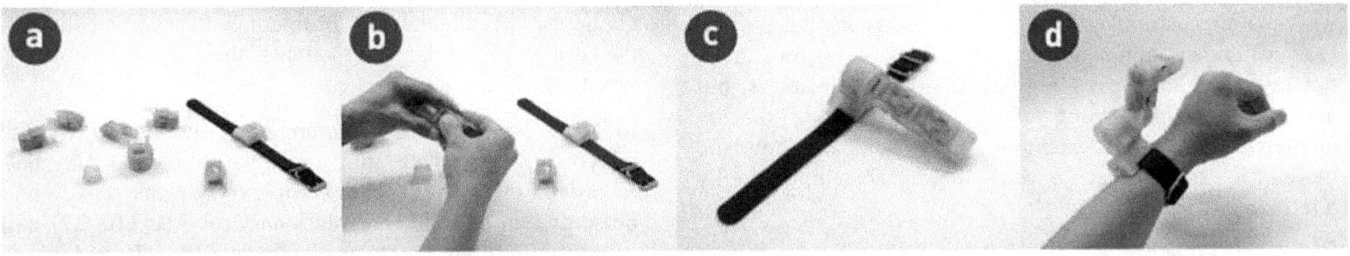

Figure 1: a) modules for robot assembly b) the modules are connected by a single clasp action c) an assembled robot connected to the wrist attachment module d) the robot in action, worn on a user's wrist

ABSTRACT
Various forms of wearable robotics challenge the notion of the human body, in that the robots render the acquired capabilities in physical forms. However, majority of such systems are designed for specific purposes, where rapidly changing environments pose a diverse set of problems that are difficult to solve with a single interface. To address this, we propose a modular hardware platform that allows its users or designers to build and customize wearable robots. The process of building an augmentation is simply to connect actuator and sensor blocks and attach them to the body. The current list of designed components includes servomotor modules and sensor modules, that can be programmed to incorporate additional electronics for desired sensing capabilities. Our electrical and mechanical connector designs can be extended to utilize any motors within afforded power, size, and weight constraints. We also show how our platform can be used in various applications, in addition to how the proposed design can be extended as well as challenges for future systems.

Author Keywords
Synergistic Interaction; Hardware Platform; Modular Robotics;

TEI '18, March 18–21, 2018, Stockholm, Sweden

ACM ISBN 978-1-4503-5568-1/18/03…$15.00
https://doi.org/10.1145/3173225.3173239

ACM Classification Keywords
• Human-centered computing~Human computer interaction (HCI)

INTRODUCTION
Research in the field of augmented human has focused on increasing human capabilities through artificial systems worn on the body. With the growing interest towards the use of physical media in Human-Computer Interaction (HCI), it is not difficult to imagine the potential of augmenting the output (or motor) capability of human users, that is highly computation-driven.

The idea of cyborgs [6] has been a popular topic in science fiction literature since the invention of the concept in the 1960s. However, when it comes to an actual realization, there is only limited space on the human body for adding robotic components. In addition to that, a specific-purpose body-integrated device may not be sufficient [4, 11, 12] for the variety of problems we encounter every day.

The modular design of the human body makes it effective at dealing with rapidly changing physical environments [5]. However, the level of versatility of the human body is often hard to achieve through robotic systems, due to how much sensor or motor technologies have to be embedded for emulating the human biomechanics. Furthermore, an extended use of the type of augmentation can be unnecessary, or even cumbersome, as robotic interfaces are often designed for a particular application.

To address that, we propose a hardware platform, a modular robotic assembly kit, that allows for customizing and building motor augmentations on demand. The process of building one is straightforward – it is simply to connect robotic modules together and attach those to a base station worn on the wrist. We implemented two types of servomotor modules, and an interchangeable tip module that can be modified to serve different sensing or effector functionalities. The mechanical/electrical connector design of the modules can be incorporated in the design of new modules with any desired features, making them compatible with the rest of the modules in our system. This paper extends on a partial report from [13], articulating the design and implementation of the system in depth.

Through implemented applications, we showcase how robotically embodied actors on the body can be used, as well as how customized shapes or functions can be utilized. Our design accommodates augmentations of various kinds, not only including conventional robotics applications, but also ones in the scope of HCI. Finally, we discuss challenges in further extending the system and how the modularity of our design could be further improved by alternative designs.

RELATED WORK

Here we discuss research in wearable robots and robotic user interfaces. Through that, we identify the gap between the state-of-the-art in robotic interfaces and what is potentially needed to realize versatile robotic augmentations of the body.

Supernumerary Robot

Supernumerary Robots (SR) [19, 25, 26] is a recently established field of research exploring extra robotic fingers or limbs added to the human body, unlike exoskeletons and prostheses that are designed for offering amplified performance [9, 15] or replacements for the loss of body parts with equivalent ones [3]. SRs are often designed in a wearable form and work in parallel with the human limbs.

While various forms of SR systems are proposed – SR fingers [25, 26], arms [19], and so on, there have been few investigations into SR systems that go beyond emulating existing limbs of a person. One example could be a shape-changing wearable robot [12] that demonstrated versatile usages. However, its fixed configuration and number of parts potentially limit its adaptability, and can be redundant when not all parts are being actively utilized.

Although not an SR system, IKO Creative Prosthetic System [2] is a platform for kids, that allows for playful customization of their own prosthetic arms using LEGO parts. All of its components are passive, however, it presents a good example of customizing the body.

Shape Changing / Robotic Interfaces

Shape displays have been utilized to create reconfigurable physical shapes for a broad range of applications: dynamically rendering data or affordances in physical forms [7], or embodying a user's body in alternate forms for telepresence applications [14]. While shape displays can support a wide range of shape rendering, their use is constrained due to their limited mobility and 2.5D representation in the current state-of-the-art.

Other shape changing mechanisms such as actuator chains [17, 18, 22, 23] can offer more 3D shapes and portability. ChainForm [17] presents a modular hardware system that contains servomotors, LEDs, and touch sensors. However, these projects focus largely on shape-changing aspects, and offer limited insight into robustness, assembly, or force actuation – that are critical for robots that perform physical operations.

Modular Hardware System

This section describes hardware systems that attempt to challenge the adaptability problem we discussed, through the use of modular components that are assembled to constitute a functional system.

In HCI, Topobo [20] is a tangible construction kit with which one can create animated assemblies and play back recorded motions. More complex systems have been presented in the field of evolutionary robotics [10, 27], self-assembling robots such as furniture [24, 27] and blocks [21]. The self-assembly or self-replicating capability of those robots show a promising potential towards realizing a fully reconfigurable hardware system. However, the actuation mechanisms offered by those systems are not suitable for wearables [21], or are too bulky in size and weight since each module requires self-contained power sources.

DESIGN CONSIDERATIONS

As discussed in the introduction section, our main goal is to achieve versatility, ease of use, and potential customizability in the design of wearable robots. The key design features we identify as required are modularity and a universal connector design across modules.

Modularity

Since different applications require different sets of actuators, sensors, and end effectors, our platform design emphasizes the combination of three interchangeable types of modules: actuator modules, sensor modules, and shape modules.

Actuator modules can be chained in series (figure 1b) (and possibly in a more complex network structure with branching modules designed), and constitute the main body of a final assembly. We demonstrate an implementation of a pitch angle module (figure 3), that offers a 1D rotational motion and an encoder that streams the motor's position to a base (master) microcontroller.

Sensor (tip) modules can accommodate up to two sensors (since the electronics design has two analog read pins available, see electronics design section) and stream sensor data back to the base microcontroller. Shape modules can take passive forms that act as effector affordances [8]. A module can also act both as a sensor and a passive shape at the same time. (figure 4)

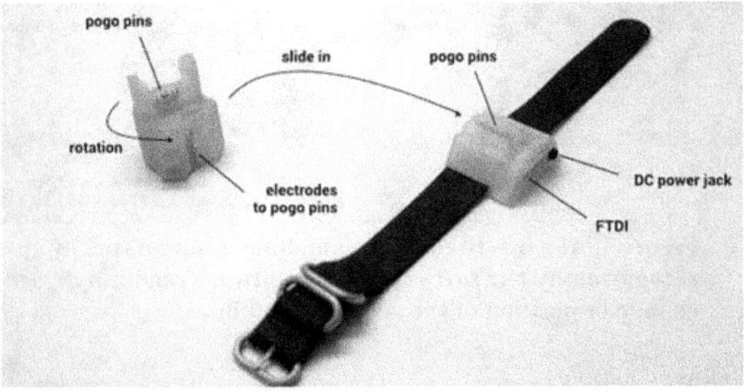

Figure 2: the wristband attachment module (right), and the rotational modules (left) that connects to the attachment module

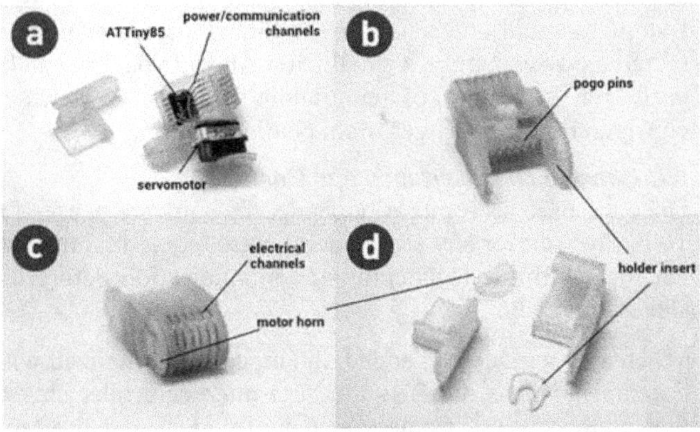

Figure 3: a) the internal view of the pitch module, the wires for the connector are embedded in channel structures b) front view: female connectors have pogo pins c) rear view: mail connectors have annular copper channels that get in contact with the pogo pins d) 3D printed parts for the module. The motor horn and the insert have clasp structures that hold connected modules together

Connector Design

A critical design requirement is to implement the same mechanical and electrical connectors across all different modules, so that users are not restricted to a specific order of assembly.

For modules that involve movements, the male connectors have annular electrical channels (figure 3c) on which pins on the female connectors (figure 3b) can slide along. In this way, moving parts can be utilized without taking up extra space for embedding the moving parts within the modules themselves.

The connector design can also be utilized in designs of new modules, by simply importing the connectors into the new model. Therefore, different actuators or modules with alternative shapes can easily be created.

Ease of Assembly and Robustness

The modules are attached to each other through a single “clasp” action (figure 1b), where electrical channels embedded in the mechanical connectors (figure 3b-c) get into contact once the modules are connected. After the electrical connection is made, our software automatically detects the change in the overall structure and update the connection map (figure 7a). Hence, there is no effort required from the user other than simply plugging the modules together (and no wires required like in other daisy chain systems [17, 18, 23]).

Figure 4: different tip module designs – (from left to right) trigger, pick holder, sensor tip, knob tip, LEGO connector

In addition to that, for the system to have force capability comparable to that of the human fingers, the mechanical connector should be able to withstand load that includes the weight of the actuators needed for the force actuation. Especially, compared to other modular interface systems discussed earlier, our system requires motors with stronger torque capacity and more reliable mechanical connector design.

IMPLEMENTATION

Physical Design

The structure of the modules is made primarily of a clear photopolymer using a Multi-Jet Modeling additive manufacturing process [1]. The robot is hereby custom-made, torque-dense, and composed of lightweight components.

Attachment Module (figure 2 right)

A small part shaped to hug the wrist; this module houses the base microcontroller. It is designed for the addition of further attachment modules alongside it as well as simple connection with a rotational module using a “dove tail” clasp.

Rotational Module (figure 2 left)

Coupled with the attachment module, the rotational module effectively performs the same function as the human forearm and wrist: rotation about the axis along the length of the fully extended fingers. This module is the starting point for further modules to be attached.

Pitch Module (figure 3)

The main building block of the robot, the pitch module functions as a human knuckle, with 180 degrees of motion relative to its base. The modules are daisy-chained together, connected via clasping structures on their motor horns and clasp inserts (figure 3d). The clasping structure and inserts allow for easy assembly while maintaining load/shock bearing capacity.

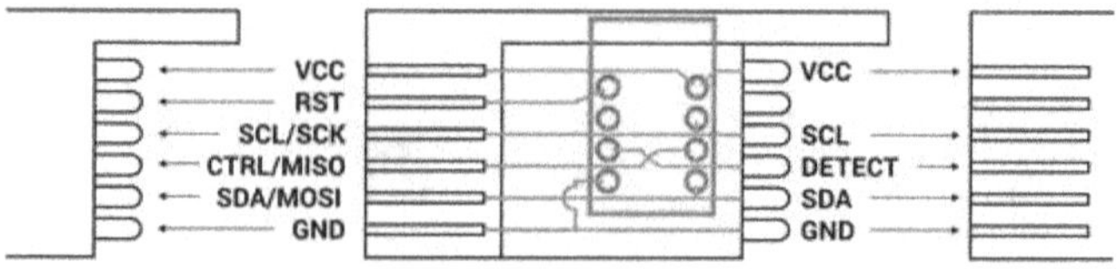

Figure 5: wire diagram for electrical connections, each module shares the same channels for power and I2C

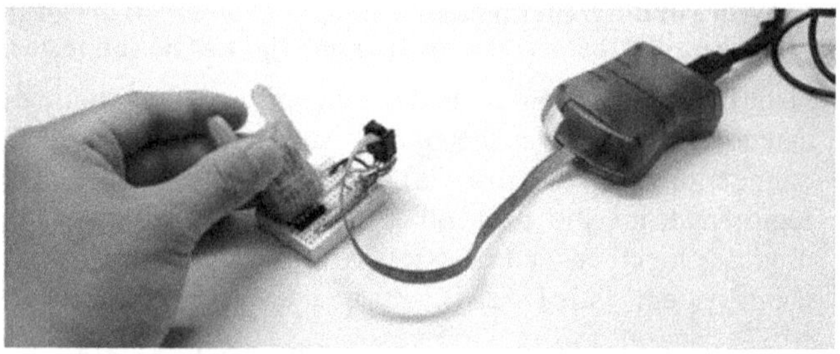

Figure 6: programming a module is done by simply placing the module on a jig connected to an ISP programmer

Tip Module (figure 4)
Possibly the most customizable part of our platform, the tip module is much like a human fingertip with sensing and effector functionalities. The design of this module, however, is not limited to a tip form. It can also have both male and female connectors and potentially be placed in the middle of a module chain.

Electronics and Software

Each module contains an ATtiny 85 microcontroller, and is powered through the module chain (figure 5). To reduce complexity and increase structural robustness, wires (except for the ones that go to other electronic components such as actuators or sensors) are enclosed in channel structures on the outside casing (figure 3a).

Power Transfer and I2C Communication
Power (input voltage, ground) and I2C communication channels are connected through pogo pins and annular copper channels (figure 3b-c, figure 5). When two modules are plugged together, the pogo pins are placed on and pushed against the copper channels - electrically, all the modules connected in parallel.

Programming a Module
The annular channels (figure 3c) are used for ISP programming as well. RST and MISO pins along with the four pins used (power and I2C) are exposed through the channels; therefore, microcontrollers on a module can be flashed simply by placing the module on a programming jig (figure 6). USB ports on the modules can be used for power if needed for programming.

The programming step defines the input/output of a specific module, and once that is done, no further programming is required. It sets the module's type, values to be read and sent back to the base microcontroller, and how the command value is utilized (e.g. angle values from the control software applied to the control of servomotors).

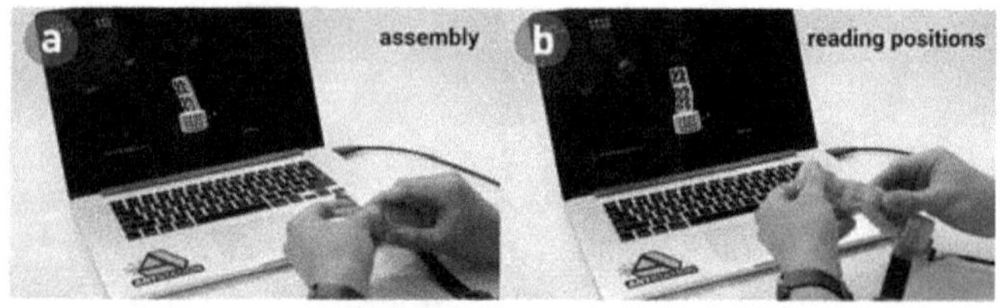

Figure 7: a) a newly connected module is automatically recognized by our software b) the software reads any change in position of the robot in real time

Power Supply
In the current implementation, power is provided through an FTDI cable or a 2.1 mm DC power jack on the attachment module (figure 2). USB 3.0 (900mA) provides sufficient power for a continuous operation of a robot with five motors and one sensor tip modules. Instead of using a tethered power supply, a small 850mAh LiPo battery can be used for an hour of continuous actions in such a configuration (and longer if not continuous).

I2C Connection Initialization and Control
Once the base servomotor boots up, the software pauses for 100ms to wait for any slave microcontrollers to initialize, as I2C may fail due to attempting communication before the slaves are ready.

When a new module is added, the module is initialized with a default address of 127 - the base microcontroller checks that address every frame. Once the module and the base establishes communication, the base assigns a new address to that module and updates the list of modules connected (figure 7). DETECT pins (figure 5) on each module is used to infer where the new module is connected to. Once a module stops responding to the base, a timeout is called and the base microcontroller updates the connection map with the module's removal.

Once the connection is established, commands from either the base microcontroller or a computer (connected through a serial channel with the base microcontroller) is sent to each individual module specified by its address. Read data from each module (such as servomotor angle or sensor data) is collected by the base microcontroller, and also streamed back to the computer for an application software to use.

Authoring Applications
Developing an application for the system requires three components: configuration, input signals, and robot behaviors. The configuration describes the number of modules used for the chain as well as the functionality of a tip module. This way the implemented application can send control signals to corresponding modules correctly, as well as interpreting received signals from each module properly. Input signals can be anything based on the application such as electromyography signal, button inputs, or any other external sensor data. Based on the information, the behavior of the robot is programmed as trajectories of angle value changes in each motor. It can be a linear mapping between

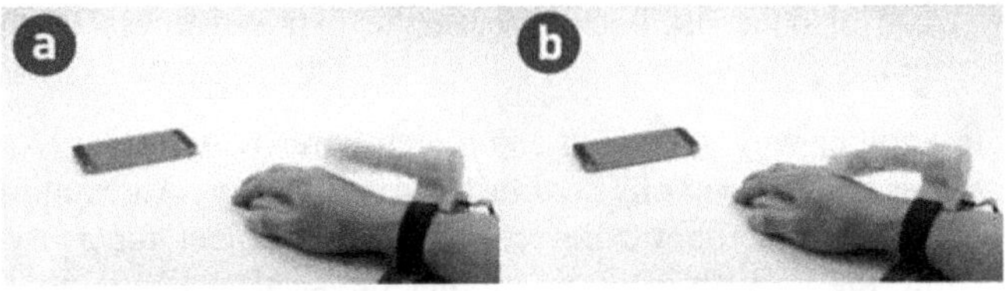

Figure 8: the robot can be used for interpersonal haptic communication – the robot taps on the hand once received a message from a friend or a family member

an input signal and motor actions as shown in [12], or automatically triggered behaviors as will be shown in the next section.

APPLICATIONS

Here we present two categories of applications using our system. The first category describes how robotic companions can assist in forms of notification, intervention, or instruction. The other category illustrates the robotic system's use in more traditional HCI contexts such as physical user interfaces. The applications also illustrate customized modules in addition to the servomotor chain, demonstrating the system's customizability in comparison to the previous iteration [12].

The use the robotic joints as prosthetic (or supernumerary) robotic actors is not covered in this manuscript since that has been studied widely in the field of robotics. We suggest referring to [12, 25, 26] for conventional SR applications and control strategies for those. However, our robotic design will certainly be effective in that context.

In the presented examples, mostly a single robotic finger on the wrist is used. However, a user can have multiple robots by wearing more than one attachment module, and the module can be mounted on different parts of the body as well (such as on a belt or the ankle).

Action-Capable Companion

In this category of application, we discuss the use of body worn robotic interfaces as a semi-autonomous agent. In the implementation of these applications, the robot is controlled through software triggers, such as sensor value changes or events defined by a user. Therefore, the robot can suggest behavior change or provide new information to the user, where it can closely engage in the user's physical space.

The robot can notify the user about an unread text message from a close friend or a family member, by a gentle tap on the hand (figure 8). The type of a notification can increase intimacy and can be an effective means in interpersonal communications. It can also be triggered differently based on the sender's ID and so on by parsing notification from the phone's operating system. Thereby, based on who is sending or how urgent the message is, the robot can render different types of physical triggers.

Similar implementation can benefit the user by helping the user to better focus through physical interventions. When set in focus-assist mode, one can set event triggers that

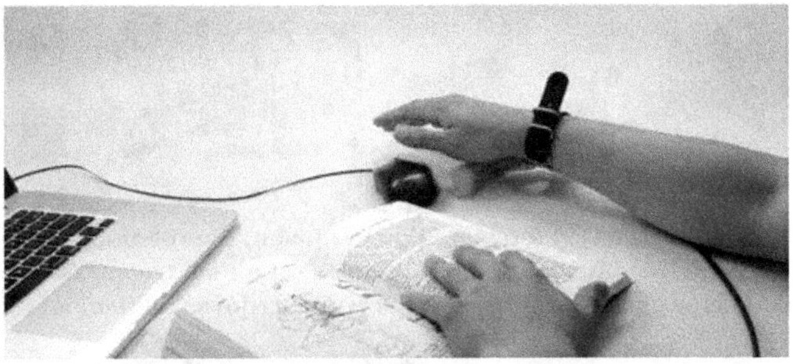

Figure 9: the robot can help the user to disengage from distraction through physical interventions

describe the distracted state of a user. Our demo software detects mouse movements on a computer, thereby, a detected operation on the computer will trigger the robot to push the mouse away from the user's hand (Figure 9). Proximity sensors can potentially be used to detect the user's hand approaching the mouse, and preemptively stop the user from using the computer (as illustrated in the video figure.)

Prescript motions of the robot can be utilized further for instruction purposes as well. A guitar stroke pattern can be downloaded to a user's robot and teach the user how to execute a certain rhythm pattern (figure 10a). The user would need to swap the finger tip of the robot to a pick holding structure (figure 10b). The learning session can be interactive and customized upon the user's initiative since the robotic behavior is programmable. For example, the user can change the speed of the demonstration, and interrupt the demonstration whenever s/he would like to try on the guitar by oneself.

A sensor tip module can also be utilized to detect potential hazard to a user and alert the user. For example, a temperature sensor embedded in the tip (figure 11) can sense areas or objects with high temperature, such as a soldering iron or a glue gun left turned on. The robot

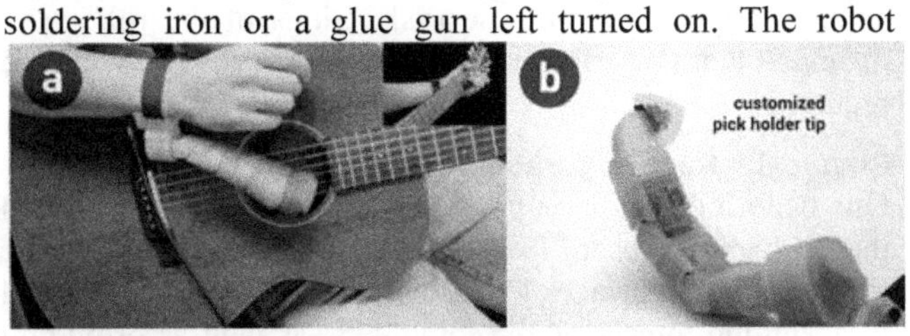

Figure 10: the tip module can be designed to perform variety of operations e.g. holding a pick (b), in turn allowing the robot to instruct a range of physical tasks such as how to play a guitar

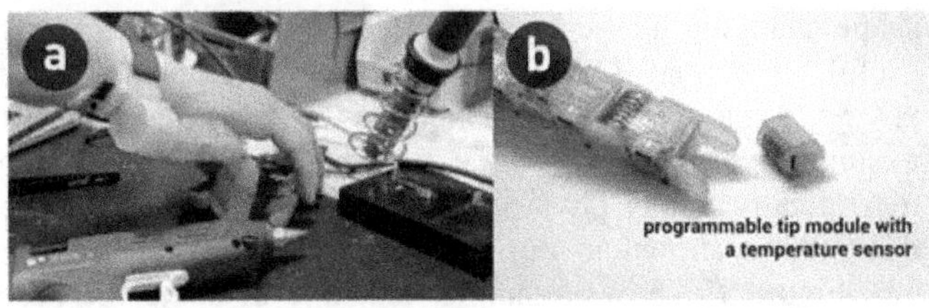

Figure 11: a temperature sensor equipped tip (b) can be used to alert the user about potentially dangerous environments, through a reflexive behavior of the robot

Figure 12: a) gun trigger tip mounted b) the robot used as a gaming interface c-d) running out of ammo triggers a shape change, notifying the user of a required action

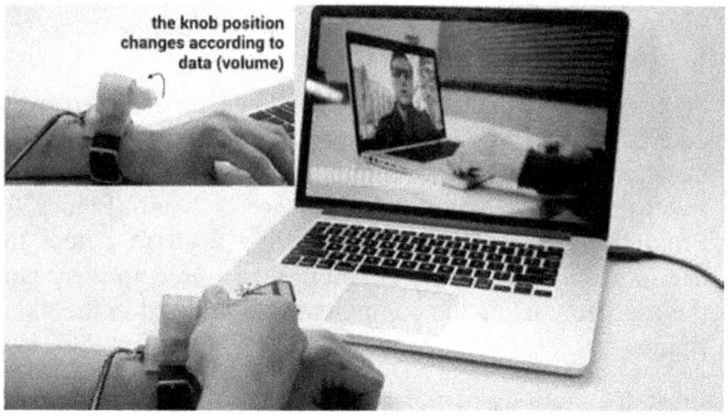

Figure 13: the wearable robot is also an always-available control interface, capable of haptic feedbacks

displays reflexive behaviors to warn the user, or the user can use the robot as a probe before touching an object. The current implementation suffers from slow response time and the need for accurate calibration of the thresholds, but potentially more quick responsive components such as IR based sensors can enable just-in-time interventions.

The implementation of robotic motions in the examples are written as reusable software snippets, therefore, our software pipeline allows for potential applications to follow IFTTT style programming. A user or a designer does not need to implement the entire control system. Only relatively simple scripts describing desired actions of the robot and the event that will trigger the motions respectively would be required.

Physically Reconfigurable Affordances

One benefit of having a physically reconfigurable system is that it can be used to render physical affordances for forming user interfaces [7]. Such capabilities can be useful in designing interfaces for computers, as well as providing opportunity to create simple robotic systems that assist in physical tasks.

One way for this system to be used is an always-available, shape changing haptic interface. This feature is particularly useful for Virtual Reality (VR) applications, since it is not always intuitive to execute commands with hand gestures or a single type of controller. A reconfigurable robot can dynamically adjust physical affordances and behaviors on demand, as shown in our gun controller example (figure 12). Figure 13 shows a simpler example of using the base rotational module as a TV controller without employing the entire chain of motors. Other fingertip form factors (Figure 4) can also be used to increase the expressiveness of the system.

In another way, the robot can be temporarily detached from a user and offload physical tasks from the user. An example would be the robotic device holding an object for a user, while the user engages in another physical task. Figure 14 shows a user learning to play a song on a guitar while reading a score. However, playing guitar requires both hands to be occupied. The robot attached to the guitar head then holds the user's phone and display the score to the user, freeing both of the user's hands.

Potentially, a detached robot can execute more complex behaviors such as fetching objects from a distant location. Such future applications would be useful for users needing to stay in a constrained space (e.g. patients in hospitals) or to pay continuous attention to a task while requiring other operations to be executed at the same time. Especially with the upcoming availability of internet-of-things platforms, a customizable robotic system can offer more ability for users to arrange their physical environments and what they can do.

DISCUSSION AND FUTURE RESEARCH

Here we provide further information on our design, including durability of the current prototypes and how to further expand the design. We also shed light on limitations and potential challenges towards realizing future systems.

Exertion Capability and Robustness

The motor we used has a relatively good torque density of 5N·cm/cm^3 (2.0 kg-cm stall torque at 4.8V power supply). The amount of force it can exert depends on the detailed configuration, but to give a rough idea, a setup of four pitch modules will provide about 0.4kg of force pulling or pinching. Human fingers have 5kg to 7.7kg of tip pinching force [16], and given that such setup is much longer than a finger, the amount of force the robot exerts is well within an order of magnitude from the human fingers. The exertion capability can significantly increase using other types of motors or actuation mechanisms (such as Bowden cables), if heavy duty operations are required.

We also tested the durability of the 3D printed structure. Our measurement shows that the motor horn (figure 3d) starts fracturing at 80N-cm on average, roughly four times

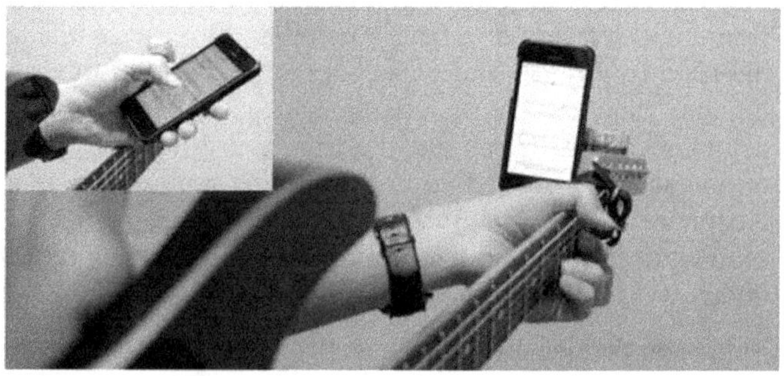

Figure 14: temporarily detached from the user and externally mounted, the robot can give an extra hand

higher than the stall torque provided by the motors. We also checked the clasping mechanism between modules, as it is required to withstand the loads that the modules may encounter along the axis of the connection. After five separate tests with a Newton meter, it is determined that an average force of 42N is required to disconnect a module.

The choice of material also determines these numbers. We initially considered casting the modules in brass for stronger structural integrity, however, the torque density of the motors used allows only maximum of four modules connected in series. Therefore, we decided to use 3D printed modules that met our durability requirements and were also lightweight.

Platform for Wearable Sensor Design

Another application domain our platform can be used for is wearable sensors. Instead of using the wristband module only as an attachment point for motors, sensors and skin contact electrodes can be embedded in the module as well. In addition to that, up to 5 base modules can be attached to the wristband side-by-side, giving room for multiple on body electronics (such as heartrate sensor, skin conductance sensor, electromyography sensor, electrical or thermal stimulators, and so on) to be integrated.

Designing Modules across Scales

One design challenge posed is how to incorporate modules in very different sizes. In our current implementation, all the modules and connectors are designed in the scale of the human hand, restricting the size of potential modules within a certain window.

Therefore, one future direction could be designing adapters for modules in different scales. The size of the current connector is ~27mm x ~17mm, where an adapter can split the connector into two smaller connectors and make room for two smaller modules to be integrated (imagine LEGO blocks having differently sized blocks). Using permutations of such adapters, more sophisticated robotic morphologies can also be achieved. For example, a connector on one end of a motor chain can be split into two smaller chains acting as extra-dexterous fingers.

Limitations and Challenges

The presented system discusses the design and engineering of a modular wearable robotic system and its potential applications. In this section, we discuss a few technical challenges towards realizing a more deployable system. First, a reliable sensing of the environment will be critical for autonomous operations by the system. The examples utilizing the context of a user (shown in the previous section), in practice, pose a critical sensing challenge. Especially for a fully mobile system, it is necessary that the sensing is embedded in a small, wearable form factor. Potentially, a camera- or radar-based inside-out tracking would be required for a real-time and reliable sensing.

Second, designing an ergonomic yet capable wearable robotic system requires further attention to the mechanical design. Most critically, there is a tradeoff between the weight of the system and the force actuation capacity. Therefore, depending on applications or user contexts, different grades of mechanical capacities have to be adopted. In addition to that, the extra weight added to the body requires a period of training or familiarization since it will affect the overall behavior of a user. It is also critical to design a system such that it does not pose too much burden or interfere with regular manipulation tasks.

CONCLUSION

In this paper, we presented a modular hardware platform for designing customizable and physically capable wearable devices. Our design aims to allow users or other designers to develop customized robotic augmentations, by simply connecting modular sensor, actuator, and shape blocks. The constructed robot is attached to a wristband worn on a user's body, and act as a physical extension or an always-available agent to the user. We showcase the capability of our platform through demonstrating servomotor modules and a range of tip modules with sensing or effector functionalities. Using those designed modules, applications are developed to illustrate how the platform can be utilized in actual application contexts. The potential of the system is not limited to what we have presented. The basic components (the universal connectors, and the basic electronic design) can be embedded in any new module design – that incorporates different types of motors or sensors, or with any alternative physical forms. We discussed the durability of our system, yet allowing easy assembly via a single step clasp mechanism, as well as limitations of the current system and potential challenges towards realizing a deployable system in the future.

REFERENCES

1. Stratasys VeroClear material. http://www.stratasys.com/materials/polyjet/transparent
2. Torres, C. IKO Creative Prosthetic System. https://vimeo.com/97877783
3. Carrozza, M. C., Massa, B., Micera, S., Lazzarini, R., Zecca, M., and Dario, P. The development of a novel prosthetic hand-ongoing research and preliminary results. IEEE/ASME Trans. Mechatronics. Aug 2002. http://dx.doi.org/10.1109/TMECH.2002.1011247
4. Clawson, J., Pater, J. A., Miller, A. D., Mynatt, E. D., Mamykina, L. No Longer Wearing: Investigating the Abandonment of Personal Health-Tracking Technologies on Craigslist. In Proc. UbiComp '15. http://dx.doi.org/10.1145/2750858.2807554
5. Clune, J., Mouret, J.B., Lipson, H. The evolutionary origins of modularity. Royel Society B. 2016. http://dx.doi.org/10.1098/rspb.2012.2863
6. Clynes, M. E. and Kline, N. S. Cyborgs and Space. in Astronautics. Sep 1960.
7. Follmer, S., Leithinger, D., Olwal, A., Hogge, A., and Ishii, H. inFORM: dynamic physical affordances and

constraints through shape and object actuation. In Proc. UIST '13. http://dx.doi.org/10.1145/2501988.2502032

8. Gaver, W. Technology affordances. In Proc. CHI 91. ACM Press: NY (1991), 79-84. http://dx.doi.org/10.1145/108844.108856
9. Herr, H. Exoskeletons and orthoses: classification, design challenges and future directions, J. of NeuroEngineering and Rehabilitation. 2009. http://dx.doi.org/10.1186/1743-0003-6-21
10. Kernbach, S., Meister, E., Scholz, O., Humza, R., Liedke, J., Ricotti, L., Jemai, J., Havlik, J., Liu, W. Evolutionary robotics: The next-generation- platform for on-line and on-board artificial evolution. IEEE CEC 2009. http://dx.doi.org/10.1109/CEC.2009.4983066
11. Lazar, A., Koehler, C., Tanenbaum, J., Nguyen, D. H. Why We Use and Abandon Smart Devices. In Proc. UbiComp '15. http://dx.doi.org/10.1145/2750858.2804288
12. Leigh, S., and Maes, P. Body Integrated Programmable Joints Interface. In Proc. CHI '16. http://dx.doi.org/10.1145/2858036.2858538
13. Leigh, S., Maes, P. Morphological Interfaces: On Body Transforming Technologies. Alt. CHI '17. http://dx.doi.org/10.1145/3027063.3052758
14. Leithinger, D., Follmer, S., Olwal, A., Ishii, H. Physical telepresence: shape capture and display for embodied, computer-mediated remote collaboration. In Proc. UIST '14. http://dx.doi.org/10.1145/2642918.2647377
15. Lemley, B. Really Special Forces. Discover 25–26. 2002.
16. Mathiowetz, V., Kashman, N., Volland, G., Weber, K., Dowe, M., Rogers, S. Grip and pinch strength: normative data for adults". Arch Phys Med Rehabil. 1985. http://www.ncbi.nlm.nih.gov/pubmed/3970660
17. Nakagaki, K., Dementyev, A., Follmer, S., Paradiso, J.A., Ishii, H. ChainFORM: A Linear Integrated Modular Hardware System for Shape Changing Interfaces. In Proc. UIST '16. https://doi.org/10.1145/2984511.2984587
18. Nakagaki, K., Follmer, S., Ishii, H. LineFORM: Actuated Curve Interfaces for Display, Interaction, and Constraint. In Proc. UIST '15. http://dx.doi.org/10.1145/2807442.2807452
19. Parietti, F., Asada, H., Chan, K., Bracing the Human Body with Supernumerary Robotic Limbs for Physical Assistance and Load Reduction. In Proc. ICRA '14. http://dx.doi.org/10.1109/ICRA.2014.6906601
20. Raffle, H. S., Parkes, A. J., Ishii, H. Topobo: a constructive assembly system with kinetic memory. In Proc. CHI '04. http://dx.doi.org/10.1145/985692.985774
21. Romanishin, J. W., Gilpin, K., Rus, D. M-Blocks: Momentum-driven, Magnetic Modular Robots. In Proc. IROS '13. http://dx.doi.org/10.1109/IROS.2013.6696971
22. Roudaut, A., Krusteva, D., McCoy, M., Karnik, A., Ramani, K., Subramanian, S. Cubimorph: Designing Modular Interactive Devices. In Proc. ICRA '16. http://dx.doi.org/10.1109/ICRA.2016.7487508
23. Sekiguchi, D., Inami, M., Tachi, S. Robotphone: RUI for interpersonal communication. CHI EA '01. http://dx.doi.org/10.1145/634067.634231
24. Sprowitz, A., Pouya, S., Bonardi, S., Van den Kieboom, J., Möckel, R., Billard, A., Ijspeert, A. J. Roombots: reconfigurable robots for adaptive furniture. In Proc. Computational Intelligence Magazine. 2010. http://dx.doi.org/10.1109/MCI.2010.937320
25. Wu, F. Y. and Asada, H. Bio-Artificial Synergies for Grasp Posture Control of Supernumerary Robotic Fingers. In Robotics: Science and Systems. 2014. http://hdl.handle.net/1721.1/88457
26. Wu, F. Y. and Asada, H. "Hold-and-Manipulate" with a Single Hand Being Assisted by Wearable Extra Fingers. In Proc. ICRA '15. http://dx.doi.org/10.1109/ICRA.2015.7140070
27. Zykov, V., Mytilinaios, E., Adams, B., Lipson, H. Robotics: Self-reproducing Machines. Nature Brief Communications. 2005. http://dx.doi.org/10.1038/435163a

TwistBlocks: Pluggable and Twistable Modular TUI for Armature Interaction in 3D Design

Meng Wang[1,2], Kehua Lei[1], Zhichun Li[3], Haipeng Mi[1], Yingqing Xu[1,2]
[1]Academy of Arts and Design, [2]The lab for Lifelong Learning, [3]Department of Automation
Tsinghua University, Beijing, China
{m-wang16, lkh16, zc-li15}@mails.tsinghua.edu.cn, {mhp, yqxu}@tsinghua.edu.cn

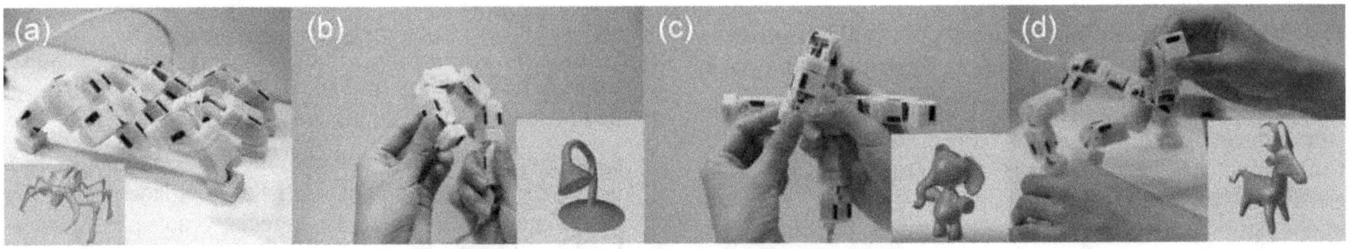

Figure 1. TwistBlocks as physical armatures.

ABSTRACT
The use of armatures is a convenient way of deforming and animating 3D digital models. However, interact with an armature is usually time-consuming, and often requires professional skills. Tangible interfaces, such as building blocks, while having improved the accessibility of digital construction, are still lacking in flexibility and present difficulties in dealing with curved armatures. This paper introduces TwistBlocks, a pluggable and twistable modular TUI that improves the accessibility of 3D modeling and animating by physical armature interaction. TwistBlocks is capable of creating complex armatures with dense branches, and supports a high DOF (Degree of Freedom) in physical manipulation. In addition, a set of software tools are provided for novice users to easily create, rig, and animate models. The global-posture sensing network sensing scheme can also measure the rotation and movement of the physical armature, and enables interaction between multiple models.

Author Keywords
Tangible Input; 3D Design; Skeletal Animation; Non-Rigid Interface; Modular Sensor Network

ACM Classification Keywords
• **Human-centered computing~Interface design prototyping**

TEI '18, March 18–21, 2018, Stockholm, Sweden

ACM ISBN 978-1-4503-5568-1/18/03…$15.00
https://doi.org/10,1145/3173225.3173231

INTRODUCTION
Creating and rigging digital 3D models is a common task in areas such as entertainment, education, and digital fabrication. However, novice users usually find doing this task challenging since it requires lots of experience, professional skill, patience, and time.

Tangible User Interfaces (TUIs) enable direct, hands-on interaction with physical objects. Tangible building blocks, which can be assembled into a complex structure, have been explored in creating both physical and digital models. Generally, 3D design often requires a high flexibility, which may not be easily supported by the traditional rigid TUIs. For example, the armature (aka skeleton) is widely used to provide deformation for a digital model. However, because it consists of many bones with a branched structure, it is not easy to use simple TUIs to control an armature. Recently, modular TUIs have been proposed to deal with the armature manipulation problem [1, 12]. Those methods adopt hierarchical local sensing techniques, limit such methods to have a wider applications.

In this paper, we present TwistBlocks, a novel modular TUI toolkit that improves the accessibility of 3D modeling and animating by physical armature interaction. Our contributions are summarized as follows:

- A pluggable and twistable modular TUI with a compact design that can be assembled into various complex physical armatures that can then be manipulated freely.
- A novel sensing scheme using a global-posture sensing network, which enables measurement of rotation and movement in a global coordinate system and the interaction between multiple armatures.
- A series of software tools that allows novice users to easily rig existing models or to create new models based on a physical armature.

RELATED WORK

Building Virtual Structures with Physical Blocks

Assembly based TUIs have been a hot topic in tangible interface research for a long time. Anderson et al. introduced a method to build virtual structures with LegoTM-like blocks [5] as early as 1999. Kitamura et al. presented ActiveCube [13], which allows for real-time 3D interaction with tangible cubes. Gupta et al. demonstrated the DuploTrack system [2] to track the assembly process of building blocks using computer vision.

Most assembly based TUIs employ rigid building blocks, which are capable for constructing rigid structures but lack flexibility to present curved shapes.

Curve Input

Curve input has been the focus of several research works. Grossman et al. introduced an input device for the manipulation of curves [14]. Rendl et al. presented FlexSense [4], a transparent self-sensing deformable surface. Bächer et al. introduced DefSense [11], an algorithm for the design and fabrication of customized, deformable input devices that are capable of continuously sensing their deformation. Nakagaki et al. demonstrated LineFORM [9], an actuated curve interface.

Sensing techniques have enabled new input methods supporting curved shape interaction in a tangible manner. However, most of them can only interact with a single curve string or an individual deformable surface.

Modular Sensing

Kahn et al. propose the concept of "Smart Dust" for mobile networking [8] in 1999, which is a prototype of modular sensing. Modular sensing is a novel way in HCI to perform a complicated sensing. Topobo [7], presents a 3D constructive assembly system embedded with kinetic memory. Siftables [6], applies wireless sensor networks to tangible user interfaces. SensorTape [3], presents a self-sensing tape and a novel way of detecting/obtaining curve input.

In these modular sensing networks, the sensor nodes are mostly in a static topology. A sensing network with dynamic topology for assembling requires more than one physical network layer in the design.

Armature Interaction

An armature is a very convenient tool for rigging a digital model. Weller et al. presents a computationally-enhanced hub-and-strut construction kit which can generate a simple digital character by physical construction for learning and play [10]. Yoshizaki et al. presented an actuated handheld puppet system for controlling the posture of a virtual character [15] in 2011. Jacobson and Glauser et al. developed a tangible input device as an armature to rig an animation [1, 12]. Their work applies a hierarchical local sensing scheme, which provides good performance in interacting with simple armatures. However, such method will encounter problems while handling a complex armature, and a local sensing system is not applicable for different characters in the same scene.

Based on previous work, we have extended the modular TUIs design for armature interactions in various aspects such as sensing, branching, rigging and modeling.

DESIGN

Considering the limitations of some related work, the following design requirements have been considered during the design process:

- **Global manipulation**. Global sensing enables physical rotation of the whole model, multiple models interaction and presents zero accumulated error in calculation.
- **Compact branching**. The modular block should serve as a polydirectional splitter itself. A compact design can better match more models, especially some with dense branches like the bug in Figure 1.a.
- **DOF of twists**. A digital armature joint has 3 DOFs for twisting. A 3-DOF physical joint (such as a ball and socket joint) can provide a better user experience for manipulation input.

Global Sensing System

The TwistBlocks sensing system consists of a set of assembling blocks and a data collector. The system architecture is shown in Figure 2.

Each block contains a 9-axis IMU (Inertial Measurement Unit), enabling them to measure the rotation in the global coordinate system. Compared with the relative rotation measuring techniques, the armature calculated using a global coordinate data can accurately reflect not only relative bending and twisting of each joint, but also a global manipulation in advance, enabling rotating and movement in one's hand. Additionally, a global coordinate sensing also removes the accumulated error that is always presented in the relative sensing systems.

The blocks, assembled together, collectively become an IMU sensing network. This sensing network consists of two physical layers: an IIC bus for data transmission, and a network between blocks for topology detection and reconstruction.

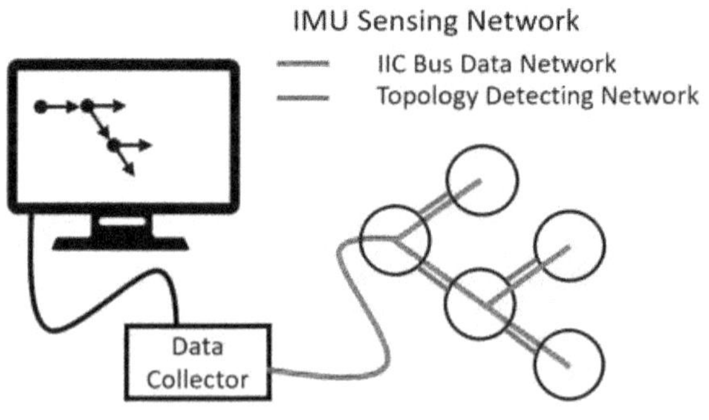

Figure 2. System architecture.

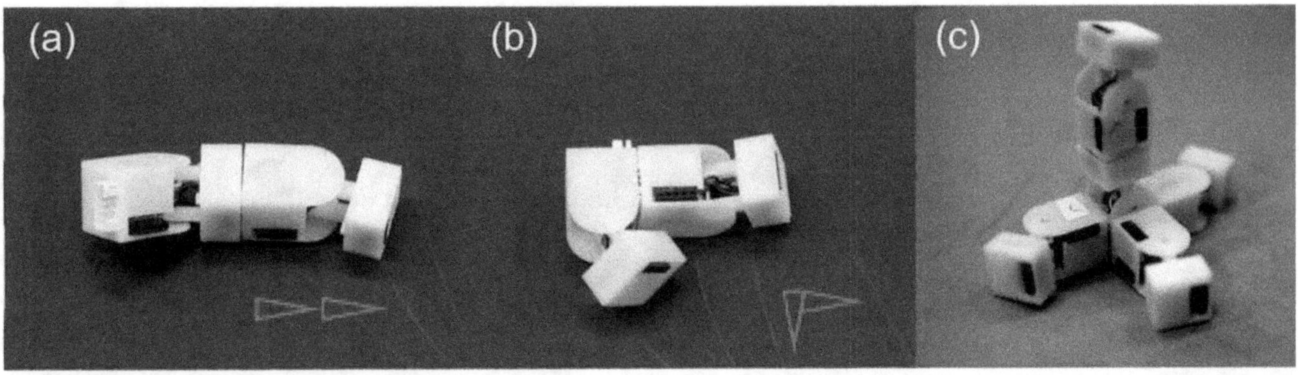

Figure 3. (a) A bottom connector plugged into a top connector, forming a chain connection; (b) A bottom connector plugged into a side connector, forming a side connection; (c) An example armature consists of one chain and three branches.

A data collector is used to consolidate the data and forward them to the computer. Sensors and the data collector simply composes a star-type communication network. Multiple data collectors can work in parallel, so that different sensing networks can work together to support multiple armatures.

Blocks

The design of TwistBlocks is based on building blocks, which has good accessibility for physical construction. Each block contains a twistable articulation and several connectors.

Figure 3 shows how the connectors work. There are three types of connectors in each block module. The *bottom connector* (white) can either match a *top connector* (black) to create a chain connection, or match a *side connector* (black) to create a branch connection. Each block module can have up to four side connectors, allowing other blocks to be connected to it simultaneously. In the latest design we replace the regular PCB connectors with a set of modular battery connectors (Figure 4.Bottom), which provides more robust electronic connection.

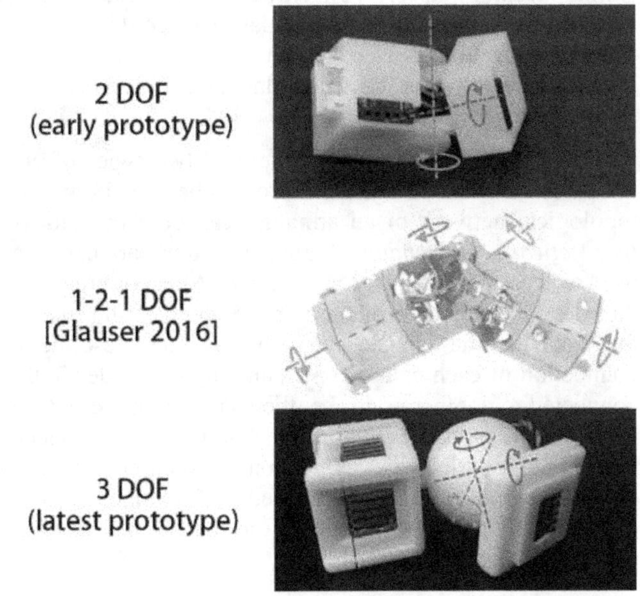

Figure 4. The articulation design of different DOF.

From 2-DOF to 3-DOF

In the first mockup of a modular block, we applied a gimbal structure that enabled two-DOF of rotation in every sensor block (Figure 4.Top). Glauser et al. presented a structure to to increase the DOF by adding two individual rotation DOFs at the end of each node (Figure 4.Middle) [12]. We then improved the joint design of modular blocks by using ball-socket joints (Figure 4.Bottom). This unique 3-DOF joint design can be implemented as the IMU sensing scheme does not need any sensing part within the articulation. With integrated 3-DOFs in one articulation, the ball-socket joints can provide better experiences than the separated 1-2-1 DOF structure.

Branching

An armature is structured as a typical tree network in topology. Each node with two or more child nodes will produce a physical branch in the network. In order to compose such a branch, a specially-designed splitter is usually required. Splitters lead to a greater *rigid area* and longer distances between branches (Figure 5). Having considered these limitations, we designed our modular blocks to be directly pluggable into the sides of one another. This splitter-free design allows for more flexibility in the physical armatures.

As is shown in Figure 5, each branch will inevitably produce a *rigid area*, in which the physical component is rigid and cannot be deformed. In order to achieve the splitter-free design, we integrated the rotation parts and branching connection parts into one block. The small size of the block is also important for hands-on interaction.

With this compact design scheme, we shrank the rigid area and reduced the minimum distance between branches without increasing the size of certain blocks. This improvement makes TwistBlocks more compact and flexible, allowing the built armatures to better match with the desired armatures, especially those with dense branches, such as insects. (Figure 1.a.)

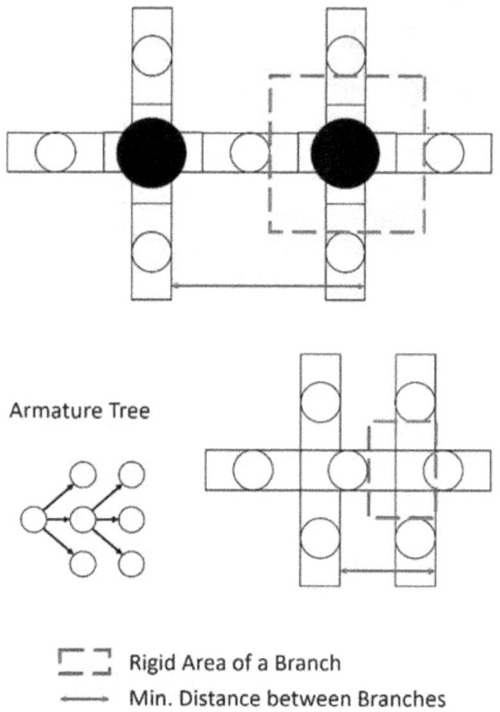

Figure 5. When matching the same armature tree, our design (bottom) shrinks the rigid area and reduces the minimum distance between branches in comparison with a splitter design (top). The two designs have the same block sizes in this figure.

Software

The data collector consolidates the data and forwards them to the computer. We used *Blender*, an open-sourced software, for creating and rigging 3D models. An add-on for *Blender* was developed, which allows the software to receive the sensing data while still maintaining compatibility with *Blender's* functions so professional users can still perform elaborate modifications on their models.

Apart from the generation of a digital armature based on the physical one, the add-on also provides many easy-to-use features, such as the relative deformation tool and the armature-based modeling tool. A detailed description is made in the following application section.

IMPLEMENTATION

Modular Block Hardware

A modular block consists of a controlling circuit board and a few connectors. Connectors are divided into two groups: chain connectors and side connectors. Each block has two chain connectors (one parent and one child), and a few side connectors (all children). Only a parent connector and a child connector can be connected. A compact design was implemented for the modular block resulting in a size of 18mm×18mm×36mm.

Figure 6. The PCB design.

The controlling circuit has a size of 15mm×15mm (Figure 6). An MCU (Micro Controller Unit, ATMEGA328P) and a 9-axis IMU (Inertial Measurement Unit, MPU9150) were integrated on the board. The IMU and the MCU are connected using a software IIC bus. The raw data from the IMU (including gyroscope, accelerometer, and magnetometer) is processed using an onboard DMP (Digital Motion Processor). Calibration is automatically done when the firmware runs for the first time. We fuse the gyroscope and compass data so that the sensor won't produce any obvious yaw drift (within 0.1°) even used continuously for hours. The AHRS (Attitude and Heading Reference System) data of each node is represented by a quaternion.

Due to the fact that the fusion calculation outputs a 3D rotation and that the accuracy/resolution differs when facing different directions, it is difficult to make a precise measurement directly. The compass sensitivity 0.3uT/LSB is roughly 0.3°, and the accelerometer sensitivity 16384LSB/g is roughly 0.003°. This basically provides similar accuracy as [1, 12]. However, in a local sensing system like [1, 12] the 0.5° angular error could produce a 5°angular accumulated error with a 10-node chain. In our global sensing system the accumulated error is always zero.

Topology Detection

In the TwistBlocks system, we defined two types of child branches in the topological network: chain and side. The topological network of an armature can be presented as a *tree network with chains* (Figure 7). Four parameters are used to locate each node: (M, S, C, N). M is a unique value that denotes the chain of the node. S denotes the index of the node in the chain. These two values describe the connection of each chain. If a chain's master node (S=0) is connected to another node (i.e. the start of a branch), C and N are used to record the value of M and S of the connected node. This describes the connection between chains so that the entire topology can be decoded and obtained from the original node data. Table 1 shows the specific description of the parameters.

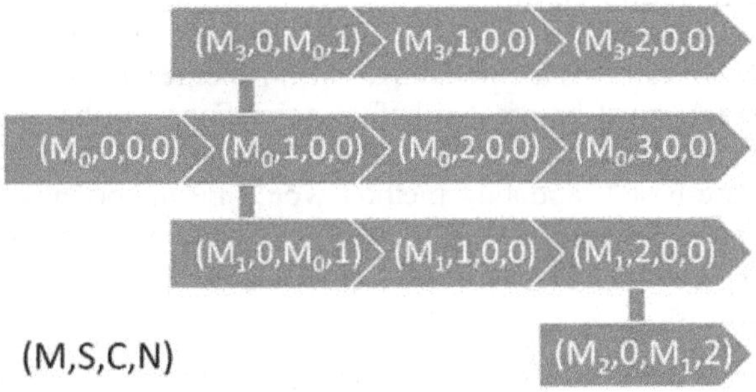

Figure 7. A typical chain tree network.

	Meaning	Value
M	Chain ID	The ID of the master node
S	Slave Index	Position in the chain
C	Connected Chain	M of the connected node
N	Connected Node	S of the connected node

Table 1. Description of the parameters.

A unique ID is burned into the firmware of each node which allows for the recognition in topological network and the avoidance of IIC address conflict. Unidirectional serial connections are used between nodes: the bottom connector contains a RX line, meanwhile the side and top connectors contain two different TX lines. Thus, a node can differentiate whether it is plugged into a side connector or plugged into a top connector. The node is able to interpret the topological parameters in the data received to know which node it is connected to.

Network Data Gathering

The connector between nodes integrates power supply, a hardware IIC bus, and a unidirectional serial interface described above. All the nodes act as IIC master devices and send data packets to a data collector which has a connection to a PC. We coded the data package as 15Bytes, so that a standard 400KHz IIC bus can in theory transmit 3000package/s. Therefore our data rate can reach 3000Hz for single node, or 300Hz for 10 nodes. In the current demo we control it at 20Hz to provide possibility for more nodes to work together at an acceptable rate.

Because we apply a multi-master IIC bus, the maximum of sensors is not restricted by the limitation of 7-bit address. However the actual number is affected by the parasitic capacitance of each device. We support at least 30 blocks under current circuit design, which is enough for most scenarios.

Armature Structure Generation

A data packet contains four topological parameters and a matching quaternion. The software will store or update the data once it receives a data packet from the data collector.

Calculations would be performed to ensure that every parent node is generated before its child node each time a new armature is generated. The armature bones can then be rebuilt one by one. Firstly, the parent bone is found using the topological relationship. Secondly, a new bone is extruded in accordance with the physical length set in the software. Thirdly, the new bone is rotated according to the AHRS data. This process is repeated until the whole armature is reconstructed.

APPLICATION

Armature Generation

Armature generation is the most fundamental function provided by the interface. The user starts by attaching the blocks together and twisting the joints to create a desired armature (Figure 8.a). Once the physical armature is created, the user can instruct the software to collect the sensing data of the armature and a digital *initial armature* will be generated automatically (Figure 8.b). This armature has the same structure, length and posture as the physical, tangible one. After the generation process, the user can still physically change the tangible armature (e.g. adding or removing a block) and the changes can be updated to the digital armature with another generation command.

Rigging Existing Models

Once the *initial armature* is generated, its posture can be changed according to the manipulations on the physical one. If an existing model is rigged with this *initial armature*, it will perform a deformation together with the armature (Figure 8.d-e).

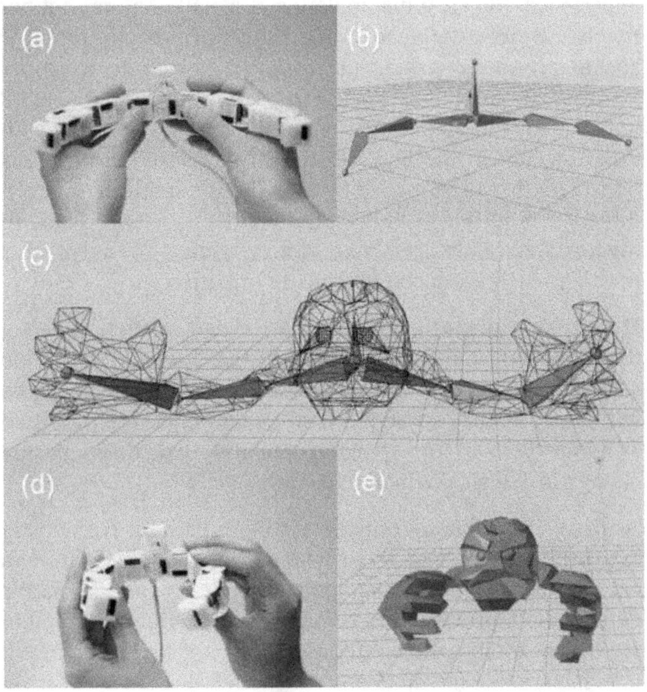

Figure 8. (a) Building a physical armature with TwistBlocks. (b) Generating a coressponding initial armature. (c) Adjusting the bones digitally to rig the model. (d)(e) Performing a relative deformation using physical manipulation.

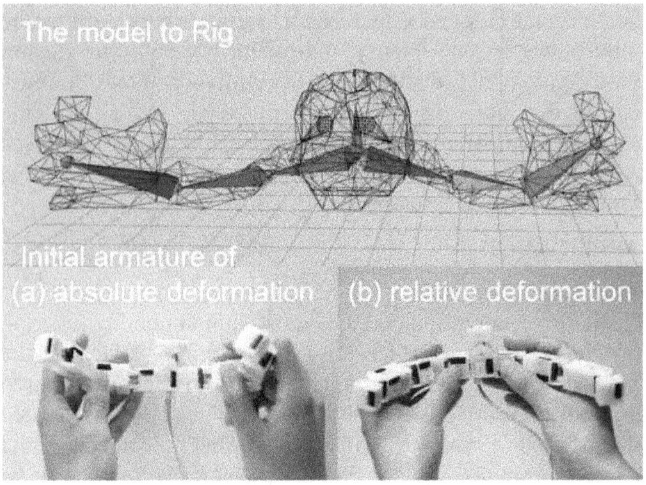

Figure 9. An initial armature with corresponding posture is required before absolute deformation. In contrast, relative deformation only needs an approximate structure.

TwistBlocks supports two types of deformations: *absolute deformation* and *relative deformation.*

Absolute deformation. With absolute deformation, the digital armature is always the same with the physical one. It provides direct imitation of the physical armature in the digital world.

Absolute deformation is widely used in most related work. However, it can still be improved if we pursue a better user experience. Physical manipulation is usually natural but not precise. Before the absolute deformation process, the user has to physically adjust the *initial armature* to a proper posture, and bind the armature to the existing model (Figure 9.a). Physical manipulation is not the best way to deal with this task, and if the user desires an armature with various bone lengths, digital modification is preferable. However, directly modifying the digital armature may lead to mismatches under absolute deformation. To solve this problem, we introduced relative deformation.

Relative deformation. With relative deformation enabled, the bones of the *initial armature* can be edited in the software (e.g. adjusting the length of certain bones), while still allowing the user to physically manipulate the modified armature with a corresponding mapping calculated by the change of physical armature posture.

Although absolute deformation is more precise, we noticed that users do not care about whether the digital armature is exactly the same as the physical one or not. Relative deformation provides faster and more flexible interaction for digital modification, and users will not feel an apparent mismatch when manipulating the model.

3D Design and Viewing

In our pilot study some novice users felt that they preferred animation rather than modeling, but it becomes an obstacle as models must be created before animations can be done on them using armatures. This indicates that an easy-to-use armature-based modeling method would be important and useful to novice users. Thus, we developed an armature-based fast modeling method consisting of the following procedures.

Initial armature. The user creates a physical armature with TwistBlocks and then an *initial armature* is generated. (Figure 10.a)

Straighten armature. Bones in the any chain can be automatically straightened (Figure 10.b), so that standard meshes (e.g. cylinders) can be easily applied to the armature.

Modeling. A function can help to generate a chosen type of mesh subdivided (producing a smooth effect) and rig it with the chosen chain (including length and position) automatically (Figure 10.c). The user can also add meshes by themselves.

Animating. All the models created can deform with the tangible armature automatically (Figure 10.d).

The TwistBlocks also allows for the design of various curved models (Figure 11). The global coordinate sensing network allows users to rotate the entire armature in their hands and view the digital model from multiple directions. A 3D curve can be better observed and adjusted in the physical space.

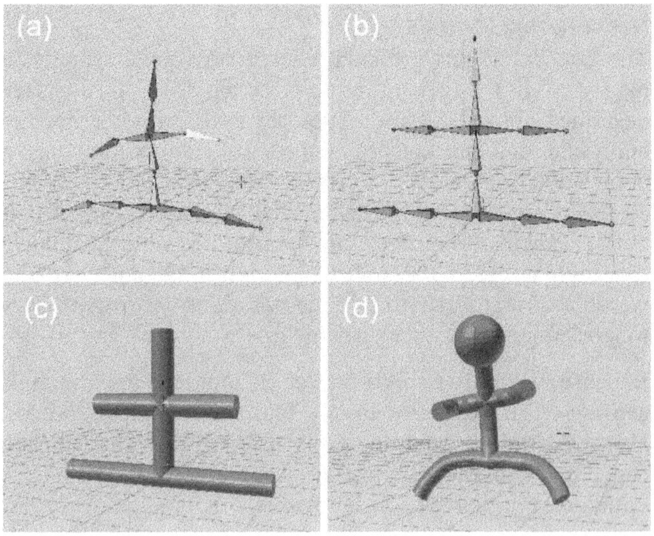

Figure 10. (a) Building with the blocks and generating an initial armature. (b) Straightening the armature. (c) Adding the cylinders automatically. (d) Adding a sphere and enabling deformation.

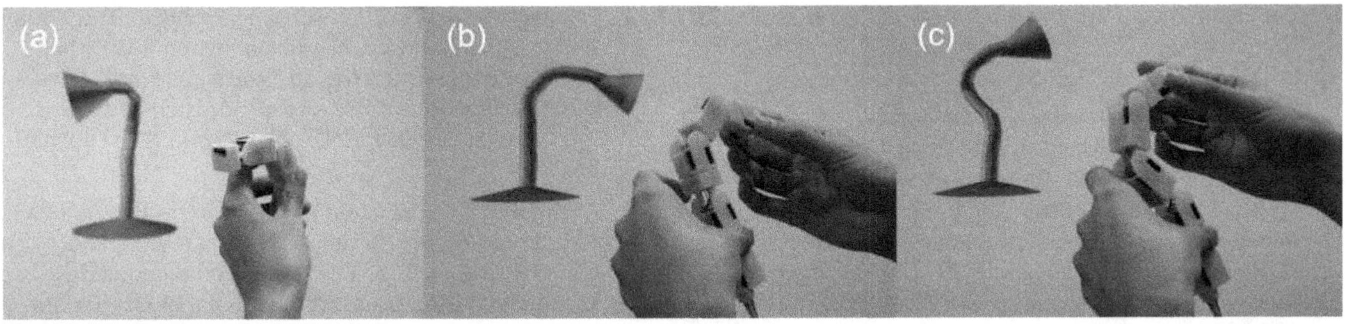

Figure 11. (a) Designing a lamp based on the physical armature. (b) Rotating the armature in order to observe the digital model from different directions. (c) Adjusting the lampstand using physical manipulation.

Interaction between Multiple Models

Interaction between multiple models brings possibilities to the creation of complex dynamic scenes such as interactive storytelling. The TwistBlocks system supports multiple physical armatures to be used simultaneously, enabling interactions between multiple digital models in real-time (Figure 12).

Since TwistBlocks uses a global coordinate system, all armatures share the same coordinate space. This means that users can easily perform face-to-face or back-to-back postures with two or more digital models. Traditional way of using a hierarchy of local sensors is not capable to sense any interaction between different models, while our sensing scheme enables the detection of global rotation, as well as global movement if we further apply a camera to calibrate the position.

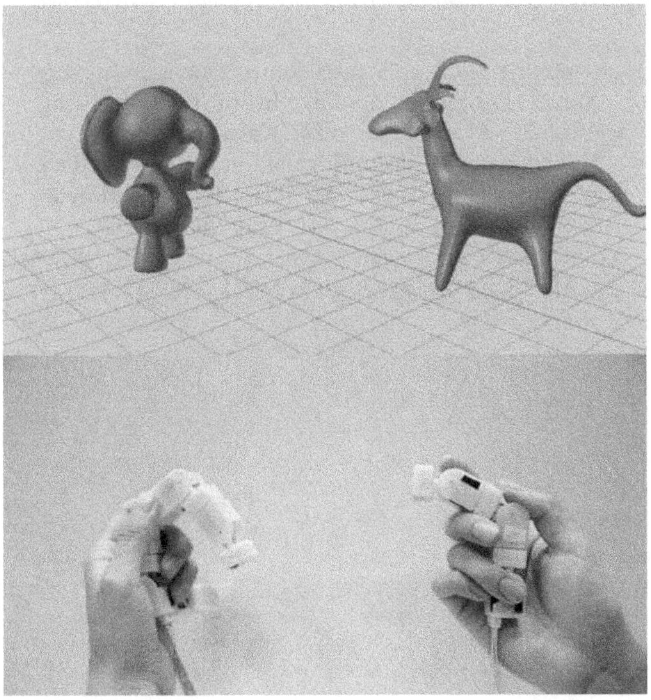

Figure 12. Multiple TwistBlocks systems can be used in the same scene for different characters.

CONCLUSION AND FUTURE WORK

We have demonstrated TwistBlocks, this easy-to-use TUI toolkit allows novice users to create digital 3D models and animate them in a simple manner. We have proposed a global coordinate sensing system, which enables physical manipulation of either a part or the whole model. A 3-DOF physical joint provides best user experience in manipulation, and interaction between multiple models brings possibilities to the creation of complex dynamic scenes such as interactive storytelling.

The design of the modular blocks can be further optimized. The armature structure is affected by the size of the block, so that a more compact design will provide more flexibility. In the next step, we are planning to optimize the demo with our latest designed mockups, and conduct a thorough user study. We are also considering interfaces for additional sensors and actuators to extend the applications.

ACKNOWLEDGEMENTS

Thank Piyush and Mr. Shaoen MA for proofreading, and Ms. Yuan YAO for producing the video. This work is supported by National Key Research & Development Plan of China under Grant No. 2016YFB1001402, and National Natural Science Foundation of China under Grant No. 61402250, 61232013.

REFERENCES

1. Alec Jacobson, Daniele Panozzo, Oliver Glauser, Cedric Pradalier, Otmar Hilliges, and Olga Sorkine-Hornung. 2014. Tangible and modular input device for character articulation. In *Proceedings of the adjunct publication of the 27th annual ACM symposium on User interface software and technology* (UIST'14 Adjunct), 45-46.
2. Ankit Gupta, Dieter Fox, Brian Curless, and Michael Cohen. 2012. DuploTrack: a real-time system for authoring and guiding duplo block assembly. In *Proceedings of the 25th annual ACM symposium on User interface software and technology* (UIST '12), 389-402.
3. Artem Dementyev, Hsin-Liu (Cindy) Kao, and Joseph A. Paradiso. 2015. SensorTape: Modular and Programmable 3D-Aware Dense Sensor Network on a

Tape. In *Proceedings of the 28th Annual ACM Symposium on User Interface Software & Technology* (UIST '15), 649-658.

4. Christian Rendl, David Kim, Sean Fanello, Patrick Parzer, Christoph Rhemann, Jonathan Taylor, Martin Zirkl, Gregor Scheipl, Thomas Rothländer, Michael Haller, and Shahram Izadi. 2014. FlexSense: a transparent self-sensing deformable surface. In *Proceedings of the 27th annual ACM symposium on User interface software and technology* (UIST '14), 129-138.
5. David Anderson, James L. Frankel, Joe Marks, Darren Leigh, Eddie Sullivan, Jonathan Yedidia, and Kathy Ryall. 1999. Building virtual structures with physical blocks. In *Proceedings of the 12th annual ACM symposium on User interface software and technology* (UIST '99), 71-72.
6. David Merrill, Jeevan Kalanithi, and Pattie Maes. 2007. Siftables: towards sensor network user interfaces. In *Proceedings of the 1st international conference on Tangible and embedded interaction* (TEI '07). ACM, New York, NY, USA, 75-78.
7. Hayes Solos Raffle, Amanda J. Parkes, and Hiroshi Ishii. 2004. Topobo: a constructive assembly system with kinetic memory. In *Proceedings of the SIGCHI Conference on Human Factors in Computing Systems* (CHI '04). ACM, New York, NY, USA, 647-654.
8. J. M. Kahn, R. H. Katz, and K. S. J. Pister. 1999. Next century challenges: mobile networking for "Smart Dust". In *Proceedings of the 5th annual ACM/IEEE international conference on Mobile computing and networking* (MobiCom '99). ACM, New York, NY, USA, 271-278.
9. Ken Nakagaki, Sean Follmer, and Hiroshi Ishii. 2015. LineFORM: Actuated Curve Interfaces for Display, Interaction, and Constraint. In *Proceedings of the 28th Annual ACM Symposium on User Interface Software & Technology* (UIST '15), 333-339.
10. Michael Philetus Weller, Ellen Yi-Luen Do, and Mark D Gross. 2008. Posey: instrumenting a poseable hub and strut construction toy. In *Proceedings of the 2nd international conference on Tangible and embedded interaction* (TEI '08). ACM, New York, NY, USA, 39-46.
11. Moritz Bächer, Benjamin Hepp, Fabrizio Pece, Paul G. Kry, Bernd Bickel, Bernhard Thomaszewski, and Otmar Hilliges. 2016. DefSense: Computational Design of Customized Deformable Input Devices. In *Proceedings of the 2016 CHI Conference on Human Factors in Computing Systems* (CHI '16), 3806-3816.
12. Oliver Glauser, Wan-Chun Ma, Daniele Panozzo, Alec Jacobson, Otmar Hilliges, and Olga Sorkine-Hornung. 2016. Rig animation with a tangible and modular input device. *ACM Trans. Graph.* 35, 4, Article 144 (July 2016), 11 pages.
13. Ryoichi Watanabe, Yuichi Itoh, Masatsugu Asai, Yoshifumi Kitamura, Fumio Kishino, and Hideo Kikuchi. 2004. The soul of ActiveCube: implementing a flexible, multimodal, three-dimensional spatial tangible interface. In *Proceedings of the 2004 ACM SIGCHI International Conference on Advances in computer entertainment technology* (ACE '04). ACM, New York, NY, USA, 173-180
14. Tovi Grossman, Ravin Balakrishnan, and Karan Singh. 2003. An interface for creating and manipulating curves using a high degree-of-freedom curve input device. In *Proceedings of the SIGCHI Conference on Human Factors in Computing Systems* (CHI '03), 185-192.
15. Wataru Yoshizaki, Yuta Sugiura, Albert C. Chiou, Sunao Hashimoto, Masahiko Inami, Takeo Igarashi, Yoshiaki Akazawa, Katsuaki Kawachi, Satoshi Kagami, and Masaaki Mochimaru. 2011. An actuated physical puppet as an input device for controlling a digital manikin. In *Proceedings of the SIGCHI Conference on Human Factors in Computing Systems* (CHI '11). ACM, New York, NY, USA, 637-646.

Digitally Enchanted Wear: a Novel Approach in the Field of Dresses as Dynamic Digital Displays

Rebecca Kleinberger
MIT Media Lab
75 Amherst Street, E14-333B
Cambridge, MA, USA
rebklein@media.mit.edu

Alisha Panjwani
SEEDS Studio Lab
5 Lowell Ave
Winchester, MA, USA
alisha@aceraschool.org

ABSTRACT
We introduce the term Digital Dresses as Dynamic Displays as an emergent field in the domains of Wearable Computing and Embodied Interactions. This recent approach consists of turning clothing into visual - and sometimes audiovisual - displays to enable novel forms of interaction between the wearer, the viewer, the tangible clothing and the embedded content. In this context, we present Enchanted Wearable, a new optimized low cost approach to create Digital Dresses as Dynamic Displays. Enchanted Wearable is a technologically embellished and augmented garment containing a portable rear dome projection system that transforms the clothing fabric into a blank canvas displaying audiovisual content. With this system, we create a new form of expression through clothing to reflect identity, personality, emotions and inner states of the wearer. In this paper we first present the growing field of Digital Dresses as Dynamic Displays, then we survey and analyse existing prior art in this field using a specific list of characteristics: display technology, wearability, interactivity, brightness, context. Finally we present the design and technology behind our new Enchanted Wearable system and explain how it brings new perspectives to the field.

CCS CONCEPTS
Human-centered computing Displays and imagers; Collaborative and social computing devices; Ubiquitous computing; Applied computing Performing arts; Hardware Emerging interfaces;

Author Keywords
Wearables, projection, wearable computing, augmented fashion

INTRODUCTION
The history of clothing reflects that the development of useful, protective, and ergonomic features coincides in parallel with the development of aesthetics and fashion. In different societies, clothes have always been at a point of tension between

https://doi.org/10.1145/3173225.3173249

Figure 1. Enchanted Wearable dress, credit to National Geographic [12] for the projected content

a liberating sense of self expression and a pressuring urge to follow social trends [21]. But whether they reveal social hierarchical status or offer the opportunity to present a unique, personal sense of aesthetic, clothes can always be seen as displaying information about the wearer [9]

In the past, personal choices of the wearer were mainly expressed through the choice of clothes they bought, the way they matched different items, added accessories or altered the clothes. But with the advent of new available technologies on the mass market, as well as the rise of the Do-It-Yourself (DIY) community, more tools and techniques have become available to create more personal, reflective and dynamic fashion. Many artists and technologists have explored ways to create new synergies between clothing and technology. Clothes are not static anymore but can be dynamic and the same piece of clothing can perform a wide range of different looks to match and represent the ever-changing inner states and desires of the wearer. Now, from one press of a button, your dress can be made longer for a work event, or shorter for an evening out, using dynamic pneumatic actuation [24]. Additionally, you can change the color of the fabric interactively using chromatic inks [30]. By adding LEDs, speakers, sen-

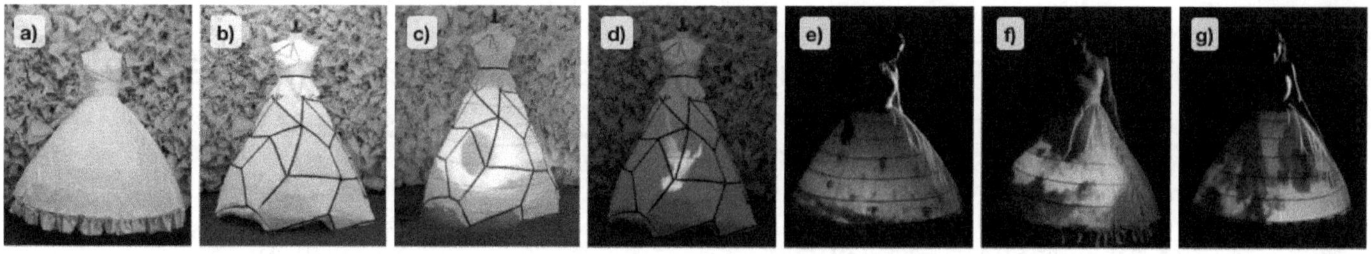

Figure 2. The two instances we build of the Enchanted Wearable system and examples of visuals content being projected. a) "Fablur" garment without projection; b) "I is Plural" garment without projection; c) "I is Plural" garment with projection of a setting sun animation, credit to wazdowls [33] for the projected content; d) "I is plural" garment with projection of an caged bird to symbolize the how clothing can become a form of opression for women, credit to dizi sever [8] for the projected content; e) "Fablur" worn by a user with projection of hot air baloons, credit to National Geographic [11] for the projected content; f) "Fablur" worn by a user with projection of fire, to represent heated mood of the wearer, credit to the Citrus Group [13] for the projected content g) "Fablur" worn by a user with projection of ink animation to represent cold mood of the wearer, credit to Abracadabra TV [29] for the projected content

sors and other electronics, users have the potential to bring a sense of empowerment to the way they dress.

This paper focuses on Digital Dresses as Dynamic Displays (D4) that use either color-changing pigments, direct lighting sources (such as LEDs), or projection to bring changing visualization on the surface of the garment. We can already see a movement to extend D4s out of the realm of performance art and into everyday life with commercial products such as T-shirts containing LED reacting to sound levels [34]. We believe that it is not only the trend of personalisation that justifies the need for the democratisation of D4 but also a need to enable users and primarly women with a sense of control, choice and potential for projection for and of the inner states.

We created two projects using the Enchanted Wearable system: "Fablur" and "I is plural" (see Figure 2). *Fablur* is a piece of clothing that performs itself revealing the inner feelings of the wearer. *I is Plural* is a participative art-fashion that reflects the diversity of a community and also the plurality present inside each of us. Both pieces are wearable tech installation that uses the Enchanted Wearable system to represent the links between individual and collective feminine conscience. With these projects, we discuss the technology behind the Enchanted Wearable system as a reproducible approach to create Digital Dresses as Dynamic Displays.

TECHNICAL BACKGROUND

Many breakthroughs have been made in the last few years in the domain of wearable technologies. The miniaturization of powerful batteries and the mass production of microchips have enabled the development of embedded systems to be worn closer and closer to the body. In the 90s, early work from Steve Mann [22] paved the way for modern embedded and embodied technologies.

In terms of general philosophy, the Enchanted Wearable system borrows from previous work in the field of projection based augmented reality. When thinking about the affordance of the interface and about gestural vocabulary, projects such as SixthSense [23], a projector based wearable gestural interface or LuminAR [20], a projector-camera system designed to use the traditional incandescent bulb interface as a power source, were inspirational. We also learned, from previous work in gestural interfaces with fabrics, how to use properties of fabric in the interface [19].

When creating the Enchanted Wearable system, our objective was to create a portable projection system by attaching a projector inside the dress. For the optics system, we drew inspiration from Hayden and Novy's Narratorium[15]. In this project, a system of mirrors and projectors reflect dynamic interactive animations on the 4 walls of a fabric tent creating an immersive environment called Dream Room. Interactions in the room are controlled by the voice to offer a novel approach to storytelling. For our project we use the same type of system to obtain rear projection on the inner surface of the fabric, kept in a dome shape by a custom made hoop skirt. This required a portable optical bench that is precise enough to create a focused high resolution image but also flexible and robust enough to allow for motion of the dress when the wearer walks and moves. We acknowledge the existence of other display technologies such as shape changing displays like Ishi's shape changing display [10] or Daniel Rozin's pompom mirror [17], but we choose not to include them as dynamic digital display because we have not yet seen wearables versions of these.

Technologies used to develop D4 systems broadly fall into three different categories: direct lighting, indirect lighting and color-changing materials. Direct lighting systems use displays generally made with LED strips or arrays. This is made possible by smart control systems such as one wire protocol of LED arrays or matrices. The recent development of lumaLive (a process that allows manufacturers to seamlessly integrate LEDs into fabrics) and Flexible Organic LED displays (FOLED) [26] offer good potential for textile based dynamic projects. Indirect lighting systems use front or rear projection to create images on a blank canvas. Finally, color-changing materials are based on electrochromic, thermochromic or photochromic pigments.

The choice of display technology will inform many other design decisions. Direct lighting systems have generally lower resolution but higher brightness. Color changing systems can have a lot of latency and generally remain low resolution but require less power. Projection systems offer better resolution but often at the cost of brightness and portability. Most projection based D4 systems use very big powerful projectors that are decoupled from the gown. These projects use projection mapping and because of this, the user's freedom of motion is constrained. Sometimes such systems even require the gown to stay absolutely immobile at a specific location.

As we can see, for an optimal result, D4 systems require a combination of design choices. We chose the following criteria to classify and evaluate our system and previous instances of D4 systems: display technology (LED/projection/color-changing); wearability (static on a mannequin/ limited range of motion/fully portable), interactivity (not interactive/reactive to inner or outer signals), brightness (low, medium, high), context (research/DIY/production/Haute Couture). We will keep those criteria in mind both in our review of previous work and in the description of the design of our system.

DIGITAL DRESSES AS DYNAMIC DISPLAYS: A SURVEY OF THE FIELD

This project draws inspiration from previous artistic and technological experiments. In this section, we review several past instances and efforts in this domain. At the end of this section, we classify the different cases according to the design criteria presented above: display technology, wearability, interactivity, brightness and context. The systems described range from haute couture dresses to performance costume to academic research projects. Because of this, it was difficult to obtain consistent and in depth information about each case.

Very early work from the 50s can be considered as instances of D4s (see Figure 3-a) [32]. Atsuko Tanaka "electric dress" worn by the artist and first exhibited at the Museum of Contemporary Art, Tokyo in 1956 uses about one hundred colored lightbulbs to create a post-modern kimono covering the artists to symbolize the gap between tradition and modernity. The piece built in the context of performing art is very bright as suggests the reconstituton of the dress in 1986 but because of the cables connecting the bulbs to power, it is not fully portable. In this system, the flickering lights are not interactive.

We believe that the first proof of concept of Digital Dresses as Dynamic Displays using projection was introduced in Jacques Demy's 1970 film Donkey Skin (see Figure 3-b) [7]. The film features a Dress colored with the weather: a magical gown whose colors and patterns look like an ever changing blue sky with moving clouds. This analogy effect is realised using an external projector on the film set. The result is bright enough to be seen in bright daylight, but the system is only portable inside a constrained area.

D4s have recently made their mark in fashion art production with the explosion of musical and theatrical shows of massive scale, they are used both as costumes and parts of the sets. For instance, while performing the ballad "Feel the Light" from the animated film Home, American singer Jennifer Lopez wears a very large circular skirt that serves as a canvas revealing special effects and images of the movie's animated characters projected onto the dress (Figure 3-c) [5]. Stylist Rob Zangardi and Mariel Haenn designed this dress that came to life as part of the singer's performance intending it to be both aesthetically pleasing and functional and allowing the animation to be projected onto the dress. The dress has only been shown in a very dark space which leads us to believe that the dress is not bright enough to be shown in daylight. Also the singer stays immobile on stage which suggests that the projection mapping on the dress is not actively tracking her position but only calibrated to a specific location.

Fashion designers Ece Ozalp (Figure 3-d) [1] and Frank Sorbier (Figure 3-e) [18] have also showcased Digital Dresses as Dynamic Display systems as a way of marrying Haute Couture with new technologies that portray projection mapping and audiovisual installation as performative fashion. In both cases, the projection mapping is not actively tracking the garment and the gown has to stay immobile. In the case of Ece Ozalp, the dress has only been showcased on a mannequin. Designers Nicola Buttari and Martino Chiti have taken this performative fashion approach to another level, adding interactivity to the design with the sonic addition (Figure 3-f). In their creation Performa [2] , the visuals react to sounds, changing patterns and formations on the surface of a white dress. This system allows the wearer to be able to change what they are wearing by making some noise. Again, in those three cases, the brightness seems to be in the medium range as the dresses have only been showcased in very dark environments.

The "Bee Dress" by Steven Guthierrez (Figure 3-g) [14] is a rare example of projected garment where the light sources are attached to the garment. In this case the dress has general illumination from a central light but only has projection on a small surface in the front part of the dress. The system does not seem to contain any interactive part and the illumination level seems to be medium level.

In recent years, direct lighting systems have gained some attention in the experimental fashion world. Hussein Chalayan's Video Dress project (Figure 3-h) [31] contains 15000 LEDs embedded beneath the fabric. The Video Dresses are portable with high brightness. However, the resolution is still very low and the current model is not interactive.

The LED galaxy dress from CuteCircuit is another example of an LED garment (see Figure 3-i) [6]. The dress is currently exhibited in the "Fast Forward: Inventing the Future" exhibit at the Museum of Science and Industry in Chicago. It contains 24000 LED and offers a high potential for interactive behaviors even though only one mode has been displayed to the public. This dress can be seen as a blank canvas of electronic components that could allow users to program different behaviours in the system.

In addition to LED and projectors, color changing inks have also been used to create dynamic digital displays on clothing, for instance, L Calder's thermochromic TUTU that is controlled by Kinect and Arduino (Figure 3-j). This garment display is low resolution and the interactions are delayed due to

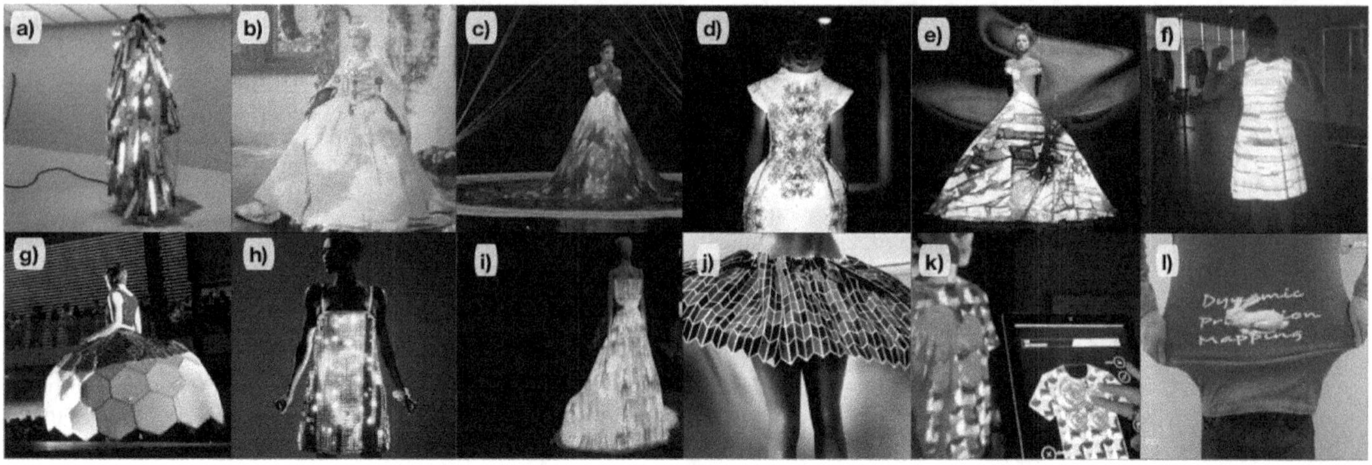

Figure 3. Examples of Digital Dresses as Dynamic Displays: a) Atsuko Tanaka "electric dress", b) Jacques Demy's Donkey skin; c) Jennifer Lopez's "Feel the Light" dress; d) Ece Ozalp's What is Real?; e) Frank Sorbier's dress; f) Nicola Buttari and Martino Chiti's Performa; g) Steven Guthierrez's "Bee dress"; h) Hussein Chalayan's Video Dress ; i) LED galaxy dress from CuteCircuit; j) L.Calder's "Thermochromic TUTU"; k) Mirror Mirror system; l) Ishikawa Watanabe Laboratory dynamic projection system

Name	Year	Display Tech	Wearability	Interactivity	Brightness	Context
Atsuko Tanaka's electric dress	1956	light bulbs	limited range	no	high	art show
Jacques Demy's Donkey Skin	1970	front projection	limited range	no	medium	show costume
Frank sorbier's dress	2012	front projection	immobile	no	medium	haute couture
Hussein Chalayan's Video Dress	2012	LEDs:15000 individual LEDs	fully portable	no	high	haute couture
CuteCircuit's LED Galaxy Dress	2012	LEDs:24000 individual LEDs	fully portable	no	high	haute couture
L.Calder's "Thermochromic TUTU"	2013	thermochromic inks	fully portable	yes: arduino controlled	high	design experiment
Steven Guthierrez's "Bee dress"	2014	rear front projection	fully portable	no	medium	art show
Jennifer Lopez's "Feel the Light" dress	2015	front/top projection	immobile	no	medium	show costume
Ece Ozalp's What is Real?	2015	front/side projection	on mannequin only	no	low	haute couture
Nicola Buttari's Performa	2015	front/side projection	immobile	yes: reacts to sounds	low	design experiment
Mirror Mirror	2016	front projection	limited range	yes: motion and action	medium	HCI research
Ishikawa Watanabe Laboratory system	2016	front projection	limited range	yes: wearer motion	medium	HCI research
Enchanted Wearable system	2017	rear dome projection	fully wearable	yes	medium	HCI research

Table 1. survey of the field of Digital Dresses as Dynamic Displays organized in chronological order

the speed of the chemical reaction but the brightness is not affected by ambient lighting [3].

HCI researchers have been developing new Digital Dresses as Dynamic Display prototypes exploring novel interactions using real-time cloth simulation. The Mirror Mirror system [25] (Figure 3-k) is a virtual fitting room containing a mirror display that allows the users to virtually draw on their T-shirt by adding colors to their reflection in the mirror. This interactive system uses live projection mapping so the user can move freely within a small area. Currently limited to t-shirts, the system is not portable but allows for a broad spectrum of interactions and for the users to generate creative ideas to personify their garment. Another system from Ishikawa Watanabe Laboratory in Japan (figure 3-l) presents dynamic projection mapping that allows projection onto deformed t-shirts [4]. The system uses a high-speed projector, which projects images up to 1000 frames per second. The t-shirt surface that is used as a screen is first marked with invisible IR ink to enable sensing of the projected images. These infrared targets restrict any distortion of the images onto the T-shirt.

While these systems create magical dynamic illumination effects on the dress, the portability remains limited such that the wearer is often unable to walk around. The ones that support projection mapping on free-moving 3D surfaces require sophisticated setup containing motion capture stage and external display or a powerful projection systems. The survey results of D4s are presented in Table 1 in a systematic way. After presenting the design of our system in the following section, we will come back to this table and discuss the uniqueness of our system. As most of the instances reviewed are not described in detail in research papers, we fill this table to the best of our knowledge and would be very grateful for any correction or comments.

DESIGN OF THE ENCHANTED WEARABLE SYSTEM

The Enchanted Wearable system is at the intersection of optics, projection mapping, computational art, wearable fashion and experience design. Each of these domains present their own design challenges that at times were in opposition to each other, and we sought to find a balance between the different criteria to construct the optimal prototype.

Optics

The design and implementation were a challenge from an optics point of view as we had to invent and build a lightweight wearable optical bench that was still precise and robust enough to produce a compelling visualization. The optical system consists of an aluminum bar to serve as optical bench, a laser projector and a half sphere concave mirror mounted on custom made adjustable mounts (see figure 4). We did an exploration of different projectors to determine the best one for our situation. We had to decide between LCD or laser projection. We reviewed and tried several models of small portable LCD projectors (UO smartbeam, AAXE, brookstone) as they offered better brightness, but they raised issues when trying to keep the image in focus. Indeed, the distance between the fabrics and the mirror needed to be constant and identical for each point. This was not possible because the fabric needs to be fluid and follow the motions of the wearer.

We decided to use a laser projector and, even though the luminosity is theoretically smaller (only 32 lumens for the Sony MP-CL1A compared to 300 lumens for the AAXA P300 Pico), the perceived brightness of laser projectors is higher than the measured brightness. For the mirror, we had to find the smallest possible radius in order to keep the distance projector-mirror as short as possible

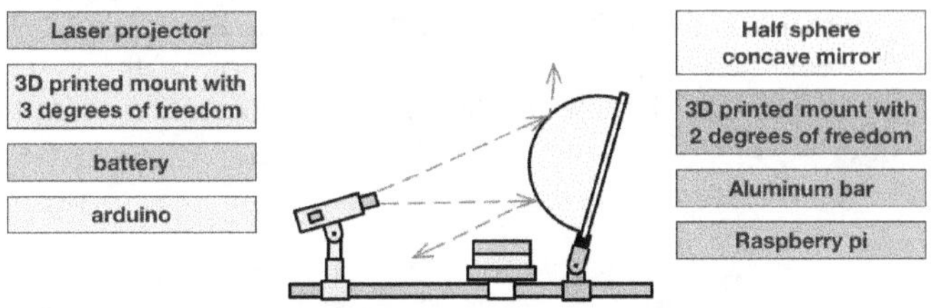

Figure 4. Optics of the Enchanted Wear system, the different elements are color coded and details of the process can be found in Figure 5

Fabrics and Dress Design

For the choice of material and textile, we had to find a compilation of material that is opaque enough to hide the inside components and to keep the laser beam from reaching the eyes of the public, but transparent enough to reveal a high quality image. The system had to project high definition image in focus and to be light, robust to the fluidity and relative motion of the different parts of the system.

The system also required to be easily stretchable to cover a half sphere. We chose a thin transparent crinoline covered by a layer of silk. The shape of the skirt had to allow for enough projection surface without reducing the wearability.

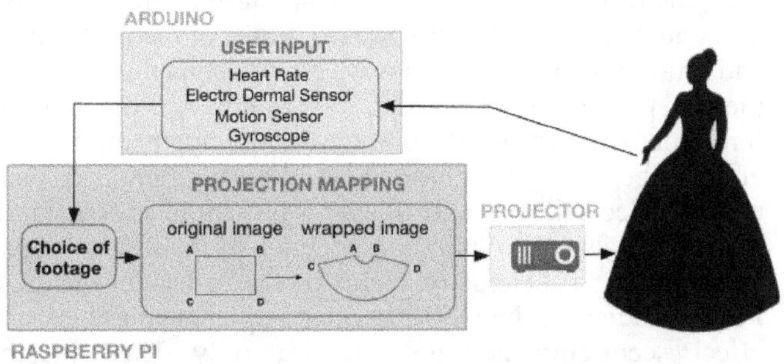

Figure 5. System diagram of the Enchanted Wear System, the input signals measured by the Arduino are processed by the Raspberry Pi to choose the footage to be projected. The footage is then warped into an arc and projected on the dress.

Software and Hardware

The project also contained a software aspects in order to map the content on the surface of the dress. We use projection mapping to warp the image around the dress while keeping the correct aspect ratio all around the 3D surface. To create the projection warp, we used the same pattern used for the pattern cut in the fabric to make the skirt. The hardware of the system uses an embedded computing system (Raspberry

Pi) and an Arduino micro-controller for sensing (see figure 5).

User Experience and Interaction Design

The system is wireless and portable and enables the wearer to walk freely with the garment. Due to the attachment, the skirt and image will slowly undulate with each step of the wearer but the whole system and focus will remain robust to motion and present a crisp image despite small variation of relative distance between the components. The rear projection system reaches about 80% of the surface of the dress (about 300 degrees) (see Figure 6) and the final position of the system avoids casting shadows of the legs when the wearer is immobile.

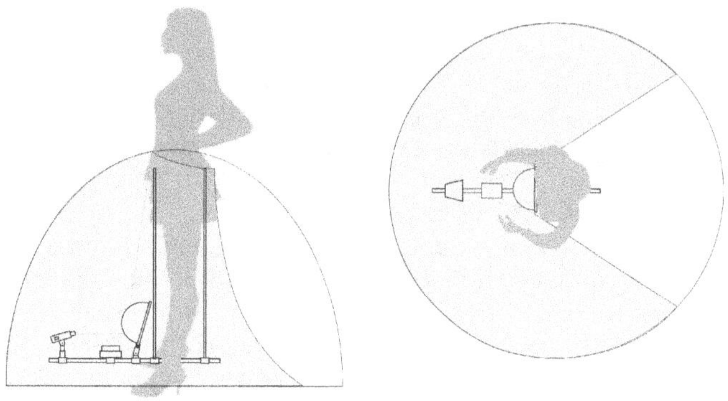

Figure 6. Side and Top view of the Enchanted Wearable system attached to a wearer with a belt, the pink area represents the surface covered by projection

The experience of the wearer and the experience of the viewer are quite different. The wearer doesn't have a full view of the dress but is in control of the system. Some of the interactions and proof of concept scenarios we have designed so far target the self perception of the user. For example, projecting different pairs of legs on the dress create an augmented reality effect of body transfer illusion [27]. Projecting multiple pairs of legs reflects the plurality of agents present inside each individual. We also play with the perception of the wearer's body by projecting a skeleton or a fetus on the surface of the dress. For the audience, the view is more complete and the illusion effects seem embodied in the user naturally. These illusion effects are not meant to be realistic but add an important interactive embodied effect to the aesthetic experience.

Using affective computing technologies [16] based on heart rate or electro-dermal activities, we can change the projected content to metaphorically match the inner state of the wearer. For example we can project blooming flowers or different seasons on the dress to represent different moods. By adding gyroscope and motion sensors to the system we can also create abstract visuals following the motions of the user and the different pan, tilt and roll motions of the dress. All those different interactions aim to bring a level of creative storytelling to clothing. The dress is telling a story which literally wraps around the main character.

Figure 7. Different seasons can be displayed on the dress to represent the mood of the wearer, credit to wazdowls [33] for the projected content

Figure 8. Augmented reality effect for body transfer illusion, credit to Rebecca Kleinberger and Eddie Talavera [28] for the projected content

EVALUATION AND DISCUSSION

In this section we come back to the variety of design criteria applicable to the conception of D4s and apply them to survey and evaluate the various previous work presented in the section *Digital Dresses as Dynamic Displays: a Survey of the Field* As we explained in the technical section, finding the balance between those criteria provides fertile ground for the creation of D4 systems.

The criteria we use to categorize previous work are: display technology, wearability, interactivity, brightness and context.

Display Technology

As described in Table1, the choice of display technology includes LEDs, projection and color-changing inks. We acknowledge the existence of other display technologies such as shape changing displays but choose to not include them in our survey. The choice of display technology informs the criteria as LED are generally brighter but with lower resolution. Projection and color changing inks also tend to blend more naturally with fabrics as they are indirect lightsources. Most examples we could find of previous D4 systems use projection over other display technologies. For our Enchanged Wearables system we also opted for projection as this allowed us to obtain better resolution and a smoother visual effect. The projector we use is a laser projector to avoid optical focus issues.

Wearability

In the previous examples shown in Table 1, we can see that the level of wearability varies a lot. Some pieces have only been displayed on immobile mannequins and never actually worn by people such as Ece Ozalp's "What is Real?" or some of Hussein Chalayan's Video Dresses. In most cases, using projection, the system is not actively tracking the wearer but is only passively targeting a specific area and the wearer has to stand immobile in that area. This is the case with Frank Sorbier's piece and Carrie Underwood's Grammy's dress. The advantage of the Enchanted Wearable system is that the projector is attached to the Garment so our system is fully wearable. The only other example of a fully wearable garment is Steven Guthierrez's "Bee dress" for which it also seems that the projector is attached under the hoop skirt. In this case the dress has general illumination from a central light but only has projection on a small surface in the front part of the dress while the Enchanted Wearable system reaches 80% of the surface of the skirt.

Interactivity

As we can see in Table 1, most examples found in haute couture and art shows are not interactive but only play back prerecorded animations. We believe that D4 systems are particularly interesting when they are interactive and allow for real time changes and modifications with the mood and the will of the wearer. We can distinguish two types of interactive systems. On the one hand, the systems that react to internal signals such as heart rate, motion, electrodermal activity, etc. On the other hand, the kind of system reacting to external signals such as ambient sound, button pressed, weather, etc. Both qualities of interaction seem interesting for the development of D4 systems. We can see in Table 1 that, currently, only examples from HCI research explore the dimension of internal interaction mainly detecting movement. Our system is the only one that seeks to express inner psychophysiological activities through dynamic display clothing. This way the user is empowered, by being in charge, regulating emotion and controlling the expression.

Brightness

The perceived brightness depends on the absolute luminosity of the system but also on other factors such as darkness of the environment, surface of projection, etc. LED systems are the brightest. Color-changing inks are not sources of light but are less influenced by outside lighting than systems using projection. We evaluated the brightness of prior works by looking at video and photographs of the systems. Generally when the garments are only displayed in a very dark environment we assume that their brightness is only low or medium. Brightness was a challenge for us as most small projectors have low luminosity. This explains why, among the designs we surveyed, most of the ones using projection decouple the projector from the dress, making the system not fully wearable.

Context

The survey of the field ranges across several disciplines, from haute couture to art show and costume creation to DIY projects and HCI research. It was important for us to consider all those contexts to survey the field as they influence each other in pushing the boundaries of wearable computing.

Limitations and Future Work

The Enchanted Wearable system was displayed at five different occasions (three times on a mannequin and twice on a live model). Each time it required either an enclosure to avoid ambient lights or to exhibit the garment outdoor at night. We received very positive feedback both from the audience and from the wearer. The quality and luminosity of off-the-shelf portable laser projecters is continuously improving and we believe that in the near future we will be able to deploy our Enchanted Wearable in brighter and brighter environments and also use darker fabric color for the garment.

We believe that the approach chosen for the Enchanted Wearable system is novel and overcomes many of the short comings of other approaches. However the versatility of the design is limited to dome-like projections, which implies the garment design is constrained to bell-like shaped skirts. Although using actrive projection mapping we were also able to cover more varieted shapes such as cones, balls or more irregular hoop skirt shapes.

From the exhibition, we received feedback regarding the ergonomy of the system. With the current system, the wearer can walk and turn but is still limited in his/her movements. With our first instance, the model gets quickly tired as they could not sit while wearing the dress. With our second instance, we changed the rotation of the system to allow the user to sit on a high top stool. For the next itteration we wish to make the system more ergonomic to be used for dancers, theatrical performances and as a more convenient real life ceremony garment

CONCLUSION

This paper introduced the term Digital Dresses as Dynamic Displays, an approach consisting in turning clothing into audiovisual displays. We surveyed the field considering prior art according to five characteristics: display technology, wearability, interactivity, brightness and context. We then presented the design and technology behind our new Enchanted Wearable system and explain how it brings new perspectives to the field.

ACKNOWLEDGMENTS

The development of the Dress Installation "I is plural" was funded in part by a Director's Grant from the Council for the Arts at MIT.

Additional we wish to thank William Collins, Sunny Jolly, Dan Novy, Yoav Reches, Diana Robinson, Shantanu Sina and Akito van Troyer for their help and support in the development of this project.

REFERENCES

1. Nathaniel Ainley. 2015. Abstract patterns and kaleidoscopic designs are projected onto Ece Uzalp's high fashions. (2015). https://creators.vice.com/en_us/article/4xqbxp/a-high-fashion-dress-meets-high-tech-projections

2. Nicola Buttari. 2012. Performa. (2012). http://www.proformavideodesign.com/about/

3. Lynsey Calder, Jose Magalhaes, Ruth Aylett, Sandy Louchart, Stefano Padilla, Mike Chantler, and Andrew MacVea. 2013. Kinect-based RGB detection for'smart'costume interaction. (2013).

4. Alvaro Cassinelli, Jussi Angesleva, Yoshihiro Watanabe, Gonzalo Frasca, and Masatoshi Ishikawa. 2012. Skin

games. In *Proceedings of the 2012 ACM international conference on Interactive tabletops and surfaces*. ACM, 323–326.

5. Stephanie Chan. 2015. Jennifer Lopez's 'American Idol' Gown, Deconstructed | Pret-a-Reporter. (2015). www.hollywoodreporter.com/news/jennifer-lopezs-american-idol-gown-783393
6. CuteCircuit. 2009. LED Galaxy Dress. (2009). http://cutecircuit.com/the-galaxy-dress/
7. Jacques Demy. 1970. Donkey Skin. (1970). http://www.imdb.com/title/tt0066207/
8. dizi sever. 2015. White bird flapping on black background shooting with high speed camera phantom flex. (2015). https://www.youtube.com/watch?v=QcKzBL216Po
9. Bonnie English. 2007. *A cultural history of fashion in the 20th century: from the catwalk to the sidewalk*. Berg Oxford.
10. Sean Follmer, Daniel Leithinger, Alex Olwal, Akimitsu Hogge, and Hiroshi Ishii. 2013. inFORM: dynamic physical affordances and constraints through shape and object actuation.. In *Uist*, Vol. 13. 417–426.
11. National Geographic. 2014a. Colorful Time-Lapse of Hot Air Balloons in New Mexico. (2014). https://www.youtube.com/watch?v=QGAMTlI6XxY
12. National Geographic. 2014b. Time-Lapse: Watch Flowers Bloom Before Your Eyes Short Film Showcase. (2014). https://www.youtube.com/watch?v=LjCzPp-MK48
13. Citrus Group. 2014. Slow Motion Fire HD Motion Background. (2014). https://www.youtube.com/watch?v=9Rnq0XtgadY
14. Steven Gutierrez. 2014. Dream Inside a Beehive a Second Before Awakening. (2014). http://www.sgevolution.com/surrealfashion.htm
15. Kasia Hayden, Dan Novy, Catherine Havasi, Michael Bove, Santiago Alfaro, and Rob Speer. 2013. Narratarium: An immersive storytelling environment. In *International Conference on Human-Computer Interaction*. Springer, 536–540.
16. Javier Hernandez, Daniel McDuff, Rich Fletcher, and Rosalind W Picard. 2013. Inside-out: Reflecting on your inner state. In *Pervasive Computing and Communications Workshops (PERCOM Workshops), 2013 IEEE International Conference on*.
17. Dan Howarth. 2015. PomPom Mirror creates "reflections" with tufts of fur. (2015). https://www.dezeen.com/2015/05/29/daniel-rozin-pompom-mirror-interactive-silhouettes-fur-tufts-descent-with-modificationbitforms-gallery-new-york/
18. Alexa Kestecher. 2012. Designer Franck Sorbier Projects An Haute Couture Fairy Tale. (2012). https://creators.vice.com/
19. Julian Lepinski and Roel Vertegaal. 2011. Cloth displays: interacting with drapable textile screens. In *Proceedings of the fifth international conference on Tangible, embedded, and embodied interaction*. ACM, 285–288.
20. Natan Linder and Pattie Maes. 2010. LuminAR: portable robotic augmented reality interface design and prototype. In *Adjunct proceedings of the 23nd annual ACM symposium on User interface software and technology*. ACM, 395–396.
21. Alison Lurie. 1991. Language of clothes. In *Human ecology forum*.
22. S Mann and R Picard. 1994. *Beingundigitalwith digital cameras*. MIT Media Lab Perceptual.
23. Pranav Mistry and Pattie Maes. 2009. SixthSense: a wearable gestural interface. In *ACM SIGGRAPH ASIA 2009 Sketches*. ACM, 11.
24. Laura Perovich, Philippa Mothersill, and Jennifer Broutin Farah. 2014. Awakened apparel: embedded soft actuators for expressive fashion and functional garments. In *Proceedings of the 8th International Conference on Tangible, Embedded and Embodied Interaction*. ACM, 77–80.
25. Daniel Saakes, Hui-Shyong Yeo, Seung-Tak Noh, Gyeol Han, and Woontack Woo. 2016. Mirror mirror: An on-body t-shirt design system. In *Proceedings of the 2016 CHI Conference on Human Factors in Computing Systems*. ACM, 6058–6063.
26. CD Sheraw, L Zhou, JR Huang, DJ Gundlach, TN Jackson, MG Kane, IG Hill, MS Hammond, J Campi, BK Greening, and others. 2002. Organic thin-film transistor-driven polymer-dispersed liquid crystal displays on flexible polymeric substrates. *Applied physics letters* 80, 6 (2002), 1088–1090.
27. Mel Slater, Bernhard Spanlang, Maria V Sanchez-Vives, and Olaf Blanke. 2010. First person experience of body transfer in virtual reality. *PloS one* 5, 5 (2010), e10564.
28. Eddie Talavera. 2012. 0 to 9 Months Journey In The Womb. (2012). https://www.youtube.com/watch?v=LcgXN5UAMOQ
29. Abracadabra TV. 2016. Color Ink Drops in Water Slow Motion HD. (2016). https://www.youtube.com/watch?v=y5auUsD6yAk
30. Akira Wakita and Midori Shibutani. 2006. Mosaic textile: wearable ambient display with non-emissive color-changing modules. In *Proceedings of the 2006 ACM SIGCHI international conference on Advances in computer entertainment technology*. ACM, 48.
31. Moritz Waldemeyer. 2015. Hussein Chalayan - Airborne - Video Dresses. (2015). http://www.waldemeyer.com/hussein-chalayan-airborne-video-dresses
32. Tracey Warr and Amelia Jones. 2000. *The artist's body*. Phaidon London.
33. wazdowls. 2009. 4 Seasons 1 Tree. (2009). https://www.youtube.com/watch?v=NK8WWcXB4j0
34. Andrew Zenoff. 2017. T-shirt with screen display. (July 11 2017). US Patent D791,443.

The Cuebe: Facilitating Playful Early Intervention for the Visually Impaired

Peter Fikar
TU Wien
Multidisciplinary Design Group
Vienna, Austria
peter.fikar@tuwien.ac.at

Florian Güldenpfennig
TU Wien
HCI Group
Vienna, Austria
florian.gueldenpfennig@tuwien.ac.at

Roman Ganhör
TU Wien
Multidisciplinary Design Group
Vienna, Austria
roman.ganhoer@tuwien.ac.at

TEI '18, March 18–21, 2018, Stockholm, Sweden

ACM ISBN 978-1-4503-5568-1/18/03.
https://doi.org/10.1145/3173225.3173263

Abstract

Cortical Visual Impairment in children is a severe issue caused by prenatal injury of the brain affecting timely development during childhood. Therapists work with affected children to foster general development, to improve their learning, and to train sensory skills. In order to support effective and playful practices in Early Intervention we designed *The Cuebe* and present a working prototype. It is a tangible device that can detect and project colors, allowing therapists to "magnify" those colors and creating a vast variety of playful interactions for and with children suffering from low vision. The exploration of the design domain and the iterative development of *The Cuebe* were driven by a co-design approach involving four therapists and 12 affected children. We describe use-cases from the field, illustrate *The Cuebe's* potential in Early Intervention sessions and discuss further improvements and directions of future developments.

Author Keywords

Therapeutic toys; children; disabilities; CVI; stimulation; playful approach

ACM Classification Keywords

• *Human-centered computing ~ Field studies* • *Human-centered computing ~ Participatory design*

Introduction

In this work-in-progress paper we present the design and exploration of *The Cuebe*, a working prototype from a one-year research project ('Schaukasten') involving 12 children with Cortical Visual Impairment (CVI) and their four Early Intervention specialists. The project's objective is to support affected children with innovative therapeutic toys (see also [3]), which fit with Early Intervention strategies.

Our main challenge in formulating fitting design proposals stems from the heterogeneity of the group of affected children and their diverging developmental goals. In order to uncover obvious and hidden needs in this challenging design space we follow a design-driven approach similar to Research through Design (e.g., [11]). Thus, we aim to add to existing Early Intervention practices by iteratively formulating design proposals, *The Cuebe* being one of them.

In this paper we focus on the design and underlying motivation of *The Cuebe*, a stand-alone tangible toy for children that "magnifies" (amplifies) visual cues, supporting play activities guided by therapists. *The Cuebe* is capable of detecting colors and projecting them onto its surface in a bright "magnified" fashion (see Figure 1).

In this way, *The Cuebe* makes visual stimuli "graspable" and thereby invites children to explore, experience, and experiment with visual cues in a playful fashion. In the following, we briefly provide background information before we describe the design process of *The Cuebe* and a preliminary field study.

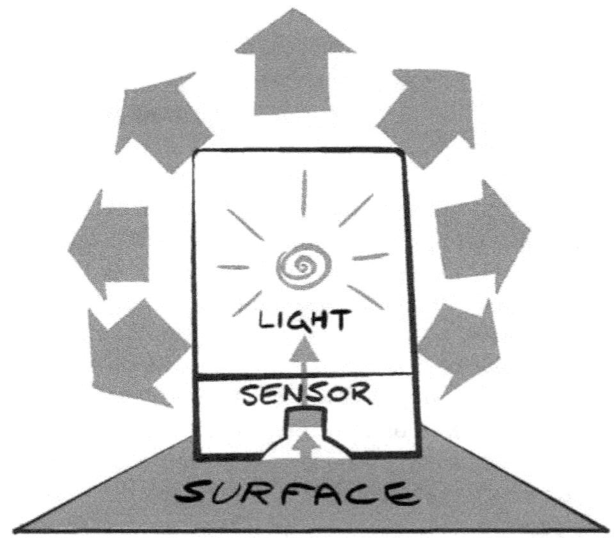

Figure 1: Concept sketch of *The Cuebe* - The sensor at the bottom detects the color of the underlying surface. The detected color is electronically amplified and the whole upper body of *The Cuebe* lights up in that color.

Background & Related Work

The term Cortical Visual Impairment (CVI) encompasses neurological impairments related to low vision. Children suffering from such impairments are not only handicapped in their development regarding visual factors, they are often also affected in their motoric and cognitive skills (like hand-eye coordination or attention and learning capabilities) [2; 7]. Hence, children with CVI suffer from a complex variety of individual symptoms, increasing the challenges for therapeutic intervention.

CVI – symptoms and support

CVI is an umbrella term for a broad variety of vision-related impairments relating to poor visual acuity, restricted field of vision, problems in visual cognition, issues with hand-eye coordination, etc. [7]

Early Intervention Services usually support affected children by offering training with special materials and toys painted with saturated colors and high-contrast patterns. In this way, children can exercise their vision in a playful fashion. At the same time, in this example, their motor system is addressed in physically playing the game (for example, throwing a yellow ball into a blue ball-run) training their hand-eye coordination. However, the number of toys that are both suitable and fun for the children is limited; thus in this paper we explore *The Cuebe*, a tangible for providing appropriate visual cues and interesting physical affordances.

Children with CVI find support in Early Intervention Services where trained professionals assess and successively build up their capabilities, for example, by exercising vision and motor control. Early Intervention Service is most effective when it supports affected children from birth on and during crucial phases of their development [2; 5]. To this end, the trained specialists accompany the children up to the age of 6 years [5]. As play is of crucial importance in a child´s development [4], Early Intervention specialists (in our case, primarily psychologists and educators by training) create playful experiences for the children. Playful interaction also offers the chance to capture a child's attention during (potentially) exhaustive intervention sessions. The info box on the left side provides more detailed information about CVI.

As children with multiple disabilities are described to play "differently", design-work should acknowledge these circumstances in order to be suitable [1]. Thus, stimuli or visual cues need to be more intense and vivid for affected children to provoke interaction. Especially tangible artifacts and interactions are promising when supporting learning and developing skills in children [6]. From the large body of literature about tangible toys we present two examples, IO-Brush [8] and Polipo [9].

IO-Brush [8] is a tangible device for children, which is capable to scan color and texture of real world objects, e.g. the favorite stuffed animal of a child. The scanned colors can then to be used as digital paint on a screen. The brush-shaped IO-Brush invites children to explore their surroundings as if it was a palette for painting and picking up colors.

Polipo [9], on the other hand, aims to improve motor skills of children in a therapeutic context. As a playful artifact Polipo allows a therapist to customize exercises for the children by offering different interactions for motor training by attaching different knobs and handles to Polipo to provide different affordances. If a child performs an exercise correctly, Polipo rewards the child by playing audio clips and light animations. The knobs and handles as well as the rewards can be customized and adapted to best fit a therapist's goal.

In contrast to the IO-Brush [8], *The Cuebe* is a standalone tangible device that is designed to be employed together with (existing) materials and equipment from the therapists. And while the Polipo [9] addresses the training of fine motor skills, *The Cuebe* targets visual exercising. *The Cuebe* is specifically designed to the requirements of our participants as a toy-like supplementary artifact supporting playful therapeutic activities (going beyond conventional interventions or games for CVI that are often just screen-based [10]).

Research Approach and User Needs

The Cuebe prototype resulted from an ongoing collaborative one-year project between the authors (experts in interaction design) and Early Intervention specialists (experts in working with children suffering visual impairment or CVI).

Initially, we explored and gathered information about the domain of Early Intervention by conducting four in-depth interviews lasting 1 to 2 hours each. Additionally, we made 18 in-situ observations of Early Intervention sessions at 12 children's homes lasting 1 hour each. Hence, we familiarized ourselves with the daily work of

Figure 2: From top to bottom: The opaque basis of *The Cuebe* housing a
a) color sensor facing down
b) Arduino Micro and
c) LiPo Battery: 3.7V 850 mAh.

our partners and their therapeutic efforts, goals and practices. In addition to the fieldwork, we held an initial design workshop, lasting about 2 hours, with the four Early Intervention specialists in order to establish common ground for further discussions and to collaboratively generate ideas.

Stemming from the analysis of these data we generated sketches and design proposals of artifacts, including the concept of *The Cuebe*. In a second workshop, again lasting about 2 hours, with the four Early Intervention specialists we discussed the sketches and selected the most promising ideas. Then we further detailed the chosen concepts and brainstormed practice-oriented interactions and use-cases.

The most promising ideas included the enhancement of visual stimuli by means of colored lights. These kind of optical cues play a central role in training visual perception and learning the colors' names. We also aimed to improve opportunities to establish play activities as we identified playing as a key motivator and often-used strategy to sustain attention and to increase training time and intensity.

To this end, visual cues and (versatile) elements of play were the most important factors in the design process for *The Cuebe*, a toy for experiencing and playing with colors and chromatic light.

The Cuebe: Design & Development

The Cuebe aims to provide a toy design that supports the goals of Early Intervention specialists and fits the needs of the visually (and often multiple) impaired children. The major goals our design pursues are:

a) **to deliver stimuli appropriate for therapeutic training** in the context of Early Intervention and b) to support Early Intervention specialists with a **toy to inspire the creation of play activities in order to uphold motivation.**

The main function of *The Cuebe* is to detect color from an underlying surface and to replicate the color through an array of RGB LED-lights. In analogy to a "reading stone" that magnifies text, *The Cuebe* intensifies the color it reads. For example, the surface of a red toy car will be "magnified" by self-emitted red light projected onto the cap of the device, which again produces visually perceivable stimuli for children with low vision who hardly can perceive the color of the original toy car (c.f., major goal a).

The latest working prototype of *The Cuebe* is a physical handheld artifact resembling a cubic shape measuring 6x6x7 centimeters fitting the hands of children of the target group well.

The bottom of *The Cuebe* acts as a button as its surface is mounted on springs and can be pushed inwards (2mm). Children can use the device by placing their hands on top of *The Cuebe*, pushing it, and thereby "updating" *The Cuebe's* color by activating the color sensor, which is located at the bottom's surface (see Figure 2). It is reading the color continuously, as long as *The Cuebe* gets pushed down. After a child releases his or her hands *The Cuebe* keeps glowing with the same color until the next push.

The top of *The Cuebe* is made of translucent material and houses an array of RGB-LEDs. When a new color is read, an Arduino microprocessor board processes the

Figure 3: From top to bottom:
a) 5 Adafruit-Neopixel LEDs attached on top of the basis
b) the translucent cap made of acrylic glass, diffusing the emitted light and
c) an alternative 3D printed cap made of semi transparent PLA material (in a test-setup).

signal, maps the electrical signal to a color and subsequently activates the array of RGB-LEDs. The cap then lights up, replicating the (read) color in bright light (see Figure 3).

Similar to frosted glass, the cap diffuses the light homogenously. This is important for many children with CVI to correctly perceive and understand the shape of *The Cuebe* as a whole. Unevenly lit parts could create an incoherent perception of the colored surface and make a correct interpretation of the shape of the cap more difficult. Figure 3c depicts the development of an alternative cap for the current iteration of *The Cuebe* with improved light diffusion.

According to the Early Intervention specialists and our observations the children can be supported in their perception by two different modalities: constant light and blinking light. These are *The Cuebe's* two basic "play modes". We go on to describe how *The Cuebe* supports Early Intervention specialists creating play with children in the field (c.f., major goal b).

Field Study & Play

In order to evaluate the design of our prototype and to gain insights for further design iterations, we observed how each of the specialists used *The Cuebe* in the field. Six of the 18 total observations (each lasting approx. 1 hour) included *The Cuebe* as a toy offered to five different children. Beside its basic functionality we provided no instructions for *The Cuebe* to minimize influence on genuine interactions. We go on and describe three exemplary cases, illustrating play scenarios we observed during different Early Intervention sessions. The names of the children are altered for anonymity.

Figure 4: Mario playing with *The Cuebe*, using a dice (arrow on the left) and a prepared set of colored discs with different shapes & colors.

Case A: Kyle was invited by one of the specialists to explore the room and find a certain color to pick with *The Cuebe*: "Will you pick something *green* for me?" Kyle was carefully navigating in the room, examining different colors.

Case B: Tim was challenged to pick colors from a colored wooden disk located inside an empty metal can. The reflective steel mirrored the emitted light and the can lit up strongly. Tim was putting the head close to the top, observing the change of color curiously. He took pride in picking colors and in putting *The Cuebe* into the can and taking it out again.

Case C: An Early Intervention specialist was setting up a board game-like play activity, combining *The Cuebe* with other common materials in therapy (see Figure 4). Colored disks and planes were spread out on a flat surface. Mario was throwing a dice with differently colored surfaces. He was then asked to find the corresponding disk. The child had to say a "magic spell"

Figure 5: Currently under development (from top to bottom):
a) cross section of the next design iteration,
b) schematics and extruded parts from robust plastics and
c) bottom-view of the new iteration's mockup including the color sensor behind protective acrylic glass.

including the color's name and then pick it with *The Cuebe* to complete the task. The spell was part of the specialist's narrative or play strategy to make the game more engaging.

These cases illustrate three different play ideas inspired by *The Cuebe*. The trained specialists seamlessly integrated the device in their sessions in various ways, highlighting its potential for creating play.

Discussion & Further Development

Throughout the field tests *The Cuebe* showed the potential to fulfill the roles it was initially designed for. It was interesting to observe how the specialists used supplementary materials (colored planes, discs and old cans) to extend *The Cuebe's* functionality.

The creation of play activities included make-believe aspects or narratives like "magic spells" to foster interaction and to connect therapeutic goals with play. The therapeutic goals/challenges integrated into those play activities demanded a variety of skills from the children, such as various ranges of vision (close to distant) and different motor-skills (fine to gross). Games like the mentioned "board-game" or the "I-spy-with-my-little-eye"-like exploration game supported different kinds of such therapeutic challenges through different gameplay experiences.

However, regarding *user needs* we also found areas for improvement covering affordances, electrical components, and product safety.

Adjustable brightness: Some children are susceptible to glaring effects, even though their visual acuity is low.

Complexity and shape: Some children did not understand that picking the color requires using a distinct side of *The Cuebe* (the bottom-one with the sensor) leading to confusion and discouragement.

Additional modalities: Vibro-tactile or auditive feedback, as well as different color mappings may add more opportunities to create meaningful play activities.

Product safety: Replacing the potentially hazardous lithium polymer battery (LiPo battery) with another type of accumulator.

Hygiene: As children tend to put toys into their mouths, the next iteration of *The Cuebe* must be easier to clean.

Finally, *The Cuebe* has to be more *robust*. The structural integrity of the last prototype was easily brought to its limits, when a child smashed it forcefully and repeatedly against a table´s surface. The resulting destruction of *The Cuebe* ultimately concluded the evaluation of the current prototype in a 'spectacular way', allowing us to proceed to the next iteration.

For the next iteration, which is not yet in a working state, we will consider the items listed above. We will extrude the device from solid plastics to improve robustness and hygiene. We will also continue the exploration of different functionalities and form factors, for example, using a cylindrical shape (see Figure 5).

Acknowledgements

This research was funded by "Gemeinsame Gesundheitsziele aus dem Rahmen-Pharmavertrag, eine Kooperation von österreichischer Pharmawirtschaft und Sozialversicherung".

References

1. Jane Brodin. 1999. Play in Children with Severe Multiple Disabilities: Play with toys - a review. *International Journal of Disability, Development and Education 46*, 1, 25-34.
2. E. Fazzi, S. G. Signorini, S. M. Bova, P. Ondei, and P. E. Bianchi, 2005. Early intervention in visually impaired children. *International Congress Series 1282,* 117-121.
3. Florian Güldenpfennig, Peter Fikar, and Roman Ganhör, 2018. Interactive and Open-Ended Sensory Toys: Designing with Therapists and Children for Tangible and Visual Interaction. In *Proc TEI'18*, ACM.
4. Karin Lifter, Suzanne Foster-Sanda, Caley Arzamarski, Jacquelyn Briesch, and Ellen Mcclure. 2011. Overview of Play: Its Uses and Importance in Early Intervention/Early Childhood Special Education. *Infants & Young Children 24*, 3, 225-245.
5. Annette Majnemer, 1998. Benefits of early intervention for children with developmental disabilities. *Seminars in Pediatric Neurology 5*, 1, 62-69.
6. Paul Marshall. 2007. Do tangible interfaces enhance learning?. In *Proceedings of the 1st international conference on Tangible and embedded interaction*, ACM, 163-170.
7. Maria B. C. Martín, Alejandro Santos-Lozano, Juan Martín-Hernández, Alberto López-Miguel, Miguel Maldonado, Carlos Baladrón, Corinna M. Bauer, and Lotfi B. Merabet, 2016. Cerebral versus Ocular Visual Impairment: The Impact on Developmental Neuroplasticity. *Frontiers in Psychology 7*, 1958.
8. Kimiko Ryokai, Stefan Marti, and Hiroshi Ishii. 2004. I/O brush: drawing with everyday objects as ink. In *Proceedings of the SIGCHI Conference on Human Factors in Computing Systems* (CHI '04). ACM, New York, NY, USA, 303-310.
9. Victoria Tam, Mirko Gelsomini, and Franca Garzotto, 2017. Polipo: a Tangible Toy for Children with Neurodevelopmental Disorders. In *Proc TEI'17*, ACM, 11-20.
10. Jonathan Waddington, Conor Linehan, Kathrin Gerling, Kieran Hicks, and Timothy L. Hodgson, 2015. Participatory Design of Therapeutic Video Games for Young People with Neurological Vision Impairment. In *Proc CHI'15*, ACM, p. 3533-3542.
11. John Zimmerman, Jodi Forlizzi, and Shelley Evenson. 2007. Research through design as a method for interaction design research in HCI. In *Proceedings of the SIGCHI Conference on Human Factors in Computing Systems* (CHI '07). ACM, New York, NY, USA, 493-502.

Soft-bodied Fidget Toys: A Materials Exploration

Peter Cottrell
University of California, Santa Cruz
Santa Cruz, CA 95060, USA
pcottrel@ucsc.edu

April Grow
University of California, Santa Cruz
Santa Cruz, CA 95060, USA
agrow@ucsc.edu

Katherine Isbister
University of California, Santa Cruz
Santa Cruz, CA 95060, USA
katherine.isbister@ucsc.edu

TEI 2018, March 18–21, 2018, Stockholm, Sweden.
ACM ISBN 978-1-4503-5568-1/18/03.
https://doi.org/10.1145/3173225.3173266

Abstract
We present an exploration of e-textile/soft materials that can be used to capture fidget traces, while providing the touch sensations that fidgeters report seeking out in everyday fidget objects [3,4,5]. We created two soft-bodied "sampler" objects with a range of smart fidgeting affordances, which we describe in this paper, along with a general outline of the range of properties explored. This work extends exploration of a novel design space introduced in [4], toward the end goal of creating smart fidget objects that aid self-regulation. We include an overview of our design process, present some preliminary insights about materials that support this design space, and conclude with current and future directions for the work.

Author Keywords
Soft materials; e-textiles; fidget traces; self-regulation tool; materials exploration.

Introduction
Fidgeting is a natural and habitual practice that people seem to use to distract themselves and focus their minds [2,3,5]. For example, people keep objects nearby for fidgeting when they are doing deskwork. A study of fidget objects [4] collected using an online Tumblr gathered examples that ranged from ready-to-hand items such as pens and paper clips, to toys such

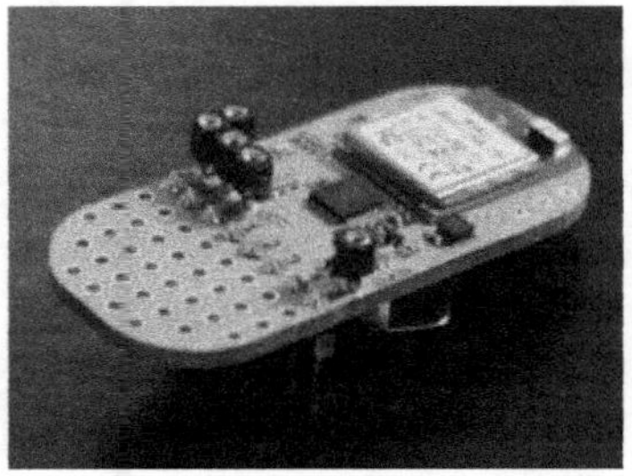

Figure 1: A LightBlue Bean microcontroller with interface sockets

as spinning tops, to desk ornaments like Newton's Cradle. It has been suggested that capturing touch traces could be beneficial in aiding fidgeters' attention management efforts—helping a person to realize when they are fidgeting a lot, and might want to take a break or shift tasks, for example [4].

The present work builds upon prior study of objects that people report fidgeting with [4], focusing on particular sensations that fidgeters are attracted to that are not provided by current commercial technology products, and looking to generate those kinds of sensations with soft electronic/e-textile materials on a soft-bodied object. We present two "sampler" objects that we created, which offer the user multiple modalities for interaction. In addition, we describe an underlying technological infrastructure we created that allows capture and storage of touch traces.

Related Work

HCI practitioners and researchers have previously engaged in some exploration of the space of handheld fidget objects that have technological augmentation. For example, Mind Spheres [8] was a pair of wooden, LED-studded spheres that the user carefully rotated in one hand, similarly to Chinese Baoding balls. Moving the spheres in the right way would cause the lights to glow in particular patterns. The *Relax!* pen attempted to track user states such as frustration, and provide some kinesthetic feedback to help prompt them to modulate their state [1]. The Skweezee system provided tools for sensing squeezing of soft materials and software that could be used to capture patterns of use [11]. Perner-Wilson et al. conducted workshops in which participants constructed textile interfaces [7], and have provided toolkits and resources that we found helpful in our research [9]. Research groups have also explored and cataloged materials used in "Smart Material Interfaces" [6,10], materials that can make expressive changes such as electrochromic or electroluminescent materials. No one that we are aware of has systematically explored the material space that we present in this paper.

Research Process

The work presented here was a materials exploration, grounded with a list of touch qualities drawn from [4]'s study of self-reported fidget objects. These included "crinkly, squishy, squash, snap, hissing, strumming, clicky-clackety, cool, smooth, rough, mush, twirl, spin, roll, bounce, shaking, braid, flipping, clicking, scrunch, squeeze, rub, and twiddle." Examining the objects and descriptors from this study led us to conclude that fidgeters seek a combination of complex sensations in fidget items, one that is not broadly available in today's technologies [3]. We set out to develop prototypes of objects that encompassed as many of these sensations as possible, which could also capture touch traces unobtrusively.

An additional constraint of our explorations was an emerging partnership with researchers interested in supporting self-regulation behaviors in children. We decided to focus our design efforts on crafting objects that could potentially appeal to children ages 8-10, to prepare us to engage with this future use case. In a companion study we are verifying that fidgeting in children presents the same heuristics of interaction that it does for adults as reported in [4]. The results from the companion study are currently under review.

We gathered two sets of materials, those that mimicked or had some traceable properties and those that would form the infrastructure around which the smart material could be integrated. Notable materials included in our collection:

- 2 varieties of conductive fabric, MedTex180 (a soft cotton-like variant) and RipStop (analogous to a stiff starch pressed shirt)
- Faux Leather to imitate Eeonyx non-woven resistive fabric
- Pressure sensors made of Velostat and conductive tape
- Knitted yarn balls with interwoven conducive tread to make squeeze sensors.

After gathering our materials, we sketched out ideas that would make for interesting repetitive use interactions drawing from fidgeting actions as described in our criteria. We aimed to envision one unique interaction for each word with some basis in traceable data. Some examples include: "squash" a ball sensor to determine grip strength, "strumming" a field of flex sensor embedded grass, "rub" the belly of a creature with embedded conductive thread strands.

By the end of our brainstorming we had several amalgamations of individual ideas including a potted plant that had bunny ears instead of leaves, which would light the pot up when the ears were squished or played with, a hedgehog that would flex its spines when threatened and relax when its belly was rubbed, and a set of conductive scales that would understand when the creature was being reshaped. We finally settled on two main fidget-able plush toys that would incorporate most of our favored sensors—a hedgehog and a dragon. We built both sampler creatures in an iterative process that is described in Research Results.

Hardware Design Parameters

As part of our effort to make objects aimed at 8-10-year-old children, we needed two key requirements in terms of hardware: 1) keep wires contained within the animal as much as possible, 2) keep the objects small so as to fit the hands of children. The limiting factor in size would be the main microchips. We evaluated then current market ready micro-controllers with the smallest possible footprint (to maintain minimum possible size) that would be able to communicate wirelessly (to keep wires contained within the toys while in use) and had an onboard battery that could last for multiple days. Rather than compact several smaller boards that each served one of these goals we found a microcontroller that had all three functions in one.

The LightBlue Bean from PunchThrough (see Figure 1) is 3 inches long, and has onboard Bluetooth, protoboard and battery which makes it suited to soft structured objects such as fidgeting toys as it reduces the chances of the board getting crushed while being manipulated. It has 2 analog channels (capable of reading in a range of values from a sensor) and 6 digital channels (capable of detecting if a switch is open or closed), which means we needed to be strategic about how many and what style of sensors we tried to integrate into a single design. However, the reduced array of sensors allowed us to get an extended battery life allowing for minimal down time. Unfortunately, the LightBlue Bean uses single-use coin cell batteries rather than the more popular rechargeable lithium batteries,

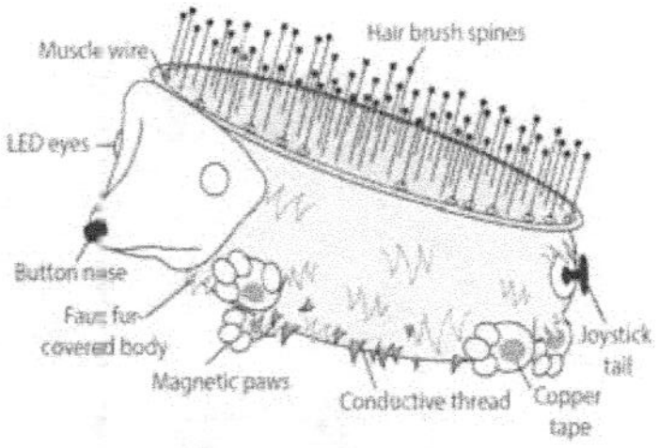

Figure 2: A diagram of the hedgehog.

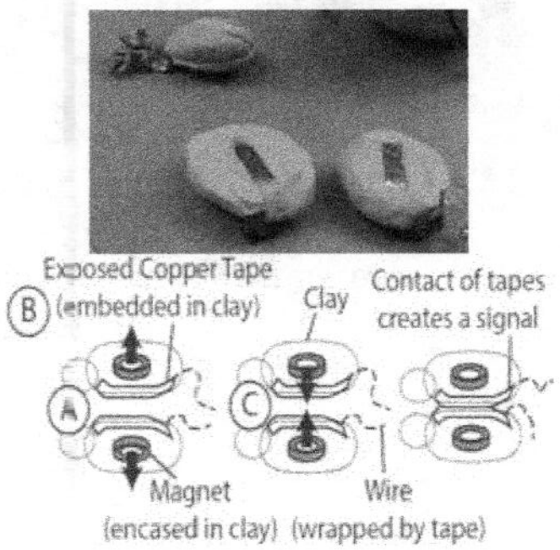

Figure 3: An initial prototype and x-ray side view of paws showing the construction of the embedded magnets and copper tape. Magnets are wrapped in polymer clay, and copper tape is anchored on surface of the clay. The orientation of the magnets directs the polarity of the object. Clay, magnet, tape, and wire are baked per clay instructions to harden. The tape must be the most protruding surface to make contact.

but with the Low-Energy Bluetooth protocols the battery lasts for multiple days of interactions before losing power. Programming was done in a mix of Arduino and Blue Bean specific coding.

Research Results

Hedgehog

Figure 2 is an illustration of the hedgehog's features (see Figure 5 for photo of final prototype). Our two planned keystone sensors for the hedgehog were a pressure sensitive squeeze ball and a prickly sheet that could detect when a user is stroking it. Due to our target audience, we replaced the prickly sheet with a child-friendly metal-spinned hairbrush with plastic nubs on the tips. We ultimately removed the pressure sensing portion of the squeeze ball so that we didn't encourage users to apply pressure to the microcontroller, but kept the plush interior to invite some light squeezing.

We then added LED eyes for interaction feedback, a push-button nose for clicking, a joystick tail for rolling under the thumb, and a field of conductive threads embedded into faux fur to detect when a user is petting the belly of the beast. The conductive thread is embroidered in two separate sections; when stroked the conductive fibers flatten and create a loose connection detectable by the microcontroller.

We combined magnets, partially embedded copper tape and clay to form paired surfaces that either attract or repulse. With the exposed copper tape and paired magnets, a detectable connection for the microcontroller is created when paws meet (see Figure 3).

As we were assembling the various sensors we realized the hair brush had a flexible foundation that when morphed could present anthropomorphized feedback to the user. Attempting to create this capability, we added a ring of muscle wire around the perimeter of the hairbrush. However, when testing we realized the muscle wire either didn't have the leverage or the physical strength to stress the brush back to create the desired feedback. In future iterations of a similar prototype, this is a feature the team would like to revisit.

Dragon

Figure 5 presents an illustration of the dragon's features, and Figure 6 shows various features in collaged photos. The initial concept for the dragon revolved around a sheet of conductive scales that could detect when the scales shifted position and a conductive-fabric-lined squeezable tail filled with a variety of beads and stones to create a smooth texture within the tail. Lacking a reliable distributor of Eeonyx resistive fabric, we substituted faux leather for the more substantive conductive material provided the flexation we were looking for to differentiate it from the rest of the body. The conductive tail was the single keystone that maintained its initial design from brainstorming to implementation (see Figure 4). We started implementing the build with an aluminum frame around which we could layer different fabrics while retaining the gangly nature of a reptile, which made the dragon distinct from that of the plush hedgehog. We draped scales around the shoulders of the dragon (H), and found scale-textured faux fur that complemented the shoulder scales and used that for the underbelly. We also implemented several similar sensors to those

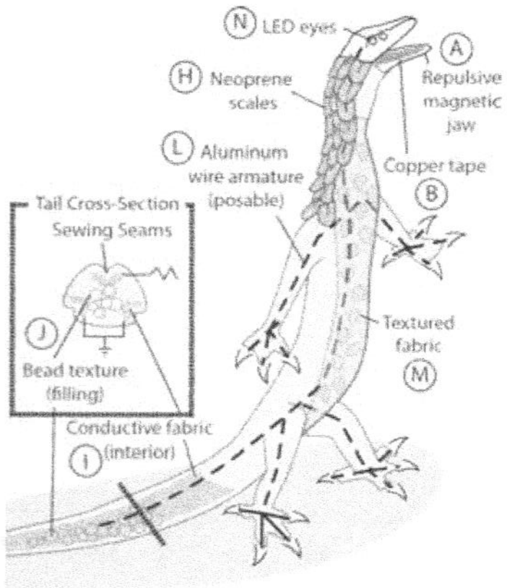

Figure 4: A diagram of the dragon. Letters correlate to smart technology embedded into the dragon.

Figure 5: Final prototypes resulted in a 9" x 5" x 5" hedgehog and a 12" x 6" x 4" Dragon both larger than expected but still approriate for children.

in the hedgehog; repellent magnet pairs, clay claws and LED eyes.

For the weighted squeeze sensor that acted as a tail, we lined two pieces of conductive fabric along the top and bottom of the tail so that as the poly-fill, rice and marbles inside the tail are moved aside the two conductive pieces of fabric meet and create a circuit, this allow the micro-controller to detect approximately how much pressure the tail is being crushed with due to corresponding variable resistor values.

Discussion

While building the exemplar animals, we initially aimed to implement multiple forms of sensors so that each sensor or feedback method was implemented uniquely. We found that what were perceived as unique implementations of sensors could ultimately be collapsed down into similar hardware design, but different perception of the hardware based on the contextualization. For instance, the embedded magnets provided different experiential properties depending on if the magnets attracted or repulsed each other. This meant we could encourage users to bring the paws of the hedgehog together by creating paws that could barely reach due to their positioning on the body, but when they do connect they stick together. Whereas the dragon's mouth refused to stay closed (due to repulsive magnets) and when a user forced its mouth shut we could use the LED eyes to react.

In the process of assembling the exemplar animals, the authors and their labmates expressed similar interest in specific experiential qualities. The hairbrush, the filled squeeze sensor, the embroidered faux fur, and the repulsive magnets evoked unique and unexpected pleasure. To help understand why people drifted to those textures and interactions, we decided to catalog their experiential qualities here.

- The hairbrush's flexible back and prickly alert spines made it pleasant to strum, squeeze, morph and poke.
- The mixture of microbeads and rice against each other and the slippery texture of the conductive fabric made the squeeze sensor pleasant to squish, roll, and pinch, and had a satisfying weight that made it pleasant to swing around in its initial detached.
- The faux fur belly was soothing with its soft fuzzy fluff.
- The magnet pair placed in the mouth of the dragon encouraged fiddling since the jaw was long enough for a comfortable thumb and forefinger to pinch easily, but with its floating drifting mid-air slip kept a pleasant resistance between your fingertips.

Overall, the team was satisfied with the evocative set of soft electronics/e-textiles options generated in this research, toward building soft-bodied fidget toys, which can enable the kinds of sensory experiences that people want in fidgets while allowing for capturing touch traces.

Every step in the production of this project, from ideation to construction, required a blend of electrical engineering and physical craft expertise. Electrical engineering provided the hard constraints for types of conductive materials and means of interaction that could produce a detectable change in analog signals. For example, while working, our crafter was looking for a sharp snap interaction and suggested solid metal snaps as would be used on overalls to create a solid connection, but was cautioned against exposing users to electric shock, and told that constant contact could easily drain the battery if used as part of a circuit. Physical craft expertise provided a library of tools, materials, and construction blueprints for embedding, disguising, and enhancing the hard constraints of electrical engineering. Without the expertise of the crafting team the engineering team would have created much rougher, simplified examples, and amalgamations like the conductive thread embedded belly would have been dismissed out of hand.

This style of prototyping heavily relies on the creators' skill sets. Well-documented smart material crafting tutorials can help improve understanding between teammates and when shared, also broaden the skillset of the community at large, as exemplified by blogs like that of Perner-Wilson and Satomi [9]. In addition, workshopping and skill share events that teach practical prototyping skills such as those hosted in the TEI Studio series greatly improve the overall skill and quality of the community. Quality work comes from not only have the right tools, but also the creators to use the tools, and it's our recommendation that smaller communities develop a series of skill share workshops when possible.

Conclusion and next steps

In our research, we conducted a materials exploration in which we examined a range of soft electronics/e-textile materials that could provide appropriate kinesthetic and tactile sensations to support everyday fidgeting based on prior research [4]. We developed two sampler objects that provide a range of sensations to fidgeters, and that have the capacity to unobtrusively track touch traces. Should this paper be accepted, we can bring the two prototypes for live demos at the conference.

We believe fidgeting with such 'smart' toys can be an opportunity for attention management awareness and skill building, through capture of and reflection upon touch trace patterns. Our exemplar objects are currently being used and refined in research with children age 8-10, to support development of smart fidget toys for self-regulation. We are using the sampler objects to help children understand the possible range of sensations, toward generating a more viable end product.

Acknowledgements

We would like to thank our post-doc Elena Márquez Segura who supported us and our lab space to allow us to keep the project moving forward.

References

1. Alonso, M.B. Relax! Inherent Feedback During Product Interaction to Reduce Stress. Delft University of Technology, 2010.
2. Cloud, J. Better Learning Through Fidgeting. *Time 173*, 2009, 61.
3. Karlesky, M. and Isbister, K. Designing for the physical margins of digital workspaces: fidget widgets in support of productivity and creativity. In *Proc. TEI 2014.* ACM Press (2014), Pages 13-20.
4. Karlesky, M. and Isbister, K. Understanding Fidget Widgets: Exploring the Design Space of Embodied Self-Regulation. In *Proc. NordiCHI 2016*. ACM Press (2016), Article 38.
5. Karlesky, M., and Isbister, K. Fidget widgets: secondary playful interactions in support of primary

serious tasks. In *CHI EA 2013*. ACM Press (2013), Pages 1149-1154.

6. Minuto, A. and Nijholt, A. Smart material interfaces as a methodology for interaction: a survey of SMIs' state of the art and development. In *Proc. SMI 2013.* ACM Press (2013), Pages 1-6.
7. Perner-Wilson, H., Buechley, L., and Satomi, M. Handcrafting textile interfaces from a kit-of-no-parts. In *Proc. TEI 2011.* ACM Press (2010), Pages 61-68.
8. Philips. Mind Spheres. *design.philips.com*. http://www.design.philips.com/about/design/designportfolio/design_futures/mind_spheres.page. [Online; accessed July-2015]
9. Satomi, M. and Perner-Wilson, H. How to get what you want. http://www.kobakant.at/DIY/, 2008. [Online; accessed July-2016].
10. Vyas, D., Poelman, W., Nijholt, A., and De Bruijn. A. Smart material interfaces: a new form of physical interaction. In *CHI EA 2012.* ACM Press (2012), Pages 1721-1726.
11. Vanderloock, K., Vanden Abeele, V., Suykens, J.A.K., and Guerts, L. The skweezee system: enabling the design and programming of squeeze interactions. In *Proc. UIST 2013.* ACM Press (2013), Pages 521-530.

NewsThings: Exploring Interdisciplinary IoT News Media Opportunities via User-Centred Design

John Mills
Media Innovation Studio
University of Central Lancashire
Preston, UK
jmills@uclan.ac.uk

Peter Bennett
University of Bristol
Bristol, UK
peter.bennett@bristol.ac.uk

Mark Lochrie
Media Innovation Studio
University of Central Lancashire
Preston, UK
mlochrie@uclan.ac.uk

Tom Metcalfe
Thomas Buchanan
Bristol, UK
tom@thomasbuchanan.eu

TEI '18, March 18–21, 2018, Stockholm, Sweden

ACM ISBN 978-1-4503-5568-1/18/03.
https://doi.org/10.1145/3173225.3173267

Abstract
Utilising a multidisciplinary and user-centred product and service design approach, 'NewsThings' explores the potential for domestic and professional internet of things (IoT) objects to convey journalism, media and information. In placing news audiences and industry at the centre of the prototyping process, the project's web connected objects explore how user requirements may be best met in a perceived post-digital environment. Following a research-through-design methodology and utilising a range of tools - such as workshops, cultural probes, market research and long-term prototype deployment with public and industry - NewsThings aims to generate design insights and prototypes that could position the news media as active participants in the development of IoT products, processes and interactions. This work-in-progress paper outlines the project's approach, methods, initial findings - up to and including the pre-deployment phase - and focuses on novel insights around user-engagement with news, and the multidisciplinary team's responses to them.

Author Keywords
Physical; objects; news; IoT; interaction; prototype; media; RtD; design; personalization; insights; journalism

Introduction
Journalism has undergone substantial disruption with the rise of digital technologies. When viewed through a Schumpeterian 'creative destruction' frame [22], the last 25 years of digital evolution has eroded traditional platforms, practice and business models that have sustained journalism and its role in democratic society throughout the 20th century, forcing it into a market and socially driven evolution. This process is continuing, and there is constant adaptation to a networked society [7] and new power systems that emerge as a result of it - this spans the relationship between editorial and audiences [5], and how revenues have shifted from print to alternative digital platforms (PEW estimates[1] one such marker, advertising in US newspapers, to have fallen from $49.4m in 2006 to $18m in 2016). These challenges come at the same time as the public's falling trust of journalism[2], and its capacity to have a positive influence on public perceptions and discourse. To combat these trends, a number of media and journalism scholars have championed collaboration, co-design and open (source) innovation as key tools in producing relevant, usable and 'successful' products and editorial output [6, 14, 17]. The disruption prompted by the web is now being joined by a whole raft of further technologies that will continue to disrupt and distort. These include the impact of Artificial Intelligence and content automation, immersive technologies, smart cities and smart home combined with ambient information transfer, and, in the form of the Internet of Things (IoT), physical-digital ubiquitous computing. All these areas are yet to be explored to their full potential in terms of new content delivery mechanisms from a news perspective. For example; an Amazon Echo simply delivers the news in an audible structured list, whereas, the BBC's R&D Future Experiences is exploring new methods for content rendered in the form of Object Based Media [3, 4] to offer greater user experience from connected objects, and the potential to enhance storytelling across multiple platforms. In some respects, post-digital futures where screens recede and smart cities, homes and ambient digital experiences become normalised, the news media industry will again be placed in a position of digital flux and change.

[1] http://www.journalism.org/fact-sheet/newspapers/
[2] https://www.edelman.com/global-results/

Background
Funded by the Google Digital News Initiative, NewsThings asks how could the news media sector respond to the potential of IoT. It deploys user-focussed methods, interdisciplinary collaborations and co-constructed development pathways create relevant and timely IoT news media products. The multidisciplinary team spans journalism industry and academia, HCI, user experience design, product design, graphic design and behavioural psychology.
NewsThings also leans on previous work on how connected and interactive printed surfaces [11, 19, 12, 18] can be used to convey news and information, and how can news be deconstructed through broadcasting via connecting objects [20]. Working with industry partner Trinity Mirror, design agency Thomas Buchanan the Media Innovation Studio at the University of Central Lancashire, it asks can IoT, connected objects, ambient design and glanceable tech produce more integrated digital news and information systems for users, and therefore new editorial, commercial and interaction opportunities? This approach aligns with a participatory

and user-centred approach to IoT innovation [16] – an emerging approach that is mirrored within media and journalism [6, 14, 17] (as well as within innovation management more generally [8, 23]). NewsThings hopes to offer a novel understanding into how users experience objects within their own home, and receive and convey emotion and meaning from them [9]. It also aims, from postmodern and post-structuralist perspectives, to understand how connected objects may create their own cultural syntax and agency, and how this agency may impact on content and interactions with it [2]. The project therefore adopts a Research through Design (RtD) approach [24] to enable researchers to better understand users, the environments news consumers inhabit and how to best shape new methods for news engagement.

NewsThings

NewsThings adopts a number of phases to its development process to provide a multi-frame/stakeholder stream of user data and insights for the design team to interpret and respond to. A core academic team initially produced a market report detailing relevant human-computer interaction, UX, design, journalism and theoretical constructs. Key findings and recommendations included focus on personalisation (and how AI may help to shape this content), peer-to-peer connectivity and a lack of

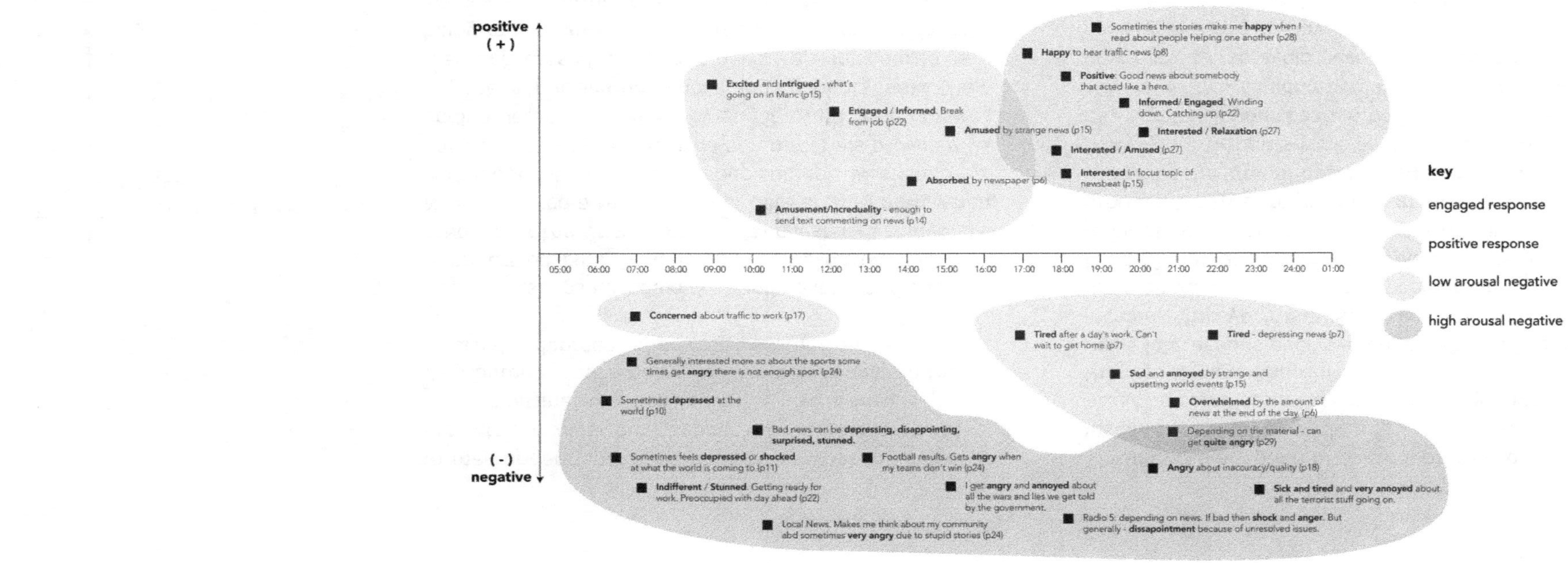

Figure 1. Emotions reported by workshop participants in response to the news throughout the day

Figure 2. Photograph of the cultural probe 'Daily Debrief'.

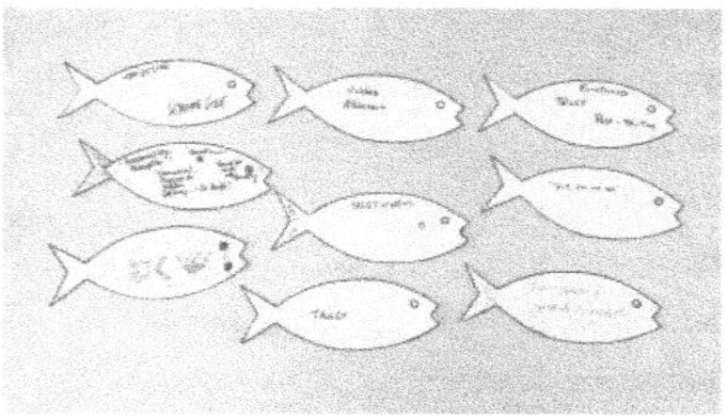

Figure 3. Photograph taken during the creative facilitation sessions around questions of 'stinky fish'

Figure 4. Photograph of the first user insights workshop.

formed understanding/recognition of what IoT objects are within a wider public sphere. It also explored IoT-specific business models, covering smart and distributed manufacturing, which may impact on the future development of physical-digital NewsThings.

User workshops including 40 Trinity Mirror audience members based in Bristol and Manchester (who locally read either the Bristol Post or Manchester Evening News) created a reach seam of data around how, when, where and why users consumed content. Workshop participants mapped their day on materials provided, adding details of media they engage with, when they engage with it and how those engagements make them feel. Concepts of media and news were introduced as being much more pervasive than just print and digital, acknowledging that media is lived in rather than lived with [10] (Figure 4 & Figure 5). User motivations for engaging with content covered a wide range of human emotions such as a desire to learn about the world, country, region and community. To experience news that had a positive impact (Figure 1) and to feel a sense of community. A workshop with a cross-section of Trinity Mirror staff, included representatives from editorial, commercial, marketing and data analysis, was also held. A range of creative facilitation techniques asked questions such as "what is 'stinky fish' of news" to identify industry problems that will just get worse. Stinky fish themes included fake news, trust and reputation, and the impact of a post-truth discourse on public debate and society more generally (Figure 3). Other topics raised during the workshop were increased competition, falling audience loyalty, interactions that move beyond touch, falling audience attention spans and a rise in niche content.

Through the adoption of cultural probes to give rich insights (or inspiration data [13]), 15 participants were asked to complete a task that explicitly encouraged them to engage and reflect upon the context of their news interactions over five days (Figure 2). Examples include: **Map your News:** Participants were asked to draw a map on the back of a postcard in any style they liked of their day's journey through the news. This led to creative responses where types of news were grouped together to form landmarks such as 'vitriol island' or the 'gulf of information'. **No News (is Good News):** Participants were asked to avoid the news for a day and 'stick your head in the sand'. They recorded any news they couldn't avoid. Users were surprised at how hard it is to avoid news as it is 'so ingrained in society' and day-to-day life. **'Paparazzi'**: Participants took pictures of people engaging with the news to build up a picture of news reading context. One participant reported back that *"I was making up ideas in my head about what I thought people were reading from a distance."* This highlights that the idea that the context of news-reading act as a signifier to other people. Photos in this task were often taken outside despite most of the other self-reports in the workshops being inside. Additionally, the probes provided insights into people's responses to being sociable with their news-reading by asking participants to discuss the articles.

Furthermore, each participant had the opportunity to attend either a 'debrief workshop' or one-to-one with a member of the research team. This allowed participants to explore the experience, and feedback directly in a supportive yet enquiring setting, which offered more in-depth discussions and insights, and allowed users and researchers to drill down into issues/ideas they raised. This data fed into the overall probe insights. Analysing

NEWSTHINGLYNESS allows us to include a wow-factor that none of the others do, or reinforce and accentuate the excellent position featured in some of the categories.

COMMERCIAL OPPORTUNITIES do concepts create new revenue streams, business opportunities or meet partner/stakeholder strategy.

USER IMPACT is based on the qualitative and quantitative data gathered. How relevant would it be to participants, audiences and users more widely? Judgements relating to social capital or community engagement are also relevant

EDITORIAL VIABILITY is the possibly for the editorial teams, or community members, to generate the content or data required to power platforms.

PRODUCT VIABILITY is it viable if built? Can it be built within budgets, timescales and skills? Will it function in users' homes or workspaces?

the user insights, it was found that local news was generally more positive than national and international topics. This suggests that our contexts can have psychologically and emotionally, but also physiologically and socially. To transform the user insights and analysis into prototypes, two ideation sessions were conducted with the entire team. Insights and analysis from the workshops and probes were shared and new concepts ideated. A range of concepts that projected from immediate opportunities to 20-year future gazing were also generated by Thomas Buchanan. Concepts were iterated and built during these sessions and subject to an assessment tool to visualise competing factors via a kitemark; dubbed NewsThings Pentonomics (sidebar). This process created a systematic approach to rating and assessing NewsThing concepts. A further round of collaborative design generated the final prototypes:

PrinterThing (Figure 6) provides a personalised and printed daily newspaper at a time that is best for the reader. Throughout the day, users select or 'Pocket' stories they discover on the web but don't have time to read at the time. These articles are stored and laid out automatically into a print newspaper layout. The user is then able to choose when their newspaper is printed, this can be set for 'an hour before bed', 'breakfast' or another time during the day. The print is A4, and prints continuously from an IoT, bespoke printer that uses a thermal printer to avoid ink refill. Once complete, the user rips it from the printer, signalling the end of the retrieval process. Probe insights showed people are more distracted reading news online compared to reading physical news and have a greater sense of fulfilment from the 'going deeper' probes over the 'skip and skimming' one, this also links closely with the ownership of the news (referred to as the endowment effect in psychology'). This prototype therefore asks questions such as: does consuming news in physical form impact on a sense of wellbeing? How often do people want to 'go deeper' into news? How sharable is physical news? And how does delayed reading affect the rhythm of collecting news?

ConeThing (Figure 7) is placed directly within a newsroom. It is a discrete, glanceable device that provides journalists with an ambient view of the public's positive and negative sentiment towards their recent articles on Facebook. It tracks a single article, such as a journalist's most recent post and then performs sentiment analysis on the comments, before rolling itself on its axis to highlight the predominant result, for example, if ConeThing rolls to the left, the reactions to that article are positive. Further details, such as the article title, sub-title and author, are displayed on an e-ink display on the device's upper surface. It moves to the next article every five seconds. Questions this prototype is exploring include: Do people report less negatively towards the end of the day? Can we spot some trends during the course of the day? How does the audience emotional state impact upon the reader? Does enhanced interaction between reporter and reader enhance trust and reduce the propensity for fake news?

RadioThing (Figure 8) allows the construction of a personalised spoken-word account of delivered based on their sentiment. RadioThing can be set to give bad news first and finish with the good news, or other custom curves such as good-bad-good, this feature was inspired by the 'and finally', feel-good news stories, at the end of local news broadcasts. The user loads

Figure 5. Photograph of the user insights and analysis workshop.

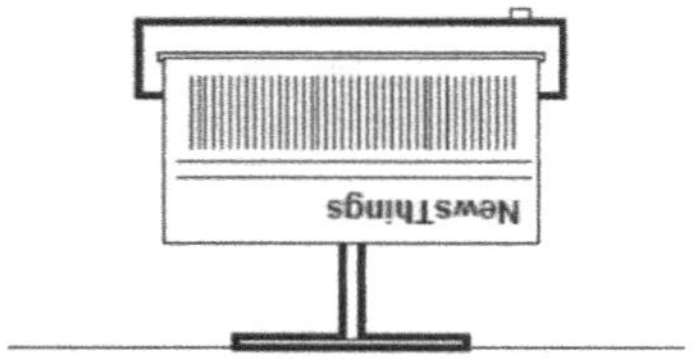

Figure 6. PrinterThing produces a physical summary of the day's news

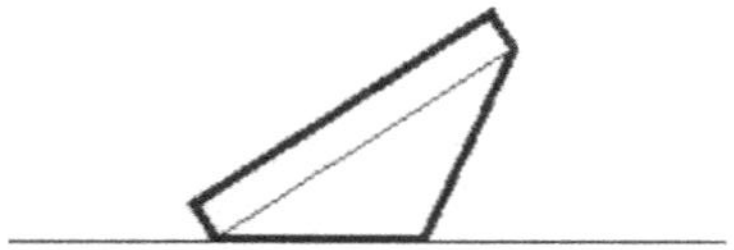

Figure 7. ConeThing's glanceable position shows audience responses

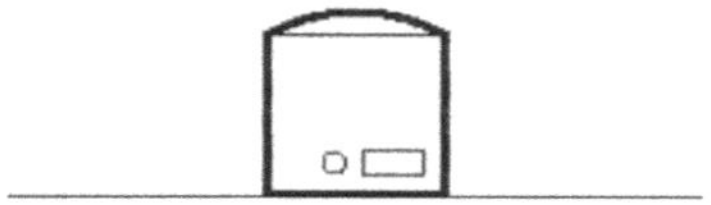

Figure 8. RadioThing allows users to physically filter content

headlines through the use of tangible RFID tags, each representing a different source. Each time a tag is tapped on RadioThing, a new story is added. In this way the user is given greater control in shaping both the content and the emotional delivery. An example would involve a user creating a short show to listen to while they have their breakfast. They tap the Bristol Post token five times to load up a few local news stories, before tapping the international news token and then a music news token once. They then turn the dial to 'bad news at the end' at which point the stories are rearranged so fit the desired 'emotional delivery curve' and played back. The ability to change the combination of the categories to have your own filtered news will be interesting to test and the level of demand for local and good news and whether there is the need for consistency or change. Something that could be correlated to personality traits. It asks if enhanced filtration can increase overall satisfaction/happiness with content to assist the identification of a user's content consumption themes, do people want good news and does user behaviour change over time?

Findings and Future Work

Initial findings demonstrate that users and audiences who consume news and information experience anger and frustration throughout the course of the day, but more emotionally receptive in the evening. We found that news media is diverse and fragmented both in a digital space and in a social space, where users' interactions provide a rich stream of data that they may not initially call 'news' but which functions in the same way. Verbal interactions around news and information, and the physical contexts in which they consume it, can impact on users' rational and emotional processing of that information. During the ideation stage, we sought to create physical objects that responding to this: ConeThing provides a visual display of emotional responses, PrinterThing hopes to capitalise on users' receptiveness to media in key times of the day, and RadioThing gives personalised control to the user. It is important to note these devices are prompts for how media is consumed in the environments we inhabit. During deployment, we will observe how these devices could 'talk' to others in the home/workspace. For instance, how could an Amazon Echo or Google Home be repurposed to include the features and services of RadioThing or would bespoke devices be preferable for users and commercial/industry partners?

Deployment in people's homes and work spaces will take place between January 2018 and May 2018, and we intend to publish more detailed results in due course. Additional areas of enquiry will span users' response to physical form, functionality, content and emotional connections generated over an extended period. The team will also explore how analytic data from the prototypes may be utilised, and what opportunities for expanding online analytics of news and information into context aware physical locations to benefit audience understanding and develop commercial opportunities.

Acknowledgements

To Alison Gow, Paul Gallagher and Mandy Brain at Trinity Mirror for their participation and support, Chloe Foy and David Haylock from Thomas Buchanan, the participants who shared their insights at the workshops and to Google Digital News Initiative for funding the project.

References

1. Tanja Aitamurto, and Seth C. Lewis. 2013 "Open innovation in digital journalism: Examining the impact of Open APIs at four news organizations." new media & society 15.2: 314-331.
2. Jean Baudrillard.1996. "The System of Objects, trans. J. Benedict." London and New York: Verso
3. BBC Research and Development, Future Content Experiences: The First Steps For Object-Based Broadcasting, retrieved November 4, 2017 from http://www.bbc.co.uk/rd/blog/2015-03-future-content-experiences-the-first-steps-for-object-based-broadcasting
4. BBC Research and Development, Object-based broadcasting, retrieved November 4, 2017 from http://www.bbc.co.uk/rd/blog/2013-05-object-based-approach-to-broadcasting
5. Axel Bruns. 2008 Blogs, Wikipedia, Second Life, and beyond: From production to produsage. Peter Lang.
6. Axel Bruns, 2009. "From prosumer to produser: Understanding user-led content creation." in Transforming Audiences 2009, 3-4 Sep, London.
7. Manuel Castells. 2011. The rise of the network society: The information age: Economy, society, and culture. Vol. 1. John Wiley & Sons
8. Henry William Chesbrough. 2006. Open innovation: The new imperative for creating and profiting from technology. Harvard Business Press.
9. Mihaly Csikszentmihalyi and Eugene Halton. 1981 The meaning of things: Domestic symbols and the self. Cambridge University Press.
10. Deuze, Mark. Media life, (2014) John Wiley & Sons.
11. Paul Egglestone and John Mills. 2012 "Interactive Newsprint: The Future of Newspapers? Printed electronics meets hyperlocal and community co-design."
12. David M. Frohlich, Philip Ely, Helen Moore, Connie Goldsteijn, Paul Eggletone, John Mills, Jon Rogers, Tom Metcalfe, Kate Stone, Maria Menicou. 2017. "Designing interactive newsprint." International Journal of Human-Computer Studies 104: 36-49.
13. Bill Gaver, Tony Dunne,and Elena Pacenti.1999. "Design: cultural probes." interactions 6.1: 21-29.
14. Jeff Jarvis.2011. What would Google do?: Reverse-engineering the fastest growing company in the history of the world. Harper Business.
15. Gerd Kortuem and Fahim Kawsar.2010. "Market-based user innovation in the Internet of Things." Internet of Things (IOT), 2010. IEEE
16. Bruno Latour. 2005. Reassembling the social: An introduction to actor-network-theory. Oxford University Press
17. Seth C. Lewis and Nikki Usher. 2013. "Open source and journalism: Toward new frameworks for imagining news innovation." Media, culture & society 35.5 602-619.
18. Mark Lochrie, John Mills and Paul Egglestone. 2015. "Paper gaming: Creating iot paper interactions with conductive inks and web-connectivity through ekko." Proceedings of the 2015 Annual Symposium on Computer-Human Interaction in Play. ACM.
19. John Mills, Paul Egglestone, Mark Lochrie and Martin Skelly. 2015. "Paper-based web connected objects and the Internet of Things through EKKO." Proceedings of the 2015 British HCI Conference. ACM.
20. John Mills, Tom Metcalfe, Mark Lochrie and Adrian Gradinar. 2016. "Rare Occurrence: Exploring IoT, news media, calm interfaces and infrequent interactions." Proceedings of the 30th International BCS Human Computer Interaction Conference (HCI 2016). Electronic Workshops in Computing (eWic).

21. Irene Ng and Susan Y.L. Wakenshaw, 2017. The Internet-of-Things: review and research directions. International Journal of Research in Marketing, 34(1), 3-21.
22. Joseph Schumpeter. 2010. "Creative destruction." Capitalism, socialism and democracy (1943), Routledge, London and New York.
23. Eric Von Hippel.2005. Democratizing innovation. MIT press.
24. John Zimmerman, Jodi Forlizzi and Shelley Evenson 2007. Research through design as a method for interaction design research in HCI. In Proceedings of the SIGCHI conference on Human factors in computing systems (pp. 493-502). ACM

Mechamagnets: Tactile Mechanisms with Embedded Magnets

Figure 1: *Mechamagnet* widgets.

Clement Zheng
ATLAS Institute
University of Colorado
Boulder, CO, USA
clement.zheng@colorado.edu

Ellen Yi-Luen Do
ATLAS Institute
University of Colorado
Boulder, CO, USA
and Keio-NUS-CUTE Center
NUS, Singapore
ellen.do@colorado.edu

TEI '18, March 18–21, 2018, Stockholm, Sweden

ACM ISBN 978-1-4503-5568-1/18/03.
https://doi.org/10.1145/3173225.3173268

Abstract

This paper presents *Mechamagnets*, a technique to rapidly prototype tactile mechanisms for tangible interfaces. We demonstrate how to embed different passive tactile mechanisms in physical systems through a combination of magnets and digitally fabricated parts. We also discuss how DIY materials and 3-axis magnetometers can instrument *Mechamagnet* interfaces into functional prototypes.

Author Keywords

Tactile; Magnets; Rapid Prototyping; Digital Fabrication; Tangible Interaction.

Introduction

Advances in digital fabrication have enabled designers to rapidly prototype physical parts for tangible interfaces—however, integrating mechanisms into these parts is still a complex process. This is compounded by the steep learning curve that many design novices face while learning computer-aided design (CAD) [7].

Mechanisms, however, are vital in making functional physical prototypes for tangible interfaces. In this investigation, we focus on passive mechanisms that also deliver tactile textures (tactile mechanisms).

Tactile feedback is a ubiquitous part of our interactions with physical interfaces; the 'click' of flicking a light switch, or the resistance of turning a door knob, accompanies our use of these objects. They play an important role in informing and guiding our actions [6].

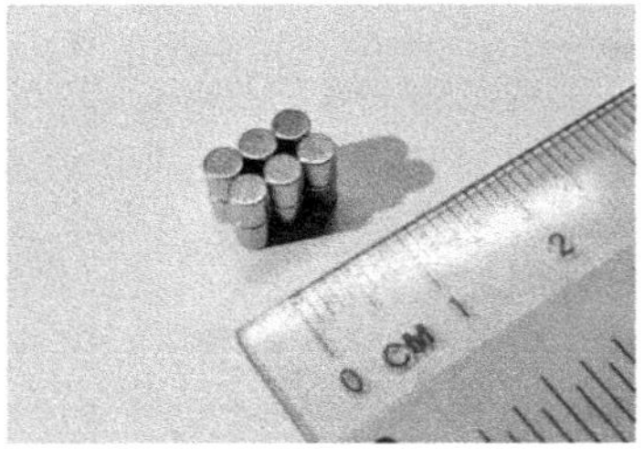

Figure 2: Neodymium magnets.

Figure 3: Printing a *Mechamagnet* part with a FDM machine.

Figure 4: Embedding a magnet into the 3D printed part.

We hypothesize that as a material paired with digital fabrication, magnets are capable of affording a wide range of tactile mechanisms, along with simplifying the process of embedding such mechanisms in tangible interactive systems. In this paper, we describe *Mechamagnets*, a work-in-progress exploring the affordances of magnets in creating passive tactile mechanisms for tangible interfaces. We demonstrate how embedding different configurations of an identical magnetic unit can give 3D printed widgets different tactile mechanisms, as well as afford physical actuation. We also outline methods of instrumenting *Mechamagnet* interfaces into functional prototypes.

Related Work

Mechamagnets is informed and inspired by research on magnets for tangible interfaces, as well as research on prototyping functional physical interfaces.

Magnets come in a variety of forms (sheets, discs, powder etc.), and they can be easily integrated with different partner materials (paper, plastic, liquids etc.). This diversity makes it an ideal material for physical prototyping. Magnets and magnetic forces have been used in various ways in the development of tangible interactive systems. Researchers have demonstrated how to create haptic textures and expressions through the use of magnets [12,13]. Combinations of static- and electro-magnets have also been used as visual and tactile cues to guide user actions [8,11]. Magnets have also been explored as a form of tangible input, in combination with hall effect sensors and 3-axes magnetometers [1,2,4,10,11]. This paper extends the body of work by demonstrating how similar magnetic units can be configured and embedded in 3D printed parts to create functional physical widgets with different tactile textures and mechanisms.

Embedding pre-manufactured mechanisms and electronic parts is a common way to prototype tangible interactive systems. This is a complicated process, as the designer has to build around off-the-shelf parts. *Makers' Marks* [9] expedites this process for designers through a computer vision system which creates inserts and recesses for electronics in a physical form. Physical computing platforms such as the *Calder* toolkit [3] offer designers a range of sensors and actuators which can be easily programmed and attached onto physical models for functional testing. However, while these systems mitigate the integration of electronics, they restrict designers to the form, structure and tactile mechanisms offered by existing components.

Mechamagnets: Design Exploration

We started by exploring the design space of embedded magnets as tactile mechanisms in digitally fabricated assemblies. We used a specific static magnet in this investigation: 3mm by 3mm cylindrical neodymium magnets (Figure 2). Different mechanisms were created from varying the polarity and spatial arrangements of this same magnet unit. All other parts were fabricated by a desktop fused deposition modelling (FDM) 3D printer in polylactide (PLA) plastic (Figure 3). To embed the magnets, holes with a negative tolerance were modelled in the 3D printed parts. Magnets are pressed into these holes, resulting in a snug fit (Figure 4). We developed a variety of widgets from this exploration.

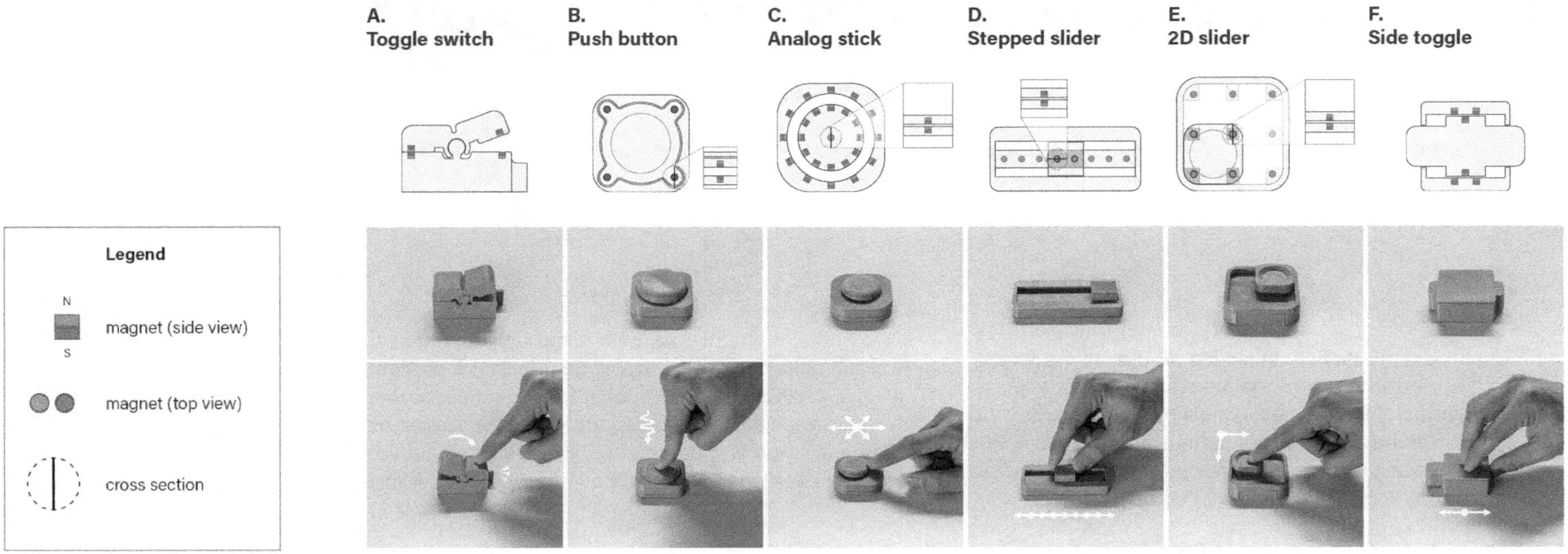

Figure 5: Input widgets— A) *Toggle switch*, attracting magnets snap between states. B) *Push button*, repelling magnets act as a spring. C) *Analog stick*, magnets repel around the perimeter while attracting magnets creates a center rest-point. D) *Stepped slider*, linearly spaced magnets attract and snap the slider into position. E) *2D slider*, a grid of magnets attract and snap the slider into position. F) *Side toggle*, repelling magnets stop the button at three different positions.

Tactile mechanisms for input

For this initial exploration, we focused on replicating the tactile textures and mechanisms found in common physical input interfaces.

1. *Toggle switch* (Figure 5A): The switch is constrained to rotate about a hinge, while a set of attracting magnets hold its state. When pressed with sufficient force, the switch flips into its new position, resulting in a satisfying snapping sound.
2. *Push button* (Figure 5B): Repelling magnets keep the button lifted off the floor. These magnets offer resistance when pushed, simulating the act of compressing a spring.
3. *Analog stick* (Figure 5C): A perimeter of repelling magnets pushes against the stick when it is off-center, while a pair of attracting magnets creates a center rest-point. The tactile texture generated resembles the stick controls found in Sony's PlayStation® Portable or Nintendo's 3DS.

4. *Stepped slider* (Figure 5D): An array of magnets is embedded along the track, corresponding to a pair placed in the slider. The slider 'clicks' as if there were detents when it is pushed along the track.
5. *2D slider* (Figure 5E): A variation of the stepped slider, the *2D slider* uses a two dimensional grid of regularly spaced magnets instead.
6. *Side toggle* (Figure 5F): A series of repelling magnets offer push back when the button is pushed along the shaft. This creates three rest positions for the button.

Physical Actuation
Our initial exploration on input widgets revealed that magnets can be easily configured in a physical part as a substitute for different physical mechanisms. This motivated our exploration for output widgets; and we focused on using magnets to translate simple physical movements into more complex actuation.

1. *Latch* (Figure 6A): This widget consists of two moving parts: a rotating arm, and an opposing pin constrained to move along its shaft. Depending on the polarity of the magnets arrayed around the arm, its rotation translates to linearly pushing or pulling the pin along its shaft.
2. *Multi-solenoid* (Figure 6B/C): A set of four pins is animated via a circular magnet array. Pins rise or fall depending on the polarity of the opposing magnet on the wheel as it rotates, and different animations can be created by rearranging the polarity of magnets around the wheel.

Characterizing tactile mechanisms
We observed that the tactile mechanisms of each widget can be characterized by two parameters: namely, the angle between its movement path and the orientation of its magnets (tangent or normal), as well as the polarity of opposing magnets (attraction or repulsion) (Figure 7).

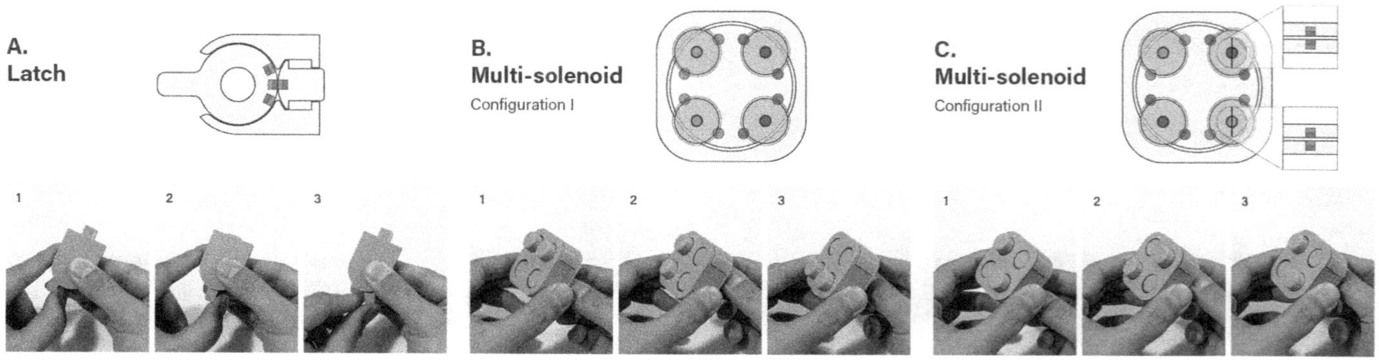

Figure 6: Output widgets— A) *Latch*, pushing or pulling a pin based on the opposing magnet's polarity. B/C) *Multi-solenoid*, the animation of the four pins is determined by the different arrangements of the magnet polarities around the wheel.

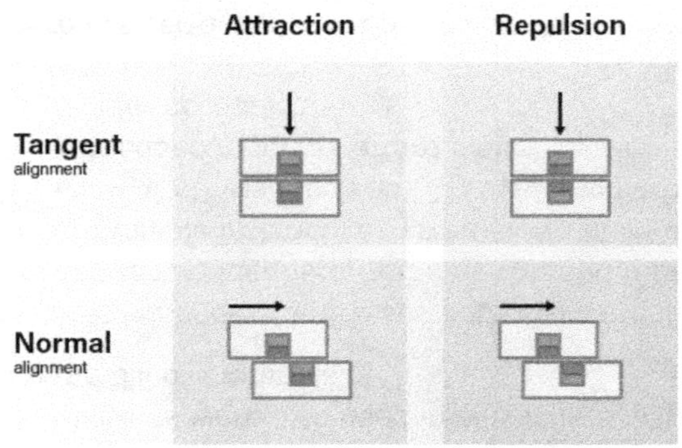

Figure 7: Matrix of fundamental tactile mechanisms.

A combination of tangent alignment and attraction creates a "hard stop". This tactile mechanism is expressed in the toggle switch widget, and feels similar to the click of a light switch. Combining tangent alignment with repulsion resembles a "spring", as observed in the push button and analog stick widgets. A combination of normal alignment and attraction creates a "detent". This tactile mechanism is demonstrated by the stepped slider and 2D slider widgets, and feels similar to dials that turn with discrete increments. Finally, combining normal alignment with repulsion creates a "soft barrier". This is expressed by the side toggle widget; repelling magnets form a barrier which is overcome with enough force.

This initial classification is an attempt at characterizing the tactile mechanisms afforded by *Mechamagnets*. Thus far, we have focused our exploration on modeling tactile mechanisms found in existing interfaces. While these four categories may not comprehensively encompass all possibilities, we believe that it serves as a useful vocabulary to guide the development of new tactile mechanisms for tangible input.

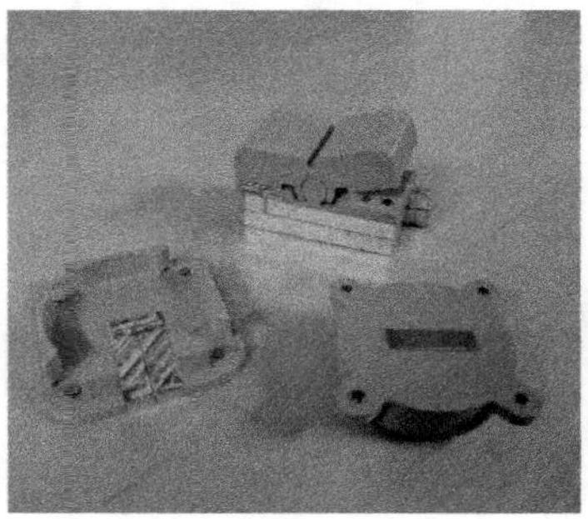

Figure 8: Using copper tape to trace circuits directly on the widgets' surface.

Instrumenting Mechamagnet Interfaces

Beside tactile mechanisms, we further investigated methods of creating functional *Mechamagnet* interfaces. We used the widgets developed from the design exploration as a platform to explore different instrumentation methods.

The "untoolkit" approach [5] to physical computing proposed by Mellis et al. was particular inspiring to us, and resonated with our material-centric perspective. They harnessed craft practices and materials to create functional tangible interfaces. In our exploration, we used copper tape to trace circuits directly on the widgets' surface. We were able to create simple contact switches to sense binary input with this method; such as to detect the state of the toggle switch and the push button widgets (Figure 8).

Magnetometers have been used to detect the identity, location and states of tangible tokens and widgets [1,2,10]. Similarly, we explored using 3-axis magnetometers to estimate the position of magnets in a *Mechamagnet* widget, thus providing an operationalization for user interaction. A rig and visualization was developed to test each widget (Figure 9A). Compared to the former method of instrumenting the widgets with copper tape circuits, the magnetometer setup was able to detect not just binary state changes, but also analog variations between a widget's states. For example, we were able to sense the depth of a push button (Figure 9B), as well as the position of an analog stick (Figure 9C).

Benefits & Limitations

Magnets provide many opportunities for the design of functional and expressive tangible user interfaces. Our

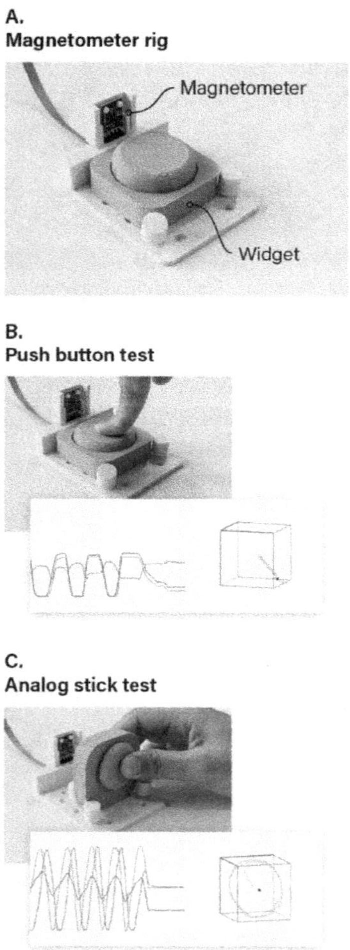

Figure 9: Testing widgets with the magnetometer rig.

work extends this body of research by demonstrating a means to embed tactile mechanisms with magnets for tangible interfaces. At this stage, we believe that *Mechamagnets* benefits the design of tangible interfaces in the following ways:

1. *Mechamagnets* offers a relatively efficient technique for prototyping tactile mechanisms. As a comparative example, creating a conventional stepped slider requires the integration of springs, ball bearings and detents; while the *Mechamagnet* stepped slider (Figure 5D) employs an array of identical magnets. Furthermore, these magnets are embedded via a simple hole feature, thus providing designers with more flexibility when considering other aspects of a tangible interface.
2. *Mechamagnets* is an economical technique. All widgets demonstrated were fabricated with a low-end 3D printer, while magnets were inserted either manually or with regular hand tools. Identical magnets were also used in all widgets, simplifying the bill of materials.
3. *Mechamagnets* addresses both instrumentation and tactile feedback in the design and fabrication of tangible interactive systems. We build on the work of others (such as [2]) by demonstrating how embedded magnets afford digital sensing as well as tactile mechanisms.

There are certainly limitations to *Mechamagnets*; primarily due to the properties of magnets themselves. The widgets demonstrated in this paper were designed as tangible interfaces for hands and fingers, and the chosen magnetic unit was able to provide sufficient force to afford different tactile textures. For applications involving greater forces (such as foot or full body interfaces), other methods might be more effective (such as springs with a larger spring constant). Magnets are also affected by magnetic materials. While this is not a concern with the 3D printed plastic parts demonstrated, this property constrains the material space of *Mechamagnet* interfaces.

Future Work

We have explored replicating the tactility of common interfaces and proposed an initial vocabulary to describe the range of fundamental tactile mechanisms afforded by *Mechamagnets*. In addition, we explored embedded magnets for physical actuation.

Moving forward, we plan to engage with other tangible interaction designers to imagine new tactile textures and mechanisms with embedded magnets. We will also work on developing more robust characterizations of magnets to understand its affordance for the *Mechamagnets* technique. Ultimately, we aim to formalize a practical approach for supporting designers as they develop tactile textures and mechanisms for tangible user interfaces with embedded magnets.

Furthermore, 3D modeling—and 3D printing by extension—remains a challenge for design novices. While we envision *Mechamagnets* as a prototyping technique, we also see an opportunity for CAD tools to facilitate the design and fabrication of interfaces with embedded tactile mechanisms. This can increase the accessibility of *Mechamagnets* to a wider range of designers. In its simplest form, such a tool could offer parametric *Mechamagnet* primitives where designers can customize different parameters associated with the form, mechanism and tactile texture of the part.

Acknowledgements
This research is supported by the ATLAS Institute, University of Colorado Boulder, USA and National Research Foundation, Prime Minister's Office, Singapore under its International Research Centres in Singapore Funding Initiative.

References

1. Andrea Bianchi and Ian Oakley. 2015. MagnID: Tracking Multiple Magnetic Tokens. In *Proceedings of the Ninth International Conference on Tangible, Embedded, and Embodied Interaction* (TEI '15), 61–68. https://doi.org/10.1145/2677199.2680582
2. Sungjae Hwang, Myungwook Ahn, and Kwang-yun Wohn. 2013. MagGetz: Customizable Passive Tangible Controllers on and Around Conventional Mobile Devices. In *Proceedings of the 26th Annual ACM Symposium on User Interface Software and Technology* (UIST '13), 411–416. https://doi.org/10.1145/2501988.2501991
3. Johnny C. Lee, Daniel Avrahami, Scott E. Hudson, Jodi Forlizzi, Paul H. Dietz, and Darren Leigh. 2004. The Calder Toolkit: Wired and Wireless Components for Rapidly Prototyping Interactive Devices. In *Proceedings of the 5th Conference on Designing Interactive Systems: Processes, Practices, Methods, and Techniques* (DIS '04), 167–175. https://doi.org/10.1145/1013115.1013139
4. Rong-Hao Liang, Liwei Chan, Hung-Yu Tseng, Han-Chih Kuo, Da-Yuan Huang, De-Nian Yang, and Bing-Yu Chen. 2014. Gaussbricks: Magnetic Building Blocks for Constructive Tangible Interactions on Portable Displays. In *CHI '14 Extended Abstracts on Human Factors in Computing Systems* (CHI EA '14), 587–590. https://doi.org/10.1145/2559206.2574776
5. David A. Mellis, Sam Jacoby, Leah Buechley, Hannah Perner-Wilson, and Jie Qi. 2013. Microcontrollers As Material: Crafting Circuits with Paper, Conductive Ink, Electronic Components, and an "Untoolkit." In *Proceedings of the 7th International Conference on Tangible, Embedded and Embodied Interaction* (TEI '13), 83–90. https://doi.org/10.1145/2460625.2460638
6. Don Norman. 2013. *The design of everyday things: Revised and expanded edition*. Basic Books (AZ).
7. Lora Oehlberg, Wesley Willett, and Wendy E. Mackay. 2015. Patterns of Physical Design Remixing in Online Maker Communities. In *Proceedings of the 33rd Annual ACM Conference on Human Factors in Computing Systems*, 639–648. https://doi.org/10.1145/2702123.2702175
8. Masa Ogata and Masaaki Fukumoto. 2015. FluxPaper: Reinventing Paper with Dynamic Actuation Powered by Magnetic Flux. In *Proceedings of the 33rd Annual ACM Conference on Human Factors in Computing Systems* (CHI '15), 29–38. https://doi.org/10.1145/2702123.2702516
9. Valkyrie Savage, Sean Follmer, Jingyi Li, and Björn Hartmann. 2015. Makers' Marks: Physical Markup for Designing and Fabricating Functional

Objects. In *Proceedings of the 28th Annual ACM Symposium on User Interface Software & Technology* (UIST '15), 103–108. https://doi.org/10.1145/2807442.2807508

10. Boris Smus and Christopher Riederer. 2015. Magnetic input for mobile virtual reality. In *Proceedings of the 2015 ACM International Symposium on Wearable Computers*, 43–44.

11. Evan Strasnick, Jackie Yang, Kesler Tanner, Alex Olwal, and Sean Follmer. 2017. shiftIO: Reconfigurable Tactile Elements for Dynamic Affordances and Mobile Interaction. In *Proceedings of the 2017 CHI Conference on Human Factors in Computing Systems* (CHI '17), 5075–5086. https://doi.org/10.1145/3025453.3025988

12. Katrin Wolf and Peter D. Bennett. 2013. Haptic Cues: Texture As a Guide for Non-visual Tangible Interaction. In *CHI '13 Extended Abstracts on Human Factors in Computing Systems* (CHI EA '13), 1599–1604. https://doi.org/10.1145/2468356.2468642

13. Kentaro Yasu. 2017. Magnetic Plotter: A Macrotexture Design Method Using Magnetic Rubber Sheets. In *Proceedings of the 2017 CHI Conference on Human Factors in Computing Systems* (CHI '17), 4983–4993. https://doi.org/10.1145/3025453.3025702

The Evolving Design of Tangibles for Graph Algorithmic Thinking

Andrea Bonani, Vincenzo Del Fatto, Rosella Gennari
Computer Science Faculty, Free University of Bozen-Bolzano
Piazza Domenicani 3, 39100 Bolzano, Italy
abonani@unibz.it, vincenzo.delfatto@unibz.it, gennari@inf.unibz.it

TEI '18, March 18–21, 2018, Stockholm, Sweden
ACM 978-1-4503-5568-1/18/03.
https://doi.org/10.1145/3173225.3173270

Abstract
Algorithmic thinking is at the core of computational thinking. Tangible interactive solutions can help children develop algorithmic thinking skills. This paper focusses on exploratory research concerning tangibles for graph algorithmic thinking for primary and middle schools. By following an action-research process, tangibles evolved through prototyping and actions-studies. The paper overviews their evolution and delves into its most recent action: an ecological study with 8 middle school children, and 5 primary school children, using tangibles for graph algorithmic thinking. It ends by reflecting on results and future work.

Author Keywords
algorithmic thinking; tangible design; action research; IoT; children; primary school; middle school.

ACM Classification Keywords
[Human-centered computing]: Interaction design theory, concepts and paradigms

Introduction
In the last decade, an increasing number of countries produced documents and guidelines for *Computational Thinking* (CT) or *Algorithmic Thinking* (AT) education [1, 8]. *CT* refers to a pool of abilities necessary to abstract away a problem, and represent it in a format amenable for comput-

ers to process. At the core of CT abilities, one can recognise the less known AT abilities [25]. Thinking algorithmically means being able to: *understand* an abstract representation; apply it to *model* a problem; *design* or employ a strategy/algorithm for solving it [11]. This paper focuses on *Graph AT* (*GAT*) for children, which requires them to: (1) understand graphs; (2) model a problem with graphs; (3) design or employ strategies for solving it.

Example problems for GAT, familiar to all and used throughout this paper, are found in social networks, e.g., of Facebook friends or classmate friends. The formal definition of a graph, adopted in the rest of the paper, is as follows: a(n undirected) *graph* is an ordered pair $G = (V, E)$, with $V = \{v_1, \ldots, v_n\}$ the set of *nodes*, and $E = \{\{v_i, v_j\} \mid v_i, v_j \in V\}$ the set of *edges* between pairs of nodes.

In the social network example, people can be modelled as graph nodes, and edges between nodes represent their friendship relations. Designing or employing graph algorithms in this context mean tackling the following example problems: is there a way to connect a person, A, to another person, B, through a path of mutual friends? Can someone connect to all the other people, and how?

Graphs are abstract constructs for primary and middle classes, and GAT may be difficult for them. This paper builds on the idea that *interactive tangible objects* (briefly, *tangibles*) can help building GAT skills of primary and middle school children, as well as of their teachers, through multi-sensory experiences, possibly collaborative.

The design and assessment of such tangibles are highly complex. Tangibles for GAT should be developed and explored in the field with children. Actions in the field should assess not only whether tangibles are usable and *engage* children and teachers, but also if they are useful, and what their effects are in terms of AT *learning*. In this paper, action-based research, which recommends the deployment of prototypal tangibles and acting with them in real-world contexts, has been chosen to design GAT tangibles, which are thus informed by repeated usage practices.

The paper starts with positioning this on-going research with respect to existing literature and giving the necessary background. Then it explains the chosen research approach for making GAT tangibles evolve over time, through evolving development of tangibles and actions in the field. The development of the most recent GAT tangible prototype is explained, and the latest action with it is described: a field study with children from primary and middle schools, reporting children's engagement and learning. The paper ends by reflecting on the experience and future work.

Background and Related Work

A systematic literature review was conducted and papers were classified in three main categories of approaches to CT/AT education.

With computers. There are numerous activities oriented to CT via coding activities, also in the early years of schooling. Block-based programming environments are mainly used, such as Scratch [15] and Alice [24]. They all require computer or mobile devices, they mainly target individual work, and mostly programming skills.

Unplugged. Experiences, inspired by the CS unplugged movement, foster CT with children through non-technology-mediated activities, e.g., [2, 26, 23, 19]. They are based on the principle that children learn best through multi-modal experiences and with the help of teachers trained to work as facilitators of the AT/CT learning process. An example unplugged AT activity concerning GAT is reported in [22], with middle school students and paper-based material.

With tangibles. As advocated by the Unplugged CS movement, multi-sensory physical activities are beneficial for learning. In this view, unobtrusive tangible solutions can further enhance the experience with interactivity, and help children and teachers engage in the learning process [18]. In the area of CT, well-known examples are instructional activities with robotics such as [3, 9], and others requiring different physical computing devices like [12, 10]. Other specific tangibles acting as probes for CT or AT education are reported in [13, 14].

The classification shows different approaches concerning CT, and specifically AT, of varying maturity. In the majority of cases, AT activities are oriented to the transmission of CT as a whole. There are relatively few proposals that focus specifically on AT scaffolding with primary or middle school children, and which assess their emotional engagement or their inclusion in the learning process, e.g., [5]. The research presented in the remainder of this paper is one of such proposals, focussed on tangibles for GAT.

The Design Process in a Nutshell

The design of GAT tangibles follows an action research paradigm. This aims at bringing benefits to all participants: novel design ideas to designers who work with the intended users of their tangibles, in their natural contexts; engagement and learning benefits to users of tangibles, that is, 9–13 years old learners, from primary and middle schools, and their teachers.

The design process spirals through three stages. The first is the (1) *development* of tangibles. The second consists in (2) *acting in the field* with tangibles and users. The final stage consists in (3) *reflecting about users' usage* of tangibles. The stages are interleaved, e.g., reflections are conducted meanwhile actions are taken, and require to develop evolving prototypal tangibles. Such prototypes are also modular, and vertical in that that they provide just few fully novel functionalities so as to explore their usage in the field, as rapidly as possible. They are conceived as intermediary objects, in the sense of [6], which are used in studies with designers and users for detecting usability issues, exploring novel design possibilities, as well as creating learning possibilities for users.

The design process of GAT tangibles started with a literature review, overviewed above, and an exploratory context of use analysis, which gave the first alternative design ideas, assessed with interaction design experts. After building a first prototype of GAT tangibles, designers and users participated in two small-scale studies, held in informal learning contexts, see [4, 16] respectively. Tangibles were rapidly assessed and redesigned, according to results of the studies. For instance, the main usability issues were fixed, new learning scenarios for primary and middle schools were developed together with teachers, and new design features were added after studies with children.

The novel GAT tangible prototypes and learning scenarios are presented in the following section.

GAT Tangibles

The current version of GAT tangibles are implemented as client-server prototypes. Software is written in Python 2.7 and uses NetworkX package for managing graphs.

The client software runs on a set of GAT tangibles: nodes and a so-called confirmation button. Each node is a wood box which embeds a Raspberry PI and other micro-electronics components, such as LEDs, buttons and power banks. The confirmation button is a 3D-printed cylinder with a large LED button for asking specific feedback about the graph

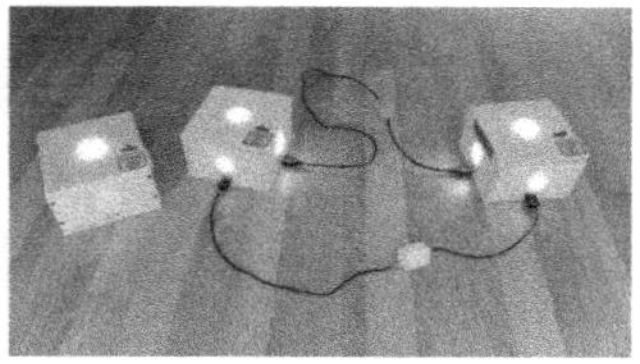

Figure 1: Red lights indicating a parallel edge error.

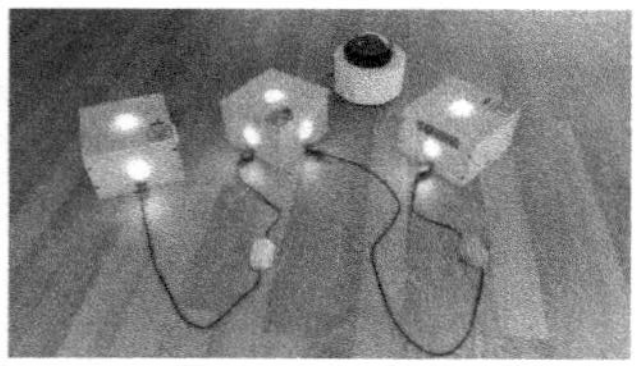

Figure 2: Connected graph, where all lights blink green.

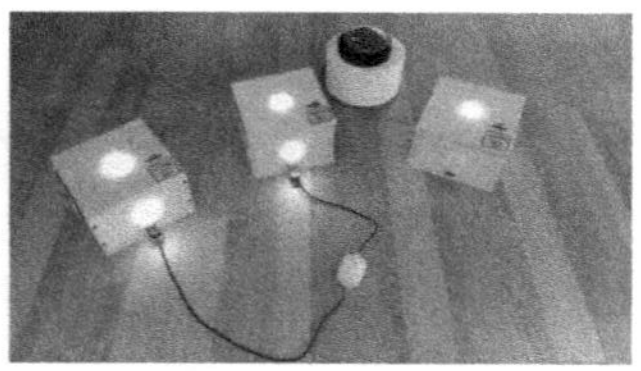

Figure 3: Light feedback concerning a disconnected graph and its connected components.

on demand. Other components are edges, currently, USB cables, for connecting nodes. See Figg. 1, 2, and 3.

By referring to the social network example, given in the introductory section, nodes represent people, and edges represent friendship relationships. Therefore, two friends are modelled with two nodes connected by an edge.

The GAT tangibles differently interact with learners, depending on the specific learning scenario. This has a learning goal and is activated through the teacher GUI, which is one of the server side functionality. Moreover, the server communicates with GAT tangibles through Wi-Fi and verifies in real-time graph properties according to the learning scenario chosen by the teacher.

The two main *learning scenarios* of this paper are: (1) *simple graphs*; (2) *simple and connected graphs.*

The former is the basic scenario for making children understand simple graphs, without loops and parallel edges, and model problems with simple graphs. In the paper example, "simple" means that "none is friend oneself". LED lights and sounds give feedback, e.g., if learners add two parallel edges between two nodes, an intermittent red light and sound indicate the property violation, as shown in Figure 1.

The simple and connected graph scenario considers graph connectivity. Once children consider the scenario over, they press the confirmation button. If the graph is connected, all nodes have green LED lights and a victory sound (see Figure 2). Else, each connected component (set of nodes) of the graph blinks with a different colour, and gives a wrong alert sound (see Figure 3).

GAT tangibles and their companion scenarios were used in the study described in the remainder of this paper.

Study Design

Research Questions

Having considered usability issues within previous small-scale studies, the novel study with primary and middle schools explores expected children's benefits: **(R1)** children's engagement; **(R2)** children's learning, specifically, in relation to graph understanding, graph modelling and, to a minor extent, graph algorithm/strategy design.

Participants and Setting

The novel small-scale study involved: 8 middle school children aged 12–13; 2 primary school children aged 10, and 3 primary school children aged 11. The study was split into different interventions, and conducted according to the school or children's timetable constraints. Each intervention lasted circa 1 hour and a half. The study also involved three researchers: one, an in-service teacher pursuing a PhD, acting as teacher and moderator; the other, with a background in child computer interaction, worked as observer; a third one acted as technician and managed the video recording apparatus. All children participated on a voluntary basis, and their parents authorised their participation, after being informed about the aim of the interventions and data collection procedure.

Data Collection

Data collected by researchers were qualitative and quantitative, concerning engagement (R1) and learning (R2).

Qualitative data. Qualitative data were gathered during the interventions in two main manners: interviews; indirect observations. Interviews with questions were led by the teacher and answers were tracked by the observer. They tackled children's graph understanding with GAT tangibles, modelling problems with GAT tangibles, and designing strategies to solve problems with GAT tangibles.

Indirect observations were gathered through videos; a video camera was positioned so as to record all children's interaction with GAT tangibles. Interview answers and videos were independently analysed by researchers and then iteratively compared for assessing: children's engagement with GAT tangibles, by considering the behavioural indicators suggested in [17]; children's learning of GAT, specifically, their answers to the teacher's interview questions.

Quantitative data. Data concerning engagement was also assessed at the end of the interventions, by using the again-and-again table and asking children whether they would like to do activities with GAT tangibles again [20]. Data concerning children's learning of GAT was also measured through a post-survey, after each intervention. The survey was constructed by two researchers and pilot tested with two teachers and two children before its administration. With the help of teachers, researchers also mapped Bloom's levels to the survey questions, like in [21]. Survey questions concentrated on the following levels of Bloom's taxonomy: **(1)** understanding of simple graphs (3 questions concerning 3 graphs, with yes-no answers); **(2)** understanding of connected graphs (3 questions concerning 3 graphs, with yes-no answers); **(3)** application, namely, GAT modelling (2 modelling exercises, with open format answers). Note that none of the participating children had any experience of graphs, algorithms or programming, and hence the survey could not be administered before the study.

Tasks
Task scenarios were used to conduct the study with children. Task scenarios refine the aforementioned learning scenarios. They describe, for all researchers and teachers, how to use GAT tangibles in the study, so as to be able to replicate and compare results across interventions; in particular, they specify what interview questions the teacher should pose in a semi-structured manner. The *first task scenario* mainly aims at making children understand simple graphs and model problems with them. The *second task scenario* aims at making children understand connected graphs, model a problem with a connected graph, and design a strategy to create a connected simple graph. Children are guided through tasks of the scenarios with GAT tangibles and teacher's questions.

Study Results
The main study findings, resulting from qualitative and quantitative data analyses, are reported in the following in relation to the two main research questions of the study: (R1) children's engagement; (R2) children's learning.

Engagement Results
According to the qualitative data analysis, all children were engaged with GAT tangibles, except one primary school child aged 10. An example behavioural indicator of engagement was that all children got close to GAT tangibles when the visual feedback was given for observing colours. According to their again-and-again table answers, all children except the aforementioned one are willing to repeat the experience for learning about GAT with tangibles.

Learning Results
According to the qualitative data analysis, primary-school children required further scaffolding support by researchers than envisioned in task scenarios in order to understand simple and connected graphs. All children succeeded in using tangibles for modelling the problem proposed by the task scenarios. In relation to the second task scenario, only one child from the middle school was able to devise a strategy for connecting a disconnected graph—by always working on a single node per connected component.

Answers to the survey were either correct (coded as 1) or not (0). Success rate was measured by considering the percentage of correct answers divided by the number of participating students. Relevant basic statistics are as follows. The average success rate related to the understanding of simple graphs was: 79% for middle school children; 93% for primary school children. The average success rate for understanding of connected graphs was: 54% for middle school children; 67% for primary school children. The average success rate for modelling was: 87% for middle school children; 29% for primary school children.

Reflections and Conclusions

This paper presented *exploratory* action-based research concerning the design of tangibles for AT, and specifically AT for graphs, that is, GAT. It presented the evolving design of GAT tangibles and the latest action with them, namely, a study with primary and middle school children using tangibles. Data, qualitative and quantitative, were collected with different methods in relation to: (R1) children's engagement; (R2) learning of GAT. Qualitative data were mainly used to interpret quantitative data results, and place them into context in relation to R1 and R2. Reflections concerning results follow and conclude this paper.

Results concerning engagement (R1), qualitative and quantitative, are overall positive. However, engagement results may also be due to the novelty factor. Further studies with GAT tangibles are needed to confirm the results.

Results for learning (R2) are reflected over in relation to the AT tasks of graph understanding, graph modelling and designing of a strategy for connecting a disconnected graph.

Quantitative survey results suggest that children understood simple and connected graphs. Surprisingly, primary school children had slightly better results concerning understanding than middle school ones. However, according to qualitative results, primary school children needed additional scaffolding support concerning graph understanding (i.e., to repeat task scenarios). Such scaffold may be the reason for the differences in survey results concerning graph understanding. Middle school children's survey results for modelling were better than primary school children's results. These differences can be explained by children's ages.

Qualitative results reveal that only a middle-school child could design a strategy to connect the graph. This task seems thus difficult for children even with GAT tangibles, in an intervention of circa 1 hour and a half.

In view of the above results, future experiences with middle school children will tackle more advanced GAT topics and create novel learning scenarios for teachers, e.g., novel scenarios with trees, which may adapt themselves to children, e.g., [7]. Future work will also seek to employ a different research design for assessing learning benefits due to GAT tangibles.

Acknowledgments
Thanks to Gabriella Dodero and Guerriero Raimato for their work on previous versions of GAT tangibles, Markus Zanker for his support, all participating children and their teachers, Claudio Benizi and Luigi Caneve of the Archimede school in Bolzano, besides the financial support of the GAPH project.

REFERENCES

1. E. Barendsen, L. Mannila, B. Demo, N. Grgurina, C. Izu, C. Mirolo, S. Sentance, A. Settle, and G. Stupurienė. Concepts in K-9 computer science education.
2. T.C. Bell, I.H. Witten, and M. Fellows. 1998. *Computer Science Unplugged: Off-line activities and games for all ages*. Computer Science Unplugged.
3. M.U. Bers, L. Flannery, E.R. Kazakoff, and A. Sullivan. 2014. Computational thinking and tinkering: Exploration of an early childhood robotics curriculum. *Computers & Education* 72 (2014), 145–157.
4. A. Bonani, V. Del Fatto, G. Dodero, R. Gennari, and G. Raimato. 2017. *First Steps Towards the Design of Tangibles for Graph Algorithmic Thinking*. Springer International Publishing, Cham, 110–117. DOI: http://dx.doi.org/10.1007/978-3-319-60819-8_13
5. M. Brondino, G. Dodero, R. Gennari, A. Melonio, M. Pasini, D. Raccanello, and S. Torello. 2015. Emotions and inclusion in co-design at school: Let's measure them! *Advances in Intelligent Systems and Computing* 374 (2015), 1–8. DOI: http://dx.doi.org/10.1007/978-3-319-19632-9_1
6. F. Cabitza, D. Fogli, and A. Piccinno. 2014. *"Each to His Own": Distinguishing Activities, Roles and Artifacts in EUD Practices*. Springer International Publishing, Cham, 193–205. DOI: http://dx.doi.org/10.1007/978-3-319-07040-7_19
7. T. Di Mascio, R. Gennari, A. Melonio, and P. Vittorini. 2012. The user classes building process in a TEL project. *Advances in Intelligent and Soft Computing* 152 AISC (2012), 107–114. DOI: http://dx.doi.org/10.1007/978-3-642-28801-2_13
8. C. Duncan and T. Bell. 2015. A pilot computer science and programming course for primary school students. In *Proceedings of the Workshop in Primary and Secondary Computing Education*. ACM, 39–48.
9. B. Ericson and T. McKlin. 2012. Effective and sustainable computing summer camps. In *Proceedings of the 43rd ACM technical symposium on Computer Science Education*. ACM, 289–294.
10. Y. Feaster, L. Segars, S.K. Wahba, and J.O. H. 2011. Teaching CS unplugged in the high school (with limited success). In *Proceedings of the 16th annual joint conference on Innovation and technology in computer science education*. ACM, 248–252.
11. G. Futschek. 2006. Algorithmic thinking: the key for understanding computer science. In *Informatics education–the bridge between using and understanding computers*. Springer, 159–168.
12. G. Futschek and J. Moschitz. 2011. Learning algorithmic thinking with tangible objects eases transition to computer programming. In *Informatics in Schools. Contributing to 21st Century Education*. Springer, 155–164.
13. R. Gennari, V. Del Fatto, E. Gashi, J. Sanin, and A. Ventura. 2016. *Gamified Technology Probes for Scaffolding Computational Thinking*. Springer International Publishing, Cham, 303–307. DOI: http://dx.doi.org/10.1007/978-3-319-33464-6_19
14. R. Gennari, A. Melonio, and S. Torello. 2017. Gamified Probes for Cooperative Learning: a Case Study. *Multimedia Tools and Applications* 76, 4 (2017), 4925–4949. DOI: http://dx.doi.org/10.1007/s11042-016-3543-7

15. Lifelong Kindergarten Group. 2003. Scratch. (2003). https://scratch.mit.edu.
16. Ó. Mealha, M. Divitini, and M. Rehm (Eds.). 2018. Springer International Publishing, Cham.
17. J. Ocumpaugh, R.S. Baker, and M.M.T. Rodrigo. 2015. Monitoring Protocol (BROMP) 2.0 Technical & Training Manual. NY, NY: Teachers College. (2015).
18. S. Papert. 1980. *Mindstorms: Children, computers, and powerful ideas.* Basic Books, Inc.
19. S. Pasterk, H. Demarle-Meusel, B. Sabitzer, and A. Bollin. 2016. Informatik-Werkstatt: Entwicklungen und Erfahrungen einer Lern-und Lehrwerkstatt für Informatik.. In *GI-Jahrestagung.* 1179–1183.
20. J.C. Read and S. MacFarlane. 2006. Using the Fun Toolkit and Other Survey Methods to Gather Opinions in Child Computer Interaction. In *Proceedings of the 2006 Conference on Interaction Design and Children (IDC '06).* ACM, New York, NY, USA, 81–88. DOI: http://dx.doi.org/10.1145/1139073.1139096
21. B. Rodriguez, S. Kennicutt, C. Rader, and T. Camp. 2017. Assessing Computational Thinking in CS Unplugged Activities. In *Proceedings of the 2017 ACM SIGCSE Technical Symposium on Computer Science Education.* ACM, 501–506.
22. B. Rodriguez, C. Rader, and T. Camp. 2016. Using student performance to assess CS unplugged activities in a classroom environment. In *Proceedings of the 2016 ACM Conference on Innovation and Technology in Computer Science Education.* ACM, 95–100.
23. M.M. Sysło and A.B. Kwiatkowska. 2014. Playing with computing at a children's university. In *Proceedings of the 9th Workshop in Primary and Secondary Computing Education.* ACM, 104–107.
24. Alice Team. 1995. Alice Project. (1995). https://www.alice.org.
25. J.M. Wing. 2006. Computational thinking. *Comm. of the ACM* 49, 3 (2006), 33–35.
26. B. Wohl, B. Porter, and S. Clinch. 2015. Teaching Computer Science to 5-7 year-olds: An initial study with Scratch, Cubelets and unplugged computing. In *Proceedings of the Workshop in Primary and Secondary Computing Education.* ACM, 55–60.

The Artistic Potential of Tactile Vision Interfaces: A First Look

Antal Ruhl
Avans University of Applied Sciences, Centre of Expertise for Art, Design and Technology
Beukenlaan 1
4854 TA, Breda, NL
a.ruhl1@avans.nl

Alwin de Rooij
Tilburg University, Tilburg center for Cognition and Communication (TiCC)
Warandelaan 2,
5037 AB, Tilburg, NL
AlwindeRooij@uvt.nl

Michel van Dartel
Avans University of Applied Sciences, Centre of Expertise for Art, Design and Technology
Beukenlaan 1
4854 TA, Breda, NL
mf.vandartel@avans.nl

TEI '18, March 18–21, 2018, Stockholm, Sweden

ACM ISBN 978-1-4503-5568-1/18/03.
https://doi.org/10.1145/3173225.3173271

Abstract
Interfaces that subvert, substitute, or augment the relationship between acting and sensing make interesting tools for experimentation in artistic research. Amongst them, tactile vision interfaces, which enable people to experience to "see with their skin", have particular appeal. However, surprisingly few such interfaces are used by artists. In the present work we take a first look at how the artistic potential of tactile vision interfaces could be unlocked. On the basis of related artistic work, we argue that an accessible, generalizable and learnable interface is needed to enable artists to explore the possibilities of tactile vision. Subsequently, we present ongoing research that revolves around the development of such a tactile vision interface. A case study is presented that informs the development of a new prototype of this interface that overcomes two key limitations in its purpose to unlock the artistic potential of tactile vision.

Author Keywords
New Media Art; Sensory Augmentation; Sensory Substitution; Tactile Vision; Cognitive Science.

Introduction

Developments in cognitive science suggest that people make sense of their environment by exploiting contingencies between their physical actions and the changes in sensory input that these actions bring about [9]. In parallel, recent developments in the domain of art suggest that art is not to look at or listen to passively, but that art should call to action to make sense of something [9]. Therefore, interfaces that subvert, substitute, or augment the relationship between acting and sensing, make interesting tools for both scientific as well as artistic experimentation [2].

Tactile vision interfaces map data from imaging sensors worn on the body to tactile sensory stimulation in real-time [1] and can be used to achieve a wide range of sensory augmentations [6]. Such augmentations enable novel and surprising ways to make sense of our environment, which makes them appealing for artistic experiences that activate and challenge audiences to make sense of something. However, surprisingly few tactile vision interfaces are being used in the domain of art. It seems that the artistic potential of tactile vision interfaces has yet to be unlocked.

In this paper, we present ongoing research on the development of a tactile vision interface that may help to unlock this artistic potential.

Tactile vision interfaces

Counteracting the cold, hard and less human world of screens, the body can be seen as a canvas where interaction takes place to explore the human-technology relationship on a much more personal level [16]. Tactile vision interfaces are designed to substitute or augment the visual sense, by mapping the sensory changes that result from the movement of an image sensor to the sensory changes in the tactile sense [6]. Such sensorimotor mappings can, for instance, enable or support sensemaking in the absence of a sufficiently functioning visual sense, i.e., *sensory substitution* [1], but may also augment sensemaking by pairing vision through the eyes with tactile vision, i.e. *sensory augmentation* [14].

Sensory substitution based on tactile vision was pioneered by Bach-y-Rita, who developed the first tactile vision interface: a chair with a camera placed over the user's shoulder, and a mapping of the camera image sensor to a grid of solenoids embedded in the backrest of a chair [1]. After training, people used the interface to estimate an object's spatial orientation and recognize the type of object, sometimes achieving remarkable detail, such as recognizing whether a person in front of them was wearing glasses or not [15]. A noteworthy observation made during these pioneering studies is that for some participants the tactile vision interface enabled the novel subjective experience of *"seeing with the skin"* [15].

Sensory augmentation through tactile vision is achieved by, for instance, making use of the specialized properties of the tactile sense to process visual information (e.g. a higher temporal resolution, cf. [4]), making use of the imaging sensor and processing capabilities that extend the human visual sense (e.g. using an infra-red image sensor [14]), or placing the image sensor on the body in an 'unnatural' configuration (e.g. an image sensor on the hands embedded in a glove [7]). These particular uses of tactile vision expand a person's sensemaking capabilities, and thus their ability to have novel personal and subjective experiences.

While anecdotal subjective experiences, such as "seeing with the skin" [15], are commonly not further explored in scientific research, such novel personal and subjective experiences are a key subject for exploration in artistic research. While anecdotal evidence points towards extremely interesting subjective experiences based on tactile vision [11], our conjecture is that this artistic potential has yet to be realized.

Unlocking artistic potential

An exploration of the artistic potential of sensory augmentation implies that novel experiences are created on the basis of a person's active contribution to the emergence of that experience. This implication aligns well with a contemporary shift in art theory that considers art a call to action to make sense of something, rather than the passive consumption of some object [9]. In line with this, much artistic work has shifted from making objects to actively intervening, subverting, and augmenting the relationship between humans and their environment [2].

Artist Carsten Höller, for instance, aims to elicit experiences that are "like an expedition, a conscious decision to get confused, to end up somewhere else", which contrasts with viewing the artist as a kind of "visionary who says 'This way, follow me!'" [13]. Such artistic work enables its audience to have novel personal and subjective experiences, based on their own active contributions. Experiences based on sensory augmentation do exactly that, which means they have substantial potential for artistic work. Although artists do incorporate sensory augmentation in their work (see [11] for examples), tactile vision is generally not the preferred means to achieve it.

We identify three potential reasons for this:

Accessibility. A noteworthy artistic achievement that involves tactile vision is *Invisible Labyrinth* by artist Jeppe Hein. In this work, Hein applies a head-band equipped with location sensors and small vibrators to indicate distance to invisible barriers, forming a labyrinth that challenges visitors to find their way out of [10]. Although the work has been widely reviewed (see, e.g., [5]), these reviews do generally not acknowledge the technological challenges involved in achieving a convincing tactile vision experience of this scale. The expertise and financial means required to implement tactile vision on such a scale lays well beyond the reach of most artists. Therefore, increased *accessibility* to tactile vision technology, e.g. by creating more affordable solutions that are 'plug-and-play', could open its potential to a wider use by artists.

Generalizability. As every artwork aims to achieve a different experience, an interface will only be widely used by artists if it allows for the exploration of diverse experiences; i.e. it should be general in its purpose by, for example, having interchangeable input sensors and output actuators to enable a wide variety of sensorimotor mappings. Similarly, *multiple* inputs and outputs could aid experimentation on new combinations of mappings, without the need to redesign the interface or reprogram the software. Therefore, *generalisability* based on modularity and multiplicity seems key for an interface to unlock the artistic potential of haptic vision.

Figure 1: Front of the haptic vision interface, with camera.

Figure 2: Back of the haptic vision interface, with solenoids.

[1] See github.com/antalruhl/Tactile-Vision for files and code.

Learnability. If conscious experience relies on the capacity to exploit contingencies between physical actions and the changes in sensory input that result from these actions, then having rich sensory experiences requires *learning* to understand these contingencies [15]. Not surprisingly, it has been proven that haptic vision based on high resolution tactile stimulation requires more practice (e.g., 20-40 hours with Bach-y-Rita's 20x20 solenoid grid [15]), than haptic vision based on a low-resolution output (e.g., one vibrating actuator on the skin connected to a distance sensor can instantly be used [3]). Therefore, a tactile vision interface should have a relatively low resolution to meet the amount of time an audience is likely to invest in an artistic experience, or should be adjustable to the preferred duration of an experience.

Prototyping a tactile vision interface

To mitigate these three reasons that may prevent artists from widely using tactile vision in their work, we are developing an interface based on accessibility, generalizability, and learnability. To have a first look at how such an interface may support the unlocking of the artistic potential of tactile vision, we created and tested a rudimentary interface that maps image sensor data to a tactile actuator in a modular way.

The input module is a 3x3 grid of motorized pixels in a lightweight wooden casing (Figure 1). A camera can be mounted on top of the casing, in which case a custom software program translates the camera's feed into a 3x3 pixel feed. The grey value of each pixel is continuously filtered, using a threshold that categorizes the input as either 'black' or 'white'. When an input is classified as 'black', the corresponding motorized pixel is activated; when an input is classified as 'white', the pixel is not activated.

Another wooden box holds an Arduino board, to which a desired mapping between the input and output can be uploaded, as well as a custom-build electrical circuit to interface the input and output (Figure 1).

The output module consists of a 3x3 grid of solenoids (Figure 2). The linear motors driving these solenoids administer local pressure on the skin when the Arduino board transmits an electrical pulse because one of the motorized pixel is activated. Together, these nine solenoids function as binary pixels, i.e., each of them either pushes against the skin or remains passive[1].

A first look at the artistic potential

To explore how such an interface may support the unlocking of the artistic potential of tactile vision, we conducted a small case study in the form of a masterclass which consisted of six parts: 1.) an introduction to the art and science of sensory augmentation, 2.) introductions to a range of sensory augmentation interfaces (including the tactile vision interface introduced above), 3.) hands-on exploration of these interfaces, 4.) the forming of subgroups around each of the interfaces, 5.) discussions within each subgroup moderated by experts instructed to steer their discussion towards possible uses of the interface, and 6.) presentations of discussion outcomes to the whole group.

The participants (n=13) consisted of a mix of students and young professionals with backgrounds in art, design and science. The masterclass was held as part of the *STRP Biennial* on March 28, 2017 [12].

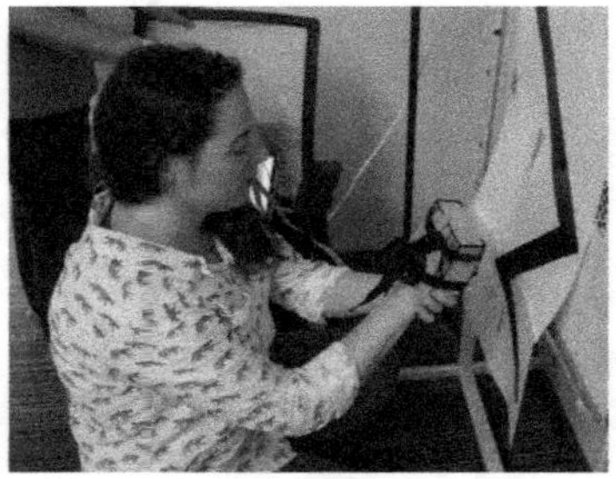

Figure 3: A rudimentary test to measure in how far haptic vision is of aid to people with impaired vision.

During the masterclass, participants focusing on inversion goggles (i.e. goggles that reverse vision, e.g., up and down), decided to work together with the subgroup that explored the tactile vision interface. This unscripted merge led the group discussion to gravitate towards the potential of combining *'inverted vision'* with *'tactile vision'*. This sparked a surprising number of ideas in which the tactile vision interface could be used to substitute inverted vision; e.g., to compensate for the difficulty of coordinating limbs while vision is inverted, or to aid the learning of new sensorimotor contingencies that result from reversing vision.

One of these ideas was a rudimentary test for the extent to which haptic vision can be of aid to people with impaired vision (Figure 3). For the demonstration of this concept, two participants were asked to wear a pair of inverted goggles; one of them was subsequently also equipped with the tactile vision interface, which was attached to the palm of his/her dominant hand. Both participants were then instructed to follow a jagged line on the wall, with one hand and starting at the same time. As both participants struggled to follow the jagged line with their hand, because their vision was inverted, it became apparent that the participant equipped *with* haptic vision interface had a significant advantage opposed to the participant who followed the line with his/her bare hand.

Due to popular demand amongst the participants, based on the competitive element of the concept, the test was performed many times with different participants. Repeating the demonstration resulted in a range of interesting descriptions of the subjective experiences that participants had while performing the test. One participant, for instance, remarked *"I had the feeling that I could feel the line"*, which suggests that the interface could unlock the potential to make 2D visual information tangible.

In summary, our case study resulted in the observation that the haptic vision interface (i) provides useful additional information when vision is impaired (ii) can be engaging and fun, and (iii) is useful in gaining insight into the subjective experience of haptic vision.

Implications for the prototype

These preliminary findings suggest that, on the basis of our rudimentary interface, (i) tactile vision can be made accessible, as it allowed novices to work with and experience haptic vision; (ii) different types of applications can be conceived, as illustrated by the diversity of ideas and experiences obtained; and (iii) the learning required can be scaled to an amount suited for art experiences, as at least one of the demonstrations was considered engaging. The case study, however, also uncovered some shortcomings of the interface.

Firstly, our findings suggest that the generalizability of the rudimentary prototype is limited: Although it prompted the exploration of different ways to map the image data to the tactile grid, and facilitated experiences of these mappings, these explorations and experiences were limited to the fixed configuration of the actuators in a grid and to the positions on the body where these actuators could be placed (cf. [7]). More flexibility in the configuration and placing of the actuators is required to generalize the purpose of the interface to a wider range of potential experiences.

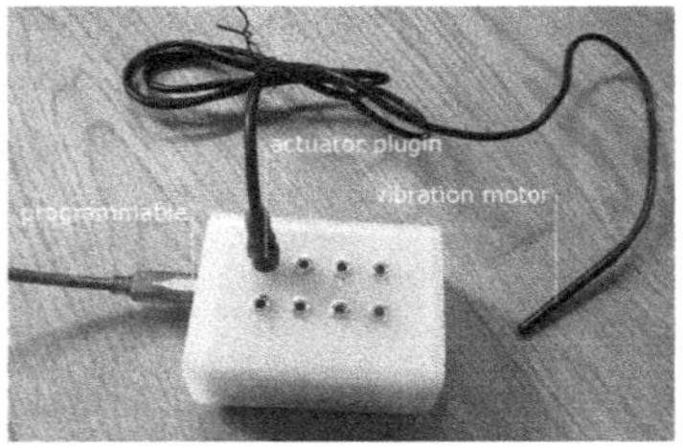

Figure 4: A new version of the tactile vision interface, with vibration motors

Secondly, our case study suggests that exploration with the interface does not automatically elicit artistic exploration, even when the exploration is conducted in the context of an art festival and participants are first introduced to related artistic work. This could be partly attributed to the set up of the masterclass (e.g., as not all participants were artists and participants were allowed to explore in any direction), yet could also be attributed to the interface itself: The binary output signal, for instance, may force participants to reason from this technological limitation (e.g., an exploration mainly targeting meaningful mappings that can be made given on/off output) rather than from the wider possibilities of haptic vision (e.g., an exploration of interesting artistic concepts that the interface may be able to facilitate). The case study therefore suggests that the masterclass, but possibly also the prototype itself, requires further work.

Work in progress

The preliminary findings above suggest that a redesign of the prototype is needed to unlock the artistic potential of haptic vision interfaces. To this end, we are currently developing a new version of the interface (Figure 4), which explicitly addresses the need for more generalizability and for better support in the elicitation of artistic concepts.

This version[2] consists of 8 vibration motors, each of which can be individually connected to the body using *velcro* straps. This design allows for a lot of freedom in the spatial configuration of the actuators and how they are placed on the body. The vibration motors can be connected to a custom-made plastic plug-and-play box, through which they can connect to a computer or to analog input sensors. The number of actuators can be varied easily this way. Also, although the actuators can still be placed in a grid on one body part, they can now also be spread over the body in different configurations. This improvement may overcome the first shortcoming that our findings suggested, as the higher flexibility in the configuration and placing of the actuators on the body generalizes the purpose of the interface to a wider range of potential experiences.

In the light of the second shortcoming suggested by our case study, the upgrade from solenoids to vibrating actuators should be noted. As vibrators allow for binary as well as nonbinary mapping, this improvement allows for the exploration of all scenarios that could be conceived on the basis of the previous version of the interface, but also opens up the possibility to explore scenarios that require more subtle mappings. For instance, the vibrating motors may allow for seeing grey scales or signal strengths "through the skin", and henceforth may better support the elicitation of artistic concepts.

Demonstration at TEI'18

TEI '18 makes for an ideal time and place to combine a discussion of our progress with the premiere demonstration of our new prototype. The demonstration will allow visitors and participants of TEI'18 to experience tactile vision and to explore potential applications on the basis of live experimentation. We expect that this will generate feedback from experts in the field of tangible interfaces, which will help us to evaluate the new prototype and to gain technical insight into the accessible, generalizable and learnable tactile vision solutions that will ultimately unlock its artistic potential.

[2] See github.com/antalruhl/Modular_Tactile_Interface for files and code.

References

1. P. Bach-y-Rita, C.C. Collins, S.A. Saunders, B. White, B. & L. Scadden. 1969. Vision substitution by tactile image projection. *Nature* 221: 963-964.
2. M.F. van Dartel. 2016. *Aesthetics in the Wild: Art and Design Practices and Pedagogies after the Situated Turn.* Avans, Breda.
3. T. Froese, M. McGann, W. Bigge, A. Spiers, & A.K. Seth. 2012. The enactive torch. *IEEE Transactions on Haptics* 5, 4: 365-375.
4. W. Fujisaki & S.Y. Nishida. 2009. Audio-tactile superiority over visuo-tactile and audio-visual combinations in the temporal resolution of synchrony perception. *Experimental Brain Research* 198, 2-3: 245-259.
5. J. Jones. 2012. Invisible: Art about the Unseen 1957 – 2012. Retrieved October 22, 2017 from http://www.theguardian.com/artanddesign/2012/jun/10/invisible-art-about-unseen-review
6. Á. Kristjánsson, A. Moldoveanu, Ó.I. Jóhannesson, O. Balan, S. Spagnol, V.V. Valgeirsdóttir, & R. Unnthorsson. 2016. Designing sensory-substitution devices: Principles, pitfalls and potentials. *Restorative neurology and neuroscience* 34, 5: 769-787.
7. S. Meers & K. Ward. 2005. A vision system for providing the blind with 3D colour perception of the environment. In *Proceedings of the Asia-Pacific Workshop on Visual Information Processing* (Hong Kong, December 2005). http://ro.uow.edu.au/infopapers/436/
8. A. Noë. 2015. *Strange Tools, Art and Human Nature.* Hill and Wang, New York, NY.
9. J.K. O'Regan. 2011. Why Red Doesn't Sound Like a Bell: Understanding the Feel of Consciousness. Oxford University Press, Oxford, UK.
10. K. O'Rourke. 2013. *Walking and Mapping.* MIT Press, Cambridge, MA.
11. A. de Rooij, M.F. van Dartel, A. Ruhl, H. Schraffenberger, B. van Melick, M. Bontje, M. Daams & M. Witter. In press. Sensory Augmentation Interfaces: A Dialogue between the Arts and Sciences. In *Proceedings of 6th EAI International Conference (ArtsIT 2017).*
12. M.F. van Dartel & A. de Rooij. 2017. STRP, The Art and Science of Expanding the Sensorium. Retrieved October 21, 2017 from http://strp.nl/en/program/the-art-and-science-expanding-our-sensorium/
13. R. Spence. 2011. "Just Höller." *The Financial Times* (16 December 2011.). Retrieved October 15, 2017 from http://www.ft.com/intl/cms/s/2/c9b0b29e-2261-11e1-923d-00144feabdc0.html#axzz1rX87CXAu.
14. E.E. Thomson, R. Carra & M.A. Nicolelis. 2013. Perceiving invisible light through a somatosensory cortical prosthesis. *Nature communications* 4: 1482.
15. B.W. White, F.A. Saunders, L. Scadden, P. Bach-Y-Rita & C.C. Collins. 1970. Seeing with the skin. *Perception & Psychophysics* 7, 1: 23-27.
16. Ava Aghakouckak. 2016. SAROTIS; The New Sense. Retrieved December 7, 2017 from http://www.interactivearchitecture.org/sarotis-the-new-sense.html

Embodied Interactions with E-Textiles and the Internet of Sounds for Performing Arts

Sophie Skach
s.skach@qmul.ac.uk

Ariane Stolfi
a.stolfi@qmul.ac.uk

Anna Xambó
a.xambo@qmul.ac.uk

Rebecca Stewart
rebecca.stewart@qmul.ac.uk

Luca Turchet
luca.turchet@qmul.ac.uk

Mathieu Barthet
m.barthet@qmul.ac.uk

School of Electronic Engineering and Computer Science
Queen Mary University of London
London E1 4NS, United Kingdom

TEI '18, March 18–21, 2018, Stockholm, Sweden
ACM 978-1-4503-5568-1/18/03.
https://doi.org/10.1145/3173225.3173272

Abstract
This paper presents initial steps towards the design of an embedded system for *body-centric sonic performance*. The proposed prototyping system allows performers to manipulate sounds through gestural interactions captured by textile wearable sensors. The e-textile sensor data control, in real-time, audio synthesis algorithms working with content from Audio Commons, a novel web-based ecosystem for re-purposing crowd-sourced audio. The system enables creative *embodied music interactions* by combining seamless physical e-textiles with web-based digital audio technologies.

Author Keywords
E-textile; Audio Commons; Internet of Musical Things; music information retrieval; technology probe; Bela

CCS Concepts
•**Hardware** → **Tactile and hand-based interfaces;** •**Applied computing** → *Sound and music computing;* •**Information systems** → Web interfaces;

Introduction
In our digital era, creating artifacts for tangible, embedded and embodied interactions becomes more and more concerned by the "humanization" of the digital. This can be addressed by looking at how analog and digital design spaces

Figure 1: Sketch of a performance, using integrated textile sensors on joints to create sound from body movement.

can be interlocked. Returning to traditional, natural materials as analog gateways to the digital world is central to the so-called *post-digital art* [1]. Applied to creative media, this is a two-way process in which access to and control of digital devices is enhanced by haptic interfaces and embodied interactions. In this work, we investigate how such a post-digital design approach can be applied to sonic and musical interactions.

Most *digital musical interfaces* [13] have been designed as objects separated from the body, often consisting of hard components such as plastic knobs. In this work we are concerned with *body-centric sonic interactions* fostering explicit action-effect loops without the barriers of screen-based media. Rather than tackling this using wearable controllers that are attached to the body, such as Myo gesture controlled armband (https://www.myo.com/), an approach traditionally used in *embodied music interaction* [24], we propose to design sonic controllers that work more closely to the body using garments incorporating electronic textile or *e-textile*, which are fabrics turned into soft sensors and actuators by using conductive material when manufacturing or manipulating a textile surface. In addition, we propose to leverage the vast amount of audio content available in the cloud and wireless network capabilities for communication of audio and sensor data. The *Internet of Things* (IoT) [2] brings cloud-based computing to everyday portable objects with the aim of improving our daily lives. In the digital audio domain, we find projects providing services for online audio content repositories and networked-based sonic interaction (which we coin as the *Internet of Sounds* (IoS)), such as Audio Commons [6] and the Internet of Musical Things [21]. Both explore the potential of cloud architecture and computing applied to audio applications for music makers, sound designers, and other types of consumers.

In this work-in-progress paper we explore the novel combination of two cutting-edge technologies, (1) e-textiles and (2) the Internet of Sounds. We present an embedded system for prototyping embodied sonic performances (see Figure 1) based on the Bela platform, designed for ultra-low latency audio and sensor processing [11]. Bringing together the e-textile and IoS domains can be of interest to several communities, from wearable and music technology designers to performing arts audiences. We aim to foster rich interdisciplinary exchanges between technology, fashion and sound art designers through the convergence of the digital and the physical domains.

Background

E-textiles

Textiles can be seen as an interface to the analog world through the sense of touch. Present on many surfaces, whether through chair covers, bed sheets, clothing, and so on, textiles are a promising and intuitive design material for HCI. In recent years, the idea of e-textiles has been explored through a growing DIY community (http://www.instructables.com/id/E-Textiles/) as well as through industrial and academic research (e.g., [15]). Especially noteworthy are applications for rehabilitation (e.g., monitoring movement in [23] and [12]), affect and event detection (e.g., [5]), as well as soft robotics (e.g., [3]). Advantages of using textile sensing systems and interfaces over other wearable devices lie in their unobtrusive character and in providing a natural interface for human interaction.

Internet of Sounds

A number of studies explore the use of Internet and networked devices for sound interaction, which we refer to as the Internet of Sounds (IoS). The Internet of Musical Things project [21] investigates interconnected *smart musical instruments* [22] and haptic wearables for performer and audience interactions [20]. The Audio Commons initiative brings Creative Commons (https://creativecommons.org/) audio content from online repositories, such as Jamendo (http://www.jamendo.com) and Freesound [7], to creatives from the music and audiovisual production industries [6]. The main goal of the Audio Commons initiative is to develop an ecosystem that promotes repurposing of crowd-sourced audio content through smooth creative workflows. This is made possible through a range of services accessible through an *Application Programming Interface* (API) [6], which addresses how to query and interact with sound files from online repositories for creative applications, and has already been tested during a workshop (http://designingsound-am2017.apps.devcloud.eecs.qmul.ac.uk/). To view the Audio Commons API, see: https://m.audiocommons.org/docs/api.html.

Embodied performative interaction with e-textiles
The performing arts have a rich history of incorporating technology to facilitate embodied interactions. As new technologies are developed, artists have used them to create new artworks and neither e-textiles nor IoT are exceptions. One such recent example is Flutter/Stutter which looked at the role of data and IoT technologies within an improvised dance performance [18]. In [14], a wearable helmet embedding sensors has been purposely designed for dancers, to unleash the potential of sonic generation from body movements.

In order to create new performances with embodied technology, tools that allow exploration and experimentation are needed. The e-textile platform presented here builds on a prototyping system designed by Anja Hertenberger and Mika Satomi for the eTextile Summer Camp in 2016 (http://etextile-summercamp.org/2016/etextile-and-performance/). Their system used a modular design to allow for easy experimentation with the placement of e-textile sensors and their mapping to audio parameters. Adding the IoS to our system brings an original contribution that can inform future e-textile sonic interaction projects.

Methodology

Technology probes
Our prototype design is inspired by *technology probes* [9]. Technology probes are a tool to understand social, engineering, and design aspects. We use the probes to elicit information on user experience to improve the next design iteration. We expect to collect such data from (1) a set of workshops (detailed in the next section); (2) showcasing our work-in-progress system to the TEI community; and (3) future performances making use of our system. We are interested in observing, from a user perspective: (1) how the tool is used to socially communicate in a performance setting; (2) what are the successes and failures of the technology; and (3) what are the creative and disruptive uses of the design.

Making workshops
The system detailed in the next section is tested during workshops welcoming both the music technology and performance art communities. A first case study at AlgoMech Festival (http://algomech.com/2017/) invites participants to explore ways of capturing body movement through textile sensors (see Figures 2, 3, 4) to create soundscapes. IoS is used to help participants to find online sound files to be used in their design artefacts. Such workshops are meant to evaluate the sensor design as well as the cycle of interaction as such. Findings are then used to develop further iterations of the system and to identify interaction and technological challenges. One of these challenges concern the type of gestures and postural cues that can be used to retrieve, modify and create sound for performative purposes.

Figure 2: Tilt sensor from woven conductive fabric and twisted yarn.

Figure 3: Pressure sensors made of different conductive fabrics (copper, silver thread and silver coating) and resistive foam.

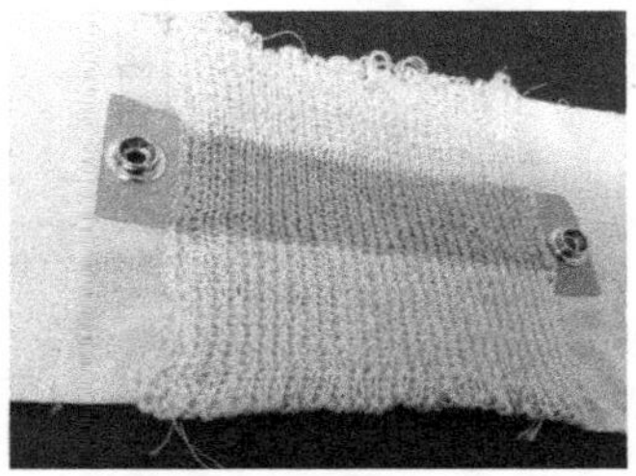

Figure 4: Stretch sensor, knitted from stainless steel and polyester yarn.

User Interaction

Conceptual design

Our tool is designed to be a seamless e-textile augmented with IoS capabilities that can be useful to both novice and expert performance artists and potential technologist collaborators. The tool should be as intuitive as possible, keeping enough degrees of freedom to move and interact with sound. Each interaction should provide a unique, distinctive user experience.

Sonic control data are generated through movement of the e-textile (e.g., press, tilt, or stretch) and voice input (e.g., a melody, an onomatopoeia). The data is mapped to audio synthesis parameters (e.g., for pitch shifting, time-stretching, delay, granular synthesis, and so on) that affect sound files retrieved from online databases. Sound retrieval can be done prior to the performance using a browser-based desktop or mobile application, or during the performance using non screen-based mechanisms, such as through vocal input recorded by a portable microphone (e.g., lavalier). Notification signals are used to provide feedback to users through the visual, haptic, and auditory channels (e.g., LEDs, haptic feedback motors, speakers), deemed to be essential to provide information on the internal system processes.

Scenario

The interactive system has been designed to revolve around two use phases, rehearsal/preparation and performance. During the preparation or rehearsal stage, users map the on-body sensors to sounds. The sounds are obtained from online content repositories from the Audio Commons ecosystem either by keyword search or audio feature-based queries. Selected files are uploaded to Bela and allocated to the textile sensors.

During the performance phase, the artist can trigger sounds as well as modulate them through gestural movement and whole-body interactions (see Figure 1). Figure 5 shows a systematic overview of the interaction cycle.

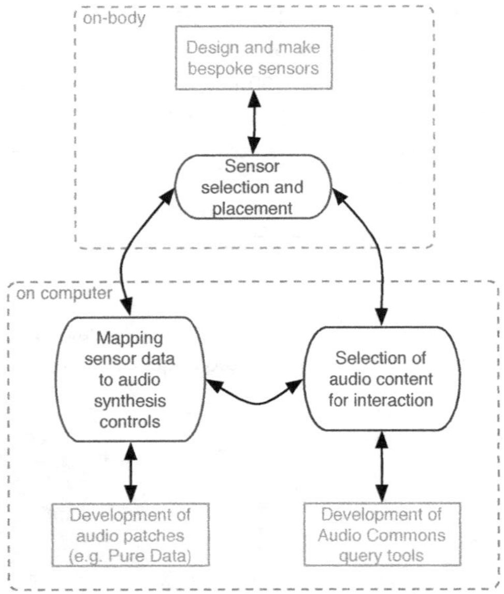

Figure 5: Rehearsal/Preparation Phase (circles: composer/performer processes, boxes: developer/maker processes).

Hardware and Software Architecture

The system architecture comprises four parts: (1) the wearable sensors and actuators; (2) the embedded computer; (3) the software running on the computer; and (4) the web services accessed by the computer. An overview of the system can be seen in Figure 6.

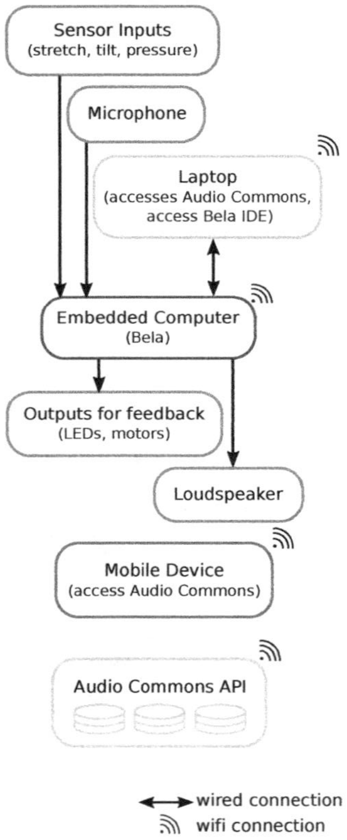

Figure 6: System architecture.

Sensors and actuators
E-textile sensors are used in order to capture body movement without inhibiting the movement or causing discomfort. While there are a variety of movements that can be captured with specific sensors, stretch, pressure and orientation/tilt are the most versatile. Knit stretch sensors are made of fabric knit from conductive yarns or from non-conductive knit fabric coated in a conductive polymer [19]. As they stretch, they change their resistance. Resistance-based pressure sensors rely on a material that changes its resistance under pressure; when two electrodes are placed on either side of the variable resistance material, the electrodes can measure the change in resistance when pressure is applied. E-textile tilt sensors use gravity and haberdashery items like metal beads to maintain an electrical connection that is correlated with a particular orientation.

For the making workshops, a kit of previously constructed handmade textile sensors (see Figures 2, 3, 4) are provided for participants to use in their prototypes. Participants are also taught how to make basic sensors so that they can construct bespoke shapes for their prototypes.

A small battery-operated loudspeaker is worn on the body to playback the generated audio. The complete prototyping system will also include actuation beyond the sound output, most likely in the form of LEDs and haptic vibration motors. These allow the wearer to know the internal state of the software, when it would not be appropriate to use sound. For example, if waiting for a search query to complete or to indicate a change in mapping between the sensors and sound.

Wearable computer
The computing system is controlled by Bela [11], a low-latency audio signal processing platform based on the Beaglebone Black. We choose this platform because it integrates both audio and sensor processing, which is suitable for performing arts projects.

Figure 7: Bela on the fabric breakout board with a textile connection cable.

Care needs to be taken when designing the connections between the flexible textile circuitry and Bela's traditional PCB construction. A fabric circuit board, seen in Figure 7, was created to provide a soft circuit breakout board for five analog inputs and two digital inputs. Snaps provide an interface between the conductive fabric pads and the fabric connection cables which attach to the sensors. Wires soldered to header pins on one end, and stitched to the conductive fabric pads on the other, provide the connections between the Bela board and the fabric breakout board.

Internet connectivity is added to the Bela board with a Wi-Fi USB dongle interfacing with a router delivering Internet to a local network. The complete system is powered by a rechargeable USB battery.

Software

Bela supports multiple audio programming languages, such as Pure Data [16] and SuperCollider [10]. Pure Data (PD) was chosen for this project as it is accessible to those new to programming and is commonly used by artistic communities. For example, in our workshop participants can easily start learning by using example PD patches that demonstrate how to map sensor data to audio playback or trigger a search query.

Web services

A client script running on Bela provides an interface to the Audio Commons API. The script allows selected files to be downloaded from the Internet to the board so that they can be played back and processed by Pure Data patches.

The Audio Commons environment provides tools that allow to search sounds using language or audio-based filters relating to technical and aesthetic characteristics. For instance, sounds can be filtered based on key, BPM, and duration, among others. The current design provides a browser-based audio content search engine for querying the sounds and sending them to Bela using Internet protocols. The software and web services modules are being developed and will be integrated next.

Final Remarks

We have proposed a new embedded system using e-textile for embodied music interaction that targets novice and expert performers as well as their technologist collaborators. Compared to other existing interactive systems that enhance sound design through wearable devices, our design innovates in the use of lightweight textile sensors directly integrated into worn garments.

As next steps, we plan to evaluate: (1) how bespoke e-textile sensors can be used in a performing arts context; (2) what mappings from the sensor to the audio synthesis domains can be implemented using sensor fusion algorithms in light of user expectations; and (3) what audio query and retrieval filters to access sound files from the Internet motivate users in a performative context.

Of particular interest for future investigations are creative queries of sound files using gesture or voice inputs. In the music information retrieval (MIR) field, textual-based search has been expanded to query-by-humming, e.g., the tune of a song [8]; or query by gesture-to-sound [4]. With the advent of the Web Audio API (https://www.w3.org/TR/webaudio/), new browser-based applications point to potential directions, such as querying Freesound with a microphone [17].

Within the overall theme of embodiment in HCI [25], this work presents several other interesting domains of applications worth investigating, including music listening of pre-recorded media, post-production, design for well-being, sports, fashion design, and affective computing.

Acknowledgements

The project Audio Commons is funded by the European Commission through the Horizon 2020 programme, research and innovation grant 688382. This work was supported by the EPSRC and AHRC Centre for Doctoral Training in Media and Arts Technology (EP/L01632X/1). Thank you to Giulio Moro for his assistance with the Bela platform and to An Liang for her help with preparing the workshops.

REFERENCES

1. Melvin L. Alexenberg. 2011. *The Future of Art in a Postdigital Age: From Hellenistic to Hebraic Consciousness* (2nd ed.). Intellect Books, Bristol, UK.

2. Luigi Atzori, Antonio Iera, and Giacomo Morabito. 2010. The Internet of Things: A Survey. *Computer Networks* 54, 15 (2010), 2787–2805.
3. Tapomayukh Bhattacharjee, Advait Jain, Sarvagya Vaish, Marc D. Killpack, and Charles C. Kemp. 2013. Tactile Sensing over Articulated Joints with Stretchable Sensors. In *Proceedings of the World Haptics Conference (WHC 2013)*. IEEE, 103–108.
4. Baptiste Caramiaux, Frédéric Bevilacqua, and Norbert Schnell. 2011. Sound Selection by Gestures. In *Proceedings of the New Interfaces for Musical Expression (NIME '11)*.
5. Lucy E. Dunne, Sarah Brady, Richard Tynan, Kim Lau, Barry Smyth, Dermot Diamond, and Gregory M.P. O'Hare. 2006. Garment-based Body Sensing Using Foam Sensors. In *Proceedings of the 7th Australasian User Interface Conference - Volume 50 (AUIC '06)*. Australian Computer Society, Inc., 165–171.
6. Frederic Font, Tim Brookes, George Fazekas, Martin Guerber, Amaury La Burthe, David Plans, Mark D. Plumbley, Meir Shaashua, Wenwu Wang, and Xavier Serra. 2016. Audio Commons: Bringing Creative Commons Audio Content to the Creative Industries. In *Proceedings of the 61st AES International Conference: Audio for Games*. Audio Engineering Society.
7. Frederic Font, Gerard Roma, and Xavier Serra. 2013. Freesound Technical Demo. In *Proceedings of the 2013 ACM Multimedia Conference*. ACM, 411–412.
8. Asif Ghias, Jonathan Logan, David Chamberlin, and Brian C. Smith. 1995. Query by Humming: Musical Information Retrieval in an Audio Database. In *Proceedings of the Third ACM International Conference on Multimedia*. ACM, 231–236.
9. Hilary Hutchinson, Wendy Mackay, Bo Westerlund, Benjamin B. Bederson, Allison Druin, Catherine Plaisant, Michel Beaudouin-Lafon, Stéphane Conversy, Helen Evans, Heiko Hansen, Nicolas Roussel, and Björn Eiderbäck. 2003. Technology Probes: Inspiring Design for and with Families. In *Proceedings of the SIGCHI Conference on Human Factors in Computing Systems (CHI '03)*. ACM, New York, NY, USA, 17–24.
10. James McCartney. 2002. Rethinking the Computer Music Language: SuperCollider. *Computer Music Journal* 26, 4 (2002), 61–68.
11. Andrew McPherson and Victor Zappi. 2015. An Environment for Submillisecond-Latency Audio and Sensor Processing on BeagleBone Black. In *Audio Engineering Society Convention 138.* Audio Engineering Society.
12. Cheryl D. Metcalf, SRI Collie, A.W. Cranny, Georgie Hallett, Christopher James, Jo Adams, P.H. Chappell, N.M. White, and J.H. Burridge. 2009. Fabric-based Strain Sensors for Measuring Movement in Wearable Telemonitoring Applications. In *Proceedings of the Assisted Living Conference*. 1–4.
13. Eduardo Reck Miranda and Marcelo M. Wanderley. 2006. *New Digital Musical Instruments: Control and Interaction Beyond the Keyboard.* Vol. 21. AR Editions, Inc.
14. Tim Murray-Browne, Di Mainstone, Nick Bryan-Kinns, and Mark D. Plumbley. 2013. The Serendiptichord: Reflections on the Collaborative Design Process between Artist and Researcher. *Leonardo* 46, 1 (2013), 86–87.

15. Ivan Poupyrev, Rodney Berry, Jun Kurumisawa, Keiko Nakao, Mark Billinghurst, Chris Airola, Hirokazu Kato, Tomoko Yonezawa, and Lewis Baldwin. 2000. Augmented Groove: Collaborative Jamming in Augmented Reality. In *Proceedings of the ACM SIGGRAPH 2000 Conference Abstracts and Applications*. 77.
16. Miller Puckette and others. 1996. Pure Data: Another Integrated Computer Music Environment. In *Proceedings of the Second Intercollege Computer Music Concerts*. 37–41.
17. Gerard Roma and Xavier Serra. 2015. Querying Freesound with a Microphone. In *Proceedings of the 1st Web Audio Conference (WAC '15)*.
18. Kate Sicchio, Camille Baker, Tara Baoth Mooney, and Rebecca Stewart. 2016. Hacking the Body 2.0: Flutter/Stutter. In *Proceedings of the International Conference on Live Interfaces (ICLI '16)*. 37–42.
19. Sophie Skach, Patrick G.T. Healey, and Rebecca Stewart. 2017. Talking Through Your Arse: Sensing Conversation with Seat Covers. In *Proceedings of the 39th Annual Meeting of the Cognitive Science Society (CogSci 2017)*. 3186–3190.
20. Luca Turchet and Mathieu Barthet. 2017. Envisioning Smart Musical Haptic Wearables to Enhance Performers' Creative Communication. In *Proceedings of International Symposium on Computer Music Multidisciplinary Research*. 538–549.
21. Luca Turchet, Carlo Fischione, and Mathieu Barthet. 2017. Towards the Internet of Musical Things. In *Proceedings of the Sound and Music Computing Conference (SMC 2017)*. 13–20.
22. Luca Turchet, Andrew McPherson, and Carlo Fischione. 2016. Smart Instruments: Towards an Ecosystem of Interoperable Devices Connecting Performers and Audiences. In *Proceedings of the Sound and Music Computing Conference (SMC 2016)*. 498–505.
23. Qi Wang. 2016. Designing Posture Monitoring Garments to Support Rehabilitation. In *Proceedings of the Tenth International Conference on Tangible, Embedded, and Embodied Interaction (TEI '16)*. ACM, 709–712.
24. Anna Xambó. 2017. In *Digital Bodies: Creativity and Technology in the Arts and Humanities*, Susan Broadhurst and Sara Price (Eds.). Palgrave Macmillan UK, London, Chapter Embodied music interaction: creative design synergies between music performance and HCI, 207–220.
25. Anna Xambó, Carey Jewitt, and Sara Price. 2014. Towards an Integrated Methodological Framework for Understanding Embodiment in HCI. In *Proceedings of the Extended Abstracts of the 32nd Annual ACM Conference on Human Factors in Computing Systems (CHI EA '14)*. ACM, 1411–1416.

Designing a Smart Reading Environment with and for Children

Pedro Ribeiro
Anna Michel
Ido Iurgel
Christian Ressel
Rhine-Waal University of Applied Sciences,
Kamp-Lintfort, Germany
pr@hsrw.eu
ami@hsrw.eu
ii@hsrw.eu
cr@hsrw.eu

Cristina Sylla
CIEC/engageLab, University of Minho, Braga, Portugal
sylla@engagelab.org

Wolfgang Müller
University of Education Weingarten, Weingarten, Germany
mueller@md-phw.de

TEI '18, March 18–21, 2018, Stockholm, Sweden

ACM ISBN 978-1-4503-5568-1/18/03.
https://doi.org/10.1145/3173225.3173274

Abstract
In this paper, we present an ongoing project named STREEN (Story Reading Environmental Enrichment). The project explores a concept of augmented reading focusing on a smart environment that is able to automatically trigger digital media enrichments depending on the reading performance and the narrative. By creating an engaging and immersive reading experience, STREEN has the potential to support early readers. In order to understand how the story reading activities can be enriched through digital media, as well as the effect of such enrichments on the reading experience, the design and development of STREEN follows a Design Based Research approach, involving teachers and primary school children along the design process. In this paper, we describe the first steps towards the construction of a smart reading environment for primary school children.

Author Keywords
Augmented Reading; Digital Media; Reading; Smart Environments; Children.

Figure 1: Conceptual rendering of an artificial environment, that is able to trigger environmental enrichments (e.g. sound or light effects) while a child reads aloud.

Figure 2: Teachers presenting their concept.

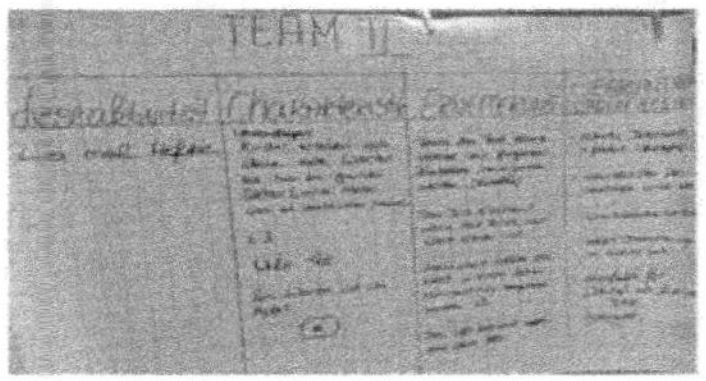

Figure 3: Flip chart with the analyses of the reading activity.

Introduction

Reading is a fundamental activity in almost every culture. The growing usage of multifunctional devices (e.g. smartphones or tablets) as a medium for reading [3], is a natural tendency in today's digital era. Although some studies [3,7] report that reading in flexible multitasking devices may contribute to the decline of reading skills, we are convinced that digital media has the potential to create superior reading experiences, in which the reader becomes completely absorbed in the reading activity. We envision that involvement, curiosity and social interaction can be promoted by literally transforming the space where reading takes place through a technical infrastructure that is able to proactively and reactively trigger environmental digital media enrichments depending on the reading performance and the narrative (Figure 1). Our target is to create a joyful reading environment that encourages children to read, increases their reading comprehension and stimulates their reading skills. In this paper, we summarize the first steps towards this goal.

The STREEN Project

The augmented reading concept described above is being currently explored in the scope of the STREEN project (Story Reading Environmental Enrichment). This project aims at exploring innovative ways of enriching the reading experience of primary school children, and follows a Design Based Research approach, involving researchers, educational practitioners and children from a local primary school in Germany in the design process. This methodology allows to adapt research to practice and bridge the gap between design and theory [1,6].

Identification and Analysis of Reading Activities

In order to identify the usage scenarios and design requirements of STREEN, we started by carrying a workshop with two groups of four teachers each (seven females and one male, age ranging from 33 to 51). The workshop had the duration of 3 hours and took place at the primary school. After presenting and discussing the concept of a smart environment for story reading, the teachers identified various curricular reading activities, such as "Lesekiste", "Lies mal! - Hefte", and "Ganzschrift" that could potentially be enriched through this smart environment (Figure 2 and 3). "Lesekiste" (reading box) is an activity where students decorate and fill a simple shoebox with objects that are related with the content of a selected book. After that, children present the story to the class. "Lies mal! - Hefte" (read! - booklet) are picture booklets that are associated with words or simple short sentences that intend to support beginning readers in reading. The "Ganzschrift" (reading book) activity implies silent or oral reading of an entire book mainly at school. This activity aims at activating reading engagement, concentration on reading a book for a long period of time, as well as reading and understanding the content of the book.

The teachers considered that the reading experience can be visually and auditory enhanced through digital media, bringing images to life, increasing motivation and involvement. Further, they mentioned that the digital media enrichments may potentially engage the listeners, increasing their motivation to discuss the story. Interestingly, the teachers see a great opportunity to motivate boys for reading, seeing the use of the technology as a strong motivational factor. The teachers also emphasized that direct feedback (through digital media enrichment) may promote individual reading success and that digital media enrichments may promote vocabulary acquisition.

Following the first workshop, we conducted semi-structured, in-depth interviews with two teachers to get a deeper understanding of the suggested reading activities and to choose the reading activity for our technological intervention. In the interviews we asked the teachers to describe in detail the reading activities, as well as the application process, problems experienced while carrying those activities and current solutions to overcome the problems.

After analysing the data we decided to target the reading activity "Ganzschrift". Contrary to the other two reading activities, "Ganzschrift" is often used at school throughout the various school grades, therefore offering more opportunities for designing and testing the STREEN technology. Additionally, the learning objectives targeted by "Ganzschrift" match our concept of augmented reading, that is, promoting reading motivation and comprehension, besides improving general reading skills. Furthermore, "Ganzschrift" is an activity that can involve different types of reading, e.g. reading silently or reading aloud, as well as take place in different contexts such as classroom, library or at home. As such, the various reading scenarios supported by the "Ganzschrift" reading activity provide the ideal space to explore the potential of the STREEN augmented reading concept. At the same time, it allows exploring other reading modalities, such as the "Reader's Theatre" [2,6]. The "Reader's Theatre" is a pedagogical activity, in which the readers read aloud for an audience. This reading variation has the potential to motivate readers, while increasing reading comprehension and reading skills. Besides being informed by the teachers and the children, the design of the STREEN environment is strongly influenced by concepts of the "Reader's Theatre" and the analysis of the design space.

Designing a Smart Environment for Story Reading with Children

The discussion of our augmented reading concept with the teachers and the analysis of the activities carried at the primary school gave us valuable insights for the design of potential usage scenarios, being the starting point for the design of a smart reading environment prototype. The prototype will be placed in the primary school's library. Our approach is to design a space for children that is able to support reading aloud activities, which are part of the "Ganzschrift" activity. These include children reading a book to other children, or teachers reading a book to the children.

The design process of the STREEN environment involved creating a core design team, which is composed by one teacher, two interaction designers and nine children aged between seven and nine years of age. The team meetings are scheduled to take place at the school's library every two weeks, for around 90 minutes. So far four meetings were held.

Session 1 – Reading Habits and the STREEN Concept
In the first design session, the members of the team got to know each other and talked about reading habits and preferences. Then, the children were introduced to the STREEN augmented reading concept. After that the children were asked to choose a book in order to explore the concept of a smart reading environment within a usage scenario. The children chose the book "Der Computer im Gartenhaus" (The Computer in the

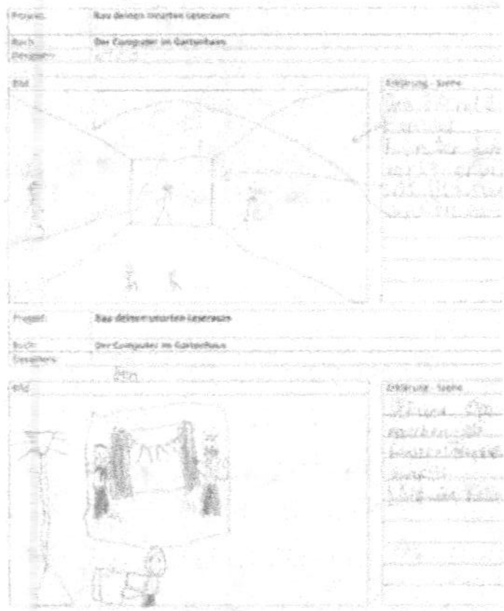

Figure 4: Example of two storyboards that the children produced.

Figure 5: The scale model of the Smart Reading Environment.

Garden House). Besides getting information about children's reading habits and preferences, an interesting outcome of this session was the realization that most children do not feel comfortable when reading aloud, which reinforces the idea that novel solutions that engage children in reading aloud activities are most welcome.

Session 2 – Smart Reading Environment Storyboards
The focus of the second design session was to deepen children's understanding of the smart reading environment and to explore the sensory dimension of the digital media enrichments. After reading a short excerpt of the selected book, each child used an A3 sheet of paper to draw a storyboard illustrating how the smart reading environment might enrich the text with images, sound and light effects (Figure 4). In general, the children tried to map all the relevant events of the narrative and characteristics of the setting to different digital media effects in the smart reading environment. For example, a child imagined that when someone in the room reads the sentence "Grandpa opens the window shutter" an image of this scene is projected on the wall, the light coming from a lamp turns more intense and the squeaking sound of an old shutter opening can be heard. All children envisioned a smart reading environment with image projection in one or more surfaces (walls, ground and ceiling). One of the children even suggested that the characters could be represented with holograms turning the environment in some way comparable with "Holodeck", the fictional room from the television series Star Trek. This tendency indicates that children imagine a smart reading environment leveraged by immersive technologies, which is consequently able to increase presence [5], this is, the perception of being physically present in the non-physical story world. Additionally, we observed that most of the children used a comic's style to represent the scenes using for example speech balloons.

Session 3 – Smart Reading Environment Scale Models
For the third design session and based on the storyboards produced in the previous session we built a scale model prototype of the smart reading environment (Figure 5). In the first part of the session we presented the prototype to the design team and generated a discussion around it using the Sticky Noting Cooperative Inquiry technique [4]. In general, children provided a positive feedback mentioning for example that the synchronization of sounds and images with reading was an enjoyable experience. Furthermore, they proposed adding music to intensify the narrative and suggested projecting an elucidative picture and/or synonyms to facilitate the understanding of unknown words.

In the second part of the session we invited children to read a different excerpt of the book and to build their own scale model prototype. The researchers provided children with A3 sheets of paper, coloured pencils and a smartphone to record audio. During this activity children suggested and created different auditory and graphical enrichments, for example, one child suggested that when someone reads the sentence "the sunflowers are already much taller than you" the room could project the animation of a sunflower growing and a sound effect. Interestingly, children considered that the excerpt of the book that they were enriching with digital media did not require any light changes, thus, suggesting that the light effects shall only map light events that take place within the narrative, e.g. a

Figure 6: Children interacting with the prototype.

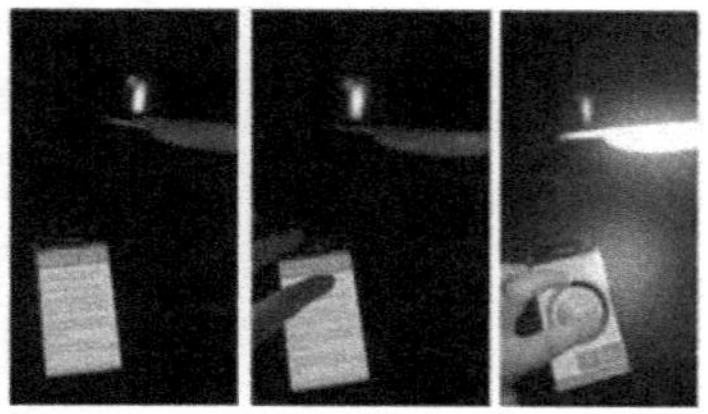

Figure 7: A user selecting a word to trigger a light effect, specifying the digital media effect.

character switching on the light. Children also enjoyed the idea of using their own drawings or audio recordings as enrichments of the smart reading environment. Finally, it was also suggested that the system should be able to emphasize some enrichments over others, for example, spotlighting a specific graphical projection or intensifying a single sound by cancelling other sounds.

Session 4 – Smart Reading environment Functional Prototype

In this design session, we presented a functional prototype and invited the children to use it (Figure 6). The prototype was composed by a smartphone, a LED bulb and a loudspeaker. The Smartphone was able to display the text of the story, identify the reading position and control the digital media infrastructures (LED bulb and loudspeaker). In order to determine the reading position, we implemented a touch-based interaction where the reader moves his/her finger along the line of text that he/she is reading. Then, depending on the specification of how the LED bulb reacts in a specific reading position, the Smartphone controls the properties of the light and plays the specified soundscape. Additionally, this prototype provides an authoring tool, which allows users to define how the digital media infrastructures, that are responsible for creating an enriched reading experience, will behave and contextually react to the narrative itself (Figure 7). After instructing children on how to use the prototype we built two groups and invited them to use the prototype to enrich an excerpt of the story. Following the interaction with the functional prototype children gave feedback on the usage experience using the Sticky Noting Cooperative Inquiry technique [4]. Children referred that they typically do not use their finger to read, however, they consider it acceptable to trigger enrichments. Regarding the functioning of the prototype, there were some technical issues with the touch based interaction, e.g. it did not work properly at the borders of the smartphone's screen and it did not always recognize a fast finger movement. Apart from that, the children enjoyed using the prototype, particularly the authoring functionalities, e.g. associate a light or a sound effect to a part of the narrative.

Finally, based on the feedback collected, the design team proposed some new functionalities:

1. The sound library should be larger and provide search, record and classification functionalities;
2. The possibility to associate graphic effects to a part of the narrative;
3. Using an active pen to provide a better user experience;
4. Determine the reading position through a speech recognition mechanism.

Conclusion and Future Work

In this paper we have presented an ongoing project, named "STREEN" (Story Reading Environmental Enrichment) that targets the design of a smart reading environment for primary school children. This environment aims to provide a joyful reading experience while stimulating reading skills. The development of STREEN follows a Design Based Research approach, involving researchers, teachers and children from a local primary school in the design of the environment. In this paper we reported the steps done so far in the design process.

Ongoing and future work involves developing an improved version of the functional prototype focusing on the development of the graphical enrichments; the improvement of the control modality to promote a more effective control and better user experience; and to evolve the authoring tool. Furthermore, we will also test the functional prototype with a focus group in order to understand if this augmented reading concept has the potential to positively influence the reading comprehension and motivation of 3rd and 4th grade students.

Acknowledgements

We would like to thank the primary school *Schule am Bienenhaus*, in Rheinberg, Germany and especially the teachers and all the children that willingly work with us in this project.

Cristina Sylla has been financed by the FCT (Portuguese Foundation for Science and technology), the European Operational Programme Human Capital(POCH), with the Postdoctoral grant SFRH/BPD/111891/2015

References

1. Terry Anderson and Julie Shattuck. 2012. Design-Based Research A Decade of Progress in Education Research? *Educational Researcher* 41, 1: 16–25.
2. Lara Beth Clementi. 2010. Readers Theater: A Motivating Method to Improve Reading Fluency. *Phi Delta Kappan* 91, 5: 85–88.
3. David M. Durant and Tony Horava. 2015. The Future of Reading and Academic Libraries. *portal: Libraries and the Academy* 15, 1: 5–27.
4. Mona Leigh Guha, Allison Druin, and Jerry Alan Fails. 2013. Cooperative Inquiry revisited: Reflections of the past and guidelines for the future of intergenerational co-design. *International Journal of Child-Computer Interaction* 1, 1: 14–23.
5. Anežka Kuzmičová. 2012. Presence in the reading of literary narrative: A case for motor enactment. *semi* 2012, 189: 23–48.
6. Pedro Ribeiro, Cristina Sylla, Ido Iurgel, Wolfgang Müller, and Christian Ressel. 2017. STREEN -- Designing Smart Environments for Story Reading with Children. *Interaction Design and Architecture(s) Journal* 2017, 32: 84–103.
7. Maryanne Wolf and Mirit Barzillai. 2009. The Importance of Deep Reading. *ResearchGate* 66, 6: 32–37.

Kniwwelino: A Lightweight and WiFi Enabled Prototyping Platform for Children

Valérie Maquil
Luxembourg Institute of Science and Technology (LIST)
5, av. des Hauts Fourneaux
L-4362 Esch/Alzette
valerie.maquil@list.lu

Lou Schwartz
Luxembourg Institute of Science and Technology (LIST)
5, av. des Hauts Fourneaux
L-4362 Esch/Alzette
lou.schwartz@list.lu

Christian Moll
Luxembourg Institute of Science and Technology (LIST)
5, av. des Hauts Fourneaux
L-4362 Esch/Alzette
christian.moll@list.lu

Johannes Hermen
Luxembourg Institute of Science and Technology (LIST)
5, av. des Hauts Fourneaux
L-4362 Esch/Alzette
johannes.hermen@list.lu

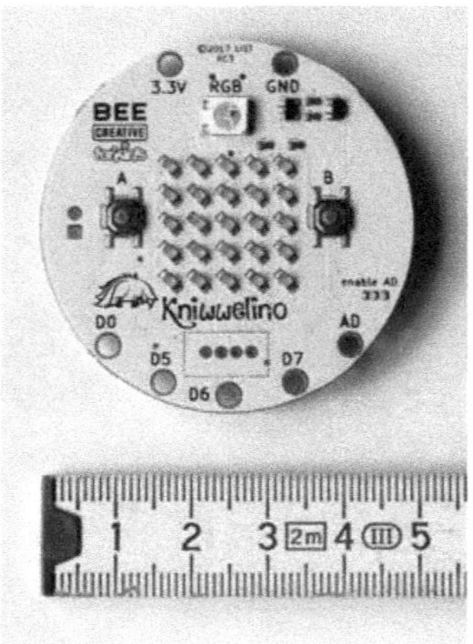

Figure 1. The size of the Kniwwelino is 5 cm of diameter.

ACM ISBN 978-1-4503-5568-1/18/03.
https://doi.org/10.1145/3173225.3173275.

Abstract
Nowadays, computational thinking skills are considered as fundamental for our future daily life and many initiatives and tools are created to foster these skills. In this paper, we present the Kniwwelino, a new platform for prototyping physical computing projects based on WiFi. The novelty of our solution lies in the use of a WiFi chip on a small, extendable board, programmable via a block based visual programming language, making the platform compact, low-cost, WiFi enabled, and accessible to children. This paper presents the design rationale and implementation of the platform as well as two simple, example projects making use of the new WiFi-based functionalities.

Author Keywords
Prototyping; Physical Computing; Digital skills; Computational thinking; Children.

Introduction
In the past years there is an ongoing discussion on how the digitalization of society will change our jobs and, more importantly, the skills required to perform these jobs. In this context, computational thinking is considered as a fundamental skill required by anyone in the future, in order to be able to understand the power

and limitations of computing processes and efficiently make use of computational power as part of our daily life [8].

Simplified approaches for learning how to program had already been proposed in the 60s with Logo [6], and became widely available through the easy-to-use web-based approach provided by Scratch [7]. To widen the focus to hardware, in the past years many low-cost electronic development platforms have been proposed, some of them being made available on the market. Examples of such projects include Arduino [9], the BBC Micro:bit [10], the Calliope mini [11], Lego Mindstorms [12], littleBits [1], or MakeMe [4]. Aim of these platforms generally is to propose an easy way of coding and making which is engaging and fun.

Typically, the challenges addressed by such projects deal with multiple aspects. First, platforms need to be versatile. They need to propose various sensors and actuators that can be combined to allow realizing any creative idea. Second, they need to be accessible and attractive to a broad range of people, hence they need to be low cost, engaging and easy to use. Finally, they need foster computational thinking and expose users to its multiple dimensions, i.e. computational concepts, practices, and perspectives [2].

To date, available platforms focus on processing power. To be able to connect devices to the Internet additional hardware needs to be added. For instance, the BBC micro:bit or the Calliope mini come with Bluetooth Low Energy (BLE) and only allow connection to the internet via a connected mobile phone or PC. However, to make people understand the power and limitations of computing processes today, it is necessary to provide a platform which supports features of the Internet of Things (IoT), i.e., communication between devices, as well as with web services.

In this paper, we present the Kniwwelino platform, a new platform for prototyping physical computing projects. The platform consist of (1) a printed circuit board (PCB), (2) a library with MQTT support, (3) a visual programming language, and (4) a web platform to handle firmware distribution and user management. The novelty of our solution lies in the use of a WiFi chip on a small, extendable board, programmable via a block based visual programming language, making the platform compact, low-cost, WiFi enabled, and accessible to children. In this paper, we present the design rationale and implementation of our platform as well as two simple, example projects making use of the WiFi-based functionalities.

Design process

To develop the Kniwwelino, we followed an iterative, user-centric design process, building upon results from previous work and taking in account current technologies available on the market.

Technology review

In a first step, requirements and inspirations for the Kniwwelino were collected. We performed, on one hand, an analysis of existing platforms where we identified best practices and of these projects: holes to connect wires or connectors, a 5x5 LED matrix as minimalistic display to show text and icons. Furthermore, we conducted a technology review to identify available low-cost electronic components. This review provided us with a list of 24 components, ranging from \$0.06 to \$2.59. Finally, we set up a list of

Figure 2. An example set of cards, each containing a topic and several electronic components

Figure 3. Participants sketching an idea with the cards.

available Do-it-Yourself projects for children, with a focus onto what these projects may be used for. We then grouped this information to proposed 8 topics which are potentially interesting for children: (1) protect your room, (2) explore space, (3) build the home of the future, (4) play music, (5) develop super heroes' powers, (6) share secrets with your best friend, (7) pimp your ride.

Brainstorming sessions

With the outcomes of the technology review, we organized two brainstorming sessions, with 11 and 3 participants each. Participants were all colleagues from our research institute, who work in the IT domain and regularly participate in ideation sessions, most of them having children on their own. For each of the identified topics and electronic components we created a separate card with an image, a title and a description (see Figure 3). In small groups of 2-3, participants were instructed to design ideas for projects for children by selecting a topic with the associated electronic components set and creating a storyboard. From these two brainstorming sessions, in total 15 project ideas were generated.

Technical development

Taking into account common features of the ideas generated in the brainstorming sessions, we selected the electronic components and created a first version of the platform, including the PCB and the library.

To test this design we ordered a first batch of 50 Kniwwelinos and used them as part of an electronic prototyping workshop with students [5]. In addition, we selected two ideas from the 15 ideas generated during the two brainstorming which were considered as most suitable by 2 informal education experts, as well as the most conform to price expectations and technical complexity. We implemented them and let children play with them within the scope of a Maker Fair.

These tests showed the need for some minor modifications in the board design, such as the need for buttons which are easier to push, as well as a USB plug with a better physical connection to the PCB. Furthermore, the library required modifications in order to better encapsulate standard functions and reduce the lines of code to be written. We then slightly improved the PCB and library, as well as implemented the visual programming tool and the firmware distribution platform. As part of this iteration, we also implemented the first two projects (see below), and adapted the blocks accordingly to make sure they are coherent and based on a child-friendly language.

The Kniwwelino platform

In the following, we will describe the details of the Kniwwelino platform: the PCB, the library, the visual programing tool, and the firmware distribution platform.

The PCB

To keep the board lightweight, but nevertheless allow children to implement interesting ideas, we chose to integrate only a minimum of sensors and actuators in the board: a 5x5 LED matrix, a RGB LED and two push buttons. All further components (e.g. additional sensors or peripherals) can be attached through additional ports (see Figure 4).

To compensate for the few possibilities provided by the components, we decided to use a System on a Chip

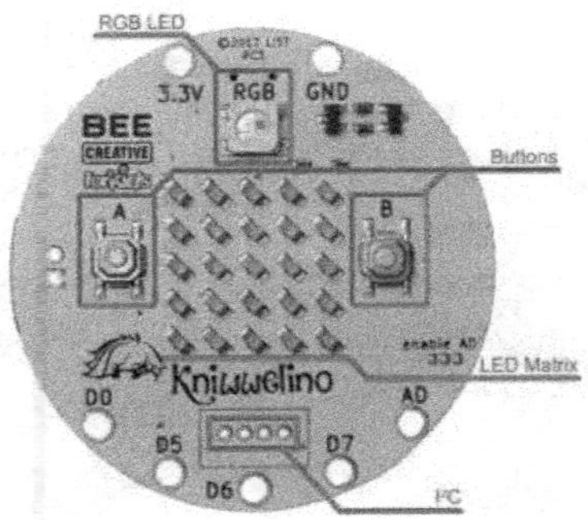

Figure 4. The Kniwwelino integrates a 5x5 LED matrix, a RGB LED and two push buttons

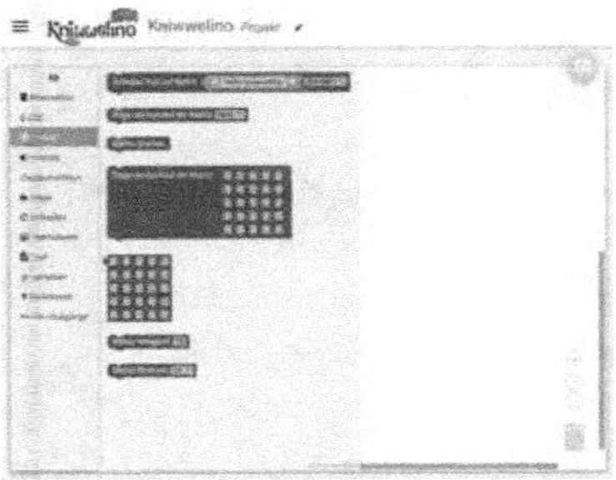

Figure 5. Screenshot of the visual programming tool.

(SoC) with an embedded WiFi stack. This then allows users, on one hand, to implement project making use of IoT concepts, such as communicating between devices or connecting to other databases such as weather channels. On the other hand, it allows us to propose a web platform to visually programming the board, and distribute the firmware wireless, without the need of installing any extra drivers or software.

The Kniwwelino PCB shape was chosen to be round with a diameter of 50mm to keep it small and easily embeddable to all kind of objects, e.g. wristwatch or flower head. The PCB size has also a positive influence on the manufacturing costs. In this way it was possible to lower the price from the first iterations to a price of $5.77.

Arduino Library with MQTT support
As the used System on a chip (SoC) is compatible and supported by the Arduino ecosystem, we decided at the beginning of the software development to use Arduino-C code and libraries. One design goal of the library was to encapsulate the functionality of the hardware as much as possible. This has the benefit to make short and understandable code. For instance, connecting predefined MQTT messages to the LED matrix or RGB LED can be done in one line of code. In addition, we wanted the library functions to be easily visualized and matched to blocks in the web programming tool, to help the children when they take the step from visual programming to coding.

Visual programming tool
As the underlying coding of the Kniwwelino is done in Arduino-C we decided to base our web development tool on the existing ArduBlockly [13] which is based on Google Blockly [14] (see Figure 5). ArduinoBlockly adds Arduino blocks and code generators to the standard Blockly. In addition we added blocks to interact with the Kniwwelino hardware and MQTT protocol. Beside the code blocks children can show the generated code and even open it directly in Arduino IDE. This helps to do the transition from blocks to code and to add features to programs that are not covered by the visual programming, e.g. use of additional libraries

Firmware distribution platform
During the design of the web-platform architecture we identified the problems of distributing demo projects and user projects to the Kniwwelino hardware. This problem was confirmed during our first workshop with adult participants [2] where we were faced with problems installing drivers and software on different versions of Windows and Mac OS X. To avoid such frustration, we decided to take advantage of the build-in WiFi-Stack of the underlying SoC and designed our firmware distribution around the the MQTT and HTTP(s) protocol. Whenever a board is powered up and connected to the Internet it connects to our MQTT broker. By default it subscribes to a topic build from its MAC address to get informed about updates and configuration changes. These messages are triggered by the server when a user associates a firmware designed in the visual programming tool with a Kniwwelino. Same is done when the program is changed later on. In these messages the Kniwwelino receives the URL to download an update. After downloading it to a free chunk of flash memory it checks the md5 against the server and installs the update and resets. After re-booting the new software is running and the children can test and further develop their project.

Figure 6. The best-friends' wristband allows children to send icons from one wristband to another one: first sketch of the idea (top) and the functional prototype (bottom).

Example projects

In the following we provide two simple example projects, which we developed to illustrate the use of the Kniwwelino platform: the digital Rock-Paper-Scissors game, and the Best Friends Wristband. These are two projects which resulted from the brainstorming sessions and achieved a high scoring in the evaluation with two experts and 50 children and which responded best to the technical requirements in term of simplicity and price. We then further specified the projects in a way that, on one hand, they show an attractive example which can be developed with only a few lines of code. On the other hand, the projects should allow for multiple ways of extending them, i.e. by adding new sensors and/or integrating them in a different object.

Best-friends' wristband

The best-friends' wristband allows children to send icons from their wristband to another one (see Figure 6). For each of the two buttons an icon or text message is preconfigured. When pushing the button, the icon or text appears on the LED matrix of the connected Kniwwelino.

With our enhanced version of the visual programming tool, we could implement this idea with 6 lines of code (see **Figure 7**). In the first line, users can define a group which is then added to all MQTT topics used within the example. In the second line, users connect the LED matrix to MQTT, meaning that all MQTT events send to MATRIX/ICON or MATRIX/TEXT will be shown automatically on the LED Matrix. The remaining code is detecting clicks on button A or B, to trigger sending a respective icon as MQTT message.

To create an extended version of this project, one possibility would be to integrate the Kniwwelino in other types of objects, such as a doll, showing the icon on its belly. Or a button can enable to navigate between several icons and the second button select the icon and sent it to the group.

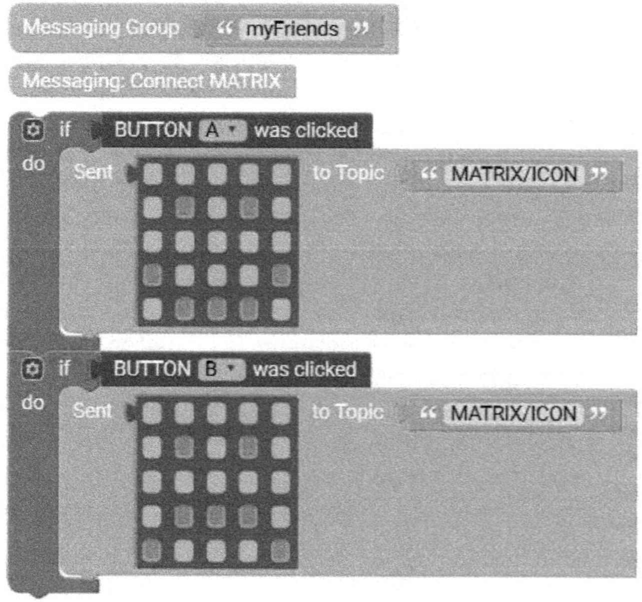

Figure 7. The blocks needed to implement the Best Friends Wristband idea.

Rock-Paper-Scissors game

The basic idea is to create a digital version of the Rock-Paper-Scissors game. Children can push button A to trigger a game. An icon representing one of the three symbols is then generated randomly. The RGB LED lights up green for the player who won, and red for the player who lost (see Figure 8).

In contrast to the previous project, the Rock Paper Scissors game requires more lines of code, in total 24.

Figure 8. The digital Rock-Paper-Scissors game.

While the random generation of icons on button press is rather straightforward (8 lines), some additional mechanisms are needed to detect when a new game starts and reset the variables (3 lines), to send the own score via MQTT (2 lines) and to interpret and visualize over MQTT who has won (11 lines).

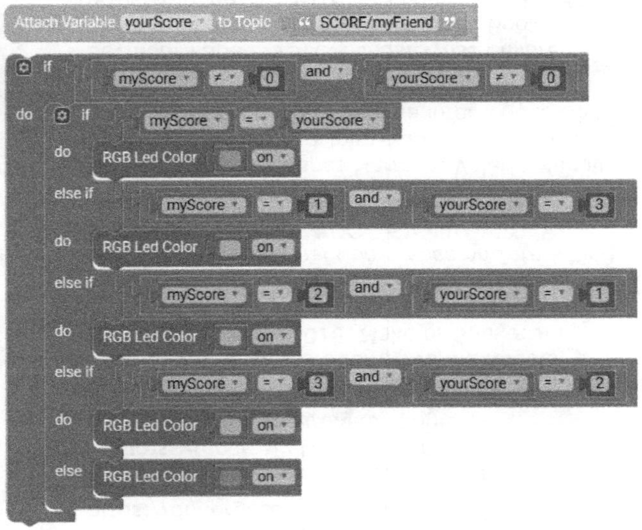

Figure 9. Excerpt of the code defining the subscription to the score of a play partner, and the related conditions to determine the resulting color code.

For the latter, we used the block subscribing to a topic (used by the partner to publish his/her score) and assigning the message to a variable. This variable can then be compared to the randomly generated score by oneself, in order to create a color code which represents who won (see **Figure 9**).

To create an extended version of this project, children could add external sensors, such as an accelerometer or a light sensor. The board could then be integrated into a cup. Instead of pressing a button, children could then trigger a new game by turning the cup upside down, or closing it with one hand to cover the light sensor.

Summary and outlook

In this work, we have presented the Kniwwelino platform as a lightweight and WiFi enabled solution for prototyping physical computing projects. We have shown how WiFi support allowed us to generate new project ideas for children and to propose a new way of distributing projects to the hardware. We have proposed a series of visual programming blocks to make use of MQTT communication as part of such a project and illustrated them in two example projects.

In future work, we will evaluate the platform with children in the scope of science and Maker fairs. Based on the insights gained in these evaluations we will then further improve the platform with the aim to address potential usability problems and refined requirements.

Acknowledgements

This project is supported by the Fonds National de la Recherche, Luxembourg. We would like to thank John-Nathan Hill and Henrique Rangel who contributed to the development of the platform as well as all the children and adults who tested the Kniwwelino and provided us with useful ideas and feedback.

References

1. Ayah Bdeir. 2009. Electronics as material. *Proceedings of the 3rd International Conference on Tangible and Embedded Interaction - TEI '09*: 397. https://doi.org/10.1145/1517664.1517743
2. Karen Brennan and Mitchel Resnick. 2012. New frameworks for studying and assessing the development of computational thinking. *Annual American Educational Research Association meeting, Vancouver, BC, Canada*: 1–25. https://doi.org/10.1.1.296.6602
3. European Commission. 2017. *Europe's Digital Progress Report*. Retrieved from https://ec.europa.eu/digital-single-market/en/european-digital-progress-report
4. Rose Johnson, Venus Shum, Yvonne Rogers, and Nicolai Marquardt. 2016. Make or Shake: An Empirical Study of the Value of Making in Learning about Computing Technology. *Proceedings of the The 15th International Conference on Interaction Design and Children (IDC '16)*: 440–451. https://doi.org/10.1145/2930674.2930691
5. Christian Moll, Johannes Hermen, Valérie Maquil, Henrique Rangel, and John-Nathan Hill. 2017. Prototyping connected tangible interactions with kniwwelino. In *CEUR Workshop Proceedings*.
6. Seymour Papert. 1980. *Mindstorms: Children, computers and powerful ideas*. Basic Books, Inc. https://doi.org/10.1016/0732-118X(83)90034-X
7. Mitchel Resnick, John Maloney, Andrés Monroy-Hernández, Natalie Rusk, Evelyn Eastmond, Karen Brennan, Amon Millner, Eric Rosenbaum, J a Y Silver, Brian Silverman, and Yasmin Kafai. 2009. Scratch: Programming for All. *Communications of the ACM* 52: 60–67. https://doi.org/10.1145/1592761.1592779
8. Jeannette M. Wing. 2006. Computational thinking. *COMMUNICATIONS OF THE ACM* 49, 3: 33–35. https://doi.org/10.1145/1227504.1227378
9. Arduino. Retrieved November 3, 2017 from https://www.arduino.cc/
10. BBC micro:bit. Retrieved November 3, 2017 from http://microbit.org/
11. Calliope mini. Retrieved November 3, 2017 from https://calliope.cc/
12. LEGO Mindstorms. Retrieved November 3, 2017 from https://www.lego.com/en-us/mindstorms
13. ArduBlockly. Retrieved November 3, 2017 from https://ardublockly.embeddedlog.com/
14. Google Blockly. Retrieved November 3, 2017 from https://developers.google.com/blockly/

CRISPEE: A Tangible Gene Editing Platform for Early Childhood

Clarissa Verish
Wellesley College
Wellesley, MA 02481, USA
cverish@wellesley.edu

Amanda Strawhacker
Marina Bers
Tufts University
Medford, MA 02155, USA
Amanda.Strawhacker@tufts.edu
Marina.Bers@tufts.edu

Orit Shaer
Wellesley College
Wellesley, MA 02481, USA
oshaer@wellesley.edu

TEI '18, March 18–21, 2018, Stockholm, Sweden
ACM 978-1-4503-5568-1/18/03.
https://doi.org/10.1145/3173225.3173277

Abstract
We present CRISPEE, a novel tangible user interface designed to engage young elementary school children in bioengineering concepts. Using CRISPEE, children assume the role of a bioengineer to create a genetic program that codes for a firefly's bioluminescent light. This is accomplished through sequencing tangible representations of BioBricks, which code for the primary colors of light (red, green, and blue) to be turned on or off. The interface and curricular supplement expose children in early elementary school to concepts traditionally taught much later in school curricula through playful interaction and exploration. We discuss CRISPEE's concept and design, and share findings from its preliminary evaluation with children and adults.

Author Keywords
Children; education; play / games.

ACM Classification Keywords
- **Human-centered computing~Interface design prototyping**

Introduction
Bioengineering is at the frontier of a wide range of scientific domains including space exploration, medicine, and food production. However, despite the relevance of bioengineering to solving pressing real-world problems, foundational

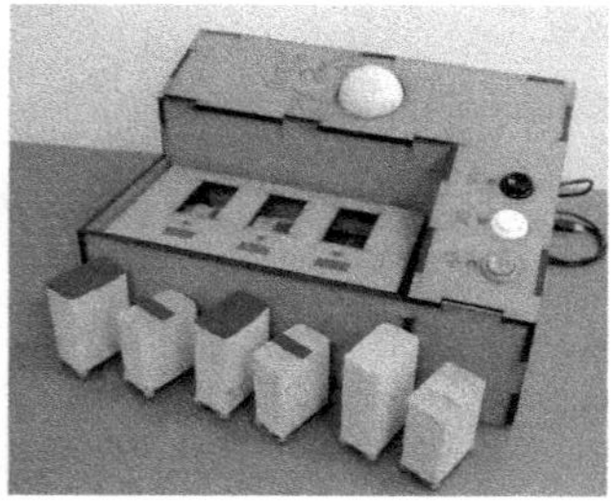

Figure 1: The current prototype of CRISPEE. Tangible blocks code red, green, and blue light to be either on (solid color) or off (colored line). Blocks are placed into the corresponding slots on the platform to create the genetic program of the firefly, with a colored output in the firefly's tail.

concepts of microbiology and genetics are not introduced to US students until middle school or later [1]. Young children (ages 5-7 years) are at a critical age to explore the world around them through a multidisciplinary lens, and educational advances in other domains (e.g. engineering, technology, computer science) have shown that children as young as age 4 are capable of learning core concepts of fields related to bioengineering [5, 4]. The goal of this work-in-progress is to describe our current efforts to develop a tangible, developmentally-appropriate tool to introduce children to foundational concepts of bioengineering. Using CRISPEE, children can explore how bioengineering can be used to solve problems in the real world.

CRISPEE is a novel tangible user interface for children to engage in bioengineering concepts, such as gene editing, through play and exploration. This paper describes CRISPEE's iterative design process, and discusses findings from preliminary evaluation with children and adults.

Background and Related Work

Bioengineering is a multidisciplinary field at the forefront of scientific progress, combining the fields of engineering and microbiology to create biologically-based solutions to real-world problems. One such solution is CRISPR/Cas9, a gene-editing tool that grants researchers the ability to make targeted changes to DNA sequences quickly and inexpensively [15]. CRISPR shows promise as a versatile method with applications in a broad array of domains, and its role in bioengineering will only grow as more applications for the technology are discovered. Gene editing protocols are not limited to CRISPR, and various methods exist for creating and inserting genetic programs into living cells. The MIT Registry of Standard Biological Parts [8] contains more than 20,000 biological parts, also referred to as BioBricks (i.e. DNA sequences with documented characteristics and functions which conform to assembly standards).

Bioengineering impacts a wide range of areas, from agriculture, to medicine, to environmental sustainability and space exploration. The advances and impact that this field offers, as well as the ethical questions that it raises, are going to become critically important in the future of today's children. However, currently, US education standards do not recommend exploring microbiology until 6th grade at the earliest [1], well after students have formed influential stereotypes and foundational ideas about STEM fields [18]. Until recently, engineering was also not taught to children before middle school, but current research has shown that young children (ages 5-7 years) can engage playfully and meaningfully in foundational concepts of engineering design [4, 6]. Engineering design is now recommended as early as Kindergarten [1]. Researchers have formed guidelines for designing technological tools that leverage children's natural ability to learn-by-doing [14], including the use of screen-free, tangible, highly-interactive platforms that support curiosity and self-directed play [2, 3, 17]. We applied the same principles in the design of CRISPEE, as we attempt to introduce children to foundational concepts of bioengineering.

This work draws upon other tangible interfaces for engaging children in bioengineering such as Synflo [13] and BacPack for New Frontiers [12], and interfaces that encourage tangible and virtual interaction with live cells [9, 10, 7]. Targeting children in grades 2-5, researchers found that students advanced their understanding of concepts like genes, DNA, and engineering [11]. Prior work on bioengineering tools for Kindergarten includes Garden G-nome, a digital workbench interface to explore genetics in plant life [16]. A major finding from this work was the importance of teacher

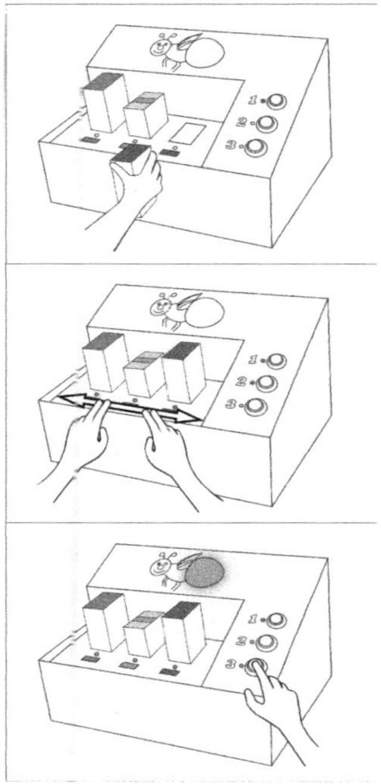

Figure 2: The three steps of interacting with CRISPEE. First, design: users place the tangible BioBricks into the corresponding slots on the platform. Next, mix: the user shakes the platform back and forth. Finally, test: the firefly lights up with the color output coded in step one.

buy-in through screen-free tangible technology. We created CRISPEE, a screen-free tangible user interfaces for children ages 5-7 years, to be used in conjunction with a developmentally-appropriate curriculum that introduces concepts such as bioengineering and gene editing in playful, story-based ways.

Design Process

CRISPEE was created through an iterative design process in which we designed a series of prototypes in increasing fidelity. The current, fully-functional prototype is shown in Figure 1. We worked with educators and children to design the interface, and observed children playing with related and early prototypes to inform the direction of our design.

The design of CRISPEE was inspired by the form of gene sequencing machines currently on the market, to give children a sense of the types of tools that bioengineers use in their labs. We created a tangible interface made of large age-appropriate components and materials (wood, felt, and Velcro). BioBricks (i.e. genes) are represented by tangible wooden blocks, and LED indicators provide guidance and feedback through light output. Early iterations included a screen for guidance, but we removed the screen to comply with design guideline for early elementary school and per a request from educators.

An important design consideration was the cost of the final interface. We sought to create a toy that could be accessible to any classroom, so we designed the tangible blocks and enclosure with affordable materials and electrical components.

Early designs emphasized the order of the BioBricks, with ten tangibles each representing an output color. CRISPEE had five output lights in the order the blocks were placed. We changed this design from five outputs to one (the firefly's tail) to better reflect the concepts of genetically programing living organisms. The tangibles now represent red, green, and blue light, with each type of light having a block for "on" and a block for "off". The children program a light for a firefly, enhancing the meaning of the task.

Interaction

Interaction with CRISPEE is illustrated in Figure 2. The goal of the interaction is to help a firefly light up by creating a genetic program. Children accomplish this task using BioBricks (i.e. genes) that produce the red, green, and blue primary light colors, and by mixing the genetic material to light up the firefly. Children are led through the process using LED indicators and buttons which indicate the three steps of the bioengineering process: design, mix, and test.

In step 1, design, children program a light color by placing red, green, and blue tangible blocks representing BioBricks into the slots in the sensor platform. Once the first button is pressed, CRISPEE checks the program and gives feedback through LEDs in front of the sensors, showing green for correct block placements and red for incorrect. The blocks must be placed in the correct red, green, and blue slots for the program to read correctly.

Once the program is correct, children proceed to step 2, mix, where they mix their genetic program to insert it into the firefly's DNA. This is accomplished by physically moving the platform back and forth until all three LEDs on the sensor platform have turned green. In the final step, test, children see the firefly light up with the color combination created by their genetic program.

Throughout the interaction, lights next to the buttons flash red to indicate the next step in the protocol, and shine green when a step has been completed. Light feedback is also included in the design step to show the correctness of the program, in the mix step to indicate mixing progress, and in the test step to indicate that the genetic program has been successfully output.

Implementation and Fabrication

CRISPEE is implemented using the ATmega1280 microprocessor connected to arcade buttons, an accelerometer, LEDs, and conductive Velcro sensors. The tangible blocks are made of wood, felt, and conductive Velcro, with a resistor embedded in each block and connected to the Velcro. When the block is placed into the receiver slot, it is identified by reading the voltage drop across the block's resistor through a voltage divider in parallel with a known resistor. The conductive Velcro replaced an earlier iteration of the blocks and sensors that used metal rails to create contact, because reliable connections between the two flat surfaces were challenging, and the blocks moved significantly when the platform was shaken. The accelerometer is used to sense the platform movement in step 2 (mix).

We made the enclosure with laser-cut medium-density fiberboard and designed it to have interlocking pieces for aesthetics and strength. We used Velcro to attach the back and the faceplate of the platform so they could be opened and the electronics shown to children. CRISPEE was designed to be durable, with drawer slides under the moving platform to provide a solid and satisfying sliding action, and resilient blocks that could withstand being dropped or thrown. The toy has a satisfying weight so that it feels solid and doesn't move when the platform is being shaken.

Pilot Testing

We conducted a preliminary evaluation of CRISPEE with four children (grades K-3), and five adults who work directly with children in this age group. For all participants, we introduced CRISPEE with a story-based task that involves helping a living organism (a firefly whose body cannot light up) by reprogramming its genes to produce light in various colors. Core concepts were introduced throughout the session, to connect playful learning with domain content. We studied the usability of the interfaces as well as participants' experience engaging with CRISPEE.

Following a brief introduction to bioengineering and genetics, participants were asked to guess what the blocks represent, and to figure out how the interface worked with prompts from researchers. Once they successfully lit up their firefly for the first time, they were asked to reflect on the blocks they had chosen, and to investigate the different colors that they could create using CRISPEE. They were then asked about their enjoyment of the interface.

Pilot Tests with Adults

We asked adults who work closely with children to place themselves into the role of the child. All participants were able to place the blocks into the slots with the Velcro down and press the indicated button, and most could figure out what those lights indicate when the blocks were placed incorrectly. No adult could figure out the mixing mechanism until shown by a researcher; some thought that mixing the blocks meant moving them around to different slots.

The adults generally enjoyed the interface and thought that children would too. Many commented that they liked the different block combinations and the output colors, and that they thought children would enjoy matching the colors to the slots and trying different combinations. All of them commented that they were confused about the mixing mechanism, but once they were shown how it worked, they enjoyed the interaction of physically sliding the platform. Two commented that the buttons should have labels instead of being numbered.

Figure 3: A kindergarten girl playing with the CRISPEE interface. She has placed the tangible BioBricks into the corresponding slots and is pressing the first button to check the accuracy of her program.

Pilot Tests with Children

We tested the interface with four children, one kindergarten girl, one second-grade girl, and two third-grade boys. Children were led through the same process as adults, and after a post-task questionnaire were asked whether they would like to keep playing with the interface. These children generally understood the first step of the interaction, placing blocks correctly in the slots and pressing the first button to check their program. Some prompting was needed to help them relate the color of the LED to the correctness of the block placement. All of the children moved the bricks around in the slots when told it was time to mix the program, rather than moving the platform back and forth. Once they were shown the mixing action, they were able to remember how to do it as they played with it longer. They all expressed excitement when they successfully lit up the firefly and wanted to continue playing with the interface after this first interaction.

The kindergarten girl (shown in Figure 3) asked to keep playing with the interface after the post-task questionnaire, and played for an additional 17 minutes. She seemed to greatly enjoy the interface, cheering when she created a correct program and exclaiming "I made my favorite color!" when she made a cyan light. She spent some time trying to make her mom's favorite color (red) and tried different color combinations to achieve this. She talked through her logic as she placed blocks, choosing carefully and saying "that should do it" when she thought she made the program that would give her the color output she wanted. Once she figured out the on and off blocks, she began stating her planned output color and how she would achieve it, saying "so first I'm going to do red, the first color in the rainbow" and placing red-on, green-off, and blue-off blocks. She also explored what different color combinations would create, saying "now I want to try mixing blue and red."

The second-grade girl also enjoyed the interface. She was able to grasp the meaning of the on- and off-bricks very quickly, and was immediately able to place the blocks into the correct colored slots. After playing with the interface, she talked about how the blocks she was combining were helping the firefly. One third-grade boy was able to relate the concepts presented by CRISPEE to other forms of life, asking "Can we use the same genes for lighting a zebrafish?", showing that the interaction prompted further exploration of bioengineering principles. The other third-grade boy commented that he thought he and his peers would be too old for CRISPEE, confirming our goal age group of K-2. Both third-grade boys thought that a screen would make the interface more fun, but they did not say they thought the interface needed this screen to be more understandable.

Results and Discussion

Initial pilot tests of CRISPEE were promising and will drive further design of the interface. We received positive feedback from the adult pilot testers, who thought that the interface would be enjoyable for the target age range. Children enjoyed working with the interface and showed understanding of the connection between the blocks they chose and the color of the firefly, and the role of mixing in the process of creating their genetic program.

Several improvements need to be made to the interface for the next iteration. It is clear that the mixing step, while satisfying, needs additional work to make the interaction more obvious. Suggestions from the adult pilot testers included adding flashing arrows to the platform to indicate horizontal movement, and using separate LED indicators for the sensors and the mixing, as having different meanings for the same lights was confusing. Other improvements include making the firefly bulb brighter, as some of the colors are hard to distinguish in bright ambient lighting conditions, and changing the action of the first button so that the program can be restarted at any point through the process.

Conclusions and Future Directions

We presented CRISPEE, a tangible user interface for engaging children in early elementary school with core concepts of biological engineering. Our goal is to expose children to domain concepts as well as to the promise and ethical concerns of this cutting-edge field at the intersection of science and technology. We believe that given developmentally-appropriate tools, young children can engage meaningfully with abstract concepts that were traditionally considered too complex for them to learn.

We plan to iterate on the design of the interface and to evaluate CRISPEE together with an accompanying curricular intervention within a classroom environment. We are also expanding the scope of CRISPEE to include a "design-a-biobrick" module, which allows children to engage more deeply with sequencing and DNA, and to program functions for BioBricks such as color value (e.g. dark or light) and sensor activation. Our curricular intervention will expand the story-based task into a full curriculum with bioengineering challenges that can be addressed with a diversity of physical and creative activities.

Acknowledgements

This work is funded by NSF IIS-1563932. A special thank you to Larry Knowles, Amy Banzaert, Thomas Verish, the members of the Tufts DevTech Lab and the Wellesley HCI lab, and our pilot testers.

REFERENCES

1. 2013. *Next Generation Science Standards: For States, By States.* The National Academies Press, Washington, DC. DOI: http://dx.doi.org/10.17226/18290
2. Shaaron Ainsworth. 2006. DeFT: A conceptual framework for considering learning with multiple representations. *Learning and instruction* 16, 3 (2006), 183–198.
3. Marina Umaschi Bers. 2012. *Designing digital experiences for positive youth development: From playpen to playground.* Oxford University Press.
4. Marina Umaschi Bers. 2017. *Coding as a playground: Programming and computational thinking in the early childhood classroom.* Routledge.
5. Douglas H Clements and Julie Sarama. 2003. Strip mining for gold: Research and policy in educational technology—A response to "Fool's Gold". *AACE Journal* 11, 1 (2003), 7–69.
6. Gerald A Goldin. 2013. *" Show Me what You Know": Exploring Student Representations Across STEM Disciplines.* Teachers College Press.
7. Zahid Hossain, Engin Bumbacher, Paulo Blikstein, and Ingmar Riedel-Kruse. 2017. Authentic Science Inquiry Learning at Scale Enabled by an Interactive Biology Cloud Experimentation Lab. In *Proceedings of the Fourth (2017) ACM Conference on Learning@ Scale.* ACM, 237–240.
8. iGem. Registry of Standard Biological Parts. (????). Retrieved November 2, 2017 from http://partsregistry.org/Main_Page.

9. Seung Ah Lee, Engin Bumbacher, Alice M Chung, Nate Cira, Byron Walker, Ji Young Park, Barry Starr, Paulo Blikstein, and Ingmar H Riedel-Kruse. 2015a. Trap it!: A Playful Human-Biology Interaction for a Museum Installation. In *Proceedings of the 33rd Annual ACM Conference on Human Factors in Computing Systems.* ACM, 2593–2602.

10. Seung Ah Lee, Alice M Chung, Nate Cira, and Ingmar H Riedel-Kruse. 2015b. Tangible interactive microbiology for informal science education. In *Proceedings of the Ninth International Conference on Tangible, Embedded, and Embodied Interaction.* ACM, 273–280.

11. Anna Loparev, Amanda Sullivan, Clarissa Verish, Lauren Westendorf, Jasmine Davis, Margaret Flemings, Marina Bers, and Orit Shaer. 2017a. BacToMars: Creative Engagement with Bio-Design for Children. In *Proceedings of the 2017 Conference on Interaction Design and Children.* ACM, 623–628.

12. Anna Loparev, Lauren Westendorf, Margaret Flemings, Jennifer Cho, Romie Littrell, Anja Scholze, and Orit Shaer. 2017b. BacPack: Exploring the Role of Tangibles in a Museum Exhibit for Bio-Design. In *Proceedings of the Eleventh International Conference on Tangible, Embedded, and Embodied Interaction (TEI '17).* ACM, New York, NY, USA, 111–120. DOI: http://dx.doi.org/10.1145/3024969.3025000

13. Johanna Okerlund, Evan Segreto, Casey Grote, Lauren Westendorf, Anja Scholze, Romie Littrell, and Orit Shaer. 2016. SynFlo: A Tangible Museum Exhibit for Exploring Bio-Design. In *Proceedings of the TEI '16: Tenth International Conference on Tangible, Embedded, and Embodied Interaction (TEI '16).* ACM, New York, NY, USA, 141–149. DOI: http://dx.doi.org/10.1145/2839462.2839488

14. Seymour Papert. 1980. *Mindstorms: Children, computers, and powerful ideas.* Basic Books, Inc.

15. Alex Reis, Breton Hornblower, Brett Robb, and George Tzertzinis. CRISPR/Cas9 and Targeted Genome Editing: A New Era in Molecular Biology. (????). Retrieved November 2, 2017 from https://www.neb.com/tools-and-resources/feature-articles/crispr-cas9-and-targeted-genome-editing-a-new-era-in-molecular-biology.

16. Orit Shaer, Marina Umaschi Bers, and M. Chang. 2011. Making the Invisible Tangible: Learning Biological Engineering in Kindergarten. *ACM CHI 2011 Workshop on User Interface Technology and Educational Pedagogy, ACM: CHI 2011.* (2011).

17. Amanda Strawhacker and Marina U Bers. 2015. "I want my robot to look for food": Comparing Kindergartner's programming comprehension using tangible, graphic, and hybrid user interfaces. *International Journal of Technology and Design Education* 25, 3 (2015), 293–319.

18. Amanda Alzena Sullivan. 2016. *Breaking the STEM Stereotype: Investigating the Use of Robotics to Change Young Children's Gender Stereotypes About Technology and Engineering.* Ph.D. Dissertation. Tufts University.

Exploring Around-Device Tangible Interactions for Mobile Devices with a Magnetic Ring

Victor Cheung
Carleton University
Ottawa, ON, Canada
victor.cheung@carleton.ca

Audrey Girouard
Carleton University
Ottawa, ON, Canada
audrey.girouard@carleton.ca

TEI '18, March 18–21, 2018, Stockholm, Sweden

ACM ISBN 978-1-4503-5568-1/18/03.
https://doi.org/10.1145/3173225.3173283

Abstract
We present our initial work on using a magnetic ring as a tangible input control to support around-device interactions for mobile devices, aiming to address touchscreen issues such as occlusion and imprecision, at the same time provides tangibility to interaction. This input mechanism allows users to use the surface on which the mobile device is placed as an extended input space, with a rotatory motion as the main form of interaction. Our technique requires no calibration, no modifications to the mobile device, and no external power for the ring, which also functions as an accessory item (a finger ring) when not in use. We discuss our design criteria, prototype implementation and illustrative applications, and directions for future work.

Author Keywords
Around-device interaction; mobile device; magnetism; magnetic ring; wearable; jewelry; tangible interaction.

ACM Classification Keywords
• Human-centered computing~Human computer interaction (HCI) • Human-centered computing~Interaction devices • Human-centered computing~Gestural input • Human-centered computing~Mobile devices

Introduction

Touch interactions with mobile devices suffer from issues such as occlusion and imprecision [13]. Around-Device Interactions (ADIs) address these by extending the interaction regions beyond the device itself [4,10], while enabling novel interaction techniques that are not possible on a display surface where contact must be maintained (e.g., mid-air 3D [11]). The extra regions also allow additional hardware to provide tactile feedback that is missing from a typically featureless touchscreen (e.g., physical widgets [10]).

However, in many cases, ADIs either require the mobile device to be augmented with special sensing hardware, for example, SideSight [4] uses an array of proximity sensors to determine finger positions; or require a custom input control, often because the control must have specific physical affordances to represent its functionality, for example, MagGetz [10] uses various physical widgets which are an embodied representation of their associated control in the mobile interface. Such requirements lead to reliance on dedicated custom components that are not easily available to average consumers and, hence, reduce practicality.

We overcome this limitation by using sensing hardware that is commonly available in modern mobile devices, and an affordable (~USD$5) and easily obtainable input control. We use magnetism through combining the built-in magnetometer of a mobile device, and a magnetic ring, which is commonly used as an inconspicuous prop in close-up magic performances[1].

[1] Also known as "PK (Psycho-Kinetic) ring", with which magicians appear to be able to manipulate objects with their minds.

Related Work

There has been active research in ADIs for mobile devices using various techniques, including proximity sensing [4,12], visual tracking [6], and acoustics [8]. We focus on those that uses magnetism as the main input detection mechanism, and group them into two categories of either using magnets only, or with other items, to compare their advantages and drawbacks.

ADI with Magnets Only

Han et al. [7] and Harrison & Hudson [9] used a finger-worn magnet, and tracked its movements using a magnetic sensor worn on the user's wrist. Both work used dedicated magnetic sensors to detect fluctuations in magnetic field to determine the magnet's position, for recognizing handwriting [7] and selecting items [9].

MagiTact [11] explores three different magnet shapes (rod, pen, and ring) for 3D gesture inputs. Nenya [2] focuses on the ring form factor to provide subtle and eyes-free input, where the user wears the ring and selects menu items with one- and two-hand gestures.

The advantage of this approach is that the magnets being used are easily obtainable and can be very small (fraction of the size of one's fingertip). However, the drawback is that the input vocabulary with magnets alone is limited to those actions that affect the magnetic field, namely, translations and rotations.

ADI with Magnets Attached to Other Items

TMotion [14] attaches a magnet and an inertial measurement unit (IMU) to a stylus to detect 3D inputs. Abe et al. [1] used a similar setup, but removed the need of an IMU by limiting the movements to the surface on which the mobile device is placed.

MagGetz [10] attaches magnets to a number of customizable controllers that mimic GUI interface components, and detects their associated actions (e.g., pressing a button, moving a slider, turning a wheel). Bianchi & Oakley [3] attached magnets of different strengths to various objects to enable identification of tokens, as well as their movements and positions.

The advantage of this approach is that the magnet-augmented items provide greater tangibility and affordance of use, for example, a stylus for drawing, a button for pressing. However, the drawback is that each item is often interface-specific and has to be swapped out for different interactions, requiring the user to carry all of them along and taking up space.

We employ the magnet-only approach, so as to keep the input control as compact and portable as possible. Additionally, we chose to use a finger ring form factor, which naturally suggests rotatory actions via its circular shape. However, instead of wearing the ring during use (as in Nenya [2]), we explored scenarios where the ring is taken off and placed parallel to the mobile device (similar to on-surface interactions by Colley et al. [5]).

Design Criteria

To lower the barriers in adopting ADIs, for example, costly and custom hardware, effort to learn and perform interaction gestures, we established the following four design criteria:

DC1: No modification to the mobile device.
The technique should be usable by most if not all modern mobile devices. This means no additional hardware attached to the device, and preferably no modification to the operating system (e.g., rooting).

DC2: Requires minimal setup/calibration.
The technique should be available for anyone. This means no elaborate and time-consuming setup (e.g., extraneous computing items that require calibration).

DC3: Input control is self-contained and -sufficient.
The technique should be available at any time. This means the input control does not rely on any external support that renders itself unusable if missing (e.g., battery). If power is needed, it has to be self-powered.

DC4: Ergonomic to use.
The technique should allow repeated activation without causing much fatigue. This means no large movements (e.g., constant mid-air gestures). Smaller movements also have the advantage of drawing less attention.

Prototype

We designed our technique to use only the built-in magnetometer of a mobile device (available in most Android devices[2], and all iOS devices except 1st-gen iPhone, iPhone 3G, and iPod Touch[3]) for sensing the magnetic field. This sensor is accessible without any modifications (DC1). The input control, a magnetic ring, is a permanent magnet shaped as a finger ring (DC3).

Input gestures are mainly performed on the same plane as the mobile device's display. Mid-air gestures are possible, but to minimize fatigue we focus on scenarios where both the device and ring are on a surface (DC4).

[2] Android's sensor overview webpage: https://developer.android.com/guide/topics/sensors/sensors_overview.html

[3] Apple's iOS device compatibility reference webpage: https://developer.apple.com/library/content/documentation/DeviceInformation/Reference/iOSDeviceCompatibility/DeviceCompatibilityMatrix/DeviceCompatibilityMatrix.html

Figure 1. Setup of the prototype. Top: Mobile device (Nexus 5), Bottom: Magnetic ring (diametrically magnetized). The ring can be placed anywhere around the device as long as its movements are within the detection range of the device's magnetometer.

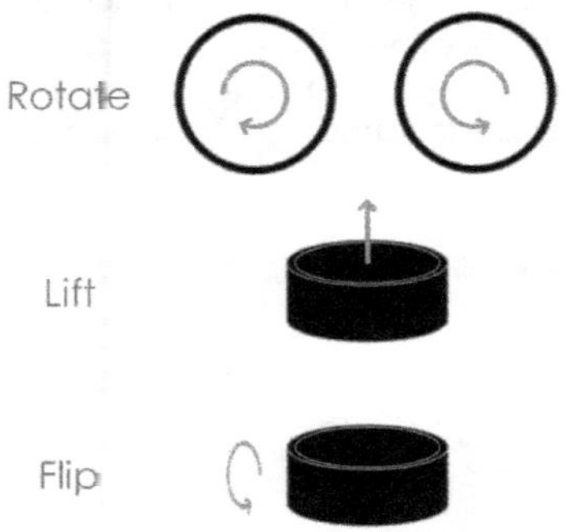

Figure 2. Three input gestures with the magnetic ring. Top: Rotate (clockwise/counter-clockwise), Middle: Lift (up), Bottom: Flip. All actions are assumed to be starting from a surface at the same plane as the devices display.

The input gestures are actions that cause discernable fluctuations in the magnetic field as detected by the mobile device. These changes are deterministic and hence can be measured without calibration (DC2).

Figure 1 shows the physical setup of the prototype demonstrating the technique. The magnetic ring can be anywhere around the mobile device as an input control.

Implementation

We tested on an LG Nexus 5 (running Android 6.0.1) as the mobile device, and a magnetic ring (diameter: 20mm, height: 7.5mm, thickness: 1mm, diametrically magnetized with strength: ~50 mT at each pole) as the input control. We implemented the sensing software using Android API 23, which measures calibrated magnetic field strength in the x-, y-, and z-axes aligned to the device's orientation.

Input Gestures

Through experimenting with our prototype, we identified three promising input gestures (Figure 2) using the following three actions. We describe their working principles and performance considerations.

ROTATE (AROUND THE Z-AXIS)

Like a dial, the circular shape of the ring naturally affords a rotate (turn) action. As shown in Figure 3, rotating the ring at a fixed position relative to the mobile device causes discernable changes along the x- and y-axes, and reverts back to the original values when a full rotation is completed. Utilizing this property, we calculate the angle created by the x- and y-values using the following formula:

$$\theta = \tan^{-1}\frac{y}{x},\ \theta \epsilon [-180°, 180°] \qquad \text{Eq. 1}$$

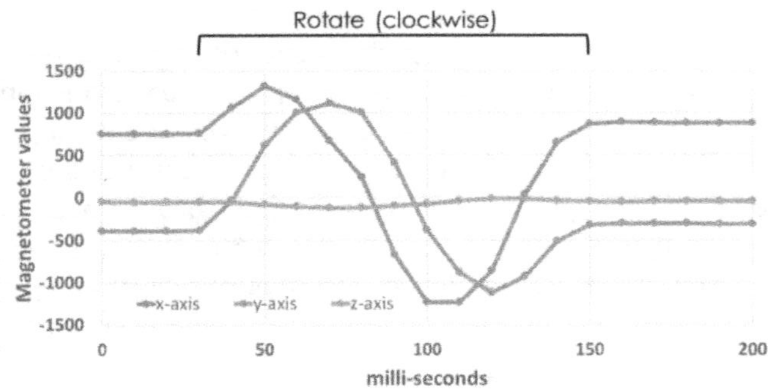

Figure 3. Magnetometer values in x-, y-, and z-axes as the ring rotates clockwise for 360 degrees at approximately 5cm away.

This value is consistent as long as the relative position of the ring remains the same. Hence, it can be mapped to any continuous input parameter within a range.

LIFT (ALONG THE Z-AXIS)

Examination of the ring's magnetic field reveals that it behaves like a typical bar magnet, with North and South poles on its opposite arcs. This means that tracking techniques employed in prior work (e.g., [1,9]) can be applied to determine the position of the magnetic ring. However, this is in conflict with the detection of the rotate gesture, as both use the same x- and y-values from the sensor. Since we want to prioritize the rotate gesture in this work as afforded by the ring's circular shape, our technique does not associate translation actions with input gestures.

Nevertheless, a lifting action causes a discernable change along the z-axis, which is not present in the rotate action, and hence can be associated with a different input gesture. In actuality, such action is equivalent to moving the ring away from the device, thus causes changes not just in z-axis but all the axes

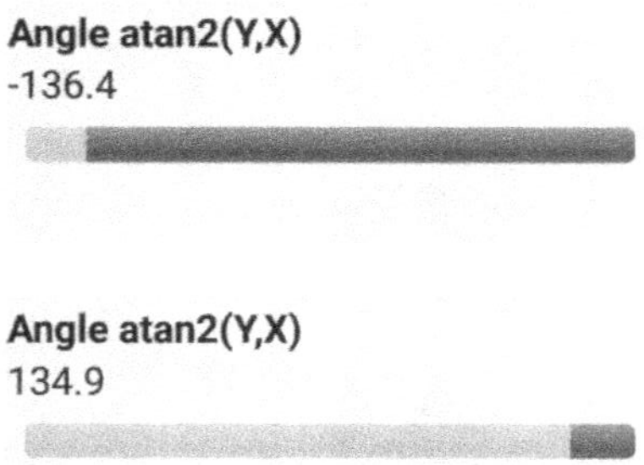

Figure 6. Example control using the angle calculated between the x- and y-values. The -180-180 range is mapped to a linear level control.

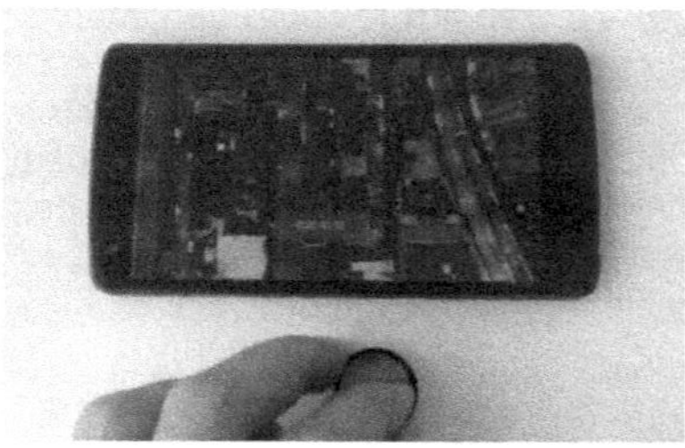

Figure 7. Example using change in angle to scrub through a video clip. Rotating clockwise advances the playback, rotating counter-clockwise rewinds the playback.

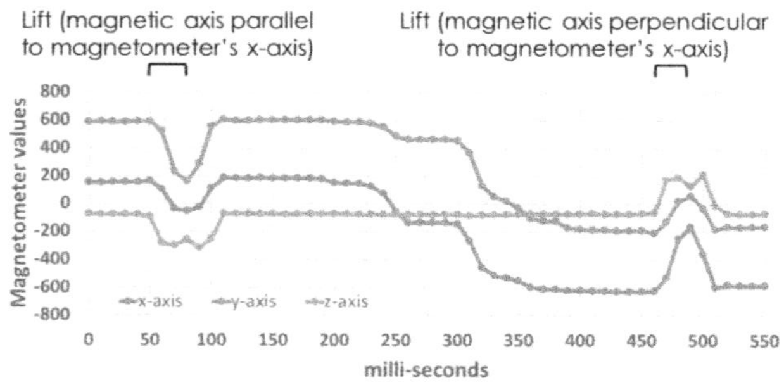

Figure 4. Magnetometer values in x-, y-, and z-axes as the ring lifts approximately 5cm upwards. Note how the orientation of the ring affects the way these values change.

(see Figure 4). One caveat, is that the orientation of the ring (magnetic axis) has an effect on how these values change, and warrants further investigation to properly recognize such gesture.

Flip

An interesting action, only possible when the ring is not worn, is flipping (turning the ring upside down). As shown in Figure 5, this action causes a drastic change in polarity in one/both of the x- and y-values, which can be mapped to a discrete input.

However, similar to the lifting action, the degree of polarity change varies with the flipping action relative to the magnetic axis of the ring: the change is the strongest if it is perpendicular to the ring's magnetic axis, and decreases as it gets closer to being parallel to the axis, which can be unnoticeable (Figure 5, left).

Illustrative Applications

We provide two examples utilizing the input gestures mentioned above to illustrate how our technique can facilitate around device tangible interaction.

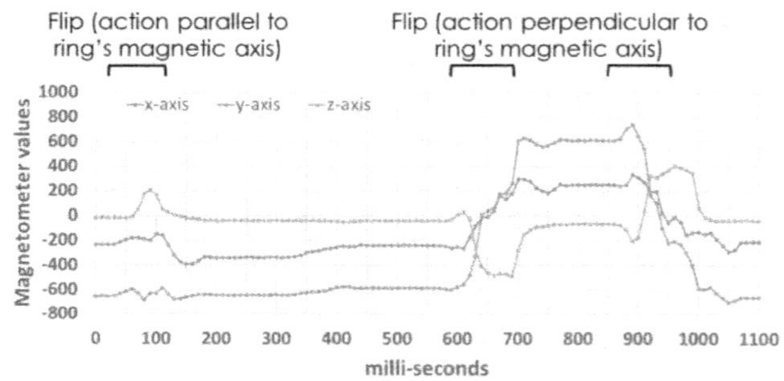

Figure 5. Magnetometer values in x-, y-, and z-axes as the ring flips. Note how the action's relative to the ring's orientation affects the degree of changes in the values.

Level Control

As mentioned above, the angle of the rotate action can be mapped into an absolute value within a range. Figure 6 shows an example of such control. To prevent wrapping around of angles (happens when the angle goes beyond -180° or 180° using Eq. 1), the device can alert the user that they are reaching the extremes, and ignore these values close to them. Other actions (lift or flip) can be incorporated as a confirmation gesture.

Media Scrubbing

Using a sliding window approach, one can determine the change in angle between two time frames. This change indicates both the direction as well as the speed of the rotation. Figure 7 shows an example of using this value as a media scrubbing parameter (clockwise advances, counter-clockwise rewinds, rotation speed proportional to frames skipped).

Discussion

We discuss the implications based on our initial observations on the current prototype.

Range Limit
Since all the actions are triggered by discernable disruptions to the measurements of the mobile device's magnetometer, there is a physical limit to the distance at which the actions can be reliably detected (approximately 8cm around the device, in all directions). This limit is dependent on the magnetic ring's strength, the magnetometer's sensitivity, as well as the magnetic field fluctuation of the surroundings.

Nevertheless, our initial tests show that once in range, the measurements are fairly stable, regardless of where the interaction takes place, as the strength of the static magnetic ring dominates all other field strengths to the magnetometer. We developed our media scrubbing prototype with this insight by using a change threshold, beyond which starts the input, and basing the play head's movement on the change in the measurements. This approach also allows the device to be tilted (for a better viewing angle), though both the ring and the device had to be in the same respective positions, and we did not investigate how large the angle could be.

Location Limit
Similar to Abe's [1] technique, our design is limited to surfaces with non-magnetic substance, as the presence of such will affect the magnetic properties of the ring. Moreover, since the ring itself is a magnet, it will adhere to a magnetic surface, making rotation difficult.

Orientation of the Magnetic Ring
We observed that all the actions except rotate are impacted by the orientation (magnetic axis) of the ring. During lifting, different orientations result in either increase or decrease in measurement along all the x-, y- and z-axes; whereas during flipping, different orientations result in either discernable (when perpendicular) or unnoticeable (when parallel) changes along the x- and y-axes. One way to mitigate this issue is to have markings on the ring to indicate orientation, though how this variation can be incorporated into the gesture recognition process requires further work.

Conclusion & Future Work
In this paper we explored the use of magnetism to enable around device interaction. Through combining the built-in magnetometer of a mobile device, and a magnetic ring, we proposed three input gestures that require no calibration, no modifications, and no external power. The shape of the ring also provides tangibility to the interaction, and is a compact item that can be worn as an accessory item when not in use.

As future work we aim to further investigate the recognition of input gestures given that some are affected by the ring's orientation, and evaluate their performance in different environments (in/outdoors). We also plan to explore other possible gestures [5], mappings between these tangible gestures and digital interactions, and evaluate their utility by replacing touch-based inputs in typical applications such as games and media players.

Acknowledgements
This work was supported and funded by the Natural Sciences and Engineering Research Council of Canada (NSERC) through a Discovery grant (402494/2011), as well as through the *Collaborative Learning in Usability Experiences* (CLUE) Create grant.

References
[1] Abe, T., Shizuki, B., and Tanaka, J. Input

techniques to the surface around a smartphone using a magnet attached on a stylus. *CHI Extended Abstracts on Human Factors in Computing Systems*, (2016), 2395–2402.

[2] Ashbrook, D., Baudisch, P., and White, S. Nenya: Subtle and eyes-free mobile input with a magnetically-tracked finger ring. *SIGCHI Conference on Human Factors in Computing Systems*, ACM (2011), 2043–46.

[3] Bianchi, A. and Oakley, I. Designing tangible magnetic appcessories. *Proceedings of the 7th International Conference on Tangible, Embedded and Embodied Interaction*, ACM (2013), 255–258.

[4] Butler, A., Izadi, S., and Hodges, S. SideSight: Multi-"touch" interaction around small devices. *User Interface Software and Technology*, ACM (2008), 201–204.

[5] Colley, A., Inget, V., Rantala, I., and Häkkilä, J. Investigating interaction with a rng form factor. *International Conference on Mobile and Ubiquitous Multimedia*, ACM (2017), 107–111.

[6] Grubert, J., Ofek, E., Pahud, M., Kranz, M., and Schmalstieg, D. GlassHands: Interaction around unmodified mobile devices using sunglasses. *Interactive Surfaces and Spaces*, ACM (2016), 215–224.

[7] Han, X., Seki, H., Kamiya, Y., and Hikizu, M. Wearable handwriting input device using magnetic field. *SICE Annual Conference*, (2007), 365–368.

[8] Harrison, C. and Hudson, S.E. Scratch input: Creating large, inexpensive, unpowered and mobile finger input surfaces. *User Interface Software and Technology*, ACM (2008), 205–208.

[9] Harrison, C. and Hudson, S.E. Abracadabra: Wireless, high-precision, and unpowered finger input for very small mobile devices. *User Interface Software and Technology*, ACM (2009), 121–124.

[10] Hwang, S., Ahn, M., and Wohn, K. MagGetz: Customizable passive tangible controllers on and around conventional mobile devices. *User Interface Software and Technology*, ACM (2013), 411–416.

[11] Ketabdar, H., Roshandel, M., and Yüksel, K.A. Towards using embedded magnetic field sensor for around mobile device 3D interaction. *International Conference on Human-Computer Interaction with Mobile Devices and Services*, ACM (2010), 153–156.

[12] Kratz, S. and Rohs, M. HoverFlow: Expanding the design space of around-device interaction. *International Conference on Human-Computer Interaction with Mobile Devices and Services*, ACM (2009), 1–8.

[13] Potter, R.L., Weldon, L.J., and Shneiderman, B. Improving the accuracy of touch screens: an experimental evaluation of three strategies. *SIGCHI Conference on Human Factors in Computing Systems*, ACM (1988), 27–32.

[14] Yoon, S.H., Huo, K., and Ramani, K. TMotion: Embedded 3D mobile input using magnetic sensing technique. *International Conference on Tangible, Embedded, and Embodied Interaction*, ACM (2016), 21–29.

Investigation of Touch Interfaces Using Multilayered *Urushi Circuit*

Koshi Ikegawa
Shuhei Aoyama
Shogo Tsuchikiri
Takuto Nakamura
Yuki Hashimoto
Buntarou Shizuki
University of Tsukuba
1-1-1 Tennodai, Tsukuba,
Ibaraki, 305-8573 Japan
ikegawa@iplab.cs.tsukuba.ac.jp
aoyama@iplab.cs.tsukuba.ac.jp
s_tsuchikiri@vrlab.esys.tsukuba.ac.jp
nakamura@iplab.cs.tsukuba.ac.jp
hashimoto@iit.tsukuba.ac.jp
shizuki@cs.tsukuba.ac.jp

TEI '18, March 18–21, 2018, Stockholm, Sweden
ACM 978-1-4503-5568-1/18/03.
https://doi.org/10.1145/3173225.3173285

Abstract
Urushi (Japanese lacquer) is a natural resin paint with electrical insulating capability. By using it as a base material and coating material for electronic circuits, it is possible to construct a circuit with an elegant appearance and feel.
It is also possible to build a multilayered electronic circuit by using *urushi* as insulation layers. In this study, we investigate techniques to construct touch interfaces using a multilayered electronic circuit (*urushi circuit*). At first, we fabricated an *urushi circuit* with a touch electrode consisting of two layers. To improve its appearance, we fabricated *urushi circuits* in which all touch electrodes are arranged on the top layer and all wires are hidden in the bottom layer. Moreover, as an extension of the touch interface, we built a grid of touch electrodes that realizes two-dimensional touch sensing.

Author Keywords
Fabrication; Japanese lacquer; lacquerware; traditional Japanese craft; visual design.

Introduction
Urushi (Japanese lacquer) is a natural resin paint, which is used in traditional Japanese crafts such as furniture and dishes. While *urushi* is famous as a beautiful paint, it also has many useful features such as electrical insulating capability and waterproofness. Owing to these properties, it

is possible to construct an electronic circuit with an elegant appearance and feel by using *urushi* as a base material and coating material of electronic circuits [11]. In addition, it is possible to build a multilayered electronic circuit (*urushi circuit*) by using *urushi* as insulation layers as shown in Figure 1. In addition, there is a technique called *makie*, which draws patterns for decoration on the surface of lacquerware (craftwork made by painting *urushi* on wood or paper) by sprinkling metal powder (e.g., gold and silver).

In this study, we are exploring techniques to add interactivity to lacquerware in a visually harmonized way with lacquer, enhancing its elegant appearance and feel. To achieve this, we investigate techniques to incorporate touch electrodes, which are made with *makie* and a multilayered *urushi circuit*, into lacquerware. In particular, circuit patterns made with makie on the *urushi* surface serve as both touch electrodes and components of visual design in our techniques. In addition, we demonstrate techniques to extend the touch interface function to detect touch positions and swipe gestures by separating circuit patterns into each layer of the multilayered *urushi circuit*.

The contributions of this paper are as follows:

1. We demonstrate techniques to construct touch interfaces using an *urushi circuit*.
2. We demonstrate that the overlapping of wires and electrodes does not affect the touch detection of the touch interface on a multilayered *urushi circuit*.
3. We demonstrate the applicability of the *urushi circuit* to a grid of touch electrodes that realizes two-dimensional touch sensing.

Related Work

Many researchers have explored approaches to incorporate a touch interface into visual design. One approach is a technique to construct a touch electrode that can also serve as a component of visual design. For example, Weigel et al. [8] and Lo et al. [1] developed an on-skin touch electrode that is thin, flexible, and visually customizable. Van de Zande et al. [7] proposed touch electrodes that can also display icons using screen printed electroluminescence and conductive ink. Olberding et al. [2] developed a cuttable capacitive multi-touch electrode that is printed with conductive ink. Another approach is supporting users in designing touch-sensitive objects and/or surfaces. For example, Zhang et al. [12] demonstrated a technique that makes various objects and surfaces touch-sensitive using electric field tomography. Savage et al. [3] demonstrated a toolkit to support the design, fabrication, and programming of flexible capacitive touch electrodes for interactive objects. Similarly, Schmitz et al. [4] showed a toolkit to help users fabricate 3D-printed objects with capacitive multi-touch sensing. As compared with these studies, we investigated techniques to incorporate touch electrodes, which are made with *makie* and a multilayered *urushi circuit*, into lacquerware.

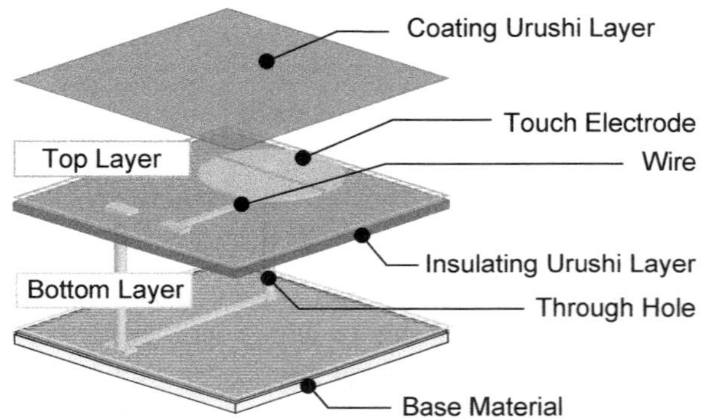

Figure 1: Construction of a multilayered *urushi circuit*.

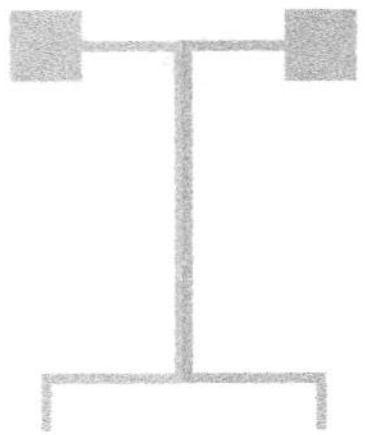

Figure 3: Design of the first prototype consisting of two layers. Two wires connected to touch electrodes were overlapped between the two layers.

Figure 4: First prototypes: top) a prototype with a thin insulating layer, bottom) a prototype with a thick insulating layer.

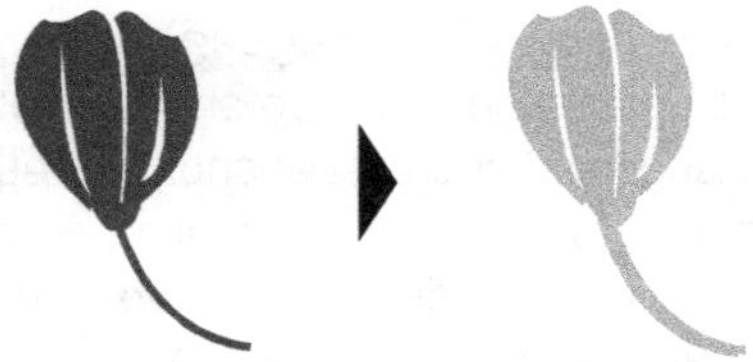

Figure 2: Example of a two-layer *urushi circuit*. Each layer has a touch electrode and wire.

Our study uses a multilayered circuit to construct a touch interface with its wiring hidden to retain beauty. A similar approach was used by Ta et al. [5] to create digital artwork; they hid wiring by connecting circuit patterns, which are printed with conductive ink on both sides of a paper, via holes. Tsuruta et al. [6] demonstrated a method to detect a touch on multiple electrodes printed on one side of a paper, which are connected with circuit patterns that are printed on the other side of the paper. By contrast, our study investigates the effects of the design of multilayered *urushi circuit* patterns based on touch detection.

Multilayered Urushi Circuit

Multilayering broadens the degree of freedom in arranging electrodes and wires and thus allows us to enrich the touch interface of lacquerware while maintaining its visual design. In our investigation, we first tested prototypes (first prototypes) consisting of two layers, each of which has a touch electrode and wire. Next, we tested four prototypes (second prototypes) that arranged all the touch electrodes on the top layer.

First prototypes

We first designed a touch interface with a single decoration (e.g., a flower with a stem) that can detect left and right touch positions and swipe gestures (Figure 2). Our idea to detect such rich touch vocabulary is to use multilayering to divide the decoration (Figure 2 left) into two parts (Figure 2 right), each of which is arranged in a layer (top and bottom layers) and has a touch electrode and wire. In this design, two wires are overlapped to form the stem of the flower. In addition, the covering thinly coating the *urushi* layer on the circuit pattern can maintain the visual design.

To test the above idea, we designed an *urushi circuit* to examine whether each touch electrode can detect a touch (Figure 3). This *urushi circuit* design has a touch electrode and wire in each layer. In addition, the wires connected to the touch electrodes were overlapped between the two layers. We fabricated an *urushi circuit* based on this design (Figure 4 top) according to the fabrication process described in [10]. In this process, the circuit pattern is printed by silkscreening with silver ink. The thickness of one urushi layer is approximately 30 μm. The cost of one *urushi circuit*, excluding the base material is approximately 6.6 USD (*urushi*: 3.5 USD, silver ink: 3.1 USD).

However, the two circuit patterns of the two layers were short-circuited due to an unevenness of the thin insulating *urushi* layer. Therefore, we constructed another *urushi circuit* (Figure 4 bottom) that has an insulating *urushi* layer thick enough to prevent a short-circuit by applying *urushi* twice. As a result, while short-circuiting was solved, this *urushi circuit* had a problem: the left and right electrodes appear different, as shown in the figure, given that the thickness of *urushi* on the two electrodes was different.

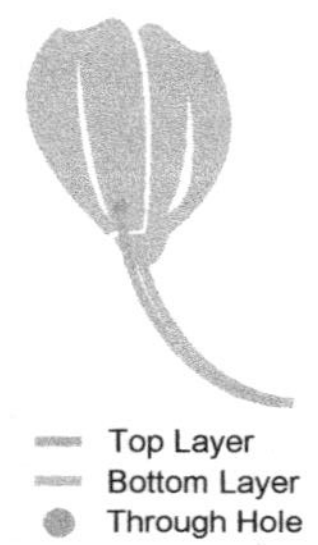

Figure 5: Example of a two layer *urushi circuit* that arranges all the touch electrodes on the top layer.

Second prototypes
To solve the first prototypes' problem, we adopted a different approach; we arranged all the touch electrodes on the top layer and used multilayering for wiring (Figure 5). To connect the electrodes on the top layer and wires on the bottom layer, we made through holes in the insulating *urushi* layer by using processing technology established by Myojin et al. [9]; it uses *urushi's* property where it can be decomposed by ultraviolet (UV) radiation.

We demonstrate the design of the *urushi circuits* (Figure 6); we designed four *urushi circuits* to investigate the effect of overlapping circuit patterns on touch detection:

- A There is no overlap between the left and right parts.
- B There is an overlap only between the wires of the two layers.
- C The wire of the bottom layer overlaps the touch electrode of the top layer.
- D The wire of the bottom layer overlaps both the wire and touch electrode of the top layer.

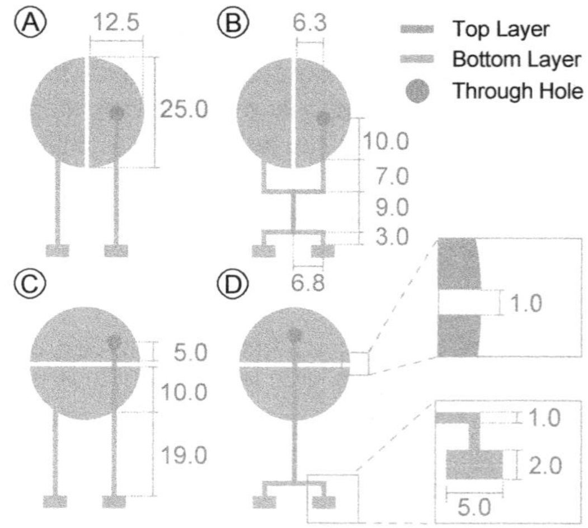

Figure 6: Design of the four *urushi circuits* and their dimensions (mm).

We fabricated the *urushi circuits* based on the design (Figure 7).

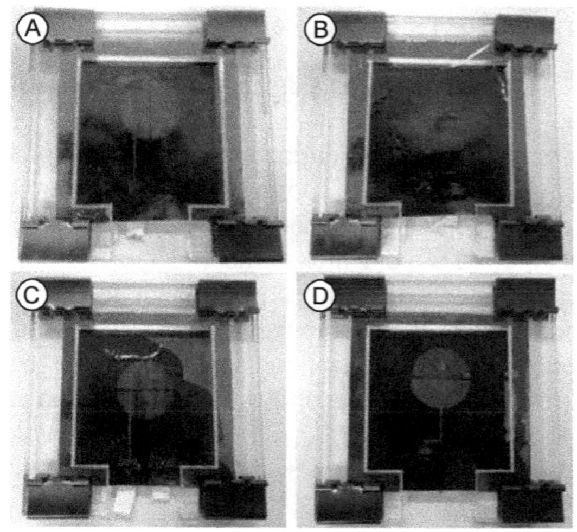

Figure 7: Four second prototypes.

Evaluation of the Urushi Circuit

We tested whether the four *urushi circuits* work as touch interfaces. We connected a capacitance meter to the edges of the two wires of each circuit and recorded the sensor values when we touched various positions of the circuit. The capacitance meter was constructed using a Capacitive Sensing Library (CapSense) operating on Arduino. To touch the circuit, we used a capacitive stylus to prevent the contact area from changing. In this experiment, we touched the four positions of the circuit: a) touch electrode connected to the bottom layer wire, b) touch electrode connected to the

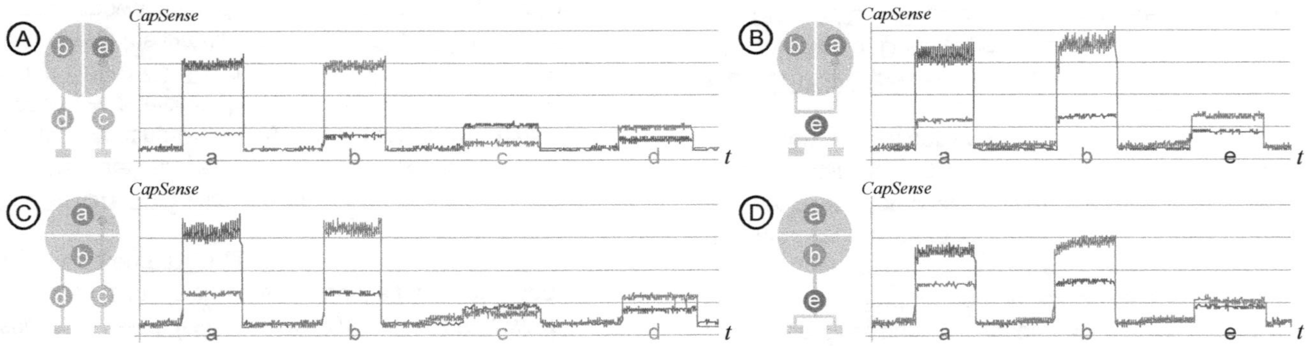

Figure 8: Capacitance waveforms measured by CapSense observed when the four *urushi circuits* were touched. The capacitances were measured at the edges of the two wires of each circuit. The a–d on the circuit design indicate touched positions: a) a touch electrode connected to the bottom layer wire, b) a touch electrode connected to the top layer wire, c) a bottom layer wire, d) a top layer wire, and e) overlapped wires. Each of a–d under the waveforms display the periods when each position of the circuits was touched.

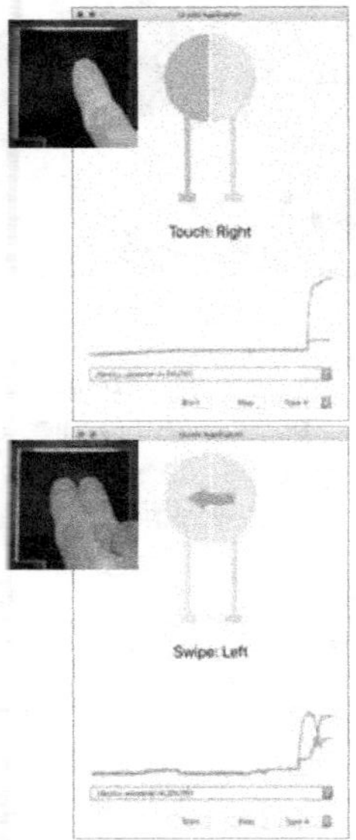

Figure 9: Test application detecting a touch on the right part (top) and left swipe (bottom).

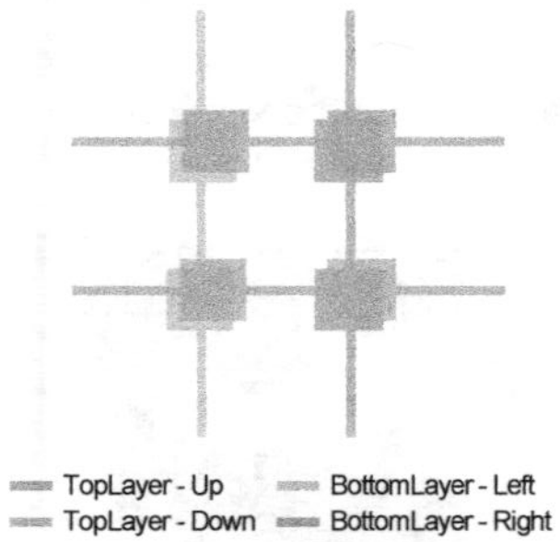

Figure 10: Design of a 2×2 grid circuit. Each of the four electrodes has two touch points which are overlapped in a grid pattern

top layer wire, c) bottom layer wire, d) top layer wire, and e) overlapped wires.

Figure 8 shows the waveforms of the sensor values measured with the capacitance meter. As the waveforms of a–b in Figures 8A-8D demonstrate, the sensor values of a touched electrode were larger than an untouched electrode. Moreover, the sensor values when a wire was touched (c–e) were smaller than the values when an electrode was touched (a–b). These results suggest that touch can be detected even if there is an overlap between the bottom layer wire and the upper layer wire, or between the bottom layer wire and the upper layer touch electrode.

Test Application

We developed a test application (Figure 9) that detects touches and swipe gestures and visualizes the results to demonstrate the potential of our second prototype as a touch interface. This application receives the sensor values from the capacitance meter and plots their waveforms. It also detects touches and swipe gestures using a threshold which was empirically defined. The swipe direction is judged from the order of touched electrodes.

Grid of Touch Electrodes

Projected capacitive touch sensing technology, which is used for two-dimensional touch sensing, consists of two layers of electrodes, which forms a grid. Given that this structure can be fabricated with a multilayered *urushi circuit*, it is possible to construct the surface of the lacquerware such that it detects the touched position. To test this, we designed a circuit that consists of a grid of two rows and two columns of electrodes with a multilayered *urushi circuit* (Figure 10). We arranged the two rows on the top layer and the two columns on the bottom layer. In this circuit, since each electrode has two touch points which are overlapped in a grid pattern, it is possible to detect four touch points.

Figure 11: A 2×2 grid electrode.

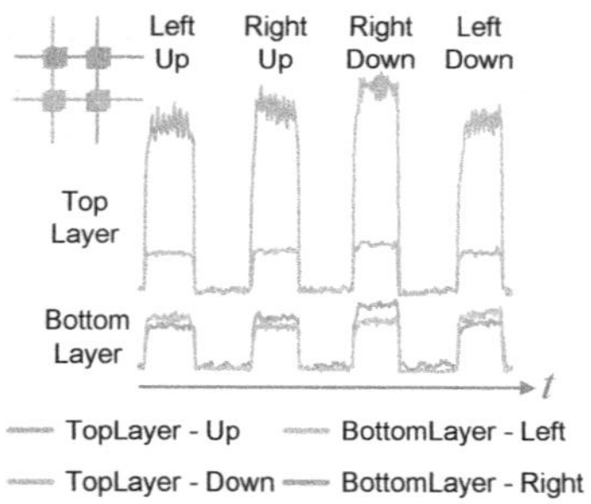

Figure 12: Four waveforms measured by CapSense when each point of a 2×2 grid circuit was touched.

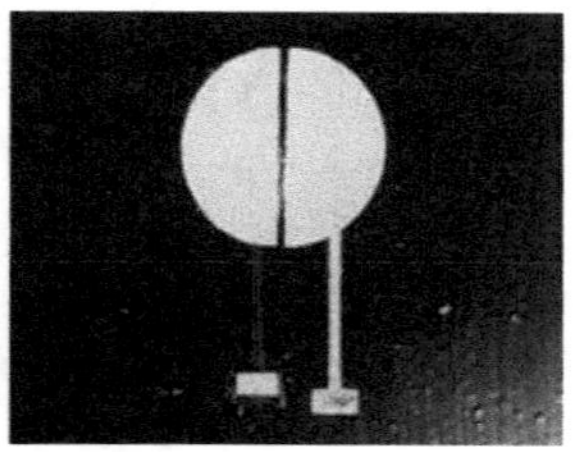

Figure 13: *Urushi circuit* without coating the *urushi* layer.

We fabricated a *urushi circuit* based on this design (Figure 11).

Figure 12 displays the waveforms obtained by the capacitance meter when each touch point was touched. In this circuit, the waveform's amplitude of the bottom layer electrodes was smaller than those of the top layer. Nevertheless, the changes in the waveform of the electrodes corresponding to the touch point were larger than the others in each layer. For example, when the Left-Up touch point was touched, the changes in the BottomLayer-Left and TopLayer-Up waveforms were larger than the others. This result suggests that detecting four touch points with a 2×2 grid of electrodes could be possible.

Limitation

We believe that the *urushi circuit* can contribute to the field of media arts thanks to its elegant appearance. Designers can select colors by mixing *urushi* and pigment. However, designers cannot use pale colors, such as white and pale blue, because pure *urushi* is translucent brown. In addition, *urushi* cannot be applied to flexible objects. This is because *urushi* becomes stiff when dried. This means that when flexible objects to which *urushi* is applied are deformed, *urushi* will deteriorate and peel off.

Discussion and Future Work

In our investigation, we coated the circuit patterns with *urushi* (i.e., coating *urushi* layer in Figure 1). However, if the coating was thicker, the pattern was less visible, as shown in Figure 7B. To solve this problem, we fabricated the circuit with the circuit pattern exposed (Figure 13). As this circuit shows, if the designer wants to clearly display the pattern, it is effective not to coat the surface. On the other hand, the designer can hide the pattern by thickening the coating or by mixing it with paint. Therefore, the designer can select one of the two methods to design the appearance of the touch interface.

In addition, we demonstrated that the two-dimensional touch electrodes can be built with a multilayered *urushi circuit.* In the future, we plan to build a touch interface that detects touch positions more finely by constructing a finer grid circuit. In this interface, we will arrange the touch electrodes without overlaps based on our investigation of this paper. Specifically, we will use a diamond-shaped grid design, which is widely used in projected capacitive touch sensing technology.

Furthermore, *urushi* is often applied to non-flat surfaces (e.g., dishes). Therefore, we plan to investigate the effect of a *urushi circuit* that is fabricated on non-flat surfaces.

Conclusions

In this study, we investigated techniques to construct a touch interface that has the elegance and feel of the Japanese traditional material *urushi.* We focus on *makie*, which is the technique of drawing patterns on *urushi*, to incorporate touch electrodes into lacquerware as components of visual design. Furthermore, utilizing the feature that the circuit pattern can be multilayered, we demonstrated how the wires connected to touch electrodes can be hidden in a lower layer. Moreover, we demonstrated a multilayered *urushi circuit* with a grid of electrodes that realizes two-dimensional touch sensing.

REFERENCES

1. Joanne Lo, Doris Jung Lin Lee, Nathan Wong, David Bui, and Eric Paulos. 2016. Skintillates: Designing and Creating Epidermal Interactions. In *Proceedings of the 2016 ACM Conference on Designing Interactive Systems (DIS '16).* ACM, New York, NY, USA,

853–864. DOI: http://dx.doi.org/10.1145/2901790.2901885

2. Simon Olberding, Nan-Wei Gong, John Tiab, Joseph A. Paradiso, and Jürgen Steimle. 2013. A Cuttable Multi-touch Sensor. In *Proceedings of the 26th Annual ACM Symposium on User Interface Software and Technology (UIST '13)*. ACM, New York, NY, USA, 245–254. DOI: http://dx.doi.org/10.1145/2501988.2502048

3. Valkyrie Savage, Xiaohan Zhang, and Björn Hartmann. 2012. Midas: Fabricating Custom Capacitive Touch Sensors to Prototype Interactive Objects. In *Proceedings of the 25th Annual ACM Symposium on User Interface Software and Technology (UIST '12)*. ACM, New York, NY, USA, 579–588. DOI: http://dx.doi.org/10.1145/2380116.2380189

4. Martin Schmitz, Mohammadreza Khalilbeigi, Matthias Balwierz, Roman Lissermann, Max Mühlhäuser, and Jürgen Steimle. 2015. Capricate: A Fabrication Pipeline to Design and 3D Print Capacitive Touch Sensors for Interactive Objects. In *Proceedings of the 28th Annual ACM Symposium on User Interface Software and Technology (UIST '15)*. ACM, New York, NY, USA, 253–258. DOI: http://dx.doi.org/10.1145/2807442.2807503

5. Tung Ta, Masaaki Fukumoto, Koya Narumi, Shigeki Shino, Yoshihiro Kawahara, and Tohru Asami. 2015. Interconnection and Double Layer for Flexible Electronic Circuit with Instant Inkjet Circuits. In *Proceedings of the 2015 ACM International Joint Conference on Pervasive and Ubiquitous Computing (UbiComp '15)*. ACM, New York, NY, USA, 181–190. DOI:http://dx.doi.org/10.1145/2750858.2804276

6. Masaya Tsuruta, Shuta Nakamae, and Buntarou Shizuki. 2016. RootCap: Touch Detection on Multi-electrodes Using Single-line Connected Capacitive Sensing. In *Proceedings of the 2016 ACM on Interactive Surfaces and Spaces (ISS '16)*. ACM, New York, NY, USA, 23–32. DOI: http://dx.doi.org/10.1145/2992154.2992180

7. Ty Van de Zande and Dan Lockton. 2017. Printerface: Screen Printed Electroluminescent Touch Interface. In *Proceedings of the 2017 ACM International Conference on Interactive Surfaces and Spaces (ISS '17)*. ACM, New York, NY, USA, 450–453. DOI: http://dx.doi.org/10.1145/3132272.3132286

8. Martin Weigel, Tong Lu, Gilles Bailly, Antti Oulasvirta, Carmel Majidi, and Jürgen Steimle. 2015. iSkin: Flexible, Stretchable and Visually Customizable On-Body Touch Sensors for Mobile Computing. In *Proceedings of the 2015 CHI Conference on Human Factors in Computing Systems (CHI '15)*. ACM, New York, NY, USA, 2991–3000. DOI: http://dx.doi.org/10.1145/2702123.2702391

9. Myojin Yu and Hashimoto Yuki. 2015. Quantification of Urushi Dissolution by Ultraviolet Irradiation for an Urushi - based Electronic Circuit. In *Proceedings of the 3rd IIAE International Conference on Intelligent Systems and Image Processing 2015 (ICISIP '15)*. IIAE, 329–336. DOI: http://dx.doi.org/10.12792/icisip2015.063

10. Myojin Yu and Hashimoto Yuki. 2017. Development of the Urushi Processing System by Ultraviolet Irradiation Method. *Transactions of the Virtual Reality Society of Japan* 22, 1 (2017), 31–40. DOI: http://dx.doi.org/10.18974/tvrsj.22.1_31 (In Japanese).

11. Hashimoto Yuki, Koizumi Naoya, Myojin Yu, Shizuki Buntarou, and Hanada Nobuko. 2015. The Urushi Circuit - Use of a Traditional Craft Material for HCI -. In *Proceedings of ACM CHI2015 Symposium on Emerging Japanese HCI Research Collection*. 8.

12. Yang Zhang, Gierad Laput, and Chris Harrison. 2017. Electrick: Low-Cost Touch Sensing Using Electric Field Tomography. In *Proceedings of the 2017 CHI Conference on Human Factors in Computing Systems (CHI '17)*. ACM, New York, NY, USA, 1–14. DOI: http://dx.doi.org/10.1145/3025453.3025842

Tangible Interaction in the Dentist Office

Frode Guribye
University of Bergen
Bergen, Norway
frode.guribye@uib.no

Tor Gjøsæter
Bryggen Research
Bergen, Norway
tor@bryggenresearch.com

TEI '18, March 18 - 21, 2018, Stockholm, Sweden

ACM ISBN 978-1-4503-5568-1/18/03.
https://doi.org/10.1145/3173225.3173287

Abstract
This paper presents the design efforts involved in making a system for supporting haptic communication between dentist and patient during dental treatment. We describe Grasp Live, a haptic interaction technology consisting of a tangible stone-like object connected to a vibro-tactile feedback device.

Author Keywords
Tangible interaction; affective interaction; haptic interaction; dental care; dental fear and anxiety

Introduction
Pain and discomfort are major sources of stress and anxiety when going to the dentist. While most people can handle the situation, some people dread going to the dentist and avoid the situation altogether and thus their dental health suffers. In this paper we describe Grasp live, a haptic interaction technology consisting of a tangible hand-held stone-like object (Figure 1), a visualization on a smartphone and vibro-tactile feedback on a smartwatch. We address how Grasp Live can be used to help alleviate distress when sitting in the dentist chair, and to support haptic interaction between patient and dentist.

Going to the dentist can be uncomfortable [8]. The patient is exposed to a salient environment in a situation that

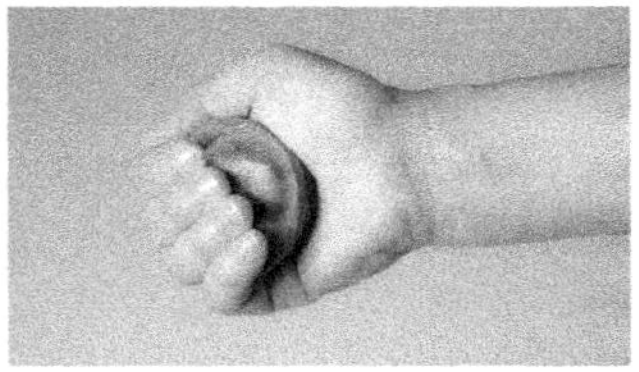

Figure 1: The Grasp being held in hand.

can induce several unpleasant feelings. Being placed in a supine position in a chair where it is hard to escape can result in a feeling of loss of control. Further, dental treatment may include sensations of pain and discomfort, and the dental professionals approach one of the most sensitive and intimate parts of the body (the mouth and the oral cavity) which can lead to feelings of embarrassment if, for example, the dentist comments on oral hygiene. Considering these factors it is not a surprise that dental fear or anxiety has a prevalence around 20 percent [21].

The relationship between dentist and patient is a key factor in oral health. A trusting and empathic relation plays a pivotal role in avoiding or controlling anxiety and to make the patient comfortable [8]. There is an inherent asymmetry in the relation between patient and dentist in that the dentist must control the situation and limit the patient's movement. In addition, the patient can for key periods of the treatment not give any meaningful verbal feedback to the dentist. In this study we explore how we can design for tangible and haptic interaction between patient and dentist to support meaningful communication during the dental treatment, and to support an empathic relation between the dentist and patient.

The paper first reviews relevant studies and designs for haptic interpersonal communication, the use of tangible interaction to express emotions and sensations. Then the design of Grasp Live is presented, with emphasis on design choices, requirements and, material and interactional qualities. Finally we reflect on the design and discuss a small-scale pilot field trial of the technology during dental treatment.

Related studies

Vibro-tactile feedback can be used to communicate information using parameters such as rythm, roughness and spacial location [4, 9, 19]. HaptiColor [5], for example, uses different spatiotemporal vibro-tactile patterns to encode different colors.

Touch can support the communication of emotion, and is not only an amplifier of other expressions of affect through voice and facial expressions [15]. The use of tangible interaction to express or register emotions and sensations have been explored in some recent studies [6, 10–13]. Simms et al. [20] have studied how pressing a digital stress-ball can be used to manage stress and anxiety in the context of adults with autism. Tasst [10] is a prototype designed to illustrate how to mediate social touch with a sleeve device. Input to sensors in one sleeve is transmitted to motors in another sleeve that give vibro-tactile feedback on the forearm. This design thus explores one way of supporting haptic affective communication with wearable technology.

Damian and André [7] have looked at how to use haptic feedback during social interaction. There are many designs to support haptic interpersonal communication. InTouch [2] explored how force and haptic interaction could emulate the feeling of interacting with a shared physical object while being at different locations. Hassental et al. [14] review how haptic interactions can mediate emotional intimate relationships. Another way of using haptic communication and vibro-tactile interaction is as an augmentation of phone calls [16] where pressing a phone in one end of the conversation leads to vibro-tactile feedback with the recipient. These "pressages" were used to express emotion, greetings and give a sense of presence between the interlocutors. More generally, haptic devices can be used to express and communicate emotions at a distance by way of virtual

Figure 2: Different membranes and 3D printed prototypes. The two rightmost halves are printed in flexible resin.

Requirements

Grasp: (G1) The Grasp should turn on and connect effortlessly to an accompanying app. (G2) The Grasp feel good and have a calming effect when held. (G3) The Grasp should respond to a wider range of squeezes. Ranging from very mild, to strong and all in between.

App: (A1) Manage connection with Grasp and Watch (A2) Visualize the squeezes in real-time

Watch: (W1) Provide haptic feedback to the wrist

interpersonal touch [1]. In this study we focus on a situation where the interlocutors are located in the same place at the same time, and where the haptic interaction is used as an additional channel of communication since the patient is hindered from verbal communication.

The design of Grasp Live

Initially the Grasp platform was designed for in situ, intentional tangible self reporting of affective states [13] with the possibility of using this data in a retrospective debriefing and therapeutic setting [18]. This paper presents a modification of the Grasp platform to support communication of distress in real time to a dentist during dental treatment.

During the initial conceptualization of Grasp Live we envisioned a system that would enable users to communicate feelings in real time to another person in a non-verbal manner. The overarching idea is to enable the user to easily report on their feelings or sensations during a situation when verbal communication might be problematic.

The target user group for the use case presented here is people that might experience dental anxiety or fear. Grasp Live is designed with the aim of allowing users with varying degrees of dental anxiety to easily report discomfort, pain, fear or anxiety to their dentist in real time during dental treatment. Additionally, the device should provide the user with a feeling of safety and connectedness to the dentist.

The basic design principles behind the materiality and shape of the Grasp device described in [13] is carried forth in to the current iteration. However, some of the design features supporting portability and the qualities of the device have been modified to support slightly different interactional attributes.

The original design of Grasp required an external device to activate the BLE (Bluetooth Low Energy) device. This was done in an effort to make the device more power efficient. The process for activation and transfer of data was somewhat cumbersome, and not necessarily compatible with a dental setting. G1 (see list of requirements in the margin) was solved by modifying the firmware to allow the BLE stack to be initiated by a light squeeze. This will consume more power, but would still be sufficient for several 30 minute sessions before needing to change the battery.

G2 reflects the need for the interaction with the tangible device to have comforting qualities when being held by the patient. This means that it should be comfortable to hold and squeeze. The squeeze should support a synchronous communication between the interlocutors during treatment. The patients should feel confident that when they squeeze the stone, the dentist is made aware of the squeezes.

In regards to G3, in the initial prototype of Grasp, the nature of the interrupt circuit and low power requirements meant some very mild squeezes disappeared in filtering algorithms. In this use case we found that we needed a more granular feedback. Further, the force sensitive resistor expresses its input in a nonlinear fashion. To have a more linear representation of the input data we implemented a function to normalize the quadratic curve.

Additionally, the membrane working as a mechanical filter for the force sensitive resistor was designed to activate at more forceful squeeze than necessary for this use context. Users of Grasp Live will try to relax in a supine position in a dental chair and squeezing hard in this position might be uncomfortable. Hence we experimented with different materials for the membrane, as well as using 3D printed flexible resin to accommodate this requirement. We quickly discovered that engineering something with flexible resin was

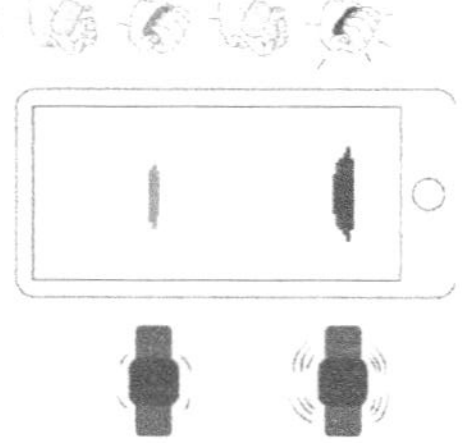

Figure 3: Illustrating how the interaction relates to a squeeze, being visualized to the user using a smart phone(see figure 5) and sent to a smart watch with fine grained haptic feedback.

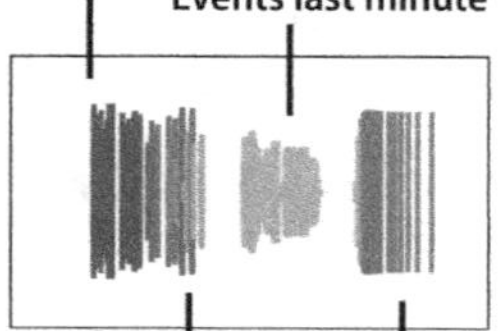

Figure 4: Screenshot from the app of the basic time line visualization seen by the user.

troublesome. The material was flexible, but creating a good squeeze experience was difficult. The flexible 3D printed casing would also quickly deteriorate and break. Figure 2 illustrates different thickness and material membrane as well as two iterations of flexible material 3D print. Finally, we chose the prototype with the thickest membrane and a soft internal padding as this allows for a more refined interaction that responds to a wider variety of squeezes.

An app running on an iPhone device actively looks for a Grasp device and manages connectivity (requirement A1). Figure 4 shows how squeezes are visualized to the user (A2). Recent events will appear as a dynamic visual rendering entering from the right side into view on the display. The most recent events (1-5 seconds) are shown and then gradually compressed on the X axis to become less visually significant (grayed out) as time passes. The events will appear and be rendered with a curve based motion timing with a quick start of motion that gradually fades to extremely slow. This allows events during a long dental session to appear in view and function as feedback and historical reference to the patient.

The requirement (W1) of providing haptic feedback on the wrist was achieved by extending the iPhone app to communicate with an Apple Watch. A preset list of haptic styles are available to developers meant to symbolize different events such as "notification", "start", "stop" and more. In this iteration we are using four of the styles available to render haptic interaction that reflects the hardness of the squeezes of the tangible device.

Haptic rendering

- light tap - Weak squeeze
- tap-tap-tap - Medium squeeze
- long vibrate - Hard squeeze
- tap-tap vibrate - Very hard squeeze

These four styles allow us to represent weak, medium, hard and very hard squeezes easily recognizable by the dentist.

Implementation

Grasp is designed around a System on a Chip (SoC) incorporating an ARM Cortex M0 CPU and BLE peripherals. The hardware and the protocol stack are managed independently from the application software, and the former are assigned protected memory areas and a separate execution context. To ensure that the device does not consume excessive amounts of power, it is vital to keep the device in a low-power idle mode whenever it is not in active use or the hardware requires CPU interaction. To that end, the firmware follows an entirely event-driven design pattern. User inputs in the form of BLE stack events and the application of pressure generate soft or hard interrupts. The interrupt handling routines transfer signals to the main application context with a First In First Out (FIFO) scheduler. To conserve power the Grasp goes into deep sleep when disconnected from the iPhone or the connection times out.

Figure 3 illustrates the basic operation of the system. When the Grasp is squeezed a basic BlueTooth connection is attempted with the iPhone if not already connected. Next, when the Grasp senses a squeeze it sends the amplitude of ongoing squeeze every 50ms to the app. The app renders the squeezes as animated bars appearing on the screen as visual feedback to patient. Squeezes are simultaneously forwarded to the connected Apple Watch. The watch interprets the received squeeze and generates haptic feedback based on a set of preset ranges.

A short and faint squeeze on the Grasp translates to a short series of slight "tap-tap" haptic signals being exhib-

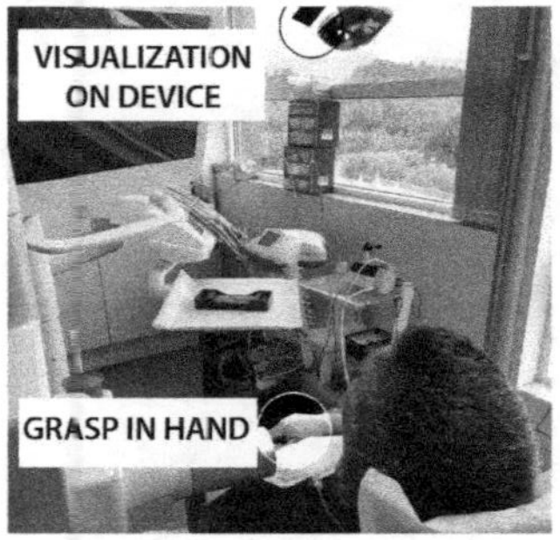

Figure 5: Photography from the field trial showing the test user holding the Grasp in his hand, while a mounted smart phone gives the user visual feedback about the squeezes.

Figure 6: Photography from the field trial showing the Apple Watch on the dentists wrist.

ited on the smart-watch. Harder and longer squeezes translate to more severe haptic feedback for the duration of the squeeze.

Pilot field trial and reflections

As an evaluation of Grasp Live we arranged a small-scale pilot field trial [3] in a dentist office with a dentist and a patient. The evaluation was held at a dental clinic with dentists specializing in treatment of patients with dental anxiety. In the trial we used Grasp Live as a technology probe [17] to look for unforeseen implications and to get an understanding of the potential uses of Grasp live in this setting. The user/patient and dentist was given a brief introduction and overview of how the technology operated. The iPhone was mounted above the user as seen in figure 5 and the dentist had the Apple Watch on his wrist as seen in 6. The devices was set to silent, to not express the sounds related to the haptic feedback styles enabled by the WatchKit SDK. During the session the squeezes with timestamps, normalized and raw amplitude was recorded and stored on an external server for review and analysis (see Figure 7).

The patient -a male aged 50 self reporting mild dental anxiety - was scheduled for a dental examination with the intent of uncovering potential cavities. During the dental examination the dentist and the patient used Grasp Live, one of the authors observed the session and had an unstructured interview with the participants after the session had ended. Figure 7 shows the real time gathering of data during the examination.

In the initial conversations with one of the dentists at the dental clinic he told us about an existing arrangement in use at the clinic that includes an unorthodox use of toothpicks. Patients with dental anxiety would be presented with the option of using a toothpick to prick the dentist in the leg if the situation becomes unbearable and no other way of communicating were feasible. This arrangement suggests that haptic interaction might be a fruitful way of communicating between patient and dentist during parts of the dental treatment.

The dentist reported that the different haptic feedback rendered was easily recognizable. During the procedure itself the wrist worn device was of no hindrance to performing the examination.

In one episode Grasp Live was used to communicate a discomforting experience. During a longer session of probing teeth to uncover cavities found in an X-ray the patient experienced a drowning sensation (see Figure 7). An excess of spit buildup in the oral cavity during this long period without the felt ability to spit led to a firm squeeze of the Grasp resulting in hard vibrations on the smart watch. This illustrates how the arrangement can serve as a "panic button" for the patient and provide a feeling of safety and comfort in this sense.

The dentist in our field trial had a very reflective relation to how he communicated with his patients, especially when the patients are suffering from dental anxiety. As an example, he usually tried to look for signs of distress in the patient such as holding their breath and closing their eyes. In some cases he did things like remove his facemask to show the patient that he was paying attention. This will of course vary between different dentists, but adding a haptic communication channel between dentist and patient can on the one hand make the dentist become more aware of the patient's wellbeing and can on the other hand calm the patient in that they know that the dentist is aware of his/hers condition. This might help build an empathic relation between patient and dentist.

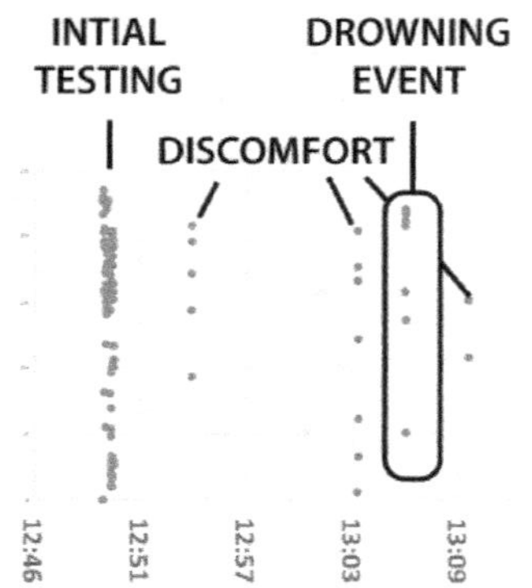

Figure 7: A graph showing the normalized squeezes during the examination. The Y axis represents the amplitude and the X axis represents the timestamps.

Furthermore, we observed some instances where the squeezes and haptic feedback allowed for the cooperation between dentist and patient for verifying cavities. It is common practice for dentists to verify or examine cavities with a probe and sometimes this might lead to pain for the patient. We observed some instances of the quick feedback from the squeeze resulted in quick conformation of cavities without excessive pain.

The visualization on the mounted smart phone was not seen as crucial in the arrangement, but may serve as a feedback mechanism where the patients can see that the squeezes actually are registered. The visualization could reportedly also function as a distraction and as a focus point for the patient.

The participants also reported that a common understanding of the representation of squeezes prior to engaging in the procedure could be helpful as the patient and dentist had no common agreement of what should happen when a forceful squeeze occurred and what this would mean. This is partly a result of using the technology as a probe in one treatment, and this is something that could be addressed further in a more extensive evaluation and field trial.

Conclusions and Future work

This study has presented the design of Grasp Live as an exploration into how we can design for tangible and haptic interaction between patient and dentist during dental treatment. Further, we have explored how to support meaningful communication during dental treatment, and how such communication might help build an empathic relation between dentist and patient. The study shows that there is a potential in this form of communication as an additional channel during treatment.

The study has uncovered some limitations in our design. One potential improvement would be create a more customizable wrist or arm worn device for providing haptic feedback. The inherent limitations of using an Apple Watch and the prescribed styles of haptic feedback available limits the types of vibrations we can generate. Secondly, a larger empirical study with more participants could uncover how Grasp Live will be experienced by a wider variety of patients with varying degree of dental fear and anxiety. An empirical study could also address to what extent the embodied interaction of squeezing the device can support a feeling of comfort and safety. Further, we will investigate how the haptic communication can induce an empathic relation between the interlocutors. There is also a need to get a firm understanding of how the haptic renderings are experienced by the dentist and that they are not interfering with the dentist's work.

Acknowledgments

A thank you to Grasp AS for lending the Grasp prototype devices used in this study. We also would like to thank the dental clinic TannDan that provided input and facilitated the pilot study and evaluation of the Grasp Live. Thanks to the anonymous reviewers who provided valuable feedback and directions for further research.

REFERENCES

1. Jeremy N Bailenson, Nick Yee, Scott Brave, Dan Merget, and David Koslow. 2007. Virtual Interpersonal Touch: Expressing and Recognizing Emotions Through Haptic Devices. *Hum.-Comput. Interact.* 22, 3 (aug 2007), 325–353. `http://dl.acm.org/citation.cfm?id=1466603.1466606`
2. Scott Brave and Andrew Dahley. 1997. inTouch: A Medium for Haptic Interpersonal Communication. In *CHI '97 Extended Abstracts on Human Factors in Computing Systems (CHI EA '97)*. ACM, New York, NY,

USA, 363–364. DOI: http://dx.doi.org/10.1145/1120212.1120435

3. Barry Brown, Stuart Reeves, and Scott Sherwood. 2011. Into the wild: challenges and opportunities for field trial methods. In *Proc. SIGCHI '11*. ACM Press, New York, NY, USA, 1657–1666. DOI: http://dx.doi.org/10.1145/1978942.1979185
4. Lorna M. Brown, Stephen A. Brewster, and Helen C. Purchase. 2006. Multidimensional Tactons for Non-visual Information Presentation in Mobile Devices. In *Proceedings of the 8th Conference on Human-computer Interaction with Mobile Devices and Services (MobileHCI '06)*. ACM, New York, NY, USA, 231–238. DOI: http://dx.doi.org/10.1145/1152215.1152265
5. Marta G. Carcedo, Soon Hau Chua, Simon Perrault, PawełWozniak, Raj Joshi, Mohammad Obaid, Morten Fjeld, and Shengdong Zhao. 2016. HaptiColor: Interpolating Color Information As Haptic Feedback to Assist the Colorblind. In *Proceedings of the 2016 CHI Conference on Human Factors in Computing Systems (CHI '16)*. ACM, New York, NY, USA, 3572–3583. DOI: http://dx.doi.org/10.1145/2858036.2858220
6. Ming Ki Chong, Umar Rashid, Jon Whittle, and Chee Siang Ang. 2014. SqueezeDiary: using squeeze gesture as a triggers of diary events. In *Proceedings of the 16th international conference on Human-computer interaction with mobile devices & services - MobileHCI '14*. ACM Press, New York, New York, USA, 427–429. DOI: http://dx.doi.org/10.1145/2628363.2633572
7. Ionut Damian and Elisabeth André. 2016. Exploring the Potential of Realtime Haptic Feedback During Social Interactions. In *Proceedings of the TEI '16: Tenth International Conference on Tangible, Embedded, and Embodied Interaction (TEI '16)*. ACM, New York, NY, USA, 410–416. DOI: http://dx.doi.org/10.1145/2839462.2856519
8. Renate Deinzer. 2015. Oral Health, Psychology of. In *International Encyclopedia of the Social & Behavioral Sciences* (second edition ed.), James D Wright (Ed.). Elsevier, Oxford, 279–283. DOI: http://dx.doi.org/10.1016/B978-0-08-097086-8.14075-9
9. Sebastian Feige. 2009. *Can You Feel It? – Using Vibration Rhythms to Communicate Information in Mobile Contexts*. Springer Berlin Heidelberg, Berlin, Heidelberg, 800–803. DOI: http://dx.doi.org/10.1007/978-3-642-03655-2_87
10. Aduen Darriba Freriks, Dirk Heylen, and Gijs Huisman. 2013. TaSST: affective mediated touch. In *Proceedings of the 15th ACM on International conference on multimodal interaction - ICMI '13*. ACM Press, New York, New York, USA, 315–316. DOI: http://dx.doi.org/10.1145/2522848.2531758
11. Carolina Fuentes, Iyubanit Rodríguez, and Valeria Herskovic. 2015. *EmoBall: a study on a tangible interface to self-report emotional information considering digital competences*. Springer International Publishing, Cham, 189–200. DOI: http://dx.doi.org/10.1007/978-3-319-26508-7_19
12. T. Gjøsæter, F. Guribye, and J. Fjøsne. 2014. The Helpstone - an interactive transitional object. *DAIMI Report Series* 41, 597 (2014).

13. Frode Guribye, Tor Gjøsæter, and Christian Bjartli. 2016. Designing for Tangible Affective Interaction. In *Proceedings of the 9th Nordic Conference on Human-Computer Interaction (NordiCHI '16)*. ACM, New York, NY, USA, Article 30, 10 pages. DOI: http://dx.doi.org/10.1145/2971485.2971547

14. Marc Hassenzahl, Stephanie Heidecker, Kai Eckoldt, Sarah Diefenbach, and Uwe Hillmann. 2012. All You Need is Love: Current Strategies of Mediating Intimate Relationships Through Technology. *ACM Trans. Comput.-Hum. Interact.* 19, 4, Article 30 (Dec. 2012), 19 pages. DOI: http://dx.doi.org/10.1145/2395131.2395137

15. Matthew J. Hertenstein, Rachel Holmes, Margaret McCullough, and Dacher Keltner. 2009. The communication of emotion via touch. *Emotion* 9, 4 (2009), 566–573. DOI: http://dx.doi.org/10.1037/a0016108

16. Eve Hoggan, Craig Stewart, Laura Haverinen, Giulio Jacucci, and Vuokko Lantz. 2012. Pressages: augmenting phone calls with non-verbal messages. In *Proceedings of the 25th annual ACM symposium on User interface software and technology - UIST '12*. ACM Press, New York, New York, USA, 555. DOI: http://dx.doi.org/10.1145/2380116.2380185

17. Hilary Hutchinson, Wendy Mackay, Bo Westerlund, Benjamin B. Bederson, Allison Druin, Catherine Plaisant, Michel Beaudouin-Lafon, Stéphane Conversy, Helen Evans, Heiko Hansen, Nicolas Roussel, and Björn Eiderbäck. 2003. Technology probes: inspiring design for and with families. In *Proc. SIGCHI '03*. ACM, New York, NY, USA, 17–24. DOI: http://dx.doi.org/10.1145/642611.642616

18. Aleksander Krzywinski, , Tor Gjøsæter, and Frode Guribye. 2016. GRASP Intervention – Review of In Situ Intentional Registration on Shared Interactive Surfaces. In *4th ESRII Meeting*. Bergen, Norway. https://esrii2016.files.wordpress.com/2016/07/abstract-book-esrii-v1-2.pdf

19. Julia Seebode, Robert Schleicher, Ina Wechsung, and Sebastian Möller. 2013. Investigating the Affective Impression of Tactile Feedback on Mobile Devices. In *Proceedings of the 27th International BCS Human Computer Interaction Conference (BCS-HCI '13)*. British Computer Society, Swinton, UK, UK, Article 4, 10 pages. http://dl.acm.org/citation.cfm?id=2578048.2578055

20. Will Simm, Maria Angela Ferrario, Adrian Gradinar, and Jon Whittle. 2014. Prototyping 'clasp': implications for designing digital technology for and with adults with autism. In *Proceedings of the 2014 conference on Designing interactive systems - DIS '14*. ACM Press, New York, New York, USA, 345–354. DOI: http://dx.doi.org/10.1145/2598510.2600880

21. Ulla Wide Boman, Viktor Carlsson, Maria Westin, and Magnus Hakeberg. 2013. Psychological treatment of dental anxiety among adults: a systematic review. *European Journal of Oral Sciences* 121, 3pt2 (2013), 225–234. DOI: http://dx.doi.org/10.1111/eos.12032

Paper Circuitry and Projection Mapping: An Interactive Textbook Approach to Veterinary Education

Margaret Cook
Texas A&M University
College Station, TX 77840, USA
atmgirl@email.tamu.edu

Annie Sungkajun
Texas A&M University
College Station, TX 77840, USA
asungkajun@tamu.edu

Jinsil Hwaryoung Seo
Texas A&M University
College Station, TX 77840, USA
hwaryoung@tamu.edu

Michelle Pine
Texas A&M University
College Station, TX 77840, USA
mpine@cvm.tamu.edu

TEI '18, March 18–21, 2018, Stockholm, Sweden

ACM ISBN 978-1-4503-5568-1/18/03.
https://doi.org/10.1145/3173225.3173290

Abstract
We present an interactive book platform that was initially developed for veterinary students. This platform provides a simple tangible book interface that users can touch, flip through pages, and read the content. Meanwhile, they experience a dynamic content display system using a projector. In this paper, we present an interactive book which specifically covers Cattle (Bovine) laminitis, a painful and widely prevalent disease in cattle. Our project aims to support students' understanding of the multi-faceted nature of bovine laminitis, through the use of an interactive book interface. We implemented the unique approach of using paper circuitry to create the electrical pathway from an actual book to the computer. Book pages with embedded paper circuitry become an interactive surface, that visualizes a progression of bovine laminitis through its stages of disease. Future development of the work will include developing content from other disciplines for the same platform.

Author Keywords
Interactive book; Bovine Laminitis; Veterinary Education; Paper Circuitry; Projection Mapping.

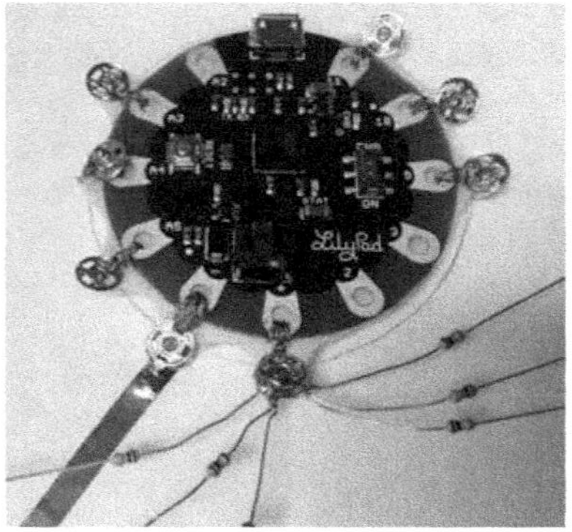

Figure 1: Snaps are soldered to resistors and the copper tape

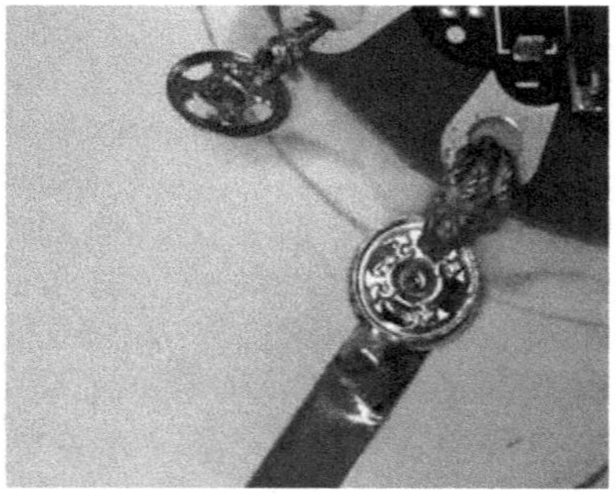

Figure 2: A Close-up view of the Arduino, conductive thread, snaps, and copper tape connections

ACM Classification Keywords
Human-centered computing~ Human computer interaction; Human-centered computing~Interaction devices; Applied Computing~Education; Applied Computing~ Interactive Learning Environments; Applied Computing

Introduction
Cattle (Bovine) laminitis is a painful and widely prevalent condition that affects the cattle industry. Although its multifactorial etiology is not fully understood, the general assumption is that environmental factors, nutrition, and vascular reactivity culminate to induce a change in the claw (hoof) anatomy of the cow, causing lameness. Claw disorders represent a significant economic impact on the cattle industry, because they account for 70-90% of lameness in cattle [7, 5]. According to veterinary professionals, it is of highest importance that new veterinary graduates are competent in recognizing, discussing, and treating diseases of dairy and feedlot cattle [4]. Therefore, it is critical to provide students with supportive, dynamic content learning materials, complete with an interactive interface. We introduce an interactive textbook using paper circuitry and projection mapping. Students learn about bovine laminitis from interactive simulations, and can take notes on the book while interacting with the content. This interactive textbook platform can be integrated with different disciplinary content which also involves processes or the progression of changes.

Paper Circuitry
Even though many digital learning tools have been developed, most popular materials in current veterinary education have a book format. Therefore, our design focuses on augmenting digital content over book page surfaces. We embedded a paper circuit in book pages and created an interactive paper surface. There are other examples in the literature which use similar circuitry: Paints, Paper and Programs by Buechley et al. [1] and Instant Inkjet Circuits by Kawahara et al. [3]. Our paper circuit deals with simple DIY materials, such as copper tape, an Arduino board, and registers, as seen in Figure 3. Conductive adhesive copper tape was soldered to metal snaps, which were in turn connected to a paired snap on the Arduino Board. The paired snaps were sown tightly to the board with conductive thread. The copper tape was laid on the pages beneath the two pages used for display, in order to hide the circuitry. The tape runs on to flaps of paper that finish the connections of the "buttons" on the pages, which act as pressure sensor signals to the LilyPad Arduino board. The visual cue for the button is drawn directly on the display pages above.

Figure 3. The interactive textbook with projection mapping occurring on the left side (top pages), with circuitry revealed beneath Design and Implementation

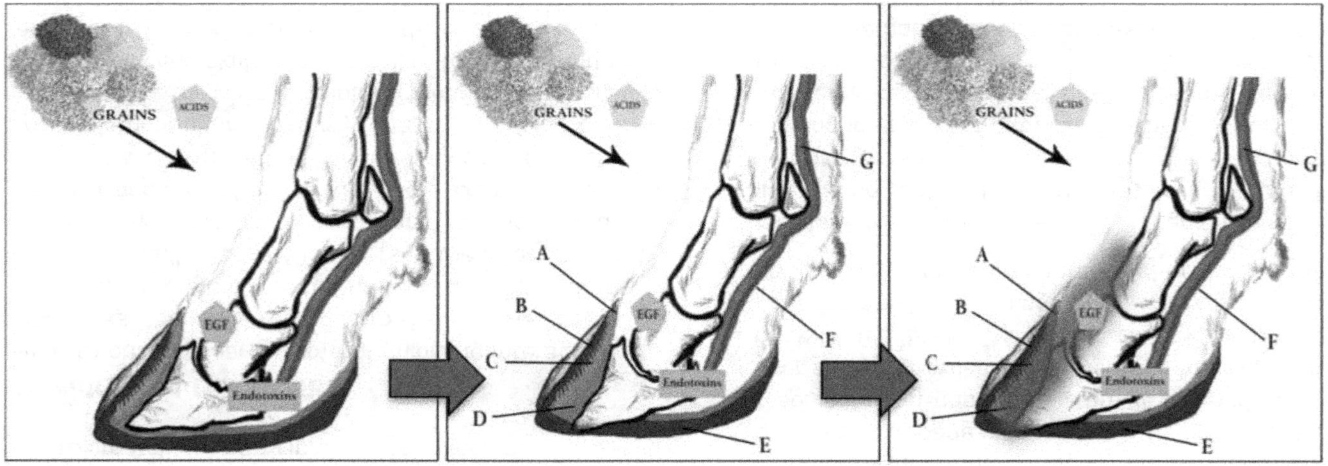

Figure 3. A sample sequence of animation for the user, showing the progression of change in hoof anatomy, as well as labels for important structures. From left to right, you can see the bottom bone sinking, and inflammation appearing (represented with pink shading).

Projection Mapping
When each button is pressed, the Arduino board sends a signal to Processing, and via Syphon and MadMapper the projection of images and text on the pages is changed. All of the visual references and animations were created in the Adobe AfterEffects. The content was compiled and approved by anatomy experts.

Application
The intent of the user interface is to begin the student with an overview and introduction section. In that module, the student can view three different anatomical layers of an ordinary cow limb, to become familiar with the general anatomy of the animal. When the student moves on to the Scenario A button, they can explore a textual and visual explanation of the classic hypothesis of the cause of the disease, as seen in Figure 4. Three different projections show the

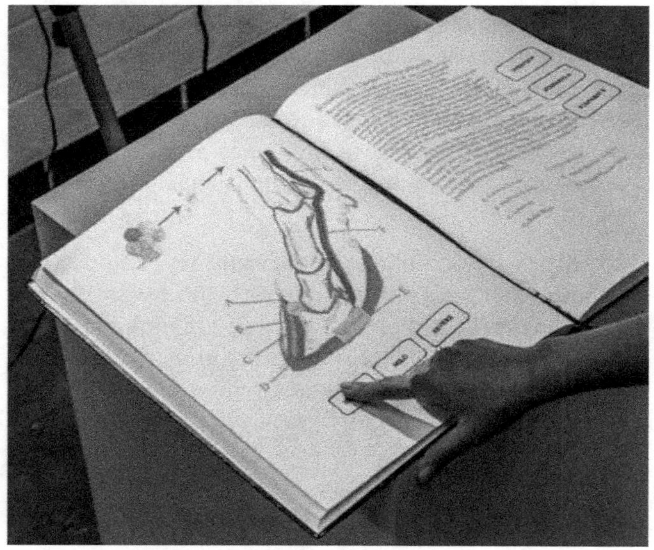

Figure 5. User interacting with the textbook animations.

student a progression of healthy, mild, and severe views of the disease caused by those circumstances. These projections are not static, but are in fact animations that play and demonstrate the process of the disease. Scenario B is very similar in set-up, with the same type of description and three different views to explore, but with an alternative explanation for the cause of the disease.

Preliminary User Interactions

The project was presented in two local venues for initial feedback. Both were interactive art installation shows, which were open to the public. The majority of users were either college students or faculty from the art department of the local university. At both times, the room was dimly lit, for ease of projection, and the book was mounted to a pedestal for stability. Feedback from approximately 30 participants was collected.

Results and Discussion

As with other research projects involving interactive textbooks, the initial response to the book has been positive, although a measurement of the impact upon learning is still needed. The users of the interface were engaged by getting to press buttons, in order to make the text and animations on the pages change. Recent studies have indicated that there is a positive potential for implementing interactivity in learning complex concepts like this, because interactivity enhances problem solving skills and the ability to understand the abstract [6]. In addition, making the textbook interactive may produce a higher user engagement level than a textbook with static images and text [2]. Users expressed a wish to see sharper contrast in the text, but really enjoyed the phenomenon of the texture of the paper being the "buttons" that they controlled the projections with. Users also expressed that the use of this platform made them more interested in anatomy than they thought that they could be. These initial responses we received have encouraged us to move beyond this first phase of development.

Future Work

Future work will include correction of user interface issues, and more conditions in interactive code, to give the user more freedom of exploration. In addition, we would like to add more pages with more content, to enrich the amount of information available to the user. Printable electronic ink is emerging as a way to enhance interactive interfaces, so we believe that adding this component will make the experience more immersive [8]. Furthermore, we wish to explore more sophisticated interactions with the played animations, i.e. zooming into images, based on the length of time a button on the page is pressed. Once all issues are resolved, an in-depth user study is planned. During the user study, we will allow students to interact with the book for feedback. Our goal is to see if the use of it provides a better learning opportunity for improving veterinary students' competency of bovine laminitis.

In addition, we would like to take steps toward integrating content from other disciplines into this platform as well. Other researchers have approached making interactive textbooks for subjects such as mathematics, biology, physics and so on. We will seek to apply those subjects to our projection mapped, interactive book platform, and explore a potential improvement to the learning process in those disciplines as well.

References

1. Leah Buechley, Sue Hendrix, and Mike Eisenberg. Paints, paper, and programs: first steps toward the computational sketchbook. Proc. *TEI 2009*, ACM (2009), 9–12.
2. Jeffrey Donnell, William Singhose, Arto Kivila. An Interactive Textbook for Introductory Engineering Design. CSEDU, Proc. *6th International Conference on Computer Supported Education*. (2014) DOI: 10.1016/S0007-1935(05)80223-4
3. Yoshihiro Kawahara, Steve Hodges, Benjamin S. Cook,Cheng Zhang,and Gregory D. Abowd. Instant inkjet circuits: lab-based inkjet printing to support rapid prototyping of ubicomp devices. Proc. *UbiComp 2013*, ACM (2013), 363–372.
4. Robert B. Miller, Laura E. Hardin, Ross P. Coward, and Mark R. Ellersieck. Practitioner-Defined Competencies Required of New Veterinary Graduates in Food Animal Practice. *JVME* 31, 4.(2004). DOI:10.3138/jvme.31.4.347
5. Christoph K.W. Mülling, and Paul R. Greenough. Physiopathology of the foot. Proc. *World Buiatrics Congress 2006*. Nice, France. (2006).
6. Claire O'Malley, and Danae Stanton Fraser. Literature Review in Learning with Tangible Technologies. *A NESTA Futurelab Research report*. Report 12. (2004). <hal-00190328>
7. J.J Vermunt and P.R. Greenough. Review: Predisposing Factors of Laminitis in Cattle. *Br.vet.J.* 150-164. (1994). DOI: 10.1016/S0007-1935(05)80223-4
8. Jürgen Steimle. Printed electronics for human-computer interaction. Magazine Interactions, 22(3), 72-75 (2015). DOI: 10.1145/2754304

Touch Connection: A Vibrotactile, Textile Prototype

Lucie Hernandez
Falmouth University
Penryn, TR10 9FE, UK
Lucie.hernandez@falmouth.ac.uk

TEI '18, March 18–21, 2018, Stockholm, Sweden

ACM ISBN 978-1-4503-5568-1/18/03.
https://doi.org/10.1145/3173225.3173293

Abstract
Touch Connection is a pair of digitally embroidered textile surfaces with vibrotactile capability. The surfaces are designed as a paired system, to enable people to connect, share touch responses and construct communal tactile experiences. It consists of two different fabric surfaces that use the textile techniques of quilting and embroidery to create dramatic volume and texture.

The work suggests that the application of textural effects and vibrotactile feedback as materials for design can be shaped and moulded to engage participants. It further explores the role these materials play in generating improvised action and emotional responses.

Author Keywords
Craft; design; e-textiles; vibrotactile stimuli; embroidery; haptic feedback.

Introduction
Touch Connection is an experimental prototype that examines how textile surfaces with embedded vibrotactile feedback can be used to facilitate shared touch experiences. Haptic feedback enables participants to sense vibrotactile sensations that

vary in waveform, length and amplitude depending on whether the surfaces connect through touch signals or not. The waveform signals escalate to correspond with an increase in the number of people engaging with the work through touch behaviour; pressing, stroking and nestling. We hope that developing these prototypes can provide insights into the role simultaneous interaction plays in invoking tactile sensations in a shared, tangible, expressive manner.

Figure 1: Digitally embroidered leatherette

Role of Craft

My doctoral research explores how craft moves beyond a dialogue with materials towards shaping an experience, understanding how people approach and explore artefacts, and examining the type of emotional responses their actions generate.

Functioning artefacts have been developed in order to uncover their potential in stimulating a material dialogue. Paul Dourish [3] describes the practical consequences of implementation, our reliance on it to get something done, assembling components into groupings and making interactions active. We can begin to distinguish the role each element plays in contributing an order of sensations that move our actions deeper into the work to construct personal, unfolding experiences. The development of *Touch Connection* engages with materials across the digital and physical spectrum to realize a mode of object making to focus on hybrid materials and techniques. As Boer et al. have outlined [1], the vibrotactile stimuli is approached as a design material, that can be manipulated and shaped around interactive potentials, for creating an experience through technological and physical means.

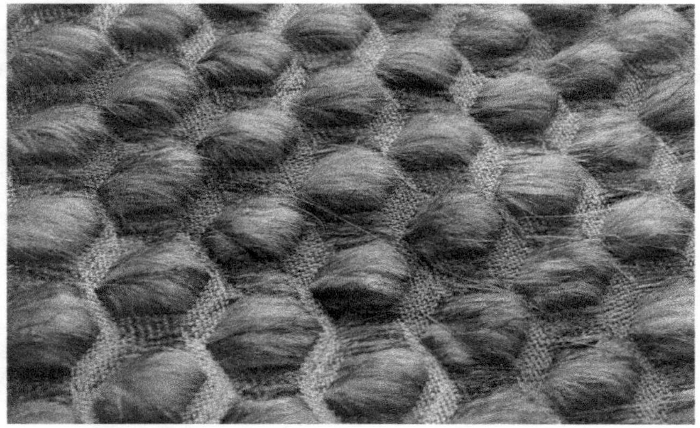

Figure 2: Digitally embroidered fur

Networked Touch

The integration of vibrotactile sensation within textile surfaces and the experiences that unfolded was evaluated by a group of people as part of the doctoral research. The results were analysed to assess their responses to the material properties and their effects. The group proposed more connected experiences, describing a context of use that would allow people to share vibrotactile sensations with others. One of the aims of *Touch Connection* was to construct a situation to facilitate communal participation using networked touch encounters that could create sensation for others.

Evaluating the Experience

During the study, the majority of people found the experience of *Touch Connection* pleasant and enjoyable. Results from a questionnaire reveal that most people scored 'look and feel' and 'attractiveness' highly, which seems to demonstrate an affinity to the textural properties, patterns and colours. Enjoyment also scored highly with comments from participants such as "*I had a natural impulse to stroke the work. I was also drawn to the pattern on the work*", and "*The materials felt lively, and warm and engaging*." These positive, initial responses seem to correlate with Normans [5] description of the visceral level of cognition and how it functions around an objects appearance, touch and feel.

Other participants were intrigued by the qualities of the materials and the manner in which the fabric surfaces were paired with the potential for bringing people together. One participant described, "*The way the work was exhibited brought together visitors. A novel experiment in digital fabric/connectivity.*"

A number of participants experienced the physical, electronic and digital materials in a holistic manner, describing the components as one, integrated form. This questions the notion of a perceived separation between analogue and digital forms to suggest the emergence of new materials for design in which separate properties have been merged. These new materials have the potential to foreground feeling and sensation within the order of experiences.

Figure 3: Playful, bodily encounters with *Touch Connection*

Behavioural Responses

Touch engagement moved beyond hand/fingertips to include other parts of the body. A small group of participants explored more intimate, playful ways to engage the surfaces, enjoying the sensations across their cheeks and upper body. They described an impulse to play with *Touch Connection* in a more immersive manner through bodily engagements that prompt enjoyment and delight. Dourish recognises the active, dynamic nature of participants who are, "improvising action by creatively responding to the setting in which they find themselves" [3, p.160].

Material Dimension

The material dimension operates in a sensory, expressive zone. As Maxine Bristow explains, "crucial to the idea of the material object as a non-discursive language is the suppressed modality of touch, a sense that is implicit in textile" [2, p.46]. *Touch connection* exists in the material domain and requires multisensory bodily engagement. The tactile nature of the work, its physical presence and textural qualities all invite touch responses. Gibson describes the concept of affordance as perceiving actions that might be possible with objects and environments [4]. The textile produces an immediate familiarity around use to suggest participation through touch. The textiles perform the role of attractor, to provoke an initial dialogue with the work, moving the participant into deeper engagements, playing and exploring its surfaces as they uncover additional layers of function and expression.

Future Developments

We are currently revising the performance of *Touch Connection* to make the physical interaction more robust. This will increase the accuracy of the system and provide more support to participants in establishing and improvising expressions and connections with others.

Reflecting on *Touch Connection* through participant evaluation suggests there may be therapeutic benefits in experiencing tactile textiles with integrated vibrotactile patterns. The work could be further developed as sensory textiles that could be used in an interior setting by people who struggle with day-to-day insecurities. The vibrotactile textiles could provide a distraction from anxieties and problems through their form, behavior and connection to others. Future work would evolve the prototypes and hope to explore these themes in greater depth, assessing the impact they could have in supporting feelings of wellbeing and enhanced connections to others.

References

1. Boer, L, Cahill, B, and Vallgårda, A. 2017. The Hedonic Haptics Player: A Wearable Device to Experience Vibrotactile Compositions. *Proceedings of the 2017 ACM Conference Companion Publication on Designing Interactive Systems*
2. Bristow, M., 2012. Continuity of touch - textile as silent witness. In J. Hemmings, ed. *The Textile Reader*. London: Berg. pp.44-51.
3. Dourish, P. 2001. Where the Action Is. MIT
4. Gibson, J.J., 2014. The Ecological Approach to Visual Perception. *Psychology Press*
5. Norman, D. 2004. Emotional Design. *Basic Books*.

Designing an Expandable Illuminated Ring to Build an Actuated Ring Chart

Maxime Daniel[1,2]
[1]ESTIA, Estia-Recherche
F-64210
64210, Bidart, France
m.daniel@estia.fr

Guillaume Rivière[1,2]
[2]Univ. Bordeaux, CNRS, LaBRI, UMR 5800, F-33405
33405, Talence, France
g.riviere@estia.fr

Nadine Couture[1,2]
n.couture@estia.fr

TEI '18, March 18–21, 2018, Stockholm, Sweden

ACM ISBN 978-1-4503-5568-1/18/03.
https://doi.org/10.1145/3173225.3173294

Abstract

Data physicalizations are growing popular in many societal domains which indicates a strong potential for fostering public engagement thanks to public exhibition (e.g. in train stations, in airports, on roundabouts, and in enterprises). We focus on dynamic physical charts for visualizing renewable energy forecasts in public spaces. To get charts readable from any point of view around, we propose a physical ring chart inspired by stone cairns. To build this physical chart, we designed an expandable and stackable illuminated ring. In this paper, we describe the design process and the limitations of the first prototype of such a ring.

Author Keywords

Tangible User Interfaces; Data Physicalization; Shape-Changing Interfaces; Actuation; Dynamic Physical Ring Charts; Renewable Energy Forecast; Shifting Energy Demand; Public spaces.

Introduction

Tangible User Interfaces "give physical form to digital information, employing physical artifacts both as representations and controls for computational media" [16]. Recently, *Data Physicalization* has emerged as a new research area at the intersection of *Data Visualization* and *Tangible User Interfaces*. In 2015, Jansen et al. [7] defined

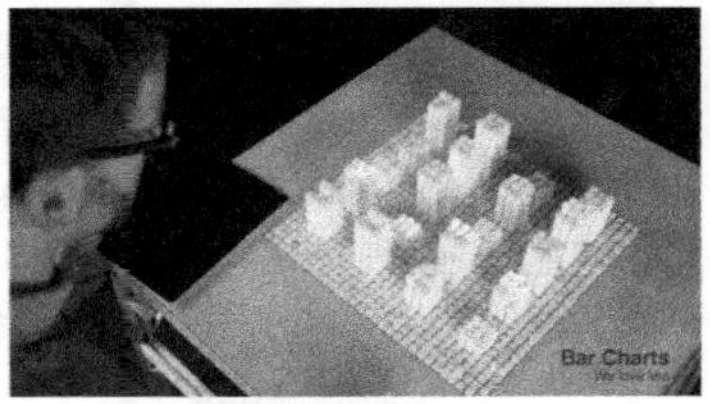

Figure 1: Bar charts displayed with InFORM [3].

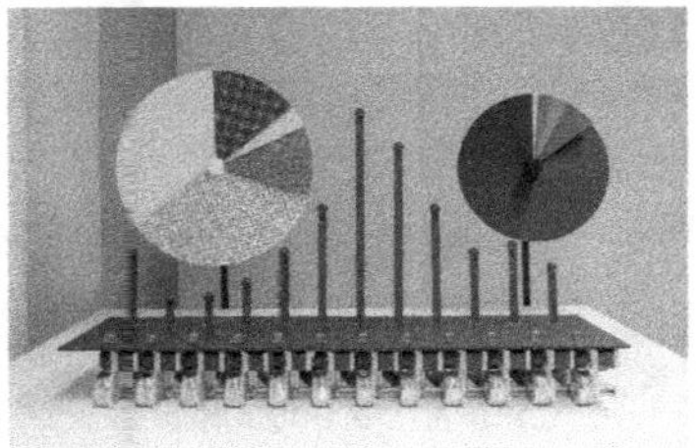

Figure 2: Physical Data [1].

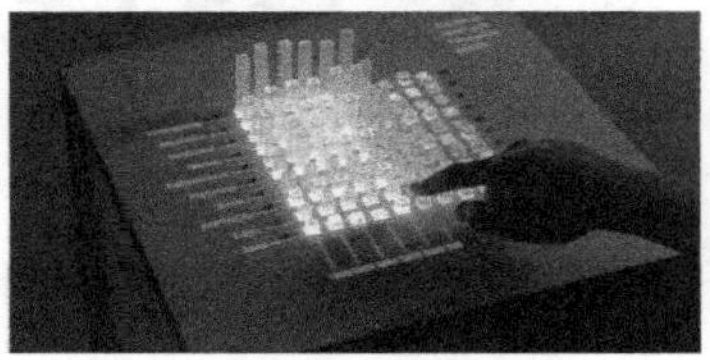

Figure 3: EMERGE [15].

a *Physicalization* as "a physical artifact whose geometry or material properties encode data" and propose to think of *Data Physicalization* as a research area that "examines how computer-supported, physical representations of data (i.e., physicalizations), can support cognition, communication, learning, problem solving, and decision making". *Static Physicalizations* are hard to modify, but the geometry or material properties of *Dynamic Physicalizations* can be modified (e.g. by computer-controlled actuators). Examples of dynamic physicalizations are physical charts, like the bar charts displayed with inFORM [3] (Figure 1), like the Physical Data [2] (Figure 2), and like EMERGE [15] (Figure 3). As noted by Jansen et al. [7], "The growing popularity of data physicalizations in many societal domains indicates a strong potential for fostering public engagement. This popularity suggests that data physicalizations pique interest, and this interest could in turn be leveraged to have people spend more time and effort exploring and understanding important and complex data".

In this paper, we explain our interest in using dynamic physical charts to foster the shift of energy demand in public spaces. We design CairnFORM, a dynamic physical ring chart, for visualizing renewable energy forecasts. One advantage of these ring charts is to be readable at 360°. They can be used to display data in public spaces where people come and go to different directions such as entrance halls, roundabouts, public places, train stations and airports. We describe the design process of a first prototype of an expandable illuminated ring which is the basis component of the dynamic physical ring chart. Finally, we list some limitations of the current prototype and we evoke future works concerning the design and the study of CairnFORM.

Using Dynamic Physical Charts to Foster the Shift of Energy Demand in Public Spaces

Using renewable energy rather than nonrenewable energy is a strategy considered as appropriate for reducing environmental impact. However, as energy generation shifts to renewables and microgeneration[1], the interplay between energy supply and energy demand becomes more complex to manage. Critical problems, such as peak demand, can lead to power outages and make the electrical grid inefficient [4]. These issues are amplified by renewable energy generation fluctuating with weather conditions (e.g. sun, wind, wave, tide) and by a limited energy storage capacity [5]. Unless energy storage becomes economically and environmentally reliable to balance energy supply against energy demand [10], we will need to synchronize the energy demand with the availability of renewables. During the last five years, researchers have designed and studied systems to encourage users in using renewable energy when there is plenty of it rather than when there is little (i.e. shifting energy demand) [1, 8, 11, 12, 13, 14]. Most of the designed systems target households and help inhabitants to plan their everyday energy usage by visualizing renewable energy forecasts using graphical charts such as clock charts [8, 13], timeline charts [13] and line charts [8, 14].

To the extent of our knowledge, no dynamic physical chart has been used for visualizing renewable energy forecasts in a public space. Yet, as evoked by Zuckerman [17], tangible interfaces have strengths that can contribute to "change what people think and do" [2]: *Visibility and Persistance*; *Situatedness*; *Tangible representation*; and *Affordances*.

[1] Microgeneration is the small-scale generation of electricity and/or heat by individuals, businesses, or communities to meet their own needs.
[2] http://dataphys.org/list/dynamic-physical-charts-to-communicate-community-data/, accessed 13/09/2017.

Figure 4: A *cairn* is a stack of stones indicating a landmark, a path, a border, or a sacred place[3].

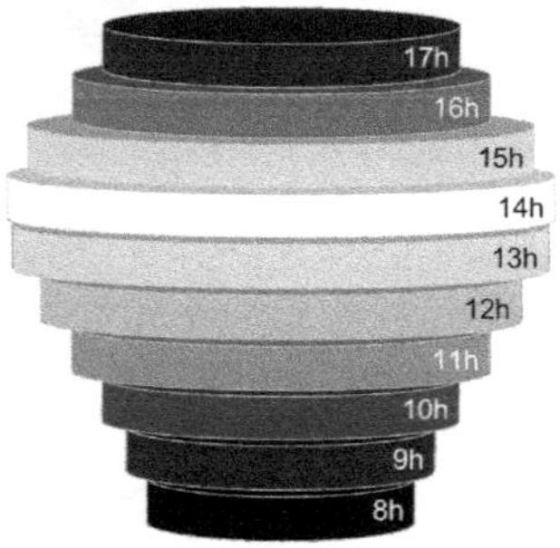

Figure 5: An illustration of CairnFORM, a dynamic physical ring chart.

Figure 6: The actuated skeleton of AMPHORM (i.e. without its skin), a cylindrical kinetic sculpture [9].

Through these properties, tangible interfaces such as dynamic physical charts can help reducing the *intangibility* and the *invisibility* of energy that drives citizens away from energy [11].

CairnFORM: a Dynamic Physical Ring Chart

Bar charts are data visualizations commonly used to perform data comparisons over time. Therefore, bar charts seem relevant for highlighting trends in renewable energy forecasts such as incoming peaks of renewable energy. In the literature, we found examples of dynamic physical bar charts such as bar charts displayed with inFORM [3] (Figure 1), Physical Charts[2] (Figure 2) and EMERGE [15] (Figure 3). However vertical bars are not readable at 360° around because of occlusion effects. This occlusion effect can be countered by moving around the interface. Nonetheless, users can hardly move around the interface in many cases: train stations, public places, airports, roundabouts are public spaces where people are in a hurry and do not have time to change their point of view.

To counter this occlusion effect, we propose to use a vertical physical chart readable at 360° around it. Inspired by *stone cairns* (Figure 4), we propose to design CairnFORM, a stack of expandable illuminated rings that can morph to different *cairn* shapes (i.e. defined by the number of rings and their diameter). For example, a ten-rings-CairnFORM can represent renewable energy forecasts for each hour of a workday (i.e. 8 am to 5 pm) (Figure 5). The ring's diameter and brightness would both be correlated to the average power forecasted to be generated in the hour: for a renewable power generation capacity ranging from 0 W to *max* W, a forecast of 0 W would be represented by a fully retracted ring with no brightness and a forecast of *max* W would be represented by a fully expanded ring with full brightness.

Designing an Expandable Illuminated Ring

The expandable illuminated ring is the basis component of CairnFORM. To design an expandable illuminated ring, we first looked for existing kinetic mechanisms allowing the expansion of a ring. In the literature, AMPHORM [9] makes use of expandable rings to shape a silicon skin: the result is a shape-changing vase (amphora). The aluminium rings of the skeleton of AMPHORM (Figure 6) are based on the Hoberman mechanism [6]. Based on three existing kinetic mechanisms, we iteratively prototyped a new expandable ring mechanism. Finally, we added illumination to the new expandable ring mechanism to obtain the current expandable illuminated ring. All along the design process, we eliminated expandable ring mechanisms that do not meet the following criteria: 1) the kinetic mechanism has inner-space available to put electronics (e.g. actuator, sensor) for actuation; 2) the kinetic mechanism maintains a regular ring-like shape during and after the expansion; and 3) the mechanism expands to a ring-like shape nearly two times larger than its initial size. We detail these steps in the following.

Existing Expandable Ring Mechanisms

We found three existing kinetic mechanisms allowing the expansion of a ring (Figure 7):

1. *HobermanRing-7points*[4] (Figure 7a) and *HobermanRing-12points*[5] (Figure 7b) are based on the Hoberman mechanism and can expand to a continuous ring-like shape two times larger than its initial size. However during the expansion, the ring shape changes in a seven-pointed star with *HobermanRing-7points* and in a twelve-pointed star

[3] https://pixabay.com/p-2082937, image under CC0 licence, downloaded 14/09/2017.

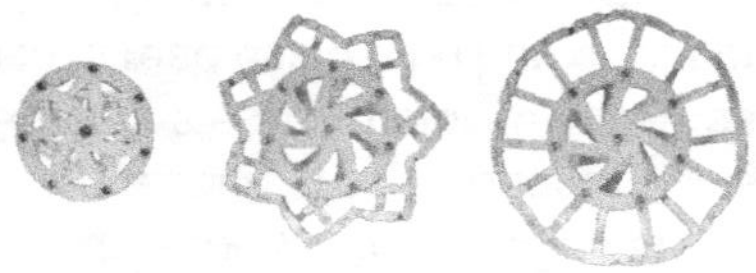

(a) HobermanRing-7points[4]

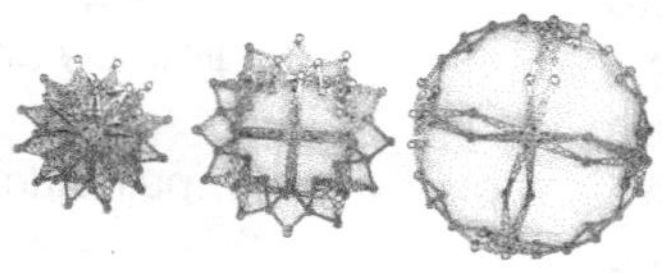

(b) HobermanRing-12points[5]

(c) DiscontinuousRing-6arms-6arcs[6]

Figure 7: Three existing expandable ring mechanisms.

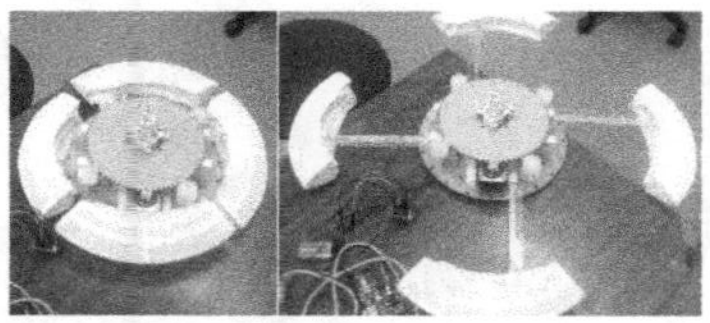

(a) DiscontinuousRing-4arms-4arcs

(b) IrregularRing-4arms-8arcs

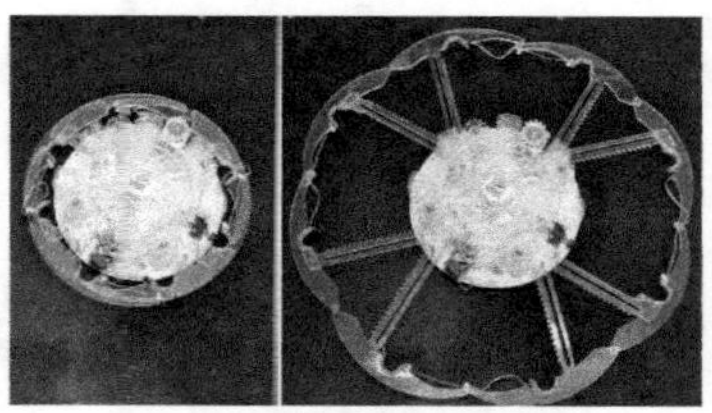

(c) RingLike-8arms-8arcs

Figure 8: The three expandable ring mechanisms made during the iterative protctyping.

with *HobermanRing-12points*. Moreover, very few inner-space is available.

2. The structure *DiscontinuousRing-6arms-6arcs*[6] (Figure 7c) maintains its ring-like shape during the expansion and there is inner-space available. However, it only expands to a discontinuous ring-like shape less than two times larger than its initial size.

Iterative prototyping of a new expandable ring mechanism
Through iterative prototyping, we designed a new expandable ring mechanism. Based on *DiscontinuousRing-6-6* and inspired by *HobermanRing-7/12*, we prototyped three different expandable ring mechanisms before obtaining the current version:

1. *DiscontinuousRing-4arms-4arcs* (Figure 8a) can expand to a shape three times larger than its initial size. However, during the expansion, the ring shape changes from a continuous ring to a discontinuous rounded square.
2. *IrregularRing-4arms-8arcs* (Figure 8b) can expand to a continuous ring-like shape two times larger than its initial size. However during the expansion, the ring shape changes from a continuous regular ring to a continuous irregular ring-like shape.
3. *RingLike-8arms-8arcs* (Figure 8c) can expand to a continuous ring-like shape two times larger than its initial size while maintaining a regular ring-like shape.

Adding illumination to the new expandable ring mechanism
Based on the *RingLike-8arms-8arcs* mechanism (Figure 9), our final prototype of an expandable illuminated ring (Figure 10) is composed of a column making the ring stackable. The ring is actuated by a TRINAMIC stepper motor QSH4218-41-10-035 with a transmission gear that activates a wheel gear. The wheel activates four pinion gears. Each pinion gear activates an axial rack and a diagonal rack. At the edge of each rack, there is an arc representing one eighth of a ø35 cm ring. When the ring is fully retracted, the arcs form the initial ring (ø35 cm). When the ring is fully expanded, the arcs form a ring-like shape nearly two times larger than its initial size (ø62 cm). The ring is illuminated by 24 NeoPixel Digital RGB LEDs (three LEDs on each arc). Furthermore, a micro-switch is used to sense when the ring is fully retracted.

[4] https://vimeo.com/32823353, accessed 13/09/2017.
[5] https://www.youtube.com/watch?v=5eOG-uEqDxU, accessed 13/09/2017.
[6] https://www.youtube.com/watch?v=KgYX9m6sG5c, accessed 13/09/2017.

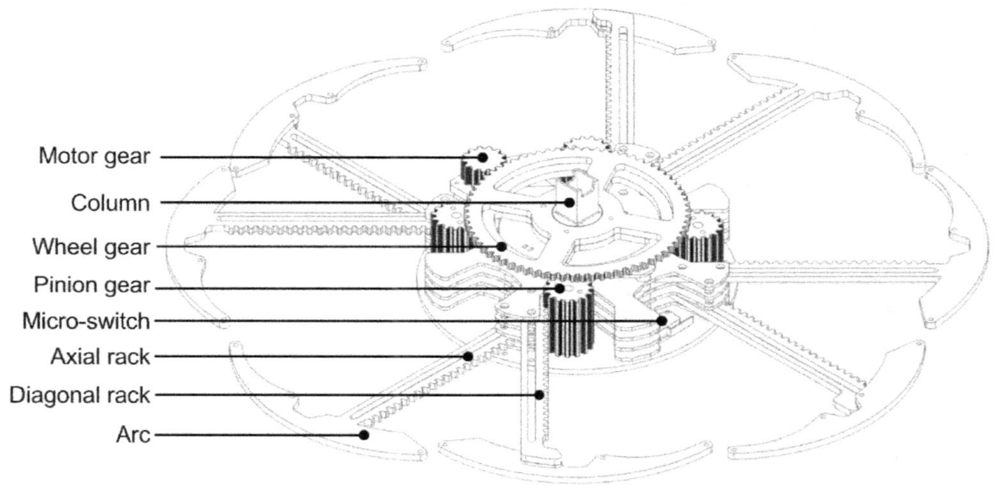

Figure 9: The CAD model of the mechanism of the final expandable ring[6], designed with OnShape, a Cloud CAD Software.

The column was manufactured in PLA material using 3D printing. All other parts were made in translucent PMMA material using 2D laser cutting and assembled using acetone. The remaining parts, mainly support parts, were made in plywood using 2D laser cutting. Bolts, nuts and washers were used to assemble all the parts together.

All LEDs and the stepper motor are powered by a ATX computer power supply. The 24 LEDs are controlled using an Arduino Mega2560. The stepper motor is controlled using an Adafruit stepper motor HAT for Raspberry Pi. The micro-switch is read using a pull-up circuit on an Adafruit perma-proto HAT for Raspberry Pi. One Raspberry Pi 3 is used to communicate with the Mega2560 (serial protocol) and the HATs (I2C protocol). The driver is written in Python 2.7.

Limitations

We identified four limitations of the current prototype:

- **Expansion range.** The current prototype expands with a 1.8 diameter scale factor (ranging from 35 cm to 62 cm). The smallest the expansion range is, the more the difference between each ring of the final ring chart will be subtle to perceive. In our case, the expansion range is 27 cm: to display a 256-point data scale, the granularity would be only ∼1 mm, would be ∼3 mm for a 100-point data scale, and would more reasonably be ∼1 cm for a 30-point data scale.

[6] The CAD model is available at: https://cad.onshape.com/documents/7d4ecae370a1e03250f148cc/w/40919688efd268263900abc1/e/6c37dd97791037a37d7dd39b, accessed 13/09/2017.

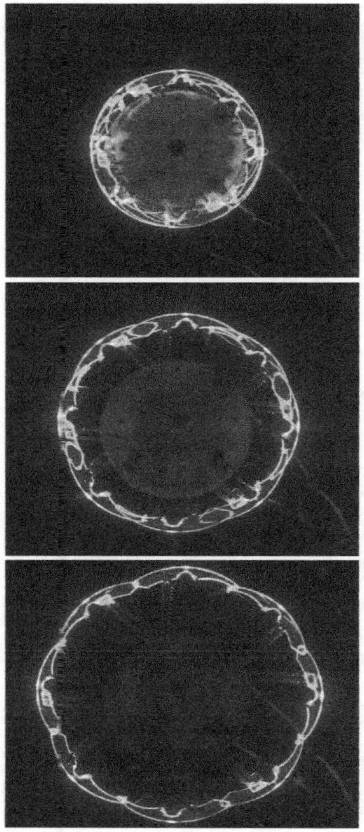

Figure 10: The final prototype of an expandable illuminated ring.

- **Motion noise.** When the ring is expanding, the overall structure generates about 60 dB at a distance of 1 meter, when the 5 V stepper motor QSH4218 is at 60 RPM in double coil mode. This noise makes the current ring intrusive: it should be used in situations where noise does not reduce usability (e.g. in an entrance hall, but not in an office or an open plan).
- **Power consumption.** In the worst case, the prototype draws up to 12.2 W (7.2 W max for LEDs and 5 W max for the stepper motor). This case occurs when actuating the ring at full brightness with the stepper motor in double coils mode (the most energy-consuming mode). This case will rarely or never occur. However, because the purpose of the final ring chart will be to engage users with an energy-related issue, this chart will have to help in saving more energy than it consumes.
- **Fabrication cost.** A ring costs about 200€ to build: 60€ of raw materials (PLA, PMMA, and plywood) manufactured using a 3D printer and a 2D laser cutter; 100€ of electronics (NeoPixel digital RGB LED, stepper motor QSH4218, and micro-switch); and 40€ of bolts, nuts, washers, aluminium profiles, and other products such as PVC glue and acetone. A prototype stacking ten expandable illuminated rings will cost approximately 2000€ for the rings plus 300€ of electronics to control it (Raspberry Pi 3, Adafruit perma-proto HATs, Adafruit stepper motor HATs, Arduino Mega2560, and ATX power supply).

Conclusion and Future Works

In this paper, we propose to use dynamic physical charts to foster shifting energy demand in public spaces. We think that the tangible properties [17] of physical charts such as the *Visibility and Persistance*, the *Situatedness* and the *Tangible representation* can help mitigating the *intangibility* and the *invisibility* of energy that drives citizens away from energy [11]. Therefore, we propose to use a dynamic physical ring chart for visualizing renewable energy forecasts. We propose the design of CairnFORM, a customizable stack of expandable illuminated rings readable at 360° around it. Inspired by existing kinetic mechanisms, we describe the design process of a first prototype of an expandable illuminated ring. Furthermore, we identify several limitations of our final prototype of an expandable illuminated ring such as the expansion range, the motion noise, the power consumption, and the fabrication cost.

In future works, we will manufacture 10 expandable illuminated rings. With this stack of 10 rings, we will conduct *in vitro* user studies to assess the readability of ring charts when asking users to retrieve incoming peaks of renewable energy production. Furthermore, we will study *in vivo* the attractiveness over weeks and months of such dynamic physical charts in a public space.

References

[1] Enrico Costanza, Joel E. Fischer, James A. Colley, Tom Rodden, Sarvapali D. Ramchurn, and Nicholas R. Jennings. 2014. Doing the Laundry with Agents: A Field Trial of a Future Smart Energy System in the Home. In *Proceedings of the SIGCHI Conference on Human Factors in Computing Systems (CHI '14)*. ACM, New York, NY, USA, 813–822. DOI: http://dx.doi.org/10.1145/2556288.2557167

[2] Brian J. Fogg. 1998. Persuasive Computers: Perspectives and Research Directions. In *Proceedings of the SIGCHI Conference on Human Factors in Computing Systems (CHI '98)*. ACM Press/Addison-

Wesley Publishing Co., New York, NY, USA, 225–232. DOI: http://dx.doi.org/10.1145/274644.274677

[3] Sean Follmer, Daniel Leithinger, Alex Olwal, Akimitsu Hogge, and Hiroshi Ishii. 2013. inFORM: Dynamic Physical Affordances and Constraints Through Shape and Object Actuation. In *Proceedings of the 26th Annual ACM Symposium on User Interface Software and Technology (UIST '13)*. ACM, New York, NY, USA, 417–426. DOI: http://dx.doi.org/10.1145/2501988.2502032

[4] Frontier Economics and Sustainability First. 2012. Demand side response in the domestic sector-a literature review of major trials. UK Department of Energy and Climate Change, Final Report, London, August. (2012). http://www.frontier-economics.com/documents/2013/10/frontier-report-demand-side-response-in-the-domestic-sector.pdf Accessed 13/06/2017.

[5] David Hafemeister. 2010. Sustainable Energy - Without the Hot Air. *American Journal of Physics* 78, 2 (2010), 222–223. DOI: http://dx.doi.org/10.1119/1.3273852

[6] Charles Hoberman. 1991. Radial expansion/retraction truss structures. (June 1991). US Patent 5,024,031.

[7] Yvonne Jansen, Pierre Dragicevic, Petra Isenberg, Jason Alexander, Abhijit Karnik, Johan Kildal, Sriram Subramanian, and Kasper Hornbæk. 2015. Opportunities and Challenges for Data Physicalization. In *Proceedings of the 33rd Annual ACM Conference on Human Factors in Computing Systems (CHI '15)*. ACM, New York, NY, USA, 3227–3236. DOI: http://dx.doi.org/10.1145/2702123.2702180

[8] Jesper Kjeldskov, Mikael B. Skov, Jeni Paay, Dennis Lund, Tue Madsen, and Michael Nielsen. 2015. Facilitating Flexible Electricity Use in the Home with Eco-Feedback and Eco-Forecasting. In *Proceedings of the Annual Meeting of the Australian Special Interest Group for Computer Human Interaction (OzCHI '15)*. ACM, New York, NY, USA, 388–396. DOI: http://dx.doi.org/10.1145/2838739.2838755

[9] David Lakatods. 2012. *AMPHORM: Form Giving through Gestural Interaction to Shape Changing Objects*. Master's thesis. Massachusetts Institute of Technology (MIT), Cambridge, MA, USA.

[10] Xing Luo, Jihong Wang, Mark Dooner, and Jonathan Clarke. 2015. Overview of current development in electrical energy storage technologies and the application potential in power system operation. *Applied Energy* 137 (January 2015), 511–536. http://wrap.warwick.ac.uk/63615/

[11] James Pierce and Eric Paulos. 2010. Materializing Energy. In *Proceedings of the 8th ACM Conference on Designing Interactive Systems (DIS '10)*. ACM, New York, NY, USA, 113–122. DOI: http://dx.doi.org/10.1145/1858171.1858193

[12] Filipe Quintal, Clinton Jorge, Valentina Nisi, and Nuno Nunes. 2016. Watt-I-See: A Tangible Visualization of Energy. In *Proceedings of the International Working Conference on Advanced Visual Interfaces (AVI '16)*. ACM, New York, NY, USA, 120–127. DOI: http://dx.doi.org/10.1145/2909132.2909270

[13] Johann Schrammel, Cornelia Gerdenitsch, Astrid Weiss, Patricia M. Kluckner, and Manfred Tscheligi. 2011. FORE-Watch – The Clock That Tells You When to Use: Persuading Users to Align Their Energy Consumption with Green Power Availability. In *Proceedings of the 2nd International Conference on Ambient Intelligence (AmI '11)*. Springer Berlin Heidelberg, Berlin, Heidelberg, 157–166. DOI: http://dx.doi.org/10.1007/978-3-642-25167-2_19

[14] Will Simm, Maria Angela Ferrario, Adrian Friday, Peter Newman, Stephen Forshaw, Mike Hazas, and Alan Dix. 2015. Tiree Energy Pulse: Exploring Renewable Energy Forecasts on the Edge of the Grid. In *Proceedings of the SIGCHI Conference on Human Factors in Computing Systems (CHI '15)*. ACM, New York, NY, USA, 1965–1974. DOI: http://dx.doi.org/10.1145/2702123.2702285

[15] Faisal Taher, John Hardy, Abhijit Karnik, Christian Weichel, Yvonne Jansen, Kasper Hornbæk, and Jason Alexander. 2015. Exploring Interactions with Physically Dynamic Bar Charts. In *Proceedings of the 33rd Annual ACM Conference on Human Factors in Computing Systems (CHI '15)*. ACM, New York, NY, USA, 3237–3246. DOI: http://dx.doi.org/10.1145/2702123.2702604

[16] Brygg Ullmer and Hiroshi Ishii. 2000. Emerging Frameworks for Tangible User Interfaces. *IBM Syst. J.* 39, 3-4 (July 2000), 915–931. DOI: http://dx.doi.org/10.1147/sj.393.0915

[17] Oren Zuckerman. 2015. Objects for Change: A Case Study of a Tangible User Interface for Behavior Change. In *Proceedings of the Ninth International Conference on Tangible, Embedded, and Embodied Interaction (TEI '15)*. ACM, New York, NY, USA, 649–654. DOI: http://dx.doi.org/10.1145/2677199.2687906

HäirIÖ: Human Hair as Interactive Material

Christine Dierk, Sarah Sterman, Molly Jane Pearce Nicholas, Eric Paulos
Electrical Engineering and Computer Sciences
University of California, Berkeley
{cdierk, ssterman, molecule, paulos}@berkeley.edu

ABSTRACT

Human hair is a cultural material, with a rich history displaying individuality, cultural expression and group identity. It is malleable in length, color and style, highly visible, and embedded in a range of personal and group interactions. As wearable technologies move ever closer to the body, and embodied interactions become more common and desirable, hair presents a unique and little-explored site for novel interactions. In this paper, we present an exploration and working prototype of hair as a site for novel interaction, leveraging its position as something both public and private, social and personal, malleable and permanent. We develop applications and interactions around this new material in HäirIÖ: a novel integration of hair-based technologies and braids that combine capacitive touch input and dynamic output through color and shape change. Finally, we evaluate this hair-based interactive technology with users, including the integration of HäirIÖ within the landscape of existing wearable and mobile technologies.

Author Keywords

wearables; cosmetic computing; ambient displays; hair.

INTRODUCTION

As wearables become increasingly prevalent and diverse, we see sites of interaction on the body expanding in creative and exciting ways. Wearable technology is no longer limited to wrist-worn forms or glasses-based interactions, or even encapsulated in stand-alone devices. Conductive inks, thermochromic pigments, and other new materials have enabled new wearables in the form of tattoos [17, 32, 11, 33], clothing [5, 21, 20], fingernails [29, 10, 23, 6], and makeup [31, 27, 12, 13], among other form factors [9]. In this paper we build on this work and related themes of Cosmetic Computing [6] and Beauty Technologies [30] to explore, design, develop, and evaluate hair-based interactive technologies.

Hair is a tangible and interactive extension of the body that allows for unique style interactions. Our approach is to directly engage with the natural and cultural affordances of hair as a material in our design. In many cultures and for many people, hair itself is both highly visible and ubiquitous. This allows people to explore a range of public and private interactions using their hair. Taking inspiration from existing material properties and cultural meanings of hair, we designed and developed HäirIÖ[1] — a hair-integrated technology that uses color and style as output, natural human touch as input, and makes use of commercially available hair extensions. HäirIÖ is performative, yet personal. Movement can be seen by an audience, or felt only by the wearer.

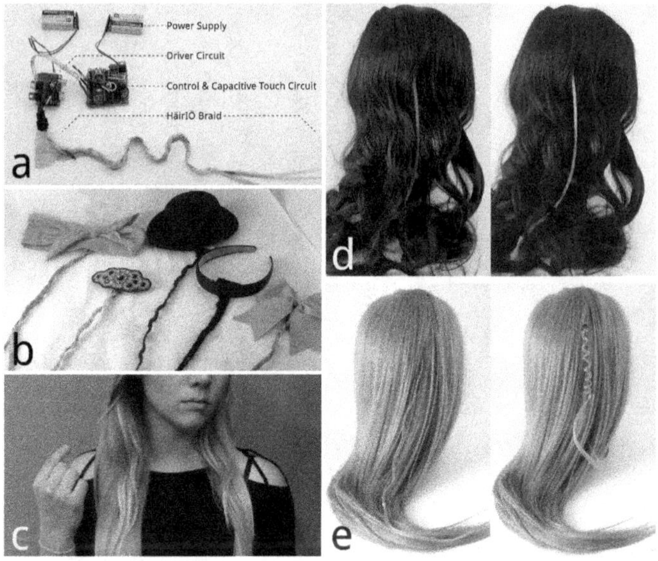

Figure 1. A) HäirIÖ prototype prior to miniaturization, B) exemplar HäirIÖ hair accessory form factors, C) HäirIÖ uses Swept Frequency Capacitive Sensing to detect natural hair interactions, D) HäirIÖ color changing properties using thermochromic pigments, and E) shape changing properties using Nitinol wire.

There is a large landscape for potential interaction design within the rich cultural history of hair. We focus first on two of the most commonly-changed aspects of hair: color and shape. These output modalities enable a wide range of expressions both public and personal, leverage existing properties and form factors of hair to facilitate embodied interaction, and find inspiration in the wide diversity of existing hair colors and shapes. This makes them appropriate choices for an initial exploration of hair. While there are many other output modalities using materials such as electroluminescent materials, LEDs, etc., our prototypes leverage Nitinol wire, commonly known as Shape Memory Alloy (SMA), and thermochromic pigments.

TEI'18, March 18–21, 2018, Stockholm, Sweden

ACM ISBN 978-1-4503-5568-1/18/03...$15.00
https://doi.org/10.1145/3173225.3173232

[1] HäirIÖ is both a reference to hair as input/output and as a disruptive medium, since it is also a Finish word meaning 'disruption.'

In this paper we define and explore a new hair-based wearable framework through the development of functional prototypes that capture and evaluate the expressiveness, interactivity, and social acceptability of hair technologies. In order to focus this work, we leave related issues of power, size, and additional materials to future work, and center our investigation into the ecology of hair. This work also sits at the intersection of traditional hair practices and wearable devices as an exemplar of Cosmetic Computing.

Cosmetic Computing

In this paper we position HäirIÖ as operating and expanding the research landscape of *Cosmetic Computing*.

Cosmetic Computing [6] is an expression of radical individuality and an opportunity for deviance from binary gender norms. It is a catalyst towards an open, playful, and creative expression of individuality through wearable technologies. Unlike many modern traditional cosmetics that are culturally laden with prescriptive social norms of required usage that are restrictive, sexually binary, and oppressive [34], we desire a new attitude and creative engagement with wearable technologies that can empower individuals with a more playful, performative, and meaningful "technique of dress."

HäirIÖ challenges gender norms and expectations of who can and how to style hair. It enhances the cultural positioning of hair as a statement of group and individual identity. It opens up a world of creativity and engagement with technology embodied in a familiar, intimate, transformative platform.

HäirIÖ

HäirIÖ augments hair with both touch input and visual output, using existing technologies and practices as a demonstration of the potential for cosmetic computing and hair as a unique platform for interaction. HäirIÖ uses thermochromic pigments and SMA to output visible change in color and shape, reflecting and enhancing the natural and cultural malleability of hair. This includes alternating between a natural color and a vibrant one, and between shaped and straight styling, creating publicly visible changes.

HäirIÖ also adds a new haptic dimension to personal interactions with hair: while people often touch their own hair, now their hair can touch them. Using shape changing capabilities, HäirIÖ can transmit subtle haptic communications by stroking or tapping. By shifting from the side of the face into the user's field of view, HäirIÖ provides lo-fi visual signals.

HäirIÖ uses Swept Frequency Capacitive Sensing to detect and interpret how users interact with the extension. Microcontrollers, sensors, Bluetooth modules, and other components are embedded in accessories or hidden in the hair itself. As such, HäirIÖ combines input with output, incorporates Smartphones and other devices into the interaction cycle, and creates novel, rich interactions. HäirIÖ provides a framework with which designers, makers, and users can craft their own unique interactions and incorporate hair in new prototypes and designs.

RELATED WORK

As technology continues to move towards the body and more diverse wearable technologies emerge, many designers and researchers have focused on creating wearable displays that are ambient, ambiguous, and abstract. New designs favor wearable displays that are subtle, slow-moving, and often ambiguous in meaning to onlookers, or even to users themselves [8]. Devendorf et al. identify and describe aspects of the complex relationship between computationally-controlled displays and personal style using thermochromic thread [5]. Other designs employ thermochromic pigments on skin [11, 12] to support rapid and early prototyping of cosmetic interfaces. Shape memory alloys have been used to explore animated, reactive, and interactive models of actuating textiles[4]. Our work extends these prior explorations in hybrid displays to a new domain: hair.

Previous work has explored the potential for hair extensions and wigs as input devices [25, 28], sites for embedded sensors [14, 25], and low-fidelity displays [3, 16]. Our work is most related to [3], where treated hair changes color in response to external temperatures, and Vega et. al's Hairware, where chemically metalized hair extensions function as capacitive touch input [28]. The path forged by these two research groups lays the foundation for the fundamental building blocks of hair interaction. Building on this foundation, our work presents a complete system in which input and output are combined and controlled. We expand output modalities presented in prior work by including shape change in addition to color change, internally actuating the changes, and incorporating capacitive touch sensing, informed by Vega et. al. By incorporating both input and output in a single braid, our system affords new interactions and applications previously unattainable. To enable future developments, we present a cohesive framework for augmenting human hair with both input and output capabilities.

DESIGN GUIDELINES

Based on salient features of hair as a design site, we developed guidelines to shape contributions and inform explorations of the design space (Table 1). We envision the following as continuing the conversation around the design of on-body wearables, while incorporating the unique features of hair.

Public/Personal

The public/personal dichotomy focuses on looks or appearance of a new on-body technology. Hair is a powerful symbol of identity, and is often employed as an indicator of gender, age, status, and wealth [18, 26]. While speaking to ones individual identity, hair also speaks to their group identity; monks, punks, hippies, skinheads, Rastafarians, and Beliebers all employ their hair as a means of expressing their identities and ideologies [24]. Hair is personal in that it is a part of the body, yet in many cultures it typically remains visible to the public. Because it is so often visible, hair may disappear into the background. This unique combination of highly visible yet inconspicuous makes on-body displays well-suited to a wide range of output modalities, and any technology that explores this space should consider the tradeoffs along the public-personal continuum.

Malleability/Permanence

Hair is malleable, supporting temporary or permanent changes in length, color, and style. The use of artificial hair is established in both traditional and modern cosmetics. The practice

Themes and Guidelines
Public / Personal – Provide a range of output modalities from subtle to spectacular. – Allow for both hidden and highly visible designs.
Malleability / Permanence – Make removable. – Provide choice of when/how much to modify. – Enable both conscious and unconscious interactions.
Social / Individual – Create opportunities for both social and individual interactions.
Embodied Interaction – Leverage existing form factors.

Table 1. Design Guidelines

is at least 5,000 years old, adopted by Ancient Egyptians, Romans, Queen Elizabeth, and the like [18]. As many cosmetic trends, artificial hair has persisted through modern times with the emergence of extensions, weaves, and modern toupees. Hair additions are culturally accepted, commercially available, and easily removed or interchanged. The natural physical affordances of hair should inform the design of hair-worn technology, allowing for both unconscious and conscious interactions, and temporary or permanent installation. Any interfaces should be removable, allowing semi-permanent versions.

Social/Individual
The social/individual dichotomy relates to behavior of the user and wearable (compared with the private/public dichotomy which describes appearance). This on-body technology is individual, yet in some contexts, it becomes an intimate, shared platform for social bonding: between children braiding hair on a playground, or close friends expressing comfort or affection. Individual use-cases should co-exist with collaborative and socially engaging ones.

Embodied Interaction
The many natural physical affordances of hair allow for a diverse range of interaction choices. Individuals have habits around their own hair; an embodied design leverages the user's existing gesture vocabulary and the physical affordances of their hair to integrate into their life and behavior. Hair can be straight, curly, kinky, wavy, and colorful; a design for the hair should be flexible enough to fit naturally into any kind of hair and any kind of behavior, merging the technology into the user's own bodily representation.

TECHNICAL ARCHITECTURE
HäirIÖ is a functional prototype that demonstrates the hair-based design guidelines presented above. Each individual HäirIÖ augmented braid has input and output capabilities. It is controlled through a connection to a single central control board that can handle up to four braids at a time. While each braid can behave independently, more compelling interactions

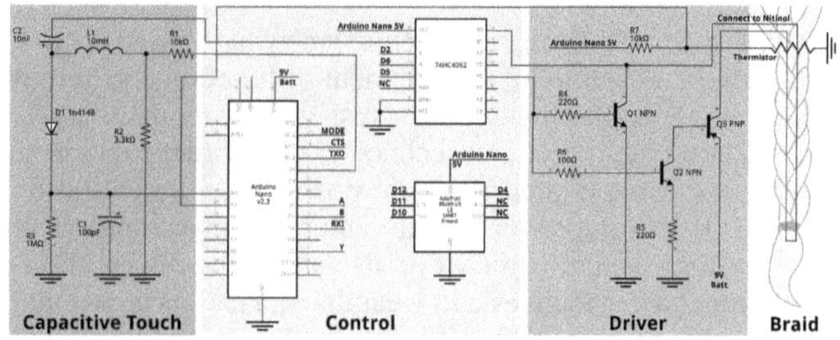

Figure 2. Circuit diagram for our system. The circuit can be extended by connecting additional braids to the available I/O pins of the multiplexer. Note: additional braids require an additional driver circuit. All ground is connected. However, the circuit requires two separate 9V batteries: one connected to the control circuit, the other to the driver circuits.

and applications are achieved by linking braid behaviors together, and connecting the onboard controller to other devices over wireless communication. What follows is a discussion of the technical choices and details of this prototype as informed by the design guidelines.

Technical details
HäirIÖ consists of a central controller, a capacitive touch circuit, a power supply, multiple driver circuits, and swappable braids (Figure 2). Each braid with output capabilities has its own driver circuit to switch power on and off, but capacitive sensing can be handled by a single sensor circuit on the main control board by using multiplexing. The control circuit in this prototype can handle sensing and actuation on four braids at a time, based on the components chosen. Two modalities of output are implemented in our prototypes: shape change and color change. Our prototypes leverage SMA and thermochromic pigments (Table 2); materials which are capable of both subtle and spectacular changes (See Table 3 for example of a braid's lifting capabilities). HäirIÖ braids can display one or both of the output modalities (color or shape change). Similarly, they can be configured for only input, only output, or integrated input/output. Integrating input and output in the same braid allows for new interaction behaviors that would be otherwise infeasible, such as immediate reactions to touch.

Material	Transition Temp	Width
Nitinol	46.1°C (115°F)	0.5mm
Thermochromic Pigments	31.1°C (88°F)	–

Table 2. Materials used in the prototype. While the transition temperature of the Nitinol seems high in comparison to the average internal temperature of the human body (37°C/98.6°F), it poses no risk to the user or their hair [1]. Commercial hair straighteners operate between 93.3°C and 204.4°C (200°F and 400°F) [15]. In addition, both the user's own hair and the hair extension provide a layer of insulation.

Heat: SMA and thermochromic pigments are both controlled through resistive heating. One battery powers the main control circuit, while a separate battery provides the resistive heating, to avoid current overloads. For safety and efficiency, we control the power shut-off for output through a thermistor mounted inside the braid. The thermistor provides real-time temperature information, enabling closed-loop temperature control. This ensures both user safety and efficient operation, as we can shut down heating when the temperature exceeds a threshold. By using pulse width modulation, we can modify the time to transition, maintain a particular temperature (and

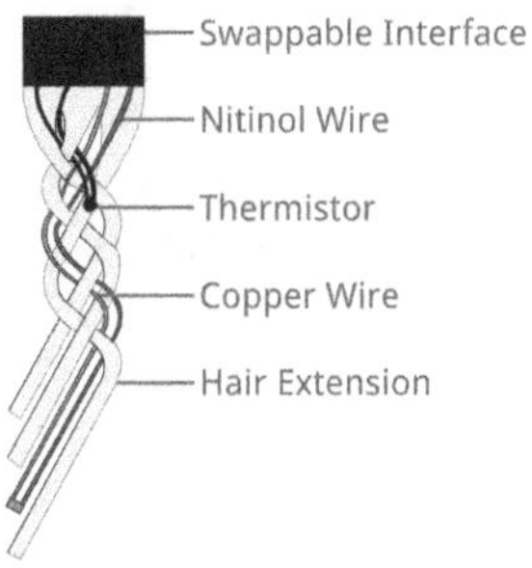

Figure 3. Diagram of a HäirIÖ braid. The connector at the top of the braid attaches directly to the driver circuit. The Nitinol and copper wires are soldered together at the end of the braid to make a single wire. The thermistor is woven into the braid to ensure accurate readings.

resulting output), and prevent overheating the hair. Ambient heat may also have an effect: thermochromic pigment may change color when exposed to environmental heat such as the sun, or physical touch due to its lower transition temperature (See Table 2). However, the transition temperature of the SMA is significantly higher, and in normal use will not actuate without additional power.

Sensing: HäirIÖ uses swept frequency capacitive sensing (SFCS), which has been shown to be capable of detecting multiple types of touches [22, 7]. We study the recognition of touch/no touch in the initial system, but by implementing SFCS we leave room in future work for such gestures as stroking or twirling the hair. Sensing and actuation occur on the same wire. Combining input and output on a single wire requires a switching driver circuit that can disconnect the wire from both power and ground, as the capacitive electrode must be floating. When choosing transistors for this purpose, check the internal capacitance: the capacitance in field effect transistors will overwhelm the signal of the human body. Instead, we implement switching with bipolar junction transistors, and recommend this for future designs. Our method of sensing requires some amount of exposed wire. To achieve this, we use a four strand braid (Figure 3); however, there are many different types of braids and ways in which the wire can be incorporated. Additionally, there are other methods for sensing capacitive touch. For example, previous work has used chemically metalized hair extensions [28]. While SMA is still necessary for shape as an output, techniques such as metalized hair extensions extend the braid design space (e.g. completely concealing SMA within the braid).

Power requirements: The actuation power requirements of the initial prototype remain quite high, due to the heat needed. Typical operation on a 2 Ω braid wire draws approximately 1.5A (Figure 4). As discussed earlier, in this paper we focus on creating and evaluating novel interaction possibilities around hair; while functional and safe, we did not focus on reducing power draw as a core goal. However, we prototype interactions that take advantage of the bi-stable potential of SMA to produce shape and style changes that require short periods of actuation for long term effects, as discussed in Applications.

Customization and Communication: Each braid is constructed with a generic connector that allows one braid to be easily swapped for any other. A wide variety of behaviors can be

Current	Time	Angle Raised
1.5 A	2min35sec	84°
2.1 A	38sec	88°

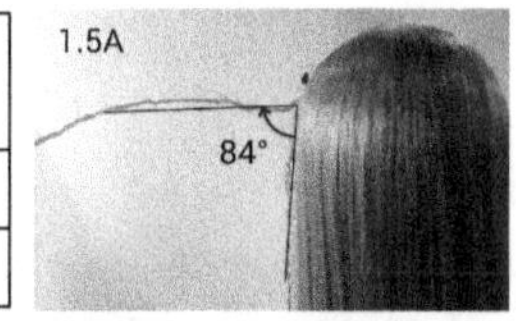

Table 3. Lifting capability of shape changing braids. The Nitinol begins hanging down, actuates to the listed angle, then relaxes to a resting angle of 44° after power is turned off. Braid specifications: 115° transition Nitinol with 0.75mm diameter, trained to a 90° bend; 1.0 Ω; 50cm total braid length (42cm after bend); 4.9g total braid mass. Though this wire is a thicker gauge than our on-head prototypes, transition time behavior and lifting capabilities are comparable.

encoded in the braids using shape and color change, allowing broad physical customization ranging from style change to haptic touch. Programmatic customization can change the control flows and timing of the behaviors. We integrate a Bluetooth module to the control circuit to allow communication with other devices. Wearables often leverage mobile phones to handle the computational heavy-lifting of networking; with Bluetooth communication we can send user-generated data to other devices or apps, or react to information shared from other wearables, IoT devices, or other users.

Transition Behaviors: The time to transition and order of transition events are key features in designing interactions. The insulating properties of natural and synthetic hair extensions mean that the outside of the hair does not heat in direct synchrony with the internal wire, leading to a more gradual color transition and varying event orderings.

To enable future designers, we provide a model of the dynamics of the heat energies of Nitinol (Q_n) and hair (Q_h):

$$\dot{Q}_n = P(t) - \frac{T_n - T_h}{R_1} \qquad T_n = Q_n/C_n \qquad R_1 = 9.1K/W$$
$$\dot{Q}_h = \frac{T_n - T_h}{R_1} - \frac{T_h}{R_2} \qquad T_h = Q_h/C_h \qquad R_2 = 16K/W$$
$$T_t = A * T_n$$

$P(t)$ is the electrical power input; T_n and T_h are the temperatures of the Nitinol and the hair, while T_t is the measured temperature at the thermistor. The parameters R_1 and R_2 are the thermal resistance of the Nitinol to the hair, and the hair to surrounding air, respectively. We determine these values through a least-squares regression on the experimental data represented in Figure 4.

These equations can be used to design approximate transition behavior based on available power input. Further tuning may be required given different braid construction or hair properties. These parameters were fit to data collected on a braid with 4g of bleached human hair, and 33cm of 0.5mm diameter Nitinol. Heat capacities C_n and C_h can be calculated from the specific heats of hair [19] and Nitinol. A, the relation between the thermistor readings, Nitinol temperature, and ambient temperature, is calculated in our system to be $A = 4/11$; this will vary based on braid construction.

Hair Extensions: The first obvious consideration for choosing hair extensions is hair color and style. Consumer hair extensions are available in all natural hair colors and seem-

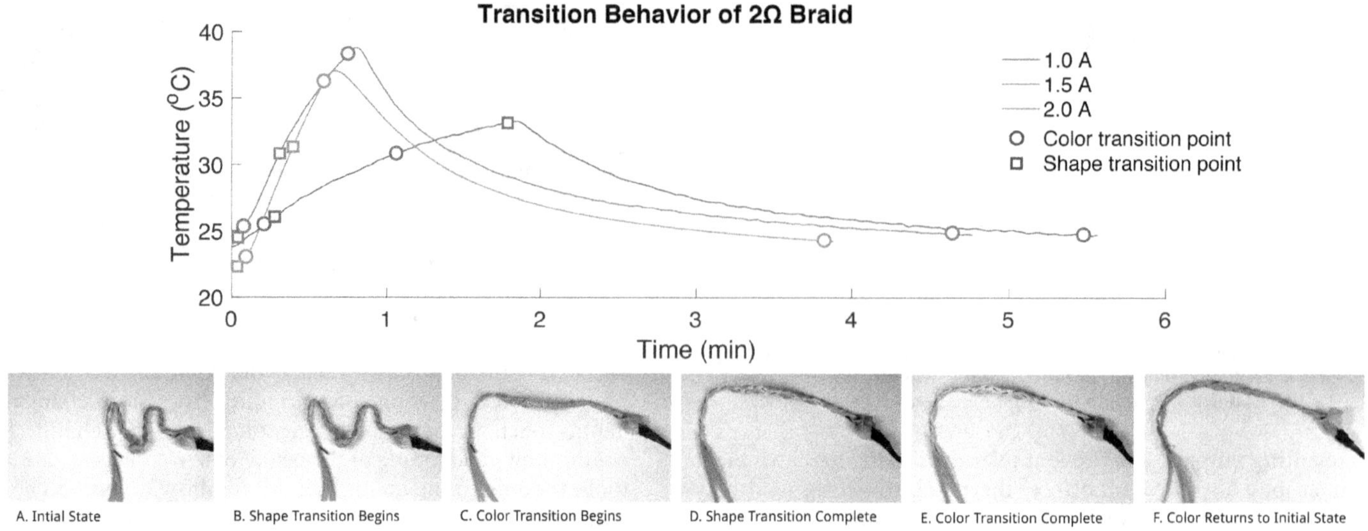

Figure 4. Transition behaviors for a HärIÖ braid with a resistance of 2Ω, at three operating currents; smoothed with a low pass filter. Typical worn operation uses a current draw of 1.5A. Photos of the braid in each transition state are of HärIÖ braid with a resistance of 2Ω at an operating current of 2.0 A; however, braids at different currents demonstrate similar effects. Note that the insulating properties of the hair affect when transitions occur; the ordering of shape and color events in transition pairs (B,C) and (D,E) switch in the 1.0A case.

ingly endless unnatural ones. They can be purchased curly, wavy, straight, and in various lengths. While paramount to intended effect and applications, the color and style of the hair extensions has minimal technical implications. Another consideration is choosing synthetic or real hair extensions. Synthetic extensions are cheaper, and are available in a wider variety of colors and styles; however, real hair extensions feel more natural to the user (see User Study) and are more robust at high temperatures. For long term applications, a user's own hair can be used instead of extensions, as long as the circuitry is protected from water.

USER STUDY

Participants

We conducted a study with eleven participants. Each had some experience styling, braiding, and touching hair (avg. age 29 yrs, 8 Female) as reported in a preliminary survey. All users had changed their hair color at least once, styled it regularly, and all but one rated themselves as proficient at French braiding, a common but more complex maneuver.

Participants were recruited from University and local mailing lists and invited to meet with us in our studio location for an hour-long workshop. They were compensated at the rate of $20/hour. We first gathered background experience with hair fashion and wearables. Participants were then invited to interact with several prototypes. These prototypes included a range of output braids, an integrated input/output braid with Bluetooth capability, and two wearable braids with specific applications: a haptic notification in which the braid subtly curls behind the users ear, and a lo-fi visual notification in which the braid slowly moves into the users field of vision. These applications are presented in more detail in the Applications section, below. Participants were encouraged to touch and stroke the braids, and given the option to wear the prototypes. We then conducted an informal interview, and finally ended with a brainstorming activity and assessment questionnaires.

Survey Results

Users reported their experience with the prototypes by answering questions on a five-point semantically anchored Likert scale (1=Strongly Agree, 5=Strongly Disagree).

Noticeability		Experience	
Ear curl	**Enter FOV**	**Comfort**	**Safety**
3.25 ± 1.4	3 ± 1.4	1.875 ± 0.6	1.1 ± 0.4

Table 4. Qualitative ranking by participants of noticeability of notification interactions, and comfort and safety.

Users rated the wearable demo as extremely comfortable and perceived it as safe. When asked to rate how safe the demos felt, all participants rated them as very safe, and no participants mentioned any discomfort from the hair interface. In fact, one participant vocalized that she expected the interface to be uncomfortable, but was pleasantly surprised by how natural it felt. The two wearable notifications received middling scores for noticeability: half of the users gave very low ratings, and half gave very high ratings. Those who didn't feel the behind-ear curling theorized that it was due to ear shape, the stems of their glasses interfering, or them moving the demo as it actuated. Those who rated the touch as highly noticeable emphasized that they "definitely would notice it". The behind-ear notification could easily be made much more dramatic, and can and should be tailored to a particular user's ear shape and around other accessories (such as glasses). Similar considerations hold for the visual notification.

Qualitative Findings

We first report survey responses (see Table 4), then present qualitative results from participant interactions with the wearable demos, and finally discuss interview responses from the end of the study. We synthesize these findings into common themes and insights for future physical design tools.

Embodied Interaction

All of our participants emphasized that the way the technology disappeared into existing form factors was very appealing. The following user immediately began twirling the hair around her fingers, as she would her real hair, saying:

P1 It doesn't feel unnatural. My body is just immediately accepting of it, like, "yes, I'd like to play with it now." My body definitely keyed into it naturally: "Oh, hair."

P6 It seems like it's a part of you.

In particular, participants appreciated the familiarity of the hair as a way to enhance the experience of the technology:

P6 Wearables can enhance your own experience of yourself.

P7 It's like a bridge between myself and the phone.

All participants confirmed that the enhanced hair felt natural and pleasantly soft.

Social/Individual

Because hair is one of the only body parts it's acceptable to interact with on another person, the shared experiences made possible by HäirIÖ were especially appealing to some:

P5 The way you swapped the braids out, it makes me think of a tradeable collectable item. I could make a braid, program it and give it to my friend who could wear it and find out what it does.

In general, when participants described interacting with other people's hair it was in extremely positive and prosocial terms:

P4 Braiding somebody's hair is more like an act of care. Something you're doing because you want to do something nice for somebody.

A participant with experience working with middle-school aged girls thought that her students would immediately be drawn to the hair as a way to connect socially:

P2 Girls that age do hair-braiding and touching as emotional and social connection.

P3 [These are] really honing in on how people react with each other, and how [they] encourage touch and creativity.

For some, the subtler versions of HäirIÖ were more appealing. Some participants liked the idea of a secretive control to surprise friends with a hidden interface control.

P7 This kind of control interface would be so hard to spot. The motion is so natural, it's so stealth.

Participants emphasized that they would sometimes like the programmed behavior to be hidden from most observers. One participant suggested that she could use the technology to train herself out of the habit of touching her hair, since she saw that as unprofessional. She did not want it to be obvious that her hair was tracking how often it was touched, and so appreciated the subtle design of the interface.

Public/Personal

From parties and costume festivals to avoiding judgment in an exercise class, participants imagined a variety of use-cases along the public-personal continuum. The majority of participants were particularly drawn to the subtle and hidden nature of our wearable technology. One participant commented on the use of inconspicuous technology as a useful tool in managing social expectations and norms around technology use. Subtlety allows for navigation of the complex social expectations that have evolved around the increasingly many ways we stay connected:

P8 I don't want them to see me responding faster to [a text message from] someone else than I do to [a text message from] them.

The surreptitious nature of the interface allowed a user to take an action without offending a friend or acquaintance. One user imagined being able to silence her phone during an exercise class, without the typical social judgment she would feel for running over to turn it off.

More than half of participants also preferred the more subtle possibilities for technology embedded in something as ubiquitous as hair. Several users' preferred display type was highly contextual, and contingent on their mood, the environment, and their goals.

The ability to vary how publicly visible HäirIÖ was allowed the technology to be imagined as integrating into a wide variety of settings, from meetings to long car rides, to parties. One saw the ability of the technology to control appearance as a potential opportunity for creating a cohesive experience at a party event:

P7 It would be amazing if you went to the party and your hair matched the theme of the party. Matched the shape or size or color and everyone in the party was doing the same thing.

Hair is a site for personal expression and style exploration and many participants immediately perceived HäirIÖ as a natural extension of that potential. They began imagining HäirIÖ as another way to experiment with different styles. All participants envisioned the hair autonomously changing color throughout the day, emphasizing how changing hairstyles affects others' perceptions of oneself. All users expressed interest in the ability to flexibly incorporate these kinds of changes into everyday life.

P9 You can't tell that it's technology but it is, so you can integrate it into your outfit.

Some participants exclusively wanted to use their hair for style or identity expression:

P11 For me hair is more an expression to everybody else, rather than it telling you to do things.

All participants recognized the potential for HäirIÖ as an engaging and eye-catching display, and imagined incorporating it into stage productions.

P2 As the frolicking innocent character enters with the creepy demon and the hair starts changing and she doesn't notice until she gets to the mirror - but the audience is seeing it.

One user imagined a specific, spectacular use-case for the hair:

P1 Drag Queens would definitely use it. They'd walk down the runway and change the color while they're going, for the spectacle of it.

Malleability/Permanence

Several participants commented on the fact that hair is a performative expression of an identity. The ability to rapidly (over the course of a day) experiment with different appearances appealed to all participants. The fact that one's hair was quickly changing would in itself become part of the identity one was performing, not just the changes themselves.

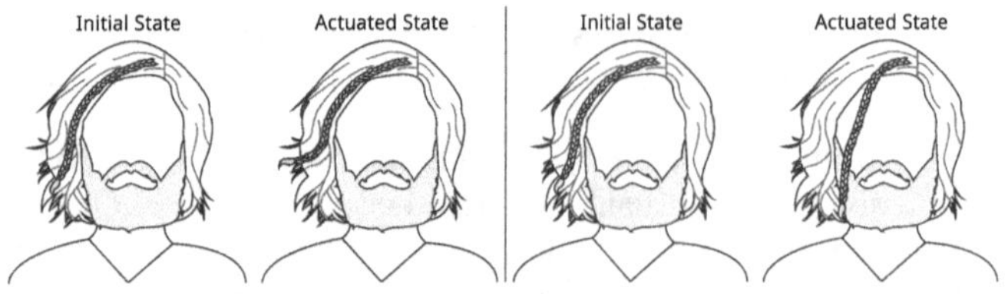

Figure 5. Illustration of two subtle notifications. Left: the actuated braid lifts slightly, protruding from the side of the head. Right: the actuated braid shifts into peripheral view. While the user would notice these subtle movements of their hair, onlookers are unlikely to notice the changes, and would likely attribute them to natural hair movement.

P10 I'm just imagining going into the bathroom with straight hair and coming out with curly hair...When you change something about your appearance, you can be perceived in a different way.

One participant commented that the extensions could be used by a developing child as a way to experiment with their growing sense of identity, and specifically focused on the temporary nature of HäirIÖ as an important piece of that exploration.

P3 I could see something like this being an extension of [gender expression]: he wants to put on his princess dress and his sparkly braid that curls.

Discussion

Overall, users expressed excitement and curiosity about the hair displays, and were intrigued by the use-cases (detailed below). The intimate nature of technology that physically blends into the body seemed particularly compelling to users, who appreciated both the possibility of a subtle interface, and the potential for more eye-catching displays. While experiencing the demos, participants described a variety of different applications, and responded to those we suggested.

APPLICATIONS

HäirIÖ leverages the unique characteristics of human hair to enable many classes of interactions. We present here a selection of proposed use cases for the initial HäirIÖ prototype.

Notifications

State changes on the head and near the face enable a wide range of notification capabilities. Depending on the location of the braid, some HäirIÖ outputs may not be visible to the user without the use of a mirror. These outputs lend themselves to unobtrusive updates and notifications that will not distract the user until they actively look for them. Besides these inconspicuous outputs, the hair can provide more intrusive outputs such as by moving itself into the user's field of view. By changing its shape, a strand of hair tucked away might slide into peripheral vision (Figure 5). This could be used for spatiotemporal cues, including hands-free navigation: the side of the head on which the hair moves would indicate the direction to turn. Participants in our study universally responded positively to this application idea, and could imagine such an interface being useful in their everyday lives.

Haptics

The shape-changing capability of the HäirIÖ braids provides both a visual and a tactile output, as the hair moves against the skin during the transition time. A HäirIÖ braid curling subtly behind the ear might not be visible to the user or an observer, but can be calibrated to be clearly felt on sensitive skin (Table 4). This can be used as an invisible, silent notification, acknowledged through capacitive sensing when the user smooths out the curl. Or, a curl may straighten itself, gently tapping a user on the shoulder or brushing their neck (Figure 7). Depending on how the hair is heated, the movement of the notification can vary – a little heat for a subtle shift, and greater heat for a more dramatic change. This variation can be achieved on the same braid, without physical modifications.

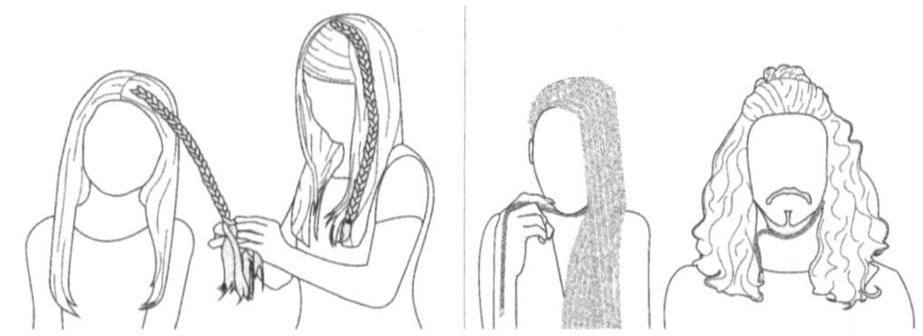

Figure 6. Illustration of two social applications of HäirIÖ . Left: interacting with a friend's HäirIÖ braid could change the color of one of your own braids. Right: Manipulating a HäirIÖ braid could cause a friend's braid to move in the same way. This application could be used for sending discreet messages during meetings, or for sending haptic messages to someone not collocated.

Most participants in our study noted that for someone who wishes to disconnect from the screen but is expecting particularly urgent messages, this kind of notification system could be very useful. Haptic interactions can extend to other use cases as well: consider a scary story enhanced by the faint tickle of hair on the back of your neck, or a comforting touch transmitted by a friend far away (Figure 6).

Public Display

Hair is often dyed and colored prior to special events. HäirIÖ confers the ability to change hair dynamically at a party or event for a more unique hair display. Changes in the braids were universally described by participants in our study as engaging, eye-catching, and interesting. Even a series of individual, small changes were considered intriguing to most participants, not just single dramatic events. During a conversation, the slow change would eventually become noticeable, prompting delight and a sense of whimsy. Changing hair might be incorporated into an intimate stage production, such as a concert or a dramatic show. One user imagined these kinds of playful displays making a big impact at a children's birthday party. Another user suggested hair could be programmed to indicate current weather conditions, or respond to mood.

With their location atop the head, HäirIÖ braids are sometimes more visible to onlookers than to the users themselves. This characteristic can be used to inform both public displays and social interactions. One participant imagined a kind of encoded side-channel: for example, hair could curl or straighten, communicating a pre-defined message during a negotiation.

Social Engagement

Interpersonal touch in hair can be both playful and intimate. Integrating input and output capabilities on the same HäirIÖ strand enables new forms of social touch. Imagine a child's braid that changes color as a friend braids it, then fades back when the interaction ends. Or imagine it maintains its color – a color unique to the friend who shaped it. Perhaps a touch on the hair causes a shape change, which invites a new touch,

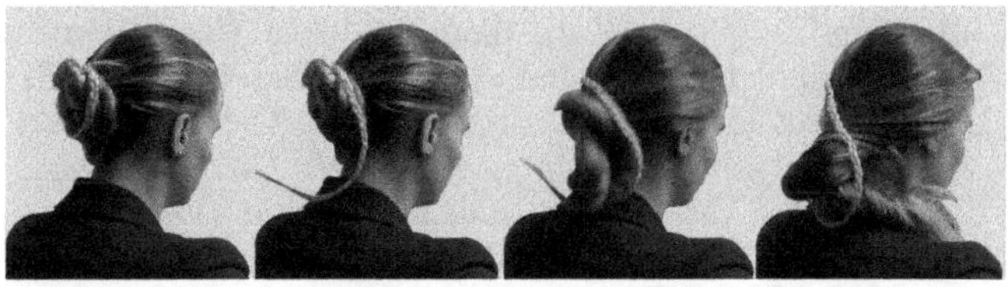

Figure 7. Physical implementation of application. HäirIÖ braid is twisted around a bun. Upon actuation, the braid begins to straighten out, unwrapping from the bun and falling on the user's shoulder. A second wire unravels similarly, and the entire bun falls down. This technique also employs haptics, as the hair movement elicits a tactile sensation.

continuing a responsive interaction. These interactions are distinct from isolated input or output: providing immediate feedback and direct output in the same interface creates a complete, self-contained world of interactions (Figure 6).

Style Changes

A final application is to enable low effort, high impact, extremely flexible hair styling. Using the bi-stable nature of SMA, we can use power only during the transition time, after which the braid will retain its new shape. Perhaps a user wants curly hair on Friday, but only to have color for the evening. Leveraging the individual strand control, the hair might change slowly over the day to build up to an exciting night-time style.

We can also use static elements, such as hair accessories and buns, to add further bi-stable features to HäirIÖ braids. For instance, a powered braid may lift and wrap around a hair clip. When the SMA is no longer being actuated and the braid releases, the static clip holds the braid in its transitioned state. Alternatively, a HäirIÖ braid may be twisted around a bun. Upon actuation, the braid could straighten out, unwrap from the bun, and fall upon the user's shoulder (Figure 7).

LIMITATIONS

The current instantiation of HäirIÖ has several practical limitations. The high power draw of the resistive heating reduces battery life, requiring frequent recharging. The heat-based actuations require careful monitoring to keep the temperatures within a comfortable range. The thermochromic pigments are not bistable and require continuous power to maintain the actuated state. Since our SMA is not currently insulated, sweat or other water could potentially cause a user to feel a tingling sensation, but this is similar to conductive thread under the same conditions. Though the size of the device can be easily reduced with smaller electronics, the size is ultimately constrained by the power source.

We implemented capacitive touch input as a proof of concept. As such, there are many limitations to our approach. We designed, implemented, and tested our system in the same laboratory under the same conditions; a calibration method is needed to generalize results. Furthermore, HäirIÖ braids are susceptible to parasitic capacitance in applications and configurations in which the braids are in direct contact with the user's neck, face, or other exposed skin. In these cases, HäirIÖ braids are liable to detect false positives for user touches. In addition, frequency of accidental touches would need to be characterized to fully assess integration into daily life, but different braiding techniques and locations could solve a variety of issues in this domain.

FUTURE WORK

We envision a world where the entire head can be responsive, autonomous, performative, or subtle. Hair that could style itself, effortlessly adjusting in response to the outside world, or computationally generating new, previously impossible fashions. It would also be possible to have someone else style one's hair, which is then remembered and replayed by the hair itself at a later time. The hair might have functional roles, such as extending into a context-dependent cellphone antenna.

We imagine a differentiated assortment of interchangeable braid designs that easily integrate and swap, and an app framework to allow individuals to author their own hair designs, surprising friends. We envision location-specific hairstyles that automatically adjust themselves. Beyond color and shape, we imagine a broad range of changing output options: polarized light, electro-luminescence, and other displays. These display options could also easily be incorporated into other hair-like objects. A stuffed animal or shaggy wall-hanging could move or change color as part of an ambient or interactive display. Fringed clothing, shoelaces, ribbons, even cables could potentially be actuated or color-changing.

While this work has tended to focus on Western styles and traditionally white hair, there are incredibly rich traditions of African braiding, weaving, and styling. Future work must expand to include other hair types, and to contextualize it within non-Western styles. We also imagine the incorporation into facial hair, such as long beards or ornate mustaches. Our current prototype uses a chalking method to apply thermochromic pigments to the braids [2]; in future iterations, we hope to utilize existing cosmetic practices to chemically dye the extensions with these pigments. If waterproofed and safely enclosed, HäirIÖ configurations could be braided into natural hair and kept/maintained for a period of time (days/weeks) such as cornrows, weaves, and other more permanent hairstyles. We hope to reduce power requirements with photovoltaics or parasitic power. As such, HäirIÖ contributes to a growing landscape of new Cosmetic Computing devices that do not need to be removed, charged, and cared for in the traditional sense [6].

CONCLUSION

HäirIÖ provides a framework for designers and individuals to create their own unique hair-based interactions, expanding the landscape of wearable devices. We hope that this work will inspire others to explore and develop across the emerging and broad palate of body sites for new interactive wearables, and that hair emerges as an exciting new body-based interactive design material.

ACKNOWLEDGEMENTS

We thank Justin Yim and Jenna Wen for their aid with implementation and fabrication, and the anonymous reviewers for their valuable feedback. This research was supported by funding from Adobe, the ARCS Foundation, and Nokia.

REFERENCES

1. 2012. Pathophysiology of thermal burn injury. (21 Nov 2012). https://www.co.pierce.wa.us/documentcenter/view/3352 [Online; posted 21-Nov-2012].
2. 2016. How to Chalk Dye Your Hair. (2016). http://www.wikihow.com/Chalk-Dye-Your-Hair
3. 2017. Fire. (17 February 2017). http://seetheunseen.co.uk/collection-archive/f-i-r-e/
4. Joanna Berzowska and Marcelo Coelho. 2005. Kukkia and Vilkas: Kinetic Electronic Garments. In *Proceedings of the 2005 Ninth IEEE International Symposium on Wearable Computers (ISWC '05)*. IEEE Computer Society, Washington, DC, USA, 82–85. DOI: http://dx.doi.org/10.1109/ISWC.2005.29
5. Laura Devendorf, Joanne Lo, Noura Howell, Jung Lin Lee, Nan-Wei Gong, M. Emre Karagozler, Shiho Fukuhara, Ivan Poupyrev, Eric Paulos, and Kimiko Ryokai. 2016. "I don't Want to Wear a screen": Probing Perceptions of and Possibilities for Dynamic Displays on Clothing. In *Proceedings of the 2016 CHI Conference on Human Factors in Computing Systems (CHI '16)*. ACM, New York, NY, USA, 6028–6039. DOI: http://dx.doi.org/10.1145/2858036.2858192
6. Christine Dierk, Tomás Vega Gálvez, and Eric Paulos. 2017. AlterNail: Ambient, Batteryless, Stateful, Dynamic Displays at your Fingertips. In *Proceedings of the 2017 CHI Conference on Human Factors in Computing Systems (CHI '17)*. ACM, New York, NY, USA. DOI: http://dx.doi.org/10.1145/3025453.3025924
7. Mads Hobye. 2012. Touche for Arduino: Advanced Touch Sensing. (2012). http://www.instructables.com/id/Touche-for-Arduino-Advanced-touch-sensing/
8. Noura Howell, Laura Devendorf, Rundong (Kevin) Tian, Tomás Vega Gálvez, Nan-Wei Gong, Ivan Poupyrev, Eric Paulos, and Kimiko Ryokai. 2016. Biosignals as Social Cues: Ambiguity and Emotional Interpretation in Social Displays of Skin Conductance. In *Proceedings of the 2016 ACM Conference on Designing Interactive Systems (DIS '16)*. ACM, New York, NY, USA, 865–870. DOI: http://dx.doi.org/10.1145/2901790.2901850
9. Oskar Juhlin. 2015. Digitizing fashion: software for wearable devices. *Interactions* 22, 3 (2015), 44–47.
10. Hsin-Liu (Cindy) Kao, Artem Dementyev, Joseph A. Paradiso, and Chris Schmandt. 2015. NailO: Fingernails as an Input Surface. In *Proceedings of the 33rd Annual ACM Conference on Human Factors in Computing Systems (CHI '15)*. ACM, New York, NY, USA, 3015–3018. DOI: http://dx.doi.org/10.1145/2702123.2702572
11. Hsin-Liu (Cindy) Kao, Christian Holz, Asta Roseway, Andres Calvo, and Chris Schmandt. 2016a. DuoSkin: rapidly prototyping on-skin user interfaces using skin-friendly materials. In *Proceedings of the 2016 ACM International Symposium on Wearable Computers (ISWc '16)*. ACM, New York, NY, USA, 16–23. DOI: http://dx.doi.org/10.1145/2971763.2971777
12. Hsin-Liu (Cindy) Kao, Manisha Mohan, Chris Schmandt, Joseph A. Paradiso, and Katia Vega. 2016b. ChromoSkin: Towards Interactive Cosmetics Using Thermochromic Pigments. In *Proceedings of the 2016 CHI Conference Extended Abstracts on Human Factors in Computing Systems (CHI EA '16)*. ACM, New York, NY, USA, 3703–3706. DOI: http://dx.doi.org/10.1145/2851581.2890270
13. Hsin-Liu (Cindy) Kao, Bichlien Nguyen, Asta Roseway, and Michael Dickey. 2017. EarthTones: Chemical Sensing Powders to Detect and Display Environmental Hazards through Color Variation. In *Proceedings of the 2017 CHI Conference Extended Abstracts on Human Factors in Computing Systems (CHI EA '17)*.
14. Nockhwan Kim, Ji Hwan Ryu, Minjae Park, Jeongho Keum, Junwoo Yoo, Jihoon Lee, and Jun Dong Cho. 2015. Smart wig for patient with chemotherapy induced alopecia: emphasis on fall detection and emergency alert. In *Proceedings of HCI Korea (HCIK '15)*. Hanbit Media, Inc., South Korea, 246–252. http://dl.acm.org/citation.cfm?id=2729522
15. Sarah Leon. 2012. Flat Iron Tips: How To Straighten Your Hair Without Damage. (3 May 2012). http://www.huffingtonpost.com/2012/03/05/flat-iron-tips_n_1316212.html [Online; posted 3-May-2012].
16. Bing Li, Dawei Zheng, Yujia Lu, Fangtian Ying, and Cheng Yao. 2017. LightingHair Slice: Situated Personal Wearable Fashion Interaction System. In *Proceedings of the 2017 CHI Conference Extended Abstracts on Human Factors in Computing Systems (CHI EA '17)*. ACM, New York, NY, USA, 1824–1828. DOI: http://dx.doi.org/10.1145/3027063.3053093
17. Joanne Lo, Doris Jung Lin Lee, Nathan Wong, David Bui, and Eric Paulos. 2016. Skintillates: Designing and Creating Epidermal Interactions. In *Proceedings of the 2016 ACM Conference on Designing Interactive Systems (DIS '16)*. ACM, New York, NY, USA, 853–864. DOI: http://dx.doi.org/10.1145/2901790.2901885
18. Desmond Morris. 2012. *Peoplewatching: The Desmond Morris Guide to Body Language*. Random House. https://books.google.com/books?id=8B_1PfLTDcMC
19. Rafael Pires-Oliveira, Franciele G. Oliveira, Tatielle S. Batista, and Inés Joekes. 2013. Specific heat capacity of cosmetically treated human hair. In *Proceedings of the 22nd Conference of the International Federation of the Societies of Cosmetic Chemists (IFSCC '13)*. 3. https://www.researchgate.net/publication/266454223_Specific_heat_capacity_of_cosmetically_treated_human_hair
20. E. Rehmi Post and Margaret Orth. 1997. Smart Fabric, or "Wearable Clothing". In *Proceedings of the 1st IEEE International Symposium on Wearable Computers (ISWC '97)*. IEEE Computer Society, Washington, DC, USA, 167–. http://dl.acm.org/citation.cfm?id=851036.856432

21. Ivan Poupyrev, Nan-Wei Gong, Shiho Fukuhara, Mustafa Emre Karagozler, Carsten Schwesig, and Karen E. Robinson. 2016. Project Jacquard: Interactive Digital Textiles at Scale. In *Proceedings of the 2016 CHI Conference on Human Factors in Computing Systems (CHI '16)*. ACM, New York, NY, USA, 4216–4227. DOI: http://dx.doi.org/10.1145/2858036.2858176

22. Munehiko Sato, Ivan Poupyrev, and Chris Harrison. 2012. Touché: enhancing touch interaction on humans, screens, liquids, and everyday objects. In *Proceedings of the SIGCHI Conference on Human Factors in Computing Systems (CHI '12)*. ACM, New York, NY, USA, 483–492. DOI:http://dx.doi.org/10.1145/2207676.2207743

23. Chao-Huai Su, Liwei Chan, Chien-Ting Weng, Rong-Hao Liang, Kai-Yin Cheng, and Bing-Yu Chen. 2013. NailDisplay: bringing an always available visual display to fingertips. In *Proceedings of the SIGCHI Conference on Human Factors in Computing Systems (CHI '13)*. ACM, New York, NY, USA, 1461–1464. DOI: http://dx.doi.org/10.1145/2470654.2466193

24. Anthony Synnott. 1987. Shame and Glory: A Sociology of Hair. *The British Journal of Sociology* 38, 3 (1987), 381–413. DOI:http://dx.doi.org/10.2307/590695

25. Hiroaki Tobita and Takuya Kuzi. 2012. SmartWig: wig-based wearable computing device for communication and entertainment. In *Proceedings of the International Working Conference on Advanced Visual Interfaces (AVI '12)*. ACM, New York, NY, USA, 299–302. DOI: http://dx.doi.org/10.1145/2254556.2254613

26. Thorstein Veblen. 1899. *The Theory of the Leisure Class*. Macmillan.

27. Katia Vega, Abel Arrieta, Felipe Esteves, and Hugo Fuks. 2014. FX e-Makeup for Muscle Based Interaction. In *Design, User Experience, and Usability. User Experience Design for Everyday Life Applications and Services (DUXU '14)*. Springer, Berlin, Heidelberg, 643–652. DOI: http://dx.doi.org/10.1007/978-3-319-07635-5_61

28. Katia Vega, Marcio Cunha, and Hugo Fuks. 2015. Hairware: The Conscious Use of Unconscious Auto-contact Behaviors. In *Proceedings of the 20th International Conference on Intelligent User Interfaces (IUI '15)*. ACM, New York, NY, USA, 78–86. DOI: http://dx.doi.org/10.1145/2678025.2701404

29. Katia Vega and Hugo Fuks. 2014a. Beauty tech nails: interactive technology at your fingertips. In *Proceedings of the 8th International Conference on Tangible, Embedded and Embodied Interaction (TEI '14)*. ACM, New York, NY, USA, 61–64. DOI: http://dx.doi.org/10.1145/2540930.2540961

30. Katia Vega and Hugo Fuks. 2014b. Beauty Technology: Body Surface Computing. *Computer* 47, 4 (April 2014), 71–75. http://dx.doi.org/10.1109/MC.2014.81

31. Katia Fabiola Canepa Vega, Patricia J. Flanagan, and Hugo Fuks. 2013. Blinklifier: A Case Study for Prototyping Wearable Computers in Technology and Visual Arts. In *Design, User Experience, and Usability. User Experience in Novel Technological Environments (DUXU '13)*. Springer, Berlin, Heidelberg, 439–445. DOI: http://dx.doi.org/10.1007/978-3-642-39238-2_4

32. Martin Weigel, Tong Lu, Gilles Bailly, Antti Oulasvirta, Carmel Majidi, and Jürgen Steimle. 2015. iSkin: Flexible, Stretchable and Visually Customizable On-Body Touch Sensors for Mobile Computing. In *Proceedings of the 33rd Annual ACM Conference on Human Factors in Computing Systems (CHI '15)*. ACM, New York, NY, USA, 2991–3000. DOI: http://dx.doi.org/10.1145/2702123.2702391

33. Martin Weigel, Aditya Shekhar Nittala, Alex Olwal, and Jrgen Steimle. SkinMarks: Enabling Interactions on Body Landmarks Using Conformal Skin Electronics. ACM Press, 3095–3105. DOI: http://dx.doi.org/10.1145/3025453.3025704

34. Naomi Wolf. 1990. *The Beauty Myth*. Chatto & Windus. https://books.google.com/books?id=D0naAAAAMAAJ

Integrating Textile Materials with Electronic Making: Creating New Tools and Practices

Irene Posch
TU Wien
Vienna, Austria
irene.posch@tuwien.ac.at

Geraldine Fitzpatrick
TU Wien
Vienna, Austria
geraldine.fitzpatrick@tuwien.ac.at

ABSTRACT
We introduce and discuss the design and use of new tools for electronic textile making. Electronic textiles, or eTextiles, are increasingly produced and used in experimental interfaces, wearables, interior design, as well as in the education and maker cultures. However, the field relies on tools specific to either the textile or the electronic domain, neglecting the distinct requirements, and potentials, of their intersection. To address this gap, we explored the design of new tools, targeted at specific needs and use cases of electronic textile making and the materials used. Three resulting prototypes have been evaluated through use in both our own practice and among a group of experts in the field. Our findings show the importance of specialized tools for routines essential to the field eTextiles, their role for the emergence of new practices, as well as for the understanding of the discipline.

Author Keywords
Crafts, Design, DIY, eTextiles, Making Cultures, Maker, Textiles, Tools, Wearables

ACM Classification Keywords
• **Human-centered computing~User studies** • *Human-centered computing~Systems and tools for interaction design* • *Human-centered computing~Ubiquitous and mobile computing*

INTRODUCTION
Recent years have been dominated by the spread of computational technologies and computer mediated interactions beyond the screen into the physical world, into growing areas of everyday life. This also includes the field of electronic textiles [3, 13, 15, 18]. Advanced technological developments [8, 19, 20] as well as educational and DIY kits [4, 22] have made electronic components accessible to the integration with textiles, fostering the expansion of computational technologies into textile domains. However, their development has been mostly discussed from a perspective of technological achievement, neglecting the processes and interactions that bring the electronic textile artefacts into being. Even the explorations of craft approaches in the domain of electronic textiles [5, 7, 16, 17] have largely been made using legacy electronic or textile crafting tools. The experiment undertaken here is to design new tools that account for both textile and electronic requirements when working on eTextiles [23]. We especially want to design for a textile making practice including electronic functionalities, rather than electronics that also incorporate some textiles. The purpose is to intervene in the existing tool space, and inquire about potential new routines, possibilities, and values within the domain.

TEI '18, March 18–21, 2018, Stockholm, Sweden
 ACM ISBN 978-1-4503-5568-1/18/03…$15.00
https://doi.org/10.1145/3173225.3173255

BACKGROUND AND MOTIVATION
Electronic textiles, or eTextiles, describe textiles or fabrics that enable digital and electronic functionalities to be embedded in them. The use of textiles for electronic and computational applications has been explored through the crafting of conductive and resistive threads in specific patterns to hold electronic functions [16, 17] and the combination of textile materials with custom electronics and circuit boards [5], among them the commercially available Arduino Lilypad [12] and the Adafruit Flora [22].

Discourse and developments in the field of eTextile kits have mostly focused on making electronic components connectable on and with textiles with the goal to incorporate the qualities inherent to the textile material - its softness, flexibility, and aesthetics - into new uses and interaction scenarios. Studies of the use of such kits have shown their potential to attract a different user group to computational technologies [4, 6]. Current instructions and kits include conductive thread and a needle for sewing conductive thread, and use the same tools electronics use for decades for electric measuring and connecting tasks [8, 22]. They propagate novel outputs combining textiles and electronics, however, they do not reference the changed production possibilities of an integrated electronic textile practice.

The design of new tools is motivated by the wish to account for the specific needs when working with electronic textiles. Tools cannot be considered neutral. Their form, function and cultural embedding explicitly or implicitly include or exclude specific experiences, insights, and goals

[14]. Examining the tools allows us to look outside the work itself, the conditions that make it possible in the first place [1]. Tools are not just important to functionally complete tasks, but often also take on a role to figuratively stand for a practice. Historically established stereotypes surface, suggesting who uses the tool, in what domain it is used, and what artefacts it brings into being [2]. In a research through design process we want to explore what tools specific to a practice of electronic textile crafts might look like? What would the availability of targeted tools mean for the practice of eTextiles?

METHODOLOGY

We approached the task giving high importance to the pondering of material cultures, aesthetics, and context of use in the design process in order to create tools that reflect the functional as well as formal needs of the practice.

The research presented here discusses the genesis, design, and evaluation of three versions of measurement/power tools, that we named *eTextile Tape*, *Travel Tester*, and *eTextile Tester*. We engaged in this work from the position of reflective practitioners in the field, using personal practice as the first point of investigation. Observation and reflection on the practice, tools, and routines regularly used by the first author over the duration of two months marked the starting point of the design process.

Within the design process, all three tools underwent several design iterations to reach the level of elaborated prototypes usable in everyday making. We base our explorations on the use of these prototypes within established eTextile practices to understand the role of specific tools.

The *eTextile Tape* and *Travel Tester* were informally tested through their integration in the personal practice of the first author. The experiences gained from this consequently informed the design of the third tool, the *eTextile Tester*. This tool was given to a group of 28 practitioners in the field with a follow-up questionnaire one year later. To probe the unbiased integration and usage of the tool into their practices, we did not announce that we might ask in the future about their experiences with the tool. The online questionnaire asked quantitative and qualitative questions about their experiences, and probed the role of the tool for the practices of this group of experts. The thematic analysis of their feedback is the basis for the discussion of our findings.

EXPLORING FORM AND FUNCTION

Reflecting on the experiences of the first author in their own making practices, we identified making contact to the textile material to measure electric continuity and to apply power as essential key routines in the making of textile electronic artefacts. In conventional electronics applications, testing continuity is done with a multimeter. Multimeters are used for testing a wide array of industrial and household devices. They have multiple measurement functions, such as electric current, voltage and resistance, to select from, and are designed to withstand high currents and rough working environments. To take the measurement, two multimeter probes are put in contact with the device under test, and the result is displayed on the meter. Electrical continuity is usually indicated through a beeping sound. Standard multimeters do not supply power.

Working in the domain of electronic textiles, creating a circuit poses different challenges than working with conventional hardware electronics. Applications are in a low-power range and the materials are soft and often delicate to handle. Conductive threads are used to construct connections rather than insulated cables. Mostly realizing custom designs, connections have to be designed and realized from scratch, including connecting hardware parts to textile elements where no standard solutions exist. Consequently, there is an increased need for testing the actual functionality of established connections, as well as to test for potential short circuits of the conductive textile materials. Applying power allows testing the circuit, or parts of it, before it is finally connected. It allows probing the functionality of electronic components that are about to be used. Integrating components in eTextile projects is often more labour intensive than in conventional electronic projects, hence knowing the component functions is especially helpful. In the following, we describe our explorations of tools to address these challenges.

Design 1: From Textile Tool to eTextile Tool

In our approach to look at eTextiles as electronic textile crafts, we turned towards textile cultures, skills, and techniques for inspiration. Studying the textile tool space we noticed the tailor's tape as omnipresent in textile craft studios to measure lengths, one of the main measuring tasks in textile making. This led us to explore interaction scenarios towards one of the main measuring tasks of electronics: electric conductivity; And so to make an *eTextiler's Tape*.

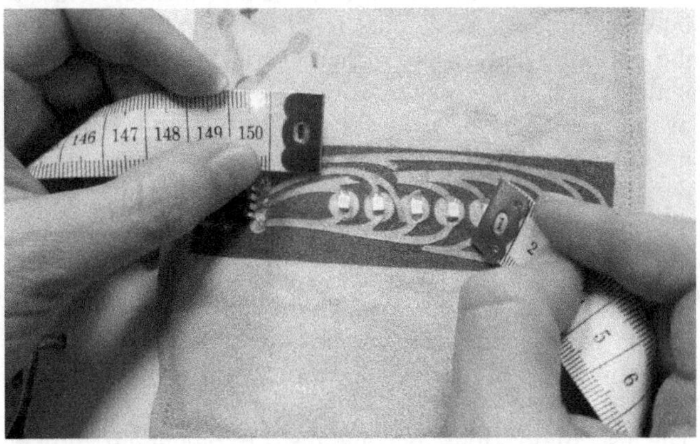

Figure 1. Testing scenario with the eTextiler's Tape. The ends of the tape touch the material under test, essentially working as a switch to the circuit. If the material is conductive the circuit closes, the LED lights up to indicate the conductivity.

The tape measure or tailor's tape is part of the standard equipment of sewing baskets. It is essentially a flexible ruler, usually 1,5 meters (or 60 inches) long and between 0,7 and 1,5 cm wide with the cm or inch measurements printed along the length. It is made of durable but flexible and light material. It most commonly features metal handles at its ends, probably to prevent fraying of the material and to clearly mark the endpoints. Since its introduction in the 19th century, it has become a ubiquitously used and iconic textile tool. Tailors often 'wear' the tape around their neck, the tape being always within fast reach of the hand even when wandering around the studio or moving around a client to take measurements.

To appropriate the tailor's tape as an eTextile tool, we used the metal fastenings at the end to make electrical contact to conductive materials. We scratched the surface for increased conductivity and connected the ends with conductive thread to form an electric circuit including an LED and a 3V coin cell integrated into the tape. The LED is mounted close to the end, lighting up when the circuit is closed – when both metal ends touch a continuously conductive material. A tool very commonly used for measuring tasks in textile practices now becomes a tool for one of the essential measuring needs of electronic work: a tool to measure the length as well as the conductivity of a textile (Figure 1).

An additional switch allows switching between two modes: testing continuity and applying 3V power. When switched to the power mode, the ends connect the device under test to the positive and negative terminal of the coin cell, applying power when the circle is closed. When switched to the testing mode, the LED lights up when there is an electrically conductive connection between the two ends.

Our own reflective usage of the tool over a year highlighted a few points worth noting: The tool fulfilled the practical expectations: We could get feedback about the conductivity of a material through the LED and apply 3V to circuits or components. The interaction with the tool was very close to interaction scenarios known from tailoring. Worn around the neck, the ends to probe the material were conveniently within reach of our hands. However, while the metal ends of the tape could be used as a connecting probe, they did not allow for high precision. Also, the tool design needed the probes to always be held manually during the measuring, as there is no possibility to fix it to the material.

Apart from these practical experiences, we also received interesting reactions from people whenever we showed the tool in workshops or presentations to audiences of makers and novices in the field. The iconic form and handling of the tool clearly placed it into the context of textile crafts. The use of the tool, making the LED light up through electric conductivity, bridged the textile context with an electronic circuit. This straightforward combination of textile aesthetics and electronic functionality embedded in the tool, prompted immediate ideas about the production space of electronic textiles.

Design 2: Adapting to New Material Contexts

The goal of the second tooling experiment was to design a 'ready at hand' tool to detect conductive materials for potential inclusion within an eTextile practice. The *Travel Tester* is a tool to always take along when on the look out for new materials that fulfil aesthetic and haptic qualities, as well as hold desired conductive properties.

Metallic materials have been produced and used in textile crafts for centuries, with early written mentions dating back to the Old Testament [10]. A variety of wires and threads spun out of gold, silver or copper, and also beads and jewellery elements, traditionally appreciated for ornamental reasons, are of potential interest for eTextile practices for their conductive properties [18]. Today these materials are a rare find. Lurex is often used as a replacement, mimicking the metallic appearance without possessing its material properties. Our experience showed, that sellers often do not know about the composition of the materials they are selling. As electric conductivity is not a prime concern for them or their customers, the materials are not sorted according to their conductivity, and sellers are not prepared or able to answer related questions.

To make it easier to find these materials and so make them accessible to the field of eTextiles, we developed a prototype consisting of a black ribbon with conductive ends. If the points touch a continuous conductive material a circuit is closed and the LED lights up (Figure 2a and 2b). Folded up it fits easily in a bag or pocket.

Figure 2a and 2b. A small travel tool in use at a market in Turkey (2a, top) and India (2b, bottom), looking for local materials of potential for electronic textile practices.

Our experiences of bringing the tool to shops to test different materials have been very positive. Often the sellers were as interested as we were to learn if a material was conductive or not, and to learn what we would do with this information. Motivated by seeing the LED light up, sellers started looking for more materials and artefacts we could test for their conductive properties. In presenting them to us and waiting for the LED to light up, they would often also talk about the 'original' use context of a specific material, or the specific purpose of an artefact we were looking at.

The *eTextiler's Tape* was an experiment to translate electronic functionality onto an existing textile tool. The *Travel Tester* aimed at making a tool for detecting conductive materials as portable as possible. Building on these two distinct approaches, the motivation for the third tool was to design a portable tool that lives within a studio practice of eTextiles.

Design 3: Designing for New Practices

The *eTextile Tester* allows for continuity testing and supplying of 3V, but in a different form than the tape tool we previously introduced. Again inspired by materials and routines of textile crafts, it uses pins to connect to the device under test. Pins have been used to fastening diverse objects or soft material together for centuries, but have an especially strong connotation of being sewing equipment, often seen symbiotically with the practice [2]. Pins, made out of thin, sharpened metal wire, are pierced through the material to hold it together or place a mark. They are a precise, firm and temporary way to connect (to) textile material. Being metal, they are also conductive. In the design of the *eTextile Tester* these formal and functional properties of a pin are repurposed: they become the probe to electrically connect to the textile material (Figure 3).

The design of the *eTextile Tester* is primarily driven by practical considerations to create a small and flexible electronic tool that integrates well with the materials and routines of textile crafts: The body of the *eTextile Tester* is a small almond shaped 3D print, holding the coin cell and the switch to choose between the two modes, with labels indicating which mode is selected. Each side of the body extends to a cord that ends with a pin. To integrate well with textile practices, the connecting cord consists of a flexible conductive core coated with a braided textile cord, producing a thin and flexible insulated textile conductor. They are long enough so that the tool can be worn around the neck, similar to the tailor's tape. The connection of the pin to the cord is covered with a 3D printed handle, enlarging the area to grasp the pin. The handles are of different size and colour, and labelled to differentiate between the anode and cathode of the coin cell. An LED, lighting up if electric continuity is detected, is integrated within the bigger, yellow pinhead. When not in use, the pins can be stuck into the felt cover of the almond shape body (Figure 4a-d).

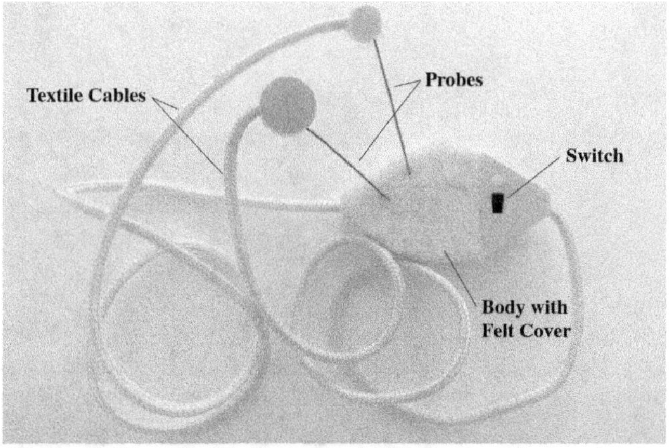

Figure 3. The eTextile Tester tool: Pins are used as probes to electrically connect to the textile material. They are connected to the battery in the body of the tool through a textile cable. A switch enables selecting between supplying 3V or measuring electric continuity. The LED indicating continuity is included in the yellow handle of the tool. When the pins are not in use they can be stuck into the felt cover.

USING AND EVALUATING THE ETEXTILE TESTER

The evaluation of the *eTextile Tester* focused on its integration within the existing practices of eTextile practitioners. The hypothesis was that, as active makers, they were the target audience.

Participants were accessed via an annual eTextile workshop meeting of practitioners in the field. Each participant was invited to contribute physical work samples to an eTextile Swatchbook in exchange for other participant's swatches [11]. The *eTextile Tester* in the form shown above was included as one such swatch, given to 28 participants. The tool was mounted in the book in a way that it could easily be taken out to use and was complemented by a brief description [9]. A practical demonstration of how to use the tool was given during the workshop. The group of recipients was predominantly female (five male participants). They came from three different continents and were of diverse ages, the majority of the group being between 30 and 40 years. They had individual backgrounds in the fields of design, textile, fashion, and engineering, but all had an established eTextile practice of their own.

The survey we sent them via email after a year included a total of ten quantitative and qualitative questions about the adoption of the tool into their routines, and the role the tool took within their practice.

Out of the 28 recipients, 16 completed the survey (P1-P16). Out of the 16, two said they never used the tool: One said they did not do any practical work in the field of electronic textiles over the past year (P1), the other one said they wanted to keep the tool in its original form within the Swatchbook (P16). Three people said they tried it but did not usually use it when working on eTextile projects because they preferred using a multimeter (P13, P15) or did not remember it at the right moment (P14).

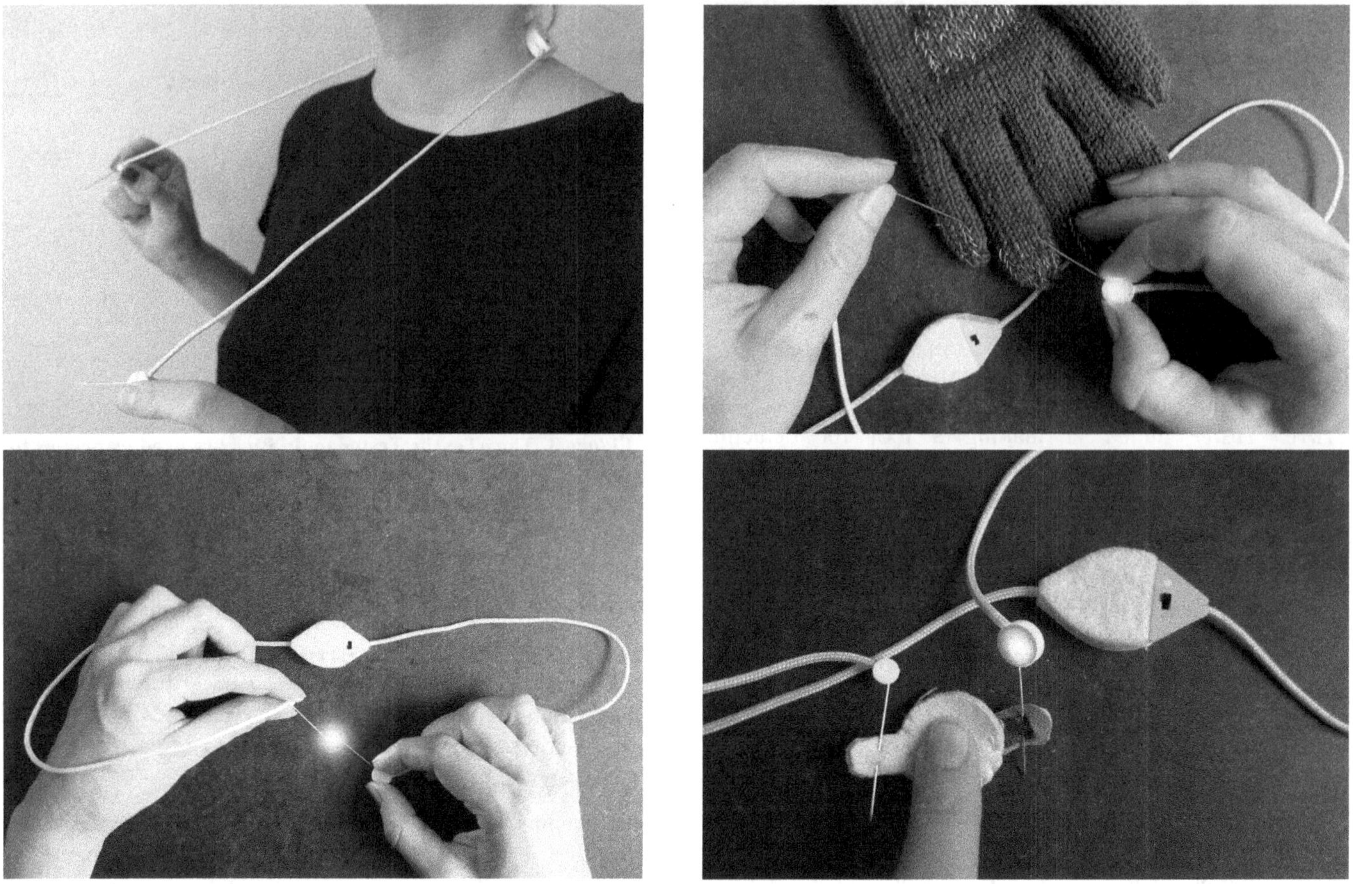

Figure 4a,b,c,d. Example scenarios of the eTextile Tester in use: interacting with the tool, testing and applying power to electronic textile projects. Top left, 4a: "Wearing" the tool around the neck, ready to use. Top right, 4b: Applying 3V to test the functionality of a small LED. Bottom left, 4c: Testing connections in a knitted circuit in touching the yarn with the pins. Bottom right, 4d: Pinning the probes to a textile artefact (here, a textile button) to test if contact is established.

The remaining 11 participants used it to various degrees: Three people said they used the tool, but mainly to demonstrate the other swatches in the book (e.g. applying power to other swatches or demonstrating conductive materials). Seven people said they used the tool on some of their eTextile projects, one said they used it on half of their projects (P5). They described using the tool with diverse conductive fibre and thread based techniques and materials: knitting, crocheting, weaving, felting, embroidering, and sewing in the making of textile sensors, circuits, and fabric circuit boards. Extending the textile domain, two of them stated they also used it on materials other than textiles (P3, P6), the small and light weight size of the tool being *"convenient for situations where [the multimeter] is too big or heavy"* (P3).

"something easy and effective to use!"

12 out of 16 participants stated the tool being beneficial to their work with eTextiles. Participants who used the tool most mentioned its small and light design (P3, P6, P9, P10, P11) and the *"handy"* (P6, P9, P11) form as most beneficial for their practice. Participants commented on its form as *"friendly to use"* (P4), *"attractive"* (P7), *"aesthetic"* (P9), and *"Nice Design!"* (P2). It was most contrasted to the multimeter, with several participants describing it as *"easy"* or *"easier"* (P7, P8, P11, 12,) for *"fast basic testing"* (P4). The additional function to supply power was positively received: *"I normally would have to put a battery in a battery holder and attach crocodile clips to it - this makes it easier!"* (P8). Users described the pins as *"pointy probes"* that they could *"securely attach to textile, but not damaging it the way alligator clips can"* (P15). This made it possible to *"pin the tester into the circuit and leave it there to test continuity over time, especially in actively moving or interactive e-textile projects. I can see how the connectivity behaves through the LED, while my hands are busy with the interaction"* (P12). The light output as feedback for connectivity was also mentioned positively: *"if you get annoyed by the beep short circuit tester [the continuity signal of the multimeter] [...] it illuminates the spot where you measure"* (P3). One participant summarized the main benefit for their practice as providing *"a sense of immediacy: it allows to quickly test sensors and debug traces, etc."* (P5).

Participants gave explicit descriptions of the scenarios of use of the tester tool in supplying 3V: testing the polarity of small LEDs (P6), testing if an LED or buzzer motor works

(P3, P9) testing specific custom made components (P7), as well as powering circuits (P3, P8). They were even more precise in providing accounts of using the continuity-testing mode within their practice: checking the connections between textile and electronic components (P9) or the continuity between two conductive lines or in complex traces (P3, P5, P9). One mentioned using the brightness of the LED as a visual indicator for the resistance (P5). Other users (P10, P11) noted they used specifically when working with (very) thin yarns. Unlike with conventional multimeter probes, they would *"pin it straight into the combined materials"*, or *"wind the pin end directly into the threads"* (P11). One said that they would pin the *eTextile Tester* to the textile artefact to have their hands free when testing the interaction of an artefact: The LED light indicates if a switch was closed properly and as reliably as intended (P12).

The analysis shows that the majority used both functions of the tool. Among those using only one function, the group using it to test continuity was slightly bigger than those using it to apply 3V. Among those who reported using the tool at least sometimes, four participants said the tool (partially) replaced the multimeter. Six people said it replaced custom constructions to apply 3V for testing components or circuits. For others, it did not replace a specific tool but was an extension to the toolkit they were already using.

The questionnaire also asked about the problems people faced when working with the tool. Most problems concerned the physical realization of the tool: the LED having a loose contact or being broken (P3, P9), the coin cell being drained (P4, P7), or the top of the body coming loose from time to time (P2, 12). One participant mentioned that the probes were too small to be grabbed quickly (P6), while another observed that the probes were not suitable to be pinned to coated materials as they left a hole there (P11). While the *"thin and pointy"* probes were predominantly mentioned as a positive feature of the tool, one person said that this shape made it hard to make good contact on certain threads or surfaces (P12). Rather a suggestion than a complaint, some participants wished for wider functionality, either the tool itself incorporating more elements of a multimeter (P4, P5) or a modular way to integrate it into a multimeter (P2, P5, P15).

"the tester is much more textile"

The questionnaire also asked about new or altered practices potentially enabled by the tool. One person specifically mentioned the portability of the tool as relevant to their practice (P6). Other descriptions focused on how the pin probes allowed for new ways to make contact with the material. Participants mentioned how the pins allowed for a *"much better"*, connection as the usually used *"crocodile clips are too clumsy"* (P11). They also mentioned being able to make contact to material *"where even small multimeter clips try to cramp"* (P11), and being able to *"place the needles more precise at the testing area"* (P9). This made the tool being perceived as "*much more textile in its use*" (P11). Another user mentioned how it influenced their actual making routine *"I use the multimeter often in a sequential manner (first make, then measure, make a change, then measure again). With the eTextile Tester, it became easier to work in a simultaneous manner (measure while making)"* (P12). On a more abstract level, another participant stated: *"It galvanized me to brainstorm and explore designing other customized tools to support my practice"* (P5). The participant further stated that being introduced to research on making of new tools for the practice of eTextiles had *"a profound impact on how I think about, describe, and approach eTextiles/eCraft as a field. Not only are they extremely helpful, but they provide a tangible provocation to discuss and problematize the space. These tool mashups embody the intersection of the fields we pull from and ground eTextiles as a separate, discrete field"* (P5).

DISCUSSION

The goals of our approach of designing and then using new tools for an emerging eTextile practice have been both to explore tools that highlight the textile material and cultures within electronic textile making practices, as well as how the availability of targeted tools influences the practice. Our user study specifically focused on the last prototype, the *eTextile Tester*, collecting feedback from a group of eTextile practitioners about its use and role. In the following we discuss the results, focusing on the themes of design, practice, and adoption in relation to a new tool.

Tools Matter

A dominant part of the feedback from participants was concerned with new possibilities to contact to textile fabrics and threads. The pointy and thin shape of the pin allowed for precision in selecting the point of contact and in piercing through the fabric for temporary, minimally invasive, hands-free connection to the textile material. It physically extended the reach to textile materials that otherwise could not, or not as easily without damage, be electrically connected. It also extended the reach of the pin, a tool strongly associated with textile crafts, into the field of electronics, becoming both literally and figuratively the point of connection between textiles and electronics, embodying the integration of textile and electronic fields.

Our goal was to value the practice and materials of the craft, a decision we see validated in the participants' feedback. They could use the tool as intended and appreciated the functionalities introduced. The approach of referencing established textile tools in the design, and functionally mapping their tasks to the field of electronics, while drawing on familiar routines, proved suitable in this endeavour. The users' feedback also reinforced our assumption that a tool is not just a physical artefact for manipulation or measuring, but also an object of identification; the availability of specific tools potentially contributing to the grounding of the practice as discrete discipline.

New Material Interactions

Apart from describing how established routines could be improved to fit the textile context, participants also described how the use of the *eTextile Tester* allowed for new routines to be included in their practice. Measuring electric continuity is foreign to textile craft, as is a continuous, physical, aesthetic driven design process to electronics. Using existing tools from either domain thus inherently ignores essential aspects of electronic textile making processes.

What one participant called "*measure while making*" points to the potential transformation tools can have on a discipline. *eTextile Tester* now render an essential quality of the artefact, electric conductivity, perceivable to the maker. This additional information enables new routines for exercising judgment, dexterity, and care in the making, essential qualities of crafting processes [21]. Not only aesthetic decisions influence the next step to be taken, but also electrical aspects not per se visible to the human eye.

Adopting New Tools

Although the feedback points to relevant contributions to the practice of those who used it, attracting new users proved more challenging than we expected. Including the tool in the eTextile Swatchbook seemed a good way to reach a target group active and interested in the field of electronic textiles as they would be able to judge the potential improvement within their practice. However, some considered the Swatchbook a precious collection they wanted to preserve and thus did not remove the tool to use it. Also worth noting is that all recipients had already an established practice, meaning they had to actively remember the new tool and change their previous routines to include it. We interpret the fact that still half of the people answering our survey did adopt the tool and adapt their practices to its use as proof of its potential to fill a gap in eTextile making routines but are also aware that changing routines can be difficult.

The tools presented here are experiments towards a practice that integrates electronics and textiles in the making. They illustrate the statement: *"Designing for the post digital does not mean blindly embracing nostalgia or turning away from technology – it means demystifying the digital through the design process and encouraging designs that equalize the status of digital and analogue, both in the materials and the practices"* [24]. Our research to date suggests that tools matter toward reaching this goal. Their design influences how we interact with the electronic and material properties in the making. They are a physical argument for an integrated practice inclusive of both textile and electronic properties. Even at the state of functional prototypes, they shaped the processes and the self-understanding of a discipline among the groups of experts that used them.

CONCLUSION

The research discussed covers the genesis and application of a new tool instantiated in three designs combining electronic functionality with traditional textile craft tools: the *eTextilers Tape* building on an established textile tool to perform eTextile measurements, the *Travel Tester* as a portable tool to easily test the conductivity of newly found materials in situ, and the *eTextile Tester* repurposing pins to not only connect materials but also electrically connect to them.

The study investigated the usage of the tool among eTextile practitioners over the duration of a year. The tool was well received by the participants. They provided positive feedback about the design and use of the tool and valuable insights into the tools new form and functional possibilities easing routines or allowing for new ways of working, as well as thinking about, in the field of eTextiles. It also pointed at possible improvements in a next design iteration, addressing parts becoming loose or breaking over time.

Future research will look at a wider set of tools relevant to the practice. While in this study we focused on practitioners, we are also specifically interested to explore how tools influence the access and understanding of a discipline among novice users, what role they play in framing the potentials and possibilities of a discipline. Directing what tools are used - how things are made - might eventually also influence what is being made, and by whom.

ACKNOWLEDGEMENTS

This research was supported by the project Stitching Worlds (www.stitchingworlds.net) funded by the Austrian Science Fund (FWF): AR 284-G21, initially developed as part of a workshop by Ebru Kurbak, Hannah Perner-Wilson, Irene Posch and Mika Satomi. We would like to thank all the participants of our study, as well as our colleagues and reviewers for helpful comments.

REFERENCES

1. Glenn Adamson. 2013. *The Invention of Craft.* Bloomsbury Academic.
2. Mary C. Beaudry. 2006. Findings: the material culture of needlework and sewing. Yale University Press.
3. Joanna Berzowska. 2005. Electronic Textiles: Wearable Computers, Reactive Fashion, and Soft Computation. *TEXTILE* 3, 1 (May 2005), 58 - 75.
4. Leah Buechley, Mike Eisenberg, Jaime Catchen, and Ali Crockett. 2008. The LilyPad Arduino: using computational textiles to investigate engagement, aesthetics, and diversity in computer science education. In *Proceedings of the SIGCHI Conference on Human Factors in Computing Systems* (CHI '08). 423-432. https://doi.org/10.1145/1357054.1357123
5. Leah Buechley and Michael Eisenberg. 2009. Fabric PCBs, electronic sequins, and socket buttons: techniques for e-textile craft. *Personal Ubiquitous*

Computing. 13, 2 (February 2009), 133-150. http://dx.doi.org/10.1007/s00779-007-0181-0

6. Leah Buechley and Benjamin Mako Hill. 2010. LilyPad in the wild: how hardware's long tail is supporting new engineering and design communities. In *Proceedings of the 8th ACM Conference on Designing Interactive Systems* (DIS '10). ACM, New York, NY, USA, 199-207. DOI:http://doi.acm.org/10.1145/1858171.1858206
7. Leah Buechley and Hannah Perner-Wilson. 2012. Crafting technology: Reimagining the processes, materials, and cultures of electronics. *ACM Trans. Comput.-Hum. Interact.* 19, 3, Article 21 (October 2012), 21 pages. DOI: https://doi.org/10.1145/2362364.2362369
8. Laura Devendorf, Joanne Lo, Noura Howell, Jung Lin Lee, Nan-Wei Gong, M. Emre Karagozler, Shiho Fukuhara, Ivan Poupyrev, Eric Paulos, and Kimiko Ryokai. 2016. "I don't Want to Wear a Screen": Probing Perceptions of and Possibilities for Dynamic Displays on Clothing. In *Proceedings of the 2016 CHI Conference on Human Factors in Computing Systems* (CHI '16). ACM, New York, NY, USA, 6028-6039. https://doi.org/10.1145/2858036.2858192
9. eTextile Tester. 2015. In *eTextile Swatchbook 2015.* Retrieved June 23 2017 from http://etextile-summercamp.org/swatch-exchange/etextiles-tester/
10. Sophie Fürnkranz. 2005. Metallstickerei im Außereuropäischen Raum: Beispiele aus der Sammlung des Weltmuseums Wien. In *Technologische Studien, Kunsthistorisches Museum: Konservierung - Restaurierung - Forschung – Technologie. Band 2.* Wilfried Seipel (ed.). KHM-Museumsverband, Wien, AT, 10 - 49.
11. Anja Hertenberger, Barbro Scholz, Beam Contrechoc, Becky Stewart, Ebru Kurbak, Hannah Perner-Wilson, Irene Posch, Isabel Cabral, Jie Qi, Katharina Childs, Kristi Kuusk, Lynsey Calder, Marina Toeters, Marta Kisand, Martijn ten Bhömer, Maurin Donneaud, Meg Grant, Melissa Coleman, Mika Satomi, Mili Tharakan, Pauline Vierne, Sara Robertson, Sarah Taylor, and Troy Robert Nachtigall. 2014. 2013 e-textile swatchbook exchange: the importance of sharing physical work. In *Proceedings of the 2014 ACM International Symposium on Wearable Computers: Adjunct Program* (ISWC '14 Adjunct). ACM, New York, NY, USA, 77-81. http://dx.doi.org/10.1145/2641248.2641276
12. LilyPad Arduino Main Board. Retreived June 30 2017 from https://www.arduino.cc/en/Main/ArduinoBoardLilyPad
13. Diana Marculescu, Radu Marculescu, Nicholas H. Zamora, Philipp Stanley-Marbell, Pradeep K. Khosla, Sungmee Park, Sundaresan Jayaraman, Stefan Jung, Christl Lauterbach, Werner Weber, Tünde Kirstein, Didies Cottet, Janusz Grzyb, Gerhard Tröster, Mark Jones, Tom Martin, Zahi Nakad. 2003. Electronic textiles: A platform for pervasive computing. *Proceedings of the IEEE*, 91, 12, (December 2003), 1995-2018.
14. Cara McCarty and Matilda McQuaid (eds.). 2015. *Tools: Extending our Reach.* Cooper Hewitt, Smithsonian Design Museum, New York, NY.
15. Kylie Peppler. 2016. A review of e-textiles in education and society. In *Handbook of research on the societal impact of digital media, Barbara Guzzetti and Mellinee Lesley (eds.).* IGI Global, Hershey, PA, 219-241.
16. Hannah Perner-Wilson, Leah Buechley, and Mika Satomi. 2010. Handcrafting textile interfaces from a kit-of-no-parts. In *Proceedings of the fifth international conference on Tangible, embedded, and embodied interaction* (TEI '11). ACM, New York, NY, USA, 61-68. http://dx.doi.org/10.1145/1935701.1935715
17. Irene Posch and Ebru Kurbak. 2016. CRAFTED LOGIC Towards Hand-Crafting a Computer. In *Proceedings of the 2016 CHI Conference Extended Abstracts on Human Factors in Computing Systems* (CHI EA '16). ACM, New York, NY, USA, 3881-3884. https://doi.org/10.1145/2851581.2891101
18. E. Rehmi Post and Margaret Orth. 1997. Smart Fabric, or "Wearable Clothing". In *Proceedings of the 1st IEEE International Symposium on Wearable Computers* (ISWC '97), 167-168.
19. E. Rehmi Post, Margaret Orth, Peter R. Russo, and Neil Gershenfeld. 2000. E-broidery: design and fabrication of textile-based computing. *IBM Systems Journal,* 39, 3.4 (July 2000), 840-860. http://dx.doi.org/10.1147/sj.393.0840
20. Ivan Poupyrev, Nan-Wei Gong, Shiho Fukuhara, Mustafa Emre Karagozler, Carsten Schwesig, and Karen E. Robinson. 2016. Project Jacquard: Interactive Digital Textiles at Scale. *In Proceedings of the 2016 CHI Conference on Human Factors in Computing Systems* (CHI '16). ACM, New York, NY, USA, 4216-4227. https://doi.org/10.1145/2858036.2858176
21. David Pye. 1968. *The nature and art of workmanship.* Cambium Press.
22. Becky Stern and Tyler Cooper. 2015. *Getting started with Adafruit FLORA*. Maker Media Inc.
23. Stitching Worlds - Connected Research: Kobakant. 2014. Retrieved Dec 6 2017 from http://www.stitchingworlds.net/experimentation/connected-research-kobakant/
24. TEI 2018 - Twelfth International Conference on Tangible, Embedded and Embodied Interactions. Retrieved July 22, 2017 from http://tei.acm.org/2018/

ShapeTex: Implementing Shape-Changing Structures in Fabric for Wearable Actuation

Jiachun Du, Panos Markopoulos, Qi Wang, Marina Toeters
Department of Industrial Design
Eindhoven University of Technology
Eindhoven, The Netherlands
jiachun_du@foxmail.com, P.Markopoulos@tue.nl, Q.Wang@tue.nl, m.toeters@gmail.com

Ting Gong
Ting Gong Studio, Amsterdam,
The Netherlands
t.gongting@gmail.com

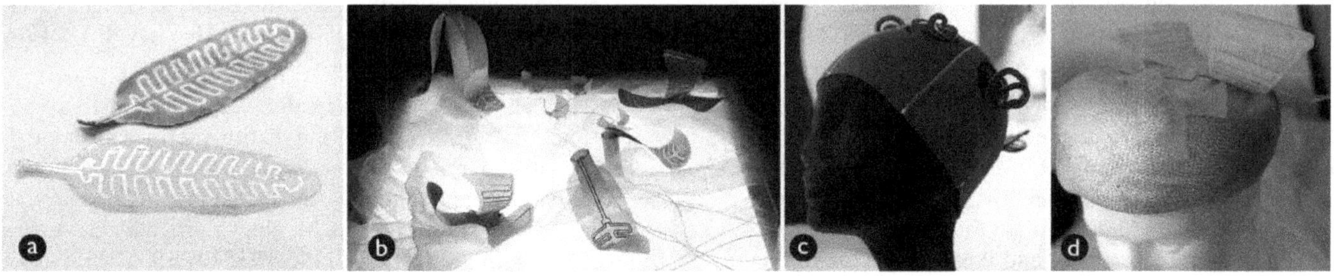

Figure 1. (a) ShapeTex samples (b) Textile Garden is an art exhibit based with several moving pieces simulating leaves and flowers with ShapeTex; (c) Crazy Coil is a fashion design exhibit where coil shaped pieces of ShapeTex that pop up in response to temperature rising in the head; (d) Botanic Hat a hat-design featuring a ShapeTex flower that blossoms in response to heartbeat variation

ABSTRACT
Research in smart textiles and garments has mostly focused on integrating sensing technology. In order to make garments that are truly interactive it is also essential to develop technologies for actuating smart garments and textiles. This paper introduces ShapeTex, a thermal shape changing fabric that uses laminate thermal expansion to actuate textiles. We present the design process and rationale for ShapeTex; we explain the fabrication process we have developed for making ShapeTex accessible to fashion designers and interaction designers. Based on co-creation sessions with designers we discuss requirements derived from this material. Finally we present a number of concept prototypes created to explore and illustrate the potential applications of ShapeTex.

Author Keywords
Shape-Changing Interface; Thermal Transformation; Wearable Actuation; Material Design

TEI '18, March 18–21, 2018, Stockholm, Sweden

ACM ISBN 978-1-4503-5568-1/18/03…$15.00
https://doi.org/10.1145/3173225.3173245

INTRODUCTION
Wearable systems, especially garments endowed with sensing and computation and garments integrating smart textiles, promise comfort and unobtrusiveness allowing users to wear them through the day and in the diverse situations where their daily activities bring them. The bulk of research on smart garments and textiles has concerned the integration of sensing technology in wearables. Relatively few efforts have been invested on novel forms of output on wearable systems. Explorations include visual output, e.g., in the form of textile displays [21,24], or vibrotactile output based on embedded vibration motors [3] or even by functional electric stimulation to provide haptic feedback [29].

Reflecting on the broader field of tangible and embodied interaction Ishii et al. [14] remark the relative absence of materiality from physical interfaces. Towards this end, recent research pertaining to the vision of organic forms of interaction [6] or shape-changing interfaces [26] indicates the broad range of possibilities for output that actuation can provide. Especially research on shape changing interfaces, with very few exceptions, has not yet considered the use of actuation on garments. When forces need to be exerted upon the human body as in the case of rehabilitation applications, solutions often need to resort to bulky and obtrusive exoskeletons. Where less force needs to be applied, e.g., for movement feedback, more limited forms of actuation like vibration are preferred, e.g. see [2,31].

Traditionally actuation on wearables relies on external mechanism such as motors, shape memory alloy and soft robotics to provide the force needed for shape transformation. However, these actuation routes do not yet provide the necessary flexibility, efficiency and are difficult to conceal but also hard to control. Thus research is needed to develop new unobtrusive mechanisms of sufficient wearability to allow integration in smart garments.

Crucially, the fabrication of such constructions requires still a lot of handwork and material engineering expertise that is not readily accessible to interaction designers. This prohibits interaction designers from applying their own skill set in developing novel forms of interactivity involving actuation in wearables. In order to lower the threshold for prototyping wearable shape-changing interfaces but also to improve the performance of such interactive materials, we need to develop fabrication approaches accessible to designers and to understand the requirements and opportunities designers find in using these new materials.

In this paper we introduce a novel thermal shape-changing fabric called ShapeTex (see Figure 1) which has a three layers structure: A thin copper/aluminum layer, a fabric and an ultra-high molecular weight polyethylene (UHMWPE). ShapeTex bends when current goes through it and recovers its original shape when it cools down.

The remaining sections summarize design driven research to develop ShapeTex. We discuss:

- The design and engineering performance of ShapeTex
- The fabrication process of ShapeTex, where we replace copper etching with vinyl cutting.
- Co-creation workshops aimed at uncovering the potential of ShapeTex for wearable shape-changing interfaces.
- Proof of concept prototypes using ShapeTex to illustrate the design space opening up at the intersection of interaction design and fashion design.

RELATED WORK

Shape-Changing Interfaces

Research on shape changing interfaces has mostly been concerned with enhancing/transforming visual displays to support shape-change as output. Fewer works examine shape change as the primary interaction modality, e.g., see Kwak [17], and often the purpose of actuation is for a partial or complementary function to a device, e.g., Hemmert [12] explores how shape changing interactions can enhance the expressiveness of notifications on mobile phones; Wrigglo [23] is a shape-changing smart phone peripheral that allows pairs of users to share wriggling movements with one another. Efforts towards miniaturization have considered thin film printed electronics. E.g., Foldio explored the fabrication of foldable interactive objects combining shape-change with thin-film printed electronics for sensing and output [20].

Wearable Actuation

If we focus on wearable actuations there are a few well-developed technologies that can be used such as, soft robotics with air pumps [1], shape memory alloy [4], vibrators [34], piezoelectric [9], thermal transformation polymer [11] and electromagnetic [8].

Air driven actuator

Air driven wearable actuators are usually made of silicone gel. When air is pumped into the gel it inflates and changes shape. Although the transformation is quite easy to perceive visually and through touch, the air pumps are noisy and large and too big to integrate into the actuating device [22].

Shape memory alloy (SMA)

Some actuators contain shape memory alloys (NiTi, for example). In robots the SMA serves as muscle and steel as bone. When heated the muscle shrinks and pulls the bone making robotic limbs move. SMAs are strong and robust but the shape-change emits substantial heat. Sprout I/O [5] presented a good example of embedding SMA in textiles. However it is only an initial exploration that has not yet been integrated in wearable applications.

Vibrator & Piezoelectric Actuator

Vibrations are achieved through electromagnetic or ferro-electricity based actuation, which pushes other objects to change shape. These devices can produce but small displacements, which are not ideal for shape-change in the scale of the human body as is needed in wearable applications.

Electromagnetic

Small electromagnetic motors are integrated into a moving structure and can drive the structure to move. Electromagnets have a binary state only, but by combining many small units they can provide higher resolution feedback [8]. A limitation for electromagnetic actuation is its size; electromagnets are rather big to be implemented on wearables.

Microorganisms

BioLogic [37] demonstrates how microorganisms can be used for wearable actuation. By adding Natto bacteria on the joint of fabric pieces researchers could demonstrate a humidity-controlled shape-changing effect. While the idea is fascinating with biological control method, the drawbacks are the difficulty to prototype with this material and the persistence of the shape change actuation.

Flexible Wearable Electronics

Other explorations have focused on making wearable electronics flexible. SkinMarks [36] enables interaction with capacity sensing input and luminescent displays output on tattoos. DuoSkin [15] purposes a rapid-prototyping on-skin user interface with skin-friendly gold leaf material. It allows for making touch sensing input, thermo chromatic displays and wireless communication by NFC in the same structure. For more traditional wearable electronics with SMD components, designers make fabric circuit boards using a vinyl cutter [13], which inspired our approach for facilitating and digitizing the fabrication process of a new shape changing fabric, as discussed below.

SHAPETEX

Design Rationale

We appreciated that building a thin-film wearable actuation would be valuable due to its unique properties in terms of thickness, lightweight and controllability. However, current thin-film shape changing structures do not fit the wearable context because of their flexibility, incompatibility on fabric and lacking of aesthetic design space. We aimed at providing an accessible solution for fashion designers by developing a novel shape changing structure for wearables. In this effort, we have been inspired by uniMorph a thin-film shape changing structure introduced by Heibeck et al [11]. It can achieve a heat-controlled deformation based on the principle of laminate thermal expansion.

We started with experiments on uniMorph which first attempted and succeeded to reproduce the performance reported by [11]. We tried to attach the fabric directly onto uniMorph; this would conceal uniMorph, a muscle wire structure, in the fabric like in a sandwich. We found that uniMorph could drive a fabric of roughly its own weight. However, attaching uniMorph to fabric decreased its flexibility and resulted in an unstable structure and an appearance that was not aesthetically acceptable for integrating in wearables. Therefore we attempted to replace the polythene tape with other materials but this compromised the ability of the material to deform. Also, we noted that attaching the polythene onto the copper can prevent exposing the user to heat and current.

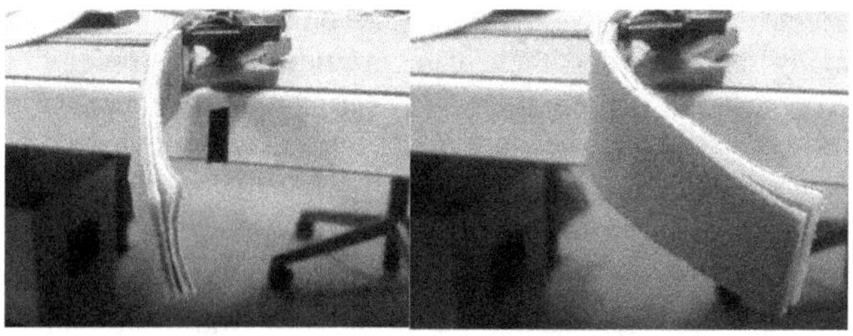

Figure 2. Attaching fabric on muscle wire pieces

At the outset of our efforts we also consulted fashion designers regarding their requirements and directions in which to develop the material. They suggested making the structure transparent. Realizing that the kapton layer was unnecessary and limiting aesthetically with its yellow color and that it made the structure inflexible and heavy, we decided against attaching this material on fabric. Thus we developed a new structure to open up more possibilities for wearable actuation.

Structure of ShapeTex

ShapeTex has a three layer structure (see Figure 3): a copper/aluminum layer with certain heating pattern; a fabric layer as the substrate; an ultra high molecular weight layer as the transformation and protection layer. Actuation is

Figure 3. Three layer structure of ShapeTex.

achieved based on the principle of laminate thermal expansion. The thermal coefficient of polythene tape and fabric are very different. When a current goes through the metal layer, ShapeTex will heat and deform (see figure 4). The speed of this deformation depends on the current, the overall weight of the piece, and the thickness of the polythene tape. ShapeTex reacts to thermal changes caused by the metal tape or even by the environment. ShapeTex can be powered by battery making it portable/wearable, though battery power also limits the size of the material that can be deformed.

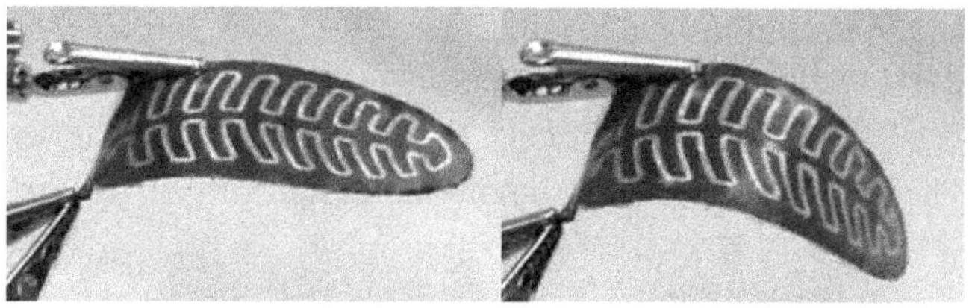

Figure 4. The shape changing effect of ShapeTex.

We made a few key decisions for enhancing the applicability of ShapeTex to wearables:

- We attach the polythene tape always on top of the metal tape; while this constrains the transformation direction it prevents users from accidentally touching the metal and creating a short circuit. Note that for a small piece of ShapeTex a shock would be tolerable since we just apply only 2.4V battery for the power. However, if one were to deform larger pieces of ShapeTex, a higher voltage would be required which could be uncomfortable or even harmful for users. By insulating the metal tape from the human body with polythene tape on top and fabric at the bottom (like a sandwich), the shock risk is significantly reduced. We separate the fabrication of three layers for better implementation. Benefitting from the tape structure of polythene and copper/aluminum, designers can make the layers individually and attach them directly on clothing. Copper tape is commonly used in electrostatic shielding, e.g., it is used in the foldable paper circuits mentioned above [20]. It is flexible and thin but still provides the conductive properties of copper. We considered it might be useful to replace the flexible printed circuit board copper substrate by a structure of copper tape and fabric combination.
- We use organza and linen and cotton as the substrate of ShapeTex. These textiles have a higher resistance to heat

which also helps protecting the user. In our experiments ShapeTex reached the temperature of 50 degree Celsius when at its maximum transformation. After reching that we can reduce the current for maintaining the transformation or let it cool down.

- We introduce aluminum tape as an alternative option to copper tape. On the one hand, aluminum tape has a relatively higher resistance, it is stiffer and harder to solder. However, fashion designers working with us found its white color more suitable and saw the potential of integrating it in semi-transparent clothing designs.
- ShapeTex integrates functional components as a flexible circuit board while also supporting shape-change. Next to actuation it can potentially support input in several ways: by turning copper tapes into capacity sensors [36], using SMD solder pads [13], or NFC wireless communication [15], etc. ShapeTex can support the actuation of the structure and complete the input/output of a fabric circuit.

LOWERING THE THRESHOLD FOR FABRICATION

Copper Etching

UniMorph is made by copper etching which is a mature technology used for making printed circuit boards. Normally ferric chloride or hydrochloric acid is used as the etching liquid. Initially we fabricated Shapetex using copper etching (see fiture 5)but using sodium thiosulfate instead of high performance hydrochloric acid for safety reasons. While this takes longer (approximately 4 hours for a 12cm*2cm copper plate), this procedure is tender, controllable and produces no gas or heat. We continued using the Kapton tape for protection during copper etching.

Copper etching has some drawbacks. The thin copper layer breaks easily. Second, the adhesive of the copper tape hinders copper etching and removing the protection layer. We had to use acetone to clean it which introduces the risk of corroding the fabric substrate. Additionally the liquids used in the process make the ShapeTex wet and wrinkle and the by-product copper sulfate is poisonous.

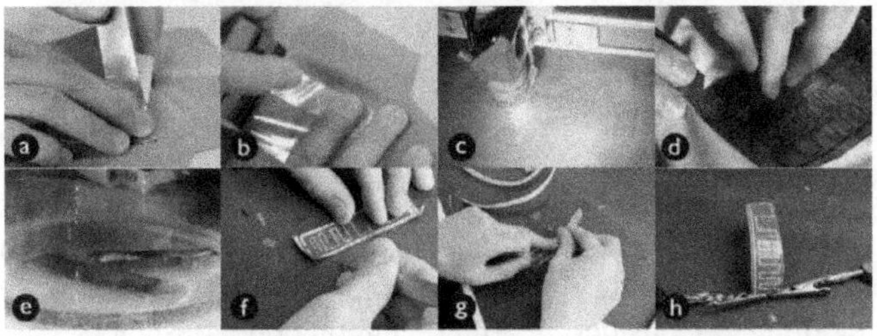

Figure 5. The fabrication of copper etched ShapeTex. First attach copper tape on the chosen fabric (a); then attach the protective layer (b); laser cut the pattern (c); remove the excessive protective layer (d); bathe in 1:5 sodium thiosulfate solution (e); wash and dry the material and remove the protection layer (f); attach the polymer tape (g) and test (h).

Vinyl Cutter

Considering the disadvantages of copper etching, we decided to attempt using a vinyl cutter to render the desired copper patterns. Unlike laser cutting, vinyl cutting is a low-temperature process using a physical blade which can cut through a thin metal sheet. We used the Roland GS-24 desk cutter; its cutting pattern is drawn using an Illustrator™ file, which makes it possible to digitalize the fabrication process.

We maintained the three layer ShapeTex structure with a fabric substrate, a copper pattern and a polythene tape on top (See figure 7). The fabrication process using a vinyl cutter is as follows:

1. Design the metal pattern and the fabric shape. The metal pattern needs to be a closed loop. For fitting the vinyl cutter we suggest putting fillets in the corner and keeping the lines wider than 0.5mm.
2. Choose a fabric that meets the design requirements, e.g., a light and heat-resistant fabric such as organza (see figure 8).
3. Pre-process the fabric with laser cutting or other traditional weaving methods. Since we do not need to attach copper, the making of the fabric and copper layers can be separate. If the shape is complex we suggest laser cutting for the polythene layer.
4. Cut the metal sheet using the vinyl cutter.
5. Transfer the metal pattern to the fabric using reusable transfer sticker. Remove excess part of the metal pattern.
6. Attach the polymer tape on the copper and test. As before leave some copper exposed for the power supply connection.

During the co-creation process (see next section) fashion designers found copper restrictive aesthetically and suggested using a white metal layer instead. For this we decided to try the same fabrication process using aluminum. The experiment was successful and a substantial shape changing effect could also be achieved. As aluminum comes in many colors, a host of opportunities open up for designers who can now choose the color of the metal pattern. However there are a few differences between the aluminum version of ShapeTex and the copper version:

- Aluminum ShapeTex is stiffer than copper ShapeTex because the aluminum tape on the market is typically thicker than copper tape or copper sheets (though this can be overcome by using thinner aluminum tape).
- Aluminum has a higher resistance and heat capacity than copper. This means that it will heat up slower than copper especially when powered by a battery.

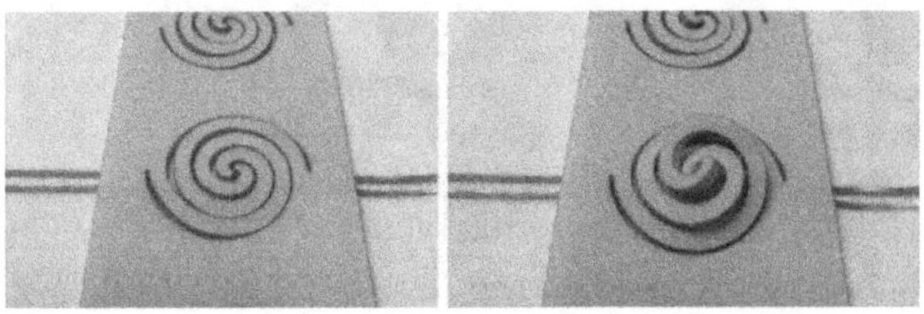

Figure 6. The shape changing effect of ShapeTex on a spiral pattern.

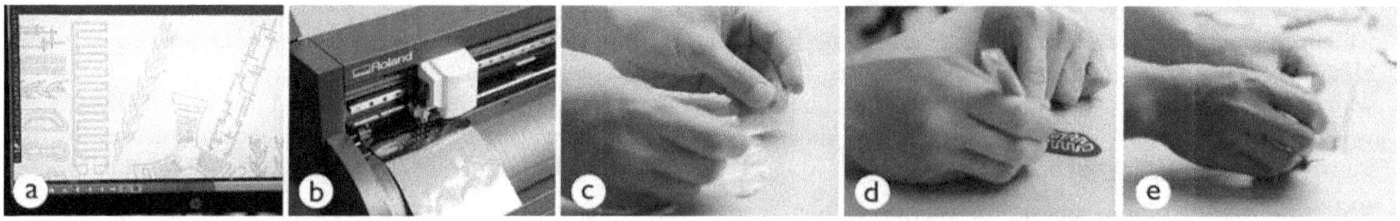

Figure 7. The fabrication of vinyl cutting ShapeTex. First design the pattern (a); then use vinyl cutter to cut on the metal sheet; after that transfer the metal on fabric; next remove the excessive part (d); finally attach the polymer tape on the top (e).

Discussion on the Fabrication of ShapeTex

We have described the three layered structure of ShapeTex and two fabrication process using etching and cutting. Compared to copper etching, cutting a metal sheet with a vinyl cutter offers a few advantages and one disadvantage:

- Cutting is safer and cleaner. Although we use tender chemicals during copper etching the by-products of this process are potentially harmful. Also during etching the fabric is immersed in a blue copper sulfate liquid for a few hours, which can affect adversely the color and the weaving structure.
- Cutting can deal with aluminum tape, which allows for ShapeTex in white or in different colors.
- Cutting is faster since designers don't need pre-processing and post-processing as in copper etching and because the etching time is saved.
- The drawback of cutting is that available vinyl cutters cannot cut very thin lines on the metal. Limited by the size of the blade the precision is less than that of laser cutting. We found that sometimes vinyl cutting results in undesired curves especially when the sheet is not flat enough or the blade is worn. Overall, copper etching is more stable and precise in making pattern lines thinner than 0.2mm.

From an aesthetic perspective, designers can explore different metal patterns that are less technical-looking. For example inspired by paintings of Mondrian we made a grid pattern that looks more rhythmic and abstract, but not strictly geometrical. Alternatively, a nature inspired pattern e.g. as leaves can be created to decorate a textile or garment. Figure 9 illustrates some explorations of the fabric variations on a classical spiral pattern and different layers on a similar fabric pattern.

Figure 8. Aluminum and copper ShapeTex pieces with organza as substrate.

From an interaction design perspective, the pattern can create a complete interactive system comprising of a fabric circuit board with input (copper or aluminum foil as capacity sensor or NFC coil), processor (SMD microcontrollers soldered on the pattern) and the output (ShapeTex as the actuator). This structure makes the fabric circuit board seamlessly attached with aesthetical patterns.

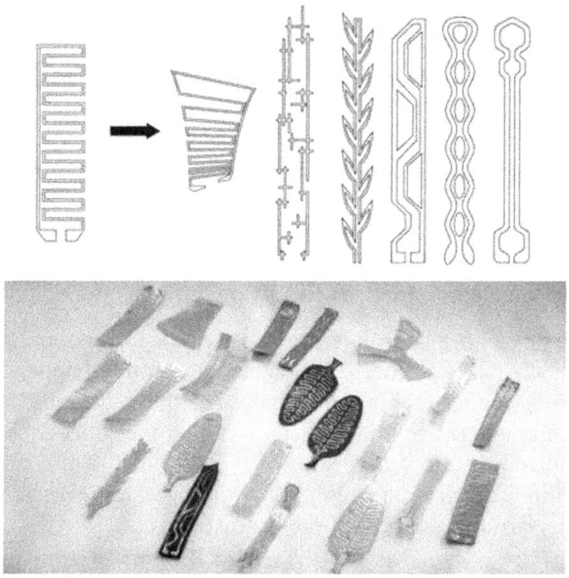

Figure 9. From engineering pattern to aesthetic patterns.

EXPLORING THE POTENTIAL OF SHAPETEX IN CO-CREATION SESSIONS

ShapeTex was developed in a design driven manner. Designers provided requirements and proposed contexts in which to illustrate opportunities for using it in interactive clothing. Considering that interaction designers are typically not expert in aesthetic aspects of garment design, we involved 4 fashion designers and 3 interaction designers in these workshops. We held a few co-creation workshops with them following a research through design approach [16] (See Figure 11). The workshops were facilitated by the first author who kept notes and also provided technical explanations to designers when needed.

The workshops followed the following process:

1. Sharing the challenge. By introducing fashion designers to wearable technology and the limitation of current designs, they got the first impression of what the challenge was.
2. Demonstrating ShapeTex. In this stage we introduced ShapeTex and showed them fabrication and demonstration videos to inspire them. We also showed them a sample book with different patterns.
3. Idea Generation. We asked designers to generate ideas on applications of ShapeTex in their respective fields of expertise.
4. Discussion. In the final step we would discuss with them how to integrate their idea into a demonstrable concept design.

Overall designers were very inspired by the new shape changing material for fabrics and excited about the design opportunities ShapeTex could bring them. For us, it was remarkable how the mindset and concerns of fashion designers differed to that of interaction designers. We summarize their feedback below.

Feedback from Designers

Interaction designers held rather pragmatic concerns with regards to the context and input/output of the system. For example, one interaction designer asked: "*Where should sensors be placed and how fast does your shape changing effect react to the data?*" Meanwhile they expressed their concern for the current and pertinent safety issues. A designer claimed "*I think this shape changing technology is not extremely promising when only technical designers are able to use it. However a software application could bridge this gap so that it becomes available for people like fashion designers.*" With this he emphasized the importance of making this new material accessible to interaction designers; this inspired us to develop simulation software for assisting interaction designers to use the material (this is discussed below).

The main concerns of fashion designers revolved around making the material as aesthetic as possible. They favored abstract patterns of the metal layer, such as the Mondrian-like grid rather than representative images such as the willow leaf (see figure 8). One fashion designer stated: "*I would like to make the shape changing clothing entirely transparent and disappear in the space.*" It was this statement that triggered us to develop white ShapeTex using aluminum tape. Contrary to our expectations, (at least from an interaction design perspective) fashion designers favoured random movements that do not carry any specific meaning for the viewer over attaching semantics to the movement. Surprising concepts such as a tie that tells the time by its position were also proposed. One experienced hat designer saw in the slow and limited range movement (at least when compared to human motion or electromechanical actuation) the possibility of expressing emotions subtly. She commented "*What if there are shape changing hats that reflect anger, love and anxiety? If it's anger it relates to a hedgehog with stiff spins lifting like an animal. For love a flower blossoms in the aspect of plant. For anxiety you can make coils popping out of the brain when you head is hot. That must be interesting.*" Another hat designer emphasized movement and figurative relations. She said "*When it opens it grows something out. It's like a magician. It can have a strange shape go out. You can have a hat open in a few pieces and something comes out like a joker box.*"

Fashion designers seemed to consider ShapeTex as a breakthrough that opens up new opportunities for their profession. Compared to interaction designers, their concept generation process stayed at a more conceptual level focusing on expressing emotions or articulating an affective narrative rather than on how information can be conveyed to users which concerned interaction designers the most.

Design Protocols from Co-Creation Session

During the co-creation sessions our role was that of smart materials scientist engaging with interaction designers and fashion designers and providing expert input on this new material. The first author assumed the dual role of a participant-observer in the design session, aiming to draw lessons regarding the design process, keeping notes and getting feedback from participants after the sessions. From this process we learnt the following lessons:

1. Accessibility and flexibility of ShapeTex. Fashion Designers have very personal preferences regarding fabric and color selection. They need to be able to choose the fabric they are familiar with and see how it behaves in combination with ShapeTex A simulation software would be very helpful and cut down prototyping time.
2. Visibility of metal patterns. Hiding the metal pattern takes a lot of time and effort; it adds weight to ShapeTex and hampers performance. On the other hand, exposing the metal pattern can have a positive aesthetic impact.
3. Interactivity. Although fashion designers prefer random movements, interaction design will benefit from adding sensors and electronic components for supporting more functional interactivity.

PROTOTYPES WITH SHAPETEX

We discuss some concept prototypes that realized some of the ideas proposed in the creative workshops. The selection of prototypes below illustrates different ways of driving the actuation and diverse applications that ShapeTex can have. The prototypes shown are not put forward as viable applications aiming to address functional user needs but as showroom prototypes [16] that are evocative and will help illustrate the relevant space of opportunities and concerns, and inspire other designers.

Willow Cap

The *Willow Cap* (see Figure 10) is a flannel hat decorated by ShapeTex. It has two leaves made of copper based ShapeTex. One acts as a capacity touch sensor; the other with the leaf outline acts as the actuator. Inside the hat there is a 1.2V NiMH battery, an Arduino Pro Mini and a N-FET to control the current. The Willow Cap supports touch input and shape-changing output: When the user touches the sensing leaf the capacity drops; when this is detected an instant HIGH signal is output on the Arduino gate; the willow leaf is then deformed. When the user stops touching the sensing leaf, the gate is closed, the heating stops and the leaf returns to its original shape.

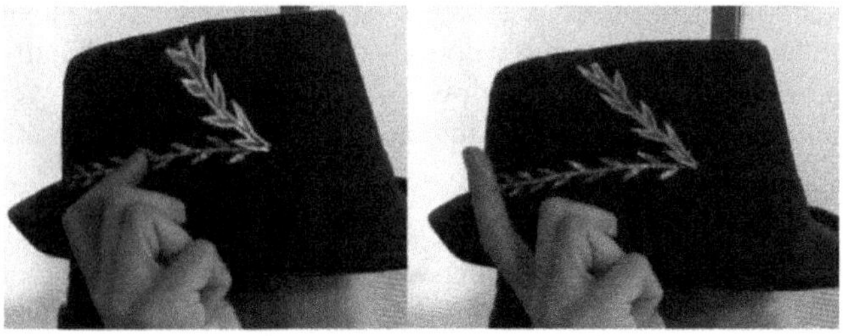

Figure 10. Willow Cap with tangible input of a touch sensor and ShapeTex as output. When user touches the sensing leaf the actuation leaf will have a shape-changing output.

Textile Garden

Textile Garden (see Figure 1(b) and Figure 11) is an interactive exhibit that we developed to demonstrate Shapetex at an art exhibition. It represents discarded fabric and metal waste that comes to life again to evoke reflections on sustainability. It comprises of ShapeTex flowers and leaves that are laid out on a lit platform with an organza cover. The flowers and leaves make random movements controlled by an Arduino Pro mini and a 5V power supply. By transforming a new thermal shape-changing textile into a soft-growing plant yard we created the sensation of a magical yet literal textile plant.

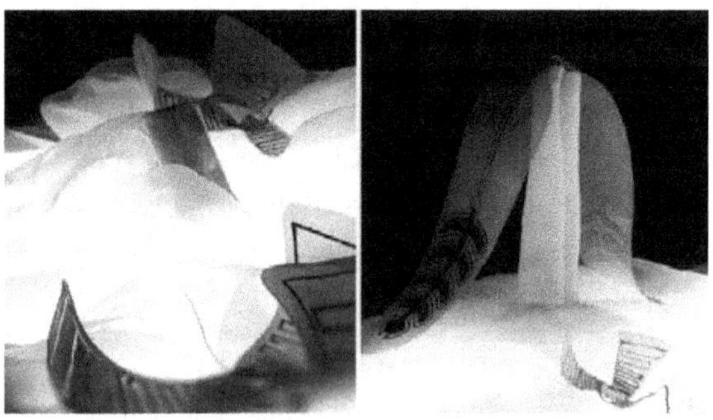

Figure 11. Shots of Textile Garden.

Crazy Coil

Crazy Coil was conceived during the co-creation session to embody the idea of an emotional shape-changing hat. Black coils with coppers are distributed evenly around the hat. Heat sensors are embedded inside the hat; when the user's temperature rises ShapeTex coils pop up visualizing and exaggerating their assumed emotional state to their surroundings (note that this was the abstract concept; we do not of course assume that a reliable emotion detection is achieved through heat sensing). By exaggerating the emotional response with a shape changing effect Crazy Coil creates a fascinating and lucid narrative.

Botanic Hat

Botanic Hat is another variation on the theme of emotional shape changing hats. With a silver base and white-yellow ShapeTex the Botanic Hat features abstract looking flowers on the hat in order to visualize affection towards one's lover. The narrative embodied in this concept design is that when the dresser sees their lover the heartbeat will increase; this is sensed by the hat, which in turn actuates the ShapeTex flowers. As a result the flower on the hat blossoms to express the love in an embodied way.

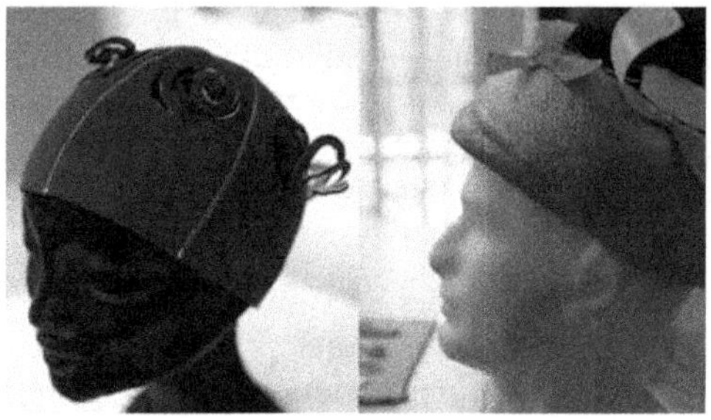

Figure 12. Crazy Coil (left) and Botanic Hat (right)

SHAPETEX SIMULATION SOFTWARE

Taking up the suggestion designers made during the co-creation session we have created simulation software that visualizes the dynamics of shape change based on the choice of material, size, voltage, etc. The simulation is based on fitting a model for the shape change on the performance data collected during the prototyping of ShapeTex. While not a full-fledged design or prototyping tool, the simulation encapsulates some of the physics and some of the experience we acquired in different sizes and shapes of ShapeTex, and can potentially reduce the need for trial and error with physical prototypes. Designers can import a vector file of the pattern and select the parameters for their design. Then they can see how fast the material combinations will move to make further decisions. This application is only meant for inspection and inspiration: To fully support design a more exact simulation and a direct link to drive cutting tools still need to be implemented.

DISCUSSION

The contribution of ShapeTex

In this paper, we have introduced a new shape-changing fabric called ShapeTex which extends the state of the art regarding the flexibility, performance and the accessibility to designers of wearable actuation. We have argued how ShapeTex improves upon its predecessor uniMorph (which did not target a wearable context) regarding its applicability

Figure 13. ShapeTex simulation software, a proof of concept.

on wearable systems and in the ease and safety of fabrication. We have demonstrated two variants of the material based on the new structure and propose a few future design directions. Perhaps most important for the wearable field is the introduction of aluminum based ShapeTex which greatly reduces costs and extends the options offered to designers.

The contribution of the paper is to:

1. A new approach to integrate a shape-changing structure directly on fabric.
2. A new combination of materials for supporting actuation in wearable systems.
3. A new fabrication procedure that is arguably cheaper, safer and more flexible (than the original procedure for fabricating UniMorph) which can potentially make this technology more accessible to designers.
4. A design driven exploration of the opportunities Shaptex presents for wearable shape-changing interfaces

The utility of these advances is perhaps more evident if we look back to the Sprout I/O [5], where SMA was knitted onto a felt. They selected a bi-state actuation method by sewing a three dimensional SMA strand onto both sides of a rectangular piece of felt. By applying similar control to ShapeTex, it becomes possible to make the felt bend as well as to control the angle, speed, and direction of the transformation.

We consider the most suitable application for ShapeTex is for small garments to provide visual feedback. The reason is that a smaller ShapeTex element is easier to power with a smaller battery, which is quite important for a portable / wearable design.

Limitations of ShapeTex

One of the main limitations of ShapeTex is the large current for heating which can cause three problems: safety, energy efficiency and heat. Due to the low resistance of the metal layers the current going through will become relatively large even though the voltage is low. We have thus put the polythene tape on top of the metal layer to prevent direct contact with the skin but in wearable interactive prototypes some metal parts are still likely to be exposed in soldering junctions where the microcontrollers are wired to the wearable electronics.

Since ShapeTex applies the principle of thermal expansion it consumes a lot of energy. For the current prototypes we use either NiMH batteries or a Mean Well power supply. Additionally the force it provides is rather small compared to the requirements for some applications of wearable actuation where force feedback is needed rather than just a shape transformation (e.g., force feedback in rehabilitation, or haptic notifications). ShapeTex can only lift its own weight thus it cannot be used as a muscle wire and cannot deliver nearly the same forces as SMA. Also the low resistance of the heating circuit makes the resistance of cables non negligible. This means that the cables connecting ShapeTex and the power supply may also heat up. To avoid this we suggest directly attaching the battery onto the ShapeTex metal layer or using thicker copper cables for the connection.

We already noted that ShapeTex becomes hot (normally around 60 Celcius) when actuating. There are two ways to deal with this: Limiting this side effect, e.g., by insulating hot areas or keeping them small or placing them where they do not cause discomfort to the user (e.g., on the shoulder). Alterantively one can utilize this side effect, e.g. to provide local thermal comfort or treatment, or to use the thermo-luminescent effect for visual output.

Future Work

Future work will further explore the integration of ShapeTex in interactive clothing together with fashion and interaction designers. Also we aim at improving the performance of ShapeTex by lowering the working current and enhancing energy efficiency. More explorations on how to better integrate ShapeTex with other fabric circuit components is necessary. Finally future development will need to extend the simulation software into a fully fledged prototyping tool that can support interaction designers in experimenting with different forms and sizes of ShapTex.

REFERENCES

1. Air-Powered Soft Robotic Gripper. (n.d.). Retrieved October 16, 2016, from http://www.instructables.com/id/Air-Powered-Soft-Robotic-Gripper/
2. Benini, M. J. S., Bruinink, M., Pekel, A. D., Talbott, W. A., Visser, A., & Markopoulos, P. (2011). Restoring Balance: Replacing the Vestibular Sense with Wearable Vibrotactile Feedback. In *Smart Healthcare Applications and Services: Developments and Practices* (pp. 283–301). IGI Global. Retrieved from http://www.igi-global.com/chapter/restoring-balance-replacing-vestibular-sense/50665
3. Bosman, S., Groenendaal, B., Findlater, J., Visser, T., de Graaf, M., & Markopoulos, P. (2003). Gentleguide: An exploration of haptic output for indoors pedestrian guidance. *Human-Computer Interaction with Mobile Devices and Services*, 358–362.
4. Coelho, M., Ishii, H., & Maes, P. (2008). Surflex: a programmable surface for the design of tangible interfaces. In *CHI'08 extended abstracts on Human factors in computing systems* (pp. 3429–3434). ACM. Retrieved from http://dl.acm.org/citation.cfm?id=1358869
5. Coelho, M., & Maes, P. (2008). Sprout I/O: a texturally rich interface. In *Proceedings of the 2nd international conference on Tangible and embedded interaction* (pp. 221–222). ACM. Retrieved from http://dl.acm.org/citation.cfm?id=1347440
6. Coelho, M., Poupyrev, I., Sadi, S., Vertegaal, R., Berzowska, J., Buechley, L., … Oxman, N. (2009). Programming reality: from transitive materials to organic user interfaces. In *CHI'09 Extended Abstracts on Human Factors in Computing Systems* (pp. 4759–4762). ACM. Retrieved from http://dl.acm.org/citation.cfm?id=1520734
7. Coelho, M., & Zigelbaum, J. (2011). Shape-changing interfaces. *Personal and Ubiquitous Computing*, *15*(2), 161–173.
8. Deng, K., Enikov, E. T., & Zhang, H. (2007). Development of a pulsed electromagnetic micro-actuator for 3D tactile displays. In *2007 IEEE/ASME international conference on advanced intelligent mechatronics* (pp. 1–5). IEEE. Retrieved from http://ieeexplore.ieee.org/xpls/abs_all.jsp?arnumber=4412457
9. Edmison, J., Jones, M., Nakad, Z., & Martin, T. (2002). Using piezoelectric materials for wearable electronic textiles. In *Wearable Computers, 2002.(ISWC 2002). Proceedings. Sixth International Symposium on* (pp. 41–48). IEEE. Retrieved from http://ieeexplore.ieee.org/xpls/abs_all.jsp?arnumber=1167217
10. Hardy, J., Weichel, C., Taher, F., Vidler, J., & Alexander, J. (2015). ShapeClip: towards rapid prototyping with shape-changing displays for designers. In *Proceedings of the 33rd Annual ACM Conference on Human Factors in Computing Systems* (pp. 19–28). ACM. Retrieved from http://dl.acm.org/citation.cfm?id=2702599
11. Heibeck, F., Tome, B., Della Silva, C., & Ishii, H. (2015). uniMorph: Fabricating Thin Film Composites for Shape-Changing Interfaces. In *Proceedings of the 28th Annual ACM Symposium on User Interface Software & Technology* (pp. 233–242). ACM. Retrieved from http://dl.acm.org/citation.cfm?id=2807472
12. Hemmert, F., Hamann, S., Löwe, M., Wohlauf, A., & Joost, G. (2010). Shape-changing mobiles: tapering in one-dimensional deformational displays in mobile phones (p. 249). ACM Press. https://doi.org/10.1145/1709886.1709936
13. HOW TO GET WHAT YOU WANT. (n.d.). Retrieved April 3, 2017, from http://www.kobakant.at/DIY/?p=1132
14. Ishii, H. (2015). TRANSFORM: Beyond Tangible Bits, Towards Radical Atoms. In *Proceedings of the 3rd ACM Symposium on Spatial User Interaction* (pp. 1–1). ACM. Retrieved from http://dl.acm.org/citation.cfm?id=2788958
15. Kao, H.-L. C., Holz, C., Roseway, A., Calvo, A., & Schmandt, C. (2016). DuoSkin: rapidly prototyping on-skin user interfaces using skin-friendly materials. In *Proceedings of the 2016 ACM International Symposium on Wearable Computers* (pp. 16–23). ACM. Retrieved from http://dl.acm.org/citation.cfm?id=2971777
16. Koskinen, I., Zimmerman, J., Binder, T., Redstrom, J., & Wensveen, S. (2012). *Design Research Through Practice: From the Lab, Field, and Showroom* (1st ed.). San Francisco, CA, USA: Morgan Kaufmann Publishers Inc.
17. Kwak, M., Hornbæk, K., Markopoulos, P., & Bruns Alonso, M. (2014). The design space of shape-changing interfaces: a repertory grid study (pp. 181–190). ACM Press. https://doi.org/10.1145/2598510.2598573
18. Lee, M., Chen, C.-Y., Wang, S., Cha, S. N., Park, Y. J., Kim, J. M., … Wang, Z. L. (2012). A hybrid piezoelectric structure for wearable nanogenerators. *Advanced Materials*, *24*(13), 1759–1764.
19. mikey77. (n.d.). Make Flexible Circuit Boards Using A 3D Printer. Retrieved from http://www.instructables.com/id/Make-Flexible-Circuit-Boards-Using-A-3D-Printer/?ALLSTEPS

20. Olberding, S., Soto Ortega, S., Hildebrandt, K., & Steimle, J. (2015). Foldio: Digital fabrication of interactive and shape-changing objects with foldable printed electronics. In *Proceedings of the 28th Annual ACM Symposium on User Interface Software & Technology* (pp. 223–232). ACM. Retrieved from http://dl.acm.org/citation.cfm?id=2807494
21. Olberding, S., Wessely, M., & Steimle, J. (2014). PrintScreen: fabricating highly customizable thin-film touch-displays. In *Proceedings of the 27th annual ACM symposium on User interface software and technology* (pp. 281–290). ACM. Retrieved from http://dl.acm.org/citation.cfm?id=2647413
22. Ou, J., Skouras, M., Vlavianos, N., Heibeck, F., Cheng, C.-Y., Peters, J., & Ishii, H. (2016). aeroMorph - Heat-sealing Inflatable Shape-change Materials for Interaction Design (pp. 121–132). ACM Press. https://doi.org/10.1145/2984511.2984520
23. Park, J., Park, Y.-W., & Nam, T.-J. (2014). Wrigglo: shape-changing peripheral for interpersonal mobile communication. In *Proceedings of the SIGCHI Conference on Human Factors in Computing Systems* (pp. 3973–3976). ACM. Retrieved from http://dl.acm.org/citation.cfm?id=2557166
24. Peiris, R. L., Fernando, O. N. N., & Cheok, A. D. (2011). Flexible, non-emissive textile display. In *International Joint Conference on Ambient Intelligence* (pp. 167–171). Springer. Retrieved from http://link.springer.com/10.1007%2F978-3-642-25167-2_20
25. Pfeiffer, M., & Rohs, M. (2017). Haptic Feedback for Wearables and Textiles Based on Electrical Muscle Stimulation. In *Smart Textiles* (pp. 103–137). Springer. Retrieved from http://link.springer.com/chapter/10.1007/978-3-319-50124-6_6
26. Rasmussen, M. K., Pedersen, E. W., Petersen, M. G., & Hornb\a ek, K. (2012). Shape-changing interfaces: a review of the design space and open research questions. In *Proceedings of the SIGCHI Conference on Human Factors in Computing Systems* (pp. 735–744). ACM. Retrieved from http://dl.acm.org/citation.cfm?id=2207781
27. Rivera, M. L., Moukperian, M., Ashbrook, D., Mankoff, J., & Hudson, S. E. (2017). Stretching the Bounds of 3D Printing with Embedded Textiles. In *Proceedings of the 2017 CHI Conference on Human Factors in Computing Systems* (pp. 497–508). New York, NY, USA: ACM. https://doi.org/10.1145/3025453.3025460
28. Roudaut, A., Karnik, A., Löchtefeld, M., & Subramanian, S. (2013). Morphees: toward high shape resolution in self-actuated flexible mobile devices. In *Proceedings of the SIGCHI Conference on Human Factors in Computing Systems* (pp. 593–602). ACM. Retrieved from http://dl.acm.org/citation.cfm?id=2470738
29. Siegel, A. C., Phillips, S. T., Dickey, M. D., Lu, N., Suo, Z., & Whitesides, G. M. (2010). Foldable printed circuit boards on paper substrates. *Advanced Functional Materials*, *20*(1), 28–35.
30. Sonar, H. A., & Paik, J. (2016). Soft Pneumatic Actuator Skin with Piezoelectric Sensors for Vibrotactile Feedback. *Frontiers in Robotics and AI*, *2*, 38.
31. Ten Bhömer, M., Tomico, O., & Hummels, C. (2013). Vigour: smart textile services to support rehabilitation. *Nordes*, *1*(5). Retrieved from http://nordes.org/opj/index.php/n13/article/view/364
32. The Social Interaction Dress. (2016, September 20). Retrieved October 16, 2016, from https://www.raspberrypi.org/blog/the-social-interaction-dress/
33. Tsubouchi, Y., & Suzuki, K. (2010). BioTones: a wearable device for EMG auditory biofeedback. In *2010 Annual International Conference of the IEEE Engineering in Medicine and Biology* (pp. 6543–6546). IEEE. Retrieved from http://ieeexplore.ieee.org/xpls/abs_all.jsp?arnumber=5627097
34. Wang, Q., Toeters, M., Chen, W., Timmermans, A., & Markopoulos, P. (2016). Zishi: A Smart Garment for Posture Monitoring. In *Proceedings of the 2016 CHI Conference Extended Abstracts on Human Factors in Computing Systems* (pp. 3792–3795). ACM. Retrieved from http://dl.acm.org/citation.cfm?id=2890262
35. Wang, Y., Luo, S., Lu, Y., Gong, H., Zhou, Y., Liu, S., & Hansen, P. (2017). AnimSkin: Fabricating Epidermis with Interactive, Functional and Aesthetic Color Animation. In *Proceedings of the 2017 Conference on Designing Interactive Systems* (pp. 397–401). New York, NY, USA: ACM. https://doi.org/10.1145/3064663.3064687
36. Weigel, M., Nittala, A. S., Olwal, A., & ürgen Steimle, J. (n.d.). SkinMarks: Enabling Interactions on Body Landmarks Using Conformal Skin Electronics. Retrieved from http://www.martinweigel.com/assets/skinmarks/2017-SkinMarks.pdf
37. Yao, L., Ou, J., Cheng, C.-Y., Steiner, H., Wang, W., Wang, G., & Ishii, H. (2015). BioLogic: natto cells as nanoactuators for shape changing interfaces. In *Proceedings of the 33rd Annual ACM Conference on Human Factors in Computing Systems* (pp. 1–10). ACM. Retrieved from http://dl.acm.org/citation.cfm?id=2702611

38. Yeo, J. C., Yap, H. K., Xi, W., Wang, Z., Yeow, C.-H., & Lim, C. T. (2016). Flexible and Stretchable Strain Sensing Actuator for Wearable Soft Robotic Applications. *Advanced Materials Technologies*. Retrieved from http://onlinelibrary.wiley.com/doi/10.1002/admt.201600018/full

39. YU, B., Arents, R., Hu, J., Funk, M., & Feijs, L. (2016). Heart Calligraphy: an Abstract Portrait Inside the Body. In *Proceedings of the TEI'16: Tenth International Conference on Tangible, Embedded, and Embodied Interaction* (pp. 675–680). ACM. Retrieved from http://dl.acm.org/citation.cfm?id=2856341

Beyond LED Status Lights - Design Requirements of Privacy Notices for Body-worn Cameras

Marion Koelle
University of Oldenburg
Oldenburg, Germany
marion.koelle@uni-oldenburg.de

Katrin Wolf
Hamburg University of Applied Sciences
Hamburg, Germany
katrin.wolf@haw-hamburg.de

Susanne Boll
University of Oldenburg
Oldenburg, Germany
susanne.boll@uni-oldenburg.de

Figure 1. For bystanders it is not always easy to determine whether state-of-the-art body-worn cameras are recording them: some devices, such as Google Glass (left) or the Narrative Clip (2nd from the left) do not provide any status indicator or privacy notice. Other devices, e.g., the Snap's Spectacles (2nd from the right), provide LED indicators. However, those can be easily overlooked, misunderstood, or hidden, e.g., by applying stickers (right).

ABSTRACT

Privacy notices aim to make users aware of personal data gathered and processed by a system. Body-worn cameras currently lack suitable design strategies for privacy notices that announce themselves and their actions to *secondary* and *incidental* users, such as bystanders, when they are being used in public. Hypothesizing that the commonly used status LED is not optimal for this use case, due to being not sufficiently understandable, noticeable, secure and trustworthy, we explore design requirements of privacy notices for body-worn cameras. Following a two-step approach, we contribute incentives for design alternatives to status LEDs: Starting from 8 design sessions with experts, we discuss 8 physical design artifacts, as well as design strategies and key motives. Finally, we derive design recommendations of the proposed solutions, which we back based on an evaluation with 12 UX & HCI experts.

Author Keywords

Augmented Reality; Wearable Cameras; Lifelogging; Privacy

INTRODUCTION

The use of personal, body-worn cameras is often problematic and controversial in social situations, as it may cause discomfort and social tension. Recent work discusses bystander privacy that might be compromised by body-worn cameras [10, 12, 17, 27]. In particular, wearable cameras create a different experience for bystanders than camera phones or CCTV cameras because they are considered subtle personal devices that can enable covert recording without consent [12, 55]. As a result of the diminutive form factor, the camera's status cannot be easily inferred from the user's body posture. Thus, bystanders are often not aware they are being captured and subjectively perceive a lack of situation awareness and control.

According to Gurrin et al. [22], an essential aspect of privacy with "always-on" cameras is that bystanders have the right and ability to choose when, where, and by whom they are recorded. Privacy notices in this case are feedback (or feedthrough) [3, 16] mechanisms that make both, primary and secondary users, aware of personal data gathered and processed by a system. While privacy indicators are well researched in the context of HTTPS web browsing [48, 36], state-of-the-art body-worn cameras (c.f. Figure 1) either do not provide any indicators or rely on binary information from point lights (status LEDs) that can be easily overlooked, misunderstood, or hidden.

Non-existent or poor feedback mechanisms are an everyday, practical privacy problem [3, 13] that also deprives bystanders of the possibility to react or possibly object to being captured. Additionally, even though actual device usage might not be a privacy violation as such (e.g., having the camera turned off), the presence of a camera that is (potentially) "always-on" is perceived as a threat to privacy [30]. This has a negative effect on both, the spectator's and the user's social acceptance (c.f. [5, 41]), which can cause the user to avoid using or wearing

TEI '18, March 18–21, 2018, Stockholm, Sweden

ISBN 978-1-4503-5568-1/18/03... $15.00

DOI: https://doi.org/10.1145/3173225.3173234

the camera device, potentially sacrificing its assistive funtion (c.f., [47]). Thus, we base our research on the assumption that privacy notices for body-worn cameras need to deal with the following user (and bystander) concerns:

Situation Awareness Is the bystander aware whether a camera device is present? Is (s)he able to verify whether this device is on or off? Does (s)he know what data is being recorded, for what purpose and by whom?

Justification Does the device show that I (the user) do not have any dishonest intentions? Does the device communicate when the camera is worn, but not turned on? Does the device communicate when the camera is turned on (e.g., for tracking) but is not persistently storing data?

In addition to potentially conflicting with penal and civil law[1], cameras that facilitate subtle recording violate privacy or privacy-by-design guidelines that demand **Openness** (OECD, [19]), **Notice** [33], or **Visibility and Transparency** [9], such that everyone involved should be able to verify what is captured and how their data[2] is handled. Providing adequate design solutions is a timely issue, as from May 2018 a revision of the EU General Data Protection Directive[3] will obligate manufacturers to implement "privacy-by-design" for both, users and potential bystanders. The directive does not detail how this privacy-by-design requirement shall be achieved. Thus, research in industry and academia will have to fill this gap by providing well thought-out procedures and design strategies.

Research Goals and Challenges

In order to satisfy the above-mentioned requirements, Openness [19], Notice [33], and Visibility and Transparency [9] for body-worn cameras, two design challenges need to be solved.

Challenge 1: Body-worn cameras should announce themselves and their actions in a noticeable, but not too obtrusive way (c.f., Flammer et al. [18]).

Conveying knowledge about usage intentions is not only demanded by existing privacy regulations, but can increase social acceptance [30]. In order to do so, privacy indicators need to show what information is used by the system [15].

Challenge 2: Body-worn cameras should publicly communicate their purpose of use to bystanders, but not impair the user's privacy.

Our research goal is to tackle these challenges by contributing to a better understanding of the weaknesses of established design strategies – particularly status LEDs – and by highlighting novel design opportunities. This paper makes two contributions: First, we present eight physical artifacts that embed design strategies addressing the problems *noticeability*, *understandability*, *security*, and *trustworthiness*, and suggest alternatives to LED status lights. They may serve as inspiration or critical designs [14] to spark innovative thinking about privacy notices. Second, we discuss the used design strategies and derive design recommendations for privacy notices and privacy mediating procedures for body-worn cameras.

Related Work

While there exists an extensive body of literature on privacy notices for *primary users* while browsing the web [48, 36], or using mobile phones [29] or fitness trackers [20], only very few researchers have targeted *secondary users* (e.g., conversation partners) or third party, *incidental users* (e.g., bystanders, c.f. [28]). Systems implementing the negotiation of privacy preferences between device users and bystanders, similar to the "Privacy Dashboard" concept (c.f., [18]) have been presented by Memon et al. [38] and Aditya et al. [1]. Krombholz et al. suggest design guidelines based on three conceptual privacy-mediating technologies, a "privacy bracelet", a "privacy fabric", and a "privacy app" [32]. These conceptual scaffolds were used to better understand bystander privacy risks and explore options to communicate user-defined privacy policies. These systems all require bystanders to own a particular device (e.g., smart phone or token) and to proactively define and communicate their privacy preferences. Although the dissemination of smart phones and BLE devices is increasing, these approaches do not render notification and announcement mechanisms obsolete, as bystanders need to be made aware of potential privacy risks in the first place. Our work aims at closing this gap by investigating privacy notices that announce to the captured person if (s)he is being captured and what the captured data will be used for.

These kinds of announcement mechanisms have been discussed in an early work by Bellotti et al. [3] who proposed design solutions, such as the "confidence monitor" (a public display showing the captured imagery) and visual and audio signals. This work, however, is based on fixed-location cameras in a work environment and does not cover concerns triggered by today's body-worn cameras, e.g., "Is this footage going to be shared on social media?" (c.f., [27, 12]).

Moreover, our work is complementary to Schaub et al.'s [51] who propose a comprehensive design space for effective privacy notices taking into account all possible stakeholders, and account for timing, channel, modality, and control. They further discuss best practices for photo and video lifelogging. Their taxonomy, however, is based on literature research and state-of-the art consumer systems, and thus, limited to existing concepts and technologies. We extend their work by asking experts to develop and critically discuss ideas for novel approaches - that then may be classified according to their taxonomy. Flammer [18] recommends a "Peacock Design" principle where information about a device and a user's actions with it are announced to bystanders. This could be achieved using actuators or physical gestures and signs to replace the current "invisible and unobtrusive" approach. However, they also highlight that announcement mechanisms should not compromise the users' impression management (e.g., being too flashy), which will require novel design solutions. To the best of our knowledge, no design strategies other than status LEDs have been suggested so far in literature or applied by industry.

[1]Legal regulations defining whether a photograph of a person requires his/her consent vary between locales. An overview is provided at http://tinyurl.com/d6b6fco, accessed 12/06/2017

[2]Photographs potentially allow to identify depicted persons, and thus are typically considered as **personal data** under the EU Data Protection Directive 1995 and derived national regulations.

[3]EU GDPD, http://ec.europa.eu/justice/data-protection/reform/index_en.htm, accessed 12/06/2017

With our work we go beyond those conceptional considerations by presenting design artifacts to serve as inspiration or starting points, as well as concrete design recommendations.

Problem Description

In order to meet any of the above mentioned guidelines, body-worn cameras would require effective announcement mechanisms that indicate (at least) whether the camera in question is recording or idle. It would also be ideal to inform the subject(s) about the intention of the recording and the information being saved. One commonly used design strategy is the use of light indicators (LEDs), which for example, is used by GoPro cameras. Despite being wide-spread and ubiquitously integrated in various types of devices with build-in cameras, this design strategy is not optimal for various reasons.

First, LED status indicators are **not well noticable**. Portnoff et al. [46] were able to show that, when focusing on a primary task unrelated to the recording device, participants were unlikely to notice the webcam indicator light of their computer turning on. They further note that it is particularly challenging to help people notice a LED status indicator when they are in the same room but otherwise occupied. We believe that this also applies to wearable cameras, particularly when there is no direct interaction between the camera user and the bystander.

Second, status LEDs might **not always be fully understood** as they are not mentally linked to the camera [46]. Particularly, when integrated into a novel and unfamiliar device, bystanders might be unsure what a point light indicates [30]. Despite point light displays providing a rich design space, their effectiveness is heavily influenced by learned conventions [24]. Since bystanders are not typically the primary users, they are often unaware of the meaning of a particular point light display. Therefore, colored LED indicators (e.g., red: recording, green: tracking) are unlikely to be optimal solutions.

Third, LED indicator lights are **not secure enough** as they are spoofable - i.e., they can be modified by their primary users to record secretly without signaling the bystanders. While hardware modifications, i.e., removing or de-wiring the LED require technical skills, LED indicators can also simply be masked[4] or painted over. In addition, malicious software might aim to take over the device and secretly record with the status LED turned off. Depending on the actual device's hardware, status LEDs are typically controlled through software, and thus could potentially be deactivated without simultaneously disabling the recording capabilities. Sophisticated counter strategies have been covered by IT Security research [40], but do not provide hundred percent protection. Aiming to prevent software attacks, other devices have the status LED hardwired in the same logical connection as the webcam. However, recent research has shown that attacks on hardwired status LEDs have also been successful [6].

Since LED indicator lights are prone to various kinds of spoofing, they are often perceived as **untrustworthy** from a user's or bystander's point of view. Prior studies have indicated that users are often unsure about the actual mode of operation of the status lights [46], and due to the perceived risk of a security breach, users often cover the camera's lens [34]. In addition, even though actual device usage might not be a privacy violation as such (e.g., having the camera turned off), the presence of a camera that is (potentially) "always-on" is perceived as a threat to privacy: a turned-off indicator light does not entirely eliminate bystander concerns of being recorded [30].

Summing up, LED status lights are not ideal for the design of effective privacy notices for body-worn cameras. Designing effective alternatives is challenging, as they would have to be *noticeable*, *understandable* without prior device-specific knowledge, *secure*, i.e. unspoofable and therefore also both, objectively and subjectively *trustworthy*.

EXPERIMENT 1: EXPERT DESIGN STUDY

To address the research challenges (1) camera presence and status, and (2) communication of the intention of use, we asked teams of experts to create concepts and design artifacts that support the user's need for *justification* and the bystander's need for *situation awareness*. This approach aims to explore requirements of privacy notices for body-worn cameras, which we believe is essential to reduce the lack of social acceptance of those devices. We do not limit privacy notices to the visual modality, but - following Schaub et al [51] - understand privacy notices as information output of interactive systems using any modality, including audio [31] and haptics [49].

Experiment Design & Participants

Design solutions developed in participatory design can produce solutions relevant to users' existing needs and desires, but may be less effective at producing innovative ideas that answer users' future or latent needs [50]. In addition, privacy notices are an abstract, non-tangible concept, and body-worn cameras not (yet) widely adopted, which makes it too challenging for non-experts to come up with novel design strategies for privacy notices. Thus, we decided to recruit experts instead of potential users for our experiments.

Working with experts promises not only to involve people that are able to reflect on needs that users are unaware of, experts also know the needs of many users from a survey perspective. Therefore, one expert can bring in the expertise of many users. In consequence, we deemed in-depth design exercises with a limited number of experts more suitable than for the particular design challenge (privacy notices of body-worn cameras) than large scale surveys, and conducted 8 design sessions (2-3h) with 2 expert participants each.

In a successful and complete product design process, iterating through analyzation, design, evaluation and redesign phases requires a lot of time [8]. In contrast, our experiments aim for incomplete, but interesting design artifacts that each address a few perspectives of the complex design challenges described beforehand. There are two reasons for this approach: first, the time frame of a single design session is too short for a fully-developed product. Second, by deliberately aiming for the incomplete and imperfect, we also allow not-fully thought out, not (yet) realizable and exaggerated or visionary ideas to be part of the created artifacts. Thus, the design artifacts' perspectives are extended towards abstract and creative thinking.

[4] How to modify & Black out Snapchat Spectacles, https://www.youtube.com/watch?v=GRN3rRqo198, accessed 12/06/2017

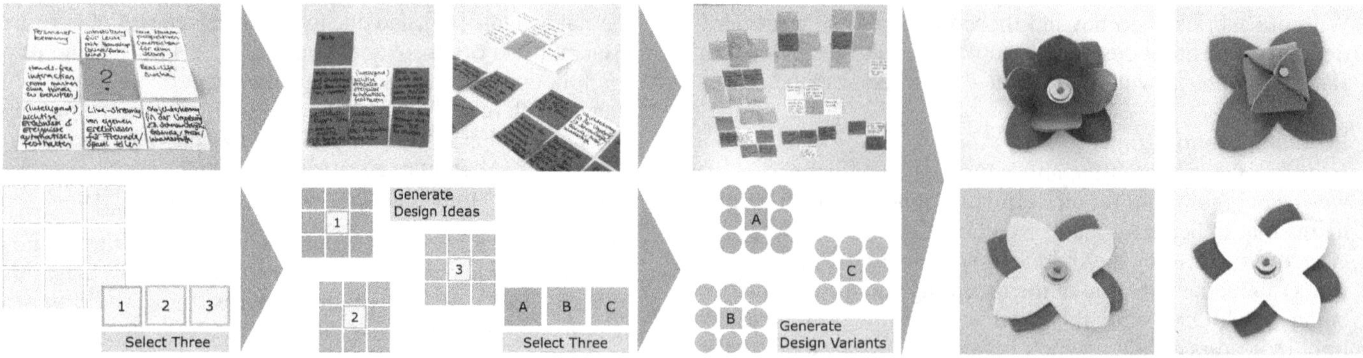

Figure 2. The design sessions were organized following the Lotus Flower Method: schematic explanation at the bottom, documentation of the design session at the top. [From left to right:] Participants started out from applications that can be enabled with wearable cameras, of which they then selected three. In two subsequent iterations they generated design ideas, selected their three favorites and elaborated on those by designing different variants. Finally, one selected idea was visualized as low-fidelity prototype (here: Prototype A, "Status Flower").

Referring to the constructivism paradigm [21, 52], which assumes that novel solutions are constructed from the learner's (here: expert's) previous knowledge, we expected the potential perspectives on the design challenges to be diverse. Thus we intentionally recruited experts with different research focuses. Each pair of experts contributes one or multiple perspectives on privacy notices of body-worn cameras from which the underlying design strategies are then reconstructed. To more holisticly understand strengths and weaknesses of each design strategy, we use the design artifacts created by experts to stimulate a discourse around our research topic [56], which, in our case, is the question how the design of body-worn smart cameras can address *justification* and *situation awareness*. This discourse will be twofold. First, the experts themselves will reflect on their designs, which happens right after they finish the design process. Second, UX experts will analyze the design artifacts, which will be described in greater detail in the section on *Experiment 2: UX Evaluation*.

We conducted 8 design sessions with 2 experts participating in each session as a design team. They were teamed up, as design is usually done in teams, and discussion often fruitfully enforces creativity [2]. To generate design artifacts that embed a wide scope of design perspectives, we recruited design research teams from our community that were covering the following expertise: (1) information retrieval (2) wearable computing (3) shape changing interfaces (4) notifications (5) ambient light displays (6) social context technologies (7) integrated media, and (8) cognitive science. They were recruited from different groups at four universities and one research institute. Our 16 experts (8 females, 8 males) were between 23 and 43 years (mean = 30, SD = 5).

Procedure & Task

Our design sessions were similarly structured like the design thinking phases [7]. Design thinking could, of course, not fully be applied as the temporal limitation of our sessions did not allow for iteration and readdressing previous phases.

First, tackling the phases *empathy* and *design*, we started with a presentation about the state of the art as well as trends and challenges of current Augmented Reality (AR) smart glasses and body-worn cameras. We also gave an overview of related research and clearly articulated our targeted problems of users' justification and bystanders' situation awareness referring to the work of Portnoff et al. [46]. Summarizing previous work's conclusions, we highlighted that LEDs do neither work for user justification nor for bystanders situation awareness, as they show significant weaknesses regarding *noticeability*, *understandability*, *security*, and *trustworthiness*.

Second, participants were instructed to ideate alternatives in a guided design process, starting from the *ideation* phase. We guided our experts through a 3-step ideation session applying the Lotus Flower Method (see Figure 2). The Lotus Flower Method [39] – or Lotus Blossom Technique [54] – is a method for group brainstorming that originated in the 1990ies. It is a problem-solving approach where each successive step provides a more in-depth look at potential solutions to the problem. Although highly structured, it fosters imagination and innovative thinking while it is at the same time easy to use and explain [25, 26, 53]. Balancing structure and flexibility, the Lotus Flower Method was ideal for our research intentions.

All experts were provided with post-its and pens. Then, using a top-down approach, we asked in step 1 *"What applications can be enabled with wearable smart cameras?"* In step 2, each team selected 3 to 4 applications and answered for them the following question: *"How and where could a smart camera communicate to spectators whether they are being captured and what the images are being used for?"*. In step 3, again 3 ideas should be selected and be brought into the next design level through developing different variations of selected ideas. The focus of that task was on *"How could the UI communicate the application kind and how the camera mode?"* For each step, we reminded the design teams to be aware of all kinds of modalities and to avoid status LEDs.

Third, we arranged a *prototype* phase. Here, each expert team chose one of their ideas generated in step 3 of the *ideation* phase. That idea was then prototyped using a material box equipped with all kinds of materials and making tools inspired by the IDEO's Tech Box[5].

Forth, we tackled the Test phase through encouraging our experts to evaluate their prototypes. The experts rated in a 7 item Likert scale *"How well the prototyped idea communicate the*

[5]A curated collection of various technologies, materials and mechanisms, source of inspiration when designers are being stuck. C.f., `https://tinyurl.com/yayvbpvq`, accessed 12/06/2017

camera status?" as well as *"How well does it communicate the kind of application?"* The ratings were intended to get the experts in the mood of critical reflecting on their ideas. Followed by that, we gathered qualitative feedback through asking for specific design elements of their prototypes. In a semi-structured interview, they were asked to name those elements particularly important/beneficial respectively problematic to situation awareness, and those elements particularly important/beneficial respectively problematic for justification. Sessions lasted 2 to 3 hours. Participants were served with sweets and beverages. There was no monetary compensation.

Measurements

We recorded the *ideation* phase by photographing the arranged post-its. Results of the *prototype* phase were captured on video and with still images of the prototypes. Ratings and answers of the *test* phase were filled in and saved in Google docs.

EXPERIMENT 2: UX EVALUATION

Nikander et al. [44] demonstrate that the outcome of concept evaluations tends to be biased, and not objective when designers evaluate a set of designs including their own concepts or ideas. For this reason, we supplement the design team's evaluations of their own prototypes (experiment 1) with a second idea evaluation, where we invited UX and HCI experts that had not taken part in our design session. The major goal of the evaluation was analyzing the meta-concepts underlying the designs from the first session and gather opinions on how well they solve the problems *noticeability*, *understandability*, *security*, and *trustworthiness*. However, as explained above, the generated design artifacts cannot take the place of ready-made product ideas. We understand them as truly subjective, and high-quality perspectives on the research challenges, which – during the design session – became physical artifacts.

Experiment Design & Participants

We conducted expert interviews aiming to capture a meta-perspective on the generated design strategies and how they target our research challenges (again, rather than aiming for finding a real product design). Hence, we interviewed UX as well as HCI experts and asked them to analyze the design artifacts created in the first experiment. We invited 12 HCI and UX experts (6 m / 6 f), aged 25 to 40 ($M = 30, SD = 4$) who had in average 7 years of experience (SD = 4).

Procedure, Task & Measurements

There are no established usability principles (heuristics) or evaluation criteria for body-worn or Augmented Reality smart cameras (yet). Nevertheless, general criteria for privacy notices, such as presented by Cranor et al. [11], Dourish et al. [13], and Bellotti et al. [3] are available and had provided the theoretical groundwork for the design requirements that were given to the experts during the first iteration of design sessions. For this reason, we re-used the design requirements and transferred them into open interview questions.

For each of the 8 design artifacts, we prepared a printed A4 design explanation card containing 3-4 pictures and a descriptive text. A short version of the explanations is shown in Table 1. To encourage our interview partners to judge the design artifacts, we asked them for rating each design regarding the pre-defined requirements, e.g. "How noticeable is the camera's status in the described design?". The ratings were measured in a 7 item Likert scale (1: "very poorly" to 7: "very well"). Again, through the provision of a numerical rating, the expert participants should be directed towards re-thinking the concepts and establishing a consolidated opinion, before elaborating. Making a decision about the rating was only used as an "opinion builder" to serve as starting point to reflect on the ideas. Then, in a second step, the participants were asked to explain their rating, which we later used as basis for analysis and discussion. The design artifacts were presented in randomized order. Ratings and interview answers were recorded using Google docs.

RESULTS

This section jointly presents results of the expert design study (Experiment 1) and the UX evaluation (Experiment 2). Each design team visualized their favorite concept from the ideation phase as a low-fidelity prototype. We denote qualitative statements and ideas by the design teams as "DT". An overview of the resulting prototypes is given in Table 1. The prototypes represent iteratively developed interaction concepts that are made physically using material and low-fi prototyping techniques. As result, we got 8 design artifacts that address the issues previously mentioned with AR and smart cameras. The design artifacts serve as base for identifying design strategies that make AR and smart cams more usable in public.

In addtion to the prototypes, we analyzed the ideas of step 2 and 3 of the *ideation* phase (Lotus Flower) using inductive category development, as suggested by Mayring [37] and extracted design ideas. Then, we compared the developed prototypes amongst each other and to the extracted ideas, and worked out overarching approaches to solve the research problem, that we subsequently present as design strategies.

Discovered design strategies were analyzed qualitatively. We carefully selected suitable qualitative comments from our expert evaluation that help reflecting on the design strategies from a meta-perspective. As explained earlier, the expert rating of the prototypes served as "opinion builder" so that the experts have a starting point from where they can explain their opinion about the ideas. Hence, we selectively report ratings that have clear scoring when describing the design strategies to show what concepts were found most or least promising. Here, we present the design strategies and substantiate them through expert ratings as well as through expert comments (denoted as "E") explaining their critical and promising aspects.

Physical Occlusion

A concept that, in contrast to software solutions, was rated trustworthy is the occlusion of the camera lens with opaque material (Prototype A & C) which is reflected by the highly rated security (Mdn=6, SD=1.8) and trustworthiness (Mdn=5, SD=1.7) of Prototype A. This idea is inspired by traditional camera lens covers ("irises"), which prevents image capturing even if the software would still be in recording state.

The occlusion ideas show that that approach allows for playfulness and physical design of, for example, a flower metaphor with opening and closing leaflets (Prototype A), or a physical "eye lid" metaphor as used in Prototype C. Both serve to

	Prototype A - DT1	Prototype B - DT2	Prototype C - DT3	Prototype D - DT4
Prototype Depiction			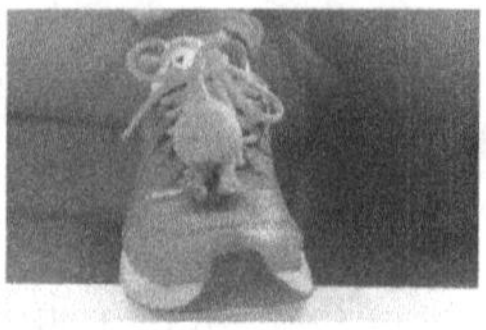	
Short Description	A flower-shaped camera enclosure covers the lens with an opaque material when no recording takes place ("closed bud" metaphor). Different types of recordings (video, still images) are visualized through color changing petals.	The camera device has an embedded printer that displays the captures as physical artifacts. The artifacts also serve as controls that can be used by the bystander to delete the recording or adjust the audience it may be shared to.	A kid's camera shaped as a character with the lens embedded in the eye. Eyelid and ears close when no video/audio is captured ("eyelid" metaphor). The necks tilting angle indicates the angle of vision.	The camera device is projecting a frustum on the floor, indicating what area is being captured. Additionally, icons are projected that indicate the nature of the recording, e.g., video/still images as well as whether (and where) the imagery might be shared.
Design Strategies	physical occlusion color-coding	transfer of control displayed camera image	physical occlusion indicated angle of vision	indicated angle of vision indicate captured area visible device actions text & icon
	Prototype E - DT5	Prototype F - DT6	Prototype G - DT7	Prototype H - DT8
Prototype Depiction				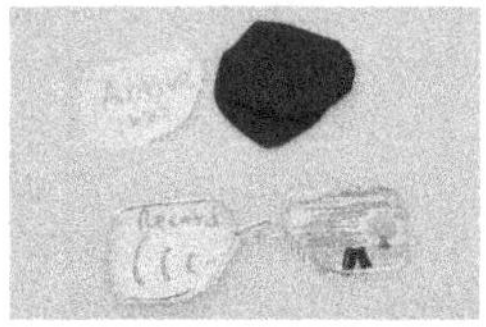
Short Description	The camera device integrates two icons, one for "analysis only" and one for "persistent storage"/"recording" associated with a color ("red" and "blue") as well as a textual label. The corresponding color is repeated as circling point light on a LED circle surrounding the lens.	The camera device depicts or "mirrors" the camera's view of the scene when the device is turned on. Its image is shown in an abstract way to visualize object or person detection/recognition (here: 3 persons) and where detected entities are located in the field of view.	The camera device (here: glasses) "mirrors" the camera view on its frame and lenses. If a face is recognized, the frame on the glasses front lights up (for the detected bystander to see) and vibrates (for the user to feel the event).	This smart glasses device for blind people acts as normal (dark) sunglasses when turned off. When turned on it shows the camera image on one side and an icon and textual description of the usage intention on the other side.
Design Strategies	text & icon color-coding visible device actions	displayed camera image visible device actions	displayed camera image visible device actions	text & icon color-coding displayed camera image

Table 1. Physical design artifacts created during the design sessions of Experiment 1. Each artifact is presented along with characteristic design strategies obtained from inductive category development and comparative analysis. Further imagery is included with the supplementary material.

reassure bystanders of what a camera can capture and what is impossible to be recorded through. This effect can also be leveraged by playing around with other physically limiting attributes of the camera, for example the FOV (through tilting the camera or using glare shields or blenders). The simplicity of that concept was very much appreciated by E10 who stated *"Metaphors ... for everybody. With open eyes, you can see, with closed eyes you can't. Same with the direction of the eye."*

Indicated Capture Area and Angle of Vision

Depicting the camera's frustum in the environment (see Prototype D) leads to high noticeability (Mdn=6, SD=1.6). Variants had been proposed also during the phases of *ideation*, where participants suggested metaphors such as "Aura", "Shine" or "Halo" to indicate capturing angle and distance or projecting an area on the floor. Consequently, if inside the captured frame, a bystander could step out of it knowing where to stand without being captured. While this concept can be easily seen (E3) and is a *"good way of giving context to other people"* (E4), the projector could be masked (E4, 5, 6, 8), and therefore, E12 even *"won't trust the projector operation"*.

Displayed Camera Image

In their final prototype, four out of eight design teams (DT) suggested to communicate to bystanders what the camera was recording by displaying the camera image (Prototypes B, F, G, H). This strategy follows a "What-you-see-is-what-you-get" approach, as appreciated by E8: *"The device is feeding back what it captures."* In consequence, this strategy becomes very understandable, which is emphasized by the two highest ratings for understandability, the understandable camera status of Prototype H (Mdn=6.5, SD=0.8) as well as of the understandable application purpose of Prototype F and H (F: Mdn=6.5, SD=1.5, H: Mdn=6.5, SD=2.0). Even though displaying the camera image may be intuitive as that method is building on what users know about digital cameras, remote display locations (e.g. on the chest) may be a problem as the connection of the camera and the camera image might not always be obvious: *"[The prototype] does not really link image and camera on a first glance."* (DT6) Moreover, even though the camera could be recording, *"The display can still be covered if I just put the camera upside down in my shirt pocket."* (E5 about Prototype

F) Another problem of this strategy (as of any but the physical occlusion) is a lack of trustworthiness. Experts mention that the device could be capturing even, despite a software controlled display indicating the opposite: *"If the displayed video was paused, it [the camera] could still capture."* (E2) However, E10 noted that *"an abstraction of the image increases the trustworthiness"*, but E8 raised the concern that it was unclear whether *"the raw image [was] saved somewhere?"*.

Visible Device Actions

While the previously discussed strategy ("displaying the camera image") replicates the captured image, other suggestions aimed to make usage intentions visible to provide a better understanding of what the image will be used for. DT6 suggested, for instance, displaying the result of image processing to both the user and the bystander, through displaying emojis on smart glasses when performing emotion detection to communicate to the bystander which sentiment has been recognized. That would allow to better show what kind of application is used (E1). Further design ideas made use of abstractions (Prototype F, G) to symbolize that objects or persons were detected, e.g., highlighting a "view finder" on successful face recognition. However, this only communicates that something has been recognized but not for what purpose (E11). The proposed solutions have been criticized for a lack of understandability (E8, E9), which could potentially be achieved better using application icons (E2), as explained in the next paragraph.

Color-coding, Text & Icon

The experts proposed established methods to visualize information, especially concepts that require only little display space, were proposed. Colors can be used to symbolize (or "code") different kinds of stati or meanings. Color-coding of some sort has been used in Prototype A, E and H. However, using color codes is easier to implement than other design strategies, experts have doubts about the understandability of such visualization as, for example, *"Blossom color change / flash does not inform us exactly of what is happening"* (E7). Such concern was already stated from the design team itself when reflecting on their prototype: *"We're not sure whether the glowing, blinking, and steady colour is intuitive."* (DT1)

Textual displays, e.g., "recording" have been suggested in Prototypes E and H, which may be easier to get but hard to read from greater distance. Moreover, various icons or pictograms were proposed to illustrate the camera's status and the purpose of recording, persistence of data storage or the targeted platform for sharing (Prototype D). Although, icons are widely-used, they *"can have different meanings if the audience is not trained for it"* (E11), and hence, *"[i]conic design could be unintuitive"* (DT5). Using well-known icons, e.g., associated with applications (E5) or social media (E6, E8), can communicate what application is accessing the image. Nevertheless, there is some vagueness, e.g., where or to whom social media would share an image (E9, E11), which would require a new consent vocabulary of icons (E5).

Transfer of Control

During *ideation*, different mechanisms to transfer control over the image to the bystander, were proposed, e.g., using gesture or voice commands such as "camera off" to disable a third party camera. Prototype B suggests to put the bystander in control and to enable him/her to consent (or object) to being recorded, for example, through deleting the image. Alternatively, (s)he can allow the user to share it via a social network. This idea also embodies the notion of a person's ownership of his/her image. While it is difficult to fully control the distribution of digital media, this is truly possible with analog media. Protoype B encapsulates the control into an analog artifact and hands the picture over to the captured person. While this idea lacks in transparency whether the camera is recording or not (E5, E6, E7), and the feedback about the recording might be given too late to be rejected by the bystander (E8), Prototype 2 presents an interesting and truly novel approach for a transfer of control over the image usage from user to bystander. However, experts also noted a lack of trust regarding both, user and used technology: *"I don't trust human beings, and this is a big factor here."* (E10), *"I cannot verify what has been recorded and if the bubble really was pressed."* (E9), The *"camera could still store images."* (E6) However, it is appreciated by E9 that – after handing over the physical control – the captured person can decide about her/his likeness. In summary, experts liked the principle of handing over control, but criticized how this aim was implemented in the Low-Fi prototype.

DISCUSSION

To derive design recommendations and to close the loop on the evaluation criteria, noticeability, understandability, security, and trustworthiness, presented in the section on *Problem Description*, we discuss how the identified design strategies address the criteria as well as how they relate to previous work.

Improving Noticeability

Noticeability, i.e., whether user's notice a privacy indicator or not is an important quality criteria [11] of privacy notices. Design strategies that made a device most noticeable were those that display the camera image or the ones indicating the capture area. A reason for the good noticeability of these strategies is surely the visual dominance of the shown content and its well visible placement. In the case of body-worn cameras, its status, e.g, recording, idle, or off, but also the camera's presence and location has to be communicated. The latter fails, if the camera is not recognized as such, as e.g, criticized for Prototype C: *"Having [a] hidden camera is not socially acceptable."* (DT3). On the other hand, privacy notices that merely inform bystanders – e.g., "Warning: CCTV in use" signs or Protoype D's "recording", but do not offer actionable and meaningful choices are not effective [51].

However, procedures or technologies realizing choice of consent or mediation of privacy preferences (c.f., [38, 45]) also need to appropriately notify bystanders of the necessity of choice in the first place. Procedures that ask for consent without prior notice, might satisfy the need for *justification*, but not the need for *situation awareness*. A lack of notice was also criticized by the UX experts: *"It's a Kinder Surprise[6] - only when you have been captured you can choose what you do."* (E7 about Prototype B) While the control card (Prototype B) provided the bystander with control over the captured imagery and the option to withdraw his/her consent to recording, this

[6]Popular sweet, a chocolate egg containing a small plastic toy, https://en.wikipedia.org/wiki/Kinder_Surprise, accessed 12/06/2017

was only after (s)he had already been recorded. Thus, the request for consent was not coupled with an appropriately timed notice: ideally, consent and notice complement each other.

Recommendation: Combine consent and notice in a meaningful way; First notify and make both, user and bystander aware of the situation, then ask for consent.

Improving Understandability

Bystanders of body-worn cameras encounter them incidentally and potentially without preparation. Hence, privacy notices targeted at bystanders need to be understandable without prior knowledge. Egelman et al. [15] note that a lack of familiarity with e.g., face detection and recognition, video recording and visual tracking, makes it difficult to design distinguishable icons presenting those concepts, which is suggested through the design strategy: visible device action. This is problematic, as according to Moyes et al. "an icon [that] is not guessable it is not necessarily an unsuccessful icon" [42]. In consequence, while icons, related techniques (e.g., earcons [4], and also color codes can be beneficial for primary users that had the opportunity to learn their meaning, they do not achieve the goal of *situation awareness* on the bystanders' side. In addition, they might be inaccessible to users suffering from color blindness. Textual displays can only partially overcome this problem, as the bystander would need to be able to see it under readable conditions (lighting conditions, glare, scale), and understand, both used language and the notices meaning. Metaphors, such as e.g., the "eye lid" (Prototype C), "iris", or "bud" (Prototype A) might be a promising approach, whose effectiveness will have to be proven by future work. Approaches from cinematography [35] could also inspire non-iconic, but simple 2D visualizations of captured regions (c.f., Gustafson et al. [23]), as outlined by Prototype D.

Recommendation: Privacy notices targeting bystanders, should avoid any element that has to be known (written language), learned (color codes) or cannot be guessed easily (complex, unfamiliar icons), as well as consider accessibility.

Improving Security & Trustworthiness

Concerning privacy notices, security and perceived trustworthiness are closely interconnected. However, an unspoofable, i.e., objectively secure technique, is not necessarily perceived as fully trustworthy. A design strategy that can achieve both is to physically block the camera lens. Evidence about webcam covering behavior [34] as well as homemade camera covers[7], suggest that this might be an intuitive and higly trustworthy option (also noted by Bellotti et al. [3]). In the context of body-worn cameras this strategy could act reassuringly by justifying both needs, *situation awareness* and *justification*. However, noticeability and understandability might largely depend on the visual design of the shutter or switch, particularly whether the camera is still recognizable as such.

Shutters and switches, but also any other enabling/disabling function of a body-worn cameras can be operated manually or automatic. Manual operation by the user might be easy to realize, but also prone to human error and dishonesty, as noted during the UX evaluation: *"If you have trustworthy users, the system is trustworthy. Utopia."* (E10 about Prototype B). For this reason, manually disabling a camera might not be predictable enough from a bystander's perspective, as they cannot be sure whether the user will actually remember or be willing to disable the camera, when e.g., entering a public bathroom or swimming pool. Moreover, notifying displays could be deliberately hidden by camera users. Hence, the location of the camera lens and of the notifying display should be at the same position, which ensures that of the display is occluded that lens is occluded as well.

Due to the mistrust in users as outlined above, automatic, software-controlled solutions, e.g., based on sensors[8] that ensure bystander privacy might be preferable. This is a challenge for future research, as they would require sensing procedures that, unlike e.g., microphones, do not infringe with the users privacy and that are robust enough to reliably react to changes regarding the privacy sensitivity of a situation.

Recommendation: Privacy notices should provide bystanders with a reassuring mechanism to rule out false positives (recording without indication), and automatically react to privacy sensitive situations in a predictable and reliable way.

Limitations

With their relatively small scale our studies do not provide a generalizable cross section of opinions. However, we believe that, as stated by Jakob Nielsen [43] that specialists can act as "double experts" with their expertise covering the kind of interface being evaluated, as well as its users, thus providing a survey perspective. Nevertheless, particularly creative or extraordinary solutions might have been missed. On the provision of their informed consent for experiment one, participants were informed that they will be asked to prototype in the end. Thus, they might have been biased towards rejecting concepts that are hard to build, e.g., the "odor emitting camera" (DT6).

CONCLUSION

LED status lights are an established option to signal whether a wearable camera is recording, but lack *noticeability*, *understandability*, *security* and *trustworthiness*. In this work, we investigated alternative announcement mechanisms in the context of body-worn cameras addressing those problems. From a UX analysis of design strategies based on 8 physical artifacts designed by experts, we derive design recommendations for privacy notices and privacy mediating technologies for body-worn cameras. Providing potential starting points for product design, our recommendations address a timely issue, as the increasing dissemination of wearable consumer cameras and the projected EU legislation (GDPD) demand effective solutions for privacy notices, that realize privacy-by-design and that are acceptable from the perspectives of all stakeholders, including users, bystanders and manufacturers.

ACKNOWLEDGMENTS

This work has been supported by the BMBF project ChaRiSma under grant number 16I1665.

[7]John Biehler, Google Glass Privacy Cover, https://www.thingiverse.com/thing:182763, accessed 12/06/2017

[8]Patent for a computing device camera view controller and shutter, https://www.google.com/patents/WO2016090351A1, accessed 12/06/2017

REFERENCES

1. Paarijaat Aditya, Rijurekha Sen, Peter Druschel, Seong Joon Oh, Rodrigo Benenson, Mario Fritz, Bernt Schiele, Bobby Bhattacharjee, and Tong Tong Wu. 2016. I-pic: A platform for Privacy-compliant Image Capture. In *Annual International Conference on Mobile Systems, Applications, and Services (MobiSys)*. ACM, 235–248. DOI:http://dx.doi.org/10.1145/2906388.2906412
2. Ernesto Arias, Hal Eden, Gerhard Fischer, Andrew Gorman, and Eric Scharff. 2000. Transcending the Individual Human Mind – Creating Shared Understanding through Collaborative Design. *ACM Transactions on Computer-Human Interaction (TOCHI)* 7, 1 (2000), 84–113. DOI: http://dx.doi.org/10.1145/344949.345015
3. Victoria Bellotti and Abigail Sellen. 1993. Design for Privacy in Ubiquitous Computing Environments. In *European Conference on Computer-Supported Cooperative Work (ECSCW)*. 77–92. http://dl.acm.org/citation.cfm?id=1241940
4. Meera M Blattner, Denise A Sumikawa, and Robert M Greenberg. 1989. Earcons and Icons: Their Structure and Common Design Principles. *Human–Computer Interaction* 4, 1 (1989), 11–44. DOI: http://dx.doi.org/10.1207/s15327051hci0401_1
5. Stephen Brewster, Roderick Murray-Smith, Andrew Crossan, Yolanda Vasquez-Alvarez, and Julie Rico. 2009. The GAIME project: Gestural and Auditory Interactions for Mobile Environments. *BRIT COMP S* (2009). http://eprints.gla.ac.uk/34242/
6. Matthew Brocker and Stephen Checkoway. 2014. iSeeYou: Disabling the MacBook Webcam Indicator LED. In *USENIX Security*. 337–352. http://dl.acm.org/citation.cfm?id=2671247
7. Tim Brown. 2009. Change by Design. (2009).
8. Tim Brown and Jocelyn Wyatt. 2010. Design Thinking for Social Innovation IDEO. *Development Outreach* 12, 1 (2010), 29–31. DOI: http://dx.doi.org/10.1596/1020-797X_12_1_29
9. Ann Cavoukian. 2009. Privacy by Design – The 7 Foundational Principles. (2009). https://www.iab.org/wp-content/IAB-uploads/2011/03/fred_carter.pdf accessed 12/06/2017.
10. Soumyadeb Chowdhury, Md Sadek Ferdous, and Joemon M Jose. 2016. Bystander Privacy in Lifelogging. In *British Human Computer Interaction Conference*. DOI: http://dx.doi.org/doi:10.14236/ewic/HCI2016.62
11. Lorrie Faith Cranor. 2006. What do they indicate?: Evaluating Security and Privacy Indicators. *Interactions* 13, 3 (2006), 45–47. DOI: http://dx.doi.org/10.1145/1125864.1125890
12. Tamara Denning, Zakariya Dehlawi, and Tadayoshi Kohno. 2014. In situ with Bystanders of Augmented Reality Glasses: Perspectives on Recording and Privacy-mediating Technologies. In *Conference on Human Factors in Computing Systems (CHI)*. ACM, 2377–2386. DOI: http://dx.doi.org/10.1145/2556288.2557352
13. Paul Dourish, E. Grinter, Jessica Delgado de la Flor, and Melissa Joseph. 2004. Security in the Wild: User Strategies for Managing Security As an Everyday, Practical Problem. *Personal Ubiquitous Comput.* 8, 6 (Nov. 2004), 391–401. DOI: http://dx.doi.org/10.1007/s00779-004-0308-5
14. Anthony Dunne and Fiona Raby. 2001. *Design Noir: The Secret Life of Electronic Objects*. Birkhauser.
15. Serge Egelman, Raghudeep Kannavara, and Richard Chow. 2015. Is This Thing On?: Crowdsourcing Privacy Indicators for Ubiquitous Sensing Platforms. In *Conference on Human Factors in Computing Systems (CHI)*. ACM, New York, NY, USA, 1669–1678. DOI: http://dx.doi.org/10.1145/2702123.2702251
16. Barrett Ens, Tovi Grossman, Fraser Anderson, Justin Matejka, and George Fitzmaurice. 2015. Candid interaction: Revealing hidden mobile and wearable computing activities. In *Annual ACM Symposium on User Interface Software & Technology (UIST)*. ACM, 467–476. DOI:http://dx.doi.org/10.1145/2807442.2807449
17. Md Sadek Ferdous, Soumyadeb Chowdhury, and Joemon M Jose. 2017. Analysing Privacy in Visual Lifelogging. *Pervasive and Mobile Computing* (2017). DOI:http://dx.doi.org/10.1016/j.pmcj.2017.03.003
18. Ivo Flammer. 2016. Genteel Wearables: Bystander-Centered Design. *IEEE Security & Privacy* 14, 5 (2016), 73–79. DOI: http://dx.doi.org/10.1109/MSP.2016.91
19. Organisation for Economic Co-operation and Development. 2013. *OECD Guidelines on the Protection of Privacy and Transborder Flows of Personal Data.* OECD Publishing. http://acts.oecd.org/Instruments/ShowInstrumentView.aspx?InstrumentID=114&InstrumentPID=312&Lang=en accessed 12/06/2017.
20. Joshua Gluck, Florian Schaub, Amy Friedman, Hana Habib, Norman Sadeh, Lorrie Faith Cranor, and Yuvraj Agarwal. 2016. How Short Is Too Short? Implications of Length and Framing on the Effectiveness of Privacy Notices. In *Symposium on Usable Privacy and Security (SOUPS)*. https://www.usenix.org/node/197281
21. Egon G Guba, Yvonna S Lincoln, and others. 1994. Competing Paradigms in Qualitative Research. *Handbook of Qualitative Research* 2, 163-194 (1994).
22. Cathal Gurrin, Rami Albatal, Hideo Joho, and Kaori Ishii. 2014. A Privacy by Design Approach to Lifelogging. *Digital Enlightenment Yearbook* (2014), 49–73. http://doras.dcu.ie/20505/

23. Sean Gustafson, Patrick Baudisch, Carl Gutwin, and Pourang Irani. 2008. Wedge: Clutter-free Visualization of off-screen Locations. In *Conference on Human Factors in Computing Systems (CHI)*. ACM, 787–796. DOI: http://dx.doi.org/10.1145/1357054.1357179

24. Chris Harrison, John Horstman, Gary Hsieh, and Scott Hudson. 2012. Unlocking the Expressivity of Point Lights. In *Conference on Human Factors in Computing Systems (CHI.* ACM, 1683–1692. DOI: http://dx.doi.org/10.1145/2207676.2208296

25. James M Higgins. 1994. *101 creative problem solving techniques: The handbook of new ideas for business*. New Management Publishing Company.

26. James M Higgins. 1996. Innovate or evaporate: creative techniques for strategists. *Long Range Planning* 29, 3 (1996), 370–380.

27. Roberto Hoyle, Robert Templeman, Steven Armes, Denise Anthony, David Crandall, and Apu Kapadia. 2014. Privacy Behaviors of Lifeloggers using Wearable Cameras. In *International Joint Conference on Pervasive and Ubiquitous Computing (Ubicomp)*. ACM, 571–582. DOI:http://dx.doi.org/10.1145/2632048.2632079

28. Giovanni Iachello, Khai N Truong, Gregory D Abowd, Gillian R Hayes, and Molly Stevens. 2006. Prototyping and Sampling Experience to Evaluate Ubiquitous Computing Privacy in the Real World. In *Conference on Human Factors in Computing Systems (CHI)*. ACM, 1009–1018. DOI: http://dx.doi.org/10.1145/1124772.1124923

29. Patrick Gage Kelley, Lorrie Faith Cranor, and Norman Sadeh. 2013. Privacy as Part of the App Decision-making Process. In *Conference on Human Factors in Computing Systems (CHI)*. ACM, 3393–3402. DOI: http://dx.doi.org/10.1145/2470654.2466466

30. Marion Koelle, Matthias Kranz, and Andreas Möller. 2015. Don't look at me that way!: Understanding User Attitudes Towards Data Glasses Usage. In *International Conference on Human-Computer Interaction with Mobile Devices and Services (MobileHCI)*. ACM, 362–372. DOI: http://dx.doi.org/10.1145/2785830.2785842

31. Gregory Kramer. 1993. *Auditory Display: Sonification, Audification, and Auditory Interfaces*. Westview Press.

32. Katharina Krombholz, Adrian Dabrowski, Matthew Smith, and Edgar Weippl. 2017. Exploring Design Directions for Wearable Privacy. In *Network and Distributed System Security Symposium (NDSS)*. DOI: http://dx.doi.org/10.14722/usec.2017.23001

33. Marc Langheinrich. 2001. Privacy by Design – principles of Privacy-aware Ubiquitous Systems. In *International conference on Ubiquitous Computing (Ubicomp)*. Springer, 273–291. http://www.vs.inf.ethz.ch/publ/papers/privacy-principles.pdf

34. Dominique Machuletz, Henrik Sendt, Stefan Laube, and Rainer Böhme. 2016. Users Protect Their Privacy If They Can: Determinants of Webcam Covering Behavior. In *European Workshop on Usable Security (EuroUSEC)*. DOI:http://dx.doi.org/10.14722/eurousec.2016.23014

35. Tim Marsh and Peter Wright. 2000. Using cinematography conventions to inform guidelines for the design and evaluation of virtual off-screen space. In *AAAI 2000 Spring Symp. Ser. Smart Graphics*. 123–127.

36. Max-Emanuel Maurer, Alexander De Luca, and Tobias Stockinger. 2011. Shining Chrome: Using Web Browser Personas to Enhance SSL Certificate Visualization. In *IFIP TC 13 International Conference on Human-Computer Interaction (Lecture Notes in Computer Science)*, Vol. 6949. Springer, 44–51.

37. Philipp Mayring. 2014. Qualitative content analysis: theoretical foundation, basic procedures and software solution. (2014). http://nbn-resolving.de/urn:nbn:de:0168-ssoar-395173

38. Mohsin Ali Memon and Jiro Tanaka. 2014. Ensuring Privacy during Pervasive Logging by a Passerby. *Journal of Information Processing* 22, 2 (2014), 334–343. DOI: http://dx.doi.org/10.2197/ipsjjip.22.334

39. Michael Michalko. 2014. *Thinkpak: a Brainstorming Card Deck*. Ten Speed Press.

40. Saeed Mirzamohammadi and Ardalan Amiri Sani. 2016. Viola: Trustworthy Sensor Notifications for Enhanced Privacy on Mobile Systems. In *Annual International Conference on Mobile Systems, Applications, and Services (MobiSys)*. ACM, 263–276. DOI: http://dx.doi.org/10.1145/2906388.2906391

41. Calkin S. Montero, Jason Alexander, Mark T. Marshall, and Sriram Subramanian. 2010. Would You Do That?: Understanding Social Acceptance of Gestural Interfaces. In *International Conference on Human-Computer Interaction with Mobile Devices and Services (MobileHCI)*. ACM, New York, NY, USA, 275–278. DOI: http://dx.doi.org/10.1145/1851600.1851647

42. Jackie Moyes and Patrick W Jordan. 1993. Icon Design and its Effect on Guessability, Learnability, and Experienced User Performance. *People and Computers* 8 (1993), 49–60.

43. Jakob Nielsen. 1992. Finding Usability Problems Through Heuristic Evaluation. In *Conference on Human Factors in Computing Systems (CHI)*. ACM, New York, NY, USA, 373–380. DOI: http://dx.doi.org/10.1145/142750.142834

44. Jan B Nikander, Lassi A Liikkanen, and Miko Laakso. 2014. The Preference Effect in Design Concept Evaluation. *Design Studies* 35, 5 (2014), 473–499. DOI: http://dx.doi.org/10.1016/j.destud.2014.02.006

45. Sarah Pidcock, Rob Smits, Urs Hengartner, and Ian Goldberg. 2011. Notisense: An Urban Sensing Notification System to Improve Bystander Privacy. *PhoneSense* (2011). DOI: http://dx.doi.org/10.1.1.390.599

46. Rebecca S Portnoff, Linda N Lee, Serge Egelman, Pratyush Mishra, Derek Leung, and David Wagner. 2015. Somebody's Watching Me?: Assessing the Effectiveness of Webcam Indicator Lights. In *Conference on Human Factors in Computing Systems (CHI)*. ACM, 1649–1658. DOI: http://dx.doi.org/10.1145/2702123.2702164

47. Halley Profita, Reem Albaghli, Leah Findlater, Paul Jaeger, and Shaun K Kane. 2016. The AT Effect: How Disability Affects the Perceived Social Acceptability of Head-Mounted Display Use. In *Conference on Human Factors in Computing Systems (CHI)*. ACM, 4884–4895. DOI: http://dx.doi.org/10.1145/2858036.2858130

48. Kenneth Radke, Colin Boyd, Juan Gonzalez Nieto, and Laurie Buys. 2013. Who decides?: Security and Privacy in the Wild. In *Australian Computer-Human Interaction Conference (OzCHI)*. ACM, 27–36. DOI: http://dx.doi.org/10.1145/2541016.2541043

49. Diego C. Ruspini, Krasimir Kolarov, and Oussama Khatib. 1997. The Haptic Display of Complex Graphical Environments. In *Annual Conference on Computer Graphics and Interactive Techniques (SIGGRAPH)*. ACM Press/Addison-Wesley Publishing Co., New York, NY, USA, 345–352. DOI: http://dx.doi.org/10.1145/258734.258878

50. Elizabeth BN Sanders. 2001. Virtuosos of the Experience Domain. In *IDSA Education Conference*. Boston, USA. http://echo.iat.sfu.ca/library/sanders_01_virtuosos.pdf

51. Florian Schaub, Rebecca Balebako, Adam L Durity, and Lorrie Faith Cranor. 2015. A Design Space for Effective Privacy Notices. In *Symposium On Usable Privacy and Security (SOUPS)*. USENIX Association, 1–17. https://www.usenix.org/conference/soups2015/proceedings/presentation/schaub

52. Thomas A Schwandt and others. 1994. Constructivist, Interpretivist Approaches to Human Inquiry. *Handbook of Qualitative Research* 1 (1994), 118–137.

53. Gerald F Smith. 1998. Idea-generation techniques: A formulary of active ingredients. *The Journal of Creative Behavior* 32, 2 (1998), 107–134.

54. Sheridan Tatsuno. 1990. *Created in Japan: From imitators to world-class innovators*. Ballinger Pub Co.

55. Katrin Wolf, Albrecht Schmidt, Agon Bexheti, and Marc Langheinrich. 2014. Lifelogging: You're Wearing a Camera? *IEEE Pervasive Computing* 13, 3 (2014), 8–12. DOI: http://dx.doi.org/10.1109/MPRV.2014.53

56. John Zimmerman, Jodi Forlizzi, and Shelley Evenson. 2007. Research through Design as a Method for Interaction Design Research in HCI. In *Conference on Human Factors in Computing Systems (CHI)*. ACM, 493–502. DOI: http://dx.doi.org/10.1145/1240624.1240704

zPatch: Hybrid Resistive/Capacitive eTextile Input

Paul Strohmeier, Jarrod Knibbe, Sebastian Boring, Kasper Hornbæk
Human Centred Computing - University of Copenhagen, Denmark
{p.strohmeier, jarrod, sebastian.boring, kash} @ di.ku.dk

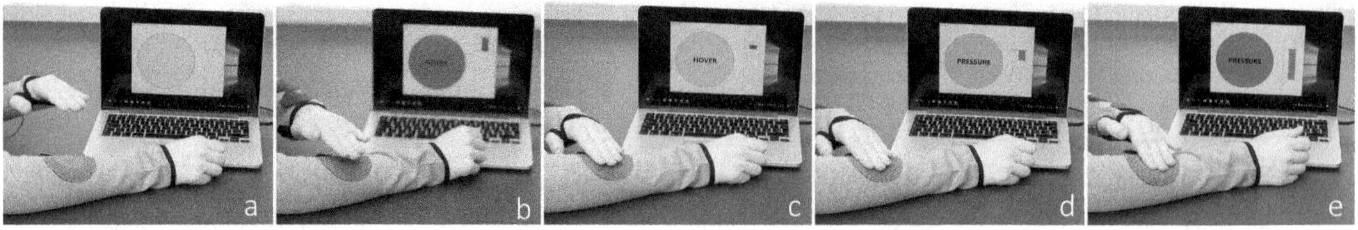

Figure 1 – Hand approaching and pressing a zPatch: (a) initially, the patch does not detect the hand, (b, c) as the hand approaches the sensor, hover is detected, (d, e) once the hand touches the sensor, the exerted pressure is reported.

ABSTRACT
We present zPatch: an eTextile patch for hover, touch, and pressure input, using both resistive and capacitive sensing. zPatches are made by layering a piezo-resistive material between silver-plated ripstop, and embedding it in non-conductive fabric to form a patch. zPatches can be easily ironed onto most fabrics, in any location, enabling easy prototyping or ad hoc modifications of existing garments. We provide open-source resources for building and programming zPatches and present measures of the achievable sensing resolution of a zPatch. A pressure based targeting task demonstrated users could reliably hit pressure targets at up to 13 levels, given appropriate feedback. We demonstrate that the hybrid sensing approach reduces false activations and helps distinguish between gestures. Finally, we present example applications in which we use zPatches for controlling a music player, text entry and gaming input.

Author Keywords
Hybrid Sensing, eTextile, On Body Input

ACM Classification Keywords
Human-centered computing~Human computer interaction (HCI) • Human-centered computing~User interface toolkits

INTRODUCTION
On-body input sensing has received much attention in HCI. For example, wearable sensors have been presented for mobile gesture input [34] and on-skin tracking has expanded the interaction space of smartwatches beyond the device [18]. These input techniques and technologies typically focus on lateral interaction across the body: Though taps, swipes and multi-touch may be used, it is their spatial distribution across the surface plane that received the most attention.

When interacting on the body, pressure and touch-dynamics are especially interesting, as we perceive the interaction both with the active hand and the passive body part that is being touched [22]. The way in which we might interact with our body is also very likely to be more complex [42] than could be detected by a simple touch-position sensor.

We have therefore designed zPatches: small fabric sensor patches that can be sewn or ironed onto existing clothing. zPatches are designed to maximize sensing capabilities to capture the dynamics of on-body touch interaction. zPatches use a hybrid sensing approach: capacitive sensing enables the measurement of approach behavior and hover interactions, while resistive sensing provides robustness and high-resolution pressure measurements.

zPatches are designed to be simple to manufacture and deploy. This simplicity does not come at the cost of sensor performance: using both sensing modalities of a zPatches provides it with the ability to distinguish between different input gestures. Additionally their hybrid sensing approach can be used to reduce false activation problems [14] typically associated with fabric sensors.

zPatches are not only easy to build, but also simple to deploy. They can be sewn or ironed onto garments, allowing for individual customization. They can also be attached with safety pins for fast prototyping.

We make the following contributions: (1) a simple workflow as well as instructions and open source code for novices and experts to create similar textile sensors; (2) evaluations of the fidelity zPatch and a demonstrate of how hybrid sensing can reduce unintentional activation and improve gesture classification; and (3) example applications of zPatches, including a music player, text entry, and gaming.

TEI '18, March 18–21, 2018, Stockholm, Sweden

ACM ISBN 978-1-4503-5568-1/18/03.
https://doi.org/10.1145/3173225.3173242

RELATED WORK

We present an eTextile sensor that enables proximity-, touch-, and pressure-based input on the body. While touch, proximity [16] and pressure [31] have been explored in rigid devices, our primary interest is to develop a platform that allows for their transfer on to the body. Our research draws upon in eTextile sensing and craft, and is inspired by our proprioceptive, kinesthetic and tactile perception.

Haptic Physiology

Our body provides us with a rich feedback channel for touch interactions. We can sense the location of a touch within around 2mm for the hands and face and around 10mm on most other parts of the body [22,43]. The tactile sensitivity of the skin has been measured to be around 0.07g for the face and hands, ~0.4g for the arms, and ~1g for the legs [1]. We present a system focusing on the latter feedback channel. Additionally, we benefit from the proprioceptive resolution of our body in understanding how our limbs are arranged relative to each other [19]. This may be of advantage for on-body hover interactions.

On-Body Sensing in HCI

Much of the existing on-body input research has focused on interacting around smartwatches (e.g.,[20]) as they provide both close-by visual feedback and a convenient housing for sensors. Prototypes have demonstrated the feasibility of IR sensors [18,24,36], capacitive touch [23], magnetic techniques [10], as well as approaches that send electrical [45] or ultrasonic [21] signals through the body for on-body input around smartwatches.

Further work has explored camera-based tracking for interaction [35,40]. Harrison demonstrated a device that allowed tapping input on the skin [12] and using computer vision expanded this work for general on-body input [11].

Others have moved interfaces even closer to the body by integrating sensing capabilities in make-up [7], beauty products [39], or temporary tattoos [38]. The latter were also explored by Weigel et al. [41], who demonstrated a series of applications for thin devices worn on the skin.

Our work situates itself in yet another approach to on body input: integrating sensing capabilities in the textiles of our clothing.

eTextile Sensors

Clothing provides a convenient location for sensor placement. This has led to the integration of various sensors into fabric, including stretch [37], biometric [25], touch [26,30], pressure [6], and even optical sensors [13]. Most eTextile approaches however are based around either capacitive or resistive sensing.

Capacitive eTextiles

A fabric keypad was one of the earliest demonstrations of capacitive eTextiles [26]. GesturePad presented a similar concept to demonstrate capacitive sensing around the body [32]. More recently, with Project Jacquard, conductive threads have been woven into textiles [30], enabling mass manufacturing of capacitive sensors. Indeed, this technique has already been used in a first product, in the form of a Levi's Jacket [47].

While these systems can be used to detect hover or near-sensor in-air gestures, they are primarily used for touch detection. A notable exception is work by Cheng et al. [3] which measures changes in the capacitance of the human body to infer the user's movements. We expand upon this work by exploring gestural input above the sensor.

Resistive eTextiles

More recently, pressure sensitive fabrics have also gained attention. For example, Roh et al., Donneaud et al., and Zhou et al. have explored pressure sensitive textiles, but primarily on rigid surfaces [5,33,46]. Although their sensing abilities are promising, research has shown the performance of users interacting with sensors worn on the body to be half as fast than on a rigid surface. Users cited task completion strategies that included 'holding ones breath' [14].

Parzer et al. demonstrate a general purpose elastic textile sensor for input on furniture, and show its applicability to the body [27]. Wearable pressure sensors have also been explicitly designed for on-body gesture input on the arm [34] thigh [14]. Here, however, pressure was used to infer touch position. Yoon et al. present a finger-worn textile used for gesture detection. Parzer et al. [28] also expand on the typical gesture vocabulary by adding fabric-deformation gestures. Continuous pressure as an input modality for eTextiles on the body has, however, received comparatively little attention. We add to this work by exploring this pressure dimension.

Robust and Hybrid Sensing

We use the term 'hybrid sensing' to describe sensors that combine two distinct information channels. This can provide additional information about dynamics of movements, or improve the robustness of the sensor [8]. Such a hybrid textile was presented by Wicaksono and Paradiso [44]. Using seven functional and two layers of non-functional fabric, they measure up to four modalities simultaneously.

Hybrid sensing was also used in iSkin to distinguish between two levels of pressure input [41]. A similar approach was used in the 'one button recognizer' to distinguish between different people based on button-push-dynamics [29]. Hybrid sensing has applications beyond improving input-resolution – an alternative use was presented by Freed and Wessel who demonstrated that hybrid sensing could improve robustness to electrode deterioration [8].

Robustness is a limitation of current fabric sensors. For example, Heller et al. [14] demonstrated that task completion time doubled when a soft sensor was moved from a flat surface on to the body. Heller and others also presented systems such as Pinstripe [17] and Grabrics [2] which bypass this problem by requiring explicit pinch or rub gestures.

Hybrid sensing helps us address the robustness problem noted by Heller [14]. Hybrid sensing also enables us to infer additional information about the input gesture, similar to the work by Pohl et al. [29] and as suggested by Cheng et al.[4]. Finally hybrid sensing enables combined touch and hover interactions [16] using zPatch.

WHAT IS A ZPATCH?

A zPatch is a thin, soft, iron-on textile patch, similar to patches used to cover a torn garment or show off one's favorite band (Figure 2). zPatches provide users with an input channel to control an app on their phone or a remote IoT device with their day-to-day clothing. We envision a user might buy a 10 pack of zPatches and iron them on their jacket, backpack, or jeans. The user would then train it to detect a set of gestures of their choosing. This supports novices to effortlessly augment their clothing and customize their input methods.

zPatches can either have a single sensor (as seen in Figure 2) or a sensor cluster (Figure 6, Figure 12c). A single sensor zPatch already supports a rich set of interactions. It provides capacitive proximity and resistive pressure sensing, with which complex gestures can be built through temporal patterns of interaction.

A zPatch with a cluster of sensors (Figure 6, Figure 12c), or multiple zPatches placed in proximity of each other (Figure 12a, b), provide a three-dimensional interaction space – adding the opportunity of spatial interaction in the x and y dimension in addition to the temporal patterns of approach behavior and pressure.

Benefits of zPatch design over Similar Sensors

a) Low Complexity

zPatches use two analog input pins and require no additional hardware. Thus, the mechanical and electrical complexity is low. This enables easy incorporation of zPatches into garments and simple interfacing to existing microcontroller platforms.

The manufacturing technique used for zPatches is less complex than yarn-based approaches, such as Jacquard [30], but can still be used to achieve professional-standard results [9]. Compared to Wicaksono's eTextile keyboard [44], the approach presented in this paper uses 3 functional fabric layers instead of 7, increasing its robustness and making it easier for novices to replicate.

b) Resolution in the Z Axis

Various pressure based textile sensors exist in the research [14,27,34] and DIY community [5,15]. These sensors are typically used to infer the location of pressure events. zPatches do not provide position information, however, unlike most existing solutions they are optimized for interaction along the z Axis.

c) Continuous Hybrid sensing in a Soft Circuit

Freed et al. [8] and Pohl et al. [29] presented rigid hybrid sensors that capture continuous input. Unlike their imple-

Figure 2 - A pack of zPatches with regular Denim patches in the background.

mentations our sensors are soft and can easily be integrated into garments. The on-skin sensors by Weigel et al. provide a similar soft form factor, however they do not offer the continuous proximity and pressure sensing of zPatch.

d) Improved resistivity to noise and improved gesture detection through Hybrid Sensing

Hybrid sensing provides the potential for discarding many forms of false activation. Typically, one would expect input from the two data sources to be correlated (Figure 3, compare also Figure 9). If they are not correlated, one might discard such activation as noise: for example, if one bumps into an object the resistive sensor is triggered, but without finding the expected approach behavior in the capacitive readings.

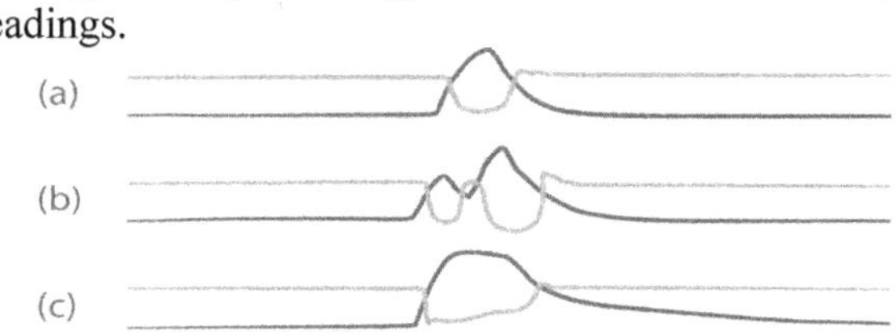

Figure 3 – Typical readings for (a) single-tap, (b) double-tap, (c) slow release. Resistive measures are yellow, capacitive blue.

While correlated, the two signals measure different things: Capacitive sensing captures the release and approach behavior, while pressure sensing provides an accurate measure once the sensor is touched. When attempting to distinguish between different input methods, this can be of advantage (Figure 3). For example, a regular tap (Figure 3a) can be distinguished from a tap where the finger lingers after the action is completed (Figure 3c). Actions with a temporal pattern (such as a double tap) can easily be identified on both sensing channels (Figure 3b).

BUILDING ZPATCH

The design of zPatches and the code used are open source. Here we present a quick overview. In depth documentation can be found online. Links to step by step instruction and code are available on the projects GitHub repo[1]

[1] https://github.com/fkeel/zPatch

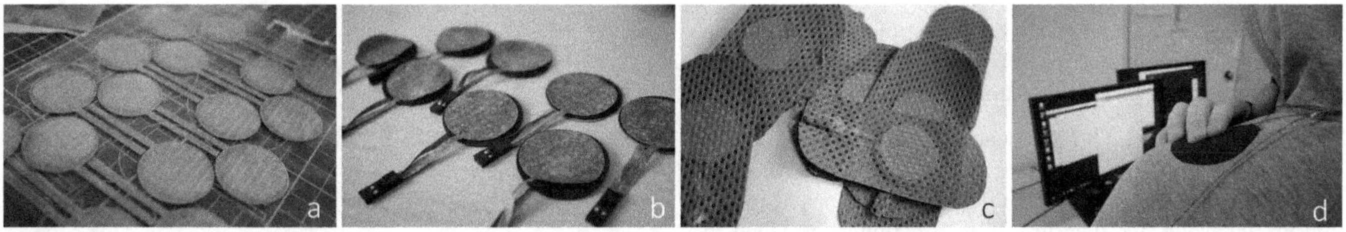

Figure 4 – (a) Laser-cut conductive fabric, (b) assembling the sensor, (c) fusing the textile to form a zPatch, (d) zPatch in Action.

Materials

zPatches are designed with simplicity and versatility in mind. They are simple to construct using a layering technique (as seen in Figure 4a-c).

zPatches use 3 materials (Figure 4a-c and Figure 5): The center layer of a sensor consists of non-woven resistive fabric by Eeonyx (20kΩ/□). Mechanically it behaves similarly to very dense felt. Electrically it is piezo-resistive: when compressed, its resistance decreases.

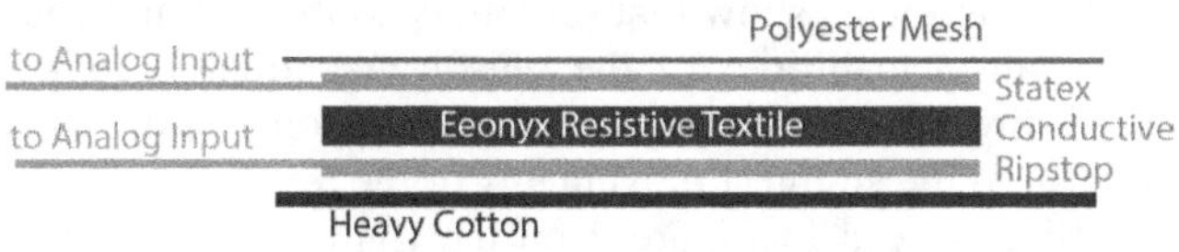

Figure 5 – Cross Section of zPatch

The resistive material is sandwiched between two conductors made of 'Bremen' ripstop by Statex, a silver-plated polyamide fabric with < 0.3Ω/□ surface resistivity. The conductive fabric is crimped to standard headers.

For mechanical stability, these three layers are encased in non-conductive textiles. Any non-conductive textile can be chosen, allowing the sensors to be tailored to the target garment. To optimize our sensors, we chose a very thin polyester mesh as the top layer (visible in Figure 5c). The mesh allows direct contact between finger and conductive material. This improves the robustness of touch sensing, and allows visual inspection of the underlying electrodes. The sensors also work with non-mesh material. We chose a relatively strong cotton fabric as a backing, to provide structural support and to lift the sensor off underlying skin.

The individual layers are heat-bonded: A sheet of double-sided fabric glue (interfacing) is placed between the layers one wishes to fuse, and subsequently heated and compressed using a household iron. Note that there should be no glue between the resistive and conductive materials, because this degrades the sensor performance.

Process

Sensor layouts can be designed in any vector-based application (we used Adobe Illustrator). Those designs are laser-cut on an Epilog Helix 60Watt laser cutter (Figure 4a). The Eeonyx resistive material was directly placed in the laser-cutter without any special preparations and cut at 50% speed, 9% power and 5000Hz.

The conductive ripstop was first fused to a layer of double sided interfacing which is fused to wax paper. The wax paper was then glued to an acrylic sheet. This made the conductive material act rigid, dispersing worries of the air-flow in the laser-cutter moving it while it is being cut. Here, we set the power of the laser-cutter to slightly engrave the acrylic underneath (50% speed, 20% power, 5000Hz).

Once cut the conductive material can be simply peeled off the acrylic. The laser-cutting process has the additional benefit that it seals all the cuts, preventing the fabric from fraying. This makes the fabric easier to work with than it would be if cut by a knife or scissors. Once all materials are cut, crimp connectors are added, the materials are fused together, layer by layer using double sided interfacing.

Configuring the microcontroller

zPatches have two symmetrical connectors – the orientation with which they are attached to a microcontroller is irrelevant, if both are connected to analog input pins. zPatches work by taking advantage of the multiple ways a microcontroller pin can be configured. The pins are configured to measure capacitance[2] and resistance alternatingly. Code examples ready to upload to an Arduino can be found on our GitHub page[1].

Multi-Sensor Synergies

zPatch configurations with more than two electrodes are also possible. In fact, combinations allow for increasing the spatial resolution beyond their sum: Figure 6a and 12c shows a layout in which four electrodes allow us to infer pressure from nine locations, based on common activation.

Flexibility with pin-configurations allows us to minimize complexity of such sensors. For example, the four electrodes shown in Figure 6a, can be pulled low sequentially and the voltage can be measured by a shared electrode at the bottom. In the depicted setup (also seen in Figure 12c),

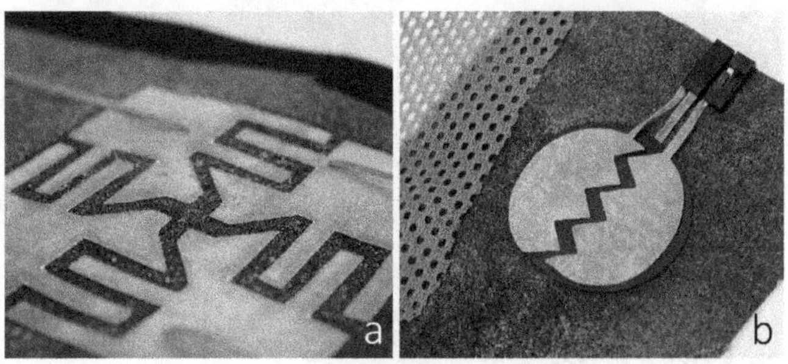

Figure 6 – (a) 4 sensors used to generate 9 touchpads as used in our text-input demo and (b) differential pressure sensor as used for our music-player demo.

[2] Code adapted from http://playground.arduino.cc/Code/ADCTouch

pressure can be measured at nine locations with a single analog input – however as all electrodes are electrically connected they act as a single capacitive sensor.

The layout in Figure 6b (also seen in Figures 12a and 12b) enables differential pressure sensing. By connecting the two visible electrodes to +5v and GND and reading from the bottom electrode, we measure 2.5v. If a finger is placed in the center of the zPatch, that voltage does not change (though we can detect the finger's presence through the capacitive readings. If the finger is rolled towards the positive or negative electrode the measured voltage will rise or sink accordingly.

EVALUATING ZPATCH

We conduct a range of evaluations of zPatch. First, we report on the sensing resolution of zPatches. Consequently, we report initial findings of a targeting task. We demonstrate that, with this resolution, we can support multi-item menu selection with pressure alone. Finally, we demonstrate that hybrid sensing improves the performance of a Random Forest algorithm for gesture classification and false positive reduction.

Sensor Performance

Resistive Sensing

We placed weights on our sensor to better understand how it reacts to pressure changes. We found the sensor could detect pressure of < 1.38 Pascal (5g with 3.5cm^2 area). We incremented the weights until 829 Pascal (3kg with 3.5cm^2 area) and found that between ~10 Pascal and ~275 Pascal the change in weight had an exponential relation to the change in resistance (R^2 = 0.95). Readings were inconsistent below, and flattened out above this range.

Capacitive Sensing

We placed and calibrated a zPatch in 3 positions relative to a user, to measure the signal response to the user's open palm. The zPatch was taped directly on the user's left arm (Figure 7, blue), attached to the left arm of a hoodie worn by that user (Figure 7, orange) and placed on a table in front of the user (Figure 7, green). We fixed the position of the left arm and varied the position of the right palm with a plexiglass spacer. Once the sensor was placed in its intended position we set the current capacitive reading as its baseline. We then measured the signal when the right palm was 0.2, 0.5, 1, 1.5, 2, 3, 4, 5, 10 and 20cm away from the zPatch. Figure 7 shows 50 samples of each combination of position and distance. The samples represent change in capacitance from the baseline.

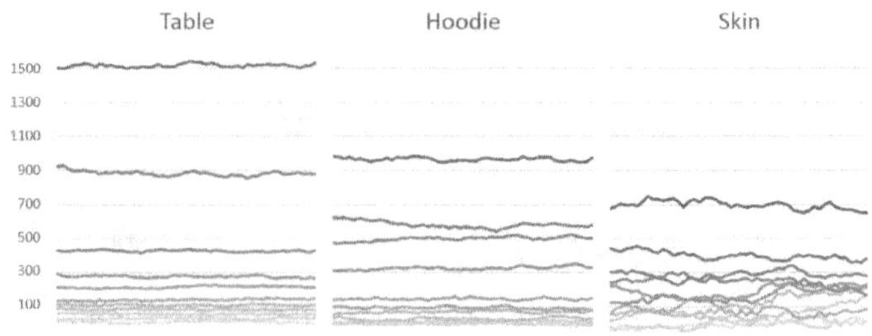

Figure 7 – 50 sample measures at 0.2 (darkest), 0.5, 1, 1.5, 2, 3, 4, 5, 10 and 20cm (lightest). Y axis is the change in capacitance, as measured using the code we provide.

Our measurements show that proximity to the skin impedes the sensing capabilities of the sensor. Additionally, when placed directly on the body, the signal becomes extremely sensitive to the slightest movements of the textile relative to the body, as seen in Figure 7 on the right. The change in response based on placement makes it difficult to correctly infer proximity. The size of the sensor influences the ability to sense proximity as well - the larger the sensor area, the more sensitive it becomes. However, while the absolute readings of the capacitive sensor are inconsistent, even when placed directly on the skin, hover and approach *dynamics* are observable.

Input Performance

While we assume the primary use of capacitive sensing will be in hover detection and gesture classification, we speculate that on-body pressure input could also be used for navigating menus and target selection. We therefore present an evaluation of user input performance in a targeting task.

We recruited 11 participants (all students, 1 female. Age: M = 26.5, SD = 5.24) for a targeting task (Figure 8a). Participants wore a hooded jacket with 8 integrated sensors (stomach, wrist, biceps, sternum, shoulder, back of hand, palm, and temple). They were shown a 700 pixel vertical linear

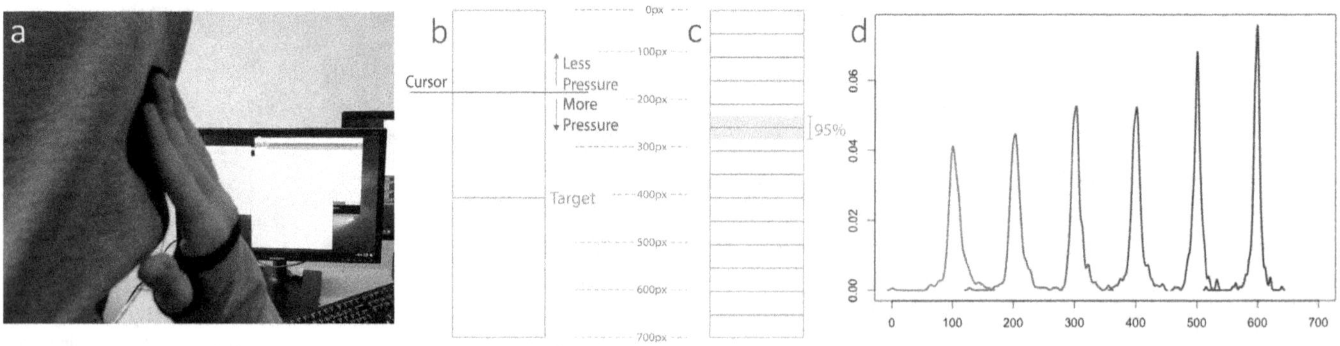

Figure 8 – (a) participant during the experiment (the UI was shown in front of them on a screen) (b), interface presented to user with single target, (c) target positions as calculated based on observed distributions (if users were to aim for the 5th target, we would expect 95% of all hits to fall within the highlighted area), (d) density plot of all observed distributions by target.

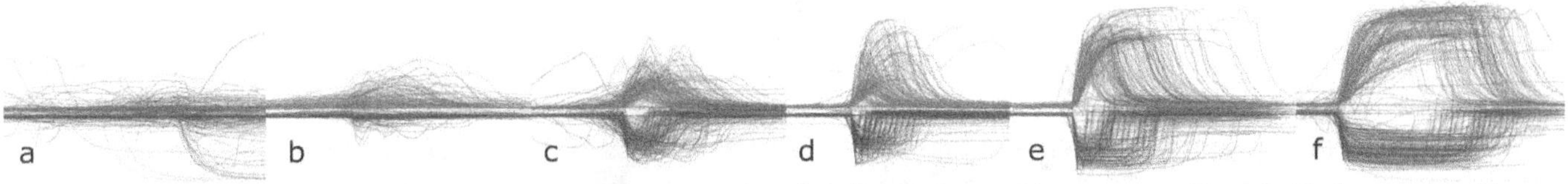

Figure 9 – Raw data sorted by class: (a) noise, (b) hover, (c) swipe, (d) gentle tap, (e) strong tap, (f) push. Reds are capacitive measures, blues are resistive measures. For visualization purposes measures are aligned so that the largest negative change in resistance lines up. Consequently, the average of the first 5 readings was set to zero, per measure type. Finally, resistive and capacitive measures were slightly vertically offset to reduce overlap. Each image shows 200 measures per sensing method.

slider. The cursor of the linear slider had its resting state at the top, and it moved towards the bottom with increasing pressure (Figure 8b). Participants were shown one-pixel targets and were instructed to move the cursor to the target as fast and precisely as possible.

We linearized the output of the sensor, and then calibrated each sensor per participant: We asked each participant to provide us with a minimum pressure (gentle touch) and their maximum comfortable pressure. These were set to the values 0 and 700. Pressure levels in between were mapped to the 700 point range proportionally, corresponding to the 700 pixels of the vertical slider. 6 targets were placed with 100 pixel distance from minimum, maximum and each other. Participants repeated each target 3 times

We collected a total of 1584 (11 *Participants* × 8 *Locations* × 6 *Targets* × 3 *Repetitions*) measures as offsets from their intended target and found that, on average, participants missed the target by 8 pixels (M = 8.95, SD = 9.56). Participants tended to overshoot (M = 9.00, SD = 9.88) more than undershoot (M = 6.55, SD = 8.38). Figure 8d shows the density functions of all trials by targets.

Based on our observed distribution of targeting offset, we calculated that we could correctly classify 95% of all trials if the targets were placed every 50 pixels (Figure 8c), 98% with a spacing of 73 pixels and 99% with targets every 85 pixels. Dividing the total pixel range by the calculated target spacing suggests that our sensor can accommodate 13, 8 or 7 targets, depending on acceptable classification error.

Our initial evaluation leaves many questions regarding the psychophysics of pressure perception and human input, as well as gender variation regarding on body interaction unanswered. While more detail is beyond the scope of this paper, we hope that future research will investigate these questions. The current study demonstrates that zPatches can be a useful tool for such explorations.

Hybrid Sensing to Improve Robustness

We imagine that if zPatches were a product, the included software might allow users to train the patch to recognize a set of gestures and how they perform them. To demonstrate that hybrid sensing can help reduce false activations and improve gesture recognition, we implemented such a system. We roughly follow an approach presented by Pohl et al. [29]. Note that we merely use machine learning as a demonstration of the benefits of hybrid sensing, the following example is by no means optimized.

Data Collection

We collected data from 10 participants. They were given a box that had a sweater tightly stuffed inside. The sweater had a zPatch attached. Participants followed instructions presented on a laptop screen. The data was collected in three phases:

1) Participants removed the sweater from the box and depending on condition either wore it or placed it on a table. During this period 'noise' was recorded. 2) Participants were then instructed to perform either a *hover*, *swipe*, *gentle tap*, *strong tap* or *push* gesture. Participants performed each gesture 10 times, whenever the screen changed color. In between these explicit inputs a random number of 2 to 4 'noise' trials were recorded. These were used to add additional variation to the 'noise' class. 3) Participants were instructed to place the sweater in the box. During this period additional 'noise' data was recorded.

This process was repeated 10 times, so that all 5 input types were performed both on the body and on the table. Participants did not receive any training or specific instructions on how to perform the gestures. Data was continuously recorded and split into 60 sample frames which were labeled according to when they were measured.

Raw Dataset

This resulted in an intentionally noise dataset containing many 'false activations' from moving the sweater. The 'hover' gesture was included to have an edge case which we anticipated to be difficult to detect. The 'swipe' gesture was included to see if lateral movement could also be captured through the approach behavior. All gestures were designed to be relatively similar – as opposed to, for example, comparing single- and double-tap.

We trimmed the dataset to 400 measures per participant, of which ~300 were 'noise' and the remaining ~100 were evenly distributed among the remaining classes. Each measurement contained 60 resistive and 60 capacitive samples. A visualization of the raw data[3] can be found in Figure 9.

Features & Final Datasets

We chose to extract 7 features describing the signal envelope: *Attack* (max change between two readings at begin of touch), *Release* (max change between two readings at end

[3] The data can be found at https://github.com/fkeel/zPatch/tree/master/data

RESISTIVE

classified as -->	Noise	Hover	Swipe	Gentle Tap	Strong Tap	Push
Noise	**2908**	27	23	11	5	6
Hover	139	**63**	0	1	0	0
Swipe	49	0	**133**	24	0	0
Gentle Tap	33	1	28	**133**	5	1
Strong Tap	10	0	2	6	**171**	12
Push	19	0	0	2	8	**179**

CAPACITIVE

	Noise	Hover	Swipe	Gentle Tap	Strong Tap	Push
Noise	**2935**	10	13	11	5	6
Hover	56	**137**	5	4	0	1
Swipe	15	3	**162**	19	5	2
Gentle Tap	13	7	19	**147**	13	2
Strong Tap	6	0	2	10	**173**	10
Push	10	0	2	4	6	**186**

HYBRID

Noise	Hover	Swipe	Gentle Tap	Strong Tap	Push	<-- classified as
2943	5	16	6	5	5	Noise
53	**144**	3	3	0	0	Hover
17	2	**173**	14	0	0	Swipe
16	3	14	**160**	5	3	Gentle Tap
6	0	2	6	**177**	10	Strong Tap
10	0	3	2	5	**188**	Push

Figure 10 – Cumulative classification results using Random Forest and 10 fold cross validation on each participant, by dataset.

of touch), *Sustain* (distance in samples between attack and Release) and *Maximum, MaxTime* (distance in samples between attack and Maximum) *Minimum* and *MinTime* (distance in samples between attack and Minimum).

We created a dataset using only resistive measures, a dataset using capacitive measures and a 'hybrid' dataset which contained both sets of features (all 'distance' measures were put in a shared frame of reference) additionally we added the difference between the resistive and capacitive measures as features.

Results

We used Random Forest in Weka (with default settings) to classify the data. We validated our approach per participant using 10 fold cross validation. The weighted F-Measures show that the resistive data performed worst followed by the capacitive data while the hybrid data performed best (see Table 1).

We were particularly interested in the effect of the datasets on the instances of false activation, specifically, noise classified as a gesture. We found the most instances of noise classified as a gesture in the resistive data (M: 7.2, SD: 3.42) followed by the capacitive data (M: 4.5, SD: 2.16). Again, the hybrid data performed best (M: 3.5, SD: 2.57). Figure 10 shows a confusion matrix of the sums of results.

To see if the results would generalize to new participants, we re-analyzed them as a whole, again using 10 fold cross validation. This time the data was split such that each fold trained on nine participants and tested on the tenth. While the results were less convincing then for the per-person training, we observed the same trends and the data generalized relatively well, weighted *F-Measure* were 0.84 for the resistive data, 0.86 for the capacitive data and 0.89 for the shared data.

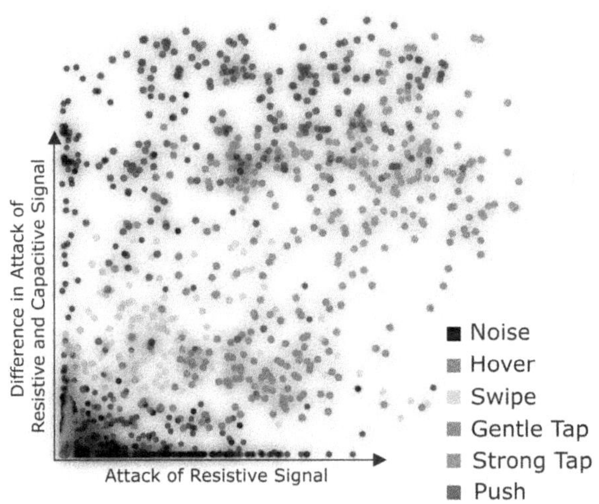

Figure 11 – Scatterplot of two features on complete dataset

	W. F-Measure		Precision		Recall	
	Mean	SD	Mean	SD	Mean	SD
Resistive	**0.89**	*0.03*	**0.89**	*0.04*	**0.90**	*0.03*
Capacitive	**0.93**	*0.01*	**0.93**	*0.01*	**0.94**	*0.01*
Shared	**0.95**	*0.02*	**0.95**	*0.02*	**0.95**	*0.02*

Table 1 – Summarized results of per person cross validation

DISCUSSION

zPatch is a hybrid sensor, providing both resistive and capacitive measures. Viewing the raw-data output we receive from either channel, the resistive readings immediately appear useful, we demonstrate participants can select from 13 pressure levels with 95% accuracy. The capacitive readings on the other hand are 'all over the place'. The extent to which their output varies based on context is a clear limitation of their utility as a continuous, absolute input channel. If we focus on discrete rather than continuous input, the situation changes. When classifying gestural input, the capacitive sensing outperforms the resistive sensing.

What we wish to demonstrate, however, is that the two approaches are complimentary and that best performance is achieved by utilizing the hybrid nature of zPatch. It should be noted that hybrid sensing not only benefits from additional data, but that the relationship between the resistive and capacitive measures provides additional information not contained in either data source. For example, using correlation based feature selection, three of the top five predictors of our 'hybrid' dataset were the *Difference in Sustain,* the *Difference in Attack* and the *Distance between Attack* of the two signals. The remaining two were *Attack* of resistive measures and *Release* of capacitive measure.

The benefit of adding the difference in signal as feature can be seen in Figure 11. While *Attack* (x-axis) is the strongest predictor of the resistive measures, it alone still does not lead to a strong result. Paired with the *Difference in Attack* (y-axis) we can see clear clustering in the data.

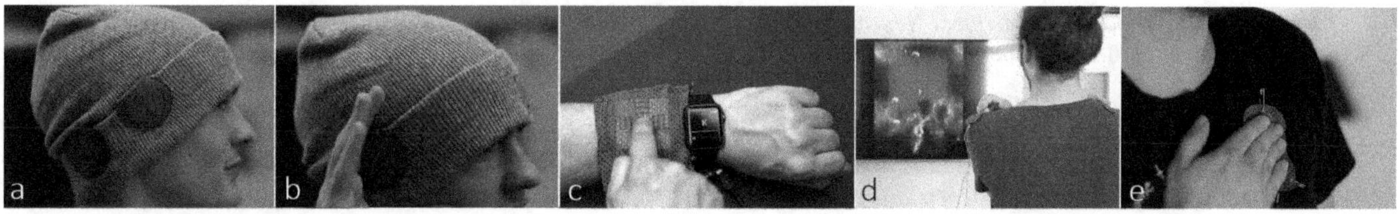

Figure 12 – (a, b) Audio player with gestural interface, (c) sweatband for spatial and pressure input for smartwatch, (d, e) users improvising on-body based interactions by pinning zPatches on various body locations for gaming.

APPLICATION SCENARIOS / DEMOS

We present three demos of zPatches in use. All sensors were sampled using Arduino Nanos, the data was received and processed by a C# application, and events were forwarded either to custom iOS applications or in the form of system-level input events (e.g., key presses/mouse clicks). Please refer to our Video Figure for full demonstration.

Combining Multiple Input Modalities

To demonstrate how multiple input modalities can be combined, we present a music player using two zPatches placed on a hat. Each zPatch features a differential sensor (see Figure 12a, b). Playing, pausing and stopping the currently selected song is controlled by hover gestures: to pause music (and thus hear the environment), users simply raise their hand to their ear; to resume the music, they then lower the hand again; to fully stop the music, they instead move their hand backward.

Controls for volume (front zPatch) and track selection (back zPatch), are based on pressure input. Differential pressure sensing, through rolling the finger forward or backward, allows for adjusting values: rolling the finger forward increases volume/skips to the next track, and rolling it backward does the opposite.

Interpolation & False Positive Removal

To demonstrate a) capacitive sensing for avoiding false activation, b) interpolated pressure sensing and c) item selection using pressure for navigation, we present a sweatband that can be used to provide text input for a smartwatch. The sweatband has a zPatch with a cluster of four sensors (2×2 matrix), which allows for nine discrete touch areas (i.e., buttons in a 3×3 grid) by sensing touch and pressure on different combinations of patches (see Figure 12c). We present a multi-tap[4] text entry variation: users select letters by adjusting the pressure level. The currently selected character is shown on the smartwatch. Once users are satisfied with their selection, they quickly release the pressure.

When putting on the sweatband or when the sweatband is in contact with other objects, changes in pressure are measured. We can distinguish between such pressure and intentional input through the secondary information provided by capacitive sensing - character selection is only possible when a touch is also present.

[4] https://en.wikipedia.org/wiki/Multi-tap

Easy customization

To show off the ease with which zPatches can be used to prototype interactions, we present a gaming scenario: Users can customize gaming experience by changing the location of zPatches. For example, mapping a steering mechanism to zPatches attached to a user's socks dramatically changes both the difficulty of the game and the attentional focus of the player.

We designed a system for controlling applications on a large display. We used a Unity sample (SpaceShooter[5]) to demonstrate our approach. We use three zPatches: one controlling the firing mechanism, and two for steering the spaceship left and right. Placements were chosen ad-hoc while filming. The first setup used zPatches on either shoulder (for steering left and right - see Figure 12d), and one zPatch in a sock underneath the foot to trigger firing. Another setup explored the firing mechanism attached on the chest (Figure 12e), and one zPatch for steering underneath each foot.

CONCLUSION

We presented zPatches: iron-on eTextile patches with hybrid resistive/capacitive sensors that capture multiple sensing modalities. This enables us to design general purpose sensing patches that can be used for various interaction techniques. We also demonstrated the fabrication process and strategies for combining individual sensors to create clusters with more complex functionality. We presented an evaluation showing that approach behavior can be detected even if the zPatch is placed directly on the skin and that, given appropriate feedback, pressure can be used to select from up to 13 targets using our sensor. We also show that the hybrid sensing approach improves the ability to distinguish between gestures and can reduce false activations. Finally, to demonstrate the versatility of zPatches, we presented three example applications.

ACKNOWLEDGEMENTS

This work was supported by the European Research Council, grant no. 648785.

REFERENCES

1. Rochelle Ackerley, Ida Carlsson, Henric Wester, Håkan Olausson, and Helena Backlund Wasling. 2014. Touch perceptions across skin sites: differences between sensitivity, direction discrimination and

[5] https://unity3d.com/learn/tutorials/projects/space-shooter-tutorial

pleasantness. *Frontiers in behavioral Neuroscience* 8: 54. https://doi.org/10.3389/fnbeh.2014.00054

2. Nur Al-huda Hamdan, Florian Heller, Chat Wacharamanotham, Jan Thar, and Jan Borchers. 2016. Grabrics: A Foldable Two-Dimensional Textile Input Controller. In *CHI Extended Abstracts on Human Factors in Computing Systems*, 2497–2503. https://doi.org/10.1145/2851581.2892529
3. Jingyuan Cheng, Oliver Amft, and Paul Lukowicz. 2010. Active capacitive sensing: Exploring a new wearable sensing modality for activity recognition. In *Lecture Notes in Computer Science (including subseries Lecture Notes in Artificial Intelligence and Lecture Notes in Bioinformatics)*, 319–336. https://doi.org/10.1007/978-3-642-12654-3_19
4. Jingyuan Cheng, Bo Zhou, Paul Lukowicz, Fernando Seoane, Matija Varga, Andreas Mehmann, Peter Chabrecek, Werner Gaschler, Karl Goenner, Hansjürgen Horter, Stefan Schneegass, Mariam Hassib, Albrecht Schmidt, Martin Freund, Rui Zhang, and Oliver Amft. 2017. Textile Building Blocks: Toward Simple, Modularized, and Standardized Smart Textile. 303–331. https://doi.org/10.1007/978-3-319-50124-6
5. Maurin Donneaud, Cedric Honnet, and Paul Strohmeier. 2017. Designing a Multi-Touch eTextile for Music Performances. In *Proceedings of the International Conference on New Interfaces for Musical Expression*, 7–12. Retrieved from http://www.nime.org/proceedings/2017/nime2017_paper0002.pdf
6. Yu Enokibori, Akihisa Suzuki, Hirotaka Mizuno, Yuuki Shimakami, and Kenji Mase. 2013. E-textile pressure sensor based on conductive fiber and its structure. *Proceedings of the 2013 ACM conference on Pervasive and ubiquitous computing adjunct publication - UbiComp '13 Adjunct*: 207–210. https://doi.org/10.1145/2494091.2494158
7. Patricia J Flanagan, Katia Vega, and Hugo Fuks. 2012. Blinklifier: The power of feedback loops for amplifying expressions through bodily worn objects. In *Proceedings of APCHI*, 641–642.
8. Adrian Freed and David Wessel. 2015. An Accessible Platform for Exploring Haptic Interactions with Co-located Capacitive and Piezoresistive Sensors. In *Proceedings of the Ninth International Conference on Tangible, Embedded, and Embodied Interaction - TEI '14*, 317–320. https://doi.org/10.1145/2677199.2680571
9. Rachel Freire, Cedric Honnet, and Paul Strohmeier. 2017. Second Skin: An Exploration of eTextile Stretch Circuits on the Body. *Proceedings of the Tenth International Conference on Tangible, Embedded, and Embodied Interaction - TEI '17*: 653–658. https://doi.org/10.1145/3024969.3025054
10. Chris Harrison and Scott E. Hudson. 2009. Abracadabra. *Proceedings of the 22nd annual ACM symposium on User interface software and technology - UIST '09*: 121. https://doi.org/10.1145/1622176.1622199
11. Chris Harrison, Shilpa Ramamurthy, and Scott E. Hudson. 2012. On-body Interaction: Armed and Dangerous. In *Proceedings of the Sixth International Conference on Tangible, Embedded and Embodied Interaction - TEI '12*, 69. https://doi.org/10.1145/2148131.2148148
12. Chris Harrison, Desney Tan, and Dan Morris. 2010. Skinput: Appropriating the Body as an Input Surface. In *Proceedings of the 28th international conference on Human factors in computing systems - CHI '10*, 453. https://doi.org/10.1145/1753326.1753394
13. Sunao Hashimoto, Ryohei Suzuki, Youichi Kamiyama, Masahiko Inami, and Takeo Igarashi. 2013. LightCloth: Sensible Illuminating Optical Fiber Cloth for Creating Interactive Surfaces. *Proceedings of the SIGCHI Conference on Human Factors in Computing Systems. ACM*: 603–606. https://doi.org/10.1145/2470654.2470739
14. Florian Heller, Stefan Ivanov, Chat Wacharamanotham, and Jan Borchers. 2014. FabriTouch: Exploring Flexible Touch Input on Textiles. *Proceedings of the 2014 ACM International Symposium on Wearable Computers - ISWC '14*: 59–62. https://doi.org/10.1145/2634317.2634345
15. Anja Hertenberger, Barbro Scholz, Beam Contrechoc, Becky Stewart, Ebru Kurbak, Hannah Perner-Wilson, Irene Posch, Isabel Cabral, Jie Qi, Katharina Childs, Kristi Kuusk, Lynsey Calder, Marina Toeters, Marta Kisand, M.T. Bhömer, Maurin Donneaud, Meg Grant, Melissa Coleman, Mika Satomi, Mili Tharakan, Pauline Vierne, Sara Robertson, Sarah Taylor, and T.R. Nachtigall. 2014. 2013 E-Textile swatchbook exchange: The importance of sharing physical work. *Proceedings - International Symposium on Wearable Computers, ISWC*: 77–81. https://doi.org/10.1145/2641248.2641276
16. Ken Hinckley, William Buxton, Seongkook Heo, Michel Pahud, Christian Holz, Hrvoje Benko, Abigail Sellen, Richard Banks, Kenton O'Hara, and Gavin Smyth. 2016. Pre-Touch Sensing for Mobile Interaction. In *Proceedings of the 2016 CHI Conference on Human Factors in Computing Systems - CHI '16*, 2869–2881. https://doi.org/10.1145/2858036.2858095
17. Thorsten Karrer, Moritz Wittenhagen, Leonhard Lichtschlag, Florian Heller, and Jan Borchers. 2011.

Pinstripe: Eyes-free Continuous Input on Interactive Clothing. *Proceedings of the 2011 annual conference on Human factors in computing systems - CHI '11*: 1313–1322. https://doi.org/10.1145/1978942.1979137

18. Jarrod Knibbe, Diego Martinez Plasencia, Christopher Bainbridge, Chee-Kin Chan, Jiawei Wu, Thomas Cable, Hassan Munir, and David Coyle. 2014. Extending interaction for smart watches. In *Proceedings of the extended abstracts of the 32nd annual ACM conference on Human factors in computing systems - CHI EA '14*, 1891–1896. https://doi.org/10.1145/2559206.2581315
19. Jürgen Konczak, Daniel M. Corcos, Fay Horak, Howard Poizner, Mark Shapiro, Paul Tuite, Jens Volkmann, and Matthias Maschke. 2009. Proprioception and Motor Control in Parkinson's Disease. *Journal of Motor Behavior* 41, 6: 543–552. https://doi.org/10.3200/35-09-002
20. Gierad Laput, Robert Xiao, Xiang "Anthony" Chen, Scott E. Hudson, and Chris Harrison. 2014. Skin buttons. In *Proceedings of the 27th annual ACM symposium on User interface software and technology - UIST '14*, 389–394. https://doi.org/10.1145/2642918.2647356
21. Shu-Yang Lin, Chao-Huai Su, Kai-Yin Cheng, Rong-Hao Liang, Tzu-Hao Kuo, and Bing-Yu Chen. 2011. PUB - Point Upon Body: Exploring Eyes-Free Interaction and Methods on an Arm. In *Proceedings of the 24th annual ACM symposium on User interface software and technology - UIST '11*, 481. https://doi.org/10.1145/2047196.2047259
22. Kimberly Myles and Mary S Binseel. 2007. The Tactile Modality : A Review of Tactile Sensitivity and Human Tactile Interfaces. *Army Research Laboratory*, May: 1–27. https://doi.org/10.1109/HAPTIC.2004.1287224
23. Ian Oakley and Doyoung Lee. 2014. Interaction on the edge. In *Proc. CHI*, 169–178. https://doi.org/10.1145/2556288.2557138
24. Masa Ogata and Michita Imai. 2015. SkinWatch: Skin Gesture Interaction for Smart Watch. *Proceedings of the 6th Augmented Human International Conference on - AH '15*: 21–24. https://doi.org/10.1145/2735711.2735830
25. OM. 2016. OMbra - The ultimate running bra that just happens to be smart – OMsignal. Retrieved April 1, 2017 from https://www.omsignal.com/
26. Maggie Orth, Rehmi Post, and Emily Cooper. 1998. Fabric computing interfaces. *CHI 98 conference summary on Human factors in computing systems - CHI '98*, April: 331–332. https://doi.org/10.1145/286498.286800
27. Patrick Parzer, Kathrin Probst, Teo Babic, Christian Rendl, Anita Vogl, Alex Olwal, and Michael Haller. 2016. FlexTiles: A Flexible, Stretchable, Formable, Pressure-Sensitive, Tactile Input. *Proceedings of the 2016 CHI Conference Extended Abstracts on Human Factors in Computing Systems - CHI EA '16*: 3754–3757. https://doi.org/10.1145/2851581.2890253
28. Patrick Parzer, Adwait Sharma, Anita Vogl, Jürgen Steimle, Alex Olwal, and Michael Haller. 2017. SmartSleeve: Real-time Sensing of Surface and Deformation Gestures on Flexible, Interactive Textiles, using a Hybrid Gesture Detection Pipeline Patrick. In *Proceedings of the 30th Annual ACM Symposium on User Interface Software and Technology - UIST '17*, 565–577. https://doi.org/10.1145/3126594.3126652
29. Henning Pohl, Markus Krause, and Michael Rohs. 2015. One-Button Recognizer: Exploiting Button Pressing Behavior for User Differentiation. *Proceedings of the Joint International Conference on Pervasive and Ubiquitous Computing and the International Symposium on Wearable Computers (Ubicomp/ISWC'15)*: 403–407. https://doi.org/10.1145/2750858.2804270
30. Ivan Poupyrev, Nan-Wei Gong, Shiho Fukuhara, Mustafa Emre Karagozler, Carsten Schwesig, and Karen E. Robinson. 2016. Project Jacquard: Interactive Digital Textiles at Scale. In *Proceedings of the 2016 CHI Conference on Human Factors in Computing Systems*, 4216–4227. https://doi.org/10.1145/2858036.2858176
31. Gonzalo Ramos, Matthew Boulos, and Ravin Balakrishnan. 2004. Pressure widgets. In *Proceedings of the 2004 conference on Human factors in computing systems - CHI '04*, 487–494. https://doi.org/10.1145/985692.985754
32. Jun Rekimoto. 2001. GestureWrist and GesturePad: unobtrusive wearable interaction devices. In *Proceedings Fifth International Symposium on Wearable Computers*, 21–27. https://doi.org/10.1109/ISWC.2001.962092
33. Jung-sim Roh, Yotam Mann, Adrian Freed, David Wessel, U C Berkeley, Adrian Freed, Arch Street, and David Wessel. 2011. Robust and Reliable Fabric and Piezoresistive Multitouch Sensing Surfaces for Musical Controllers. *Proceedings of the International Conference on New Interfaces for Musical Expression*, June: 393–398. Retrieved January 19, 2017 from http://www.nime2011.org/proceedings/papers/L01-Roh.pdf
34. Stefan Schneegass and Alexandra Voit. 2016. GestureSleeve: using touch sensitive fabrics for gestural input on the forearm for controlling smartwatches. *Proceedings of the 2016 ACM*

International Symposium on Wearable Computers - ISWC '16: 108–115. https://doi.org/10.1145/2971763.2971797

35. Jie Song, Gábor Sörös, Fabrizio Pece, Sean Ryan Fanello, Shahram Izadi, Cem Keskin, and Otmar Hilliges. 2014. In-air gestures around unmodified mobile devices. *UIST 2014*: 319–329. https://doi.org/10.1145/2642918.2647373
36. Paul Strohmeier. 2015. DIY IR Sensors for Augmenting Objects and Human Skin. In *Proceedings of the 6th Augmented Human International Conference on - AH '15*, 181–182. https://doi.org/10.1145/2735711.2735802
37. Paul Strohmeier, Roel Vertegaal, and Audrey Girouard. 2012. With a flick of the wrist: Stretch Sensors as Lightweight Input for Mobile Devices. *Proceedings of the Sixth International Conference on Tangible, Embedded and Embodied Interaction - TEI '12*: 307. https://doi.org/10.1145/2148131.2148195
38. James Tribe, Dumtoochukwu Oyeka, John Batchelor, Navjot Kaur, Diana Segura-Velandia, Andrew West, Robert Kay, Katia Vega, and Will Whittow. 2015. Tattoo Antenna Temporary Transfers Operating On-Skin (TATTOOS). In *Proceedings, Part II, of the 4th International Conference on Design, User Experience, and Usability: Users and Interactions - Volume 9187*. Springer-Verlag New York, Inc., 685–695. https://doi.org/10.1007/978-3-319-20898-5_65
39. Katia Fabiola Canepa Vega and Hugo Fuks. 2013. Empowering electronic divas through beauty technology. In *Lecture Notes in Computer Science (including subseries Lecture Notes in Artificial Intelligence and Lecture Notes in Bioinformatics)*, 237–245. https://doi.org/10.1007/978-3-642-39238-2_26
40. Cheng-Yao Wang, Wei-Chen Chu, Po-Tsung Chiu, Min-Chieh Hsiu, Yih-Harn Chiang, and Mike Y. Chen. 2015. PalmType. In *Proceedings of the 17th International Conference on Human-Computer Interaction with Mobile Devices and Services - MobileHCI '15*, 153–160. https://doi.org/10.1145/2785830.2785886
41. Martin Weigel, Tong Lu, Gilles Bailly, Antti Oulasvirta, Carmel Majidi, and Jürgen Steimle. 2015. iSkin. In *Proceedings of the 33rd Annual ACM Conference on Human Factors in Computing Systems - CHI '15*, 2991–3000. https://doi.org/10.1145/2702123.2702391
42. Martin Weigel, Vikram Mehta, and Jürgen Steimle. 2014. More Than Touch : Understanding How People Use Skin as an Input Surface for Mobile Computing. *Proceedings of the 32nd annual ACM conference on Human factors in computing systems - CHI '14*: 179–188. https://doi.org/10.1145/2556288.2557239
43. S. Weinstein. 1968. Intensive andd extensive aspect of tactile sensitivity as a function of body part, sex, and laterality. In *First International Symposium on the Skin Senses, held at the Florida State University in Tallahassee, Florida*, 195–218.
44. Irmandy Wicaksono and Joseph A Paradiso. 2017. FabricKeyboard : Multimodal Textile Sensate Media as an Expressive and Deformable Musical Interface. In *NIME*, 348–353. Retrieved July 31, 2017 from http://homes.create.aau.dk/dano/nime17/papers/0066/paper0066.pdf
45. Yang Zhang, Junhan Zhou, Gierad Laput, and Chris Harrison. 2016. SkinTrack: Using the Body As an Electrical Waveguide for Continuous Finger Tracking on the Skin. In *Proceedings of the 2016 CHI Conference on Human Factors in Computing Systems*, 1491–1503. https://doi.org/10.1145/2858036.2858082
46. Bo Zhou, Jingyuan Cheng, Mathias Sundholm, and Paul Lukowicz. 2014. From smart clothing to smart table cloth: Design and implementation of a large scale, textile pressure matrix sensor. In *Lecture Notes in Computer Science (including subseries Lecture Notes in Artificial Intelligence and Lecture Notes in Bioinformatics)*, 159–170. https://doi.org/10.1007/978-3-319-04891-8_14
47. Function Meets Fashion: Levi's® Commuter x Jacquard by Google - Levi Strauss. Retrieved April 1, 2017 from http://www.levistrauss.com/unzipped-blog/2016/05/function-meets-fashion-levis-commuter-x-jacquard-by-google/

COLORISE: Shape- and Color-Changing Pixels with Inflatable Elastomers and Interactions

Juri Fujii
Keio University
5322, Endo, Fujisawa
s15763jf@sfc.keio.ac.jp

Takuya Matsunobu
Keio University
5322, Endo, Fujisawa
t15829tm@sfc.keio.ac.jp

Yasuaki Kakehi
Keio University
5322, Endo, Fujisawa
ykakehi@sfc.keio.ac.jp

ABSTRACT
We propose a new method for shape- and color-changing display called COLORISE. Our "COLORISE" system has inflatable shape changing pixels that can change their colors without using any light-emitting type devices. The array of the modules enables various color patterns, making full use of the characteristics of the material. Each pixel also has a touch sensing function that enables users to interact with it intuitively. This paper describes the design and mechanism of our system, explores interactions with users, and presents technical evaluations of the proposed pixel modules.

Author Keywords
Shape-changing display; Color-forming; Touch interactions; Inflatable Materials.

ACM Classification Keywords
• Applied computing→ Arts and humanities→ Media Arts

INTRODUCTION
In the physical environment, shape-changing displays and interfaces have attracted much attention as a means of enabling intuitive expression and interactions[13]. While many displays still show images on a static 2D surface, these shape-changing displays can express 2.5- or three dimensional information physically by changing their shape. From the human-computer interaction point of view, shape changing media also functions as intuitive interfaces, providing not only visual but also tactile feedback to users. So far, various methods for developing shape-changing displays/interfaces have been proposed. To provide richer information on the display, efforts have also been made to integrate other modalities, such as color change, to pixels and surfaces. For example, inFORM adopts the method of superimposing an image on the surface by a projector attached to the ceiling[2]. In Lumen, each pin has an LED at the tip that changes color and expresses animations of 2.5D shape and light change[12]. Since these are based on light-emitting displays, in places where outdoor or external lighting is strong, their lighting conditions are constrained. Another disadvantage is that the entire system becomes large scale when external devices are used, like projectors. For these issues, especially in the field of media art, several types of color-forming displays have been proposed. For examples, Daniel Rozin's Penguins Mirror and PomPom Mirror[1,14] express pixel-like animation using the movement of materials or objects.
For color forming techniques, systems using materials such as thermochromic and photochromic materials have been proposed.

* The first two authors contributed equally to this work

TEI '18, March 18–21, 2018, Stockholm, Sweden

ACM ISBN 978-1-4503-5568-1/18/03...$15.00
https://doi.org/10.1145/3173225.3173228

Figure 1. COLORISE shape- and color-changing pixels with inflatable elastomers.

From these backgrounds, we propose a new substantial pixel system that can control both size and color called COLORISE. In this system, we can control pixel sizes by inflating a film membrane. Inflating different colored membranes while switching colors makes it possible to change the appearance of the membrane to multiple colors. By arranging such membranes two-dimensionally, it is possible to create animations with shape and color expressions and add interactivity to the animation. We also added an interactive function to the pixel. In this paper, we will describe the color changing system, its design and implementation, and interaction mechanism.

RELATED WORK

Organic User Interfaces and Shape-Changing Displays
In the concept of Organic User Interface proposed by Holman et al[5], importance of changing the shape of

interfaces depending on functions and situations was pointed out. They also discussed the shape-changing interfaces should also work as not only expression tools but also input tools from surroundings to realize natural interactions.

From these viewpoints, shape-changing displays and interfaces, which can transform their surfaces, have attracted much attention and various implementations have been attempted. Many projects are based on mechanical methods. Typical works are pin array displays arranging linear actuators[6,9]. A more user-friendly configuration made of soft materials using deformation methods like inflating and stretching has been proposed[8,15].

Besides shapes, there are several approaches to add color changeability to a shape changing display, such as combining it with a projector and attaching a large number of LEDs.[2,7,10]. For a projector, there are limitations in scale as the device becomes lager. The use of light-emitting devices such as LEDs is limited to dark places, and in order to maintain softness, it is necessary to consider restrictions on the installation position. Nojiri et al. has focused on color-changing displays made of inflatable shape-changing soft material[11]. However, the number of colors in this system was quite limited.

Color-Forming Display

Color-changing methods that do not rely on luminescence have some precedents in research. A representative approach uses a color-changing material that responds to heat or light called thermochromic ink or photochromic ink. For example, the hand rewriting system of Hashida et al. utilizes the characteristics of thermochromic ink to interactively erase the lines drawn with the user's pen, and provides information based on color development on the canvas using an ultraviolet projector[4]. The group has also developed a volumetric display with a laminated structure type that takes advantage of the characteristic that color is carried by the wavelength of invisible light [3]. In artworks, Transience refers to color-changing letters written by ink mixed with liquid crystal ink and thermochromic ink that can change color according to temperature [17]. Controlling the discoloration of these inks contributes to the creation of colors different from that of a projector. However, the main disadvantage is that it takes time to change color. Depending on the environment, it may take several minutes to change colors and return to original. Though thermochromic ink can shorten the time depending on the composition, it is necessary to keep the temperature constant and the durability of the material is weakened. There are electric discoloration control methods, such as E-ink, that can improve the speed of discoloration. Among them, a thin display corresponding to some bending and folding has been proposed [16]. While E-ink can change multicolor, it is difficult to implement on materials with large stretching and express height information.

OUR APPROACH: COLORISE

Our COLORISE system consists of an array of pixel modules onto which a membrane-like material is attached. We can control the physical size of each pixel module by inflating this membrane with air. By spatially arranging these modules, the shape-changing function can be realized.

In this system, membranes of different colors incorporated in the layer structure are arranged in the module. By changing the air flow path of this module and switching the inflatable membrane, we can quickly control the apparent color of the material.

Inside the module, a sensor for acquiring the user's touch is built in, enabling both input and output to be realized in the module.

We will describe below how pixel animation and interaction are realized using the design and implementation of such a device.

SYSTEM DESIGN

Design of Pixel Module

Figure 2 shows the basic design of the pixel module. Pumps and valves are connected to each membrane and each membrane can be inflated (separately). With regard to the color changing mechanism, Figure 3 shows the A, B, and C tubes connected to the blue, red, and white membranes, respectively. Pumps and valves are connected to the opposite side of the tube. When we turn on pump A and close the valve A, the blue membrane bulges and pushes up the red and white membranes. At this time, the membrane viewed from above becomes blue. When we release air from the blue membrane and put in air from pump B, the red membrane bulges while pushing up the white membrane. At this time, the red membrane appears through the white membrane. When we release air from white membrane and put in air from pump C, the white membrane bulges. COLORISE changes to three colors as shown in Figure 4.

Membrane Part

We adopted an elastomer as the material of the rubber membrane because of its high durability among stretching materials and low viscosity. Elastomers, unlike ordinary balloons, can control film thickness and produce durable films. We adopted Smooth-on Ecoflex 00-30 as the material of the membrane and Silc Pig as the pigment, and we added the pigment upon mixing the Ecoflex and spread the color by stirring. The white (top layer), red (middle layer), and blue (bottom layer) elastomers were formed into a thin membrane. Each elastomer was unified with a thickness of 0.5 mm, and the amount of pigment was 1%, 1%, and 4% as going under the layer structure. This pixel changes its color by pushing up the top layers. While the top layer is inflating, they become thinner than usual. Then, the bottom layer goes through the top layer and the color changes. It is necessary to make the bottom layer visible to change multicolor. Hence, the amount of pigments for the bottom layer is higher than for the top layers.

In order to use it for display, it is necessary to inflate all the pixels equally. Therefore, the elastomer was made uniformly.

In the fabrication process, we created a mold with 0.5 mm thickness and poured the elastomeric liquid mixed with pigment into it. As a result, all films can be made with uniform thickness and errors in swelling can be minimized.

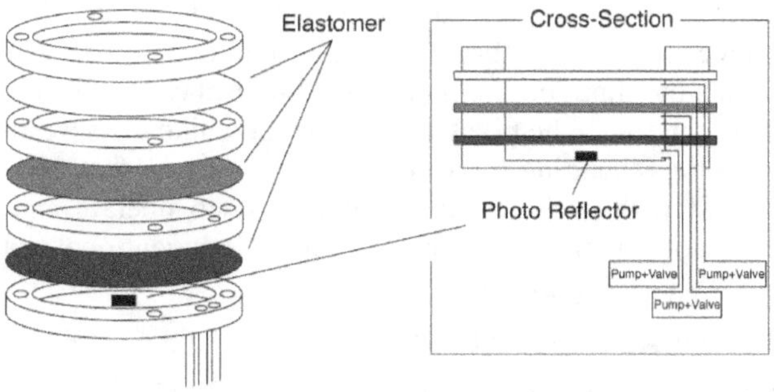

Figure 2. Basic design of the pixel module. Each layer has a pump and valve. When it is inflated, the pump is moving and the valve is closed.

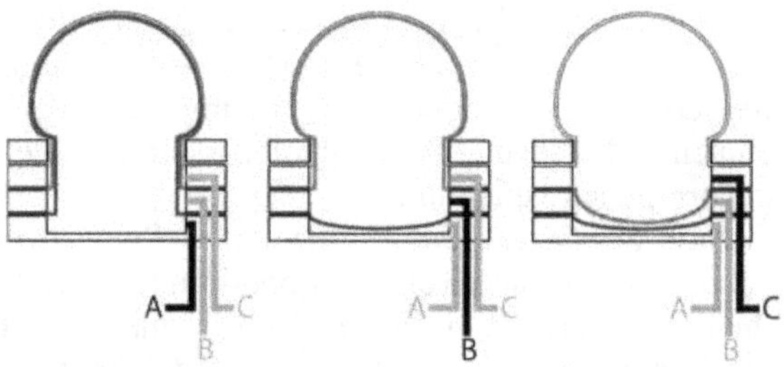

Figure 3. How to inflate each layer. A, B, and C have pumps and valves. When A is actuated, the bottom layer becomes visible. When B is moving, the middle layer is visible. When C is on, the top layer become visible.

Figure 4.COLORISE can change 3 colors: white, red, blue.

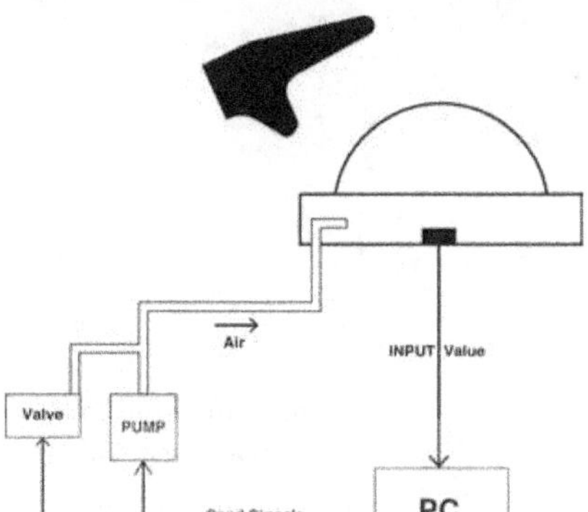

Figure 5. Touch sensing on the pixel.

Sensing Part

By attaching a photoreflector to the bottom of each module, it enables us to interact with the pixels. It is possible to sense that the user touched the pixel irrespective of the degree of bulging of the membrane. It can prompt the user an intuitive operation rather than just changing the pixel's appearance. If the bulge is small, we can use four photoreflectors and calculate the center of gravity of each sensor value. Then, the pixel enables us to sense the touched location. However, when the pixel is significantly inflated, there is no difference between sensor values, and it can only sense what is eventually touched. For this reason, we implemented sensing with one photoreflector. By using sensors, we made it possible to express more interactive.

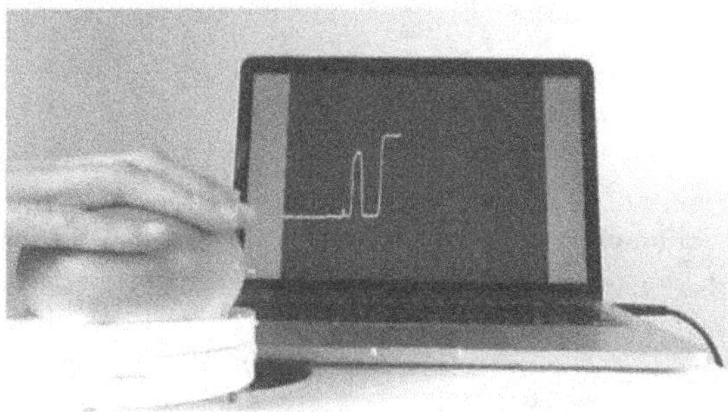

Figure 6. Photoreflector can detect the touch.

IMPLEMENTATION

Prototyping of 5 × 5 Pixel Display System

We implemented an array of 5 × 5 pixel modules shown in Figure 7. In this prototype, each pixel module has three air pumps to control each layers independently. We utilized rfp32b03r (Oken Seiko) for the air pump. We also connected air valves (PS-1015W, Takasago Electric, Inc.) to each pixel module to control the release of air. To control the air pumps and valves, we used Arduino and openFrameworks. We also developed a program to control the behavior of pixels through a graphical user interface.

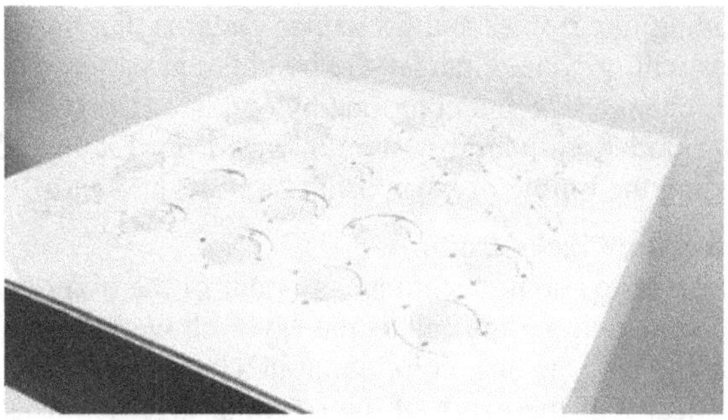

Figure 7. COLORISE prototype model. We implemented 5 × 5 array modules (25 pixels).

Figure 9. COLORISE can change the color without changing height.

Figure 8. COLORISE motion pattern. The top is the gradation pattern and the bottom is the firework pattern.

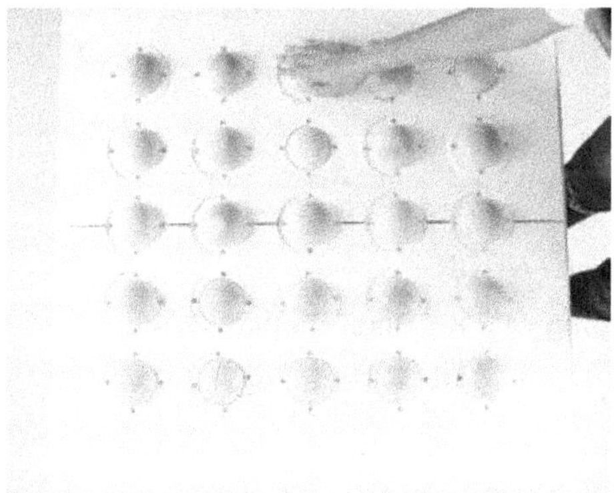

Figure 10. We can touch and interact with pixels.

Pixel Pattern Samples

We tested several animation patterns on this display system. Various patterns can be implemented, such as patterns spreading like ripples and fireworks, patterns that move like waves with gradual changes the height, and patterns where pixels change size and color one by one in order. It can also show gradation patterns, as illustrated in Figure 8, by changing the timing of when inflation starts and ends.

Control the Pixel's Color

We also tested some techniques to control the pixel colors. We found that adding air to the layer above the swelling layer can change the color without changing the height. Specifically, if the pump of the swelling layer is turned off and air is added to the next layer for 1 second, the next layer inflates. Then, the next color becomes visible without changing the height. (see Figure 9). It also accomplishes the aesthetic color change that do not seem like usual color change.

Interaction System

We put in a pattern that can be used for touch input by sensing. It is possible to sense that a hand touched the surface of the membrane using a photoreflector, which reflects the input on the motion of the display. At this time, when you touch the pixel, the pixels move like the spread of fireworks, changing their colors. The interface that can be touched with such soft material is easy to operate and is gentle on human skin compared to conventional hard displays (see Figure 10).

TECHNICAL EVALUATION

The Range of Color change

We investigated the changes in size and color due to air injection time. In order to measure color, we used CS-100A (KONICA MINOLTA) as the color luminance meter. Size was measured from the side of the pixel, and the color luminance meter was set at the top 650 mm of the pixel. The measurement of each color was performed in the same environment. The change in each color is represented by a CIE xy chromaticity diagram.

As shown in Figures 11 and 12, the size and color became larger and darker, respectively, in proportion to time. As red and blue membranes became larger, the brightness decreased and color density increased. From these measurements, it was possible to confirm how color and size changed by overlapping and inflating the elastomer.

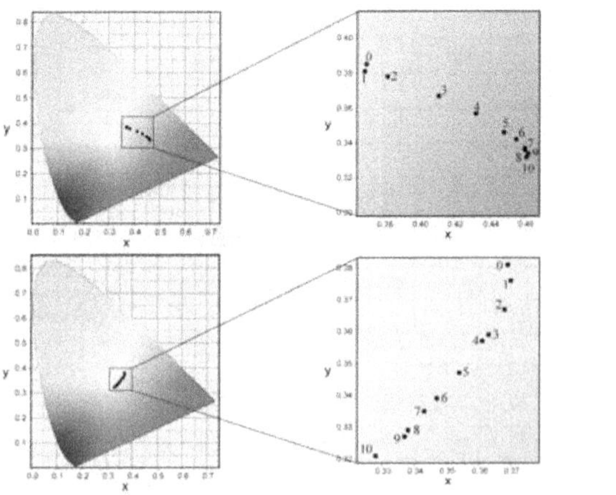

Figure 11. CIE XY color space of color change ranges of the COLORISE sample. It measures color per 1000 ms.

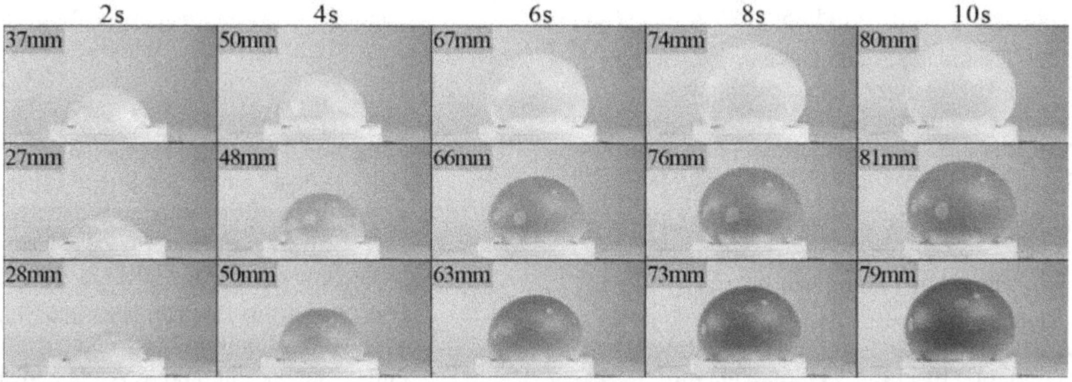

Figure 12. The size of COLORISE is changed by air between 0 mm and 81 mm.

Durability Test of Pixel Material

We tested the durability of the elastomer we created for the COLORISE system. In this test, we counted the number of times the elastomer can be inflated and deflated without deterioration of the shape and damage. In one cycle, the elastomer was inflated for 10s, then the air was released for 18s. Under this condition, the height of the inflated elastomer was approximately 80 mm, the maximum size of the pixel.

The results show that the blue (bottom), red (middle), and white (top) layers were inflated 1026, 1469, and 2796 times, respectively, without breaking. As the lower film requires a pushing up force, the durability is lower as the lower layer. We also observed the chronological change in the shape of elastomer surfaces. During this test, the elastomers maintained a flat shape when deflated, without being affected by the continuous inflations and deflations. For comparison, we conducted the same test using the material of commercially available balloons. The balloon developed holes after being inflated 600 times on average. As for the surface, the balloon material gradually stretched and lost its flat shape during the inflations.

DISCUSSION & LIMITATIONS

In this study, we changed the color of pixels by overlapping rubber films and mixing them by expanding and contracting each with air. As the method of color-changing of the pixel, photochromic ink and E-ink exists. There are usual multicolor changing methods like thermochromic ink and E-ink. However, it is difficult to control the range of changing color. Also these inks do not have high stretchability. In contrast, our method made it possible to change one color into two by overlapping rubber films. We could overlay colors by overlapping layers. However, as the color becomes darker with the lower layer, not all color can be made out due to the transparency problem. In the method of color change by the layer structure, a color region that can be expressed according to the amount of deformation is compulsorily determined. In this method, the strength of color and height information cannot be separated. Therefore, in order to produce strong color, the films need to be greatly inflated. When bubbles enter between each layer, the colors red and blue are not seen clearly. We have tried using oil and dust powder between the elastomers, but no noticeable effects have been observed. Also this pixel was actuated by a small pump. Because of this, it takes time to expand the pixel. The pixel inflation and deflation process also takes a long time. Therefore, although the pixel can sense the user's touch, the response takes time.

CONCLUSION AND FUTURE WORK

In this paper, we proposed new multicolor and volume changing pixel system called COLORISE. COLORISE enables gradual information representation by making full use of the properties of the material. The system has great potential for applications in future displays given the softness of the elastomer used and its ability to change color owing to its layered structure. In the future work, we plan to increase the color variations of the pixel. The range of expressions will be expanded by enriching the colors.

Also we will make it possible to read various input forms such as push as well as touch. Atmospheric pressure sensor is an effective method in taking advantage of the characteristics of air, and we would like to use the difference in atmospheric pressure for input in the future work.

ACKNOWLEDGEMENT

This work was partially supported by JST ERATO Grant Number JPMJER1501, Japan. We would like to express our gratitude to Professor Kawahara for supporting projects and discussions for this project.

We also thank Satoshi Nakamaru and Fuka Nojiri for their advices.

REFERENCES

1. Rozin Daniel. 2015. bitforms gallery » Penguins Mirror. Retrieved August 4, 2017 from http://www.bitforms.com/rozin/penguins-mirror
2. Sean Follmer, Daniel Leithinger, Alex Olwal, Akimitsu Hogge, and Hiroshi Ishii. 2013. inFORM: Dynamic Physical Affordances and Constraints through Shape and Object Actuation. *Proceedings of the 26th annual ACM symposium on User*

interface software and technology - UIST '13: 417–426. https://doi.org/10.1145/2501988.2502032

3. Tomoko Hashida, Yasuaki Kakehi, and Takeshi Naemura. 2011. Photochromic Sculpture: Volumetric Color-forming Pixels. *ACM SIGGRAPH 2011 Emerging Technologies*: 11:1--11:1. https://doi.org/10.1145/2048259.2048270
4. Tomoko Hashida, Kohei Nishimura, and Takeshi Naemura. 2012. Hand-rewriting: automatic rewriting similar to natural handwriting. *Proceedings of the 2012 ACM international conference on Interactive tabletops and surfaces*. https://doi.org/10.1145/2343456.2343466
5. David Holman and Roel Vertegaal. 2008. Organic user interfaces: Designing computers in any way, shape, or form. *Communications of the ACM* 51, 6: 48–55. https://doi.org/10.1145/1349026.1349037
6. Hiroshi Ishii, Daniel Leithinger, and Sean Follmer. 2015. TRANSFORM: Embodiment of " Radical Atoms " at Milano Design Week. *CHI'15 Extended Abstracts*: 687–694. https://doi.org/10.1145/2702613.2702969
7. Daniel Leithinger, S.a Follmer, A.b c Olwal, and H.d Ishii. 2014. Physical Telepresence: Shape capture and display for embodied, computer-mediated remote collaboration. *UIST 2014 - Proceedings of the 27th Annual ACM Symposium on User Interface Software and Technology*: 461–470. https://doi.org/10.1145/2642918.2647377
8. Shuo Li, Bryan N. Peele, Chris M. Larson, Huichan Zhao, and Robert F. Shepherd. 2016. A Stretchable Multicolor Display and Touch Interface Using Photopatterning and Transfer Printing. *Advanced Materials* 28, 44: 9770–9775. https://doi.org/10.1002/adma.201603408
9. Ken Nakagaki, Luke Vink, Jared Counts, Daniel Windham, Daniel Leithinger, Sean Follmer, and Hiroshi Ishii. 2016. Materiable: Rendering Dynamic Material Properties in Response to Direct Physical Touch with Shape Changing Interfaces. *Proceedings of the 2016 CHI Conference on Human Factors in Computing Systems*: 2764–2772. https://doi.org/10.1145/2858036.2858104
10. Akira Nakayasu and Akira. 2016. Luminescent Tentacles. *Proceedings of the 29th Annual Symposium on User Interface Software and Technology - UIST '16 Adjunct*: 33–34. https://doi.org/10.1145/2984751.2985695
11. Fuka Nojiri and Yasuaki Kakehi. 2014. BelliesWave : Color and Shape Changing Pixels Using Bilayer Rubber Membranes. *SIGGRAPH '14: ACM SIGGRAPH 2014 Posters*: 4503. https://doi.org/10.1145/2614217.2633390
12. Ivan Poupyrev, Tatsushi Nashida, Shigeaki Maruyama, Jun Rekimoto, and Yasufumi Yamaji. 2004. Lumen: interactive visual and shape display for calm computing. *SIGGRAPH '04: SIGGRAPH 2004 Emerging technologies*: 17. https://doi.org/10.1145/1186155.1186173
13. Ivan Poupyrev, Tatsushi Nashida, and Makoto Okabe. 2007. Actuation and tangible user interfaces: the Vaucanson duck, robots, and shape displays. *Proceedings of TEI 2007*: 205–212. https://doi.org/10.1145/1226969.1227012
14. Daniel Rozin. 2015. bitforms gallery » PomPom Mirror. Retrieved August 4, 2017 from http://www.bitforms.com/rozin/pompom-mirror
15. Andrew Stevenson, Christopher Perez, and Roel Vertegaal. 2011. An inflatable hemispherical multi-touch display. *Proceedings of the fifth international conference on Tangible, embedded, and embodied interaction - TEI '11*: 289. https://doi.org/10.1145/1935701.1935766
16. Aneesh Tarun, Peng Wang, Paul Strohmeier, Audrey Girouard, Derek Reilly, and Roel Vertegaal. 2013. PaperTab. *CHI '13 Extended Abstracts on Human Factors in Computing Systems on - CHI EA '13*: 2881. https://doi.org/10.1145/2468356.2479559
17. Kohei Tsuji and Akira Wakita. 2013. Transience: Aesthetics of Dynamic Colors Inside Japanese Calligraphy. *Proceedings of the 7th International Conference on Tangible, Embedded and Embodied Interaction*: 387–388. https://doi.org/10.1145/2460625.2460706

Plux: Exploring Light Settings through Hybrid Control

Tom van Rooij and Saskia Bakker
Industrial Design Department, Eindhoven University of Technology, Eindhoven, the Netherlands
t.j.a.v.rooij@alumnus.tue.nl; s.bakker@tue.nl

ABSTRACT
Connected lighting solutions are replacing traditional lightbulbs in the home environment and offer unlimited numbers of light settings, varying in color, brightness, saturation and more. Interaction design for such systems is challenging: simple switches no longer suffice, and asking users to specify all parameters of all lightbulbs separately is time-consuming and requires them to understand the desired outcome. This paper presents Plux, a tangible light controller which employs a hybrid control approach. Plux generates light settings of pseudo-randomized color palettes, while users control the saturation and brightness directly. Plux is intended to enable serendipitous exploration of new light settings using a peripheral interaction design approach. A field deployment in which 5 people used Plux for 3 weeks in their homes revealed that using Plux easily became a part of the everyday routine. Plux's hybrid control approach was particularly valuable for users who struggle to determine the desired light setting.

CCS Concepts
• **Human-centered computing ~ Field studies** • *Human-centered computing ~ User interface design* • *Human-centered computing ~ Interface design prototyping*

Author Keywords
Lighting; Smart Lighting; Hybrid Control; Tangible Interfaces; Peripheral Interaction; Design Research.

INTRODUCTION
In recent years, various developments have been seen in the domain of artificial lighting, bringing new lighting opportunities to the home environment. Modern LED-based systems enable control of many parameters such as hue, brightness and saturation, and given the miniaturization of LED technology one armature can contain large amounts of light sources. Moreover, modern light sources are no longer mechanically coupled to one switch per light source, but are wirelessly connected and can be operated remotely.

TEI '18, March 18–21, 2018, Stockholm, Sweden

ACM ISBN 978-1-4503-5568-1/18/03…$15.00
https://doi.org/10.1145/3173225.3173240

While these developments led to a great amount of freedom and light combinations, designing successful interfaces to operate such systems remains a challenge [18]. Commercially available connected lighting systems for the home environment (e.g. Philips HUE [20], MiLight [16] and LIFX [12]) mostly use smartphone applications. These enable users to either set each light source to a particular hue, saturation and brightness individually, or to create and select light presets. Since this latter functionality demands minimum effort, it seems to be most used. As a result, people often use only a limited number of light settings even though they likely have more diverse light preferences in different situations [18]. These light preferences however, are often tacit, and are constructed when being confronted with multiple different settings regularly [17]. Given the routineness usually associated with turning on the light, people unlikely regularly explore alternative options, even though this could lead to more satisfactory lighting.

We present Plux, see Figure 1, a tangible interface for connected lighting systems. Plux is a research artifact designed to explore if being confronted with alternatives regularly enables users to have a better understanding of their light preferences in different settings and ultimately a more satisfactory user experience. When pressing Plux, it generates light settings of pseudo-randomized color palettes, while users control the saturation and brightness of the light by applying different levels of pressure. Plux thereby employs a hybrid control approach [19], intended to enable serendipitous exploration of new light settings while also preserving user control. Plux's interaction design is based on the principles of peripheral interaction [4], and is thereby intended to demand minimum attention to fit fluently into the user's routines.

This paper reports on the design of Plux and on an exploratory qualitative field study in which 5 people used a working prototype version of Plux for three weeks in their living room environment.

RELATED WORK
With connected lighting systems making their way to the home environment (e.g. [5,6,8,12,16,20]), several related works have explored new ways to interact with such systems. Many explorations aim to make interactions with modern lighting systems more effortless, such that these operations might shift to the periphery of attention. By employing *peripheral interaction* [4], using lighting systems can become a more seamless part of everyday life [2].

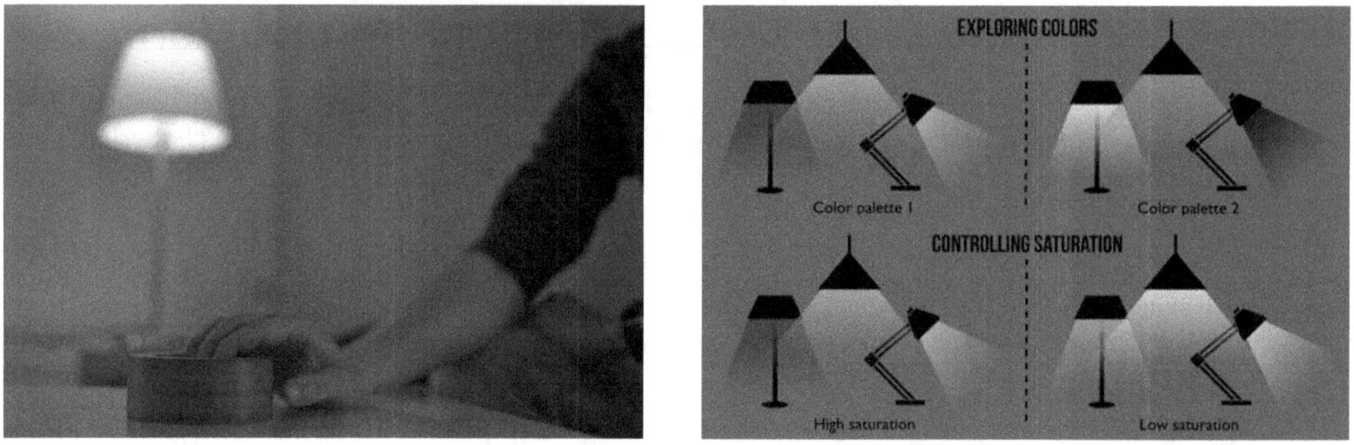

Figure 1. Plux lighting controller (left), illustration of random color pallets (top right) and user control of saturation (bottom right).

Magielse and Offermans [15,18], for example, present a touch sensitive light switch: pressing the pad gently activates a warm light setting while pressing it harder triggers a bright light setting. This allows controlling both color temperature and brightness in one straightforward action. Lappalainen et al. [10] present an aesthetical interface to control light colors, aimed at fitting light controllers better in the home. Similar challenges have been addressed by commercially available light controllers, such as the m!QBE [7], a cube that triggers preprogrammed light settings by turning it to one of its sides.

Since peripheral interfaces usually allow only imprecise control [3], employing hybrid control [19] (mixing system- and user control) is suggested as a suitable approach to enable peripheral interaction while still using the opportunities offered by connected lighting [2]. Offermans et al. [18], for example, proposed several physical and app-based light controllers, addressing different degrees of freedom and different types of hybrid control. Bakker and Niemantsverdriet [3] explored tangible interfaces to peripherally control connected lighting in the living-room. Their 'Swivel' concept uses automatic system behavior by adjusting lighting to user's routines automatically and revealing these adjustments on the tangible interface to enable direct adjustment by the user. The interfaces discussed in [3] however, are merely conceptual designs and form explorations rather than functioning prototypes.

Lucero et al. [13] studied touch-based interfaces for bathroom lighting, which used metaphors to reduce complexity, and presets to guide the user Lucero et al. [14] suggest to reduce complexity in controlling lighting and to enable users to play with and enjoy light through simple and accessible interfaces. We see Plux as such a simple and accessible interface. The study presented in this paper contributed to these related studies by exploring hybrid control through peripheral interaction in the home environment.

PLUX DESIGN

This paper explores if being frequently confronted with diverse light settings leads to an improved experience of connected lighting systems and an improved understanding of one's own light preferences. We designed Plux, a peripheral interaction design which randomizes colors, but allows users to control brightness and saturation, of the lights in their living room to enable serendipitous exploration of light as part of the daily routine.

The Plux controller (see Figure 1), which contains pressure sensitive foam in the center, is wirelessly connected to a user's Philips Hue [20] lighting system, consisting of up to five connected light bulbs. When pressing the foam, a dedicatedly developed algorithm creates a new light setting consisting of one dominant color and up to four recessive colors. The algorithm uses two parameters to compose the color palette. The first parameter describes the primary color angle on the hue color wheel. The second parameter describes the deviation angle from the primary color in both positive and negative directions. The deviation angle is multiplied by two to create the last two color angles. This algorithm is inspired by color palette creation software (e.g. Adobe Color [1]) and results in a set of colors that fit well together based on analogous color relations. When the color palette is created, each individual Philips Hue light bulb is randomly assigned one of the computed colors, which form the hue mappings for the light setting.

The brightness and saturation of the lights is determined by the user through the amount of pressure applied when pressing the tangible Plux controller, see Figure 1. Pressing the foam gently will result in a dimmed setting with high saturation. The firmer the foam is pressed, the lower the saturation and the higher the brightness. A firm press will therefore result in a bright white light setting showing almost no color. Each time a user presses Plux, a new setting is created, with brightness and saturation levels relating by the pressure applied. Light settings are directly implemented when Plux is pressed, allowing users to directly evaluate their choice.

A tangible user interface was chosen, because tangible interactions are generally easy to initiate and may therefore be more likely than graphical user interfaces to blend into a user's everyday routine [4]. We hypothesized that the pressing-interaction described would be quick and easy for users to perform during their daily routines.

To decrease the need of other controllers and thus, a better integration of Plux in the daily routine, the controller supports turning off the lights by a firm long press and it is portable so that it can be moved around in the living room.

USER STUDY SETUP

To evaluate the experience of serendipitous exploration of pseudorandom light settings through Plux, we conducted a field study. To ensure that participants would be confronted with various settings in different situations, and to overcome novelty effects, we deployed Plux 'in-the-wild' [9] in the homes of five participants for three weeks.

All of the five participants owned a Philips Hue light system and had used it in their living room for at least 10 months before participating in this study. We selected these participants to avoid novelty effects of using a connected lighting system in general. All participants were male students, aged 23 to 25 years old, who lived alone. Four lived in a studio apartment (P1, P2, P4 and P5) and one participants had a separate bedroom and used Plux in his living room (P3). The participants used between 2 and 9 Philips Hue lightbulbs (see Table 1). Every lamp got randomly assigned to one of the five colors of the composed color palette by Plux. Due to this random assignment, multiple lamps could receive the same color. Next to the Philips Hue lightbulbs, participants P2 and P4 had other light sources installed in their living rooms which could not be controlled by Plux.

Participants were encouraged to use Plux as their main lighting controller, although they could also use other controllers (such as the Philips Hue app).

Data gathering

To gain insights into the usage of Plux, interaction moments with Plux were logged during the deployment, with a 15 second interval. Due to technical limitations, when two or more interactions occurred within this 15 second timeframe, only the first interaction was logged. We logged both touch (when Plux was touched or moved but not pressed) and press interactions.

Each participant was asked to fill out an online questionnaire before the start of the experiment focusing on participant's usage and experience of the Philips Hue system. We also sent participants online questionnaires about the usage of Plux during the three-week deployment. However, since these were very irregularly filled out by the participants, we decided to exclude them from analysis. After the deployment, a semi-structured one-hour interview was held with each participant. At the start of the interview, each participant was asked to rate the mental effort they needed to use Plux and the Philips Hue app on the Rating Scale Mental Effort (RSME) [21]. The remainder of the interview focused on the experience of using Plux as part of their everyday routine, how it compared to the interactions normally used to operate the lighting system (using the Philips Hue application) and how the generated light settings were experienced. During the interview, data-visualizations of the individual's usage of Plux were used as input for discussion.

Qualitative data analysis

The semi-structured interviews were audio recorded and transcribed verbatim. From these transcripts, 161 quotes were selected which related to the user experience of Plux. To avoid bias in the analysis of these data, the 161 quotes were divided over the first author and a researcher who was not previously involved in the study. Both researchers independently clustered their quotes using open-coding [11], and subsequently discussed their insights and agreed to one final set clusters.

FINDINGS

To gain insights into the experience and effects of Plux, we first present quantitative data gathered in our user study, and subsequently discuss qualitative data gathered from the interviews.

Quantitative findings

Table 1 reveals the number of times each participant touched and pressed the Plux prototype during the three weeks of deployment. As evident from this table, usage differed considerably among participants; while participant P5 used Plux 38 times to create a light setting, P4 pressed Plux a total number of 113 times. The participants did not use Plux every day during the deployment, this ranged from 5 days (P5) to 18 days (P3) in three weeks.

Participant	# Of Hue lamps	Logged # times Plux was used		RSME rating *(0 to 150 scale)*	
		Touching	Pressing	Plux	App
P1	2	42	103	55	35
P2	3	*	41	44	61
P3	9	89	99	28	50
P4	3	*	113	38	76
P5	3	96	38	80	25

Table 1. Number of Hue lamps controlled by Plux (Left), number of times Plux was touched and pressed (Middle) and the rating scale mental effort (RSME) rating of using Plux and the Philips Hue app (right) for each participant. *Due to a technical error, the number of touch interactions could not reliably be established for P2 and P4.

Table 1 furthermore shows the participants' RSME ratings of interaction with Plux and interactions with the Philips Hue app. RSME [21] uses a 0 to 150 scale, where 2 means 'absolutely no effort' and 114 means 'extreme effort'. As seen in this table, participants P1 and P5 indicated that their perceived mental effort for using Plux was higher than for using the Philips Hue app to turn on the lights. On the contrary, P2, P3 and P4 perceived the mental effort required to use the Philips Hue app higher compared to Plux. Using the RSME, P2, P3 and P4 described Plux as requiring 'a little effort' or 'some effort', whereas P1 and P5 rated Plux as requiring 'rather much effort' (P1) and 'great effort' (P5).

Qualitative findings

The analysis of interview data revealed three clusters describing the participants' experiences of using Plux.

Using Plux to create light settings

The interviews revealed clear differences in how participants experienced using Plux to create light settings. Both participants P1 and P5 indicated that they found it hard to create a particular light setting which they had in mind. For example, P5 indicated *"the white balance that came out of it was never what I was looking for, if there was a small hint of green in it, I already thought 'this is not what I want'"*. Both P1 and P5 mentioned that not finding the right setting caused frustration, particularly when it took longer to find an acceptable setting. *"It was difficult because I always searched for a preset that I had in mind, so the longer it took to find it, the more irritating it was"* (P1). Similarly, P5 mentioned that he often did not appreciate random light settings: *"I almost always have in mind what kind of lighting I want, it is almost never like 'give me something random'"*. P5 also mentioned that when he could not find an acceptable light setting, he used the Philips Hue app instead. *"When I know you cannot find that setting with this controller [Plux], than I am not even going to start using it"* (P5).

P2, P3 and P4 had quite contrary experiences with Plux. All three found it easy to find acceptable light setting using Plux. P3, for example, indicated that the created light settings *"always seemed to be something that fit"*. P4 indicated that he found acceptable light settings easily, often ones which he would normally not use. As if talking to Plux, he mentioned *"Ah is that what you make of it? Fine, I can live with it"*. Similarly, P2 mentioned *"Some shades of lighter blue, for example, which I would normally never choose, than I was like 'wait, this is actually also fine'"*. These participants also enjoyed the diversity in light settings Plux created: *"It is nice that it is not always the same"* (P2), and *"I liked the different colors, it created an atmosphere in a low-threshold way"* (P4). They furthermore indicated that they usually did not have a specific light setting in mind: *"It is rarely the case that I want to create a very specific setting"* (P3).

P2, P3 and P4 furthermore agreed that using Plux was easier than using Philips Hue app: *"in general I needed 2 or 3 clicks [interactions to find an acceptable setting]"* (P3). P2 indicate that *"I prefer this controller [Plux, over the app], just because it is much more easy"*, while he also mentioned *"but I get to the desired result more quickly if I would do it with the app"*. P4 furthermore indicated that Plux helped overcome a problem he experienced with the app: *"The problem of the Philips Hue app is that if I 'sit down' for it and I must say what I actually want with the light, yes that is the problem, because I actually really don't know [what lighting I want]"*.

Experience of interaction with Plux

Different from controlling the lights through the Philips Hue app, all five participants indicated that they were able to look at the lights rather than the controller while interacting with Plux: *"I mainly paid attention to the lights [..] to see what kind of lighting the room gets"* (P4). *"That was the nice part, you directly looked at the lighting"* (P2).

P2 and P4 mentioned that in the beginning it took some effort to find the right amount of pressure he had to apply to Plux. However, the participants found it easy to understand the mapping of the pressure sensitive foam. *"It is understandable that subtle actions lead to subtly lighting"* (P4). Participants furthermore mentioned they often pressed Plux multiple times: *"it invited to press multiple times"* (P1). *"When I really did not like it [the lighting], I pressed another time, and another time, and another time"* (P4).

Regarding the hybrid control implemented in Plux, P4 mentioned that it felt that he was in control of the lighting together with Plux: *"A bit of you and a bit of that thing"*. P4 furthermore indicated that he liked Plux's help in coming up with creative new light settings: *"This controller does the creative work for you, you do not have to think about it"*. Participant P1 liked that he was able to press Plux and have the feeling that he also had some control over the lighting output *"I liked that you had to press it and that that gave you the feeling that you were in control over the lamps and brightness"* (P1). However, P4 also mentioned that he would have liked more control in some cases: *"I would have liked to have influence on amount of influence I had, [..] in some cases you just want it a bit warmer or a bit colder. Then I would like to not have to press three times because than you feel a bit like a fool, you don't feel understood"*.

Integration in everyday life routines

One of the aims of Plux was to enable exploration of light settings to become a more regular part of the everyday routine. All participants mentioned a limitation of the controller, which could influence its integration into routines: since the design was portable, energy consumption needed to be limited, which was realized by bringing Plux to sleep mode automatically when not used. This also meant the controller needed a few seconds to boot after a user grabbed it. During these seconds, the participants could not interact with Plux. Interestingly, participants easily found solutions to fit this delay in their routine. P3: *"Often I resolved it by [..] briefly touching that thing [Plux], then I put my coat on the rack, and then I pressed it [Plux] [..], it became a part of my routine within a day"*.

Despite these technical difficulties causing some annoyance among participants, all indicated that they were able to fit Plux to some extend into their everyday routines. P2 indicated that he almost immediately got used to use Plux as his main lighting controller: *"It [Plux] was in a central place, I was almost immediately used to the fact that I needed to use this controller instead of the app".* P1 mentioned it became part of his routine: *"in the end it becomes something of the daily rhythm, like a post-it note that you do not notice anymore at a certain moment".* P4 indicated he could use Plux while doing other things *"I could simply press it while working".*

However, some participants also mentioned that they used Plux as a more focused activity at certain occasions. For example, P2 mentioned *"if people are coming over, [..] then I am going to try something out [with Plux]".* P5 mentioned that he liked playing with the controller, *"It is always nice to play with the light [..], I used it when I needed a distraction".*

DISCUSSION AND CONCLUSION

The research presented in this paper explored if being regularly confronted with pseudorandom light settings could enhance the user experience of connected lighting systems, and whether it might result more diverse light preferences. To promote integration into users' everyday routines, our dedicated light controller Plux implemented a hybrid control approach and relied on principles of peripheral interaction [4]. Plux was used in five participants' living rooms for three weeks.

As evident from both quantitative and qualitative findings, the experience differed considerably among our five participants. It seems that P1 and P5 usually started interactions with their lighting with a rather particular lighting setting in mind. Since Plux pseudo-randomly created light settings, P1 and P5 often did not find what they were looking for, as indicated during the interviews. This lead to frustration and caused these participants to switch to the app, with which they could directly set particular lighting. This might explain the fact these two participants rated their interactions with Plux as demanding higher mental effort compared to the Philips Hue app (see Table 1), as the latter led to the desired result more quickly.

P2, P3 and P4, on the other hand, did not seem to have very concrete settings in mind when interacting with their lights, or even found it hard to use the app because it demands indicating exactly what kind of lighting you want. As a result, these participants were generally satisfied with the light settings created by Plux, as revealed in the interviews. This difference of approach to using connected lighting systems might also explain that these participants used Plux more regularly and that they indicating lower mental effort needed for Plux compared to the app (see Table 1).

P1 and P5 evidently already had clear light preferences, while P2, P3 and P4 did not. These latter three participants also indicated they used light settings during the deployment, which they would normally not have chosen with the app. This indicates that, for these participants, Plux enabled a broader exploration of light settings than the app normally did. We hypothesized that being confronted with alternative light settings regularly would improve people's understanding of their own preferences and potentially support the process of constructing these preferences. However, we did not find evidence for this from our three week field-study. A longer term deployment amongst more diverse participants would be needed to verify if and how such effects can be achieved with light controllers such as Plux.

Although P1 and P5 did not see much benefits of using Plux over the app, they did indicate that interactions with Plux were easy enough to fit into their everyday routine. Despite practical limitations which caused the controller to require a few seconds to boot before it could be used, operating Plux seemed to fit particularly well into the routines of the other three participants, as indicated in the interviews and evidenced by their RSME ratings (Table 1). These participants quickly accepted Plux as their main light controller. This seems to have been afforded by Plux's interaction design, which allows it to be manipulated in a straightforward manner, without requiring visual focus, and located anywhere that suits the user's routine.

Concluding, it is clear that pseudorandom lighting, even when a user could still control brightness and saturation of the light, was not experienced as beneficial by users who have very clear light preferences. It simply cost too much effort to achieve the settings they had in mind. Those who did not have such clear preferences however, had a positive user experience: they used and were satisfied with various different light settings and the interaction required to operate the lights became more effortless.

Modern connected lighting systems offer virtually limitless light settings. This raises challenges in interaction design: using these options often requires too much effort to fit in users' everyday routines and exploring all possibilities is practically impossible. Our findings indicate that serendipitous exploration of settings, through straightforward interactions as part of the everyday routine, seems a promising direction to address these challenges, which exist in connected lighting, but likely extend to other domains when Internet of Things solutions make their way to the home environment.

To further explore how hybrid control approaches might support users in exploring new light settings while preserving user control, our future work will explore the application of machine learning combined with tangible peripheral interaction to learn and improve a users' preferred light settings.

ACKNOWLEDGEMENTS

We would like to thank all participants in the study for the effort they put in using Plux and providing feedback on it. We also would like to thank Berry Eggen, Koen Beljaars and David Verweij for their help and feedback during the design and research process.

REFERENCES

1. Adobe. Color. Retrieved July 27, 2017 from https://color.adobe.com/nl/create/color-wheel/
2. Dzmitry Aliakseyeu, Bernt Meerbeek, Jon Mason, Remco Magielse, and Susanne Seitinger. 2016. Peripheral Interaction with Light. *In Peripheral Interaction.* (March 2016), 207–235. http://dx.doi.org/10.1007/978-3-319-29523-7_10
3. Saskia Bakker, and Karin Niemantsverdriet. 2016. The Interaction-Attention Continuum: Considering Various Levels of Human Attention in Interaction Design. *International Journal of Design* 10, 2:1-14.
4. Saskia Bakker, Elise van den Hoven, and Berry Eggen. 2014. Peripheral interaction: characteristics and considerations. *Personal and Ubiquitous Computing* 19, 1: 239–254. http://doi.org/10.1007/s00779-014-0775-2
5. Belkin. Wemo. Retrieved July 27, 2017 from http://www.belkin.com/nl/Products/c/home-automation/
6. Elgato. Avea. Retrieved July 27, 2017 from https://www.elgato.com/en/avea
7. Forpow. (2015, March 5). M!Qbe controls lighting with a roll of the die – forpow-We make your ideas come to life. Retrieved July 27, 2017, from http://www.forpow.com/mqbe-controls-lighting-with-a-roll-of-the-die/
8. Ikea. TRÅDFRI. Retrieved July 27, 2017 from http://www.ikea.com/us/en/catalog/categories/departments/lighting/smart_lighting/
9. Rose Johnson, Yvonne Rogers, Janet van der Linden, and Nadia Bianchi-Berthouze. 2012. Being in the Thick of In-the-wild Studies: The Challenges and Insights of Researcher Participation. *Proceedings of the SIGCHI Conference on Human Factors in Computing Systems*: 1135–1144. http://doi.org/10.1145/2207676.2208561
10. Tuomas Lappalainen, Johanna Korpela, Ashley Colley, and Jonna Häkkilä. 2016. Experiential tangible UI for controlling lighting. In *Proceedings of the 2016 ACM International Joint Conference on Pervasive and Ubiquitous Computing: Adjunct* (UbiComp '16), 317-320. https://doi.org/10.1145/2968219.2971380
11. Pranee Liamputtong, and Douglas Ezzy. 2005. *Qualitative research methods*. Oxford University Press.
12. LIFX. Retrieved July 27, 2017 from https://www.lifx.com/
13. Andrés Lucero, Tatiana Lashina, and Jacques Terken. 2006. Reducing complexity of interaction with advanced bathroom lighting at home (Reduktion der Interaktionskomplexität bei hochentwickelten Badezimmerbeleuchtungssystemen für die Heimanwendung). *i-com*, *5*(1), 34-40. https://doi.org/10.1524/icom.2006.5.1.34
14. Andrés Lucero, Jon Mason, Alexander Wiethoff, Bernt Meerbeek, Henrika Pihlajaniemi, and Dzmitry Aliakseyeu. 2016. Rethinking our interactions with light. *Interactions*, *23*(6), 54-59. http://dx.doi.org/10.1145/3003334
15. Remco Magielse and Serge Offermans. 2013. Future lighting systems. *CHI 13 Extended Abstracts on Human Factors in Computing Systems on - CHI EA 13* (2013). http://dx.doi.org/10.1145/2468356.2479545
16. Milight. Retrieved July 27, 2017 from http://www.milight.com/
17. Karin Niemantsverdriet, Harm Essen, and Berry Eggen. 2017. A perspective on multi-user interaction design based on an understanding of domestic lighting conflicts. *Personal Ubiquitous Comput.* 21, 2 (April 2017), 371-389. https://doi.org/10.1007/s00779-016-0998-5
18. Serge Offermans, Harm van Essen, and Berry Eggen. 2014. User interaction with everyday lighting systems. *Personal and Ubiquitous Computing* 18, 8 (January 2014), 2035–2055. http://dx.doi.org/10.1007/s00779-014-0759-2
19. Serge Offermans, Harm van Essen, and Berry Eggen. 2013. Exploring a hybrid control approach for enhanced user experience of interactive lighting. In Proceedings of the 27th International BCS Human Computer Interaction Conference (BCS-HCI '13). http://dx.doi.org/10.1007/978-3-319-20889-3_17
20. Philips. Hue. Retrieved July 27, 2017 from http://www2.meethue.com/nl-nl/
21. Fred Zijlstra. 1993. *Efficiency in work behaviour: A design approach for modern tools*. Ph.D Dissertation. Delft University Press.

Screenprinting and TEI: Supporting Engagement with STEAM through DIY Fabrication of Smart Materials

Stacey Kuznetsov[1], Piyum Fernando[1], Emily Ritter[2], Cassandra Barrett[3], Jennifer Weiler[1], Marissa Rohr[1]

[1]School of Arts, Media, and Engineering
Arizona State University
{kstace, pfernan4, jjweiler, marissa.rohr}@asu.edu

[2]School of Art
Arizona State University
Tempe, AZ USA
eritter1@asu.edu

[3]School of Biological and Health Systems Engineering
Arizona State University
Tempe, AZ USA
cmbarre6@asu.edu

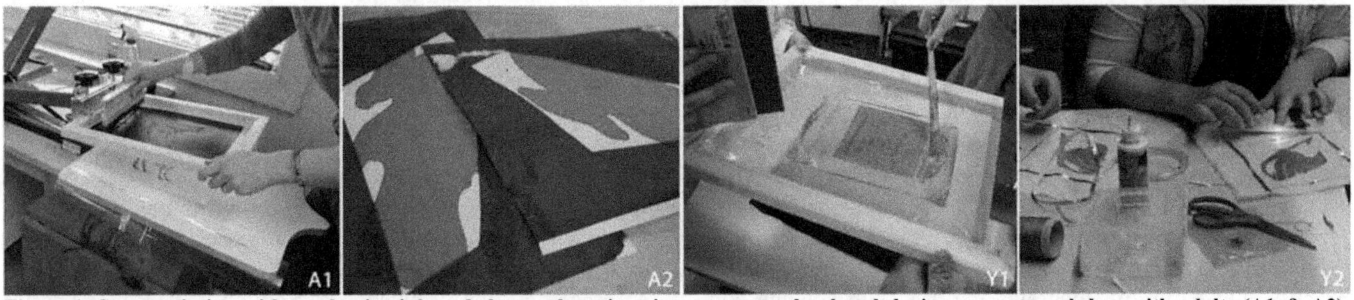

Figure 1. Screenprinting with conductive ink and thermochromic prints on paper developed during our art workshop with adults (A1 & A2); children screenprinting and assembling foldable circuits on fabric during our STEAM class for junior highschool youths (Y1 & Y2).

ABSTRACT
This paper focuses on manual screenprinting as a DIY fabrication technique for embedding interactive behavior onto a rage of substrates such as paper, fabric, plastic, wood, or vinyl. We frame screenprinting as a process that operates at the intersection of art, technology, and material science and iteratively examine its potential in two STEAM contexts. We conducted youth and adult workshops whereby participants worked with our low-cost thermochromic, UV-sensitive, and conductive screenprinting inks to develop a range of concepts and final projects. Our findings highlight several unique features of screenprinting: it affords a low barrier to entry for smart material fabrication, supports a collaborative maker practice, and scaffolds creative engagement with STEAM concepts. By being widely-accessible and substrate-agnostic, screenprinting presents exciting opportunities for TEI: DIY fabrication of smart materials in domains such as fine arts, information visualization, and slow technology; and bridging diverse disciplines through STEAM screenprinting initiatives at youth and adult levels.

TEI '18, March 18–21, 2018, Stockholm, Sweden

ACM ISBN 978-1-4503-5568-1/18/03...$15.00
https://doi.org/10.1145/3173225.3173253

Author Keywords
Screenprinting, DIY fabrication, STEAM, smart materials.

INTRODUCTION
Recent HCI research has innovated a number of printing methods to create interactive materials such as printable touch sensors, biosensors, hydrogels, and thin-film displays [27, 38, 43]. This work has contributed towards the evolution of "smart" materials, whereby instead of using external components, responsive behavior and/or visualization is incorporated into the material itself. In this paper, we focus on screenprinting as a DIY fabrication process that can be used to embed interactive properties into a range of substrates including paper, fabric, vinyl, wood, or acrylic.

We focus on screenprinting not only because it has not been previously studied widely in HCI literature, but also because it has several unique advantages. First and foremost, screenprinting is extremely versatile as it can be applied to a variety of substrates. Second, screenprinting supports different stencil-making methods: the images to be printed can be created by vinyl cutting, hand-drawn with screen filler and drawing fluid, or developed with photo-emulsion, to name a few. Because of its versatility, screenprinting also has a low barrier to entry. DIY-level screenprinting set-ups are accessible to amateurs and screenprint designs can be easily replicated and altered. When coupled with interactive or conductive inks, screenprinting operates at the crossroads of traditional art practice, technology, and material science. Therefore, when framed as a DIY fabrication method for smart materials, screenprinting presents a novel platform for creative STEAM initiatives in TEI.

Research Contribution

Our work applies manual screenprinting to support DIY fabrication of smart materials in STEAM contexts. We begin by describing the low-cost screenprinting inks we developed, which demonstrate consistent reproducibility of photochromic, thermochromic, and conductive properties across different substrates. We then present findings from iterative STEAM workshops with adult and youth makers. In our adult workshop, local artists experimented with our screenprinting methods and applied them to their practice. The workshop resulted in two interactive pieces showcased at a local gallery and revealed a host of application areas for interactive arts, ambient displays, and ultra-low-cost sensing. Insights from the workshop led us to develop a summer camp course for junior highschool youths. Our key contribution lies in uncovering unique features of screenprinting when compared to other methods of making with responsive inks. We found that due to its reproducibility and versatility across almost any substrate, screenprinting supports a highly collaborative maker practice and naturally integrates the arts with science and technology. We conclude with broader implications for screenprinting as a DIY fabrication method for smart materials and a platform STEAM engagement.

RELATED WORK

HCI has been exploring the intersection between art and technology through venues such as the ACM Creativity and Cognition Conference, the Art.CHI workshop series [2], a DIS workshop on multidisciplinary participation [48], or this year's TEI Arts Track. Printmaking has been of particular interest in design research, with digital and analog technologies being used to embed prints into a variety of mediums [3], or serigraphy being proposed in a number of capacitive touch-sensing projects [22, 43]. Our work with screenprinting is especially aligned with two related work domains: smart material fabrication and STEAM.

Smart materials and DIY fabrication

Smart materials perceptibly change in response to their environment and recent HCI examples include odor, color, and shape-changing substances that visualize pH [26], a flexible and stretchable sensor network in the form factor of tape [15], stretchable proximity sensors [51], moisture-sensitive garments [51], and shape-changing foods [50], haptic interactions with piezo-resistive sensors [19], as well as new liquid-based and hydrogel printing technologies [49]. In most of these cases, however, specialized domain knowledge or equipment is needed to create these materials. Screenprinting presents a low-cost and widely accessible platform for embedding responsive elements onto a range of substrates—from wood to fabric, vinyl, and paper.

Similar to our work, recent DIY fabrication methods have incorporated paper into a range of interactive computing projects [5, 22]. Existing techniques include hacking Inkjet printers for rapid prototyping of electronics [27], using consumer level printing methods for fabricating interactive components [38], screenprinting with off-the-shelf conductive paint [7, 22], or painting circuits by hand [10, 13]. In addition, thermochromic inks have been used to produce ambient display technologies [36, 37] with external heating elements such as peltiers. Our work with screenprinting extends these techniques by embedding interactive elements as printed layers on a range of materials and exploring the versatility of the process with adult and youth makers.

STEAM initiatives and HCI

Our research integrates practices from the fine arts with fabrication of interactive and smart materials, and we orient our work within the STEAM movement. STEAM (STEM + the Arts) incorporates art and design into science, math, technology, and engineering fields, particularly in K-20 education [45], and has been backed by methodological HCI research [6, 18, 47]. STEAM principles have been implemented many computer clubhouses, which focus art and design through technology use [e.g., 25, 40, 41], and embraced by platforms such as Scratch [40], Robot Diaries [32], Modkit [33], LilyPad Arduino [9, 10, 16, 31], and EduWear [28], to name a few. More recently, STEAM research has explored sketching [11, 29], theatrical performance [24], music remixing [17], and sound composition [20], as platforms for science and tech learning. We contribute to this work by focusing on screenprinting—a previously unexplored approach in STEAM, which combines traditional printmaking, digital design, and fabrication of interactive materials.

ABOUT SCREENPRINTING

Screenprinting is one of the most popular DIY printing methods, which has been, for many years, used to produce static visual representations in various scales and forms. In this method of printmaking ink is transferred through a mesh screen onto an underlying material. A stencil on the screen makes sections of the mesh impermeable to the ink, thereby creating the desired patterns on the substrate. Screenprinting studios range from basic, at home DIY setups to professional level studios. Our screenprinting set-up is lower cost and could be easily implemented in makerspaces or private art studios and homes. Our process is fully manual process, using materials such as vinyl stencils, polyester meshes, off-the shelf inks, and several powdered pigments that are easily available for affordable prices (below $50).

To develop robust thermochromic, photochromic, and conductive screenprinting inks, we relied on expertise from our entire multidisciplinary research team, which included a screenprinting expert, a computer engineer, a biologist, and an interaction designer. Below, we describe three types of interactive screenprinting inks we developed: resistive, thermochromic, and UV-responsive. These were tested by

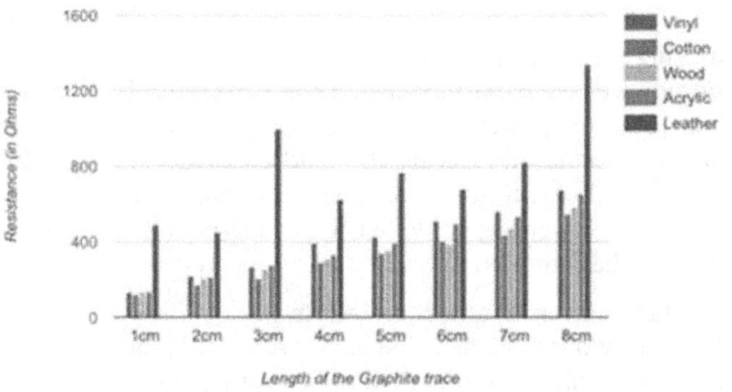

Figure 2. Resistance values of graphite traces printed on different materials (Average values of 2 samples of each material)

all members of the team to examine the reproducibility of the work by non-experts.

Low-cost, consistent resistive traces

There are many off-the-shelf conductive inks available for screenprinting, with resistive, (e.g., graphite-based) inks costing upwards of $18/oz [3] and conducive (e.g., silver-based) inks costing upwards of $60/oz [30]. Since screenprinting usually uses a large quantity of ink than hand-drawn or inkjet printed circuits we developed our own, ultra low-cost custom-made ink. The ink was made by mixing Graphite powder (General's pure powdered graphite), extender base (Speedball screenprinting gel polymer) and water at a 8:1:1 ratio by volume, costing under $2 per oz. We tested the resistance of graphite traces screenprinted on various materials including wood, leather, vinyl, and paper and measured resistance values across the ends of traces. Traces of similar length produced consistent resistance values on evenly-textured materials (except leather, which has an uneven surface) (Fig 2). Overall, this shows that screenprinting is a reliable method for embedding conductive traces onto woods, acrylics, and fabrics—substrates that have not been previously explored by prior research, which focused predominantly printing circuits on paper [22, 27].

Thermochromic prints

While our conductive inks can of course be paired with traditional electronics components (e.g., LEDs, sensors, etc.) to prototype interfaces, we also examined thermochromic actuation as a form of expressive output. Thermochromic pigments are heat sensitive compounds that temporarily change color with exposure to heat. There are many commercially available powders with different color choices and temperature sensitivities [17], and in our work we used pigments from [46] that change from color to clear at 77F. For screenprinting, we mixed these powders with

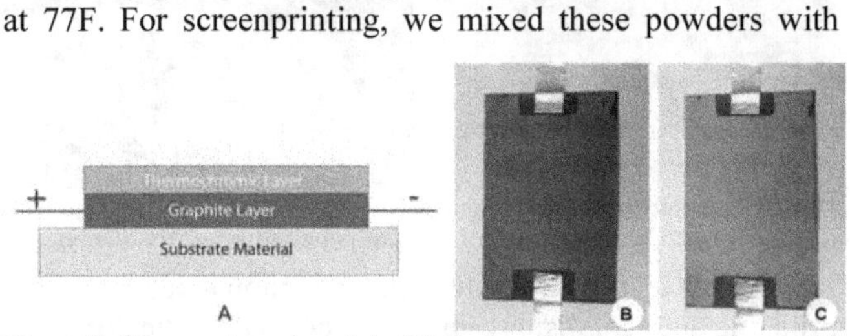

Figure 3. Thermochromic prints (A) Composition of printed layers (B) Normal state (C) After applying a voltage

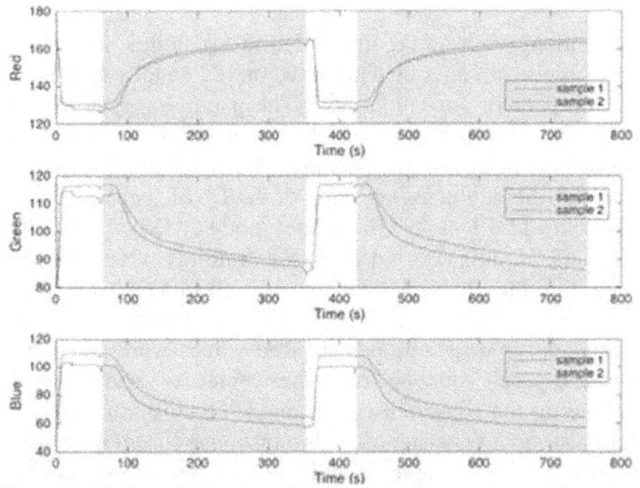

Figure 4. R,G and B values(0-255) of each samples against time (Shaded area = Voltage supply OFF)

extender base and water at a 10:1:1 ratio by volume. To confirm consistency, we tested the response of our prints to voltage actuation. We used 2 samples, where a thermochromic layer was printed on top of a graphite layer on 163GSM paper (Fig. 3). When voltage is applied across the graphite layer, it heats up causing the thermochromic layer to become clear. For the purposes of our tests, we used a voltage of 20V, kept ON for 1 minute in the beginning of the test and turned OFF for 5 minutes until the samples returned to their original colors. Color changes were video recorded using a Canon 550D DSLR camera at 60FPS with controlled lighting. Every 60th frame of the video (one data point per second) was read into the Matlab video reading function. Average RGB values of a 250-pixel square at the center of each selected frame was calculated using Matlab Image processing toolbox (Fig. 4). Our overall findings demonstrate consistent RGB responses in both samples.

UV sensitive prints

Photochromic pigments change color when exposed to an ultraviolet source (e.g., sunlight or UV flashlight). As with the thermochromic powders, there are many commercially available options with varying color changes. We used "solar drops"—concentrated liquids—that change from white to a color (e.g., white to red) when exposed to UV. We made UV-sensitive screenprinting ink by mixing solar

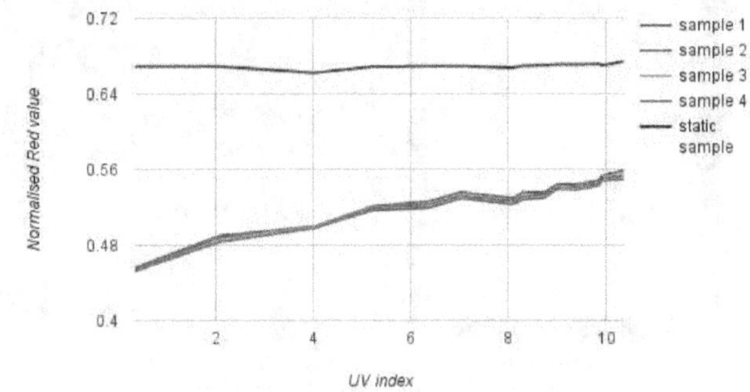

Figure 5. Normalized Red values against UV index reading

drops with extender base [42] in 40:1 ratio by volume. We tested 4 samples printed on 90GSM paper, mounted on a panel along with an Adafruit SI1145 UV index sensor [1]. A red piece of paper also mounted on the panel was used as a control color for calibration. The panel was placed in a stationary outdoor location that was exposed to natural sunlight. Photos of the samples were taken at different times of the day using a Canon 550D DSLR camera with a 17-55mm f2.8 lens in full manual mode at f5.0, 1/200, 200 ISO and 50mm. UV index sensor readings were recorded each time the photos were taken and all images were RGB normalized. Using the same MATLAB libraries as in the thermochromic set-up, average Red values were calculated for 250-pixel squares from the center of each sample (including the static red color paper). Overall, our findings demonstrate a consistent R-value response for all 4 samples at different UV levels, and a near-linear relationship between normalized Red value and the UV index (Fig. 5).

In summary, we used a fully manual screenprinting process and ultra low-cost, homemade inks to produce consistent thermochromic, UV-sensitive, and conductive prints. We continue to examine the potential of screenprinting as a DIY fabrication method in two STEAM contexts: a workshop with adults from arts community, and summer camp course we developed for junior highschool students.

SCREENPRINTING WORKSHOP WITH LOCAL ARTISTS

To explore how our interactive screenprinting inks might be applied in art domains, we conducted a workshop with 5 local artists (2 male) who were interested in interactive screenprinting techniques. Participants were recruited from various art disciplines, ranging from printmaking to dance, sculpture, and photography. During the workshop, which lasted about 4 hours, participants were presented with an overview of our inks and shown basic electronic concepts (e.g., connecting LEDs and switches to a battery using the Circuit Scribe kit [13], connecting battery powered heating elements etc.). Most of the time was used as an unstructured work session, whereby participants experimented with the inks, made prints, and provided feedback on how these materials could enhance their practice.

The workshop resulted in two finished pieces (Fig. 6) that were showcased at a Mixed Medium-themed art exhibit at a

Figure 6. Workshop outcomes: participants' thermochromic prints with electronic heat actuation, showcased at local gallery.

local gallery, drawing interest from the general public. These pieces consisted of heat-sensitive screenprints, heating elements and simple electronic circuits, which were introduced to the participants at the workshop. In addition, we audio-recorded the informal conversations that happened naturally during the work session. Transcription of the audio recording together with notes taken by the researchers were open-coded, and emergent themes were affinity diagrammed to reveal two application areas.

DIY fabrication of smart materials

In our workshop, participants were able to replicate consistent photochromic, thermochromic, and conductive prints on materials ranging from paper, to fabric, wood, and acrylic. Interestingly, the participants viewed these resulting materials—and not just the prints—as interactive. While participants were aware of commercially available thermochromic and photochromic products, all participants noted that the ability to customize visual designs and print it on any substrate material would essentially enable them to create their own smart materials to incorporate into their art practice. The discussed ideas included: screenprinting interactive costumes for dance performances, making temperature-responsive sculpture installations, augmenting indoor spaces with prints that were actuated at different times of the day based on sun exposure, and combining screenprinted circuits with traditional photography to create touch-sensitive and responsive images.

In addition to these art domain-specific ideas, participants also discussed how DIY smart materials could aesthetically respond to the environment or visualize information. For instance, as screenprinting can be done on a range of substrates, participants suggested location-specific visual expressions (e.g., solar-sensitive designs in areas that received varying levels of sunlight to produce unique visual experiences throughout the day). Likewise, when working with the voltage-actuated conductive-thermochromic prints, participants discussed the ability to break away from the constraints of premade electronic components (e.g., screens or LEDs of fixed size) and suggested various ambient displays that would more aesthetically "blend" into the underlying material. These ideas were particularly inspiriting to the interaction designers on our research team, and working with one of the artists after the workshop, we

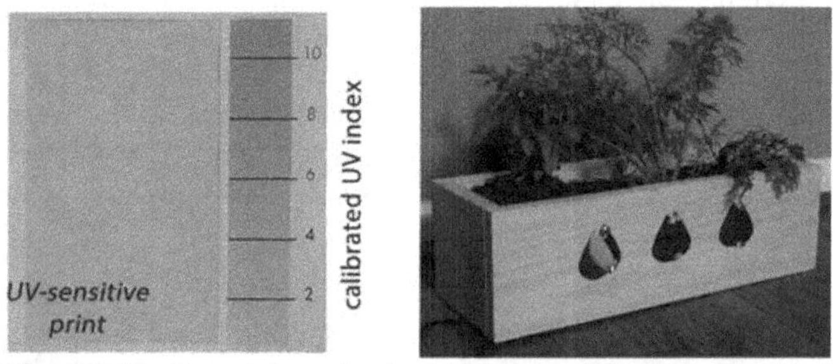

Figure 7. Rapid prototypes inspired by our workshop: screenprinted ultra low-cost UV indicator and non-emissive soil moisture display.

rapidly prototyped two potential application areas for TEI: a printable ambient display and a low cost UV indicator.

Printable ambient displays

Drawing on discussions from the workshop, we wanted to explore how new types of replicable information displays could be printed directly on materials such as woods, plastics, or textiles. To demonstrate this idea, we developed a rapid prototype that visualizes soil moisture on a wooden plant tray (Fig. 7). Data from a moisture sensor [44] embedded in the soil is processed by the Arduino microcontroller. Blue thermochromic water droplets printed over a graphite resistive layer directly on the tray are actuated, effectively changing from blue to white as the soil dries. Reflecting on this prototype, our team was particularly intrigued by the inherent slowness of thermal actuation. Unlike the near-instant response rates of most digital displays, the slow transitions between thermochromic colors mimicked the slower organic processes taking place inside the plant tray.

Printable UV indicators

Drawing on our participants' ideas to create location and time-specific prints, as well as the fact that our inks and methods produce consistent UV responses, we developed an ultra low-cost, printable UV index indicator (Fig. 7). By utilizing the results of our earlier analysis of UV sensitive prints, we found this indicator to be accurate when cross-referenced with the Adafruit UV sensor. While our rapidly-prototyped visual design is rather simple, future designs could more aesthetically engage viewers with UV exposure in different locations (e.g., murals on buildings) or on an individual level (e.g., prints on personal items).

Screenprinting as a platform for STEAM

In addition to applying interactive screenpring methods to their own practice, participants suggested using our inks and methods to teach art and science. Being from the fine-arts community, participants themselves used the workshop to learn about and experiment with simple heating elements (eg: DC powered heating pads, muscle wires) to actuate their heat sensitive screen prints. These explorations resulted in discussions around screenprinting as a way of integrating art and engineering activities. For instance, participants suggested a different workshop for novices to learn both printmaking techniques and circuit design through the use of thermal and conductive inks.

The accessibility of DIY screenprinting and the interest shown by our participants to work with electronic components suggests screenprinting as an entry point for STEAM. We continue by examining this direction through a youth summer camp course we developed.

STEAM COURSE OF JUNIOR HIGHSCHOOL YOUTHS

We developed a week-long summer camp module for junior highschool youths as part of a Digital Culture outreach program at our university. The camp teaches a breadth of creative skills, ranging from digital music design, to programming for games, and DIY fabrication using makerspace tools (e.g., 3D printing, laser cutting). Our module consisted of a 2-hour long class that ran Monday-Friday and for each project, students used low-fidelity sketching to brainstorm ideas individually and then worked on designing and screenprinting the chosen project in groups of 3 or 4.

Course curriculum

During the first day, students explored photochromism by mixing UV-responsive pigments with screenprinting inks and observing the colors with a UV light and sun exposure. Students also worked in groups to set up screens from pre-cut vinyl stencils and made their first prints using the photochromic inks they created. Days 2 and 3 focused on basic electronic concepts and students worked on designing their own stencils in Adobe Fireworks and screenprinting a folding switch circuit. This project also introduced the concept of "registering" or aligning multiple printed layers on the same material. The resulting print included a conductive strip that served as part of a folding switch, an LED and coin cell battery that completed the circuit, and a thermochromic image that was printed to decorate the switch. Days 4 and 5 were used to create a screen-printed storyboard that illustrated a narrative developed by the entire class. The inks and concepts learned in the class served as prompts for each frame of the storyboard and served as action points in the story (the final story consisted of four frames which used regular, photochromic, thermochromic, and conductive elements). Table 1 summarizes the structure of our curriculum and the art and science concepts that were covered each day through the activities. The majority of the activities were hands-on except for a longer presentation on electronic.

Day	Activities	STEAM concepts
1	Transfer pre-cut vinyl stencils onto screens, mix photochromic inks, make first print, experiment with UV light.	Screenprinting methods, photochrometry, light perception, visible light spectrum.
2	Introduction of circuits, stencil design in Adobe Fireworks.	Circuits, electronics, digital stencil design.
3	Register (align) and print conductive and thermochromic prints onto foldable material, assemble switch circuit.	Vinyl cutting, registering layered prints, debugging circuits, conductivity of materials.
4	Ideate story using interactive screenprinting elements as prompts; design storyboard stencils in Adobe Fireworks.	Structured brainstorming, storyboarding, collaborative storytelling.
5	Screenprint storyboard; film class narration of story with prints.	Review class concepts, collaborative making.

Table 1. Interactive screenprinting STEAM course curriculum for junior highschool youths.

About the students

18 students (11 female) enrolled in the class, which was one of the most popular in the camp. Of all the students, only two had some prior knowledge of screenprinting and three have previously created basic circuits with wires, but none have worked with interactive inks, stencil making vinyl cutting, or screenprinting in depth.

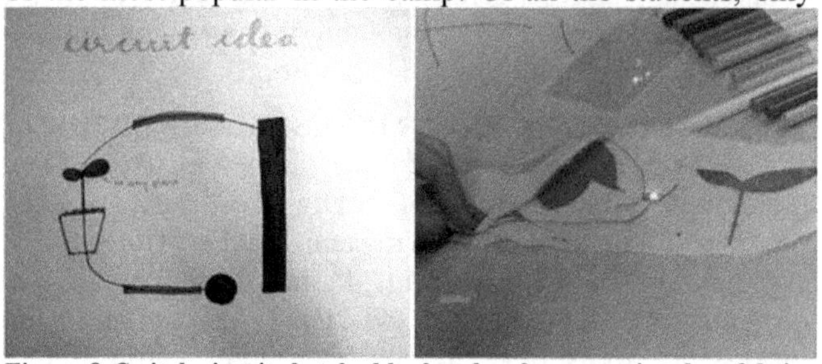

Figure 8. Switch circuit sketched by hand and screenprinted on fabric.

Data analysis and key takeaways

We obtained permission from parents and students to audio record our classes and gather select photos and images. Our classes were organized to embrace informal learning principles of exploratory play, hands-on experimentation, collaborative interactions with other people—principles that are also being increasingly associated with makerspaces in informal learning literature [7, 23]. In informal learning environments, traditional evaluation of science learning (e.g., pre and post tests) may undermine participants' confidence or even deter participation [34]. Similar to prior work that analyzed behavior and dialogue to infer learning patterns [4, 12], our data analysis focused on conversations and behavior during our classes. We audio-recorded and transcribed select aspects of the classes (logistical aspects of the class such as students washing screens were not recorded). We also documented our own in-situ observations at the end of each class, along with audio, photographs, and video recordings. Open coding was applied to relevant portions of the documentation (we did not transcribe or open code parts of the classes where students chatted about irrelevant topics such as their favorite video games or gossip about other students). Open codes were then grouped into themes and we affinity diagramed these to reveal two emergent areas: screenprinting as an integration of art and science; and smart materials as prompts for collaborative making.

Screenprinting as an integration of art and science

Throughout both classes nearly all students commented on how they perceived the class to be a blend of art and science. Certain parts of our curriculum served as particularly salient—and in some cases surprising—prompts for students to engage with STEAM. For instance, during the first day, we expected the students to mix photochromic inks quickly and proceed to screenprinting, since during our initial introductions most of them expressed more interest in the artistic aspects of the class (e.g., designing their own Tshirts). However, the process of adding photochromic pigments engaged the group for over an hour: the students experimented with various paint ratios, tested their results with UV lights or by stepping into the sun, and examined how different background colors of paper affected their color perception. In addition to general comments (e.g., "this is like science"), these experiments also led to many informal discussions about how humans perceive color and why materials change color. We used these conversations as opportunities to explain the concepts of photochromism, color perception, wavelengths of the visible and UV light, the atomic structure of materials, and the process of scientific discovery (scientific method).

Another instance when traditional screenprinting intersected with science and engineering concepts in our class was during the screenprinted circuit assembly. Our class workspace was arranged as an art studio, with a variety of different conductive materials (threads, paint, fabric, glue, etc.) available the same way regular craft materials are laid out during a find arts course. What we observed during days 2 and 3 of the course were children's seamless transitions between work with screenprinting, traditional craft activities, and circuit prototyping. During day 2, we asked the students to sketch out what their print and foldable switch would look like, and this "circuit diagram" guided each group in designing their stencils (Fig. 8). When adding LED's and batteries to their screenprints, the majority of the students informally talked about fundamental circuits concepts with each other, including conductivity, resistance, power, electron transfer, switches, and short circuits. Our set-up, where a variety of digital and fine arts materials were readily available, also led students to experiment with how different conductivities of inks, threads, and copper affected the brightness of their LEDs. Our wrap-up conversations with students asked them to describe what they were doing, and the children characterized their activities as "art and science". This blending of disciplines was further demonstrated by students who used conductive tape or thread to connect extra LEDs to their circuit, and then drew with regular paints or pencils to augment their screenprinted designs.

Screenprinting as a prompt for collaborative making

In our class, the screenprinting process naturally supported collaborative work among the students. On one hand, there

Interactive ink	Brainstorming prompt	Example brainstormed plot point
Any	____ is a ____	Kate is a swan
Photochromic	____ appears the character____	A ghost appears and Kate reaches for the door
Conductive switch	____opens and the character ____	The door opens and Kate steps inside
Thermochromic	____heats up and the character____	The room heats up and Kate regains her superpowers

Table 2. Interactive screenprinting inks as class prompts for collaborative storytelling. Inks were used to illustrate action points in storyboards.

are many steps involved, starting from designing a stencil and vinyl cutting it, to transferring it onto a screen, preparing the ink, printing (this step in particular required students to help each other with the printing press), and washing the screens. On the other hand, since screenprinting can be replicated many times without additional work, every group member can make a copy of the design on any desired material, thereby keeping a customized version of the group project. The last two days of our class supported a collaboration among the entire class of 18 students by using the interactive aspects of our inks as prompts for creative storytelling by the entire group. On day 4, the class was asked to brainstorm four storyline points, which were to be illustrated using each of the screenprinting inks and techniques from class (Table 2). After a collective brainstorming session, students selected their favorite plot line and worked in groups to design storyboards to illustrate each point with the specified inks. When these designs were printed, the students narrated the class story in a short video.

All the students themselves commented on the collaborative nature of our class—e.g., "this class is more interactive [than the other computer-based classes in the summer camp]", "this is fun"—and many perceived the group activities as a way of "hanging out" with their friends while doing the classwork. In addition, there were many instances when we observed groupwork to be particularly beneficial in supporting creative making practices: students built on each others' ideas to develop more complex stencils, suggested alternative ways of routing circuits, and, during the last two days of class, worked together to develop a narrative. Moreover, the informal conversations that occurred while working together often resulted in engagement with scientific concepts.

DISCUSSION AND IMPLICATIONS FOR TEI

Our research examined screenprinting as a platform for STEAM engagement with DIY smart material fabrication. To this end, we developed our own ultra low-cost thermochromic, photochromic, and conductive screenprinting inks and ensured they produced consistent responses across a range of substrates. Using these inks in an interactive screenprinting workshop with adult artists revealed future opportunities for material-agnostic displays and custom-made smart materials for different art domains. Moreover, discussions with adult artists inspired us to develop a STEAM summer camp course whereby junior high school students creatively engaged with fine arts, digital design, electronics, and science concepts through screenprinting.

Our work highlights two key advantages of screenprinting when compared to existing projects with responsive inks (e.g., freehand drawing or inkjet printing). First, the versatility and reproducibility of screenprinting across a range of substrates—wood, fabric, cardstock, etc.—presents new opportunities for low-cost and widely accessible smart material fabrication. Second, by being a highly collaborative practice and by integrating techniques from fine arts, material science, and electronics, screenprinting is a novel and powerful platform for STEAM. Below, we elaborate on these two ideas as future directions for applying screenprinting in TEI research.

Screenprinting and DIY fabrication of smart materials

Smart materials present a new and exciting research area for interaction design [e.g., 14, 15, 26, 50, 51]. DIY screenprinting has several unique advantages: it is ultra low-cost, widely accessible in terms of equipment, and does not require specialized domain knowledge. Also, while many smart material fabrication methods are substrate-specific, screenprinting has the additional capability of embedding responsive elements onto most evenly-textured materials. By being widely-accessible and material-agnostic, screenprinting can be used in domains such as dance, photography, sculpture, and information visualization, as our work has shown.

From another perspective, the inherent slowness of thermal actuation and organic color transitions of our inks, as well as the ability to print on most surfaces, are aligned with the recent trend towards calm computing and slow technology [35]. This body of work focuses on slowing down information consumption and presenting users with technologies that are reflective rather than instantly gratifying. Approaches described in our paper can serve as prototyping techniques for the slow technology agenda by embedding deliberately slow interactivity into everyday objects. Moreover, while our research focused on thermochromic, photochromic, and conductive printing, other materials such as biofilms, organic cells, and

Figure 9. Screenprinting as a highly collaborative maker practice: children transferring vinyl stencil onto a frame, exploring photochromic properties of DIY ink with UV light, making a print, and the final photochromic storyboard illustrating a plot point from the class story.

electroluminescent paint could be supported using screenprinting in the future.

Screenprinting as a platform for STEAM

We see screenprinting as parallel to many existing, successful initiatives that incorporate tangible media into art and science curriculums (e.g., textile or paper computing [8, 29]) or integrate computation with more traditional art forms such as glass blowing [21]. However, when compared to these existing methods, screenprinting offers several unique advantages.

First, screenprinting seamlessly combines elements from the fine arts, including one of the oldest forms of printmaking, with modern technologies such as vinyl cutting, and advancements in material science. Another particularly exciting feature of screenprinting is that it naturally supports collaborative making because of the physical aspects of the printing process and the reproducibility of the prints, such that everyone can make and keep a copy of the group project. Collaborative exploration is a tenet of informal learning, whereby participants pursue projects that are of personal interest, learn by doing, and collaboratively exchange ideas [34]. In our summer course, we saw many examples of this—e.g., when children informally discussed concepts of photochromism, thermochromism, conductivity, or human, color perception, during their collaborative troubleshooting of circuits, and class brainstorming and storyboarding.

These aspects of screenprinting—namely the blending of disciplines and the collaborative practice—render it as a particularly powerful platform for STEAM TEI research. Similar to other initiatives that support creative engagement with technology, future work can continue to explore screenprinting in informal learning contexts such as design studios, art-spaces, and makerspaces. Building on the preliminary insights from our studies, future work can more formally evaluate learning outcomes or compare screenprinting with existing STEAM approaches.

Limitations

Our analysis of the prints was carried out using consumer-level equipment—an entry level DSLR camera, regular multimeters and relatively low cost (below $30) sensors. While these lower-cost tools may limit the accuracy of our results, our findings were sufficient for speculating on the potential applications of screenprinting as a DIY fabrication method. While in this paper we focused on analyzing shorter-term performance and consistency, our future and ongoing work investigates longer-term ink stability in order to produce durable interactive systems. For example, some UV and temperature-responsive inks may fade over time, and we noticed a ghosting effect when exposing our prints to extreme heat and sunlight for several weeks. This exposure causes the inks to become less vibrant, but can be reduced by applying a fixative over the top of the prints and/or creating systems that actuate the inks for limited amounts of time. We suspect that these effects may also be reduced by experimenting with different types of pigments (e.g., different commercially available distributors).

CONCLUSION

In this work, we examined screenprinting as a new method for DIY fabrication of smart materials and a platform for STEAM. We first described three types of screenprinting inks we developed for embedding conductive, thermal, and photochromic properties onto most substrates. Our analysis shows that our inks and printing methods produce consistent outcomes across various materials even within a fully manual and basic screenprinting setup. We then studied the opportunities afforded by screenprinting in two STEAM contexts: a workshop with adult artists and a course for junior highschool youths. Our findings demonstrate several unique features of screenprinting: a low barrier to entry for smart material fabrication, a collaborative maker practice, and a creative integration fine arts, material science, and electronic concepts. We suggested that by being widely accessible and substrate-agnostic, screenprinting can be applied to new TEI research in interactive arts, information visualization, and STEAM education. Above all, we hope to have shown that by operating at the intersection of fine arts, material science, and technology, screenprinting bridges diverse disciplines through collaborative making at youth and adult levels.

REFERENCES

1. Adafruit SI1145 Breakout Board - UV index. https://learn.adafruit.com/adafruitsi1145-breakout-board-uv-ir-visible-sensor/overview
2. Art.CHI. Digital Art in a Post-Digital World. http://art-chi.org.
3. Bare Conductive. http://www.bareconductive.com.
4. Bell, P., Bricker, L. A., Reeve, S., Zimmerman, H. T., & Tzou, C. (in press). Discovering and Supporting Successful Learning Pathways of Youth In and Out Of School: Accounting for the Development of Everyday Expertise Across Settings. In B. Bevan, P. Bell, & R. Stevens (Eds.), Learning about Out of School Time (LOST) Learning Opportunities: Springer.
5. Bishop, L., and Paternoster, N. Inspirations in digital fine art printmaking. In *ACM SIGGRAPH 2014 Studio*, SIGGRAPH '14, 33:1–33:1.
6. Guy A. Boy. 2013. From STEM to STEAM: toward a human-centred education, creativity & learning thinking. In *Proceedings of the 31st European Conference on Cognitive Ergonomics* (ECCE '13). ACM, New York, NY, USA, , Article 3 , 7 pages.
7. Brahms, L. & Crowley, K. (in press). Making Sense of Making: Defining Learning Practices in MAKE Magazine. In Y. Kafai & K. Pepler (Eds). Makeology.
8. Buechley, L., Eisenberg, M., Catchen, J. and Crockett, A. (2008). The LilyPad Arduino: Using Computational Textiles to Investigate Engagement, Aesthetics, and

Diversity in Computer Science Education. In SIGCHI 2008.

9. Buechley, L., Elumeze, N., and Eisenberg, M. (2006). Electronic/Computational Textiles and Children's Crafts. In Interaction Design and Children (IDC), June 2006.
10. Buechley, L., Hendrix, S., and Eisenberg, M. Paints, paper, and programs: First steps toward the computational sketchbook. In *Proceedings of the 3rd International Conference on Tangible and Embedded Interaction*, TEI '09, ACM (New York, NY, USA, 2009), 9–12.
11. Rui Chen, Po-Jui (Ray) Chen, Rui Feng, Yilin (Elaine) Liu, Andy Wu, and Ali Mazalek. 2014. SciSketch: a tabletop collaborative sketching system. In *Proceedings of the 8th International Conference on Tangible, Embedded and Embodied Interaction* (TEI '14). ACM, New York, NY, USA, 247-250.
12. Chi, M. T. H., & Menekse, M. (2015). Dialogue patterns that promote learning. In L. B. Resnick, C. Asterhan, & S. N. Clarke (Eds.), Socializing intelligence through academic talk and dialogue (Ch. 21, pp. 263-274). Washington, DC: AERA.
13. Circuit Scribe kit. http://www.electroninks.com.
14. Artem Dementyev. 2016. Towards Self-Aware Materials. In Proceedings of the TEI '16: Tenth International Conference on Tangible, Embedded, and Embodied Interaction (TEI '16). ACM, New York, NY, USA, 685-688.
15. Artem Dementyev, Hsin-Liu (Cindy) Kao, and Joseph A. Paradiso. 2015. SensorTape: Modular and Programmable 3D-Aware Dense Sensor Network on a Tape. In *Proceedings of the 28th Annual ACM Symposium on User Interface Software & Technology* (UIST '15). ACM, New York, NY, USA, 649-658.
16. Eisenberg, M. and Buechley, L. (2008). Pervasive Fabrication: Making Construction Ubiquitous in Education. Journal of Software.
17. Shelly Engelman, Brian Magerko, Tom McKlin, Morgan Miller, Doug Edwards, and Jason Freeman. 2017. Creativity in Authentic STEAM Education with EarSketch. In *Proceedings of the 2017 ACM SIGCSE Technical Symposium on Computer Science Education* (SIGCSE '17). ACM, New York, NY, USA, 183-188.
18. Jill Fantauzzacoffin, Joanna Berzowska, Ernest Edmonds, Ken Goldberg, D. Fox Harrell, and Brian Smith. 2012. The arts, HCI, and innovation policy discourse: invited panel. In *CHI '12 Extended Abstracts on Human Factors in Computing Systems* (CHI EA '12). ACM, New York, NY, USA, 1111-1114.
19. Adrian Freed and David Wessel. 2015. An Accessible Platform for Exploring Haptic Interactions with Co-located Capacitive and Piezoresistive Sensors. In *Proceedings of the Ninth International Conference on Tangible, Embedded, and Embodied Interaction* (TEI '15). ACM, New York, NY, USA, 317-320.
20. Jamie Gorson, Nikita Patel, Elham Beheshti, Brian Magerko, and Michael Horn. 2017. TunePad: Computational Thinking Through Sound Composition. In *Proceedings of the 2017 Conference on Interaction Design and Children* (IDC '17). ACM, New York, NY, USA, 484-489.
21. Holman, D. Glassblowing: Forming a computational glass material. In *Proceedings of the Sixth International Conference on Tangible, Embedded and Embodied Interaction*, TEI '12, ACM (New York, NY, USA, 2012), 379–380.
22. Holman, D., Fellion, N., and Vertegaal, R. Sensing touch using resistive graphs. In *Proceedings of the 2014 Conference on Designing Interactive Systems*, DIS '14, ACM (New York, NY, USA, 2014), 195–198.
23. Honey, M., Kanter, D. E. Design, Make, Play. Growing the next generation of STEM innovators. Routledge, 2013.
24. Myounghoon Jeon, Maryam FakhrHosseini, Jaclyn Barnes, Zackery Duford, Ruimin Zhang, Joseph Ryan, and Eric Vasey. 2016. Making Live Theatre with Multiple Robots as Actors: Bringing Robots to Rural Schools to Promote STEAM Education for Underserved Students. In *The Eleventh ACM/IEEE International Conference on Human Robot Interaction* (HRI '16). IEEE Press, Piscataway, NJ, USA, 445-446.
25. Kafai, Y. B., Peppler, K. A., Chapman, R. N. "The Computer Clubhouse: Constructionism and Creativity in Youth Communities". Teachers College Press (July 1, 2009)
26. Viirj Kan, Emma Vargo, Noa Machover, Hiroshi Ishii, Serena Pan, Weixuan Chen, and Yasuaki Kakehi. 2017. Organic Primitives: Synthesis and Design of pH-Reactive Materials using Molecular I/O for Sensing, Actuation, and Interaction. In *Proceedings of the 2017 CHI Conference on Human Factors in Computing Systems* (CHI '17). ACM, New York, NY, USA, 989-1000.
27. Kawahara, Y., Hodges, S., Cook, B. S., Zhang, C., and Abowd, G. D. Instant inkjet circuits: Lab-based inkjet printing to support rapid prototyping of ubicomp devices. In *Proceedings of the 2013 ACM International Joint Conference on Pervasive and Ubiquitous Computing*, UbiComp '13, ACM (New York, NY, USA, 2013), 363–372.

28. Katterfeldt, E., Dittert, N., Schelhowe. H. 2009. EduWear: smart textiles as ways of relating computing technology to everyday life. Interaction Design and Children (IDC '09).

29. Joanne Lo, Cesar Torres, Isabel Yang, Jasper O'Leary, Danny Kaufman, Wilmot Li, Mira Dontcheva, and Eric Paulos. 2016. Aesthetic Electronics: Designing, Sketching, and Fabricating Circuits through Digital Exploration. In *Proceedings of the 29th Annual Symposium on User Interface Software and Technology* (UIST '16), 665-676.

30. MG Chemicals. Silver Print. https://www.mgchemicals.com

31. Ngai, G., Chan, S. C., Cheung, J. C., and Lau, W. W. 2009. The TeeBoard: an education-friendly construction platform for e-textiles and wearable computing. In Proc. of CHI 2010.

32. Nourbakhsh, I. 2009. Robot Diaries: Creative Technology Fluency for Middle School Girls. In IEEE Robotics and Autonomous Systems.

33. Modkit, http://www.modk.it/

34. National Research Council. (2009). Learning in Informal Environments: People, Places, and Pursuits. Bell, P., Lewenstein, B., Shouse, A. W., and Feder, M. A., Editors.

35. Odom, W., Selby, M., Sellen, A., Kirk, D., Banks, R., and Regan, T. Photobox: On the design of a slow technology. In *Proceedings of the Designing Interactive Systems Conference*, DIS '12, ACM (New York, NY, USA, 2012), 665–668.

36. Peiris, R. L., and Nakatsu, R. A temerature-based touch-sensor for non-emissive textile displays. In *CHI'13 Extended Abstracts on Human Factors in Computing Systems*, CHI EA '13, ACM (New York, NY, USA, 2013), 1605–1610.

37. Peiris, R. L., and Nanayakkara, S. Paperpixels: A toolkit to create paper-based displays. In *Proceedings of the 26th Australian Computer-Human Interaction Conference on Designing Futures: The Future of Design*, OzCHI '14, ACM (New York, NY, USA, 2014), 498–504.

38. Olberding, S., Wessely, M., and Steimle, J. Printscreen: Fabricating highly customizable thin-film touch-displays. In *Proceedings of the 27th Annual ACM Symposium on User Interface Software and Technology*, UIST '14, ACM (New York, NY, USA, 2014), 281–290.

39. Poupyrev, I., Nashida, T., Maruyama, S., Rekimoto, J., and Yamaji, Y. Lumen: Interactive visual and shape display for calm computing. In *ACM SIGGRAPH 2004 Emerging Technologies*, SIGGRAPH '04

40. Resnick, M. Computer as Paintbrush: Technology, Play, and the Creative Society. In Play = Learning: How play motivates and enhances children's cognitive and social-emotional growth. Oxford University Press. 2006.

41. Resnick, M. 2007. Sowing the seeds for a more creative society. International Society for Technology in Education

42. Screen printing. Speedball, https://www.speedballart.com/our-products.php?cat=21

43. Shorter, M., Rogers, J., and McGhee, J. Practical notes on paper circuits. In *Proceedings of the 2014 Conference on Designing Interactive Systems*, DIS '14, ACM (New York, NY, USA, 2014), 483–492.

44. Soil Moisture Sensor. https://www.sparkfun.com/products/13322

45. STEM to STEAM. http://stemtosteam.org/

46. Thermochromic powder. http://solarcolordust.com/t/thermal-shop.

47. Brygg Ullmer. 2012. Entangling space, form, light, time, computational STEAM, and cultural artifacts. *interactions* 19, 4 (July 2012), 32-39.

48. Vines, J., Clarke, R., Leong, T. W., Wright, P., Light, A., and Iversen, O. S. Perspectives on participation: Evaluating cross-disciplinary tools, methods and practices. In *Proceedings of the Designing InteractiveSystems Conference*, DIS '12, ACM (New York, NY, USA, 2012), 799–800.

49. Guanyun Wang, Lining Yao, Wen Wang, Jifei Ou, Chin-Yi Cheng, and Hiroshi Ishii. 2016. xPrint: A Modularized Liquid Printer for Smart Materials Deposition. In *Proceedings of the 2016 CHI Conference on Human Factors in Computing Systems* (CHI '16). ACM, New York, NY, USA, 5743-5752.

50. Wen Wang, Lining Yao, Teng Zhang, Chin-Yi Cheng, Daniel Levine, and Hiroshi Ishii. 2017. Transformative Appetite: Shape-Changing Food Transforms from 2D to 3D by Water Interaction through Cooking. In *Proceedings of the 2017 CHI Conference on Human Factors in Computing Systems* (CHI '17). ACM, New York, NY, USA, 6123-6132.

51. Michael Wessely, Theophanis Tsandilas, and Wendy E. Mackay. 2016. Stretchis: Fabricating Highly Stretchable User Interfaces. In *Proceedings of the 29th Annual Symposium on User Interface Software and Technology* (UIST '16). ACM, New York, NY, USA, 697-704.

52. Lining Yao, Jifei Ou, Chin-Yi Cheng, Helene Steiner, Wen Wang, Guanyun Wang, and Hiroshi Ishii. 2015. bioLogic: Natto Cells as Nanoactuators for Shape Changing Interfaces. In *Proceedings of the 33rd Annual ACM Conference on Human Factors in Computing Systems* (CHI '15). ACM, New York, NY, USA, 1-10

W.O.U.S.: Widgets of Unusual Size

Zann Anderson
Brigham Young University
Provo, UT, USA
zann@byu.edu

Michael Jones
Brigham Young University
Provo, UT, USA
mike.jones@byu.edu

Kevin Seppi
Brigham Young University
Provo, UT, USA
kseppi@byu.edu

ABSTRACT
Recent work in tangible interfaces, including widget sets like .NET Gadgeteer and Phidgets, has enabled prototyping of rich physical interaction at a handheld or tabletop scale. But it remains unclear how participants respond to physical widgets at larger scales. What kinds of interaction would larger widgets enable, and what kinds of systems—if any—can or should be built with them? We built unusually-sized widgets, or "mega-widgets" in order to explore this territory. We present the results of two iterations of building mega-widgets and accompanying user studies designed to help understand participants' reactions to mega-widgets and probe possible applications. Responses indicated, among other things, a correlation between widget size and the perceived size or importance of what it might control. Mega-widgets were also perceived as increasing the precision of user input control and providing a fun and playful element. We hope that knowledge gained from this exploratory work can help lay groundwork for further exploration of widgets at larger scales.

INTRODUCTION
Over the past two decades, much work has considered how to build tangible interfaces in which physical widgets, rather than virtual widgets in a GUI, control a system. To that end, many collections of physical widgets have been built and discussed, such as Phidgets [5], .NET Gadgeteer [7], Sauron [16], and others [18, 6, 19]. However, in each case, the physical widgets work at the scale of a finger: a knob is sized to be grasped and rotated by fingers, as are other controls like buttons and sliders.

It remains unclear how people react to and imagine using tangible widgets at larger scales ranging from a handspan to an armspan. We call widgets at this scale "mega-widgets". Mega-widgets are commonly used in a small number of applications such as automobiles, industrial control panels and children's playgrounds. See, for example, controls for a ship in Figure 1.

While Fitts's law is widely used and understood, and much research has explored the effects of widget size in GUI interfaces, large *physical* widgets have not been adequately explored within an HCI context, and pose a number of interesting questions such as: how might mega-widgets be used? Are they useful or merely impractical? How might participants respond to mega-widgets? Do mega-widgets provide affordances which may differentiate them from regular-sized widgets? What types of new interactions might they enable? In what situations might mega-widgets make sense? How can mega-widgets be constructed?

We anticipate that knowing how people react to and imagine using mega-widgets may be useful within the tangible user interface community because it allows people designing and implementing new systems to work from a deeper understanding of how widget size impacts tangible interface design.

In order to begin understanding the response created by mega-widgets and exploring their possible applications, we conducted two exploratory user studies. In the first, we sought to understand participants' initial reactions to mega-widgets and their impressions about what mega-widgets might be used for. In the second, we further refined our understanding of themes uncovered in the first study and explored potential applications for mega-widgets on a deeper level.

In the initial study, we fabricated mega-widgets and invited people to interact with them, and then to share with us their reactions and imagine possible uses for mega-widgets. We carried out an analysis of user responses by clustering their comments using "word embeddings" [15]. We found themes related to novelty, as might be expected, as well as others suggesting a correlation in the size of the physical control and the size of the phenomenon being controlled, and play. The applications suggested by participants included both serious and playful, and emerging themes of interest included play and visibility, among others.

Following up on the initial study, a second study was conducted using another set of mega-widgets with designs based on insights gained in the first study. This study aimed to further refine our understanding of themes identified in the first study and explore possible applications for mega-widgets. In this study, participants were invited to interact with mega-widgets and then pair applications with a specific widget type and size. We interviewed each participant asking them why they had made certain pairings, and conducted thematic analysis of participants' answers. Themes in this study had some overlap with those of the first study, while new themes also emerged, such as mega-widgets increasing the precision with which something can be controlled.

TEI '18, March 18–21, 2018, Stockholm, Sweden

DOI: https://doi.org/10.1145/3173225.3173246

Figure 1. A ship's steering wheel is a mega-widget sized knob larger than a handspan but smaller than an arm span. (Image by dreamstime.com contributor Eugenesergeev.)

Through two exploratory studies involving two sets of mega-widgets, we have begun to explore unusually-sized physical widgets, individuals' reactions to them, and their possible uses. We hope this paper and the studies it details will be effective groundwork for further exploration in this area.

The primary contributions of this paper are:

- a definition of the "mega" scale for physical widgets,
- exploration of how people react to and imagine using mega-widgets, and
- directions for future exploration of unusually-sized widgets

RELATED WORK

Widget Sets

Much prior work has been done in building and testing widget sets at "normal" scale for use with fingers. In this paper, we will refer to these as "finger-sized" widgets. Phidgets [5], an early pioneering work in this area, lays out the underlying motivations and conceptual framework behind such efforts. Namely, physical widgets aim to do for physical devices and interfaces what software widgets do for on-screen user interfaces: provide modularity, hide of implementation details, and simplify design and implementation.

Since Phidgets was published, many others have created physical widget sets and methods of adding them into physical devices. .NET Gadgeteer [19] combined "solder-less modular electronic hardware; object-oriented managed software libraries accessed using a high-level programming language and established development environment; and 3D design and construction tools" with the goal of providing flexibility, accessibility, and versatility.

Still other work explores physical widgets in the context of a physical housing. This includes forming the shape of housing using cardboard [8], foam [12, 1], and clay [9] or other sculpting media [17]. We have opted to leave exploration of integrating mega-widgets with a physical housing or other context for future work.

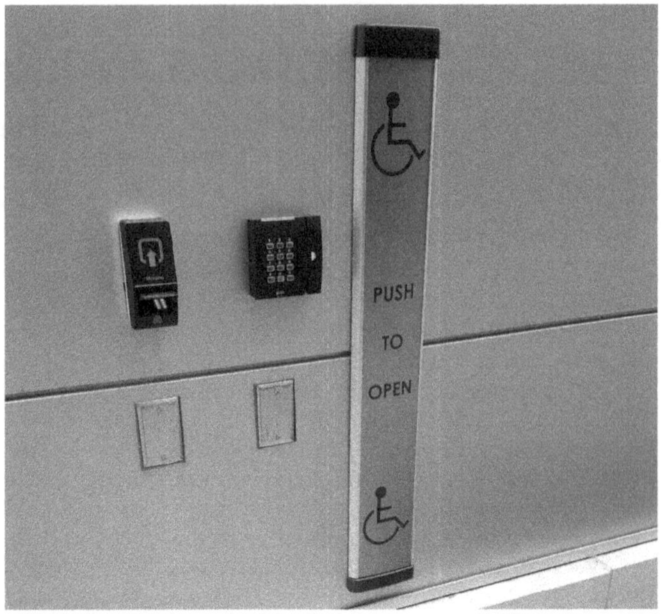

Figure 2. An example of a mega-widget intended for accessibility purposes.

Large Controls

Controls of larger sizes occur in some real-world situations, such as the aforementioned ship controls in Figure 1. In the past, one motivation for mega-widget scale controls was due to controls being connected to mechanical linkages. Although most modern controls use hydraulic or electronic linkages rather than mechanical, many such controls retain their larger size. This is presumably for other reasons such as to convey importance, to enable precise control by providing a larger range of motion, or to allow use of the control from a wide range of positions.

In other applications, large size is used for a fun and playful effect, such as in the construction of a giant-sized Nintendo controller[1] and remote control[2]. This type of application of size seems to recall childhood, where the entire world seems larger and curiosity abounds.

Accessibility for those with disabilities is also often accomplished via size, such as in the mega-widget-sized door open panel in 2. In this case, the larger size eases use for individuals for whom small buttons might be difficult to reach or press. While accessibility is an important application area for mega-widgets, we leave accessibility to future work.

BUILDING MEGAWIDGETS

We begin with a brief discussion of the "handspan to armspan" scale previously defined. For our purposes, a handspan is the distance between the tip of the little finger to the tip of the thumb when the fingers are fully extended. An armspan is the distance between middle finger tip to middle finger tip

[1] http://www.popsci.com/diy/article/2011-12/you-built-what-worlds-largest-videogame-controller

[2] http://www.guinnessworldrecords.com/news/2016/1/video-indian-brothers-build-14-ft-tv-remote-control-and-prove-it-actually-works-411614

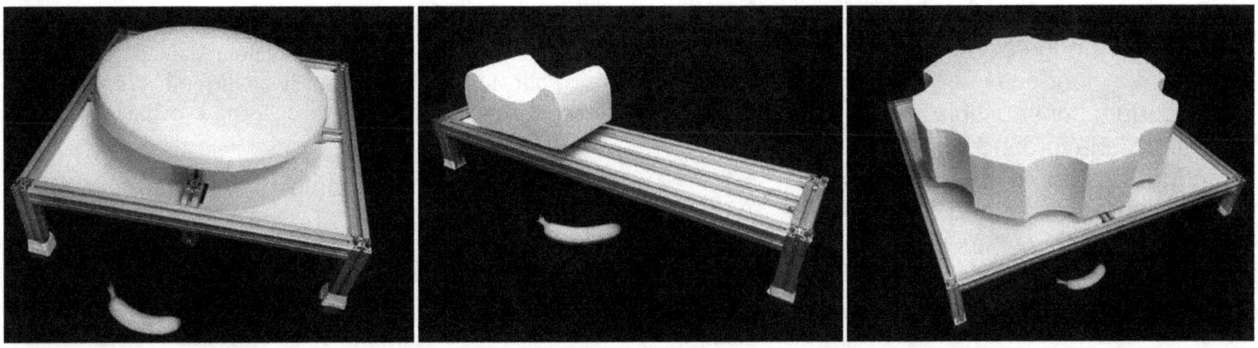

Figure 3. Widgets used in the first study were intended to represent a blank slate on which participants could project their thoughts and reactions.

when the arms are extended horizontally. We chose these as lower and upper bounds because they are sizes large enough that multiple hands are likely required for operation but not so large that a user will have to take a step during operation.

3D printing has made fabrication at the scale of normal-sized widgets quick, easy, and flexible. 3D printing is not yet easily applied to problem of fabricating a mega-widget. Thus fabrication of objects at the scale covered by mega-widgets requires application of more traditional forms of craftsmanship.

In order to make mega-widget construction simpler and more efficient, we have broken construction of an individual mega-widget into four separate modules: frame, mechanism, sensor and cap. This modularity allows for greater flexibility and ease in design and construction.

The *frame*, as its name suggests, is the housing or base which holds the other parts of the mega-widget. We used slotted aluminum bars from 80/20 Inc[3] to construct frames. This material was useful for this application as it is sturdy, tools are available for working with it, and the slots provided flexibility in assembly and expansion points for affixing mechanisms.

The *sensor* bridges the gap between physical motion and digital signals. We used three kinds of sensors which vary depending on the mega-widget type. For sliders and knobs we used ArUco (fiducial) markers as presented by Garrido-Jurado [4] in a camera system. For buttons, we used a packaged leaf button.

The *mechanism* in a mega-widget connects the frame to the cap. The mechanism allows the cap to move and provides haptic feedback. For sliders, the mechanism is a base which slides in the 80/20 slots. For knobs, the mechanism is a turntable bearing with one side anchored to the frame and the other side attached to the cap. The button mechanism is a spring system which allows the button to be depressed. To provide haptic feedback, we added pieces of felt to mechanisms for both sliders and knobs, thus providing friction-based resistance to the user's motion.

The *cap* is the object which the user sees and grasps, moves, or touches to interact with the mega-widget. The cap can be replaced without modifying the mechanism or sensor. We fabricated caps from foam and plywood but a wide range of cap fabrication methods and materials are possible. Fabrication of the cap involves craftsmanship in the creation of a tangible experience.

We fabricated two sets mega-widgets with different caps and used one set in each of the user studies described below. The first set of caps, shown in Figure 3, were intended to represent a blank canvas on which participants could project their thoughts about mega-widgets. Caps were shaped like scaled-up versions of finger-size widgets and painted white. For example, the knurls on a finger-sized knob give the fingers grip as they grasp and spin the knob. Those knurls scaled up to mega-widget size become larger than a finger or even a hand.

The second set of caps, shown in Figure 5 used color and shape to make the purpose and position of the widget more obvious. The caps used white markings on a grey background to indicate position and to prompt movement. We shaped the caps to make them graspable and usable. On the large knob cap, for example, graspable ridges on the edge of the cap invite the user to grab and turn the knob. This was a departure in design from the first set of mega-widgets, which were simply mega-scale versions of regular widgets.

We call mega-widgets "large," "very large," or "enormous" depending on their size. A *large* mega-widget is about the size of a handspan. A *very large* mega-widget is in between the sizes of a handspan and armspan. The *enormous* widgets are the size of an armspan. All widgets in Figure 3 are *enormous*, and all three sizes are depicted in Figure 5.

USER STUDIES

We conducted two exploratory user studies in order to gain an understanding of how participants respond to physical widgets at unusual sizes and to lay a foundation for future work.

In the first study, we sought to understand initial reactions by presenting participants with mega-widgets, allowing them to interact with them, and asking them to describe their reactions to them and to give us their ideas for possible uses.

Based on themes derived from responses and uses suggested by participants in the first study, we conducted a second study to explore participants' feelings about mega-widgets as it relates to their application to different usage scenarios.

[3]https://www.8020.net/

awkward unintuitive interesting fun
playplace huge overbearing fun natural
intuitive clear easy large restricted
important constructible fun exploring
curious playground fun easy clear
curiosity smooth instinctive cool
interesting interesting ginormous
useless why youthful discovery fun new
large light mindless resistant

Figure 4. The forty words generated when 10 participants were each asked to give 4 words to describe the mega-widgets shown in Figure 3. We used a clustering algorithm on word embeddings of these words to identify themes.

Study 1: Gauging Reactions and Imagining Applications

Assuming that widgets at "mega" scale would be a new experience for most individuals, our first study was aimed at understanding initial reactions. In order to do this, we invited 10 people (5 male, 5 female) to interact with mega-scale button, slider, and knob models shown in Figure 3. Interactions largely involved exploring the mega-widgets' size, shape, and range of motion by touching and moving them. Participants were recruited via convenience sampling on a college campus and were college-aged. Majors reported by participants were Computer Science, Economics (pre-med), Chemical Engineering, Math, Chemistry, Family Home and Social Sciences, Accounting, and Early Childhood Development.

Four Word Descriptions

In an effort to capture visceral reactions, we asked each participant to give us 4 words to describe their reaction to mega-widgets. These words are shown in Figure 4. This list includes opposites, like "unituitive" vs. "intuitive" and "awkward" vs. "natural". It also contains words which require interpretation like "youthful" and "cool". We asked for one-word responses with an algorithmic approach in mind, which we hoped would be a fast and simple method for analysis without introducing bias. This approach is described below.

The understanding of words in context is a fundamental objective of natural language processing (NLP)[13]. Common techniques in NLP, such as latent semantic analysis and the related information retrieval technique, latent semantic indexing [2], assume that "a word is characterized by the company it keeps" [3], and have been in use for some time.

In analyzing the data from this study, we have chosen to use a more recent, faster implementation of the "Word Embedding" idea, known as word2vec[15]. Embedding maps words with similar meaning to points that are near each other in the embedding space. Arithmetic operations in the word embedding space often correspond to their meaning the training corpus. For example, in an embedding space based on Wikipedia articles, the embedding of "king" minus "man" plus "woman" is approximately the embedding for "queen." We used a 300 dimensional embedding space trained on English Wikipedia articles[4].

Clustering Results

Using this embedding, we evaluated each of the words given by our study participants. Given the embedding values for each word we clustered the words using k-means to find clusters in the embedding space[5].

We employed cosine similarity as the distance metric for k-means clustering. Given a and b which are the semantic embeddings of two words, the cosine similarity between the embeddings is:

$$\text{similarly}(a,b) = \frac{\sum_i a_i b_i}{\sqrt{\sum_i a_i^2}\sqrt{\sum_i b_i^2}}$$

where i ranges over the dimensions of the embedding space.

Using these methods, we arrived at 5 clusters of words. In our testing, different numbers of clusters yielded less productive results. Further exploration of this approach in contrast to techniques such as open coding is warranted but outside the scope of this paper. Our approach proved very useful in our early exploratory study.

The clusters we identified are as follows, using the 3 words nearest the centroid of each as descriptors:

Fun, Enjoyable, Easy—This cluster expresses one of the sentiments that was widely discussed among researchers in the initial stages of this project: having such large widgets seems to evoke a fun and playful feeling.

Clear, Visible, Obvious—This may indicate that participants thought the purpose of the widgets or what type of controls they were was clear, or it may be related to the fact that it is easy for others to see widget operation from a distance.

Interesting, Curious, Intriguing—This cluster seems fairly obvious given the novel nature of mega-widgets, and probably captures the novelty effect as it seems that this is a common reaction when participants see something new and interesting.

Large, Huge, Massive—This is probably a reaction to the physical size of the mega-widgets, although the results of the second study seem to suggest that it may also relate to participant perceptions about the size of things that might be controlled by mega-widgets.

Mindless, Useless, Brainless—This may be an indication that the mega-widgets are simple and easy to use, or it may be that participants felt they were unnecessarily large (hence the word "useless"). It may also reflect the fact that the mega-widgets were not connected to any actual functionality for this study.

Applications

We also asked participants to imagine applications of the mega-widgets. We did not use word embeddings to identify themes in these responses because we were seeking more thoughtful discussion of application ideas rather than initial gut reactions, as facilitated by the one-word responses.

We employed a thematic analysis approach in which multiple study team members performed open-coding on participant

[4] As found at https://github.com/turbomaze/word2vecjson

[5] http://scikit-learn.org/stable/modules/generated/sklearn.cluster.KMeans

responses and subsequently discussed findings, coming to a shared agreement on points of disagreement and deriving major themes from frequently occurring code points. Four significant themes emerged from responses:

Misunderstood Shape Cues—6 of 10 participants made comments which seemed to indicate that they misunderstood the cues intended by the shape of the caps. For example, participant P5 thought the dip in the slider cap looked like "it would fit a leg." Two participants, P1 and P7, thought the button cap should twist and three participants, P1, P8 and P10, thought the knob cap looked like a gear that might be used in a gear system.

Big Things Need Big Widgets—Four participants (P3, P4, P6 and P9) said that big widgets must control big or important things. Participant P4 said "these are big devices so they should control big things." Big applications of mega-widgets included controlling the sky (P9), turning on the sun (P9), emergencies (P3), operating stadium lights (P6) and operating a theater curtain (P6).

Play—6 of 10 participants suggested applications or made comments related to play. Participant P5 said "I feel like I'm on a playground" while interacting with the mega-widgets. Applications included television game shows (P6 and P8) and playgrounds (P2, P5, and P9). Participant P7 recalled amusement parks such as LEGO Land and Disneyland.

Visibility—Three participants (P1, P2 and P4) noted that the value of mega-widgets was that people could easily see the widget move from a distance. Participant P2 said the mega-widget "shows off what you are doing." While we found this theme in only 3 responses, we considered it significant insofar as it describes a feature of mega-widgets not found in finger size widgets. This theme may also relate to the "clear, visible, obvious" theme from the word embedding analysis.

Study 2: Matching with Applications

In the second study, we invited 20 people (7 female, 13 male) to pair widgets of different types and sizes to applications. As with the first study, convenience sampling was used in a campus setting, and participants were of college age. There was no overlap in participants between the two studies.

The goal of this study was to further explore participants' responses to mega-widgets by asking them to pair mega-widgets with possible applications, both realistic and whimsical. We opted for pairing with imaginary applications rather than actually building systems for participants to control because it allowed for greater breadth, as construction of systems using mega-widgets would have limited a study with real-life applications to only a few modest use-cases. The full list of applications used in the second study appears in Table 1.

The 20 applications were imagined by the research team based on three of the themes identified in the first study: *Big Things Need Big Widgets*, *Play*, and *Visibility*. Our intent was to measure pairings between widgets and applications in a way that would help us further understand these themes. We also expected that other themes might emerge.

Roller Coaster Sprayer	Lights: Bedroom
Lights: Concert/Club	Lights: City
Pong	Temperature: Room
Temperature: Dorm	Temperature: Skyscraper
Emergency/Alarm Button	Tune Radio
Interest Rate: Branch	Interest Rate: Bank
Interest Rate: Federal	Dam Water Flow
Admissions GPA	Class Grade Curve
Spice Level	Car Vending Machine: Model
Car Vending Machine: Color	Car Vending Machine: Buy

Table 1. List of possible applications used in the second user study. "Spice Level" refers to a control to set how mild or spicy one would like their food to be at a restaurant. "Pong" refers to the classic videogame. "Car Vending Machine" is an imaginary vending machine that vends actual full-size cars.

The fourth theme in the first study of mega-widget applications, *misunderstood shape cues*, was addressed in the second study by redesigning caps to make their use more clear. This was done using color to represent position and adding appropriately-sized physical elements such as graspable ridges.

Applications were chosen which explored each of the themes, including some specifically designed to be playful (*Roller Coaster Sprayer, Pong*), some where visibility might be important (*Interest Rate, Spice Level, Alarm Button, Temperature*), and multiple sizes of some, intended to determine how strong the correlation between mega-widgets and the size of what they should control might be in participants' minds (*Interest Rate, Temperature, Lights*).

We also included baseline applications for which people already use finger-size widgets. The purpose of the baseline was to determine whether or not the presence of mega-widgets influenced people to pick them regardless of the application.

The mega-widgets shown in Figure 5 were used in the study along with finger-size widgets as a control. The finger size widgets were small devices constructed from commodity button, slider and knob parts with caps that had the same shape and color scheme as those in Figure 5.

During the study, participants were given a packet with one sheet of paper for each application. Each sheet included the name of the application and a description, such as "Dam Water Flow: Imagine controlling the flow of water through a dam." A table of widget images appeared at the bottom of each page showing photographs for each widget type and size. Participants were then introduced to a room containing the mega-widgets and regular-sized widgets pictured in the table of images. Participants interacted with the mega-widgets by pushing buttons, sliding sliders, and turning knobs. Participants circled the photograph of the widget type and size they paired with each application. Some participants interacted with widgets mainly at first prior to making assignments, others interacted to one extent or another during the process of making assignments, and still others hardly interacted with widgets at all beyond brief time spent looking them over prior to making assignments.

Figure 5. Widgets used in the second user study were designed based on insights gained in the first study. White markings on sliders indicate directions of travel and markings on the knob indicate position. Widget caps are shaped to invite gasping and motion.

The Pairings

The chart in Figure 6 summarizes the pairings of widget size and application for 20 participants and 20 applications. The six bars which are shorter reflect where participants missed making a pairing for that application. The columns in Figure 6 are sorted by the sum of very large and enormous widgets.

We expected that applications with large physical components (dam control, car vending machine) and important applications (including the Federal interest rate, city lights, skyscraper temperature) would be paired with large wigdets. For the most part, this was true. However, the class grade curve, which affects a relatively large number of people, was paired with finger-size widgets 14 of 20 times and the alarm, which is fairly important and could also benefit from increased visibility was paired with large and finger-size widgets all but once.

We also expected the two playful applications (roller coaster water sprayer and pong) to be paired with large widgets. The roller coaster sprayer was paired with very large or enormous widgets 10 times and with finger-size widgets only 3 times, as expected. But the pong game was paired with finger-size widgets 9 times and very large or enormous widgets only twice. It may be that previous pong or videogame experience with finger-sized widgets caused participants to lean that direction. It may also be that the increased energy expended and distance to be covered using a mega-widget dissuaded participants from choosing them in this case.

We expected the baseline applications (room temperature, bedroom lights and radio dial) to be paired with finger-size widgets as they are in normal usage. Room temperature and bedroom light controls were paired with the usual finger-size controls 37 of 39 times. The radio controls were paired with finger-size widgets 14 of 19 times.

Rationale for Pairings

Before the study we selected 8 applications of interest to discuss in more detail with participants. To avoid interview fatigue, each participant was asked about 4 of the 8. The Latin squares method was used to assign which participants to ask about which applications. Applications which were discussed were selected to cover a broad swath of the concepts which were encapsulated by the overall application list. The applications selected were: *Lights: City*, *Temperature: Skyscraper*, *Temperature: Dorm*, *Interest Rate: Federal*, *Car Vending Machine: Model*, *Roller Coaster Sprayer*, *Class Grade Curve*, and *Dam Water Flow*. For each pairing we asked two questions: Why did you pair this application with that widget? Why did you not pick a different size? We asked the questions whether the participant had selected a mega-widget or a finger-sized widget for the given application. Interview notes were analyzed using the same thematic analysis approach as the previous study of mega-widget applications.

We found three dominant and two secondary themes. The three dominant themes were precision, size and importance and a sense that some of the widgets were too big. The two other themes which appeared less frequently were games and accidentally bumping the widget to change the value.

Precision—Participants paired applications with mega-widgets in order to give more precise control in the application. 23 pairings involving mega-widgets were justified in terms of precision. For example, P6-2 selected a very large knob for "Temperature: Dorm" because it is "more detailed" and "gives better control." Participant P4-2 selected a large knob for "Temperature: Skyscraper" because it was "bigger for fine tuning."

Size and importance—As in the first study, participants made a connection between physical size or application importance and the size of the widget. 21 pairings of mega-widgets were justified based on the relationship between size and importance. In some cases, particularly for "Dam Water Flow", participants picked a mega-widget for an application in order to gain mechanical advantage. For example, P11-2 picked the enormous knob for the dam flow control application because "there's more power behind it."

In other cases, participants picked a mega-widget because the underlying application was important. P7-2 picked the large slider for the city light application because "for something as big as a city use something industrial." Similarly, P15-2 picked the enormous slider for city lights control because "a lot more people care" and "it matters more."

Participants picked mega-widgets for applications based on the importance of the application even when the application had no physical component. P14-2 picked the enormous slider for "Federal Interest Rate" because "the largest scale problem should have the largest slider possible" and P16-2 picked the large knob for the class grade curve because it was "slightly bigger to account for the importance level" of the application.

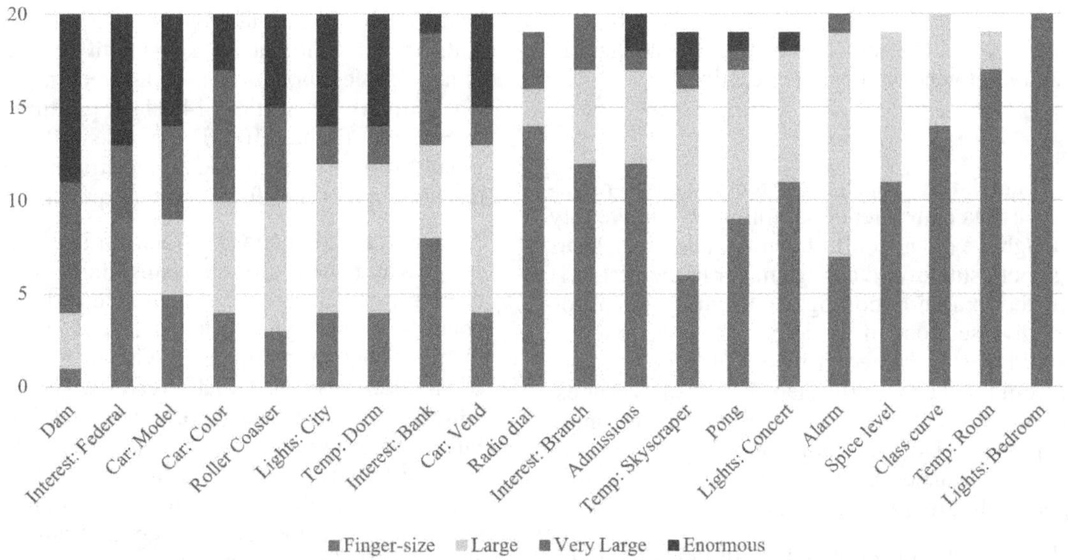

Figure 6. Pairings of widgets with applications generated by 20 people for 20 applications. Columns are sorted by the sum of very large and enormous widgets with "enormous" widgets at the top of each stacked bar and finger-size widgets at the bottom. (One participant did not make a pairing for six applications.)

Some widgets were too big—This was a reason *not* to pick a larger mega-widget for an application and was given as a justification 21 times. Larger widgets were not selected because they would be a "hassle" (P4-2), "impractical" (P19-2), "obnoxius" (P16-2) or "intimidating" (P12-2). 7 participants simply said that mega-widgets were "too big."

Games—Fun and games were mentioned in 5 responses with 3 of those responses related to the roller coaster sprayer. The other 2 references to fun and games came up in the context of the car vending machine model selector. In both cases, the participant compared the process to a "game show."

Accidental Input—Six mega-widget pairings were made because the participant wanted to prevent accidental input. They felt that a larger widget would be more difficult to change accidentally. For example, P3-2 picked the large knob for "Temperature: Dorm" because the finger size knob was "easy to knock around." P13-2 picked the enormous knob for the dam flow controller because it was a purposeful movement that is is "less likely to be an accident."

DISCUSSION

Interesting Results

A key result seems to be that people imagine "big widgets control big things," for different interpretations of "big things" as either physically large or conceptually important. This is an application area for further exploration with mega-widgets, perhaps involving studies to attempt to tease out to what extent the size of a control is able to communicate something about the importance or physical size of what it is controlling, and whether this is able to add meaningful context in interaction design.

In our studies, we observed participants often considering precision as a driving factor in using a mega-widget. This may be connected to the idea of importance, possibly indicating the notion that in some applications, the user would like to get the setting precisely right. Similarly, participants also used the size of mega-widgets to make sure that the widget was not accidentally adjusted through a bump or careless movement. Those who mentioned this, however, tended not to use the "enormous" mega-widgets for these pairings, presumably because beyond some point a larger widget begins to lend itself to being more easily bumped. Further exploration may yield controls which produce a larger range of motion in order to aid in precision while being more ergonomically designed and less prone to accidental input.

Whereas we had largely discounted the idea of physical leverage, some of our participants did not, and for physical or metaphorical reasons still wanted to use mega-widgets to apply leverage. It may be intersting to explore increased resistance or other more pronounced haptic feedback in connection with this notion of leverage.

We were not surprised that fun and playfulness came up in our studies. The value of this characteristic should not be overlooked, because it can be a key enabler of engagement and be very valuable in some settings. A toolkit implementing mega-widgets in an easy-to-use prototyping fashion a may prove valuable for educational or similar applications.

One surprising result was that visibility, which was a theme in results from the first study, did not emerge during the second study. It is hard to tell whether this is due to the applications used in the study or some other factor. Because of the increased visibility mega-widgets provide over finger-sized widgets, this is an area worth further consideration.

It is not part of the scope of this work to explore specific hypotheses concerning the construction or efficacy of mega-widgets. However it seems clear from the word embedding-based cluster characterized by the words "mindless, useless, brainless" that some people may respond poorly to mega-widgets. Future work will need to put a finer point on this reaction, so as to avoid the application of mega-widgets in contexts which might generate negative reactions.

Weaknesses

A weakness of our study approach is our recruitment of participants, which was via convenience sampling on a university campus. Although we did not collect demographic data apart from gender in both studies and college major in the first, it is likely that this led to a fairly homogeneous group of participants. A more diverse group of participants may have led to data which would have contained insights which we were not able to glean from the data we collected. Future efforts at exploring mega-widgets would do well to recruit a broader, more diverse participant set. Different and interesting results may also be gathered from studies involving specific demographics such as designers, children, and educators.

While we did construct a working version of the game Pong which used the enormous knob, we did not include it or other working applications of mega-widgets in our studies. Instead, we asked participants to imagine using mega-widgets in applications. We still felt it important to build working mega-widgets in order to prove the concept and provide a physical experience for participants. A very important next step in future work is to study their use in actual working applications.

We only constructed three types of widgets for each study. While this may have limited the ability of participants in our studies to imagine applications, we felt that a button, slider, and knob were fairly representative of the broader world of physical widgets, and sufficient for exploratory work in this area.

Future Work

We found our use of word embeddings and clustering effective for our purposes. We intended it as an approach which would be fast and avoid researcher bias, and we felt that it accomplished both of these goals as well as producing results which seemed reasonable and accurate. But this does seem to be a new approach, and as such there is need for more exploration and testing.

In future work we would like to address the way in which designers might use these results to elicit specific feelings, which might be useful in specific settings. As with the prior work related to the creation of physical widgets, designers likely need a toolkit that would allow them to experiment at the mega-widget scale for the purpose of designing systems that use the reactions we explored here to achieve their desired ends. Properly executed, a tool kit for mega-widgetscale devices could make the process of designing constructing them much easier.

A barrier to implementing such a toolkit, and to implementing mega-widgets in general, is the heavily manual and labor-intensive process by which objects of this size are crafted. Mega-widgets simply require more work and material than finger-sized widgets. While our decision to modularize mega-widget construction helps, there is much more work that can be done to enable rapid prototyping and construction of mega-widgets. An obvious avenue to simplifying this process is work in large-scale fabrication, such as breaking larger objects into smaller parts for printing [14, 11] or printing joining members to construct frames [10]. These and similar approaches could greatly simplify mega-widget construction, helping to move research in this area forward more quickly.

An important distinction between our implementation of mega-widgets and "naturally-occurring" large-scale controls is the driving motivation behind their size and shape. Large-scale controls in existing applications take on a size and shape which fits their context, while mega-widgets are scaled-up versions of smaller controls, which creates an entirely new context which is, to this point, largely divorced from usage context. Future work with mega-widgets will need to navigate the balance between making widgets, which are by definition widely applicable in many different contexts, and purpose-built controls whose size, shape, and range of motion more closely fit their usage context.

The large size of mega-widgets also lends itself to exploration of the aesthetic and ergonomic aspects of their construction, which was not a focus of our work thus far. The phenomenon we called out as *Misunderstood Shape Cues* in our first study may in fact point to an opportunity within mega-widgets to explore new shapes and motion profiles in conjunction with larger-sized controls, rather than simply magnifying smaller controls. Such work may also address ergonomics and accessibility, which are both areas for future exploration with mega-widgets.

Also, while we made attempts to provide haptic feedback, this is an area where a great deal of progress could be made. The physical and mechanical properties of the mechanisms, including the haptic feedback they provide, becomes an interesting design and engineering question at larger scales.

The visibility aspect of mega-widgets may also be a fruitful area for further research. Mega-widgets can provide visibility of the actions performed with a control and its present setting, without need for external visualizations such as screens. This may prove to be a useful application in certain situations.

CONCLUSION

We have presented the concept of unusually-sized widgets, which we have termed mega-widgets. Through two iterations of construction and user studies, we have begun to understand user responses to mega-widgets and possible uses for them. Based on responses from user studies, we have identified this as an interesting new avenue for exploration and have helped to set directions for future study. While much work and study remains to be done in this area, we hope that this paper and our work can serve to open the door to inquiry in this area and lay a foundation on which we ourselves and others can build in exploring the world of mega-scale physical interaction.

ACKNOWLEDGEMENTS

This work supported by the National Science Foundation under grant IIS-1406578.

REFERENCES

1. Daniel Avrahami and Scott E. Hudson. 2002. Forming Interactivity: A Tool for Rapid Prototyping of Physical Interactive Products. In *Proceedings of the 4th Conference on Designing Interactive Systems: Processes, Practices, Methods, and Techniques (DIS '02)*. ACM, New York, NY, USA, 141–146. DOI: http://dx.doi.org/10.1145/778712.778735

2. Scott Deerwester, Susan T. Dumais, George W. Furnas, Thomas K. Landauer, and Richard Harshman. 1990. Indexing by latent semantic analysis. *JOURNAL OF THE AMERICAN SOCIETY FOR INFORMATION SCIENCE* 41, 6 (1990), 391–407.

3. John R. Firth. 1957. A synopsis of linguistic theory 1930-1955. In *Studies in linguistic analysis*. Oxford:Blackwell, 1–32.

4. Sergio Garrido-Jurado, Rafael Muñoz-Salinas, Francisco José Madrid-Cuevas, and Manuel Jesús Marín-Jiménez. 2014. Automatic generation and detection of highly reliable fiducial markers under occlusion. *Pattern Recognition* 47, 6 (2014), 2280–2292.

5. Saul Greenberg and Chester Fitchett. 2001. Phidgets: Easy Development of Physical Interfaces Through Physical Widgets. In *Proceedings of the 14th Annual ACM Symposium on User Interface Software and Technology (UIST '01)*. ACM, New York, NY, USA, 209–218. DOI:http://dx.doi.org/10.1145/502348.502388

6. Chris Harrison and Scott E. Hudson. 2009. Providing Dynamically Changeable Physical Buttons on a Visual Display. In *Proceedings of the SIGCHI Conference on Human Factors in Computing Systems (CHI '09)*. ACM, New York, NY, USA, 299–308. DOI: http://dx.doi.org/10.1145/1518701.1518749

7. Steve Hodges, Stuart Taylor, Nicolas Villar, James Scott, and John Helmes. 2013. Exploring Physical Prototyping Techniques for Functional Devices Using .NET Gadgeteer. In *Proceedings of the 7th International Conference on Tangible, Embedded and Embodied Interaction (TEI '13)*. ACM, New York, NY, USA, 271–274. DOI: http://dx.doi.org/10.1145/2460625.2460670

8. Scott E. Hudson and Jennifer Mankoff. 2006. Rapid Construction of Functioning Physical Interfaces from Cardboard, Thumbtacks, Tin Foil and Masking Tape. In *Proceedings of the 19th Annual ACM Symposium on User Interface Software and Technology (UIST '06)*. ACM, New York, NY, USA, 289–298. DOI: http://dx.doi.org/10.1145/1166253.1166299

9. Michael D. Jones, Kevin Seppi, and Dan R. Olsen. 2016. What You Sculpt is What You Get: Modeling Physical Interactive Devices with Clay and 3D Printed Widgets. In *Proceedings of the 2016 CHI Conference on Human Factors in Computing Systems (CHI '16)*. ACM, New York, NY, USA, 876–886. DOI: http://dx.doi.org/10.1145/2858036.2858493

10. Robert Kovacs, Anna Seufert, Ludwig Wall, Hsiang-Ting Chen, Florian Meinel, Willi Müller, Sijing You, Maximilian Brehm, Jonathan Striebel, Yannis Kommana, Alexander Popiak, Thomas Bläsius, and Patrick Baudisch. 2017. TrussFab: Fabricating Sturdy Large-Scale Structures on Desktop 3D Printers. In *Proceedings of the 2017 CHI Conference on Human Factors in Computing Systems (CHI '17)*. ACM, New York, NY, USA, 2606–2616. DOI: http://dx.doi.org/10.1145/3025453.3026016

11. Manfred Lau, Akira Ohgawara, Jun Mitani, and Takeo Igarashi. 2011. Converting 3D Furniture Models to Fabricatable Parts and Connectors. In *ACM SIGGRAPH 2011 Papers (SIGGRAPH '11)*. ACM, New York, NY, USA, Article 85, 6 pages. DOI: http://dx.doi.org/10.1145/1964921.1964980

12. Johnny C. Lee, Daniel Avrahami, Scott E. Hudson, Jodi Forlizzi, Paul H. Dietz, and Darren Leigh. 2004. The Calder Toolkit: Wired and Wireless Components for Rapidly Prototyping Interactive Devices. In *Proceedings of the 5th Conference on Designing Interactive Systems: Processes, Practices, Methods, and Techniques (DIS '04)*. ACM, New York, NY, USA, 167–175. DOI: http://dx.doi.org/10.1145/1013115.1013139

13. Omer Levy and Yoav Goldberg. 2014. Dependency-Based Word Embeddings.. In *ACL (2)*. 302–308.

14. Linjie Luo, Ilya Baran, Szymon Rusinkiewicz, and Wojciech Matusik. 2012. Chopper: Partitioning Models into 3D-printable Parts. *ACM Trans. Graph.* 31, 6, Article 129 (Nov. 2012), 9 pages. DOI: http://dx.doi.org/10.1145/2366145.2366148

15. Tomas Mikolov, Ilya Sutskever, Kai Chen, Greg S Corrado, and Jeff Dean. 2013. Distributed Representations of Words and Phrases and their Compositionality. In *Advances in Neural Information Processing Systems 26*, C. J. C. Burges, L. Bottou, M. Welling, Z. Ghahramani, and K. Q. Weinberger (Eds.). Curran Associates, Inc., 3111–3119.

16. Valkyrie Savage, Colin Chang, and Björn Hartmann. 2013. Sauron: Embedded Single-camera Sensing of Printed Physical User Interfaces. In *Proceedings of the 26th Annual ACM Symposium on User Interface Software and Technology (UIST '13)*. ACM, New York, NY, USA, 447–456. DOI: http://dx.doi.org/10.1145/2501988.2501992

17. Valkyrie Savage, Sean Follmer, Jingyi Li, and Björn Hartmann. 2015a. Makers' Marks: Physical Markup for Designing and Fabricating Functional Objects. In *Proceedings of the 28th Annual ACM Symposium on User Interface Software & Technology*. ACM, 103–108.

18. Valkyrie Savage, Andrew Head, Björn Hartmann, Dan B. Goldman, Gautham Mysore, and Wilmot Li. 2015b. Lamello: Passive Acoustic Sensing for Tangible Input Components. In *Proceedings of the 33rd Annual ACM Conference on Human Factors in Computing Systems (CHI '15)*. ACM, New York, NY, USA, 1277–1280. DOI: http://dx.doi.org/10.1145/2702123.2702207

19. Nicolas Villar, James Scott, Steve Hodges, Kerry Hammil, and Colin Miller. 2012. .NET Gadgeteer: A Platform for Custom Devices. In *Proceedings of the 10th International Conference on Pervasive Computing (Pervasive'12)*. Springer-Verlag, Berlin, Heidelberg, 216–233. DOI: http://dx.doi.org/10.1007/978-3-642-31205-2_14

Tailor-made Accessible Computers: An Interactive Toolkit for Iterative Co-Design

Florian Güldenpfennig
Vienna University of Technology (TU Wien)
Vienna, Austria
florian.gueldenpfennig@tuwien.ac.at

ABSTRACT
An increasing number of people with little experience in technology desire to use the Internet and web related services like social networking or online information research. However, the way most computers are designed today does not allow many older people to participate in this key technology due to their lack in computer-literacy compared with younger generations. Age-related impairments and disabilities can further complicate or deny the use of conventional computers. To remove existing barriers, we created a series of tailor-made computers, which met specific needs like improved accessibility or particular aesthetics. To accomplish this, we used a co-design toolkit that we created (a) to provide senior users with early tangible experiences of their future systems and (b) to iteratively convert it into the final implementation. In this paper, we demonstrate both the toolkit and the resulting designs of accessible Internet computers.

Author Keywords
Co-design toolkit; accessible computing; prototyping;

ACM Classification Keywords
• Human-centered computing~User interface toolkits • Human-centered computing~Systems and tools for interaction design

INTRODUCTION AND SCOPE
Older adults are an age group in expansion that has a low adoption rate of technology compared to younger adults [16]. While the TV is widely spread among older people and constitutes the most popular media device, Internet use is progressively decreasing with increasing age, and only 45% of all people older than 69 years in Germany have access to the Internet according to a recent representative study [8]. In contrast, about 80-90% of all teenagers, young adults or mid-aged adults are online regularly. Still, senior people too can benefit significantly from having access to computers and the Internet, for example, to research information, for entertainment or to fight social isolation and loneliness, which is a severe problem among older people [1]. Access to such technologies can help them stay independent and continue living in their own homes [2]. However, many devices are poorly designed [7], and there are only a few commercial companies that created desktop or tablet computers specifically to meet older people's needs, for example [9; 13; 15].

TEI '18, March 18–21, 2018, Stockholm, Sweden

ACM ISBN 978-1-4503-5568-1/18/03…$15.00
https://doi.org/10.1145/3173225.3173237

To support the adoption of new technology by older adults, researchers in HCI and TEI have investigated the design of technology for this particular user group (see Rebola's research [11] for a range of exemplary devices). Today, user-centred and participatory or co-design approaches are increasingly employed to make devices both more usable and useful for older people [2; 12]. Nevertheless, a number of researchers stated that they had difficulties on some occasions in exchanging ideas with older participants [18].

To add to the research about accessible Internet computers for older users (or users with physical impairments), we drew on tangible interaction design and created a series of tailor-made computers. To reveal the requirements of the prospective users, we employed a prototyping kit (*Infobricks*) that we introduced to support the participants in imagining the possibilities technology can afford, hence, to make technology more tangible for them.

We seek to contribute two different types of insights with our demonstration. First, we share new forms or tangible designs for accessible devices, which extend the conventional idea of personal Internet computers (commercial products for older users mostly rely on touch screens or mouse/keyboard based interaction [9; 13; 15]). Second, we reflect about co-design or participatory design processes with older adults and how these approaches can be augmented with new interactive toolkits, taking into account that electronic prototyping and rapid product design is available at low cost now.

Our target group is primarily comprised of older adults that have no or only little prior experience with computers and difficulties in using this technology. While this latter characteristic (a lack in computer-literacy) is what all of our four participants (abbreviated with P) have in common, the age varies significantly between our participants (65, 70, 75, and 91 years old). Their physical abilities too differ between no physical impairment and age-related problems with (fine) motor control. Hence, the devices we build are adapted to the participants' needs and customized to a high degree. Accordingly, these designs can be classified as somewhere between novel, tangible, and accessible (Internet) computers and assistive technology. In the next section, we detail our design approach.

DESIGN APPROACH

It is a known problem that technologies, designed particularly for people with special needs, are abandoned on a regular basis. In a seminal survey, Phillips and Zhao [10] found that important reasons for unused or unusable devices were that people haven't been involved close enough in the process of device selection and also that people experienced a change in abilities over time.

To avoid such pitfalls in the design of accessible computers, we involve our participants closely in the design process. To be able to account for their ideas and needs, we created an interactive prototyping toolkit (*Infobricks*) as mentioned in the introduction. The kit allows a high amount of flexibility to support the collaborative exploration of form and function between participants and designers or researchers. After the completion of the prototype, it is still possible to (re-)configure aspects of the software or some tangible components to account for potential changes in user needs.

The use of such an interactive kit distinguishes the work presented in this paper from most other research into accessible computers for older people. It involves prototypes that can be assembled together with the participant into working systems, and in further iterations these can again be reassembled as needed. This procedure usually demands a number of meetings and several weeks of time, since the participants are encouraged to take their interim prototype home to test it in their natural environment. Once a stable set of requirements is established, the resulting design is transferred into a final prototype (which also can be re-configured to some extent if needed at some point in time). Thus, the overall design process can broadly be divided into two parts. (1) Co-design sessions with interactive prototyping are followed by (2) the assembly of the final system in our workshop using tools like 3D-printing, laser-cutting or CNC-milling.

PROTOTYPING TOOLKITS IN CO-DESIGN

Designing useful technologies for older people requires a deep understanding of their issues and needs (see e.g. [17]). This can be hard to obtain for designers who probably experience a different life context [6; 14]. Older people again might experience difficulties in imagining what actually can be created using technology [12; 18].

To overcome this gap, Rogers et al. introduced the *MaKey MaKey* invention kit to senior workshop participants and invited them to create future input devices [12]. Being provided with this tangible experience, the participants learnt what was possible in principal, and moreover, they were able to reconfigure the *MaKey MaKey* components into an innovative piece of technology. Hence, the *MaKey MaKey* kit allows the users to create their own computer input devices without knowledge of programming and electronics or design craftsmanship.

In contrast to Rogers et al. [12], who introduced tangibles as a powerful means to temporarily explore quite fragile and limited prototypes for input devices, we are interested in co-designing accessible Internet computers that last and are actually deployed or used for years. For this reason, we adapted parts of the *MaKey MaKey* concept and created our own toolkit *Infobricks* for the co-design of accessible Internet computers. In a prior publication [5], we described the requirements gathering of a predecessor version of *Infobricks* including a case study where one *maker* used one provided *Infobricks* kit to build a DIY computer for her mother.

In the present paper, in contrast, we make use of *Infobricks* as an intermediate step to provide the prospective users with interactive experiences to make an informed selection of functions. Subsequently, if the design met their expectations, we finalize the prototype into a tailor-made personal and accessible Internet computer (see Figure 3-6 for examples).

Prototyping Toolkit Infobricks

Infobricks is comprised of several components (see Figure 1), a main module and optional peripherals. This modularity enables us to collaboratively explore together with the senior users what functions or characteristics their computer should have and to quickly adjust the design proposal accordingly. (Note, further details about the *Infobricks* system can be found in the description of the toolkit's predecessor implementation [5].)

Hardware. The extension board (displayed in Figure 1, labeled with 2) is connected to the main module using

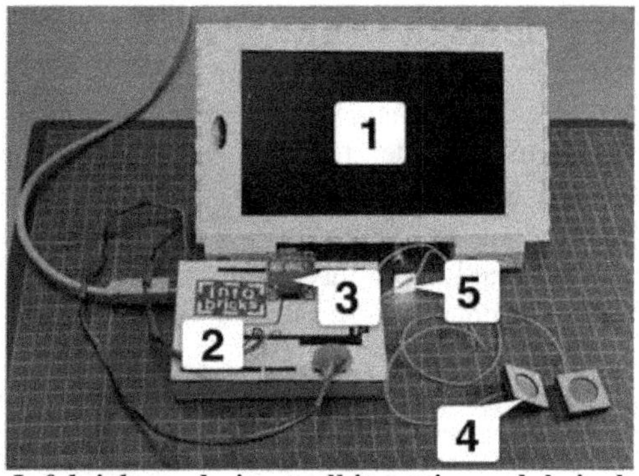

Figure 1. *Infobricks* co-design toolkit: main module incl. screen (1), extension-board (2) for optional components like small OLEDs for displaying text (3), up to twelve extra capacitive buttons (4), feedback LEDs (5), etc. The screen is available in different sizes. The kit can be configured into a working system. Sticky tape, glue, plywood boxes, and cardboard are used to temporary connect all chosen components (see also Fig. 2).

Bluetooth or USB, and again, provides ports for connecting additional user interfaces with wire like small OLEDs for displaying additional contextual information (e.g., "you have received a new message"), buttons or feedback lights (for indicating important events like an incoming message etc.). A RFID reader (e.g., Figure 4 left) can also be attached, should the participant wish to work with RFID tokens that trigger certain user-defined actions (e.g., the presence of a token can be set to open the browser app).

Software. As the main module is based on a modified (rooted) version of Android, regular Android applications that ship with this operating system are available to the user. Moreover, we provide a number of custom apps to improve accessibility. Our photo app, for example, can automatically receive photos and associated annotations that are sent to the system externally by using a corresponding smartphone app. These received images are then presented on the main module as if it was a digital photo frame.

Similarly, we created a simplified e-mail client or chat application that allows the users to exchange text messages in an easy way. It offers more accessible user interface elements and interactions compared with conventional e-mail clients. Messages can be sent to a set of predefined users, who can reply using a smartphone application or another *Infobricks* system.

For (quick) customizations, custom background screens, audio recordings, text messages, and videos can be uploaded to the main module. In this way, the designer can for example upload a custom design for the start screen. In addition, *Infobricks* can be configured to show a welcome text message displayed on a small OLED screen on boot-up together with this start screen. At the same time, a custom audio recording could welcome the user and give instructions for how to operate the system.

Moreover, a configurator app can be employed to assign different functions/apps to different buttons and RFID tags, given the corresponding components are supposed to be integrated into the design. This behaviour is accomplished by using a simple scripting language that we defined and which features different keywords and variables so that physical buttons, custom text/audio-messages, feedback lights, and system events can all be linked quickly in a useful manner.

Overall, the modularity and high degree of customizability described above are key factors that enable our hands-on and tangible design process. Usually, within the duration of one co-design workshop, *Infobricks* can be adjusted according to the elaborated user needs. To this end, we bring cardboard and plywood boxes with prepared mounting holes etc. to the workshops (see Figure 2). After a period of user testing, the prototype is transferred into a permanent installation (as displayed in Figure 3-6), should the setup be satisfactory. In that case, components of

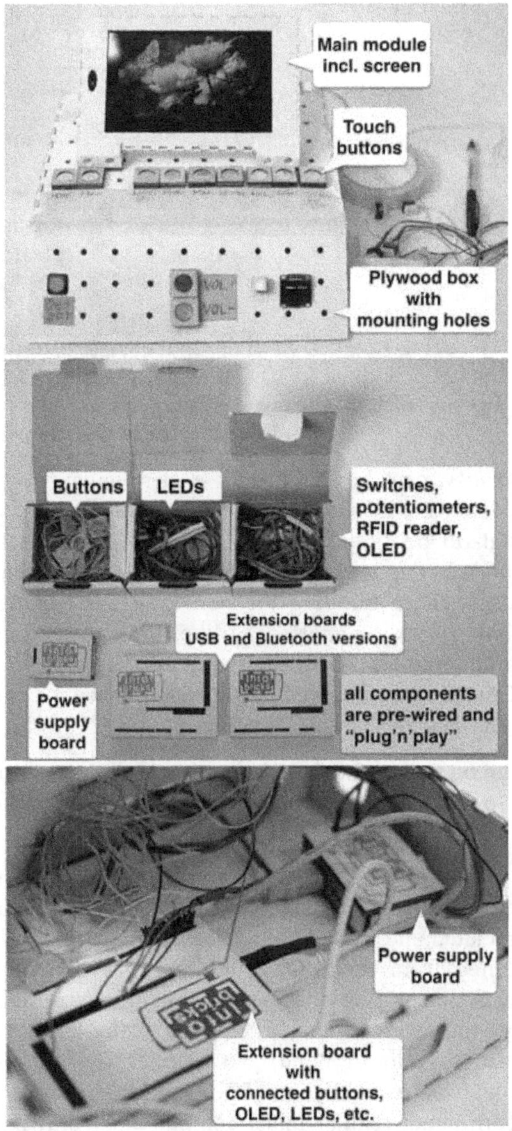

Figure 2. Top: toolkit temporary assembled using a plywood box and glue/tape. Middle: different toolkit components. Bottom: Extension and power supply boards revealed in opened plywood box.

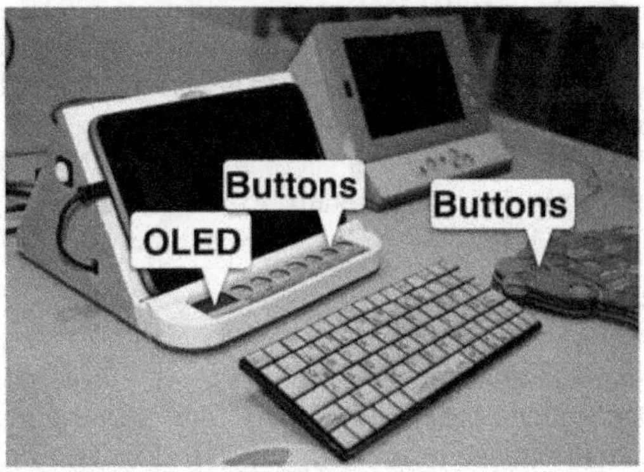

Figure 3. Two completed prototypes for accessible Internet computers resulting from the design sessions. The arrows point at features for displaying text messages and providing quick access to important functions like opening the email or shutting down the system.

Figure 4. Detailed views of input devices resulting from the design process drawing on *Infobricks*. Left: polaroid portraits including hidden RFID tags can be placed onto the reader device to open the email client with the corresponding addressee already filled in. Customized computer keyboard (partially visible). Right: quick access button board in the shape of a sheep to be connected to the accessible computer for triggering favorite apps and functions.

Infobricks can be built into a permanent casing. The extension board (including other components) is small enough to be fit into the computer bodies (see Figure 2 bottom). In this way, the effort for creating the final system is restricted to building the new case for the electronics (including user interfaces like touch buttons etc.). Programming is not necessary, as the final system is configured with the same *Infobricks* software components as described earlier in this section.

We go on to present some indicative findings resulting from this co-design approach to create tailor-made computers.

INSIGHTS AND REFLECTIONS

Infobricks proved (and still is proving) to be valuable in exposing participants to technology and finally to create appreciated and accessible devices. In particular P2 and P4 benefited from their new computers, as they have been using them for over one year now on an almost daily basis. They too were the participants with least computer experience (almost none). To date, P1 is still using her computer occasionally, and P3 is working towards her goal to learn about regular tablet computers by drawing on her *Infobricks* design (as explained below in *item 1)* and *2)*).

In the co-design process, the physical and interactive artefacts served as "a common frame of reference between participants and designers" [7, p.1201], helped computational concepts to become more tangible [7], and took away computer-shyness. The participants showed a high amount of motivation in co-designing and later in using their systems. Coleman et al. [4] also found that older participants were generally more likely to accept technology if they were able to see a direct benefit from it.

Throughout all design processes, we conducted informal interviews and made a variety of observations. Drawing on a thematic analysis approach [3], we clustered design-related salient observations into four themes in order to present these insights in a structured fashion as follows.

1) Physical appearance of the designs: In the course of the co-design process, it became apparent that the participants favoured to have their own individual designs regarding the aesthetics of their accessible computers. Most important to all of them was a friendly, "non-techy", and familiar design that matched well with their homes and personal preferences. The design process of *Infobricks* allowed us to consider such preferences.

Figure 3, for example, shows a conventional Android tablet in the front of the picture, because P3 conceived her computer as a "smart dock" to which a regular Android device (running *Infobricks* software) could be connected. The dock featured quick access buttons and an information OLED to facilitate use. By having the regular tablet visible and unmasked, the participant aimed at creating an accessible Internet computer with a conventional, non-stigmatizing appearance.

2) Adaptability: Additionally, this feature of making the tablet detachable aimed at allowing *making adaptations* to the system. One day, with increasing computer-literacy, paricipant P3 anticipated to "transform" the accessible computer into a conventional tablet by waiving smart dock functions or even by completely removing the smart dock. Figure 5 shows P2's prototype where the main computer could also be detached from the dock. In summary, making the systems adaptable was a strength of *Infobricks* not least because of its software components. In this way, we addressed an agenda as proposed by Wobbrock and colleagues: "In making the shift to ability-based design, we move away from assisting human users to conform to inflexible computer systems, and instead consider how systems can be made to fit the abilities of whoever uses them." [19, p. 2]

One way to accomplish this design philosophy, besides building smart docks etc., is to make use of RFID tokens as input devices similar to work by Ylirisku et al. [20]. By employing this wireless technology, our systems could be extended easily with tangible elements. Figure 4 (left) shows RFID cards with portraits of people to open the email client ready to mail the corresponding addressee. In addition, RFID could be used to trigger different apps and functions as defined in the configurator application. In the same way, the interface could conveniently be extended into the homes of the users by configuring RFID tokens (or touch buttons) to remote-control power outlets (via 433 MHz transceiver technology) with additionally connected appliances (e.g., floor lamps).

3) Input modalities: In analogy to different physical appearances, participants preferred different user input modalities. While some participants preferred tangible user interfaces (e.g. RFID cards or objects with RFID tags), others preferred the touch screen (depending also on the specific task). Moreover, Android's built-in language processing capabilities were well received by the older users. Making use of the system by giving voice commands worked well for certain tasks (e.g., requesting the weather forecast for a specific place on a particular date). Thus, we see great potential in such natural user interfaces in the context of accessible computing.

We also co-designed a number of customized computer keyboards (see Figure 3 and 4 left) with different colour codes and labels engraved. It turned out beneficial to print short instructions with a summary of the most important functions, e.g., how to use voice commands, on the backside of the keyboard (see Figure 6). This served as an excellent reminder, and when the user felt overwhelmed by the system's complexity, the keys could be covered by placing the board on the table upside down.

4) Design as a method for inquiry: One interesting aspect of our research approach using the interactive toolkit was that the insights described above were generated by relatively quick design iterations in which the participants were exposed to the artifacts. That is, design was employed as a method for inquiry ("research through design"), and here the strategy was to "focus on the *right* thing; artifacts intended to transform the world from the current state to the preferred state" [21, p.497]. Hence, through an iterative process of design and feedback the problem was repetitively reframed and looked at from different angles, and the final prototypes embody findings and design knowledge that were created in the process.

Figure 5. P2's Internet device where the main computer can be removed from the docking station featuring quick access buttons, OLED, and notification light. Computer and dock are connected via Bluetooth.

Figure 6. P4 studying the backside of her computer keyboard which contains hints and "tool tips" (e.g., how to turn on/off the computer, navigate using quick access buttons, etc.).

CONCLUSION

More than the half of older people (aged 69 years and above) are still excluded from the Internet [8], even though this group of people could benefit strongly from Internet related services (gathering information, entertainment, overcoming social isolation, communication, etc.)[2; 12]. Providing more accessible Internet computers can help overcome a lack in computer-literacy as well as compensate physical impairments in order to enable more senior people to get access to useful applications [2].

As older users are a very diverse group of people, designers or researchers can have difficulties in understanding their particular situation and user needs. Older people again can experience difficulties in anticipating technology that is yet to be implemented or intangbile [7; 12].

To bridge this gap, we introduced an interactive prototyping toolkit (*Infobricks*) for accessible computers to our co-design sessions. This provided us and the participants with a tangible tool for communication. Instant interactivity proved as a powerful device for older people to understand technology, and at the same time, it was valuable for us to understand what was needed. After a number of design iterations, and after some time between iterations to "let technology settle", the initial designs were eventually implemented into stable and final prototypes also making use of the *Infobricks* engine.

This iterative and interactive approach enabled us to understand and react to user needs, which we would not have uncovered in the same way following a different research method (e.g., observing and asking people about what they want to have or studying technology that already existed). We expect this prototyping approach to gain more importance in the near future, when accessible computers and Internet devices (or technology in the home in general) will increasingly "lose" their stable appearances, and interfaces will be found in new shapes and places. This will make imagining technology even harder for participants as well as for designers, and tools are needed to move from the abstract to the concrete.

This paper constitutes a prototype demonstration including some indicative findings. Future research will investigate in depth in which ways *Infobricks* can facilitate co-design, how the completed computers are used, and how accessibility can be operationalized in order to measure the effect of our Internet computers.

REFERENCES

[1] Ron Baecker, Kate Sellen, Sarah Crosskey, Veronique Boscart, and Barbara Barbosa Neves. 2014. Technology to reduce social isolation and loneliness. In *Proc ASSETS'14*, ACM, 27-34.

[2] Ronald M. Baecker, Karyn Moffatt, and Michael Massimi. 2012. Technologies for aging gracefully. *interactions 19*, 3, 32-36.

[3] Virginia Braun and Victoria Clarke. 2006. Using thematic analysis in Psychology. *Qualitative Research in Psychology 3*, 2 (2006/01/01), 77-101.

[4] Graeme W. Coleman, Lorna Gibson, Vicki L. Hanson, Ania Bobrowicz, and Alison Mckay. 2010. Engaging the disengaged: How do we design technology for digitally excluded older adults? In *Proc DIS'10*, ACM, 175-178.

[5] Florian Güldenpfennig. 2017. Making a customized DIY-Computer with Infobricks. In *Proc British HCI'17*, ACM.

[6] Florian Güldenpfennig, Francisco Nunes, Eva Ganglbauer, and Geraldine Fitzpatrick. 2016. Making space to engage: An open-ended exploration of technology design with older adults. *International Journal of Mobile Human Computer Interaction (IJMHCI) 8*, 2, 1-19.

[7] Stephen Lindsay, Daniel Jackson, Guy Schofield, and Patrick Olivier. 2012. Engaging older people using participatory design. In *Proc CHI'12* ACM, 1199-1208.

[8] ARD/ZDF-Arbeitsgruppe Multimedia, 2016. ARD/ZDF-Online Studie. http://www.ard-zdf-onlinestudie.de/index.php?id=563. Last accessed 01 Augst 2017.

[9] MyGait. 2017. Senior computing made easy. https://www.mygait.com. Last accessed 26 November 2017.

[10] Betsy Phillips and Hongxin Zhao. 1993. Predictors of assistive technology abondonment. *Assistive Technology 5*, 1 (1993/06/30), 36-45.

[11] Claudia Rebola. 2015. *Designed technologies for healthy aging*. Morgan & Claypool Publishers.

[12] Yvonne Rogers, Jeni Paay, Margot Brereton, Kate L. Vaisutis, Gary Marsden, and Frank Vetere, 2014. Never too old: engaging retired people inventing the future with MaKey MaKey. In *Proc CHI'14*, ACM, p. 3913-3922.

[13] A Plus Computers For Seniors. 2017. Easy to use computers for seniors. http://www.aplusseniorcomputer.com. Last accessed 26 November 2017.

[14] Özge Subasi, Lone Malmborg, Geraldine Fitzpatrick, and Britt Östlund. 2014. Reframing design culture and aging. *interactions 21*, 2, 70-73.

[15] Telikin. 2017. A simpler, easy to use computer. http://www.telikin.com. Last accessed 26 November 2017.

[16] John Vines, Mark Blythe, Stephen Lindsay, Paul Dunphy, Andrew Monk, and Patrick Olivier, 2012. Questionable concepts: Critique as resource for designing with eighty somethings. In *Proc CHI'12*, ACM, p.1169-1178.

[17] Nicole Wagner, Khaled Hassanein, and Milena Head. 2010. Computer use by older adults: A multi-disciplinary review. *Computers in Human Behavior 26*, 5 (2010/09/01/), 870-882.

[18] Jenny Waycott, Sonja Pedell, Frank Vetere, Elizabeth Ozanne, Lars Kulik, Alan Gruner, and John Downs, 2012. Actively engaging older adults in the development and evaluation of tablet technology. In *Proc OzCHI'12* , ACM, p. 643-652.

[19] Jacob O. Wobbrock, Shaun K. Kane, Krzysztof Z. Gajos, Susumu Harada, and Jon Froehlich. 2011. Ability-based design: Concept, principles and examples. *ACM Trans. Access. Comput. 3*, 3, 1-27.

[20] Salu Ylirisku, Sian Lindley, Giulio Jacucci, Richard Banks, Craig Stewart, Abigail Sellen, Richard Harper, and Tim Regan, 2013. Designing web-connected physical artefacts for the 'aesthetic' of the home. In *Proc CHI'13*, ACM, p. 909-918.

[21] John Zimmerman, Jodi Forlizzi, and Shelley Evenson, 2007. Research through design as a method for interaction design research in HCI. In *Proc CHI'07*, ACM, p. 493-502.

Augmented Metacognition: Exploring Pupil Dilation Sonification to Elicit Metacognitive Awareness

Alwin de Rooij
Tilburg University
Warandelaan 2, Tilburg, NL
alwinderooij@uvt.nl

Mathijs Bontje
Tilburg University
Warandelaan 2, Tilburg, NL
mathijsbontje@gmail.com

Hanna Schraffenberger
Tilburg University
Warandelaan 2, Tilburg, NL
h.k.schraffenberger@uvt.nl

TEI '18, March 18–21, 2018, Stockholm, Sweden

ACM ISBN 978-1-4503-5568-1/18/03.
https://doi.org/10.1145/3173225.3173265

Abstract
Metacognitive awareness enables people to make conscious decisions about their own cognitions, and adapt to meet task performance goals. Despite the role of metacognition in task performance, technologies that effectively augment metacognition are scarce. We explore a novel approach to augment metacognition based on making the eye's pupil dilations, which associate with a variety of cognitions, audible via sonification in real-time. In this exploratory study, we investigated whether pupil dilation sonification can elicit metacognitive awareness. Our findings suggest that correlations between a variety of cognitions, e.g., attentional focus and depth of thinking, and sounds generated by the sonification can emerge spontaneously and by instruction. This justifies further research into the use of pupil dilation sonification as a means to augment metacognitive abilities.

Author Keywords
Augmented Metacognition; Biofeedback; Embodied Information; Metacognition; Pupil Dilation; Sonification.

Introduction
Awareness about your own thinking, or *metacognitive awareness*, enables you to adapt cognitions to meet

task demands [12]. It can help compensate for lower IQ [31], improve learning [33], and benefit self-confidence [18]. However, technologies that augment metacognition are scarce [16]. We propose that by making pupil dilations audible in real-time with a *pupil dilation sonification* [cf. 35], correlations can emerge between the sounds generated by the sonification, and the cognitions that associate with changes in pupil dilation [8, 21]. When such correlations emerge, changes in the sound can bring changes in cognition into awareness, i.e., elicit metacognitive awareness. In this paper, we explore the potential of pupil dilation sonification to elicit metacognitive awareness; as a first step toward a novel way to augment metacognition.

Metacognition and its augmentation

Metacognition can be defined as the awareness and control of one's own cognitive processes [1]. When changes in cognitive processes enter awareness, decision making about one's cognitive behaviour, e.g., for task performance goals, can take place. For example, awareness about sustained attentional focus can aid in the appraisal of what kind of task requires such focus [cf. 36]. This, in turn, can be used to exert control over one's own cognition in order to effectively adapt to changing task demands [11].

However, *technologies* that effectively augment metacognition are scarce [16]. Typically, closed-loop systems that classify cognitions based on physiological data [23] are used to select and present feedback to support metacognitive awareness and control [25]; and thus, in turn, affect cognition. However, such classification models are error prone [14], and generalise poorly to situations not contained in the data these models are developed from [22]. Even if cognitions could be classified accurately [14], other information that is necessary to enable metacognition [12], such as task performance appraisals, may not be available to the technology [cf. 5, 6, 7]. Overcoming these issues may be necessary to truly enable metacognitive augmentation. This study presents a first step toward that aim. We build on the fact that people themselves have access to the necessary information, as it resides in their own mental environment; and focus on bringing this information into people's awareness; empowering them to adapt and control their cognitive processes.

The pupil dilation-cognition link

Technologically augmented metacognition could be based on the eye's *pupil dilations*. The pupil is a circular opening that dilates and constricts [3] to regulate the amount of light that falls onto the retina [36]. Pupil dilation also associates with the type and amount of allocation of *cognitive resources* [26] and tracks changes in cognition rapidly [24]. Task-evoked pupil dilation associates with the allocation of cognitive resources to a task, e.g., attentional focus [15] and mental effort [8]; task-independent pupil dilation associates with the allocation of cognitive resources to task-irrelevant information, e.g., distractibility [15] and mind wandering [28]. Similarly, the association between pupil dilation and depth of thinking [2] and cognitive load [17] can be explained in this way.

Being able to perceive one's own physiological changes can serve as *embodied information* about the cognitions these changes associate with [30]. For example, mechano- and thermoreceptors in the skin enable us to sense when we are sweating [10], and when engaging in a difficult exam, this may elicit

Figure 1 Setup used in the experiment. Participants solve a mathematics problems presented on a computer screen; while listening to a sonification of their own pupil dilation data that is captured and streamed by an eye-tracker in real-time.

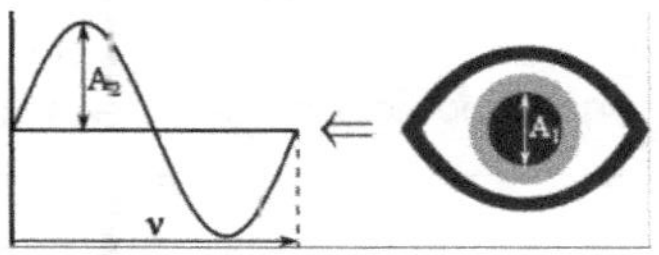

Figure 2 Illustration of the pupil dilation-to-sound mapping. The size of the pupil (A_1) is mapped in real-time to the amplitude (A_2) of a continuously playing sine wave (v=440Hz), and presented to the user during a problem solving task.

metacognitive awareness about the difficulty of the exam [29]. As pupil dilation tracks changes in a variety of cognitions rapidly [8, 24], it could be a rich source of embodied information [11]. However, one can normally not perceive one's own pupil dilations. Therefore, it could be that a technology that makes a person's own pupil dilation perceivable can be used as a basis for a new way to *augment metacognition*.

Using pupil dilation sonification to augment metacognition

We propose a novel way to augment metacognition via *pupil dilation sonification.* We conjecture that perceiving one's own pupil dilations can elicit *metacognitive awareness*. As cognitions change, associated pupil dilations rapidly follow [24]. When these changes are perceived via audible sound, it might enable one to learn correlations between one's own pupil dilations and related cognitions [cf. 21]. These correlations then potentially can function as embodied information about if, when, and what cognitions change during a task [cf. 30], i.e., help elicit metacognitive awareness [11].

In this study, we take the first steps to explore whether, what, and when correlations emerge between sound generated based on pupil dilation and related cognitions *spontaneously*; and we check whether people can experience *instructed* relations between the sound and pupil dilation related cognitive processes.

Method

An exploratory study was conducted to investigate the conjectures developed in the above.

Participants

Twenty people participated (M_{age}=22.68, SD_{age}=5.11, $Range_{age}$=18-38, 16♀, 4♂). Participation required (past) involvement in higher education. They were Dutch. Participants' self-reported mathematical expertise was above average (M=6.58, SD=1.29, Range=2-7). Course credit was offered where appropriate.

Pupil dilation sonification

Sonification [35] was used because of the high temporal resolution of the auditory sense [20] and because it allows us to make pupil dilation changes perceivable in detail [19]. The Eye Tribe eye-tracker streamed the mean pupil size of both eyes at 60 Hz [32] to a custom sonification program made in Cycling '74 Max 7 [4]. To scale the streaming data to a 0-1 range a 15 micrometre minimum pupil size was assumed and a maximum was captured while darkening the room. Signal loss (e.g., due to blinking) was handled by retaining the last data point before signal loss until new data was received. The data stream was resampled at 44.1 KHz and interpolated. See Figure 1 for the setup used.

The pre-processed *pupil dilation* data controlled the *amplitude of a sine wave* (*v*=440Hz, Figure 2). Pupil dilations linearly increased, whereas constrictions linearly decreased the volume of the sine wave. Initial pilot testing suggested that this yielded more clearly discernable results and was less intrusive than other combinations that varied in type, i.e., mapping to volume and frequency, and in wave form, i.e., noise, sine, saw, and square waves. The sounds were presented through headphones. Dimmed lighting conditions (room, screen) were used to minimize interference from the pupil's light reflex [36].

T_1	1	2	3	4	5	6	7	8	9	10	11	12
	E	M	M	M	E	M	M	H	E	H	H	E

T_2	1	2	3	4	5
	E	M	H	H	E

Table 1 Presentation order of mathematics problems in part one (T_1) and part two (T_2) of the task. Presentation index (numbers) and difficulty level (E=easy, M=medium, H=hard).

T_1	*Did you notice anything particular about the sound*
	If so, what behaviours correlated with the sound
	When did you notice a correlation between the sound and your behaviour
T_2	*Were you able to correlate the change in sound with your state of mind now that you know that it was directly influenced by it*

Table 2 Questions asked after part one (T_1) and part two (T_2) of the Presentation order of mathematics problem solving

Problem solving task
A *mathematics problem solving task* was developed during which the sonification was used. Mathematics involves cognitions that associate with pupil dilation, e.g., attentional focus [8]; and can be manipulated by varying the mathematics problems' difficulty [13]. Participation required (past) involvement in higher education so that three difficulty levels could be based on educational norms: *easy*, problems people can solve after primary school; *medium*, problems people can solve after high school; *hard*, problems at a behavioural sciences undergraduate level. The difficulty of the problems was gradually increased, and interspersed with easy problems (Table 1). Pilot tests suggested this affected the pupil dilation-cognition link more effectively compared to e.g., random presentation.

The first part of the task consisted of twelve mathematics problems (Table 1 and cognition. , T_1). No information was given about the link between the sounds heard and cognition. This was done to explore if and what correlations between the sound and cognitive processes emerge *spontaneously*. The second part was preceded by the instruction that there exists a link between "...the amount of cognitive resources allocated to the task and the changes in volume of the sound". Participants were then instructed to try to solve an additional five problems (Table 1, T_2). This was done to explore whether *instruction* enabled experiencing a given link between the sounds and cognition.

Questionnaire
To explore whether changes in the sounds generated by the pupil dilation sonification elicited awareness about related cognitions *spontaneously*, we asked participants to elaborate on whether, what, and when correlations between their behaviour and the sounds emerged after the first part of the task (T_1). Responses were clustered into categories based on (a) type of response (e.g., deep thinking', 'when staring'), and (b) whether the responses related to cognitions (e.g., 'concentrating'), oculomotor behaviours (e.g., 'blinking'), or no associations. After the second part (T_2) we explored whether changes in the sounds brought changes in the *instructed* relationship between the sound and cognition into awareness, by inquiring about the participant's ability to perceive the instructed correlation. The questions are presented in Table 2.

The *qualities of the sound* itself may also affect the participants. We thus asked to describe the sound itself. Responses were clustered by (a) type (e.g., '*annoying*'), and (b) valence (e.g., '*negative*'). This was done to gather data to help improve future versions of the sonification. To gain some insight into the socio-demographics of the sample, participants were asked to report their age, gender, and education level, but also mathematical ability (very poor=1, very good=10).

Procedure
Participants were seated behind a computer screen and introduced to the study. Information that could reveal the purpose of the study was withheld. Participants reported their socio-demographics and signed informed consent. Task instructions followed, the eye-tracker (9-point calibration) and sonification were calibrated. Participants put on headphones and adjusted loudness to comfortable levels. They then engaged in part one and two of the mathematics problem solving task while hearing the sounds generated by the pupil dilation sonification. After part one and two they filled in the questionnaires, were debriefed, and sent on their way.

Results

The results suggest that people can correlate sounds generated based on pupil dilation with their cognitions.

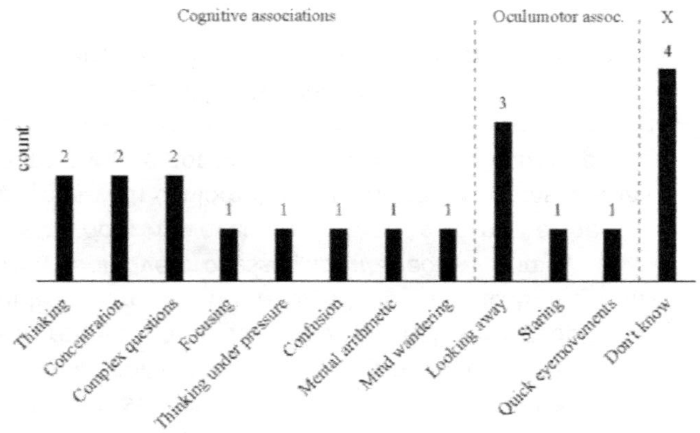

Figure 3 Correlations reported between the sounds generated by the pupil dilation sonification and behaviours.

Eighteen participants (90%) reported they noticed a link between the sound and their behaviour, two (10%) did not. Eleven (55%) suggested a correlation with a cognitive processes, including thinking, concentration, focus, and dealing with complex questions (Figure 3); five (25%) correlated the sound to oculomotor behaviours, such as looking away, staring, and moving the eyes quickly; whereas four participants (20%) did not uncover such correlations *spontaneously*. Relatedly, fifteen participants (78%) reported that the sounds changed when there was a change in cognition or related behaviour (Figure 4); whereas two participants (11%) thought the sound changed due to oculomotor activity only; and two (11%) did not think the sound changed at any particular moment. When *instructed* that the sounds correlate with the amount of cognitive resources allocated, fifteen participants (75%) experienced this correlation, whereas five (25%) did not. These findings indicate that some people are likely to correlate the sounds to oculomotor behaviours, whereas for some it may not be possible to experience such correlations at all. However, most people are able to correlate the pupil dilation sonification sounds with cognitive processes *spontaneously* and by *instruction*, which suggests pupil dilation sonification has the potential to help elicit metacognitive awareness.

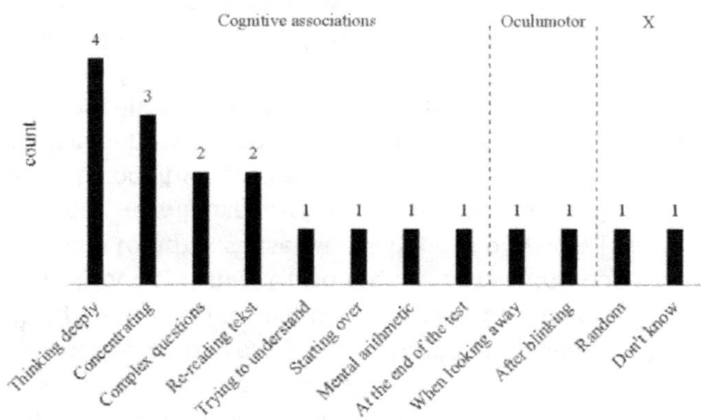

Figure 4 Indication of when the sounds generated by the pupil dilation sonification changed during the problem solving task.

However, there were issues with the quality of the sounds generated by the pupil dilation sonification (Figure 5). Fifteen negative responses (68%), e.g., that the sound was annoying or distracting, seven neutral responses, e.g., that it sounds like a radar (32%), and no positive responses (0%) were reported. Despite its apparent ability help elicit metacognitive awareness, the findings also suggest issues with the use of (our) pupil dilation sonification, which requires further study.

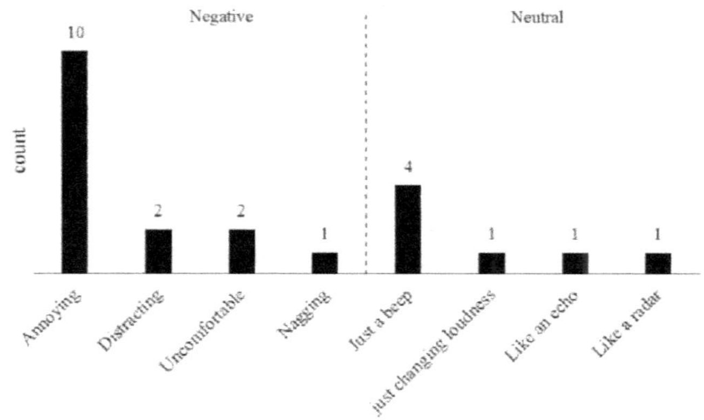

Figure 5 Experiences and attribution to the sound itself.

Discussion and conclusion

In the present study we explored the potential of pupil dilation sonification for eliciting metacognitive awareness. The results showed that most people are able to correlate the pupil dilation sonification sounds with cognitive processes *spontaneously* and by *instruction*. However, some tend to correlate the sounds with oculomotor behaviours, whereas a small minority was not able to perceive a correlation at all. This preliminary evidence suggests that pupil dilation sonification could potentially be a novel way to augment metacognition, but more work is needed.

There are of course limitations. For example, the full range of possible correlations between the pupil dilation sonification sounds and cognition has not yet been explored because a) the mathematics task mostly manipulated task-evoked rather than task-independent pupil dilations [8], and b) light can cause larger dilations than cognition, biasing correlations between sound and oculomotor behaviour [3]. Second, negative responses to the sound itself may have influenced metacognitive awareness (Figure 5), introducing uncertainty about the validity of our approach. Third, caution about any conclusions about using pupil dilation sonification to eliciting metacognitive awareness and augment metacognition is needed as no control group was used and task performance was not measured.

Future work will address these limitations. First, we will explore how to mitigate negative responses to the initial version of the sonification, by a) exploring sparsity, e.g., by sonifying change in pupil dilation, b) using non-intrusive sounds, e.g., café-sounds or waves; but c) it might also require translating pupil dilations to other senses, e.g., haptics or vision [9]. Second, we will explore how to improve the elicitation of metacognitive awareness, by a) developing a sonification that emphasizes differences in task-evoked and task-independent pupil dilations, which signify different cognitions [8]; and (b) test these in a wider range of tasks fully the range correlations between pupil dilation and cognition. Third, replication is advised with a control (fake sonification) to further confirm the theoretical assumptions that underlie our approach.

The contribution of this study is thus preliminary evidence that making pupil dilation audible can elicit metacognitive awareness. Given the role of such awareness in task performance, it may have potential to develop a novel technological approach that can augment metacognition to help people to get the most out of their own cognitive capabilities.

References

1. Baker, L. (2010). Metacognition. *International encyclopedia of education*, 204-210.

2. Beatty, J., & Wagoner, B. L. (1977). Pupillometric signs of brain activation vary with level of cognitive processing (No. TR-9). University of California.
3. Campbell, F. W., & Gubisch, R. W. (1966). Optical quality of the human eye. *The Journal of Physiology*, 186(3), 558-578.
4. Cycling '74 (2017). Retrieved at 26-07-2017 from https://cycling74.com/products/max
5. de Rooij, A., Corr, P. J., & Jones, S. (2015). Emotion and creativity: Hacking into cognitive appraisal processes to augment creative ideation. In *Proceedings of the 2015 ACM SIGCHI Conference on Creativity and Cognition*, 265-274.
6. de Rooij, A., & Jones, S. (2015). (E) motion and creativity: Hacking the function of motor expressions in emotion regulation to augment creativity. In *Proceedings of the Ninth International Conference on Tangible, Embedded, and Embodied Interaction*, 145-152.
7. de Rooij, A., van Dartel, M., Ruhl, A., Schraffenberger, H., van Melick, B., Bontje, M., Daams, M., & Witter, M. (2017). Sensory Augmentation: Toward a Dialogue between the Arts and Sciences. In Proceedings of the 6th EAI International Conference: ArtsIT, Interactivity & Game Creation.
8. Eckstein, M. K., Guerra-Carrillo, B., Singley, A. T. M., & Bunge, S. A. (2017). Beyond eye gaze: What else can eyetracking reveal about cognition and cognitive development?. *Developmental cognitive neuroscience*, 25, 69-91.
9. Ehlers, J., Strauch, C., Georgi, J., & Huckauf, A. (2016). Pupil size changes as an active information channel for biofeedback applications. *Applied psychophysiology and biofeedback*, 41(3), 331-339.
10. Filingeri, D., Fournet, D., Hodder, S., & Havenith, G. (2014). Why wet feels wet? A neurophysiological model of human cutaneous wetness sensitivity. *Journal of neurophysiology*, 112(6), 1457-1469.
11. Flavell, J. H. (1979). Metacognition and cognitive monitoring: A new area of cognitive–developmental inquiry. *American psychologist*, 34(10), 906.
12. Fleming, S. M., & Frith, C. D. (Eds.). (2014). *The cognitive neuroscience of metacognition*. Springer Science & Business Media.
13. Fuchs, L. S., Compton, D. L., Fuchs, D., Paulsen, K., Bryant, J. D., & Hamlett, C. L. (2005). The prevention, identification, and cognitive determinants of math difficulty. *Journal of Educational Psychology*, 97(3), 493
14. Gerjets, P., Walter, C., Rosenstiel, W., Bogdan, M., & Zander, T. O. (2014). Cognitive state monitoring and the design of adaptive instruction in digital environments: lessons learned from cognitive workload assessment using a passive brain-computer interface approach. *Frontiers in neuroscience*, 8, 385.
15. Gilzenrat, M. S., Nieuwenhuis, S., Jepma, M., & Cohen, J. D. (2010). Pupil diameter tracks changes in control state predicted by the adaptive gain theory of locus coeruleus function. *Cognitive, Affective, & Behavioral Neuroscience*, 10(2), 252-269.
16. Goldberg et al., (2014). Enhancing self-regulated learning through metacognitively-aware intelligent tutoring systems. In *Proceedings of the 11th International Conference of the Learning Sciences*.
17. Kahneman, D., & Beatty, J. (1966). Pupil diameter and load on memory. *Science*, 154(3756), 1583-1585.
18. Kleitman, S., & Stankov, L. (2007). Self-confidence and metacognitive processes. *Learning and Individual Differences*, 17(2), 161-173.
19. McLaren, J. W., Erie, J. C., & Brubaker, R. F. (1992). Computerized analysis of pupillograms in

studies of alertness. *Investigative ophthalmology & visual science*, 33(3), 671-676.

20. Moore, B. C. (2012). An introduction to the psychology of hearing. Brill.
21. Novich, N. (2015). *Sound-to-touch sensory substitution and beyond*. Doctoral thesis. Rice University.
22. Ocumpaugh, J., Baker, R., Gowda, S., Heffernan, N., & Heffernan, C. (2014). Population validity for Educational Data Mining models: A case study in affect detection. *British Journal of Educational Technology*, 45(3), 487-501.
23. Omurtag, A., Aghajani, H., & Keles, H. O. (2017). Decoding human mental states by whole-head EEG+FNIRS during category fluency task performance. *Journal of neural engineering*, pre-print.
24. Reimer, J., McGinley, M. J., Liu, Y., Rodenkirch, C., Wang, Q., McCormick, D. A., & Tolias, A. S. (2016). Pupil fluctuations track rapid changes in adrenergic and cholinergic activity in cortex. *Nature communications*, 7, 13289.
25. Roll, I., Aleven, V., McLaren, B. M., & Koedinger, K. R. (2011). Improving students' help-seeking skills using metacognitive feedback in an intelligent tutoring system. *Learning and instruction*, 21(2), 267-280.
26. Rondeel, E. W., Van Steenbergen, H., Holland, R. W., & van Knippenberg, A. (2015). A closer look at cognitive control: differences in resource allocation during updating, inhibition and switching as revealed by pupillometry. *Frontiers in human neuroscience*, 9, 494.
27. Schraw, G. (1998). Promoting general metacognitive awareness. *Instructional Science*. 26, 113-125.
28. Smallwood, J., Brown, K. S., Tipper, C., Giesbrecht, B., Franklin, M. S., Mrazek, M. D., & Schooler, J. W. (2011). Pupillometric evidence for the decoupling of attention from perceptual input during offline thought. *PloS one*, 6(3), e18298.
29. Spielberger, C. D., Anton, W. D., & Bedell, J. (2015). The nature and treatment of test anxiety. *Emotions and anxiety: New concepts, methods, and applications*, 317-344.
30. Storbeck, J., & Clore, G. L. (2008). Affective arousal as information: How affective arousal influences judgments, learning, and memory. *Social and personality psychology compass*, 2(5), 1824-1843.
31. Swanson, H. L. (1992). The relationship between metacognition and problem solving in gifted children. *Roeper Review*, 15(1), 43-48.
32. The Eye Tribe (2017). Retrieved at 26-07-2017 from http://www.theeyetribe.com
33. Thiede, K. W., Anderson, M., & Therriault, D. (2003). Accuracy of metacognitive monitoring affects learning of texts. *Journal of educational psychology*, 95(1), 66.
34. Walcher, S., Körner, C., & Benedek, M. (2017). Looking for ideas: Eye behavior during goal-directed internally focused cognition. *Consciousness and Cognition*, 53, 165-175.
35. Walker, B. N., & Nees, M. A. (2011). Theory of sonification. *The sonification handbook*, 9-39.
36. Woodhouse, J. M., & Campbell, F. W. (1975). The role of the pupil light reflex in aiding adaptation to the dark. *Vision research*, 15(6), 649-653.

Designing Bimanual Tangible Interaction for Stroke Survivors

Mikko Kytö
David McGookin
Wilfried Bock
Aalto University
02150 Espoo, Finland
mikko.kyto@aalto.fi
david.mcgookin@aalto.fi
wbock@kth.se

Héctor A. Caltenco
Charlotte Magnusson
Lund University
221 00 Lund, Sweden
hector.caltenco@certec.lth.se
charlotte.magnusson@certec.lth.se

TEI '18, March 18–21, 2018, Stockholm, Sweden

ACM ISBN 978-1-4503-5568-1/18/03.
https://doi.org/10.1145/3173225.3173269.

Abstract

Stroke is a significant cause of long-term disability, impairing over 10 million peoples motor function, primarily on one side of the body every year. Whilst effective rehabilitation exercises can help recover and maintain some affected motor function, stroke survivors often do not carry out enough of these. Instead relying on their `good' side to carry out tasks. However, this leads to poor recovery limiting the ability to carry out everyday bimanual tasks (such as dressing or cooking). We present work that seeks to support stroke survivors to engage in bimanual rehabilitation through interaction with augmented tangible objects that can be used to control everyday devices. Through a user-centered design process, we uncovered how bimanual rehabilitation can be supported. This led to the development of the ActivSticks device that allows bimanual rehabilitation and interaction with other devices and services.

Author Keywords

Stroke Rehabilitation; Bimanual; Tangible Interaction; Home; Activities of Daily Living.

Occupational Therapist (OT2): "*For the enhanced upper limb thing, what we do is we put a splint on the healthy hand. And we force you to do everything with the paralysed hand...If the therapist looks the other way, you'll soon have the splint off and you'll do it with that hand.*"

Stroke survivor (S5): "*I think in my case it's more about being lazy. Because everything is so easy with this right hand, I'd rather use that. Whereas my left hand is still a bit clumsy and so on so, why use it? I think in my case that's the most common reason.*"

Stroke survivor (S6): "*Before the stroke I used to write very fast using ten fingers. Now I have only five fingers. I would be able to type using the left hand too but, if the speed of the right hand is ten, the speed of the left hand is 0.5. Their paces are completely different.*"

Figure 1. Initial interviews helped illustrate the importance of bimanual interaction for stroke survivors.

Introduction and Background

Every year over 10 million people survive a stroke [17]. Stroke causes a wide range of physical and psycho-social impairments, with approximately half of all stroke survivors having to rely on assistance to carry out basic activities of daily living (ADLs), such as dressing, walking and eating [13]. Stroke impacts primarily one side of the body, causing significant motor and cognitive impairments, while leaving the other side of the body more unaffected. Thereby requiring many ADLs (e.g., dressing and cooking) that would normally be carried out bimanually, to be performed mainly one handed [12], leading to frustration. Recovering the ability to perform ADLs independently requires regular performance of simple exercises (e.g., squeezing a ball). However, their repetitive nature has been found to reduce motivation and adherence, leading to reduced recovery of affected limbs [16].

Our approach is to create tangible user interaction devices that support both the effective execution of existing bimanual ADL exercises and support interaction with everyday devices, encouraging stroke survivors to engage with rehabilitation. Skill recovery using bimanual upper limb training has been found to be helpful [6,11,15]. However, the majority of the work within HCI has focused on supporting single-handed interaction, where the simultaneous use of both upper limbs is not required [3,4,9,20]. For example, Kirk *et al.* [9] developed a tangible music creation device for between hands). Simultaneous inter limb coordination (for example when tying shoe laces) has been shown to paresis [11], which is our main target group stroke bimanual movements (e.g. users hit drum pads using one hand at a time without having physical interaction rehabilitation. Although their device supported use of both upper limbs, it did not require simultaneous.

The closest to our work on bimanual interaction with stroke survivors is a study by Hijmans et al. [8]. They enabled simultaneous bimanual interaction attaching a standard games controller to a custom handle bar. Whilst they found this improved motor performance, the games controller limited how the impaired limb could be incorporated into interaction, as nearly one third of the stroke survivors were not able to press keys with their impaired hand. In this study, we take another approach by designing bimanual tangible devices without the limitations of existing controllers.

Design Process

We employed a user-centered design process to investigate how best to motivate and support stroke survivors in rehabilitating bimanual movement. Interviews with patients and rehabilitation professionals led to initial brainstorming and exploration of the design space. Discussion around video prototypes of early concepts were then used to help develop a tangible bimanual device (ActivSticks) to support integration of bimanual use in everyday tasks.

Initial Interviews with Therapists and Patients

We conducted initial individual semi-structured interviews (lasting around 1 h) with 6 stroke survivors (aged 25-75, 3 female), and one group interview (lasting about 1.5 h) with 7 physical and occupational rehabilitation therapists. This provided an in depth understanding of challenges in stroke rehabilitation, and covered how stroke affected participants in

Movement: What the person is doing with her/his upper limb? This can be *Pushing, Pulling, Squeezing, Releasing, Moving, Rotating and/or Twisting.*
Manipulated Object/Device: What object or device the person is interacting with? These can be *Existing Mobile* (e.g., vase and hat), *Existing Semi-Fixed* (e.g., *table* - This lies between mobile and fixed as things that can be moved, but aren't very mobile), *Existing Fixed* (e.g. door handle and handrail), *New* (e.g., dedicated ball) or *None* (sensed arm only e.g. kinect sensing – basis for existing exergames)
Collaboration: Is the activity done with someone? *Individual, Partner, Group or social.*
Effect: What is the outcome of the exercise? *Independent Living* (e.g., encourage someone to use their upper limb when cooking). *Utilitarian* (change TV channel), *Playful* (create and play a game)
Output Device/Object: What device/object provides feedback?
Progress monitoring: How can improvement be quantified? *Implicit* (e.g. ambient light)/*Explicit* (e.g. line chart of progress)
Advancement: How can development be supported? Do you have to do more, increase challenge (i.e. make the same thing more challenging)

Figure 2. The design aspects taken into consideration in creating initial design concepts.

everyday life, as well as how often participants engage their impaired limb in ADL exercises.

Interviews highlighted the fact that stroke survivors are often either reluctant to use or forget to use their impaired upper limb (see Figure 1). Using the unimpaired hand is often faster and easier. In particular, this means that the impaired hand is often not used between formal rehabilitation sessions (such as with a rehabilitation professional). For example, it is rare that a stroke survivor will interact with a desk top computer using their impaired hand, although they are designed for bimanual interaction. 4 of the stroke survivors did not use their impaired upper limb for interacting with any device at home. However, recovering skills where both upper limbs are needed is motivating (Occupational therapist, OT2: "*I have this one patient who likes photographing, a lot...So there's a lot of things I can link to that.*"). As such, the bimanual training should be linked to something that motivates stroke survivors or is part of their ADLs.

Initial Design Concepts
Based on the interviews, four interaction designers carried out a structured brainstorming activity to identify potential everyday tasks around the home that could be augmented to support bimanual rehabilitation. Each researcher generated initial ideas independently, before discussing all ideas as a group. Researchers rotated around rooms in a typical home (kitchen, living room, bedroom, bathroom and hallway). With each, images of typical rooms were used to identify objects in those rooms, movements performed with them, and how those movements could be augmented to support performing ADLs. In discussions we aimed to focus on adjustability and modularity of the activities, so that movements could be mapped to many things. In order to achieve this, we used modular structure for the initial design concepts (shown in Figure 2).

Video Prototypes
From initial design concepts, five were selected to represent the design space. These included different types of bimanual movements (e.g., squeezing and rotating), as well as with and without (e.g. gesture) an object. In order to get feedback and to inspire patients and therapists to generate more ideas, we made video prototypes of these five concepts (see Figure 3).

We showed video prototypes to 10 stroke survivors, aged from 44 to 60, 6 females. Whilst stroke survivors were able to tell us if they liked the prototype or not, (S7: "*I could order one of those.*"), the majority saw the video prototypes as concrete solutions rather than as a starting point to develop further ideas (S8: "*Yes I liked it but I don't really know how to put it in words. "Oh my, my, I can't really put it in words."*). Therefore, feedback was largely related to the prototypes as shown. Encouraging bimanual activities on the bed divided opinions (S9: "*This didn't impress me at all. Here, the idea is clearly that person stays at home within four walls, staring at your own bedroom ceiling.*" and S10: "*I'm the kind of person who stays indoors, so those are good. It's really hard to do anything. If I'm given a task, I don't really, I just sit still. These are really good.*"). As such the use of video prototypes among stroke survivors seem to work well for communicating our concepts (similar finding with [10]) and for confirming if the individuals liked the concepts or not, but did not (at least for stroke survivors) act as starting points to support co-design of solutions. Stroke often has a significant negative impact on cognitive

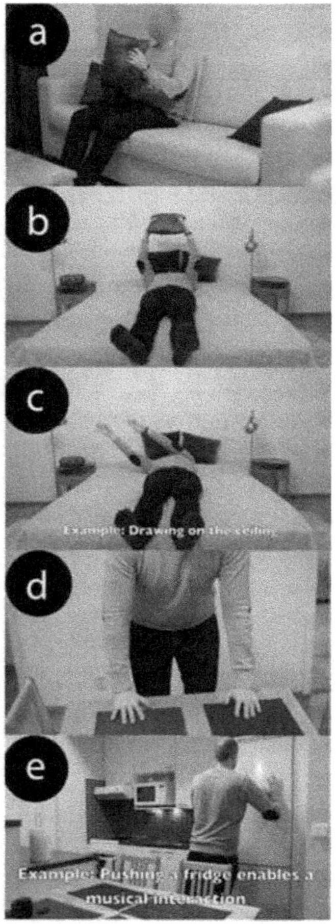

Figure 3. Screenshots from the video prototypes where a user is required to use both of their upper limbs. (a) Using a pillow for controlling the TV, (b) using a pillow for exploring in Google Street view, (c) using two hands for drawing on a ceiling, and using two-hands for playing a song by pushing a (d) table or (e) fridge.

capabilities, and developing ideas beyond what was shown, may have been too demanding for participants.

From therapists (1 physical and 4 occupational therapists) we received a lot of valuable feedback for developing our ideas further in terms of movements. Therapists emphasized the importance of symmetry, having both limbs carry out the same movement at the same time. This ensures that the movement range of the impaired upper limb is extended by the healthier upper limb, and the movement trajectory is natural. Symmetry should be guaranteed by having an object that can be held by both hands (OT2: *"from the pillow that it's good, there's the bilateral control system"* and OT3: *"This is good, this steering a wheel type of movement"*). In addition to symmetry, instant feedback should be given describing how much the impaired limb is incorporated into the movement, as stroke survivors' self-awareness of their impaired limb is affected.

The number of repetitions of an exercise was also highlighted as important (Physical therapist, PT1: *"...there should be a lot of these activities, even small ones or any kind of, activity that is done with the impaired hand, as long as it's repeated enough. No matter what kind of... It can be squeezing, it can be tapping...as long as they do it a lot."*). Therapists also highlighted that the tangibles should be firm enough to support easy grasping, with the pillows used in the prototype being seen as too compliant.

Designing and Building Initial Prototypes

Based on this feedback we started developing a device that requires bimanual interaction (see Figure 4). We aimed at supporting various general interactions such as rotation, squeezing and releasing, and the simultaneous movements seen as important by the therapists. The movements could then be mapped onto various outputs (such as controlling TV). To meet these requirements, we build a light ring using plastic pipe and rounding it with a foam. We chose to use a ring form due to it is familiarity among stroke survivors and rehabilitation professionals, and the necessity to use both upper limbs to hold and rotate it. We measured hand squeezes from three different locations with a pressure sensitive fabric (velostat [1] using the method described in [21]). We used an accelerometer [2] to detect rotation. Although we had a lot of ideas of mapping outputs to many different things (see Section *Initial Design Concepts*), we decided to map the manipulations of the ring to standard mouse and keyboard controls (shown in Table 1). As stroke patients had difficulties in extrapolating beyond the video prototypes, this allowed fast prototyping of different interactions through standard PC applications (e.g. surfing the Internet or controlling a Netflix). Having bimanual rehabilitation linked with such a general task enables good number of repetitions and it would fit larger portion of stroke survivors than games (e.g., [7,8]) and/or musical interaction (e.g., [5,9]).

Feedback about the Initial Prototypes

We collected feedback about the initial prototype from 1 physical and 4 occupational therapists. Therapists were able to interact with the ring, and it was mapped to navigate in Google Street view, to read a magazine through issuu.com service and to control Netflix.

Therapists were positive about the ring being both lightweight and requiring the use of both hands. The form of the ring was also positively commented on being a natural and familiar shape (e.g. the therapists

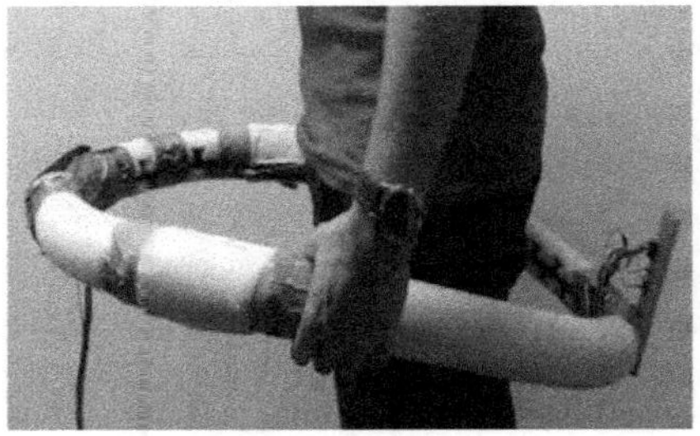

Figure 4. The initial prototype. The gyroscope (at the back) was used to detect rotations, with pressure sensitive fabric detecting grip. The ring was so flexible it was not possible to hold it in this position with one upper limb only.

	Mouse	Keyboard
Tilt right	Move right	Right key
Tilt left	Move left	Left key
Tilt up	Move up	Up key
Tilt down	Move down	Down key
Squeezing and releasing on the left	Click left button	Space
Squeezing and releasing on the right	Click right button	

Table 1. The mappings of movements for the initial prototype (see figure above) when mapped to a mouse and keyboard.

discussed how they used a hula hoop) and being able to be held close to one's body when inside the ring. However, the ring shape was also found to be problematic, being difficult to put on (either by standing in or putting over the head) for stroke survivors. The ring is also difficult to use when sitting, as the rear of the ring presses the back. Although the ring is lighter and thicker (making it easier to grasp) than rings already used in therapy, it is still difficult to use for a prolonged period, and it might be easy to lose grip.

Although bimanual interaction was seen as valuable, the initial approach of using left/right tilting of the ring was not as useful as expected. An impaired arm often suffers from spasticity, meaning the impaired hand would act as a pivot point, with the unimpaired hand lowering or raising the ring. Raising only one arm at a time was not considered good movement, instead having symmetrical lifting and lowering movements (where the ring stays level) would be better. The rotational movements originating from the shoulders, and having both arms fully extended would be more relaxing for the impaired hand, as it would not require flexing the muscles of the arm continuously. The range and length of movements should also be adjustable, and be able to be tailored to an individual's capabilities (OT5: *"The possibility to adjust the range of motion is essential in order to enable meaningful training. Because I am thinking that this [tilting and squeezing] is very challenging."* and OT7: "*One needs to squeeze pretty long here. Many of our stroke survivors would not be able to do such a challenging movement*"). As such the sensitivity to detect squeezes and releases should be higher. Therapists also highlighted how the ability to release a grip was often more important than being able to grip. Due to spasticity, stroke survivors must often learn to relax their arm and release a grip, before learning to grip.

Designing and Building ActivSticks
Based on this feedback we redesigned the prototype, changing the form from a ring to a scissor device (see Figure 5). This is easier to take into use than ring, as it does not require standing inside. The adjustable angle enables the upper limbs to be close to the user's waist, and the angle allows additional movements, such as abduction (decreasing the angle) and adduction (increasing angle). ActivSticks can also be used as a straight bar. We replaced the non-ergonomic asymmetrical tilt movements with yaw rotations (rotating the tip of the ActivSticks to left and right while having it in balance), which were detected with a sensor having magnetometer, accelerometer and gyroscope fixed to the end of the sticks [5]. ActivSticks is easier to use than the ring when sitting or supported (for example on a table). When supported, the user can interact with it one handed. In order to increase the detectable pressure range and to detect whether the stroke survivor is using the device with both hands we replaced the velostat with a higher pressure sensitive fabric using the method described in [14]. This zebra fabric (see Figure 5) allows detection of spatial movements of the pressure as well, as the pressure is detected from the intersections of vertical and horizontal stripes.

Stroke Survivors and Therapist Feedback on ActivSticks
Two stroke survivors (1 female) and 7 physical and occupational therapists were able to interact with the final ActivSticks prototype. All were positive towards the design changes, with the ability to set the stick angle allowing more gross motor movements (including

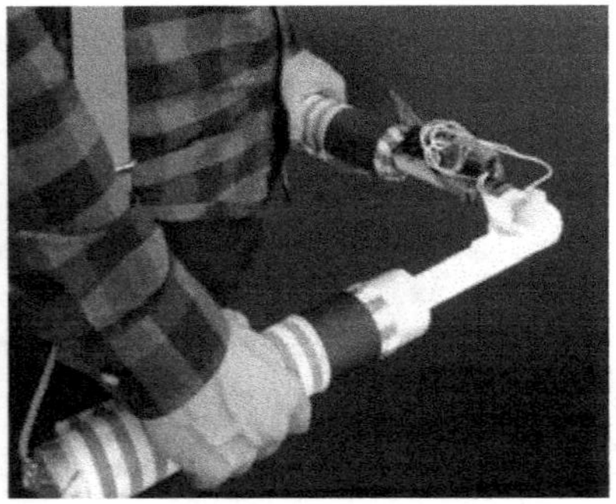

Figure 5. User holding ActivSticks. The zebra fabric was used to detect squeezing and releasing. We added braces in order to prevent it falling down.

	Mouse	Keyboard
Rotate right	Move right	Right key
Rotate left	Move left	Left key
Tilt up	Move up	Down key
Tilt down	Move down	Up key
Squeezing and releasing on the left	Click left button	Space
Squeezing and releasing on the right	Click right button	

Table 2. The mappings of movements for ActivSticks.

rowing when used as straight bar), as well as fine motor movements, such as grasping and releasing both hands along the vertical bar. As such our existing mappings (shown in Table 2) can be extended by these new movements (e.g., using adduction and abduction for making selections). As our new design uses a grid that allows pressure measurement of individual fingers, we can provide more detailed feedback about the bimanual grip. Physical therapist specialised in grip suggested that the less impaired hand could be used to act as a reference point for defining the pressure levels for interaction (e.g. the user can make selections by matching the grip strengths between hands). So far, using the less impaired hand as a reference has been used in clinical work to measure maximum grip [19], but has not been used for interacting with tangibles with varying grip strength levels.

Discussion

Designing rehabilitative tangible interaction for stroke survivors is demanding. Stroke survivors can have widely diverging needs in training. Whilst some may need to keep up a general activity level to improve strength, others should focus more on decreasing spasticity in their upper limb. As such, it is important that designs should enable as a set of movements as wide as possible, with a range of outputs from which the most relevant can be chosen and customised to individually fit the individual. Although this is a laborious way, it seems to be the most valuable.

As the training needs and motivations of stroke survivors are so divergent, different ways to encourage bimanual interaction are needed. The requirement of using both upper limbs can be designed through physical properties of the tangible, so that it is not physically possible to use it one handed. Whilst we implemented this in the first prototype, the ActivSticks can be also taken into use one-handed (e.g., supporting it on a lap or on a table), and the bimanual use is guaranteed through sensors. As such ActivSticks is more adaptive for a larger range of stroke survivors than the first prototype. The third approach is to provide affordance for bimanual interaction, but not to force it. This would require reminders and motivation to use the impaired hand, e.g., through including gamified elements to interaction, such as getting scores when using bimanual input device, to motivate the bimanual interaction in everyday tasks.

Our future work is focused on the tailoring of the movements and outputs those movements generate to better fit with individual needs and motivations. In order to investigate the use beyond novelty effect, we will carry out longer term studies where stroke survivors will use the ActivSticks in day-to-day life. By doing so we will significantly advance understanding of how tangible user interfaces can enhance bimanual rehabilitation for stroke survivors.

Acknowledgements

The authors gratefully acknowledge NordForsk for the support given to the project ActivABLES. We wish to thank all the stroke survivors and health care professionals in Finland and Sweden taking part in the research, and all the researchers in ActivABLES project, especially Laura Maye, Steinunn A. Ólafsdóttir, Ingibjörg Hjaltadóttir and Thóra B. Hafsteinsdóttir.

References

[1] Adafruit. Pressure-Sensitive Conductive Sheet (Velostat/Linqstat). *https://www.adafruit.com/product/1361*, 2017.

[2] Adafruit. ADXL345 - Triple-Axis Accelerometer. *https://www.adafruit.com/product/1231*, 2017.

[3] Alankus, G., Proffitt, R., Kelleher, C., and Engsberg, J. Stroke therapy through motion-based games: a case study. *ACM Transactions on Accessible Computing (TACCESS) 4*, 1 (2011), 3:1-33.

[4] Balaam, M., Rennick Egglestone, S., Fitzpatrick, G., et al. Motivating mobility: designing for lived motivation in stroke rehabilitation. *Proceedings of the SIGCHI Conference on Human Factors in Computing Systems*, (2011), 3073–3082.

[5] Caltenco, H.A., Bjartmarz, I., Olsson, A., et al. Designing Interactive Systems for Balance Rehabilitation after Stroke. *Proceedings of the Tenth International Conference on Tangible, Embedded, and Embodied Interaction - TEI '17*, (2017), 511–516.

[6] Van Delden, A.E.Q., Peper, C.E., Kwakkel, G., and Beek, P.J. A systematic review of bilateral upper limb training devices for poststroke rehabilitation. *Stroke Research and Treatment*, (2012), 17:1-17.

[7] Dukes, P.S., Hayes, A., Hodges, L.F., and Woodbury, M. Punching ducks for post-stroke neurorehabilitation: System design and initial exploratory feasibility study. *IEEE Symposium on 3D User Interface 2013, 3DUI 2013 - Proceedings*, (2013), 47–54.

[8] Hijmans, J.M., Hale, L.A., Satherley, J.A., McMillan, N.J., and King, M.J. Bilateral upper-limb rehabilitation after stroke using a movement-based game controller. *The Journal of Rehabilitation Research and Development 48*, 8 (2011), 1005.

[9] Kirk, P., Grierson, M., Bodak, R., and Stewart, L. Motivating Stroke Rehabilitation Through Music : A Feasibility Study Using Digital Musical Instruments In The Home. *SIGCHI conference on Human factors in computing systems*, (2016), 1781–1785.

[10] Magnusson, C., Caltenco, H.A., McGookin, D., et al. Tangible Interaction for Stroke Survivors: Design Recommendations. *Proceedings of the Tenth International Conference on Tangible, Embedded, and Embodied Interaction*, (2017), 597–602.

[11] McCombe Waller, S. and Whitall, J. Bilateral arm training: why and who benefits? *NeuroRehabilitation 23*, 1 (2008), 29–41.

[12] Michielsen, M.E., Selles, R.W., Stam, H.J., Ribbers, G.M., and Bussmann, J.B. Quantifying nonuse in chronic stroke patients: A study into paretic, nonparetic, and bimanual upper-limb use in daily life. *Archives of Physical Medicine and Rehabilitation 93*, 11 (2012), 1975–1981.

[13] Miller, E.L., Murray, L., Richards, L., et al. Comprehensive overview of nursing and interdisciplinary rehabilitation care of the stroke patient: A scientific statement from the American heart association. *Stroke 41*, 10 (2010), 2402–2448.

[14] Parzer, P., Probst, K., Babic, T., et al. FlexTiles: A Flexible, Stretchable, Formable, Pressure-Sensitive, Tactile Input Sensor Patrick. *Proceedings of the 2016 CHI Conference Extended Abstracts on Human Factors in Computing Systems - CHI EA '16*, (2016), 3754–3757.

[15] Pollock, A., Farmer, S.E., Brady, M.C., et al. Interventions for improving upper limb function after stroke. *Cochrane database of systematic reviews (Online) 11*, 11 (2014), CD010820-CD010820.

[16] Shaughnessy, M., Resnick, B.M., and Macko, R.F. Testing a model of post-stroke exercise behavior. *Rehabilitation Nursing 31*, 1 (2006), 15–21.

[17] Stroke association. *State of the Nation, Stroke statistics*. 2016.

[18] Summers, J.J., Kagerer, F.A., Garry, M.I., Hiraga, C.Y., Loftus, A., and Cauraugh, J.H. Bilateral and

unilateral movement training on upper limb function in chronic stroke patients: A TMS study. *Journal of the Neurological Sciences 252*, 1 (2007), 76–82.

[19] Sunderland, a, Tinson, D., Bradley, L., and Hewer, R.L. Arm function after stroke. An evaluation of grip strength as a measure of recovery and a prognostic indicator. *Journal of neurology, neurosurgery, and psychiatry 52*, 11 (1989), 1267–1272.

[20] Vandermaesen, M., Weyer, T. De, Luyten, K., and Coninx, K. PhysiCube : providing tangible interaction in a pervasive upper - limb rehabilitation system. *Proceedings of 8th International Conference on Tangible, Embedded and Embodied Interaction (TEI'14)*, (2014), 85–92.

[21] Handcrafting Textile Sensors from Scratch. *https://cdn-shop.adafruit.com/datasheets/HandcraftingSensors.pdf*, 2017, 0.

MacroScope: First-Person Perspective in Physical Scale Models

Dorothé Smit
University of Salzburg
Salzburg, Austria
dorothe.smit@sbg.ac.at

Vincent van Rheden
University of Salzburg
Salzburg, Austria
vincentvanrheden@gmail.com

Thomas Grah
University of Salzburg
Salzburg, Austria
thomas.grah@sbg.ac.at

Manfred Tscheligi
University of Salzburg,
Salzburg, Austria
manfred.tscheligi@sbg.ac.at

Martin Murer
University of Salzburg
Salzburg, Austria
martin.murer@sbg.ac.at

TEI '18, March 18–21, 2018, Stockholm, Sweden

ACM ISBN 978-1-4503-5568-1/18/03.
https://doi.org/10.1145/3173225.3173276

Abstract
Traditionally, architects and designers have used scale models to explore, communicate, and evaluate concepts and ideas in large-scale, spatial projects. These scale models offer the user a bird's eye perspective and often tangible ways of interacting with the model. Nevertheless, they lack a realistic, first-person view on the effects that the design solutions have in the space. In this paper, we explore MacroScope, a tool that aims to support collaborative spatial design by providing a real time, 360° first-person perspective in a physical scale model, by means of a virtual reality head-mounted display. We reflect on the usage potentials in collaborative creative processes, before describing next steps for the development of MacroScope.

Author Keywords
Virtual reality; mixed reality; scale models; collaborative design; creative processes; first-person perspective.

Introduction
Prototyping is a way to consider the effects of design solutions, to test their validity and usability, and to communicate ideas. In large-scale, spatial projects, constructing full-size prototypes is often an expensive undertaking, requiring many resources and plenty of man-power. Therefore, architects and designers alike

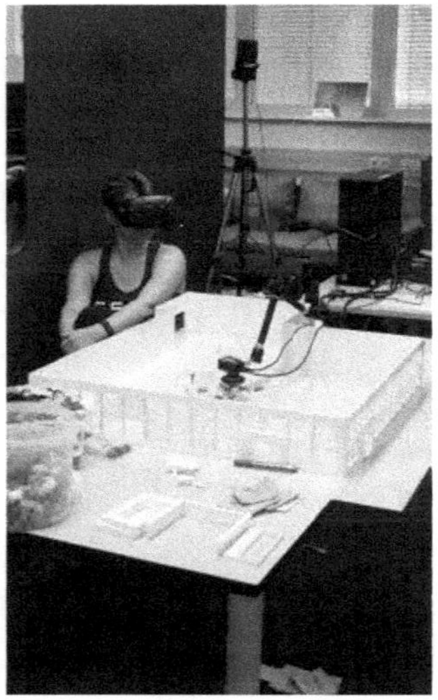

Figure 1: The MacroScope system provides a first person perspective in a physical scale model

make use of scale models to grasp, evaluate and communicate the impact of their ideas on the physical space in which they are situated [11,13]. Nevertheless, scale models offer the user only a single perspective: a top-down look on the design space, rather than a realistic view on what effects creative ideas and concepts in the space may have from a first-person perspective.

In architecture, the first-person perspective in conjunction with physical scale models is a common theme [10]. To achieve this perspective, the use of endoscopes was popular in the 80s and 90s. However, the development of CAD tools for digital 3D models reduced the use of physical scale models, and the underwhelming images (in terms of quality and field of view [8]) from endoscopes were replaced by digital walkthroughs [9]. Recently, due to the advances in rapid prototyping, physical scale models have regained relevance in the architectural field [10] due to their ease of use in multi-stakeholder, collaborative creative processes [4,12].

In this paper, we introduce an improved version of the first-person perspective in physical scale models by means of *MacroScope* (figure 1). MacroScope consists of a fully immersive head-mounted display (HMD) featuring a real-time 360° video stream from the first-person perspective in a scale model. Based on explorations of respectively a basic and a more elaborate immersive system, we reflect on how the use of a first-person perspective in physical scale models can facilitate collaborative, creative processes in large-scale spatial projects.

Related Work

In the realm of the combination between a virtual first-person perspectives and tangible tools, Stoakley et al. [14] introduced 'World-in-Miniature' (WIM) in 1995. WIM is an individual user interface that combines a fully immersive HMD, displaying a virtual environment, with a hand-held, miniature version of the virtual environment, used to navigate the environment and manipulate objects in the environment. They found that holding the physical copy of the virtual environment helps the immersed user orient, plan pathways, locate objects in the space, and estimate distance.

In 1999, Underkoffler and Ishii [15] created Urp, a system for urban planning. The system allows architectural scale models to be placed on any ordinary table to, e.g., simulate wind flow, by means of projections on the scale model. Users of the system responded well to the use of physical architectural models as the system's primary interface. The tangible tools support the communication of ideas to others on the design team, as well as outsiders.

More recently, Ibayashi et al. [5] created Dollhouse VR, consisting of a multi-touch tabletop screen, displaying a 2D view on a miniature interior paired with an HMD. The tabletop provides a bird's eye view for designers, and the HMD provides a first-person perspective for occupants. They found that efficient communication between the occupants and the designers is crucial, but particularly difficult, as HMDs usually cover the eyes and a large part of the face.

Efforts have also been made recently to create point-of-view 360° live streams (e.g. [6]). These systems are often applied in dislocated situations in which two persons work towards a shared goal. The difficulties of integrating these systems often involve the contradiction between quality and latency, the complexity of live stitching multiple camera feeds into one 360° image, and motion sickness of the (stationary) viewer of the footage.

MacroScope

Considering the work previously done in this field, we set out to explore the first-person perspective in a physical scale model as an alternative or addition to the bird's eye perspective. The system we describe in this paper, MacroScope, is an immersive virtual reality system, constructed to explore the creative and interactive possibilities of the first-person perspective in a physical scale model. It allows users to take advantage of the combination between the bird's eye perspective, and the first-person perspective. Its application goes beyond creative processes related to (interior) architecture, but could conceivably support education, manual labor, stage design, etc. In the current version of MacroScope, only one user at the time can have the first-person perspective. Other users will have the bird's eye perspective, with no visual indication of what the immersed user is seeing. The aim of the system is to provide a realistic viewpoint on design interventions made in the scale model.

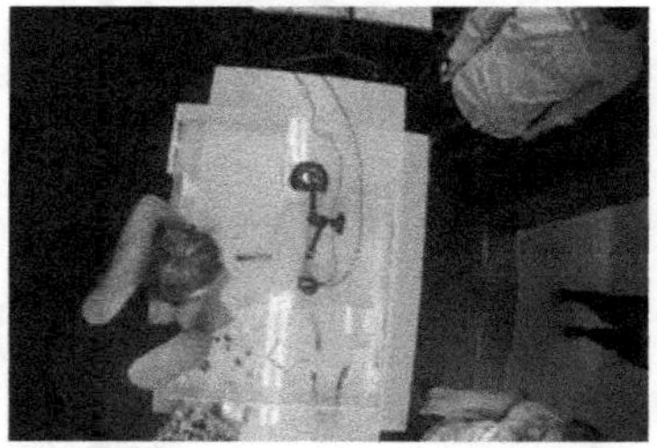

Figure 2: The top-view recordings of the design cases from the GoPro.

Figure 3: Three participants explore a scale model, with one person using the first version of MacroScope to gain a first-person perspective.

We have explored the first-person perspective using two different setups. The first setup was studied as a proof of concept, before a second, more elaborate setup was realized. The proof of concept was explored with one group of three participants in three 20-minute design cases. The second setup was explored with two groups of three participants. Both of these groups also took part in three 20-minute design cases, respectively. During each design case, only one of the participants wore the HMD, while the other participants interacted with the scale model from a bird's eye perspective. Each participant wore the HMD once, each for the duration of one of the total of three design cases that each group of participants performed.

All creative sessions were recorded on video via a GoPro camera mounted above the scale model (see figure 2). Semi-structured group interviews, to gather anecdotal feedback on the system, were conducted with the participants after each exploration.

Proof of Concept

In this first setup, video was captured by a HD wide-angle webcam in the scale model. The camera lens was positioned at the height of an average male at a scale of 1:43, in order to match the scale of the model. The video stream from the scale model was sent to the Oculus Rift DK1.

Creative Sessions - Three participants explored the first setup in three twenty-minute creative sessions (figure 3). The participants had backgrounds in interaction design, game design, and communication science, respectively. In the sessions, the participants collaboratively worked on three design cases pertaining to the design of the interior of a car showroom. The participants used miniature furniture models, cars, and puppets; and LEGO™ blocks to construct concepts and ideas in the scale model. They were also provided with markers to draw on the floors and the walls of the scale model.

Technical Limitations - In the first setup of MacroScope, the HMD that was used has an effective resolution of 640 x 800 per eye and a maximum frame rate of 30

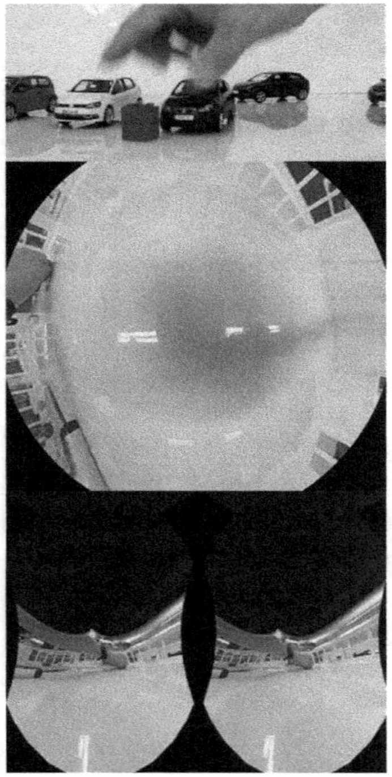

Figure 4: From top to bottom: The first person perspective as seen from the HMD in the first setup; the fisheye footage from the second setup; and the equirectangular footage that was streamed to the HMD in the second setup.

fps. It also suffers from the 'screen-door effect', causing the pixels in the image to look like they are bordered by black lines. The field of view of this setup was limited to 120° due to the webcam that was used. As a consequence, whenever a participant turned his or her head further than the available field of view, he or she would be confronted with a vertical black bar on the side of the screen.

Second Setup

In the second setup, we used a GoPro Hero 4 fitted with a 280° fish-eye lens, mounted on an arm and turned face-down (figure 1), so as to provide participants with a 360° viewing angle around the scale model, effectively leaving out the 'sky above', (figure 4, bottom). The fish-eye video was then projected onto a virtual 360° dome and fed to an HTC Vive, increasing both the frame rate and resolution of the video stream viewed by the participants wearing the HMD. The head-tracking of the HTC Vive allows the user to look around in the virtual scene by turning the head.

Creative Sessions - The second, more elaborate setup was explored by two groups of three participants, with backgrounds in information technology, geo-informatics, communication science, and psychology. Again, both groups were introduced to the first-person perspective in three twenty-minute creative sessions. This time, the creative sessions were focused on the development of diverse, creative workspaces. In these sessions, participants used miniature furniture models, puppets, whiteboard markers and LEGO™ blocks, as well as Playcorn and colored cardboard.

Technical Limitations - The video stream in the second setup is monoscopic, so although the users are presented with an HD stereoscopic rendering through the HMD, they not fully benefit from the stereoscopic capabilities of the used HMD. Furthermore, the current setup doesn't allow the user to move their view throughout the scale model, other than through head movements.

Reflections

In the next section, we detail our reflections on the use of MacroScope, based on the analysis of the recorded video of the sessions, the interviews with participants and the researchers' observations. The reflections are divided into five themes.

Embodiment in the Virtual Environment
In the real world, humans act as embodied beings: through our senses, our bodies provide us with feedback about our presence, activity, attention, capabilities and many other factors [2] in the environment in which we act. Wearing an HMD has a great effect on the way a user connects to his surroundings, including the way he communicates to other people in his vicinity [3]. For example, users reported a sense of 'bodilessness', i.e., when wearing the VR headset in the particular setting as previously described, the user becomes 'a pair of eyes', floating in space, rather than an embodied being capable of physically interacting with and moving around in the space. As a result, the wearer of the HMD often took on an assessing role in the creative process, overseeing the design concepts built by the other participants, rather than actively constructing. Contributions to the creative sessions were mainly of a verbal nature (sometimes supplemented with gestures), discussing the effects of the concepts from the immersed perspective.

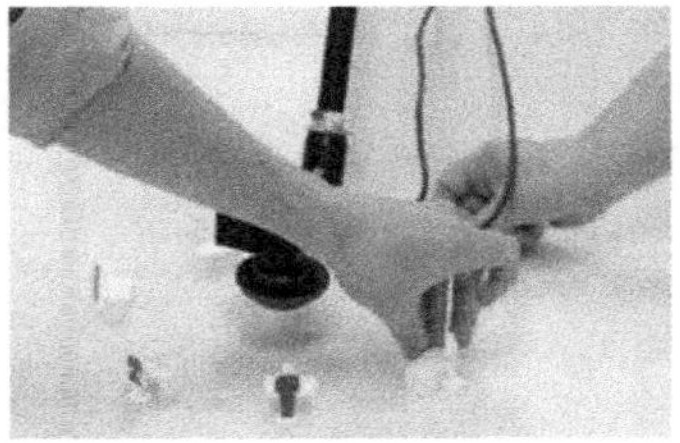

Figure 5: Participants placing markers around the camera as references.

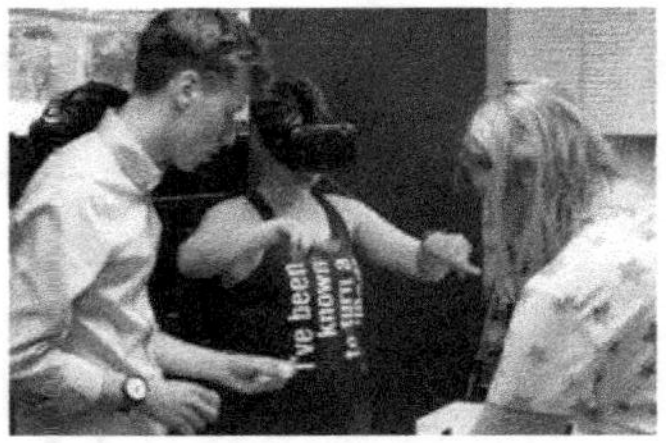

Figure 6: The immersed person instructing the other participants on how to construct an idea.

Figure 7: The large viewing angle in the second setup caused the wearer of the HMD to sometimes completely turn away from the other participants.

Proportions and Orientation in the Model

Initially, users wearing the HMD had difficulty determining size and proportions of the scale model, and orienting themselves in the scale model (P4: *"I found the scale felt a lot bigger in VR."*). The participants that were not immersed quickly noticed that they could help orient the wearer by placing visual references (e.g., the miniature cars or colored cardboards) in view for the wearer of the HMD to give him a sense of proportion, and by showing the wearer points of reference in the space (figure 5).

In each of the exploration, it was noted that during the second and third design case each group did, the participants who had experience with wearing the HMD from the previous cases, used that experience to provide visual references in the model for the (new) wearer of the HMD. This awareness increased the efficiency of orientation in the scale model for (new) HMD wearers. Visualizing the perspective of the immersed participants to the other participants (e.g., via an external screen or a projection of the field of view onto the scale model) may lead to a more efficient shared understanding between participants.

Eye-contact, Gesturing and Orientation

Eye gaze, facial expressions and gesturing are key to efficient interpersonal communication in co-located settings [2,7]. Similar to the findings in [5], we found that, although the immersed participants still use gestures to communicate ideas (figure 6), covering the eyes by the HMD hinders communication between participants. This is due to the fact that the wearer of the HMD cannot visually confirm whether he is being addressed, and the other participants cannot visually confirm whether the wearer of the HMD is paying attention to the situation at hand. This situation was especially present after incorporating a 360° camera in the second exploration because the gaze direction of the participant wearing the HMD could not be deducted from the orientation of the camera. Additionally, because of the full 360° viewing angle, the wearer of the HMD would often completely turn away from the physical scale model and his/her team mates, to look at something placed 'behind' him/her (figure 7). As a result, the wearer may gesture towards something that lines up with the visual image provided to him/her through the HMD, but in reality will be pointing in a completely different direction.

Constructing a Shared Understanding

Bringing different points of view together in a shared understanding is crucial in co-creative processes [1]. To create a shared understanding, it is imperative that all participants know what the others are seeing. When one participant is wearing an HMD, this knowledge cannot be derived from eye-contact or gaze direction. The participants were therefore forced to quickly devise new ways of aligning their perspectives. We noticed that participants who were not wearing the HMD did so by asking specific questions about the viewpoint of the wearer of the HMD (P2: *"Can you see the blue car in the corner?"*) or by asking the wearer to describe the viewpoint (P9: *"What can you see? Can you see around the corner?"*). The wearer of the HMD confirmed his viewpoint to the other participants by relaying information about his field of view (P1: *"On the far left, I can see the wall, and on the far right I can see the cars."*; P8, gesturing: *"No, I can't see, there is sort of a wall in the way."*). Participants were not introduced to the immersed perspective at the beginning of the exploration, nor were they provided an on-screen view of

Figure 8: The wearer of the HMD instructs the two other participants.

the video stream that was visible in the HMD. Shared understanding was established more quickly in the second and third design cases of each session, as the participants who had worn the HMD previously could better imagine what the current wearer of the HMD was seeing.

Roles during the Collaborative Creative Process
From the observations during the exploration, and the interviews conducted afterwards, we can deduce that the roles the participants took on during the design cases greatly differed depending on their state (i.e., wearing the HMD or not wearing the HMD). The wearer of the HMD becomes a 'contractor' of sorts, verbally assessing the design solutions and concepts that the 'builders' create for him (figure 8). During the exploration, it became apparent that the contractor had the deciding vote on the concepts, deeming them suitable or unsuitable.

In the explorations, we saw the building participants often *relay reflective assessment* of their ideas to the wearer of the HMD. As P1 described: *"It did make me [...] have less of a boundary of, 'okay, this idea is bad anyway'. But you just want to figure out whether it is bad [...] by placing it and then asking [the wearer of the HMD]: what do you think?"* Each idea the builders came up with was thus discussed externally, rather than potentially being dismissed internally, giving the other participants the opportunity to use, transform and build on those ideas.

Conclusion & Future Work
Consumer-grade VR systems have advanced rapidly since the launch of the Oculus DK1 in 2012, but research into communication and interaction between immersed and non-immersed people in mixed reality settings is still fairly sparse. A system like MacroScope can help inform the development for VR tools in collaborative, co-located settings. We continue to explore the implications of the first-person perspective in physical scale models in several application areas.

We are working towards a system that allows the wearer of the HMD to move the camera autonomously, solving one of the issues that may contribute to a feeling of 'bodilessness' users experienced while wearing the headset. The current system makes use of a monoscopic camera feed, as 360° cameras that are small enough to simulate stereoscopic view at a 1:43 scale do not currently exist. A possible solution is to use two smaller cameras with a limited field of view mounted on a panning mechanism, that moves synchronously with the HMD. To stimulate constructive contribution, and increase shared understanding during the creative session, we are exploring the possibility of giving the wearer(s) of the HMD the option to switch from a bird's eye perspective when building, to a first-person perspective when assessing the design solutions and concepts. Additionally, we will construct means of communicating gaze direction and viewpoint of the immersed user to other participants in the creative session (e.g., by mapping a projection of the field of view of the immersed user in the scale model).

Acknowledgements
We gratefully acknowledge the support by the Automotive Retail Lab (hci.sbg.ac.at/ARL).

References

1. Ernesto Arias, Hal Eden, Gerhard Fischer, Andrew Gorman, and Eric Scharff. 2000. Transcending the individual human mind -- creating shared understanding through collaborative design. *ACM Transactions on Computer-Human Interaction (TOCHI)* 7, 1: 84–113.
2. Steve Benford, John Bowers, Lennart E. Fahlén, Chris Greenhalgh, and Dave Snowden. 1995. User embodiment in collaborative virtual environments. *Proceedings of the SIGCHI conference on Human factors in computing systems*, ACM Press/Addison-Wesley Publishing Co., 242–249.
3. Frank Biocca. 1997. The Cyborg's Dilemma: Progressive Embodiment in Virtual Environments [1]. *Journal of Computer-Mediated Communication* 3, 2: 0–0.
4. Eva Brandt. 2007. How tangible mock-ups support design collaboration. *Knowledge, Technology & Policy* 20, 3: 179–192.
5. Hikaru Ibayashi, Yuta Sugiura, Daisuke Sakamoto, et al. 2015. Dollhouse VR: a multi-view, multi-user collaborative design workspace with VR technology. ACM Press, 1–2.
6. S. Kasahara, S. Nagai, and J. Rekimoto. 2017. JackIn Head: Immersive Visual Telepresence System with Omnidirectional Wearable Camera. *IEEE Transactions on Visualization and Computer Graphics* 23, 3: 1222–1234.
7. Kristine Lund. 2007. The importance of gaze and gesture in interactive multimodal explanation. *Language Resources and Evaluation* 41, 3-4: 289–303.
8. Bob Martens. 1999. A Rennaissance of Architectural Endoscopy? Retrieved November 4, 2017 from http://info.tuwien.ac.at/eaea/Renaissance/rae.html
9. Bob Martens and Wolf-Michael Tschuppik. 2003. Displaying Spatially Complex Constellations. *6th EAEA-Conference Proceedings, Bratislava (Slovakia)*, SUT Publishing, 101–107.
10. Bob Martens, Wolf-Michael Tschuppik, and Alexander G. Keul. 2008. Endoscopy without Endoscopes: Alternatives for Gaining Shared-IN-sights at an Eye-level. *Special Issue AMIT (Intern. Journal of Architecture and modern Information Technologies) - April 2008 - Proceedings of the 8th EAEA Conference 2007.*
11. Andrea Mina. 2009. intimate immensity, an interior architecture. Retrieved August 30, 2016 from http://researchbank.rmit.edu.au/view/rmit:6161.
12. Mark Morris. 2006. *Models: Architecture and the Miniature*. Academy Press.
13. Albert C. Smith. 2004. *Architectural model as machine: a new view of models from antiquity to the present day*. Architectural Press, Oxford.
14. Richard Stoakley, Matthew J. Conway, and Randy Pausch. 1995. Virtual reality on a WIM: interactive worlds in miniature. *Proceedings of the SIGCHI conference on Human factors in computing systems*, ACM Press/Addison-Wesley Publishing Co., 265–272.
15. John Underkoffler and Hiroshi Ishii. 1999. Urp: a luminous-tangible workbench for urban planning and design. *Proceedings of the SIGCHI conference on Human Factors in Computing Systems*, ACM, 386–393.

SENSE-SEAT: Challenging Disruptions in Shared Workspaces Through a Sensor-Based Seat

Nils Ehrenberg
Madeira-ITI, Funchal, Portugal
nils.ehrenberg@m-iti.org

José Luís Silva
Madeira-ITI, Funchal, Portugal
Instituto Universitário de Lisboa (ISCTE-IUL), ISTAR-IUL, Lisboa, Portugal
jose.l.silva@m-iti.org

Pedro Campos
Universidade da Madeira
Madeira-ITI, Funchal, Portugal
pedro.campos@m-iti.org

TEI '18, March 18–21, 2018, Stockholm, Sweden
ACM 978-1-4503-5568-1/18/03.
https://doi.org/10.1145/3173225.3173278

Abstract
Creative industries' workers are becoming more prominent as countries move towards intellectual-based economies. Consequently, the workplace needs to be reconfigured so that creativity and productivity can be better promoted at shared workspaces. We report on a study based on diaries, interviews and probes, with 8 creative industries' professionals at a co-working space, with the goal of understanding their advantages and disadvantages, and causes for cognitive disruptions. Findings indicate that temperature, noise and coworkers' requests are the main causes for disruptions in the work processes. The insights are used to inform the design process of SENSE-SEAT, a seat with embedded sensors and tangible actuators, as a contribution to reimagining the role of tangible and embedded interaction in intelligent furniture. We are currently at a prototyping stage, with 3D prints and 3D renders and we explain the design process and outlining the early results.

Author Keywords
Tangible interaction; sensor-based furniture; interaction design;

Introduction
This paper introduces the design and prototyping of a new seat for relaxation and productivity, which fuses the digital and the analog in a futuristic piece of furniture, targeted

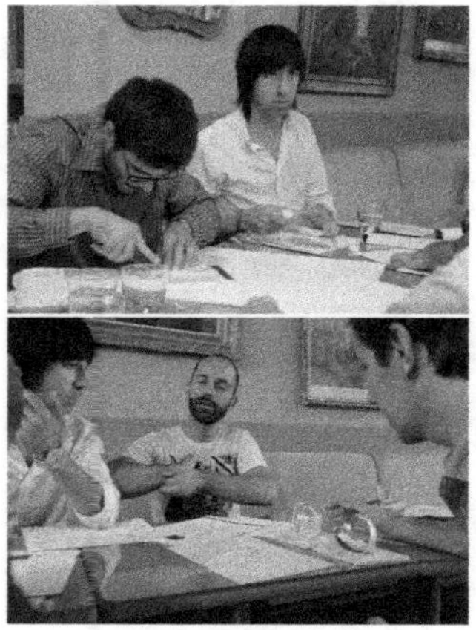

Figure 1: Prototyping in the co-creative workshop

at workspaces, in particular creative co-working spaces. This interactive seat, with embedded sensors and actuators, aims at reimagining the role of interactive technologies in the workspace of the future by challenging disruptions in shared workspaces through a multi-sensory design approach. SENSE-SEAT aims to explore the balance between social interruptions and social benefits of the creative workspace. Creative industriesâĂŹ workers are becoming more prominent as countries move towards intellectual-based economies. Consequently, the nature and essence of the workplace needs to be reconfigured so that creativity and productivity can be better promoted at these spaces. We will introduce initial interview studies, a co-creative workshop - both of which informed the design - and early renders and 3D prints of our prototype. We also present the rational for how the design has been developed and our initial findings from the prototyping efforts.

Related Work

There has been great progress in terms of gaining a better understanding of the interplay between the work environment and the creativity, or productivity, of office workers. Creativity is the production of novel and potentially useful ideas for solving problems, developing new artifacts and accomplishing tasks. In organizations, employee's creativity can be translated into innovative products, services, processes, systems, work methods, etc. [3]. Workplace creativity is usually seen as a result of a creative personality or individual skillsets [4], dependent on intrinsic motivations, such as personal interest, satisfaction, or the challenge of the work itself. However, there are also studies that suggest that other factors, such as socio-organizational (e.g., job design, team work, rewards, time pressure, and leadership) are also factors in motivating creative work [3][1][4], even in contexts such as kindergarten [2]. Typical physical environment improvements, that affect employee's creativity in a positive way, as suggested by various researchers, are: a non-crowded workspace, presence of plants, the use of inspiring colors on the walls, a new carpet in the office, more pictures and posters on the walls, windows with outside view, privacy, dim lightning, etc. [1]. Aiello and his team [1] did research on the effects of workspace crowding over employee's creativity, and they concluded that crowding could have negative effects, regardless of crowded subjects interpersonal distance preference, which showed a lower level of creativity than their non-crowded counterparts. Also, Stokols and his team [5] observed that high levels of environmental distraction, such as noise or prolonged exposure to crowded environments, were associated with less perceived support for creativity at work, and they furthermore suggested that private or non-overcrowded workspaces could have a counter effect, i.e. it could boost employee's creativity. Zelinksky [7] underlines the importance of recognizing that workspaces need to be inspiring places. Vischer's [6] research shows how people are affected by the environment on their workplace. Many factors contribute to these quite subjective productivity levels. Sometimes it is the room temperature, other the surrounding noise but even visuals play a role (e.g. if the work desk is messy and cluttered). Previous work has also explored how technological artifacts could be used to address work interruptions, e.g. Züger [8] who proposes FlowLight, a device that combines a physical traffic-light like LED with an automatic interruptibility measure based on computer interaction data, which exhibited very good results, having reduced the interruptions of participants by 46%. As well as industry work such as LiveOS[1] which collect data to optimize the workspace, and the Kokon[2] stress reduction pod. The approach of SENSE-SEAT is to provide a tool for reducing stress in

[1] https://www.hermanmiller.com/products/smart-office/smart-furnishings/live-os/

[2] https://thekokon.com

tasks that require focus, or when the work environment is too chaotic.

Challenging Disruptions in Shared Workspaces

The original idea for building SENSE-SEAT was to provide a place for relaxation, focus and creativity, something extremely difficult in today's fast-paced offices. To gain an initial understanding of these factors, we conducted a pilot study with eight participants (six men and two women) from a local co-working space, who we invited to take part in an interview, four (two men and two women) of which agreed to also submit a diary over disruptions in their work over two weeks' time. We distinguish between interruptions and disruptions because of the negative connotation which is typically inherent to interruptions - a disruption can actually be positive for the user, whereas it is never a positive thing to be interrupted. Each of the interviews took approximately 30 minutes and were conducted with two interviewers, one leading the interview and one recording, taking notes, speaking the local language and translating as needed. The study aimed to explore what they perceived as both positive and negative factors with working in a co-working space. As all participants were currently working in a co-working space, it should be expected that they feel that the positive aspects outweigh the negative. In the interview, they were asked about what they perceived as interrupting their work, but also how they interact with others in the space. In the diary that followed the interview, we compared how their perception of interruptions match up with how their documented interruptions. The comparison was done by looking at what kind of disruptions they mentioned in the different inquiries, as well as how severe they were by the description.

The participants focused on two areas, the physical and the social space. The majority of the frustrations expressed was in regards to the physical space, too warm, noisy, uncomfortable, or otherwise not suited for certain tasks, such as calls or meetings, while the spaces dedicated for meetings were not deemed sufficient due to both lack of availability and the air-quality. In the discussion of the social space, where the majority of participants expressed that the coworkers were a major positive factor, they also expressed that it was the largest distraction, though not always a negative one. Joining others for a coffee when struggling with a difficult or tedious task helped maintain focus, although some would have offices that allowed them to close the door when needed. The pilot study suggests that there is a conflict between the public and private in interactions, where the social aspects is at the same time a source of inspiration and motivation, but also interruptions.

Prototyping and Co-creative Workshop

In a second phase, we started our prototyping, working together with a team of interior designers, architects, HCI researchers, software and hardware engineers (See Figure 1). We held a 1-day co-creative workshop which employed brainstorming and product ideation techniques with 16 participants, six of them part of the SENSE-SEAT project team, the remaining were creative industries' professionals who had no previous contact or any information about the project. Figure 1 shows the overall aspect of this co-creative workshop, as well as some of the low-tech prototyping tools and materials which were used.

In this workshop, we brought together design professionals, researchers, and developers with the explicit goal of creating concepts together. We asked them to explore their view on smart furniture through a multi-sensory approach, using sketching, and low fidelity prototyping. While the type of furniture was left open-ended, a seat or bed was the general topic of discussion, rather than furniture that was acted

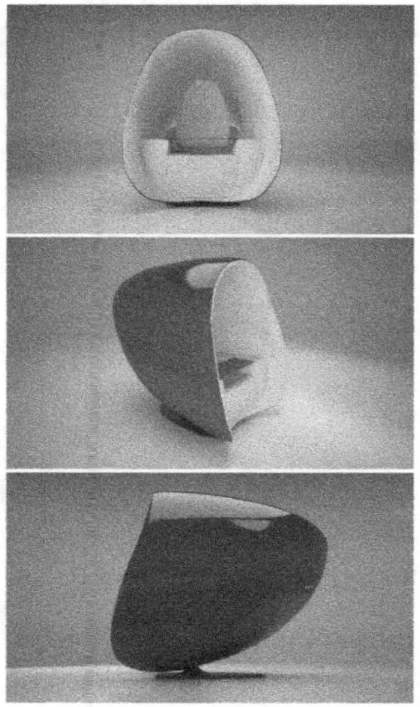

Figure 2: 3D-renders of the design

on, such as desks. The participants each set out to individually create multiple concepts that were then explored in groups where they combined their ideas, and prototyped them using low-fidelity materials such as paper, foam-core and pencils. The final concepts which were produced by the different groups of participants involved:

- a Work-life chair, a semi-open pod which can be adjusted for relaxation, lighting, as well as placed into groups for collaboration;
- an all-in-one chair that focuses on the physical comfort, such as sitting still for too long, or on resting when needed;
- a 'sleeper bed' that senses both the environment and the position of the sleeper, but also communicates with its surrounding environment.

The common theme expressed by the participants is relaxation or stress, this suggests that a future design could reflect the need to be able to relax, rather than stressing productivity or focus. Both the work-life chair and the sleeper bed are intended as parts of a larger environment, rather than as a stand-alone piece.

A multi-sensorial approach

SENSE-SEAT has the overall goal of promoting user focusing and the ability for temporary separation through the use of a pod-like chair (see Figure 2 for 3D renders). The aim is a design that allows the user to remain in the office, and approachable if necessary while also communicating that they are working on something that requires focus. Sensors and smart technology can detect and respond to the person seated, what they are working on (which software they are using, posture, or focus).

When exploring solutions for the challenges of creative workspaces, we have taken a multi-sensorial approach, in order to explore how different senses, such as hearing or sight can affect productivity. Our design approach is ground in terms of function, technology and form. While the function concerns are relatively straightforward (connected workspace, relaxing, personal), the form concerns we are addressing include achieving a contemporary, versatile, modular piece of technological furniture that can also bring a timeless, elegant comfort to the workplace. In terms of technology, a reclining seat will provide body positions values that can provide ergonomic feedback to the user. Directional sound provides relaxing soundtracks according to the user's preference, the same applies to the LED interior 'mood' lighting.

By sensing the position of the user, the SENSE-SEAT can improve the ergonomics of the chair using adjustable seating, it can also remind the user to take a break through gently adjusting the internal lighting. It helps the user manage interruptions by letting others know externally through outside LED-lighting that a person is working. The aim is to provide simple, effortless interactions.

For the final prototype, we are using pressure-sensitive conductive sheets (Velostat) sewed to woven conductive fabric with a thin conductive thread to build two squares (matrix) for the seat and its back. These allow to track the user's posture and presence. Afterwards, we added an electret microphone amplifier and an air-quality sensor. Both will be used to check if external factors such as noise and oxygen levels polluted would interfere with the productivity of users. A temperature and humidity sensor was added so that the system can check the outside air temperature and trigger a ventilation to adjust the inside temperature. In terms of actuators, we added programmable RGB-LED strips to the

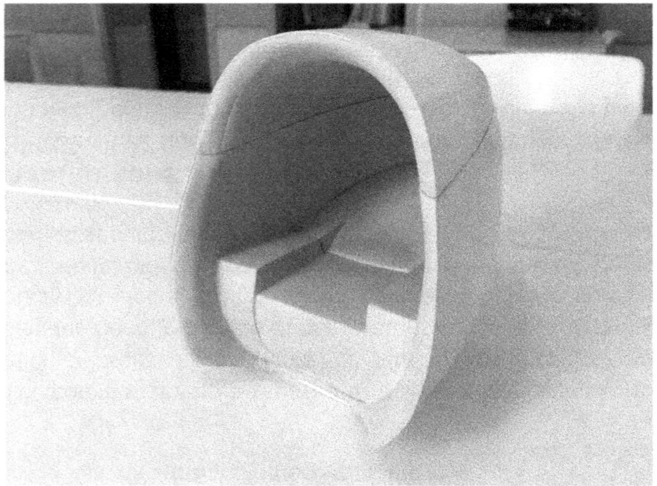

Figure 3: *SENSE-SEAT's 3D print.*

sides and back of the chair as well as a directional sound beacon just above. Overall, the final prototype will register when a user is sitting down, the ergonomic posture (if posture is correct, the pressure will be distributed along the pressure-sensitive pads), the noise, outside air temperature and air quality (this data would then be cross-checked by the team in terms of minutes against the times when a user would be writing or typing, to see if those had any influence). Finally, the ambient sound and the LED coloring will be adjusted to test what users would prefer for their two main activities (relax and work). Figure 3 exhibits a 3D print of the prototype, including a cross section that includes a 'cap'. This can be used to allow different configurations of the seat, e.g. relaxing configuration, 'Conference-call' configuration, etc.

Conclusions

SENSE-SEAT brings up several research questions which will be assessed once it becomes a fully usable product: firstly, it introduces tangible and embedded systems as an approach to resolve the challenge of the physical challenges found at creative workplaces. Secondly, how do we explore the balance between social interruptions and social benefits of the space? Interactive furniture could play a decisive role in the near future (e.g. a smart meeting table could invite other people to join an interesting discussion). Thirdly, it raises some privacy issues: what happens when the office place has a seat like this, where ergonomics data from users is being constantly gathered? In any workspace, there's a dichotomy between the company and the private. How much time and effort does the employee owe the company, what loyalty? Personal calls during work hours are often frowned upon, but if the call is important the borders soften. If the employer supplies a phone, the employee may receive work email and calls even after hours. While there is no obligation to answer, it is common for employees to respond if they feel it's urgent, or if not, the mere existence causes mental workload.

In a co-working space, there is an added dimension of what is public. There are many aspects that can be explored; for example, which spaces may be used by anyone? Where is it appropriate to chat and to have coffee? To what extent should one share advice or thoughts with someone from another company? When creating technology for Smart Workspaces, the intent of various stakeholders shape the needs and requirements for new technology. Small changes in existing designs, sometimes drastically change the nature of the product. Thus, within collaborative workspaces, there's a need to find the right balance between the need for privacy and support for social interaction. As such, collaborative work environments require spaces, furnishings and technologies that facilitate, not only for collaborative work, but also to focus work that fosters solo creativity and productivity.

Future Work

The next step of the SENSE-SEAT project is to establish the final technical requirements to build a full-scale prototype. This work will require taking the 3D-model from prints and building first a full-scale paper prototype, and after that adjust and build a seat in fiberglass. Aside from the physical prototype, we will also set the technical requirements for an initial set of sensors, and assemble the electronics. The physical seat and the initial sensors will be tested and calibrated to explore the how the pod affects work in a creative workspace.

Acknowledgements

This project was funded by Regional and European funds through IDE-RAM (ProCiência), project reference M1420-01-0247-FEDER-000001.

REFERENCES

1. John R. Aiello, Donna T. DeRisi, Yakov M. Epstein, and Robert A. Karlin. 1977. Crowding and the Role of Interpersonal Distance Preference. *Sociometry* 40, 3 (sep 1977), 271–282. DOI: http://dx.doi.org/10.2307/3033534
2. Pedro Campos and Sofia Pessanha. 2011. Designing Augmented Reality Tangible Interfaces for Kindergarten Children. Springer, Berlin, Heidelberg, 12–19. DOI: http://dx.doi.org/10.1007/978-3-642-22021-0_2
3. Jan Dul and Canan Ceylan. 2014. The Impact of a Creativity-supporting Work Environment on a Firm's Product Innovation Performance. *Journal of Product Innovation Management* 31, 6 (nov 2014), 1254–1267. DOI: http://dx.doi.org/10.1111/jpim.12149
4. Beth A. Hennessey and Teresa M. Amabile. 2010. Creativity. *Annual Review of Psychology* 61, 1 (jan 2010), 569–598. DOI: http://dx.doi.org/10.1146/annurev.psych.093008.100416
5. Daniel Stokols, Chip Clitheroe, and Mary Zmuidzinas. 2002. Qualities of Work Environments That Promote Perceived Support for Creativity. *Creativity Research Journal* 14, 2 (apr 2002), 137–147. DOI: http://dx.doi.org/10.1207/S15326934CRJ1402_1
6. Jacqueline C. Vischer. 2008. Towards an Environmental Psychology of Workspace: How People are Affected by Environments for Work. *Architectural Science Review* 51, 2 (jun 2008), 97–108. DOI: http://dx.doi.org/10.3763/asre.2008.5114
7. Marilyn Zelinsky. 2002. *The Inspired Workspace: Interior Designs for Creativity & Productivity*. Rockport Publishers. 160 pages.
8. Manuela Züger, Will Snipes, Christopher Corley, André N. Meyer, Boyang Li, Thomas Fritz, David Shepherd, Vinay Augustine, Patrick Francis, and Nicholas Kraft. 2017. Reducing Interruptions at Work. In *Proceedings of the 2017 CHI Conference on Human Factors in Computing Systems - CHI '17*. ACM Press, New York, New York, USA, 61–72. DOI: http://dx.doi.org/10.1145/3025453.3025662

EMS Painter: Co-creating Visual Art using Electrical Muscle Stimulation

Ashley Colley
Aki Leinonen
Meri-Tuulia Forsman
Jonna Häkkilä

Faculty of Art and Design
University of Lapland
Rovaniemi
Finland

firstname.lastname@ulapland.fi

Figure 1: (top to bottom) An audience member activates EMS stimulation on the artist's lower arm, causing the artist's brush stroke to deviate. Note the visual feedback provided by the LEDs attached to the contact EMS pads.

ACM ISBN 978-1-4503-5568-1/18/03.
https://doi.org/10.1145/3173225.3173279

Abstract
We present a work in progress, enabling an audience to influence a painter, through electrical muscle stimulation (EMS) to co-create visual art works. Two sets of EMS pads are positioned on the painter's arm such that stimulation pulses, triggered on a collocated tablet interface by audience members, cause deviation in the ongoing brushstroke. LEDs co-located with the EMS pads provide additional visual feedback to the audience of stimulation delivery. In an initial trial, rather than focusing on co-creation, the audience amused themselves by mischievously diverting the painter from his work.

Author Keywords
EMS; electrical muscle stimulation; co-creation; painting; visual art.

CCS Concepts
• **Human-centered computing→Human computer interaction (HCI)**

Introduction
Through participatory co-creation with an artist members of the public can gain enjoyment and deeper understanding of the creative process involved. Electric Muscle Stimulation (EMS), whilst well known as a tool for physiotherapy, offers the potential to remotely

manipulate an artist's hand movements, modifying his creation. In this work, we apply the concept to the process of painting, with a collocated audience able to influence the artist's strokes. We contribute by extending the range of applications to which the potential of adding EMS has been explored [3-8,11,13]. To the best of our understanding, we present the first work on EMS that integrates visual feedback at the location a stimulation pulse is delivered.

Related Work

Relevant prior works for our topic fall in the areas of art collaborations utilizing computational elements as a mediating element and applications of EMS, beyond those related to physiotherapy.

Collaborative Art

Prior work on utilizing HCI to enable collaborative creation of art has utilized a wide variety of approaches and formats. For example, in their *WiiArts* work Lee et al. [1] explore gesture based drawing on a digital display, with several participants simultaneously able to draw on the canvas. In Weiley and Adcock's *Lamposcope*, the drawing canvases of two remotely situated artists are superimposed, by means of picoprojection, enabling collaborative sketching [14]. Davis et al. consider co-operation between a human artist and an autonomous agent, which makes changes and additions to the artist's drawing in real-time as it is being drawn [2]. In common with Davis et al. [2], and in contrast to most prior work considering human-human art collaboration, the collaborator roles in our concept are not equal. The painter maintains primary control over the artwork, whilst the audience members add nuances, attempting to influence the ongoing work.

Electrical Muscle Stimulation

Since Tamaki et al.'s early work on the *PossessedHand* [13], Electrical Muscle Stimulation (EMS) has been applied to a variety of applications in the HCI field. For example, providing haptic feedback in virtual reality [7], guiding pedestrian navigation [11] and remotely communicating emotional states [5]. An overview of the potential of EMS for actuating human bodies is given by Duente et al. [3], whilst a further work, led by the same author, explores the potential granularity of movement that the approach may yield [4].
Interpersonal kinesthetic communication using EMS has been demonstrated in Nishida & Suzuki's *BioSync* [10]. Guiding drawing via EMS is demonstrated in Lopes et al.'s Muscle Plotter, where the user's hand is manipulated to draw mathematical charts on paper [6]. Perhaps the closest works to ours are the *conductive ensemble* where the audience manipulate band musicians via connected smartphone apps that trigger EMS pads [8] and Stelarc's *PingBody* [12]. Differing from these works, we explore other artistic media and add the additional audience feedback of LED lighting, when EMS pulses are applied.

EMS Artist

Concept and System Design

To explore the concept of enabling an audience to influence a painter through EMS, we implemented a prototype system (Figure 1).

The system was built around a commercial EMS massage device which was connected to 2 sets of electrode pads positioned on the artist's arm. An Arduino microcontroller controlled switch was connected between the high voltage EMS device and the pad sets. Thus, with the EMS source continuously

Figure 2: An audience member guiding the artist's brushstrokes by pressing a button on a connected tablet to activate one of the sets of EMS pads worn by the artist.

on, controlled pulses could be sent to either set of pads. The setup connected to an audience interface via Bluetooth, which consisted of an Android tablet mounted on a plinth. The tablet's interface contained two buttons, which when pressed caused a short pulse (600 ms) of EMS to be delivered to the pad associated with each button (Figure 2). To provide additional feedback to the audience, LED strips were attached on top of the electrode pads and were illuminated when an EMS pulse was delivered (Figure 1).

Public Trial

To evaluate the EMS painter concept, we conducted a trial in the lobby area of [removed for review]. The location was adjacent to a cafeteria and had many passersby. For the trial, we set up an easel with paper and provided our volunteer artist with a brush and paints. The audience interface tablet was mounted on a plinth to the side of the artist (Figure 2). Before beginning the trial the EMS electrode pads were attached to the artist's arms and their position was adjusted, such that an EMS pulse created a large movement in the painter's arm. The painter was instructed to paint abstract figures, such as lines and circles, such that deviations induced by the audience interaction would be clearly visible.

Figure 3: Artist with the finished painting. After a pilot trial, an apron to protect the artist's clothes from pain splashes was an essential addition.

Observations

In general, people passing by our trial were fascinated by the concept, and it immediately drew a small crowd. Whilst the majority were content to be passive observers, those that chose to interact with the system became fully engaged with it, seeking to find the limits of their influence on the artist and painting. With this initial evaluation, there was not yet any feeling of co-creation between the participants and artist. Rather, for some participants, the possibility to mischievously divert the painter from his work caused great amusement.

Discussion & Conclusions

Similarly to other EMS augmented performance pieces such as Lopes' *Conductive Ensemble* [8], the EMS influenced artist must, at least in part, play a role such that the overall audience experience is engaging and entertaining for the audience. Here, the interaction between the painter and co-creator is broader than just through the EMS channel, with also verbal and visual communication taking place. This of course depends in part on the details of the setup environment, alternatives with the painter remotely connected via a video only link would restrict some elements of interaction.

The influence of the visualization of EMS shocks through situated LEDs is of particular interest. We believe this to be a key element in establishing the co-creator's feeling of control over the painter. Without this visualization element, the association between EMS activation button presses on the tablet and resulting movements of the artist's arm and brush appeared somewhat weak. Further from the point of view of an interactive piece performed in front of an audience, the shock visualization adds greatly to the performance. It would be interesting to explore the addition of such visual clues in other formats of EMS performance e.g. [8]. Whilst building our setup we considered the addition of audible feedback for EMS shock delivery, however we considered this would be too distractive from the main output mechanism of muscle movement.

Whilst our study setup raised some parallels with Milgam's obedience test [9], from the artist's demeanor during our trial, it is clear to the audience members that they are not inflicting pain through their button presses. However, from observations it was apparent that many of the audience found inflicting disruption on the artist to be a fun experience. In this respect, our work raises the question - what would be required to create a serious collaboration between the parties?

Limitations

We present our work as a work in progress, highlighting the novelty of the collaborative artistic use case, rather than aiming to present state-of-the-art in EMS systems.

Future Work

As the next steps of our work, we aim to explore the degree of deft with which it is possible to control the painter's brushstrokes via EMS. We will also further explore the participant interface, towards the use of tangible input mechanisms. With a more general scope, we plan to study the impact of in situ visualization of EMS pad activation, such as the LEDs in our setup, when applied to previously presented EMS use cases.

Acknowledgements

This research has been supported by a grant from Tekes – the Finnish Funding Agency for Innovation as part of 'The Naked Approach – Nordic perspective to gadget-free hyperconnected environments' programme. We also thank Pedro Lopes for his help with the EMS equipment.

References

1. Hyun-Jean Lee, Hyungsin Kim, Gaurav Gupta, and Ali Mazalek. 2008. WiiArts: creating collaborative art experience with WiiRemote interaction. In *Proc. TEI '08*. ACM, 33-36. http://dx.doi.org/10.1145/1347390.1347400
2. Nicholas Davis, Chih-PIn Hsiao, Kunwar Yashraj Singh, Lisa Li, Sanat Moningi, and Brian Magerko. 2015. Drawing Apprentice: An Enactive Co-Creative Agent for Artistic Collaboration. In *Proc. C&C '15.* ACM, 185-186. http://dx.doi.org/10.1145/2757226.2764555
3. Tim Duente, Stefan Schneegass, and Max Pfeiffer. 2017. EMS in HCI: challenges and opportunities in actuating human bodies. In *Proc. MobileHCI '17.* ACM, Article 67, 4 pages. https://doi.org/10.1145/3098279.3119920
4. Tim Duente, Max Pfeiffer, and Michael Rohs. 2017. Zap++: a 20-channel electrical muscle stimulation system for fine-grained wearable force feedback. In *Proc. MobileHCI '17*. ACM, Article 1, 13 pages. https://doi.org/10.1145/3098279.3098546
5. Mariam Hassib, Max Pfeiffer, Stefan Schneegass, Michael Rohs, and Florian Alt. 2017. Emotion Actuator: Embodied Emotional Feedback through Electroencephalography and Electrical Muscle Stimulation. In *Proc. CHI '17.* ACM, 6133-6146. https://doi.org/10.1145/3025453.3025953
6. Pedro Lopes, Doǎa Yüksel, François Guimbretière, and Patrick Baudisch. 2016. Muscle-plotter: An Interactive System based on Electrical Muscle Stimulation that Produces Spatial Output. In *Proc. UIST '16.* ACM, 207-217. https://doi.org/10.1145/2984511.2984530
7. Pedro Lopes, Sijing You, Lung-Pan Cheng, Sebastian Marwecki, and Patrick Baudisch. 2017. Providing Haptics to Walls & Heavy Objects in Virtual Reality by Means of Electrical Muscle Stimulation. In *Proc. CHI '17.* ACM, 1471-1482. https://doi.org/10.1145/3025453.3025600
8. Pedro Lopes, 2015. Conductive Ensemble: http://plopes.org/project/conductive-ensemble-art-piece/ Last accessed 1 November 2017.
9. Stanley Milgram, 1963. "Behavioral Study of Obedience". Journal of Abnormal and Social Psychology. 67 (4): 371–
8. PMID 14049516. doi:10.1037/h0040525
10. Jun Nishida and Kenji Suzuki. 2017. bioSync: A Paired Wearable Device for Blending Kinesthetic Experience. In Proc. CHI '17. ACM, 3316-3327. https://doi.org/10.1145/3025453.3025829
11. Max Pfeiffer, Tim Dünte, Stefan Schneegass, Florian Alt, and Michael Rohs. 2015. Cruise Control for Pedestrians: Controlling Walking Direction using Electrical Muscle Stimulation. In *Proc. CHI '15.* ACM, 2505-2514. https://doi.org/10.1145/2702123.2702190
12. Stelarc Ping Body http://www.artelectronicmedia.com/document/stelarc-ping-body Last accessed 1 November 2017.
13. Emi Tamaki, Takashi Miyaki, and Jun Rekimoto. 2011. PossessedHand: techniques for controlling human hands using electrical muscles stimuli. In *Proc. CHI '11.* ACM, 543-552. https://doi.org/10.1145/1978942.1979018
14. Viveka Weiley and Matt Adcock. 2013. Drawing in the lamposcope. In *Proc. C&C '13.* ACM, 382-383. http://dx.doi.org/10.1145/2466627.2481213

Mobile, Exercise-agnostic, Sensor-based Serious Games for Physical Rehabilitation at Home

Ana Vasconcelos
Fraunhofer Portugal AICOS
Rua Alfredo Allen 455/461
4200-135 Porto, Portugal
ana.vasconcelos@fraunhofer.pt

Catarina Correia
Fraunhofer Portugal AICOS
Rua Alfredo Allen 455/461
4200-135 Porto, Portugal
catarina.correira@fraunhofer.pt

Francisco Nunes
Fraunhofer Portugal AICOS
Rua Alfredo Allen 455/461
4200-135 Porto, Portugal
francisco.nunes@fraunhofer.pt

Alberto Carvalho
Fraunhofer Portugal AICOS
Rua Alfredo Allen 455/461
4200-135 Porto, Portugal
alberto.carvalho@fraunhofer.pt

TEI'18, March 1821, 2018, Stockholm, Sweden.

ACM ISBN 978-1-4503-5568-1/18/03.
https://doi.org/10.1145/3173225.3173280

Abstract

Serious games can improve the physical rehabilitation of patients with different conditions. By monitoring exercises and offering feedback, serious games promote the correct execution of exercises outside the clinic. Nevertheless, existing serious games are limited to specific exercises, which reduces their practical impact. This paper describes the design of three exercise-agnostic games, that can be used for a multitude of rehabilitation scenarios. The developed games are displayed on a smartphone and are controlled by a wearable device, containing inertial and electromyography sensors. Results from a preliminary evaluation with 10 users are discussed, together with plans for future work.

CCS Concepts

•**Software and its engineering** → **Interactive games;**
•**Human-centered computing** → *Mobile devices;*
•**Applied computing** → *Consumer health;*

Author Keywords

Serious games, Physical rehabilitation, EMG, IMU, Mobile health, Health

Introduction

Physical rehabilitation commonly takes place in clinics, where physiotherapists supervise the correct execution of exercises [3]. Patients are also advised to continue exercising at home, for a speedier recovery. However, performing exercises at home can be challenging, because exercises must be carefully executed. At home, the physiotherapist cannot monitor exercises and offer feedback, thus there is the need for simple, portable, and easy-to-use technological solutions that extend physiotherapy programs to the home.

Serious games[1] have been used in a variety of rehabilitation settings, including: balance and mobility [5, 4, 9], limb functionality [6, 10], back and neck afflictions [11], respiratory rehabilitation [12], and posture training [2]. These serious games used different sensors for evaluating the execution of the physiotherapy exercises, including Microsoft Kinect [2, 11], the user's smartphone [4, 12], or inertial and optical sensors combined [9].

Some serious games have been evaluated in preliminary field trials showing good potential to increase exercise adherence and performance [8]. However, in general, serious games tend to be limited to well-defined scenarios. In particular, the literature lacks examples of serious games that can be used to train a variety of exercises, as is often the case in physiotherapy rehabilitation. Apart from demonstration purposes, it is hard to make an impact if serious games are tied to specific exercises. This was the main purpose of developing a mobile, exercise-agnostic platform for the *Physio@Home* project.

This paper proposes a solution based on a smartphone and a wearable device containing an electromyography

[1]Serious games consist of game systems for purposes other than solely entertainment [7], in this case, physical rehabilitation at home. Serious games are increasingly common and have been used to support different purposes in healthcare, including health education, physical activity, self-management, and physiotherapy [8].

Figure 1: The goal of the 'Gates Game' is to open the gates and let the circle go through them. Contracting the muscle makes the gates open, while relaxing it enables the ball to move forward.

(EMG) sensor, and an inertial measurement unit (IMU) sensor. The sensors track the execution of the movements, and the smartphone displays intuitive games that guide the user through the execution of the exercises (see screenshot of the Gates Game in Figure 1). The metrics collected during the games are stored and made available to the physiotherapist through a web portal, guaranteeing a second layer of quality assessment.

By being exercise-agnostic, the developed serious games can adapt to a multitude of exercises, which can improve the adoption of serious games for physical rehabilitation at home, beyond demonstration purposes.

Game Design

Context

The target audience for the developed serious games is very broad since it includes anyone who is undergoing physical rehabilitation sessions. This means that the game should be appropriate for children, teenagers, stroke patients, athletes with any kind of neuromuscular injury, or older people. In addition, each one of these individuals will be in a very particular exercise regimen, highly dependent of their goals.

The developed games needed as well to be abstract enough to support different exercises. Physiotherapists planned to use the *Physio@Home* project platform to prescribe more than one hundred different exercises, and developing a game for single one of them would be impossible in the available time. Thus, we decided to design games that adapt to multiple exercises.

Developed solution
The proposed solution is a game module that supports the execution of rehabilitation exercises, by presenting them in a more dynamic and entertaining "package". So far, games were designed to be controlled by an EMG sensor that is connected via Bluetooth to the smartphone running the game. Metrics extracted from the sensor's signal control the game. If the values that are being measured are above the threshold defined by the physiotherapist in the clinic, or, in other words, if the player is contracting the muscle appropriately, they will be able to move the object and advance in the game. With values bellow the threshold, the player will be relaxing the muscle and the object won't move. There are also moments in the game in which the player is expected to relax the muscle, and the game promotes that activity.

The developed games are modular and designed to integrate well with the work of physiotherapists. These professionals can easily define the number of series, number of repetitions, relaxation time, and contraction time, in their platform at the clinic, knowing that the games of the patient will adapt to the characteristics that they defined[2]. At the end of each game, therapists receive all the session data, to accompany their patient's progress and, if necessary, adapt their exercise prescription.

The game environment reflects itself the modular design. It is also for that reason that it is shaped with geometric and simple forms that challenge the user to move and interact with it, in order to unlock paths or complete puzzles. Such a minimal environment was designed to be used by a diverse range of players, for a wide array of exercises, and also due to the constraints of the mobile form factor.

Bridges Game
The goal of this game is to make the circle move to the right, until it reaches its final end point. The game has several rectangular platforms that are raised when the user contracts the required muscle (see bars of Figure 2 at the bottom of the screenshot). When the platform reaches the top, the circle element advances. After contracting the muscle to raise the platform, the user needs to rest for some seconds, while the circle advances to the right.

The player needs to respect the contraction and rest times, as otherwise the game does not proceed. If the user stops contracting the muscle, for example, the platform starts falling, to remember the user to contract. Similarly, if the user does not respect relaxation times, the circle stops advancing. This way, the system ensures that the exercises are performed correctly.

The number of platforms are defined by the therapist, when setting the number of series and repetitions.

[2]The platform for physiotherapists is called *physioplux* and was developed by Plux, Portugal.

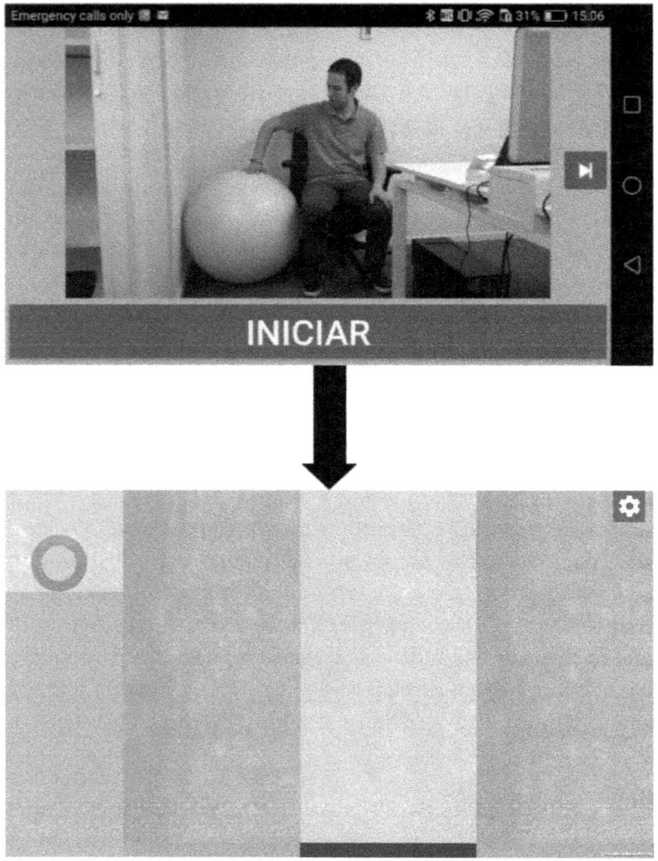

Figure 2: The top screenshot shows the video the player sees before starting an exercise session. On the bottom the 'Bridges Game' is displayed. The goal of this game is to raise the bridges, so that the circle can advance.

Figure 3: In the 'Labyrinth Game' the player contracts the correct muscles to make the circle advance through the maze.

Labyrinth Game
In this game the user guides a circle throughout a labyrinth path. Contraction advances the circle on the right direction to follow the labyrinth path. If the user relaxes the muscle before reaching a checkpoint, the circle will move backwards. The checkpoints are semi circles where the circle fits and stops its motion. The checkpoint will only release the circle once the user relaxes the muscle for a period of time. This guarantees that the player respects the contraction and relaxation times defined by the therapist.

The number of obstacles is also defined by the therapists in their platform, when setting the series and repetitions.

Gates Game
In this game the player needs to open gates in order to advance and reach the final destination. The execution of a contraction will open each gate. After the gate is opened the circle will automatically move to the next one.

In order to maintain the mandatory relaxation phase of the game, there is a numerical countdown before each gate that will only progress if the user keeps the muscle relaxed.

Similar to the previous games, the player needs to respect the contraction and relaxation times, as otherwise the game does not advance.

Moreover, the game always presents a singular experience, as the five different gates are randomly distributed, according to the number of series and repetitions defined by the therapist beforehand.

Preliminary evaluation

As a first trial test, before testing the solution with actual rehabilitation patients, a testing session was organized with a convenience sample of participants. The goal was to evaluate their first impression while playing the games and identify any possible usability issues. Emphasis was given to understanding: i) if the mechanics of the games was easy to comprehend; ii) if the instructions were clear; and iii) if the users could read all the on-screen elements.

Methods

Ten people, 5 women and 5 men, with an average age of 33 years were recruited for this test. No specific recruitment criteria were used; it was assumed that anyone is a potential physiotherapy patient. Therefore, participants were randomly selected among our colleagues. Six researchers, two designers, and two administrative professionals were involved in the tests. Only one participant was undergoing physiotherapy treatments and another one had done so in the past. Participants were asked to complete the three different games, after watching a video of an exercise (a different exercise for each game). Participants were asked to place a Jawbone[3] bracelet on their wrist and were told that the games were controlled by the movement of their wrist.

The game itself was controlled by one of the facilitators, who had a mobile application to emulate the sensor's response, and thus trigger the elements to move. The chosen exercises involved ample arm movements, to enable the facilitator to easily identify them. The reason for using the Wizard-of-Oz method [1], was due to the limited availability of the EMG sensors to use as part of the tests. Moreover, since the main focus of this evaluation were the developed games and the user interaction promoted by them, it was enough to mock the detection of the movements, as long as the facilitators enforced the game mechanics through their use of the app (i.e., contraction and relaxation times).

Results

The developed games were successfull. Participants understood how to play with little to no help. Participants were extremely concentrated while playing the game and there were no clear signs of annoyance. The errors while performing the exercises (e.g. not knowing if there was a number of repetitions vs number of seconds) can be explained by participants inexperience. In a real context, participants would have already performed similar exercises at the clinic, together with a therapist, therefore these errors would be easily removed in a real setting.

Still, there is room for improvements. The first aspect is the lack of consistency between the game elements the player controls in a given game (raising bar, moving ball, barrier gates), and in the countdown made during different

[3] Jawbone is an activity monitor. Refer to: https://jawbone.com/ for further information.

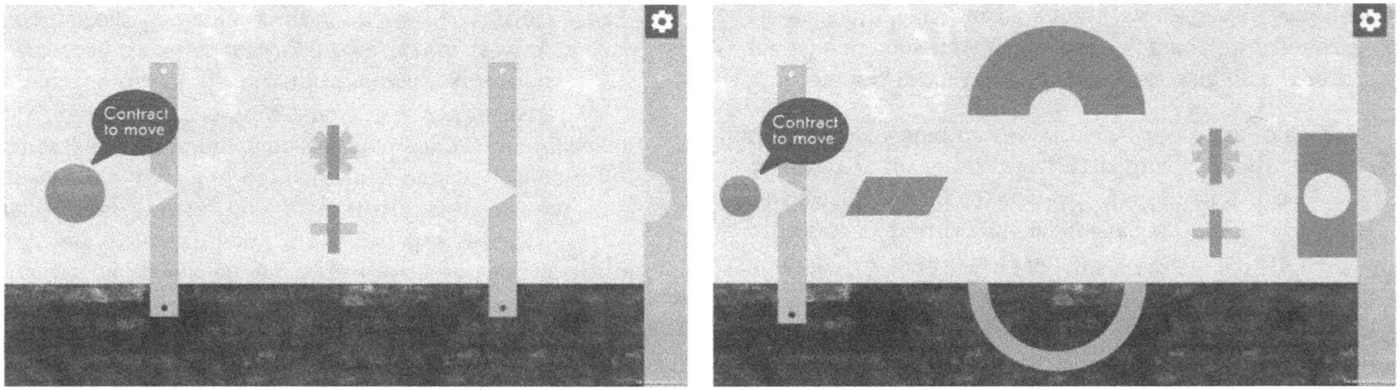

Figure 4: Gates Game with 3 repetitions/gates (left) and 5 repetitions/gates (right) - the number of repetitions the players needs to perform is defined by the physiotherapist.

games with different purposes (game 1 - contraction time, game 2 - relaxation time) or the lack of a countdown in the third game. It was also mentioned that gravity was an inconsistent element. Sound was pointed out as the missing component that could bring a new dimension to the games, even increasing their usability level.

The Wizard-of-Oz method was also a success as no user noticed that they were not controlling the game directly. While we performed the tests with participants with high technological literacy, and in some cases, even development background with inertial measurement units, none of them questioned how they could be moving the game with a proprietary wristband as the Jawbone.

Conclusions and Future Work

Three exercise-agnostic mobile games were developed and initially evaluated with potential users. The success of the evaluation suggests that exercise-agnostic games may cater for multiple exercises used in physical rehabilitation.

Future work will focus on developing games and organizing feasibility pilots with patients and physiotherapists, in both clinic and home scenarios.

Acknowledgements

We would like to thank the volunteers who participated in the usability tests. The serious games would not be possible without the work of the developer João Madureira. Moreover, we thank the interesting discussions we had with Plux, who are our partners in the project.

We acknowledge the financial support obtained from the project *Physio@Home: Extending Physiotherapy Programs to Peoples Home*, co-funded by Portugal 2020, framed under the COMPETE 2020 (Operational Program Competitiveness and Internationalization) and European Regional Development Fund (ERDF) from European Union (EU), with operation code POCI-01-0247-FEDER-017863.

REFERENCES

1. Steven Dow, Blair MacIntyre, Jaemin Lee, Christopher Oezbek, Jay David Bolter, and Maribeth Gandy. 2005. Wizard of Oz Support Throughout an Iterative Design Process. *IEEE Pervasive Computing* 4, 4 (Oct. 2005), 18–26. DOI: http://dx.doi.org/10.1109/MPRV.2005.93
2. Brook Galna, Dan Jackson, Guy Schofield, Roisin McNaney, Mary Webster, Gillian Barry, Dadirayi Mhiripiri, Madeline Balaam, Patrick Olivier, and Lynn Rochester. 2014. Retraining function in people with Parkinson's disease using the Microsoft kinect: game design and pilot testing. *Journal of NeuroEngineering and Rehabilitation* 11, 1 (14 Apr 2014), 60. DOI: http://dx.doi.org/10.1186/1743-0003-11-60
3. S.J. Geffen. 2003. Rehabilitation principles for treating chronic musculoskeletal injuries. *Med J Aust* 178, 5 (2003), 238–242.
4. Maureen Kerwin, Francisco Nunes, and Paula Alexandra Silva. 2012. Dance! Don't Fall - preventing falls and promoting exercise at home. *Studies in health technology and informatics* 177 (2012), 254259. http://europepmc.org/abstract/MED/22942064
5. K. Laver, S. George, J. Ratcliffe, S. Quinn, C. Whitehead, O. Davies, and M. Crotty. 2011. Use of an interactive video gaming program compared with conventional physiotherapy for hospitalised older adults: a feasibility trial. *Disability and Rehabilitation* 34, 21 (2011), 1802–1808.
6. Gwyn N. Lewis, Claire Woods, Juliet A. Rosie, and Kathryn M. Mcpherson. 2011. Virtual reality games for rehabilitation of people with stroke: perspectives from the users. *Disability and Rehabilitation: Assistive Technology* 6, 5 (2011), 453–463. DOI: http://dx.doi.org/10.3109/17483107.2011.574310
7. Simon McCallum. 2012. Gamification and serious games for personalized health. *Stud Health Technol Inform* 177 (2012), 85–96.
8. Brian A. Primack, Mary V. Carroll, Megan McNamara, Mary Lou Klem, Brandy King, Michael Rich, Chun W. Chan, and Smita Nayak. 2012. Role of Video Games in Improving Health-Related Outcomes: A Systematic Review. *American Journal of Preventive Medicine* 42, 6 (2012), 630 – 638. DOI: http://dx.doi.org/https://doi.org/10.1016/j.amepre.2012.02.023
9. A. Santos, V. Guimares, N. Matos, J. Cevada, C. Ferreira, and I. Sousa. 2015. Multi-sensor exercise-based interactive games for fall prevention and rehabilitation. In *9th International Conference on Pervasive Computing Technologies for Healthcare (PervasiveHealth)*. 65–71.
10. Devinder Kaur Ajit Singh, Nor Azlin Mohd Nordin, Noor Azah Abd Aziz, Beng Kooi Lim, and Li Ching Soh. 2013. Effects of substituting a portion of standard physiotherapy time with virtual reality games among community-dwelling stroke survivors. *BMC Neurology* 13, 1 (13 Dec 2013), 199. DOI: http://dx.doi.org/10.1186/1471-2377-13-199

11. Jan David Smeddinck, Marc Herrlich, and Rainer Malaka. 2015. Exergames for Physiotherapy and Rehabilitation: A Medium-term Situated Study of Motivational Aspects and Impact on Functional Reach. In *Proceedings of the 33rd Annual ACM Conference on Human Factors in Computing Systems (CHI '15)*. ACM, New York, NY, USA, 4143–4146. DOI:http://dx.doi.org/10.1145/2702123.2702598

12. Gabriele Spina, Guannan Huang, Anouk Vaes, Martijn Spruit, and Oliver Amft. 2013. COPDTrainer: A Smartphone-based Motion Rehabilitation Training System with Real-time Acoustic Feedback. In *Proceedings of the 2013 ACM International Joint Conference on Pervasive and Ubiquitous Computing (UbiComp '13)*. ACM, New York, NY, USA, 597–606. DOI:http://dx.doi.org/10.1145/2493432.2493454

Feeling Virtual Worlds: An Exploration into Coupling Virtual and Kinaesthetic Experiences

Joey Campbell
University of Bristol
joey@joeycampbell.ie

Trevor Hogan
Cork Institute of Technology
Trevor.Hogan@cit.ie

Mike Fraser
University of Bristol
fraser@cs.bris.ac.uk

ACM ISBN 978-1-4503-5568-1/18/03
https://doi.org/10.1145/3173225.3173281

Abstract

In this paper we describe an exploratory study that incorporates the design, implementation and study of a system that utilises virtual reality, tangible interaction and force feedback[1]. The approach we take is to design a VR system that incorporates a moveable tangible interface (wheelchair), which overlaps seamlessly with a 3d counterpart in the virtual world. The user interacts with the virtual environment by pushing the physical wheelchair, which simultaneously controls the virtual avatar. In the virtual world we place objects that once collided with trigger force feedback by stopping the physical wheelchair. In this paper we discuss the design rationale and technical implementation and follow by describing the next phase of this work in progress.

[1] To view demo video see https://vimeo.com/216675981

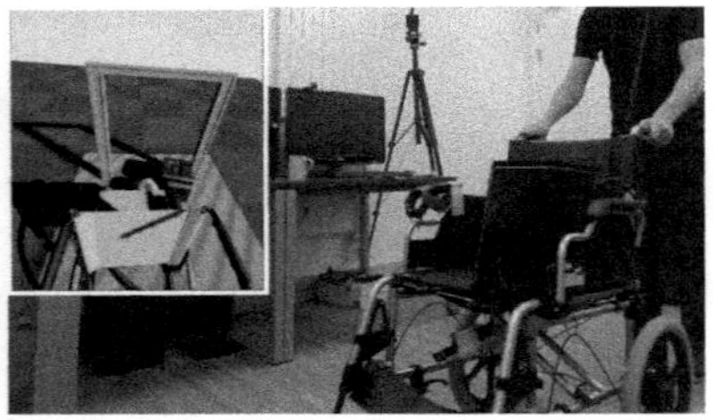

Figure 1. Feeling virtual collisions in the real world. Feeling the real world interface in the virtual world.

Author Keywords
Visual-Kinaesthetic Experience; Embodied Interactions; Mixed Reality; TUI; Passive Haptics; Force Feedback; Resistance.

Introduction
VR researchers are seeking to add extra 'reality' into their immersive experiences by taking a more holistic approach. Projects are now emerging which delve beyond the exclusive use of visual and aural modalities to achieve a more embodied interactive experience [15] and heightened stimulation [11].

While it is clear that research is needed to explore the benefits of combining VR and TUI systems, there are now many tools and technologies available that can facilitate research across the two disciplines by providing tactile feedback in VR systems[2]. In this work-in-progress we present the design and implementation of a hybrid TUI/VR system. Furthermore, we present initial findings from a user study conducted to evaluate people's experience of the system. This research is based on the belief that a fully embodied kinaesthetic experience will enhance people's sense of presence in the virtual environment.

Related work
The research we present here transcends a number of different domains within HCI research, including immersive environments [3], TUI [4] and haptic feedback [13]. To date, much research has been conducted that explores aspects of responsive tactile hardware in an attempt to add enhanced realism into tangible interfaces (cf. [10]) and interactive simulations (cf. [7]). Recently, however, we are seeing increased attention from the research community that moves beyond utilising haptics solely dedicated to real world conventions and instead incorporating their usage into more immersive scenarios (cf. [17]).

Insko has shown that the use of passive haptics in his experiments [8] significantly enhances Virtual Environments. In our research however, while we have tightly *coupled* the real and virtual interface to maximise presence we have also *decoupled* human haptics and haptic technology. This has been achieved through implementing adaptive/dynamic controls in the virtual world over resistance in the real world.
Moving beyond passive haptics, Gu and colleagues utilise active passive force feedback via a glove based exoskeleton in order to provide the user with a sense of realistic grasp gestures whilst interacting in a virtual environment [5]. Mehra and colleagues also integrate hand-based interactions for use with VR headsets but focus on touch sensitivity [12]. In a similar vein, Benko and colleagues found that high-fidelity shape output rendered by mechanically-actuated hand-held controllers led to an increased accuracy of VR interaction. The authors of this paper concluded their study emphasising '*a clear need for haptic solutions that offer more than simple buzzing and rumbling to the hand*' [1].

Israr et al's Surround Haptics project [9] is an example of integrating full body haptics by means of tactile illusions. In line with this, an aspect of Mixed Reality research has recently begun to place more emphasis on kinaesthetic aspects, such an example can be seen in Tennent et al's work, which explored the integration of passive haptics in the form of a playground swing [14].

[2] For further reading see https://tinyurl.com/vr-peripherals

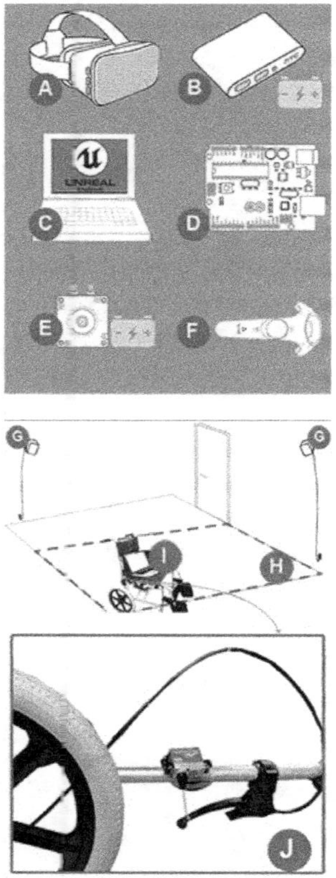

Figure 2. Embodied Tangible-Virtual Interface system design. (A) VR HMD, (B) Battery operated link box, (C) Laptop running Unreal Game Engine, (D) Arduino, (E) Battery powered high torque servo, (F) Vive controller, (G) Vive tracking station, (H) Pre-calibrated space, (I) Wheelchair and laptop, (J) Close up of mounted servo attached to brake lever.

The use of a physical wheelchair in a virtual space is not entirely unique. Harrison et al. combined wheelchairs, haptics and virtual space in order to facilitate the design of more accessible buildings [6]. Comparisons can also be seen in the choice of interface used in our project and that of Byagowi et al's VRNChair [2] however while their research focuses on assessing kinetosis (motion sickness) our research has focused on integrating virtual collisions as well as the decoupling of human and machine haptics.

Design Rationale

The primary design aim of our study was to create a tangible-virtual interface that facilitates a heightened sense of realism when undertaking physical activity within an immersive environment. We sought to achieve this by designing a system that would seamlessly integrate a tangible interface and virtual counterpart. In doing so, we also envisioned utilising haptic feedback as part of the virtual world by means of passive haptics, and correspondingly, immersive traits would be integrated into the physical control via simulated resistance based on in game collisions. In the end, we developed a tightly coupled tangible mobile interface which featured passive haptics as well as force feedback. The avatars position was controlled by its physical counterpart and resistance based on collisions encountered within the immersive environment were replicated in the real world using wheel based friction (see fig.1).

Implementation

The first aspect of the implementation involved the integration of real time variable and automated resistance. In the initial stages we conducted numerous experiments using components such as pneumatics, actuators, stepper motors, electromagnetics and robotics, however, we encountered numerous issues with latency, which resulted in these being impractical to implement. In the end, we chose to utilise friction based dynamic resistance; by using a high torque servo to pull a bicycle brake lever. This allowed us to use predefined levels of resistance, which could be generated consistently on the wheel. In the current version the wheelchairs resistance can be dynamically adjusted in order to simulate real-world collisions with the virtual obstacles in our scene. Colliding with the sphere model triggers 30% of the maximum brake power where as the cube model (which is more rigid) triggers a brake power of 70%. When both objects are collided with simultaneously or when the wheelchair collides with the doorframe the brake power is set to 100%. We should point out that while the brake friction does simulate the collision force it does not simulate the friction force between the moving objects and the ground in the virtual world. This is an aspect which we are currently looking at implementing.

The next phase involved synchronising the location and position of a virtual model and real-world object. For this we used a single HTC Vive hand controller (see fig. 2F) to enable real time tracking in a pre-calibrated space (see fig.2 G & H). We developed and tested a prototype using an office chair and a virtual representation of this chair. In the Unreal Game Engine[2] a motion controller tag was placed onto the centre of the virtual chair, in addition the physical vive controller was secured in place on the matching location of the physical chair. When tested, the user could move the physical chair and view the corresponding virtual chair move in real time without latency, generating a tightly coupled interface.

The overall look and feel of the TUI evolved during the implementation process and changes were made as result of the array of technologies explored while attempting to fulfil our design criteria. Initial explorations led us to consider the use of a cube, based on its simplistic form, however, the necessity to integrate wheels into the final physical design influenced us to use a more common wheel mounted object. Thus, we chose to use a wheelchair, as it offered a high level of affordance, as well as offering the user to engage tactically through the simple combination of reach, touch, grasp and push. The servos were then mounted on servo brackets bolted to the aluminium tubing (see fig. 2J). The servos (see fig. 2E) were connected to an Arduino (see fig. 2D), which was connected to an Alienware laptop (see fig. 2C) located on the seat of the wheelchair (see fig. 2I). Another key aspect of this criteria was to allow the tangible interface to be as mobile as its virtual equivalent. We achieved this by powering the Vives linkbox using a 12V battery (see fig. 2B) and substituting a desktop with a Laptop which would be mounted on the tangible interface. Using the UE4Duino plugin[3] within the Unreal Engine[4] the servos could be variably adjusted based on in game collisions allowing incremental brake friction to be applied in real time.

Evaluation

The main purpose of this evaluation was to investigate the usability and user experience of our system. In particular, we sought to explore whether the dual-tangibility and embodied interactive experience heightened their sense of virtual presence. For this study we developed a virtual environment comprising of a doorframe, a football and a safe, which had been created with the Unreal Engine and combined with our tangible/virtual interface (see Fig. 1). We then designed a task that involved the participant using the interface to push the safe and the ball through the doorframe. When each model successfully passed through the doorframe it would trigger a corresponding audio sound. In total, 12 participants took part in the study (aged 20 to 42, 6 male).

Based on our user study we noted that there were no tracking issues and that the real time positioning of the physical and 3D models remained synchronised without any latency. The untethered setup and smooth alignment of real and virtual had provided each user with a sense of autonomous navigation as we had hoped for. All users successfully completed the task with 10 of the 12 users continuing to engage with and explore the immersive world even when both the ball and safe had been pushed out of the scene. While most of the technical implementation had been successful, there was one outstanding issue, which we had let go unnoticed. One participant remarked 'its a bit of a pain to have to lift it back'; he was referring to having to pull or jerk the wheelchair back a few centimetres from the virtual object they had collided with. The issue was that the collision event remained triggered in the game engine for as long as the avatar and object were in the same proximity. This is something that will need to be rectified in the near future.

Synchronicity

The decision to use a wheelchair metaphor during the implementation phase proved successful with all users instinctively initiating contact through the reach, touch, grasp combination we had envisaged, however,

[3] https://github.com/RVillani/UE4Duino

[4] https://www.unrealengine.com

interaction with the environment wasn't immediate. While some pushed/pulled the physical wheelchair several centimetres, in a curious manner, to ensure that it controlled its virtual counterpart, all users chose to explore the quality of the interfaces coupling before fully engaging with the task. When engaging with the task participants typically remarked on aesthetics of the virtual world, in particular, how the VR world represented, in great detail the real world. These aspects seem to show that accurate and detailed passive haptics in our experiment had narrowed the gap between the tangible and virtual by bringing the user physically and psychologically closer to the controlling mechanism.

Virtual Calibration

We noticed that upon completion of inspecting the interface seven of the twelve users had lifted their headsets temporarily. When probed as to why they were doing so they responded that they wanted to get an idea of how much space they had in the physical world to move in. We highlight this as the participants had already been informed that a virtual 'chaperone' would become visible if they were in danger of colliding with any physical objects beyond the 'play zone'. But in referencing the real world it was as though they wanted to correlate the real and physical environment before they committed to embodied avatar interaction. We believe that the unique aspect of the embodied immersive mobile navigation was a contributing factor to the reluctance shown by these seven participants.

Convincing Experience

One participant was so surprised at the initial collision with the virtual soccer ball that he removed the VR HMD and commented while doing so "Did you put a ball there, am I hitting something?". In the demo there is currently no resistance generated when the wheelchair collides with the virtual frame yet the same user (when they accidentally bumped into the physical metal leg of an office table) commented, "Ok, is that your desk that's being hit or is it just me hitting the frame". In a way this felt like a compliment seeing as the user in question was unable to decipher between simulated and regular collisions. Again, the user wanted to take off the VR HMD when this collision happened, almost as if they didn't trust the researchers feedback and seeing as this was a new type of intermodal experience they needed to remove the virtual layer in order to decipher the sensation. Force feedback based on virtual collisions such as these facilitated convincing scenarios realising our hypothesis that a fully embodied kinaesthetic experience would enhance people's sense of presence in the virtual environment.

Conclusion and Future Work

We designed this system to generate a heightened sense of realism when undertaking physical activity within an immersive environment by tightly coupling virtual and kinaesthetic experiences. Users can engage in an immersive environment and simultaneously appreciate the tactile qualities of virtual objects and interactions through a combination of passive haptics and automated resistance. A preliminary exploration of the system shows a link between presence and mobile embodied immersive interaction as well as the potential effectiveness of a dually tangible mixed reality.

Our future line of enquiry will focus on exploring the relationship between this type of tangible-virtual interface and physical exertion through the collection and analysis of physiological data. We intend to use electromyography to gather comparable user data with the aim of measuring body compensation when dynamic resistance is integrated into a physically navigated immersive environment. We envisage that decoupling human and machine haptics when undertaking physical activity, in an embodied tangible-virtual environment, may facilitate increased physical output. We also intend to provide real-time feedback of the users exertion levels on the immersive heads up display and examine whether using such physiological data impacts on the users physical output. As well as gathering this quantitative data we would also like to gather further information by means of a presence questionnaire [16].

References

1. Hrvoje Benko, Christian Holz, Mike Sinclair, and Eyal Ofek. 2016. NormalTouch and TextureTouch. *Proceedings of the 29th Annual Symposium on User Interface Software and Technology - UIST 16*
2. Ahmad Byagowi, Danyal Mohaddes, and Zahra Moussavi. 2014. Design and application of a novel virtual reality navigational technology (VRNchair). *Journal of Experimental Neuroscience* 8, 1: 7–14.
3. Lung-Pan Cheng, Thijs Roumen, Hannes Rantzsch, Sven Köhler, Patrick Schmidt, Robert Kovacs, Johannes Jasper, Jonas Kemper, and Patrick Baudisch. 2015. TurkDeck: Physical Virtual Reality Based on People. In Proceedings of the 28th Annual ACM Symposium on User Interface Software & Technology (UIST '15). ACM, New York, NY, USA, 417-426
4. Sean Follmer, Daniel Leithinger, Alex Olwal, Akimitsu Hogge, and Hiroshi Ishii. 2013. inFORM. *Proceedings of the 26th annual ACM symposium on User interface software and technology - UIST 13* (2013).
5. Xiaochi Gu, Yifei Zhang, Weize Sun, Yuanzhe Bian, Dao Zhou, and Per Ola Kristensson. 2016. Dexmo. *Proceedings of the 2016 CHI Conference on Human Factors in Computing Systems - CHI 16* (2016).
6. Colin S. Harrison, Mike Grant, and Bernard A. Conway. 2004. Haptic Interfaces for Wheelchair Navigation in the Built Environment. Presence: Teleoperators and Virtual Environments 13, 5: 520–534.
7. Milan Ikits and J.Dean Brederson. 2005. The Visual Haptic Workbench. *Visualization Handbook* (2005), 431–447.
8. Brent Edward Insko. 2001. Passive Haptics Significantly Enhances Virtual Environments. Ph.D. Dissertation. The University of North Carolina at Chapel Hill. Advisor(s) Frederick P. Brooks, Jr. AAI3007820.
9. Ali Israr et al. 2011. Surround Haptics. *ACM SIGGRAPH 2011 Emerging Technologies on - SIGGRAPH 11* (2011).
10. Jinha Lee, Rehmi Post, and Hiroshi Ishii. 2011. ZeroN. *Proceedings of the 24th annual ACM symposium on User interface software and technology - UIST 11* (2011).
11. Pedro Lopes, Sijing You, Lung-Pan Cheng, Sebastian Marwecki, and Patrick Baudisch. 2017. Providing Haptics to Walls & Heavy Objects in Virtual Reality by Means of Electrical Muscle Stimulation. Proceedings of the 2017 CHI Conference on Human Factors in Computing Systems - CHI '17: 1471–1482.
12. Ravish Mehra, Christoph Hohnerlein, David Perek, Elia Gatti, Riccardo Desalvo, and Sean Keller. 2016. HapticWave. *ACM SIGGRAPH 2016 Emerging Technol`ogies on - SIGGRAPH 16* (2016).
13. Rajinder Sodhi, Ivan Poupyrev, Matthew Glisson, and Ali Israr. 2013. Aireal. *ACM Transactions on Graphics* 32, 4 (January 2013), 1.

14. Paul Tennent, Joe Marshall, Brendan Walker, Patrick Brundell, and Steve Benford. 2017. The Challenges of Visual-Kinaesthetic Experience. *Proceedings of the 2017 Conference on Designing Interactive Systems - DIS 17* (2017).
15. Joseph Volpe. 2016. A virtual reality game that's good for you and scientist-approved. (July 2016). Retrieved July 27, 2017 from https://www.engadget.com/2016/04/28/a-virtual-reality-game-thats-good-for-you-and-scientist-approve/
16. Bob G. Witmer and Michael J. Singer. 1998. Measuring Presence in Virtual Environments: A Presence Questionnaire. Presence: Teleoper. Virtual Environ. 7, 3 (June 1998), 225-240.
17. Mounia Ziat, Taylor Rolison, Andrew Shirtz, Daniel Wilbern, and Carrie Anne Balcer. 2014. Enhancing virtual immersion through tactile feedback. In Proc.of UIST14 Adjunct (2014). ACM. 65-66.

Your Body of Water: A Display that Visualizes Aesthetic Heart Rate Data from a 3D Camera

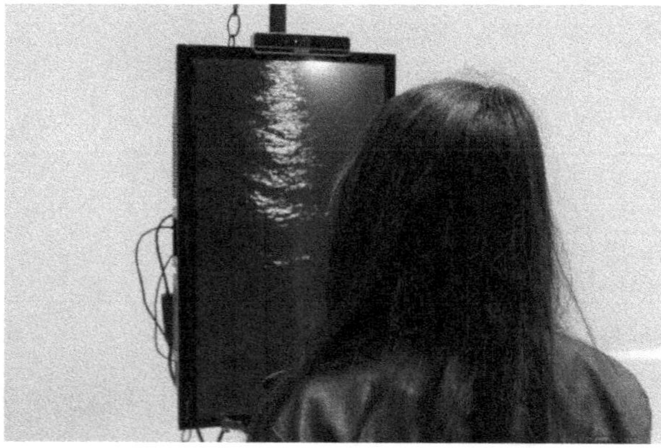

Figure 1: *Your Body of Water* aesthetically visualizes a visitor's heart rate from a 3D camera.

Lee Jones
Carleton University
Ottawa, Canada
Lee.Jones@carleton.ca

Paula Gardner
McMaster University
Hamilton, Canada
gardnerp@mcmaster.ca

Nick Puckett
OCAD University
Toronto, Canada
NPuckett@faculty.ocadu.ca

TEI '18, March 18–21, 2018, Stockholm, Sweden

ACM ISBN 978-1-4503-5568-1/18/03.
https://doi.org/10.1145/3173225.3173284

Abstract

We present the design and implementation of *Your Body of Water*, a display that wirelessly gathers heart rate data using a 3D camera and then visualizes the viewer's heart rate as water. As heart rate goes up the water gets livelier (with larger and faster waves) and as heart rate goes down the water gets calmer. The purpose of the display is to use aesthetic biofeedback data to help participants reflect on their felt bodily experience. The device went through system critique using somaesthetic appreciation design heuristics, and we describe the design themes that arose from those critiques.

Author Keywords

Biofeedback; Heart Rate; Pulse; Somaesthetics; Heuristic Evaluation; Display; Visualization; Information Visualization; Embodiment; Aesthetics

ACM Classification Keywords

- Human-centered computing~User studies

Introduction

In this study, we explored whether wireless heart rate sensors could encourage embodied somaesthetic introspection (Figure 1). By reading heart rate wirelessly we hoped to encourage participants to reflect

Somaesthetics: an interdisciplinary field with roots in philosophy that combines the soma (the living body) with aesthetics (our sensory perception)[2].

Somaesthetic Appreciation Design Characteristics[3]

Subtle Guidance: The design's ability to subtly and slowly direct a participant's attention inward.

Making Space: The design's ability to create both temporal and physical space within a participant's day for self-reflection.

Intimate Correspondence: How closely the interaction follows how the participant is feeling and what they are experiencing.

Articulation: The design's ability to give participants a way to articulate how they are feeling, as well as to make sense of their experience.

on how they are feeling, rather than focusing on their heart rate. This artwork display uses water as an aesthetic and calming way of visualizing real-time biofeedback data and aims to show how heart rate can help participants reflect on their experience and felt bodily states. The artwork aims to respond to how the user is feeling, but at the same time gives room for participant's subjective interpretation and to reflect on their own experience.

Theoretical Grounding: Design for Somaesthetic Experience

In this research project, we used somaesthetic philosophy to design a display that responds to heart rate and aims to help viewers get more in touch with their body. The main premise of somaesthetics is that we can train our body to become more aware of itself. Somaesthetics explores how we can improve and cultivate our senses through a better understanding of our sensory appreciation (*aesthesis*) [2].

This project is inspired by a psychophysical model of the body where our thoughts influence our body and focuses on how heart rate is connected to our emotional response. For example, much research has been done on how heart rate increases when humans feel stressed or excited, and how it lowers when one is calm. Slovak et al [10] have also shown that participants interpret heart rate as signaling emotional state.

In their paper "Somaesthetic design", Hook et al [2] discuss how they translated somaesthetic theory into practice. The main goal of somaesthetics in design is to create devices and systems that encourage participants to look inward and focus on their own bodily sensations rather than external stimuli [2]. In terms of how to design for somaesthetic experience, they developed somaesthetic appreciation design characteristics[3].

The four characteristics of somaesthetic appreciation design include ***subtle guidance*** in how they encourage bodily inquiry, ***making space*** by shutting out the outer world and encouraging inward focus, ***intimate correspondence*** in how the feedback follows the rhythms of the body, and ***articulation*** in how the design helps participants understand, learn, and become more aware of their bodies and lived experience[3].

Contributions

This paper contributes a heuristic evaluation, using somaesthetic appreciation design characteristics and system critiques, of a display that aesthetically visualizes heart rate data from a 3D camera. This paper is the first to evaluate an aesthetic display that gathers heart rate with a 3D camera.

Related Work: Aesthetic Heart Rate Artworks

Sun et al. [11] looked at the different ways that heart rate biofeedback can be visualized: graphical, illustrative, artistic, and ambient. They found that the metaphors in artistic and ambient displays helped viewers make a connection between themselves and what they saw, and created a "deeper impression".

Previous research in the area of aesthetic heart rate biofeedback has included projects such as CubeLife[1] Cardiomorphologies[6], LivingSurface [14], Heart Calligraphy [13], Metaphone[9], and StressTree[15]. Each of these projects mapped heart rate to aesthetic

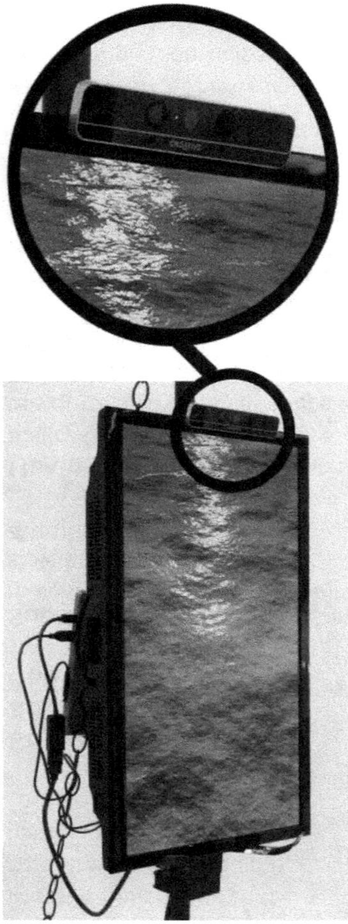

Figure 2: The Intel RealSense camera sitting on top of the display.

visuals. These projects have demonstrated the importance of real-time feedback, accurate sensors, room for reflection and environment to aestheticized heart rate visualizations. Among the biofeedback artworks that visualize aesthetic heart rate data, most of them gather pulse from the hand, and the Arduino pulse sensor[7], which attaches to an individual's index finger. During each of these projects participants were tethered to the device and in doing so the design itself signaled that it was reading heart rate.

Prototype: ***Your Body of Water***

For this display, we wanted to evaluate the somaesthetic appreciation design characteristics of a display that gathers heart rate wirelessly with a 3D camera. During initial prototyping with the Intel RealSense 3D camera[4], we found that the device could gather an accurate heart rate reading while participants were moving, when they were turned to the side, and even when their face was partially covered. Gathering heart rate wirelessly is part of the Intel RealSense software development kit (SDK). For this project, we placed the camera on top of a large display that visualized the data (Figure 2).

The water simulation was purchased on Unity[12], and we programmed the measures of wave height, wave speed, wind speed, and foam to all gradually increase and decrease as heart rate increased or decreased (Figure 3).

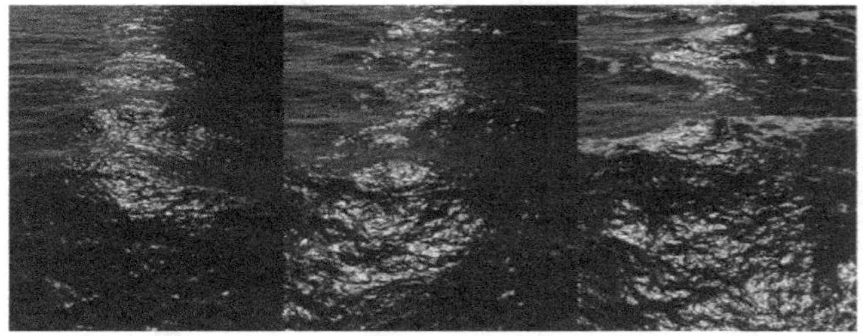

Figure 3: Changes in the water as heart rate goes up.

Method: Heuristic Evaluation with Somaesthetic Design Characteristics

For the evaluation of interactive artworks, Hook et al[3] recommend using "system critics". Similar to how art criticism has a culture of experts doing art critiques, the system critique would involve interaction designers who can evaluate a system using their background knowledge. These types of system critiques have been useful for discovering and identifying problematic areas of an interaction as well as for discussing possibilities for improvements to the work[5]. As a result, we used system critique using somaesthetic appreciation design characteristics.

To implement this evaluation method, we had individual critique sessions with 10 graduate students studying interaction design. For each of these sessions, a participant got to use the system for as long as they liked while being asked for their informed critique of the work based on the somaesthetic design characteristics. The first author gave each participant a sheet with the definitions of each of the characteristics, and briefed the participant on each one. Participants wrote down and discussed their critiques and the first author also took notes.

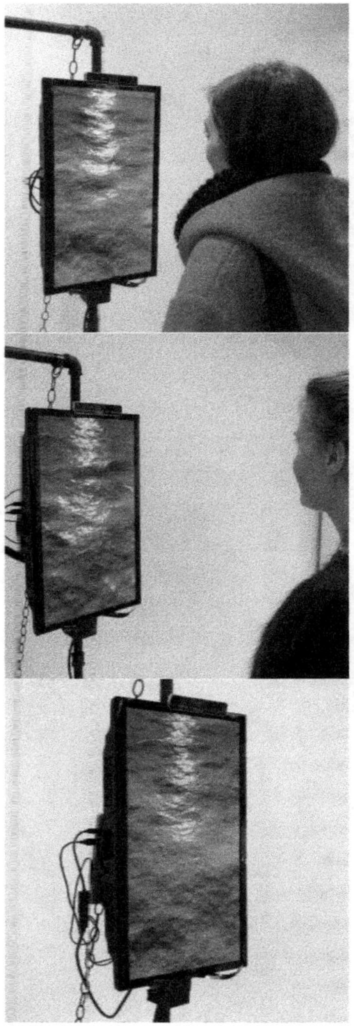

Figure 4: *Your Body of Water* display set up.

Results

Subtle Guidance: Subtle guidance is the design's ability to subtly direct a participant's attention inward. During the system critique sessions participants noted that the interaction was subtle, but at times too subtle. Participants stated that at times they decided to explore the work by jumping up and down, or thinking about uncomfortable thoughts, and at these times expected the water to be really stormy, but instead only noticed subtle changes in the water.

Making space: Making space is the design's ability to create both temporal and physical space within a participant's day for self-reflection. Every system critic involved said that this characteristic was met. Some said that the soothing imagery acted as a reminder to relax and reflect, and some mentioned that by simply having an object like this in one's home they would be more inclined to reflect on how they are feeling (Figure 4). Seven system critics mentioned locations either within the home, or in offices, where it would be useful to place an object like this to encourage reflection.

Intimate Correspondence: Intimate correspondence is how closely the interaction follows how the participant is feeling and what they are experiencing. This is where the accuracy of the sensors and how the responding visualizations aesthetically represent the data becomes important. In the critique sessions, the characteristic of intimate correspondence was only met to a certain extent. As mentioned in the critique of subtle guidance, the visualization changes were thought to be too subtle. A few participants explored how they could raise their heart rate, but the changes in the water did not seem to reflect their exertion or stress level. All participants discussed the display in relation to how they were feeling, suggesting that the display encouraged them to reflect on emotional and physical state rather than heart rate alone.

Participants also wanted an explicit sign as to whether the device was reading them or not. Since the water was always moving, participants had some difficulty differentiating when the device was not reading them and when the water was calm (a low heart rate).

Articulation: Somaesthetic articulation means to create responses that support bodily reflection. It gives participants a way to articulate how they are feeling, as well as to make sense of their experience. All participants found the choice of water to be an effective visual for thinking about how they were feeling. Participants described the water as soothing and an apt metaphor for states of feeling. Participants understood how water moves, and the concept of it getting livelier or stormier as heart rate went up was a metaphor that made sense.

Discussion

Using somaesthetic design appreciation characteristics in system critiques was an effective way of finding problematic areas in the interaction as well as for discussions on how the display could be improved. The main issues that impeded somaesthetic reflection included the subtlety of the water and the inability to differentiate when the system was picking up (or reading) a participant's heart rate.

One of the major challenges was designing the display so that the changes in the state were both subtle and recognizable. Based on the system critiques the visualization was programmed to show more dramatic changes in wave height, wave speed, wind speed and amount of foam.

The second issue with the display demonstrates some of the new challenges that arise when using wireless sensors. Participant wanted to know when they were being "read" by the wireless camera. At times participants found it difficult to recognize when the camera was reading them and when they went out of range. As a result, system critics suggested using an on/off visualization in the water so that participants could immediately recognize when they were being read by the sensor. Several system critics suggested changing the environmental lighting from night to day when a participant was in range (Figure 5). This is similar to how a computer goes into sleep mode when not being used.

Another issue this brings up is gathering data and consent. When someone puts on a pulse sensor there is implicit consent that by putting it on they know it will gather their heart rate. With wireless sensors there isn't this opportunity. Researchers looking at large displays, such as Rodriguez et al [8], have begun to look at how users can signal consent with large displays, but research is still in early stages. As a result, for this project the program didn't save any data, but this is an important area for future research.

Finally, participants suggested several locations that they thought would be useful environments to have moments of reflection. These included waiting rooms, lobbies, and when you enter or exit your home. Our next steps include *in situ* testing of the work in these locations.

Figure 5: The display signaling when it is reading a participant by going from night to day

In the Wild Evaluation and Exhibition

After the system critique sessions, suggested alterations were made to the display, it received a final group critique, and was shown to the public in a one-week exhibit. These iterative changes mentioned in the discussion, (more dramatic changes in the waves and a sleep mode when the sensor is not reading a participant) were both well received during the critique and week-long exhibition.

Conclusion

We presented the design and initial heuristic evaluation of an ambient display that aesthetically visualized heart rate data as gathered from a wireless sensor. Though participants focused on how they were feeling and their bodily state rather than heart rate alone, our heuristic evaluation stressed the importance of showing when a participant was being read by the sensor, as well as other issues of consent when using wireless sensors.

References

[1] Edmonds, E., Everitt, D., Macaulay, M. and Turner, G. 2004. On physiological computing with an application in interactive art. *Interacting with Computers*. 16, 5 (2004), 897–915.

[2] Höök, Kristina, Ståhl, A., Jonsson, M., Mercurio, J., Karlsson, A. and Johnson, and E.-C.B. 2015. Cover story: Somaesthetic design. *interactions*. 22, 4 (2015), 26–33.

[3] Höök, K., Jonsson, M., Ståhl, A. and Mercurio, J. 2016. Somaesthetic Appreciation Design. *Proceedings of the 2016 CHI Conference on Human Factors in Computing Systems* (2016).

[4] Intel RealSense Technology: 2017. *https://software.intel.com/en-us/realsense/*.

[5] Mankoff, J., Dey, A.K., Hsieh, G., Kientz, J., Lederer, S. and Ames, M. 2003. Heuristic Evaluation of Ambient Displays. *Proceedings of the SIGCHI conference on Human factors in computing systems* (2003), 169–176.

[6] Muller, L., Turner, G., Khut, G. and Edmonds, E. 2006. Creating Affective Visualisations for a Physiologically Interactive Artwork. *IEEE Tenth International Conference on Information Visualization* (2006).

[7] Pulse Sensor: *https://pulsesensor.com/*. Accessed: 2017-01-01.

[8] Rodriguez, I.B. and Marquardt, N. 2017. Gesture Elicitation Study on How to Opt-in & Opt-out from Interactions with Public Displays. *ISS'17 ACM International Conference on Interactive Surfaces and Spaces* (2017), 32–41.

[9] Šimbelis, V., Lundström, A., Höök, K., Solsona, J. and Lewandowski, V. 2014. Metaphone: Machine Aesthetics Meets Interaction Design. *Proceedings of the SIGCHI Conference on Human Factors in Computing Systems*. (2014), 1–10.

[10] Slovák, P., Janssen, J. and Fitzpatrick, G. 2012. Understanding Heart Rate Sharing : Towards Unpacking Physiosocial Space. *Proceedings of the SIGCHI Conference on Human Factors in Computing Systems* (2012), 859–868.

[11] Sun, Z., Cao, N. and Ma, X. 2017. Attention , Comprehension , Execution : Effects of Different Designs of Biofeedback Display. *Proceedings of the 2017 CHI Conference Extended Abstracts on Human Factors in Computing Systems* (2017), 2132–2139.

[12] Unity: *https://unity3d.com/*. Accessed: 2017-01-01.

[13] Yu, B., Arents, R., Hu, J., Funk, M. and Feijs, L. 2016. Heart Calligraphy : an Abstract Portrait Inside the Body. *Proceedings of the TEI'16: Tenth International Conference on Tangible, Embedded, and Embodied Interaction* (2016), 675–680.

[14] Yu, B., Bongers, N., Asseldonk, A. Van, Hu, J., Funk, M. and Feijs, L. 2016. LivingSurface : Biofeedback through Shape-changing Display. *Proceedings of the TEI'16: Tenth International Conference on Tangible, Embedded, and Embodied Interactio* (2016), 168–175.

[15] Yu, B., Funk, M., Hu, J. and Feijs, L. 2017. StressTree : a Metaphorical Visualization for Biofeedback- assisted Stress Management. *Proceedings of the 2017 Conference on Designing Interactive Systems* (2017), 333–337.

Charged Utopia VR: Exploring Embodied Sense-making in the Virtual Space

Rosa van der Veen
RISE Interactive and
Eindhoven University of
Technology
rosa.v.d.veen@ri.se

Jeroen Peeters
RISE Interactive
Umeå, Sweden
jeroen.peeters@ri.se

Ambra Trotto
RISE Interactive and
Umeå School of Architecture
Umeå, Sweden
ambra.trotto@ri.se

TEI '18, March 18–21, 2018, Stockholm, Sweden

ACM ISBN 978-1-4503-5568-1/18/03.
https://doi.org/10.1145/3173225.3173286

Abstract
This paper reports on preliminary results of a design research project that explores how spaces in virtual reality may be designed to build on qualities of embodied sensemaking. The project forms a basis for the exploration of an ethical dimension to interactions in virtual reality. This publication focuses on identifying qualities of embodied sense-making in an existing physical space, the interactive exhibition *Charged Utopia.* These qualities are transposed into a virtual interactive space. The translation of the qualities is done through the three main themes: Physical Movement, Resistance and Ambiguity. We present the design research process to describe how these themes were identified and transposed. We conclude with reflections that sketch ways in which we might capitalise on the opportunities offered by a virtual space, while respecting human skills in embodied sensemaking.

Author Keywords
Virtual Reality; Embodied Interaction; Ethics

ACM Classification Keywords
- Human-centered computing~Virtual reality
- Human-centered computing~Interaction design

Introduction

Similar to many others within the TEI community, our constructive design research [5] builds on theories of Ecological Psychology [4], American Pragmatism [2] and Phenomenology [7]. These foundations share the notion of embodiment, asserting that our perception is born from action: we make sense of the world by acting in it [3]. To design interactions based on a notion of embodiment means to design for active perception, using our 'being in the world' to allow meaning to arise. Such a stance emphasises the role of our body and physical engagement in sensemaking. However, the physicality of our world is not as straightforward as it once was. Virtual layers are becoming more intertwined with our physical world. The boundary between technologies and the physical world around us becomes increasingly vague [6]. As a result, reality is in many cases not only interpreted as merely the physical world around us, but consists out of physical and virtual aspects. So the question that arises here is: if embodiment in the physical world is the way we make sense of the world around us, how can we make sense of this emerging virtual world around us? In this article, we present the design research project *Charged Utopia VR* (Virtual Reality), where we take embodiment as a means to design meaningful interactions within a virtual space. Our aim is to explore the possibilities of designing for embodiment in a virtual space by building on qualities of a physical space.

Related Work and Motivation

Several scholarly efforts have studied our perception of the world through VR technology. Our main focus here is not on the VR technology itself, but on the possible impact of such technologies on society as a whole. Ethics and morality start to play a role in this discussion. As Madary and Metzinger write: *"VR technology will eventually change not only our general image of humanity but also our understanding of deeply entrenched notions, such as 'conscious experience,' 'selfhood,' 'authenticity,' or 'realness'"* [6]. When looking at this from a phenomenological perspective, we see that this constitutes the idea that we cannot place ourselves outside the virtual layers that we have created for ourselves, since the perception of ourselves is situated in the point of view from which we perceive objects in the world [7]. This new perception of ourselves influences our perception of the world, and thus influences our visions, actions and decisions. This phenomena was clearly illustrated in the study of Peck, Seinfield, Aglioti and Slater [8], where implicit racial bias was found to be fluctuating when VR technologies were used to *"generate an illusion of body ownership through first person perspective of a virtual body that substitutes their own body"*. Madary and Metzinger describe this phenomena as a *"complex convolution, a nested form of information flow in which the biological mind and its technological niche influence each other in ways we are just beginning to understand"* [6]. Their focus lays strongly on the importance of thinking about ethics in VR when looking at the consequences it has on our perceptions: both of ourselves and the world around us. They have created a first list of ethical concerns that might arise while using and doing research about VR, as well as a list of concrete recommendations that might overcome these risks [6]. In the *Charged Utopia VR* project we have started to explore these concerns from a design perspective. We approach this by building on an existing physical interactive design: the exhibition *Charged Utopia*, which leveraged embodied interactions to address ethical concerns.

Figure 1 Several visitors interacting with one of the installations of the Charged Utopia exhibition.

Context

The interactive exhibition *Charged Utopia* [9, video: 14] was an event designed and curated by RISE Interactive on the islands of Norrbyskär in Northern Sweden during August of 2016. The exhibition consisted of a series of interactive installations (See Figure 1) on the islands that told stories of the islands' past as the home of a large sawmill and worker community, in the late 1800's and the first half of the 1900's. These installations were designed to use the past as a lense for the present and vice versa: visitors were confronted with both the history of the islands, as well as issues of a more contemporary nature, such as the European refugee crisis. Through embodied interactions with the installations, visitors were triggered to form personal reflections regarding complex societal topics such as immigration. In the exhibition, embodiment was key in order to elicit engagement and trigger personal reflections [11].

In the project presented here, *Charged Utopia VR*, we have started to explore how we may transpose the aspects of morality, ethics and decision making that were embedded in the exhibition's physical interactive design into a new, virtual experience based on VR.

Approach

The approach for the *Charged Utopia VR* project is based on constructive design research, summarised by Koskinen et al. as *"...research that imagines and builds new things and describes and explains these constructions"* [5]. In this approach, design explorations, iterative prototyping and reflections on (intermediate) results form the core of the research methodology. For *Charged Utopia VR,* this meant that a practical approach was used to start ideating and creating interactive VR experiences. Through the development of various interactive prototypes, and through iterations and reflections on these prototypes, characteristics and qualities of embodied sensemaking were refined and transposed into VR.

Design Research Process

The design explorations took place in both the virtual space and the physical space. Alternating explorations between these different spaces made it possible to compare experiences and see how the inherently different qualities of both spaces - the physical and virtual space - may be used to create experiences where ambiguity, reflection, nuance and difficult questions could be addressed effectively.By reflecting on the physical installations of the *Charged Utopia* exhibition and by prototyping new experiences, we defined qualities that were found to elicit embodied sensemaking on issues with ethical dimensions. These qualities were translated into three different themes: *physical movement*, *ambiguity* and *resistance*. These themes were used as a starting point for the design of virtual interactions. Different prototypes were created to explore how interactions in a virtual space, based on these themes, could elicit a similar experience to their counter parts in the exhibition's physical space. We wish to emphasise here that our effort to transpose the physical interactions in the exhibition towards interactions in the virtual space should not be considered as a one to one, direct translation. This translation was done in terms of qualities, rather than the concrete actions and environment that were created in the physical interactive design, since the virtual world and the physical world, inherently possesses different possibilities of interaction.

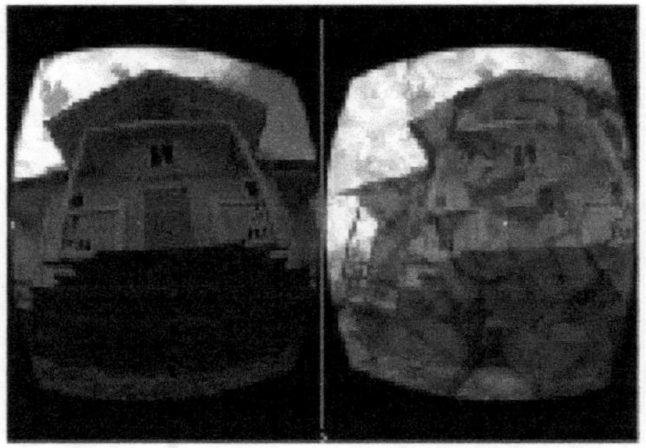

Figure 2 *This screenshot from the Charged Utopia VR experience shows an example of different images being presented to the*

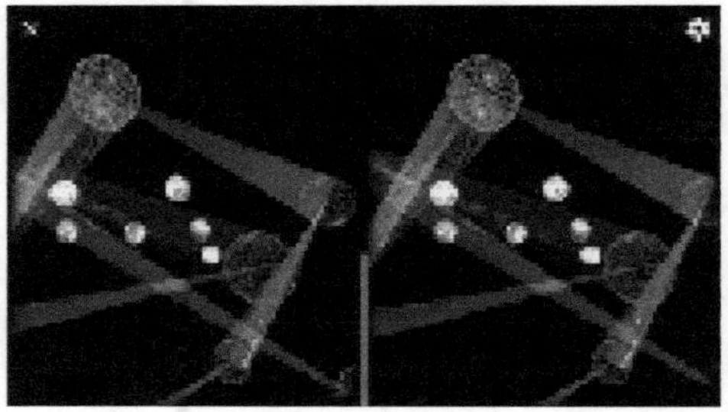

Figure 3 *This screenshot from the Charged Utopia VR experience shows a virtual space with several interconnected elements. The user is able to create a new composition by changing their position, yet experiences resistance through their interconnectedness.*

Technical Description

The game development platform *Unity* [12] was used to create virtual interactions and spaces, and eventually to bring together all the different interactions into a coherent full experience. The hardware that was used to test and experience the created software was a Google Cardboard headset and a smartphone running Android. This choice had been made to make this experience available for anyone interested in VR by removing dependency on more advanced hardware.

Charged Utopia VR

The final design, *Charged Utopia VR* (Please refer to [13] for a video impression of the design), is a virtual reality experience that questions the users identity. What it is to have roots and what it is to long for something better? Upon starting the experience, users are transported to the islands of Norrbyskär. Here, they can move around a map of the island to enter six locations, where they can listen to poems and are shown images that ambiguously address both the past of the island as well as its current state. From a focus on the past and local, the experience gradually moves to the present and global, again through images and poems. To conclude their virtual journey, users are able to craft a desired future - a Utopia - by creating and giving meaning to a composition of interconnected virtual objects in the space around them. This space is captured and printed for the user at the end of the experience, allowing them to take a physical reminder with them into the real world.

Interaction

Charged Utopia VR is a personal and unique experience that is designed to create space for ambiguity, interpretation and reflection. This experience elicits users to create their own reality by affording interpretation and decision making. For example, upon entering one of the six locations on the virtual map of the island, a different image is presented for the user's left and right eyes (one of the past, one of the present). The dominance of the user's eyes (being more dependent the right or left eye) determine what is seen, creating a unique setting for everybody (See Figure 2). Looking through both eyes, the images are overlaid and difficult to discern from one another. While, if the user closes one eye, he or she can focus on one part of the story. Users's are thus able to alter what they see in the space around them, and create their own experience. In the final part of the experience, the user is given the opportunity to express her thoughts by creating a space in which virtual elements can be re-ordered to paint a personal future. The elements can be explored by looking at them, moving them and dragging them around by holding a button and physically moving one's body. The user will find the elements to be attached to one another, resulting in the visualisation of connected aspects when the user gives form to the virtual space, illustrating the consequences of decision making and prioritising certain desires at the cost of others (See Figure 3).

Exploring embodied sensemaking in the context of VR touches upon a fundamental problem, since the physical and the social dimensions, fundamental to embodied sensemaking [3], are typically not directly present in a virtual space. In *Charged Utopia VR,* we have started to explore how to create interactions in VR that allows us to make sense of the virtual space in a similar way as we do when being embodied in a physical space, while touching on the ethical dimension of being in a virtual space. We have found that VR spaces offer new qualities of interaction that provide us with the possibility to create interactions in which embodied sensemaking is still present, but afforded in different ways that it would be in the physical space. These qualities will be set out through reflections around three main themes that we identified over the course of the project. These themes have been identified by starting from the qualities of the physical space (in this case, the exhibition *Charged Utopia*) and the role of these qualities in the process of embodied sensemaking. These themes are: *Physical Movement*, *Resistance*, and *Ambiguity.* In the following section we will set out these three different themes, and relate to them firstly in the physical space, to point out how and why there is a fundamental difficulty in transposing these themes into a virtual space. Then, we will illustrate how this case study has started to identify ways in which the virtual space offers new opportunities for creating elements that take over (parts of) the role these themes have in making sense of a physical space.

Physical Movement
In the physical space, physical movement is present in everything we do. We engage physically with the space around us to feel objects and we are able to identify where we are, what we are doing and know how we can use the world around us. This fundamental element of being in the world is not directly present in the virtual space, since one does not have a physical body. Although more advanced VR headsets are optimizing the possibilities of using real objects to create the sensation of 'being in the world', the more easily available VR soft- and hardware (for example Google Cardboard) do not contain such possibilities yet. In *Charged Utopia VR*, we have found that by creating the possibility of zooming in and out within the virtual space, users were able to shift to different perspectives. This allowed them to choose what position they wanted to have within the virtual space. The transition from a sense of 'greatness' to a perspective from which everything seems uncontrollable and larger than life, has shown to be useful for reflections on what users' position in a space means in terms of what they are able to see and do. Benford et al. describe this as physical transcendence *"a desire to use media to move beyond the limits of body and sensory channels"* [1]. The ability to zoom in and out, and position oneself in the VR space can thus be a means to create this physical transcendence, and create a different form of physical movement in a virtual space.

Ambiguity
With ambiguity we refer to the grey areas between two (or more) choices and possibilities [10]. Within the complexity of our world, nuance and ambiguity are things that everyone is confronted with. Questions like: "*What would you rather do? This or that?"* Would normally be answered with *"It depends on.."* Or, *"I can only make that choice if I knew this and this..".* The complexity of the world is captured in these answers, since the answers illustrate that decisions have consequences reaching further than the topic at hand. Within the virtual world, this complexity is usually not present, which means that deciding and choosing will not contain this nuance. This often results in a black and white world, where things *are*, or *aren't*, and there is little space to explore the grey area of what things *could be*. Within *Charged Utopia VR*, we found that the virtual space provides opportunities to create such sense of ambiguity. VR offers possibilities to create

unique experiences for every user in the virtual space, while providing them with the exact same virtual reality space. The unique experiences were created by using the fact that humans use both eyes to have 3-D vision. Through the presentation of different images to each eye, the space was perceived differently by every individual, because of the difference in dominance between the two eyes and thus the way the two separate images are mixed (See Figure 2). We have also seen that when users started to understand how this effect was initiated, they closed and opened their eyes individually, in order to play with new emerging perceptions of the space around them. This interaction allowed the interpretive abilities of people to contribute in sensemaking of the virtual space.

Resistance

In the physical space, there are physical and social aspects of resistance [10]. The place where we are in the world determines our action possibilities and the people around us might provide us with new perspectives and insights. Furthermore, physical constraints (like gravity and the characteristics of our bodies) make us be where we are and feel what we feel. In the virtual space, resistance cannot be interpreted directly as such. The complexity of the world cannot be captured in full, and the presence of others is not always possible. A social aspect is thus missing when being in a virtual space. Furthermore, the physical constraints like gravity, having our body to interact with the world around us, and the borders of our being are not evident in the same way they are in the physical world. Within *Charged Utopia VR*, we found that especially because of the 'blank' sheet that a virtual space in fact is before it is programmed to be something, any forces can be applied on the objects created in it. We found that resistance emerges when objects are related to each other and create a complex network, where interaction with one of the objects might affect the movement or position of many other elements in the VR space. This makes the dependencies and relations around oneself experienceable and brings a part of the complexities in our physical world into the VR world (See Figure 3).

Future Work

Many of the key characteristics of the physical space, on which we depend to make sense of the world from an embodied perspective, are not typically present in a VR. However, one could argue that it is exactly the absence of these key characteristics that creates the potential of VR. One could also argue, that to make use of this potential, our understanding of the virtual world and how we make sense of it, should reflect to a certain extent the way in which we make sense of the real world. The *Charged Utopia* VR project has started to explore how to create a VR space that allows us to make sense in a similar way as we do when being embodied in a physical space. Ultimately, the goal of this project is to explore how this can contribute to a better understanding how we may design to afford an ethical dimension which is not yet fully explored in the virtual space. In this publication, we have started to sketch design opportunities in which we might capitalise on both sides of this coin: to afford embodied sense-making in Virtual Reality akin to those we use in our Physical Reality, by exploiting qualities offered by the virtual that are inspired by the real. Further development of the *Charged Utopia VR* experience will focus on more clearly identifying such qualities and effective ways to transpose experiential qualities from the physical and real, into the digital and virtual.

References

1. Benford, S., Bowers, J., Fahlén, L. E., Greenhalgh, C., & Snowdon, D. (1995, May). User embodiment in Collaborative Virtual Environments. In *Proceedings of the SIGCHI conference on Human Factors in Computing Systems* (pp. 242-249). ACM Press/ Addison-Wesley Publishing Co.
2. Dewey, J. (1934). *Art as Experience*. New York, NY: Perigree
3. Dourish, P. (2001). *Where the Action is*. Cambridge: MIT Press.
4. Gibson, J.J. (1979). *The Ecological Approach to Visual Perception*. London, UK: Lawrence Erlbaum.
5. Koskinen, K., Zimmerman, J., Binder, T., Redstrom, J., & Wensveen, S. (2011). *Design Research through Practice: From the Lab, Field, and Showroom*. Elsevier.
6. Mandary, M., & Metzinger, T.K. (2016). Real Virtuality: a code of ethical conduct. Recommendations for good scientific practice and the consumers of vr-technology. *Frontiers in Robotics and AI*, 3, 3.
7. Merleau-Ponty, M. (1962). *Phenomenology of Perception*, trans. Collin Smith. New York: Humanities Press.
8. Peck, T.C., Seinfeld, S., Aglioti, S.M., & Slater, M. (2013). Putting yourself in the skin of a black avatar reduces implicit racial bias. *Consciousness and cognition*, 22(3), 7790-787
9. Peeters, J., Papworth, N., Glaser, P., Collevecchio, C. Betancour, A., Trotto, A. (2017) No Man is an Island. Situated Design Research and Wicked Impact, *The Design Journal*, 20:sup1, S3354-S3367, DOI: 10.1080/14606925.2017.1352840
10. Sennett, R. (2008). *The Craftsman*. Yale University Press.
11. Van der Veen, R., Hakkarainen, V., Peeters, J., & Trotto, A. (2018). Understanding Transformations through Design: Can Resilience Thinking Help? In *Proceedings of the Twelfth International Conference on Tangible, Embedded, and Embodied Interaction* (TEI '18). ACM, New York, NY, USA, 21-28.
12. Unity 3D Game Development Platform: https://unity3d.com/ (Accessed 24th of December, 2017)
13. Video impression of the *Charged Utopia VR* design: https://vimeo.com/247610036
14. Video impression of the *Charged Utopia* Interactive Exhibition: https://vimeo.com/181787781

Designing the Interaction with the Internet of Tangible Things: A Card Set

Leonardo Angelini
HumanTech Institute
University of Applied Sciences and Arts Western Switzerland
1700, Fribourg, Switzerland
leonardo.angelini@hes-so.ch

Elena Mugellini
HumanTech Institute
University of Applied Sciences and Arts Western Switzerland
1700, Fribourg, Switzerland
elena.mugellini@hes-so.ch

Nadine Couture
ESTIA LaBRI, UMR 5800
64210 Bidart, France
n.couture@estia.fr

Omar Abou Khaled
HumanTech Institute
University of Applied Sciences and Arts Western Switzerland
1700, Fribourg, Switzerland
omar.aboukhaled@hes-so.ch

TEI '18, March 18–21, 2018, Stockholm, Sweden

ACM ISBN 978-1-4503-5568-1/18/03.
https://doi.org/10.1145/3173225.3173288

Abstract
Current interactions for the Internet of Things are often constrained behind a screen. With the Internet of Tangible Things (IoTT) we aim at promoting the design of richer interactions, embodied in physical IoT objects. To this purpose, we propose a card set for the design of tangible interaction with IoT objects, which contains 8 cards for tangible interaction properties and 8 for IoT properties, in order to explore how tangible properties can be exploited for enhancing the interaction with IoT objects. We tested the card set in a dedicated workshop, observing that participants were able to explore most of the tangible and IoT properties. To complement the IoT card set, a hardware prototyping toolkit with examples for each of the 8 tangible properties is currently under development.

Author Keywords
Internet of Tangible Things; IoTT; Internet of Things; Tangible Interaction; Design Cards.

Introduction
The popularity of the Internet of Things (IoT) exploded in the last 5 years, as one can see searching this term on Google Trends. Although IoT has only recently become a buzzword, researchers are working in this domain since more than 20 years, focusing mostly on the supporting technological infrastructure that allows

things to be connected to and through the *Internet*. Technological advances have brought the miniaturization of electronics and an increased energy efficiency, which in turn led to the possibility to bring the Internet of Things to the mass. Nowadays, many electronic appliances and everyday objects are able to communicate through Bluetooth or Wifi connectivity with our smartphones or with the Internet. Such IoT objects offer to the user novel services and interaction opportunities. While some of them are futile and are suddenly abandoned, others can be disrupting for our life. In both cases, the interaction with such IoT objects could be not straightforward for the user. Indeed, as pointed out by Rowland [21], the interaction with the Internet of Things is often complex and goes beyond the already-known mental models of the users. As Rowland, also Knutsen et al. [16] highlight the fact that we are facing a new era of products that are hybrids, i.e., that are at the same time "tangible atoms and digital bits", referring to the digital services that are nowadays tightened to physical products. While consistent efforts should be done to improve the user experience with Internet of Things, Koreshoff et al. [17] highlighted that, as of 2013, few researchers investigated the field of the Internet of Things from a Human-Computer Interaction perspective. This trend is slightly changing, and a search on the ACM Digital Library shows that a continuously increasing number of papers deals with IoT and HCI in the last 3 years. However, Koreshoff et al.'s analysis [17] shows also that most of interactions designed for commercial products are based on smartphone or web interfaces. This trend has not changed much and still many current IoT products tend to remove physical controls from the IoT object in favor of smartphone interfaces. In this complex interaction context, we argue that tangibility can bring important benefits for the user, facilitating the grasp of intangible concepts and properties of the Internet of Things. To highlight the importance of a paradigm shift in the design of interactions with IoT, we adopt the term Internet of Tangible Things, introduced for the first time by Gallacher during a keynote talk at ETIS'16 [12] and discussed more in depth by Angelini et al. [5]. In order to contribute to this new research field, in this paper, we aim at exploring how to support the design of tangible interaction applied to the Internet of Things. To this purpose, we propose a custom card set (Figure 1) for matching tangible interaction properties to IoT properties and supporting the design of IoTT objects. After discussing the positioning of this research in respect to related work, we present the card set and the 16 proposed properties. We also present a preliminary evaluation of the card set and future work for complementing the card set with a set of hardware prototyping samples.

Related Work

Few researches have been conducted until now on tangible interaction applied to the IoT. A recent systematic review [5] shows that only 18 articles considered tangible interaction with the internet of things and that among them, only the work of Ambe et al. [4] provided grounded support to the benefits of tangible interaction for the design of IoT products. In particular, Ambe et al. [4] presented an analysis of three IoT systems that foster social connection. The analysis has been conducted adapting part of tangible interaction properties proposed in Hornecker and Buur's framework [15] in order to discuss the importance of technology individuation (through habituation, appropriation and personalization) for those particular IoT objects. Different frameworks have been proposed

Figure 1. The IoTT card set, 8 cards for tangible interaction properties, 8 cards for IoT properties. In the middle, back side of the "Persistency" card.

for supporting the design of tangible interactions for different application domains [18]. Hornecker and Buur's tangible interaction framework [15] is arguably the reference work in this field, which deserves the credits for having broadened the field by considering as tangible interactions that goes beyond direct manipulations. Indeed, Hoven et al. [22] considered designing richer digital interactions that exploit better human-sensorimotor skills and that are situated in the physical world as a foundation for tangible interaction.

While theoretical frameworks are useful as a reference for the designer, specific techniques are needed for supporting the interaction design process. Iterative design processes are well-known in design thinking [20], where iterating across divergent and convergent phases is key for obtaining innovative ideas that meet user's expectation. To support iterative processes, especially during design workshops, specific techniques such as design cards have been included in the iterative processes by Halskov and Dalsgård [13] and Dibitonto et al. [11]. Card games are powerful tool for inspiring the interaction design process, especially in the brainstorming phase. In tangible interaction design, it is worth mentioning the Hornecker's card set [14], which materialize Hornecker and Buur's framework [15] into cards with the different concepts, supported by illustrations and design questions for stimulating reflection during the brainstorming phases or evaluation phases of the design process. Card sets are popular also in IoT interaction design. Mora et al. [19] presented recently a design toolkit for supporting the participatory design of interactions with everyday objects augmented with IoT capabilities. The card set is divided in different categories, which are used at different moments of a structured design process. In particular, interactions proposed by Mora et al. [19] are divided in human actions and feedback and are based on intuitive interaction primitives (e.g., shake; vibrate), in order to support the design process also for non-expert users. Also Dibitonto et al. [11] recently presented a card deck for supporting the co-design of IoT interactions, in early phases of the design process, i.e., from the conception phase to experience prototyping. This deck is still a development phase. Individuals and design companies have released on the Internet other card sets and toolkits for the design of IoT objects. Interesting examples are Know-Cards [6], Thingclash[10] and IoT Service Kit [9]. All previous card sets in this field aims at supporting the understanding of the Internet of Things and at supporting the design of IoT services, but offer limited support for exploiting tangible interaction properties in the IoT. Indeed, examples proposed by Tiles [19] are based on interaction primitives that exploit poorly physical object affordances for grasping IoT concepts.

The IoTT Card Set

The card set presented in this article has been developed to support the design of IoTT objects, i.e., IoT objects that embody a tangible interface. The card set (Figure 1) is inspired partially from Hornecker's card set[14]. It proposes a selection of 8 tangible properties and 8 IoT properties, which are discussed in detail in the following sections. The main purpose of the card set is supporting the designers' reflection on how tangible interaction properties can be used in relationship to IoT properties, in particular for improving the user experience with IoT objects. Each card shows on the front side an illustration and the name of the property, while the back describes the property and presents two questions to drive the reflection on how it can be

Figure 2. Front side of the cards for the first four tangible interaction properties (T1 to T4). Please refer to annex material for the other cards.

applied. Inspiring metaphoric images have been selected to illustrate properties, with the purpose to retrieve rapidly the card from the set, without reading the property name, but also to stimulate reflection on the property. Image selection has been discussed by three HCI and IoT experts, with the purpose to individuate easy-to-understand and worldwide-known metaphors, avoiding metaphors belonging to a particular religion or culture. Images have been retrieved from Pixabay [1] and are copyright free, under Creative Commons CC0 License. Cards have been printed in A6 format and plasticized.

Tangible Properties

Tangible Interaction offers several benefits over traditional Graphical User Interfaces. Such properties have been highlighted in several tangible interaction frameworks and papers. Hornecker and Buur's [15] proposed several concepts that can be exploited during tangible interaction design. These concepts were grouped around 4 themes: tangible manipulation, spatial interaction, embodied facilitation and expressive representation. Ambe et al. [4] suggested that Hornecker and Buur's themes were mostly oriented to exploit spatiality in public installation and they provided a different interpretation of these properties in the context of daily routines and personal rearrangements. In order to describe the current direction of tangible interaction, Van den Hoven at al. [22] highlighted three main generic qualities for tangible interaction: meaningful representations and controls, direct representations and controls, integrated representation and controls. Since tangible interaction properties may vary consistently across the different application domains, we have chosen to adopt the tangible interaction properties that Angelini et al.'s explicitly elicited for the IoTT domain [5]. The authors selected the 8 properties from tangible interaction literature review and analyzed their presence in 18 papers in the IoTT domain, evidencing that 7 of the 8 properties were cited in several IoTT papers. Therefore, we built our cards on these 8 properties. In the following list, we report the 8 tangible properties (title in italic), with the corresponding description. Further details, such as the design questions for driving design reflections on this property, can be found in the complementary material.

- T1: *Meaningful representations and controls* of the IoT object functions and parameters.
- T2: *Rich interactions* with IoT objects that are situated in the real world, exploiting the natural human skills and senses, such as haptics and hand manipulations.
- T3: *Persistent* physical representations that could last in case of power or connectivity outrage, allowing the user to control the state of an IoT object even when no Internet connection is available.
- T4: *Spatial interactions* that support collaborative setups with multiple IoT objects.
- T5: *Immediacy and intuitiveness* of the interaction, facilitating the understanding and control of IoT objects with minimal learning time.
- T6: *Peripheral interactions* with IoT objects that are integrated in the daily routines, that free users' cognitive resources and do not disrupt attention.
- T7: Facilitated *reflections* on IoT object meaning and working principles, as well as support for associating and sharing *memories*.
- T8: *Long-lasting interactions* with IoT objects exploiting *emotional* durable designs, to cope with electronic waste due to technological obsolescence.

Figure 3. Front side of the cards for the first four IoT interaction properties (I1 to I4). Please refer to annex material for the other cards.

IoT Properties

Few works in literature have elicited IoT properties that should be considered from a human-centered perspective, in particular for the design of interactions with IoT objects. At the best of our knowledge, no work until now elicited which IoT properties should be considered by considered for the design of tangible interaction with IoT objects. Our properties are partially grounded on existing IoT literature and in particular on the book of Rowland [21] and on Bellotti and Sellen's [8] and Bellotti and Edwards' [7] frameworks. In the following list, we report the 8 IoT properties (Figure 3):

- I1: The IoT main *functions* are clear to understand for the user.
- I2: The IoT object can be easily switched on/off and *power* consumption is under control.
- I3: Current *state*/activity of the IoT object is under control.
- I4: IoT object *connectivity* can be easily switched on/off and the network links are intelligible.
- I5: User has full control and understanding of the environmental/personal *information acquired* by the IoT object.
- I6: The user knows and controls to whom acquired *information* is *sent*.
- I7: The user knows and control which *information* is *stored*, where, and for how long.
- I8: The user knows who has *access* to the IoT object functions and information.

Preliminary Evaluation of the IoTT Card Set

We evaluated the proposed IoTT card set during a full-day workshop conducted with researchers and practitioners from the field of tangible interaction, in the context of the European Tangible Interaction Studio [2] (See Figure 4). 21 people actively participated to the workshop. 6 groups of 3 or 4 people each were formed. Before the workshop, participants were informed about the purpose of the activity, with a short introduction to the Internet of Tangible Things and to the IoTT card set. Participants were asked to design one or more IoTT object for an application domain of their choice, using the IoTT card set as a support. The workshop was divided in three parts, 1) definition of the IoTT object idea and creation of a storyboard, 2) creation of a low-fi (cardboard) prototype for illustrating the functions and the interaction with the IoT object and 3) creation of a functional IoT prototype using Kniwwelino [3]as hardware IoT platform. Participants could use the IoTT card deck as a support for reflection during the whole activity. We asked to participants to keep track of the tangible and IoT properties explored during the different phases and to individuate the links among tangible and IoT properties. 6 different prototypes where realized during the workshop, which allowed to explore almost all tangible interaction and IoT properties. Only the "rich interactions" property (T2) was not explored by any group. All other tangible properties were explored at least by 3 groups. Concerning IoT properties, "Function" and "state" were explored by all groups, while "power" and "access control" only by one group. Workshop participants engaged with design cards especially in the first phase of the workshop, as a support for the ideation of the user interactions with the IoTT objects. The next phases concentrated in the materialization of the initial concepts and therefore users engaged less with the design cards. Engagement and perceived usefulness of design cards varied consistently across groups and across single participants. Some participants spent much time reviewing and analyzing the IoTT cards and underlined

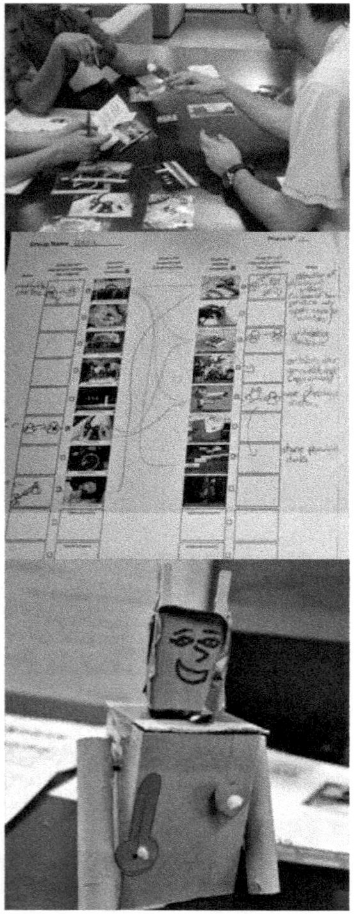

Figure 4. Top: ETIS'17 workshop participants using the IoTT card set. Middle: IoTT properties annotated by the Bobby group (T1,T6,T8, I1,I3,I5,I7). Bottom: Prototype realized by the Bobby group.

the usefulness of the card set for the ideation phase. Other participants, instead, spent less time discussing about tangible and IoT properties, focusing their discussion on the functionalities of the IoTT object.

Future Improvements and Hardware Dev Kit

From the observations conducted during the workshop about the IoTT card set usage we can conclude that the card set was useful for exploring tangible and IoT properties in the design of the interaction with an IoT object. Participants considered the proposed properties as exhaustive and did not propose additional tangible or IoT properties that they would like to explore with their object. However, the IoTT card set did not provide any support on the initial ideation of the IoT object functionality, because it focuses mainly in the design of the interaction. Other IoT card sets, such Mora et al.'s Tiles, could be used in the first part of the ideation phase, while the IoTT card set could be used once the participants have a first idea of the IoT object they would like to develop. From the workshop we also noticed that participants did not engaged anymore with the design cards during the hardware prototyping phase. Moreover, in some cases, participants were not able to implement with the hardware platform the tangible interaction properties that they originally conceived in their design concept. In order to better support reflection on IoTT properties also in this phase, we are working on ready-to-use and hack IoTT hardware examples (one per tangible interaction property) that participants can use as inspiration or starting point for prototyping IoTT objects.

Conclusion

The Internet of Things is a compelling application domain for human-computer interaction research. In particular, tangible interaction with IoT objects is still largely unexplored. Our motivation is driven by the users' need to get a grasp on a technology that is rapidly evolving and is offering new digital interaction possibilities that go beyond existing mental models of the users. Since most commercial IoT objects offer interactions based on smartphone or web apps, our efforts aims at facilitating the design of interactions that are situated in the real world, exploiting the affordances of physical objects, supporting collaboration and emotional/sensory rich interactions. To this purpose, we developed a card set as a support for bridging tangible interaction and IoT properties. The IoTT card set proved to be a valid tool for supporting the design of tangible interaction with IoT objects, but can still benefit of other tools for supporting the design and development of IoTT objects, such as existing IoT design cards and a prototyping toolkit. Further tests will be conducted in order to evaluate if the IoTT card set is effectively able to improve the tangibility of the designed interactions with IoT, compared to traditional IoT card sets. Our effort is currently concentrated in the development of a prototyping toolkit and we plan to bring at the TEI'18 conference a working example for each of the 8 tangible interaction properties. The IoTT card set and the hardware prototyping examples will be released publicly on a web site.

Acknowledgments

We thank ETIS workshop participants and all the Luxembourg Institute of Science and Technology (LIST) members that helped in the organization of ETIS'17.

References

1. Pixabay. https://pixabay.com
2. The Third European Tangible Interaction Studio. http://etis2017.lu/
3. Luxembourg Institute of Science and Technology (LIST). Kniwwelino. http://www.kniwwelino.lu/en/
4. Aloha Hufana Ambe, Margot Brereton, Alessandro Soro and Paul Roe. 2017. Technology individuation: The foibles of augmented everyday objects. in *Proceedings of the 2017 CHI Conference on Human Factors in Computing Systems*, ACM, 6632-6644.
5. Leonardo Angelini, Nadine Couture, Omar Abou Khaled and Elena Mugellini. Submitted. Internet of Tangible Things (IoTT): Challenges and Opportunities for Tangible Interaction with IoT. *MDPI Informatics* (Special Issue "Tangible and Embodied Interaction"). 1-28.
6. Tina Aspiala. KnowCards. https://know-cards.myshopify.com
7. Victoria Bellotti and Keith Edwards. 2001. Intelligibility and accountability: human considerations in context-aware systems. *Human–Computer Interaction*, 16 (2-4). 193-212.
8. Victoria Bellotti and Abigail Sellen. 1993. Design for privacy in ubiquitous computing environments. in *Proceedings of the Third European Conference on Computer-Supported Cooperative Work 13–17 September 1993, Milan, Italy ECSCW'93*, Springer, 77-92.
9. Ricardo Brito and Paul Houghton. IoT Service Kit. http://iotservicekit.com/
10. Changeist. Thingclash http://www.thingclash.com/
11. Massimiliano Dibitonto, Federica Tazzi, Katarzyna Leszczynska and Carlo M Medaglia. 2017. The IoT Design Deck: A Tool for the Co-design of Connected Products. in *International Conference on Applied Human Factors and Ergonomics*, Springer, 217-227.
12. Sarah Gallacher. Internet of Tangible Things - Talk during the Second European Tangible Interaction Studio. http://www.etis.estia.fr/etis-2016/articles/program-etis-2016.html
13. Kim Halskov and Peter Dalsgård. 2006. Inspiration card workshops. in *Proceedings of the 6th conference on Designing Interactive systems*, ACM, 2-11.
14. Eva Hornecker. 2010. Creative idea exploration within the structure of a guiding framework: the card brainstorming game. in *Proceedings of the fourth international conference on Tangible, embedded, and embodied interaction*, ACM, 101-108.
15. Eva Hornecker and Jacob Buur. 2006. Getting a grip on tangible interaction: a framework on physical space and social interaction. in *Proceedings of the SIGCHI conference on Human Factors in computing systems*, ACM, 437-446.
16. Jørn Knutsen, Einar Sneve Martinussen, Timo Arnall and Andrew Morrison. 2011. Investigating an "internet of hybrid products": Assembling products, interactions, services, and networks through design. *Computers and Composition*, 28 (3). 195-204.
17. Treffyn Lynch Koreshoff, Toni Robertson and Tuck Wah Leong. 2013. Internet of things: a review of literature and products. in *Proceedings of the 25th Australian Computer-Human Interaction Conference: Augmentation, Application, Innovation, Collaboration*, ACM, 335-344.

18. Ali Mazalek and Elise Van Den Hoven. 2009. Framing tangible interaction frameworks. *AI EDAM*, 23 (3). 225-235.
19. Simone Mora, Francesco Gianni and Monica Divitini. 2017. Tiles: A Card-based Ideation Toolkit for the Internet of Things. in *Proceedings of the 2017 Conference on Designing Interactive Systems*, ACM, 587-598.
20. IDEO. org. 2015. The Field Guide to Human-Centered Design, IDEO Canada.
21. Claire Rowland, Elizabeth Goodman, Martin Charlier, Ann Light and Alfred Lui. 2015. *Designing Connected Products: UX for the Consumer Internet of Things*. " O'Reilly Media, Inc.".
22. Elise van den Hoven, Evelien van de Garde-Perik, Serge Offermans, Koen van Boerdonk and Kars-Michiel H Lenssen. 2013. Moving tangible interaction systems to the next level. *Computer*, 46 (8). 0070-0076.

Sew-Flow: A Craft Interpretation of a Digital Game

Kinneret Itzhak
Department of Textile Design
Shenkar College, Israel
kinneretshenkar@gmail.com

Shachar Geiger
Kadar Media Lab
Shenkar College, Israel
s.geiger.s@gmail.com

Kamila Kantek
School of Industrial Design
SWPS University, Poland
kkantek2@st.swps.edu.pl

Shoval Nir
Department of Interior Design
Shenkar College, Israel
shoval.omer@gmail.com

Dafna Levi
Department of Interior Design
Shenkar College, Israel
Dfnlevi7@gmail.com

Michal Rinott
Kadar Media Lab
Shenkar College, Israel
michalrin@gmail.com

TEI '18, March 18–21, 2018, Stockholm, Sweden

ACM ISBN 978-1-4503-5568-1/18/03.
https://doi.org/10.1145/3173225.3173289

Abstract
We present "Sew-Flow", a craft interpretation of the Digital Game "Flow Free" that is played on smartphones and computers. In Sew-Flow the screen is replaced by a fabric interface that is played by a process of sewing with conductive yarn. Feedback to the game play is presented by thermo-chromic colors that gradually appear. We lay out the motivations for slowing down the game experience and moving it into the material world. The crafting of the game elements and the game experience are described in detail, as well as the technological implementation. Insights from initial trials are described, showing that children and adults perceived the game in different ways. Future directions involve solving a number of challenges involving the thermo-chromic materials and conductive yarn.

Author Keywords
Tangible Interfaces; Textile Design; Digital Craft; Computer Games; Game Controllers

ACM Classification Keywords
- Human-centered computing~Interaction paradigms

Figure 1: The original digital game: a correctly solved stage in Flow Free

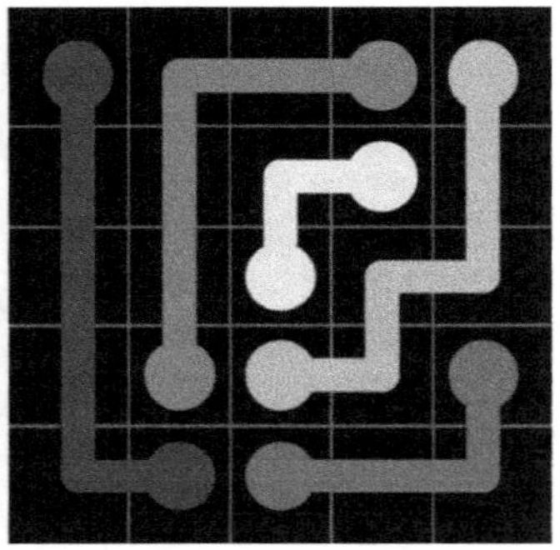

Figure 2: Playing Flow Free on a touch screen; the blue path remains to be solved

Introduction

Computer games are the second highest grossing branch in the entertainment industry after television, and show great advances in graphics, audio and game mechanics. However, the controllers that accompany them are still quite limited in their materiality [6].
Sew-Flow is a material interpretation of a game that currently exists on a screen, created in the hopes of offering a more intimate, craft-like, rich material playing experience. Using textile as the medium of interaction, and slowing down the game by using slow input and gradually appearing feedback, we wish to propose an alternative to the fast-paced, materially-poor controllers currently typical of computer games.
Sew-Flow is thus both an exploration of a novel game experience and an interface based on textile and new material behaviors.

Related Work

Slow Technology

In their highly influential paper, Hallnäs and Redström [3] call for technological experiences to be slow - in learning, understanding and presence, giving people time to think and reflect. They propose that the experience of slow time can introduce new forms of aesthetics, eschewing efficiency, bringing technology in new ways into the living environment. Since coining the term in 2001, many projects have undertaken slow technology, as do we in Sew-Flow.

Sewing Interfaces

Schoemann and Nitsche [4] combined interaction design and the craft of sewing in their "Stitch Sampler". Like our project, Schoemann and Nitsche took advantage of the needle being made of a conductive material, and worked with the technology of soft circuits. However, since they wanted the user to focus on the action of sewing, audible sounds were used as outputs [2]. This is unlike "Sew-Flow"'s output of thermo-chromatic dye, which is inherently connected to fabric and to the textile world.
Numerous projects have used fabric as a tangible interface. Chang and Ishii's "Zstretch" [1] is a fabric music controller that focuses on the "flexibility of gesture and expressive range" that is used while playing an instrument. Their choice of medium has to do with the elastic properties of fabric, and the input of stretching and pulling is inherent to the material of the controller, just as the input of sewing is inherent to the interaction in "Sew-Flow". Chang and Ishii raise an issue that our project has come across as well, and that is the effectiveness of the output dulling, as the use of the game increases.
Post, Ortho, Russo, and Gershenfeld write of the "E-broidery" technique, and give examples of projects, such as the "Electronic Tablecloth", that prove that this technique is the best for integrating electronics into textile interfaces [5]. While the projects they present require less purposeful interaction than in "Sew-Flow", it was equally important for us to choose an input that integrates the electronic elements of our project into the fabric board as naturally as possible.

Sew-Flow Description

Sew-Flow is a material interpretation of the digital game "Flow Free" [2]. In Flow Free, a single player must connect between two same-colored dots on a square grid presented on a screen, in order to form one continuous path (fig 1). This must be done so that all the different colored paths fit into the board just so, while making sure not to interrupt, and thus

disconnect, existing paths. Flow Free is usually played on touch screen interfaces (fig 2), using the finger to draw the paths, and is also offered on PCs using the mouse.
In Sew-Flow, the playing board is made of textile, and the paths are sewn into the textile using a pin and yarn (fig 3). We now describe SewFlow in detail.

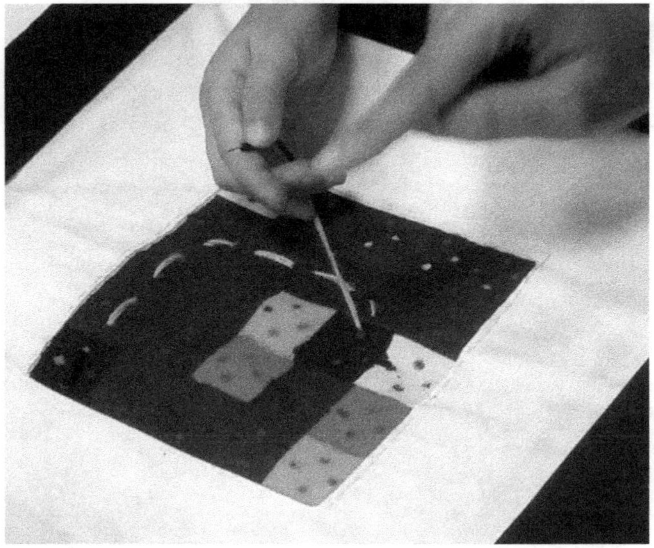

Figure 3: Sewing the solution to the blue path in Sew-Flow

The Experience
Sew-Flow is a fabric interface. In the prototype, the fabric is stretched on a wooden board, with the wires and electronic components hidden under the board. In future implementations we envision it integrated into a cushion or other fabric element that can be a held on the lap.

On each square of the board there are four holes - two lengthwise and two crosswise - to allow an easy sewing gesture (figure 3).

The player uses a piece of silver colored conductive yarn to sew each path. On one side of the yarn there is a metal pin, on the other, a curved "needle". The pin is stuck into one edge and the path to the other edge is sewn using the needle. Finally, the needle is stuck into the ending edge. If the path is correct, the heating process begins, activating the thermo-chromic black dye which gradually disappears to reveal the correct color, taking about a minute to reach full color.

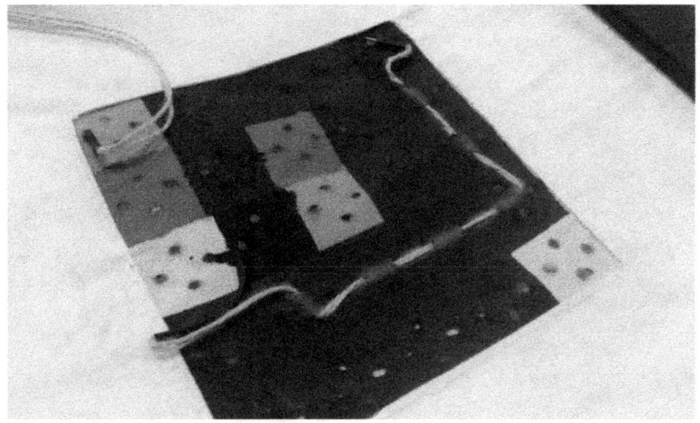

Figure 4: Revelation of the blue color when the path is correctly solved

As the player continues to solve the paths, the colors are revealed. If a wrong path is sewn, there is no change in color. If the paths cross, both colors are turned off.

Craft and game-play

Below is a graphic description of how the game elements are crafted, and the game play that they afford.

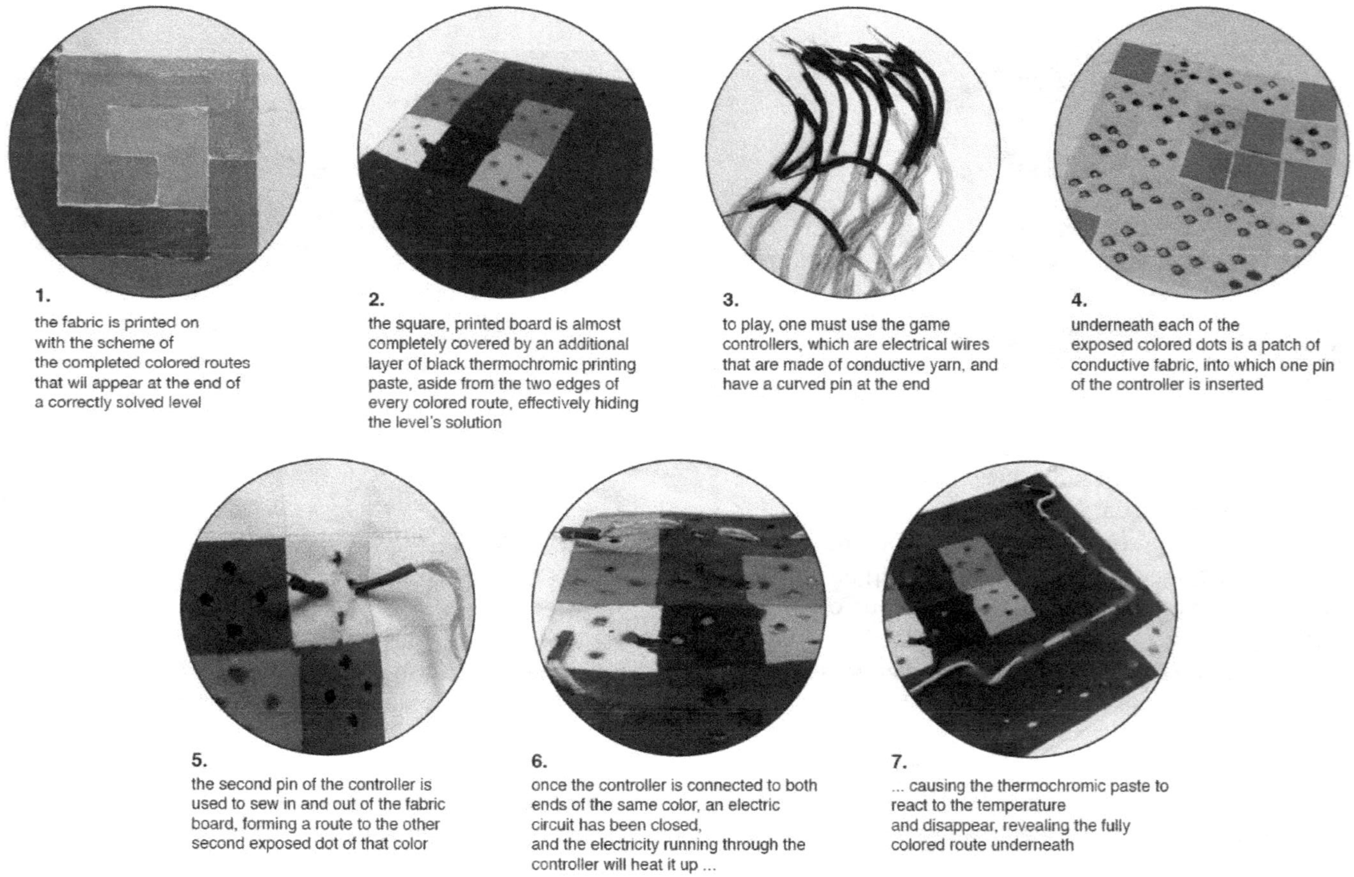

Figure 5: The stages of crafting the Sew-Flow game, and the craft of playing Sew-Flow

Technical Implementation

We used an Arduino board to test the connections and to drive the electricity through the yarn (fig 6). The voltage and current required to heat the conductive yarn (12V, ~0.5A) are too high to run directly through the Arduino. This required a 'switching' solution using transistors (in this case, a MOSFET). In Sew-Flow, the conductive materials are used both for system input (detecting correct sewn connections) and for system output (heating the conductive yarn). The following circuit was built for each color path: one color edge (designated as positive) is connected to the high voltage supply through a switch (P-Channel MOSFET), which is controlled by an Arduino digital output pin. The other color edge (designated as negative) has two connections to a second Arduino digital pin:

1. as an input, for detecting connection to any edge (through a voltage divider, reducing the 12V to 4.5V)
2. through another switch (N-Channel MOSFET) to ground, to allow current flow when the correct connection is discovered, heating the yarn.

The Arduino program runs a sequential scan of all positive edges (each edge sequentially turned HIGH while leaving the other edges LOW), and checks if any negative edge is HIGH - meaning the player made a connection between the HIGH positive edge and the HIGH negative edge. If the connection is correct (both edges are of the same color), both switches of both edges are turned on, allowing the conductor to heat. The sequential scan repeats every 1 second; during the scan, all conductors cease to heat, but the scan only lasts a few millisecond. In case an incorrect connection is read (an edge is connected to an edge of a different color), all heating is disabled.

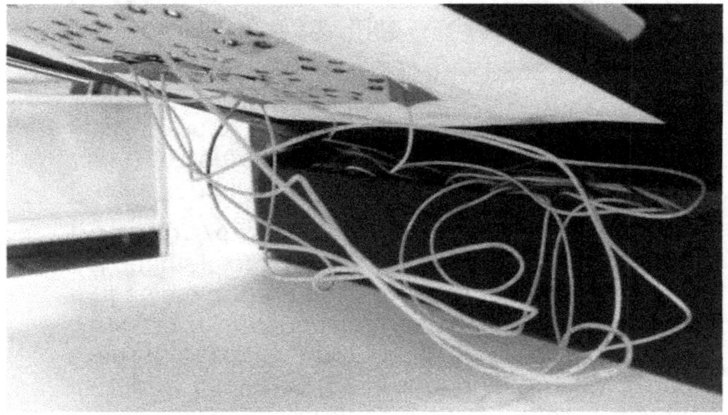

Figure 6: wires connecting each color edge to the Arduino, housed in a compartment under the board

Initial user testing

We made an initial trial of Sew-Flow within an exhibition on the topic of novel game controllers. While we envision 'Sew-Flow' being used within a different scenario - a quiet and homely ambience where patience and concentration are natural - putting the game in use by many different users generated many insights.

It was apparent that the experience was rewarding for players. Those who tried the 'sewing' got engaged into finishing the path, being curious about the result. We observed the most positive reactions during the crucial point of playing - the heating up of the thread and appearance of the colored path. Users of all ages were enthusiastic about the 'Sew-Flow' prototype, although for different reasons. The children perceived it as an enjoyable toy; their parents pointed out the potential of the game to strengthen their children's focus and manual skills. Adult users valued the 'Sew-Flow' experience as an occasion to focus and relax after constant contact with electronic devices. It was associated with pleasing sentiments related with sewing and embroidery. For all, it was an interesting and enjoyable alternative, that raised a discussion with the creators about the predominance of on-screen gaming.

Future Work

A number of technical issues need to be solved in future versions of Sew-Flow. In this version we doubled the conductive yarn in order to have it heat up in the time frame we desired. This sometimes caused the conductive yarn to overheat. The yarn we choose and current used will need optimization to prevent this. The thermo-chromic paste we used disappears at 31 degrees Celsius, which means it also starts disappearing at the long touch of a hand or finger, revealing the color underneath. The other paste we could access disappears at 45 degrees, which was too hot for the conductive yarn to carry. We will optimize these materials and parameters in future versions. Another issue with the thermo-chromic paste we used is that it does not disappear completely at a high temperature, but rather leaves a gray film which causes the colors below to look darker, making the color change less vivid. We plan tests to discover whether this is due to the constant reheating of the thermo-chromic layer, and how this can be rectified. The current Sew-Flow prototype has been created as an experiment in materials and craft interaction, and as an alternative to the norms of speed and of hard materials typical of digital games. While we envision Sew-Flow integrated with the home environment, we need to define how it will be presented at home (e.g., on a pillow?) and how more game levels can be added. Beyond Sew-Flow, we will explore ways to extend the uses we have made of fabric, sewing and dynamic color change to the design of other slow, interactive experiences. Different puzzle games in which a solution needs to be revealed slowly, and other narrative and learning experiences in which a path needs to be discovered, and information revealed - are good candidates.

References

1. Angela Chang and Hiroshi Ishii. 2007. Zstretch: A Stretchy Fabric Music Controller. In Proceedings of the 7th International Conference on New Interfaces for Musical Expression. NIME '07. New York, NY, USA: ACM, 46–49. DOI:http://dx.doi.org/10.1145/1279740.1279746
2. Flow Free game: http://www.bigduckgames.com/flowfree/.
3. Lars Hallnäs and Johan Redström,. Slow Technology; Designing for Reflection, Journal of Personal and Ubiquitous Computing. Springer-Verlag, 2001.
4. Michael Nitsche, Sarah Schoemann. 2017. Needle as Input: Exploring Practice and Materiality When Crafting Becomes Computing. In *Proceedings of the Eleventh International Conference on Tangible, Embedded and Embodied Interaction*. TEI '17. Yokohama, Japan: ACM, 299-308. DOI:http://dx.doi.org/10.1145/3024969.3024999
5. Ernest Rehmi Post, Margaret Orth, P.R. Russo, and Neil Gershenfeld. 2000. E-broidery: Design and Fabrication of Textile-based Computing. IBM Syst. J. 39, 3-4, 840–860. DOI:http://dx.doi.org/10.1147/sj.393.0840
6. Paul Skalski, Ron Tamborini, Ashleigh Shelton, Michael Buncher, Pete Lindmark. Mapping the Road to Fun: Natural Video Game Controllers, Presence, and Game Enjoyment. Sage New Media & Society J. 13, (2011), 224-242. DOI:10.1177/1461444810370949

Full Body Interaction beyond Fun: Engaging Museum Visitors in Human-Data Interaction

Swati Mishra
Department of Human-Centered Computing,
IUPUI,
Indianapolis, Indiana,
United States,
mishrasw@iupui.edu

Francesco Cafaro
Department of Human-Centered Computing,
IUPUI,
Indianapolis, Indiana,
United States,
fcafaro@iu.edu

TEI '18, March 18–21, 2018, Stockholm, Sweden

ACM ISBN 978-1-4503-5568-1/18/03.
https://doi.org/10.1145/3173225.3173291.

Abstract

Engaging museum visitors in data exploration using full-body interaction is still a challenge. In this paper, we explore four strategies for providing entry-points to the interaction: instrumenting the floor; forcing collaboration; implementing multiple body movements to control the same effect; and, visualizing the visitors' silhouette beside the data visualization. We discuss preliminary results of an in-situ study with 56 museum visitors at Discovery Place, and provide design recommendations for crafting engaging Human-Data Interaction experiences.

Author Keywords

Full-Body Interaction; Human-Data Interaction; Museums

Introduction

In recent years, the wide availability of motion tracking devices, such as Nintendo Wii and Microsoft Kinect, has opened a range of opportunities for the design of full-body installations in museums and public spaces. One of the argument in support of the use of gestures and body movements to control museum installations is that they create engagement and fun [5]. For example,

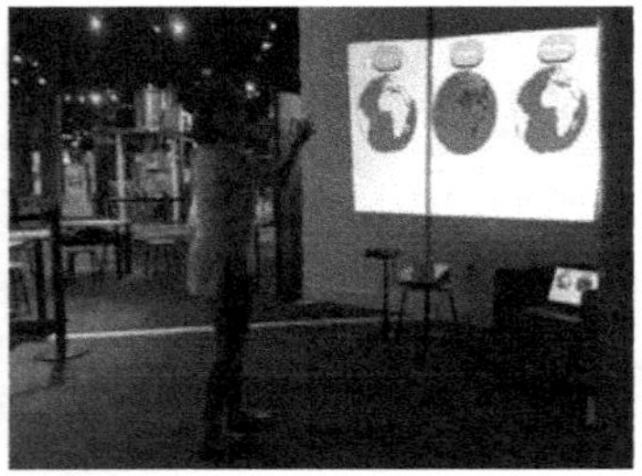

Figure 1: A museum visitor interacts with a prototype data visualization using gestures.

Puppet Parade[1] allows children to puppeteer creatures that are displayed on large projected walls [8]; Metamorphosis allows visitors to go through the stages of a butterfly's metamorphosis using "engaging ubiquitous technologies" [7]; Word Out! is an interactive game (designed to facilitate the learning of alphabet letters) that uses full-body technologies to "stimulate fun and engagement" [11].

The assumption that full-body technologies themselves are engaging for people, however, is not always true. People generally interact with museum exhibits for less than two minutes [14] and, if they are not able to quickly understand how to operate with a full-body installation, they often leave thinking that the system is broken [3]. This is particularly problematic when visitors are exposed to interactive installations for data exploration, as in the case of Human-Data Interaction (HDI) [1,2] -an example is illustrated in Figure 1. Exploring data offers a deep contrast with being a puppeteer or playing with butterflies: it is not a stereotypical example of "fun" activity, especially for young visitors. If we want HDI installation to be self-standing, and to attract visitors of different age groups without the help of museum docents, we need to identify engaging entry-points to the interaction. In this paper, we report preliminary results and observations from a study that we conducted at Discovery Place, a science museum in Charlotte, NC. Specifically, we explored four strategies for providing entry-points to the interaction: instrumenting the floor; forcing collaboration; implementing multiple body movements to control the same effect; and, visualizing the visitors' silhouette beside the data visualization. We provide design recommendations and outline future research for crafting self-standing, engaging HDI installations.

[1] http://design-io.com/projects/PuppetParadeCinekid/

Related Work

Human-Data Interaction (HDI)

Human-Data Interaction (HDI) is a term that was initially introduced in [2] and [1] to refer to interactive museum installations that allow multiple people to collaboratively explore large sets of data using hand gestures and body movements. Subsequently, the definition of HDI has been extended in [9], [6] and [93] to include the process of making big sets of data (e.g., data streams that generally undergo long data mining processes) accessible to a broader audience. This democratization process aims to move large datasets out of research labs (the domain of data scientists), into public spaces and informal learning settings, such as museums.

Personalization as an Entry-Point to HDI

Personalization has been used as a way to provide an entry-point to interacting with data. It incorporates the idea that allowing visitors to select "their own" data that they want to explore creates a personal connection with the data, which facilitates engagement [4] and learning [13]. This strategy, however, requires visitors to spend some time at a kiosk, before entering the main interactive space. This may disengage visitors because of the length of the "preliminary" configuration work that they have to undergo, or simply not be feasible in some exhibit spaces.

Using Silhouettes to Support Engagement

Snibbe et al. suggest to use bodies to control projected shadows in social spaces [16]. Shoemaker et al. propose to incorporate users' silhouettes on top of the

Figure 2: Experimental setup that we used for this study. Our system (IDEA) included a data visualization projected on a 65" screen, a Microsoft Kinect, and some instrumentation of the interaction space (e.g., we use a yoga mat to highlight the area in which users were able to control the timeline).

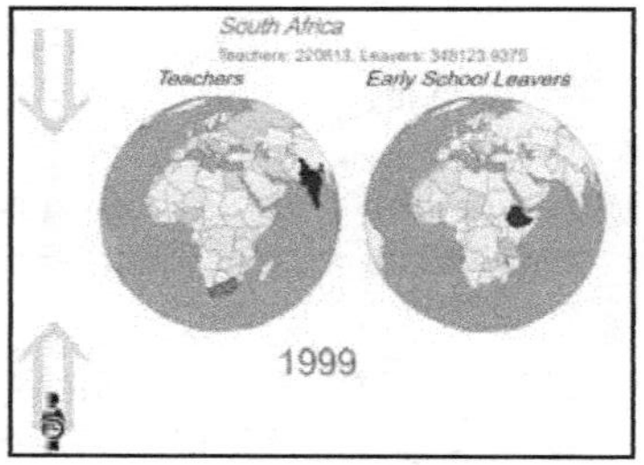

Figure 3: Screen shot of the interactive data visualization for IDEA. It can be accessed at Visualization Web Link.

user interface [15]. Although engaging, this approach covers a portion of the visualization, which would limit the learning opportunities offered by HDI installations (for example, it would be difficult to compare two datasets, if one is covered by the user's shadow). Looking Glass [10] recommends to incorporate people's silhouettes in order to design engaging shop windows. In this paper, we explore how the idea of incorporating visitors' silhouettes can be applied to the design of engaging HDI experiences for informal learning.

Application Scenario: IDEA

"Interactive Data and Embodied Analysis" (IDEA) is a prototype installation that allows museum visitors to use their body to explore large datasets -see Figure 2. IDEA comprises of interactive data visualization on a large screen and a 4mx4m interaction space in front of the screen. We used C++ (to control the Kinect) and JavaScript (for the data visualization) to create a custom-made application. Visitors can move within the interaction space to interact with the artifact.

IDEA: Data Visualization

The screen contains the geospatial representation of data projected on a globe with color gradations across countries (Figure 3): a darker color for a country represents a higher value of the corresponding data. The datasets include variables of general interest like forest coverage, GDP, tourism, number of school teachers, number of early school droppers, and number of literate people for a country. These variables were selected from United Nations Environment Program database[http://geodata.grid.unep.ch/]. All variables are available from year 1999 to 2014. Each variable is represented on individual globe, two at a time.

The visualization is interactive and allows the following functionalities:

- *Rotation (start and stop):* The globes continue to rotate at a predefined speed. They can be stopped to focus on a particular country, and the rotation can again be re-started by the user.
- *Time-line (move forward and backward in time):* The time line depicts all the data for a particular year. As the time line is moved, the data on the globe gets updated, adjusting the color gradients corresponding to the data values.
- *Exploration (Get Detailed Data about One Country)*: Navigating over a country displays the precise values of the variables for that country and the selected year in textual format.

The users are assigned different controls. User 1 is assigned control of Rotation and Time-line, while user 2 is assigned control of Exploration. The assignment takes place on first-to-enter-the-space basis.

IDEA: Interaction Space

The interaction space is an isosceles trapezoidal space in front of the projected screen, with the shorter base length at 1.0 meters and longer base length at 2.7 meters from the Kinect sensor. The height of the sensor is 1.0 meter. We marked three zones on the floor (Figure 2). The zones are labeled using colored non-slippery yoga mats and textual labels indicating the functionality that people can control in that area. For instance, the zone that enables the change in years (time-line) is marked as "TIME" as well as covered with a yellow colored mat and the user who is assigned the time-line control moves *only* in her/his zone. Visitors can move from one location to another, within a zone or across zones (depending on the control assigned). In

IDEA Functionalities	Controlling Body Movements
Stop the Globe Rotation	Stand Still on the "STOP" zone
Start the Globe Rotation	Stand Still just outside the "STOP" zone
Increase the Year Value	Take Forward steps in "TIME" zone
Decrease the Year Value	Take Backward steps on "TIME" zone
Hover over Country and Obtain Detailed Valued about that Country	Walk within the Interaction Space

Table 1: Body Movements used to Control IDEA

IDEA, we focused on movements from left to right, front and back, staying still at one location (Table 1).

Methodology

The goal of this work is to identify the challenges that users face when using the system with minimum instructions, in order to provide design recommendations for crafting interactive installations for data exploration that visitors can find engaging, even without the intervention and support of museum interpreters. In order to do that, we explore four alternative strategies for providing entry points to the interaction:

(1) instrumenting the floor;
(2) forcing collaboration;
(3) implementing multiple body movements to control the same effect;
(4) visualizing the visitors' silhouette beside the data visualization.

We conducted naturalistic observations of visitors' interaction with the prototype. The interaction between researchers and visitors was minimal: a notice that visitors were entering a video-recorded area and a study information sheet were on display at the entrance of the interaction, and two moderators were available to answer questions that visitors may have about the study or the installation. Specifically, we let the people explore the system all by themselves and observed and video recorded their interaction. We used a semi-experimental design, in order not to interfere with the way in which visitors generally experience museum installations: people were able to interact with the variation of the IDEA prototype that was on display during their visit. We then used the videos from the study sessions to find the *Interaction Time,* defined as the time spent by the users with IDEA. Ideally, we would like visitors to interact with IDEA for as long as possible, in order to discuss data to a larger extent.

Results & Discussion

A total of 56 visitors participated to this study, which we conducted at Discovery Place, a science museum in Charlotte, NC. All study sessions were videotaped. In the following, we report preliminary results and observations from our study, which we believe can be useful for the design of engaging HDI experiences.

The First Fifteen Seconds are Crucial for the Interaction
As we expected, users spent some time understanding how the artifact would respond, before being able to instrumentally operate with IDEA. In particular, we called *On-Boarding Time* of the participant the time taken by the user to understand how the interaction works. This allows the users to understand the mapping between their movement within the interaction space, and the artifact response. We observed that, even though the interaction seemed novel, the users who were not able to guess how to operate with the system after attempting for 10 to 15 seconds all gave up, frustrated that the system could not map their movements to the visualization. Thus, the first 15 seconds are crucial when creating engaging HDI installations. It is worth noting that this time is significantly shorter than the two minutes visitors generally spend with traditional exhibits [14].

Floor Controls are not an Entry-Point to the Interaction
We found that all our participants initially did not understand that the floor was the interaction media. Even though we placed some colorful mats and labeled the location (see Figure 2) people did not look at the

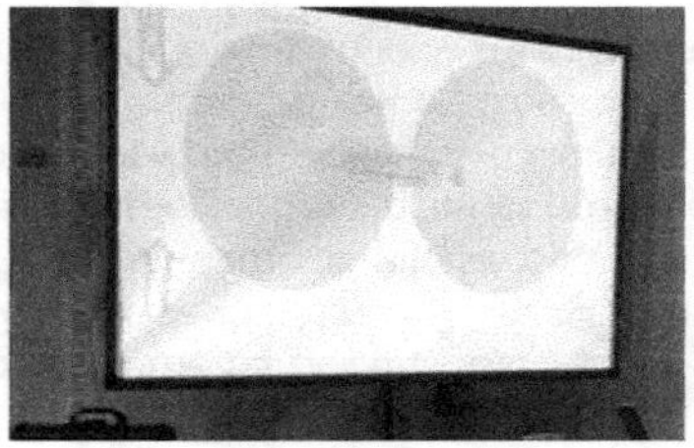

Figure 4: In the "Forcing Collaboration" strategy, the screen becomes active only when there are 2 users in the interaction space.

Figure 5: Silhouette that we used as mouse cursor in the Avatar condition (Image Link)

floor in the first instance. The data visualization was the primary focus even though areas of the floor were clearly marked and color coded. Thus, instrumenting the floor does not seem to be a viable entry-point to the interaction: it was not enough for our participants to understand that the system was interactive (rather than being static data visualization).

Forcing Collaboration is not an Entry-Point to the Interaction
Fostering collaboration and conversations among diverse groups of visitors is essential to create engaging learning experiences in museums [12,13]. Thus, we designed IDEA to encourage collaboration among two users at any given time. The start/stop and time-line control is given to one user, while navigation control is given to another user. The user entering the interaction space first is assigned the controls of start/stop and time-line; the second user is assigned the navigation control. In the case where two users enter the space simultaneously, the controls are assigned randomly. We programmed IDEA to track 2 users and send corresponding signals to the data visualization (Table 1). Because of the benefit of supporting collaboration, we tested two variations of the IDEA prototype: Forced Collaboration, and Non-Forced Collaboration. In the Forced Collaboration condition, we wanted to explore if forcing collaboration since the beginning of the interaction would be a viable entry point to the interaction itself (see Figure 4). The system initially forced the participants to enter in groups of two (we tested this system configuration with 26 visitors). If the sensor detected less than 2 users on the floor, a message was displayed on the screen saying "I *cannot see 2 users on the floor*". This experimental condition was aimed to enforce collaboration and team based data exploration. We expected visitors would have actively looked for a friend or companion to be able to "activate the system." Contrarily to our expectation, forcing collaboration was not a viable entry-point to the interaction. We observed that this did not encourage users to interact with IDEA. Some of the users left the interaction space instead of calling for a partner: out of 26 participants, eight left without even interacting with IDEA. In the Non-Forced Collaboration condition, we allowed people to operate with the system even as solo users. In this latter condition, we did not observe this phenomenon anymore.

Implementing Multiple Controlling Actions for the Same Functionality is an Entry-Point to the Interaction
In IDEA, the time-line displays the icon of a person (see Figure 3). Our original idea was to make the icon move up and down as the user moves forward and backward on the time-line area on the floor. We decided, however, to use the Kinect to track the neck joint rather than the torso, so that people were potentially able to control the timeline also with more subtle head movements. Interestingly, we observed that 6 users figured out alternative ways to move the timeline, which was by jumping up and down, swaying side by side, or rocking back and forth without moving their feet. Thus, including multiple ways of interacting with the same system functionality seem to be an effective entry-point to the interaction, as people have more chances to guess how to operate with the system.

Displaying the Visitors' Silhouette is an Entry-Point to the Interaction
When people move through the interaction space a navigation control (i.e., a cursor) moves with visitor up,

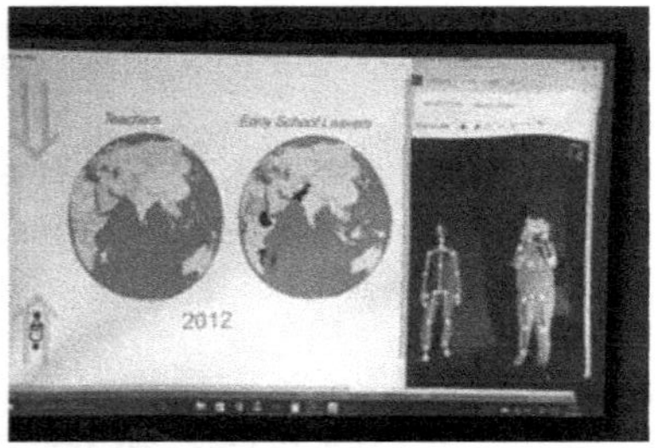

Figure 6: The "Mirror" condition showing the digital reflection of the users on the side of IDEA visualization.

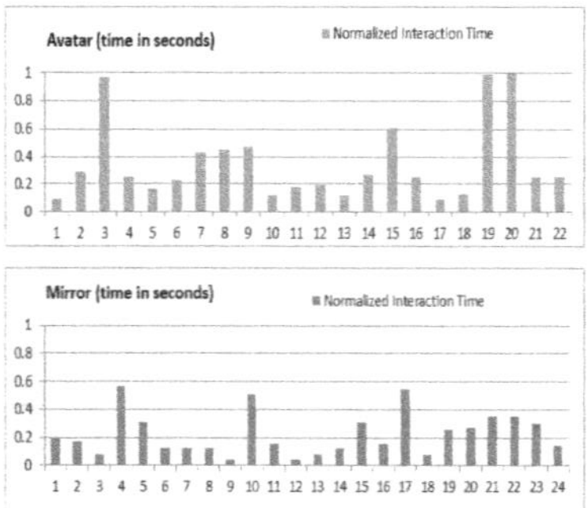

Figure 7: Interaction Time for Mirror and Avatar conditions. The X-axis contains the participant IDs: Avatar – 22 participants; Mirror-24 participants. The actual data value in second for each participant has been normalized to lie between 0 and 1 by dividing with the highest noted value across both groups, primarily to show the trend of increase in time.

down, left, right. When the user walks (i.e., moves the cursor) on a country, IDEA visualizes a popup screen with additional data for that country. We tested two alternative ways of incorporating a representation of the visitor into the data visualization interface, in order to create a correspondence between visitors' movements and navigation control: *Avatar*, and *Mirror*.

In the *Avatar* condition, we replaced the mouse cursor with a standard picture, with a person silhouette (Figure 5). We observed that the user could barely see the cursor moving. It took several attempts for the user to point out where the cursor was on the map. User responses like, *"where am I going?", "How does this thing work?"* and *"Is anything happening?"* along with random movement on the floor, demonstrated that the cursor, which works well for desktop systems, failed to provide the feedback for body movements.

In the *Mirror* condition, we displayed visitors' silhouette (together with tracking information), in real-time, beside the main data visualization (Figure 6). The users could see their own silhouettes on the right side of the screen with the rest of interactive visualization on the left side of the screen. An paired t-test was conducted to compare users' interaction time in the Mirror vs. Avatar conditions; there was a significant difference in interaction time under Avatar (X=28.29, SD=19.58) and Mirror (X=45.41, SD=36.31) conditions, $p<0.03$. Thus, we observed that the average interaction time with the system was significantly higher in the *Mirror* condition (Figure 7). In general, higher interaction with the system denotes that people are spending more time with it, which could maximize data exploration. We noticed, however, that visitors were more interested in seeing themselves on the screen rather than with the exploring the artifact: e.g., people tended to spend more time dancing and moving their bodies with minimal intention to interact with data.

Thus, introducing a live representation of the users (rather than a standardized avatar) provides an effective entry point to the interaction. It may, however, be distracting. Using silhouettes that mimic the user's body movements on the screen, but that are just slightly bigger than traditional mouse cursors, may provide an interesting compromise. Such silhouettes should appear immediately as the user enters the interaction space and should leave with the user, and may be displayed on a side portion of the screen, or used as an alternative to more traditional navigation controls. These design ideas should be further investigated in future work.

Conclusion and Future work

In this paper, we observed that engaging museum visitors in data exploration is an open challenge, and we explored different strategies to provide an entry-point to the interaction with HDI installation. In the upcoming work, we will generate alternative prototypes to further evaluate the entry-points that we identified in this paper. We would also like to experiment with different technologies (e.g., displaying the data visualization on the floor), and assess the relationship between engaging and learning when visitors interact with data.

References

1. Alissa N Antle, Paul Marshall, and Elise van den Hoven. 2011. Embodied Interaction: Theory and Practice in HCI. *Proceedings of CHI 2011*.
2. Francesco Cafaro. 2012. Using embodied allegories

to design gesture suites for human-data interaction. *Proceedings of the 2012 ACM Conference on Ubiquitous Computing*, ACM, 560–563.

3. Francesco Cafaro, Leilah Lyons, Raymond Kang, Josh Radinsky, Jessica Roberts, and Kristen Vogt. 2013. Framed Guessability: Using Embodied Allegories to Increase User Agreement on Gesture Sets. *Proceedings of the 8th International Conference on Tangible, Embedded and Embodied Interaction*, ACM, 197–204.
4. Francesco Cafaro, Alessandro Panella, Leilah Lyons, Jessica Roberts, and Josh Radinsky. 2013. I see you there!: developing identity-preserving embodied interaction for museum exhibits. *Proceedings of the 2013 ACM annual conference on Human factors in computing systems*, ACM, 1911–1920.
5. Alma Leora Culén. 2012. Transforming Children's Museums by Designing Exhibits with Children. *The Transformative Museum*: 87.
6. Heiko Hornung, Roberto Pereira, M Cecilia C Baranauskas, and Kecheng Liu. 2015. Challenges for Human-Data Interaction–A Semiotic Perspective. In *Human-Computer Interaction: Design and Evaluation*. Springer, 37–48.
7. Annie Kelly, Matt Whitlock, Brielle Nickoloff, Angel Lam, Danielle Albers Szafir, and Stephen Voida. 2017. Becoming Butterflies: Interactive Embodiment of the Butterfly Lifecycle. *Proceedings of the 2017 ACM International Joint Conference on Pervasive and Ubiquitous Computing and Proceedings of the 2017 ACM International Symposium on Wearable Computers*, ACM, 93–96.
8. Lu'\is Leite and Veronica Orvalho. 2012. Shape Your Body: Control a Virtual Silhouette Using Body Motion. *CHI '12 Extended Abstracts on Human Factors in Computing Systems*, ACM, 1913–1918.
9. Richard Mortier, Hamed Haddadi, Tristan Henderson, Derek McAuley, and Jon Crowcroft. 2014. Human-data interaction: The human face of the data-driven society. *Available at SSRN 2508051*.
10. Jörg Müller, Robert Walter, Gilles Bailly, Michael Nischt, and Florian Alt. 2012. Looking glass: a field study on noticing interactivity of a shop window. *Proceedings of the SIGCHI Conference on Human Factors in Computing Systems*, ACM, 297–306.
11. Felicia Clare Paul, Christabel Goh, and Kelly Yap. 2015. Get Creative With Learning: Word Out! A Full Body Interactive Game. *Proceedings of the 33rd Annual ACM Conference Extended Abstracts on Human Factors in Computing Systems*, ACM, 81–84.
12. Deborah L Perry. 2012. *What makes learning fun?: principles for the design of intrinsically motivating museum exhibits*. Rowman Altamira.
13. Jessica Roberts, Leilah Lyons, Francesco Cafaro, and Rebecca Eydt. 2014. Interpreting Data from Within: Supporting Humandata Interaction in Museum Exhibits Through Perspective Taking. *Proceedings of the 2014 Conference on Interaction Design and Children*, ACM, 7–16.
14. Cody Sandifer. 1997. Time-based behaviors at an interactive science museum: Exploring the differences between weekday/weekend and family/nonfamily visitors. *Science Education* 81, 6: 689–701.
15. Garth Shoemaker, Anthony Tang, and Kellogg S Booth. 2007. Shadow Reaching: A New Perspective on Interaction for Large Displays. *Proceedings of the 20th Annual ACM Symposium on User Interface Software and Technology*, ACM, 53–56.
16. Scott S Snibbe and Hayes S Raffle. 2009. Social immersive media: pursuing best practices for multi-user interactive camera/projector exhibits. *Proceedings of the SIGCHI Conference on Human Factors in Computing Systems*, ACM, 1447–1456.

Prototyping and Simulating Complex Systems with Paper Craft and Augmented Reality: An Initial Investigation

Seokbin Kang
Dept. of Computer Science
University of Maryland
sbkang@cs.umd.edu

Leyla Norooz
Coll. of Information Studies
University of Maryland
leylan@umd.edu

Virginia Byrne
Coll. of Education
University of Maryland
vbyrne@umd.edu

Tamara Clegg
Coll. of Information Studies
Coll. of Education
University of Maryland
tclegg@umd.edu

Jon E. Froehlich
School of Computer Science
and Engineering
University of Washington
jonf@cs.washington.edu

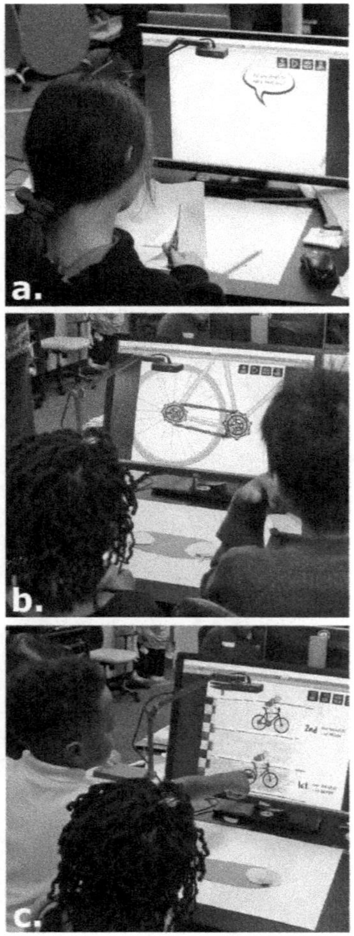

Figure 1: With *Rainbow,* children **(a)** make lo-fi prototypes of complex systems (*e.g.,* bike gears), **(b)** which are digitized into virtual models, and **(c)** tested in a digital simulation environment. See supplementary video for a demonstration.

ACM ISBN 978-1-4503-5568-1/18/03.
https://doi.org/10.1145/3173225.3173264

Abstract
We present early work developing an Augmented Reality (AR) system that allows young children to design and experiment with complex systems (*e.g.,* bicycle gears, human circulatory system). Our novel approach combines low-fidelity prototyping to help children represent creative ideas, AR visualization to scaffold iterative design, and virtual simulation to support personalized experiments. To evaluate our approach, we conducted an exploratory study with eight children (ages 8-11) using an initial prototype. Our findings demonstrate the viability of our approach, uncover usability challenges, and suggest opportunities for future work. We also distill additional design implications from a follow-up participatory design session with children.

Author Keywords
Augmented reality; prototyping; simulation; children

Introduction
With advances in computer vision, increases in the performance and availability of GPUs, and new, emerging platforms such as *HoloLens* [25] and *ARKit* [1], there is renewed interest in the role of Augmented Reality (AR) in learning (*e.g.,* [17,38]). While there is

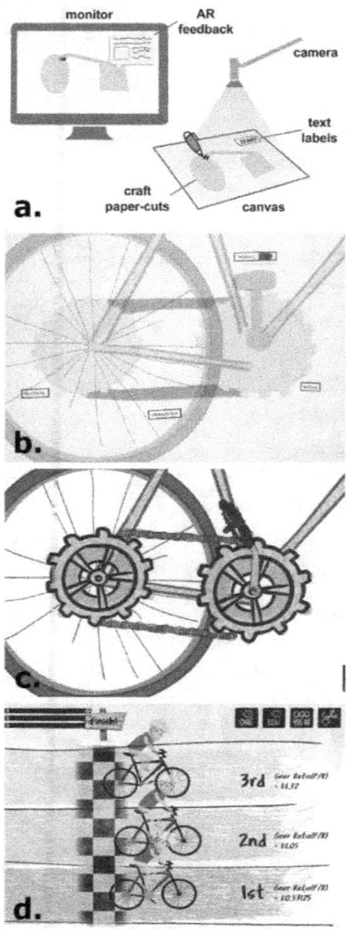

Figure 2: (a) An overview of *Rainbow.* **(b)** An example paper prototype of the bike gear system as visualized in the AR environment; **(c)** the resulting virtual models; and **(d)** a bike race simulation to test the gears.

rich literature exploring how AR may support learning and *in situ* training dating back to the early 2000s—*e.g.,* by providing contextual information via head-mounted displays [21,22] or by mobile devices [7,20]—this work is primarily aimed at adults [14,37] or high school students [7,8,28,30]. In our research, we are interested in developing and exploring new AR systems for younger learners, grades K-5, who are still developing cognitively, socially, and emotionally, and who draw primarily on direct physical and social experiences to construct understanding [39].

In this paper, we introduce *Rainbow,* an AR-based "smart desk" that allows children to rapidly prototype complex systems using paper and then to test their designs in an accompanying digital simulation environment (Figure 1). As a child builds a prototype, *Rainbow* actively analyzes the work surface using computer vision to provide *in-situ* computer-mediated scaffolds. The scaffolds provide timely feedback and bridge connections to existing knowledge to help the child solve problems that otherwise might be too difficult [29]. Because the testing environment is digital, there is tremendous flexibility in how a design can be simulated and used for scientific inquiry (*e.g.,* by dynamically changing experimental variables, modifying the testing context).

Our work is informed by the pedagogical theories of *Constructionism* [19,27] and the *Learning by Design* framework [5]—both which emphasize that learning is enhanced when children construct physical artifacts and collaboratively reflect on and share their work. To support this constructive learning experience, our work focuses on providing a creative design interface—which can be shared by multiple users—to facilitate collaborative design, rapid prototyping, and prompt evaluation of ideas.

Below, we provide background on AR-based learning systems, outline the current *Rainbow* prototype, and describe a preliminary evaluation. Our primary contributions include the initial design and implementation of *Rainbow*, key findings drawn from our user study, and a distillation of future work informed by a follow-up participatory design session.

Related Work

While many Augmented Reality (AR) systems have been developed to support interactive design tasks [2,9,24,36] and simulation-based experiments [8,21,30], there is little work targeting young children who are still developing their understanding of the world and often struggle to grasp abstract concepts (*e.g.,* cause-and-effect) [11]. Prior work has demonstrated the educational potential of AR simulation in various subjects, including physics [21,22], electronics [18,30], and science literacy [7]. For example, *Augmented Chemistry* [8] helps learners understand and explore molecular structures via AR-enhanced tangible manipulations. While *Rainbow* also augments low-fidelity materials with digital representations, we engage the user in the entire design process—from ideating and prototyping to testing and analysis. Moreover, we scaffold the user through computer-mediated prompts to bridge knowledge gaps and address design problems.

Lo-fi prototyping using paper, sketches, or wireframes can be useful for quick iteration of design and engineering ideas at a minimal cost [3]. Lo-fi materials, which require less time and design skills, are

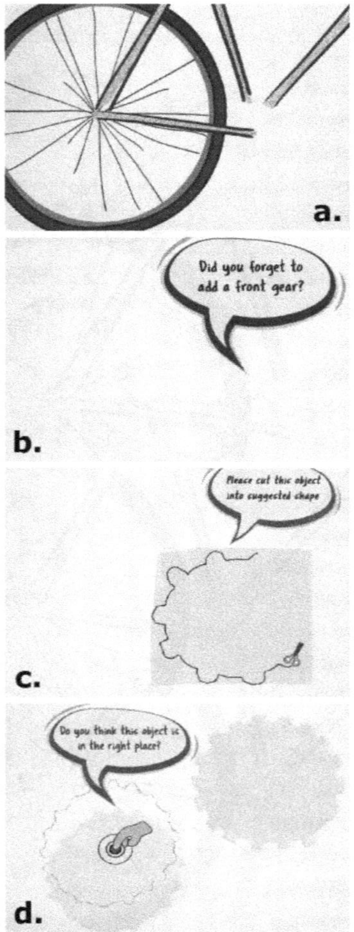

Figure 3: (a) Augmentation of a design prompt; suggestive feedback indicates **(b)** a missing object, **(c)** an inappropriate shape, and **(d)** a wrong position.

particularly suitable for young children to give tangible form to their creative ideas [6,15,31]. Many interactive prototyping systems employ tangible lo-fi materials to support the creation of virtual 3D models and 3D-printable mock ups. For example, *DuploTrack* [16] and Miller et al.'s work [26] use Lego building blocks to construct 3D models with the help of visual guidance. *Maker's Marks* [32] and *KidCad* [10] take advantage of sculpting materials to rapidly build 3D-printable mockups and reconstruct physical models, respectively. Also, paper and sketches have been used for editing 3D CAD models [33] and designing living spaces [23]. However, there is little work aimed at helping young children design and understand complex systems, which is our goal. In addition, *Rainbow* uses a novel lo-fi prototyping interface to represent physical structures, program objects' functions, and specify logical connections (Figure 2b).

System Design

Rainbow is designed to facilitate creative prototyping of systems, scaffold learning during the design process, and engage young children in personalized scientific inquiry. Our initial implementation offers a table design workspace in which user can interact with both physical materials and an AR visualization. The system is comprised of a canvas to construct prototypes with lo-fi materials (*e.g.,* craft paper, scissors, markers), a top-down document camera to recognize the prototype, and a monitor to display AR visualizations and the simulation environment (Figure 2). We describe three major parts of our approach: (1) prototyping with the lo-fi design interface; (2) design assessment and AR feedback for scaffolding; (3) functional simulation to support testing and scientific inquiry (Figure 2). See the supplementary video for a demonstration.

Lo-fi prototyping interface

The lo-fi prototyping interface leverages the tangibility and flexibility of craft material in order to engage young children in rapid prototyping of ideas. It encourages externalizing creative ideas into concrete representations that can be refined through iterations. Our initial implementation supports paper prototyping. The prototyping interface allows the child to specify common features needed to build a system, which includes the *structure*, *function*, and *logical connections* [12,13,34]. We describe each below.

Designing *Structure*. The initial AR canvas shows a design prompt (*e.g.,* "create your own bicycle gears"). An accompanying background image is superimposed on the canvas to help children think about the layout and position of system components (Figure 3). Users create each component object by choosing a color paper and cutting it into a shape—the color of paper determines the object type (*e.g., yellow* for a front gear). Then, users place the objects on the canvas, aligning them with the AR image.

Designing *Function*. Users specify the primary behavior of each *structure* by naming it (*e.g., rotate* for a wheel object) and describing related variables (*e.g.,* rotational speed for the rotate behavior). The user selects a behavior from a provided deck of printed text labels and places it near the corresponding object on the canvas. Then, the system augments the label with a caption illustrating the definition and how to describe its function variable values (Figure 4a, 4c). The user can specify a numerical value by filling a horizontal level bar (Figure 4b) or select a categorical value by marking a check box on the label (Figure 4d).

a.

b.

c.

d.

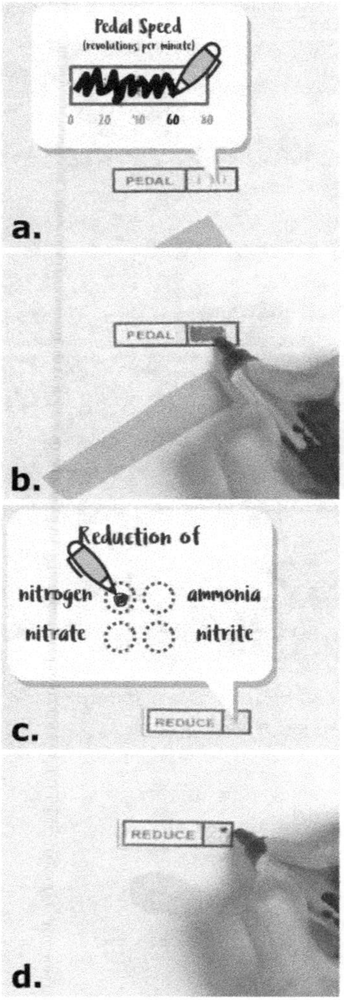

Figure 4: (a, b) Numerical function variable design; **(c, d)** categorical function variable design.

Designing *Logical Connections*. Users describe the relationship between *structure* components and behaviors such as cause-and-effect, synchronization, and parallelism. Our current implementation does not yet support designing these logical connections.

Automatic machine assessment and scaffolding
Repeatedly throughout the prototyping process, the machine assesses the validity of the prototype and provides contextualized feedback. The physical prototype is first translated into a computational model by computer vision techniques. The parallel processing of the image captured by the camera—including filtering, color clustering, blob analysis, text recognition, and variable recognition—generates a computational model of structures, behaviors, and logical connections in the prototype. Then, the system evaluates the model by comparing it to the standard model and identifies potential problems (*e.g.,* an object is placed in the wrong position). In the end, the AR renderer visualizes feedback that can help resolve identified problems (Figure 3b-d). The visualization includes both textual and graphical messages tailored to suggest corrective actions. For example, if an object is too far from its desirable position, the AR feedback shows a message (*e.g.,* "*Do you think this object is in the right place?*") and an animation moving it toward the correct position (Figure 3d).

Functional simulation
Key to any design activity is the ability to test and iterate on one's design. Functional simulation offers personalized inquiry activities in which children can test their designs, learn from these tests, and update their designs accordingly. The simulation supports learning about the functional mechanisms but also serves as a design prompt motivating iterations on prototypes. Once the user selects a set of previously built prototypes to compare (Figure 5b), the visualization converts each prototype into a virtual model that represents the design variables of the prototype. The final simulation is designed to highlight the functional difference across the virtual models through animated visualizations, possibly making it easier for children to make observations about the relationship between a specific design variable and functional phenomena. More importantly, it presents details of functional parameters (*e.g.,* a gear ratio of a bike gear prototype) to support in-depth analysis of the results (Figure 5c).

Preliminary Study
To gain a preliminary understanding of how children interact with Rainbow and future design ideas, we conducted a two-session participatory design study with eight children (ages 8-11). The study was part of a Collaborative Inquiry [6] design program in which children collaborate with adult researchers to design and develop technologies for children's learning and play. The participants were split into three groups of 2-3 children along with adult partners who captured and analyzed the children's interactions and ideas.

The first session was designed to evaluate the usability of our Rainbow prototype, which included: (i) a 15-minute overview of our prototype; (ii) 40 minutes of prototyping a bicycle gear system and reporting likes, dislikes, and design ideas [35]; (iii) 20 minutes of answering usability questions; and (iv) the adult partners' observation debrief. We used a reduced version of Rainbow with one design prompt—building bike gears—that supported designing structures but not

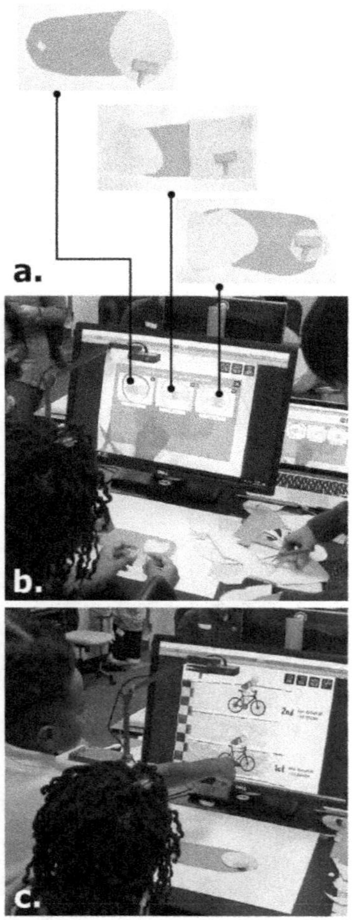

Figure 5: Children experiment with **(a, b)** previously built prototypes and **(c)** observe differences in their functions.

functions or logical connections (these were set automatically by the system).

In the second design session, children did not use Rainbow but, instead, engaged in lo-fi prototyping activities to help brainstorm future directions. The session started with a 15-minute overview of the design activity in which children chose sample systems to design (*e.g.,* a camera lens system). Then, children were divided into three groups and engaged in a 45-minute lo-fi prototyping activity. In the end, children presented their design ideas along with the prototypes.

Data and analysis

We collected system log including images of children's prototypes, a written summary of design ideas [6,15], the adult partners' reflections, and audio/video recordings of the entire activity. We used a mixed deductive and inductive approach, following Chi's eight-step process [4], to validate our approach, understand children's interaction, and identify future design ideas. Two researchers developed the initial themes including reported user experience, observed usability issues, and emerging interaction ideas. Key findings were verified by reviewing qualitative (*e.g.,* quotes) and quantitative (*e.g.,* the number of logged design iterations) data. We present our findings below.

Findings

Creation, testing and simulating. Overall, children learned how to use Rainbow and liked the core features such as the use of craft (*e.g.,* "*making our own shapes*"), responsive augmentation (*e.g.,* "*the gears mirror the paper size*"), and personalized simulation (*e.g.,* "*we can race our gears*") (Figure 1). From the beginning, children built creative designs with unexpected shapes and layouts using the lo-fi interface. Then children rapidly iterated on their prototypes, making use of testing and suggestions shown in the AR scaffolding feedback. The system log shows that each group iterated on prototypes an average of 17 times during the 40-minute activity. Children created a variety of designs with different characteristics (*e.g.,* different gear ratios), which they tested with simulated experiments. For example, a group simulated three bike prototypes of high-, mid-, and low-gear ratios and reported, "*the yellow [rear gear] is so small and it still won*" (Figure 5).

Challenges. Though children appreciated the usefulness of the suggestive feedback (*e.g.,* a child stated "*Yes it was helpful ...[to] tell you where to move it*"), some complained about the sensitivity of machine assessment (*e.g.,* "*It was picky*"). Children struggled at the beginning to understand what they were supposed to do and the extent of Rainbow's functionality (*e.g.,* "*No idea what to do*" and "*[did not know] we could choose our own gears*"). We also observed tension between promoting creativity in prototypes and controlling variables in experimentation. To test a hypothesis, all design variables (*e.g.,* chain and pedal) need to be controlled with the exception of an independent variable (*e.g.,* gears). However, children occasionally changed multiple aspects of a prototype at a time (*e.g.,* comparing two gear prototypes that differ in both gear sizes and pedal sizes), which complicated the experimental setup and subsequent analysis. A child noticed the problem, stating, "*if you are trying to prove something ... then you want to keep your variable the same ... science class taught me that.*"

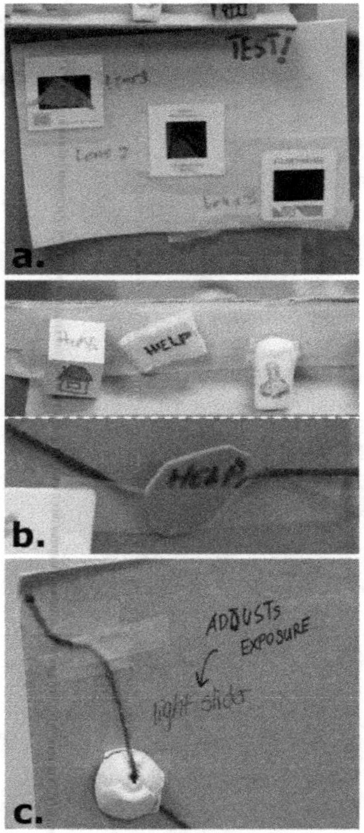

Figure 6: Children suggested design ideas of **(a)** including a simulation panel to test their prototypes while designing, **(b)** help buttons to receive scaffolding feedback as needed, and **(c)** a tangible slider to control a numerical variable.

Design ideas. From the two design sessions, we were able to distill key design ideas related to scaffolding, the lo-fi prototyping interface, and the use of AR. First, children preferred testing their own designs *first* before receiving suggestive feedback. They stressed the importance of having control over *when* to open a scaffolding or "hint" dialogue (Figure 6b). Second, children came up with novel design features for future systems, including one group who designed an intelligent doll attached a speech function to the prototype that the doll could tell about itself (*e.g.*, "*Once built, he can talk to you [to help you design]*"). Another group designed a camera system that included a tangible slider control to manipulate a hidden property (*e.g.*, the exposure value of a lens, Figure 6c). Lastly, two groups shared an idea of using immersive technologies (*e.g.*, VR goggles) rather than an external display. A child stated, "*VR is more fun. Looking in the computer, you can get more distracted but, in the VR, you can just focus on one entire thing.*"

Discussion and Conclusion

We presented early research on combining lo-fi prototyping and AR visualization to promote a new model of computer-mediated learning. Children learn through making physical prototypes, receive feedback from machine intelligence, and conduct personalized experiments with virtual simulation.

While our initial work demonstrates the viability of our approach, revealed usability issues, and offered insights into future work, our evaluation was limited to examining high-level user experience and soliciting design ideas. We did not examine how technical problems could arise from children's unexpected design activities (*e.g.*, when one child created a very tiny object to represent a gear, the computer vision algorithm simply recognizes this as noise).

In our future work, we plan to: (i) expand Rainbow to accommodate a broader range of lo-fi materials; (ii) implement improved scaffolds that better direct scientific experiments and are not seen as intrusive; (iii) develop multiple example applications in other domains (*e.g.*, biology or ecology); (iv) employ AR technologies such as a projected display or AR goggles to promote new forms of interaction; and (v) conduct expanded user studies in a range of learning contexts (*e.g.*, classrooms or afterschool programs).

Acknowledgements

We thank the children and researchers in the Kidsteam program at the University of Maryland, College Park. This work was supported by an NSF Grant IIS-441184.

References

1. Apple Inc. 2017. ARKit. Retrieved from https://developer.apple.com/arkit/
2. Ryan Arisandi, Yusuke Takami, Mai Otsuki, Asako Kimura, Fumihisa Shibata, and Hideyuki Tamura. 2012. Enjoying virtual handcrafting with ToolDevice. In *Adjunct proceedings of the 25th annual ACM symposium on User interface software and technology* (UIST Adjunct Proceedings '12), 17. https://doi.org/10.1145/2380296.2380306
3. Bill Buxton. 2010. *Sketching user experiences: getting the design right and the right design*. Morgan Kaufmann.
4. Michelene T H Chi. 1997. Quantifying qualitative analyses of verbal data: A practical guide. *The journal of the learning sciences* 6, 3: 271–315.

5. Bill Cope and Mary Kalantzis. 2015. *A pedagogy of multiliteracies: Learning by design*.
6. Allison Druin. 1999. Cooperative Inquiry: Developing New Technologies for Children with Children. In *Proceedings of the SIGCHI Conference on Human Factors in Computing Systems* (CHI '99), 592–599. https://doi.org/10.1145/302979.303166
7. Matt Dunleavy, Chris Dede, and Rebecca Mitchell. 2009. Affordances and limitations of immersive participatory augmented reality simulations for teaching and learning. *Journal of Science Education and Technology* 18, 1: 7–22. https://doi.org/10.1007/s10956-008-9119-1
8. Morten Fjeld, Jonas Fredriksson, Martin Ejdestig, Florin Duca, Kristina Bötschi, Benedikt Voegtli, and Patrick Juchli. 2007. Tangible User Interface for Chemistry Education: Comparative Evaluation and Re-design. In *Proceedings of the SIGCHI Conference on Human Factors in Computing Systems* (CHI '07), 805–808. https://doi.org/10.1145/1240624.1240745
9. Sean Follmer, David Carr, Emily Lovell, and Hiroshi Ishii. 2010. CopyCAD: Remixing Physical Objects with Copy and Paste from the Real World. In *Adjunct Proceedings of the 23Nd Annual ACM Symposium on User Interface Software and Technology* (UIST '10), 381–382. https://doi.org/10.1145/1866218.1866230
10. Sean Follmer and Hiroshi Ishii. 2012. kidCAD : Digitally Remixing Toys Through Tangible Tools. In *Proceedings of the SIGCHI Conference on Human Factors in Computing Systems* (CHI '12), 2401–2410. https://doi.org/10.1145/2207676.2208403
11. Rochel Gelman and Kimberly Brenneman. 2004. Science learning pathways for young children. *Early Childhood Research Quarterly* 19, 1: 150–158. https://doi.org/10.1016/j.ecresq.2004.01.009
12. J.S. Gero. 1990. Design Prototypes: A Knowledge Representation Schema for Design. *AI Magazine* 11, 4: 26. https://doi.org/10.1609/aimag.v11i4.854
13. Ashok K Goel, Swaroop S Vattam, Spencer Rugaber, David Joyner, Cindy E Hmelo-silver, Rebecca Jordan, Sameer Honwad, Steven Gray, and Suparna Sinha. 2009. Learning Functional and Causal Abstractions of Classroom Aquaria The SBF Theory of Understanding of Complex Systems ACT : Interactive Construction of SBF Models. *Science*, August: 2128–2133.
14. Michihiko Goto, Yuko Uematsu, Hideo Saito, Shuji Senda, and Akihiko Iketani. 2010. Task support system by displaying instructional video onto AR workspace. In *2010 IEEE International Symposium on Mixed and Augmented Reality* (ISMAR '10), 83–90. https://doi.org/10.1109/ISMAR.2010.5643554
15. Mona Leigh Guha, Allison Druin, and Jerry Alan Fails. 2013. Cooperative Inquiry revisited: Reflections of the past and guidelines for the future of intergenerational co-design. *International Journal of Child-Computer Interaction* 1, 1: 14–23. https://doi.org/10.1016/j.ijcci.2012.08.003
16. Ankit Gupta, Dieter Fox, Brian Curless, and Michael Cohen. 2012. DuploTrack : A Real-time System for Authoring and Guiding Duplo Block Assembly. In *Proceedings of the 25th Annual ACM Symposium on User Interface Software and Technology* (UIST '12), 389–401. https://doi.org/10.1145/2380116.2380167
17. Tien Chi Huang, Chia Chen Chen, and Yu Wen Chou. 2016. Animating eco-education: To see, feel, and discover in an augmented reality-based experiential learning environment. *Computers and Education* 96: 72–82. https://doi.org/10.1016/j.compedu.2016.02.008

18. María Blanca Ibáñez, Ángela Di Serio, Diego Villarán, and Carlos Delgado Kloos. 2014. Experimenting with electromagnetism using augmented reality: Impact on flow student experience and educational effectiveness. *Computers and Education* 71: 1–13. https://doi.org/10.1016/j.compedu.2013.09.004
19. Yasmin B Kafai and Mitchel Resnick. 1996. *Constructionism in practice: Designing, thinking, and learning in a digital world*. Routledge.
20. Amy M. Kamarainen, Shari Metcalf, Tina Grotzer, Allison Browne, Diana Mazzuca, M. Shane Tutwiler, and Chris Dede. 2013. EcoMOBILE: Integrating augmented reality and probeware with environmental education field trips. *Computers and Education* 68: 545–556. https://doi.org/10.1016/j.compedu.2013.02.018
21. Hannes Kaufmann and Bernd Meyer. 2008. Simulating Educational Physical Experiments in Augmented Reality. In *ACM SIGGRAPH ASIA 2008 Educators Programme* (SIGGRAPH Asia '08), 1–8. https://doi.org/10.1145/1507713.1507717
22. Hannes Kaufmann and Dieter Schmalstieg. 2003. Mathematics and geometry education with collaborative augmented reality. *Computers and Graphics (Pergamon)* 27, 3: 339–345. https://doi.org/10.1016/S0097-8493(03)00028-1
23. Han-Jong Kim, Ju-Whan Kim, and Tek-Jin Nam. 2016. miniStudio: Designers' Tool for Prototyping Ubicomp Space with Interactive Miniature. In *Proceedings of the 2016 CHI Conference on Human Factors in Computing Systems* (CHI '16), 213–224. https://doi.org/10.1145/2858036.2858180
24. Manfred Lau, Masaki Hirose, Akira Ohgawara, Jun Mitani, and Takeo Igarashi. 2012. Situated Modeling: A shape-stamping interface with tangible primitives. In *Proceedings of the Sixth International Conference on Tangible, Embedded and Embodied Interaction* (TEI '12), 275–282. https://doi.org/10.1145/2148131.2148190
25. Microsoft. 2017. HoloLens. Retrieved from https://www.microsoft.com/en-us/hololens
26. Andrew Miller, Brandyn White, Emiko Charbonneau, Zach Kanzler, and Joseph J. Laviola. 2012. Interactive 3D model acquisition and tracking of building block structures. *IEEE Transactions on Visualization and Computer Graphics* 18, 4: 651–659. https://doi.org/10.1109/TVCG.2012.48
27. Seymour Papert and Idit Harel. 1991. Situating Constructionism. *Constructionism* 36, 2: 1–11. https://doi.org/10.1111/1467-9752.00269
28. Remo Pillat, Arjun Nagendran, and Robb Lindgren. 2012. Design requirements for using embodied learning and whole-body metaphors in a mixed reality simulation game. In *2012 IEEE International Symposium on Mixed and Augmented Reality - Arts, Media, and Humanities* (ISMAR-AMH '12), 105–106. https://doi.org/10.1109/ISMAR-AMH.2012.6484003
29. Chris Quintana, Brian Reiser, Elizabeth Davis, Joseph Krajcik, Eric Fretz, Ravit Golan Duncan, Eleni Kyza, Daniel Edelson, and Elliot Soloway. 2004. A Scaffolding Design Framework for Software to Support Science Inquiry. *The Journal of the Learning Sciences* 13, 3: 337–386. https://doi.org/10.1207/s15327809jls1303_4
30. Teresa Restivo, Fátima Chouzal, José Rodrigues, Paulo Menezes, and J. Bernardino Lopes. 2014. Augmented reality to improve STEM motivation. In *2014 IEEE Global Engineering Education Conference (EDUCON)*, 803–806. https://doi.org/10.1109/EDUCON.2014.6826187
31. Jochen Rick, Phyillis Francois, Bob Fields, Rowanne Fleck, Nicola Yuill, and Amanda Carr. 2010. Lo-Fi

Prototyping to Design Interactive-Tabletop Applications for Children. *Capital & Class2* 36, 1: 77–95. https://doi.org/10.1016/j.jbusres.2014.06.013.The

32. Valkyrie Savage, Sean Follmer, Jingyi Li, and Björn Hartmann. 2015. Makers' Marks: Physical Markup for Designing and Fabricating Functional Objects. In *Proceedings of the 28th Annual ACM Symposium on User Interface Software & Technology* (UIST '15), 103–108. https://doi.org/10.1145/2807442.2807508
33. Hyunyoung Song, François Guimbretière, Chang Hu, and Hod Lipson. 2006. ModelCraft: capturing freehand annotations and edits on physical 3D models. In *Proceedings of the 19th Annual ACM Symposium on User Interface Software and Technology* (UIST '06), 1–10. https://doi.org/10.1145/1166253.1166258
34. Y. Umeda, H. Takeda, T. Tomiyama, and H. Yoshikawa. 1990. Function, behaviour, and structure. *Applications of Artificial Intelligence in Engineering V 1*, 177–193.
35. Greg Walsh, Elizabeth Foss, Jason Yip, and Allison Druin. 2013. FACIT PD: a framework for analysis and creation of intergenerational techniques for participatory design. In *Proceedings of the SIGCHI Conference on Human Factors in Computing Systems* (CHI '13), 1–10. https://doi.org/10.1145/2470654.2481400
36. Christian Weichel, Manfred Lau, David Kim, Nicolas Villar, and Hans W. Gellersen. 2014. MixFab: A Mixed-Reality Environment for Personal Fabrication. In *Proceedings of the 32nd annual ACM conference on Human factors in computing systems* (CHI '14), 3855–3864. https://doi.org/10.1145/2556288.2557090
37. Giles Westerfield, Antonija Mitrovic, and Mark Billinghurst. 2015. Intelligent augmented reality training for motherboard assembly. *International Journal of Artificial Intelligence in Education* 25, 1: 157–172. https://doi.org/10.1007/s40593-014-0032-x
38. Hsin-kai Wu, Silvia Wen-yu Lee, Hsin-yi Chang, and Jyh-chong Liang. 2013. Computers & Education Current status , opportunities and challenges of augmented reality in education. *Computers & Education* 62: 41–49. https://doi.org/10.1016/j.compedu.2012.10.024
39. Peta Wyeth and Helen C Purchase. 2003. Using developmental theories to inform the design of technology for children. In *Proceedings of the 2003 conference on Interaction design and children* (IDC '03), 93–100. https://doi.org/10.1145/953536.953550

Flyables: Exploring 3D Interaction Spaces for Levitating Tangibles

Pascal Knierim
LMU Munich, Germany
pascal.knierim@ifi.lmu.de

Alexander Achberger
University of Stuttgart, Germany
st100158@stud.uni-stuttgart.de

Thomas Kosch
LMU Munich, Germany
thomas.kosch@ifi.lmu.de

Markus Funk
TU Darmstadt, Germany
funk@tk.tu-darmstadt.de

Figure 1: Left: User performing touch interaction with a levitating tangible. **Right:** Grabbing and repositioning of a levitating tangible.

TEI '18, March 18–21, 2018, Stockholm, Sweden
ACM 978-1-4503-5568-1/18/03.
https://doi.org/10.1145/3173225.3173273

Abstract

Recent advances in technology and miniaturization allow the building of self-levitating tangible interfaces. This includes flying tangibles, which extend the mid-air interaction space from 2D to 3D. While a number of theoretical concepts about interaction with levitating tangibles were previously investigated by various researchers, a user-centered evaluation of the presented interaction modalities has attracted only minor attention from prior research. We present Flyables, a system adjusting flying tangibles in 3D space to enable interaction between users and levitating tangibles. Interaction concepts were evaluated in a user study(N=17), using quadcopters as operable levitating tangibles. Three different interaction modalities are evaluated to collect quantitative data and qualitative feedback. Our findings show preferred user interaction modalities using Flyables. We conclude our work with a discussion and future research within the domain of human-drone interaction.

Author Keywords

Tangible user interfaces; actuated tangible interfaces; 3D interaction; quadcopter; Human-Drone Interaction

CCS Concepts

•Human-centered computing → Haptic devices; Interaction techniques;

Introduction and Background

The vision of Tangible User Interfaces (TUIs) embodying digital information was proposed decades ago [9]. Holman and Vertegaal envisioned a future of Organic User Interfaces [8], where all physics act as display and interaction can be triggered by shape changes. In Radical Atoms [10], Ishii described a future in which all digital information is linked to some physical matter to enable direct interaction. For the most part, these works are rather theoretical and only scratch the surface regarding implementation.

On the roadmap to Radical Atoms, various TUIs have been developed and studied extensively. Reactable [11], a musical instrument, allows users to mix and control sounds by placing, moving, or rotating building blocks on an interactive surface. Since tangibles are passive, there are limited possibilities to indicate changes of digital information introduced by software processes. This breaks the illusion of a tight coupling of digital information and the physical matter. To overcome this limitation, Nowacka et al. [13] developed actuated physical objects for interacting with interactive multi-touch tabletops. These active tangibles can move around the surface and keep the link between digital and physical information even on software processes or remote input. However, the interaction remained limited to the 2D interaction space. Gravity inhibits tangibles from being set freely in the 3D space. 2.5D shape changing displays partly tackle this challenge, by allowing the actuation of passive objects and enabling dynamic affordances [6]. To make tangibles usable in 3D space, quadcopters have recently attracted attention in the research domain of TUIs. Gomes et al. [7] proposed BitDrones, a toolbox to model 3D tangible interaction leveraging quadcopters. This theoretical concept includes touching, dragging, picking, and throwing quadcopters as interaction modality. Various researchers showed how quadcopters could be used as floating touch interfaces [2] or to generate force feedback [1]. Recently, we used quadcopters to facilitate tactile feedback in immersive virtual environments [12] or to support blind people during guidance and navigation [3, 4]. Previous work shows the applicability of using quadcopters in practical scenarios. However, a user study evaluating the presented interaction modalities was not conducted. Ongoing research about levitating tangibles, designing spaces of quadcopters as input or output modality for TUIs has scarcely been explored. Previous research concentrated on gestural input [5, 14], and on theoretical [7] or technical [15] concepts, leaving user-centered evaluations behind.

In our work, we present Flyables, a system capable of regulating levitating tangibles in 3D space. Using Flyables, we study the design space of tangible levitating devices. This is achieved by building self-levitating tangible cubes using computer controlled quadcopters, similar to Gomes et al. [7]. We conducted a user study with 17 participants to investigate the usability of *touch* and *draw* interaction, as well as the physical interaction space reached by users executing a *drag* interaction using Flyables. Results show a high acceptance for *touch* and *drag* interaction, where participants actively controlled quadcopters. However, participants were challenged to notice *draw*, an output modality in which the quadcopter generates forces in a certain direction. The contribution of this work comprises (1) the evaluation of the three prior mentioned interaction modalities in a user-centered study and (2) the presentation of potential future research that can be derived from the conducted user study.

Interaction Modalities

Adopting flying quadcopters as levitating user interfaces allows to cover 3D interaction spaces. Input and output modalities can be communicated between the user and quadcopter.

Input Modalities
In the following, we describe two gestures to communicate user input through quadcopters. We present *drag* and *touch* as input modality.

The first user input modality is *drag*, where the quadcopter is grasped by a user and positioned to a different point in space. The quadcopter retains its position until the next user input or moves to its default position after a timeout.

The second input modality is *touch* interaction. A *touch* is recognized when the quadcopter realizes a shift into a single direction. After recognizing a *touch*, quadcopters return immediately to their original position. User touch can be performed from different sides of the quadcopter, such as touching the front or sides.

Output Modality
Similar to communicating input, quadcopters can communicate output by drawing the user into a direction upon a grasp. The grasped tangible *draws* the hand of the user into a direction, where the direction indicates the kind of feedback. In combination with *drag*, feedback can be instantly delivered by a draw gesture.

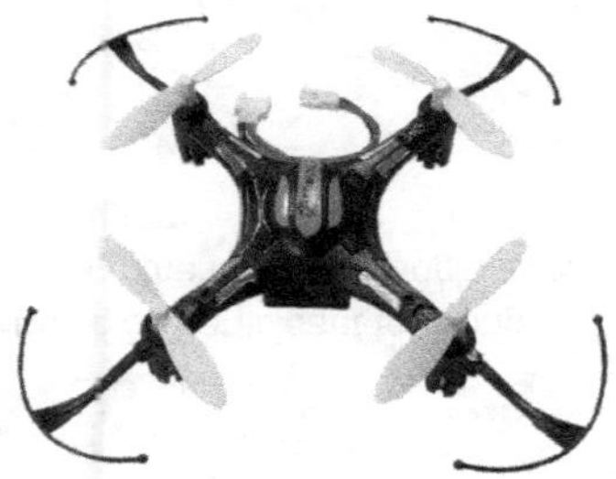

Figure 2: Quadcopter used as levitating tangible device.

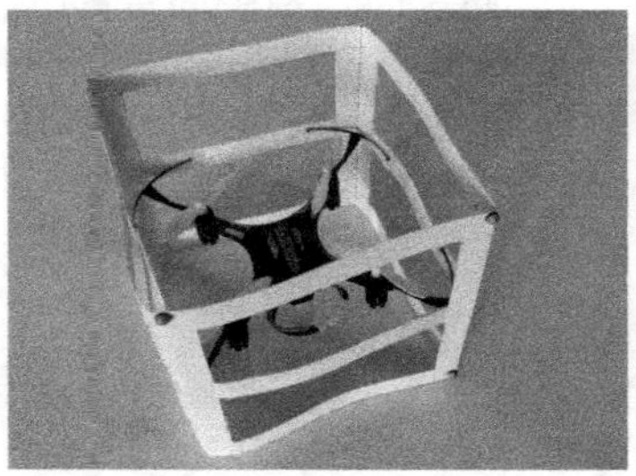

Figure 3: Quadcopter equipped with a cage to enhance tangible interaction.

Technical Overview
To evaluate physical interaction spaces using levitating tangible user interfaces, we constructed a system capable of tracking and controlling quadcopters. In the following, we present the implementation of *Flyables*.

Quadcopter
An Eachine H8 Mini is used as levitating interaction component (see Figure 2). To make quadcopters graspable, a small cage consisting of light but solid cardboard has been built around it (see Figure 3). We ensured that the cardbox was stable enough to provide protection from the rotors while being graspable at the same time. The top and bottom of the cubic cage is not covered to ensure unrestrained airflow. Reflective markers are attached on the cage to enable accurate motion tracking. Including the cage, the dimensions of the quadcopter comprise 11 cm × 11.5 cm × 11 cm. The overall weight of the levitating tangible is 26 grams.

Tracking System
An OptiTrack system is used as tracking system for our flyable framework. Eight OptiTrack Prime 13W infrared cameras are used to cover a space of 2.7 m × 2.4 m × 2.5 m. The tracking system recognizes tracking markers mounted on the cage, thus delivering the current 3D position in real-time. Position data are processed with a refresh rate of 240 Hertz.

Flight Control
To control the 3D position of the quadcopter, we connected an Arduino UNO to a remote control compatible with the quadcopter. The Arduino UNO is connected to a computer, which simultaneously receives position data of the quadcopter. A flight control software calculates the steering commands for the quadcopter to stay at a defined position. Using a PID loop, the position of the quadcopter is automatically reset to its origin if the position was changed manually.

Study
Using our system, we evaluate the interaction space and usability of levitating tangibles using our *Flyables* framework. By conducting a user study, quantitative and qualitative data is collected to evaluate the usability and user experience when using levitating tangibles as interaction

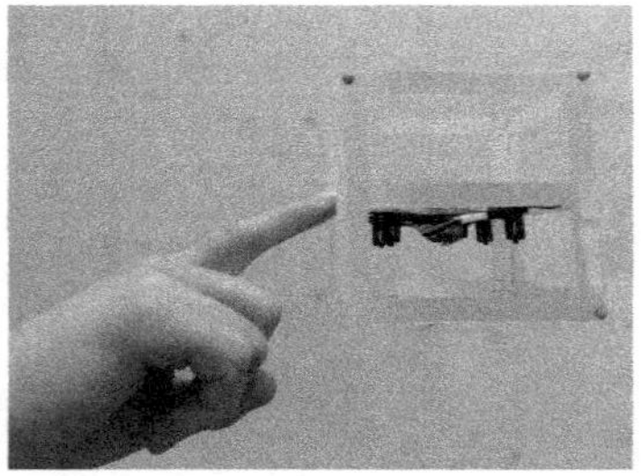

Figure 4: Participant touching the levitating tangible with the index finger.

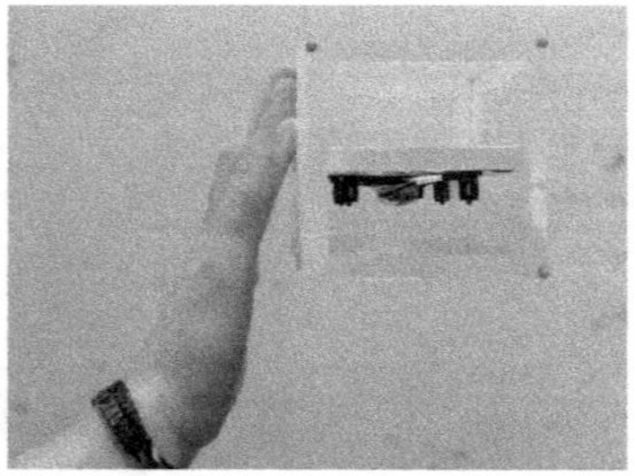

Figure 5: Participant touching or pushing the levitating tangible with four fingers.

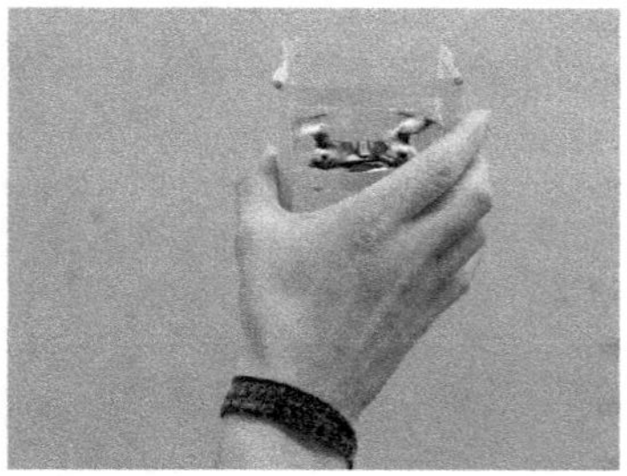

Figure 6: Levitating tangible grabbed by the user to be dragged to another physical location.

devices. The quantitative part of the study consisted of a *touch*, *drag*, and *draw* task. Qualitative data was collected during follow-up semi-structured interviews.

Method
The study was divided into three parts, each requiring participants to use one of the three prior mentioned modalities. Accordingly, two tasks comprised the usage of quadcopters as input device corresponding to the *drag* and *touch* gesture. The third task evaluated the *draw* modality to communicate output.

We analyze a subset including *touch*, *drag*, and *draw* of the previously described interaction modalities. A continuous stream of position data of a single quadcopter was collected during all tasks of the study. The experimenter instructed the participant during the study about their current objective.

During the evaluation of *touch*, participants were required to touch the levitating tangible. Participants were also instructed to perform *touch* interaction as they would prefer to. *Touch* has been evaluated for three different heights above the ground (120 cm, 140 cm, 160 cm), resulting in 15 *touch* interactions. Participants rated the interaction comfort for different heights on a 7-point Likert scale.

The second input task dealt with dragging the tangible to one of nine directions (up, up right, right, down right, down, down left, left, up left, and forward). Participants had to *drag* the quadcopter to a specific position according to spoken commands from the experimenter. We recorded the 3D position in space of the tangible with respect to the origin (140 cm above the ground in front of the participant) as well as the way participants grabbed the quadcopter. The quadcopter was moved twice in each direction in a random order. We did not explain how far the tangible should be moved as we aimed to get unbiased measures. During the *drag* condition, participants were instructed to remain their initial position.

The last task focused on the feasibility of using our levitating tangible as haptic output interface. Participants were asked to grab the tangible with their right hand while holding a wireless controller in the other hand. The tangible started to *draw* the participant in a direction (forward, backward, left or right) after a randomized delay. Each time the participant noticed a *draw* by the quadcopter, they were requested to press a button and communicate the direction they felt. Every direction was presented three times during this task. The time participants reacted to the draw as well as errors such as incorrect *draw* or wrong direction were recorded.

Qualitative data, such as user feedback and further ideas for using levitating tangibles were collected at the end of the study through semi-structured interviews and questionnaires.

Procedure
After participants signed a consent form, we explained the prototype including a flight demonstration to the participants and informed participants that are allowed to abort the experiment at any time. The tasks were performed in a counterbalanced order to prevent sequence effects. All participants were in an upright position. Furthermore, we asked them to keep their initial position during the experiment.

Participants
We recruited 17 participants (6 female) with a mean age of $M = 21.6$ years ($SD = 1.62$). Participants were recruited through university mailing lists and by asking acquaintances for participation. 14 participants had a technical background. All participants are right-handed and had an

average height of $M = 178$ cm ($SD = 10.94$ cm). Twelve participants had no prior experience with quadcopters. The overall duration of the study was 50 minutes. Participants provided their demographics upon completion of the study.

Results
We compared the ratings for the different heights above the ground while interacting but could not find any statistically significant differences. However, 53% of the participants stated in the interview that they liked the altitude of 140 cm most. In detail p03 and p09 agree on a preferred height of 140 cm since "the tangible is not on eye level" and "most easy to grasp" (p05, p07, p13). Interestingly, there are two equally used techniques to touch the tangible. Eight participants used their index finger of the right hand to touch the tangible in the center (see Figure 4) while nine participants used all four fingers of the open hand to interact (see Figure 5). All participants used their whole hand during *drag* interactions (see Figure 6).

We recorded 306 individual drag interactions in nine different directions. The derived physical interaction space users naturally tend to use is illustrated in Figure 7. The space is almost rectangular with a median height of 93 cm to 189 cm above the ground and a width of 109 cm. Participants dragged the tangible in average 5 cm further to the right than left. The median forward movement is 50 cm.

Caused by the lightweight construction of the levitating tangible the induced draw is very gentle. From the 204 draw signals, only 127 (62%) were noticed. The average delay of realizing the draw was 1.36 sec. Participants stated in 50% that they prefer the draw in forward direction because "it was most perceptible" (p10) and they were "not concerned, that the quadcopter (tangible) would crash into them" (p08).

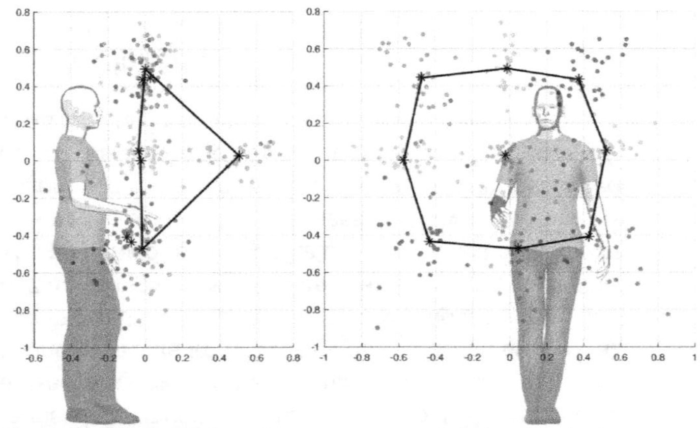

Figure 7: Physical interaction space covered during the study. Key: Up ●, Up Right ●, Right ●, Down Right ●, Down ●, Down Left ●, Left ●, Up Left ●, forward ●, Median ∗

During the course of the study and the follow-up semi-structured interview participants mentioned that they enjoyed the interaction. Five participants presented the idea to use levitating tangibles to control smart home devices. Further, one participant (p05) proposed to combine this tangible with virtual reality applications to enable haptic feedback. Beside this positive feedback participants had three major concerns. Precisely, they stated the noise and battery life as a drawback. Further, participants criticize the weak drag emitted by the tangible.

Discussion
Based on our findings, we discuss the implications of our results for future research in human-drone interaction.

Interaction Design
Results show great potential for *touch* and *drag* interaction. When designing *drag* interactions, we suggest staying within the described physical interaction space to prevent users from walking while holding levitating tangibles. When

possible, the tangible should idle at an altitude between elbow and breast (140 cm) to enable a comfortable use. Unfortunately, *draw* as output modality did not provide convincing results. Due to the light design of the tangible and the low-powered engines, the haptic feedback was not sufficient to be noticed by the users. From a technical view, we will investigate how the *draw* gesture can be improved by using draw gestures which would not be expected by the user. Furthermore, stronger engines will be incorporated in the current prototype to amplify *draw* gestures.

Hardware Design

For a satisfying user experience, the size of the cage should consist of a size between 10 cm$\times$10 cm and 12 cm$\times$12 cm. This makes it easy to grasp levitating tangibles even with small hands. We learned from our user study, that quadcopter and cage interfered together, thus creating a noisy environment. Furthermore, quadcopter frames should enclose levitating tangibles as good as possible to avoid injuries due to spinning rotor blades. These design limitations will be addressed for future development of the *Flyables* framework.

Limitations

Our current implementation is limited to unimodal interactions, which means that quadcopter can communicate single input or one output at the same time. However, *Flyables* can orchestrate multiple quadcopters and can thus extend the interaction space. Finally, the systems PID Loops are only capable of controlling tangibles within an accuracy of approximately ± 5 cm. Additionally, minor tracking inaccuracies can occur.

Future Work

Our preliminary results explore the feasibility of using quadcopters as levitating tangible interfaces. Our findings revealed spots to improve, such as fine-tuned PID controller, a more rigid frame to reduce vibrations, noise, and a visually blocking enclosure to avoid the doubt of touching the rotor blades. In future work, we want to evaluate *drag* interaction with a heavier quadcopter to improve output modalities communicated by levitating tangibles. This enables bimodal interaction between the user and levitating tangible, where feedback is communicated immediately after user input. Also, we will explore more complex interactions with more than one levitating tangible. Possible interactions could be *dragging* two tangibles at the same time to trigger rotation or resizing of digital objects. Moreover, we see enormous potential to create diversely shaped cages and investigate the affordance in learning scenarios as well as to control home appliances in a smart home environment.

Conclusion

We designed an actuated self-levitating tangible based on a quadcopter and studied potential interaction spaces in terms of communicating input and output. We conducted a user study with 17 participants to gather qualitative and quantitative data from participants interacting with levitating tangibles. Our prototype supports two input and one haptic output interaction, which were evaluated in the user study. The presented results facilitate a better understanding of how to use 3D tangible interfaces and how feasible interaction modalities can be designed. We further described guidelines on how to design levitating tangibles on basis of quadcopters, including appropriate interaction design.

Acknowledgment

This work was supported by the German Federal Ministry of Education and Research as part of the project Be-greifen (grant no. 16SV7527) and KoBeLU (grant no. 16SV7599K).

REFERENCES

1. Muhammad Abdullah, Minji Kim, Waseem Hassan, Yoshihiro Kuroda, and Seokhee Jeon. 2017. HapticDrone: An Encountered-Type Kinesthetic Haptic Interface with Controllable Force Feedback: Initial Example for 1D Haptic Feedback. In *Adjunct Publication of the 30th Annual ACM Symposium on User Interface Software and Technology (UIST '17)*. ACM, New York, NY, USA, 115–117. DOI: http://dx.doi.org/10.1145/3131785.3131821
2. Parastoo Abtahi, David Y. Zhao, L. E. Jane, and James A. Landay. 2017. Drone Near Me: Exploring Touch-Based Human-Drone Interaction. *Proc. ACM Interact. Mob. Wearable Ubiquitous Technol.* 1, 3, Article 34 (Sept. 2017), 8 pages. DOI: http://dx.doi.org/10.1145/3130899
3. Mauro Avila, Markus Funk, and Niels Henze. 2015. DroneNavigator: Using Drones for Navigating Visually Impaired Persons. In *Proceedings of the 17th International ACM SIGACCESS Conference on Computers & Accessibility (ASSETS '15)*. ACM, New York, NY, USA, 327–328. DOI: http://dx.doi.org/10.1145/2700648.2811362
4. Mauro Avila, Markus Funk, Matthias Hoppe, Robin Boldt, Katrin Wolf, and Niels Henze. 2017. DroneNavigator: Using Leashed and Free-Floating Quadcopters to Navigate Visually Impaired Travelers. In *Proceedings of the 19th international ACM SIGACCESS conference on Computers & Accessibility*. ACM, New York, NY, USA. DOI: http://dx.doi.org/10.1145/3132525.3132556
5. Jessica R Cauchard, Jane L E, Kevin Y Zhai, and James A Landay. 2015. *Drone & me: an exploration into natural human-drone interaction*. ACM, New York, New York, USA. DOI: http://dx.doi.org/10.1145/2750858.2805823
6. S Follmer, D Leithinger, A Olwal, A Hogge, and H Ishii. 2013. inFORM: dynamic physical affordances and constraints through shape and object actuation. *UIST* (2013), 417–426. https://pdfs.semanticscholar.org/724e/c59ad61124d1561f5b2a3edb917b1f9c9f22.pdf
7. Antonio Gomes, Calvin Rubens, Sean Braley, and Roel Vertegaal. 2016. *BitDrones: Towards Using 3D Nanocopter Displays as Interactive Self-Levitating Programmable Matter*. ACM, New York, New York, USA. DOI: http://dx.doi.org/10.1145/2858036.2858519
8. David Holman and Roel Vertegaal. 2008. Organic user interfaces: designing computers in any way, shape, or form. *Commun. ACM* 51, 6 (June 2008), 48–55. DOI: http://dx.doi.org/10.1145/1349026.1349037
9. Hiroshi Ishii. 2008. *Tangible bits: beyond pixels*. ACM, New York, New York, USA. DOI: http://dx.doi.org/10.1145/1347390.1347392
10. Hiroshi Ishii, Dávid Lakatos, Leonardo Bonanni, and Jean-Baptiste Labrune. 2012. Radical atoms: beyond tangible bits, toward transformable materials. *interactions* 19, 1 (Jan. 2012), 38–51. DOI: http://dx.doi.org/10.1145/2065327.2065337
11. Sergi Jordà, Günter Geiger, Marcos Alonso, and Martin Kaltenbrunner. 2007. The reacTable. In *the 1st international conference*. ACM Press, New York, New York, USA, 139–146. DOI: http://dx.doi.org/10.1145/1226969.1226998

12. Pascal Knierim, Thomas Kosch, Valentin Schwind, Markus Funk, Francisco Kiss, Stefan Schneegass, and Niels Henze. 2017. Tactile Drones - Providing Immersive Tactile Feedback in Virtual Reality through Quadcopters. In *Proceedings of the 2017 CHI Conference Extended Abstracts on Human Factors in Computing Systems (CHI EA '17)*. ACM, New York, NY, USA. DOI: http://dx.doi.org/10.1145/3027063.3050426

13. Diana Nowacka, Karim Ladha, Nils Y Hammerla, Daniel Jackson, Cassim Ladha, Enrico Rukzio, and Patrick Olivier. 2013. *Touchbugs: actuated tangibles on multi-touch tables.* ACM. DOI: http://dx.doi.org/10.1145/2470654.2470761

14. Kevin Pfeil, Seng Lee Koh, and Joseph LaViola. 2013. *Exploring 3d gesture metaphors for interaction with unmanned aerial vehicles.* ACM, New York, New York, USA. DOI: http://dx.doi.org/10.1145/2449396.2449429

15. Toshiya Yui and Tomoko Hashida. 2016. *floatio: Floating Tangible User Interface Based on Animacy Perception.* ACM, New York, New York, USA. DOI: http://dx.doi.org/10.1145/2984751.2985699

TUIst: A Collaborative and Computationally Enhanced Game Board

Trisha Garcia
Wellesley College
Wellesley, MA 02481, USA
tgarcia@wellesley.edu

Shannon Brown
Wellesley College
Wellesley, MA 02481, USA
Sbrown3@wellesley.edu

Siona Dev
Wellesley College
Wellesley, MA 02481, USA
sdev@wellesley.edu

TEI '18, March 18–21, 2018, Stockholm, Sweden
2018 Copyright is held by the owner/author(s).
ACM ISBN 978-1-4503-5568-1/18/03.
https://doi.org/10.1145/3173225.3173282

Abstract
TUIst is an interactive game board that hopes to improve collaboration and team building. Based on the familiar and popular game of Twister, TUIst is an interface of multiple circles that have lights and sounds mapped to the sensors to create an audible and visual reaction when an object (most likely a foot or hand) is placed on the corresponding circle. The game controller will allow for audience interception and participation; they will be able to change the rules of how the game is played, such as making players place their right hand on any red circle. This will increase the difficulty of the game. Our hope is that this board will be incorporated in popular and busy spaces, such as campus centers and offices. Our goal is to create an interface that will help foster engagement in communities.

Author Keywords
Graphical User Interface; Team Building; Computationally Enhanced; Light Emitting Diode;

ACM Classification Keywords
• Human-centered computing~Human computer interaction (HCI)

Introduction
Team building activities does not have a great reputation. Traditionally, awkward ice breaker games and long meetings are how people think about team building activity. However, it fosters trust, builds

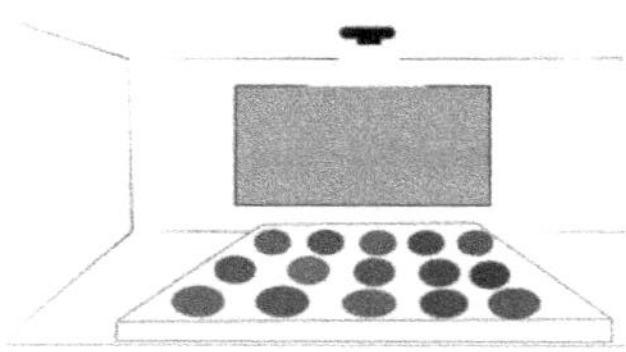

Figure 1: Mock-up designs of TUIst gameboard

communication, increases collaboration and can end conflict. Team building has helped in boosting group morale and improving creativity. Team building activities can become a more enjoyable and exciting experience when they stem away from leadership lessons and learning practical skills, it can. Unfortunately, team building as it exists is awkward and boring, which leads to it not being done not nearly enough.

Our solution to making team building a more enjoyable activity is TUIst, a game board based off two popular games: Matching and Twister. TUIst is a tangible interface that consists of a board of circles that recognizes touch and relays that signal to the game. TUIst allows users to work as a team both physically and mentally to meet a common goal. We believe that working towards a common goal while partaking in a physical activity allows for a more organic bonding to happen than by playing common ice breaker games.

Related Works

Prior works have included Table Tennis for Three [2] a tennis table that has a built-in display, where three players can remotely play tennis against one another. Table Tennis for Three contains a similar physical aspect to our concept; both games improve social interactions through physical activity. Where Table Tennis differs from TUIst is that it does not promote team building. This is primarily because Table Tennis is not a game where the players communicate with one another to meet their objective, which is the main aspect of TUIst.

Unruly Splats [1] is a Kickstarter product made up of a composition of interactive floor pieces that allow children to play, learn, and code. Unruly Splats has a similar concept to TUIst in that its primary form of interaction is through users' feet and hands. Unruly Splats, like TUIst, allows for creativity, collaboration, and audience involvement. In addition, the dynamic nature and ability to change the rules is a future goal in implementation of TUIst.

The most similar game to our project is People Pretzel [3]. People Pretzel is an enhanced game board that encourages social interaction and collaboration within public spaces. People Pretzel engages the whole body and promotes social interaction through informal collaboration. People Pretzel, like TUIst, builds upon the Twister game that prioritizes full body interaction, multicolored circles, and outside audience control to direct the nature of play. Moreover, the People Pretzel system utilizes a HandyBoard microcontroller, which is also an important implementation in our game board. The micro controller allows for the audience to interact with the game as well for the players to choose which version of the game they want to play.

Solution

Our proposed solution is a tangible user interface game board that will help with team building, shown in Figure 1. We want to create an interactive board based on the concepts of a Matching and Twister game. The board will have 24 touch panels placed in a 6x4 pattern. Each panel will have lights and sounds mapped to the sensors to create an audible and visual reaction when an object, a hand or foot, is placed on the corresponding panel. The objective of the game is for the users to match the color chosen randomly by the game, or the audience. When a user steps or places their hand on the panel, the panel will consecutively

Figure 2: Demonstrates color-changing interaction in response

emit a green, red, blue or yellow light. Since the objective of the game is to have all of the circles be the same color we envision that this product will help build communication between the users in a fun and creative way. This game forces users to physically work together in a team to improve collaboration.

We expect for "TUIst" to be engaging to a variety of users, but our target audience young adults. We see it being an opportunity for individuals gathered in public spaces to work together to match all the spots to one color. This board will provide the opportunity for adults to engage and collaborate in a visual and actionable manner, all while involving both the players and the audience at once.

We envision this interface in an easily accessible and frequently visited space within a given community. This includes university campus centers, city centers, gym entrances, office lobbies, or museum exhibits among other considerations. We see this as being a center spot within the space, something that is inviting to many at once and captures the attention of those walking by.

Game Design

The objective of TUIst is to re-invent a well-known and well understood childhood game, but in a more collaborative, engaging, and inventive way. TUIst builds on the integration of trust, interaction, and collaboration within people. The task at hand is to complete a game of twister, understanding that the game cannot be completed alone and requires teamwork to fully achieve a successful result

- Board Design
    a. Although we drew our original inspiration from the concept of a flat surface with multiple different polka dots—or game circles, we wanted to make sure that our design was simpler by using four primary colors: red, blue, yellow and green. We wanted to create a product that wasn't intimidating and can encourage spontaneous participation.
- Controller
    a. The audience uses a controller, Figure 2, to decide the nature in which the game will be played. This allows for a dynamic, ever-changing design so that the game at play is continuously different. The controller will also allow the audience to interfere in the game play by allowing the audience member to determine what color the players want to match during the game. To make this game as tangible as possible, the users will interact with controller to start a new game, and to choose the color they want to match.

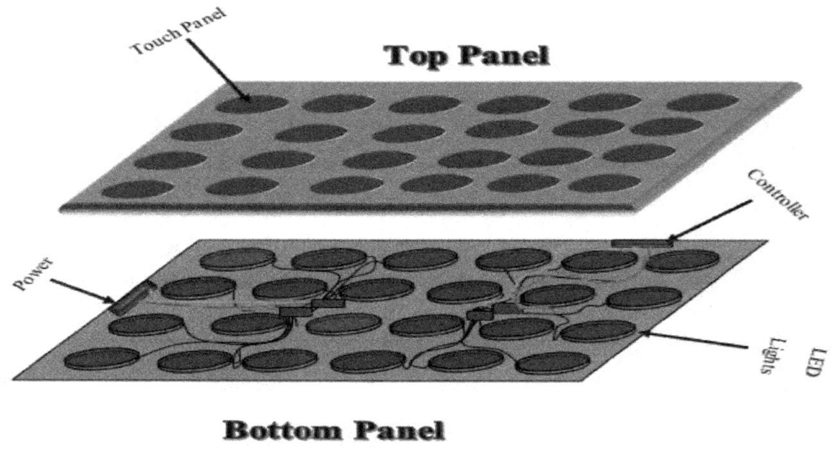

Figure 3: Structure and Components of the Game Board

Horizontal Architecture

We created the game board itself from wood by cutting 12 16″x24″ panels and using a laser cutter to replicate the image shown in Figure 3. The board will measure 5.33′ x 6′, closely following the original design of a Twister mat. The board will include 4 rows of 6 eclipsed shaped dots. The dimensions of the dots are 7″x8″ to allow for the eclipse shaped so that the user has plenty of space to place their foot and hands.

We ideally want up to four people to be able to play at once. Because the original Twister game, from which

we drew inspiration, is meant to feel crowded, we also didn't want to make the surface too large by adding too many dots because we want this game to be able to be played with smaller groups. We believe that two to four players are the perfect amount because it allows more intimate teamwork and collaboration. We decided to make the gameboard into a platform rather than a mat like the original Twister board because we wanted the surface to:

1) Stand out on the floor of a building
2) Act as a stage in a sense to encourage people to watch
3) Allow room for the electronic hardware such as lights, microcontrollers and potentially sound.

Each 16″ x 24″ panels contain two acrylic eclipse dots connected to a Force Sensitive Resistor. Underneath the panels are two Neopixels light emitting diodes, LEDs, that will consecutively emit a blue, red, green, or yellow light when the sensor is activated.

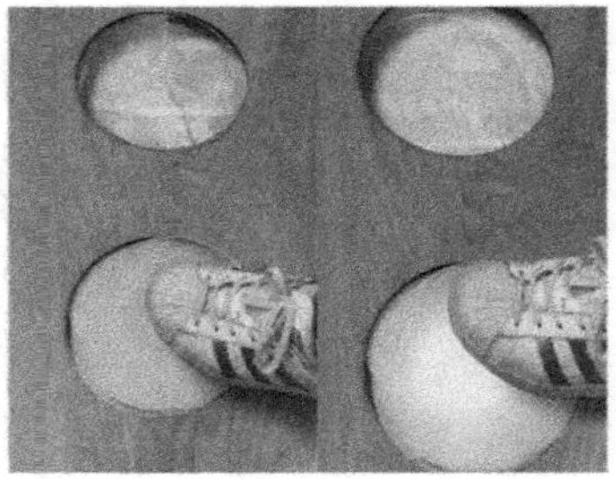

Figure 4: Demonstrates the color-changing interaction in response to a touch

Vertical Architecture

will have a passive mode in which there will be a light show that will emit a rainbow pattern while it is not being used. The game itself will start off with the users having the option to pick the number of players. After the user has inputted the number of Players, they will than choose what color they want to match. The board will than emit the four different colors for all 24 spots in a random pattern. The players can than choose which spot to place their hand or foot, see Figure 4, based on the body part that the game announced by a randomly generated algorithm. The audience members can interfere in the game by pressing the interfere button, which will give them the ability to choose which color they want the players to match. The game will than announce that there has been an interference and continue the game. When all spots are changed to the right color, the game has been won. If the players take longer than fifteen minutes to match the color, the controller will issue the game over sequence and go into passive mode.

Methods and Future Works

TUIst has been tested on primary school aged children to test for ease of play. While the test users were able to catch on to the game quickly, the lag in the light changing after users touched the panel caused the test users to become inpatient and move out of turn. Also, because the game allowed for multiple moves per round, the game was won quickly when the users did not follow the rules.

To correct the problems and issues that aroused during our first test, we will have to implement a shorter lag time to make the game run faster. We will also have to correct our programming to only register one move at a time. There is also discussion on either including a penalty of a loss of a minute when two moves our registered in one round, or to just have the game register the first movement. We also want to test this game on an 18 - 25 age group and an older demographic. We also aspire to hold a final testing in a campus center to monitor usability and user engagement.

Conclusion

The goal of TUIst is to engage people in a physical activity to promote collaboration. We imagine TUIst being in a very public setting, such as the lobby of the campus center. We believe that through the engineering of the gameboard to look like a platform combined with the passive mode option will draw users to investigate and engage with the board. The game will also be accessible to must people to play, primarily because you can either be a player or an audience participant.

Our is that this interface will give people the opportunity to meet and connect in a fun and active way. TUIst will give players the opportunity to play a fun game that leads to team building, and teaching players communication skills. We see this as a very strong opportunity for people to engage and collaborate in a non-competitive, easy-to-use, and exciting manner.

References

1. Bryanne Lemming. 2017. Unruly Splats: Active STEM Play. Retrieved September 23, 2017 from solution https://www.kickstarter.com/projects/bryanneleeming/unruly-splats-active-stem-play
2. Mueller, F. F., & Gibbs, M. R. 2007. Evaluating a Distributed Physical Leisure Game for Three Players (pp. 143-150, Tech.). doi:10.1145/1324892.1324919
3. Orit Shaer, Babak Ziraknejad, Ken Camarata, Ellen Yi-Luena, Mark D. Gross. A COMPUTATIONALLY ENHANCED PLAY BOARD FOR GROUP INTERACTION.
4. Patricia Yollin. 2008. Tangible fun at UC Berkeley's Virtual Projects. Retrieved September 23, 2017 from http://www.sfgate.com/bayarea/article/Tangible-fun-at-UC-Berkeley-s-virtual-projects-3258241.php

Crimson Wave: Shedding Light on Menstrual Health

Figure 1. The Crimson Wave smart mirror.

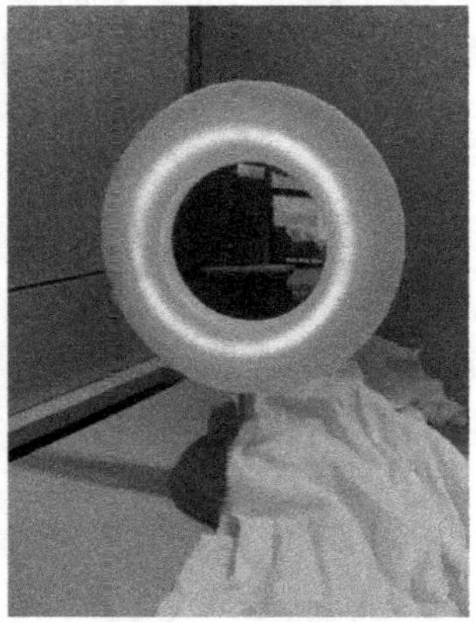

Figure 2. The user's sensor registers an elevated BBT, and the smart mirror calculates that they are on their period, causing the LED lights to shine red.

Margaret Flemings
Wellesley College
106 Central Street
Wellesley, MA 02481 USA
mfleming@wellesley.edu

Shanzay Kazmi
Wellesley College
106 Central Street
Wellesley, MA 02481 USA
skazmi2@wellesley.edu

Rachel Pak
Wellesley College
106 Central Street
Wellesley, MA 02481 USA
rpak@wellesley.edu

Orit Shaer
Wellesley College
106 Central Street
Wellesley, MA 02481 USA
oshaer@wellesley.edu

TEI '18, March 18–21, 2018, Stockholm, Sweden.

ACM ISBN 978-1-4503-5568-1/18/03.
https://doi.org/10.1145/3173225.3173292

Abstract

Crimson Wave is a personal tangible user interface that generates and displays information about its user's menstrual cycle. Basal Body Temperature (BBT) is an individual's temperature at rest, which fluctuates throughout menstruation. Crimson Wave tracks the user's BBT through the wearable armband and then displays the data visually on a separate smart mirror. Specifically, the mirror lights up a color corresponding to the menstrual stage the user is experiencing.

Crimson Wave offers a novel method of keeping track of one's health and integrating one's own menstrual information seamlessly into daily life. The combination of live and aggregated personalized data helps users optimize each day. Crimson Wave is helpful to people who are interested in being more informed about their cycles, especially when they are irregular. In this paper, we describe the concept behind Crimson Wave, as well as its implementation and iterations.

Author Keywords

Tangible interaction; physiological sensor; menstruation; wearables

ACM Classification Keywords

Human-centered computing~User interface design

General Terms

Design, Human Factors, Health

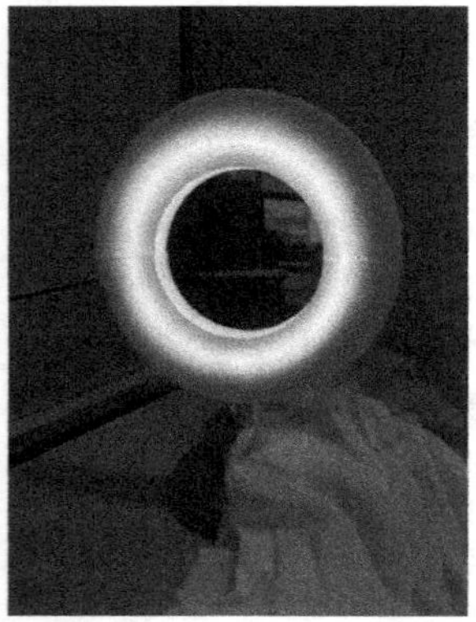

Figure 3. The user's sensor registers a BBT that has dropped from a high; thus the mirror indicates that the user's period is over.

Figure 4. The user's sensor registers a relative drop in BBT. The smart mirror calculates that the user is ovulating, which it indicates with a pink light.

Introduction

Every menstruating person's period is completely unique. One's menstrual cycle can be affected by stress, illness, medicine, pregnancy, etc. Period tracker apps on the market today attempt to estimate periods based on a standardized 28 day long cycle, but they require users to manually record data and rarely account for the aforementioned factors. Is there a better, more convenient way to get an accurate picture of menstruation? We address this question by using a sensor to track BBT over time. BBT provides more accurate and personalized data, as it rises and falls throughout an individual's menstrual cycle. During the menstrual cycle, two hormones circulate through the body: estrogen and progesterone. Estrogen stimulates the release of an egg from the ovaries and is active during the menstruation and follicular phase of the cycle. During the luteal phase, which lasts from ovulation to menstruation, progesterone production increases. This increase in progesterone causes a small, but easily measurable increase in BBT [9]. We offer a wireless, wearable armband with an integrated temperature sensor that automatically collects user's data. A separate smart mirror then displays the collected information. Depending on where the user is in their menstrual cycle, the mirror will output a different color. By using familiar objects such as a wearable and smart mirror, users can easily integrate their menstrual data into day to day life in a non-intrusive manner. This is significant as one's menstrual cycle impacts every aspect of their daily lives (weight, acne, moods, energy level, etc.). Many people who experience periods have to rearrange their lives around their menstrual cycles. Yet, due to both a lack of thorough sexual education in schools and general knowledge of menstruation, people are often unable to holistically understand their bodies. As Kannabiran et al. states, work involving sexual health is "much needed and can have immediate and positive effects on human life" [7]. Our goal is to create a tangible user interface aimed towards individuals who experience menstruation, so that they better understand their own bodies. On a larger scale, we hope Crimson Wave will stimulate discussion about the stigma surrounding menstruating bodies.

Related Work

Mobile application stores are inundated with various period, fertility, and birth control tracker apps that help users track a niche aspect of their menstrual health. In general, these apps are not based upon the user's day-to-day physical changes. Instead, these apps simplify the concept of a menstrual cycle, espousing the idea that there is a "perfect", regular period that is 28 days long on average. These apps also happen to be overwhelmingly coded with traditionally feminine characteristics. For example, the user interfaces are adorned with flowers and text that assume the user's gender by making "she/her/hers" the default pronouns. In our project, we seek to include everyone who experiences menstrual cycles, regardless of gender identity. Another characteristic of these types of mobile apps is that they send a great deal of push notifications to the user to remind them to record their daily menstrual happenings. The sheer number and frequency of these notifications can annoy users, particularly when they are busy.

While researching menstrual health we found a limited number of relevant papers. As discussed in *Hacking Women's Health*, women's health appears to be treated as a taboo topic in research [11]. Here, we recognize that many health issues associated with women's health, notably menstruation, affect more than those who identify as women, such as those who are transgender or intersex. Devices and technologies that are related to women's health appear to distance

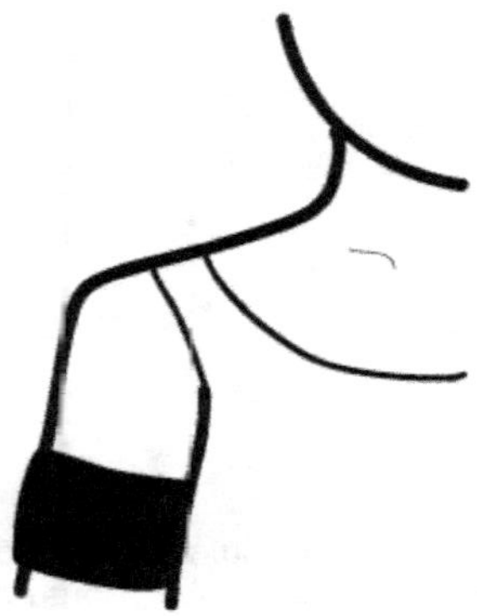

Figure 5. The user is wearing the soft armband that records the user's BBT.

themselves from the "'dirty work' of women's health" [13]. 'Dirty work' is defined as intimate care, usually associated with "personal hygiene, bodily functions and bodily products, which demand direct or indirect contact with or exposure of the sexual parts of the body as defined culturally by the individual" [13]. Instead of this more intimate care, more peripheral assistance is provided, such as advice about maintaining health throughout pregnancy and improving how health records are shared [13]. Avoidance of the body, as if it were taboo, has implications for the future of HCI [13].
A few papers deal with the role technology can play in helping a person track their menopause [10] [14]. One is an analysis of users' needs in designing the user interface of mHealth [10]. Another paper discusses functional aspects and interactions that should be integrated in mobile apps to empower people in monitoring their menopause [14]. Others consider personal informatics with respect to menstrual health. They indicate that while mobile apps can be convenient as a means of logging information, they are largely unhelpful in predicting periods as well as taking into consideration biological milestones in the life of a person who is designated female at birth (DFAB) [2]. These papers are relevant because they show a need for more research and development of technology directed towards the different stages of menstruation. Additionally, they show the flaws in conventional methods of predicting periods based on formulas.
Currently, there is a product on the market called Lady-Comp that might appear to accomplish the same goal as Crimson Wave; however, there are key differences between the two systems [9]. While both Crimson Wave and Lady-Comp rely on BBT to help users gain an understanding of their unique menstruation cycles, Crimson Wave makes the temperature recording process faster and easier. Lady-Comp requires the user to take their temperature using a thermometer and input their menstruation days manually, while Crimson Wave's wearable will record the user's BBT at the appropriate time without the user having to put in effort to do so. The goal of Lady-Comp is to help the user predict their fertile window, while Crimson Wave strives to give users a more holistic picture of their full menstrual cycle. For that reason, the outputs of Lady-Comp and Crimson Wave are very different. Finally, Lady-Comp is coded for ciswomen, and the product is very exclusionary. Crimson Wave is more inclusive of all people who may experience menstruation and fertility.
Regarding smart mirrors, Impressions Vanity Company designs their mirrors with features such as Bluetooth audio, dimmable lights, and hands-free phone call capability [5]. While these are certainly attractive features, the Crimson Wave mirror is designed with the AmbientROOM philosophy in mind, so a periphery experience is the goal [6]. Crimson Wave's mirror functions as both a mirror and physical representation of one's menstrual cycle. It would, in fact, detract from the purpose of Crimson Wave if more functions were added. Unlike the smart mirrors from Impressions Vanity Company, our mirror is intended to naturally integrate into the user's environment.

Design

Crimson Wave is designed as a circular mirror that is surrounded by LED lights (Fig. 6). The LEDs use different shades to indicate where the user is in their menstrual cycle based on the red color intensity. For example, if the LEDs are a deep red, the user is menstruating (Fig. 2). Additionally, Crimson Wave is comprised of a wearable armband that is worn at night (Fig. 5). This armband is made of a soft material and has a biosensor that tracks the user's BBT. BBT is impacted by physical activity as movement causes a rise in the body's core temperature. Thus, measuring

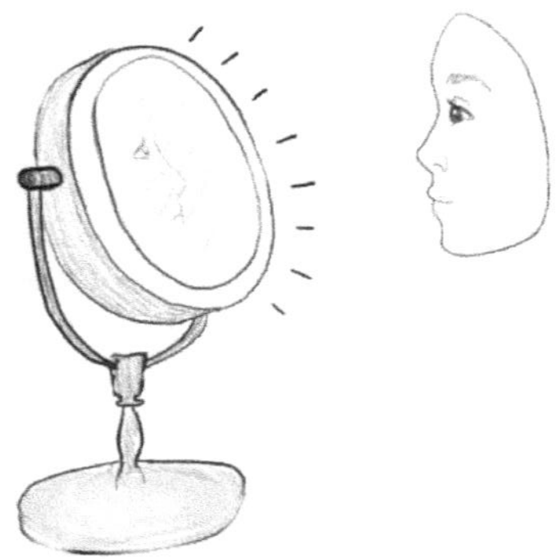

Figure 6. The Crimson Wave user interface is inspired by the AmbientROOM and based upon Fishkin's "embodied" and "metaphor" taxonomy. The relationship between the Crimson Wave's input and output is "environmental", and the metaphor is founded on the verb "to reflect", the common action of looking into a mirror.

BBT automatically at night, when the user is least active, allows the sensor to collect the most accurate resting core temperature. BBT is a non-invasive way of monitoring a person's menstrual cycle and can be mapped to a time series that helps predict what is going on in the menstrual cycle [8] [4]. BBT drops during ovulation, rises during periods, and hangs around the user's baseline BBT for the rest of the cycle [8]. The user's data is sent wirelessly to a computer that tracks and stores BBT readings to develop a personal and clear analysis of their menstrual cycle.
The wearable is portable and can be worn constantly if the user prefers not to take it off. We believe that this project is especially useful because it gathers data in a way that does not interrupt the user's routine. For example, by displaying visual updates of the user's menstrual cycle on the smart mirror, the TUI is effectively integrated into the user's movements in a room without turning its use into a task or something the user must worry about. It also engages a certain level of privacy by presenting information in the user's personal space using colors rather than disruptive audio or notifications.

Concept

The concept of the AmbientROOM from Hiroshi Ishii and Brygg Ullmer's *Tangible Bits: Towards Seamless Interfaces Between People, Bits and Atoms* strongly impacted the design of the Crimson Wave tangible user interface [6]. Crimson Wave is designed to activate the user's private space, whether that be their bedroom, bathroom, or vanity. The user will not have to consciously keep track of their menstrual cycle, instead the Crimson Wave wearable and smart mirror provides peripheral information. The user will position Crimson Wave where they would put a normal mirror; in this way, Crimson Wave is embedded within the user's environment and does not dominate their attention in the same way a mobile app would.
Based off AmbientROOM, the framework that structures the Crimson Wave interface is the taxonomy proposed by Kenneth P. Fishkin in *A Taxonomy for and Analysis of Tangible Interfaces*, which uses "embodiment" and "metaphor" as its two axes [3].The wearable relays data to the smart mirror within the same room; however, the input from the wearable and the output of colored light emitted from the mirror are viewed as two separate entities. Crimson Wave relies on a metaphor based on the verb "to reflect." When a person looks into a mirror, they see information about themselves. The Crimson Wave interface expands this idea so that when a user looks into the mirror, they see information about their menstrual cycle "reflected" there.

Implementation

The wearable is designed to be a flexible and comfortable band worn on the upper arm, allowing the temperature sensor to touch the user's skin and collect data while the user sleeps. The upper arm provides a more accurate reading of BBT because it is closer to the body's core. The armband is comprised of a LightBlue Bean+, which comes with a rechargeable battery and integrated temperature sensor. The LightBlue Bean+ was chosen for its built-in sensor and the ability to easily transfer wireless data to a computer. Upon reading the data, our computer program isolates the user's BBT based on the time of the data collection and the average temperature.
The mirror has a complete circle of 60 ultra bright smart LED NeoPixels surrounding it [12]. A 3D printed outer ring is set on top to create a glowing effect from the lights. The NeoPixels are connected to an Arduino Uno that is connected to the computer receiving the data input [1]. Based on the temperature that is recorded in the log, the NeoPixels RGB values change.

As the temperature decreases, the lights become redder, indicating an approaching period. The user will transition through various menstrual stages: follicular phase, ovulation, and the luteal phase. Their BBT will climax during ovulation and, as their temperature shifts, the lights will change in saturation from white to pink.

Conclusion and Future Work

Crimson Wave is a mirror with a light display that informs users where they are in their menstrual cycles based on a temperature sensor in the wearable. Crimson Wave will show users a holistic view of their menstrual cycles, beyond just their period and ovulation. This project highlights the need for more products that focus on menstrual health and teaching the public about the different stages of menstruation. Interaction with the product is effortless and easily integrated into normal daily activities. We plan to evaluate the wearable's accuracy in measuring BBT, improve our formula for collecting data, strengthen the way our tangible user interface interacts with the database where user information is stored, and expand the information presented by the mirror. The Crimson Wave prototype was presented in a classroom setting and received a positive response. Suggestions included: allowing collected data to be easily presented to health professionals, presenting calendars and graphs with the user's data, and adding touch screen capabilities. In the future we will evaluate Crimson Wave in home settings. We intend to explore how perceptions of the mirror might change depending on the number of people in the environment, specifically people who live alone versus people who share their space with a partner or roommate.

Ultimately, menstrual cycles are a given in users' lives. While their cycles impact their day to day health, they should not dominate users' routines. Therefore, the technology that optimizes their menstrual health should reflect this. Crimson Wave seamlessly integrates data into familiar objects, so that users may subconsciously remain informed about their bodies.

Acknowledgement

We thank our classmates and the HCI lab at Wellesley College for their valuable feedback and advice.

References

[1] Arduino http://arduino.cc

[2] Daniel A. Epstein, Nicole B. Lee, Jennifer H. Kang, Elena Agapie, Jessica Schroeder, Laura R. Pina, James Fogarty, Julie A. Kientz, and Sean Munson. 2017. Examining Menstrual Tracking to Inform the Design of Personal Informatics Tools. In Proceedings of the 2017 CHI Conference on Human Factors in Computing Systems (CHI '17). ACM, New York, NY, USA, 6876- 6888. DOI: https://doi.org/10.1145/3025453.3025635

[3] Kenneth P. Fishkin. 2004. A Taxonomy for and Analysis of Tangible Interfaces. Pers Ubiquit Comput (2004) 8: 347–358 DOI: https://doi.org/10.1007/s00779-004-0297-4

[4] Keiichi Fukaya, Ai Kawamori, Yutaka Osada, Masumi Kitazawa, and Makio Ishiguro. 2017. The Forecasting of Menstruation Based on a State-Space Modeling of Basal Body Temperature Time Series. Statistics in Medicine, 36(21): 3361–3379. DOI: 10.1002/sim.7345.

[5] Impressions Vanity Co. impressionsvanity.com

[6] Hiroshi Ishii and Brygg Ullmer. 1997. Tangible bits: towards seamless interfaces between people, bits and atoms. In Proceedings of the ACM SIGCHI Conference on Human factors in computing systems (CHI '97). ACM, New York, NY, USA, 234-241. DOI=http://dx.doi.org/10.1145/258549.258715 </bib>

[7] Gopinaath Kannabiran, Jeffrey Bardzell, and Shaowen Bardzell. 2011. How HCI Talks about

Sexuality: Discursive Strategies, Blind Spots, and Opportunities for Future Research. Proceedings of the SIGCHI Conference on Human Factors in Computing Systems (CHI '11). ACM, New York, NY, USA, 695-704. DOI: https://doi.org/10.1145/1978942.1979043

[8] Jeong-Hwan Kim, Sang-Eun Park, Gyeo-Wun Jeung, Jeong-Whan Lee, Heejung Choi, and Kyeong-Seop Kim. Estimation of a Menstrual Cycle by Covariance Stationary-Time Series Analysis on the Basal Body Temperatures. Journal of Medical and Bioengineering. 5.1: 63-66.

[9] Lady-Comp lady-comp.com

[10] Mirim Lee, Bon-chang Koo, Hee-seok Jeong, Joongsin Park, Juhee Cho, and Jun-dong Cho. 2015. Understanding Women's Needs in Menopause for Development of mHealth. Proceedings of the 2015 Workshop on Pervasive Wireless Healthcare (MobileHealth '15). ACM, New York, NY, USA, 51-56. DOI=http://dx.doi.org/10.1145/2757290.2757295

[11] Madeline Balaam, Lone Koefoed Hansen, Catherine D'Ignazio, Emma Simpson, Teresa Almeida, Stacey Kuznetsov, Mike Catt, and Marie L. J. Søndergaard. 2017. Hacking Women's Health. In Proceedings of the 2017 CHI Conference Extended Abstracts on Human Factors in Computing Systems (CHI EA '17). ACM, New York, NY, USA, 476-483. DOI: https://doi.org/10.1145/3027063.3027085

[12] NeoPixel https://www.adafruit.com/product/1768

[13] Teresa Almeida, Rob Comber, and Madeline Balaam. 2016. HCI and Intimate Care as an Agenda for Change in Women's Health. In Proceedings of the 2016 CHI Conference on Human Factors in Computing Systems (CHI '16). ACM, New York, NY, USA, 2599- 2611. DOI: https://doi.org/10.1145/2858036.2858187

[14] Amaury Trujillo and Maria Claudia Buzzi. 2016. Participatory User Requirements Elicitation for Personal Menopause App. In Proceedings of the 9th Nordic Conference on Human-Computer Interaction (NordiCHI '16). ACM, New York, NY, USA, Article 102, 6 pages. DOI: https://doi.org/10.1145/2971485.2996737

Smart Toys Design Opportunities for Measuring Children's Fine Motor Skills Development

Svetlana Mironcika
Amsterdam University of Applied Sciences
Amsterdam, The Netherlands
s.mironcika@hva.nl

Antoine de Schipper
Amsterdam University of Applied Sciences
Amsterdam, The Netherlands
a.w.de.schipper@hva.nl

Annette Brons
Amsterdam University of Applied Sciences
Amsterdam, The Netherlands
a.e.brons@hva.nl

Huub Toussaint
Amsterdam University of Applied Sciences
Amsterdam, The Netherlands
h.toussaint@hva.nl

Ben Kröse
Amsterdam University of Applied Sciences
Amsterdam, The Netherlands
b.j.a.krose@hva.nl

Ben Schouten
Amsterdam University of Applied Sciences
Amsterdam, The Netherlands
b.a.m.schouten@hva.nl

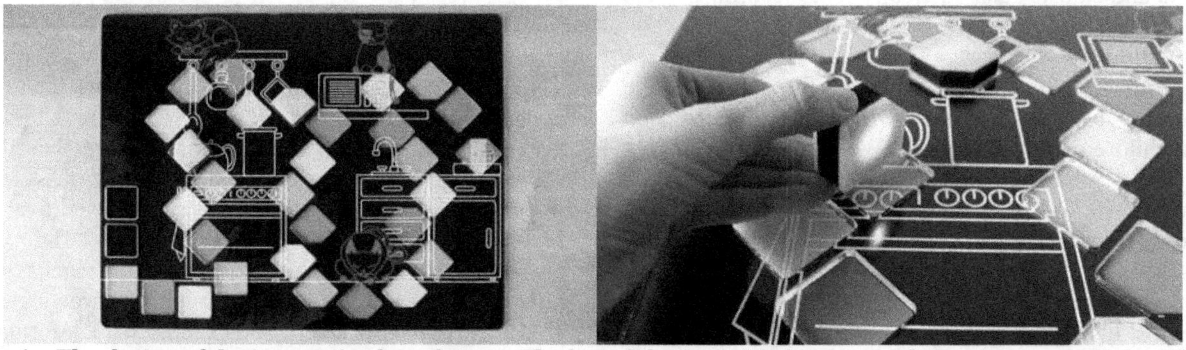

Figure 1a: The design of the interactive board game. The board depicts a kitchen, several sleeping cats and slots for the token-mouse placements that are deepened in the board and guide the player's actions in the game.
Figure 1b: Interaction with the token.

ABSTRACT

Smart tangible toys, designed for hand manipulation, can transform fine motor skills assessment into enjoyable activities which are engaging for children to play (partially) unsupervised. Such toys can support school teachers and parents for early detection of deficiencies in motor skills development of children, as well as objectively monitor the progress of skills development over time. To make a game enjoyable for children with different skills level, these smart toys could offer an adaptive game play. In this paper we describe the design and deployment of a digital board game, equipped with sensors, which we use to explore the potential of using smart toys for fine motor skills assessment in children.

TEI '18, March 18–21, 2018, Stockholm, Sweden

ACM ISBN 978-1-4503-5568-1/18/03…$15.00
https://doi.org/10.1145/3173225.3173256

Author Keywords

Tangibles for play, serious games, fine motor skills, adaptive games, toy design.

INTRODUCTION

Children's performance at school depends on a number of skills where fine motor skills are one of the strong predictors of their later achievement in math, reading, and science scores [5]. Fine motor skills require small muscles of the hand to work together in order to perform precise and refined movements [4]. Each child develops fine motor skills at his own pace and, arguably, an individualized attention in skills training could be beneficial to a child's development. Teachers at schools and parents at home may help children in their fine motor skills development by providing appropriately difficult tasks. Moreover, it is important to early detect development delays and address them timely with the help of a child physiotherapist. However, parents may not have expertise in assessing and training motor skills and teachers at schools may lack time for highly personalized training.

Various non-digital assessment tools are used to assess children motor skills (for example Movement ABC-2 [2]).

These tools require a trained specialist to guide the assessment process, equipment kits and assessment time may take from 15 up to 60 minutes [2]. To save time and effort required for assisted fine motor skills assessment, the use of smart technologies may be considered. Digital technologies, together with the analysis of acquired sensor data, may allow (partially) unsupervised fine motor skills assessment. To make the process of (partially) unsupervised skills assessment appealing and enjoyable for children we investigate the idea of turning this process into a game play. Moreover, to ensure that a child is playing at a level that matches his fine motor skills abilities, the game will dynamically adjust its levels based on the movement data collected while a child plays the game.

In this paper we describe the design and deployment of the tangible interactive board game, called *Get that cheese*. While children play and manipulate sensor-augmented token in their hands, the token collects children's fine motor skills data and adjusts game difficulty level according to the skills of each child. Here, we report on a first user study with 30 children where we evaluated whether children interact with toys as expected, whether the game has the potential for use in fine motor skills assessment, and whether children enjoy the game. We show that, *Get that cheese* has a promising potential in this field. Children enjoy using it, and the collected data correlates with standard fine motor skills proficiency test. Whereas more work is needed to improve its sensitivity and selectivity, *Get that cheese* inspires us to further work on smart toys for fine motor skills assessment.

RELATED WORK

Sensor-augmented toys for children have been proposed in several previous works. Vonach et al. [15] present a toy for measuring physiological parameters such as pulse, temperature, blood oxygen saturation and others. Sensor information is gathered while the child listens to a fairy tale and interacts with cubes following audio prompts. Westeyn et al. [16] have developed toys with integrated wireless sensors to monitor children's development progress based on object play interactions. These two works demonstrate that a child will participate in the monitoring of his health and development progress, through interactions with toys. These toys are designed in a way that a child easily understands how to use them and finds them engaging. Data, generated while the child interacts with these toys, allows assessing health parameters and development progress of the child. A similar approach can be adopted for fine motor skills assessment.

We see three categories of works that describe sensor-augmented toys and tools for fine motor skills training and assessment. The first category describes tangible toys or tools that aim to train fine motor skills while playing the game during the therapy setting. For instance, van Delden et al. [3] and Li et al. [9] describe tangible interactive toys for the repetitive training of fine motor skills for children with Cerebral Palsy.

The second category of works describes toys for automated fine motor skills assessment with the aim of conducting studies for fine motor proficiency. Rivera et al. [12] describe a smart toy system, that consists of cubes with wireless sensors and a mobile computing platform to collect the information sent from the cubes, allowing later analysis by development professionals to verify normal behavior or to detect a potential disorder. Jeong et al. [7] presente a play-based assessment tool, called *TaG-Games*, for measuring cognitive problem-solving skills and fine motor proficiency. Sensors (accelerometer and optical sensor) integrated into cubes and a host computer allow observing behavior and manipulation patterns during assembly type of play. *DataSpoon* by Zuckerman et al. [17] is an instrumented spoon that monitors movement kinematics of children with motor disorder during self-feeding. Sander et al. [13] propose to use a commercially available motion controlled gaming cube, called Futurecube, for studies on movement feature selection and they found that several data features can be used for distinguishing between children with normal and delayed motor skill development.

The last category of works describes tools that not only assess motor skills with the help of digital technologies but also adapt the task to the appropriate level based on the assessment result. Kim et al. [8] proposed a sketch-based interface, called *EasySketch2*, that can be used for both fine motor skills assessment and training. The interface classifies children's fine motor skills and teaches children how to draw, practice and improve their drawing skills as well as provides teachers and parents with information on the maturity of children's fine motor skills. This work is very interesting for us since it integrates both fine motor skills assessment and training, although it does not provide opportunities for play.

From the described research work we found that some toys and tools measure fine motor skills proficiency, others aim at skill training and some of the tools do both. Little work has been done in integrating fine motor skills assessment process and game play.

Tangible toys for motor skills should be enjoyable for children with a wide range of differences in motor skills. Based on the significant skill differences in the target group, it is important to make games more adaptive [14] so that a game or play environment can automatically change [11] within the limits of a specific user. In our vision game adaptability to player's skills, especially in assessing motor skills, is essential and we specifically defined this aspect as a requirement for our game design.

In the last year we have conducted research in the assessment of motor skills of children between 7-9 years old, in a research project called Smart Play Sets. The research is supported by Dutch game industry and intended to spin off in a company, designing health related games. In this paper we describe an interactive board game that we use to explore the design space for games and toys for computerized fine motor skills assessment.

GAME DESIGN PROCESS

Prior to the game design, we would like to present in this paper, we will describe requirements that informed the tangible toy and the game design. Two contextual interviews with child physiotherapists were conducted to find out what tasks therapists give children when assessing their fine motor skills. During fine motor skills assessment child physiotherapists often use small objects (for example coins, pegs, cubes) to evaluate how well a child can manipulate them by using one hand only. For example, therapists give a child a task (for example, hold the coin horizontally and rotate the coin with finger tips 180°) and evaluate how a child manipulates the object during this task [2]. Among other movements, therapists are looking at how children can perform picking the object with one hand, rotating it in the hand, flipping the object around while holding it in the hand, placing it precisely into the slot. One of the parameters that therapists assess is the overall smoothness of movements.

Smooth movements are characteristic for healthy and well-trained motor behavior and it shows how well a child is in control of his or her hand movements [1]. Such movements are characterized by little changes in accelerations and decelerations. In their work Sander et al. [13] used accelerometers to collect hand movement data of children and they concluded that smooth movements can be used to distinguish between children fine motor skills.

Based on before mentioned findings, the smoothness of hand movement and small object manipulations were selected to become core elements of the toy and the game design.

Requirements

For the design of our smart toy, the following three requirements were defined:

Requirements on Affordances

Based on the tasks that child physiotherapists give the children for fine motor skills assessment, our tangible toy should afford several types of manipulations: picking up the token with one hand, flipping it around while holding it in one hand, and precisely placing it in a designated place, e.g. into a slot. The size and the form of the tangible should afford the aforementioned interactions.

Sensor Data Feature Requirements

To assess smoothness of movement the toy should contain sensors such as an accelerometer sensor. Next to that, the game should encourage a player to make smooth hand movements. Therefore this smoothness of hand movement should become an essential parameter of the game.

Game Adaptability Requirements

The toy and the game should be enjoyable for children with different levels of fine motor skills, thus the game should have an adaptation mechanism to the current fine motor skills level of a player.

To sum up, the mechanics of the game should encourage players to make smooth movements while manipulating the toy with one hand. During the game the toy should capture child's movement data and adapt the game level according to the skill level of the child.

Board Game Design

Taking the above mentioned requirements into account, we have developed a game for one-hand manipulations where players move small tokens that represent mice. The children have to compete to bring their mouse to the cheese first. Each child should move his token-mouse as smoothly as possible, otherwise he will wake up cats and the token-mouse should be returned to its previous position on the board.

We will first describe the design of the game elements, such as interactive tokens and the board and then how these elements are used within the game play.

Game Elements

The board game consists of two small tokens and a board that depicts a kitchen, sleeping cats and a plate with a cheese. The tokens have the shape a quadrat with a cut off corner (to stimulate in-hand rotation before placing the token precisely into the designated slot). Each of the tokens carries a Light Blue Bean microcontroller with built-in accelerometer and two RGB LEDs. LEDs are placed behind two semi-transparent facets with engraved images of mice and they provide visual feedback to players during the game. Given the size of the sensor, tokens were made as small as possible. Dimensions of each token are 38 mm by 38 mm by 18mm (Figure 2). The tokens were shown to two child physiotherapists to assess their dimensions for interaction suitability for 7-9 year old children. Therapists expected that dimensions of tokens will be suitable for children to pick tokens up and precisely place them on the board. And that some children may have difficulties with flipping the token in one hand, although they suggested that the user study is necessary to confirm that.

The board, where the tokens should be placed on, consists of a 5 millimeter thick transparent acrylic plate with cut out slots and a printed illustration of the kitchen and sleeping cats (Figure 1a).

Game Play

The game is turn based and is played by two players. Each player moves the token which represents a mouse in a kitchen that is walking near sleeping cats and tries to get to the cheese. The goal of the game is to take the mouse to the cheese faster than another player. Each player cautiously moves the interactive token (mouse) from the start of the board to the finish by placing the token on colorful

Figure 2. Design of the tokens. The top and back facets of the token are made from a semi-transparent plastic that allows players to see light feedback from the token.

segments printed on the board. Every time that a player picks up the token and flips it around the token randomly lights up in one of three colors (green, yellow or blue) that corresponds to the colorful segments printed on the board (Figure 1b). If the player makes rapid movements while moving the token it will light up in red color (cats woke up) and this means that the token should be returned to its previous location on the board.

In this game scenario the players are stimulated to pick up the token, flip it around (to see the color which appears on the opposite side of a token), and precisely place the token to the corresponding slot. The context of the game (mice walking near sleeping cats) encourages the players to move the tokens as smoothly as possible.

Adaptability of the described game was designed in the following way: during the game tokens constantly generate data from the accelerometer sensor that is used to calculate smoothness of hand movement. We assess smoothness of movement by calculating the mean squared jerk feature that is a common measure of smooth and coordinated movements [13]. We set a threshold for the mean squared jerk, so that when the threshold is exceeded the rapid movement is detected and a player gets immediate feedback (the token will light up in red color, which means that the mouse woke up the cats).

After each move performed by the player the threshold for that token is recalculated. If a player succeeds his turn without making rapid movements, in his next turn he will need to move the token even more carefully (threshold for this token will be lowered). If a player makes a rapid movement during the turn and "wakes up cats" in his next turn it will be easier for a player to succeed (the threshold for this token will be increased).

The board game was reviewed by two child therapists and the received feedback was generally positive. Therapists said that interactions with tokens in the game are relevant for children age 7-9 years old and that they expected that children will enjoy playing the game.

USER STUDY

A user test was set up with the following three goals to be evaluated: 1) whether the children interacted with the tokens as it was expected, 2) whether sensor data collected during the game would correlate with a standard movement proficiency test scores, 3) whether the children would enjoy the game.

Study Design

The board game was deployed in a primary school in Amsterdam, the Netherlands. 30 children between seven and nine years old took part in the study. This age group was selected over younger children for their ability to articulate their opinions about game. The school was chosen where a high prevalence of deficiencies was expected. 30 children were selected from four classes. Teachers were asked to select children that in their opinion are likely to have motor issues. This was done to ensure that in the user study there are children with a spectrum of fine motor skills level. Both qualitative and quantitative observations were performed by the interdisciplinary team consisting from an experienced child physiotherapist, a game expert, two movement scientists and a game designer. Before and during the game play children were interacting with a test administer, who first explained children the rules of the game and then in the course of the game was available to answer children's questions.

To gather children opinions about the game we have used Five Degrees of Happiness Likert scale by Hall et al. [6]. It is a pictorial 5-point Smiley Face Likert scale consisting of a variation of five happy faces. This tool aims to increase the variance in children answers comparing to the often used scales (e.g. 'Smileyometer' [10]) where smiley faces range from negative to neutral to positive. A game expert was observing children playing and made notes related to children play experiences.

Both the game expert and the child physiotherapist were observing children interacting with tokens during the game play and after the study they gave their feedback in a semi-structured interview.

The children's fine motor skills proficiency level was collected by two trained movement scientists using the standard motor skills proficiency test called Movement ABC-2 test. Movement ABC-2 test is used to identify and describe impairments in motor performance of children and adolescents and consists from three parts Manual Dexterity, Aiming and Catching, and Balance. For the user study children took Manual Dexterity part of the test that consists of three tasks such as placing pegs, threading lace, and drawing trail. All tasks were timed, scored and compared with the standard percentile rank.

All sensor data from each token was transmitted over Bluetooth.

Study Procedure

All children were divided by their teacher into couples taking into account their friendship tendencies. Each couple of children was invited into a test room one by one. Children were seated at a table where the test administer showed them the game and explained the rules. Then children were given tokens to try out interactions. Once children understood how to interact with tokens, the game session started. During the game eight couples of children were allowed to interact with tokens as they liked (e.g. they were allowed to use both hands regardless the initial instruction to use one hand only) and the other seven couples of children were allowed to use only one hand when playing. This separation was done to find whether children on their own initiative would use one hand during the play, and if they use both hands, whether we can still differentiate children skill levels in the collected data. Each game session lasted for approximately 10 minutes. After the game was finished, children proceeded to separate tables where they rated the game with the help of the Smiley Face Likert scale and then took Movement ABC-2 test which lasted around 10 minutes. After approximately 20 minutes children returned to their class.

RESULTS

In this section we will present the results of our user test with respect to 1) the observed interactions with the tokens, 2) the correlation between collected sensor data and the Movement ABC-2 motor skills proficiency test and 3) the level of enjoyment of the children.

According to the Movement ABC-2 test, children who participated in the study had the following distribution in fine motor skills proficiency: 53% (n = 16) had age appropriate skill development, 20% of children (n = 6) were at risk of having movement difficulties, and 27% of children (n = 8) had significant movement difficulties.

Interactions with the Tokens

According to observations of child physiotherapist children quickly understood how to play the game and did not experience considerable issues when interacting with tokens. All children were able to easily perform such interactions as picking the token up with one hand and placing it in the designated slot. Flipping the token around by holding it in one hand was more difficult for most of the children. Some children who experienced difficulties in flipping the token while holding it in one hand (and who were allowed to use both hands during the game) applied coping strategies such as helping themselves with another hand. Although interactions were not difficult it was more challenging for children to perform these interactions smoothly.

Based on the observations done by child physiotherapist the size of the tokens should be a bit smaller to allow more comfortable manipulation in one hand.

According to the game expert observations, for six children the game was too difficult and they were struggling to accomplish their turns successfully (they were shaking tokens too much while manipulating it and they quickly exceeded set threshold) and this caused their decrease of interest in the game. As soon as the game became too challenging these children started adopting coping strategies in order to succeed. Therefore the scaffolding range for game difficulties should be increased to accommodate children with big variance in fine motor skills.

The physiotherapist and the game expert admitted that several pairs of children were showing very competitive behavior and this distracted their attention from the tasks that needed to be performed with the token (children looked agitated during the game and experts observed them making less smooth movements). According to the experts, more cooperative behavior during the game play could help children to better focus on the tasks in the game (especially when tasks require concentration). We see that the category of playful experiences that the game elicits (in our case it is a victory-oriented competition) may have an influence on how children interacted with tokens and may have an effect on collected movement data and potentially on predictiveness of the collected data. In this way game experiences should be taken into account when designing games for fine motor skills assessment.

We found that all children were able to perform interactions with tokens, although many of them were trying to use compensatory movements. Experts recommended making tokens a bit smaller and transforming the game into cooperative game, however it is unknown yet whether such changes will result in more predictive data set.

Sensor Data and Movement Proficiency Test Correlation

According to the requirements the smoothness of movement was the essential parameter of the game and the game encouraged children to make smooth hand movements. During the game the common measure of smoothness (mean squared jerk feature) was collected.

For the user study all children were divided into two groups where the first group was allowed to move the tokens as they liked and the second group was allowed to use only one hand to move the token.

For children who were asked to play only with one hand (n = 14) a correlation was found between sensor data (the average of all collected mean squared jerk values over the whole game) and Movement ABC-2 test (correlation coefficient = -0.563; p-value = 0.045) (Figure 3). This result shows that the smoother the children move the token while holding it in one hand the better their fine motor skills are.

For children who were not told to manipulate the token with one hand only, in other words, it was up to them to decide how to interact with the token, (n = 16) there was no significant correlation between sensor data (the average of all collected mean squared jerk values over the whole game) and Movement ABC-2 test results (correlation coefficient = -0.191; p-value = 0.494) (Figure 4).

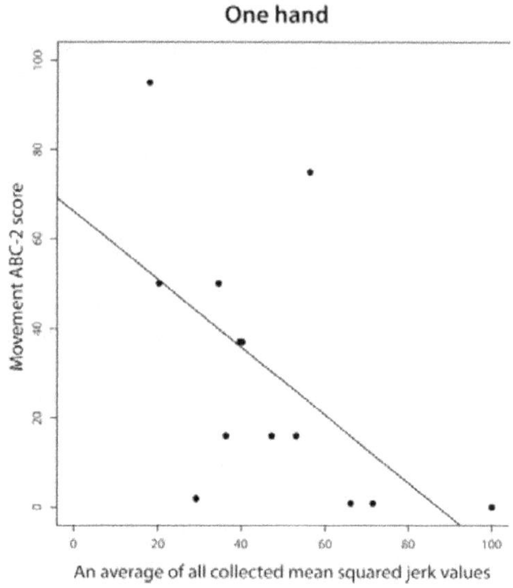

Figure 3. Scatter plot for children who manipulated the token in one hand only.

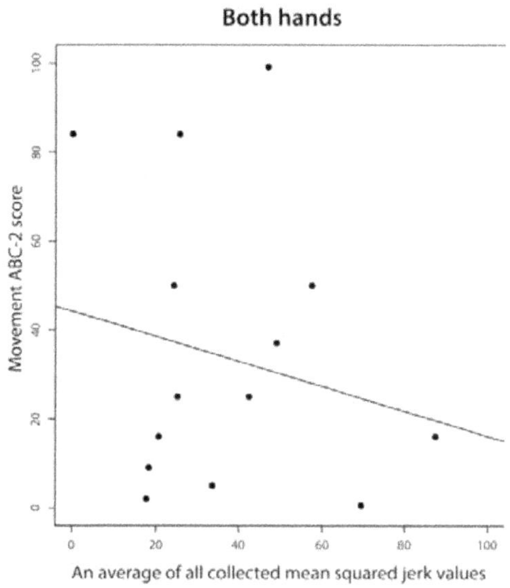

Figure 4. Scatter plot for children who manipulated the token as they preferred.

Enjoyment of the Game

Children gave the game a high evaluation despite the level of their motor skills. Figure 5 shows the overall enjoyment of the game, for which 63% (n = 19) of all children who participated in the study including 75% (n = 6) children with significant movement difficulties choose the most positive smiley. The mean rating from the Smiley Likert Scale is 4.33 (SD: 1.14). Correlation between the smiley rating and Movement ABC-2 measurements is not significant (correlation coefficient = 0.301; p-value = 0.105) and that shows that children liked to play the game regardless of their fine motor skill proficiency level. The fact that 75% children who had significant difficulties highly rated the game is an interesting result to us. We might hypothesize that we succeeded to challenge especially those children to play our game and that is

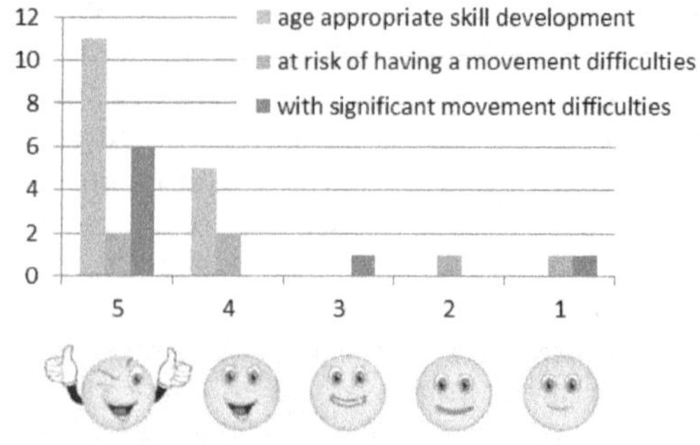

Figure 5. Smiley Face Likert scale rating for the enjoyment of the game.

exactly what we hoped for.

When asked why they have chosen smileys 4 and 5 children commented *"I liked the game"*, *"The game is exciting and you had to be careful"*, *"You must be careful as ninja"*, *"A bit difficult but nice"*, *"I felt that I was a mouse"*, *"I like the game, where to buy it?"*. Several children based their positive rating on the fact that they won the game *"I like that it was challenging and I won"*. Two children, being at risk or having significant (fine motor skill) difficulties gave the lowest score to the game admitted and that they have lost the game and it was difficult for them: *"The game is not so nice and I had to be very careful"*, *"I lost and I do not like the game"*.

According to the observations carried out by the game expert most of the children looked genuinely excited while playing the game. There seem to be a natural gameplay, the children were concentrated on the tasks and most of them did not pay attention to the experts (the physiotherapist and the game expert). The story and visual elements such as images of the kitchen, the sleeping cats, and the cheese helped children to understand the context of the game.

Children felt that the game was getting progressively more difficult expressing that *"Game becomes more difficult!"* and that *"I think it will become harder later"*. Apparently the designed adaptive scaffolding in relation to the skill proficiency of the individual child worked well. Only a few children looked frustrated and their interest in the game decreased. The system adaptation was not coping well enough with the behavior of these children. The issues were mainly related to the speed of token manipulation as well as the precision of the placement of the tokens. According to the physiotherapist, for a small fraction of children, these tasks will always be hard to perform well.

We found that children performed interactions with the tokens as it was initially expected, although several children were compensating movements by using the second hand to help themselves. Children gave high evaluation to the game and looked genuinely excited while playing the game. The correlation between collected sensor data and standard motor skills proficiency test Movement ABC-2 was found for children who were using only one hand during the game play.

LIMITATIONS AND FUTURE WORK

This is a preliminary work where we explored the possibility to assess children fine motor skills with the help of a tangible game. In the future more games and tangibles will be designed and tested with children to generate more evidence that fine motor skills can be reliably assessed with the help of smart tangible toys.

Get that cheese is, as we have shown, a promising step in the direction of creating automatic and fun tests for assessing children fine motor skills. Nevertheless, more research has to be done. As it is now, standard tests like Movement ABC-2 require the presence of a skilled observer, and *Get that cheese* is not yet sensitive enough to work unattended. Furthermore, to be fully reliable when played while unsupervised, *Get that cheese* should be able to detect whether a child is manipulating a token with one or two hands, as interactions in one hand showed correlation with the standard fine motor skills proficiency test.

Therapists admitted that they would have wanted smaller tokens, but this wasn't really feasible due to the sensor size. Following the advice of the therapists, the future version of the tokens will be smaller in size.

As we duly acknowledge these limitations, we take them as an encouragement to iterate further on our system. A combination a slightly different physical shape of the token, and some improved game rules will likely increase the accuracy of our system, which will need further testing before being able to function in a clinical and therapeutic setting.

DISCUSSION AND CONCLUSIONS

While this study is exploratory and preliminary, nevertheless we successfully gathered qualitative and quantitative insights supporting our work on tangible board games for partially unsupervised fine motor skills assessment. We still don't have a way to test children without any intervention from a movement scientist, but these exciting initial results encourage us to proceed in our research and design on tangibles and games, with the objective of developing smart toys to assess motor skills and detect early development delays.

For the design of the board game we have defined requirements such as requirements on affordances, sensor data feature requirement and game adaptability requirement. All children were able to perform such interactions as picking the token up with one hand and placing it in the designated slot. Flipping the token around by holding it in one hand was more difficult for most of the children. According to observations during the user study the tokens should have been slightly smaller to afford more comfortable flipping. Requirement for sensor data feature was met as smoothness of movement became an essential part of the game. The game encouraged players to make smooth hand movements while interacting with the tokens. The requirement of game adaptability was met in the game design so that the game was adapting its difficulty levels according to a child's motor skills level. Observations during the user study showed that the range of adaptability should be adjusted to accommodate children with big variance in fine motor skills.

A range of toys and games can be developed for fine motor skills assessment. In our case, such movement feature as smoothness informed the design of the tangibles (tokens), the board and game theme and it was the only movement feature that was assessed during the game. There are various other movement features that may be considered when designing toys and games for fine motor skills assessment. It is not clear yet what movement features may have a stronger predictive power for fine motor skills and it opens opportunities for future research. Moreover, it is also interesting to research whether other game concepts for evaluation of smooth movements would generate more predictive data for fine motor skills of children.

In this work the age appropriateness of the game concept was not fully addressed in the design process since our priority was to find whether selected interactions with tokens would generate necessary data that will have some predictive power about children fine motor skills. Therefore we have based the choice of the game theme on experts' views. In the future we will involve children in the design process to ensure that games are fun for children of different ages. It may be an interesting research opportunity to explore what kind of game themes may result in most predictive data.

When children were allowed they were playing the games with two hands although that interaction did not result in useful data set. When the game was getting to difficult for children, they were trying their best to succeed their turn and accomplish the move without waking up cats. We observed that children were using both hands to help themselves shake the token less and to move it more smoothly. Such coping strategies allowed children to perform better than they would have done using only one hand. Thus compensatory strategies that children used to succeed their turn had an influence on the collected data. It is an interesting design challenge to design games that are fun to play and on the other side children would not use compensatory movements. We will address this in our future work.

Clearly, the shape, the size and, and most likely also the weight of the token have an effect on the way a child manipulates it and therefore on the data that is being generated during the play. In our study we have seen that the size of the token could have been a bit smaller to allow more comfortable manipulation. Although it is not clear whether manipulation of a smaller size token would result in more predictive data. It is interesting to investigate further whether the shape, the size and the weight of the token have an influence on the collected data and in what way. Therefore we see opportunities for new studies addressing mentioned points.

ACKNOWLEDGMENTS

This research/publication was supported by COMMIT/.

REFERENCIES

1. Sivakumar Balasubramanian, Alejandro Melendez-Calderon, Agnes Roby-Brami, and Etienne Burdet. 2015. On the analysis of movement smoothness. *Journal of neuroengineering and rehabilitation*, 12(1),112.
2. Wouter Cools, Kristine De Martelaer, Christiane Samaey and Caroline Andries, 2009. Movement skill assessment of typically developing preschool children: A review of seven movement skill assessment tools. *Journal of sports science and medicine*, 8(2), 154-168.
3. Robby van Delden, Pauline Aarts, and Betsy van Dijk. 2012. Design of tangible games for children undergoing occupational and physical therapy. *In Proceedings of the 11th international conference on Entertainment Computing* (ICEC'12), Marc Herrlich, Rainer Malaka, and Maic Masuch (Eds.). Springer-Verlag, Berlin, Heidelberg, 221-234.
4. Fingergym Fine Motor Skills. Fingergym Fine Motor Skills School readiness program. 2011. Available from: www.fingergym.info/downloads/Finemotordevpp1-4.pdf
5. David Grissmer, Kevin J. Grimm, Sophie M. Aiyer, William M. Murrah, and Joel S. Steele. 2010. Fine motor skills and early comprehension of the world: two new school readiness indicators. *Developmental psychology*, 46(5), 1008.
6. Lynne Hall, Colette Hume, and Sarah Tazzyman. 2016. Five Degrees of Happiness: Effective Smiley Face Likert Scales for Evaluating with Children. In *Proceedings of the The 15th International Conference on Interaction Design and Children* (IDC '16). ACM, New York, NY, USA, 311-321.
7. Donghwa Jeong, Kerci Endri, and Kiju Lee, K. 2010. TaG-Games: tangible geometric games for assessing cognitive problem-solving skills and fine motor proficiency. IEEE International Conference on *Multisensor Fusion and Integration for Intelligence Systems*, 32-37.
8. H. Kim, P. Taele, J. Seo, J. Liew, T. Hammond. EasySketch2: a novel sketch-based interface for improving children's fine motor skills and school readiness. Proceeding Expresive '16 Proceedings of the *Joint Symposium on Computational Aesthetics and Sketch Based Interfaces and Modeling and Non-Photorealistic Animation and Rendering*, 2016, pp. 69-78.
9. Ying Li, Willem Fontijn, and Panos Markopoulos. 2008. A Tangible Tabletop Game Supporting Therapy of Children with Cerebral Palsy. In *Proceedings of the 2nd International Conference on Fun and Games*, Panos Markopoulos, Boris Ruyter, Wijnand Ijsselsteijn, and Duncan Rowland (Eds.). Springer-Verlag, Berlin, Heidelberg, 182-193.
10. Janet C. Read. 2008. Validating the Fun Toolkit: an instrument for measuring children's opinions of technology. *Cogn. Technol. Work* 10, 2 (March 2008), 119-128.
11. Pepijn Rijnbout, Mark de Graaf, Tilde Bekker, Ben Schouten. 2016. The Introduction of IMO, an integrated model for designing open-ended play. In: *Journal of Entertainment Computing* (2016).
12. Diego Rivera, Antonio García, Bernardo Alarcos, Juan R. Velasco, José Eugenio Ortega, and Isaías Martínez-Yelmo. 2016. Smart Toys Designed for Detecting Developmental Delays. *Sensors*, 16(11), 1953.
13. Jörg Sander, Antoine de Schipper, Svetlana Mironcika, Annette Brons, Huub Toussaint, Ben Schouten, and Ben Kröse. Detecting delays in motor skill development of children through data analysis of a smart play device. In *Proceedings of the 10th EAI International Conference on Pervasive Computing Technologies for Healthcare*(PervasiveHealth '16).
14. Ben Schouten, Menno Deen, Tilde Bekker (2014). Playful Identity in Game Design and Open-ended Play. *In Playful Identities, The Ludification of Digital Media Cultures*, V. Frissen et al. (Editors), Amsterdam University Press.
15. Emanuel Vonach, Marianne Ternek, Georg Gerstweiler, and Hannes Kaufmann. 2016. Design of a Health Monitoring Toy for Children. In *Proceedings of the The 15th International Conference on Interaction Design and Children* (IDC '16). ACM, New York, NY, USA, 58-67
16. Tracy L. Westeyn, Gregory D. Abowd, Thad E. Starner, Jeremy M. Johnson, Peter W. Presti, and Kimberly A. Weaver. 2012. Monitoring children's developmental progress using augmented toys and activity recognition. *Personal Ubiquitous Comput.* 16, 2 (February 2012), 169-191.
17. Oren Zuckerman, Tamar Gal, Tal Keren-Capelovitch, Tal Karsovsky, Ayelet Gal-Oz, and Patrice L. Tamar Weiss. 2016. DataSpoon: Overcoming Design Challenges in Tangible and Embedded Assistive Technologies. In *Proceedings of the TEI '16: Tenth International Conference on Tangible, Embedded, and Embodied Interaction* (TEI '16). ACM, New York, NY, USA, 30-37.

ClassBeacons: Designing Distributed Visualization of Teachers' Physical Proximity in the Classroom

Pengcheng An [1] **Saskia Bakker** [1] **Sara Ordanovski** [3] **Ruurd Taconis** [2] **Berry Eggen** [1]

[1] Department of Industrial Design, Eindhoven University of Technology, the Netherlands

[2] Eindhoven School of Education, Eindhoven University of Technology, the Netherlands

[3] Department of Experimental Psychology & Helmholtz Institute, Utrecht University, the Netherlands

[1, 2] {p.an, s.bakker, r.taconis, j.h.eggen}@tue.nl; [3] s.ordanovski@students.uu.nl

ABSTRACT

As necessary for creating a learner-centered environment, nowadays teachers are expected to be more mindful about their proximity distribution: how to spend time in different locations of the classroom with individual learners. However feedback on this is only given to teachers by experts after classroom observation. In this paper we present the design and evaluation of ClassBeacons, a novel ambient information system that visualizes teachers' physical proximity through tangible devices distributed over the classroom. An expert review and a field evaluation with eight secondary school teachers were conducted to explore potential values of such a system and gather user experiences. Results revealed rich insights into how the system could influence teaching and learning, as well as how a distributed display can be seamlessly integrated into teachers' routines.

CCS Concepts

• Human-centered computing ~ Field studies • Human-centered computing ~ Displays and imagers • Applied computing ~ Computer-assisted instruction

Author Keywords

Ambient information system; distributed display; teacher proximity; learner-centered education; classroom.

INTRODUCTION

Secondary school teachers' work has been recognized as dynamic, complex and busy [3,10,17]. While teaching, with different students to serve, multiple goals to achieve, and unpredictable situations to deal with, a teacher often needs to perform tasks in quasi-parallel manner, or switch back and forth between tasks [3]. Thereby, their perceptual and cognitive resources are and continually occupied, making their attention precious and limited.

TEI '18, March 18–21, 2018, Stockholm, Sweden

ACM ISBN 978-1-4503-5568-1/18/03…$15.00

https://doi.org/10.1145/3173225.3173243

The teaching practice in secondary schools is shifting from *teacher-centered* to *learner-centered* [15]. Today's educators are increasingly expected to function as facilitators who can provide differentiated instructions and punctual guidance [26] to each learner. This means more interpersonal interactions between teacher and students are needed in the classroom. As a result, teachers have to more mindfully distribute their time and spatial presence in a lesson to offer each student *closer physical proximity* [26]. This imposes even more mental load on teachers since it requires them to be more reflective [46] while working. Given already a lot of things to pay attention to in a lesson, keeping track of their distribution of proximity to students (i.e., how they wander in the classroom or how much time they have spent in different locations) cannot always be an explicit task in the center of teachers' minds. We hypothesize that this reflective task could be supported by an ambient information system [36] which can inform without overburdening teachers [45]. We developed ClassBeacons, a novel tangible ambient system visualizing teachers' physical proximity through wireless lamps distributed over the classroom (see Figure 1).

Figure 1. ClassBeacons: Each lamp on students' desks indicates how much time the teacher has spent around it through color ranging from yellow (no time spent) to green (440 seconds spent). ©Eindhoven University of Technology

Adopting a methodology inspired by *research-through-design* [49], we developed and evaluated ClassBeacons with two research goals. Firstly, since very limited research is known on physical proximity of teachers in classrooms [26], and no existing ambient information system is known to visualize teacher proximity, this study means to explore the potential values of tracking and visualizing teacher proximity to pedagogical activities. Secondly, by gathering and analyzing user experiences of ClassBeacons, this study aims to inform the design and development of tangible ambient information systems for the classroom. To achieve these research goals, an expert review with four educational researchers and a field evaluation, in which eight secondary school teachers used the ClassBeacons working prototype during two of their lessons, were conducted.

RELATED WORK

Ambient Information Systems for Classrooms

Besides interacting with individuals, or physical tools (pen, textbook, etc.), teachers also need to increasingly interact with computing devices (e.g., PC, smart phone, interactive whiteboard) [13] while teaching. Although technologies benefit pedagogical activities in many aspects [38], use of technologies in teaching seems to be restricted because the interaction is often time-consuming and effortful [4,8,16]. Today's computing devices usually require *focused attention* [7] from teachers, which means teachers need to visually attend to the graphical user interfaces (GUIs) of those devices continuously while interacting. This does not fit well in the teachers' complex and intensive routines. *Ambient information systems* [36], which display relevant but non-crucial information in an unobtrusive manner [45], are recognized as a promising direction to fit information more seamlessly into teachers' busy everyday routines [3].

A number of ambient information systems have been designed for classrooms. For example, Lamberty et al.'s [28] system displayed challenges different students were working on in the lesson to create peer awareness. ClassSearch [33] presented web search behaviors in the classroom to ease teacher-led discourse and group awareness. Lernanto [2] displayed students' real-time performance to inform the teacher during differentiated instruction. Sturm et al. [42] introduced a system to support lecturers by displaying attention/interest level of students.

Above mentioned related designs are *centralized* ambient information systems which present information through a single display on the wall of the classroom [2,28,33]. Given the distributed nature of proximity information, however, ClassBeacons is designed as a *distributed* ambient information system whose display media are physically distributed in a classroom. Few related studies on distributed ambient information systems are known in the classroom context. Lanterns [1] aim to support group working scenarios by showing the status of each group on multiple luminous devices. FireFlies [6] supports short and quiet teacher-student communication by enabling a teacher to control the color of each student's individual light-object. Although relatively fewer design explorations can be found in this sub-area, the mentioned studies have suggested that distributed display is a meaningful approach to present information in the classroom settings. Such displays enable a direct mapping between the information and the student (or location) in the large space of a classroom. According to the theory of *distributed cognition* [24], this way of displaying information makes perception intuitive and effortless. As a result, we aim to further explore the design of distributed ambient information systems in classrooms. Moreover, as the mentioned two studies targeted university level education [1] and primary schools [6], the secondary school classroom remains a new context to explore.

Teacher Proximity

A quantity of studies involving educator proximity can be found in educational research, targeting various educatee groups such as pre-school children [19,27,47], school-age learners in classrooms [11,12,18,48], or remote learners [9,43]. The term 'proximity' is used differently in different studies. An emerging cluster of studies addresses teacher proximity in virtual learning environments [9,43]. Alternatively, a relatively large body of work [11,12,18,48] has investigated teacher-student proximity through a subjective-report approach [48] to assess the quality of interpersonal relationships: i.e. how cooperating /opposing a teacher is to his/her students. Nearness between teachers and students in a classroom has not specifically been assessed in these studies. However, some studies on pedagogical interaction [29,30,35] suggest that physical proximity influences mental proximity. For example, students sitting near the teacher may have more opportunities to receive caring.

Rather than virtual proximity, or perceived closeness in relationships, this work focuses on a teacher's physical proximity to his/her students: the spatial distribution of the teacher's presence in the classroom over time. As recognized by [26], few studies can be found in this direction. However, research conducted in the second half of the 20th century [21,22,32] emphasized that physical proximity plays a significant role in communicating non-verbal messages to people (e.g. a feeling of rejection or acceptance), and therefore should be paid careful attention to by educators. A framework of proxemics patterns described in these works were used by [40] and [26] to study physical proximity of teachers for understanding different learning environments [40] and for evaluating online video-cases instructing preservice teachers [26] (to be mentioned, this framework was also utilized in HCI realm by *proxemic interaction* [31]). While these two studies directly analyzed physical proximity, a number of works [14,20,39] has studied teachers' intentional use of the *proximity-control technique* to achieve desired behavior changes of students (e.g. reduced inappropriate behavior, or increased engagement). These studies suggest that teachers' physical proximity to students can influence their behavior.

Although physical proximity between teacher and students has not been frequently studied, results of the studies mentioned above reveal its significance. However, teachers only get feedback on their proximity performance after a trained observer has attended their lesson. No technology is known to track teacher proximity and provide real-time feedback. Such technology could influence teaching and learning. Our work aims to explore the potential values of tracking and visualizing teacher's physical proximity to pedagogical activities, as well as to probe insights into how such displays can be successfully designed.

DESIGNING CLASSBEACONS

To study the value of, and design considerations for, tangible ambient information systems which reveal teachers' proximity information, ClassBeacons was designed, see Figure 1 and 2. ClassBeacons continuously collects data of a teacher's positioning and heading in the classroom through a wearable sensor, see Figure 3. Based on these data a set of small physical lighting devices distributed over the classroom shows the teacher's proximity distribution. Each lighting device changes gradually from yellow to green, indicating how long the teacher has been around that device: the more time the teacher has spent around it, the more towards green it will change (see Figure 2).

Figure 2. ClassBeacons in a classroom. ©Pengcheng An.

Beacons originally refer to the luminous objects signaling or guiding ships in the sea. ClassBeacons is also intended to provide supportive information to teachers in their intensive and complex journey of teaching in the classroom. In order to evaluate this concept in a real classroom setting, we developed a working prototype of ClassBeacons, presented in detail in the upcoming sections.

Wearable Tracking Technique

Teacher's physical proximity to students could be reflected by the teacher's location distribution in space over time. A wearable solution was designed to track teachers' real-time location. These location data were gathered using an indoor positioning sensor kit [37]. The kit consists of four 'anchors' placed on stands in four corners of the classroom and one 'tag' which is implemented in a garment worn by the teacher, see Figure 3. The tag and anchors communicate through ultra-wideband communication [25] to sense positioning of the tag in a constructed Cartesian space (coordinate value of X, Y). This kit was chosen because of its high accuracy (close to 10cm level [37]), compared to other approaches (e.g. Bluetooth, Wi-Fi, or RFID).

Next to location information, the tag also tracks teachers' heading (between 0 to 360 degrees in reference to the magnetic South), which informs the system of the direction the teacher is facing to. As Figure 3 shows, the wearable solution positions the tag on the upper-back of the teacher. The upper-back direction adequately reflects the teacher's facial direction, since we found that teachers' facial direction was mostly in accordance with their upper-body direction from informal observations on classroom videos. Additionally, comparing to other wearable approaches such as headsets, or harnesses, the present solution was expected to be less obtrusive, and therefore less distracting to teacher tasks and more socially acceptable in this context. An adjustable Velcro structure was added beneath the tag unit to tighten or loosen the garment for different teachers.

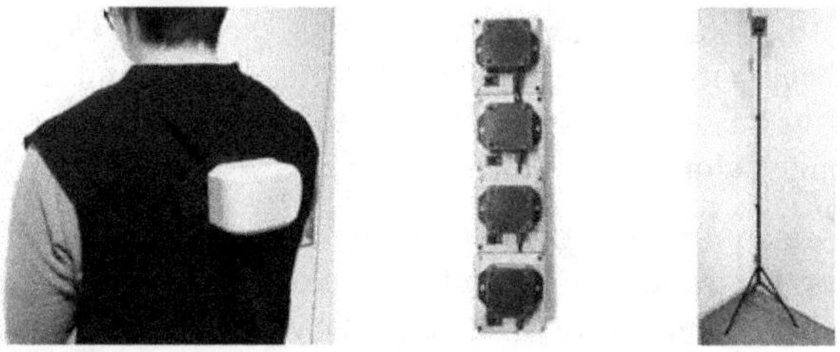

Figure 3. Left: the tag unit on the teacher garment. Middle: four anchors. Right: an anchor mounted on a stand.

Distributed Display

Inspired by studies of [6] and [1], which implemented distributed displays in educational contexts, we identified the value of leveraging distributed tangible devices for ambient display in secondary school classrooms. Therefore, we developed a set of LED devices (introduced in [44]) as the display media of ClassBeacons. As shown in Figure 2, each LED device, called a Beacon, has a frosted and semitransparent lampshade which enables an effect of color blending. All Beacons are wirelessly connected to a control hub. The control hub receives positioning and heading data transmitted by the wearable, and commands each Beacon to update its color accordingly. During deployment in classroom, Beacons were placed on the student desks. If the desks were located very close to each other, two students would share one Beacon put in the middle of the two desks, see Figure 2. Positions of the individual Beacons needed to be input into the system beforehand using the wearable tag.

Visualization of Teacher Proximity

The perception of brightness of the LEDs in a Beacon can be influenced by the existing natural or artificial light in a classroom. Therefore we decided not to indicate the amount of time a teacher spent around a Beacon by the brightness of that Beacon. Instead, we decided to use solely hue as indicator of proximity. To make the color code semantically understandable, we firstly used red-yellow-green spectrum. But to avoid connotations with positive and negative behavior, we avoided using red. Instead we chose to use a *yellow-green spectrum*, where yellow means the teacher has not spend time around that Beacon, while greener colors indicate the teacher has spent more time around that Beacon. This made the visualization less judgmental while still semantically intuitive (see Figure 2). The yellow-green color shifting of Beacons has been set in *nine discrete degrees*, which we experienced to be sufficient to enable gradual and subtle color changes while also retaining a certain level of ambiguity. Additionally, we chose to use discrete changes rather than a continuous change, because we wanted each change to be still subtly perceivable, potentially affording time awareness for the users.

Interpersonal proximity is defined in related literature [22,32] in four levels: *intimate* (0-1.5 ft ≈ 0-0.5 m), *personal* (1.5-4 ft ≈ 0.5-1.2 m), *social* (4-12 ft ≈ 1.2-3.7 m), and *public* (12-25 ft ≈ 3.7-7.6 m). Teacher proximity at the intimate and personal levels are considered as 'closer proximity' in [26]. Based on these works, as well as our informal observation, we defined the range of *close proximity* to be recognized by this system as 1.6m. Beacons within this *close proximity* range to the teacher will start to change color from yellow to green.

To determine at which speed the Beacons should change color, we decided to look closely at the types of interactions teachers might have with students when they are in close proximity. Next to being *engaged* in direct conversation, instruction or observation, more subtle interactions are also brought by teacher proximity. For example, when the teacher is walking around, he/she could glance at students close by to get an idea of their performance, while at the same time, knowing that the teacher is around, or that the teacher may be looking at them, students may also get more engaged in their activities or encouraged to initiate asking questions. Similarly, a study by [3] found that while performing a main task, teachers also try to listen to the students around or behind them to know their status. A review by [20] reported '*spill over*' effects which were found in several studies: a teacher's reinforcement or reprimands to a target student potentially influences non-targeted students sitting adjacently. To better portray teacher proximity, we argue that it is important to reflect various influences brought by teacher proximity including these non-verbal/implicit interactions. Therefore we designed the mechanism of display as follows, distinguishing three levels of interactions:

- *Engaging*: This level is activated when the teacher is standing still, one (or more) Beacon(s) is within *close proximity* to the teacher, and it is in the central area of the teacher's angle-of-view. At this level, a Beacon will take 55 seconds before changing from the current color to the next greener color on the preset nine-degree spectrum.
- *Surrounding*: This level is activated when the teacher is standing still, and one (or more) Beacon(s) is within *close proximity* and in the periphery of the teacher's angle-of-view. At this level, a Beacon will take 110 seconds before it changes to the next color.
- *Wandering*: This level is activated when either the teacher is standing still with one or more beacons in *close proximity* behind the teacher, or the teacher is walking with any Beacon in *close proximity.* At this level, a Beacon will take 220 seconds to change to the next color.

The Beacons change color from yellow to green over the course of one lesson and are reset to yellow before the start of a new lesson. This means that the Beacons can only become greener over the course of one lesson and the information is presented in a cumulative fashion.

METHODOLOGY

Adopting a research-through-design methodology [49], we developed and evaluated ClassBeacons, a distributed ambient information system visualizing teacher proximity in the classroom. Our exploration aims to answer two research questions:

- *RQ-1*: What could be the potential values of proximity visualization for pedagogical activities in the classroom?
- *RQ-2*: How will ClassBeacons be experienced by teachers and students in the secondary school classroom?

To answer these questions, we evaluated ClassBeacons using a mixed-method approach in which we conducted an expert review of ClassBeacons, and a field deployment with eight secondary school teachers. The conducting of both of them will be described in this section. The goal of the expert review is to address RQ-1, and to gather assumptions for RQ-2, while the field evaluation aims to address RQ-2.

Expert Review

We conducted an expert review of the ClassBeacons design with four educational experts (2 male, 2 female, ages 47 to 63), whom we will refer to as E1, E2, E3 and E4. They work at an educational research institute at a University in the Netherlands. All experts were conducting educational research targeting secondary school pedagogy. The jobs of E1, E2, and E3 also contained guiding and coaching preservice/novice secondary school teachers to help those teachers improve their teaching performance. All the experts had ample experiences of observing in secondary school classrooms for teacher performance improvement or research data gathering. All of them had worked as a secondary school teacher for between 6 and 30 years in their career. E2 and E4 were at the moment of the study still teaching part-time. Each expert participated in a semi-structured one-on-one interview of approximately 60 minutes, conducted in an office environment.

In the first part of the interview, the experts were asked to describe their understanding of the role of teacher proximity in secondary education. In the second part of the interview, the design of ClassBeacons was shown to them and they were asked to envision potential values of proximity display to pedagogical activities (RQ-1), and discuss possible user experiences of ClassBeacons (RQ-2). To stimulate the interviewees' imagination and to ensure they saw our design as a concept open for debate rather than as a finished product, we used a storyboard rather than the working prototype to convey the concept of ClassBeacons (see Figure 4). To trigger the experts to consciously speculate on the distributed nature of ClassBeacons, we created another storyboard presenting a screen-based display of the same information through a heatmap (see Figure 4). Experts were asked to give feedback on both and compare the two.

Figure 4. One frame of the storyboards. Left: ClassBeacons. Right: 'heatmap'. ©Pengcheng An.

The interviews were audio-recorded and transcribed verbatim for a *conventional qualitative content analysis* [23]. This standard qualitative analysis approach systematically analyzes textual data, in order to gain thorough and deep understandings about the data [23]. Following the detailed procedures described in [23], the analysis was carried out by two of the authors. 133 quotes were selected which related to (one of) the two research questions. The quotes were coded first individually and then jointly by the two researchers. Through discussion, a detailed categorization of quotes was finalized.

Field Deployments

To gather user experiences of ClassBeacons (RQ-2), the working prototype of ClassBeacons was deployed during lessons of 8 secondary school teachers from 4 different secondary schools. As Table 1 shows, we recruited a group of teachers that were diverse in gender, teaching experience and subject to cover a relatively wide range of pedagogical styles. The prototype was implemented in the classroom of each teacher for two lessons.

Teacher	Gender	School	Experience	Subject
T1	M	S1	8	Computing
T2	M	S1	17	Computing
T3	F	S2	32	English
T4	F	S2	8	English
T5	M	S2	3	English
T6	M	S3	5	Chemistry
T7	F	S4	12	Humanity
T8	F	S4	16	English

Table 1. Basic information about teachers recruited for field evaluation. 'Experience' indicates years of teaching.

Short 20-minute interviews were carried out right after each lesson: teachers were asked to quickly report specific moments in which they looked at or noticed the Beacons, and to indicate why they noticed them and which tasks they were engaged in at those moments. These short interviews aimed to capture detailed examples about how teachers used the ClassBeacons when they still kept a fresh memory about the lesson. After the last lesson of the deployment, each teacher participated in a longer interview of 30 to 60 minutes. These interviews included more in-depth questions on their experiences, such as why they felt the system had or had not helped them, how their students reacted to the system, why they thought the system had or had not brought extra workload to them, how they experienced the information display, and what other benefits, disadvantages, opportunities or risks they thought the system had. Some questions were based on assumptions we gained from the expert reviews (which will be discussed in the upcoming findings section). All the interviews were conducted in the secondary schools, and most of them took place in the classrooms where the prototype had been implemented.

The interviews were audio-recorded and then transcribed verbatim. A phenomenological approach [34] was used to analyze these textual data. This approach was chosen to understand the essence of peoples' experiences on studied phenomena [41], in accordance with the purpose of this field evaluation (to answer RQ-2). The analysis was carried out following the procedure described in [5]. The findings of the analysis will be addressed in next section.

FINDINGS AND DISCUSSION

Expert Review

After the analysis on the data from expert interviews, a categorization of the 133 selected quotes has emerged, under two main topics: the *potential values of proximity visualization* in classrooms (to address RQ-1), and the *possible benefits/challenges of ClassBeacons* (to address RQ-2).

Potential Values of Proximity Visualization (RQ-1)

Reflecting personal interaction: All four experts mentioned that while observing a lesson, they paid considerable attention to the personal interaction between the teacher and individual students. As E4 mentioned, "*education is about interaction, tuning your behavior to the needs of the individuals in your classroom.*" And according to them, there are various types of interactions that are best achieved in close proximity to the students, such as talking (E1), observing a student's work, being around to show willingness of help (E2), or passing by to maintain students' engagement (E3). E1 and E3 pointed out that proper personal interaction could activate students in learning. As indicated by E1, "*if you can create a learning environment where you have more interactions, I think the learning process is more effective... the students are more activated to learn and they also like to learn.*" Moreover, E2 and E4 thought that having sufficient personal interaction helps the teacher keep track of a student's performance ("*what they've done*" (E4)), rather than only knowing the general status of the whole class (such as if "*they're quiet*" (E2)). Given the above mentioned reasons, the experts agreed that providing real-time feedback about the teachers' whereabouts is meaningful. As E1 concluded, "*It's very important from an educational perspective that the teachers get feedback on how they interact with their students.*"

Facilitating Attention distribution: The expert review revealed that it is highly relevant, but also difficult, for teachers to provide a proper amount of attention to each student. In principal, teachers try to "*give attention to all the students*" (E1) with no one left behind. However, it is challenging to "*see all the students*" (E2), especially for teachers who have "*a big classroom*" (E2), or "*30 children*" (E1); and there might be "*a blind spot*" (E2) which the teacher has not visited during the whole lesson. According to the experts, an ideal distribution of attention among students does not necessarily mean the teacher has to spend an equal amount of time with each student. "*Every student is different, so one needs perhaps more attention than the other*" (E4). It is natural that the teacher would "*give more attention to the students who have more problems with learning*" (E1). However, E1, E2 and E4 all noticed that teachers sometimes paid too much attention to some of the students while ignoring the others. "*You sometimes realize that you've paid a lot of attention to 1 or 2 students in the lesson, and the other students have not gotten your attention. That happens, for sure*" (E4). Two types of students normally capture more attention from the teacher: "*Pupils that are making a lot of noise*" (E4), and "*The children who ask questions*" (E2). Sometimes, these active students "*somehow end up in one side of the classroom and that means the other side of the classroom, they don't get so much attention*" (E2). Thusly, with attention caught by these louder or more active students, teachers may easily ignore those reticent students. "*A difficult problem is that sometimes students* [who] *have questions or* [who] *do not understand do not even realize that they should have a question. So asking* [for] *help is not something that all the students do.*" (E4) and therefore E1 identified the benefit of making teachers more aware of their attention assigned to students: "*I think that's very nice* [...] *that you can see: where and what is the attention the teacher gives? That can be some feedback for the teacher, he can realize* [...]"

Creating immediate awareness: The experts confirmed the complexity of teaching. As E4 reported, when interacting with a student, "*there was a lot more going on and you should keep your eyes and ears open to what's going on*". A teacher often needs to have multiple tasks in mind concurrently, Such as attending to "*sound levels*" (E4), having an "*overview*" (E3) of the class, or adapting teaching plans to changes (E2). All these tasks impose cognitive load on teachers. Therefore it is difficult for them to pay continuous attention to the details of their own performances while teaching, including keeping aware of their own "*movement*" (E3) in the classroom. As experienced by E4, "*usually when you're observing the classroom, you see other things* [more] *than the teacher sees* [...] [Because] *you're not managing the class you have more time to observe*". Feedback about personal interaction or attention distribution of the teacher is often provided by the observers afterwards. The experts indicated that they thought a real-time visualization could disburden teachers' reflection and help them gain immediate awareness about their proximity distribution so far. For example, a teacher could easily notice that he/she has spent too much time with a group of students: "*if I get the feedback then I realize that I have to stop* [offering] *the feedback or the intervention for that group and I have to go to the other group*"(E1). The experts thought that a real-time visualization of proximity information could help teachers improve their performances immediately. "*When you have real time feedback you can adjust your behavior instantly, not afterwards* [...] *wait for a second lesson* [...] *So that's valuable.*" (E3)

Possible Benefits and Challenges of ClassBeacons (RQ-2)

Benefits: The most mentioned benefit by the experts was that as a public visualization ClassBeacons might create self-awareness among the students, especially for those who "*are not even aware that they should ask a question*" (E4) With this awareness, they might be encouraged to ask more attention from the teacher. Furthermore, a public display is expected to create transparency. "*I like to have a transparent situation and all students can see how much time there is given to the other students.*" (E1) As a result, the lights could be a justification for the teacher to go on to the next student, "*if you are explaining something to one student and you can say: 'Sorry, but I have to help the other students as well'*" (E4). Unlike a single device, ClassBeacons is distributed (E2) and therefore can serve as a visual cue. Being distributed over the space, ClassBeacons "*would be easier* [to perceive] *because you just see whose light is brighter than the other*" (E2). Since "*it's visible right away*" (E3), there is no need to go back and forth. "*You don't have to walk to the* [teacher's] *desk to have a look.*" (E2) And the ClassBeacons offer flexibility in how to use them: "*you could just take 4 or 5 of these lights and then put the seats together and say okay this is one group and this is the other group* [...]" (E2).

Challenges: There are also some concerns from experts about ClassBeacons. The lights might be a distraction or disruption to students, "*Maybe they give attention to the light and not* [to] *what they are doing*" (E1). Some students may complain if this feedback information is visible for them. E.g., "[a student might say:] '*His light is much brighter than mine; you should pay attention to me. It's unequal*'" (E4). Also students might have their own interpretation of the ClassBeacons with negative consequences. E.g., "*I cannot ask any questions anymore because my light is so bright*" (E3). E2 was concerned that "*if you would do this in lower* [grades of] *secondary education,*" those younger students might fiddle around with the Beacons. In a distributed manner, it can be more difficult "*to get some overview*" of the proximity distribution (E1). Comparing to a heatmap which shows the proximity information on screen, the experts expect that ClassBeacons is less beneficial for reflection afterwards (E2). And it was also estimated by E2 that with a centralized device, attention could be paid only when the teacher wanted to.

Field Evaluation (RQ-2)

In this sub-section we report the results of the analysis on eight teachers' experiences of using ClassBeacons in their classrooms to address RQ-2.

Influence on Teaching

All the teachers except T3 reported that ClassBeacons had brought them more awareness about their own proximity distribution. For instance, as T4 reported, "*I could actually see that I didn't spend that much time or I spent more time* [in this group] *than in another group*". The newly gained awareness seemed to have different meanings to them. T1 found it supportive to his decision-making: "*when multiple students were raising their hand, I checked the Beacons to see what color it was, so more towards yellow then that would be the first to go to*". T2 experienced the awareness triggered reflection: "*I saw there was the light* [that was] *a little bit yellow. Then you reflect to yourself: did that student need more attention? No, that student is okay.*" T6 reported that the information helped him to confirm his execution of plans "*In my head those* [students] *are the ones I want to give* [extra] *attention,* [...] *and now I can actually see that they also get that extra attention.*" While T3 and T5 did not think that the display could make a difference in their teaching ("*I can't imagine that it would change my behavior at all*" (T3)), the other teachers indicated that it could potentially facilitate their attention distribution and personal interaction with the students. For example, T8 felt it was "*quite useful because* [...] *you can be sure that you are dividing your time with everybody in the classroom.*" T7 thought ClassBeacons reminded her to wander more, which motivated students to ask for help.

Social Awareness

Teachers identified both benefits and risks of the social awareness created by the ClassBeacons' public visualization of the teacher's proximity. T7 found it "*a benefit for the students because some of them maybe are going to realize that they don't ask enough questions, so they don't ask for the attention of the teacher enough*". T4 experienced that it could activate students in a playful way, because they liked to have their lamps turned green: "*It's more like a reward and they become aware of their participation as well*". After being asked, no teacher reported that they had been stressed by the social awareness in their lessons (e.g., "*Does it give you any pressure?* [...] *No, it doesn't.*" (T4)). However, they could imagine that teachers might experience pressure in some occasions. One concern was that students might use it to complain about their teaching. For example, students might say: "*'my light is always yellow. I didn't get the attention I needed.'*" (T2) or "*students use it as a reason to say that the teacher is picking on me*" (T3). At the same time, T2 and T6 considered that it could also be justification for teachers: "*'I always spend time with you: look at the system, your light is always green.'*" (T2) Another possible pressure on teachers could be that the data of ClassBeacons might be abused by the school management or parents to (mis-)judge teachers. Therefore "*It would have to be made very clear to that teacher what the system was used for*" (T3).

Distraction Level

The participating teachers experienced that the students showed curiosity and interest at the beginning of the lessons when they first encountered ClassBeacons. "*At first they wanted to know why the lamps were on the table and what they were doing. So the first five minutes they were focused on the lamps* [...] *after that, that was okay*" (T7). "*They were quite excited. After a bit they stopped bothering*" (T3). None of the teachers considered ClassBeacons as a serious distraction to the learning activity. As T4 indicated, "*they find it very interesting but it's not like they're constantly aware of it*". Some teachers tended to attribute this to the novelty effect of the system: "*it's the same with the mobile phones. Once they were used to seeing them all the time, they will not notice them.*" (T8) Contrarily, T6 reported that the lamp was quite distractive to one student who he knew to be quite sensitive to distractions in general.

Perception of Information

Teachers considered the perception of information from ClassBeacons as effortless and direct. T4 experienced her perception was "*quick, because it's got the color so unconsciously... I think it's a split-second or something that you actually think about it*". T6 found that the system could show an understandable pattern by color difference: "*when at first it was all a bit yellowish, all the same, but after a while I started to see patterns, and the patterns were for me an indication.*" Some teachers also reported that they could easily ignore the display when focusing on their main tasks. "*I kind of deliberately forgot them* [...] *I was busy looking what they were writing*" (T8) Examples described by teachers indicate that they could obtain relevant information from ClassBeacons while performing other teaching tasks, sequentially or in quasi-parallel. "*You look around: is everybody okay? And then you can see, then you look at the lights and think: okay, do I have to go somewhere?*" (T2). "*So I try to observe some obvious clues: students raising their hands or students talking to each other and not working* [...] [looking at] *ClassBeacons are also part of that observation*" (T1). This seamless integration of the perception into teaching routines was appreciated by teachers. "*I think that's the best point, that you can use it at the moment.* [...] *you are just doing regular things, what you're used to do*" (T7). And compared to a visualization on a screen, "*it's direct, and it doesn't require a lot of reading.*" (T4) Additionally, a benefit brought by physicality was mentioned. As T7 experienced, her teaching was influenced not only because of the information presented to her, but also because of the physical presence of the Beacons served as a cue. "*In the first place because the system is there, it's not like this light is orange so I have to go.*" T8 had a similar comment: "*if they weren't there, there is no visual sign* [reminding me to] *go to the back* [...]"

DISCUSSION

To assess what the value of showing real-time proximity information might be to educational practice and to study the user experience of the ClassBeacons' implementation, we conducted an expert review and a field deployment.

From the expert review it became clear that close teacher-student proximity is beneficial for individual support, and activating students, which confirms views from related educational research [29,30,35]. Knowing how much time teachers have spent in different areas could help them to more mindfully distribute proximity. However, in current practice, feedback on teacher proximity is only subjectively and sporadically provided by professional observers. The experts considered objective real-time feedback as a valuable addition, which could enable teachers to reflect more often and more directly on their time and attention distribution over students. As a confirmation to this, most of the participating teachers experienced that the immediate feedback given by ClassBeacons could benefit them during teaching. They indicated that it helped them in decision-making (e.g. which students to help first) or reflection (e.g. to check if they were doing the right thing). Such reflective activities are considered important for teachers [46], especially in the context of learner-centered education [15]. Both findings indicate that teacher proximity visualization can be meaningful to classroom pedagogy. Nonetheless, T3 perceived little usefulness from the system. And she also happens to have the longest career among the teachers (see Table 1). This may suggest that a future study could focus on the differences of the system's perceived usefulness to and actual impact on the teachers with different levels of teaching experience and technology acceptance.

The ClassBeacons' distributed display makes proximity information visible to everyone in the classroom. We therefore explored the possible social effects of ClassBeacons. The experts and the participating teachers identified both benefits and risks of the design. Both experts and teachers addressed that teacher choices could be justified by the display, that information about teacher proximity could encourage 'reticent' students to ask the teacher for support, and that the engagement of students could be increased as a result of knowing that the teacher is wandering more. This echoes some findings in educational science literature [14,20,39] which show that a teacher's physical proximity positively influences student engagement. Although the number of participants in our field-study was limited and experts merely voices expected effects of ClassBeacons, a display like ClassBeacons might be able to extend the effect proximity has on student engagement. When the teacher is no longer close to the student, but a display reminds the student of a teacher's proximity earlier in the lesson, or of upcoming teacher's proximity, this might also result in increased engagement. Longer and more elaborate field evaluations would be needed to further examine such an effect of ClassBeacons.

With the ClassBeacons' display accessible to all, some experts were concerned by its distraction to students. However, through observation, none of the participating teachers found it a serious distraction to the students despite the "curiosity" during the first minutes of use. Some teachers attributed this extra attention from students at the beginning as novelty effect of a new technology. Moreover, both experts and teachers were concerned that students might complain to the teacher for receiving too much or too little attention, or misinterpret the display. Besides this, teachers also expressed the concern that the data from the system might be abused by schools or parents. Hence a careful consideration of possible social effects is needed when designing similar systems. Given that privacy concerns are appropriately dealt with, we believe to make this feedback also visible to the students is constructive for creating learner-centered dynamics in the classroom.

Teachers considered the display to be effortless and direct. Although E1 estimated that it might be difficult to have "*some overview*" of the displayed data with this distributed system, T6 experienced that an understandable pattern emerged in the space through the colors. Different from what E2 had assumed, the display was not experienced as demanding: Beacons could be easily discarded when the teachers were busy. Because of its distributed nature, a location and its related information were co-located. Teachers indicated they could use the system sequentially or in quasi-parallel with student observation (which commonly exists in teacher routines [3]). As compared to centralized displays, ClassBeacons did not require teachers to go back and forth, or read information from a screen. Therefore it seems less interrupting to the task flow of teaching. The teachers' experiences of ClassBeacons confirmed our assumption that distributed tangible displays have the potential to seamlessly integrate relevant information into teachers' everyday routines.

CONCLUSION

We presented the design, expert review, and field evaluation of ClassBeacons, a distributed ambient tangible display that visualized teacher proximity in secondary school classrooms. Our findings show that access to real-time information about the teacher's proximity over the duration of a lesson could be valuable for both teachers (to support decision-making and immediate reflection) and students (to possibly increase engagement and encourage active participation). Furthermore, the distributed and ambient nature of ClassBeacons enabled the design to potentially seamlessly blend into the classroom routines.

ACKNOWLEDGEMENT

We thank all the experts, teachers, students, and secondary schools for voluntarily participating in our research. We also thank Dr. de Putter, Dr. Paffen, Dr. Offermans, Ms. Niemantsverdriet, Mr. Bangaru, Mr. van Overbeeke (photographer of Figure 1) and other colleagues of ours who kindly supported this work.

REFERENCES

1. Hamed S. Alavi and Pierre Dillenbourg. 2012. An ambient awareness tool for supporting supervised collaborative problem solving. *IEEE Transactions on Learning Technologies* 5, 3: 264–274. https://doi.org/10.1109/TLT.2012.7
2. Erik van Alphen and Saskia Bakker. 2016. Lernanto. In *Proceedings of the 2016 CHI Conference Extended Abstracts on Human Factors in Computing Systems - CHI EA '16*, 2334–2340. https://doi.org/10.1145/2851581.2892524
3. Pengcheng An, Saskia Bakker, and Berry Eggen. 2017. Understanding teachers' routines to inform classroom technology design. *Education and Information Technologies* 22, 4: 1347–1376. https://doi.org/10.1007/s10639-016-9494-9
4. Pengcheng An, Saskia Bakker, and Berry Eggen. 2017. FeetForward: On Blending New Classroom Technologies into Secondary School Teachers' Routines. In *Lecture Notes in Computer Science (including subseries Lecture Notes in Artificial Intelligence and Lecture Notes in Bioinformatics)*, 327–347. https://doi.org/10.1007/978-3-319-67684-5_20
5. Elizabeth H Anderson and Margaret Hull Spencer. 2002. Cognitive representations of AIDS: a phenomenological study. *Qualitative health research* 12, 10: 1338–1352. https://doi.org/10.1177/1049732302238747
6. Saskia Bakker, Elise van den Hoven, and Berry Eggen. 2013. FireFlies: physical peripheral interaction design for the everyday routine of primary school teachers. In *Proceedings of Tangible and Embodied Interaction, TEI 2013, Feb 10-13, 2013, Barcelona*, 8 pages. Retrieved from http://dl.acm.org/citation.cfm?id=2460634
7. Saskia Bakker and Karin Niemantsverdriet. 2016. The interaction-attention continuum: Considering various levels of human attention in interaction design. *International Journal of Design* 10, 2.
8. Henry Jay Becker. 2000. Findings from the teaching, learning, and computing survey: Is Larry Cuban right? *Education Policy Analysis Archives* 8, 51: 1–31. https://doi.org/10.14507/epaa.v8n51.2000
9. Karin Bolldén. 2016. Teachers' embodied presence in online teaching practices. *Studies in Continuing Education* 38, 1: 1–15. https://doi.org/10.1080/0158037X.2014.988701
10. Göran Brante. 2009. Multitasking and synchronous work: Complexities in teacher work. *Teaching and Teacher Education* 25, 3: 430–436. https://doi.org/10.1016/j.tate.2008.09.015
11. Perry den Brok, Darrell Fisher, Theo Wubbels, Mieke Brekelmans, and Tony Rickards. 2006. Secondary Teachers' Interpersonal Behaviour in Singapore, Brunei and Australia: A cross-national comparison. *Asia Pacific Journal of Education* 26, 1: 79–95. https://doi.org/10.1080/02188790600608208
12. Perry den Brok and Jack Levy. 2005. Teacher-student relationships in multicultural classes: Reviewing the past, preparing the future. *International Journal of Educational Research* 43, 1–2: 72–88. https://doi.org/10.1016/j.ijer.2006.03.007
13. Alfons ten Brummelhuis, Martine Kramer, Philip Post, and Chris Zintel. 2015. Vier in balans-monitor 2015. *Kennisnet*. Retrieved from https://www.kennisnet.nl/fileadmin/kennisnet/publicatie/vierinbalans/Vier_in_balans_monitor_2015.pdf
14. Judith Caldwell. 1979. Basic Techniques for Early Classroom Intervention. *Pointer* 24, 1: 53–60. Retrieved July 3, 2017 from https://eric.ed.gov/?q=teacher+physical+proximity&id=EJ223628
15. J. Cornelius-White. 2007. Learner-Centered Teacher-Student Relationships Are Effective: A Meta-Analysis. *Review of Educational Research* 77, 1: 113–143. https://doi.org/10.3102/003465430298563
16. L. Cuban, H. Kirkpatrick, and C. Peck. 2001. High Access and Low Use of Technologies in High School Classrooms: Explaining an Apparent Paradox. *American Educational Research Journal* 38, 4: 813–834. https://doi.org/10.3102/00028312038004813
17. Walter Doyle. 1977. Learning the Classroom Environment: An Ecological Analysis of Induction Into Teaching. Retrieved November 10, 2015 from http://eric.ed.gov/?id=ED135782
18. Darrell Fisher, Bruce Waldrip, and Perry den Brok. 2005. Students' perceptions of primary teachers' interpersonal behavior and of cultural dimensions in the classroom environment. *International Journal of Educational Research* 43, 1–2: 25–38. https://doi.org/10.1016/j.ijer.2006.03.004
19. Marilyn Fleer. 2015. Pedagogical positioning in play ? teachers being inside and outside of children's imaginary play. *Early Child Development and Care* 185, 11–12: 1801–1814. https://doi.org/10.1080/03004430.2015.1028393
20. Philip L. Gunter, Richard E. Shores, Susan L. Jack, Shirley K. Rasmussen, and Julia Flowers. 1995. On

the Move Using Teacher/Student Proximity to Improve Students' Behavior. *TEACHING Exceptional Children* 28, 1: 12–14. https://doi.org/10.1177/004005999502800103

21. Edward T. Hall. 1963. A System for the Notation of Proxemic Behavior. *American Anthropologist* 65, 5: 1003–1026. https://doi.org/10.1525/aa.1963.65.5.02a00020

22. Edward T. Hall, Ray L. Birdwhistell, Bernhard Bock, Paul Bohannan, A. Richard Diebold, Jr., Marshall Durbin, Munro S. Edmonson, J. L. Fischer, Dell Hymes, Solon T. Kimball, Weston La Barre, Frank Lynch, S. J., J. E. McClellan, Donald S. Marshall, G. B. Milner, Harvey B. Sarles, George L Trager, and Andrew P. Vayda. 1968. Proxemics [and Comments and Replies]. *Current Anthropology* 9: 83–108. https://doi.org/10.2307/2740724

23. Hsiu-Fang Hsieh and Sarah E Shannon. 2005. Three approaches to qualitative content analysis. *Qualitative health research* 15, 9: 1277–1288. https://doi.org/10.1177/1049732305276687

24. Edwin Hutchins. 2005. Distributed cognition. *Cognition, Technology & Work* 7, 1: 5–5. https://doi.org/10.1007/s10111-004-0172-0

25. S.J. Ingram, D. Harmer, and M. Quinlan. UltraWideBand indoor positioning systems and their use in emergencies. In *PLANS 2004. Position Location and Navigation Symposium (IEEE Cat. No.04CH37556)*, 706–715. https://doi.org/10.1109/PLANS.2004.1309063

26. Ugur Kale. 2008. Levels of interaction and proximity: Content analysis of video-based classroom cases. *The Internet and Higher Education* 11, 2: 119–128. https://doi.org/10.1016/j.iheduc.2008.06.004

27. April Kendrick, Maria Hernandez-Reif, Carmen Hudson, Hyun-Joo Jeon, and Charlotte Horton. 2012. Coding group behaviours for preschool children in the playground and the effects of teachers? proximity on preschool children?s playground behaviours. *Early Child Development and Care* 182, 6: 665–682. https://doi.org/10.1080/03004430.2011.569544

28. K. K. Lamberty, Katherine Froiland, Jason Biatek, and Stephen Adams. 2010. Encouraging awareness of peers' learning activities using large displays in the periphery. In *Proceedings of the 28th of the international conference extended abstracts on Human factors in computing systems - CHI EA '10*, 3655. https://doi.org/10.1145/1753846.1754034

29. Nikos Macheridis and Alexander Paulsson. 2016. Governance of higher education – the role of proximity in teaching quality. *Tertiary Education and Management* 22, 3: 202–217. https://doi.org/10.1080/13583883.2016.1183036

30. M. Tim Mainhard, Mieke Brekelmans, and Theo Wubbels. 2011. Coercive and supportive teacher behaviour: Within- and across-lesson associations with the classroom social climate. *Learning and Instruction* 21, 3: 345–354. https://doi.org/10.1016/j.learninstruc.2010.03.003

31. Nicolai Marquardt and Saul Greenberg. 2012. Informing the design of proxemic interactions. *IEEE Pervasive Computing* 11, 2: 14–23. https://doi.org/10.1109/MPRV.2012.15

32. Patrick W. Miller. 1988. *Nonverbal communication.* NEA Professional Library, National Education Association. Retrieved July 18, 2017 from https://eric.ed.gov/?id=ED293190

33. Neema Moraveji, Meredith Morris, Daniel Morris, Mary Czerwinski, and Nathalie Henry Riche. 2011. ClassSearch: Facilitating the Development of Web Search Skills Through Social Learning. In *Proceedings of the SIGCHI Conference on Human Factors in Computing Systems*, 1797–1806. https://doi.org/10.1145/1978942.1979203

34. Clark Moustakas. 1994. *Phenomenological research methods.* Retrieved from http://scholar.google.com/scholar?hl=en&btnG=Search&q=intitle:Phenomenological+research+methods#0

35. Robert C. Pianta. 2012. Implementing Observation Protocols: Lessons for K-12 Education from the Field of Early Childhood. *Center for American Progress.* Retrieved July 31, 2017 from https://eric.ed.gov/?id=ED535604

36. Z. Pousman and J. Stasko. 2006. A taxonomy of ambient information systems: four patterns of design. *Proceedings of the working conference on Advanced visual interfaces*: 67–74. https://doi.org/10.1145/1133265.1133277

37. Pozyx. in-door positioning sensor kit. Retrieved from https://www.pozyx.io/

38. Kenneth Ruthven, Sara Hennessy, and Sue Brindley. 2004. Teacher representations of the successful use of computer-based tools and resources in secondary-school English, mathematics and science. *Teaching and Teacher Education* 20, 3: 259–275. https://doi.org/10.1016/j.tate.2004.02.002

39. Richard E. Shores, Philip L. Gunter, and Susan L. Jack. 2017. Classroom Management Strategies: Are They Setting Events for Coercion? *http://dx.doi.org/10.1177/019874299301800207*. https://doi.org/10.1177/019874299301800207

40. Toni M. Sills-Briegel. 1996. Teacher-Student Proximity and Interactions in a Computer Laboratory and Classroom. *The Clearing House: A Journal of Educational Strategies, Issues and Ideas* 70, 1: 21–23. https://doi.org/10.1080/00098655.1996.10114351

41. Helene Starks and Susan Brown Trinidad. 2007. Choose your method: a comparison of phenomenology, discourse analysis, and grounded theory. *Qualitative health research* 17, 10: 1372–1380. https://doi.org/10.1177/1049732307307031

42. Janienke Sturm, Rahat Iqbal, and Jacques Terken. 2006. Development of Peripheral Feedback to Support Lectures. In *Machine Learning for Multimodal Interaction*, S Renals and S Bengio (eds.). Springer Berlin Heidelberg, Berlin, Heidelberg, 138–149. https://doi.org/10.1007/11677482

43. Chryssa Themeli and Anna Bougia. 2016. Tele-proximity: Tele-community of Inquiry Model. Facial Cues for Social, Cognitive, and Teacher Presence in Distance Education. *The International Review of Research in Open and Distributed Learning* 17, 6. https://doi.org/10.19173/irrodl.v17i6.2453

44. David Verweij, Saskia Bakker, and Berry Eggen. 2017. FireFlies2: Interactive Tangible Pixels to enable Distributed Cognition in Classroom Technologies. In *ISS '17 Proceedings of the 2017 ACM International Conference on Interactive Surfaces and Spaces*, 260–269. https://doi.org/10.1145/3132272.3134122

45. Mark Weiser and John Seely Brown. 1997. The Coming Age of Calm Technology. In *Beyond Calculation*. 75–85. https://doi.org/10.1007/978-1-4612-0685-9_6

46. Chad West. 2013. Developing Reflective Practitioners. *Journal of Music Teacher Education* 22, 2: 11–19. https://doi.org/10.1177/1057083712437041

47. Elizabeth Jayne White and Bridgette Redder. 2015. Proximity with under two-year-olds in early childhood education: a silent pedagogical encounter. *Early Child Development and Care* 185, 11–12: 1783–1800. https://doi.org/10.1080/03004430.2015.1028386

48. Theo Wubbels and Mieke Brekelmans. 2005. Two decades of research on teacher-student relationships in class. *International Journal of Educational Research* 43, 1–2: 6–24. https://doi.org/10.1016/j.ijer.2006.03.003

49. John Zimmerman, Jodi Forlizzi, and Shelley Evenson. 2007. Research through design as a method for interaction design research in HCI. *Proceedings of the SIGCHI conference on Human factors in computing systems - CHI '07*: 493–502. https://doi.org/10.1145/1240624.1240704

Evolving Tangibles for Children's Social Learning through Conversations: Beyond TurnTalk

Rosella Gennari
Faculty of Computer Science,
Free U. of Bozen-Bolzano
Bolzano, Italy
gennari@inf.unibz.it

Alessandra Melonio
Faculty of Computer Science,
Free U. of Bozen-Bolzano
Bolzano, Italy
alessandra.melonio@unibz.it

Mehdi Rizvi
Faculty of Computer Science,
Free U. of Bozen-Bolzano
Bolzano, Italy
SRizvi@unibz.it

ABSTRACT

Social learning curricula teach children social norms for managing conversations, such as the norm of not overlapping in talking turns. Interactive tangible objects (briefly, tangibles) can help teachers in the scaffolding of such norms. Such tangibles should be created for the specific social learning contexts of their users, and evolve according to their requirements. An ideal design process for tangibles for children's conversations is meta-design, based on action-research: evolving tangible prototypes are developed, with natural material and easy-to-use micro-electronics components; tangibles are adopted by their users in ecological studies, and their usage is reflected over with designers to stir design directions or uncover design possibilities, which are developed and again used by users. This paper reports on such an evolutionary design process, concerning tangibles for children's conversations. It shows how new design ideas emerged by making users adopt design solutions and moving designers into ecological settings.

ACM Classification Keywords

Human-centered computing: Interaction design theory, concepts and paradigms

Author Keywords

Tangible; Meta-design; Action Research; Social Learning; Conversation; Children; Teachers; School

INTRODUCTION

Nowadays, several researchers are aware of the importance of social learning through conversation, which makes children learn how to communicate and interact with others, with positive effects that go beyond improvements in social skills, e.g., [18]. Several social learning curricula aim at teaching specific social norms for conversation, starting with primary schools. Examples are the social norms of taking turns and not overlapping in turns in a group-based conversation, by no means easy to master for primary school children [34].

TEI '18, March 18–21, 2018, Stockholm, Sweden

ISBN 978-1-4503-5568-1/18/03. . . 15.00

DOI: https://doi.org/10.1145/3173225.3173248

Interactive tangible objects, briefly *tangibles*, can sustain children's learning of social norms for conversations. Tangibles are a natural way of bringing children together, as they mirror the collaboration that occurs with physical objects and promote multi-sensory experiences, reinforcing learning [26]. Tangibles for conversation can trace conversation data, and hence help children reflect about their conversation behaviours against social norms, e.g., [17, 33].

The design of tangibles, which tackle specific social norms for conversation, should not be "in the vacuum": it should crucially consider the school context they are meant for, and over time [33]. Meta-design approaches that make users appropriate tangible solutions, which deploy and explore the usage of solutions in real-world contexts, continuously, can help design technologies informed by repeated usage practices and gain insights from the users' unique viewpoint [8].

This paper purports that tangibles are a natural way for promoting conversation social norms, and that meta-design is a suitable approach for designing and making them evolve over time. It starts by exploring related work, and then it motivates the rationale of the chosen design approach. Then the paper comes to its core matters. For the first time, it explores the evolution of tangibles for conversation in primary schools across 2017, through evolutionary development, actions with designers and users in ecologically-valid studies, and by means of joint reflections about the study results. It concludes by pondering over the entire design process of 2017, and by discussing possible future work.

RELATED RESEARCH AND BACKGROUND

Tangible Solutions for Conversation

Tangibles for Adults' Meetings

Meeting tangible solutions for adults exploit several modalities for feedback about conversation progress, e.g., [32, 21]. The latter is a tangible prototype of an inflatable table with a ball, which rolls on the inflated surface and signals when someone speaks longer than the others on average. However, at present, the visual modality is the one mainly exploited by meeting solutions. Examples are *Second Messenger* [16] and *Conversation Clock* [5]. *ConversationVote* extends the latter by allowing participants to assign a binary vote (yes, no) to conversation items [6].

However, visual metaphors adopted for meetings, and explaining conversation behaviours to adults, tend to be abstract and hence not adequate for primary school children. More generally, group conversations with children in classrooms are different than adult conversations, because children are different than adults and primary school classrooms are specific environments, to the point that at school it is very difficult to have the technical facilities and accurate logging needed by meeting solutions, e.g., [7, 10]. More generally, solutions for adults' meetings cannot be directly used for schools, and hence specific ones have been developed.

Tangibles for Learning Contexts

Collaborative learning research has developed touch-screen solutions for monitoring or mediating learners' conversations. A summary of this work is beyond the scope of this paper. An example of a generic screen-based solution, but for university students, is reported in [30]: students collaborate through a shared screen on any joint topic, and teachers assess their collaboration on another screen. Recent screen-based solutions for children with tangible objects employ games for promoting collaborative learning on a specific topic, e.g., pollution. For instance, in [29], a touch-screen game, augmented with physical pawns, allowed children to visualise the impact of their conversation choices on the climate. Similarly, Youtopia is a multi-touch game concerning environment sustainability. Children interact with Youtopia through physical stamps, and Youtopia shows whether their conversation decisions support or not land preservation. In [3], authors observed that Youtopia as well as similar tangible digital solutions can help promote desirable social behaviours, besides other learning gains.

Tangibles in this paper also aim at promoting positive social behaviours but they do it by targeting specific social norms for conversation. Such tangibles do not employ touch-screens but diverse interactive tangible objects. They do not focus on a particular topic (e.g., pollution), but aim at facilitating children's conversation about any topic and their reflections about their conversation behaviours. General solutions with similar tangible objects and without screens exist for younger children than primary-school children, but they tend not to focus on conversation. An example for all is *Ely the Explorer* [2], which fosters the exchange of physical objects, such as dolls, rotary knobs and RFID cards, through a shared surface.

Design Approaches for Tangibles

The above literature outline shows different tangibles for conversation, with varied purposes and users. Most solutions tend to focus on different purposes than supporting social norms for conversation, and few of them target primary schools, which have their own characteristics and requirements [7]. Thus the design of tangibles for conversation in primary schools, supporting specific social norms, seems an open area of research.

There are different approaches to the design of tangibles, which, in principle, may be adopted for designing tangibles for conversation in primary-schools. In general, it seems that tangibles tend to be assessed in short-term studies in controlled environments, and hence their assessment tends to be a usability or user experience evaluation. However, tangibles for conversation, in particular, and social contexts, in general, cannot be "evaluated in the vacuum of a laboratory" and "it is necessary to provide realistic conditions for the exploration of complex design spaces in order to enable constructive interactions between designers and users" [4]. User-oriented design approaches, such as participatory design [22], or other meta-design approaches, such as [13], have been recently (re)proposed as ideal design approaches for them [19]. An interesting study of meta-design of products for social contexts (physical objects interacting with social medias) is reported in [20]. Another one with children is in [12].

Tangible solutions for social contexts, moreover, are also subject to evolution. Meta-design and other end-user development approaches do not provide fixed solutions but a framework within which end users and designers alike can continuously contribute to the development. However, in spite of their potentials, so far meta-design and other end-user development approaches have been scarcely used for developing tangibles over long periods of time in a continuous manner, as done for instance in [15, 27]. The former describes the CoDICE software for tracing the rationale of co-design decisions. The latter is a participatory design study with elderly people.

Thereby meta-design seems to have the potentials for developing evolving tangibles for conversation in primary school classrooms, as advanced for the first time in [23]. This paper pursues this line of research, as explained next.

EVOLVING TANGIBLES FOR CONVERSATION

The Design Approach

In the work reported in this paper, tangibles evolve through meta-design, based on action research e.g., [14]. This spirals through *reflections* about the need and usages of tangibles, *evolutionary development* of tangibles and *actions* with tangibles in ecologically valid settings. Actions trigger new reflections, which potentially uncover novel development possibilities and actions. Details follow.

Reflections and Purpose

In this paper, each tangible has a specific social norm as purpose. In the early reflection stage, social learning experts help identify the purposes of tangibles (which social norms to target). Once tangibles are developed and used in actions in school contexts, children and teachers reflect with designers on results of actions [9]. Joint reflections trigger decisions about the evolution of tangibles: if tangibles are re-purposed, adapted or abandoned for others, all developed as follows.

Development

Tangibles are developed as vertical prototypes based on reflections: they have few new critical functionalities to explore through actions in the field. They are also modular and blend "green" natural materials that children are familiar with, such as cartoon and wood, with economic and easy-to-program IoT micro-electronics components, such as Arduino [1]. All such development choices help designers replicate tangibles for a context with many children, as well as rapidly re-purpose, adapt or discard tangibles.

Actions

Actions mainly take the form of ecologically valid studies, which involve, over time, designers and users, who adopt thc

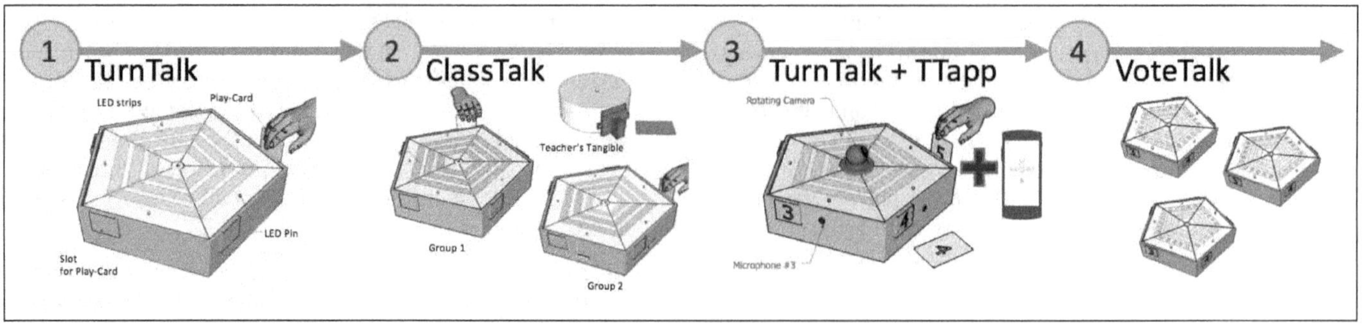

Figure 1. The evolution of tangibles starting with TurnTalk and ending with VoteTalk

developed tangibles in their context. Designers are experts of interaction design with and for children, and are present in actions to study the usage of tangibles in real contexts; users present in actions are mainly teachers and primary school children, and possibly social learning experts [11].

The Design Process in 2017

The action-research meta-design, presented in this paper, was initially carried over for designing preliminary versions of a specific tangible, namely, TurnTalk. Its purpose is the scaffolding of *turn-sharing* norms in conversations of small groups of primary school children: one child should speak at a time, without overlaps; each child should take (at least) a turn; turn frequency and times should be "balanced" across group members. The development and main actions with earlier versions of TurnTalk are all outlined in [23].

In 2017, a mature version of TurnTalk was used in different contexts. In particular, actions with it in a cooperative primary school led to reflections that uncovered new design possibilities, explored for the first time in this paper. The first is an evolution of TurnTalk for class usage: ClassTalk, in which different TurnTalk prototypes are re-purposed and adapted for class turn sharing, instead of group turn sharing. The second evolution is TurnTalk for blended turn sharing, which makes TurnTalk available to distant children through a dedicated mobile app, TTapp. The third evolution is VoteTalk, which completely re-purposes and adapts TurnTalk for the scaffolding of different voting norms for taking decisions concerning results of conversations. The remainder of this paper explores their evolution for the first time, starting with TurnTalk. See Table 1 and Figure 1 for their overview.

Tangible	Purpose
TurnTalk	norms for turn sharing in group
ClassTalk	norms for turn sharing in class
TurnTalk+TTapp	norms for blended turn sharing in group
VoteTalk	norms for voting in group/class

Table 1. The main purpose of each 2017 tangible

TURNTALK FOR GROUP TURN SHARING

Reflections and Purpose

TurnTalk is for groups of 3 to 5 children for co-located, simultaneous, face-to-face conversations in classroom. Its purpose is the scaffolding of the aforementioned turn-sharing social norms. It was inspired by the gamified probes for collaboration presented in [22, 24]. Early versions of TurnTalk have been used in actions and reflections with different education experts, teachers and children in different learning environments, reported in [23, 25, 31]. The essential features of the mature version of TurnTalk, presented in this paper, are based on those actions and reflections, and are detailed in the following.

Developed Features

TurnTalk is a wood pentagon-shaped tangible, with 3D printed components and Arduino IoT MKR1000 micro-electronics [1]. It stimulates different learning modalities—visual, tactile, kinaesthetic—primarily by means of a *play-card mechanism* and a *progression feedback*. See Figures 1 and 2.

The *play-card mechanism* is as follows. The cover of TurnTalk is split into 5 sectors, one per child. Children tangibly play a card to take or reserve their turn to speak. This mechanism is enforced by a visual feedback of LED pins, which relies on the semaphore metaphor: the current speaker's LED pin flashes green; the next speaker's LED pin flashes yellow; any other LED pin flashes red. See Figures 1 and 2 (left part).

The *progression feedback* is about the conversation behaviour. In the end of the conversation, the progression in conversation is visually displayed on the TurnTalk cover: firstly, LED strips light up according the number of turns taken by each child; secondly, they light up according to the amount of time taken to talk, with a different color. See Figures 1 and 2 (right part).

Actions

In 2017, this mature version of TurnTalk was used repeatedly by a class of a cooperative primary school. These actions, which are unpublished, are described in the following.

The cooperative learning school is a mainstream school, with heterogeneous classes. Classes are used to working in small groups, of 3 to 5 members, and discussing topics of shared interest in class. The class, designers worked with, is composed of 18 children, 9 to 10 years old, and two teachers.

Before entering the school, designers met teachers and explained the rationale of their design approach; one of the teachers was already involved in past action-research experiences with designers. Teachers explained children and their parents what the research was and its rationale. Thus all children participated on a voluntary basis, and their parents authorised their participation through a written consent form.

Initially, designers entered the classroom without TurnTalk to observe and video record how the class behave in conversations, split into groups of 3 to 5 members. There was one designer or teacher per group; one designer did the technical support and managed the video-recording apparatus. Designers and teachers observed different behaviours related to turn-sharing and used their observations to fine-tune TurnTalk, such as the timing of its progression feedback.

Then designers brought in classroom TurnTalk, repeatedly, in different days. After making children explore TurnTalk, designers asked children to use it so as to manage group conversations through the play-card mechanism. At the end of a conversation, TurnTalk displayed the aforementioned progression feedback, which children could reflect over.

In classroom, children's conversation behaviours were logged by TurnTalk micro-electronics components and video-recorded; relevant observations were also traced in notes by designers and complemented by teachers' observations, gathered through interviews. Logged data were later analysed and reflected over, together with observation and interview data. The results of the analyses were explained and presented to teachers and, again, reflected over with teachers, children and designers. Such joint reflections stirred the evolutions of TurnTalk, detailed in the remainder of this paper.

Figure 2. The used TurnTalk tangible, one per group of children of a primary school class; the left photo shows the play-card mechanism for taking a turn (green LED pin) and reserving a turn (yellow LED pin); the right photo shows the progression feedback with blue LED strips for conversation times

CLASSTALK FOR CLASS TURN SHARING

Reflections and Purpose

The study in the cooperative learning school allowed designers to improve over the design of TurnTalk but also to open up a novel design possibility: turning TurnTalk into a tangible for orchestrating class conversations, after group discussions.

Specifically, during the study, the following school practice emerged. When the time for the group conversation is over, all groups have to present the results of their conversation to the class and teachers, one of whom often acts as moderator or appoints a child to act as moderator. During the class conversation, children take the talking turn on the behalf of their group by raising hands. A pebble is also given by the moderator to assign talking turns.

However, turns are often shared unfairly among groups, in spite of raised hands or pebbles. As teachers remarked, "pebbles are not sufficiently attractive for children"; designers also observed that pebbles are immediately forgotten by children

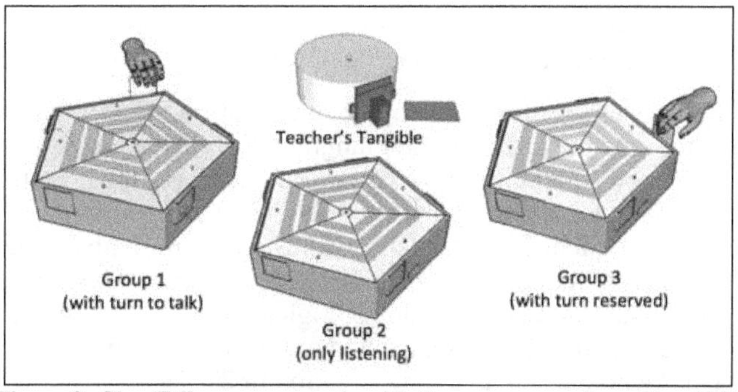

Figure 3. ClassTalk usage example with three groups and one TurnTalk per group, plus a master tangible for teachers. The group with the taken turn is indicated with green LED strips. The group with the next turn (with a reservation) is indicated with yellow LED strips.

and rarely used. Moreover, groups with dominant members in conversation tend to get more speaking turns than others. Moderators do not give turns to children out of their line of sight or whom they do not relate well with.

Such reflections made TurnTalk evolve into ClassTalk, a solution for sharing turns at the class level, as fairly as possible, and for reflecting over them, as explained in the following.

Main Developed Features

In ClassTalk, the class has again one TurnTalk per group. TurnTalk tangibles are connected to a master tangible, which is 3D printed and enhanced with micro-electronics. This tangible helps the moderator orchestrate the class conversation.

The play-card mechanism of TurnTalk is adapted as follows. Since children are spread in the class, LED strips are used instead of LED pins for visibly showing, at a distance, turn takings and reservations. A group member can take the turn in speaking on the behalf of her or his group by placing the card in the group's TurnTalk tangible. If the child's LED strips in TurnTalk flash green, then the child has the turn on behalf of her or his group; the entire TurnTalk surface becomes green and remains so until the child removes his or her card. If the child's LED strips flash yellow, then the child has reserved the next turn for her or his group; the entire TurnTalk surface becomes yellow and remains so until it is time for the group to speak, then it becomes green. Otherwise the group has to await for the other groups to finish their interventions. See the example illustration in Figure 3.

When they wish, moderators can activate the progression feedback concerning sharing of turns at the class level, by means of their master tangible. As in the case of TurnTalk for group conversations, the TurnTalk tangibles of groups will show how many turns each group had during the class conversation, proportionally, and their timing.

Actions

A first version of the ClassTalk prototype was brought into the aforementioned primary school classroom and used in the class conversation, after groups' conversations. Teachers were most willing to continue the study with ClassTalk and commented on the need of a device that can take care of the burden of distributing turns. The usage stirred new design possibilities, related to the role of teachers.

For instance, during the class conversation, a class teacher acted as moderator with her tangible. She wished to stop and reflect on a point made by a group but the ClassTalk prototype, at that stage, did not allow for that. The newer version picks up the challenge and implements this option through a special teacher card and an improved master tangible. This version was tested in a small-scale ecological study with adults and children. In 2018, it is expected to be used once more by the class who participated in its creation in 2017.

TURNTALK AND TTAPP FOR BLENDED GROUP TURN SHARING

Reflections and Purpose

During the aforementioned study in the primary school, a child was absent for three weeks and could not profit from using TurnTalk; teachers informed designers that the situation occurred frequently with the child. That made designers think of adapting TurnTalk for blended turn sharing, for allowing a child who is often distant from the class to participate in group conversation and train in turn sharing.

A first adaptation of the TurnTalk design for blended group turn sharing was assessed with education experts. A refined version was presented in a PhD student contest, with a jury of teachers and other educators, and it entered the short-list of winning projects, gaining the third position. Thereby the current version emerged, as explained in the following.

Figure 4. A conversation session in progress: TurnTalk in classroom (left) and the remote participant with TTapp mobile app (right)

Main Developed Features

This evolution adapts TurnTalk, and complements it with the TTapp mobile prototype for blended turn sharing. TurnTalk is used in classroom while the TTapp is used at the remote location of the distant child. See Figure 4.

The technical enhancements for TurnTalk are as follows. The adapted TurnTalk has a ring of 5 microphones, one per side facing children. A rotating camera is also added on top of the TurnTalk cover. See Figure 1. In case the speaker is in classroom, the predominant mic and the camera focus on the child with the taken turn, that is, the one with the play-card inserted and with the LED pin flashing green in TurnTalk. This way the remote user can focus on the voice and facial expression of the person who is talking. In case it is the remote user speaking, the non-muffled mic and the camera in TurnTalk focus on the child with the reserved turn to talk, e.g., so as to catch visual cues concerning his or her willingness to continue the conversation. In case there are no reservations, the non-muffled mic and the camera remain on the most recent speaker in classroom.

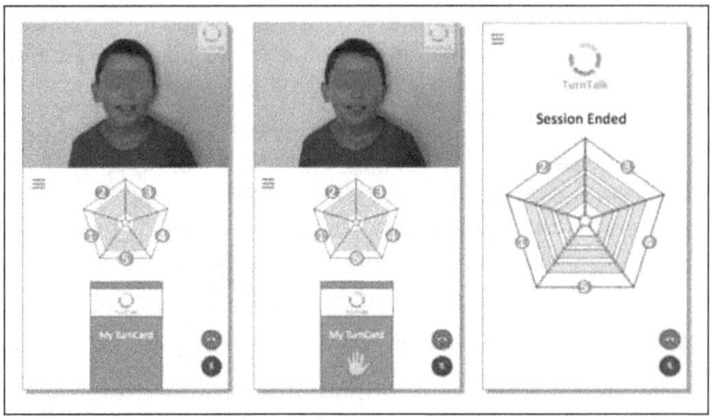

Figure 5. Interface design of the TTapp mobile app: (1) child #2 is speaking with no turn reservation; (2) child #2 speaking and child #5 (the remote user) has reserved the turn, by tapping the play-card on the mobile screen; (3) the progression feedback concerning the number of taken turns at the end of the conversation

The TTapp has a play-card mechanism and progression feedback resembling those of TurnTalk, and are synchronised with it as follows.

While TurnTalk has a tangible play-card per child, the TTapp has a play-card area for the remote child: the child taps on it to take a talking turn or reserve the next. The TTapp also shows a pentagon with the same shape as the physical TurnTalk, indicating who has the current or next turn with coloured (green, yellow) numbers instead of LED pins. See the left and central parts in Figure 5.

The progression feedback for the conversation session is also mirrored on both TurnTalk and TTapp, in terms of proportional numbers of turns and turn times, like in the original TurnTalk. See the right part of Figure 5 for the numbers of turns.

Actions

Studies with the re-purposed TurnTalk and TTapp are limited so far. A mock-up version of TTapp and TurnTalk were used by children in a small-scale study in the kid-space area of the authors' universities. Usability issues emerged but no new major design possibilities were disclosed. Novel studies with children in class may disclose more valuable information.

TURNTALK FOR VOTING CONVERSATION RESULTS

Reflections and Purpose

The repeated-measure study in the cooperative learning primary school showed that children have troubles when they have to vote results of group or class conversations. For instance, at the end of one of their group conversations, children had to vote games they would like to have during their school breaks, which they had discussed during their conversation. They voted a game (the result of their conversations) by raising hands, and counting raised hands. That was done rather unfairly at points, e.g., it happend in some groups that one decided on behalf of the others, who could not vote.

This and a subsequent interview with a voting-theory expert disclosed a new design possibility: turning TurnTalk into a tangible for engaging all children into voting and, possibly, teaching children different voting norms.

After the 2017 study in the school, designers discussed with teachers scenarios related to norms for voting in class. It came out that voting is generally done publicly, by raising hands or using pebbles or other objects for rating conversation results. Designers further met the voting-theory expert and made the expert try an adapted TurnTalk for allowing each group member to vote on a conversation result and then aggregating the results of the group. Two novel scenarios were then conceived, related to two different voting mechanisms: yes-no voting; star-like rating. TurnTalk was again re-purposed and re-adapted for them into VoteTalk.

Main Developed Features

TurnTalk was adapted and re-purposed into VoteTalk, with adapted play-card mechanisms for voting, and adapted types of progression feedback for displaying the vote outcomes.

The novel play-card mechanisms work as follows. See also Figure 6. In yes-no voting, children have at their disposal red voting cards for “no”, yellow cards for abstention, green cards for “yes”. Children vote by playing their card in their own allocated slots in VoteTalk, in order to choose between either “no”, “yes” or abstention. They can change their mind anytime by re-inserting a card. Their vote is displayed with red LED strips for “no”, green for “yes”, and yellow for abstention. In star-like rating, each child has one voting card, which they can insert in their allocated slot in VoteTalk as many times as they wish to rate conversation results. That is done in line with visual metaphors of standard rating systems, e.g., [28], and rates are displayed as follows: if the child wishes to rate an option with n, then the child's LED strip in VoteTalk lights up n bullets, with n usually ranging from 1 to 5.

The novel progression feedback concerning the voting outcomes works as follow. See also Figure 7. In case of yes-no voting, VoteTalk encodes a “no” vote with -1, a “yes” vote with 1 and an abstention with 0. Then vote encodings are summed up across all voters. If the sum is positive, all LED strips are green; if the sum is negative, all LED strips are red; else, LED strips are all yellow. In case of star-like rating, LED strips of VoteTalk light up with the approximate average rate across all voters.

Similarly as TurnTalk was adapted into ClassTalk for conversations at the class level, the VoteTalk's voting prototype is expandable at the class level with each group acting as sort of local voting district.

Actions

The novel tangible has been used in small-scale studies with 4 adults, a teacher and three designers, 2 children from primary schools, 10–11 years olds. The available results show that the tangible is usable and able to convey children the considered voting norms. Children mainly addressed the colour features of the novel tangibles, whereas the teacher highly appreciated the purpose of bringing different kinds of voting into schools, where “voting is often used but never reflected upon”.

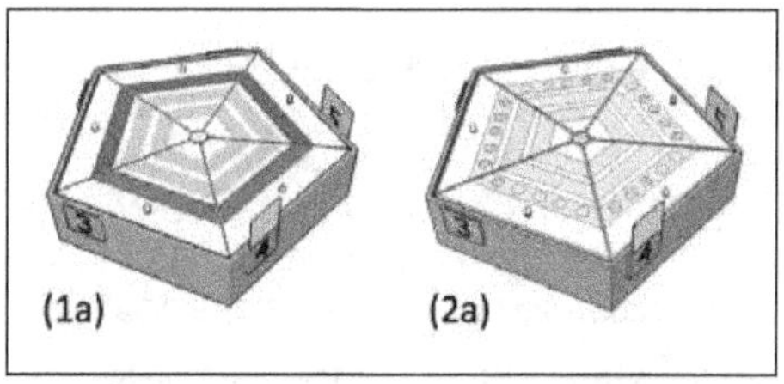

Figure 6. Play-card mechanisms for yes-no voting (1) and rating (2)

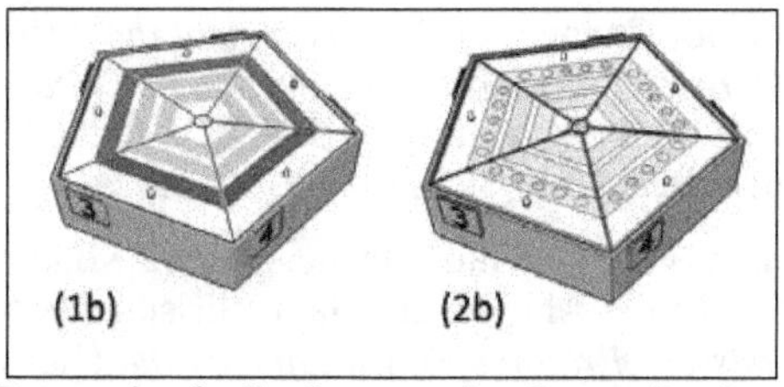

Figure 7. Progression feedback concerning the results of yes-no voting (1) and rating (2)

CONCLUSIONS

There are conversation norms for children's social learning, such as turn taking, but they are not easy for children. This paper posits that tangibles, mixing natural material and digital components, can help in the scaffolding of norms for children's conversation and social learning. The paper reports on research work concerning such tangibles.

The other paper contribution is the meta-design approach chosen for tangibles, based on action research: design spirals through evolutionary *development* and *actions* in the field, where users use tangible prototypes and designers *reflect* with users over their usage, so as to uncover design possibilities.

The paper starts by presenting a mature version of a tangible, namely, TurnTalk, for turn-sharing norms for group conversation. The paper reports on unpublished actions of repeated usages of TurnTalk in a primary school class in 2017, with children, aged 9–10, and teachers. It shows how designers' reflections with them and other relevant participants uncovered design possibilities for tangibles for conversation, which were rapidly developed and explored again with their intended users in further actions: an evolution of TurnTalk into a tangible, ClassTalk, for turn sharing at the class level; an evolution with an app, TTapp, for blended turn sharing and including distant learners in group conversation; a final evolution, VoteTalk, for differently voting conversation results, in group or class.

Therefore, the paper brings insight into both a design process and a learning area (the social one) in which tangibles can be useful.

Acknowledgements

We thank participating children, teachers, in particular Stefania Marsich and “Betty”, experts, e.g., Santina Torello and Daniele Porello. Finally, we acknowledge the financial support of the GOST project.

REFERENCES

1. *What is Arduino?* Available at https://www.arduino.cc/en/Guide/Introduction.

2. Diana Africano, Sara Berg, Kent Lindbergh, Peter Lundholm, Fredrik Nilbrink, and Anna Persson. 2004. Designing Tangible Interfaces for Children's Collaboration. In *CHI '04 Ext Abs on Human Factors in Comp Sys (CHI EA '04)*. ACM, NY, USA, 853–868. DOI: http://dx.doi.org/10.1145/985921.985945

3. Alissa N. Antle, Jillian L. Warren, Aaron May, Min Fan, and Alyssa F. Wise. 2014. Emergent Dialogue: Eliciting Values During Children's Collaboration with a Tabletop Game for Change. In *Proceedings of the 2014 Conference on Interaction Design and Children (IDC '14)*. ACM, New York, NY, USA, 37–46. DOI: http://dx.doi.org/10.1145/2593968.2593971

4. Andrea Bellucci, Giulio Jacucci, Veera Kotkavuori, Bariş Serim, Imtiaj Ahmed, and Salu Ylirisku. 2015. *Extreme Co-design: Prototyping with and by the User for Appropriation of Web-connected Tags*. Springer International Publishing, Cham, 109–124. DOI: http://dx.doi.org/10.1007/978-3-319-18425-8_8

5. Tony Bergstrom and Karrie Karahalios. 2007a. Conversation Clock: Visualizing Audio Patterns in Co-located Groups. In *Proc of 40th Annual Hawaii Int Conf on System Sciences (HICSS '07)*. IEEE Computer Society, Washington, DC, USA, 78–. DOI: http://dx.doi.org/10.1109/HICSS.2007.151

6. Tony Bergstrom and Karrie Karahalios. 2007b. Conversation Votes: Enabling Anonymous Cues. In *CHI '07 Extended Abstracts on Human Factors in Computing Systems (CHI EA '07)*. ACM, New York, NY, USA, 2279–2284. DOI: http://dx.doi.org/10.1145/1240866.1240994

7. P. Blatchford, A.D. Pellegrini, and D. Baines. 2016. *The Child at School*. Routledge.

8. A. Botero, K.H. Kommonen, and S. Marttila. 2011a. Design from the everyday: continuously evolving, embedded exploratory prototypes. In *Proceedings of DIS 2010*. ACM, 282–291.

9. A. Botero, K.H. Kommonen, and S. Marttila. 2011b. Expanding design space: design-in-use activities and strategies. In *Proceedings of the DRS 2010*.

10. Margherita Brondino, Gabriella Dodero, Rosella Gennari, Alessandra Melonio, Margherita Pasini, Daniela Raccanello, and Santina Torello. 2015. *Emotions and Inclusion in Co-design at School: Let's Measure Them!* Springer International Publishing, Cham, 1–8. DOI: http://dx.doi.org/10.1007/978-3-319-19632-9_1

11. Federico Cabitza, Daniela Fogli, and Antonio Piccinno. 2014. "Each to His Own": Distinguishing Activities, Roles and Artifacts in EUD Practices. In *Smart Organizations and Smart Artifacts*. Springer, 193–205.

12. Sharon Lynn Chu and Brittany M. Garcia. 2017. Toward Wearable App Design for Children's In-the-World Science Inquiry. In *Proceedings of the Eleventh International Conference on Tangible, Embedded, and Embodied Interaction (TEI '17)*. ACM, New York, NY, USA, 121–130. DOI: http://dx.doi.org/10.1145/3024969.3025008

13. M. F. Costabile, D. Fogli, P. Mussio, and A. Piccinno. 2007. Visual Interactive Systems for End-User Development: A Model-Based Design Methodology. *IEEE Transactions on Systems, Man, and Cybernetics - Part A: Systems and Humans* 37, 6 (Nov 2007), 1029–1046. DOI: http://dx.doi.org/10.1109/TSMCA.2007.904776

14. Tania Di Mascio, Rosella Gennari, Laura Tarantino, and Pierpaolo Vittorini. 2017. Designing visualizations of temporal relations for children: action research meets HCI. *Multimedia Tools and Applications* 76, 4 (01 Feb 2017), 4855–4893. DOI: http://dx.doi.org/10.1007/s11042-016-3609-6

15. Paloma Díaz, Ignacio Aedo, and Merel van der Vaart. 2015. *Engineering the Creative Co-design of Augmented Digital Experiences with Cultural Heritage*. Springer International Publishing, Cham, 42–57. DOI: http://dx.doi.org/10.1007/978-3-319-18425-8{_}4

16. Joan Morris DiMicco, Katherine J. Hollenbach, Anna Pandolfo, and Walter Bender. 2007. The Impact of Increased Awareness While Face-to-face. *Hum.-Comput. Interc.* 22, 1 (2007), 47–96.

17. P. Dourish. 1999. Embodied Interaction: Exploring the Foundations of a new Approach to HCI. Retrieved online from http://www.ics.uci.edu/~jpd/publications/misc/embodied.pdf. (1999).

18. Joseph A. Durlak, Roger P. Weissberg, Allison B. Dymnicki, Rebecca D. Taylor, and Kriston B. Schellinger. 2011. The Impact of Enhancing Student's Social and Emotional Learning: A Meta-Analysis of School-Based Universal Interventions. *Child Development* 82, 1 (2011), 405–432.

19. Gerhard Fischer and Thomas Herrmann. 2015. *Meta-design: Transforming and Enriching the Design and Use of Socio-technical Systems*. Springer London, London, 79–109. DOI: http://dx.doi.org/10.1007/978-1-4471-6720-4_6

20. Daniela Fogli, Elisa Giaccardi, Alessandro Acerbis, and Fabio Filisetti. 2015. *Physical Prototyping of Social Products Through End-User Development*. Springer International Publishing, Cham, 217–222. DOI: http://dx.doi.org/10.1007/978-3-319-18425-8{_}19

21. Carolyn Fu, Kritika Dhanda, Marc Exposito Gomez, Haeyoung Kim, and Yan Zhang. 2017. TurnTable: Towards More Equivalent Turn-Taking. In *Proceedings of the Eleventh International Conference on Tangible, Embedded, and Embodied Interaction (TEI '17)*. ACM, New York, NY, USA, 609–615. DOI: http://dx.doi.org/10.1145/3024969.3025079

22. R. Gennari, A. Melonio, D. Raccanello, M. Brondino, G. Dodero, M. Pasini, and S. Torello. 2017c. Children's emotions and quality of products in participatory game design. *International Journal of Human Computer Studies* 101 (2017), 45–61. DOI: http://dx.doi.org/10.1016/j.ijhcs.2017.01.006

23. R. Gennari, A. Melonio, and M. Rizvi. 2017a. The Participatory Design Process of Tangibles for Children's Socio-Emotional Learning. In *Proceedings of the 6th International Symposium on End-User Development (IS-EUD 2017) (LNCS)*, Simone Barbosa, Panos Markopoulos, Fabio Paternò, Simone Stumpf, and Stefano Valtolina (Eds.). Springer International Publishing, Cham, 167–182. DOI: http://dx.doi.org/10.1007/978-3-319-58735-6_12

24. R. Gennari, A. Melonio, and S. Torello. 2017b. Gamified Probes for Cooperative Learning: a Case Study. *Multimedia Tools and Applications* 76, 4 (2017), 4925–4949. DOI: http://dx.doi.org/10.1007/s11042-016-3543-7

25. R. Gennari, F. Pavani, and M. Rizvi. 2017d. Tangible Design for Inclusive Conversations with Deaf or Hard-of-Hearing Children. *In Proceedings of the 1st International Symposium on Emerging Technologies for Education (SETE 2016), LNCS, Springer, Rome* (2017). DOI:http://dx.doi.org/10.1007/978-3-319-52836-6_29

26. Juan Pablo Hourcade. 2015. *Child-Computer Interaction.*

27. Suhas Govind Joshi and Tone Bratteteig. 2016. Designing for Prolonged Mastery. On involving old people in Participatory Design. *Scandinavian Journal of Information Systems* 28, 1 (2016), 3–36.

28. Romina Kühn, Mandy Korzetz, Lukas Büschel, Christina Korger, Philip Manja, and Thomas Schlegel. 2016. Natural Voting Interactions for Collaborative Work with Mobile Devices. In *Proceedings of the 2016 CHI Conference Extended Abstracts on Human Factors in Computing Systems (CHI EA '16)*. ACM, New York, NY, USA, 2570–2575. DOI: http://dx.doi.org/10.1145/2851581.2892300

29. Valérie Maquil, Eric Tobias, and Thibaud Latour. 2015. *Tangible Voting: A Technique for Interacting with Group Choices on a Tangible Tabletop*. Springer International Publishing, Cham, 79–86. DOI: http://dx.doi.org/10.1007/978-3-319-22723-8_7

30. Roberto Martinez Maldonado, Judy Kay, Kalina Yacef, and Beat Schwendimann. 2012. *An Interactive Teacher's Dashboard for Monitoring Groups in a Multi-tabletop Learning Environment.* Springer Berlin Heidelberg, Berlin, Heidelberg, 482–492. DOI: http://dx.doi.org/10.1007/978-3-642-30950-2_62

31. A. Melonio and M. Rizvi. 2017. The Design of TurnTalk for The Scaffolding of Balanced Conversations in Groups of Children. *In Proc. of the 1st International Symposium on Emerging Technologies for Education (SETE 2016), Rome* (2017). DOI: http://dx.doi.org/10.1007/978-3-319-52836-6_28

32. Jacob Sikker Remin, Marcin Ignac, and Sarasiff Kjaergard. 2016. Interactive Benches. Retrieved online from http://ciid.dk/education/portfolio/py/courses/physical-computing/projects/interactive-benches/. (2016).

33. Petr Slovák and Geraldine Fitzpatrick. 2015. Teaching and Developing Social and Emotional Skills with Technology. *ACM Trans. Comput.-Hum. Interact.* 22, 4, Article 19 (June 2015), 34 pages. DOI: http://dx.doi.org/10.1145/2744195

34. John M. Wiemann and Mark L. Knapp. 1975. Turn-taking in Conversations. *Journal of Communication* 25, 2 (1975), 75–92. DOI: http://dx.doi.org/10.1111/j.1460-2466.1975.tb00582.x

Come and Play: Interactive Theatre for Early Years

Roma Patel, Holger Schnädelbach, Boriana Koleva
Mixed Reality Laboratory, School of Computing Science, University of Nottingham
Nottingham, UK
{firstname.lastname}@ nottingham.ac.uk

ABSTRACT
The convergence of theatre and digital technologies can play a valuable role in theatre for early years, but, how an audience of under-5's experiences and engages with these spaces is largely unexplored. We present an interactive performance installation and demonstrate how concepts from early years practice, in particular schemas, children's repeated play patterns, can be used as a design framework. We integrated sensors and microcontrollers into objects, puppets, and scenography and invited eight groups of very young children and their grownups to explore the performance. We discuss how schemas useful as a design and analysis tool in TEY, how schemas need to be expanded to include multi-sensory interactions with hybrid physical-digital objects, and how designers need to consider the roles of adults who scaffold interaction between very young children and their surroundings.

Author Keywords
Performance; interaction design; early years; tangible; children; theatre

ACM Classification Keywords
• Human-centered computing~Interaction design theory, concepts and paradigms

INTRODUCTION
Theatre for Early Years (TEY) refers to theatre for the under-5s and is often more challenging and experimental than other forms of children's theatre [35]. The way young children process interactions through their embodied experience call for a performance where the senses are central to the design. For that reason, alone children's theatre cannot be a simplified version of adult's theatre. Recent research in neuroscience and developmental psychology shows that babies and toddlers have a remarkable capacity to learn and comprehend much beyond what was originally thought [5,9,15]. This challenges previous assumptions about the cultural and psychological value of theatre for very young children [35]. Children at this age engage with the world through doing, watching, touching and imitating. TEY audiences are therefore unpredictable, and they have no concept of theatre conventions. However, these conventions are changing even in mainstream theatre. Interactive and immersive theatre has emerged, breaking down the barriers between audience and performer. It is more dynamic and is often preferred by TEY companies, but can be challenging and cost prohibitive [6]. An interactive format usually requires smaller audience numbers, tangible props, and spaces that can sustain curiosity, allow freedom of expression, surprise and time to play. Technologies and tangibles extend agency and imagination to an audience. And create unexpected and novel experiences that merge the tactile and the visual [10, 24, 28]. Digitally enhanced tactile objects could be a valuable addition to TEY because they appeal to young children. They encourage embodied mixed reality experiences beyond the screen and can have additional learning benefits [19].

Potential producers of TEY face multiple challenges. Interactive tangible technologies have not yet been closely investigated in TEY, and many theatre practitioners do not know how to make use of them. The challenge is how to design experiences when there is very little related research, with the exception of [13, 20, 28]. Knowledge developed in education and psychology concerning children's cognitive development, while theoretically available, has not found broader re-use in TEY production, and by itself, would not be enough for the development of more dynamic and grounded experiences. Finally, it is a challenge to break away from the concept of theatre in education is based on learning (often the motivation for TEY) and create professional children's theatre with an emphasis on aesthetic and interactive experiences [35].

In this paper, we address the emerging research around TEY by first introducing how children's play patterns (or schemas) apply as a design and analytical framework for interactive props and scenography. We discuss how this approach can extend and support very young children's play and interactions. We also consider how tangible technologies can move interaction beyond on-screen, in particular how DIY technologies can potentially extend agency in TEY and how finding the right balance between the performer and child interaction, materials and aesthetics require us to reframe our thinking.

TEI '18, March 18–21, 2018, Stockholm, Sweden

ACM ISBN 978-1-4503-5568-1/18/03…$15.00
https://doi.org/10.1145/3173225.3173251

RELATED RESEARCH

There are few examples of related research with children under four years in TEY or HCI it is largely conducted with older children within a learning context. However, an approach that draws on practices and theories in early years, interaction design and children's theatre, can help us better design tangible interaction for very young children in TEY.

Play and Exploration

Until around the age of seven, children's brains are like 'a sensory processing machine' [5]. They make meaning primarily through direct sensing and interacting with the world. Strong sensory integration is a basis for all intellectual activity [9]. Children are intrinsically motivated to play, are naturally curious and programmed to explore and master their world [37]. How they play with objects through trial and error, imitation and imagination are significant and age-dependent. A one-year-old will usually imitate how an object is used, and by two years the same object becomes disassociated from reality, and its purpose becomes imaginative [33, 36]. Weininger furthers this notion by proposing that pretend play is the effect of an 'as if' situation and imagination is the 'what if' or the thinking function behind pretend play [36]. Theatre optimises the connection of the 'as if' and the 'what if' but this can become challenging in a performance with a mixed target group. Children's play can be understood through observing repeated behaviours which can be formalised in play patterns or schemas [3, 4, 18] (Table 1). They provide early years practitioners with a tool for analysing and making sense of what children do when playing. They are the foundation for the design framework that we will discuss further in the 'Interactive Design for Performance' section.

Interaction Design for Children

Children's toys can be endowed with lifelike qualities through their movement and sound. Ackermann points out those affordances are not enough, toys need to capture our imagination, enchant and have holding power. She recommends that designers consider the user's psychological points of view and design for 'conviviality' where there is a dialogue between the child and the smart toy [1]. This notion of 'Intelligent object' is now more realistic. Tangible 'smart' toys are now available for very young children. They are either interactive standalone plush toys or one that augments screen based interaction [24, 25]. However, toy manufacturers' research has found that parents are less interested in the latter as they become more wary of mainstream media messages about the negative impact of screen time [12]. The development and availability of technologies to make physical objects interactive lies at the heart of the practical work conducted in this research.

Interactive Theatre

The experience economy and the desire for agency, physical and sensory experiences underpin the rise of interactive and immersive theatre seen in the last decade in the UK [7]. It rejects linear storytelling for the more episodic and directors draw on contemporary culture like computer games and gamification formats to inspire interactive elements [7]. Digital technology has come to shape many aspects of performance. Projection design is now a common feature of stage aesthetics, and live interactive technology is more prevalent in dance [17]. There are very few examples of this interactivity appearing in TEY. But one stand-out example is the 'cheering carpet' by children's dance company Compagnia T.P.O. Via touch sensors and motion tracking, footsteps and body movements trigger sounds and digital projections [24, 32]. When invited, the young audiences join the stage and follow the dancers' lead. Despite this demonstrating the potential for providing richer experiences and more agency for children, these technologies remain underexplored.

To the best of our knowledge, early years' practices and interactive, tangible technologies have not yet been evaluated in TEY. Next, we present our research that brings together all three areas discussed. We outline the process that led up to the performance installation by describing the creative design and application of the play pattern design framework.

INTERACTIVE DESIGN FOR PERFORMANCE

We created an interactive performance installation for toddlers (18 to 48 months) and their grownups, staged at the Lakeside Arts Centre in Nottingham, UK. We opted for an improvised immersive theatre approach (no script), as it allowed us to explore the freedom and spontaneity between the audience, performers, interactive prototypes and theatrical space. We used technologies available to digital DIY maker communities [11] such as the Arduino platform because it provides open source support networks and a variety of hardware solutions, given the economic and time constraints encountered by theatre-makers.

Design Process, Concept & Strategy

The performance installation design aimed to explore both the novel and the familiar with the scenography/spatial design and to promote agency and whole-bodied and intimate experiences. It was designed by one of the researchers who is a professional scenographer. The design process employed an artistic working method that relies on an intuitive approach to design, the tacit knowledge of the scenographer and the application of the Schema design framework. It also included several consultations with a creative team made up of HCI researchers, arts venue personnel, an object theatre artist and the performer. The design process began with an exploration of the natural world and reflected on the sensory and tactile nature of the woods. It involved experimentation and exploration of material and visual ideas around the conceptual theme, experiments with different DIY technology, prototype iterations and employ play patterns as a design framework, which we consider in the next section. Play Patterns as a Design Framework Schemas are natural play patterns that tend to occur over and over again in children. They were originally used by Piaget in his early research to describe the cognitive development of children under five. He was concerned with how schemas affect problem-solving and operational thinking. Our research employs the Chris Athey interpretation of schema, defined as a pattern of behaviour and thinking in children [3], which has since been extended by other researchers [18, 22]. The set used here is explained in table 1. These patterns of behaviour play an important role in the development of children's brain structure and understanding of spatial organisation [15, 4]. Repeated research has demonstrated they are common and observed in all children [26]. Play patterns help make sense of a very young child's repeated action, which may sometimes seem aimless to an adult; for example, turning round and round demonstrates the child's preoccupation with a circular motion – the rotation schema. Linking objects together are about making connections; den making is associated with wanting to be enclosed, inside, outside etc. [15].

Patterns of Play	Illustrative Examples
Transporting	Picking & moving up things and self
Rotation	Exploring circular things lines, turning self
Transformation	Exploring things that change
Connection	Joining, separating, scatter or tie things up
Enclosure	Covering self or other items, making dens
Trajectory	Vertical, horizontal, diagonal movement
Orientation	Looking at things from different angles
Positioning	Placing objects or self in particular places

Table 1. Common Patterns of Play / Schemas

Many early years' settings in the United Kingdom find Schemas useful to observe children's play. We propose that they can be used for a new purpose in design to help make sense of children's actions and help inspire, generate and analyse design features. In the next section, we demonstrate the use of play patterns as a design framework.

Application of Play Patterns in the Design Process

Play patterns can be employed as a framework either to initiate new designs or to adapt an existing concept or product. We utilised them in the design process during both the ideation and the prototyping phases. Both methods facilitate active change and adaptation of ideas and designs to afford one or more play patterns. Our design method was inspired by the Design Thinking model [14], and Gordon's 'Synectic Think Cycle' which interconnects thinking approaches to problem-solving the three 'Rs' referring, reflecting and reconstructing [34]. Our application of this new play pattern framework involves the following processes:

1. **Selection:** Select a play pattern based on a design requirement or make a random choice.
2. **Ideation:** Begin a process of divergent thinking to generate creative ideas for a new or an existing prototype bearing in mind the schema affordances. Then explore the solutions and the kind of interactions they facilitate. For example, how well does it work with the narrative and concept? How can it promote agency, sensory interaction in children?
3. **Construction:** Sketch and prototype your ideas or add or adjust an existing prototype.
4. **Combining:** Then consider the other schemas from table 1 and repeat the process and think about how they combine with your original idea.

When using the play pattern framework, it is important to bear in mind how it supports and is compatible with other criteria in a design brief. For the interactive performance, we considered the affordances of touch, tangible objects, space, materials, narrative, the performer's role and technologies as another design materials that can activate sounds, lights, vibrations and smells, all of which we discuss further in the prototypes presented below.

1) Suspended Discs

The suspended discs vary in size and are detachable, flat, lightweight, flexible structures that can be hung (Figure 1).

Selection: Rotation

Ideation: We began the design process by exploring leaf-shaped and circular objects, and we looked at the round and round scribbles of a two-year-old's mark making [21]. Seed pods and mobiles can afford rotation.

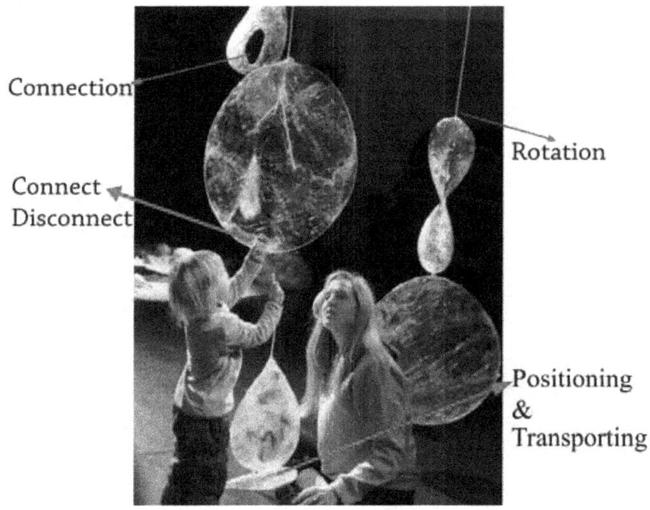

Figure 1. A suspended disc being connected by a participant. Multiple schemas applied to a simple round shape.

Construction: The circular fame was made from lightweight carbon and glass fibre rods and wrapped in several layers of clear shrink-wrap plastic and tape. The material is translucent and creates an aesthetic effect under theatrical lights. The disk was suspended from one point to afford kinetic movement similar to a mobile.

Figure 2. Prototypes: 2 Tactile Mats, 3 Musical Fruits& Vegetable, 4 Felt Creatures, 5 Malleable objects: gel beads and gloves

Combination: Further exploration of the *Connection and Positioning* play patterns was afforded by magnets around the circle, which enabled connect, detach and reposition. Some discs had small holes cut out on the surface areas to afford connections through playful interaction and peekaboo games. Others had tactile material added to the surface such as feathers, fabric and small strips of plastic to afford more tangible interactions.

2) Stepping stones

The stepping stones are force sensing tactile mats that trigger sounds when jumped or stepped on (Figure 2-2).
Selection: Trajectory
Ideation: We started the design process with an initial idea to create an experience that the participant can activate. We considered using sound as it is usually operated backstage and is not in audiences grasp. Then, we chose the *Trajectory schema* to explore ideas around children's movement, such as the affordance of full-bodied interaction, i.e. jumping and running. This led to visual research that explored stepping stones in rivers, forest floor textures, and dance mats, which in turn led to technology explorations of floor and force sensors.
Construction: We made twelve circular stepping stones from black felted mats and inserted a simple force sensor made from foil and copper wire. They attached to the 'Touch Board' a microcontroller soundboard. When stepped on, it triggered different sound effects. For haptic and exploratory play the surfaces had different tactile materials such as hard buttons, heat sensitive materials for making handprints, soft pom-poms, cold metal washers, rough fabrics, etc. The design of the mats afforded both 'whole body' interactions and more intimate exploration through touching, pressing and stroking.

3) Musical Fruits and Vegetables

A large tray of fruits and vegetable that activate sounds when touched (Figure 2-3).
Selection: Connection
Ideation: Influenced by projects that used microcontrollers and sensors with real objects, we decided to use real fruits and vegetables as they are familiar to children and are not expected to make sounds. TEY found using familiar objects and stories connected to very young children's everyday reality can increase engagement [10].
Construction: Ten common fruits and vegetables were converted into tactile capacitive sensing interfaces that enabled pre-recorded sounds, that can be heard when out in the woods and in urban areas (birds, child's voice, trains, etc.), to play when touched. The fruits were in a large tray covered with a sheet of artificial grass. Wires were attached to the fruits and connected directly to the 'Touch board.'

4) Puppets: Felt Creatures

A series of small felted creatures using wearable technologies to animate various characteristics (Figure 2-4).
Selection: Transformation
Ideation: Inspired by the shape of a trumpet and tulip, we crafted small white felted cone-shaped objects with stems, using wet felted craft techniques. We considered *Transformation* schema and experimented with LEDs to explore ideas around animation and then led to transforming the felted shapes into hand puppets to help promote storytelling and pretend play.
Construction and Combination: We used soft circuits/ wearable technology [11] designed to be flexible and lightweight to be grasped by tiny hands. A tilt sensor activated the LED eyes. Puppets were all mobile and also embodied the *transportation schema.* Inspired by this we then developed other ideas around *transformation* lights and felt, such as a larger caterpillar shaped puppet with an accelerometer connected to an 'Arduino lily pad' to activate the frequency and brightness of the lights. A sound-activated creature in a cardboard suitcase box was inspired

by the *enclosure* schema and made from felt and Little Bits modules – sound sensors, vibration module, and LEDs.

5) Malleable and sensory objects

The malleable and sensory objects provided opportunities to explore and manipulate material qualities.

Selection: Transformation, Transportation & Connection
Ideation: We were interested in observing young children's use of sensory material that can transform, stretch, mould and be easily deformed.
Construction: A series of malleable objects were provided, such as conductive Playdoh, wet gel-like water beads, ice cubes with embedded objects, inflated blue surgical gloves with LEDs (Figure 2-5), finger LEDs, stretchy fabric.

The Performance Space

The performance studio contained black drapes, a piano, theatre lights and no rigged seating. We divided it into four distinct areas for each of the prototypes. We interconnected the areas by hanging the suspended disc along the centre. The participants stood or sat on the floor mats provided.

THE PERFORMANCE STUDY

Study Participant and Procedure

The performance study took place over two and half-days. There were eight performances, 45 minutes in length with a maximum of five children in each. A total of 40 participants took part of which nineteen were children: 7- 1 year olds, 7- 2 year olds, 2- 3 year olds, 3- 4 year olds. They were recruited through the theatre's audience and social media network. The installation performance was free. The first four performances had one performer while the last four had two. They initiated improvised play and facilitated the group and child-led interactions. On arrival at the theatre, the participants were briefed by a researcher then completed a consent form for data collection and a short survey about their child's play activities. Then the audience was led down a well-lit corridor to the performance space entrance, where a researcher explained that they could freely interact with all the props supported by the performers. The performer introduced herself and invited them to explore the space. Before opening the doors, to increase the children's anticipation, she encouraged them to peek through the glass panel. After 45 minutes of playing, the house lights were switched on, and the participants left.

Data Collection and Analysis

Video recordings of the performances, field notes and a short pre-show survey (children's current play activities) were used for data gathering. A fixed camera recorded a wide angled view from the front of the room and a second roving camera captured close up selective interactions. If a child seemed uncomfortable when filmed close up, we moved away. From the video recordings, we made an index of events each indicated the number of participants involved, their position in the performance space, the object(s) that they were playing with, schemas that were recognised and a summary of what happened. From this data we identified some episodes for detailed observation using Flanagan's critical incident technique 1) to report the facts of the behaviour and 2) to report the significant behaviours of the observed activity [27]. A multimodal transcription [13, 15] of the recordings with a description of what happened was produced together with an account of the 'non-verbal signifiers' and embodied interactions (gaze, gesture, body position, and sound) which are particularly important when observing pre-verbal participants.

RESULTS

The open, playful, relaxed nature of the performance installation encouraged the child participants to freely explore the space and engage with the objects and performers. An interesting finding was that only three out of the nineteen children stayed very close to their parents and did not communicate directly with the performer. Nonetheless, they watched and then imitated the activities, suggesting they were very much active [28].

Prototypes	Schema in design process	Children's interaction	Schemas in the performance
Suspended Disc	Transporting Connection Positioning Rotation	Carried, touched, worn as hats, used as wings. Jumped and walked on. Used as a mirror, lake, train, for hiding and seek, hitting, head-butting, pulled, dragged. Attach, detach.	Transporting, Connection, Positioning Rotation, Enclosure, Enveloping, Trajectory
Stepping Stones	Trajectory	Step, walk, jump, touch, pick. Sat on, turned	Trajectory; Connection, Rotation
Musical Fruits & Vegetables	Connection	Touch, pick up, examine, move, smell, taste, stepped on, worn	Connection, Positioning, Transport
Puppets	Connecting Transporting	Carried, smell, touched, threw, friend, prop, used to peek a boo game, put in a line	Connecting, Transporting Positioning.
Malleable/ Sensory Objects Gel water beads & Playdoh gloves, LEDs	Transporting Connection Transformation	Squeeze, thrown, step on, touch, drawing Stretch, pulled and dragged. Den making, swing Squeeze, carried, thrown, hide and seek	Transporting, Connection Transformation Enveloping, Enclosure, Positioning

Table 2. Schemas designed for vs observed in the prototypes

In most of the sessions, there were sounds of laughter heard around the musical fruits & vegetables. There was a disregard for boundaries when the children tried to taste the fruits, move and pick them and even sat in the large tray. Overall, we observed more play patterns during the study than we considered in the original design, seen in Table 2. The suspended discs were the most popular object. The ambiguous design permitted more varied types of interactions and patterns of play. For instance, a child wore one around her neck and pretended to be inside a train while the actor used it as a hat. Some children were more occupied with a particular play pattern and exercised their agency by repeatedly coming back to play with that object. We now present three episodes that give a more detailed account of how the play patterns are revealed.

Episode 1: Construction & Connecting

This episode was initiated by a young male participant who came to the performance pretend-playing being a dog, he moved around on all fours and barked for attention. He spent his first ten minutes crawling around the perimeter of the room alone.

The young boy and the performer are on the floor connecting discs, he crawls forward towards the tactile mats, the performer then moves away, he stops, then turns his head and looks behind him, he moves a bit more and then turns his head and looks behind him. He then crawls, behind the performer and glances at her a few times, before he utters "woof" and moves towards the middle of the room. He stops, on all fours, he looks forward and notices something, he lifts his body upright and scuffles on his knees to a column of discs, he reaches for the large disc at the bottom, with one hand he holds the desk and pulls it away from the column of discs. He turns around holding the disc with both hands and shuffles on his knees to the performer. The young boy reaches the performer, looks directly at her, he is holding a large disk in his right hand, he tries to hand it to her, but there are other children with her, he drops the disk on the floor in front the performer. She asks him something (not audible), both her hands are open with her palm facing upwards resting on her knee as if she asks a question-what shall we do with it?

3. Positioning and connecting the discs

The boy crawls back to the centre of the room where they last played and looks directly at her, the performer pushes the large disc towards him, and he reaches for it with one hand and positions it at the bottom of the line of the discs. (Figure 3) The performer then gets up and moves toward him to resume their former play. (Day 1, session 1.)

Schemas: Transporting, Connecting and Positioning

This extract reveals a young participant's sustained interest and determination to play with a particular object as well as demonstrates how a combination of schemas can work together – first *disconnecting* a disc, *transporting* it, then *positioning* it and *connecting*. Crawling away was part of his role play, he wanted the performer to follow him. The performer did not seem to recognise this and walked away. To get her attention, he loudly uttered 'woof!' and when that didn't work, he *transported* the disc to her. He gained a sense of confidence and *connected* with the performer. He was interested in playing with the discs, although she disconnected from their original play, he took the bold initiative to get her attention. They continued to play the game of connecting for ten minutes in different areas of the room. Interestingly, in the last four minutes, he started running upright, but still fully engaged with the combination of schemas. His schema play could be seen to propel him out of his role-playing to constructive play.

Episode 2: Knock, Knock – Schemas and sound

Episode two took place on day three. There were two performers and a mixed group of five child participants with their grownups. The interaction is between the male performer and an 18-month-old participant. The young child is very confident and plays away from his father. The extract has begun just after he played a few keys on the piano.

The child moves towards the fruits and vegetables. He bends over and slaps a Swede with his right hand; it triggers a train whistle. He crouches on his knees and slaps the celeriac twice and the sound of a hard hat echoes, he slaps the swede, and it triggers the train whistle, then he moves to the melon, and the sound of a baby's voice says 'Mama, mama ah ha'. The male performer is standing near him and then lounges to the floor opposite the boy (getting down to his level). The boy looks at the performer, who points to an avocado, and the performer looks directly at the child and touches the avocado with one finger, and it triggers the sound of a knocker. The performer lifts his hand away, then slowly touches it three times with his finger, the boy looks on, then the performer hits it with his knuckles and says: 'hello anyone at home?' 'hello anyone at home?' As he moves his hand away, the boy slaps the melon with his palm and the sound ''mama, mama, ah woo" is heard. The performer repeats the action and says, 'hello anyone at home?' Then the boy imitates the performer and touches the melon with one finger that activates the sound again. The performer then touches another fruit, and the child stands up, moves a few steps, then points at the avocado, and he says something inaudible. The performer says 'Melon?', and then the boy touches the melon, four times and pushes it towards the performer, he turns around and sees his father then looks down at the tray, reaches in and picks up a pompom then turns around and walks away singing 'Mama.... Mama.... Mama''... (Day 3, session 5).

Schemas: Transformation and Connecting Vygotsky found that using a physical object helps very young children to pretend play [33]. But what the object represents, in reality, does not seem to matter for symbolic play to occur. In this episode, the sound transforms the avocado into a door knocker and the melon into a baby. It demonstrates a simple example of how the *transformation* schema with sound can play a role in imaginative and symbolic play. The child's encounter with the performer further enriched his experience by *connecting* the sound to an imaginative narrative as the sound took precedence over the material object. Secondly, the moments of interaction between the child and the performer demonstrate the very young child's awareness of the performer's question and turn taking. When the performer touched another object, the boy's response was to stand up and point to the avocado (knocker) it seems as if he wants to continue with the previous activity. The performer misreads the child's action, the child perceives this and move on. The young child's turn-taking and imitation of subtle gestures and sounds can be indicative of an intelligibility of action.

Episode 3: Tuning In – schema and dramatic play

Fantasy and sociodramatic play are common with children at this age. Our pre-show survey found that 17 out of 19 children engaged in role play such as being, a hairdresser, shopkeeper, doctor, etc. In the performance, the felted hand puppets became the catalyst for sociodramatic and symbolic play (Figure 4). The following extract was the longest pretend play (14 minutes) episode during the study.

Figure 4. The LED light transforms the inanimate felt object into a 'live' hand puppet.

Child: 'That does not work if you stand it up.' Performer: 'Oh, right,' 'Flop flop' (she flicks her finger, and the standing puppet falls onto the green mat) Child: (stares at it holding it in both hands, he presses it and slightly moves it, so the tilt switch is triggered.) Child: 'Ahh! I switch it on. I switch it on and off' and proceeds to put his left hand into the hand puppet. The performer leans over to look at the puppet's eyes turning on and off. The boy names all the puppets 'Peter' and as the play continues, he takes one of the puppets to the shop. He acts as the puppet, and the performer is the shopkeeper. She refers to the puppets by their name 'Peter'. The boy interchanges himself with the puppet by saying 'I want' instead of 'Peter wants', and as the play continues it shifts, and he talks directly to the shopkeeper rather than through the puppet. The performer responds using his real name. The boy orders a packet of salt and vinegar crisps for himself and his mum and dad. Once he gets the pretend crisp packet, he runs over to his mum. First, he takes the crisp packet, and the second time he explains, how he used a credit card. Then he and his puppet join the shopkeeper at the back of the shop (Figure 5), *and he makes his puppet jump up and down on the clouds (wool in a basket) saying 'Boing-in, Boing -in' with a smile.*

Figure 5. 'Boing -in, Boing -in' making the puppet jumping up and down on the carded wool in the basket

Schemas: Transformation and Trajectory

The tilt switch affords the puppet a *transformative* state, awake or asleep. In this extract, the child had a strong motivation for exploratory play, which led him to try and figure out how the tilt switch works. We also observed his curiosity to discover how things worked with the other prototypes. His enjoyment and engagement in play was noticeable by his laughter, especially when bouncing the puppet up and down (*trajectory*). Seeing the child as an active participant can shift the adult's role of leading to being a partner or a facilitator. This shift of roles also occurs when the child's real and imaginative world *transform* as the child takes over the role of the puppet.

DISCUSSION

No previous study has used play patterns as a design framework for digitally enhanced TEY. We reflect on our use of the play pattern framework, multisensory, tangible technologies and the role of adults in TEY.

Play Pattern Framework

Each play pattern represents a naturally occurring behaviour in children that affords the designer a specific way of thinking about and extending ideas for interaction design. The results presented in this study are encouraging: the play patterns applied to the design were evident in the children's interactions, and additional patterns were also observed (Table 2), even if not every child experienced all patterns presented. We see the opportunities offered by multiple, overlapping play patterns (designed and experienced) as the key reason for the suspended discs being the most popular item. Our results demonstrate how a combination of patterns that support a logical sequence of actions works well together. The ambiguous form of the suspended discs may be a complementary reason for their popularity. Ambiguity in design can free an object and open it up to the participants' imagination, permitting a wider variety of interpretation and interaction [16]. The play pattern framework presents a new approach to design for TEY beyond its original purpose to analyse (rather than design for) the play of children. There are other performance frameworks [7, 21] that have been proposed for both design and analysis of HCI experiences. A crucial limitation of this framework is that it does not address important areas such as multisensory interactions (e.g. sound and lights enabled through tangible technologies) and the role of the performer is also outside its object-focused remit, both of which we will address below.

Multi-sensory Tangible Technology

Arguably, the boundaries between very young children and technology have never been more porous and for the current generation of toddlers, swiping a screen is as normal as shaking a rattle. Beyond this screen-focused interaction the combination of interactive sound, lights and tangible props creates novelty in an object and adds to its performativity as demonstrated in the work presented here. It can create fun, playful, tactile and embodied interactions that fill the entire theatre stage. For this, we have combined familiar objects and themes, which young children respond to [10], with the 'unexpected' playful interaction afforded by multisensory, tangible technologies with the aim of creating 'richer and more varied experiences' [29]. We found that embedded electronic components can be seen as a material rather than a tool and can afford more agency to young participants as they were for example, able to activate sounds. Typically the choices of sound and lights are not in an audience's control. Episode 2 has provided examples of how interactive sound can play a role in introducing narrative and how vocal repetition of digital sounds resulted in children having a deeper relationship and connection with a particular sound. We also note that relatively cheap and brittle technologies such as conductive threads, embedded LEDs, and washable microcontrollers were suitable for props and provided a robust short-term solution. However, whether they will stand the rigours of a typical touring TEY production will need to be explored in the future. As multisensory tangible technologies become even more widespread, accessible and reliable, there will be a need for HCI designers and theatre practitioners to work collaboratively to understand better how to design and make these spaces more conducive for interactions for this age group. To achieve this, teams of designers should draw on an expanded set of play patterns that captures interactions with multisensory tangible technologies.

The Adult and Child

The children in all three episodes responded to the devised and impromptu invitations from the performers to play. In turn, they were sensitive to the children, supported their interests by imitating their actions, following their stories, being part of their imaginative play and gained their trust as a result. In episode 3 for example, the performer left moments of silence to give the child time to think and to take the initiative, make choices and lead the 'play' while she remained engaged in storytelling throughout. By being alert and following his lead, she was valuing what he had to say. However, at times the performers missed some of the children's reactions; devising in a live situation is very challenging for actors, especially with such an unpredictable and authentic audience. Beyond leaving enough space for play, another strategy that performers employed was that of engineering surprise. Previous studies with two year olds found that if the functions of a physical object are introduced to a child as if it is found by accident or in a playful manner, then they tend to be more exploratory than if the functions were introduced formally [30]. In addition to the performer, parents play a central role in scaffolding. An adult's reaction to a child's behaviour is important because, from a very young age, children are responsive to the values and judgment of adults, especially those familiar to them [15]. Connecting to a parent or carer by touching base and sharing an experience, as we found in episode 2, was important to many of the participating children. In episode 1, for example, it was only after the child was introduced to the female performer while sitting on his mother's lap, that he played with her. So a parent/ carer's role cannot be underestimated, and available space must be given to the minority of children who may hesitate or decline to play with a performer, so they feel confident to interact. If a child refuses an invitation from a performer and only engages with a parent, she should not be considered as passive or as missing out. Whether designing an interactive performance or object, our findings provide evidence that when interacting with very young children the role of the adult needs further consideration. An implication of this is that HCI researchers should consider using a performer or theatrical methods for testing interactive toys and objects with very young children (those under 36 months of age) because children at this developmental stage are expected or tend to play with adults who provide the appropriate framing and support.

CONCLUSION

Research on how very young children act in interactive performance spaces is limited. In this paper, we presented how schemas can be used as a framework to design an interactive performance installation that incorporates children's natural play patterns. Studying how young children experienced this performance installation enabled us to reflect on the opportunities offered by tangible technology and the role of adults in TEY.

ACKNOWLEDGMENTS

This work was supported by the Horizon Centre for Doctoral Training at the University of Nottingham (RCUK Grant No. EP/G037574/1) and by the RCUK's Horizon Digital Economy Research Institute (RCUK Grant No. EP/G065802/1). The authors would additionally like to thank the performers Sophie Johnson-Hill and Sean Myatt and the staff at the Lakeside Arts Centre.

REFERENCES

1. Edith K. Ackermann. 2005. Playthings that do things: a young kid's "Incredibles"!. *In Proceedings of the 2005 conference on Interaction design and children* (IDC '05). ACM, New York, NY, USA, 1-8. DOI=http://dx.doi.org/10.1145/1109540.1109541
2. Kristina Andersen. 2004. 'Ensemble': playing with sensors and sound. In CHI '04 Extended Abstracts on Human Factors in Computing Systems (CHI EA '04). ACM, New York, NY, USA, 1239-1242. DOI=http://dx.doi.org/10.1145/985921.986033
3. Chris Athey. 2007. *Extending Thought to Young Children.* Sage Publications, Thousand Oaks, Calif.
4. Frances Atherton, Cathy Nutbrown. 2013. *Understanding Schemas and Young Children* (1st Ed). Sage Publications Ltd.
5. Jean Ayres. 2005. *Sensory Integration and the Child* Western Psychological Services.
6. Steve Ball, Jo Belloli, Selene Burn and Peter Wynne-Willson. 2007. Let's Pretend. *Charting Antarctica: Another stepping-stone across the landscape of early years theatre.* Conference Report. Retrieved April 13, 2015, from, http://bigcitizens.smallsize.org/imgup/Charting%20 Antarctica.pdf .
7. Steve Benford and Gabriella Giannachi. 2011. *Performing Mixed Reality.* MIT Press, Cambridge, MA.
8. Catherine Bouko. 2014. Interactivity and immersion in a media-based performance. *Participation - Journal of Audience & Reception Studies* 11, 1: 254–269.
9. John Brierley.1994. *Give Me A Child Until He Is 7: Brain Studies And Early Childhood Education* (2nd Ed). Routledge
10. Mark Brown. 2012. *Oily Cart: All Sorts of Theatre for All Sorts of Kids*, Trentham Books Ltd
11. Leah Buechley and Hannah Perner-Wilson. 2012. Crafting Technology: Reimagining the processes, materials, and cultures of electronics. ACM Trans. Comput. -Hum. Interact. 19, 3, Article 21 (October 2012), 21 pages. DOI: https://doi.org/10.1145/2362364.2362369
12. Zoe Corby. 2016. *The future of smart toys and the battle for digital children* (September 2016) Retrieved October 24, 2016, from https://www.theguardian.com/technology/2016/sep/22/digital-children-smart-toys-technology
13. Kate Cowan. 2014. Multimodal transcription of the video: examining the interaction in Early Years classrooms. *Classroom Discourse* 5, 1: 6–21. DOI= http://doi.org/10.1080/19463014.2013.859846.
14. Nigel Cross. 2011. *Design Thinking: Understanding How Designers Think and Work.* Bloomsbury Academic.
15. Mary Fawcett, 2009. *Learning through Child Observation* (2nd.ed). Jessica Kingsley Publishers, London. John Wiley & Sons; 1 edition (15 Dec. 2009)
16. William W. Gaver, Jacob Beaver, and Steve Benford. 2003. Ambiguity as a resource for design. In Proceedings of the SIGCHI Conference on Human Factors in Computing Systems (CHI '03). ACM, New York, NY, USA, 233-240. DOI=http://dx.doi.org/10.1145/642611.642653
17. Berto Gonzalez, Erin Carroll, and Celine Latulipe. 2012. Dance-inspired technology, technology-inspired dance. In Proceedings of the 7th Nordic Conference on Human-Computer Interaction: Making Sense Through Design (NordiCHI '12). ACM, New York, NY, USA, 398-407. DOI: https://doi.org/10.1145/2399016.2399078
18. Susan Harper. 2004. Schemas in Areas of Play. *Playcentre Journal.* Issue 121: 18-19.
19. Bart Hengeveld, Caroline Hummels, Hans van Balkom, Riny Voort, and Jan de Moor. 2013. Wrapping up LinguaBytes, for now. In *Proceedings of the 7th International Conference on Tangible, Embedded and Embodied Interaction* (TEI '13). ACM, New York, NY, USA, 237-244. DOI=http://dx.doi.org/10.1145/2460625.2460664
20. Juan Pablo Hourcade, Sarah L. Mascher, David Wu, and Luiza Pantoja. 2015. Look, My Baby Is Using an iPad! An Analysis of YouTube Videos of Infants and Toddlers Using Tablets. *In Proceedings of the 33rd Annual ACM Conference on Human Factors in Computing Systems.!*
21. Sus Lundgren, Joel E. Fischer, Stuart Reeves, and Olof Torgersson. 2015. Designing Mobile Experiences for Collocated Interaction. *In Proceedings of the 18th ACM Conference on Computer Supported Cooperative Work & Social Computing* (CSCW '15). ACM, New York, NY, USA, 496-507. DOI: http://dx.doi.org/10.1145/2675133.2675171
22. Stella Louis, Clare Beswick, Liz Magraw, Lisa Hayes. 2013. *Understanding schemas in young children: Again! Again* (2nd). Featherstone Education
23. Antonio Machón. 2013.*Children's Drawings.* Machón (1st ed) Durango, Antonio
24. Jackie Marsh, Lydia Plowman, L., DylanYamada-Rice, Julia Bishop, Jamal Lahmar, Fiona Scott, Andrew Davenport, Simon Davis, Kate French, Maddalena Piras, Sally Thornhill, Peter Robinson and Peter Winter, *Exploring Play and Creativity in*

*Preschoolers Use of Apps.*2015. Retrieved January 30, 2016, from http://www.techandplay.org

25. Emily McReynolds, Sarah Hubbard, Timothy Lau, Aditya Saraf, Maya Cakmak, and Franziska Roesner. 2017. Toys that Listen: A Study of Parents, Children, and Internet-Connected Toys. In Proceedings of the 2017 CHI Conference on Human Factors in Computing Systems (CHI '17). ACM, New York, NY, USA, 5197-5207. DOI: https://doi.org/10.1145/3025453.3025735
26. Cathy Nutbrown. 2011. *Threads of Thinking, Schemas and Young Children's Learning*, Fourth Edition, SAGE Publications Ltd.
27. Helen Spencer-Oatey. 2013. *Critical incidents. A compilation of quotations for the intercultural field. GlobalPAD Core Concepts*. Retrieved March 20, 2015, from GlobalPAD Open House http://go.warwick.ac.uk/globalpadintercultural
28. Mark Reason. 2010. *The Young Audience: exploring and enhancing children's experiences of youth theatre*. Trentham Books Limited
29. Yvonne Rogers, Mike Scaife, Silvia Gabrielli, Hilary Smith, Eric Harris. 2002. A Conceptual Framework for Mixed Reality Environments: Presence, Vol 11, No 6, 677-686.
30. The TPO Company and Interactive Theatre, retrieved, April 11, 2016, from http://www.tpo.it/down/stampa/pubblicazioni/tpo_pubblicazione_2009.pdf
31. Laura Shneidman, Hyowon Gweon, Laura E. Schulz and Amanda L. Woodward. (2016). *Learning from Others and Spontaneous Exploration: A Cross-Cultural Investigation.* Child Development, Volume 87, Issue 3, 723–735, DOI: 10.1111/dev. 12502
32. Davide Venturini and Francesco Gandi. 2010. CCC trilogy: the Italian garden. In Proceedings of the 18th ACM international conference on Multimedia (MM '10). ACM, New York, NY, USA, 1407-1408. DOI: https://doi.org/10.1145/1873951.1874229
33. Lev Vygotsky. 2004. *Imagination and creativity in childhood.* Journal of Russian and East European Psychology, 42 (1), pp. 7-97.
34. Warren K. Wake (2009*). Design Paradigms: A Source for Creative Visualization.* John Wiley & Sons
35. Manon Van de Water. 2012. *Theatre, Youth, and Culture: A Critical and Historical Exploration.* Palgrave Macmillan, New York.
36. Otto Weininger. 1986. "What If" and "As If": Imagination and Pretend Play in early childhood, International Journal of Early Childhood.Vol: 18 (1) pp: 22-29
37. Donald Winnicott. 2005. *Playing and Reality.* London, Routledge.

Sensory VR: Smelling, Touching, and Eating Virtual Reality

Daniel Harley[2], Alexander Verni[1], Mackenzie Willis[1], Ashley Ng[1], Lucas Bozzo[1], Ali Mazalek[1]
Synaesthetic Media Lab, Responsive Ecologies Lab
Ryerson University[1] York University[2]
Toronto, ON, Canada Toronto, ON, Canada
dharley@ryerson.ca, alexander.verni@ryerson.ca, mackenzie.willis@ryerson.ca,
ashley.ng@ryerson.ca, lucas.bozzo@ryerson.ca, mazalek@ryerson.ca

ABSTRACT
We present two proof of concept sensory experiences designed for virtual reality (VR). Our experiences bring together smell, sound, taste, touch, and sight, focusing on low-cost, non-digital materials and on passive interactions. We also contribute a design rationale and a review of sensory interactions, particularly those designed for VR. We argue that current sensory experiences designed for VR often lack a broader consideration of the senses, especially in their neglect of the non-digital. We discuss some implications of non-digital design for sensory VR, suggesting that there may be opportunities to expand conceptions of what sensory design in VR can be.

Author Keywords
Tangible and embodied interaction; virtual reality; interactive narratives; diegetic design; sensory design; non-digital.

ACM Classification Keywords
• **Human-centered computing~Virtual reality** • *Human-centered computing~Interaction design theory, concepts and paradigms* • *Software and its engineering~Interactive games.*

INTRODUCTION
As the visual and aural fidelity of consumer virtual reality (VR) continues to improve, recent industry and academic work has examined digitally-mediated touch, taste, and smell in VR. Citing the effects of immersion [32], presence [60, 76] or engagement [8], physical experiences are often said to lend a sense of realism in VR (cf. Denisova et al. [14], who suggest that there are overlaps and gaps in the ways we assess these effects). However, sensory experiences within digitally-mediated virtual environments can lack broader considerations of bodies and environments. Active haptic interactions with physical objects, for example, may neglect the passive haptics of that same object, let alone its other sensory characteristics, such as its taste and smell. While we do not expect all virtual environments to be touched, smelled, or tasted, we argue that design for the virtual can include a consideration of the rich affordances of the non-digital world.

In this paper, we contribute two proof of concept sensory experiences designed for VR that include smell, sound, taste, touch, and sight. We draw on the notions of diegetic [21, 22] design and intersensory [39] design, asking how a contextually situated interplay of sensory qualities might contribute to the overall narrative experience. Our two VR environments each explore the sensory qualities of a moment: a moment at the beach, including heat, sunscreen, sand underfoot, and a fruit drink; and a moment in a forest inspired by the storyworld of Little Red Riding Hood, with the looming presence of a virtual wolf, real wind, grass underfoot, and freshly baked bread in a basket nearby.

We argue that low-cost, non-digital, diegetic interactions (e.g., Figure 1) can help to reconceptualize sensory VR design practices, offering a contrast to technologically-driven VR experiences. We also contribute a review of several current trends in digitally-mediated design for the senses, a design rationale, and lessons learned from our sensory workshops. We conclude with a discussion of some of the implications of our work, suggesting that sensory VR could allow players to co-construct experiences that take into account the multiple variations of their sensory needs and preferences, and the sensory variations of their real-world environments.

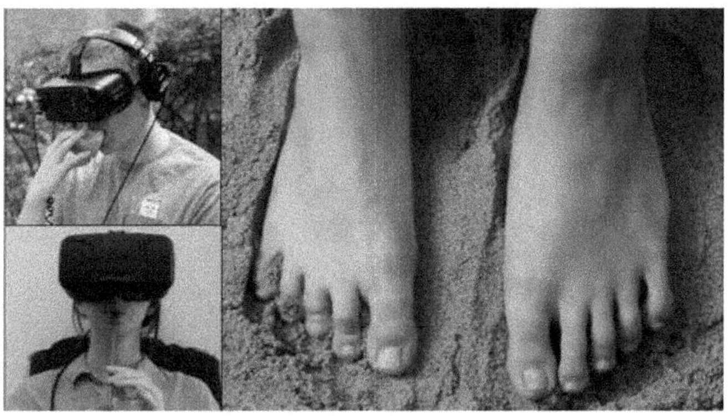

Figure 1. Engaging with the non-digital for sensory VR.

TEI '18, March 18–21, 2018, Stockholm, Sweden

ACM ISBN 978-1-4503-5568-1/18/03...$15.00
https://doi.org/10.1145/3173225.3173241

RELATED WORKS

While consumer VR is primarily a visual and aural medium, it also includes the tracked, embodied actions of players' head and hand movements. These sensory, embodied modalities—the visual, the aural, and some physical movement—form the basis of consumer VR. In this section, we review some work that attempts to fill in VR's missing modalities. In later sections, we reflect on how these trends appear to conceptualize the body, and what this may mean for sensory VR design.

Smell & Taste

For Ghinea et al., smell is a modality that is yet to be "conquered" by multimedia [18]. As the authors note, designers face the challenge of a modality that can be perceived in different ways based on age, gender, culture, and lived experience. In the attempts to address the challenge of smell as controlled "data" that will "drift, diffuse, and linger," the work reviewed by the authors implicitly suggests neutral, smell-free environments modified by the planned "emission of scents." Under this conceptualization, the environment, and the people in it, are part of the design problem. Murray et al. also note the unpredictability of human olfactory perception in their review of "olfaction-enhanced multimedia" [42], but argue that the inclusion of smell and taste will "make multimedia applications more reflective of reality." As "olfactory displays" (e.g., pumps, fans, and cannons that blow or shoot smells) have a relatively tenuous connection to reality, the goal may be, more accurately, a "sense of reality" [18].

Narumi's review of taste in VR echoes this conception with its focus on the "pseudo-gustatory" [46]. In MetaCookie+, for example, the headset overlays a virtual cookie onto a plain cookie and then pumps a scent into the user's nose through a set of tubes, resulting in a reported change in taste [47]. The fallibility of human perception is similarly exploited in projects such as the "tongue interface" [54]. With a design inspired by other "objects that people use to interact with their mouths," the tongue interface uses two electrodes, one under the tongue and the other on top, to produce sour, bitter, sweet, and salty sensations. Just as smell interfaces appear to exclude organic materials, taste interfaces appear to exclude food, although some examples of food in VR do exist. You Better Eat to Survive is a two-player game in which one player in VR must occasionally eat or the screen fades to black. A second non-VR player acts as the VR player's arms, feeding them when necessary. A microphone picks up the sound of chewing, restoring the VR player to life [3] (cf. the eat, chew, smile interaction sequence of the non-VR Food Practice Shooter [33]).

Touch

Generally, we can categorize touch in VR as employing either passive or active haptics. In Metaspace II [63] and Real Virtuality [9], the passive haptics are the physical characteristics of an object, like its weight or texture, are said to lend realism to a virtual environment. In Metaspace II, the user carries a large box that represents a shining virtual cube; in Real Virtuality the player carries a rod that represents a virtual torch. Active haptics, like the vibrotactile feedback of a mobile phone or a VR controller, are more common. Systems can combine passive and active haptics, as in Tangible VR, using a stuffed animal for the passive haptics of its fur and weight, and the active haptics of a "heartbeat" and head movement triggered by the interaction [22]. Zenner and Krüger [78] suggest the additional category of dynamic passive haptics, in which active haptics change the passive haptic properties of an object. This is demonstrated by a handheld rod that shifts its weight depending on the corresponding virtual object.

Touching virtual objects can employ haptic controllers and wearables, as with the handheld "haptic shape controller" of TextureTouch and NormalTouch [7]. Holding the controller, the user puts a finger on a 6 DOF pad that moves to simulate the contours of a virtual object. Similarly, Schorr and Okamura [58] present two fingertip-mounted devices that press on the pads of the user's fingers to simulate a change in the virtual object's weight and texture. The authors suggest that such work could enable users to interact more "directly" with virtual environments, with their "bare hands" rather than a "physical tool" (cf. the "real contact" of VR Touch [19]).

Since handheld, worn, and mounted devices constrain the user's hands, tangible proxies offer an alternative approach. Snake Charmer [2] uses a robot arm with an attached tangible object to present physical proxies in place of virtual counterparts. The authors demonstrate examples of tangible objects outfitted with textures, buttons, Peltier pads, or fans (cf. the "realistic touch sensations" of Axon VR [4]). The authors show that these tangible "endpoints" of the robot arm can be exchanged and used as passive, active, or input-based interactions. Leveraging the affordances of both the virtual and physical is also a design goal of Sparse Haptic Proxy [13], in which a wall-like prop is used as a surface for virtual content as well as for its passive haptic qualities.

Flying objects can also act as proxies. Knierim et al. [35] present quadcopters as proxies for virtual objects that hit the user: first virtual bumblebees and arrows, then virtual bricks, wood, and skulls. While there is no mention that the user may want to swat the quadcopter away, a cage around the quadcopter helps to shield the user from the propellers. The potential for physical pain in virtual worlds is also explored with Impacto, a wearable device that simulates the impact of a hit using electrical muscle stimulation (EMS) to trigger involuntary muscle contractions [37].

Movement

Many touch-based interactions imply additional movement on the part of the user: reaching, grasping, pointing, even kicking. The same can be said of the physical movement implied by the tracked controllers of consumer VR. The wearable puppet of VRSurus [16] is an extension of this kind of movement, with the user's arm controlling an in-game character. As with passive haptics, physical actions are often said to lend a degree of embodied realism. Shadow Shooter [77], aims to align embodied actions with virtual feedback using a real archery bow modified with sensors and a mobile projector to project virtual content onto a wall (cf. the movement implied with the physical proxies of VR Zone [74], or VIRZOOM [69]).

Consumer VR [e.g., 29] can track the user's position to allow walking and kneeling, but not climbing. Solutions for climbing appear to range from the passive haptics of small ridges on the floor to simulate stepping on virtual stairs [43] to boots connected to motorized stilts to simulate climbing steps in VR [56]. In the latter case, some users did report that the heavy prototypes made regular walking feel "less natural" (cf. the "natural movement" of Virtuix [68]). These interactions contrast non-VR foot-based interactions, which appear to conceptualize the feet and legs as input devices [67]. Kickables [57], for example, presents tangible interactions for the feet using common interaction models like sliders and buttons, striving for precision and control.

Movement in VR must include a consideration for the available physical space (compare, e.g., the tracked walking in Anvio VR [1] with the pod-like chair of VRGo [72]), while also addressing medium-specific design challenges: with 360-degree movement, users can potentially look or walk away from the designed experience. In response, the SwiVRChair directs the user's gaze by automatically rotating or halting rotation to point the user in the direction of story content [20], with scenarios that include spinning the user, or having monsters sneak up and surprise the user with a virtual punch to the face. A larger-scale example of working within constraints is TurkDeck, in which a group of people move a set of wall panels around to simulate physical rooms and corridors for a VR user [12]. The system consists of 65 physical props in all. With the "workers" moving the pieces in tandem with player movement, the physical space can appear larger than it is. This illusion echoes the contributions of redirected walking in VR [38, 64] with the added opportunity to touch the virtual world.

Ambient effects

Ambient effects, including simulated wind and heat, have been explored for added "realism," as demonstrated by the felt heat and wind of a virtual desert, volcano, living room, chimney, and a train [31]. The authors use eight axial fans and three infrared lamps that can reach temperatures up to 100 degrees Celsius, with sensors that trigger a shut off if the temperature rises higher than 45 degrees Celsius. Similarly, Ambiotherm seeks to simulate "real-world conditions" with two fans mounted on a Gear VR and two Peltier elements secured to the back of the user's neck with a strap around the throat [53]. The authors claim that this placement of the Peltier elements was chosen for its "high levels of comfort" and for the "perception of overall temperature change (similar to the effects of induced hypothermia)." The VaiR prototype uses a head mounted set of 10 nozzles that can blow short blasts of air or steady streams up to 25km/h while rotating around the user's head [55]. As the authors note, however, the head is not the only part of the body to experience wind (cf. work that focuses only on the "frontal region of the head" to examine the perception of wind direction [45], or ViveNChill [70] for another motivation: to cool a sweaty player down).

Mixed Reality VR

In their attempts to draw on physical as well as virtual affordances, much of the work already described could be classified as mixed reality. There are some advantages to this approach. As suggested by the makers of Oscillate, a physical swing within a virtual environment, "physical reality is replete with interesting kinaesthetic experiences" [65]. Like passive haptics, mixed reality interfaces can include the sensory, embodied qualities of the physical environment. CarVR leverages the kinaesthetic motion of a passenger in a car with virtual content mapped to a predefined route [25] (cf. VR roller coasters [36, 59]). Meehan et al. [40] use a wooden plank above a virtual pit, grounding the experience with a low-cost, tangible object (cf. the physical props of Project iCan [52], or the props and ambient effects designed for The Void [71]). Annexing Reality predicts possible overlays of virtual objects onto the nearest physical match in the player's view, like a bottle representing a light-saber [24]. IRIDiuM+ includes the active and passive "walkable haptics" of vibrating carpet-like materials and the "air haptics" of actuated fans [34]. Work that considers both the user and the environment begins to resemble interactive theatre (e.g., Sleep No More [51]), in which a user interacts within the bounds of a constructed space. Flatland [75] is a recent example, using a tangible object to guide the user through darkened spaces with particular smells and tactile qualities.

DESIGN RATIONALE

Within the work we reviewed, we found conceptual gaps that reflect implicit and explicit decisions made prior to design. We noticed that, first, much of the research simulates sensory experiences using digitally-mediated solutions. Second, the designer often creates structured experiences for a neutral body in a neutral environment. And third, a focus on one or two sensory modalities often ignores the rest of the body or the environment. A naive reading could suggest a common set of design assumptions: i.e., that (a) a digital solution (with its implicit promise of control and reproducibility) is better than a non-digital solution; (b) we need not consider the multiple variations of a player's sensory needs and preferences, or the variations of their environment; and further, (c) design that focuses on discrete sensory experiences will not be affected by our environment or our other senses. As a design prompt, we propose to challenge these apparent assumptions.

We draw on the field of tangible, embedded, and embodied interaction (TEI), for the reminder to better assess the physical medium of the digital experience. In her critique of Paul Dourish's conception of embodied interaction, Hornecker argues that "the human body is strangely missing, as well as the materiality of the world we live in." Hornecker broadens the scope of "tangible" interaction, attempting to include embodied interactions within shared physical spaces [27]. The notable absence of the digital in design tools like Ideating in Skills [61], or the focus on the physical form of a "hybrid object" [50] is an attempt to draw attention to the situated, embodied practices with tangible objects as well as the interplay between digital and non-digital. In their theoretical framework, van Dijk and Hummels [15] argue for design that "radically rejects" the Cartesian frame, which undergirds "the bulk of interactive technology." They aim to reconceptualize "embodied" design in TEI as something that requires a consideration of the physical and social interplay between people, places (what they refer to as the "lifeworld"), and things (e.g., artifacts), with an emphasis on open-ended design that can respond to changing contexts.

Our designed experiences, therefore, attempt to challenge the taken-for-granted theoretical stance suggested by related VR work. We draw on tangible and embodied design in order to include a consideration of the sensory experience as shaped by the digital and the non-digital. To consider the people, places, and things that create the interplay between the digital and non-digital, we also draw on notions of "intersensory" design and "diegetic" design. McBride and Nolan [39] emphasize that any individual sense must be understood as part of an "intersensory" whole, not just within our bodies but also as "a relational and contingent part of the total social, cultural and environmental ecology" (190). Diegetic design [21, 22] conceptualizes all aspects of the designed, narrative experience as belonging within its story world. Bringing these perspectives together in our design process, we asked: "What are the intersensory characteristics of these narrative environments?"

In the following sections, we describe the interaction scenarios and implementation of our two proofs of concept in more detail. We sought to examine non-digital sensory interactions within a digitally-mediated environment in order to better understand how we might conceptualize sensory VR. For this preliminary work, we chose to design around the sensory qualities of a single narrative moment to narrow and constrain the sensory interactions in each proof of concept.

INTERACTION SCENARIOS

Our two proofs of concept explore sensory experiences for VR focusing on a single moment. The first is a moment at the beach and the second is a moment in Little Red Riding Hood. Both scenarios suggest a number of sensory characteristics that are not typically available in VR. There are smells and tastes, things to feel and touch, ambient effects, and embodied actions. In addition to the constraint of the narrative moment, the experience is constrained by the technology: in both experiences, the player is seated and cannot move within the virtual environment, and because of the limitations of the Oculus DK2 and the Gear VR, they do not see a representation of their body or the objects.

Despite the similarity of interactions in our environments, both scenarios are also open-ended, i.e., we conceptualize experiences that players co-create: modifying, replacing, or using the sensory affordances of their environments. For example, in the beach experience, the sand replaces the feeling of tiles underfoot, while the forest environment uses the wind and grass of a nearby park. Finally, both scenarios conceptualize some planning on the part of the player. We present possible choices here; note that these choices are provocative rather than prescriptive. As we discuss later, a narrative moment can contain many sensory qualities, which can be shaped by players' own lived experiences.

The Beach

The goal of this scenario is to recreate some of the sensory qualities of being at the beach. The player prepares sunscreen, a drink of choice, a lawn chair, a space heater, and a plastic storage container of sand to accompany their VR experience. The player adjusts the temperature and the placement of the space heater to simulate the warmth of the wind, and sits in a lawn chair. The player puts on sunscreen. The smell is reminiscent of a hot day at the beach. In advance, the player has warmed some of the sand separately and spread it as the top layer of sand in the container. The player puts their feet in the sand, puts on the headset and the headphones. They see an empty beach and hear the waves and the seagulls (Figure 2). To match their virtual drink, the player has a drink in the cup holder of their chair.

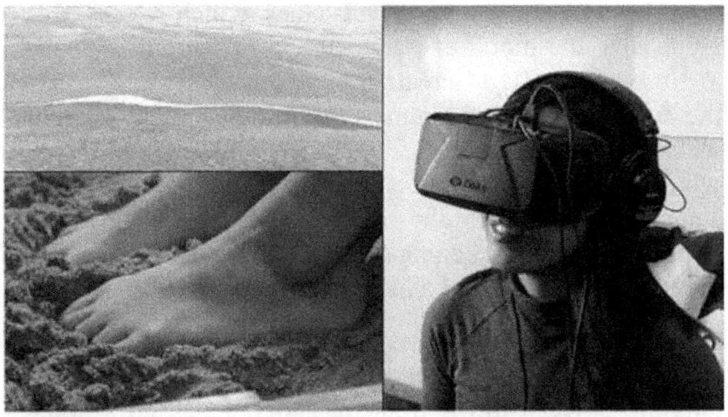

Figure 2. The beach environment, featuring sand underfoot.

Little Red Riding Hood

This interaction scenario draws inspiration from Little Red Riding Hood, recreating the moment before Red's encounter with the Wolf in the forest. Red stops to sit a while to rest and pick flowers. The player prepares the basket of food that is meant for Grandma, and walks to an outdoor area that has some of the sensory qualities of the story. Being in the city, this version uses a nearby park. The player takes off their shoes and puts their bare feet in the grass. It is summer and it is warm. There is a gentle breeze and the smell of the fresh air. The player puts on a mobile headset and headphones, transforming the sights and sounds of the park into the sights and sounds of the fairy tale forest (Figure 3). The player dawdles as Red does and eats the bread, even though it is meant for Grandma. Virtual fog rolls in and the sky darkens. The mood changes: there is the sound of breathing in the woods nearby and eyes looking out at Red. The wolf is nearby.

Figure 3. The forest environment, with wind, grass, and the smell of the outdoors "simulated" by a city park.

IMPLEMENTATION

We designed our VR experiences to work alongside technology, using non-digital solutions for sensory interactions. We used an Oculus DK2 for the beach environment and a Gear VR for the forest environment. Out of the box, neither headset supports hand tracking or object tracking. In keeping with the focus on low-cost materials, we did not add any peripheral tracking to match the placement of the real and virtual objects, though each of the physical objects did have a virtual counterpart. Players wore headphones for the soundscapes, which we created to emphasize the mood and atmosphere of the environments. We used Unity3D to create the environments and to place the spatialized sound sources. For the beach environment, we sampled and looped sounds of waves, seagulls, and wind; for the forest environment, we sampled and looped sounds of a forest and the creaking sounds of wind through trees. The fog, a darkening sky, and the sound of the wolf's breathing nearby signal a mood change.

Sensory objects of the forest environment included a basket with fresh bread and apples, and in one iteration, various tangible objects drawn from the story, like Red's hooded cloak, pine needles, and dirt from outside. In this environment, the breeze of the wind, the temperature, and the feeling of grass on bare feet are all from reality. In the city, these sensory characteristics are even more readily available than those we used for the beach environment. These are examples of the simplest non-digital solutions: the wind simulates the wind. Sensory objects for the beach environment included a lawn chair, a space heater, fruit juice, sunscreen, and a plastic storage container filled with sand. Each of these allows for embodied, sensory actions: the act of putting on sunscreen, with its characteristic scent; the act of settling into the deep seat of a lawn chair; the warm "wind" of a space heater; the taste of a fruit juice; and the feeling of sand between toes (Figure 4). Together, these objects create a relatively complex VR environment that engages several senses at once. Trying the environment ourselves for the first time, we noticed one thing did not feel "right." The sand was too cold, so we warmed a few cups in the microwave. Now the top layer was warm, as if exposed to the sun, with cool layers below.

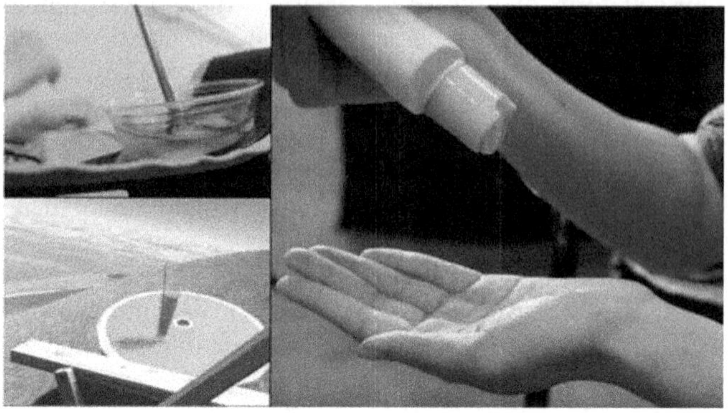

Figure 4. A tropical drink to match the drink in VR, and the smell and embodied action of putting on sunscreen.

SENSORY DESIGN WORKSHOPS & EVALUATION

We began our design process by brainstorming the sensory details of particular moments and environments in our own lives. We used the concept of diegetic design to think about how each sensory detail might contribute to an overall narrative whole, and the concept of intersensory design to think about how each sensory detail might work with or against another. To examine the varied and interdependent contexts of sensory interactions, we organized several informal design workshops, often including members of our lab. Workshops with our lab included as many as 25 people. We make no claims of generalizability as to our process or the feedback we received; instead, we discuss this preliminary design process in order to document how it challenged our own design assumptions and to better understand how we might conceptualize sensory VR. In our first set of workshops, we set aside VR to focus on the non-digital. In our second set of workshops, we focused on the ways that the non-digital could contribute to VR design.

Workshops without VR

Inspired by guidelines outlined in McBride and Nolan's work [39], our goal in our first set of workshops was to examine our own sensory practices, expectations, and beliefs. In one workshop, we reflected on the tangible, sensory qualities of oranges, smelling, peeling and tasting the fruit. We discussed the smell of the rind on our fingers, the stickiness of the juice. When we repeated this exercise with members of our lab, conversations turned to a variety of culturally situated food practices that were beyond those that we had discussed—a reminder of individual preferences and experiences. The reminder that a single organic object has a number of sensory characteristics, though obvious in retrospect, was necessary. It was a reminder that any single distilled smell, like that of an essential oil, is also a removal of several other sensory, embodied characteristics, like the act of peeling an orange.

We continued these conversations in the following workshops, discussing and smelling several essential oils. We hoped to critically examine our own assumptions about these smells: where do they come from, what might these smells communicate about a narrative environment, and what are the other sensory qualities of this smell in its original context? We did the same with tangible objects in another workshop. We brought in and discussed the physical attributes of several objects, asking what they might communicate. These ranged from a dried seahorse found on a beach to a packaged latex condom. Conceptualizing individual objects as diegetic was a design prompt: what do these objects tell us about their environments or their story worlds? Engaging with the non-digital in these workshops became a valuable resource for design, offering low-cost sensory explorations. When we prepared to include VR, we found that the same questions applied: what are the sensory characteristics of our VR environments and what might we gain or lose by introducing a particular modality?

Workshops with VR & informal user feedback

When we began prototyping our proofs of concept, we organized additional workshops with members of our lab to elicit informal feedback. For the first iteration of the forest environment, we presented all the modalities separately: a red cloak; apples; dirt, grass, and pine needles; a soundscape; and a VR forest. We discussed the sensory qualities of each, asking for feedback on the modalities and the narrative mood. Some guessed that it was based on Little Red Riding Hood; for those who did not, we noted how reactions varied. Some were drawn to the sounds, some were drawn to the smell of the dirt and pine needles. We realized that like much of the work reviewed above, we were still choosing the sensory modalities for the player, asking them to ignore one thing while paying attention to another, with the implicit promise of immersion.

In industry rhetoric about "immersion" (e.g., Holovis's "immersive" and "transformative journeys" [26] or VRCade's "immersive gaming experiences" [73]), it is the system that immerses the player. The player's suspension of disbelief is assured by the power and illusion of the system. Disconnected and embodied aspects of the experience, like the awkwardness of donning a heavy headset, must be ignored. For Murray [41], this could be an opportunity to use the headset as a "threshold object"; i.e., using it as a stand-in for a physical object worn by the player-character, like an astronaut's helmet. But what about environments in which a headset is not diegetic, like a beach or a forest? A large VR sunhat, or Red's hood could help make the headset a threshold object, but the weight and heat of the headset would still have to be ignored by the player, which is also to say that the weight and heat are not diegetic.

These reflections led us to reconceptualize "immersion" as player-driven rather than system-driven. If the player chooses the sensory qualities that they want to experience, the interaction can begin before the player puts on the headset. This can help to break down other taken-for-granted assumptions about the designed experience. Since we do not know the sensory qualities of the player's home, the players can look to include particular sensory aspects of their own environments. This also suggests that the experience does not have to happen in one place, and does not have to happen exclusively indoors. The player could become an active participant in their own immersion, knowingly co-constructing their virtual reality experience. As this also requires players to make choices that impact the story, designers could help create more player-driven experiences by offering suggestions for sensory modalities or by helping to scaffold the experience.

Similarly, when showing the beach environment to our lab colleagues in another workshop, we found that our efforts in controlling the experience and acting as helpers were largely unnecessary. After putting on sunscreen, the headphones, and the headset, each volunteer looked around briefly, sat back in the chair and then curled their toes in the sand. Like the helpers in TurkDeck [12] and You Better Eat to Survive [3], we had focused on the player's experience rather than on that of the helpers. (The helpers' experience is, however, a consideration in work that provides the "human actuators" with goals and feedback of their own [10, 11], suggesting that their role(s) could also be made diegetic.) While there are certainly occasions for heavily structured and monitored experiences, in this sensory moment, the sand was enough. Seeing a virtual drink on a virtual table, one player said, "All I need now is that drink over there." We promptly handed him a fruit punch.

DISCUSSION

VR presents an opportunity for TEI because virtual reality is never merely a visual/aural experience. The embodied negotiation of the potential mismatch between what we see and what we feel is, in many ways, a question for the TEI community. We have made a point to include industry work in an effort to show trends and similarities between industry and academia. In both, we find "sensory" attachments for headsets, vibrating wearables that claim to increase "immersion," and finger-mounted haptic devices for "realistic" touch. As we have noted in our design rationale, these parallels suggest several design assumptions that, in turn, suggest gaps. In this section, we return to these apparent assumptions: (a) digital solutions are superior to non-digital solutions; (b) we should design for a neutral body in a neutral environment; and (c) we should design for discrete sensory experiences. Challenging these assumptions, we find opportunities to reconsider the non-digital as a design resource, leading to a reconceptualization of players, their environments, and their roles within sensory VR. These considerations can be a fruitful avenue as the TEI community continues to contribute an examination of the whole body within digitally-mediated environments, raising important questions: how much of our bodies and our physical environments do we include and how much do we exclude? How do we conceptualize the body in VR design?

Limitations

As our work was tested in informal settings, we make no claims of generalizability or reproducibility. We suggest the value of our contribution is primarily in its "criticality" [5] in the sense that it questions current design trends in VR and requires us to confront our own taken-for-granted assumptions. In the same vein, the overall goal in our exploratory workshops, both with core members of the design team and with members of our lab, was to better understand how we might conceptualize sensory VR. We do not suggest that it will be possible or advisable to recreate what we have created, nor do we suggest that every player or every designer will have the same experiences that we document. Such recommendations are beyond the scope of this work and beyond our design intentions. For example, while we suggest that "co-constructed" experiences may offer opportunities for VR design, these are, at present, conceptual rather than practicable suggestions as we did not engage in participatory design practices. Nevertheless, we do suggest that a consideration for the non-digital, for player-driven experiences, for an examination of how we simulate the senses and what technologies we use, are each a potential opportunity to examine and expand on current design practices.

The non-digital as design challenge

As our related work suggests, digitally-mediated sensory simulations are assumed to offer control and reproducibility, often negating the prospect of the non-digital. Challenging such taken-for-granted assumptions in our design process led us to reflect on some the broader ramifications of conventional reproducibility: Must reproducibility necessarily include technology? Must every interaction be planned or controlled? From an interaction design perspective, our inclination is often to provide feedback to "confirm" the user's actions, guiding them towards the "right" actions, and helping the user "know what to do" [49]. But there is no need to think about technologically enabled feedback in the case of one's feet in the grass—the feedback of the cool passive haptics of the grass in the heat of the afternoon sun is immediate and complex (Figure 5).

Similarly, the idea of "knowing what to do" implies knowing what to do next: a procession from one interaction to another. There is nothing to "do" in our beach environment. There is no sequence of planned interactions with planned results. Presenting our proofs of concept in our workshops, we were aware of the potential for shallow engagement with novel technologies [28] and our players' potential expectation of wanting to know what they were supposed to "do" next. Yet, as demonstrated by the player who requested a fruit punch to go with the beach experience, there may be an opportunity to allow the player to co-construct their experience (e.g., by placing the heater, warming the sand, or preparing a drink). Reflections such as these helped us to reconceptualize "immersive" experiences as player-driven rather than system-driven.

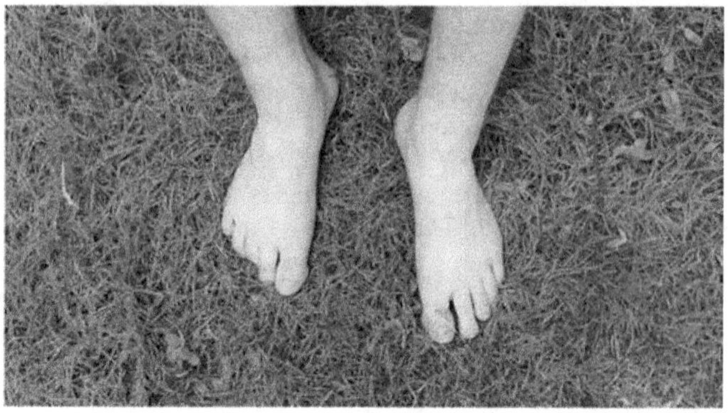

Figure 5. Using grass for the feedback of its passive haptics.

Including the player

We chose to explore a single narrative moment in order to constrain the experience and narrow our focus. Yet, as our proofs of concept suggest, one narrative moment can have several sensory qualities and can last as long as the player wants to experience them. Designers face additional challenges if they hope to create longer narratives with distinct transitions between sensory experiences. Smell, for example, is a difficult modality to work with, having numerous practical and ethical challenges [see, e.g., 23]. Related work that assumes a neutral body within a neutral environment might bypass these challenges by disregarding the complex contexts of a designed experience. For us, challenging this assumption started with the admission that we could not assume to know the needs and preferences of the player or the sensory conditions of their environment.

Conceptualizing the experience as player-driven allows us to reintegrate the player and the player's sensory environment. Designing interactions in which the player chooses for themselves what diegetic smells, tastes, atmospheres, and tangible objects accompany a narrative could help to personalize the experience while also helping to circumvent some of the difficulties that designers face when attempting anything to do with smell or taste, like the risk of an allergic reaction. Integrating the player begins to overcome some of the challenges of the reproducibility of the non-digital. A video game that plans for a player to eat baked goods does not have to provide baked goods as long as the player knows to get the ones that suit them ahead of time. In this way, designers can work to enable players to co-construct a variety of possible narratives in ways that are most meaningful to them.

Reconsidering the bounds of sensory VR

A reconsideration of the beginning of the designed experience to include any preparatory actions (e.g., putting on sunscreen, or choosing an appropriate time and location outside, or eating baked goods) could go still further. The interaction could begin when the player contemplates the available sensory affordances of their own environment. With some foreknowledge of a desired experience, the player can ask, as we did, "What are the sensory qualities of the environments available to me? What are the diegetic qualities of my environment?" In turn, the designed experience could help players to incorporate their physical environments. This begins to suggest a spectrum of sensory, diegetic possibilities that could be available to the player. In our version of Little Red Riding Hood, for example, a player with a nearby forest might have a more diegetic sensory experience than our player in a city park. Yet both experiences are valid if they meet the player's needs and preferences.

Giving the player more control over a designed experience acknowledges some of the uncontrollable aspects of those spaces, while also offering more opportunities for design. The assumption that discrete sensory experiences will not be affected by our environment or our other senses limits the designed experience, both intentionally and unintentionally. For example, it is probably safe to assume that most video games designed for VR make no consideration for what is in the player's mouth, or what the player is tasting. This is to say that the player and the designer have implicitly agreed that what the player might be tasting is outside the story world. The player must implicitly agree to ignore some senses and pay attention to others. How might designed experiences change if players did not have to ignore some of their senses? How might these experiences change if both players and designers implicitly agreed that all of the player's senses and their environments could be diegetic? Every physical space lends its ambient sensory qualities to virtual worlds, just as every player has differing needs and preferences within those spaces.

Reconsidering technology

The absence of any technological innovation in our proofs of concept is not intended as a dismissal of technology. Rather, using low-cost sensory materials is an attempt to (re)consider the real-world aspects of a designed experience, filled with organic and inorganic materials. As VR is a digital simulation, work that explores other digital simulations appears to be a natural fit. Attempts, for example, to deliver "augmented" or "electric" taste [44] complement work that aims to "digitize" smell and taste [62] (cf. the "super realistic smells" of Vaqso [66] or the "deep immersion" and "simulated effects" of the Feelreal helmet and mask [30], or the "new senses" of the Neo Sensory Vest [48]). However, some of the trends in VR that we have touched on in this paper suggest an ironic turn away from the body in order to achieve embodiment. Our proofs of concept are a reminder that the design of sensory VR should include a consideration of sensory experiences that are non-digital, readily available, and chosen by users.

Examining the taken-for-granted in the technologies we use offers opportunities for future work. Following van Dijk and Hummels [15], it can be "radical" to focus on the sensory affordances of an environment before a technological intervention. For embodied experiences, it can also be practical. For those working on technological solutions to sensory VR, explorations like ours may be useful for prototyping digitally-mediated sensory design. Contrasting a contextually situated sensory experience with its digital, virtual, or synthetic counterpart can simply be an exploration of what we gain or lose in the process of mediation. At the very least, the non-digital can allow designers to better assess the sensory, embodied qualities of a particular environment. As Gaver et al. suggest, it can be useful to consider the ambiguous, open-ended experience as it may help to position the user in an active, interpretive role [17]. Open-ended experiences in VR could also benefit from a consideration of the "trajectory" of the user's experience: what are the possible paths through which the user navigates physical/digital spaces, as well as through planned moments of an experience? [6]

CONCLUSION

We have argued that much of the current work that aims to bring sensory experiences to VR does so while ignoring the non-digital. Drawing on design practices that strive for an interrelated conception of our bodies and environments, we created two proof of concept sensory VR experiences. We offer a consideration for taste, touch, and smell, as well as ambient effects like heat and wind to the more conventional modalities of sight and sound. Both experiences are barefoot and open-ended, one indoors, the other outdoors, exploring the sensory details of a moment. In our VR and non-VR workshops, we used diegetic and intersensory considerations as design prompts: how does a particular modality contribute to the environment, the story, and the player? In response, we emphasize the inclusion of the passive, experiential aspects of the non-digital. Neither experience requires sophisticated programming or physical prototyping, yet both deliver an array of sensory affordances that are rarely offered in VR. Technological solutions to these sensory interactions would be prohibitively complex and expensive, for our lab and for a general audience. We conclude by suggesting that the incorporation of the non-digital is a challenge to sensory design and technology, but not a dismissal of either. Instead, it offers opportunities to expand the design space, allowing players to co-construct designed experiences that best suit their own environments and their own bodies.

ACKNOWLEDGEMENTS

This research was undertaken, in part, thanks to funding from the Canada Research Chairs program, Canadian Foundation for Innovation, and the Ontario Ministry of Research and Innovation. We also thank: Melanie McBride for her guidance and collaboration; Laura Garrido-Beltran for her collaboration; and the students and researchers in the Synaesthetic Media Lab for their valuable feedback.

REFERENCES

1. Anvio VR. 2017. Retrieved from: https://en.anviovr.com/
2. Bruno de Araujo, Ricardo Jota, Varun Perumal, Jia Xian Yao, Karan Singh, and Daniel Wigdor. 2016. Snake Charmer: Physically Enabling Virtual Objects. In Proceedings of the TEI '16: Tenth International Conference on Tangible, Embedded, and Embodied Interaction (TEI '16). ACM, New York, NY, USA, 218-226.
3. Peter Arnold. 2017. You Better Eat to Survive! Exploring Edible Interactions in a Virtual Reality Game. In *Proceedings of the 2017 CHI Conference Extended Abstracts on Human Factors in Computing Systems (CHI EA '17).* ACM, New York, NY, USA, 206-209. DOI: https://doi.org/10.1145/3027063.3048408
4. AxonVR. 2017. Retrieved from: https://axonvr.com/
5. Jeffrey Bardzell and Shaowen Bardzell. 2013. What is "critical" about critical design?. In *Proceedings of the SIGCHI Conference on Human Factors in Computing Systems* (CHI '13). ACM, New York, NY, USA, 3297-3306. DOI: https://doi.org/10.1145/2470654.2466451
6. Steve Benford, Gabriella Giannachi, Boriana Koleva, and Tom Rodden. 2009. From interaction to trajectories: designing coherent journeys through user experiences. In *Proceedings of the SIGCHI Conference on Human Factors in Computing Systems (CHI '09).* ACM, New York, NY, USA, 709-718. DOI: https://doi.org/10.1145/1518701.1518812
7. Hrvoje Benko, Christian Holz, Mike Sinclair, and Eyal Ofek. 2016. NormalTouch and TextureTouch: High-fidelity 3D Haptic Shape Rendering on Handheld Virtual Reality Controllers. In *Proceedings of the 29th Annual Symposium on User Interface Software and Technology (UIST '16).* ACM, New York, NY, USA, 717-728. DOI: https://doi.org/10.1145/2984511.2984526
8. Jeanne Brockmyer, Christine Fox, Kathleen Curtiss, Evan McBroom, Kimberly Burkhart, and Jaquelyn Pidruzny. 2009. The Development of the Game Engagement Questionnaire: A Measure of Engagement in Video Game Playing: Response to Reviews. Journal of Experimental Social Psychology 25, 4 (March 2009), 624-634. DOI:http://dx.doi.org/10.1016/j.jesp.2009.02.016
9. Sylvain Chagué and Caecilia Charbonnier. 2016. Real Virtuality: A Multi-User Immersive Platform Connecting Real and Virtual Worlds, VRIC 2016 Virtual Reality International Conference - Laval Virtual, Laval, France, ACM New York, NY, USA.
10. Lung-Pan Cheng, Patrick Lühne, Pedro Lopes, Christoph Sterz, and Patrick Baudisch. 2014. Haptic turk: a motion platform based on people. In *Proceedings of the SIGCHI Conference on Human Factors in Computing Systems* (CHI '14). ACM, New York, NY, USA, 3463-3472. DOI=http://dx.doi.org/10.1145/2556288.2557101
11. Lung-Pan Cheng, Sebastian Marwecki, and Patrick Baudisch. 2017. Mutual Human Actuation. In *Proceedings of the 30th Annual ACM Symposium on User Interface Software and Technology* (UIST '17). ACM, New York, NY, USA, 797-805. DOI: https://doi.org/10.1145/3126594.3126667
12. Lung-Pan Cheng, Thijs Roumen, Hannes Rantzsch, Sven Köhler, Patrick Schmidt, Robert Kovacs, Johannes Jasper, Jonas Kemper, and Patrick Baudisch. 2015. TurkDeck: Physical Virtual Reality Based on People. In *Proceedings of the 28th Annual ACM Symposium on User Interface Software & Technology (UIST '15).* ACM, New York, NY, USA, 417-426. DOI: https://doi.org/10.1145/2807442.2807463
13. Lung-Pan Cheng, Eyal Ofek, Christian Holz, Hrvoje Benko, and Andrew D. Wilson. 2017. Sparse Haptic Proxy: Touch Feedback in Virtual Environments Using a General Passive Prop. In *Proceedings of the 2017 CHI Conference on Human Factors in Computing Systems* (CHI '17). ACM, New York, NY, USA, 3718-3728. DOI: https://doi.org/10.1145/3025453.3025753
14. Alena Denisova, A. Imran Nordin, and Paul Cairns. 2016. The Convergence of Player Experience Questionnaires. In *Proceedings of the 2016 Annual Symposium on Computer-Human Interaction in Play* (CHI PLAY '16). ACM, New York, NY, USA, 33-37. DOI: https://doi.org/10.1145/2967934.2968095
15. Jelle van Dijk and Caroline Hummels. 2017. Designing for Embodied Being-in-the-World: Two Cases, Seven Principles and One Framework. In Proceedings of the Eleventh International Conference on Tangible, Embedded, and Embodied Interaction (TEI '17). ACM, New York, NY, USA, 47-56. DOI: https://doi.org/10.1145/3024969.3025007
16. Ruofei Du and Liang He. 2016. VRSurus: Enhancing Interactivity and Tangibility of Puppets in Virtual Reality. In *Proceedings of the 2016 CHI Conference Extended Abstracts on Human Factors in Computing Systems* (CHI EA '16). ACM, New York, NY, USA, 2454-2461. DOI: https://doi.org/10.1145/2851581.2892290
17. William W. Gaver, Jacob Beaver, and Steve Benford. 2003. Ambiguity as a resource for design. In *Proceedings of the SIGCHI Conference on Human Factors in Computing Systems* (CHI '03). ACM, New York, NY, USA, 233-240. DOI=http://dx.doi.org/10.1145/642611.642653
18. Gheorghita Ghinea and Oluwakemi A. Ademoye. 2011. Olfaction-enhanced multimedia: perspectives and challenges. *Multimedia Tools Appl.* 55, 3

(December 2011), 601-626. DOI=http://dx.doi.org/10.1007/s11042-010-0581-4

19. GotouchVR. 2017. Retrieved from: https://www.gotouchvr.com/
20. Jan Gugenheimer, Dennis Wolf, Gabriel Haas, Sebastian Krebs, and Enrico Rukzio. 2016. SwiVRChair: A Motorized Swivel Chair to Nudge Users' Orientation for 360 Degree Storytelling in Virtual Reality. In *Proceedings of the 2016 CHI Conference on Human Factors in Computing Systems* (CHI '16). ACM, New York, NY, USA, 1996-2000. DOI: https://doi.org/10.1145/2858036.2858040
21. Daniel Harley, Jean Ho Chu, Jamie Kwan, and Ali Mazalek. 2016. Towards a Framework for Tangible Narratives. In Proceedings of the TEI '16: Tenth International Conference on Tangible, Embedded, and Embodied Interaction (TEI '16). ACM, New York, NY, USA, 62-69. DOI=http://dx.doi.org/10.1145/2839462.2839471
22. Daniel Harley, Aneesh P. Tarun, Daniel Germinario, and Ali Mazalek. 2017. Tangible VR: Diegetic Tangible Objects for Virtual Reality Narratives. In *Proceedings of the 2017 Conference on Designing Interactive Systems* (DIS '17). ACM, New York, NY, USA, 1253-1263. DOI: https://doi.org/10.1145/3064663.3064680
23. Victoria Henshaw, Dominic Medway, Gary Warnaby, and Chris Perkins. 2016 Marketing the 'city of smells'. 16 2 (June 2016), 153-170. DOI: http:dx.doi.org/https://doi.org/10.1177/1470593115619970
24. Anuruddha Hettiarachchi and Daniel Wigdor. 2016. Annexing Reality: Enabling Opportunistic Use of Everyday Objects as Tangible Proxies in Augmented Reality. In *Proceedings of the 2016 CHI Conference on Human Factors in Computing Systems* (CHI '16). ACM, New York, NY, USA, 1957-1967.
25. Philipp Hock, Sebastian Benedikter, Jan Gugenheimer, and Enrico Rukzio. 2017. CarVR: Enabling In-Car Virtual Reality Entertainment. In *Proceedings of the 2017 CHI Conference on Human Factors in Computing Systems* (CHI '17). ACM, New York, NY, USA, 4034-4044. DOI: https://doi.org/10.1145/3025453.3025665
26. Holovis. 2017. Retrieved from: http://www.holovis.com/
27. Eva Hornecker. 2006. Physicality in tangible interaction: bodies and the world. First Steps in Physicality, 21.
28. Eva Hornecker. 2008. "I don't understand it either, but it is cool"-visitor interactions with a multi-touch table in a museum. In Horizontal interactive human computer systems, 2008. TABLETOP 2008. 3rd IEEE International Workshop on, pp. 113-120. IEEE, 2008.
29. HTC Vive. 2017. Retrieved from: https://www.vive.com
30. Feelreal. 2017. Retrieved from: http://feelreal.com/.
31. Felix Hülsmann, Julia Fröhlich, Nikita Mattar, and Ipke Wachsmuth. 2014. Wind and warmth in virtual reality: implementation and evaluation. In *Proceedings of the 2014 Virtual Reality International Conference* (VRIC '14). ACM, New York, NY, USA, Article 24, 8 pages. DOI=http://dx.doi.org/10.1145/2617841.2620712
32. Charlene Jennett, Anna L. Cox, Paul Cairns, Samira Dhoparee, Andrew Epps, Tim Tijs, and Alison Walton. 2008. Measuring and defining the experience of immersion in games. *Int. J. Hum.-Comput. Stud.* 66, 9 (September 2008), 641-661. DOI=http://dx.doi.org/10.1016/j.ijhcs.2008.04.004
33. Takayuki Kosaka and Takuya Iwamoto. 2013. Serious dietary education system for changing food preferences "food practice shooter". In *Proceedings of the Virtual Reality International Conference: Laval Virtual* (VRIC '13). ACM, New York, NY, USA, Article 23, 4 pages. DOI: https://doi.org/10.1145/2466816.2466841
34. Maggie Kosek, Babis Koniaris, David Sinclair, Desislava Markova, Fraser Rothnie, Lanny Smoot, and Kenny Mitchell. 2017. IRIDiuM+: deep media storytelling with non-linear light field video. In *ACM SIGGRAPH 2017 VR Village* (SIGGRAPH '17). ACM, New York, NY, USA, Article 10, 2 pages. DOI: https://doi.org/10.1145/3089269.3089277
35. Pascal Knierim, Thomas Kosch, Valentin Schwind, Markus Funk, Francisco Kiss, Stefan Schneegass, and Niels Henze. 2017. Tactile Drones - Providing Immersive Tactile Feedback in Virtual Reality through Quadcopters. In *Proceedings of the 2017 CHI Conference Extended Abstracts on Human Factors in Computing Systems* (CHI EA '17). ACM, New York, NY, USA, 433-436. DOI: https://doi.org/10.1145/3027063.3050426
36. Kuka. 2017. *Kuka Coaster*. Retrieved from: https://www.kuka.com/en-ca/industries/other-industries/entertainment/kuka-coaster
37. Pedro Lopes, Alexandra Ion, and Patrick Baudisch. 2015. Impacto: Simulating Physical Impact by Combining Tactile Stimulation with Electrical Muscle Stimulation. In Proceedings of the 28th Annual ACM Symposium on User Interface Software & Technology (UIST '15). ACM, New York, NY, USA, 11-19. DOI: https://doi.org/10.1145/2807442.2807443
38. Keigo Matsumoto, Yuki Ban, Takuji Narumi, Yohei Yanase, Tomohiro Tanikawa, and Michitaka Hirose. 2016. Unlimited corridor: redirected walking

techniques using visuo haptic interaction. In *ACM SIGGRAPH 2016 Emerging Technologies* (SIGGRAPH '16). ACM, New York, NY, USA, , Article 20 , 2 pages. DOI: https://doi.org/10.1145/2929464.2929482

39. Melanie McBride & Jason Nolan. (2016). “Including smell: An intersensory curriculum, by design.” In Victoria Henshaw, Kate MacLean, Dominic Medway, Chris Perkins, & Gary Warnaby (eds.). *Designing with smell: practices, techniques and challenges*. New York: Routledge.

40. Michael Meehan, Brent Insko, Mary Whitton, and Frederick P. Brooks, Jr. 2002. Physiological measures of presence in stressful virtual environments. In Proceedings of the 29th annual conference on Computer graphics and interactive techniques (SIGGRAPH '02). ACM, New York, NY, USA, 645-652. DOI: http://dx.doi.org/10.1145/566570.566630

41. Janet Murray. 2005. Did it make you cry? Creating dramatic agency in immersive environments. In Virtual Storytelling. Using Virtual Reality Technologies for Storytelling (pp. 83-94). Springer Berlin Heidelberg.

42. Niall Murray, Brian Lee, Yuansong Qiao, and Gabriel-Miro Muntean. 2016. Olfaction-Enhanced Multimedia: A Survey of Application Domains, Displays, and Research Challenges. *ACM Comput. Surv.* 48, 4, Article 56 (May 2016), 34 pages. DOI: http://dx.doi.org/10.1145/2816454

43. Ryohei Nagao, Keigo Matsumoto, Takuji Narumi, Tomohiro Tanikawa, and Michitaka Hirose. 2017. Infinite stairs: simulating stairs in virtual reality based on visuo-haptic interaction. In *ACM SIGGRAPH 2017 Emerging Technologies* (SIGGRAPH '17). ACM, New York, NY, USA, Article 14, 2 pages. DOI: https://doi.org/10.1145/3084822.3084838

44. Hiromi Nakamura and Homei Miyashita. 2011. Augmented gustation using electricity. In *Proceedings of the 2nd Augmented Human International Conference* (AH '11). ACM, New York, NY, USA, , Article 34 , 2 pages. DOI=http://dx.doi.org/10.1145/1959826.1959860

45. Takuya Nakano, Shota Saji, and Yasuyuki Yanagida. 2012. Indicating wind direction using a fan-based wind display. In *Proceedings of the 2012 international conference on Haptics: perception, devices, mobility, and communication - Volume Part II* (EuroHaptics'12), Poika Isokoski and Jukka Springare (Eds.), Vol. Part II. Springer-Verlag, Berlin, Heidelberg, 97-102. DOI=http://dx.doi.org/10.1007/978-3-642-31404-9_17

46. Takuji Narumi. 2016. Multi-sensorial virtual reality and augmented human food interaction. In *Proceedings of the 1st Workshop on Multi-sensorial Approaches to Human-Food Interaction* (MHFI '16), Anton Nijholt, Carlos Velasco, Gijs Huisman, and Kasun Karunanayaka (Eds.). ACM, New York, NY, USA, Article , 6 pages. DOI: https://doi.org/10.1145/3007577.3007587

47. Takuji Narumi, Shinya Nishizaka, Takashi Kajinami, Tomohiro Tanikawa, and Michitaka Hirose. 2011. Augmented reality flavors: gustatory display based on edible marker and cross-modal interaction. In *Proceedings of the SIGCHI Conference on Human Factors in Computing Systems*(CHI '11). ACM, New York, NY, USA, 93-102. DOI: https://doi.org/10.1145/1978942.1978957

48. Neo Sensory. 2017. Retrieved from: http://neosensory.com/

49. Don Norman. 2013 The design of everyday things: Revised and expanded edition, New York City, NY: Basic Books.

50. Daniela Petrelli, Alessandro Soranzo, Luigina Ciolfi, and John Reidy. 2016. Exploring the Aesthetics of Tangible Interaction: Experiments on the Perception of Hybrid Objects. In Proceedings of the TEI '16: Tenth International Conference on Tangible, Embedded, and Embodied Interaction (TEI '16). ACM, New York, NY, USA, 100-108. DOI: https://doi.org/10.1145/2839462.2839478

51. Punchdrunk. 2017. *Sleep No More.* Retrieved from: https://www.punchdrunk.org.uk/sleep-no-more/

52. ProjectiCan. 2017. Retrieved from: https://project-ican.com/

53. Nimesha Ranasinghe, Pravar Jain, Shienny Karwita, David Tolley, and Ellen Yi-Luen Do. 2017. Ambiotherm: Enhancing Sense of Presence in Virtual Reality by Simulating Real-World Environmental Conditions. In *Proceedings of the 2017 CHI Conference on Human Factors in Computing Systems* (CHI '17). ACM, New York, NY, USA, 1731-1742. DOI: https://doi.org/10.1145/3025453.3025723

54. Nimesha Ranasinghe and Ellen Yi-Luen Do. 2016. Digital Lollipop: Studying Electrical Stimulation on the Human Tongue to Simulate Taste Sensations. *ACM Trans. Multimedia Comput. Commun. Appl.* 13, 1, Article 5 (October 2016), 22 pages. DOI: https://doi.org/10.1145/2996462

55. Michael Rietzler, Katrin Plaumann, Taras Kränzle, Marcel Erath, Alexander Stahl, and Enrico Rukzio. 2017. VaiR: Simulating 3D Airflows in Virtual Reality. In *Proceedings of the 2017 CHI Conference on Human Factors in Computing Systems* (CHI '17). ACM, New York, NY, USA, 5669-5677. DOI: https://doi.org/10.1145/3025453.3026009

56. Dominik Schmidt, Rob Kovacs, Vikram Mehta, Udayan Umapathi, Sven Köhler, Lung-Pan Cheng, and Patrick Baudisch. 2015. Level-Ups: Motorized Stilts that Simulate Stair Steps in Virtual Reality. In

Proceedings of the 33rd Annual ACM Conference on Human Factors in Computing Systems (CHI '15). ACM, New York, NY, USA, 2157-2160. DOI: https://doi.org/10.1145/2702123.2702253

57. Dominik Schmidt, Raf Ramakers, Esben W. Pedersen, Johannes Jasper, Sven Köhler, Aileen Pohl, Hannes Rantzsch, Andreas Rau, Patrick Schmidt, Christoph Sterz, Yanina Yurchenko, and Patrick Baudisch. 2014. Kickables: tangibles for feet. In *Proceedings of the SIGCHI Conference on Human Factors in Computing Systems* (CHI '14). ACM, New York, NY, USA, 3143-3152. DOI=http://dx.doi.org/10.1145/2556288.2557016
58. Samuel B. Schorr and Allison M. Okamura. 2017. Fingertip Tactile Devices for Virtual Object Manipulation and Exploration. In *Proceedings of the 2017 CHI Conference on Human Factors in Computing Systems* (CHI '17). ACM, New York, NY, USA, 3115-3119. DOI: https://doi.org/10.1145/3025453.3025744
59. Six Flags. 2017. *Galactic Attack.* https://www.sixflags.com/overtexas/newsroom/galactic-attack-vr-coaster
60. Mel Slater. 1999. Measuring Presence: A Response to the Witmer and Singer Presence Questionnaire. *Presence: Teleoper. Virtual Environ.* 8, 5 (October 1999), 560-565. DOI=http://dx.doi.org/10.1162/105474699566477
61. Dorothé Smit, Doenja Oogjes, Bruna Goveia de Rocha, Ambra Trotto, Yeup Hur, and Caroline Hummels. 2016. Ideating in Skills: Developing Tools for Embodied Co-Design. In *Proceedings of the TEI '16: Tenth International Conference on Tangible, Embedded, and Embodied Interaction* (TEI '16). ACM, New York, NY, USA, 78-85. DOI: https://doi.org/10.1145/2839462.2839497
62. Charles Spence, Marianna Obrist, Carlos Velasco, and Nimesha Ranasinghe. 2017. Digitizing the chemical senses: possibilities & pitfalls. *International Journal of Human-Computer Studies* (2017), 1071-5819. DOI:http://dx.doi.org/https://doi.org/10.1016/j.ijhcs.2017.06.003
63. Misha Sra, and Chris Schmandt. 2015. MetaSpace II: Object and Full-body Tracking for Interaction and Navigation in Social VR. arXiv preprint arXiv:1512.02922. DOI: http://dx.doi.org/10.1145/2815585.2817802
64. Evan A. Suma, Mahdi Azmandian, Timofey Grechkin, Thai Phan, and Mark Bolas. 2015. Making small spaces feel large: infinite walking in virtual reality. In *ACM SIGGRAPH 2015 Emerging Technologies* (SIGGRAPH '15). ACM, New York, NY, USA, Article 16, 1 pages. DOI: https://doi.org/10.1145/2782782.2792496
65. Paul Tennent, Joe Marshall, Brendan Walker, Patrick Brundell, and Steve Benford. 2017. The Challenges of Visual-Kinaesthetic Experience. In Proceedings of the 2017 Conference on Designing Interactive Systems (DIS '17). ACM, New York, NY, USA, 1265-1276. DOI: https://doi.org/10.1145/3064663.3064763
66. Vaqso. 2017. Retrieved from: https://vaqso.com/
67. Eduardo Velloso, Dominik Schmidt, Jason Alexander, Hans Gellersen, and Andreas Bulling. 2015. The Feet in Human--Computer Interaction: A Survey of Foot-Based Interaction. *ACM Comput. Surv.* 48, 2, Article 21 (September 2015), 35 pages. DOI=http://dx.doi.org/10.1145/2816455
68. Virtuix. 2017. Retrieved from: http://www.virtuix.com/
69. VIRZOOM. 2017. Retrieved from: https://www.virzoom.com/
70. ViveNChill. 2017. Retrieved from: https://www.indiegogo.com/projects/vivenchill-vr#/
71. The Void. 2017. Retrieved from: https://www.thevoid.com/
72. VR Go. 2017. Retrieved from: http://www.vrgochair.com/
73. VR Studios. 2017. *VRCade.* Retrieved from: https://www.vrstudios.com/vrcade/
74. VR Zone. 2017. Retrieved from: https://vrzone-pic.com/en/
75. Sarah Wiseman, Janet van der Linden, Ad Spiers, and Maria Oshodi. 2017. Control and Being Controlled: Exploring the use of Technology in an Immersive Theatre Performance. In *Proceedings of the 2017 Conference on Designing Interactive Systems (DIS '17).* ACM, New York, NY, USA, 3-14. DOI: https://doi.org/10.1145/3064663.3064694
76. Bob G. Witmer and Michael J. Singer. 1998. Measuring Presence in Virtual Environments: A Presence Questionnaire. *Presence: Teleoper. Virtual Environ.* 7, 3 (June 1998), 225-240. DOI=http://dx.doi.org/10.1162/105474698565686
77. Masasuke Yasumoto and Takehiro Teraoka. 2015. Shadow Shooter. In *Proceedings of the 2015 Virtual Reality International Conference* (VRIC '15). ACM, New York, NY, USA, Article 17, 2 pages. DOI: https://doi.org/10.1145/2806173.2806193.
78. Andre Zenner and Antonio Kruger. 2017. Shifty: A Weight-Shifting Dynamic Passive Haptic Proxy to Enhance Object Perception in Virtual Reality. *IEEE Transactions on Visualization and Computer Graphics* 23, 4 (April 2017), 1285-1294. DOI: https://doi.org/10.1109/TVCG.2017.2656978.

"You Better Eat to Survive": Exploring Cooperative Eating in Virtual Reality Games

Peter Arnold
Exertion Games Lab
RMIT University, Australia
peter@exertiongameslab.com

Rohit Ashok Khot
Exertion Games Lab
RMIT University, Australia
rohit@exertiongameslab.com

Florian 'Floyd' Mueller
Exertion Games Lab
RMIT University, Australia
floyd@exertiongameslab.com

ABSTRACT
"You Better Eat to Survive" is a two-player virtual reality game that involves eating real food to survive and ultimately escape from a virtual island. We sense eating actions of players by analyzing chewing sounds captured by a low-cost microphone attached to the players' cheek. Our interest in using cooperative eating as a way of interacting in virtual reality is driven by the possibilities of creating a cross-modal gameplay experience that benefits social interactions. A user study with 22 players showed that eating real food improved players' feeling of presence, challenged trust dependencies and made the survival aspect of the game feel more *"real"*. We use these insights to articulate three design themes that can guide designers in creating virtual reality games that incorporate cooperative eating. Ultimately, our work aims to guide design thinking towards using underexplored interaction methods in virtual reality games, thereby reiterating the *post-digital design* theme of TEI 2018.

Author Keywords
Virtual reality games; Cooperative Eating; FoodCHI; Human-Food Interaction (HFI); Multisensory Games.

Categories and Subject Descriptors
• Human-centered computing~Virtual reality • Human-centered computing~Collaborative interaction • Human-centered computing~Interaction techniques • Software and its engineering~Interactive games

INTRODUCTION
Virtual Reality (VR) games are increasingly becoming popular [31] and companies like Google, Facebook and Oculus are building platforms and hardware to support the development of VR games. In most VR games, software technology is used to build replicas of the real world through simulations and such experiences are visualized using head-mounted displays (HMDs) [51]. Although VR games can offer an immersive and exciting new way of gaming, interaction options within VR games are still limited [31]. Since commonly used game controllers do not offer an easy and convenient way of interaction in VR, researchers are looking into other ways to interact in a VR environment [13,18,40]. The majority of these works investigate visual and auditory interfaces for interactions in VR [13,40], whereas gustatory and olfactory interfaces have been underexplored, even though studies suggest that supporting the associated senses would benefit VR in facilitating richer gameplay experiences [20,42].

In this work we investigate the use of a gustatory interface, in particular the chewing of food, to control actions in VR games. Eating can offer a rich multisensory social experience [24] that so far has rarely been used in a VR gaming context. Our work also aims to address the feeling of social disconnect in VR environments through cooperative eating, which could add excitement [50] and the feeling of social presence [3] to the VR experience. Drawing on this, we designed and studied *You Better Eat to Survive,* a two-player VR game in which a player has to chew real food (fed by the other player) to survive and ultimately escape from a virtual island (see Figure 1). We detect chewing by analyzing the chewing sounds captured by a low-cost microphone attached to the player's cheek.

TEI '18, March 18–21, 2018, Stockholm, Sweden

ACM ISBN 978-1-4503-5568-1/18/03…$15.00
https://doi.org/10.1145/3173225.3173238

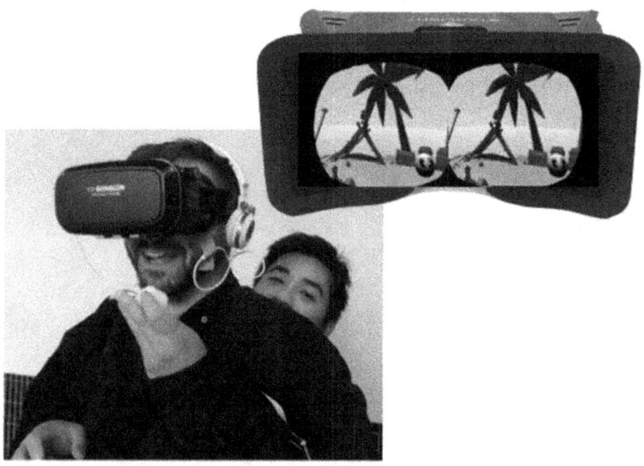

Figure 1. In *You Better Eat to Survive,* the non-VR player feeds the VR player from behind to survive on a virtual island

We conducted a study with 22 players to understand the user experience of playing *You Better Eat to Survive*. The study findings highlight that eating real food increased players' feeling of presence, challenged trust dependencies and made the survival aspect of the game feel more *"real"*.

Our work makes the following contributions: 1) By presenting *You Better Eat to Survive*, we introduce the opportunity of combining food with virtual reality for an engaging cross-modal gameplay experience that transforms the loss of a sense (i.e. not seeing the food) into an exciting game element. 2) We contribute a first conceptual understanding of the interrelationship between VR and cooperative eating by presenting a descriptive account on the design and user experience of the *You Better Eat to Survive* game. 3) We articulate three design themes to help designers in creating engaging VR games that incorporate eating as a control mechanism.

RELATED WORK

While we use all our bodily senses in everyday life, when it comes to technology design, *"we mostly rely on vision and audition, increasingly harnessing touch, whilst taste and smell remain largely underexploited"* [38]. According to LaValle [31], visual and auditory interfaces become popular in VR because the underlying organs are close to each other in a human body, they are easy to combine with low-cost head tracking and the digitization of audio and sound might be easier as they are measured in frequency [38,48]. Interestingly, Gallace et al. [20] point out advantages of increasing the number of senses stimulated in VR to increase enjoyment, memorability and sense of presence, drawing onto the unique qualities of the gustatory and the olfactory senses, such as inducing positive mood [53] and contributing to long lasting memory [15]. In particular, within the field of *Human-Food Interaction (HFI)* [37] there have been numerous works that explore the relationship between technology and the gustatory as well as the olfactory sense [8,34,38].

Human-Food Interaction

Many works within HFI have focused on altering food perception to improve the consumption experience. For example, Ranasinghe et al. [43] developed the *Spoon+* and *Bottle+* prototypes that can be used to virtually manipulate the taste of food or drinks and may help to replace possibly harmful artificial flavorings. A similar approach to alter the gustation sense was done by Narumi et al. [36] through *MetaCookie+* that uses augmented reality and smells to overlay a cookie with visual and olfactory information thereby changing the perceived taste of the cookie. *Project Nourished* artificially stimulates all senses to offer eating experiences without caloric intake [41].

Playful interactions with food

HFI works also looked into utilizing existing foods to offer playful new experiences [34]. Maynes introduced *Edible User Interfaces* [33] through a system called *TasteScreen*, where users interact with a system by licking liquid residue of different flavors that dripped onto the LCD screen. Khot et al. explored the use of food as a celebratory technology [24] through mixing sports drinks [28] and printing motivational slogans and smileys in chocolate [27] based on an individual's physical activity data. Murer et al. [35] created a haptic input device, *LOLLio* (lollipop) that dynamically changes its flavors thereby offering playful experiences around taste. Not using food but related through its focus on input through the mouth is the work by Tennent et al. [49]. The authors developed a gas mask that utilized the player's breathing as a game mechanic for a computer game where the players had to control their breath at certain points to progress in the game. These works demonstrate that games can benefit from allowing an additional bodily action to be sensed in order to control gameplay and led us to the idea of utilizing eating as a technique to interact with a VR game.

Rationale: Why combine cooperative eating with VR?

Food is not just a source of energy it is also a medium that defines our social and cultural identity [17]. The processes of cooking and eating food together offer opportunities for social bonding [19] and intergenerational play [16] while also supporting a rich multisensory experience. French gastronome Brillat-Savarin [10] notes that pleasures associated with eating and drinking constitute some of the life's most enjoyable experiences. Grevet et al. further highlight the social benefits of commensal mealtimes and their ability to support connectedness [23]. To the best of our understanding, the games research field has yet to explore these benefits particularly in a VR gaming context, which motivated us to do this work. In particular, we were motivated to research the following two opportunities:

1. Utilizing loss of vision in VR as a positive game element

Combining VR running on HMDs and eating leads to the condition that people would not see what they are eating. While this might seem problematic at first glance, our interest is to explore this as an advantage for novel gameplay. Several restaurants are already using VR and the absence of vision of the food to create novel dining experiences [46]. Drawing on this, we explore the design of a VR game that explores eating without seeing what we eat.

2. Bridging VR and the real world through cooperative eating

Wetzel et al. [50] found that adding a social element in a mixed reality environment could enable the sharing of thoughts about the game and thus could prevent players from feeling lonely or disconnected from the real environment. Eating food is an activity that most people enjoy doing with others [39], feeding food to each other is also quite common. However, in most cases, the people who dine together are part of or viewing the same world. We wondered what if the diners view different worlds? For example, one of them is exploring a VR world and the other one is viewing the real world. Drawing on this, we are motivated to create a VR experience that uses the act of feeding to build a bridge between the virtual and the real world [6].

DESIGN PROCESS

You Better Eat to Survive was the result of many explorations, extensive prototyping and iterative game development spanning over half a year. We conducted brainstorming sessions and focus group discussions with members of the research lab to gather diverse insights on how to detect eating behavior, how to relate food to VR and how to inform design decisions on the gameplay.

1) Choosing the VR technology

Our aim was to develop a low-cost VR game to allow a broad audience to experience it. To achieve this, we used mobile virtual reality, i.e. a smartphone paired with a HMD as a gaming device. We further used the Google VR SDK along with Unity 3D to develop our game [22].

2) Detecting eating

In games such as *Minecraft* [52], simulation of eating is used to regain health of the game character. However, our aim was to capture and use a real eating behavior. At first, we considered augmenting kitchen utensils with thermal or sound sensors, similar to the *Context-Aware Kitchen Utilities* [30]. We further developed a prototype of a food detection system that distinguishes between different kinds of food based on electricity flow and then putting these foods on weight measuring scales with an assumption that removing food items from the plate means they are being eaten. However, these approaches did not give consistent results. We therefore looked into capturing a particular eating behavior directly: *chewing*.

Several approaches exist in the literature to sense chewing. For example, Zhang et al. [54] used glasses with integrated skull vibration sensors to sense vibrations caused by chewing. Another approach was developed by Amft et al. [1] who designed earpad sensors measuring air-conducted vibrations to sense chewing. While these approaches can offer more accurate detection of chewing actions, they need costly and sophisticated devices that may not easily integrate well into a mobile gaming scenario. To address this, we came up with the approach of using sound to sense chewing. We attached a microphone to the players' cheek (Figure 2) and measured the variation in sounds during a chewing and non-chewing action to interpret if the person is eating or not.

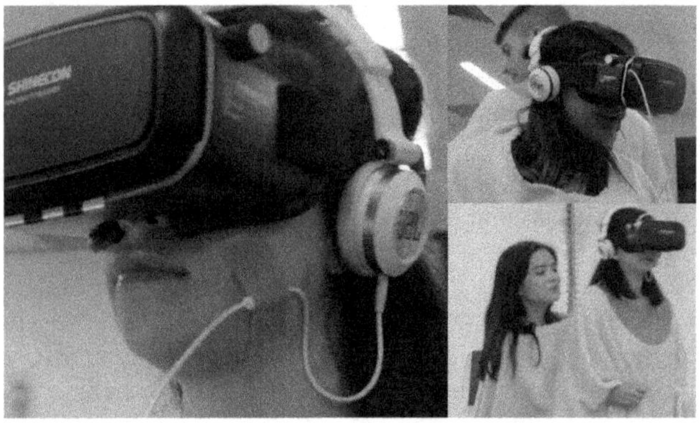

Figure 2. The game setup for *You Better Eat to Survive*

The microphone captures the audio from the player's cheek to generate a loudness variable. When the loudness variable exceeds a certain threshold it means the player just chewed on something thereby starting the chewing mechanism and the action is counted as one chewing action. When the loudness variable afterwards drops under another threshold and a certain time passed since the chewing began, the chewing process is finished and the program is ready to capture the next chewing action.

3) Relating eating to VR

After deciding on the VR technology and eating actions, we focused our attention on the mapping between the two. After reviewing the literature, we found that there could be three ways in which food and VR can be combined.

Same food in VR and reality

The first approach presents the same food in VR that people consume in reality. The purpose of VR in this case is to augment the food by altering other senses such as the visuals or the smell to have an effect on the perceived taste of the food. One example of this approach is *MetaCookie+*, which alters the smell and appearance of food through augmented reality [36]. Similarly, Ganesh et al. [21] developed a system to augment the plate of children's meals by digitally projecting sad smileys on the plates when healthy food was avoided.

Different food in VR and reality

The second approach is to use different foods (or its representations) in VR and reality. An example of this approach is *Project Nourished*, a multisensory VR system that plays with people's perception by displaying appetizing high calorie food in VR but actually allowing them to consume 3D printed low calorie food [41]. Although the confusion caused by the difference of the food can be an interesting gameplay element, we decided to go with the third approach that shows no food in VR.

No food in VR but food in reality

In this work, we went with not displaying any food in VR but still requiring people to eat food in reality. We find the lack of vision of the food quite intriguing to support new eating experiences as explored in VR restaurants [46]. This approach goes well with the cooperative eating and survival theme of the proposed game, which we describe in the next section.

4) Deciding on the gameplay

The final decision was to identify the right gameplay that connects eating behavior with a VR game. To help us in gaining this understanding, we conducted a two-hour long brainstorming session with 7 participants (3 female, age 23-38) from a research lab with diverse academic backgrounds. In the session we asked the participants to playtest two single player games that demonstrate early concepts of the gameplay. The first game utilized eating as interaction to break down game obstacles in a maze style game. The other game was a 3D platform game in which players could restore health by looking at health icons and simultaneously eat real food. We further discussed how to enrich the gameplay.

Participants enjoyed playing these games and found eating based interaction novel and exciting. The use of a microphone to detect chewing was not considered uncomfortable or obstructive while playing. However most of the participants felt that the games could utilize more social interactions or some way to connect players with the audience. Some participants stated they felt awkward playing while the others are just watching them not knowing what is happening in the game. This led to the decision to make the game a two-player game that utilizes cooperative eating as an interaction technique within a VR game. Participants also mentioned the contrast between eating and gaming where one can play games for hours but cannot eat for the whole duration. Furthermore, the concept of satiety (i.e. feeling full) after the consumption of food was also debated. The discussion further brought up the topics of using a natural environment as opposed to abstract worlds, and identifying a strong link between the VR world and the eating. These topics guided us in the development of our game. *You Better Eat to Survive* is a multiplayer game that takes advantage of cross-modal gameplay, having two players, one inside VR and the other outside in the real world. Finally, we went with fruit based snacks instead of heavy foods to allow for longer duration of play without feeling full. We explain the gameplay next.

YOU BETTER EAT TO SURVIVE

You Better Eat to Survive is a two player VR game. In this game, one player puts on the VR headset and tries to find a way to call for help after being stranded on a virtual island. This game uses the narrative of a survival adventure game, where the main character has not eaten for days and he/she is on the brink of passing out, thereby constantly losing his/her vision in the game. We refer to the loss of vision as blackout phases and represent them using a steadily shrinking view (Figure 3). The blackout phases are activated throughout the game. The objective of the VR game is to move around the island and find and use different objects via gaze interaction that ultimately lead to a flare gun that is hidden on the island. Once found, the player fires it to call for help and wins the game. Once a blackout phase starts the only way to regain vision in the game is by eating.

Figure 3. Transition of vision during a blackout phase

We use auditory feedback (digital chewing noises) and visual feedback (virtual crumbs falling down) to visually portray the chewing activity in the game. With every chew, the player's view gets increasingly restored until he/she has full vision again. When the vision is restored fully the microphone is deactivated until the next blackout phase to avoid accidental triggering of the microphone through players' chatting. In case not enough food was eaten or there is no food left, the player dies and loses the game.

A major problem for the VR player is that he/she does not see the food because he/she is wearing the HMD (Figure 1). The food is prepared and rationed on three tables set up in a triangle around the players resembling the playing field. The job of the second player is to lead the VR player around the playing field and both guide him/her to the food and then feed him/her. This creates an intriguing game setup of two players playing the same game but one in the virtual and one in the real world. This setting is enforced by requiring the players to play as one *"shared body across both worlds"* that combines the abilities of the two players: the VR player cannot see the real world or the food but sees the virtual world, while the real world player does not see the virtual world but sees the food and is able to interact with it. In order to win the players need to cooperate: While the VR player tries to discover a way to get help in the game the real world player is in charge of feeding his/her companion to prevent him/her from losing vision in the game. Physically, the players resemble one body because the real world player embraces the VR player from behind and uses his/her own hands as it would be the VR player's hands to feed him/her while the VR player is not allowed to use his/her hands (Figure 1). This confronts the players with the challenge of collaboration and working as a team. To this end, our game aims to facilitate a rich social experience that promotes teamwork. Our game was showcased to a large number of people in the course of the student game competition at CHI 2017 in Denver and won in the category *Innovative Interfaces* [2].

USER STUDY

We conducted a study with 22 participants (9 male, 13 female) to gather insights on the user experience of playing our game. The participants' ages ranged from 18-34 years with an average age of 26 and a standard deviation of 5.

Participants played the game in pairs of two. Each session involved two participants playing the game twice, once as a VR player and once as a feeder. Prior to each session we prepared fresh food and we cleaned and disinfected the HMD and microphone that come in contact with human skin. The participants then received an oral introduction to the game and were asked to choose either the role of the VR player or the role of the feeder and alternating afterwards. The playing session ended when players finished the game or when the food ran out and the participants thereby lost. If the VR player died before the food ran out because the feeder did not manage to feed the food on time, we allowed them to restart the game and try again. At the end of the study, we asked the participants to fill out the game experience questionnaire (GEQ) [26] and partake in a semi-structured interview that lasted for about 20 minutes.

FINDINGS

We now describe the study findings collected from the three sources of data: 1) video analysis of the gameplay 2) GEQ questionnaire 3) post-study semi-structured interviews.

Video Analysis of Gameplay

To gain insights about player behavior we video recorded all gameplay sessions. This helped us to discover behavioral patterns as described below.

Effective food management

In *You Better Eat to Survive,* the only way to regain vision during blackout phases was to eat real food, which made food an important resource that had to be managed well. Since the food was laid out on a table before the actual game started, both players knew how much food was available to eat. Since the number of blackout phases and their occurrences within the game was unknown, the participants needed to be skilful in determining how much food to eat and how much food to keep for next the blackout phase. Our participants came up with interesting strategies to use the food efficiently: Six players chew food really slowly and stopped when the vision was restored. Four participants continued mimicking the chewing actions even when the food was almost gone in their mouth. Three other participants asked their partners to keep some food pieces ready in their hands as preparation for the next blackout phase.

Winning strategies

We also found that participants were willing to cheat or *"act smartly"* in the game in order to win. In total three different core strategies were observed: one method often used was to illicitly pick food from the same table two or more times before moving to the next table thereby saving precious time to explore the island further. Some VR players cheated and used their own hands to grab and eat the food to save time putting it in their mouth. Lastly, after realizing that chewing is captured via sounds, several participants mimicked the chewing without having any food in their mouth (i.e. by clicking their teeth) in a fashion that would be falsely detected as eating. An interesting fact that came out of the analysis was that the VR players started most forms of cheating. One explanation could be given that the high immersion in the VR game unknowingly prompted the participants to cheat in the game because they forgot that we were observing them.

GEQ Data

We used the GEQ questionnaire [26] to provide us with numerical data about perceived game experiences to supplement the qualitative data from interviews and the video analysis of the observed gameplay. This questionnaire has four different modules: the core module, in-game module, post-game module and social presence. By asking module specific questions, each module provided us with numerical data (on a scale from 1 to 5) about the general game, in-game, post-game and social experiences, which we utilized to understand players' experience of the game [11].

In the core module, the five positive components: *competence, flow, immersion, challenge* and *positive affect* received high ratings (2.67 – 3.95) while the negative components: *tension* and *negative affect* got a 1.50 and 1.23 rating. The post-game module revealed that participants rated the experience as more positive (2.67) than negative (1.97) and inflicted hardly any tiredness (1.27). The results of the social presence module showed high behavioral involvement (3.57) and a psychological involvement with an empathy character (3.20) rather than negative feelings (1.97).

The GEQ results demonstrate that *You Better Eat to Survive* was perceived as a positive game experience that offers behavioral involvement, high immersion and good flow without annoying or tiring the participants. This finding is supported by the qualitative data gathered from the interviews, which we detail next.

Analysis of Interviews

The semi-structured interviews were transcribed using NVIVO [4] with footage coded and transcribed following thematic analysis [9]. Each question asked by the interviewer and the associated answers represented one unit of data generating 199 data units in total. We read and reread all units several times to create a codebook. These codes helped to identify the most interesting features of the data unit to help grouping them together afterwards. In the first iteration of this phase of the thematic analysis we developed 50 codes, for example *"Understanding game mechanics"* or *"Auditory eating feedback"*. In a second iteration we discussed the 50 codes and re-examined them to merge similar codes into broader codes to reduce the complexity. Through this process we decreased the number of codes to 17. Those remaining codes were again re-examined, refined and categorized into groups with the help of two senior researchers. The final outcome of these analytic and evaluative processes is a set of three overarching themes, which we present below.

T1: Using eating to promote feeling of presence in VR

This theme describes how the eating interaction influenced the feeling of presence. There are two aspects to it: Improved feeling of presence through eating and preference of bodily actions.

Improved feeling of presence through eating

The participants felt that eating strengthened their feeling of presence in the game. Participants enjoyed the fact that eating and gameplay are not separated but interlinked as P12 said in the interview, *"using one of your senses, chewing, to do something in a game, definitely feels more immersive."* P15 similarly said, *"Best bit was how doing things affected the game. Normally when you are playing a game and you sit on the couch and you eat food nothing happens. But when you are playing this game, your eating directly impacts the game it's decidedly odd but in a good way of course."* Participants also appreciated the use of the survival narrative making it a struggle to find the food and eating real food gave them an extra element to connect with the world outside of VR bridging the gap between VR and the external world. As P19 mentioned, *"I was not sort of sealed away in the avatar world, I was still very much part of the real world (through eating)"*. Participants also enjoyed the connection between real world actions of chewing food with a virtual world reaction of regaining vision. For instance, P7 mentioned, *"it was satisfying to hear the crunch sound in your mouth and then your vision repairing in VR as a result of it, it snaps you back to the real world."*

Preference of bodily actions

Although participants liked how eating allowed them to regain energy in a game, they felt that interaction with virtual objects in the game could be further improved. In particular, they found it challenging that they cannot use their body as you would normally use it in the real world. For example P4 disliked the gaze-based interaction with objects: *"Interacting with an object just by looking at it felt a bit weird. I was hoping that I could interact with the objects with my hands. I don't know how that would be done, but may be through external body tracking methods."* P3 also thought that a movement sensor that can track hand movements would be ideal in this scenario. She added, *"It would be cool if there would be a cable going to your hand and capturing your hand movements on screen."* Three participants also suggested integrating walking directly in the game. P14 said *"Yes I would prefer if it was moving in the game so you move sort of yourself. Being able to go everywhere instead of the three different places. And maybe go in the water as well, that would be nice."*

Implications for design

While the two words immersion and presence are often used interchangeably, Slater [47] defines immersion as the objective level of sensory fidelity provided by a VR system and presence refers to the user's subjective response to a VR system. In other words, presence is a personal feeling of *"being there"* that can vary from person to person. Earlier research found that utilizing bodily interactions such as walking within VR helps in creating presence [29,45]. So far, most of the research on bodily interactions in VR is happening around transforming bodily interactions such as gestures [44] or walking [45] in the virtual world to increase presence in VR.

In our study, participants also expressed their wish to use their legs to move around or their arms to interact with objects in the game because using their own body, as they did while eating increased their feeling of presence. Drawing on this, designers could consider implementing traditional bodily interactions, such as hand gestures, to support the feeling of presence. However, as pointed out by Cummings et al. [14], designers would then need to think of the trade-off between the desired level of presence and the associated costs. Besides any monetary expenditure, any high end tracking system would also make the system more complex and cumbersome for users [7,14]. Drawing on these implications, designers can think of using low cost tracking techniques to capture bodily actions such as eating and support the feeling of presence through an engaging game narrative.

T2: Building trust by creating dependencies around cooperative eating activities

This design theme describes the interplay of trust and cooperative eating activities and how it contributed to social engagement among players. The game setup of *You Better Eat to Survive* has one person not seeing what happens in the virtual world and the other person not seeing what happens in the real world. This automatically creates an environment in which players have to depend on each other to stay alive in the game. For the participants, the aspect of feeding was challenging at first, but it also resulted in an enjoyable trust exercise. P21 reflected: *"Having another person feed you with their hands was funny. Something I haven't experienced before."*

Having a partner in the game offered comfort

Participants appreciated the fact that they got to play the game with another person, even though they engaged in different worlds. Having another person allowed the VR players to feel more comfortable and less isolated to explore the island and complete the required goals. P21 added, *"The connection with the real world was really good. It really elevated the game."* Similarly, P15 said, *"I am glad that it is not just like another game where you are isolated in the virtual world."* Participant P22 had a similar experience: *"So when I was going blind in any situation whether you know it is virtual or if it's real it's still scary and there is still a moment of anxiety. So having someone there calms you down immediately and I think that is really helpful and it also drives you to finish the game and you want to do it for the team not just for yourself."*

Eating interaction helped to build trust

The success in the game depended on the proper synchronizations of eating between the two players as P6 said, *"your partner is your eyes to the outside world, helping you survive in the virtual world."* In the beginning, it was frustrating for the players to know that they do not share the same world and do not have the same audio-visual cues. As a result, effective communication became a critical element. For P18, this activity however challenged his trust with the other player: *"It is a real big trust exercise letting somebody guide you and you are basically blind to things you are going to eat. You also have to be really good in communication with somebody else to tell them when to feed and how much."* Participant P22 also agreed that the survival in the game heavily depended on getting fed at the right moment. She said, *"You must completely put your trust into another person and hope the person behaves in the right way. But it is also a really cool feeling when things work out."*

Coordination of food led to bonding between players

P18 reflected that through the dependencies created by the feeding act, she bonded with her partner while playing: *"So there was a lot of partner work involved which was good because that sort of creates a bonding effect which is really cool. I found it helped me to get to know a stranger much quicker. Even though you are not talking about personal things, you feel like you're bonding because you are helping each other in a situation where you have to communicate and help the other person to survive."*

Implications for design

The study findings reveal that the coordination of feeding and eating activity allowed players to connect even if they were in different worlds (in and outside of VR). Even though eating in the real world might seem to be disadvantageous for the feeling of presence we found that the participants did not feel a break in immersion but rather an increase in immersion through the eating. This might be due to the fast paced nature of the game and the immersive survival theme of the game. We encourage longitudinal in-depth studies on this topic to unfold the correlation between the feeling of presence and eating.

We also found that the food served as a bridge between the two worlds and encouraged a cooperative play experience that values trust. Since 16 of the 22 participants knew each other beforehand, it was easier for them to trust each other on food-related decisions in the game. The situation could be different if the game is played between strangers and could have challenged the trust and dependencies between players. However, as identified in the study, the game narrative and mutual interest of succeeding in the game encouraged players to trust each other right away. Participants also felt rewarded when cooperation led to positive outcomes (i.e., regaining of vision) within the game. Drawing on this, when creating VR experiences that utilize eating as an interaction, designers should consider utilizing the benefits of cross-modal gameplay and having several people playing together even if they are not sharing the same VR game world.

So far, the majority of VR games found in the app stores today are played alone. Research happening around VR and food is also focussed on an individual's food consumption and dining patterns (for examples, see [36,41,46]) while, despite the rich social history of eating, the social aspect of cooperative eating seems underexplored. Eating and feeding interaction as explored in this work could offer possibilities to interact and bond with other people over engaging cross-modal social VR experiences that challenge their trust but also afford moments of comfort through cooperation and coordination.

T3: Encouraging uncomfortable interactions around loss of vision in VR

This theme describes the effects of losing the vision within the game and how cross-modal gameplay helped participants to overcome the challenges of the limited vision.

Losing the vision led to improved focus

In our game, the VR player was constantly on the brink of losing vision in the game. This, at first, caused discomfort among players but also allowed the participants to be more reflective and determined about how they should proceed in the game. P22 mentioned, *"Slowly your vision, from the outside in, starts to be destroyed. Beginning with your peripheral and then moving into your direct line of sight. It was more like an emptiness that came towards me and it snapped me back into the thought of the real world. Since you are losing what you are seeing in front of you, it pushes you to think hard on how you can get back into the game and what you should do to fix this."*

The unpredictability of losing vision caused discomfort but in a good way

Participants found the gameplay challenging and a test of their skills. On the one hand, the act of losing vision caused some anxiety but on the other hand the recovery through eating also resulted in joy and relief. P6 reflected on how the game caused a variety of feelings by saying, *"I had frustration, happiness when the scene lights up again and you get to see the island. You also become excited when you grab objects and complete the required missions. But panic also kicks in when the blackout phase starts. You will then constantly be thinking: 'Am I going to survive? Will the other players be able to feed me at the right time?' So you are excited but you also fear, fear for the things that are not in your control."* P22 described similar changes in emotions during the game. She said, *"So the game starts off and you are all curious to explore the island. But then the anxiety kicks in with the blackout phase and you feel the pumping of your heart."* Most participants however were happy with the discomfort and the sudden rush in adrenalin as P3 described, *"I guess it is a good kind of anxiety and adrenalin. You feel like after you been on a ride or done something a bit crazy that you usually wouldn't do. It's like a healthy amount of fear and that can be a deliberating good feeling."*

Reduced real world cues posed additional challenges

The participants found it difficult to navigate without seeing their surroundings to reach the food but they trusted the non-VR players to guide them in right direction. P13 described her experience: *"I felt strange because I know you had to walk for the food so I was ready to walk but I don't know maybe you should let the other person guide you or you walk on your own. But I think I learned it quite quickly to move with the other person because obviously you don't know which way the food is."* Participant P11 found the time criticality of walking and eating quite exciting. He mentioned: *"I like the time pressure element of it: 'Oh okay I need to go but oh crap! I have to eat!' That added an extra level of excitement."*

Loss of vision led to perceived feeling of real hunger

During the gameplay, the sight of the food was never visible for the VR players but they knew that during the blackout phase they would be getting some food to eat. Surprisingly, this anticipation for food even led to a perceived feeling of hunger. P10 said, *"I liked the fact that when my eyes getting closed it actually made me feel hungry. It made me hunt for food."*

Implications for design

Using the loss of vision as a game element, as explored in our game, lends itself to earlier works around creating *"uncomfortable interactions"* [5,32]. Traditionally uncomfortable feelings, such as apprehension, are considered *"bad"*. Benford et al. [5] however state that uncomfortable interactions, if carefully applied, can offer benefits for entertainment, enlightenment and social interactions. Following this approach, Brown et al. [12] created *Thaphobos*, a two-player game where one player is *"buried alive"* in a coffin but the coffin acts as the VR gaming environment utilizing discomfort as an enjoyable game element. In another work, Huggard et al. [25] developed a game called *Musical Embrace* where players have to hug a pillow together to control the game, thereby creating uncomfortable interactions that can help to overcome social awkwardness. The study findings support the argument of creating discomfort for positive benefit while interacting in VR environments. Participants did not treat the anxieties of constantly losing the vision within VR and having no vision of the food as negative, rather these aspects were perceived as exciting and crucial parts of the engagement possibly because of the involvement of another player and the consumption of real food. Drawing on this, designers could consider creating an engaging cross-modal narrative that allows players to deal with their anxieties of not having the vision of the food and sensory void by coupling them with another player.

FUTURE WORK

In the next iterations of this work, we aim to work on the following three aspects:

1) Improving detection of chewing.

Although chewing can be captured through sounds as explored in this study, this solution does not work well in loud environments such as public exhibits and game arcades where it would be hard to separate background noise from chewing sound. Moreover, as the chewing is detected through sound, sometimes a simple mimic of a chewing sound rather than the actual chewing is also enough to play the game. To tackle this problem, designers could build systems that utilize noise cancellation to prevent interference through background noise and allow for better detection of chewing. Another option is to use special devices, such as the glasses capturing chewing through muscle movements [54] although this would increase the detection complexity since they require elaborate prototypes.

2) Explore the full design space of eating in VR

As described in our work we implemented cooperative eating to create a novel gaming experience that utilizes the cross-modal gameplay to connect VR players with non-VR player in a playful way, making the focal point of our work cooperative eating in VR games limiting our insights to this subset of eating. To gather more information about the relation between food and VR in a gaming context in general we aim to explore the full design space in the future, including non-cooperative eating experiences and exploring the two approaches that our work did not investigate, namely, showing either the same or different food in VR and in reality. Exploring these two options would help improving our understanding on how eating can influence the other senses while playing a VR game. However, using eating as a game mechanic in VR could lead to players strategically over-eating or remaining hungry in order to win in the game. To avoid this, designers could collaborate with dietitians to sketch out a proper in-game meal plan to restrict over- and under-eating.

CONCLUSION

In this paper, we described the design and study of *You Better Eat to Survive*, a two-player multisensory VR game that offers an underexplored way of interaction - eating - by requiring eating real food to survive and escape from a virtual island. Our aim was to demonstrate that cooperative eating can be an intriguing interaction technique to enrich VR experiences while offering complementary benefits of social interactions around food. Along with the details of the design process, we also described the insights collected from interviews, the questionnaire and the video analysis of gameplay. Through thematic analysis we developed three themes we hope will help designers in creating engaging VR games with cooperative eating as a control mechanism.

To conclude, the technology used to play VR games has been rapidly improved in recent times. The big question is: Can we, as designers, keep up with this swift development and provide VR users with novel interactions that help foster social interactions, provide a high level of presence and utilize the circumstances of HMD gameplay to benefit the experience? As a first step to address this question, we illustrated how eating can be an intriguing interaction technique that enriches VR experiences while offering complementary benefits of social interactions around food. We invite more explorations on cross-modal VR gameplay experiences with eating and provide designers with an initial understanding on how to begin such explorations.

ACKNOWLEDGMENTS

We want to thank all members of the Exertion Games Lab for their participation in our brainstorming and focus group sessions and their viable general feedback.

REFERENCES

1. Oliver Amft, 2010. A wearable earpad sensor for chewing monitoring. In *Sensors, 2010 IEEE*, 222-227.

2. Peter Arnold, 2017. You Better Eat to Survive! Exploring Edible Interactions in a Virtual Reality Game. In *Proceedings of the 2017 CHI Conference Extended Abstracts on Human Factors in Computing Systems* ACM, 206-209.

3. Pollie Barden, Rob Comber, David Green, Daniel Jackson, Cassim Ladha, Tom Bartindale, Nick Bryan-Kinns, Tony Stockman, and Patrick Olivier, 2012. Telematic dinner party: designing for togetherness through play and performance. In *Proceedings of the Proceedings of the Designing Interactive Systems Conference* (Newcastle Upon Tyne, United Kingdom2012), ACM, 2317964, 38-47. DOI= http://dx.doi.org/10.1145/2317956.2317964.

4. Patricia Bazeley and Kristi Jackson, 2013. *Qualitative data analysis with NVivo*. Sage Publications Limited.

5. Steve Benford, Chris Greenhalgh, Gabriella Giannachi, Brendan Walker, Joe Marshall, and Tom Rodden, 2012. Uncomfortable interactions. In *Proceedings of the SIGCHI Conference on Human Factors in Computing Systems*, 2005-2014.

6. Steve Benford, Carsten Magerkurth, and Peter Ljungstrand, 2005. Bridging the physical and digital in pervasive gaming. *Communications of the ACM 48*, 3, 54-57.

7. Doug A. Bowman and Ryan P. Mcmahan, 2007. Virtual reality: how much immersion is enough? *Computer 40*, 7.

8. Marius H. Braun and Adrian D. Cheok, 2015. Using Scent Actuation for Engaging User Experiences. In *Proceedings of the 12th International Conference on Advances in Computer Entertainment Technology* ACM, 54:51-54:53.

9. Virginia Braun and Victoria Clarke, 2006. Using thematic analysis in psychology. *Qualitative research in psychology 3*, 2, 77-101.

10. Jean Anthelme Brillat-Savarin, 2009. *The physiology of taste: or meditations on transcendental gastronomy*. Vintage.

11. Jeanne H. Brockmyer, Christine M. Fox, Kathleen A. Curtiss, Evan Mcbroom, Kimberly M. Burkhart, and Jacquelyn N. Pidruzny, 2009. The development of the Game Engagement Questionnaire: A measure of engagement in video game-playing. *Journal of Experimental Social Psychology 45*, 4, 624-634.

12. James Brown, Kathrin Gerling, Patrick Dickinson, and Ben Kirman, 2015. Dead fun: uncomfortable interactions in a virtual reality game for coffins. In *Proceedings of the 2015 Annual Symposium on Computer-Human Interaction in Play*, 475-480.

13. David Chu, 2016. Toward immersive mobile virtual reality. In *Proceedings of the Proceedings of the 3rd Workshop on Hot Topics in Wireless* (New York City, New York2016), ACM, 2980123, 54-54. DOI= http://dx.doi.org/10.1145/2980115.2980123.

14. James J. Cummings and Jeremy N. Bailenson, 2016. How immersive is enough? A meta-analysis of the effect of immersive technology on user presence. *Media Psychology 19*, 2, 272-309.

15. Vanessa Danthiir, Richard D. Roberts, Gerry Pallier, and Lazar Stankov, 2001. What the nose knows: Olfaction and cognitive abilities. *Intelligence 29*, 4, 337-361.

16. Hilary Davis, Frank Vetere, Martin Gibbs, and Peter Francis, 2012. Come play with me: designing technologies for intergenerational play. *Universal Access in the Information Society 11*, 1, 17-29.

17. Lupton Deborah, 1996. Food, the Body and the Self London, Thousand Oaks, CA: Sage.

18. Rae A. Earnshaw, 2014. *Virtual reality systems*. Academic press.

19. Hasan Shahid Ferdous, Bernd Ploderer, Hilary Davis, Frank Vetere, and Kenton O'hara, 2016. Commensality and the social use of technology during family mealtime. *ACM Transactions on Computer-Human Interaction (TOCHI) 23*, 6, 37.

20. Alberto Gallace, Mary K. Ngo, John Sulaitis, and Charles Spence, 2012. Multisensory presence in virtual reality: possibilities & limitations. In *Multiple sensorial media advances and applications: New developments in MulSeMedia* IGI Global, 1-38.

21. Sangita Ganesh, Paul Marshall, Yvonne Rogers, and Kenton OĥAra, 2014. FoodWorks: tackling fussy eating by digitally augmenting childrenś meals. In *Proceedings of the 8th Nordic Conference on Human-Computer Interaction: Fun, Fast, Foundational*, 147-156.

22. Google, 2017. Google VR SDK for Unity | Google VR | Google Developers, Retrieved July 27, 2017 from https://developers.google.com/vr/unity/.

23. Catherine Grevet, Anthony Tang, and Elizabeth Mynatt, 2012. Eating alone, together: new forms of commensality. In *Proceedings of the Proceedings of the 17th ACM international conference on Supporting group work* (Sanibel Island, Florida, USA2012), ACM, 2389192, 103-106. DOI= http://dx.doi.org/10.1145/2389176.2389192.

24. Andrea Grimes and Richard Harper, 2008. Celebratory technology: new directions for food research in HCI. In

Proceedings of the SIGCHI Conference on Human Factors in Computing Systems, 467-476.

25. Amy Huggard, Anushka De Mel, Jayden Garner, Cagdas Chad Toprak, Alan D. Chatham, and Florian Mueller, 2013. Musical embrace: facilitating engaging play experiences through social awkwardness. In *CHI13 Extended Abstracts on Human Factors in Computing Systems*, 3067-3070.
26. W. A. Ijsselsteijn, Y. A. W. De Kort, and K. Poels, 2013. The game experience questionnaire: Development of a self-report measure to assess the psychological impact of digital games. manuscript in preparation.
27. Rohit Ashok Khot, Deepti Aggarwal, Ryan Pennings, Larissa Hjorth, and Florian'floyd' Mueller, 2017. EdiPulse: Investigating a Playful Approach to Self-monitoring through 3D Printed Chocolate Treats. In *Proceedings of the 2017 CHI Conference on Human Factors in Computing Systems* ACM, 6593-6607.
28. Rohit Ashok Khot, Jeewon Lee, Deepti Aggarwal, Larissa Hjorth, and Florian'floyd' Mueller, 2015. Tastybeats: Designing palatable representations of physical activity. In *Proceedings of the 33rd Annual ACM Conference on Human Factors in Computing Systems* ACM, 2933-2942.
29. Alexandra Kitson, Bernhard E. Riecke, Abraham M. Hashemian, and Carman Neustaedter, 2015. NaviChair: Evaluating an embodied interface using a pointing task to navigate virtual reality. In *Proceedings of the 3rd ACM Symposium on Spatial User Interaction*, 123-126.
30. Matthias Kranz, Paul Holleis, and Albrecht Schmidt, 2010. Embedded interaction: Interacting with the internet of things. *IEEE internet computing 14*, 2, 46-53.
31. Steven M. Lavalle, 2016. Virtual reality. *Champaign (IL): University of Illinois*.
32. Tim Marsh and Brigid M Costello, 2012. Experience in Serious Games: Between Positive and Serious Experience. In *SGDA* Springer, 255-267.
33. Dan Maynes-Aminzade, 2005. Edible bits: Seamless interfaces between people, data and food. In *Conference on Human Factors in Computing Systems (CHI05)-Extended Abstracts*, 2207-2210.
34. Christiane Moser and Manfred Tscheligi, 2013. Playful taste interaction. In *Proceedings of the 12th International Conference on Interaction Design and Children* ACM, 340-343.
35. Martin Murer, Ilhan Aslan, and Manfred Tscheligi, 2013. LOLL io: exploring taste as playful modality. In *Proceedings of the 7th International Conference on Tangible, Embedded and Embodied Interaction*, 299-302.
36. Takuji Narumi, Shinya Nishizaka, Takashi Kajinami, Tomohiro Tanikawa, and Michitaka Hirose, 2011. Augmented reality flavors: gustatory display based on edible marker and cross-modal interaction. In *Proceedings of the SIGCHI Conference on Human Factors in Computing Systems*, 93-102.
37. Marianna Obrist, Alexandre N. Tuch, and Kasper Hornbaek, 2014. Opportunities for odor: experiences with smell and implications for technology. In *Proceedings of the 32nd annual ACM conference on Human factors in computing systems*, 2843-2852.
38. Marianna Obrist, Carlos Velasco, Chi Thanh Vi, Nimesha Ranasinghe, Ali Israr, Adrian D. Cheok, Charles Spence, and Ponnampalam Gopalakrishnakone, 2016. Touch, taste, & smell user interfaces: The future of multisensory HCI. In *Proceedings of the 2016 CHI Conference Extended Abstracts on Human Factors in Computing Systems*, 3285-3292.
39. Elinor Ochs and Merav Shohet, 2006. The cultural structuring of mealtime socialization. *New directions for child and adolescent development 2006*, 111, 35-49.
40. Iana Podkosova, Michael Urbanek, and Hannes Kaufmann, 2016. A Hybrid Sound Model for 3D Audio Games with Real Walking. In *Proceedings of the Proceedings of the 29th International Conference on Computer Animation and Social Agents* (Geneva, Switzerland2016), ACM, 2915948, 189-192. DOI= http://dx.doi.org/10.1145/2915926.2915948.
41. Projectnourished, 2017. Project Nourished - A Gastronomical Virtual Reality Experience, Retrieved July 27, from http://www.projectnourished.com/.
42. Nimesha Ranasinghe, Kasun Karunanayaka, Adrian David Cheok, Owen Noel Newton Fernando, Hideaki Nii, and Ponnampalam Gopalakrishnakone, 2011. Digital taste and smell communication. In *Proceedings of the 6th International Conference on Body Area Networks*, 78-84.
43. Nimesha Ranasinghe, Kuan-Yi Lee, Gajan Suthokumar, and Ellen Yi-Luen Do, 2016. Virtual ingredients for food and beverages to create immersive taste experiences. *Multimedia Tools and Applications 75*, 20, 12291-12309.
44. Siddharth S. Rautaray and Anupam Agrawal, 2015. Vision based hand gesture recognition for human computer interaction: a survey. *Artificial Intelligence Review 43*, 1, 1-54.

45. Roy A. Ruddle, 2013. The effect of translational and rotational body-based information on navigation. In *Human walking in virtual environments* Springer, 99-112.

46. Samsung, 2017. Using Samsung Gear VR to Revolutionize the Restaurant Experience, Retrieved July 27, 2017 from https://insights.samsung.com/2015/11/12/using-samsung-gear-vr-to-revolutionize-the-restaurant-experience/.

47. Mel Slater, 2003. A note on presence terminology. *Presence connect 3*, 3, 1-5.

48. Charles Spence, Marianna Obrist, Carlos Velasco, and Nimesha Ranasinghe, 2017. Digitizing the chemical senses: Possibilities & pitfalls. *International Journal of Human-Computer Studies*.

49. Paul Tennent, Duncan Rowland, Joe Marshall, Stefan Rennick Egglestone, Alexander Harrison, Zachary Jaime, Brendan Walker, and Steve Benford, 2011. Breathalising games: understanding the potential of breath control in game interfaces. In *Proceedings of the 8th International Conference on Advances in Computer Entertainment Technology*, 58-58.

50. Richard Wetzel, Rod Mccall, Anne-Kathrin Braun, and Wolfgang Broll, 2008. Guidelines for designing augmented reality games. In *Proceedings of the 2008 Conference on Future Play: Research, Play, Share*, 173-180.

51. Alan Wexelblat, 2014. *Virtual reality: applications and explorations*. Academic Press.

52. Ea Christina Willumsen and Hansjoachim Backe, 2015. How to Approach Health Packs in the Wild. Metaontological Reflections.

53. Christine Youngblut, Rob E. Johnston, Sarah H. Nash, Ruth A. Wienclaw, and Craig A. Will, 1996. *Review of Virtual Environment Interface Technology*.

54. Rui Zhang and Oliver Amft, 2016. Regular-look eyeglasses can monitor chewing. In *Proceedings of the 2016 ACM International Joint Conference on Pervasive and Ubiquitous Computing: Adjunct*, 389-392.

Situated Game Level Editing in Augmented Reality

Gary Ng[1] **Joon Gi Shin**[1] **Alexander Plopski**[2] **Christian Sandor**[2] **Daniel Saakes**[1]
Industrial Design, KAIST[1]
Daejeon, Republic of Korea
{garykcng,jshin,saakes}@kaist.ac.kr
Nara Institute of Science and Technology[2]
Ikoma, Japan
{plopski,sandor}@is.naist.jp

Figure 1. Augmented reality games make use of the unique characteristics of the players' physical space where players must overcome both virtual and physical obstacles (1). Virtual objects, such as a rock, are spatially aware and fall down the stairs when the player enters a trigger volume (2). Our system enables end-users to design personal games with virtual objects and define game logic through spatial trigger-action programming (3).

ABSTRACT

Level editors let end-users create custom levels and content within a given video game. In this paper, we explore the concept and design of Augmented reality game level editors. These new types of editors are not only spatial and embodied, but also situated, as they enable users to tailor games to the unique characteristics and emotional value of their own space.

We present the design and implementation of a prototype level editor that runs on the Microsoft HoloLens. The editor enables users to add virtual content in their homes and add interactions through spatial trigger-action game-logic programming. We had pairs of students create games with the prototype and play each other's games. They reported that games are fun to make, play, and watch others play. Based on the design and evaluation, we propose guidelines for Augmented reality game-authoring tools for end users.

CCS CONCEPTS

• Human-centered computing → user studies; Collaborative Interaction; • Computing methodologies → Mixed augmented reality;

Author Keywords

Augmented Reality; Game Design; Level Editor; Spatial Programming; Trigger-Action Programming

TEI '18, March 18–21, 2018, Stockholm, Sweden

© 2018 ACM. ISBN 978-1-4503-5568-1/18/03...15.00

DOI: https://doi.org/10.1145/3173225.3173230

INTRODUCTION

Video game design is a complex task that requires highly technical tools and skills from a variety of fields, including computer science, interaction design, and the arts [20]. Level layout is an important aspect of game design [1, 16] since storytelling and levels guide users through a game. In-game level editors let artists and designers create game content such as layouting game levels by placing objects and scripting interactivity. The key is that these editors do not require the advanced programming skills needed for making the game engine, and so facilitate development. Several games ship such an editor with the game to let players (end users) make their own levels in the game [29]. End-user editors are available for several genres ranging from first-person shooters [53], to strategy games [9], puzzle games [52], and racing games [42]. For other games, such as Super Mario Maker [38] and MineCraft [36], the main activities are content creation and sharing games with other players and in online communities.

In this paper, we look into the design of video game level editors for emerging Augmented Reality (AR) games. Whereas video games currently take place in a virtual environment that is played through a 2D display, games in AR and Virtual Reality (VR) immerse the users in the game and allow for natural and embodied interactions with the virtual content.

Compared to VR, AR games take place in the real world and bring the additional challenge of the game having to adapt to the physical space of the user. For example, a star topology could be applied to a player's living room which turns it into a hub for several challenges in adjacent rooms. A linear story (bus topology) could unfold through the house from the entrance to the stairs and then to the bedroom. In addition, spaces might have emotional significance, such as grandpa's special chair, and this could be applied to personalize games. That leads to our question: How can we let users personalize or create games that are unique to their living space?

Whereas traditional editors for games support WYSIWYG editing, authoring immersive experiences for VR games challenges the imagination. Therefore, game creation platforms such as Unreal [19] and Unity [50] have started to include level editors that let users design in-situ, in VR. AR game editors bring additional challenges as they are situated in a real space. Therefore, in our design, we address the challenges of 1) in-situ design: The player is in the game when making the game, as opposed to traditional, screen-based level editors that make use of several views such as maps and third and first-person views; and 2) situating and personalizing game content in the user's home. We look specifically at how to create interaction through the use of 3D spatial trigger-action programming (Figure 1).

The contributions of this paper are: 1) the design and implementation of a prototype game level editor for head-worn AR and the considerations that went into it; 2) a formative evaluation with users both playing and designing games; and 3) guidelines for AR game level editors which are useful for game developers. The limitations consists of the small size of the user study that was performed in a laboratory environment instead of the users' homes, the limitations in game content and interaction, and the limitations of using the Microsoft HoloLens.

RELATED WORK

To the best of our knowledge, there is no related work that discusses AR level editors for making interactive games that make use of the user's physical location. The closest is i.Ge [39] in which the virtual game characters interact with ad-hoc manipulation of walls, such as drawing or adding objects.

Content creation in AR differs from other content creation as it adds (or removes) content to the world and there is no need for creating architectural structures like walls or ceilings [48]. Several projects employ Augmented Reality to bring computer games into the real world. Early examples utilized backpack computers and Head-Mounted Displays (HMD) for outdoor games, such as Human Pacman [12] and ARQuake [48], and newer examples employ wearable computers with cameras [27]. Typically, these projects transform gameplay designed for screen and keyboard interaction to spatial user interfaces. Other examples employ Mobile AR [8, 32] on the smartphone, such as Pokemon Go [37].

Although several game genres empower the player with superhuman abilities, there are many design limitations in AR. For example, the game cannot teleport the user back to the start position or require the user to jump off a roof. While changing the user's virtual position in VR could lead to a break in presence, it is not possible in AR. Storytelling techniques relying heavily on controlling the camera, such as cut-scenes, might need new equivalents in AR.

In AR, virtual content can be freely added and moved around, but physical items cannot be rearranged without the aid of human helpers [12] or robotics [41]. Interaction with the physical environment is also possible through IoT enabled objects, such as opening doors or turning on lights [5]. Everyday objects could function as tangible proxies [23] in the game. In this paper, however, we focus on the layouting and programming of virtual game objects in physical space.

Recent advances in hardware make AR games spatially aware. A few projects [6, 26, 54] employ projector-based systems to situate games in the living room. Fragments [3], a commercial game released for the Microsoft HoloLens, adapts to the user's environment and recognizes objects such as chairs, which allows the virtual characters to sit on them. Situating virtual content to fit to the user's environment is a key challenge of AR gaming that we address in our design. We aim for direct manipulation [47] for object creation and therefore build on work that deals with interior design in AR [13, 30, 31] and 3D content creation [28]. These projects unify action and feedback [17, 49] and employ embodied interaction [18].

Interactivity is important in game design and is typically created in game editors using scripting languages. However, programming in VR [14] or AR [43] suffers from the same problems as programming IoT devices [51] as these interfaces are typically not situated, there is a spatial disconnect between the user and the objects they are working with. To solve this disconnect, some projects [40, 46] and the Reality Editor [24] visualize cause and effect relationships by visualizing virtual connections with directed lines [15]. Another tangible approach to dataflow programming is shown with Spatial Physical Computing [11] in which sensor and actuator modules' relationships are programmed through physical touch. Visual and tangible programming can be applied for beginners or non-technical users to create their own interactive applications [45] and are applied in our design of the AR level editor.

AUGMENTED REALITY LEVEL EDITOR

In this paper, we focus on first-person game experiences [1] in which the player is inside the game world and interacts from the viewpoint of the player's character. This type of game leverages the strengths of the immersive and embodied interactions of head-worn AR (such as the Microsoft HoloLens). Several game genres are available for first-person interactions, such as shooters, construction, and simulations. We selected adventure and puzzle genres to explore the design of an AR editor because they require causal relationship scripting and embed the gameplay in the physical space.

The editor is designed around the concept of visually programming the cause and effect relationships that is common in level editors [7, 29]. For example, as shown in Figure 3, a trigger could be activated when the user enters or exits a space, touches an object, executes a voice command, performs a gesture, or changes their pose. Triggers can cause actions which influence the behavior of non-player characters, start an animation, hide or show objects, or let the user win or lose the game. However, unlike existing end-user programming editors (such as Scratch [44]), we employ situated programming (such as [24, 46]). We define triggers as (collision) volumes in space that are either visible, such as virtual objects, or invisible boxes indicating a space around a real object.

Figure 2. In play mode (top), touching the fire will make the player lose the game, but the fire can be extinguished using the button. In edit mode (bottom), the button has a trigger applied to it which disables the fire. The fire has a game over action applied to it.

AR game editors range from allowing the full authoring of new games to applying templates to an existing space, for instance through the use of wizards. Since, AR games are a new genre, we focus on a basic, but versatile editor, to be employed in a user study. The core functionality of an authoring environment consists of: 1) a library with virtual content and tools to position virtual content in a given location; 2) a scripting environment to program interactivity, non-player character behaviors, and animations; and 3) seamless switching between playing and editing as it allows for explorative design and iteration. In this section we describe the design of a first-person in-situ editor. The editor has an "edit" mode and "play" mode and users switch back and forth with a voice command: *"switch mode"* to facilitate iterative design with stages of making, testing, and playing. A visual comparison of the two modes is shown in Figure 2. As we focus on the game design process, we base our interaction design decisions on the Apple AR Human Interface Guidelines [2] and the Microsoft mixed reality design guidelines [35] and use a combination of gaze, in-air gestures, and voice commands. Iterative prototyping further guided decisions and helped work around hardware limitations. For instance, because of the narrow Field of View of the HoloLens, we avoided small virtual objects because they are easily missed and reduced the size of the virtual Head Up Display.

Edit Mode

In the edit mode, users design the game by layouting objects and creating relationships between them. Virtual objects can be spawned from a diegetic menu and then selected, moved, rotated, or scaled by performing a selection gesture. Objects that are being moved, are moved relative to the user's gaze and are aware of the physical environment. Objects slide over the floor and stick on walls (but do not go through walls). Some objects, such as the lasers, automatically adjust orientation to match the normal vector of the surface they are placed on.

Figure 3. A treasure chest is set up as a trap. When the player walks over to the treasure chest, it disappears and causes a rock to fall from the sky.

We included a library with standard game content. The library consists of three themes (selected for no particular reason): a farm theme with objects such as pigs, haystacks, and a campfire; a pirate theme with skeletons, a treasure chest, and a rock; and a space theme with lasers and spaceships.

Any virtual object can become a trigger (using its bounding box as a volume) and the user can add any number of triggers to the object by staring at it and saying *"On Enter"* or *"On Exit"* to create a trigger that responds to whether the user is entering or exiting it. After the trigger type has been assigned, an action must be assigned to it by performing another voice command. We designed four actions, one for winning the game, one for losing the game, one action for showing an object, and one for hiding an object. An example is shown in Figure 2. The button ignites or extinguishes the fire, and touching the fire means "game over". In edit mode this behavior is scripted with two trigger actions. An **on-enter** trigger is applied to the fire and assigned to a **game over** action. Another **on-enter** trigger is applied to the button with an action to **disable** the fire. A directed line shows the relationship between the button and the fire in edit mode.

Objects can also be set to be disabled when the game starts and need to be activated with an enable trigger in order for them to be shown. Disabled objects do not invoke their triggers, and thus allow for sequential events. Disabling objects is useful for scenarios such as the one shown in Figure 3: a rock becomes visible and falls down when the player reaches the treasure chest.

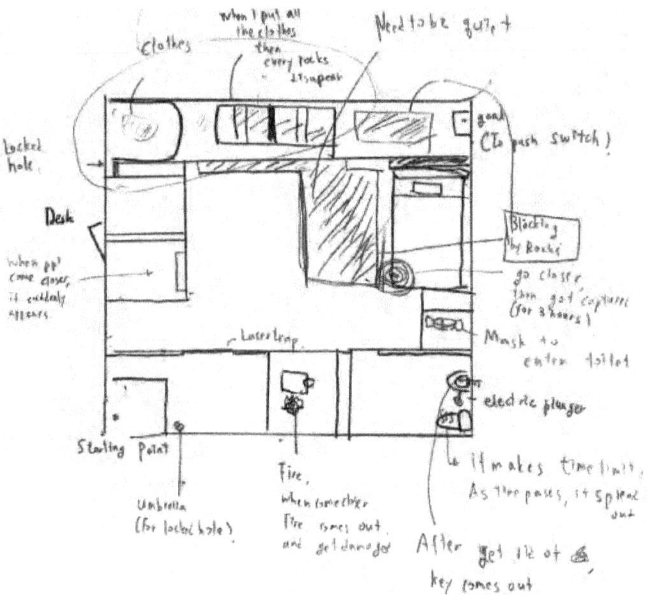

Figure 4. To prepare participants for the user study, we made a sensitizing probe with activities to be completed before the user study. The second-day activity asked to draw a top-down perspective of their space with added game elements. Participant 3A drew an action-adventure game spanning their entire apartment which includes spatial triggers and events.

Play Mode

In play mode, the disabled objects, trigger areas, and UI elements are hidden. The triggers of the enabled objects are also activated, meaning that whenever the user enters or exits an object collider, the linked trigger actions will activate. If the player wants to reset the game, everything will be set back to its initial state when the player says *"Reset Game"*.

The physical position of the HMD is used to check for collisions with virtual objects in the play mode. When the player enters or exits an object's collision volume, the triggers are activated, as shown in Figure 3. We defined a $0.5 \times 0.5 \times 2.0$m collision volume that extends downwards from the player's head. This allows for the simulation of the player's body colliding with virtual objects and also makes it possible for the user to duck below objects. This approximation was necessary because the HoloLens is not capable of tracking the user's posture and only provides the information about the pose of the user's head.

EVALUATION

We expect that AR games will be played together within families and with friends. Therefore, in a formative user study we let pairs of participants make games and play each others' games. From the user study we aimed to discover how participants design games, and how they work with virtual objects in the physical space.

We implemented a prototype as described above. However, during informal tests and a pilot study, we discovered that non-native English speaking participants struggled with issuing voice commands. Since the goal of the study was to explore game play and creation rather than usability, we provided an alternative way of entering voice commands by use of the Wizard of Oz technique [21]. Participants issued voice commands as described earlier, but instead of speech recognition, one of the researchers entered the command on a wireless keyboard. We also noticed that because the voice commands are not self-discoverable, participants needed help during the design session. Therefore, during the study we provided a small card that listed all of the voice commands.

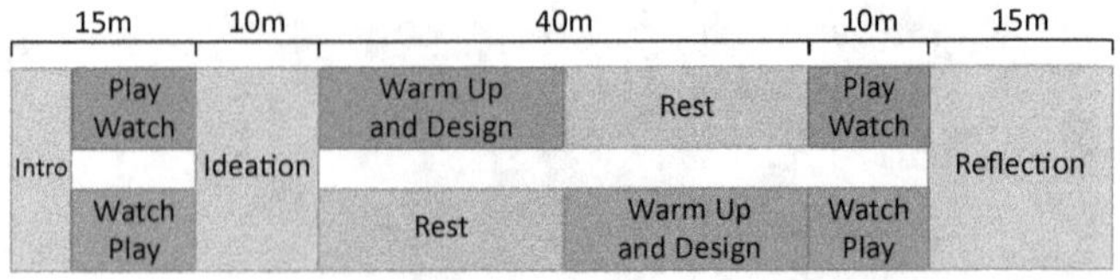

Figure 5. We asked pairs of friends to participate in the user study. After an introduction the pair brainstormed together for ideas. One by one, participants made a game while the other waited in another room. When both designs were completed, participant played each other's games. The study concluded with a reflection interview.

Sensitizing Probe

Because the participants were new to game design, we employed a sensitizing probe [34] to familiarize them with the topic one week prior to the study. The probe consisted of exercises to be executed over two days. For the first-day activity, we tasked the participants to think back to a memorable moment in a recent game they played or a movie they watched and describe how a physical obstacle was overcome and why it was memorable. We designed the second-day activity to get the participants to draw their own space and think about how they would make a game for it. An example of this activity is shown in Figure 4. Participant 3A sketched an adventure game that spanned multiple rooms in his apartment.

All participants completed the probe and they designed a variety of games for their homes. Most games were either of the escape room genre, in which players had to solve a puzzle (e.g. find items) to get out, or action games (e.g. shoot enemies behind a desk, avoiding falling objects). All participants had made the game personal and included elements of their space or physical items they owned. For instance, one participant made a puzzle game in which the player had to find objects in her room that she hid in her desk and wardrobe. The results were not further analyzed but strengthen the idea of personalizing games by situating the game in the user's space.

Procedure

We recruited four pairs of friends from a local university who did not have game design experience (n=8, avg. age=23.25, SD=1.03). The study took 90 minutes per pair and we compensated each participant with the equivalent of 9 USD.

The user study took place in a lounge area at a university and attempted to simulate an apartment. The area was L-shaped and contained furniture items that are typically found in living rooms. We set up two video cameras in opposite corners of the room to document the participants' movements. A laptop captured the first-person video stream from the HoloLens using screen capturing software. We logged users' actions and movements in Unity (visualized in Figure 7). Adjacent to the

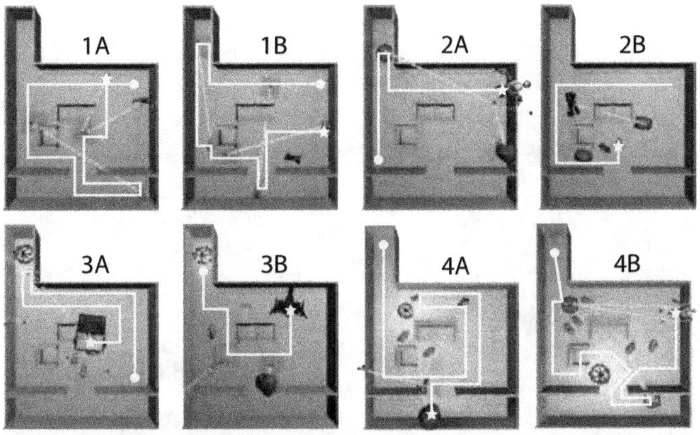

Figure 6. Each of the eight participants made a game during the user study. The green lines are the trigger-action links and the yellow lines represent the path the player was expected to take. The circle indicates the start position and the star marks the goal.

"living room" we created a "design" area with a whiteboard, pens, and paper.

The user study had five phases: introduction, ideation, design, play, and reflection, as shown in Figure 5. The study was designed in a way so that participants could both design and play games. We started by letting the participants play (and watch) an introduction game. During the ideation phase, the participants brainstormed game ideas together without the use of the system.

The design phase was conducted twice. One participant designed while the other rested in a separate room where we provided refreshments. During the design phase, the researcher walked the participant through two warm-up exercises to familiarize them with the interface and functionality. Then, the participants had 20 minutes to design their game.

Once both participants completed their design, they played each other's games. The designer started by introducing the goal of the game to the player and indicated the starting position of the game. We gave players multiple attempts to beat their partner's game. We recorded both the player's and designer's reactions, as shown in Figure 8.

The final phase of the user study was the reflection phase. We interviewed both participants to discuss their experiences using the system, in both design and play aspects. We based the interview structure on the NASA Task Load Index which was designed to evaluate interface designs and augmented vision [22].

Each session resulted in three video recordings and a user actions and movement log. We synchronized and transcribed the video recordings. We also visualized the design flow of the participants using the log, as shown in Figure 7. Two researchers independently analyzed the probes, transcribed data, videos and metrics and extracted key moments from the study by means of printed screenshots and transcriptions [10]. They identified themes through affinity diagramming [33]. In a second round, the two jointly discussed overarching themes that emerged from the study and are described below.

RESULTS

All of the participants enjoyed designing and playing games and a few participants mentioned that they would like to make games for their family members. Participant 3A said: *"I'm going make a game for my parents. For them, our home is more like a sitting place but I want to give it a special meaning for them"*. The participants also mentioned how watching someone play their game is also entertaining, especially since they designed the game. Participant 4B said, *"When you're playing this, people can make fun of you and there's more friendship and interaction... I think they'll be freaking out but in reality we don't see anything"*. Participant 2B also echoed a similar sentiment, saying, *"Since I'm watching her playing the game I wanted to force her to do funny things"*.

All participants successfully created games with a victory condition except for participant 1A who forgot to place the victory condition, but notified her partner when she fulfilled it. All games are shown in Figure 6. The eight participants spawned a total of 81 objects (mean = 10.13, SD = 3.09) in total with 59 of them (mean = 7.38, SD = 2.39) present in the final games. Participants mostly used "On Enter" triggers, with 88% (61/69) of all created triggers and 96% (54/56) of all triggers in the final game designs being set to "On Enter".

None of the participants encountered difficulties playing or making games. Additionally, the NASA TLX and exit interviews did not reveal usability issues. However, the participants frequently mentioned that the in-air gestures in the edit mode were physically demanding and frustrating. Occasionally, when playing the games, touching (or kicking) objects did not trigger events and resulted in a break in presence because objects did not react as expected. This was because the HoloLens only tracks head position and not the user's limbs. Future HMDs should support full-body tracking to support embodied interaction and natural behavior.

The participants all agreed that the ability to place game objects in a real space was a novel and entertaining task, with participant 4B commenting that the system *"was also a bit empowering. I had this kind of fantasy as a kid. Being able to turn your home into a game place, and then, this is exactly what that is"*. When participant 1B was playing through the game her partner made for her, she said *"it's actually scary"* and was visibly spooked when a skeleton appeared in front of her.

The participants typically made interactions based on the affordance of an object. For example, most of the participants tended to be cautious around items that were perceived to be dangerous, like the lasers. However, since the current prototype allows for the designers to create any trigger on any object, any interaction can be created, even if it is unintuitive. Participant 2A mentioned that she could make an event where *"if you touch the pig, a rock falls down. You can make it because the system allows you to do it. But it doesn't really make sense"*. Half of the participants (2A, 2B, 4A, 4B) said that it was difficult to determine the object functionality when playing a game. For example, some games used pigs as a victory condition whereas others had them as dangerous objects.

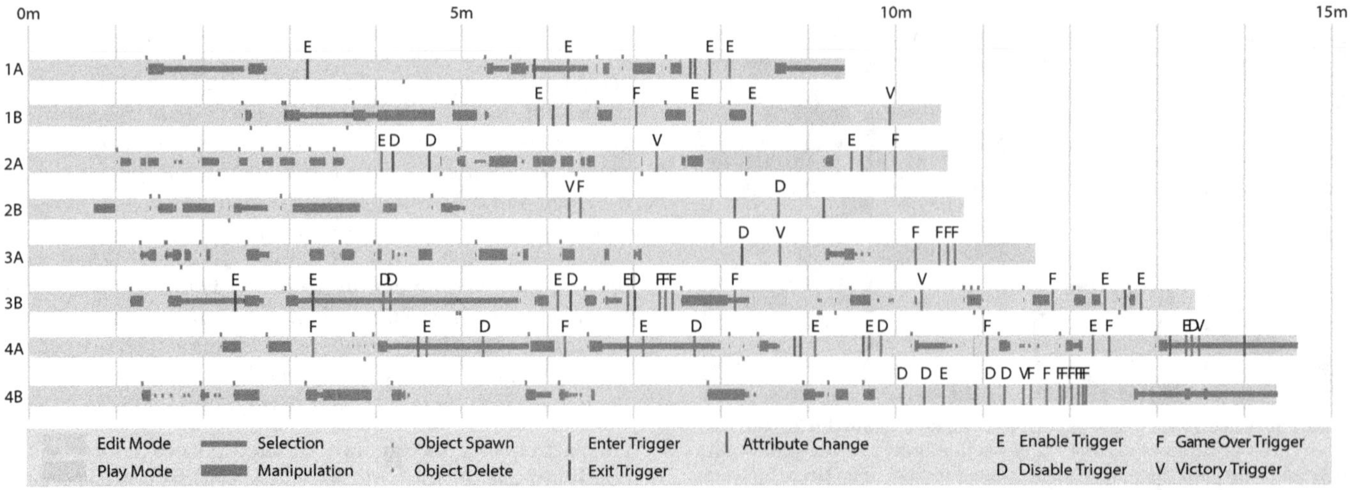

Figure 7. We captured users' actions during their individual design session to understand their design process. Participants 2A, 3A, 3B, 4A, and 4B utilized an iterative design process by switching between the editor and play mode to test and refine their games, whereas the others first made their entire game before testing it.

Making Use of the Real World

When designing AR games, the participants built their game to fit the physical space. During the ideation phase, two pairs (1 and 4) walked around the physical space to think of game ideas and they commonly used spatial gestures and play acting to express and explain their ideas to their partner. For example, participant 1B walked around the room and pointed out potential walking paths that the player might take and then her partner proposed ideas for where objects should be placed.

The fourth pair also manipulated different physical elements within the space when thinking of ideas. They opened and closed the patio door to explain a trap they could make and even moved some chairs around to define gameplay boundaries and physical obstacles.

The participants expected and enjoyed movement in AR games and so they tried to design games that would include as much physical movement as possible. Participant 3B specifically said that he "*wanted to make it physically challenging so [his partner] had to jump*" so he placed a dangerous object in the corridor between a wall and an armchair which blocked off the path and prompted his partner to try and jump over the object. Participant 1A also mentioned that "*you're supposed to move. If there was more movement it would be good*".

Additionally, the participants typically focused on the virtual elements more than the physical environment. Half of the participants (1A, 1B, 3A, 3B) accidentally bumped into something, like the camera or sofa, because they were not paying attention.

Game Design Process

The metrics data, shown in Figure 7, revealed that participants generally take two approaches when making games, an iterative approach alternating editing and playing, and a big-bang approach, designing the entire game followed by a short testing session. Five of the participants (1A, 1B, 2A, 3B, 4A) created the triggers for the objects as they spawned them while the others (2B, 3A, 4B) first layouted all of the objects in the scene before creating all of the triggers at once. Three of the participants (1A, 1B, 2B) were focused on the act of placing objects and creating triggers and so only tested their games once and did not make many changes based on their testing. However, the other participants (2A, 3A, 3B, 4A, 4B) used an iterative process with the play mode to test their designs and discover logic errors or mistakes, which resulted in relatively more complex and complete games.

Figure 8. Several participants mentioned how it was entertaining to not only design and play games, but also to watch their partner play the game they designed.

All of the participants said that it was not too difficult to create a game, with participant 2A saying that "*you can't really program other games by yourself*", referring to traditional game creation methods. However, some participants mentioned that they had difficulty remembering everything they had done or forgot what they needed to do. Participant 1A notably forgot to disable a trap and later mentioned that "*at the end there were so many objects and things that I didn't think about until [my partner] started playing*" and participant 4A also said something similar, commenting "*sometimes it just tricked my mind because I can't really remember what I did before so I had to pause and think for a while*".

Figure 9. AR gaming blends the virtual with the physical. Virtual objects (the laser and pig) were combined with the physical armchair to block the way of the participant so he decided to climb over the armchair to proceed through the game.

DISCUSSION

Based on the design, implementation and evaluation with users, we propose guidelines for the design of future Augmented reality game level editors. We hope that our findings are directly applicable for first-person games and editors and are useful for developers. Usability issues we attributed to the HoloLens (such as speech and gesture recognition, limited Field of View, and body tracking) are excluded from this discussion.

During the user study, we saw participants duck under lasers and jump over both virtual and physical objects, as shown in Figure 9. The participants expected and enjoyed physical activity when playing AR games. Therefore, we propose that future editors and games should **encourage different types of locomotion and actions**, such as jumping, running, and climbing as it would create a more unique and immersive experience that is suitable for AR. However, care needs to be taken to remove unnecessary movement from the game and to highlight areas that could lead to injuries in both modes. In traditional games, characters can be teleported or moved where they need to be, but it is not possible in AR due to the situated context. This means that the understanding of things like the start and end positions in games must be rethought in order to minimize tedious movements.

AR games are played in the real world which means that game content has to "fit" the physical space. Although it is possible to use objects as tangible proxies [23], it is not possible to turn a living room into an expansive desert nor a house into a rabbit hole. Deeper integration is needed with the room's unique characteristics, perhaps with IoT sensors, so that triggers can be mapped to environmental events. For example, opening a door or moving furniture could serve as a trigger for an in-game event, similar to the connections between virtual objects in the editor.

Some participants found it difficult to start designing since they had no idea what could be done. Game templates that act as tutorials can teach them how to design and assist the users in getting started. Some systems, like Scratch [44], encourage remixing existing programs in order to explore new ideas [25] and a similar system can be implemented for AR game editors. **Templating functions** could speed up the design process and help new users. Templates could consist of pre-configured modules containing networks of objects and logic can be applied to a physical space and could range from simple interactions, such as buttons that activate doors, to entire games.

Tools and smart guides should be implemented to reduce or eliminate common errors and give users a quick way to holistically view and assess their designs. Game design is a complex task that typically requires several iterations to expose logic errors. In the study we identified a few approaches that users take which indicates that supporting an iterative design process could be beneficial. Additional view modes, such as an overview mode that shows the entire design from a top-down perspective, could also be beneficial to remind users what they have done so far [4].

Augmented reality games should also **facilitate social interaction**. Since AR games are played in context, collocated game modes, such as co-op or competitive modes, are suitable. A "dungeon master" mode, similar to the role of game masters in tabletop role-playing games, can also be implemented where a game master facilitates the game flow using authoring tools while other players play the game. Another avenue would be to let users make games together or in teams.

CONCLUSIONS AND FUTURE WORK

In this paper, we made a first step towards the design of situated level editors in AR that aim to let users design games in their homes. Based on our experience, we provided guidelines for situating the game in the user's environment and how to use the first-person perspective to program basic interactive content. Our user study indicated that both creation and play can be part of the game experience and suggest multi-user games that make use of both aspects as a next iteration.

The formative user study was performed with only a few users in a laboratory that resembled a living room. Hence, we could not study the intimacy and emotional values of designing in a personal space that are to be expected based on the probe study. Therefore, in the future we intend to perform long-term evaluations "in the wild" in people's homes where we can investigate how the editor performs on a larger scale with multiple rooms and longer scenarios. Additionally, as the first prototype of its kind, we implemented a subset of the functionality that is required for full-fledged games. Future iterations will include functions such as object and logic grouping and templating. We will also extend the trigger system to include temporal and physiological triggers to enable users to design more complex games. Another avenue that we would like to explore is competitive and collaborative design and play.

ACKNOWLEDGEMENTS

This project was supported by JSPS and NRF under the Japan-Korea Basic Scientific Cooperation Program. This research was supported by Basic Science Research Program through the National Research Foundation of Korea (NRF) funded by the Ministry of Science, ICT & Future Planning (NRF-2017K2A9A2A08000200)

REFERENCES

1. Ernest Adams. 2014. *Fundamentals of Game Design, 3rd Edition*. New Riders.
2. Apple. 2017. Human Interface Guidelines: Augmented Reality. (2017). https://developer.apple.com/ios/human-interface-guidelines/technologies/augmented-reality
3. Asobo Studio. 2016. Fragments. (2016). http://www.asobostudio.com/games/fragments
4. Blaine Bell, Tobias Höllerer, and Steven Feiner. 2002. An Annotated Situation-awareness Aid for Augmented Reality. In *Proceedings of the 15th Annual ACM Symposium on User Interface Software and Technology (UIST '02)*. ACM, New York, NY, USA, 213–216. DOI: http://dx.doi.org/10.1145/571985.572017
5. Andrea Bellucci, Telmo Zarraonandia, Paloma Díaz, and Ignacio Aedo. 2017. End-User Prototyping of Cross-Reality Environments. In *Proceedings of the Tenth International Conference on Tangible, Embedded, and Embodied Interaction - TEI '17*. ACM Press, New York, New York, USA, 173–182. DOI: http://dx.doi.org/10.1145/3024969.3024975
6. Hrvoje Benko, Andrew D. Wilson, and Federico Zannier. 2014. Dyadic Projected Spatial Augmented Reality. In *Proceedings of the 27th Annual ACM Symposium on User Interface Software and Technology (UIST '14)*. ACM, New York, NY, USA, 645–655. DOI: http://dx.doi.org/10.1145/2642918.2647402
7. Blender Foundation. 2017. Blender Game Engine: Game Logic. (2017). https://docs.blender.org/manual/en/dev/game_engine/logic/introduction.html
8. Blippar Group. 2009. Layar. (2009). https://www.layar.com/
9. Blizzard Entertainment. 2002. Warcraft III. (2002). http://us.blizzard.com/en-us/games/war3/
10. Jacob Buur and Astrid Soendergaard. 2000. Video Card Game: An Augmented Environment for User Centred Design Discussions. In *Proceedings of DARE 2000 on Designing Augmented Reality Environments (DARE '00)*. ACM, New York, NY, USA, 63–69. DOI: http://dx.doi.org/10.1145/354666.354673
11. Alvaro Cassinelli and Daniel Saakes. 2017. Data Flow, Spatial Physical Computing. In *Proceedings of the Tenth International Conference on Tangible, Embedded, and Embodied Interaction - TEI '17*. ACM Press, New York, New York, USA, 253–259. DOI: http://dx.doi.org/10.1145/3024969.3024978
12. Adrian David Cheok, Xubo Yang, Kok Hwee Goh, Wei Liu, Farzam Farbiz, Sze Lee Teo, Hui Siang Teo, Shang Ping Lee, Yu Li, and Siew Wan Fong. 2004. Human Pacman. In *Proc. ACE '04*. ACM Press, New York, New York, USA, 360–361. DOI: http://dx.doi.org/10.1145/1067343.1067402
13. Foong-Yi Chia, Bokyung Lee, and Daniel Saakes. 2016. Collaboration in the Living Room or How Couples Design Together. In *Proceedings of the 9th Nordic Conference on Human-Computer Interaction - NordiCHI '16*. 1–6. DOI: http://dx.doi.org/10.1145/2971485.2996734
14. Matthew Conway, Steve Audia, Tommy Burnette, Dennis Cosgrove, and Kevin Christiansen. 2000. Alice: Lessons Learned from Building a 3D System for Novices. In *Proceedings of the SIGCHI Conference on Human Factors in Computing Systems (CHI '00)*. ACM, New York, NY, USA, 486–493. DOI: http://dx.doi.org/10.1145/332040.332481
15. R. Dauenhauer and T. Mï£¡ller. 2016. An Evaluation of Information Connection in Augmented Reality for 3D Scenes with Occlusion. In *2016 IEEE International Symposium on Mixed and Augmented Reality (ISMAR-Adjunct)*. 235–237. DOI: http://dx.doi.org/10.1109/ISMAR-Adjunct.2016.0083
16. Sjoerd "Hourences" de Jong. 2008. *The Hows and Whys of Level Design - Second Edition*. Self Published.
17. Tom Djajadiningrat, Kees Overbeeke, and Stephan Wensveen. 2002. But How, Donald, Tell Us How?: On the Creation of Meaning in Interaction Design Through Feedforward and Inherent Feedback. In *Proceedings of the 4th Conference on Designing Interactive Systems: Processes, Practices, Methods, and Techniques (DIS '02)*. ACM, New York, NY, USA, 285–291. DOI: http://dx.doi.org/10.1145/778712.778752
18. Paul Dourish. 2004. *Where the action is: The Foundations of Embodied Interaction*. MIT Press.
19. EPIC Games. 2012. Unreal Engine 4. (2012). https://www.unrealengine.com/
20. James Paul Gee, Elizabeth Hayes, Robert J. Torres, Alex Games, Kurt R. Squire, and Katie Salen. 2008. Playing to learn game design skills in a game context. *ICLS'08: Proceedings of the 8th international conference on International conference for the learning sciences - Volume 3* 3 (2008), 368–374. http://dl.acm.org/citation.cfm?id=1600040
21. Paul Green and Lisa Wei-Haas. 1985. *The Wizard of Oz: A Tool for Rapid Development of User Interfaces*. Technical Report. 21 pages. https://deepblue.lib.umich.edu/bitstream/handle/2027.42/174/71952.0001.001.pdf?sequence=2
22. Sandra G. Hart. 2006. Nasa-Task Load Index (NASA-TLX); 20 Years Later. *Proceedings of the Human Factors and Ergonomics Society Annual Meeting* 50, 9 (oct 2006), 904–908. DOI: http://dx.doi.org/10.1177/154193120605000909
23. Anuruddha Hettiarachchi and Daniel Wigdor. 2016. Annexing Reality: Enabling Opportunistic Use of Everyday Objects As Tangible Proxies in Augmented Reality. In *Proceedings of the 2016 CHI Conference on Human Factors in Computing Systems (CHI '16)*. ACM, New York, NY, USA, 1957–1967. DOI: http://dx.doi.org/10.1145/2858036.2858134

24. Valentin Heun, James Hobin, and Pattie Maes. 2013. Reality editor. *Proceedings of the 2013 ACM conference on Pervasive and ubiquitous computing adjunct publication - UbiComp '13 Adjunct* (2013), 307–310. DOI:http://dx.doi.org/10.1145/2494091.2494185

25. Benjamin Hill and Andres Monroy-Hernández. 2013. The Cost of Collaboration for Code and Art: Evidence from a Remixing Community. *Collaboration in Creative Communities* (2013), 1035–1045. DOI: http://dx.doi.org/10.1145/2441776.2441893

26. Brett Jones, Rajinder Sodhi, Michael Murdock, Ravish Mehra, Hrvoje Benko, Andrew Wilson, Eyal Ofek, Blair MacIntyre, Nikunj Raghuvanshi, and Lior Shapira. 2014. RoomAlive: Magical Experiences Enabled by Scalable, Adaptive Projector-camera Units. In *Proceedings of the 27th Annual ACM Symposium on User Interface Software and Technology (UIST '14)*. ACM, New York, NY, USA, 637–644. DOI: http://dx.doi.org/10.1145/2642918.2647383

27. Georg Klein and David Murray. 2007. Parallel Tracking and Mapping for Small AR Workspaces. In *2007 6th IEEE and ACM International Symposium on Mixed and Augmented Reality*. 225–234. DOI: http://dx.doi.org/10.1109/ISMAR.2007.4538852

28. Max Krichenbauer, Goshiro Yamamoto, Takafumi Taketomi, Christian Sandor, and Hirokazu Kato. 2014. Towards Augmented Reality user interfaces in 3D media production. In *2014 IEEE International Symposium on Mixed and Augmented Reality (ISMAR)*. IEEE, 23–28. DOI:http://dx.doi.org/10.1109/ISMAR.2014.6948405

29. David Kushner. 2003. *Masters of Doom: How Two Guys Created an Empire and Transformed Pop Culture.* Random House.

30. Manfred Lau, Masaki Hirose, Akira Ohgawara, Jun Mitani, and Takeo Igarashi. 2012. Situated modeling. *Proceedings of the Sixth International Conference on Tangible, Embedded and Embodied Interaction - TEI '12* (2012), 275. DOI: http://dx.doi.org/10.1145/2148131.2148190

31. Bokyung Lee, Minjoo Cho, Joonhee Min, and Daniel Saakes. 2016. Posing and Acting As Input for Personalizing Furniture. In *Proceedings of the 9th Nordic Conference on Human-Computer Interaction (NordiCHI '16)*. ACM, New York, NY, USA, Article 44, 10 pages. DOI:http://dx.doi.org/10.1145/2971485.2971487

32. Blair MacIntyre, Alex Hill, Hafez Rouzati, Maribeth Gandy, and Brian Davidson. 2011. The Argon AR Web Browser and standards-based AR application environment. In *2011 10th IEEE International Symposium on Mixed and Augmented Reality*. 65–74. DOI:http://dx.doi.org/10.1109/ISMAR.2011.6092371

33. Bella. Martin and Bruce M. Hanington. 2012. *Universal methods of design : 100 ways to research complex problems, develop innovative ideas, and design effective solutions*. Rockport Publishers. 207 pages. https://books.google.co.kr/books?hl=en

34. Tuuli Mattelmäki. 2005. Applying probes – from inspirational notes to collaborative insights. *CoDesign* 1, 2 (2005), 83–102. DOI: http://dx.doi.org/10.1080/15719880500135821

35. Microsoft. 2017. Design: Learn the Fundamentals of designing mixed reality experiences. (2017). https://developer.microsoft.com/en-us/windows/mixed-reality/design

36. Mojang. 2009. Minecraft. (2009). https://minecraft.net/en-us/

37. Niantic. 2016. Pokémon Go. (2016). http://www.pokemongo.com/

38. Nintendo. 2015. Super Mario Maker. (2015). http://supermariomaker.nintendo.com/

39. Patrick Oswald, Jordi Tost, and Reto Wettach. 2014. The real augmented reality: real-time game editor in a spatial augmented environment. *Proceedings of the 11th Conference on Advances in Computer Entertainment Technology - ACE '14* (2014), 1–4. DOI: http://dx.doi.org/10.1145/2663806.2663853

40. Heonjin Park, Kyle Koh, Yuri Choi, Han Joo Chae, Jeongin Hwang, and Jinwook Seo. 2016. Defining Rules Among Devices in Smart Environment Using an Augmented Reality Headset. *Proceedings of the Second International Conference on IoT in Urban Space* (2016). DOI:http://dx.doi.org/10.1145/2962735.2962746

41. Tetiana Parshakova, Minjoo Cho, Alvaro Casinelli, and Daniel Saakes. 2016. Ratchair. In *ACM SIGGRAPH 2016 Emerging Technologies on - SIGGRAPH '16*. ACM Press, New York, New York, USA, 1–2. DOI: http://dx.doi.org/10.1145/2929464.2929473

42. PlayStation Mobile. 2015. GT6 Track Path Editor. (2015). https://play.google.com/store/apps/details?id=jp.co.polyphony.GTCourseMaker

43. Iulian Radu and Blair MacIntyre. 2009. Augmented-reality Scratch: A Children's Authoring Environment for Augmented-reality Experiences. In *Proceedings of the 8th International Conference on Interaction Design and Children (IDC '09)*. ACM, New York, NY, USA, 210–213. DOI: http://dx.doi.org/10.1145/1551788.1551831

44. Mitchel Resnick, John Maloney, Andrés Monroy-Hernández, Natalie Rusk, Evelyn Eastmond, Karen Brennan, Amon Millner, Eric Rosenbaum, Jay Silver, Brian Silverman, and Yasmin Kafai. 2009a. Scratch: Programming for All. *Commun. ACM* 52, 11 (Nov. 2009), 60–67. DOI: http://dx.doi.org/10.1145/1592761.1592779

45. Mitchel Resnick, Brian Silverman, Yasmin Kafai, John Maloney, Andrés Monroy-Hernández, Natalie Rusk, Evelyn Eastmond, Karen Brennan, Amon Millner, Eric Rosenbaum, and Jay Silver. 2009b. Scratch. *Commun. ACM* 52, 11 (nov 2009), 60. DOI: http://dx.doi.org/10.1145/1592761.1592779

46. Christian Sandor, Alex Olwal, Blaine Bell, and Steven Feiner. 2005. Immersive Mixed-Reality Configuration of Hybrid User Interfaces. In *Proceedings of the 4th IEEE/ACM International Symposium on Mixed and Augmented Reality (ISMAR '05)*. IEEE Computer Society, Washington, DC, USA, 110–113. DOI: http://dx.doi.org/10.1109/ISMAR.2005.37

47. B. Shneiderman. 1983. Direct Manipulation: A Step Beyond Programming Languages. *Computer* 16, 8 (Aug 1983), 57–69. DOI: http://dx.doi.org/10.1109/MC.1983.1654471

48. Bruce Thomas, Ben Close, John Donoghue, John Squires, Phillip De Bondi, Wayne Piekarski, and Michael Morris. 2000. ARQuake: An Outdoor/Indoor Augmented Reality First Person Application. *Personal and Ubiquitous Computing* 6, 1 (2000), 75–86. DOI: http://dx.doi.org/10.1007/s007790200007

49. John Underkoffler, Brygg Ullmer, and Hiroshi Ishii. 1999. Emancipated Pixels: Real-world Graphics in the Luminous Room. In *Proceedings of the 26th Annual Conference on Computer Graphics and Interactive Techniques (SIGGRAPH '99)*. ACM Press/Addison-Wesley Publishing Co., New York, NY, USA, 385–392. DOI: http://dx.doi.org/10.1145/311535.311593

50. Unity. 2005. Unity. (2005). https://unity3d.com/

51. Blase Ur, Elyse McManus, Melwyn Pak Yong Ho, and Michael L Littman. 2014. Practical trigger-action programming in the smart home. *Proceedings of the 32nd annual ACM conference on Human factors in computing systems - CHI '14* (2014), 803–812. DOI: http://dx.doi.org/10.1145/2556288.2557420

52. Valve. 2011. Portal 2. (2011). http://www.thinkwithportals.com/

53. Valve. 2012. Counter-Strike: Global Offensive. (2012). http://blog.counter-strike.net/

54. Andrew Wilson, Hrvoje Benko, Shahram Izadi, and Otmar Hilliges. 2012. Steerable Augmented Reality with the Beamatron. In *Proceedings of the 25th Annual ACM Symposium on User Interface Software and Technology (UIST '12)*. ACM, New York, NY, USA, 413–422. DOI: http://dx.doi.org/10.1145/2380116.2380169

Ani-Bot: A Modular Robotics System Supporting Creation, Tweaking, and Usage with Mixed-Reality Interactions

Yuanzhi Cao*, Zhuangying Xu*, Terrell Glenn, Ke Huo, Karthik Ramani
School of Mechanical Engineering, Purdue University, West Lafayette, IN 47907 USA
[cao158, xu970, glenn3, khuo, ramani]@purdue.edu

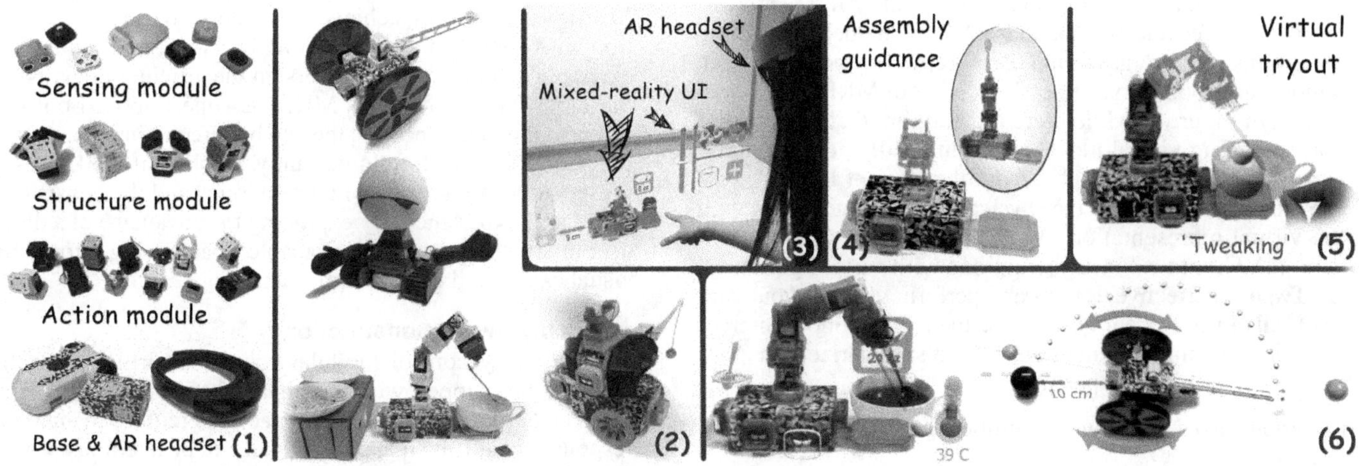

Figure 1. Ani-Bot system overview: Ani-Bot provides users with (1) a modular kit that allows them to (2) assemble and construct robots with crafted DIY objects, and (3) use mixed-reality interaction to perform direct manipulation, sensor driven programming, and animation authoring. (4) The system can assist users in the assembly process, and (5) help them tweak ineffective designs through virtual tryout. (6) Taking advantage of mixed-reality, users can easily program their robots to perform environmentally interactive tasks, such as adding sugar to a teacup or shooting objects into a bowl.

ABSTRACT

Ani-Bot is a modular robotics system that allows users to control their DIY robots using Mixed-Reality Interaction (MRI). This system takes advantage of MRI to enable users to visually program the robot through the augmented view of a Head-Mounted Display (HMD). In this paper, we first explain the design of the Mixed-Reality (MR) ready modular robotics system, which allows users to instantly perform MRI once they finish assembling the robot. Then, we elaborate the augmentations provided by the MR system in the three primary phases of a construction kit's lifecycle: Creation, Tweaking, and Usage. Finally, we demonstrate Ani-Bot with four application examples and evaluate the system with a two-session user study. The results of our evaluation indicate that Ani-Bot does successfully embed MRI into the lifecycle (Creation, Tweaking, Usage) of DIY robotics and that it does show strong potential for delivering an enhanced user experience.

*Yuanzhi Cao and Zhuangying Xu contributed equally to this paper.

TEI'18, March 18-21, 2018, Stockholm, Sweden

ACM ISBN 978-1-4503-5568-1/18/03...$15.00
https://doi.org/10.1145/3173225.3173226

ACM Classification Keywords

• **Information systems∼Multimedia content creation**

Author Keywords

Modular robotics; Mixed-reality; Human-robot interaction; DIY robotics; User interface.

INTRODUCTION

DIY modular robotics has a strong appeal to makers and designers since it can be used in quickly designing, building, and animating their own creation which opens the thrilling possibility of bringing imagination to life. The physical modular units inherently serve as tangible interactive interfaces within a DIY robotics process. Thus, developing a robotics kit with embedded Tangible User Interface (TUI) shows the potential to allow intuitive interaction in the DIY process [3, 37]. However, the versatility and malleability of such TUI's are limited when it comes to programming complex tasks involving a fine level of control [40]. To provide comprehensive controllability for the robotics kit, a Graphical User Interface (GUI) design has been adopted by commercial products such as Lego Mindstorms [5]. This separate digital interface, however, breaks the bridge between the physicality and the virtuality which are built through the TUIs [22]. To prevent inconsistent and fractured user experiences in the DIY robotics process, we seek for a seamlessly integrated workflow in which the intuitive tangible interactions are enhanced by a coherent spatially situated and contextually relevant digital interface.

The newly emerging Mixed-Reality (MR) technology enables the embedding of a versatile and malleable digital interface in the DIY robotics process without impeding the inherent tangibility. Previous researches have attempted mainly in either assisting the assembling of passive building blocks [47, 31, 48] or controlling a pre-defined robot/machine [18, 24, 12, 20, 21]. Although we are inspired and motivated by these efforts, we focus on extending mixed-reality interaction to the whole lifecycle of modular robotics, namely **Creation**, **Tweaking**, and **Usage** [29]. Therefore, we propose Ani-Bot, a modular robotics system embedded with MRI. As demonstrated in Figure 1, while users are building their robots, the corresponding virtual model is automatically generated and superimposed with the robot from the view of HMD. Users can then visually control the physical robot by interacting with the virtual representation. With the Ani-Bot system, users can: (1) **Create** robot constructions with virtual guidance; (2) **Tweak** ineffective designs and perform virtual tryout; and (3) **Utilize** mixed-reality to make their DIY robots interact with the surrounding environment. To summarize, the main contributions of this paper are:

1. *System workflow*, which embeds MRI with modular robotics.
2. *Design of the Ani-Bot system*, including the mixed-reality ready 'plug-and-play' hardware and the incorporated MR features that promote a novel interaction experience.
3. *Evaluation results*, including the constructive feedback summary from our user studies that guides future endeavors.

RELATED WORK

Interacting with DIY Robots

Due to the inherent tangibility in the DIY robotics process, previous works have developed several TUI approaches. Topobo and VEX robotics adopted the Programming-by-Demonstration method with kinetic memory to play back user-defined motions and animate the robot [37, 8]. Since only actuation modules can be programmed, this approach has a limited level of controllability. On the other hand, the Programming-by-Assembly approach requires no further programming once the robot is constructed, thus encouraging users to try different assembly configurations [40]. Therefore, this highly engaging TUI approach has been widely used in the area of childhood robotics education by Cubelets, LittleBits, MakerWear, etc. [3, 11, 2, 35, 25]. However, because each module is pre-programmed for a specific function, complex robots require a large number of modules, which increases both the physical size and the difficulty of assembling. Furthermore, since the TUI robots are assembled and programmed for designated tasks, changing a task usually results in re-assembling a new robot architecture, which lowers the versatility and malleability.

Due to the limitations in TUI's controllability, many commercial robotics kits have adopted an additional GUI to control the robot, such as Lego Mindstorms, Tinkerbots, VEX Robotics, etc [5, 7, 8, 1, 6]. However, most of these GUIs have been separated from the physical robot targets, thereby creating a gap which results in an inconsistent user experience. Alternatively, researchers have been exploring the merging of other interaction methods with DIY robotics. KIWI used scannable image-target-covered cubes to tangibly program the robot [43]. Handimate [39] and PuppetX [17] used hand and body gestures to control the crafted DIY robots, respectively.But although these control modalities show good interactivity, the lack of a fine level of controllability still remains an open issue. Mirror Puppeteering achieved user-defined playback animation with hands-on manipulation [41], yet it still required an external camera to track markers on the articulating parts. On the other hand, Ani-Bot's MRUI is superimposed onto the physical target that bridges the gap by directly interacting with the target object. More importantly, a coherent MRUI design preserves the tangibility of DIY robotics and the consistency of the user experience. By exploiting the advantage of a digital user interface, our system is capable of achieving informative visualization and complex programming.

Assembly-Aware Construction

To effectively control modular robots, a virtual controller needs to be mapped with the physical target. Both GUI designs and controller-enabled interactions require manual correspondence for the mapping, which can be a tedious process for users. For example, when using Handimate [39], users need to manually set the gesture-actuator mapping configurations on a mobile application before controlling the robot. This problem can be solved if the modular kit can be made aware of its own assembly configuration and can therefore accomplish the mapping automatically. Such an assembly-aware concept already exists in many TUI construction kits, including Cubelets and MakerWear [3, 25]. However, they address only electronic communication logics without geometric information of the physical assembly. In our case, geometric assembly-awareness is essential for deploying a mixed-reality user interface. Prior works have explored the subject via hardware connection [26, 46, 10] and computer vision approaches [32]. But most of these works only applied assembly-awareness to passive building blocks that involved no motions. In comparison, the Ani-Bot system provides a virtual geometric model of robotic modules that update and coincide with the physical assembly, thus allowing responsive interactions and active visual feedback.

Assembly and Design Guidance with MRI

Utilizing MRI, different modalities of virtual guidance have been explored to assist users in the assembly process. Henderson et al. overlaid instructions from the view of users' Augmented Reality (AR) headset [19], while Makris et al. displayed the corresponding virtual CAD model [31]. In terms of interaction media, some researchers used a virtual interactive tool [47], while others chose to directly manipulate the virtual model with bare hands for assembly guidance [44] and design simulation [45]. These works focused on providing assembly guidance for robotics/machines with pre-defined designs. Furthermore, without an external monitoring system on the assembly procedure, the guidance remained non-interactive. By embedding an RFID tag in each of the construction modules, Zhang et al. achieved real-time tracking and monitoring for non-mobile passive blocks that enabled interactive guidance [48]. Moreover, researchers have been coupling MRI with interactive design processes, including participatory design [33], decision making [36], and design evaluation [34]. Driven by the needs from the creation and tweaking phases, we focused on incorporating suggestive design guidance for functional robot design. By achieving assembly-awareness, Ani-Bot provides users with interactive mixed-reality assembly guidance for re-configurable modular robotics construction.

Robot Operation with MRI

MRI has been investigated for interacting with robots. TouchMe and exTouch have demonstrated the process with mobile robots [18, 24]. Utilizing MRI with robotics, researchers have achieved human-robot collaboration for object manipulation [15], object delivery [23], and household sequential task instruction [16]. Besides being viewed through an AR tablet device [28, 20, 21], the control interface can also be projected directly onto [38] or near the physical target [42, 30] for ease of mixed-reality interaction. Furthermore, MRI is applied in industrial robotics for path planning [14, 12], spatial programming [27], and trajectory planning [13]. However, the above work utilized mixed-reality primarily for programming movements for robots with determined designs and configurations. Instead, we aim at investigating an MRUI with higher malleability for DIYing a re-configurable robot with both output and input modules. To the best of our knowledge, no prior work has attempted to or explored embedding MRI with DIY robotics; this, is our primary contribution of this paper.

DESIGN PROCESS AND GOALS

To design and fabricate the Ani-Bot system, we followed a user centered design process. We first developed a preliminary system with a few basic modules and MRI features. Then, by conducting a participatory design study with the preliminary system, we elicited critical design principles for our mixed-reality modular robotics system.

Participatory Design Activity

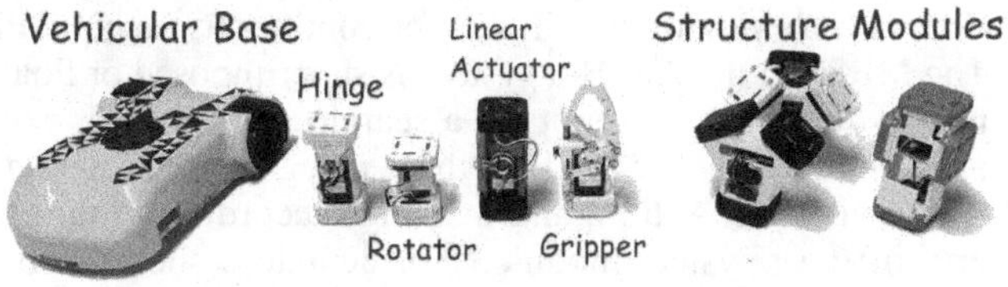

Figure 2. Preliminary modular kit for the Ani-Bot system.

Our preliminary system is demonstrated in Figure 2 with basic 'on-target' direct manipulating UI (Figure 6 (1)). We recruited 5 participants (3 male) who had substantial experience in DIY robotics and asked them to use the system. We encouraged the participants to think out loud. Also, a semi-structured post-study interview was conducted. We focused on investigating the design of a mixed-reality ready modular robotics kit, a coherent user interface, and appropriate interactions. After the study, we found that participants unanimously requested more modules with various structures and functionalities in order to fully support the element of DIY. In terms of the design of UI and the interaction methods, users suggested that we fully exploit the advantage of the digital interface by displaying more informative and visually dynamic user interfaces with appropriate operations to interact with them.

System Design Goals

Based on the feedback about our participatory design activity as well as our own experience in designing the preliminary prototype, we have synthesized the following key design goals:

- **Plug and play.** The system should be mixed-reality ready for users as they play with the modules, with no configuration/preparation time so as to ensure fluid user experiences.
- **Low floors and high ceilings.** The MR system should be intuitive and easy to start, but provide high a ceiling for the level of control capability.
- **Visually intuitive.** The system's MRUI should be informative, provide active feedback, and be self-explanatory. Moreover, it should not be distractive and obstructive between users and their robots.
- **Support creative exploration** As a DIY platform, the system should support users' creative interactive exploration via both hardware and software designs.

THE ANI-BOT SYSTEM DESIGN

System Workflow

Ani-Bot embeds MRI with DIY modular robotics; the workflow is illustrated in Figure 3. All modules in the system have processing power and can be physically connected with each other to establish network communication. By organizing the configuration data from each device, the robot is aware of its own assembly configuration and sends the data to the AR headset (Microsoft HoloLens [4]) to generate the corresponding virtual model. By detecting and tracking an image marker (Vuforia [9]) on the Base Module, the virtual model is superimposed onto its physical target for the mixed-reality interaction. The kinematics data of the virtual model are constantly transmitted to drive the physical robot. In this way, users interact with the physical robot by manipulating the virtual representation from the view of the AR headset.

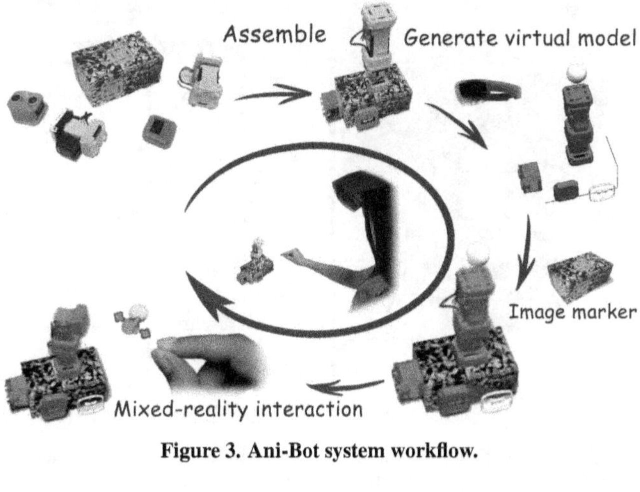

Figure 3. Ani-Bot system workflow.

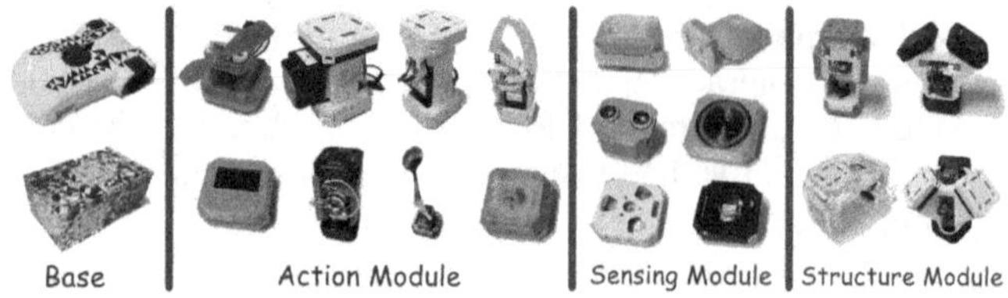

Figure 4. Module library of the Ani-Bot system.

Module Design

As shown in Figure 4, we expanded our preliminary module library based on feedback from the participatory design activity. **Base Modules** are the starting point of users' DIY construction, and they have three purposes: 1) realize tracking and detection of the virtual model via the image marker; 2) organize and transfer data between devices and the AR headset as a communication hub; and 3) provide a power supply for the connected devices. **Action Modules** provide various types of actions for users to interact with the real world. **Structure Modules** increase the structural diversity of the modular robot's configuration. They help the Ani-Bot system to better support users' DIY creation process. **Sensing Modules** read the environmental data, which are visualized in the MRI and used to program the robot behaviors. Together, all these modules compose the hardware modular kit that works coherently with the corresponding software interface to constitute Ani-Bot's mixed-reality modular robotics system.

Hardware Implementations

The modular design is illustrated in Figure 5 (2), using the Hinge Module as an example. The physical connection of the Ani-Bot's module is a Male-Female surface connection setup (42mm * 42mm), which is positioned by four cylindrical pins and secured by two embedded magnets (K&J Magnetics: DC1-N52). Most of the modules in the system have one pair of Male-Female connection surfaces to pass the power supply as well as an electric signal via four pins. All modules in Ani-Bot have only one Male surface, containing a customized PCB and a Bluetooth Microcontroller (RFduino). By reading from the *Sequence pin* and *Orientation pin*, the MCU knows its current position and orientation in the whole robot's assembly. The Base Module, as shown in Figure 5 (1), contains a Bluetooth MCU that receives the configuration data from all the connected devices. By integrating the data from all the devices, the Base is aware of the whole robot's assembly configuration instantly. The assembly configuration data are then transmitted to the HMD via an on-board WIFI MCU (ESP8266) to generate the corresponding virtual representation of the physical robot. When receiving action data from the HMD, the Base Module organizes the incoming data and feeds them to the corresponding receiver device for action.

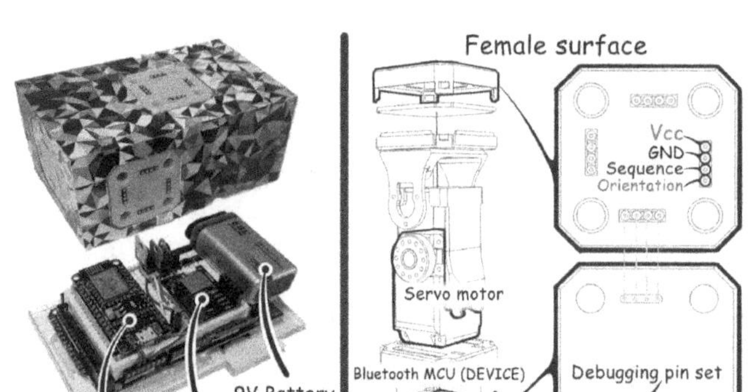

Figure 5. Hardware design of Ani-Bot's module. (1) Cuboid Base module design setup. (2) Exploded view of the Hinge Module.

Interface and Interaction Design

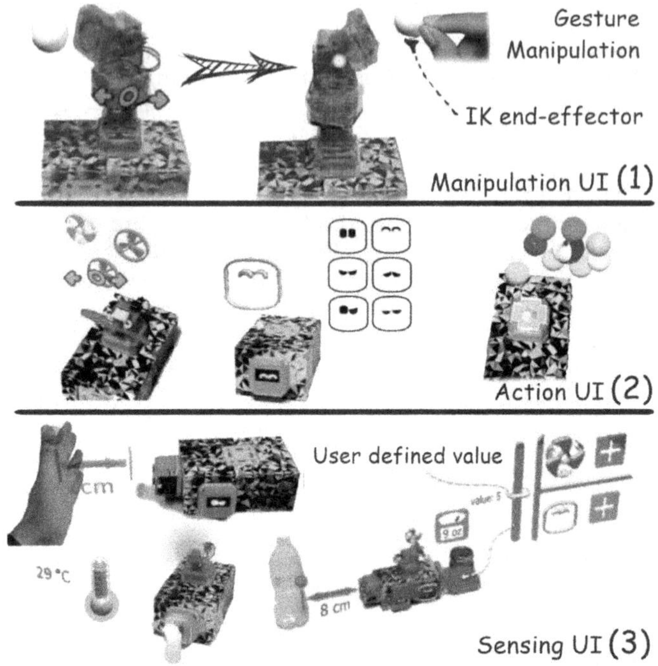

Figure 6. MRUI in the Ani-Bot system consists of (1) Manipulation UI for actuators, (2) Action UI for the other action modules, and (3) Sensing UI for visualizing and programming the sensing modules.

The Ani-Bot system utilizes gesture-based interactions for most of its control and programming. These interactions are supported by the HMD (Microsoft HoloLens) and they require an *air tap* with one finger for clicking and selecting, and a *drag and drop* with two fingers for continuous manipulation. The MRUI in the Ani-Bot system is superimposed or floating nearby the physical robot for a seamless interaction experience. Our UI is designed for three categories of interaction (Manipulation, Action, and Sensing) according to the property of the physical module. For actuators such as Hinge, Rotator, Linear Actuator, and Gripper, we superimpose the corresponding semi-transparent virtual model directly onto the physical module, as shown in Figure 6 (1). Users control these modules by manipulating the virtual models. They can achieve one DOF motion by manipulating each individual module or achieve multi-DOF motions by manipulating the auto-generated Inverse-Kinematics (IK) end-effector on top of the assembly tree. For the other action modules with discrete mode switching, a list-like UI is designed individually according to the module's function. As shown in Figure 6 (2), users can access these UIs to switch on/off the Fan module, change the facial expression on the Face module, and change the light color on the LED module, etc. In terms of the sensing modules, each environmental sensing value (distance, temperature, weight, etc.) is dynamically displayed as shown in Figure 6 (3). Moreover, users can program logic events by setting a user-defined threshold value and accessing the currently connected action modules. An example is illustrated in Figure 6 (3 right), where the user just programs the Fan module to turn ON when the weight sensing value is above 5 and the Face module to display 'happy' when the value is below 5.

Besides gesture-based interactions, the Ani-Bot system also exploits the HMD's multimedia capabilities to create immersive user experiences with active feedback. To avoid being overwhelming and distracting, we utilize voice commands and audio feedback for functions which have no explicit need to visualize, such as mode transition and menu navigation.

MODULAR ROBOTICS WITH MRI

In this section, we demonstrate and discuss the augmentation offered by MRI in the Ani-Bot system. Specifically, we illustrate the system's designated features for the three phases of a construction kit's lifecycle: **Creation**, **Tweaking**, and **Usage**, respectively. We showcase how these embedded MR features can enhance the user experience for DIY robotics.

Creation

The process of playing with a modular robotics kit begins with the assembly. Ani-Bot encourages users to freely explore different assembly configurations by providing a rich module library. In addition, the system can also fully or partially assist users in the assembly process. Utilizing MRI, Ani-Bot provides users with *mixed-reality assembly guidance* for existing designs (Figure 7 (1)). The virtual guidance is interactive and gives real-time assembly feedback. For example, the color of the virtual model will change when the corresponding physical module is correctly assembled. Besides the full assembly manual, the system can also provide partial functional structure suggestions according to the key input module. For example, in Figure 7 (2), upon detecting the 'Distance Sensor,' users can activate the *functional suggestion guidance* by voice command, and the system will display a 2-DOF thrower setup with default adjustable structure parameters.

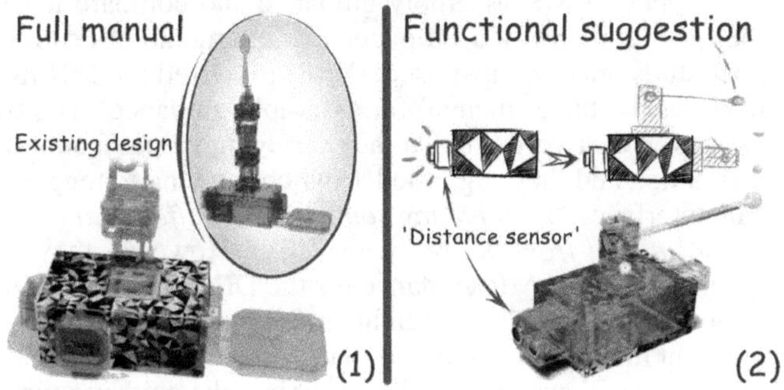

Figure 7. Creation with MRI: mixed-reality assembly guidance. (1) Full MR assembly manual for existing design. (2) Suggestive guidance based on key input device.

Tweaking

When encountering ineffective designs, users will start the iterative process in order to explore and find a working solution, namely Tweaking. Instead of physical tweaking, which requires effort for iterations with real robots, Ani-Bot provides a virtual tryout feature for users to tweak the ineffective designs into a working configuration. As demonstrated in Figure 8, upon removing the end-effector, users can activate the *'Tweaking Mode'* through a voice command. The system will then display a series of suggested derivative configurations based on the current physical setup. Users can try different virtual assemblies and compare their performance in the mixed-reality simulation to find better solutions.

Figure 8. Tweaking with MRI: virtual tryout for functional improvement. Tweaking a robot manipulator setup so that the spoon tip can reach inside the bowl.

Usage

One of the main advantages of mixed-reality is its ability to the merge of a virtual interface with its corresponding physical target. By exploiting this property, Ani-Bot allows users to easily control their robots to effectively interact with the surrounding environment. For instance, Ani-Bot's sensing modules expressively visualize the input data (temperature, distance, force, etc.) from the surrounding environment (Figure 1 (3,6)). In addition, each sensing module offers the ability to program sensor-driven logic events with the programming UI (Figure 1 (3)). In this case, the user just programs the 'Fan Module' to turn on when the weight exceeds the set value, otherwise the 'Face Module' displays a smiling expression.

Besides the sensing programming, Ani-Bot allows users to create and manage keyframe animations that enable their robots to execute automatic actions. As illustrated in Figure 9, after activating the *'Animation Mode,'* users can manipulate the virtual model to set the keyframes (the physical robot will not move in *'Animation Mode'*). Upon playing the animation, the robot will automatically transit through the defined keyframe positions and complete the action. Each animation can then be saved as an interactive *'Action Sphere,'* which floats near the physical robot and plays back the animation when tapped. Users can create multiple animations and intuitively manage them. By dragging an *'Action Sphere'* into another one, users can merge them together and create a new *'Action Sphere'* which has the combined animation. In this way, users can easily achieve complex animation authoring to create environmentally interactive and storytelling like animations.

EXAMPLE APPLICATIONS

Figure 10 demonstrates the four use cases we have created to showcase the diversity and controllability of our system, including two service robots (1,3) assisting environmentally interactive daily practice and two storytelling robots (2,4) with expressive emotions and stylish actions. The **Robot Thrower**

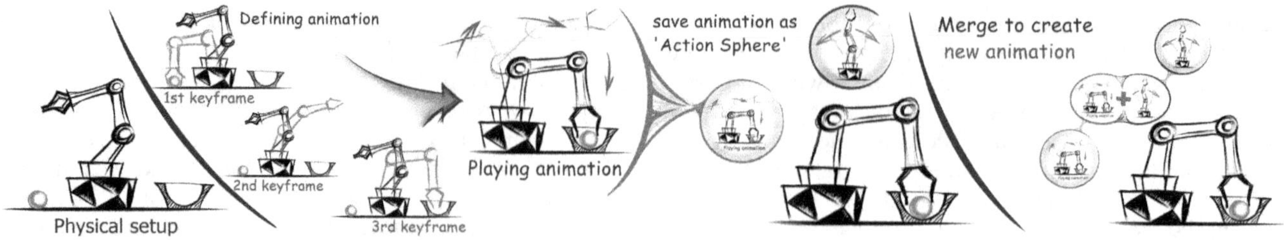

Figure 9. Mixed-reality animation authoring and management.

(1) is able to display the predicted shooting projectile to guide users to manually hit the targets with pinpoint accuracy. The thrower can also utilize the distance sensor to automatically adjust the shooting angle based on the distance reading from the target. The **Emotional Fire Fighter (2)** is a fully equipped vehicular robot with a front temperature sensor for detecting candle fire. He is never too shy to show his emotions via the face modules and he shows no hesitation in using his head-mounted fan and hanging hammer to put out a fire. The **Tea Maker (3)** is a smart service robot with an arm. By visualizing the temperature and weight of the teacup, users can customize their favorite beverage by programming the Tea Maker to automatically add sugar and keep stirring until the tea is ready to serve, which is detected by the temperature sensor and indicated by the blinking LED and the smiling face. The **Dancing Robot (4)** is a DIY character with a big head and gloomy expression. Users can program him to make numerous amazing dance moves.

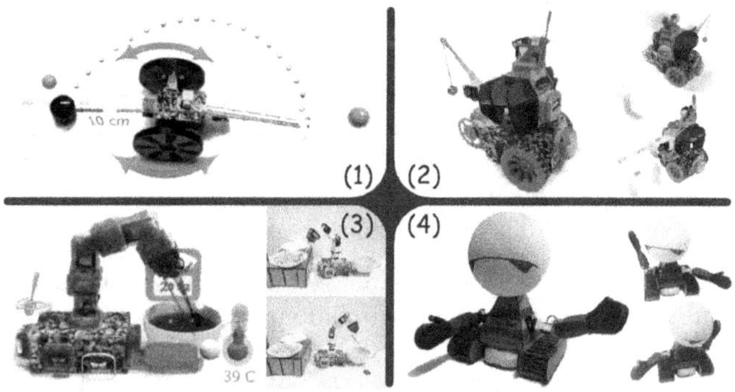

Figure 10. Use cases demonstration of the Ani-Bot system. (1) The Robot Thrower. (2) The Emotional Fire Fighter. (3) The Smart Tea Maker. (4) The Dancing Robot.

SYSTEM EVALUATION

To evaluate the Ani-Bot system, we invited 20 users to participate in our two-session user study (10 for each).

Session 1: System Usability Evaluation

We designed four tasks for the first study session featuring the key functions of the system. We invited 10 users (7 male), 7 of them in the 20-25 age range and 3 in the 25-30 age range, with varies backgrounds. The goal of this study session was to evaluate the usability of the Ani-Bot system and explore the user experience of DIY robotics with MRI.

Procedure. Session 1 took about 1.5 hours for each user, including a tutorial to introduce the HMD device and the Ani-Bot system (20 mins). We adopted one of our use cases ('Tea Maker') as the evaluation prototype due to the comprehensiveness of its functionality and the complexity of its physical structure. We dissected the prototype into four manageable tasks focusing on the three phases: **Creation**, **Tweaking**, and **Usage**. Users were given a questionnaire with Likert-type items and subjective questions after each task. Some of the more representative results are intuitively displayed as a colored scale bar for each task. Each Likert-type item is graded by users from 1 to 5, where 1 means strongly disagree and is colored in red, while 5 means strongly agree and is colored in green. The scale bars are aligned with positive answers (yellow, yellowgreen, green) on the right and negative answers on the left (red, orange). (N = number, U = user)

Task 1: Assembly Guidance, Paper Manual vs MR Manual
For a design configuration with seven modules (Figure 11), we asked users to complete the assembly using both a paper manual and an MR manual as a guidance (random order).

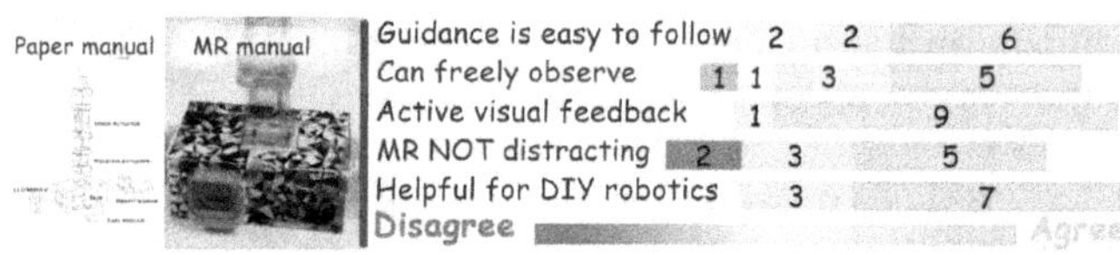

Figure 11. Task 1: Assembly guidance. Paper manual vs MR manual.

Feedback and Discussion. Due to the simplicity of this design, users were able to complete the assembly almost equally rapidly (less than 30 s) and accurately with both manuals. It is noted that the point of this task was not to systematically study the time efficiency and accuracy between the two approaches. Rather, we tried to focus on exploring the user experience of MR assembly guidance and compare it with the most commonly used paper manual method. From the post-study survey, most users (N=8) preferred the MR manual over the paper manual for assembly guidance. The two users who disagreed felt that the overlaying virtual model was distracting and they suggested a switch function to toggle the MR interface. *"I am having some trouble differentiating the virtual model from the real one (U2)."* However, they still admitted that the MR guidance for the DIY robot was useful (reporting 5 and 4). The assembly process included identifying the right module and putting it in the right location. Ani-Bot's MR system allows users to freely observe the guidance virtual model from different perspectives for module identification. One user disagreed with this because of the limited field-of-view of the HMD device. *"It is hard for me to see the whole guidance model without moving my head (U7)."* We found that the virtual feedback for confirming the assembly correctness was particularly appreciated by the users. *"The color* *change feedback really assures me about my assembly and makes me confident."* Overall, we found that the expressive visual feature as well as the interactivity of the MR guidance provided an engaging and entertaining assembly experience. *"I really like it, it's fun and makes me want to try more. (U5)"*

Task 2: Design Tweaking, Physical vs Virtual Tryout

In this task, users were asked to improve the performance of the initially ineffective robot design by changing its assembly configuration. The goal was for the robot arm's end-effector (spoon) to get inside the bowl (Figure 12). Users were asked to perform tweaking in both ways with a randomized sequence.

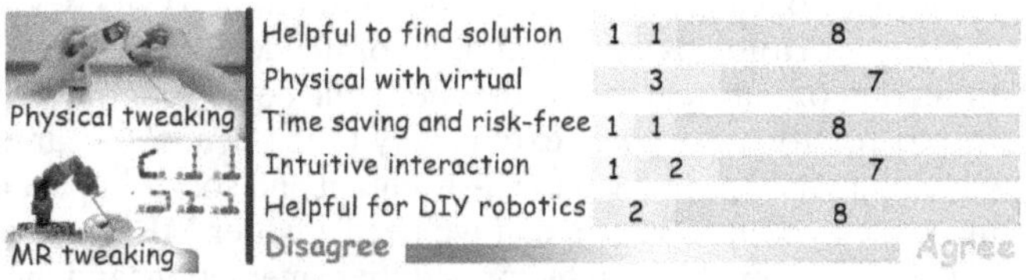

Figure 12. Task 2: Hands-on tweaking vs virtual tryout.

Feedback and Discussion. After this task, most users reported that they preferred MR tweaking over the physical tweaking (N=8). They particularly liked the grafting of the virtual model on the physical modules, while both moved together corresponding to users' simulating manipulation. *"I think the virtual/reality simulation really helps me to understand the dynamics of the robot (U7).".* According to the survey and our observation, users generally enjoyed the MR tweaking due to its time-saving effectiveness and risk-free characteristics. *"MR is fast and easy to try. I enjoy testing different options (U4).". "The MR tweaking reduces the cost and risk for revising physical robots (U1).".* As for the two users who preferred hands-on tweaking, they believed the added complexity of the MR tweaking was unnecessary, but they still appreciated the visualization and simulation ability offered by the MR tweaking. To summarize, the system's virtual tryout feature effectively helped users to identify the configuration for performance improvement. *"With MR, I know it works and I do not need to finish assembling something to test (U8)."*

Task 3: Programming Sensor Driven Events

During this task (Figure 13), users were given a simple setup with two action modules (Fan, Face) and two sensing modules (distance, weight). They were asked to interact with the sensing modules and define the logic events triggered by the environmental data to drive the action modules. Users were first given a brief demonstration and then asked to freely explore the feature and define the logic events by themselves.

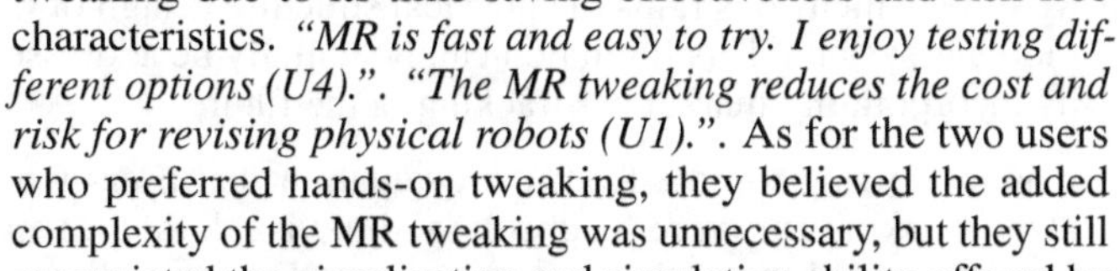

Figure 13. Task 3: Programming sensor driven events.

Feedback and Discussion. All the users found it easy to program a logic event except for U4, who answered 1 in this question. She initially struggled to understand the working mechanism and suggested adding more text or audio instructions to guide users. Despite this, she still agreed that the feature was useful for DIY robotics (score=5). Users generally enjoyed the sensing visualization, which presented the environmental information in a tangible and interactive way. *"This feature makes reading from a sensor so intuitive and entertaining (U3)!"* From the survey results as well as the subjective comments, we found users particularly appreciated the system's fast and easy approach to programming fairly complex events (N=9), which could even elicit and promote interest in DIY robotics. (*"I like this instant programming. It is easy and can make people more interested in DIY robots (U8)."*)

Task 4: Creating Environmentally Interactive Animations

In this task, users evaluated the animation authoring feature in the system. They were asked to define the keyframe animations that facilitated the 3-DOF robot arm with a spoon end-effector to automatically add sugar to the teacup (Figure 14). The average time cost for this task was about 15 min.

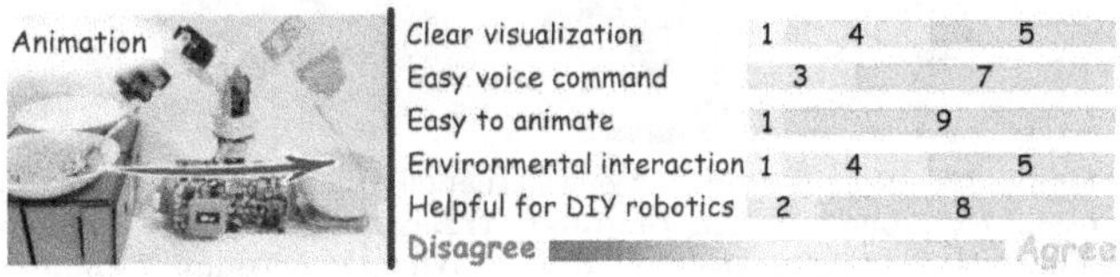

Figure 14. Task 4: Creating mixed-reality keyframe animations.

Feedback and Discussion. Considering the difficulty of task 4, we were surprised to find that most users (7/10) successfully accomplished the task with just one shot. We observed great excitement from the users when they have achieved this complex animation with just a few operations. *"I have never programmed a robotic arm so quickly and easily (U10)!".* Based on the survey results, we found that users were highly satisfied with the MR animation authoring feature in the system. They appreciated the system's ability to create automatic actions *"Animation is useful to do repetitive work (U1)"* that enabled them to quickly explore their ideas with physical robotic movements. *"I like to set several actions at one time and make it keep doing what I want it to do (U9)."* Furthermore, they found the system to be very helpful for programming environmentally interactive tasks due to the active visual feedback from the mixed-reality view. *"I can use the surrounding objects as references when I define the animations; this makes it so easy for me to program my robot around them (U1)."*

Summary. After this session, users generally agreed that the interaction of the system was intuitive and effective (avg=4.6) with well integrated functions that help to provide elevated user experiences in DIY modular robotics (avg=4.56). The System Usability Scale (SUS) survey was also deployed after the study session to evaluate the system with an average score of 83.25 and a standard deviation of 6.8, which indicated high usability of the proposed system.

Session 2: Creating and Animating DIY Robots

The element of DIY is significant to Ani-Bot as the system is designed to support add-on DIY creativity by providing a modular platform and an effective method for controlling and programming. To evaluate this, we invited 10 users from diverse backgrounds for the second session of the study (7 male), with 8 of which in the 20-25 age range and 2 in the 25-30 age range.

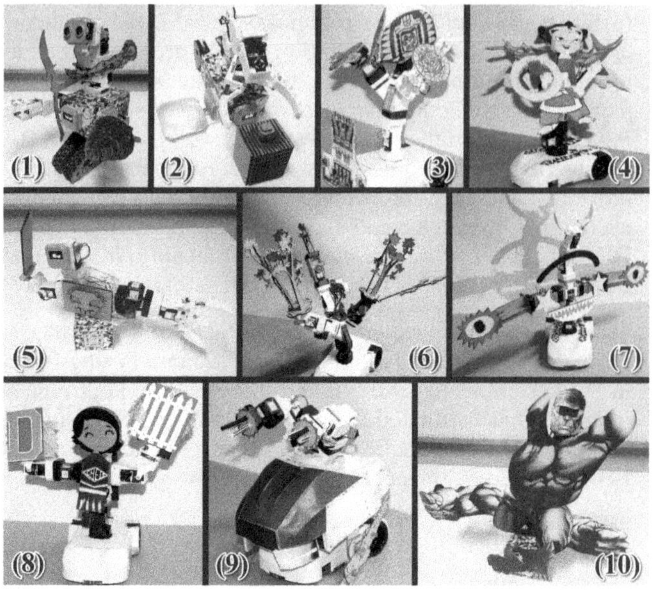

Figure 15. Results from the open creation study session showcasing users' DIY robot. (1) Mr. Destroyer (2) Box Porter (3) Peru Totem (4) 3-head Nezha (5) Robot Bandit (6) The Whomping Willow (7) Sun-eye Monster (8) Cheerleader (9) Robo-Cop (10) The Hulk

Process. Session 2 lasted about 80 min including a 20 min system tutorial. Users had full access to the system's modular kit, as well as various DIY crafting tools and materials to create their own robot. During the session, they were asked to design, craft, assemble, and animate their own DIY robot.

Results. Figure 15 showcases all the DIY robots created by the users during the open creation session. We observed a large variety from the end results, ranging from humanoid characters (4,8,10), to mechanical characters (1,2,5,9), to object-based characters (3,6,7). Each user's DIY robot consisted of 7-9 modules, which indicated high complexity involving multiple degree-of-freedom movements. All animations were created by the users uniquely for their characters which truly brought the robots to life. For example, Mr. Destroyer (1) does not hesitate for one bit to shred anything he sees (detected by the distance sensor) with his blade, claw, and drill bit. The Box Porter (2) is a diligent fellow that specializes in moving anything delivered to him (activated by the weight sensor) to the designated area. The Cheerleader (8) is a lovely girl waving 'De-Fence' for her team, while the Whomping Willow (6) furiously bashes the 'flying car' trapped on its trunk.

Feedback and Discussion. From the post-study survey, we found that most users appreciated the system's coherent workflow to create and animate the DIY robots. *"It was especially fun to make the cheerleader and then see her actually move and do things."* From our observation, we found that the idea of combining DIY with robotics really promotes users' interest in exploring more features and functionalities of the system. *"Just being able to add skin for a better appearance on my robots also encourages me to explore more designs and shapes."* During the ideation process, many users liked to test-play with multiple modules and put on the HMD to quickly test the animation performance. *"It responded well to what I wanted it to do."* The plug-and-play seamless user experience as well as the real-time responsive mechanism was highly appreciated by the users. *"You don't need to worry how you are going to articulate your model for creating the control code. You just plug and play."*

LIMITATION AND DISCUSSION

During our user study, the most common complaints we received were about the HMD device, specifically, its form factor and interaction modality. *"It is too heavy and makes me feel dizzy after some time." "The display view is too small that I have to move my head to see the whole scene." "I don't like the mid-air gesture interaction; it feels awkward and is not very accurate."* Because our system was built on the HMD device (Microsoft Hololens), the limitation of the device became the limitation of our system. Furthermore, the device confined the mixed-reality experience exclusively to the headset wearers, which inevitably impeded the distribution and social impact of the system. This suggests that we need a better MR platform with a user-friendly form factor, intuitive interaction, and most importantly, public viewing and/or accessibility.

Another limitation of the system is caused by the MR tracking mechanism. The Ani-Bot system is currently implemented with an image marker on the Base Module. This requires an initializing detection and tracking process each time users start a new assembly. Moreover, the tracking results can be corrupted by occlusion from other connected modules. *"The virtual model is sometimes mis-aligned with the robot."* The tracking mechanism is the key reason for requiring the Base Module, which constrains the physical structure design of the modular system. This limitation can potentially be addressed by incorporating markerless tracking in the future.

It is interesting to note from the evaluation that users were always asking for more feedback (audio, visual, tactile) and natural control methods (gesture, voice). Future endeavors should therefore focus more on the modality of the interaction approaches to achieve comprehensive control with minimum cognitive load. Furthermore, the system should better understand its users and execute low level operations automatically. With the rapid development of AI technology, a new balance can be established and constantly adjusted between robot intelligence and user-involved controllability.

CONCLUSION

In this paper, we present a novel mixed-reality modular robotics system, called Ani-Bot. We explore and investigate embedding a coherent MRI for DIYing a modular robot. Our use cases as well as the system usability study have evaluated and verified the augmentations for modular robotics by embedding the mixed-reality interaction. The results from the open creation study have demonstrated the Ani-Bot system's capability to support both creating and animating DIY robotics. To this end, our system has shown a strong potential for delivering in-situ and novel user experiences for DIY robotics.

ACKNOWLEDGMENT

This work was partially supported by the NSF under grants CMMI (EAGER) 1547134, IIS (NRI) 1637961 and IIP (PFI:BIC) 1632154. The contents of this manuscript do not necessarily reflect the views or opinions of the funding agency.

REFERENCES

1. 2017. CageBot. (2017). https://www.cagebot.com/shop/.
2. 2017. Code-a-pillar. (2017). http://fisher-price.mattel.com/shop/en-us/fp/think-learn-code-a-pillar-starter-gift-set-fgn83.
3. 2017. Cubelets. (2017). http://www.modrobotics.com/cubelets/cubelets-twenty/.
4. 2017. HoloLens. (2017). https://www.microsoft.com/en-us/hololens.
5. 2017. Lego Mindstorm. (2017). https://www.lego.com/en-us/mindstorms.
6. 2017. MOSS. (2017). http://www.modrobotics.com/moss/programming/.
7. 2017. Tinkerbots. (2017). https://www.tinkerbots.com/.
8. 2017. VEX Robotics. (2017). https://www.vexrobotics.com/.
9. 2017. Vuforia. (2017). https://www.vuforia.com/.
10. David Anderson, James L Frankel, Joe Marks, Aseem Agarwala, Paul Beardsley, Jessica Hodgins, Darren Leigh, Kathy Ryall, Eddie Sullivan, and Jonathan S Yedidia. 2000. Tangible interaction+ graphical interpretation: a new approach to 3D modeling. In *Proceedings of the 27th annual conference on Computer graphics and interactive techniques*. ACM Press/Addison-Wesley Publishing Co., 393–402.
11. Ayah Bdeir. 2009. Electronics as material: littleBits. In *Proceedings of the 3rd International Conference on Tangible and Embedded Interaction*. ACM, 397–400.
12. Jonathan Wun Shiung Chong, SK Ong, Andrew YC Nee, and K Youcef-Youmi. 2009. Robot programming using augmented reality: An interactive method for planning collision-free paths. *Robotics and Computer-Integrated Manufacturing* 25, 3 (2009), 689–701.
13. HC Fang, SK Ong, and AYC Nee. 2012. Interactive robot trajectory planning and simulation using augmented reality. *Robotics and Computer-Integrated Manufacturing* 28, 2 (2012), 227–237.
14. HC Fang, SK Ong, and AYC Nee. 2014. A novel augmented reality-based interface for robot path planning. *International Journal on Interactive Design and Manufacturing (IJIDeM)* 8, 1 (2014), 33–42.
15. Jared A Frank, Matthew Moorhead, and Vikram Kapila. 2016. Realizing mixed-reality environments with tablets for intuitive human-robot collaboration for object manipulation tasks. In *Robot and Human Interactive Communication (RO-MAN), 2016 25th IEEE International Symposium on*. IEEE, 302–307.
16. Richard Fung, Sunao Hashimoto, Masahiko Inami, and Takeo Igarashi. 2011. An augmented reality system for teaching sequential tasks to a household robot. In *RO-MAN, 2011 IEEE*. IEEE, 282–287.
17. Saikat Gupta, Sujin Jang, and Karthik Ramani. 2014. PuppetX: a framework for gestural interactions with user constructed playthings. In *Proceedings of the 2014 International Working Conference on Advanced Visual Interfaces*. ACM, 73–80.
18. Sunao Hashimoto, Akihiko Ishida, Masahiko Inami, and Takeo Igarashi. 2011. Touchme: An augmented reality based remote robot manipulation. In *21st Int. Conf. on Artificial Reality and Telexistence, Proc. of ICAT2011*.
19. Steven J Henderson and Steven K Feiner. 2011. Augmented reality in the psychomotor phase of a procedural task. In *Mixed and Augmented Reality (ISMAR), 2011 10th IEEE International Symposium on*. IEEE, 191–200.
20. Valentin Heun, James Hobin, and Pattie Maes. 2013a. Reality editor: Programming smarter objects. In *Proceedings of the 2013 ACM conference on Pervasive and ubiquitous computing adjunct publication*. ACM, 307–310.
21. Valentin Heun, Shunichi Kasahara, and Pattie Maes. 2013b. Smarter objects: using AR technology to program physical objects and their interactions. In *CHI'13 Extended Abstracts on Human Factors in Computing Systems*. ACM, 961–966.
22. Hiroshi Ishii. 2008. The tangible user interface and its evolution. *Commun. ACM* 51, 6 (2008), 32–36.
23. Kentaro Ishii, Yoshiki Takeoka, Masahiko Inami, and Takeo Igarashi. 2010. Drag-and-drop interface for registration-free object delivery. In *RO-MAN, 2010 IEEE*. IEEE, 228–233.
24. Shunichi Kasahara, Ryuma Niiyama, Valentin Heun, and Hiroshi Ishii. 2013. exTouch: spatially-aware embodied manipulation of actuated objects mediated by augmented reality. In *Proceedings of the 7th International Conference on Tangible, Embedded and Embodied Interaction*. ACM, 223–228.
25. Majeed Kazemitabaar, Jason McPeak, Alexander Jiao, Liang He, Thomas Outing, and Jon E Froehlich. 2017. MakerWear: A Tangible Approach to Interactive Wearable Creation for Children. In *Proceedings of the 2017 CHI Conference on Human Factors in Computing Systems*. ACM, 133–145.
26. Yoshifumi Kitamura, Yuichi Itoh, Toshihiro Masaki, and Fumio Kishino. 2000. ActiveCube: a bi-directional user interface using cubes. In *Knowledge-Based Intelligent Engineering Systems and Allied Technologies, 2000. Proceedings. Fourth International Conference on*, Vol. 1. IEEE, 99–102.
27. Jens Lambrecht, Martin Kleinsorge, Martin Rosenstrauch, and Jörg Krüger. 2013. Spatial programming for industrial robots through task demonstration. *International Journal of Advanced Robotic Systems* 10, 5 (2013), 254.

28. Daniel Leithinger, Sean Follmer, Alex Olwal, Samuel Luescher, Akimitsu Hogge, Jinha Lee, and Hiroshi Ishii. 2013. Sublimate: state-changing virtual and physical rendering to augment interaction with shape displays. In *Proceedings of the SIGCHI conference on human factors in computing systems*. ACM, 1441–1450.

29. Joanne Leong, Florian Perteneder, Hans-Christian Jetter, and Michael Haller. 2017. What a Life!: Building a Framework for Constructive Assemblies.. In *Tangible and Embedded Interaction*. 57–66.

30. Natan Linder and Pattie Maes. 2010. LuminAR: portable robotic augmented reality interface design and prototype. In *Adjunct proceedings of the 23nd annual ACM symposium on User interface software and technology*. ACM, 395–396.

31. Sotiris Makris, George Pintzos, Loukas Rentzos, and George Chryssolouris. 2013. Assembly support using AR technology based on automatic sequence generation. *CIRP Annals-Manufacturing Technology* 62, 1 (2013), 9–12.

32. Andrew Miller, Brandyn White, Emiko Charbonneau, Zach Kanzler, and Joseph J LaViola Jr. 2012. Interactive 3D model acquisition and tracking of building block structures. *IEEE transactions on visualization and computer graphics* 18, 4 (2012), 651–659.

33. Lai Xing Ng, SK Ong, and AYC Nee. 2010. ARCADE: a simple and fast augmented reality computer-aided design environment using everyday objects. (2010).

34. Lai Xing Ng, SW Oon, Soh Khim Ong, and A YC Nee. 2011. GARDE: a gesture-based augmented reality design evaluation system. *International Journal on Interactive Design and Manufacturing* 5, 2 (2011), 85–94.

35. Hyunjoo Oh and Mark D Gross. 2015. Cube-in: A Learning Kit for Physical Computing Basics. In *Proceedings of the Ninth International Conference on Tangible, Embedded, and Embodied Interaction*. ACM, 383–386.

36. SK Ong, Yu Pang, and AYC Nee. 2007. Augmented reality aided assembly design and planning. *CIRP Annals-Manufacturing Technology* 56, 1 (2007), 49–52.

37. Hayes Solos Raffle, Amanda J Parkes, and Hiroshi Ishii. 2004. Topobo: a constructive assembly system with kinetic memory. In *Proceedings of the SIGCHI conference on Human factors in computing systems*. ACM, 647–654.

38. Philipp Schoessler, Daniel Windham, Daniel Leithinger, Sean Follmer, and Hiroshi Ishii. 2015. Kinetic Blocks: Actuated Constructive Assembly for Interaction and Display. In *Proceedings of the 28th Annual ACM Symposium on User Interface Software & Technology*. ACM, 341–349.

39. Jasjeet Singh Seehra, Ansh Verma, Kylie Peppler, and Karthik Ramani. 2015. Handimate: Create and animate using everyday objects as material. In *Proceedings of the Ninth International Conference on Tangible, Embedded, and Embodied Interaction*. ACM, 117–124.

40. Orit Shaer and Eva Hornecker. 2010. Tangible user interfaces: past, present, and future directions. *Foundations and Trends in Human-Computer Interaction* 3, 1–2 (2010), 1–137.

41. Ronit Slyper, Guy Hoffman, and Ariel Shamir. 2015. Mirror Puppeteering: Animating Toy Robots in Front of a Webcam. In *Proceedings of the Ninth International Conference on Tangible, Embedded, and Embodied Interaction*. ACM, 241–248.

42. Masanori Sugimoto, Tomoki Fujita, Haipeng Mi, and Aleksander Krzywinski. 2011. RoboTable2: a novel programming environment using physical robots on a tabletop platform. In *Proceedings of the 8th International Conference on Advances in Computer Entertainment Technology*. ACM, 10.

43. Amanda Sullivan, Mollie Elkin, and Marina Umaschi Bers. 2015. KIBO robot demo: Engaging young children in programming and engineering. In *Proceedings of the 14th international conference on interaction design and children*. ACM, 418–421.

44. X Wang, SK Ong, and Andrew Yeh-Ching Nee. 2016. Multi-modal augmented-reality assembly guidance based on bare-hand interface. *Advanced Engineering Informatics* 30, 3 (2016), 406–421.

45. ZB Wang, SK Ong, and AYC Nee. 2013. Augmented reality aided interactive manual assembly design. *The International Journal of Advanced Manufacturing Technology* 69, 5-8 (2013), 1311–1321.

46. Michael Philetus Weller, Ellen Yi-Luen Do, and Mark D Gross. 2008. Posey: instrumenting a poseable hub and strut construction toy. In *Proceedings of the 2nd international conference on Tangible and embedded interaction*. ACM, 39–46.

47. ML Yuan, SK Ong, and AYC Nee. 2008. Augmented reality for assembly guidance using a virtual interactive tool. *International Journal of Production Research* 46, 7 (2008), 1745–1767.

48. J Zhang, SK Ong, and AYC Nee. 2011. RFID-assisted assembly guidance system in an augmented reality environment. *International Journal of Production Research* 49, 13 (2011), 3919–3938.

Tquencer: A Tangible Musical Sequencer Using Overlays

Martin Kaltenbrunner
University of Art and Design
Linz, Austria
martin.kaltenbrunner@ufg.at

Jens Vetter
University of Art and Design
Linz, Austria
jens.vetter@ufg.at

ABSTRACT

This article discusses the design and implementation of the Tquencer, a tangible musical sequencer device. The tangible interaction paradigm for musical sequencers has been explored previously trough the arrangement of simple tangible tokens within time-based physical constraints. While this initial approach allows for the creation of basic rhythmic or melodic loops, it sometimes lacks the musical depth required for professional live performance. Therefore we introduce several additional physical design elements that allow the development of musical complexity, while maintaining the overall simplicity of tangible interaction. These tangible elements include single-step, multi-step and resizable tokens, which can be arranged to trigger musical events, multi-step sound effects and more complex sequence patterns. Furthermore the device also allows the dynamic assignment of the content and behavior of physical tokens through dedicated configuration tokens. We also introduce tangible overlays, which allow the handling and arrangement of multiple musical configurations in various layers. This token configuration and layer management is facilitated by an additional control step, which allows for the overall tangible configuration of a musical setup. Apart from its primary musical application scenario, the Tquencer also provides a generic tangible controller platform for time-based sequencing applications.

Author Keywords

Musical Instrument; Tangible Interaction; Interaction Design; Tangible Programming; Sequencer; RFID Sensing

INTRODUCTION

Token-based sequencing[10], which allows the arrangement of digital data embodied within physical tokens, is already a well established paradigm in tangible interaction design. Sequencing is conceptually grounded in the musical domain and has therefore been implemented in a vast variety of musical instruments, starting with the musical automata in the 18th century. Today this also includes several examples of tangible sequencer applications[1], since tangible interaction promised to resolve some of the performance limitations of contemporary digital music practice. Compared to commonly used software-based laptop instruments, tangible interfaces can provide a more expressive musical interaction bandwidth through direct physical manipulation to the performers, and therefore a more engaging performative experience to the audience. Nevertheless we can also observe that apart from a few exceptions such as the table-based modular synthesizer Reactable[7], most tangible musical interfaces often still lack the necessary musical depth for live performance, in spite of their innovative interaction design approach. Our Tquencer design therefore intends to provide a portable and low-cost musical device, which combines several advanced tangible interaction techniques in order to achieve sufficient musical complexity, while maintaining the overall simplicity of token-based interaction.

TEI '18, March 18–21, 2018, Stockholm, Sweden

ISBN 978-1-4503-5568-1/18/03...$15.00

DOI: https://doi.org/10.1145/3173225.3173233

Our tangible interaction design primarily includes the sequential arrangement of physical tokens in combination with tangible overlays in order to expand the spatial limitations of a basic 8-step sequencer layout. We also focus on a fundamental tangible programming principle, which includes the static and dynamic assignment of musical content and functionality to tokens and overlays within the principal tangible domain. Therefore we provide single step tokens for musical events and resizable multi-step tokens e.g. for sound effects, as well as dedicated configuration tokens for dynamic content assignment. For the placement of these configuration tokens as well as the tangible overlays we expanded the eight sequencer steps with an additional control position.

RELATED WORK

There already exist several examples of tangible user interfaces, which individually implement some of the interaction design elements mentioned above. Verplank's et.al. early Tile-Sorting Board[11] from 1994 has been later also adapted to a musical application context. Bennet's Beat Bearing[2] device for example constitutes an elementary form of a tangible sequencer, where the positioning of uniform metal tokens within a physical multi-track configuration determines the content and timing of musical events. Hesse's Bubblegum Sequencer[5] on the other hand introduces colored tokens with statically linked musical content, which is independent of the vertical track position. Alonso's Scoretable[6] implements a circular token sequencer, which is a common alternative to the standard linear topology. Newton Dunn's BlockJam[8] design on the other hand allows the programming and arrangement of independent tangible sequencer blocks without the need for an external physical constraint. Costanza's Audio D-Touch[3] allows the swift exchange of various sequencer topologies by using application sheets. A further non-musical example for the sequential tangible programming paradigm is Gallardo's Turtan[4], which transfers the procedural Logo programming language into the tangible domain. Ullmer's Casiers[9] introduce the concept of tangible overlays, which constitute context-dependent and exchangeable physical constraints for interactive surfaces. This concept has been recently also adopted by the Sensel Morph[1] device, which provides various controller overlays for its force-sensitive surface.

HARD- AND SOFTWARE DESIGN

The central interactive element of the Tquencer device consists of an array of eight+one RFID reader modules, which are each capable of detecting the simultaneous presence of two ISO14443 (Mifare) tags operating at 13,561 MHz. The individual RFID reader modules are based on the MFRC-522 chipset, already include a PCB antenna and are interconnected through a serial SPI bus configuration. In order to avoid cross-detection problems between nearby readers, we employ a time-multiplexed sensing method by sequentially activating and reading from each module individually. The actual number of usable RFID tags is virtually unlimited, and we can statically (by design) and dynamically (by configuration) assign an individual tag UID to the actual token functionality.

Hardware Components

The overall interactive input and visual feedback is managed by an Arduino Micro (Leonardo compatible) micro-controller board, which includes an ATmega32U4 running at 16MHz. We use almost all available I/O pins for connecting the various hardware elements. As mentioned above the RFID reader array is connected through the SPI bus and uses nine additional digital selector pins. A complementary capacitive touch controller based on the MPR121 chipset is connected via the I2C bus and provides twelve individual touch points. Furthermore we use three analog pins for connecting the potentiometer knobs required for the control of global parameters. The visual feedback is provided by an array of nine Neopixel RGB LED modules, which are connected serially through single digital pin. The whole device setup is powered by a 5V2A power supply connected to a Micro USB port.

The micro-controller board processes the input data from all connected modules in real-time and also calculates the according states and events. This includes the detection of presence and removal of all RFID tokens, the analysis of capacitive touch button gestures as well as the precise sequencer timing and volume control from the potentiometer values. The resulting control values, events and states are encoded and transmitted through a custom serial protocol. Thus the micro-controller board already provides the full I/O functionality and can operate independently.

For the integrated musical functionality we employ a NanoPi Single Board Computer (SBC) running Ubuntu 16.04 with a real-time Linux Kernel. This devices sports a quad core ARM CPU running at 1GHz and 512MB RAM, and therefore provides sufficient computing power for real-time sound synthesis at a low cost and embedded form factor. The board also provides the necessary integrated sound output as well as an onboard Ethernet port, which we use for overall configuration purposes and external control capabilities. Additional USB ports also allow the connection of arbitrary USB devices, such as external sound cards or MIDI converters, while the integrated Micro USB port is used for the power supply. The overall internal hardware components are shown in Figure 1.

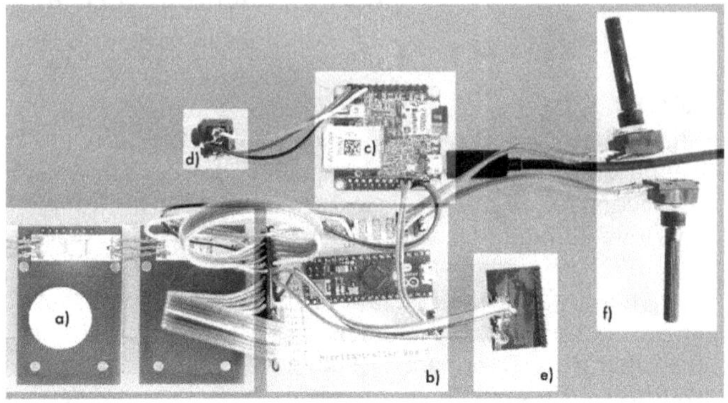

Figure 1. The internal hardware components of the Tquencer: a) RFID array b) micro-controller c) single board computer d) audio output e) touch controller f) controller knobs

Software Components

In conjunction with the basic I/O firmware on the micro-controller, we developed a simple background application, which constantly reads the provided interaction data from the serial port and translates the according states and events to a custom protocol based on Open Sound Control.[12] The according OSC messages are primarily used for the control of the internal synthesizer, and are simultaneously broadcasted to any device connected via Ethernet for alternative external control purposes.

The central synthesizer engine of the Tquencer has been implemented using the Supercollider[2] sound programming language, which not only provides the core musical sequencer functionality but also allows the design of simple programmable extensions. The audio output is managed by the Jack audio daemon, which in conjunction with the real-time Linux kernel ensures a minimal audio latency.

We also employ various integrated Linux system components for overall configuration purposes, such as the Samba daemon for file management via Ethernet as well as the Lighttpd server for a web-based configuration interface. Connected devices are automatically configured using DHCP and Zeroconf.

TANGIBLE INTERACTION DESIGN

The core musical interface of the Tquencer consists of a simple eight-step sequencer design, where the basic sonic events for each individual step can be configured through the placement of a tangible token. Due to the technical constraints of the chosen RFID sensing method described above, each step can detect two simultaneous tangibles, allowing a total of 16 musical events within each loop. While this allows the straightforward tangible programming of simple musical sequences

[1] http://www.sensel.com

[2] https://supercollider.github.io/

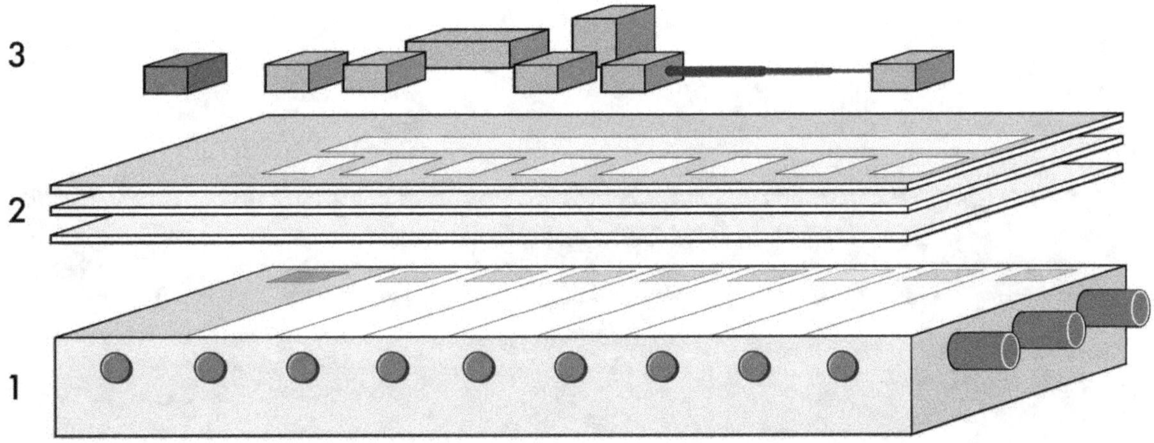

Figure 2. Diagram of interactive elements of the Tquencer: 1) sequencer 2) overlays 3) tokens

such as drum and melody loops, this of course only provides a rather minimal musical functionality in its basic configuration. Therefore we introduced several additional tangible design elements, which allow for the development of more complex musical structures, while maintaining the overall simplicity.

Tokens

From a musical point of view the Tquencer employs three different types of tokens: Event tokens, Effect tokens and Pattern tokens. Event tokens trigger simple musical events, such as sample playback, midi notes and algorithmic sound generators. Effect tokens on the other hand apply sound effects to single or multiple musical events, such as reverb, delay and distortion. Pattern tokens are altering the course of the sequencer sweep, such as reverse, repeat and local loop. In addition to that, we also provide dedicated configuration tokens, which allow the dynamic content assignment to Event and Effect tokens.

From a physical point of view, we provide three different token designs: Single-step tokens, Multi-step tokens and resizable Multi-step tokens.(see Figure 2.3) This allows the physical assignment of musical events and effects to single or multiple steps using a single token only, which covers the selected area. Resizable tokens are an extension of rigid two- and three-step tokens allowing the configuration of four- to eight-step tokens.

Overlays

Since a simple eight-step sequencer with a static configuration would not provide the necessary musical depth for professional musicians, we designed a physical approach for the selection of alternative musical programs and the management of multiple musical layers. We therefore employ physical overlays in the form of transparent plastic sheets, which are tagged with an RFID sticker on one end.(see Figure 2.2) Placing this overlay on the device with its sticker over the dedicated configuration step, thus will select the according musical program that has been associated with this overlay, such as a drum computer, note sequencer or more complex algorithmic behaviors.

Hence these overlays constitute a physical form of tangible windows, which allow the development of multi-layered musical structures, while maintaining the overall simplicity of our token-based sequencer design. Once such a configuration (e.g. drum loop) has been arranged, it can be converted to a continuous background loop by pressing a dedicated hold-button while removing the overlay including all active tokens. In order to facilitative the distinction and handling of the various overlays, we use differently colored sheets, was well as graphical (printed) and physical (engraved) design elements.

On the other hand the physical persistence of such a token-overlay configuration also imposes some conceptual constraints, since a previously configured background loop cannot be physically called back into operation. Thus we only can delete previous iterations of such a configuration, and have to rearrange a particular overlay if any changes are required.

Controls

In addition to the core token-overlay interaction, the Tquencer also provides several complementary controls, which consist of three lateral knobs (potentiometers), three lateral touch buttons (capacitive) as well as nine frontal touch buttons for each individual step (eight steps plus configuration step).

Two of the controller knobs are statically linked to the global tempo and volume controls, while the third knob is dedicated to a layer-specific global effect control, such as a reverb for example. The frontal touch buttons allow for additional gestural control of the tangible sequencer content, such as keeping an individual Event-token after removal (hold) or deleting all virtual content (double tap). The same touch gestures (hold and double tap) are applied to the button in front of the configuration step for the holding and deleting of overlays. The additional three lateral buttons are reserved for global configurations and mode changes.

Feedback

In order to facilitate its overall handling and interaction stability, the Tquencer also provides basic visual feedback in the form of an individual RGB color LED for each step including the configuration step. At the moment we defined several

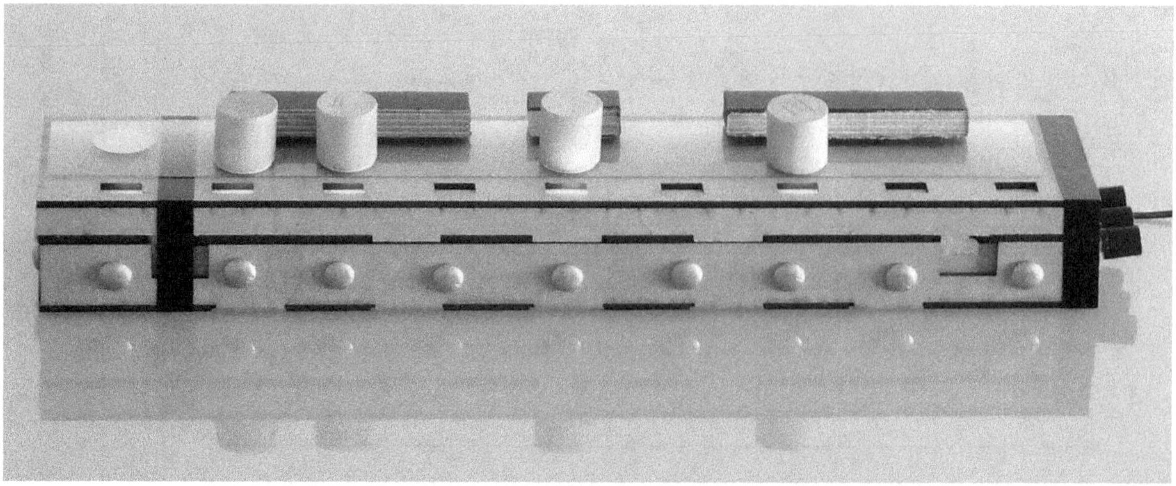

Figure 3. The current iteration of the Tquencer hardware prototype.

color codes which represent the various states of each individual step. This includes the basic feedback of the number of recognized tokens as well as the visualization of the moving sequencer sweep. The configuration step changes its color according to the currently active physical overlay.

As a musical instrument the Tquencer naturally provides acoustic feedback for all interactions, depending on the currently active musical configuration. It does not provide any additional acoustic feedback (such as tempo ticks), since this would interfere with the overall musical experience. Due to its asynchronous sequencer design, it also does not provide immediate acoustic feedback for each interaction, such as the placement of a new token. Therefore the visual cues play an important role for the real-time feedback for these interactions as well as for the overall tempo representation.

MUSICAL INTERACTION DESIGN

The Tquencer has been primarily designed as a standalone musical instrument, but can be also used as controller for external musical equipment, such as software applications (via OSC), digital synthesizers and effect devices (via MIDI) as well as analog synthesizers (via CV). In the following we will concentrate on the musical interaction design of the provided internal synthesizer, which is based on SuperCollider.

Tangible Programming

The initial default configuration after switching on the Tquencer is a generic drum sequencer. The sequencer loop starts with a default tempo, which is visualized by the moving sweep on the LED array, and can be adjusted through the primary tempo potentiometer on the right side.

Generic Sequencing

In this configuration all available tokens can be used to trigger various drum samples. Placing an Event token on an individual sequencer step will trigger the according pre-assigned drum sound as soon as the tempo sweep crosses that position. The overall arrangement of these drum tokens therefore allows the creation of simple rhythmic structures, with a maximum of two drum events per step. This physical control allows the direct manipulation of all present drum events, removing or adding further Event tokens affects the according drum sequence and results in immediate rhythmic changes.

Effect Sequencing

In addition to the generic sequencing of musical events, the Tquencer also allows three different ways to apply additional sound effects to the complete or parts of the sequence: Dedicated Effect tokens apply additional musical effects (such as delay or distortion) at their actual position in a sequence. Single-step Effect tokens only apply to an individual step, while multi-step Effect tokens cover a certain range of the sequence. Resizable multi-step Effect tokens allow for the rapid adjustment of the effect range. A global sound effect (such as reverb) can be adjusted with the dedicated effect potentiometer on the right side, while the frontal touch buttons can be used to de/activate that global effect for an individual step.

Pattern Sequencing

For the creation of more complex sequence topologies we provide a collection of preconfigured Pattern tokens, which are distinguishable from Event and Effect tokens by their shape. Pattern tokens can affect the course of an entire sequence with behaviors such as reversing, randomizing and resizing the overall sweep, but can be also employed locally for the creation of loops and repetitions.

Layer Management

As we can see, the maximum amount of simultaneously usable Event, Effect and Pattern tokens is significantly limited by the spatial and technical constraints of our basic device layout. Tangible overlays therefore allow the configuration and handling of various musical behaviors, which can be easily exchanged by the placement of an accordingly marked transparent sheet onto the device surface. Currently there are three default overlays available: a drum computer, a melody stave and an algorithmic synthesizer, which can be individually configured as explained further below. Additional blank layers can be configured for the development of complex effect sequences and pattern behaviors in order to liberate the active tangible configuration for musical interaction. Holding the touch button in front of the configuration step when removing an overlay, allows to keep any musical content in the background, while new sequences can be arranged on top of these existing loops. Double-tapping the according touch button erases any background content, and only physically present tokens will continue to trigger musical output.

Token Assignment

While we can distinguish the fundamental token classes by their physical design (currently cylinders for Event tokens, cubes for Effect tokens, and hemispheres for Pattern tokens), the creation of a physical representation for token subclasses (for example based on color) would result in a very large collection of individual tokens to represent all possible musical content or sound effects. Therefore only Pattern tokens are actually hardcoded to their specific functionality, while we rely on the dynamic content association for Event and Effect tokens. Placing a special Programming token onto the configuration step turn the device into programming mode, which allows the assignment of context (layer) dependent musical content to Event tokens or individual sound effects to Effect tokens. Placing an Event or Effect token onto the device, will in this case assign the predefined content or effect of the selected slot to the token. This configuration is maintained after the removal of the Programming slot as is only valid in conjunction with the currently present overlay.

Software Configuration

While the core musical interaction and the fundamental configuration of the Tquencer can be fully handled within the tangible domain, we provide various additional configuration layers for the individualization and customization of the internal synthesizer.

Alternative musical content such as samples and sound fonts can be simply uploaded to the device via the integrated file sharing when connected to an external computer through Ethernet. This content can be then associated to the eight slots of an individual overlay via a simple web-based configuration interface, and then subsequently assigned to an individual token using the method described above.

Advanced users will be also able to extend the functionality of the internal synthesizer through a dedicated plugin interface for the realization of additional sound effects or algorithmic synthesizer elements. Since the actual source code of the complete synthesizer component is also exposed via file sharing, we also allow its full customization if required.

Performance Observations

As mentioned above tokens are placed on the surface of the Tquencer in order to arrange a musical sequence. Since this is a very direct way to generate and manipulate sequences, playing the Tquencer feels organic and familiar. This tangible approach to musical intervention immediately encourages advanced physical interactions, such as grabbing multiple tokens at once and moving them step by step. Involving the touch buttons e.g. for additional effects fits in easily, even while moving a token on the surface. The tempo controlled by the tempo potentiometer ranges from 30 bpm to 240 bpm, which allows for radical changes in the musical output. While may initially be a challenge to keep track of the various tokens, it quickly becomes clear that the interaction based on arranging tokens is very intuitive and playful.

Connecting external equipment (for example via MIDI, OSC) works simple and uncomplicated. Here the Tquencer can be used as a MIDI-sequencer and tempo-sync master device. The individual tokens then trigger MIDI notes, which can be assigned pre-configured either in the programming mode, or individually in the web-based configuration interface (see below). This allows software synthesizers, digital audio workstations, analog synthesizers and other devices to be included. Using the Tquencer along with other musical equipment and instruments is probably more common from a musical and performative point of view, rather than considering it as a standalone solo instrument.

TANGIBLE INTERACTION PLATFORM

The overall modular design of the Tquencer also allows its usage as a generic tangible controller device for arbitrary time-based sequencing application scenarios. Although our current configuration includes an integrated synthesizer for our specific musical application, the generic OSC encoding of the overall sequencer state and user interactions also allows for the control of alternative internal (on the SBC) or external applications (via Ethernet). One possible example would be the control of a DMX driven light performance through tangible sequencing.

Following the Open Design philosophy we are also planning to provide all software and hardware elements including a comprehensive documentation of the Tquencer internals under an open licensing scheme. This includes the open source code of the micro-controller firmware, interaction daemon and synthesizer application as well as the open hardware design of the employed PCB boards and other physical components.

This open design approach not only allows the full reproduction of our device, but more importantly will also facilitate modifications of our original design for customized application scenarios as well as the improvement of our design itself by the community.

CONCLUSION AND FUTURE WORK

We presented the hardware, software and interaction design of the Tquencer device. The current iteration of this tangible musical sequencer is already quite mature, but is still subject to ongoing development and improvement both from a technical and musical perspective. The future work will mainly concentrate on the performative aspects of our tangible interaction design, which will most-importantly include its on-stage evaluation in a live performance scenario. Furthermore we are planning to refine the overall hardware design of the device towards production quality, including the possibility of a subsequent crowd-funding campaign.

REFERENCES

1. R. Arar and A. Kapur. 2013. A History of Sequencers: Interfaces for Organizing Pattern-Based Music. In *Proceedings of the Sound and Music Computing Conference (SMC2013)*. Stockholm, Sweden.
2. P. Bennett. 2010. The Representation and Control of Time in Tangible User Interfaces: (Summary of PhD Research). In *Proceedings of the Fourth International Conference on Tangible, Embedded, and Embodied Interaction (TEI '10)*. Cambridge, Massachusetts, USA.
3. E. Costanza, S. B. Shelley, and J. Robinson. 2003. D-touch: A Consumer-Grade Tangible Interface Module and Musical Applications. In *Proceedings of the Conference on HumanComputer Interaction (HCI03)*. Bath, UK.
4. D. Gallardo, C. F. Julià, and S. Jordà. 2008. TurTan: A tangible programming language for creative exploration. In *Third IEEE International Workshop on Tabletops and Interactive Surfaces (Tabletop 2008)*. Amsterdam, The Netherlands.
5. H. Hesse and A. McDiarmid. 2008. *The Bubblegum Sequencer*. Technical Report. UC Berkeley School of Information.
6. S. Jordà and M. Alonso. 2006. Mary Had a Little scoreTable* or the reacTable* Goes Melodic. In *Proceedings of the 2006 Conference on New Interfaces for Musical Expression (NIME '06)*. Paris, France.
7. S. Jordà, G. Geiger, M. Alonso, and M. Kaltenbrunner. 2007. The reacTable: Exploring the Synergy Between Live Music Performance and Tabletop Tangible Interfaces. In *Proceedings of the 1st International Conference on Tangible and Embedded Interaction (TEI '07)*. Baton Rouge, Louisiana.
8. H. Newton-Dunn, H. Nakano, and J. Gibson. 2002. Block Jam. In *ACM SIGGRAPH 2002 Conference Abstracts and Applications (SIGGRAPH '02)*. San Antonio, Texas.
9. B. Ullmer. 2011. Casier: Structures for Composing Tangibles and Complementary Interactors for Use Across Diverse Systems. In *Proceedings of the Fifth International Conference on Tangible, Embedded, and Embodied Interaction (TEI '11)*. Funchal, Portugal.
10. B. Ullmer and H. Ishii. 1999. mediaBlocks: Tangible Interfaces for Online Media. In *CHI '99 Extended Abstracts on Human Factors in Computing Systems*. Pittsburgh, Pennsylvania.
11. M. Withgott. 2015. What Do Objects Mean?: Early Tangibility in and Around Interval Research. In *Proceedings of the Ninth International Conference on Tangible, Embedded, and Embodied Interaction (TEI '15)*. Stanford, California, USA.
12. M. Wright, A. Freed, and M. Ali. 2003. OpenSound Control: State of the Art 2003. In *Proceedings of the 3rd Conference on New Instruments for Musical Expression (NIME '03)*. Montreal, Canada.

Real-time Recognition of Guitar Performance Using Two Sensor Groups for Interactive Lesson

Yejin Shin, Jemin Hwang, Jeonghyeok Park, Soonuk Seol
School of Electrical, Electronics & Communication, Korea University of Technology & Education
Cheonan, South Korea
{yepp1252, zpdltusl, 2011161058, suseol}@koreatech.ac.kr

ABSTRACT
The accurate recognition of guitarist performance is challenging compared with other instruments because a guitar player typically plays several notes at once and uses both hands in different ways. In this paper, we propose a sensor-based guitar that consists of two groups of sensors. One sensor is used to recognize the fingering positions of the fretting hand, and the other is used to detect the guitar strings that are played by the picking hand. We design an embedded system for accurate sensing and propose a data analysis mechanism to precisely figure out the played pitch and the duration of notes using the sensed data. We realize our scheme as a high-quality prototype that detects guitarist performance with accuracy sufficient for the transcribing of a performance. We also present real application examples such as a rhythm game for interactive lessons and a music sharing feature with user created musical scores.

Author Keywords
Music transcription; automatic note inference; guitar; sensors; fingering position detection; performance feedback

ACM Classification Keywords
• *Applied computing~Sound and music computing*
• *Applied computing~Interactive learning environments*
• *Hardware~Tactile and hand-based interfaces*

INTRODUCTION
With the development of ICT and multimedia technology, many fields are changing. Things that were unimaginable in the past, even things unrelated to IT, are now connected to the Internet, and various data analyses are becoming a driving force of the changes in society.

Convergence of musical instruments and IT is one such trend. The development of an IT guitar to assist beginning guitar players is one example of this trend. These products mainly focus on providing a guide, for fingering or playing technique, on the fretboard by using embedded LEDs. Fretlight [4] is a product that uses LEDs installed on the fretboard of the guitar to provide a fingering position guide by turning on the LEDs. Fret Zealot [5] is another product, comprising an LED strip and controller attached to the guitar. Still, existing products do not provide feedback through identification of correct playing. Therefore, research into providing feedback on user's playing through analysis of multimedia data from musical instruments has conducted.

A number of techniques are being developed to sense the performance of musical instruments to transcribe musical scores or give feedback to players. Techniques for analyzing audio by recording sounds from instruments [1,3,17,18] have been traditionally widely studied. However, there is a limitation in that the audio-based approach is applicable to fixed-tuned musical instruments. In addition, it is difficult to estimate pitches when multiple sounds are played at the same time, such as a chord, and even harder when there is noise from the microphone used. Another approach proposed in [19] analyzes violin fingering through video analysis. However, the match ratio for the onset, offset, and pitches elements is only 65%, which is limited for practical applications. Moreover, a string instrument has the characteristic that even if the fingerboard is fingered, it does not make a sound unless the strings are actually plucked. Therefore, judging the onset and offset depending on whether the fingerboard is fingered may result in a difference from the actual performance.

To increase sensing accuracy, approaches that involve physically embedded sensing circuits in musical instruments have been studied. Pianos with embedded sensors [6,10] are such studies. However, these pianos require only one kind of sensor and thus detecting a key press is relatively simple. More complicated approaches are required in the case of string instruments. One study [14] proposed an approach to judge the accuracy of a musical performance on a cello. The approach includes a sensing circuit on the fingerboard and combines sound recording data through a microphone and motion sensing data via a video. Other approaches [2,7,8,12] involved attaching sensors to the fingerboard and bow of a violin to sense the fingering and bowing of the strings. However, such approaches are difficult to apply to guitars. A guitar is played by fingering the chord with one hand and plucking

TEI '18, March 18–21, 2018, Stockholm, Sweden

ACM ISBN 978-1-4503-5568-1/18/03…$15.00
https://doi.org/10.1145/3173225.3173235

the strings with the other hand or a pick. Therefore, both the left and right hand motions, which cause the vibrations of the strings, should be sensed to recognize guitar performance. Similar to a sensor-attached bow in the case of a violin, a sensor circuit can be configured by wiring a metal guitar pick [15,16] However, this approach causes discomfort to players and limits guitarists from playing in various styles (e.g., fingerstyle), particularly in acoustic guitar. These difficulties have imposed limitations on transcribing music from an acoustic guitar and eliminating the gaps that have to be overcome to actually apply it to real instruments.

In this paper, we propose a sensor-based guitar. We add sensors to an LED-based guitar [13] that allows guitar students to practice guitar by lighting LEDs on the corresponding positions on the guitar fingerboard. Our sensor-based guitar consists of two groups of sensors. One sensor is used to recognize the fingering positions of the fretting hand, and the other is used to detect the guitar strings that are played by the picking or plucking hand. We design an embedded system for accurate sensing and propose a data analysis mechanism to precisely figure out the played pitch and the duration of notes by using the sensed data. The proposed method realizes music transcription with a very high level of accuracy through a sensor- and circuit-based approach. We realize our idea as a high-quality prototype and conduct experiments to evaluate the accuracy of the detection. In the evaluation, we analyze and compare the sound recorded in audio and the data sensed in the prototype. To the best of our knowledge, the proposed guitar is the first attempt to accurately recognize performance information by sensing both the fingered position and plucked strings when playing a guitar. We also present real application examples such as a rhythm game for interactive lessons and a music sharing feature with user created musical scores.

DESIGN AND IMPLEMENTATION OF SENSING CIRCUIT

Figure 1. Sensor-based guitar

We design sensing circuits and implement a commercial-grade guitar prototype by integrating the sensing circuits. The guitar is composed of a main controller as an embedded system, a fingerboard-sensing circuit, and a string-sensing circuit. The external appearance of the guitar is shown in Fig. 1. We implement an embedded system using Atmel SAM3A8C as a Micro Controller Unit (MCU), which is connected to the fingerboard-sensing circuit and string-sensing circuit.

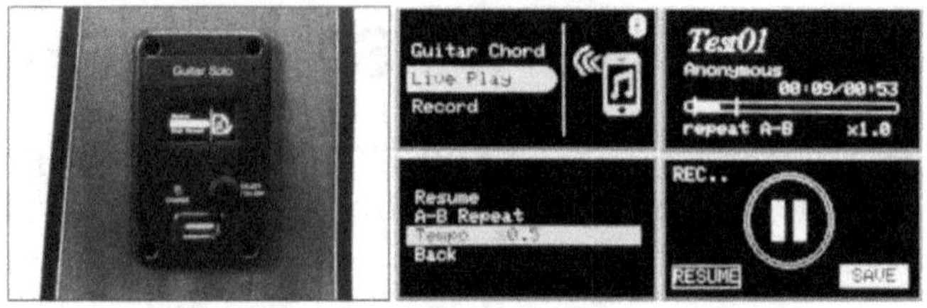

Figure 2. Various features of the embedded system

The embedded system has been significantly improved to adapt sensing features while providing all the existing useful features from our previous study [13]. For example, with the LED guidance feature, a user can easily find fingering positions on the fingerboard. The user can also search for songs from a music server and download them to the embedded system through a smartphone application. Then, without a smartphone, the user can practice the stored songs with LED guidance. In addition, the user can quickly master a certain song by using the efficient practice features, such as Rewind, Fast-Forward, and AB Repeat, provided in the embedded system. By newly employing sensors, the system can recognize the pitches and duration of the notes played. Fig. 2 shows the embedded system and some displayed menus. In this paper, we focus on the design and implementation of the fingerboard-sensing circuit and string-sensing circuit.

Fingerboard-Sensing Circuit

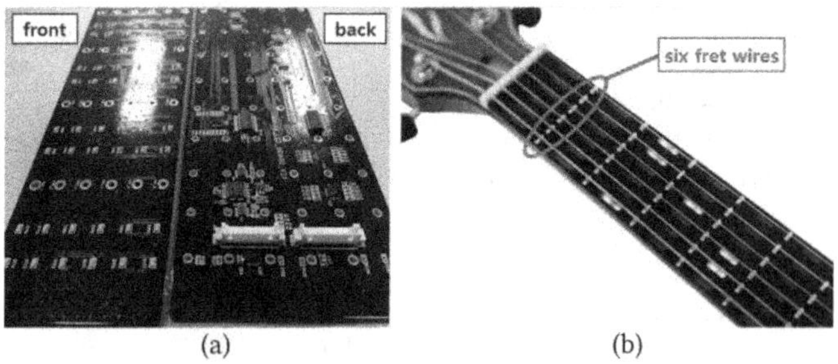

Figure 3. The fingerboard of the sensor-based guitar: (a) PCB embedded under the fingerboard, (b) the fingerboard with fret wires

To detect fingering positions, we have integrated a sensing circuit with an LED circuit, as shown in Fig. 3(a), and placed it under the fingerboard, as shown in Fig. 3(b). We have split a conventional fret wire into six fret wires, which are parts of the sensing circuit. This allows a total of 120 fret wires to play a role as individual switches when they are in contact with conductive strings.

We use each string as a part of the circuit so that if a particular string and fret wire touch, a closed loop between the fingerboard and the string is made and the position can be electrically recognized. Information on simultaneous multiple positions is input into the main controller in the form of a bit stream. By using 16 8-bit shift registers, it is possible to sense various combinations of fingering information for 120 fret wires with only six data input pins.

String-Sensing Circuit

The guitar employs six piezo sensors to recognize whether the strings have been plucked. The piezo sensors are located under the saddles, which sense the change of vibration. However, to prevent the vibrations from transmitting to other piezo sensors through the saddle, we divide the saddle into six and attach the piezo sensors under each separated saddle, as shown in Fig. 4.

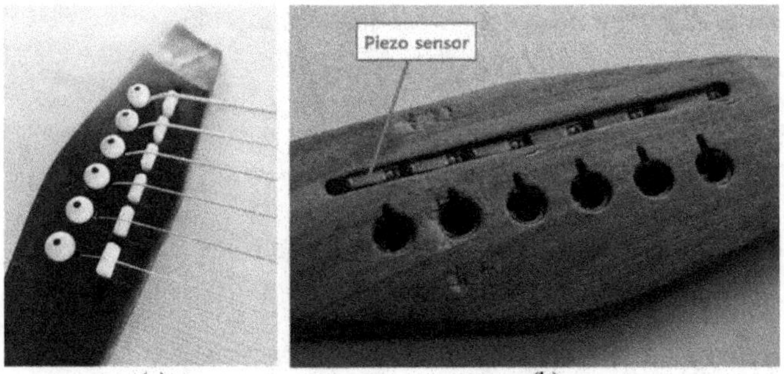

Figure 4. The bridge of a sensor-based guitar: (a) six separate saddles, (b) six piezo sensors located under the saddles

The six sensors are connected to the analog input pins of the embedded system. The string sensing is determined by comparing an analog input value with a certain threshold value. Details on how to determine the duration of a note played are explained in the following section.

SENSING DATA ANALYSIS MECHANISM

When a user plays the guitar, recognizing the user's performance is accomplished through two sensing mechanisms. Fret sensing recognizes the fingering positions. String sensing recognizes the onset and offset for each string that is plucked. The sensed data are further processed by the embedded system to obtain meaningful information. In this section, we explain the mechanisms of analyzing the sensed data.

Fingering Position Sensing

Because we use each string as part of the circuit, if a particular string touches a particular fret wire, the MCU reads a high value for the fret wire; otherwise, it reads a low value. The MCU scans each fret wire every 2ms and finds fingering positions as a set of coordinates that express string and fret numbers. Therefore, even if multiple frets are fingered at once, the fingering position can be recognized with high accuracy. In a stringed instrument, if a user plucks a string while pressing two or more frets on the same string, the actual sound is generated by the vibration of a string length from the nearest fret to the guitar body to the saddle in the guitar body. Therefore, we consider the nearest fret to the saddle a meaningful fingering fret during the data-processing step shown in Fig. 5.

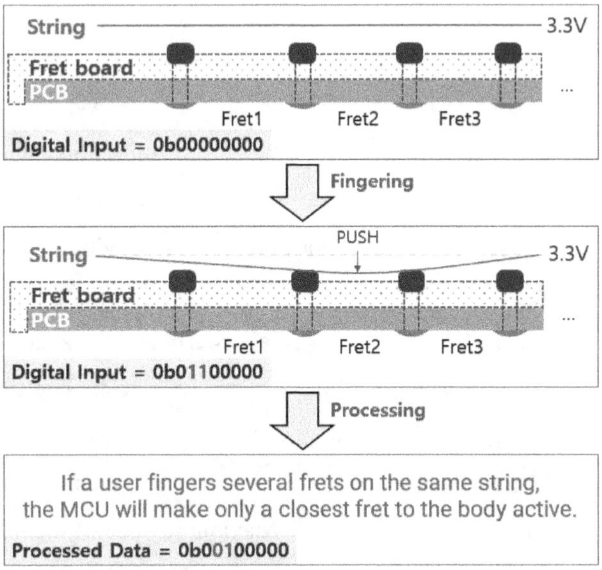

Figure 5. Fret-sensing mechanism

Recognizing the duration of a note

This section describes how to process the sensed data to recognize the duration of notes played by the user. We calculate the envelope of the analog data and compare it with the threshold to recognize the onset and offset of a note. Table 1 explains variables used for recognizing the duration of a note.

Envelope calculation mechanism

The MCU reads analog input data from the piezo sensors every 2ms ($Sample\ Rate = 500\ Hz$). The sample rate can be increased with a higher performance MCU. When a user plucks a string, the raw input data (V_{raw}) gradually decreases in amplitude, repeating positive and negative values. Therefore, if the raw data itself is used in the sensing mechanism, it is recognized that the string is plucked several times because V_{raw} repeatedly crosses the threshold. Therefore, we do not use V_{raw} directly, but calculate $V_{shifted}$ by $|V_{raw} - V_{baseline}|$, where the $V_{baseline}$ is the measured as an average vibration value of the string in the absence of any vibration. We calculate an envelope ($V_{envelope}$) of $V_{shifted}$ and compare it with the threshold to recognize the onset and offset of the note. The following equations are used to calculate the envelope.

$$g_{Attack} = e^{-\frac{1}{SampleRate \times t_{Attack}}} \tag{1}$$

$$g_{Release} = e^{-\frac{1}{SampleRate \times t_{Release}}} \tag{2}$$

$$V_{envelope(n)} = g \times V_{envelope(n-1)} + (1-g) \times V_{shifted(n)}$$
$$\begin{cases} g = g_{Attack}, V_{shifted(n)} > V_{envelope(n-1)} \\ g = g_{Release}, V_{shifted(n)} \leq V_{envelope(n-1)} \end{cases} \tag{3}$$

Variables	Descriptions
V_{raw}	Raw vibration data from piezo sensor.
$V_{baseline}$	Average V_{raw} value when there is no vibration.
$V_{shifted}$	Vibration value shifted by baseline, i.e., $\lvert V_{raw} - V_{baseline}\rvert$.
$V_{envelope}$	Vibration value from the envelope of the oscillating signal.
t_{Attack}	Time for initial run-up of vibration level from nil to peak, beginning when the string is first plucked.
$t_{Release}$	Time for the level to decay from peak to zero.
g_{Attack}	Gain coefficient for attack time calculated by the time-constant equation, Eq. (1).
$g_{Release}$	Gain coefficient for release time calculated Eq. (2).
Th_{onset}	Threshold value of the envelope to determine onset.
Th_{offset}	Threshold value of the envelope to determine offset.
I_{max}	Maximum value of the influence on the envelope due to plucking other strings.

Table 1. The variables used for calculating the duration of a note

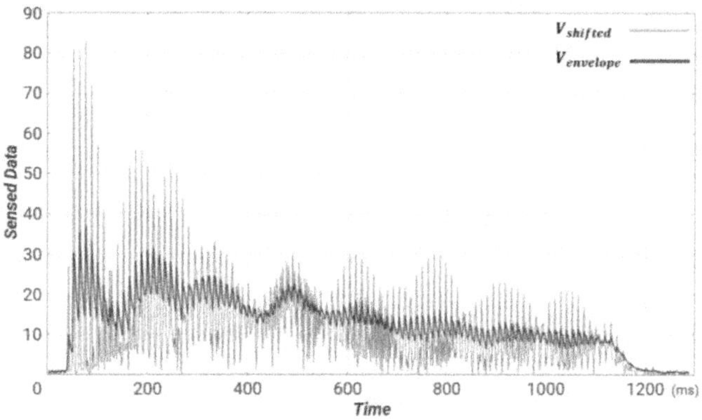

Figure 6. $V_{shifted}$ vibration waveform and $V_{envelope}$ calculation result

t_{Attack} in Eq. (1) is the time from when the sound begins to emerge until it reaches the peak, and it allows the user to specify how quickly the envelope follows a higher value. In contrast, $t_{Release}$ in Eq. (2) represents how quickly the envelope follows a smaller value. g_{Attack} and $g_{Release}$ are the gain factors that determine the rate of reflection and retention of the sampling data, respectively. Eq. (3) indicates that $V_{shifted(n)}$ is updated by reflecting the new $V_{shifted(n)}$ at the $(1-g)$ ratio and maintaining $V_{envelope(n-1)}$ at the g ratio. The g value is calculated by substituting the g_{Attack} calculated in Eq. (1) when $V_{shifted(n)}$ value increases to a larger value than $V_{envelope(n-1)}$ and the $g_{Release}$ calculated in Eq. (2) when decreasing to a smaller value than $V_{envelope(n-1)}$. t_{Attack} and $t_{Release}$ can be used to adjust the sensitivity according to the user's preference. In this paper, t_{Attack} of 5ms and $t_{Release}$ of 10ms are set as default values. Fig. 6 shows an example of $V_{shifted}$ and $V_{envelope}$ as a result of applying the above formula.

Setting a threshold through a calibration process

Using $V_{envelope}$, we determine the onset and offset of the note. The criterion is the threshold set by analyzing the intensity of vibration. There is an onset threshold (Th_{onset}) and offset threshold (Th_{offset}). When the value of $V_{envelope}$ exceeds Th_{onset}, it is judged to be the onset time. When it falls below the Th_{offset} value, it is judged to be the offset time.

The threshold needs to be set differently for each string and may be adjusted depending on the user's sensitivity preference or the change of string tension due to the environment (e.g., temperature, humidity). Therefore, we provide a calibration feature for each string.

At the beginning of calibration, the embedded system will instruct the user not to touch the strings for 2 seconds. During this time, an average value of the input analog data is derived and set as $V_{baseline}$. When $V_{baseline}$ setting is completed, the embedded system guides the user to pluck the six strings one by one. If the user plucks the strings according to the instructions, the vibration values of the six strings are input into the MCU. The MCU analyzes the input vibration values from each string. The vibration caused by one string may influence to the other five sensors due to the resonance phenomenon, vibration transmission, and so on. Therefore, We use I_{max}, which is maximum value of the influence on the envelope due to plucking other strings. For example, the I_{max} of string 1 is the maximum value of the influence when strings 2 to 6 are plucked. This allows the error of certain strings being mistakenly sensed when playing another string to be avoided.

Th_{onset} is set to 1.2 times I_{max}. Th_{offset} is set to an average value of $V_{envelope}$ for 200ms from time when $V_{envelope}$ becomes smaller than $\sqrt{I_{max}}$. If $V_{envelope}$ value of a particular string is equal to or greater than Th_{onset}, we determine that the string has been plucked, and when the $V_{envelope}$ value of the string is less than Th_{offset}, we determine that the note of the string is no longer playing.

EVALUATION

In this section, we evaluate the performance of the guitar that we proposed in terms of the sensing success rate and the error in duration of the note. The performance for the evaluation is performed by the experimenter who is an intermediate guitar player. We evaluate the success rate of multipitch detection for seven basic guitar chords shown in Fig. 7. The experimenter plucks each chord 10 times with various strengths. The plucking strengths are varied from the minimum for generating an audible pitch to the maximum strength of the experimenter. We use log data generated in our embedded system to check the result. The log data include times and sets of a fret number and a string number. The performance is also recorded with a microphone to find a ground truth for the duration of a note.

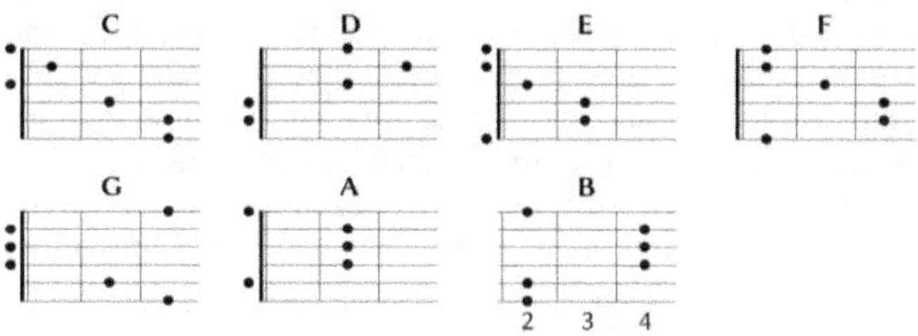

Figure 7. The seven guitar chords used to measure a sensing success rate

The sensing success rate is evaluated as passing or failing regarding whether the user's performance is sensed. The sensing success rate is determined as a "pass" if the performance is sensed well. On the other hand, if it is not sensed correctly, sensed many times, or sensed from other strings, then it is determined as a "fail." This sensing success rate is calculated as in Eq. (4).

$$Sensing\ success\ rate = \frac{The\ Number\ of\ Passes}{The\ Number\ of\ Attempts} \times 100(\%) \quad (4)$$

A sensing success rate has been measured as 100% in this experiment. Note that if a user plucks guitar strings too weakly, making almost no sound, it cannot be sensed accurately. The sensing success rate may also be affected when the tension of strings changes as time goes, or due to temperature and humidity. In these cases, the user should reset Th_{onset} and Th_{offset} through a calibration process for accurate sensing.

The frequency of calibration depends on the user's preferred sensing accuracy and the degree of change in the guitar strings' state. Normally, the user should recalibrate when the user is tuning the guitar, such as if the user installs new guitar strings or adjusts the tuning of the strings. The guitar will provide constant accuracy, even without recalibration for several weeks, if the tensions of the guitar strings remain constant.

The error in duration of the note is evaluated by checking the difference between the duration recognized by our guitar and the duration found in the recorded audio file. The amplitude scale of audio goes from positive to negative repeatedly within the range between -1.0 and +1.0. We use absolute value of the amplitude ($|amp|$) for defining onset and offset times. When $|amp|$ of the recoded audio is more than 0.1 (white noise) and maintained for 2ms, we consider it the onset of the note. When $|amp|$ is below 0.1 and maintained for 10ms, we define it as the offset of the note. The duration between the onset time and the offset time from the recorded audio is used a ground truth.

The range of the errors in duration of the note for each string is shown in Fig. 8. In this evaluation, the experimenter plucks each string 10 times at various strengths and then mutes after a random time between about 250ms and 850ms. The duration of most common notes (e.g., a quarter note, an eighth note) belongs to this range. The error value in Fig. 8 is the absolute value of the original error value. The average error for all strings is 15.6ms and in most cases the errors are within 40ms. These errors will have to be improved to satisfy instrumentalists and electronic musicians in terms of the perceived quality for action-to-sound latency to be maintained less than 10ms [9]. However, such errors can be ignored in a music transcription application where we map a recognized duration of a note into one of the known durations for common notes. In order words, it is less likely to judge a note as a wrong note because the duration difference between two different notes is sufficiently large. For example, in moderato (bpm=90), a quarter note, an eighth note, and sixteenth note are 666.6ms, 333.3ms, and 166.6ms, respectively.

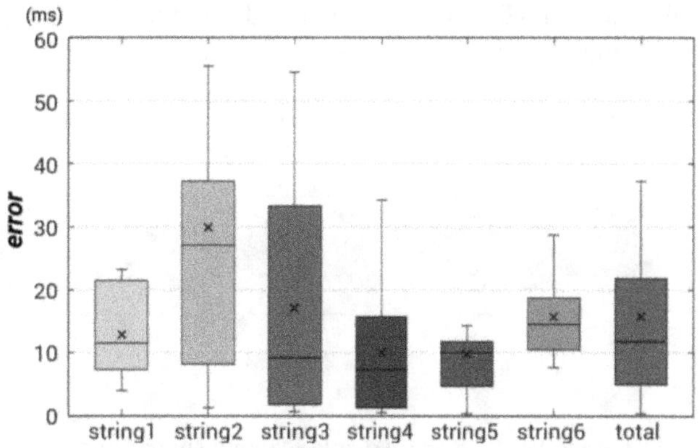

Figure 8. The range of errors in duration of the note in each string

APPLICATIONS

In this section, we introduce various utilization methods of the proposed guitar. A typical application creates musical scores. Using our guitar, musical scores can be generated with performance information by using the results of the pitches and durations of notes detected. After the performance information is analyzed by our scheme, post-processing is required to make the sensed data a musical score. Since people cannot play with a perfect beat when performing, the duration of the actually played note is mapped to the closest typical note duration. For example, if a user sets the bpm to 90 and plays a note for 700ms, it is determined as a quarter note. Note that the duration of a quarter note with a bpm of 90 is 666.7ms and a dotted quarter note is 1,000ms, so the duration of 700ms should be categorized as a quarter note.

Even if a user plays the same song, created musical scores may differ depending on the style of the user's performance. If a user plays four bars of Mozart's "Twinkle, Twinkle, Little Star" and plays each note similar to the duration of the original notes of the musical score, the generated musical score will be like that of Fig. 9(a). However, if the user plays a note for a shorter duration, an eighth note and a rest may be inserted for a quarter note, as shown in Fig. 9(b). Depending on the implementation of the application, it can also be judged as staccato.

Figure 9. Result of musical score creation depending on performance style

As an extension to the application, after creating one's own musical scores, the user can also share them on the Web using a sheet music sharing platform [12]. Shared musical scores can be downloaded through a smartphone application, and the user can receive LED guidance. In addition, if a user plays the guitar in connection with our smartphone application, TAB score is displayed on the smartphone application in real time, as shown in Fig. 10.

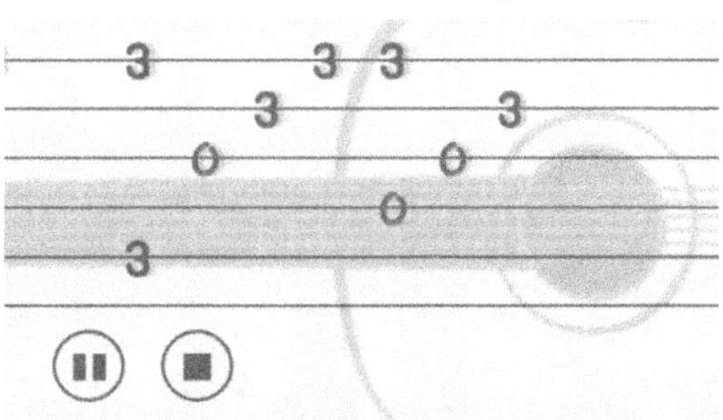

Figure 10. TAB score displayed on a smartphone

Another very useful application is a feedback system. The proposed guitar can analyze the sensed data to determine whether the user is performing correctly and provide feedback in real time. Performance feedback is provided through the LEDs on the guitar's fingerboard, where the fingering position that user has to adopt is illuminated in green. The fingering position LED lights turn yellow if the user performs correctly, while they turn red when the user performs incorrectly. The performance feedback with LED color changes and the feedback scheme for the user's performance result are shown in Fig. 11.

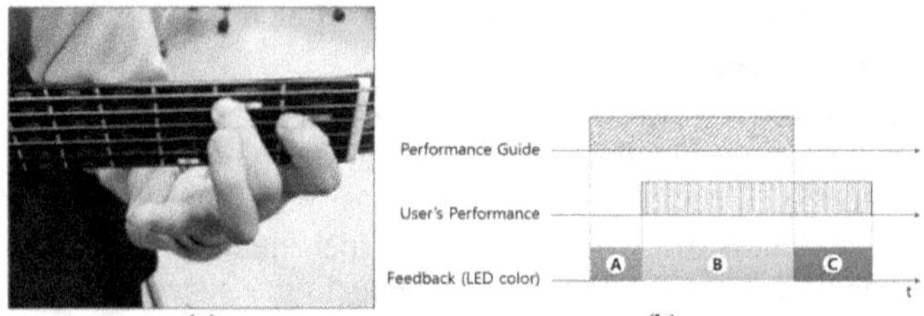

(a) (b)

Figure 11. Feature of real-time feedback: (a) performance feedback by changing LED color, (b) feedback scheme by LED color change

In the case of playing the guitar in connection with the smartphone application, real-time performance feedback is provided through the smartphone, as shown in Fig. 12. Through an interface like a rhythm game, the application displays information about the strings and frets to be fingered, and since the user can check the accuracy and combo scores of their performance, they can gain not only skill improvement, but also enjoyment. Such interactive lessons help guitar learners learn more effectively. In addition, it is expected that various applications will be possible by using sensed data. A video clip that introduces the various features provided by our proposed guitar can be found in [11]

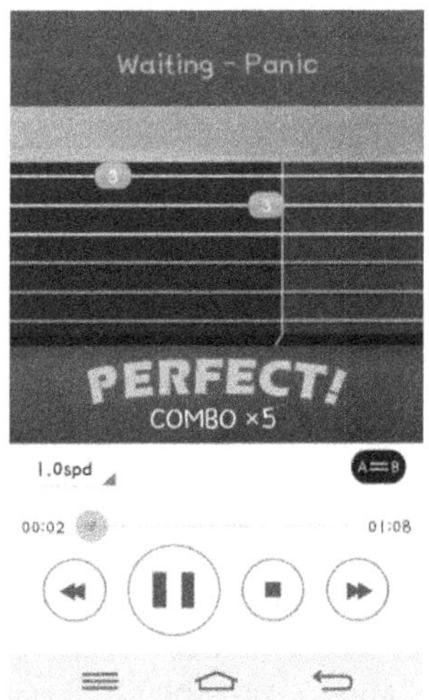

Figure 12. Feature of real-time performance feedback with smartphone

CONCLUSIONS AND FUTURE WORK

In this paper, we have proposed a sensor-based guitar that consists of two groups of sensors. The proposed guitar employs a sensing circuit in the fingerboard to recognize the fingering positions of the fretting hand, and includes attached piezo sensors under the saddles to detect the guitar string that are played by picking hand.

Many studies have employed theoretical approaches to recognize musical instrument performance information by analyzing multimedia data such as video and audio.

However, these approaches have to process large amounts of data for analysis which is difficult for a resource constrained embedded system to process in real-time. Therefore, there are still limitations to apply them to real guitars. We have reduced the amount and type of data to be analyzed, with which the existing approaches still could not get sufficient accuracy. Instead, we have designed appropriate sensor circuits. Fingering positions and plucked string judgments for multipitch estimation were made recognizable by hardware circuitry. This was yet a challenging task for an embedded system with limited number of input/output pins. The analog data from the piezo sensor was analyzed together with digital data from the hardware circuitry to precisely calculate the onset time, offset time, and duration of the note. This is one of our main contributions in this paper. Other contributions for the interactive learning environment and tactile interface can be found in our developed features or applications such as music transcription, a sheet music sharing platform, an LED feedback guitar, and a smartphone rhythm game.

In the future, one may study how to utilize only one of two sensor groups or re-design a hardware circuitry to get partial information, for example, the fret number without knowing the string number. This may improve the accuracy of existing audio-based analysis with a relatively simplified hardware configuration. We also plan to evaluate user satisfaction with our guitar.

ACKNOWLEDGMENTS

This work (Grants No.C0238987) was supported by Business for Cooperative R&D between Industry, Academy, and Research Institute funded Korea Small and Medium Business Administration in 2015.

REFERENCES

1. Juan Pablo Bello, Laurent Daudet, Samer Abdallah, Chris Duxbury, Mike Davies, and Mark B. Sandler. 2005. A Tutorial on Onset Detection in Musical Signals. IEEE Transactions on Speech and Audio Processing. 13, 5: 1035-1047. http://dx.doi.org/10.1109/TSA.2005.851998
2. Frédéric Bevilacqua, Nicolas Rasamimanana, Emmanuel Fléty, Serge Lemounton, and Florence Baschet. 2006. The augmented violin project: research, composition and performance report. In *Proceedings of the international conference on New Interfaces for Musical Expression* (NIME '06), 402-406. http://nime.org/proceedings/2006/nime2006_402.pdf
3. Giovanni Costantini, Massimiliano Todisco, and Giovanni Saggio. 2011. A sensor interface based on sparse NMF for piano musical transcription. In *Advances in Sensors and Interfaces (IWASI)*, 157-161. https://doi.org/10.1109/IWASI.2011.6004708
4. Fretlight. 2017. Wireless Guitar. (Dec 2017). http://fretlight.com/collections/guitars
5. Fret Zealot. 2017. Fret Zealot. (Dec 2017). http://fretzealot.com/
6. Tobias Grosshauser, and Gerhard Tröster. 2013. Finger Position and Pressure Sensing Techniques for String and Keyboard Instruments. In *Proceedings of the international conference on New Interfaces for Musical Expression* (NIME '13), 479-484. http://nime.org/proceedings/2013/nime2013_286.pdf
7. Tobias Grosshauser, and Gerhard Tröster. 2013. Optical bow position, speed and contact point detection. In *Proceedings of the 2013 ACM conference on Pervasive and ubiquitous computing adjunct publication* (UbiComp '13), 211-214. https://doi.org/10.1145/2494091.2494159
8. Tobias Grosshauser, and Gerhard Tröster. 2014. Musical instrument interaction: development of a sensor fingerboard for string instruments. In *Proceedings of the 8th International Conference on Tangible, Embedded and Embodied Interaction* (TEI '14), 177-180. https://doi.org/10.1145/2540930.2540956
9. Robert H. Jack, Tony Stockman, and Andrew McPherson. 2016. Effect of latency on performer interaction and subjective quality assessment of a digital musical instrument. In *proceeding of the Audio Mostly* (AM '16), 116-123. http://dx.doi.org/10.1145/2986416.2986428
10. Andrew McPherson. 2012. TouchKeys: Capacitive Multi-Touch Sensing on a Physical Keyboard. In *proceedings of the 12th international conference on New Interfaces for Musical Expression* (NIME '12), 195-198. http://nime.org/proceedings/2012/nime2012_195.pdf
11. NSERLAB. 2017. Real-time Recognition of Guitar Performance Using Two Sensor Groups for Interactive Lesson. Video. (November 28, 2017). Retrieved November 28, 2017 from https://youtu.be/dpJqdGgdPVc
12. Laurel S. Pardue, Christopher Harte, and Andrew P. McPherson. 2015. A Low-Cost Real-Time Tracking System for Violin. Journal of New Music Research. 44, 4: 305-323. http://dx.doi.org/10.1080/09298215.2015.1087575
13. Soonuk Seol, Yejin Shin, and Kangwon Lee. 2016. Learning Guitar with an Embedded System. Contemporary Engineering Sciences. 9, 12: 553-560. http://dx.doi.org/10.12988/ces.2016.6441
14. Fabian-Robert Stöter, Michael Müller, and Bernd Edler. 2015. Multi-Sensor Cello Recordings for Instantaneous Frequency Estimation. In *Proceedings of the 23rd ACM international conference on Multimedia* (MM '15), 995-998. https://doi.org/10.1145/2733373.2806384

15. Nick Summers. 2014. gTar: This iPhone-powered guitar isn't the educational instrument you've been dreaming of. (January 25, 2014). Retrieved August 2, 2017 from http://tnw.to/q3Fnh

16. Tim Vets, Jonas Degrave, Luc Nijs, Federica Bressan, and Marc Leman. 2017. PLXTRM: Prediction-Led eXtended-guitar Tool for Real-time Music applications and live performance. Journal of New Music Research. 46, 2: 187-200. https://doi.org/10.1080/09298215.2017.1288747

17. Kazuki Yazawa, Daichi Sakaue, Kohei Nagira, Katsutoshi Itoyama, and Hiroshi G. Okuno. 2013. Audio-based guitar tablature transcription using multipitch analysis and playability constraints. In *Acoustics, Speech and Signal Processing* (ICASSP '13), 196-200. https://doi.org/10.1109/ICASSP.2013.6637636

18. Jun Yin, Ye Wang, and David Hsu. 2005. Digital violin tutor: An integrated system for beginning violin learners. In *proceedings of the 13th annual ACM international conference on Multimedia*, 976-985. http://dx.doi.org/10.1145/1101149.1101353

19. Bingjun Zhang, Jia Zhu, Ye Wang, and Wee Kheng Leow. 2007. Visual analysis of fingering for pedagogical violin transcription. In *Proceedings of the 15th ACM international conference on Multimedia* (MM '07), 521-524. https://doi.org/10.1145/1291233.1291361

Loominary: Crafting Tangible Artifacts from Player Narrative

Anne Sullivan
University of Central Florida
Orlando, FL, USA
anne@ucf.edu

Joshua McCoy
University of California, Davis
Davis, CA, USA
jamccoy@ucdavis.edu

Sarah Hendricks
American University
Washington, DC, USA
slynnhendriks@gmail.com

Brittany Williams
American University
Washington, DC, USA
brisywill@gmail.com

ABSTRACT
While game narrative provides a story for the player to experience, the moment-to-moment decisions made by the player are just as important to the experience. These decisions make up a personal narrative that the player creates through their choices and actions within the game. These stories describe the player's experience, and are the stories that often get shared and retold by the player. However, these narratives are rarely captured by the game and instead rely on the player to memorize and retell them. In response to this, we designed Loominary, a game platform that plays Twine games using a rigid heddle table-top loom as a controller. Not only does this provide a new method of interacting with a game, but also records each of the player's choices into a tangible object that is created by interacting with the game. Loominary is a working prototype and in this paper, we discuss the design considerations and areas for improvement.

Author Keywords
Computational craft; game narrative; physical interface; tangible artifacts.

ACM Classification Keywords
• *Applied computing~Media arts* • *Applied computing~Computer games*

INTRODUCTION
In many story games, players are invited to explore a story world and work their way through the narration. In the process of interacting with the game and story, the player and the game designers are co-creating a narrative as a product of play. The authors and designers impose a set of constraints on the general shape of the outcome, but the details of the final crafted narrative are in the hands of the player.

Crawford [5] describes the moment-to-moment choices of a player as the basis of interactive storytelling. These player narratives are frequently more interesting and important to the player than the story created by the designers. Prominent game designer Wright [18] said in his talk at SXSW in 2007, "Players invariably come up with stories about what they did in games. They're never describing a cut scene." We posit that players have more personal investment in the narratives they have crafted than the ones they have been given, and often these crafted stories are unique to the player which increases their ownership of the story.

TEI '18, March 18–21, 2018, Stockholm, Sweden

ACM ISBN 978-1-4503-5568-1/18/03…$15.00
https://doi.org/10.1145/3173225.3173249

While players create their own narratives, the final product is rarely captured by the game, and instead it is up to the player to memorize or capture the details of their choices. There are places that exist such as websites like Obsidian Portal [19] and forums such as Giant in the Playground [20] which have dedicated areas for players to post their stories from their gaming adventures. Player narratives have also been captured in visual formats such as Let's Play videos, twitch streaming, and fan art. However, all of these methods rely on the player to create the retelling of their story.

Loominary was created to capture player narrative in a visual way through the creation of a tangible artifact as part of play. The game uses a small table-top rigid heddle loom as the interface to the game, with the player's choices being made by taking actions through the use of the loom. Through play, the player creates a tangible artifact, with their choices represented through the colored yarns they weave with. The crafted traces of the player's choices are diegetic artifacts that provide a record of the improvised outcome of play. The artifact can also provide a way to visually compare experiences between players, and work as a visual aid for the retelling of their narrative.

This paper describes the design and details of Loominary, and the method employed to capture the player's narrative in a tangible way.

RELATED WORK
We situate this game in the field of computational craft, which broadly focuses on ways computation and craft can both co-exist and inform each other. Weaving is only one of many forms of craft, but the domain of computational craft is small enough that we looked outside of weaving for inspiration for our game.

Loominary generates a pattern in the woven artifact through the actions of the player and from the physical action of playing the game. The specific pattern is co-created from both the game and the player making choices. Crafts created from computational pattern generators are not new, and work such as Elliot's [21] Processing pattern generator and Grow's [7] blackwork pattern generator generate patterns for quilts and blackwork fill patterns for computerized embroidery machines, respectively. Both of these works utilize the generative power of computation for creating new crafted works. Unlike our work, these programs generate an entire pattern that is then followed by a human creator. However, we drew inspiration from Elliot and Grow's work by studying the volume and variety of possible outcomes and considering how that could be modified to support possible player narratives.

Using crafted materials as interfaces to games has been done before in games such as eBee [4] and Addie's Patchwork Playground [16]. eBee uses hexagonal quilted pieces, each with a pathway across the piece made of conductive fabric sewn on the surface. The players take turns laying the pieces on a board to try to connect the power source to a light source and completing a circuit. In Addie's Patchwork Playground, a quilt with conductive fabric buttons uses capacitive sensing to turn the quilt into a controller for a platform style game. The digital game uses fabrics and stitch motifs to connect with the aesthetic of quilted controller. Our work was inspired by the crafted and tactile nature of the interfaces for these games, although we chose to incorporate the act of crafting as part of our control scheme instead of using a finished product, as we are interested in a personalized artifact from play.

Games also exist in which the player has access to, or is able to get personalized artifacts of their play session. One such example is Firewatch [3], an adventure game in which the player moves through beautiful scenery and takes in-game photos while following the story goals. The player then has the option of spending money to purchase physical "photos" matching the pictures they took in game. In the game Threadsteading [1], players take turns controlling a computerized embroidery machine or a computerized quilting machine in a strategy game where they battle for resources. Through play, the pre-printed fabric board has the game output sewn on it and the board with the final design is available for the winner to keep. Both of these games make use of physical artifacts as reminders of the player's game session and were inspirational in the making of Loominary. However, in Loominary the player is more directly making the artifact, and the finished woven piece does not specifically look like a game artifact, and in fact can even be worn as a scarf.

There also exist a number of games that use artifacts to tell stories. In the Intimate Fields [2] game there are a series of

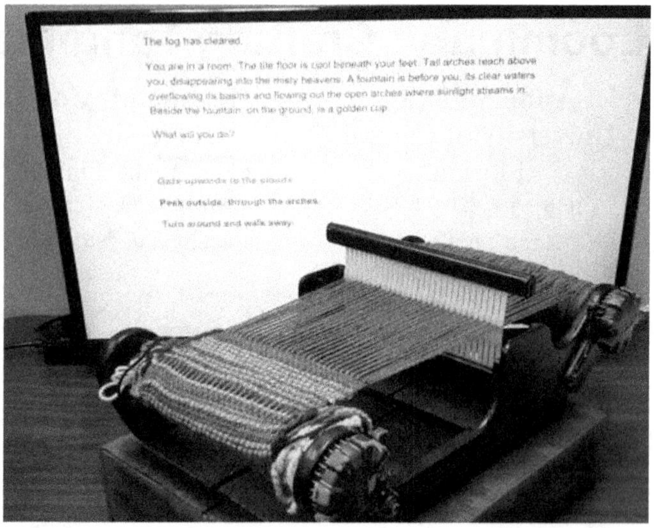

Figure 1. The loom controller with the game displaying behind it. The electronics are hidden in the base.

items, each associated with a different posy, or small love poem. As the player interacts with each item, the posy is printed out on a thermal printer.

The Reading Glove [17] gives the player a glove to use to interact with various storied items. When picking up each item, they hear a piece of a story, with the narrative sequence being chosen based on the ordering in which the player interacts with the items. Games and experiences such as these led us to be interested in story artifacts. In our work we used this as a starting point for creating Loominary which creates a story artifact through play.

LOOMINARY

Loominary is a game in which the player creates a tangible narrative artifact through the process of play. The game is a Twine game, which looks similar to a Choose Your Own Adventure style game. In the Twine games for Loominary, all the choices in the game are assigned specific colors.

The game controller is a physical table-top rigid heddle loom as shown in Figure 1. To make a choice in the game, the player weaves a row in the artifact with yarn the same color as the choice they want to make. In this way, the player's choices are literally woven into a physical record of their play session.

Two of the Twine games we have created for Loominary are retellings of Greek myths, in which the player takes on the role of the Fates and weaves the fates of the characters. One game looks at the story of Medusa, while the other follows Oedipus. While these games were created specifically for Loominary, any appropriately color-coded Twine game could be adapted to work with the system.

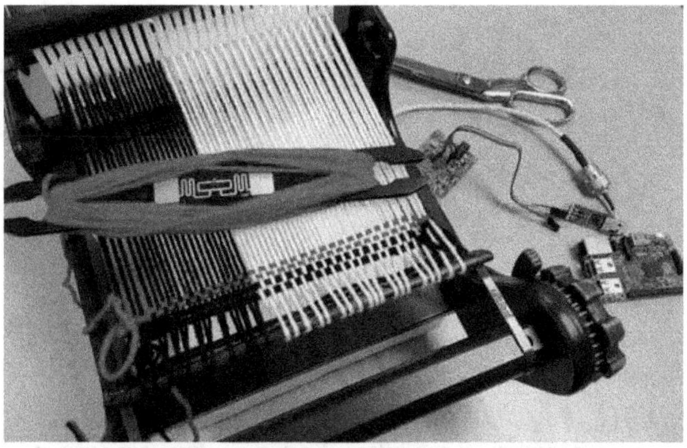

Figure 2. The shuttles (the sticks that hold the yarn) are pre-wound with specific colors and each is tagged with an RFID sticker.

We also have two other experiences for Loominary. One is a tutorial which walks the player through the process of weaving. The second is a child-friendly game in which the player spends the day with Posey the Pony, exploring the landscape, eating berries, and brushing hair.

Mechanically, the loom is unaltered. However, the shuttles (flat wooden sticks that the yarn is wound around) each have a unique RFID tag as shown in Figure 2. Each shuttle is pre-wound with a unique color and the system is calibrated to match the RFID to that yarn color.

The hardware and software for the project consists of several parts as shown in the architectural diagram in Figure 3. The first is a large RFID antenna connected to a RFID reader module. The antenna registers the RFID tags located on the shuttles as they pass in range and sends the data to the RFID reader module. We have set a delay between readings as the shuttles are in range of the reader for some length of time while weaving, which varies between players. However, players may weave with the same color multiple times in a row, and we needed a way to differentiate between one or multiple weaving actions.

The RFID reader module translates the data from signal to code and sends it to a Raspberry Pi. The Pi is the computer for the system as a whole and handles the interaction between the software programs. A monitor is connected to the Pi to show the game on screen.

There are three major programs in the project. The first is a NodeJS server which hosts the Twine games as an HTML page. The second program handles receiving the RFID signals from the RFID reader module. This program takes the encoded signal and sends it via JSON to the server. The server then sends this signal via sockets to the Twine game, where the color choice is handled in JavaScript within the Twine story. This Twine HTML page is viewed by the third program, a standard web browser.

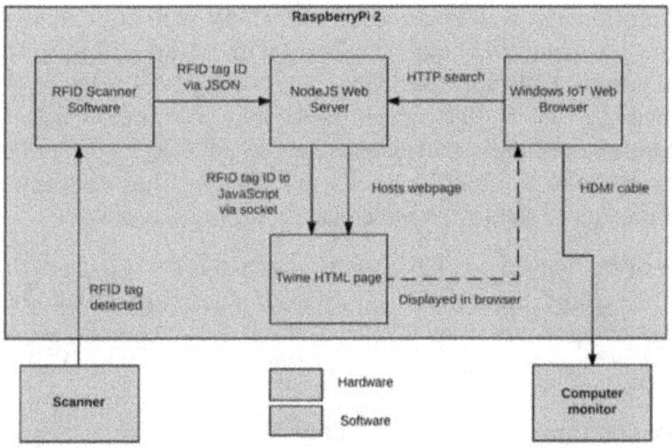

Figure 3. Architecture and software diagram of the Loominary system.

The project is open source, and information about materials, source lists, tutorials, and code are all available at the following link: http://www.loominary.info.

Interface Design

In building Loominary, we designed the interface first and then built a game to leverages its affordances. We surveyed different forms of creation in art, craft, and maker domains. While CNC (computer numerical control) machines are common in makerspaces (e.g. 3D printers and laser cutters) and were initially appealing as it is less of a logical leap to work with a computer game, we discounted them as we wanted to give the player the experience of using their hands to create the object that represented their story. This led us towards arts and crafts.

While the line between arts and crafts has evolved and shifted over time to the point where it is beyond a simple classification [11], we chose to define our interface as a crafting interface, as the current iteration of the game does not allow for much artistic expression. When looking at the history of crafting, there is a long and rich history of both subversive and overt storytelling [6,8] which we are only scratching the surface of, but gives us many interesting areas to explore in further work.

Based on the decision to utilize a crafting interface, it was important to choose an appropriate craft form for the player to interact with. There are many crafts from which to choose from, but we began by assuming the player has no prior knowledge. We therefore wanted to select a craft with a low barrier to entry.

We chose a rigid-heddle loom as the controller for a number of reasons. While weaving is a skill-based craft, rigid-heddle loom weaving has a smaller form factor and is straightforward to learn and teach the basics of the plain weave. This style of weaving also does not require complex hand dexterity such as that required by knitting or crochet, and the loom itself is portable, has minimal moving parts, and doesn't require safety equipment unlike some other craft forms.

Additionally, weaving has a long history with computation, and a centuries-long history with storytelling. The importance of more intricate designs in weaving led to the Jacquard loom [9], which used long punched cards to control the hooks that determine the pattern. Using punch cards to "program" the loom became the conceptual precursor to the use of punch cards in programming.

Woven tapestries have and are still being used for storytelling throughout the world, such as the Angers Apocalypse tapestries [12] from the late 14th century, which depict scenes from the Book of Revelations, to the Andean textiles [10] still being woven in Peru. Tapestry and Andean weaving are both more elaborate forms of textile creation than what we use in Loominary, but it was part of the inspiration that led us to using a loom as the controller for our game.

One of the more difficult aspects of weaving is setting up the loom by warping it – running the length-wise yarns in a way that has consistent tension and is appropriately wound around the roller. We have worked around this by preparing the loom ourselves ahead of exhibitions, but this does cause some issues that we cover in more depth in the discussion section.

We also considered the aesthetics and form factor of the loom. The table-top loom we are using is small and unimposing, but still retains the aesthetically pleasing appearance of a wooden, well-crafted item. Furthermore, we chose to hide away the majority of the electronics and cables inside a rustic-looking box. This helped set the "magical" tone for the game as well as beautify the appearance of the system since players would not be distracted by modern machinery or flashing lights, aside from the monitor displaying the Twine story.

Once the loom was chosen, the next step was finding a way to indicate the player's choices. Color was determined to be best suited for this purpose. Color is familiar to many people, as a selective visual variable it can quickly communicate choice, and it is not domain specific. While changes in weave types or yarn types can also be used, these require more specific domain expertise which worked against our assumption that the player would have no previous knowledge.

Color also gives us the ability to code game decisions with cultural meaning, which can be used as shortcuts and to indicate consequence in our design. For instance, in the game following the story of Medusa, certain sequences depicting Poseidon's rape of Medusa are captured in dirt brown, signifying the distastefulness of the act. While color significance is culturally dependent, it is still useful for the game designers to consider in the creation of the games.

Due to the lack of domain specificity, using color also eased the mapping between the weaving and the game interface. Using different weaves or yarn types would have required introducing unfamiliar interfaces to the player.

Figure 4. A portion of a woven scarf after multiple play sessions during an exhibition. Each time there are at least 3 grey weft yarns in a row, it signals the beginning of a new play session.

Given the use of an already unfamiliar controller, we wanted to minimize the amount of translation and knowledge gains required to play the game.

With these choices in mind, the final artifact created in the game is a scarf with the color of each row correlating to a choice that the player made. As the loom is pre-prepared with the warp (lengthwise) yarns, the game designers choose the color of the warp, while the weft (widthwise yarns) is added by the player. Generally neutral colors are used for the warp to allow the focus to be on the weft colors, but this is an area for future design exploration. See Figure 4 for an example of a section of a woven artifact created through play.

While using a loom and color as the interface to our game gives us many novel affordances, we do recognize that there are extra limitations imposed by these choices. For instance, the loom requires two hands to operate, and the use of color means that it does not work well if the player has color-blindness. Accommodations could be made to increase accessibility in these respects by choosing colors that have contrasting value, and using a loom that has been modified for use with one hand.

Game Design

The game's interface naturally influenced the game design; crafting is often a slow, meditative process. On the other hand, real-time video games tend to be fast-paced and twitch-based. Because of our choice to use a crafting interface, these types of games were not appropriate for our use. While this does have some limitations on what games are possible to create using this interface, we find the affordances of a crafting interface to be worth the constraint in game design.

To accommodate the loom as an interface, we looked at turn-based and slower game styles. Because the impetus of the project was looking at player narratives, narrative-centric forms of game play seemed the most appropriate for our use. Twine was a natural fit given that the games are text-based, not timed, and have built-in support for color-

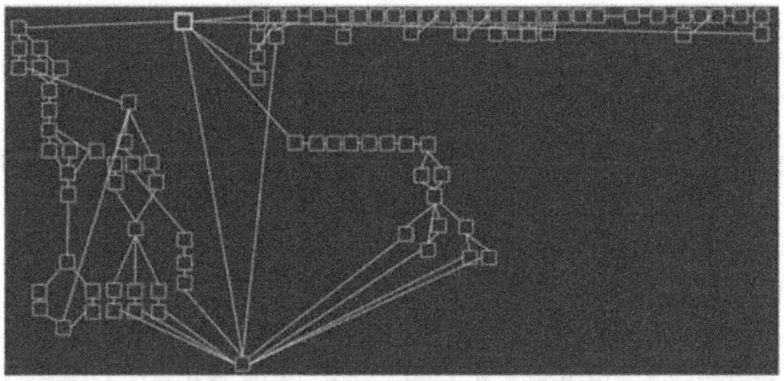

Figure 5. The graph structure of our Twine games. The left section represents the story of Medusa and has more branches than the other two stories. The middle section is the tutorial which is fairly linear until the end. The right section is quite linear but has many inter-dependencies.

coded options. Even the name is a good match for the project given that the player would be working with yarn.

For the development of the game, we initially looked at adaptations of Greek myths where the player takes the role of the Greek Fates and weaves the lives of the characters in the stories. We have completed initial versions of three games and a tutorial. Two of the stories deal with Greek myths of Medusa and Oedipus and the tutorial fits thematically with these stories. The third story was created in response to the number of young children who were interested in trying our game, as our stories were not appropriate for children. We created a shorter experience that allows the player to spend a game day with Posey the Pony and is appropriate for all ages.

We chose this Greek myth genre as an attempt to integrate the weaving with the game. Weaving the fates of mankind is a metaphor that many people are familiar with, and many of our adult players understood the reference to The Fates. To strengthen the integration, the colors of the options (and therefore color of the yarn the player is working with) were chosen to work with the story. For instance, the story of Medusa uses greens, greys, and brown which are fitting to the content and characters in the story given that Medusa herself is often depicted in these colors.

In the creation of the game, the designers also had to keep the tangible artifact design possibilities in mind. We created games in which the options would have real consequences on the storyline. While there are some events that are unchanged based on the player's choices, the different possibilities are tied together. For instance, some narratives are unavailable unless the player has explored a different narrative pathway in an earlier play session. We chose to create the games with this type of structure because it would lead to more variation in the final artifacts.

The graph structure of the games is shown in Figure 5. The longer the game play is, the more the differences in player choices can be seen. For instance, the differences in the artifact created by playing the story about Posy the Pony are minimal while those created by playing the story of Medusa are more noticeable. Additionally, the more branches that are available within the story, the more variation there is between artifacts. For instance, the fairly linear nature of the Oedipus story leads to locally similar artifacts, whereas the story of Medusa can lead to a larger variety of colors in the final artifact. Given that a linear story would produce no variation, this is not a surprising outcome.

In some cases, the game designers also used color strategically while creating options in the game. Important choices used special colors so that they stand out in the final design of the artifact. We also relied on American cultural implications of color to signify things that were happening in the games, such as greys and purples being used for the calm and mystical feel for the tutorial.

We further considered the ease of which the colors could be differentiated when appearing in the text. For instance, while having multiple shades of green may be aesthetically pleasing, it did not work in practice to have players attempting to differentiate whether an option was kelly green, fern green, or grass green. Instead we needed to limit our color scheme to colors that were more easily differentiated. This somewhat limited our color options as we balanced a pleasing final artifact with the need for players to correctly recognize which colors they needed to be picking between.

While this paper discusses the stories we created, Loominary was designed to be a platform for storytelling with a loom as the interface device. The technical architecture allows for any number of stories to be authored and easily played using the loom interface. Authors can produce a story in Twine, modify passage links to be bound to a color of yarn, and export the story to the hardware. Given this ease of authoring paired with the entire project being open source, we hope that others will use Loominary to create their own experiences.

DISCUSSION

Loominary is exploratory and has many details that could be improved by future design and technical iteration, and many directions that we intend to explore further.

Player Narrative

As stated previously, we looked at player choice carefully when creating the games for Loominary. We are interested in making sure the player has interesting and meaningful choices; to create playable stories [15].

Figure 6. Young players of Loominary learn how to use the controller. They then went on to teach the controller to their other family members after learning.

Looking at the possible traces through the games, we feel that we have managed to create some interesting and meaningful choices, but that this could be pushed further in future games. We feel that this is, in part, due to using Greek mythology as the foundation for our stories. Because these stories have been told and retold for centuries, there is a strong understanding of the narrative structure and how the stories should proceed. This led to over-constraining the space for the narratives to develop, and we have already begun creating stories in different spaces which rely on less constrained story settings.

Another area of improvement is in creating longer experiences. Currently, a single play through of the Medusa storyline takes about 10-15 minutes, and creates about 5" of woven material. While the story is meant to be played multiple times, and the length of play is appropriate for exhibitions, it would take many repeated games to create woven material of significant length. We attempt to remedy this with the Oedipus game, which is longer and requires multiple plays before the player accomplishes their goal. However, a full playthrough of this game still comes short of a significant woven piece.

Given the nature of sharing stories between players and on the internet, it seems clear that players feel a connection to the narratives they have created in the games they play. However, the ownership of the story is murky given that the game designers are co-creating the player's narrative through the constraints of their game. With Loominary, the player is still co-creating a narrative, but they are also solo-creating the woven artifact, which we hypothesize the players will feel greater ownership towards. We are interested in exploring further what differences may exist between how the players view the narratives they've created in traditional games versus the games played on Loominary where they have created their own narrative-based artifact. We hope to research this further with longer stories and more choices available. Making this possible is discussed in further detail in the following section.

Interface

In use, we have found that the loom is compelling to audiences, and met our goals of ease of learning and use. We found that both children and adults were able to learn the control mechanism quickly. In some instances, including the one pictured in Figure 6, the users felt confident enough to teach the controls and how to weave to their friends and family members after they themselves had learned.

However, the loom does require significant effort to set up for play. Warping a loom requires skill and space, and needs to be done for the game to be playable. We have worked around this by pre-warping the loom before exhibitions with a length that is suitable for many play sessions, but it is a significant limitation given our eventual goal of creating tangible artifacts for each player. It means that after play we have a single artifact with many people's stories woven into it, instead of each player being able to take their own piece.

Finishing techniques for a woven piece also requires time and skill, although techniques exist that are novice friendly. To address both the set up and finishing issues with using Loominary, we plan to include links to video tutorials of how to warp a loom and how to finish a woven piece on our github page to assist those who wish to create their own versions for play at home.

Given the amount of time that making a scarf would take, we have found that an exhibition is not an appropriate setting for having each player create their own artifact. This limits the testing we can do to study whether the artifact has personal meaning to the player and whether it retains that meaning after time has passed. Given the time constraints of finishing a piece, we will likely address this by finding ways to make the game available for longer play sessions in a quieter, solo setting.

In future games, we are addressing this by designing the systems from the ground up to be appropriate for an exhibition setting (since that is the most likely way people will interact with these games) with each player being able to keep the piece they have created while still contributing to a collaborative story. We are also investigating ways in which a collaborative storytelling artifact can be experienced and appreciated by everyone that helped create it, such as having it displayed in a public space.

For the electronics, we rely on RFID and a long-range RFID reader to capture what color the player is weaving with. Because the player can weave with the same color multiple times and the RFID reader is so sensitive, this can lead to a difficult balance in properly capturing the act of weaving. Additionally, RFID interference can be an issue given the strength of our antenna.

A more mechanical solution may help with this, but we initially had a goal to keep the loom as unaltered as possible for aesthetic reasons. However, this will need to be addressed in future iterations of the hardware, as it is a limitation with play that can make the controller feel unreliable. It is possible that making our own shuttles with accelerometers or other sensors available could solve these issues.

Aesthetics

While the loom is aesthetically pleasing and compelling, there is still room to improve the aesthetics of the game and artifact. We are already working on creating new games that use fonts and backgrounds other than the defaults as a step of refinement. Twine also supports the use of graphics, which could also be used to improve the visual quality of the stories.

The artifact itself is a mixture of stripes of color based on the player's choices (see Figure 4). The stories were not created with the finished aesthetic in mind beyond the initial color scheme. The stories could be written to take different player tendencies in mind. For instance, if the description text was created to always use cool colors, and plot point descriptions used warm colors, players who explore all the description text would create a bold, striped artifact, while those who skipped descriptive text would create a more solid looking artifact.

Along with improvements, there are areas of interest that we wish to explore further with this work. We are currently driving the aesthetic of the woven artifact by the game play alone. That is, the game does not take the player's own interest in color and color choice into account. This ignores the fact that players may be interested in the artistic expression of the woven piece itself. Creating games set in worlds with recognizable scarf patterns (Harry Potter, Dr. Who, etc.) could lead to experiences in which players may be drawn towards a certain aesthetic of woven artifact. Matching this with player modeling and prediction systems would allow us to see how far players can be pushed out of their preferred play style when driven towards a specific outcome and can be used to measure the strength of the player's aesthetic versus in-game goals.

Creating visual and tangible play traces for each player gives us a novel way to compare the uniqueness of the game's possible narratives. Looking at play traces to measure the expressive range of a system [14] as well as using play traces to find the most used paths through a game [13] is a common method of study. However, having tangible play traces allows players and observers to easily compare how different the outcomes might be without needing specialized skills or knowledge, or access to data.

CONCLUSION

Games provide a sandbox for players to explore, and through gameplay, the players create a personal narrative based on their choices in the game. These narratives are generally ephemeral, and rely on the players to remember and retell the story. In this paper, we presented Loominary, a narrative game experience with a physical loom controller in which players create a physical and tangible artifact recording their choices through the process of play. The woven artifact uses color to represent the player's choices in the game as a color-coded play-trace.

There is still much to be learned and explored in this space, and we are excited to continue working with crafting interfaces to investigate the ways tangible artifacts support and grow our understanding of player narratives.

REFERENCES

1. Lea Albaugh, April Grow, Chenxi Liu, James McCann, Gillian Smith, and Jennifer Mankoff. 2016. Threadsteading: Playful Interaction for Textile Fabrication Devices. *Proceedings of the 2016 CHI Conference Extended Abstracts on Human Factors in Computing Systems*, ACM, 285–288.
2. Heather Burgess. 2017. *IntimateFields.* .
3. Campo Santo. 2016. *Firewatch.* Panic.
4. Isabella Carlsson, Jeanie Choi, Celia Pearce, and Gillian Smith. 2017. Designing eBee: A Reflection on Quilt-Based Game Design. *Proceedings of the 2017 Foundations of Digital Games Conference.*
5. Chris Crawford. 2012. *Chris Crawford on interactive storytelling.* New Riders.
6. Judy Elsley. 1996. *Quilts as Text (iles): The Semiotics of Quilting.* Peter Lang Pub Inc.
7. April Grow. 2017. Blackwork Embroidery Pattern Generation Using a Parametric Shape Grammar. *Proceedings of the 8th International Conference on Computational Creativity.*
8. Fiona Hackney. 2013. *Quiet Activism and the New Amateur: The Power of Home and Hobby Crafts.* .
9. F. G. Heath. 1972. ORIGINS OF THE BINARY CODE. *Scientific American* 227, 2: 76–83.
10. Andrea M. Heckman. 2003. *Woven stories: Andean textiles and rituals.* UNM Press.
11. Grace Lees-Maffei and Linda Sandino. 2004. Dangerous Liaisons: Relationships between Design, Craft and Art. *Journal of Design History* 17, 3: 207–219.
12. James J. Rorimer. 1947. The Museum's Collection of Mediaeval Tapestries. *The Metropolitan Museum of Art Bulletin* 6, 3: 91–98.
13. Serdar Sali and Michael Mateas. 2011. Using Information Visualization to Understand Interactive Narrative: A Case Study on Façade. *ICIDS*, Springer, 284–289.

14. Gillian Smith and Jim Whitehead. 2010. Analyzing the expressive range of a level generator. *Proceedings of the 2010 Workshop on Procedural Content Generation in Games*, ACM, 4.
15. Anne Margaret Sullivan. 2012. The Grail Framework: Making Stories Playable on Three Levels in CRPGs. Retrieved December 4, 2017 from https://escholarship.org/uc/item/004129jn.
16. Anne Sullivan and Gillian Smith. 2016. Designing craft games. 24, 38–41.
17. Karen Tanenbaum, Joshua Tanenbaum, Alissa N. Antle, Jim Bizzocchi, Magy Seif el-Nasr, and Marek Hatala. 2011. Experiencing the Reading Glove. *Proceedings of the Fifth International Conference on Tangible, Embedded, and Embodied Interaction*, ACM, 137–144.
18. Will Wright. 2007. Will Wright Keynote. .
19. Obsidian Portal. *Obsidian Portal.* Retrieved from http://www.obsidianportal.com/.
20. Giant in the Playground Forum. Retrieved from http://www.giantitp.com/forums/.
21. About. *Libs Elliott.* Retrieved from http://www.libselliott.com/about/.

Interactive and Open-Ended Sensory Toys: Designing with Therapists and Children for Tangible and Visual Interaction

Florian Güldenpfennig
HCI Group
TU Wien, Vienna

Peter Fikar
Multidisciplinary Design Group
TU Wien, Vienna

Roman Ganhör
Multidisciplinary Design Group
TU Wien, Vienna

{florian.gueldenpfennig, peter.fikar, roman.ganhoer}@tuwien.ac.at

ABSTRACT
Treating neurological conditions like cerebral visual impairment (CVI) and related disabilities is a complex challenge where the needs of the affected persons have to be considered individually. It is also commonly agreed that stimulating the body's senses, as part of early intervention programs, is a crucial activity in therapy. With this paper, we add to the literature on how tangible and embodied interaction can facilitate such stimulation of the body and provide engaging experiences for children with (multiple) disabilities. Our report entails a detailed description of a co-design process involving early intervention specialists and affected children over the course of six months and multiple prototype iterations. According to our participants, the strengths of the resulting products or therapeutic toys are their open-endedness and versatile applicability, meeting individual needs and making therapeutic sessions both enriching and fun for the children.

Author Keywords
Therapeutic toys; children; disabilities; CVI; stimulation; body perception; playful approach; design case study.

ACM Classification Keywords
• *Human-centered computing ~ Field studies* • *Human-centered computing ~ Participatory design*

INTRODUCTION
Tangible and embodied interaction can leverage the user experience of many applications, for example, by making controls more intuitive and natural [19]. In this paper, we are interested in tangible interaction as a facilitator of stimulating bodily experiences for children with (multiple) disabilities in order to support developmental and sensory competencies. This interest is justified by (a) the strength of tangible interaction design to address the users' full body in interactive applications and (b) the usefulness of stimulating the body in the management of certain disabilities [10].

The results in this paper stem from a six months design-research endeavor with early intervention specialists (abbreviated as EIS from now on) as co-designers. EIS are social care professionals – often additionally educated in related fields like pedagogy or psychology – trained in supporting children with disabilities. In the context of our research, all children had a form of visual impairment (primarily cerebral visual impairment - CVI), in some cases causing only mild problems, in others having a more severe effect on life. In addition to vision problems, most children suffered from comorbidities like cerebral palsy, which can often be found in individuals with these kinds of vision impairments as both are consequences of neurological damage in related brain regions [6].

The EIS' task of supporting and treating these children is complex, because the children's conditions are manifested through a vast variety of symptoms [6; 17]. Hence, individual treatment plans differ significantly and have to be established on a case-by-case basis. Still, it is commonly agreed upon that interventions should start as early as possible and expose the affected child to appropriate sensory stimuli in order to spur growth, either on a cellular level where new synapses are established or on a personal level to foster developmental competencies [10]. Much of the exercising takes place in a playful age-appropriate manner using (therapeutic) toys in the children's homes.

In this kind of setting, our project was established to co-design novel interactive and therapeutic toys. As we will outline in the following, there was a demand for toys with specific but not yet clearly articulated and implemented affordances. We saw an opportunity for interactive and tangible technology to leverage conventional (therapeutic) toys. Thus, we created our own prototype family of therapeutic and sensory toys that we named BoostBeans.

The paper on hand contributes a detailed description of BoostBeans (see Figure 1 for an overview in advance). It constitutes a design case study providing fellow designers or researchers with firsthand insights into a demanding, however, rewarding design space that, in our opinion, deserves further explorations by the TEI/HCI community.

TEI '18, March 18–21, 2018, Stockholm, Sweden

ACM ISBN 978-1-4503-5568-1/18/03…$15.00
https://doi.org/10.1145/3173225.3173247

We are *not* aiming to provide summative evaluations of our products involving metrics for success or failure. Rather, we focus on describing the setting, the process and the motivation of the design decisions. A prior publication of the concept without implementation or evaluation can be found in [5].

We go on to briefly provide further information regarding the needs of the children in the project from a therapeutic perspective and review related TEI/HCI works.

THERAPEUTIC CONTEXT

Early intervention programs as offered in many countries support children with neurological issues starting from the first weeks of life and accompanying the children until about aged six years [10]. Within these programs, the primary objective is to prevent or minimize developmental delays [10]. Since the affected children can have a broad variety of symptoms (as opposed to one clearly circumscribed problem), we go on to describe what these programs aim to accomplish on an *abstract level* in order to support developmental and sensory competencies, applicable for most of the affected children.

In the literature, these abstract goals are summarized as *to improve the children's orientation and mobility, to build-up play skills* as well as *to develop daily living skills* [8]. Certainly, in practice, there will be different priorities depending on the care providers' philosophy and, of course, on the children's individual needs. Still, these goals clearly resonate with the approach of the EIS who were involved as co-designers in the research project described in this paper.

To accomplish these objectives, it is essential to provide the children with appropriate experiences, that is, stimuli that are geared towards their specific situation, allowing them to progress at the given point of time. The EIS then need to identify and deliver these appropriate experiences and assess the children's progress by maintaining a lasting relationship. A child generally does not change his or her EIS over the course of the six years of intervention.

In the case of our research project, relevant stimuli were often visual experiences, since all children suffered from a form of visual impairment like CVI [11], as mentioned in the introduction. CVI "is clinically defined as a significant visual dysfunction caused by injury to visual pathways and structures occurring during early perinatal development [... and is associated with] a myriad of visual deficits" [11, p.1]. The motivation of the EIS for engaging with the children with CVI is – besides creating an emotional bond and providing warmth and care – to recover visual function, a motivation which is supported by scientific evidence [3]. To this end, it is crucial to provide the children with sensory experiences to stimulate cellular growth and the wiring-up of new neuronal pathways [3]. Similarly, other conditions and comorbidities like cerebral palsy need stimulation for teaching the body to integrate different sensory inputs [17]. Training hand-eye coordination is an important challenge in both supporting children with CVI and/or cerebral palsy.

Having described the broad project setting from the perspective of the needs of the children, we go on to review related works from TEI/HCI that have addressed similar issues. Here, we focus on playful approaches and games, as our objective was to indeed develop novel interactive toys.

RELATED RESEARCH IN THE TEI/HCI LITERATURE

In this section, we highlight exemplary related work and appreciate their contributions to the TEI/HCI community. We start by describing prototypes with a clearly prescribed intention, that is, objects that were designed to be used in a specific way. In the course of the section, we then move on to report research that enables the user to customize parts of the product in order to meet individual needs.

Linehan et al. [9] and Waddington et al. [23] created a videogame for children, which aimed at mitigating the negative effects of CVI. They engaged in a participatory design process to come up with appropriate and interesting visual stimuli for exercising the visual pathway. While their videogame is not a tangible application, it is one of the rare examples in HCI explicitly targeting CVI.

ChillFish [20], in contrast, is a tangible game controller for a health-related computer game that was presented recently at TEI'16. It was created by Sonne and Jensen [20] in order to explore a videogame-based biofeedback application for children suffering from attention deficit hyperactivity disorder (ADHD). ChillFish is operated by a mouthpiece that can sense the players' respiratory rate. In this way a character in a *jump'n'run*-like videogame is controlled. The game constitutes a relaxing breathing-exercise that should make children with ADHD more focused and concentrated.

PhonoBlocks by Antle et al. [1] is also a typical tangible user interface, but not a game. By means of smart and illuminated letters the product supports children with dyslexia in decoding letters utilizing sound and multicolor LEDs. Kiteracy as proposed by Jadan-Guerrero et al. [7] is based on tangibles as well and aims to support children with Down Syndrome in improving their literacy.

Polipo is a research prototype for improving the motor skills of children's hands, introduced recently at TEI'17 by Tam et al. [21]. While not a toy or game per se, Polipo utilized electronic elements to make this hand-held device more engaging and fun for children when fulfilling exercises for fine motor skills. For example, on completion of a task (e.g., positioning a rotary knob mounted to the Polipo), the device rewarded the children with light animations and prerecorded audio clips. The designers of Polipo were careful to implement a "cause and effect model" in their prototype as well as different means that allowed the therapists to customize the device [21]. They could, for example, mount different knobs or handles on it, and they could copy their own audio files to the Polipo system as customized rewards.

Figure 1. Concept of BoostBeans. The prototype consists of four actuator modules (A: LightBean [in an old jar], B: BuzzerBean, C: PowerBean [with connected fan], and SoundBean [not displayed]) that can be triggered remotely with puzzle remotes (D) or conventional remote controls (E). BoostBeans was designed to be incorporated freely and flexibly into exercises or games, to augment conventional objects and toys, to make exercising more interesting, and most importantly, to address the children's senses.

While the Polipo supported (optional) adaptations, Moraiti et al. [14] created a Do-It-Yourself (DIY) toolkit for occupational therapists which made customization the main feature and a necessity. The motivation of the researchers was to empower therapists to design and create their own tailor-made assistive technologies to be handed to their clients. More specifically, the electronic toolkit enabled the transformation of everyday objects like pillows into tangible interfaces for computer applications such as games.

Verhaegh et al. [22] and Garzotto and Gonella [4] proposed tile-based (board) games for children to support their learning. Both groups of researchers carefully implemented high degrees of adaptability in their tangible applications. While Verhaegh, Fontijn and Hoonhout [22, p.187] supported "fine-grained and wide ranged difficulty levels [... and] address[ed] a range of skills including fine motor skills, cognitive and social skills", Garzotto and Gonella [4] designed their system to be completely open, allowing the users to reprogram or customize all tangible elements.

As evident from previous paragraphs, there is a lot of inspiring research currently being conducted within the TEI/HCI community. We have seen a range of different concepts involving tangible interaction in order to support children with disabilities. We can coarsely divide the reported research prototypes into two groups: devices that have been designed for one particular purpose (e.g., ChillFish [20] to calm children down) and toolkit prototypes that were conceived for customizations (e.g., as proposed by Moraiti, Abeele, Vanroye and Geurts [14] to support occupational therapists).

With the design case study of BoostBeans presented in the next section, we describe a concept that differs from the existing prototypes with respect to customizability, but also regarding tangible interaction design. As we will show, BoostBeans cannot be customized as a device, but the EIS can use it to (re-)frame situations during therapy in custom ways, that is, re-appropriate meaning. For example, our participants utilized it to alter or customize existing objects, and they incorporated it into unguided play activities. In this way, the paper also contributes to discussions about open-endedness and re-appropriation in design (e.g., [15; 16; 18]).

DESIGN CASE STUDY: BOOSTBEANS

BoostBeans were created as part of an applied research project involving four early intervention specialists over a timespan of six months. The project goal was to bring interaction design to therapeutic toys or equipment and to come up with innovative design solutions that can be used to support children with special needs. We found ourselves in the comfortable situation to have no content-related constraints, except that the outcome should be a fully functional interactive and engaging toy or object to be used in therapy. As we will see in the following, not having constraints can, however, also be a challenge as this freedom implies a huge design or solution space.

To tackle the design challenge, we broke it down into three activities (Phase 1-3). Firstly, we familiarized ourselves with the general setting by engaging in observational fieldwork. Secondly, we conducted a number of design workshops with the EIS (e.g., see Figure 2). Eventually, we iteratively prototyped, refined and deployed the final design concept (BoostBeans) in a series of field tests. Figure 1 provides a preview of this concept, but it will also be introduced in the course of this section.

Before we detail these three design phases, we provide some more information about the people who participated in the project and about the recruitment process.

Informants

As stated before, the project involved four EIS. They were recruited through a local special needs organization (partners in the research project) and they received financial remuneration for their efforts. All of the EIS had several years of professional training, and each one had more than ten years of experience in working with disabled children.

The nine children in this design case were affected by CVI and in some cases by additional conditions as described in the Therapeutic Context section. They were recruited by the four EIS. Inclusion criteria for the children were approval by the parents as well as being likely to enjoy the visits of researchers and potentially benefitting from the engagement from a therapeutic perspective. The children or their parents did not receive financial compensation, but the children received free sessions of training. In order not to distract the children or to exhaust them, only one researcher at a time came to the training sessions. All encounters with the children took place in the presence of one or two parents, and all instructions were given by the EIS only. The researcher acted as an observer, taking field notes as unobtrusively as possible, and in rare occasions photos on the approval of the parents. All involved parties, including the researchers, signed a contract. The participants gave their written informed consent, and the researchers guaranteed not to publish any personal information without permission.

During the six months, we visited the homes of nine children and particularly engaged with four of them in the design process (i.e., we visited them multiple times and focused on their needs), because of their suitability and interest as participants. We go on to briefly introduce these four children using pseudonyms.

- Mario is five years old and has a big heart for animals. He regularly meets his horse-friend Henry in hippotherapy. He likes to chat with people and tries to get away from exercising by involving the EIS in a conversation. In addition to low acuity, Mario has particular difficulties in identifying shapes and hand-eye-coordination.
- Monica is six years old. She is always very cheerful, but when she gets frustrated she likes to throw her toys. However, this is not as bad as it might sound. She is happy again in the next second. She has a severe form of cerebral palsy, a cognitive delay and slightly impaired vision.
- Michael is four years old and loves to operate his parents' TV remote control. Switches and buttons are his passion. And he likes to tickle people and being tickled gently. In addition to impaired vision, Michael has a moderate form of cerebral palsy and a cognitive delay.

Figure 2. Snapshot from a design workshop showing several lo-fi props and two of the participating early intervention specialists (abbreviated as EIS in this paper).

- Muhammad is six years old who likes to get people involved in a little chat. His favorite topic is the current weather. Muhammad lives together with his parents and three siblings in a small apartment. Due to increased intracranial pressure, Muhammad suffers from multiple neuronal disabilities like low vision and a general lack of motor-control.

Phase 1: Familiarization with the Setting

Since we, as interaction designers, were not familiar with early intervention with children, we started the project by exposing ourselves to the work environment of the EIS. We began with an investigation of their organization's special needs inventory of therapeutic toys and studied their rooms and additional equipment (waterbeds, light installations, optical assessment instruments, vibrating floor mats, etc.). Then, we accompanied the EIS during their home visits to the children's houses. In this phase, we made a total of fifteen visits, which each lasted between 60 and 90 minutes. We attended three additional sessions, which took place at the rooms of the special needs organization, but usually therapy takes place at the children's homes. Phase 1 lasted about 8 weeks. About four weeks in, we conducted in-depth and semi-structured interviews with the four EIS in order to further capture their work experience and what kind of therapeutic toys they preferred. Moreover, in this phase we talked to twelve additional EIS who worked for the organization and asked them to showcase their favorite toys and equipment for us.

We transcribed the audio recordings of the interviews and analyzed them for salient patterns or observations, which we rendered into a hierarchical mind map. We employed our field notes from the home visits and other observations for the same analysis. Note, the purpose of this analysis was to inform the subsequent design process and not to serve as the foundation for a detailed qualitative research paper. For this reason, we pinned the gathered materials (mind map, notes, photos) clearly visible on the wall of our office as a source for inspiration. We do not provide a detailed analysis of the material as this is out of scope for this design case paper.

Insights from Phase 1 to inform Phase 2

During Phase 1, two facts soon became evident. First, the EIS already possessed a huge stock of conventional and therapeutic toys. Second, the work practices of the EIS were shaped by permanent improvisations to respond to changing situations, all for the good of the children.

Huge stock of toys: The inventory catalogue of the organization featured over 1000 pieces of toys or similar equipment. This stock was approximately split half between special educational materials/toys and conventional toys that could be bought at any toy store, designed without considering special needs. While some of the conventional toys made use of electronics to enhance their experience, for example, by adding audio effects, a lot of the special needs toys were designed according the principles of

Montessori [13]. EIS2 stated: "We have an amazingly huge amount of toys, many of them get lost for years in the storage room until they are re-discovered."

Interestingly, the EIS often favored rather *simple things* in contrast to elaborate and expensive equipment. For example, simple and colorful boxes or cans with slots in different sizes were very popular utensils among the EIS. As they stated, they often instruct children to throw little objects (e.g., old bottle caps) into the cans. This was an excellent exercise for hand-eye coordination and it made insightful accompanying sounds, in particular for children with low vision. They also made use of magnetic objects attracted by the outside of metal cans, inviting the children to "pluck" them before throwing them into the can, hence, adding a more interesting motoric component.

Most of these simple toys and objects were self-made and customized according to the needs of individual children and to make rather dull exercises more interesting. This fact leads to our second observation regarding improvisations in the daily work of the EIS.

Improvisations: As documented in the literature, to work with disabled children can be challenging because of their heterogeneous needs, which moreover can change at a fast pace [4]. Also, most sessions took place at the children's home and consequently the EIS needed to get along with the situation they found there, for example, little space or bad lighting. We have observed this directly at the children's homes and indirectly through the improvisation skills that the EIS have acquired. Often the children did not like or were not able to solve one particular exercise that they were supposed to do, and in this case the EIS needed to find (on the fly) an alternative to train the child. Thus, when the children rejected a particular exercise or toy, the EIS tried to keep the attention of the children by offering variations in form and decoration, which they created and collected over the years. When asked about what kind of tinkering or DIY-practice they would engage in most often to create or upgrade equipment, EIS1 answered:

"Reduction. Reducing a toy is what we do most often in terms of tinkering. Often the toys are too complex, too many functions, too many distracting images. Then we remove stuff, we cover things with tape, we make things simpler so everyone can use them. And sometimes we also enhance things, e.g., coloring old cans and boxes to enhance the contrast and to make them look more interesting." [EIS1]

Overall, from Phase 1 we learned that the EIS already possess a large number of toys, that they have to react to a multitude of different and unforeseen situations, and that they are quite inventive and hands-on in approaching these situations. Consequently, we set ourselves the goal to create a toy that was different from the ones they already had, and that was not realizable by their own DIY skills. In addition, we aimed at creating a toy that would be useful for children with different preferences or interests and disabilities.

Phase 2: Design Workshops

To initiate the co-design phase, we invited the EIS to a hands-on design workshop. The aim of this workshop was to introduce the therapists to interaction design as performed by us and to give them an idea of what kind of designs we were capable to produce with respect to time constraints and budget. We demonstrated and explained tools for digital fabrication like 3D printer, laser cutter, and CNC mill. We initiated a 3D print and let them cut some plywood pieces with the laser. Moreover, we let them interact with prototype designs that we had created earlier in the context of other research projects. These prototypes were selected based on their affordances and represented exemplary work that might also be interesting for the EIS. In addition, we invited the EIS to 'play' with littleBits [2], a platform designed for children for creating very simple electronic prototypes by snapping together magnetic sensor and actuator modules. We concluded the workshop with a discussion of what the EIS would like to create with the tools they learned about that day, if they had an assistant helping them to bring their designs to life.

Following the design workshop, we rendered the impressions we gained as well as the insights from Phase 1 into a number of design proposals. Those were captured in a mix of sketches, storyboards, and scenarios, exploring divergent concept directions. In this course, the initial, less elaborated concept for BoostBeans was formed.

We discussed the proposals with the EIS in another meeting in order to receive feedback and narrow down the space of potential solutions. After two weeks, we scheduled yet another workshop meeting where we brought refined sketches and some lo-fi prototypes and materials for play-acting scenarios. The photo in Figure 2 was taken on this occasion.

Final decision for the BoostBeans concept

We decided collectively with the EIS that the design proposal of BoostBeans should be explored as prototypes in Phase 3.

As we learned from our investigations, one of the biggest challenges for the EIS is to motivate children and to improvise in this course. For this reason, the EIS asked us to come up with a toy, which they can build into their daily exercises with different children and different needs. Interestingly, it was not important to them that the novel toy should be designed for one particular purpose, for example, to improve hand-eye coordination, but to afford a certain degree of versatility. This is de facto what BoostBeans is aiming at as described in the next section.

Phase 3: Conceptual Design, Iterative Prototyping, and Field Deployment

Following the insights from Phases 1 and 2, we decided to focus on the design concept, which is illustrated in Figure 1 (BoostBeans). The activities as described in the following took place over the course of approximately four months. It might be to little surprise that the proposed design is not an interactive toy in a conventional sense. However, in accordance with the EIS, we opted for creating a modular system to be used to *augment* existing toys and everyday objects. That is, instead of adding yet another toy to the stock of 1000+, we designed an interactive and open-ended technology to add extra value to existing materials.

BoostBeans (see also Figure 3) is comprised of small actuator modules that can light up (LightBean), vibrate (BuzzerBean), and record and replay audio clips of six seconds (SoundBean). Later on we also added PowerBean as described subsequently. The kit comes with corresponding remote controls to wirelessly trigger the actuator modules on the push of a tactile button. In the case of the red remote control for the likewise red SoundBean, a brief touch of the button will replay the sound, and a long touch (>5secs) will record a new clip with the built-in microphone.

In the following we describe affordances of BoostBeans. While some of them were implemented by intention, others emerged during field tests.

Augmentation of existing objects and toys

The initial idea of BoostBeans was that the EIS would prepare an object with BoostBeans, for example, by putting a LightBean into an empty jar as illustrated in Figure 1A. Whenever the visually impaired child would reach out for the jar, the EIS would (secretly) operate the remote control acting as a "Wizard of Oz". In this way, the eyes of the child would be exposed to a bright stimulus (wanted behavior for wiring up visual paths), and the jar would show interesting interactive behavior without the need for fully implementing the action-reaction mechanism thanks to the Wizard of Oz/remote control.

Motivational aspects and rewards

Another idea was to use BoostBeans as rewards between training tasks, which might feature boring exercises. Then, the children should be allowed to engage in whatever activity suited them best with BoostBeans. Figure 5 (left), for example, shows a container with old bottle caps collected by the EIS. They placed BuzzerBean between the caps and offered the container to the children to stick their hands and feet into it. The result was a fun sensory impression, which at the same time was an important lesson for the children with respect to body perception. Thus, the EIS made use of the system to create holistic experiences addressing multiple senses, which again had motivational effects due to an increased variation of exercises.

Making up own games

Interestingly, it did not take long until the children wanted to operate the remote controls themselves although we originally created them for the adults. They made up their own games with them. Figure 5 (right) shows Mario using the remote control to locate the SoundBean. The SoundBean was prepared beforehand by EIS2 who recorded funny horse sounds and hid it between Mario's soft toys also shown in Figure 5 (middle). Mario used the remote again and again until he located the SoundBean. He used both his hearing and his poor vision to find the toy, which made the fun game a good exercise, as well.

Cognitive challenges and solving puzzles

Inspired by such observations, we decided, in accordance with the EIS, to create remote controls specifically for the children in the shape of puzzles (Figure 4). The pieces had to be put into place to complete the control, because they represented tactile buttons for triggering BoostBeans. In this manner, the children had to solve a cognitive puzzle involving hand-eye coordination, before they could use the device to trigger the desired action. We were inspired by the design of the LEA symbols [24], a common non-verbal eye-assessment test. The motivation was to prepare the children for the LEA test by introducing them to the symbols in a playful way.

The puzzle remote was well received by both the children and the EIS. Figure 6 (left) shows Monica holding the BuzzerBean to her head and the remote control with the other hand. Since she liked the vibration, she had to use both hands simultaneously to trigger it. This was a good exercise for her coordination and also for motivating her to make use of her "weaker" right hand. Figure 6 (middle) displays Muhammad experimenting with BoostBeans, and Figure 6 (right) shows Michael who liked the tickling feeling of BuzzerBean while holding his foot against it.

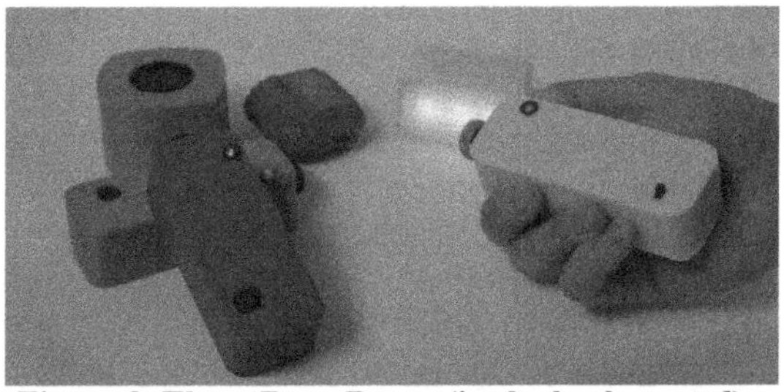

Figure 3. Three BoostBeans (in the background): SoundBean (red), BuzzerBean (blue), LightBean (yellow) and three remote controls for triggering the corresponding BoostBean of the same color.

Figure 4. Puzzle remote control for triggering the LightBean (yellow), SoundBean (red), and BuzzerBean (blue). The puzzle pieces are the buttons and have to be put into place.

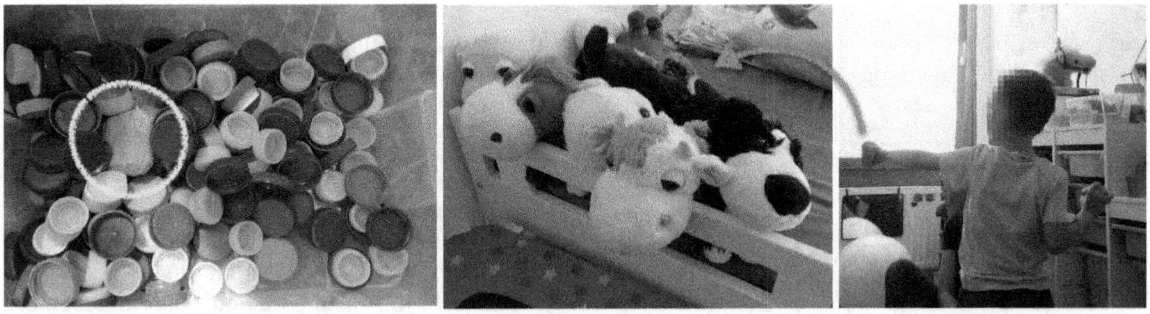

Figure 5. Container with old bottle caps and BuzzerBean (left; encircled). Mario's soft toys as a hiding place for AudioBean (middle). Mario triggering the remote control while searching for AudioBean (right; indicated with an arrow).

Figure 6. Monica engaging with the puzzle remote control (left). Muhammad examining BuzzerBean (middle). Michael holding his foot against BuzzerBean, because he enjoyed the feeling (right).

Redesign of puzzle remote control

Due to the success of the puzzle remote control and BoostBeans as a whole, we created a redesign (see Figure 7) that was extended by one additional BoostBean. We named it PowerBean (see Figure 8) as it basically constitutes an energy source with connecting port, which can be switched on and off remotely. By this means, the EIS are enabled to connect USB gadgets of their choice like LED strips or small fans to the port and incorporate these gadgets in their training sessions with the children.

DISCUSSION

Since we presented BoostBeans as a design case study, we discussed many of our design decisions as part of the main body of the paper. Here, we want to take some space to address a couple of observations and issues that we found remarkable during the project.

Motivating the children

One important lesson that we learned was about how much work in the daily practices of the EIS was about *motivating* the children to fulfill their exercises. As summarized in the Therapeutic Context section, it is crucial for the children's development to work with all of their senses. However, vision exercises, for example, can be dull as we have learned, since they require a child to iteratively look at abstract and high-contrast patterns [9; 23]. For this reason, the EIS became very inventive to engage the children in their exercises. Hence, we decided to give broad agency to the EIS during the design process and to support their great talent for improvisations and creativity through BoostBeans. This observation about their practices is in line with the literature. Metatla [12] spoke of "maker culture" when reporting on a study of the work of special education teachers for visually impaired children. He explained: "The maker culture seems to be naturally nurtured by two reoccurring factors; first the difficulty of reusing materials and resources; second, by the heterogeneity of needs of children with [visual impairments]." [12, p.5]

Sheer number of toys

To respond to this heterogeneity of needs, the EIS already obtained a large number of therapeutic toys. While a few of their 1000+ toys featured electronic components, almost no toy made use of more elaborate interactive technology or interaction mechanisms. In most cases, electronics were used to illuminate a toy to make it more visible or interesting. Sometimes, toys would also play sounds in certain situations. However, these features were used to enhance the toy, they did not define it per se and with empty batteries, most of them were still useable whilst not that interesting anymore.

These considerations should not imply that we argue "the more technology, the better". We are far from this belief; still, we identified an opportunity to draw on the tangible and embodied interaction paradigm to leverage toys for children with disabilities. Despite the great heterogeneity of their clients [11], the EIS provided beneficial sensory experiences for all of them according to their current needs. To some surprise, these experiences did not only involve encounters with visual stimuli. The reason for this is that the children are treated in a holistic way addressing all senses, so that the children can learn to integrate them. This is a challenge, we argue, where tangible and embodied interaction, and BoostBeans in particular, can be helpful and even excel.

In summary, we opted for an open-ended toy like BoostBeans as we soon found out that designing a toy, which all children of our study would accept or even cherish was nearly impossible. Children can have very particular flavors when it comes to toys, and this might be the reason why there are so many "contextual" [15] toys in the collection of the EIS (i.e., toys for one particular purpose). BoostBeans, on the contrary, constitutes an unadorned set of modular components that do not define or even suggest a particular way to be played with.

This leads to our final considerations in this paper regarding open-endedness in therapeutic toy design.

On open-endedness in therapeutic toy design

During the review of related work we found that a number of researchers offered broad options for customizing their designs to meet user needs (e.g., [21]). In a way, BoostBeans depicts a similar yet different mode for customization. In our case, the EIS did not reconfigure the shape or application, but they used BoostBeans to (re-)arrange therapeutic exercises in a meaningful way.

Seeing these 're-appropriations' by the EIS poses some interesting questions for further research. These questions center around how far we can 'push the envelope' in creating therapeutic toys and devices that are "open to interpretations" [18]. It is widely acknowledged that "designing a technical object also typically entails designing, or prescribing, its use" [16, p.411]. In designing BoostBeans, we tried to avoid prescribing a specific way of how to use them. Still, at some point we had to make a number of very specific design decisions regarding their

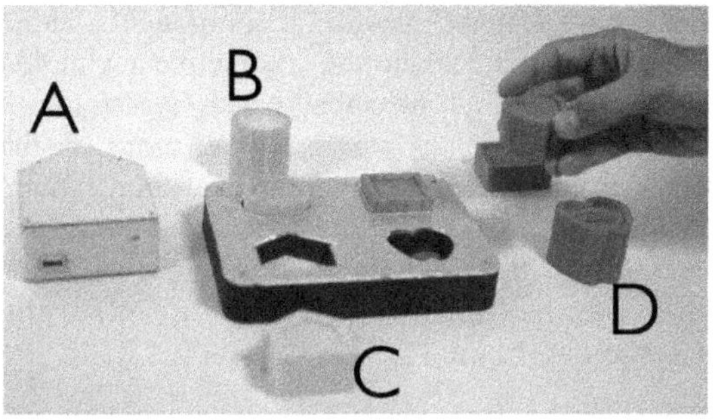

Figure 7. Redesign of the puzzle remote control. PowerBean (A) was added as a fourth actuator element. B: LightBean. C: puzzle button for PowerBean. D: SoundBean.

Figure 8. PowerBean with connected USB gadget (fan).

forms and functions. For a future research agenda, it might be interesting to look into research that consistently elaborates open-ended design (e.g., [15]) and investigate the boundaries of creating open-ended therapeutic toy design.

Limitations

The present work constitutes the description of the design case of BoostBeans. The prototype was created in a co-design process with a small number of therapists and children. In this paper, we don't aim to generalize findings. Its purpose is to describe the design process, to explain design decisions, and to show how the BoostBeans were used.

Further research is needed to evaluate the benefits of BoostBeans and map out different ways for using it. With respect to open-ended designs which have multiple interpretations, Sengers and Gaver suggest that "[...] systems might best be evaluated by gathering and presenting a variety of assessments from a diverse population of interpreters, allowing outsiders to get a rich and layered view of how the system is used, the roles it plays, and the cultural implications it suggests." [18, p.106] We agree with this evaluation strategy and plan to observe more participants interacting with BoostBeans in additional situations to be able to unpack a rich description of its use. Moreover, we want contrast observations of the EIS' use of conventional toys with that of BoostBeans.

CONCLUSION

We created BoostBeans in the course of a six months research endeavor involving four EIS and nine children. The prototype is a result of a co-design process, which revealed a potential for interactive and playful technology during early intervention programs with disabled children. BoostBeans constitutes a design case study where rather simple interaction mechanisms (controlling actions and reactions) could create valuable experiences by drawing on tangible and embodied interaction.

Through its open-endedness and tangibility, BoostBeans features a number of attributes that can be utilized in different ways. The system can be used *stand-alone*, but it can also be used *together with existing objects*, for example, toys. In this case, BoostBeans can be used to *augment* the toy or to *modify* it. Certain stimuli or characteristics of the toy could be *enhanced* or *reduced*. BoostBeans was also created to *inspire* or *enable* new exercises or (therapeutic) play activities. Finally, BoostBeans supports making the practices of early intervention even more *flexible* when responding to the children's needs.

ACKNOWLEDGMENTS

This research was funded by "Gemeinsame Gesundheitsziele aus dem Rahmen-Pharmavertrag, eine Kooperation von österreichischer Pharmawirtschaft und Sozialversicherung".

Many thanks to our participants and to Geraldine Fitzpatrick for comments on the draft of the paper.

REFERENCES

[1] Alissa N. Antle, Min Fan, and Emily S. Cramer, 2015. PhonoBlocks: A Tangible System for Supporting Dyslexic Children Learning to Read. In *Pro TEI'15*, ACM, p. 533-538.

[2] Ayah Bdeir, 2009. Electronics as material: littleBits. In *Proc TEI'09*, ACM, p. 397-400.

[3] E. Fazzi, S. G. Signorini, S. M. Bova, P. Ondei, and P. E. Bianchi, 2005. Early intervention in visually impaired children. *International Congress Series 1282* (2005/09/01), 117-121.

[4] Franca Garzotto and Roberto Gonella, 2011. An open-ended tangible environment for disabled children's learning. In *Proc IDC'11*, ACM, p. 52-61.

[5] Florian Güldenpfennig, Peter Fikar, and Roman Ganhör, 2017. Towards Interactive and Motivating Stimuli for Children with Visual Impairments. In *Proc BSC-HCI'17*, BSC.

[6] Richard Huo, Susan K Burden, Creig S Hoyt, and William V Good, 1999. Chronic cortical visual impairment in children: aetiology, prognosis, and associated neurological deficits. *British Journal of Ophthalmology 83*, 6, 670-675.

[7] Janio Jadan-Guerrero, Javier Jaen, Maria A. Carpio, and Luis A. Guerrero, 2015. Kiteracy: a kit of tangible objects to strengthen literacy skills in children with down syndrome. In *Proc IDC'15*, ACM, p. 315-318.

[8] A. Dolunay Kesiktas, 2009. Early Childhood Special Education for Children with Visual Impairments: Problems and Solutions. *Educational Sciences: Theory & Practice 9*, 2 (2009), 10.

[9] Conor Linehan, Jonathan Waddington, Timothy L. Hodgson, Kieran Hicks, and Robert Banks, 2014. Designing games for the rehabilitation of functional vision for children with cerebral visual impairment. In *Proc CHI '14 EA*, ACM, p. 1207-1212.

[10] Annette Majnemer, 1998. Benefits of early intervention for children with developmental disabilities. *Seminars in Pediatric Neurology 5*, 1 (1998/03/01), p. 62-69.

[11] Maria B. C. Martín, Alejandro Santos-Lozano, Juan Martín-Hernández, Alberto López-Miguel, Miguel Maldonado, Carlos Baladrón, Corinna M. Bauer, and Lotfi B. Merabet, 2016. Cerebral versus Ocular Visual Impairment: The Impact on Developmental Neuroplasticity. *Frontiers in Psychology 7*, 1958 (2016-December-26).

[12] Oussama Metatla, 2017. Uncovering Challenges and Opportunities of Including Children with Visual Impairments in Mainstream Schools. In *Proc BSC-HCI'17*, BSC.

[13] Maria Montessori, 2014. *The Montessori Method.* Transaction Publishers, New Brunswick, New Jersey.

[14] Argyro Moraiti, Vero Vanden Abeele, Erwin Vanroye, and Luc Geurts, 2015. Empowering Occupational Therapists with a DIY-toolkit for Smart Soft Objects. In *Proc TEI'15*, ACM, p. 387-394.

[15] Francesca Ostuzzi, Lieven De Couvreur, Jan Detand, and Jelle Saldien. 2017. From Design for One to Open-ended Design. Experiments on understanding how to open-up contextual design solutions. *The Design Journal 20*, sup1 (2017/07/28), p.3873-3883.

[16] Johan Redström. 2008. RE:Definitions of use. *Design Studies 29*, 4 (2008/07/01/), 410-423.

[17] Peter Rosenbaum, Nigel Paneth, Alan Leviton, Murray Goldstein, Martin Bax, Diane Damiano, Bernard Dan, and Bo Jacobsson. 2007. A report: the definition and classification of cerebral palsy April 2006. *Developmental Medicine & Child Neurology 49*, 8-14.

[18] Phoebe Sengers and Bill Gaver. 2006. Staying open to interpretation: engaging multiple meanings in design and evaluation. In *Pro DIS'06*, ACM, 99-108.

[19] Orit Shaer and Eva Hornecker. 2010. Tangible User Interfaces: Past, Present, and Future Directions. *Found. Trends Hum.-Comput. Interact. 3*, 1-2, 1-137.

[20] Tobias Sonne and Mads Møller Jensen, 2016. ChillFish: A Respiration Game for Children with ADHD. In *Proc TEI '16*, ACM, p. 271-278.

[21] Victoria Tam, Mirko Gelsomini, and Franca Garzotto, 2017. Polipo: a Tangible Toy for Children with Neurodevelopmental Disorders. In *Proc TEI'17*, ACM, p. 11-20.

[22] Janneke Verhaegh, Willem Fontijn, and Jettie Hoonhout, 2007. TagTiles: optimal challenge in educational electronics. In *Proc TEI'07*, ACM, 187-190.

[23] Jonathan Waddington, Conor Linehan, Kathrin Gerling, Kieran Hicks, and Timothy L. Hodgson, 2015. Participatory Design of Therapeutic Video Games for Young People with Neurological Vision Impairment. In *Proc CHI'15*, ACM, p. 3533-3542.

[24] Lotte G. Welinder and Kirsten L. Baggesen, 2012. Visual abilities of students with severe developmental delay in special needs education – a vision screening project in Northern Jutland, Denmark. *Acta Ophthalmologica 90*, 8, p. 721-726.

MOD: A Portable Instrument for Mixing Analog and Digital Drawing for Live Cinema

Ali Momeni
Carnegie Mellon University
Pittsburgh, USA
momeni@cmu.edu

Daniel McNamara
CalArts
Valencia, USA
danielmcnamara@alum.calarts.edu

ABSTRACT

This paper describes the design and fabrication of MOD (Mobile Object for Drawing)–a portable instrument for combining analog and digital drawing. MOD is intended for live performance and content creation efforts that mix common analog drawing interfaces (i.e. paper, transparency, pencil, marker) with digital cameras (webcams, scientific imaging cameras, digital magnifiers and microscopes), custom software (for keying, thresholding, looping, layer) and digital projectors. The iteration of the instrument described here combines all of these components into a single portable battery powered package that embeds the computation on a small linux computer, includes a small laser projector, and integrates custom tactile controllers. The intended uses of this instrument include experimental performance and rapid content creation; the instrument is intended to be suitable for formal (concert hall, theater) and informal (street performance, busking, parade, protest) settings, classrooms and maker spaces.

ACM Classification Keywords

H.5.m Information Interfaces and Presentation (e.g. HCI): Miscellaneous; H.5.1 Information Interfaces and Presentation (e.g. HCI): Animation

Author Keywords

Drawing; Animation; Live Cinema; Project; Projection Mapping; Performance; Interactive; Mobile; Portable; Intervention; Instrument

INTRODUCTION

This paper describes the design and fabrication of MOD (Mobile Object for Drawing)–a portable instrument for combining analog and digital drawing (see Figure 1). The instrument's design resulted from a decade of collaborative "live-drawing" performance practice by the author and Jenny Schmid, an artist with expertise in drawing and illustration. These performances were primarily achieved by combining common analog drawing interfaces (i.e. paper, transparency, pencil, marker) with digital cameras (webcams, scientific imaging cameras, digital magnifiers and microscopes), custom software on a laptop (for keying, thresholding, looping, layer) and digital projectors. The iteration of the instrument described here combines all of these components into a single portable battery powered package that embeds the computation on a small linux computer (Raspberry Pi 3), includes a small laser projector, and integrates custom tactile controllers (knobs, buttons, other sensors). The intended uses of this instrument include experimental performance and rapid content creation; the instrument is intended to be suitable for formal (concert hall, theater) and informal (street performance, busking, parade, protest) settings, classrooms and maker spaces.

TEI '18, March 18–21, 2018, Stockholm, Sweden

DOI: https://doi.org/10.1145/3173225.3173254

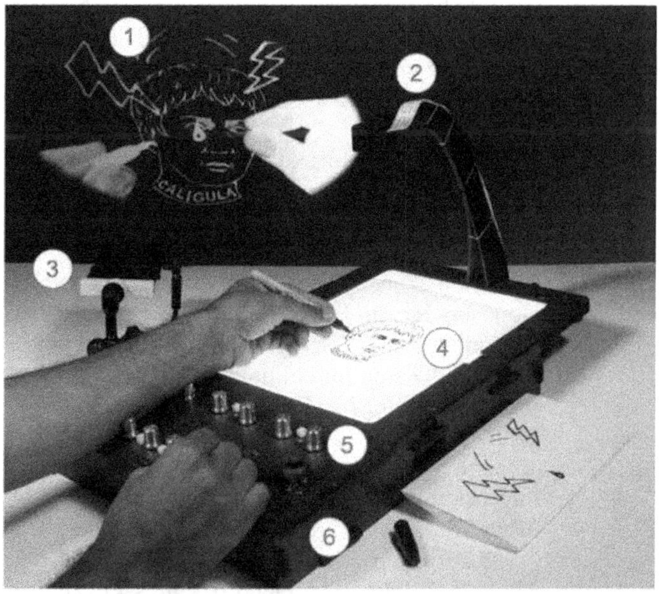

Figure 1. MOD (Mobile Object for drawing): 1) Projected image, can show live camera feed as well as three recorded layers, 2) Camera module, connected to Raspberry Pi with ribbon cable, 3) Pico projector attached with miniature magic arm, 4) back-lit drawing area, suitable for paper or transparency and pencil or marker, 5) UI panel with knobs, buttons, LEDs, power switch, 6) space between base and top surface contains Raspberry Pi, battery and voltage regulation

BACKGROUND

Motivation

The author–a musician, designer and software developer–and the collaborating artist–a master printmaker, drawer, illustrator, animator–developed a style of live performance that combines drawing, real-time video processing, sound and an outdoor

Figure 2. Performance of *Gutless Warrior* by Momeni and Schmid: (Top) Architectural projection, combining short recorded video loops of participants, and drawings made on-site; (Bottom) Networked collaborative drawing table

public setting; elements of this performance genre have been described as "live cinema" by [10]. MOD's development is also a continuation of a decade of instrument building, set into motion by an urban projection collective named MAW [1] which Momeni founded in 2007. MAW performed several hundred outdoor projection performances throughout the country and abroad. In creating these events, the MAW collective created a range of mobile instruments for participatory projection events; they included mobile projection bikes, tricycles, trailers, baskets and backpacks, as well as mobile video capture instruments for gathering drawings and mugshots[2].

The author has produced a number of site-specific participatory live projection works whose documentations delve more deeply into the aesthetic, social and technical concerns of this medium. The Battle of Everyouth [3] utilized multiple mobile and wireless media capture devices intended for allowing audience participation and was conducted by 15-16 year olds (see Figure 3); Exquisite Corpse/Lavish Martyr [4] utilized three mobile device for gathering and processing paper/marker drawings from audience members during a street performance at a festival; Gutless Warrior [5] required a panoramic projection system coupled with multiple live cameras with video sampling capabilities (see Figure 2).

While the contents and the venues for these performances varied a great deal, the goals and methodologies were consistent: to activate public spaces by using playful and collaborative technologies with large-scale architectural video projections. Of all the interfaces for public engagement that MAW's performances tried, one persisted as uniquely and reliably accessible, intuitive, expressive, and limitless: Drawing. Performances usually consisted of an artist drawing with pens and markers on white paper or transparency, a camera for digitizing the image, and custom software enabling recording, playback, layering, scaling and various visual effects. Several iterations of this hybrid hardware-software system for interactive drawing and performance were developed and tested over the course of dozens of performances.

Throughout these performance experiences, the system's complexities posed many challenges for live performance in public spaces. This system used a wide range of off-the-shelf and custom pieces of hardware, including professional photography rigging equipment, climbing and maritime fasteners, digital and analog cameras and digitizers, specialized lighting equipment, game and gestural controllers, and personal computers. The wide variety of devices and interfaces was a weak-point in the system; changes in computing platform or system updates often affected system performance in unforeseen ways; professional rigging/climbing/sailing equipment required considerable practice before mastery. Similarly, the responsiveness and latency were difficult to solve challenges. Similarly, initial versions of the software enabling video capture, processing and playback was created in Cycling '74 Max. While Max allowed for considerable flexibility and rapid development, it too posed challenges in performance (e.g. framerates), compatibility (moving from Mac, to Windows to Linux) and updatability (e.g. new Max updates often affected system performance).

MOD's design responds to these limitations by implementing all functionality onto a low-cost embedded platform, and coupling the platform with custom hardware that provides all the necessary I/O. The embedded platforms and custom hardware in MOD offer a trade-off: we gain in affordability, reliability, size and ease-of-use, while we lose in overall system flexibility and computational horsepower.

Related Works

Drawing, as an interface, has received limited attention within the TEI community. [8] and [1] describe interfaces for musical composition and performances based on drawing. [18] proposes an interface for programming that uses crayon-drawn colors, and a color-sensor based real-time system. [16] proposes a novel interface for capturing and manipulating drawings made with ink that combines the versatility of the analog interface, with the extensibility of digital image manipulation techniques. [19] describes a method for creating large-scale pictures in public spaces using directional reflections and a custom roller device. Outside the TEI community, a wide range relevant of contributions highlight the advantages of physical interfaces to digital or hybrid content creation or design processes. [9], [15] provide an overview of the theoretical framework for designing and analyzing such interfaces, as well consideration of specific use cases like video-collage, low-fidelity prototyping or user-interface design.

As an autonomous hybrid drawing interface, the MOD is inspired by the versatility of a traditional overhead projection. This omnipresent interface has seen multiple digital makeovers in devices like the digital document viewers by Epson or Elmo (e.g. Epson DC-21 or Elmo MX-1/P30HD); the most recent innovation in this area may be the HP Sprout, a hybrid interface for manipulating physical and digital worlds that combines

[1] http://maw.c-uir.org

[2] http://alimomeni.net/projection-instruments

[3] http://alimomeni.net/bey

[4] http://alimomeni.net/eclm

[5] http://alimomeni.net/gutless

a high resolution camera, a touch interface and 2D and 3D scanning. The medium of urban projection builds on interventionist [21] and situationist [11] practices that regard the urban environment as a site for activation, serendipitous interactions [17] and a canvas for visual expression [13]. This medium owes a great deal to several contemporary artists with a body of works that define this territory. Krzysztof Wodiczko (b. 1943) is a Polish/American artist renown for large-scale architectural projection works; notable in his practice is the use of custom instruments for public interactions, or what he calls the "thing-in-between" [24]. The experience of being *alien* or *strange* dominates Wodiczko's early works like the *Alien Staff (1996)* or the *Mouth Piece (1997)* [24] exemplify his recurring strategy of using tangible and embedded interactive systems as a mechanism for engaging the people in public spaces.

Jenny Holzer (b. 1950) is an iconic media artist with a wide range of large scale architectural projection works [22]. Holzer's works are particularly relevant here in two ways: first, they re-purpose features of the urban landscape that are typically at the service of capitalist messaging (i.e. road signs, buildings facades, billboards), to instead trigger the imagination and invite reflection on the state of society. Second, they often employ a graphic style consisting of block text and white-on-black. This design choice allows for a heightened visibility and legibility of projected text on non-ideal surfaces, an implied objectivity through reference to journalistic and scientific texts [6].

Graffiti Research Labs (GRL) [7] builds on the the site specificity that is at the core of Wodiczko and Holzer's work, by adding mobility into the equation. In this regard, GRL's mobile projection tricycle represents an important step in the evolution of mobile projection devices [20]. Other artists with relevant works include Rafael Lozano-Hemmer, Karolina Sobecka, Rebecca Smith, Pablo Valbuena, Chris O'Sheo, The Illuminator.

In addition to the above artistic works within the medium, numerous academic publications have identified opportunities for public engagement offered by interactive projections and media facades ([2], [12], [23], [7], [5], [3], [4]).

DESIGN PROCESS

This section describes the MOD's design requirements and iterative development process, which were derived from many software and hardware iterations informed by live performance experiences by the authors and feedback from collaborators and participants in public performance.

Design Requirements

Interactive instruments for engaging broad audiences in some creative and performative activity pose a unique set of technical and social challenges and design requirements. Our analysis of these design requirements are divided into three categories: Affordances, Mobility and Robustness, and Customizability.

[6]http://unprojects.org.au/magazine/issues/issue-4-1/jenny-holzer/
[7]http://www.graffitiresearchlab.com/blog/

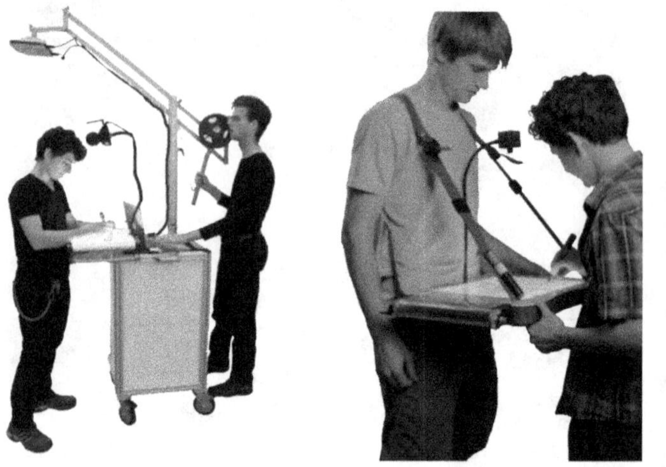

Figure 3. (Left) Drawing Case: Portable wireless interface used for gathering drawings from audience members; used in *Battle of Everyouth* by Momeni and Schmid; (Right) Projection/Drawing Jib: Mobile projection and drawing interface; used in *Musée Itinerant* by Momeni and David Bithell

Affordances

In his 2003 response to Norman's seminal 1999 publication problematizing the concept of affordance [14] Hartson outlines four types of affordances for interaction design: Cognitive, physical, sensory and functional [6]. The MOD's design has been accordingly concerned with affordances because they all impact the experience for the performers, the participating audience members and the bystanders. Regarding cognitive and functional affordances, the key consideration is the threshold for cognitive overload for a performer or participating audience member when interacting with a multi-channel system. Expert performers engaged in high-end media work for a large-scale concert or Broadway show may comfortably use a video projection system with several dozen content layers. On the other hand, the impromptu, ephemeral and outdoor nature of our use-case is often satisfied with a much smaller number of layers, combined with greater variety of physical interaction and image manipulation techniques. To make for an instrument that can be "played" while "drawing", the MOD opts for physical interfaces (real pen/makers/paper/transparency as opposed to a digital pen, physical buttons and knobs as opposed to a screen) that need no explanation, and can be manipulated intuitively and in the dark.

Mobility and Robustness

The physical and sensory affordances of our design are motivated by the range of real-world situations in which performances occur, including situations with limited lighting, unfavorable weather, overcrowded spaces, no power from the grid, or the need to clear out of the performance space very quickly. Instruments for street performances and on-the-go shows impose additional design constraints concerning weight and portability, power usage, robustness and repairability. In order to meet these requirements, the MOD uses a highly modular design in which different components are each relatively low-cost and easy to replace. Special attention was paid to making the device easy to repair (i.e. components are all easily accessible, thickness-pitch-drive of all hardware is consistent across the entire design, each module is easy to vary or customize),

Customizability

MOD was developed to not only meet the needs of the author and his collaborators in a public performance practice, but also as a versatile and extensible architecture for creating other hybrid instruments. To these ends, the hardware allows for independent real-time control of multiple continuous and discrete parameters. The software allows for independent control of multiple layers of video, each with a set of transformation and visual effects. The modular hardware and software design (see Modular Design section below) allows makers to mix-and-match components and functionalities to meet the project's needs, and to design and build new compatible modules.

Precursors and Iterative Design

The MOD is an evolution of a number of precursor instruments for achieving similar goals. Previous versions of the instrument have relied on custom software (in Cycling 74 Max, OpenFrameworks, TouchDesigner, Quartz Composer and Millumin) on a powerful personal computer, coupled with digital cameras capable of high resolution low-latency capture. The first iteration of this system created in 2008 (see Figure 4) utilized a fluorescent slide-viewing light-box , an Imaging Source scientific digital camera, a laptop and custom software that allowed for recording, playback, scaling, and masking of several layers of video (see Figure 5).

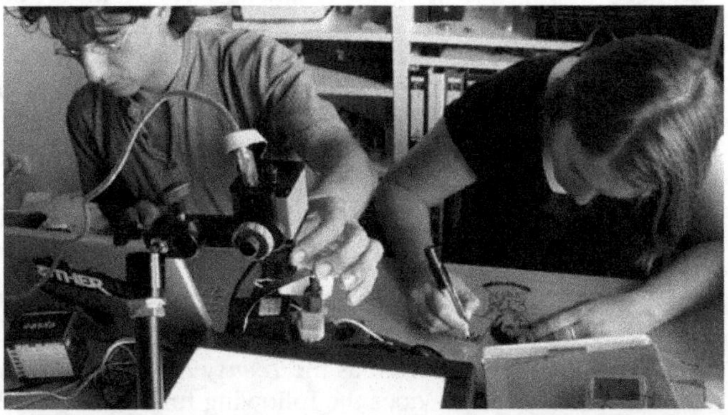

Figure 4. Livedraw Hardware v1: Momeni (left) and Schmid (right) collaborating on a livedrawing performance; System consists of a light box, digital camera with C-Mount lens and custom software. Schmid draws with pens/markers on transparency paper; digital camera captures image for manipulation in software

Later iterations of the instrument reconsidered the drawing interface (see Figure 6). This version leveraged advances in LED lighting, low-cost webcams and affordable digital fabrication to create an instrument that integrated the capture device, the mounting mechanism and the back-lighting all into a single object that was light-weight, collapsible and low-cost. By stabilizing the lighting and rigging, this iteration dramatically improved the reliability of high-quality image capture from drawings.

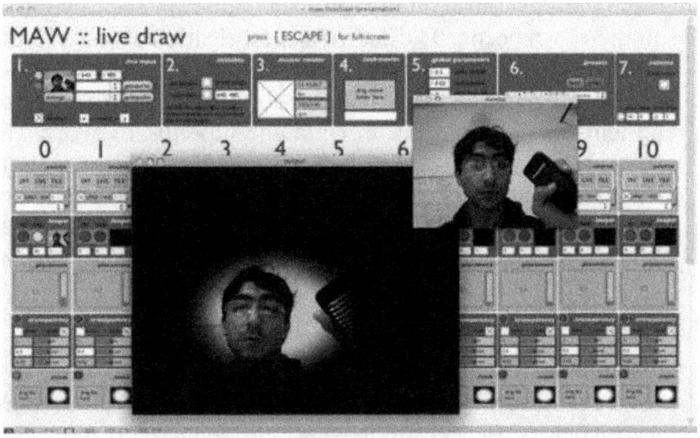

Figure 5. Livedraw Software v1: Screenshot of software developed in Max to allow for recording and manipulation of multiple multiple layers of video (labeled 0-10). Digital camera input ("monitor" window) is masked, scaled and placed on a video layer ("output" window).

Figure 6. Livedraw 2015; System consists of a thin USB-powered LED lightbox, encased in a custom fabricated casing made of Masonite that includes an appendage for holding the camera in the ideal location, and a USB HD Webcam

Opensource Hardware and Software and Mostly In-House Fabrication

The MOD is designed with makers, hackers and students in mind. All hardware and software developments for the project are shared with an opensource license on GitHub, and readers are encouraged to view, make or vary the designs to suit their own needs. The design and fabrication process for the MOD relied on flipping back-and-forth between in-house rapid prototyping and outsourced fabrication; *In-house:* all software elements prototyped in PureData and OpenFrameworks, all sculptural elements made with 3d printers and lasercutters, all circuit boards designed as 1-layer boards with Eagle and fabricated using an OtherMill small CNC-router; *Outsourced:* 2-layer printed circuit boards.

HARDWARE DESIGN

Overview

MOD's hardware is implemented as a modular system around the Raspberry Pi 3 computer and the Teensy 3.6 microcontroller (MCU). The Pi provides all video processing functionalities (video capture, layering, processing), while the Teensy provides all physical computing capabilities (buttons, knobs, joysticks, actuator control). A small LED projector handles video output, and power is provided to the entire system from a 12000mAH rechargeable Lithium Polymer battery.

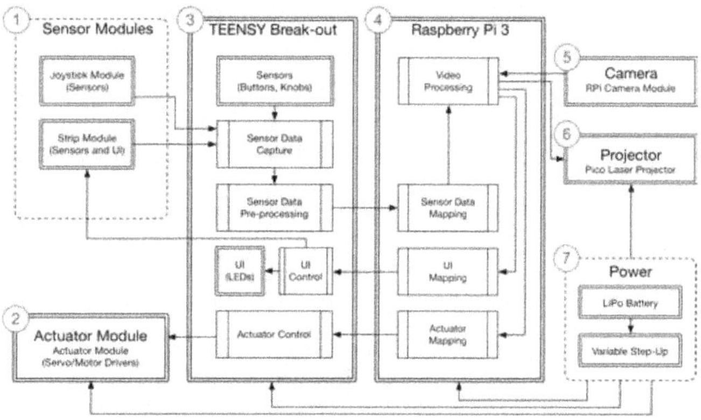

Figure 7. Hardware Overview; Double-stroke boxes labeled indicate discrete hardware components: 1) Custom PCB with sensors and UI elements, 2) Custom PCB with voltage regulation and motor drivers, 3) Custom PCB with Teensy 3.6 microcontroller, sensors and UI elements, driving circuitry for all UI elements, and connectors for secondary modules; 4) Raspberry Pi 3B, 5) Raspberry Pi Camera module, 6) Pico Projector, 7) Power management including LiPo battery and high-current voltage regulator

Physical Computing

A Teensy 3.6 Microcontroller (MCU) is used as a bridge between the software processes running on the Raspberry Pi, and physical inputs (sensors) and outputs (user interfaces and actuators) in the physical world (see Figure 10). In order to achieve these I/O requirements, the Teensy is used as a USB MIDI device slave to the Raspberry Pi that manages incoming and outgoing "Note" (discrete) and "Control Change" (continuous) MIDI Messages. Specifically, all sensor inputs are interpreted as incoming MIDI messages, while UI and actuator controls are achieved via outgoing MIDI messages. This implementation offers two notable advantage: 1) MCU programming is simplified thanks to the Teensy 's existing C/C++ classes for handling incoming and outgoing MIDI messages, 2) MIDI messages are handled with relatively low-latency/jitter by the operating system and provided to many software environments with little development overhead. This approach is also burdened by the typical disadvantages of MIDI: continuous controls are limited to the MIDI protocol's 7-bit resolution regardless of the specifications of the ADC.

Figure 8. Modular Hardware Design: Custom printed circuit boards for the physical computing subsystem; top and bottom rows show top and bottom of circuit boards respectively. From Left to Right: A) *Teensy breakout* board; includes MCU, transistor for driving circuitry, knobs, buttons, LEDs, and ribbon cables for connecting with the *Strip* and *Actuator* modules; B) *Strip module*, includes two knob-LED-Button sets and an additional status LED; C) *Actuator module*: Includes TB6612FNG dual-motor driver and terminals; D) *Joystick modules*

Modular Design

The physical computing subsystem designed around the Teensy is implemented in several modules: a *Teensy Breakout Module*, multiple *Strip Modules* and *Joystick Modules*, and an *Actuator Module* (see Figure 8). The modular design significantly reduces fabrication costs (smaller boards are much cheaper), while allowing a wider variety of future applications where individual interface elements can be redesigned or placed differently without impacting the Teensy breakout board. Together, these modules offer many input and output possibilities (see 9). These modules can be interchangeably combined to create a unified interface for the user (see Figure 10).

Teensy Breakout Module

The main board (referred to as the *Teensy Breakout* containing the MCU itself provides the following functionalities: 1) Connect all I/O pins of the Teensy to other components and/or connectors, 2) provide high-current LED driving capability with two 8-channel source driver IC's (Allegro Systems 2982) that can deliver up to 500mA to any of the PWM outputs; this allows the system to avoid drawing too much current from the MCU itself, 3) provide ribbon-cable interconnects between the *Teensy Breakout* and three other modules that implement various sensor input, UI and actuator output capabilities. The *Teensy Breakout* provides the following:

- 4 x analog inputs (for knobs)
- 4 x 3-pin connectors for additional analog sensors
- 4 x digital inputs (for buttons)
- 4 x PWM outputs (for button LEDs)
- 6 x 10-pin ribbon connectors for *Strip Modules*

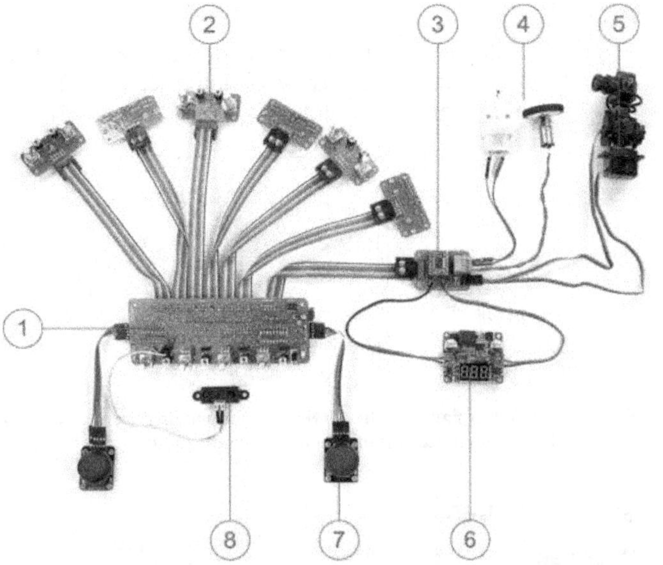

Figure 9. MOD modular design: 1) ***Teensy Breakout*** **board, includes micro controller, buttons, knobs, LEDs, power switch, and ribbon connectors to other modules; 2)** ***Strip Module*****, includes two knobs, two buttons, three LEDS; connects to breakout board with 10-conductor ribbon; 3)** ***Actuator Module*****, includes dual motor driver, and connectors to/from step-up module, 10-conductor ribbon to breakout board; 4) two DC motors; 5) two hobby servos (here used in a pan-tilt configuration for a camera); 6) High-current Step-up regulator for DC actuators; 7)** ***Joystick modules*****; 8) an IR distance sensor connected directly to the breakout board**

- 1 x 10-pin ribbon connector for *Actuator Module*
- 2 x 5-pin ribbon connectors for *Joystick Modules*
- Barrel connector for 5V power from the LiPo battery
- Main power switch and indicator LED
- 2 x 8-channel source drivers

Strip Module

Based on the analogy of a "channel strip" found in audio mixers, this module is intended to be used in multiples to control "layers" or "voices" of a multi-channel system. This module connects to the *Teensy Breakout Module* with a 10-pin ribbon, and incorporates the following:

- 1 x 10-pin ribbon connector for the *Teensy Breakout*
- 2 x analog inputs (for knobs or continuous analog sensors)
- 2 x digital inputs (for buttons or discrete sensors)
- 2 x pwm outputs (for button LEDs)
- 1 x digital output (for status LED)

Actuator Module

Our performance experiences showed that props, including simple robotic gadgets combine well with drawings to create interesting imagery. This feature allows the user to generate and control continuous visual motion without the need to continually interact with objects under the camera. This instrument allows for independent bi-direction and variable-speed of two DC actuators (motors, solenoids) and two hobby-servos via MIDI note and control-change messages. The *Actuator Module* PCB is built around the TB6612FNG motor driver IC and controls are provided from the microcontroller using a 10-pin IDC connector. All actuators are powered by a variable high-current step-up regulator (see Figure 11) in order to allow control of actuators that require more than the 250mA the Teensy can provide. The actuator module consists of the following

- 1 x 10-pin ribbon connector for the *Teensy Breakout*
- 1 x TB6612FNG dual DC motor driver
- 1 x logic-inverter IC (to save an MCU pin)
- 2 x 3-pin connectors for attaching hobby servos
- Spring-loaded quick connectors for attaching actuators

Joystick Module

This module is built around the common and low-cost thumb-joystick found in PlayStation controllers. The module connects with the *Teensy Breakout* with a 5-pin ribbon and provides two continuous controls (horizontal and vertical joystick movement) and one digital input (joystick button).

Video Input and Output

In order to optimize performance, a Raspberry Pi Camera Module V2 is used. [8]. This modules offers a Sony IMX219 8-megapixel sensor capable of 1080p30 and decent low-light performance, and a high-speed CSI interface for connecting to the Pi with a ribbon cable.

A Sony MP-CL1A pico projector with an LED light-source is used as video output. While this projector is far less bright than a full-sized home- or pro-theater projector, it offers a number of invaluable features that make it well suited to our use-case: very small and lightweight (77.0 x 149.5 x 13.0 mm , 210 g), battery powered (2 hours at 5V/1.5A; rechargeable), short throw (range 1.1 - 3.4 m) and infinite focus (as with all laser projectors). MOD also includes an optional HDMI-splitter that allows the Pi's HDMI output to be routed to a larger projector if needed.

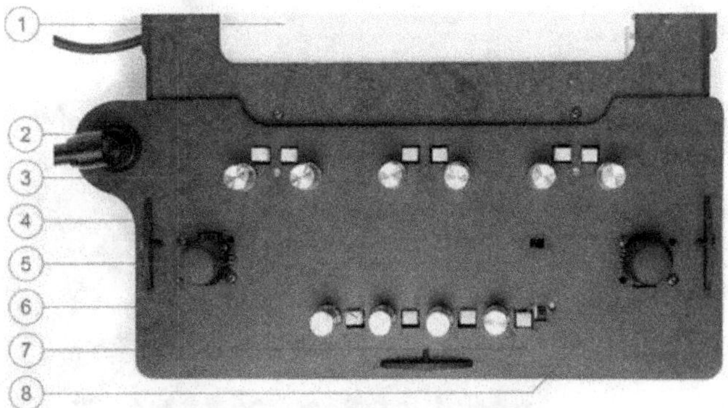

Figure 10. MOD UI Panel: 1) Back-lit drawing area; 2) mounting hole for projector; 3) knobs; 4) LED; 5) servo connectors; 6) Illuminated buttons; 7) Power button; 8) Thumb joystick

Power Management

The MOD is powered from an off-the-shelf 5V 12000mAh rechargeable LiPo battery.

[8]https://www.raspberrypi.org/products/camera-module-v2/

Table 1. Hardware modules for MOD Physical Computing Modules

Module	*Components*	#	Function
Teensy Breakout	Teensy 3.6	1	IO
	A2982	2	Drive LEDs/actuators
	Knob	4	User Input
	ButtonLED	4	User Input/Interface
	Strip Connector	6	Connect to strips
	Actuator Connector	1	Drive actuators
	Servo Outputs	2	Control Servos
	Switch	1	Power Switch
	Power	1	Power from battery
Strip Module	Knob	2	User Input
	Button LED	2	User Input User Interface
	LED	1	User Interface
Actuator Module	TB6612FNG Motor Driver	1	Actuator Control
	Variable Step-up	1	Convert 5V to 5-30V
	Servo Connectors	2	Drive two servos
	Motor Connectors	1	Drive two motors
Joystick Module	Playstation ThumbJoystick	1	User Input (continuous controls)
	Button	1	User Input (switch)

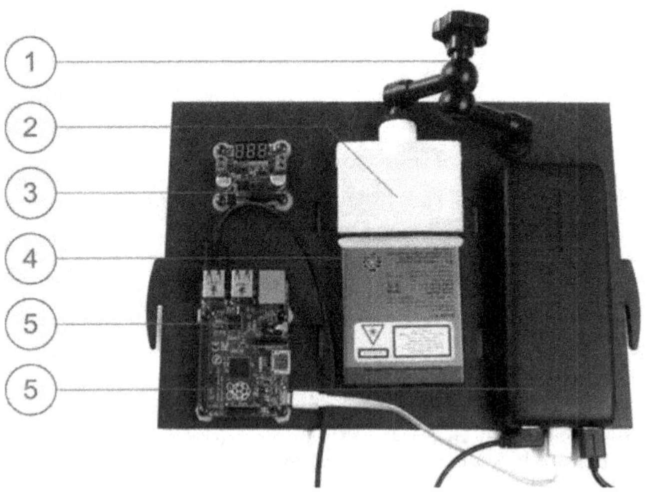

Figure 11. Hardware inside the MOD: 1) small "magic arm", 2) custom printed projector mount, 3) step-up voltage regulator for high-voltage actuators, 4) Pico laser projector, 5) Raspberry Pi 3, 6) LiPo Battery

Enclosure

The body of the instrument is fabricated from Masonite that is cut to form using a laser cutter (see Figure 12. Total material cost for the shell of the instrument is under $5.

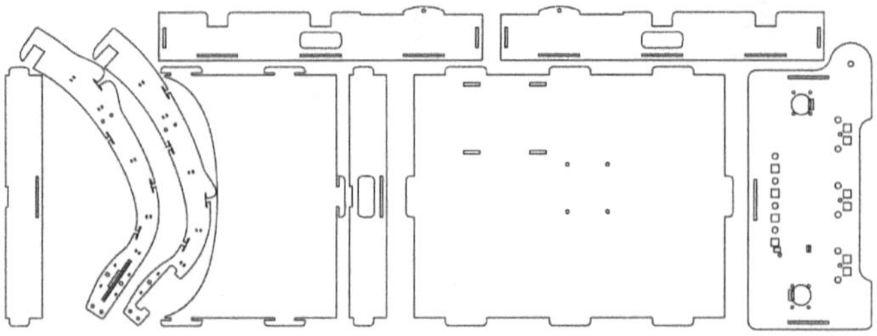

Figure 12. CAD designs for the MOD: all components are lasercut from low-cost 1/8" sheet material; minimal hardware is required for assembly

SOFTWARE DESIGN

Overview

Software for this system is developed using three environments:

1. Autodesk Eagle: Primarily used to design PCBs; also used to define the relationship between MCU hardware pins and MCU software variables; as well as the relationship between physical input devices and UI elements, and their corresponding MIDI note and control-change numbers. This feature is described in the section titled "Linking Hardware and Software Design".

2. Arduino IDE: Used to program the Teensy MCU; requires the *Teensyduino* add-on that allows programming Teensy MCUs, and provides USB-MIDI device functionality

3. OpenFrameworks: A C++ framework used to program all video processing

4. GLSL: OpenGL shader language, used to optimize video processing with GPU-based hardware acceleration

Figure 13 shows the software sub-processes and the hardware platforms that manage them.

Video Processing

The video processing functionality of MOD is based on *Livedraw* [9], a visual performance software developed by the author over the last decade. *Livedraw* offers the following core capabilities:

1. Managing multiple layers: This includes independent control of scale and position for layers of superimposed video
2. Keying and Thresholding: GPU-based image processing that renders parts of the image transparent so as to allow overlaying multiple video layers on top of one another
3. Live Looping: CPU- or GPU-based recording and looping of video frames
4. Controller mappings and UI: Triggers and parameters for the system are mapped to physical controllers and UI elements in order to allow the user to interact with the system gesturally

[9] http://maw.c-uir.org/software/

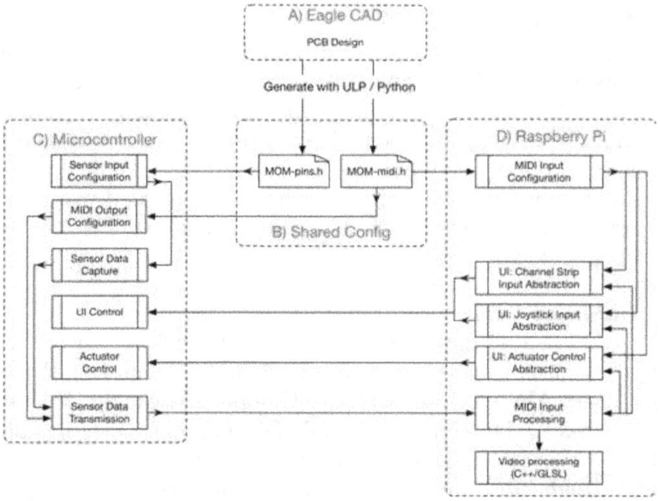

Figure 13. Software Overview; dashed-boxes indicated independent programming environments: A) Autodesk Eagle CAD was used to design all custom circuit boards; B) two header files are generated by a python script post processor a text file that describes signal connections in the "Teensy Breakout" board; C) Microcontroller code (in C on a Teensy 3.6) uses the two header files to configure sensor capture and MIDI-output configuration; D) The video processing engine (implemented in C++ with OpenFrameworks on the RPi) uses the MIDI header file to configure all MIDI I/O from system

The openFrameworks implementation of this graphics engine is built around a custom class (`vidLayer.cpp` and `vidlayer.h`), which is instantiated once for the live video layer and once for each looping video layer. This class optimizes performance by making use of the openGL `framebuffer` for all recording and processing. This class also defines the initialization and rendering behavior of each video layer, applies the openGL shader interactions. The shaders (`livedraw.frag` and `livedraw.vert`) are implemented in GLSL ES2 for compatibility with embedded platforms, and manage thresholding, keying, inverting and alpha-transparencies for all video layers.

Development Environment

Creative work with embedded systems is a mixed blessing. The ability to design, customize and build one's own hardware is rewarding. The ability to create robust and reliable turn-key systems that are unaffected by regular software updates, virus infections, or interruptions from email or the like also rewarding. Ideally, such systems lead to more fulfilling creative experiences as the user's time is mostly spent working with the tools and the content, as opposed to developing and repairing them. That said, creating complex instruments with embedded systems is considerably more difficult and error-prone than a straight-forward software development task for personal computers. For this reason, several design considerations and development tools were utilized to make the overall workflow more stream-line and less prone to human error. These areas are briefly outlined below

Networking and Configuration Management

The Raspbian distribution of Linux comes with a range of Debian tools that facilitate development on the Pi, and/or the ability to quickly install additional packages using `apt-get`. The following packages were critical to building an efficient development environment:

- samba: debian package that enables easy networking between personal computers and the Pi
- ansible: debian package that enables configuration-management, application deployment, cloud provisioning, ad-hoc task-execution, and multinode orchestration

Linking Hardware and Software Design

From the user's perspective, each tangible interaction element in MOD is represented by a MIDI note- or control-change-input or output message. This association, however, must be persistently maintained in several disparate development environments: 1) The PCB Schematic and Board files that define the hardware modules, 2) the MCU code running on the Teensy that samples sensors and sends out MIDI messages, or receives MIDI messages to control lights and actuators, 3) the graphics code running on the Raspberry Pi that receives incoming MIDI messages from the MCU and maps them to various processing parameters. In order to maintain consistency across these environments and reduce chances of human error, a series of python text-processing scripts were created that automatically generate header files for the Arduino code and an XML file for the openFrameworks application with all the necessary I/O information. Specifically, we employ the `pinlist.ulp` script that ships with Eagle CAD to generate a text file that describes which signals are connected to which pins of the MCU. We then process this text file with a custom python script that uses regular expressions to create a well-formatted C header file for the Arduino program with all the necessary signal-to-MIDI-message mappings. At the same time, the script also generates a well-formatted XML file that is used to initialize the settings of the openFrameworks application; calibrating it to correlate the incoming MIDI information with its proper functionality control.

EVALUATION

The technical functions of this instrument were evaluated in a laboratory setting for hardware and software performance. According to our tests, the physical computing hardware is easily capable of handling all 58 channels of analog and digital input and output that enable buttons, knobs, additional analog sensors, and actuator control. Timing performance is comparable to off-the-shelf MIDI-devices. Software performance is dramatically reduced as compared with a personal computer–as expected. With a performance requirement of at least 15fps for rendering, the current iteration of the video processing software can accommodate 2 layers of video at 1080p, 3-4 layers at 720p and 5-10 layers at 640x480.

The creative potential of this instrument was evaluated by four performing artists with an active live cinema practice. The first two artists, who often perform as a pair and integrate traditional drawings, sand drawings, and puppetry into their work pointed to several strengths and weaknesses of this instrument. They identified the most desirable feature of this instrument to be its reliance on analog drawing (as opposed to a digitizing tablet), its portability and its autonomy (no need for a laptop). The ability to to combine analog drawing with digital effects, layering and transformation was deemed highly desirable, although the performers saw many occasions where some of these features would not be necessary. More specifically, the artist identified a distinct advantage in using ink and markers for mark making, as it allows them to build on their existing drawing skills, while allowing them to improvise with mark making in ways that are not possible with digital drawing interfaces. This group also identified opportunities to use this interface as a more generalized digital viewer, akin to a a traditional overhead projector. Building on this function, they fashioned a small container for sand and water that allowed them to use the instrument to capture, layer and project sand drawings as well as ink-and-water visual compositions. The third artists had similar positive feedback, but was more cognoscente of the computational limitations of this system as compared with the laptop-based live cinema system with which she typically performs. Specifically, limitations in the number of layers and the length of recorded video loops that are imposed by the memory limitations of our small embedded computer. All artists agreed on a user-interface weaknesses in the system: specifically, while the instrument portends to function as a one-person device, simultaneous drawing, looping and manipulation requires more hands than a single person has available. All artists also agreed that while the pico-projector that is included in the system may be effective for rehearsal or prototyping, real-world performance situations impose requirements (distance, brightness, etc) that will rarely be met by our small projector.

CONCLUSION AND FUTURE WORK

With the development of this mobile and easy-to-use hybrid drawing instrument, we expect this type of production to continue and expand in the coming year. We are presently in the process of fabricating multiple MODs for field experimentation: One unit will travel to the celebrated Bread and Puppet festival with artist Davey Steinman who has a practice of media-rich puppetry. A set of MODs will be used in an upcoming research project in collaboration with the Children's Museum of Pittsburgh to study the possibilities of integrating drawing into the workflow of a maker space situated in a museum. We are actively seeking new collaborations and opportunities for experimenting with new use-cases of this instrument.

Our design allows for a range of future applications that we have yet to explore. In particular, the actuation possibilities of the MOD in combination with live video processing present a promising area of exploration in creating live animations. Moreover, since the *Teeny Breakout board* is capable of driving up to 16 actuators (in addition to the dedicated *Actuator Module*), we expect a range of new module designs that focus on miniature robotics.

We envision the MOD as part of a family of portable performance and content creation instruments that leverage embedded computing, gestural interaction, and intuitive interfaces. A similar instrument for music-making (named MOM for Mobile Object for Music[10]) is currently in its fourth iteration and will be further iterated to leverage the developments from the MOD.

[10]http://alimomeni.net/MOM

ACKNOWLEDGMENTS

This work is dedicated to all members, collaborators, and fans of MAW–Minneapolis Art On Wheels. Special thanks to Drew Anderson whose early work as a research assistant on mobile project instruments helped set this project in motion. Special thanks also to Jenny Schmid, Andrew Steudel, Sinan Goknur and Davey Steinman whose on-the-road work with urban projection within and beyond the context of MAW was invaluable and inspiring.

REFERENCES

1. Chiang Chenwei, Shu-Chuan Chiu, Anak Agung Gede Dharma, and Kiyoshi Tomimatsu. 2012. Birds on Paper: An Alternative Interface to Compose Music by Utilizing Sketch Drawing and Mobile Device. In *Proceedings of the Sixth International Conference on Tangible, Embedded and Embodied Interaction*. 1–4.
2. Peter Dalsgaard and Kim Halskov. 2010. Designing urban media façades: cases and challenges. In *Proceedings of the SIGCHI Conference on Human Factors in Computing Systems*. ACM Press, New York, New York, USA, 2277.
3. Claude Fortin, Steve DiPaola, Kate Hennessy, and Jim Bizzocchi. 2013. Medium-specific properties of urban screens: towards an ontological framework for digital public displays. In *Proceedings of the 9th ACM Conference on Creativity Cognition*.
4. C Fortin and K Hennessy. 2015. The dual skins of a media façade: Explicit and implicit interactions. *ACM SIGGRAPH Art Papers* (2015).
5. Claude Fortin, Kim Hennessy, and Hughes Sweeney. 2014. Roles of an interactive media façade in a digital agora. In *Proceedings of The International Symposium on Pervasive Displays*.
6. Rex Hartson. 2003. Cognitive, physical, sensory, and functional affordances in interaction design. *Behaviour & Information Technology* 22, 5 (Sept. 2003), 315–338.
7. Luke Hespanhol, Martin Tomitsch, and Oliver Bown. 2014. Using embodied audio-visual interaction to promote social encounters around large media façades. In *Proceedings of the 2014 conference on Designing interactive systems*.
8. Kazuhiro Jo. 2008. DrawSound: A Drawing Instrument for Sound Performance. In *Proceedings of the nd international conference on Tangible and embedded interaction*. 1–4.
9. Adriaan Ianus Keller. 2005. For Inspiration Only; Designer interaction with informal collections of visual material. (2005).
10. Michael Lew. 2004. Live Cinema: designing an instrument for cinema editing as a live performance. In *Proceedings of the 2004 conference on New interfaces for musical expression*.
11. Tom McDonough. 2004. *Guy Debord and the Situationist International: Texts and Documents (October Books)*. The MIT Press.

12. David Molyneaux and Hans Gellersen. 2009. Projected interfaces: enabling serendipitous interaction with smart tangible objects. *TEI '09: Proceedings of the 3rd International Conference on Tangible and Embedded Interaction* (Feb. 2009).
13. Ali Momeni and Stephanie Sherman. 2015. A Manual for Urban Projection.
14. Don Norman. 2004. Affordances and Design; Affordance, Conventions and Design (Part 2)–Two Essays on Design.
15. Daniel Saakes. 2005. Material light: exploring expressive materials. *Personal and Ubiquitous Computing* 10, 2-3 (Oct. 2005), 144–147.
16. Kayato Sekiya and Shinpei Chihara. 2011. iNkDraw: Physical Ink-Based Interface for Capturing and Manipulating Drawings on Digital Display. In *Proceedings of the fifth international conference on Tangible, embedded, and embodied interaction*. 1–4.
17. Mark Shepard. 2009. Sentient City Survival Kit: Archaeology of the Near Future. *Digital Arts and Culture 2009* (Dec. 2009).
18. Jay Silver and Eric Rosenbaum. 2010. Twinke: Programming with Color. In *Proceedings of the fourth international conference on Tangible, embedded, and embodied interaction*. 1–2.
19. Yuta Sugiura, Koki Toda, Takashi Kikuchi, Takayuki Hoshi, Youichi Kamiyama, Takeo Igarashi, and masahiko Inami. 2017. Grassffiti. In *the Tenth International Conference*. ACM Press, New York, New York, USA, 413–417.
20. Abigail Susik. 2012. Sky Projectors, Portapaks, and Projection Bombing: The Rise of a Portable Projection Medium. *Journal of Film and Video* 64, 1 (2012), 79–92.
21. Nato Thompson, Gregory Sholette, Joseph Thompson, Arjen Noordeman, and Nicholas Mirzoeff. 2004. *The interventionists*. The MIT Press.
22. Diane Waldman. 1989. *Jenny Holzer*. Solomon R Guggenheim Museum.
23. Alexander Wiethoff, Thomas Bauer, and Sven Gehring. 2014. Investigating multi-user interactions on interactive media façades. *Proceedings of the 2nd Media Architecture Biennale Conference* (2014).
24. Krzysztof Wodiczko. 1999. *Critical Vehicles*. The MIT Press.

SWAY – Designing for Balance and Posture Awareness

Simon Asplund
Royal Institute of Technology/KTH
Stockholm, Sweden
asplund.simon@gmail.com

Martin Jonsson
Södertörn University
141 89 Huddinge, Sweden
martin.jonsson@sh.se

ABSTRACT
This paper presents the SWAY prototype that encourages people to explore aspects around balance and posture in a playful way. The prototype senses small movements and shifts in posture using a Kinect sensor, and translates these movements to the tilting of a platform holding a set of marbles, and to haptic feedback in the form of vibrations. The prototype provides an interactive experience focusing on building body awareness with a particular focus on balance and posture. The design inquiry provided new insights with respect to reinforcement of bodily experiences and how different modalities affect the guiding of attention.

Author Keywords
Bodily interaction; balance; posture; somaesthetics; body awareness.

ACM Classification Keywords
• Human-centered computing~Interaction techniques

INTRODUCTION
Aspects of body awareness have recently been brought to the fore in HCI, and how we can design interactive experiences that promote an increased understanding and mastery of our bodies - our "indispensable tool of tools" [10], aiming for increased wellbeing in our everyday interactions in the world. There are numerous examples of interactive, sensor based devices aiming to improve health and wellbeing. Most of these devices are however based on a rather instrumental view of health and wellbeing, and on the assumption that our bodies are there to be trimmed, perfected, and kept free from illnesses and bad influences [7]. In this work, we aim for an alternative stance, promoting reflection rather than having the technology judge the user. The interactions should not force the user to act or move the body in a specific way, but allow for and encourage certain movements by providing an interesting and pleasant interactive experience. The more specific domain we explore is how to design for body awareness with a specific focus on balance and posture. The notion of balance has previously been explored to some extent within HCI, in particular in relation to balance training for physical rehabilitation. In this work, we are not interested in addressing any specific medical conditions, but rather in how technology designed to promote reflection around posture and balance can support an increased general sense of wellbeing. The paper presents a design exploration resulting in the SWAY prototype - a mechanical installation that balances a set of marbles in correspondence with your posture.

TEI '18, March 18–21, 2018, Stockholm, Sweden

ACM ISBN 978-1-4503-5568-1/18/03…$15.00
https://doi.org/10.1145/3173225.3173262

BACKGROUND
Recently there has been an increased interest in the somaesthetics philosophy in HCI, and how it can inform the design of bodily aesthetic interactive experiences [4, 8]. somaesthetics is an interdisciplinary field grounded in pragmatist philosophy and phenomenology [9]. By combining soma, the body, with aesthetics (understood as our sensory appreciations), the attention is drawn to our bodily movements as part of our ways of being and thinking. A key premise of the somaesthetic philosophy is the insight that all our experiences and interactions with the world happen with and through our body. To improve our somaesthetic appreciation, we thus need to break our everyday habitual patterns of walking, breathing, standing, etc. By actively creating breakdowns in these patterns and consciously putting them under scrutiny, allows for adaption and change of these unconscious dimensions of our everyday lives.

Höök et al. [4, 5] explored how somaesthetics can be addressed through interaction design and notes that when designing a Somaesthetic experience the experiential quality of *turning inwards* becomes an important factor. To support designers engaging in somaesthetics, Höök et al. suggest a strong concept called the Somaesthetic Appreciation Concept that addresses designing interactive experiences where attending to the felt experiences of the body is an integral part of the experience. The concept suggests that a design following Somaesthetic Appreciation should encompass certain characteristics such as; *subtle guidance* (directing attention without stealing focus), *making space* (designing space for reflection, in physical space and in time), *intimate correspondence* (carefully synchronized bio-feedback loops), and *articulating experience* (designing opportunities to articulate and verbalize the experiences).

The Somaesthetic Appreciation concept was instantiated in two design exemplars: The related Soma Mat and Breathing

Light prototypes [4, 5] aims to promote somaesthetic appreciation and increased body awareness. The Soma Mat supports the ability to direct your attention by providing heat feedback to different parts of the body while following the voice instructions of a pre-recorded body awareness session. The mat heats up slowly and leaves slowly underneath the body parts that are currently addressed by the guiding voice. The Breathing Light prototype consists of an enclosure made of fabric and string curtains that you position yourself under, creating a room within a room, effectively shutting out the external world. Inside this enclosure is a breathing sensor that measures the movements of your chest. The sensor controls a lamp inside the module, creating an ambient light that will dim in cadence with your breathing.

Balance and Posture awareness

There are also a number of commercial and research prototypes that more specifically address aspects of balance and posture. One example is *TruPosture* [1], a smart shirt designed to reduce back pain by measuring the posture and providing tactile feedback as reminders to straighten the back. There are also some examples from research, which rather than telling the user how to act, instead focus on means for promoting reflection. *The Slow Floor* [2] takes the form of six timber and foam interactive walking pads with embedded force sensors that measures the changing weight of a person's footsteps. This force and weight data is converted to sound sent to speakers that surround the prototype. The force sensor has an effect on a generated sound tone creating a "decelerating engine" sonic effect. This setup encourages reflections around the practice of walking and unlocks a creative agency by bringing this habitual practice of shifting body weight in a form of controlled falling to conscious reflection. The interactive installation *Surging Vertically* [6], explores aspects of balance by having a bystander actively pulling a standing person off balance while the shifts in pressure from the person's feet affects a soundscape. This setup allows for a negotiation of balance and involves sensations or feelings of centering, shifting weight, being supported and lifted or fear of falling. Other work has focused on the notion of *kinesthetic awareness*, referring to a general awareness of how our bodies move and is oriented in space. In the interactive installation *Still, moving* [3], subtle muscular activities in the legs of a participant was sensed and formed the basis of an audio feedback in the form of a soundscape. This feedback allowed for the participants to explore, and become aware of the subtle micro movements involved in the ongoing activities of keeping balance, when standing, walking, and dancing.

THE SWAY PROTOTYPE

The SWAY prototype aims to create a somaesthetic experience that encourages reflection around your posture and the continuous unconscious subtle movements and changes in center of mass. Small movements and shifts in posture are detected by a Kinect depth camera controlling a mechanical platform that holds a set of plastic marbles (See Figure 1). Shifts in posture tilts the platform in corresponding direction making the marbles roll around on the platform. These movements create a visual feedback, but more importantly an audio feedback from the plastic balls marbles on the wooden platform, creating a soothing soundscape that could be compared to the sound of rolling waves. Except from the visual and audio feedback, there is also a tactile feedback channel, where the shift in posture is translated to vibrations provided to the user's feet through a platform that the user stands on. Together these modalities aim to create a playful experience that encourages exploration of small bodily movements and reflection on the bodily sensations in relation to the provided feedback channels.

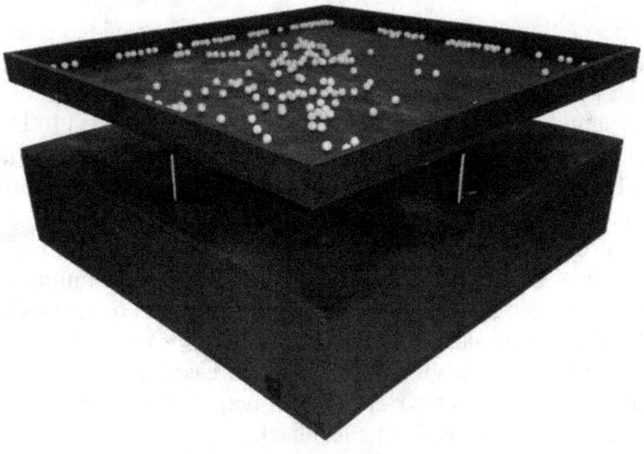

Figure 1. The Sway prototype

The qualities of the designed interaction partly correspond to the Somaesthetic Appreciation strong concept [4], and its constituting characteristics discussed above. The physical manifestation of the design relates to the notion of *making space*, and the design of audio and tactile feedback corresponds to the aim of *subtle guidance*, by directing attention to posture and balance, without requiring full attentiveness. The design however in particular aims to encompass the notion of *intimate correspondence*. Intimate correspondence puts an emphasis on carefully designed bio-feedback loops, where meaningful and immediate feedback is provided in response to different bodily functions or actions. The feedback thus serves as a form of amplifying mirror, where the reinforced sensations can form a basis for reflection around that particular bodily function, as nicely exemplified in the design of the *Still, moving* installation [3]. The feedback loops in the SWAY prototype is designed to have a similar function, providing additional stimuli that corresponds with and mirrors sensations corresponding to balance and posture.

Physical and digital design

The sensing of user movements is performed using a Kinect V2 sensor, which allows for distance measurements with an accuracy of 0.99 millimeters. By utilizing the Kinect software libraries for skeleton tracking, a specific point in the middle of the user's chest is identified, and the movements of that point along the Z and X axis (leaning forward/backwards vs sideways) is used as the control signal for the tilting of the platform. Some filtering is required to achieve a smooth and stable signal. The platform part of the prototype is made of plywood with a thickness of 6 mm and a side length of 400 mm. The total height of the platform, from bottom to the top of the balance plate edges, is 185 mm. The tilting motions of the platform is controlled by two servo motors, and the supporting structures and mounts for the motors and platform are created using a 3D-printer. Pieces of memory foam are integrated in the mount to damp the vibrations. On the platform, there are between 50-100 plastic marbles with a diameter of 6 mm (originally airsoft gun ammunition).

The haptic vibration feedback to the feet was provided using two vibration speakers and an amplifier. The speakers where integrated into a contraption made of wood and foam rubber as shown in Figure 2. The speakers were set to play 110 Hz sinusoidal waves and the amplitude was adjusted so that the vibrations did not produce a discernible sound at maximum output. The output amplitude of the two speakers is controlled by the user's tilting. Leaning back or forth affects the two speakers identically, with an increased amplitude corresponding to forward or backwards tilting. For sideways leaning the speakers behave differently. If the user is leaning to the left, the left speaker output is increased and leaning to the right increases the right speaker output. Standing upright results in little or no haptic feedback.

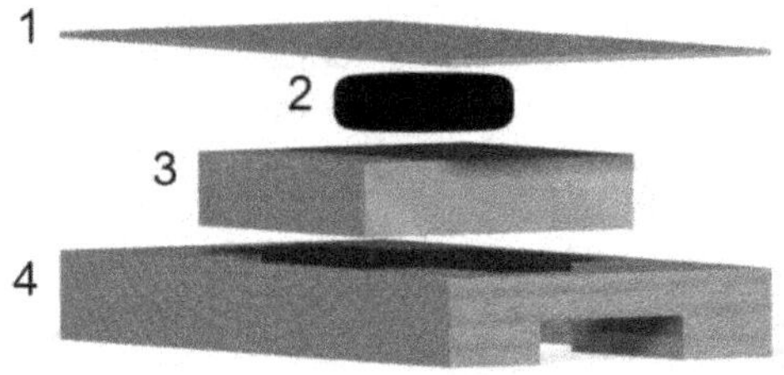

Figure 2. Exploded-view of the vibration contraption. 1 is the cover plate that the user stands on, 2 is the vibration speaker. 3 is the memory foam and 4 is the wooden frame

DESIGN INQUIRY

The method used to explore this design space can be broadly categorized as Research through Design (RtD) [11]. In an RtD research process, design work in the domain will drive the exploration of both problem and solutions – that is, we gain new knowledge via the act of making, through a design inquiry involving a combination of experiences from design work and results from tests with users. This particular design exploration started out from an idea of providing mechanical feedback loops based on biometric data and microscopic movements. In early design prototypes, the Kinect camera was used for sensing heartbeat and breathing rhythm, which were then translated to mechanical motion. Figure 3 shows an early prototype of a pillow that moves in synch with breathing. The explorations based on breathing and heartbeat

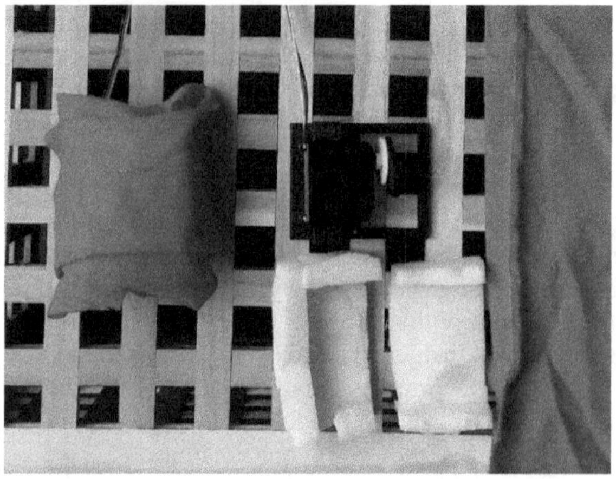

Figure 3. Pulsating pillow that moves in accordance with breathing.

were however abandoned, due to the difficulty in acquiring accurate and precise enough sensor data, in particular since we were aiming for immediate real-time feedback, and not mean estimates over time. Although the Kinect camera showed some promise for acquiring in particular breathing data, for it to work in a reliable we had to impose restrictions on the placement of the user, materials in clothing etc. that made the solution impractical.

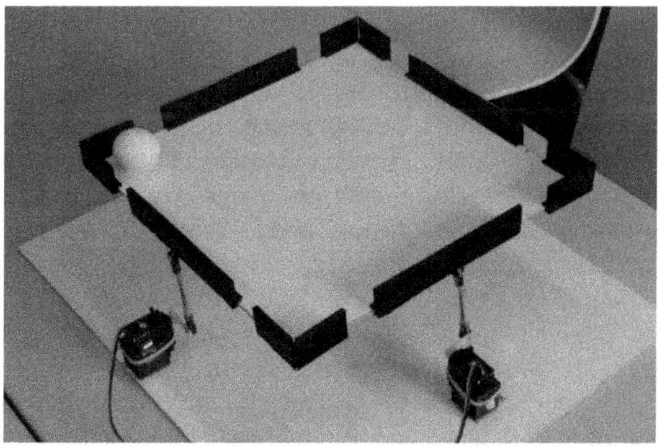

Figure 4. The initial SWAY prototype

Focus then shifted towards working with balance and posture, and the SWAY concept started to take shape. The first version of the prototype (Figure 4) had a similar design as the final prototype with the main difference that it used one single larger ball (a table tennis ball), instead of the marbles in the final prototype. The idea was that by mapping the tilt of the board to the movements of the user, the same movements would be amplified in the form of the ball moving. The user controls the ball using tilting movements and the small changes would be reflected by the movements on the ball. By designing certain tasks and exercises in the experience the user is instructed to use small movements to control the ball effectively.

Initial User Test

A small study with seven participants was conducted to investigate how the initial prototype performed in terms of evoking body reflection. The participants consisted of students and researchers from the research group. In the initial stage of the test the participants were instructed to play around freely with the prototype to get a feel of the prototype – how to control it and how responsive it was. The participants were allowed to do this for as long as they pleased and was encouraged to do this until they felt comfortable that they had full control over the prototype. Initially the table tennis ball was placed on the board from the start, but this was later changed so that the ball was added after the participant had gained control over the prototype.

The second part of the test consisted of different tasks that the participants were asked to perform. These tasks included: trying to make the ball stay in the center of the board, drawing circles using the ball while avoiding the sides, and controlling the prototype with closed eyes, and by only moving different body parts – hips, legs, or upper body. The different exercises served to encourage the users to explore different ways of interacting with the prototype and reflect upon the differences. Asking the users to close their eyes, served to encourage the user to engage other senses to explore the feedback from the prototype. The final part of the test consisted of a dialogue around the experience based on a set of questions relating to the experience of the interaction, including more specific questions such as if they felt in control of the prototype and if their movements were mapped in a satisfactory way, coupled with more open questions concerning their perception and awareness of their bodies.

Insights and Redesign

The user test revealed some major flaws with the proposed design. The aim with the prototype was to create a somaesthetic experience helping to direct focus to aspects of the body and its functioning. The tests, however, showed that the proposed design resulted in an interactive experience where the focus was very much placed on the ball and its movements, and not so much on any bodily sensations. The interaction thus became similar to that of typical representationally oriented computer games, where skillful bodily interaction is required to control an external representation. The results led to some changes in the design aiming to shift the focus of the interaction more towards the bodily sensations. One design decision was to replace the table tennis ball with 50 small plastic marbles. This change served to take away the single point of focus, but also had an unexpected effect that turned out to be very important. The plastic marbles rolling on a wooden board created a distinct soundscape that provided an audible feedback corresponding to the user movements. The other design decision concerned adding an additional haptic feedback channel to further put the focus on bodily sensations. In the final prototype the user thus stands on a platform with embedded vibration actuators that responds to the user movements.

Final User Test

In a user test with the final prototype (See Figure 5), five individuals, all students in their mid-twenties participated. The test lasted approximately 30 minutes and consisted of three parts. The first part was a dialogue regarding the purpose of the project and prototype. The basics behind how the prototype and feedback worked was explained so that the participants were aware of how the interaction would work before initiating the test. The participants were also introduced to the reasoning behind using somaesthetics and body awareness as the basis for the design. This introduction served to place the users in a specific mindset, more attentive to the bodily experiences than to the behavior of the prototype.

Figure 3. The entire SWAY prototype setup (top), in use (bottom)

The second part of the test functioned as a warm-up. The participants were asked to take off their shoes, stand comfortably on the floor and lean gently in different directions while keeping their eyes closed. Asking the participants to start reflecting on what they experienced before testing the prototype, aimed to evoke a reflective state of mind. This also gave the participants an experience they could later compare to the prototype interaction. In the last part, the participants interacted with the prototype. The participants were first asked to familiarize themselves with the prototype and were encouraged to explore how it responded to different kinds of leaning motions. When the participants felt that they had tried the interaction for a satisfactory amount of time they were asked different questions, aiming to start a dialogue regarding the experience and how the feedback was received. The participants were encouraged to elaborate on issues that came to mind during the interaction with the prototype, for example on specific bodily experiences, or how certain parts of the interaction felt.

The results from the study revealed that most of the test subjects were not used to reflect on their felt experiences: *"The truth is that you have never reflected on this, how your muscles feel when you do these [movements]"*. This realization occurred during multiple user tests. All participants stated that the prototype and user tests helped them reflect on their own body and increase their body awareness. The vibration feedback delivered to the user's soles was considered to be the most important part of the interaction by one of the participants, but was not supported by the remaining four. Despite this, the feedback was considered pleasant. When the participants were asked to step down from the prototype and control the board without vibration feedback, each participant stated that the experience was more pleasant with vibration feedback included. The consensus was that the haptic feedback helped them identify how they were positioned. By exchanging the table tennis ball used in the initial study 50-100 plastic marbles, the focus was placed on the prototype's entire motion instead of a single ball's behavior. Each of the test participants experienced the sound created by the pellets to be soothing; despite it being louder. This sound also covered the servo motor noise which disturbed the experience in the previous prototype.

DISCUSSION AND CONCLUSIONS

The design exploration resulting in the SWAY prototype generated important insights with respect to designing interactive experiences for body awareness in general, and experiences to address issues of posture and balance in particular. The most prominent findings point to the importance of designing for user attention to be directed towards the felt experiences of the body. The experiences from the first prototype highlight that visual feedback runs a high risk of moving attention out from the body, towards external objects and representations. Tactile and audio feedback on the other hand shows more potential for guiding attention towards felt bodily experiences. This aligns with previous research on guiding attention using different modalities [4, 5]

The prototype also highlights how interactive technologies for body awareness can utilize the approach of reinforcing bodily signals in order to make them available for scrutiny. The SWAY prototype reacts to very small shifts in posture, pointing to the fact that we are seldom entirely motionless, but are always engaging in more or less voluntary continuous movements. Finally, the prototype aligns with some of the findings from the study with the Slow Floor [4], regarding how the combination of tactile sensations on the soles of the feet, and audio feedback based on shifts in center of weight, may create a reinforced perception of balance, and thus may support an increased body awareness with respect to balance.

REFERENCES

1. Adela Health Inc (n.d.) *Products:* Available: <http://www.adelahealth.com/products/> 2017-08-09
2. Frank Feltham, Lian Loke, Elise van den Hoven, Jeffrey Hannam, and Bert Bongers. 2014. The slow floor: increasing creative agency while walking on an interactive surface. In *Proceedings of the 8th International Conference on Tangible, Embedded and Embodied Interaction* (TEI '14). 105-112. DOI: http://dx.doi.org/10.1145/2540930.2540974
3. Jules Françoise, Yves Candau, Sarah Fdili Alaoui, and Thecla Schiphorst. 2017. Designing for Kinesthetic Awareness: Revealing User Experiences through Second-Person Inquiry. In *Proceedings of the 2017 CHI Conference on Human Factors in Computing Systems* (CHI '17). ACM, New York, NY, USA, 5171-5183. DOI: https://doi.org/10.1145/3025453.3025714
4. Kristina Höök, Martin Jonsson, Anna Ståhl, and Johanna Mercurio. 2016. Somaesthetic Appreciation Design. In *Proceedings of the 2016 CHI Conference on Human Factors in Computing Systems* (CHI '16). ACM, New York, NY, USA, 3131-3142.
5. Martin Jonsson, Anna Ståhl, Johanna Mercurio, Anna Karlsson, Naveen Ramani, and Kristina Höök. 2016. The Aesthetics of Heat: Guiding Awareness with Thermal Stimuli. In *Proceedings of the TEI '16: Tenth International Conference on Tangible, Embedded, and Embodied Interaction* (TEI '16). ACM, New York, NY, USA, 109-117. DOI: https://doi.org/10.1145/2839462.2839487
6. Lian Loke and George Poonkhin Khut. 2010. Surging verticality: an experience of balance. In *Proceedings of the fifth international conference on Tangible, embedded, and embodied interaction* (TEI '11). ACM, New York, NY, USA, 237-240. DOI: http://dx.doi.org/10.1145/1935701.1935747
7. Stephen Purpura, Victoria Schwanda, Kaiton Williams, William Stubler, and Phoebe Sengers. 2011. Fit4life: the design of a persuasive technology promoting healthy behavior and ideal weight. In *Proceedings of the SIGCHI Conference on Human Factors in Computing Systems* (CHI '11). ACM, New York, NY, USA, 423-432. DOI: https://doi.org/10.1145/1978942.1979003
8. Thecla Schiphorst. 2009. soft(n): toward a somaesthetics of touch. In *CHI '09 Extended Abstracts on Human Factors in Computing Systems* (CHI EA '09). 2427-2438. DOI: http://dx.doi.org/10.1145/1520340.1520345

9. Richard Shusterman. 2008. *Body Consciousness: A Philosophy of Mindfulness and Somaesthetics*. Cambridge University Press.
10. Richard Shusterman. 2013. Somaesthetics. *The Encyclopedia of Human-Computer Interaction, 2nd Ed. Soegaard, Mads, and Rikke Friis Dam.*
11. John Zimmerman, Jodi Forlizzi, and Shelley Evenson. 2007. Research through design as a method for interaction design research in HCI. In *Proceedings of the SIGCHI Conference on Human Factors in Computing Systems* (CHI '07). 493-502. DOI: http://dx.doi.org/10.1145/1240624.1240704

Hard and Soft Tangibles: Mixing Multi-touch and Tangible Interaction in Scientific Poster Scenarios

Alexandre G. de Siqueira [1,2]
gomesde@clemson.edu

Brygg Ullmer [1,2]
bullmer@clemson.edu

Mark Delarosa [4,2]
delarosa.mark.j@gmail.com

Chris Branton [3,2]
cbranton@drury.edu

Miriam K. Konkel [1]
mkonkel@clemson.edu

[1]Clemson University, [2]Louisiana State University, [3]Drury University, [4]Solano Community College

ABSTRACT

Research on tangible user interfaces commonly focuses on tangible interfaces acting alone or in comparison with multi-touch or graphical interfaces. In contrast, hybrid approaches can be seen as the norm for established "mainstream" interaction paradigms. This paper proposes interfaces that support complementary use of physical and virtual interaction modalities with tangible and multi-touch interactions. We describe prototypes involving capacitively-sensed surfaces combined with laser-cut and 3D-printed dial-like tangibles. We employ them in the context of several computationally-mediated scientific poster scenarios, which we argue to have a number of attractions for such deployments. We present two platforms: one templated, the other highly customizable, supporting both tangible and multi-touch interactions across horizontal and vertical displays. We explore users' interaction modality choice among the options presented, draw lessons and challenges from posters developed by students, and consider future directions.

Author Keywords

Computationally-mediated scientific poster; poster presentation; tangible user interfaces; tangible interaction; multi-touch interaction; cyberphysical interfaces; passive tokens; hard and soft tangibles.

ACM Classification Keywords

Human-centered computing~Interface design prototyping; Human-centered computing~Touch screens; Human-centered computing~haptic devices.

INTRODUCTION

The topic of tangible interfaces has experienced great vitality in recent decades. Within the tangible interaction field, research often focuses on tangible interfaces acting by themselves, or tangible interfaces in comparison with "competing" interaction techniques (especially graphical and multi-touch interfaces [76, 20]). In contrast, when considering established "mainstream" interaction paradigms, hybrid approaches can be seen as more the norm than the exception. Reflecting upon the Xerox Star system, its creators warned not to be dogmatic about the direct manipulation on Desktop metaphors [36]. Contemporary operating systems and desktop computer applications tend to combine both graphical user interfaces and textual/command-line interfaces. Smartphone platforms typically blend multi-touch with more "traditional" applications (e.g., web browsers).

TEI 2018, March 18–21, 2018, Stockholm, Sweden.
Copyright © 2018 ACM ISBN 978-1-4503-5568-1/18/03 ...$15.00.
http://dx.doi.org/10.1145/3173225.3173252

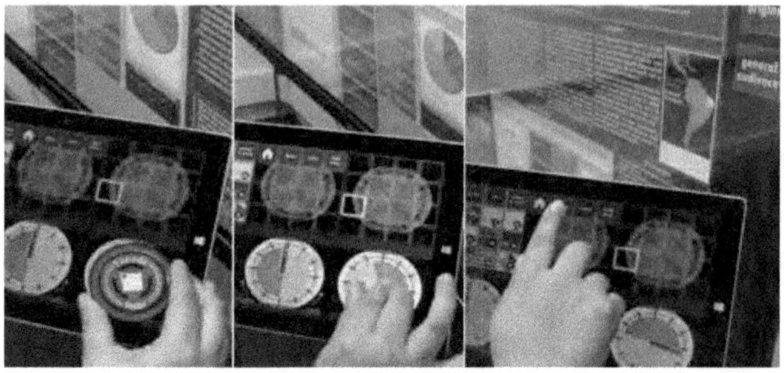

Figure 1. User interacting with an Entrada platform poster. Operations can be performed by multi-touch, hard and soft tangibles.

In this paper, we propose systems that offer functionality with and without physical tangibles[1] and with and without virtual/"soft" interactors, including combinations of both. Here, we regard "pure-multitouch" and "pure-tangible" variants, as well as hybrids thereof, all as "first-class citizens." In this sense, our system is not strictly speaking a "tangible interface" alone, but rather (inspired by [41, 42, 40]) what we and others have begun to consider as a cyberphysical interface (CPI) – a system designed to integrate support for both physical and virtual interaction modalities.

Our systems implement computationally-mediated scientific posters, leveraging on the existence of several communities of content generators that are engaged in various areas of research. We developed two platforms. Poster developers were alternatively asked to adapt their content to the constraints of a tightly-coupled platform or offered basic building blocks (e.g., methods to identify tangibles on a multi-touch screen) with more freedom to design and build their own interactive presentations. We describe posters developed for these two groups of interfaces by undergraduate students, discuss some interaction aspects, and explore lessons and challenges from

[1] tangible interfaces' physical interactors of tangible interfaces are often called tangibles [60].

Figure 2. Variations of soft tangibles arranged on a knob-tray.

the posters created. Finally, we consider future directions of the current work.

One contribution of this work is the addition of computationally-mediated scientific posters to the growing number of domains toward which tangible interaction approaches have been employed. More broadly, we contribute by exploring novel combinations of physical and virtual interactors which we expect can generalize beyond our own examples. Last, we enhance poster presentations (with our systems) by employing tangible interfaces toward promoting collaboration and learning [58].

SCIENTIFIC POSTER CONTEXT

Paper posters – whether used for (e.g.) advertising movies, food, health and political campaigns, or scientific results – have long been widely deployed. In some respects, posters are not an obvious low-lying fruit for tangible interaction. That said, we found them an intriguing and promising target for a number of reasons.

First, both in educational and professional (e.g., conference) contexts, the production and sharing of posters is very common. Posters are a proven tool for conveying knowledge quickly, with visual communication as a key facet. Within several universities where our work has been developed, more than a hundred undergraduate students each summer are required to produce scientific posters communicating their research. While advertising and informational displays have largely migrated to digital signage, educational and conference posters have remained mostly paper-bound. With large, high resolution (esp. 4K), relatively inexpensive displays, increasing engagement by academic posters with digital displays seems not a question of "if," but "when" and "how."

We and others [28, 56] see this as driven not only by technological availability, but also by opportunities for interaction. Broadly viewed, the visual real estate of academic posters can be divided into blocks of text and figures. Still figures invite dynamic (e.g., video and animation) and interactive content. Text blocks also seem promising for interactivity. One variation might be hyperlinkage – whether to greater depth (e.g., cited literature) or breadth (e.g., Wikipedia articles and YouTube videos providing background concepts and context). Another might be tailoring text for different audiences: e.g., for faculty experts vs. the general public.

One avenue for such interactivity is direct touch interaction with a digital poster display itself. This has the benefit of greatest consistency with traditional posters, and some level of "compactness," especially when mindful of present contexts where hundreds or thousands of traditional-scale physical posters are simultaneously presented [56, 50]. Direct interaction also brings a number of tradeoffs. While this will likely change, poster-scale (e.g., >=55"/140cm diagonal) displays supporting multi-touch input are presently on the order of 10x more expensive than display-only units.

An alternative or complement for direct touch interaction is indirect interaction. One such variant is with digital tablets or other devices that display complementary meta-information. Another is with tangibles. During poster presentations, whether a presenter is present or not, tangibles might offer implicit "invitations to interaction, " or even "interaction takeaways" (i.e., artifacts that can be brought away by visitors following an interaction). They could facilitate both transfer of control between presenter and one or more audience members. If horizontal tablet or tabletop displays are used, tangibles could provide greater kinaesthetic awareness for navigating in eyes-busy situations (whether gaze is toward the vertical display or audience members).

BACKGROUND AND RELATED WORK

In this section, we present background work on tangible interfaces. Next, we turn to background and related work concerning posters, and in particular, computationally-mediated scientific posters.

Tangible interfaces

Tangible interfaces represent a subfield of human-computer interaction concerned with approaches for giving physical, interactively manipulable form to digital information. The topic is also referred to as tangible user interfaces (TUIs), in the context of broader research investigating tangible interaction [34, 60].

A number of tangible-enabled systems employ dial-like tangibles as representations and controls for cyberphysical associations. The use of knobs in computational systems has a long history. The electromechanical interfaces of the 1946 ENIAC computer incorporated hundreds of radial dials [32]. The mid-1950s SAGE system [22], Sutherland's 1960s SketchPad system [63], and many other early graphical interfaces prominently incorporated interaction via mechanical dials. These early uses employed permanently mounted physical dials either statically mapped to specific digital functions, or reassigned by the GUIs to which they were coupled.

In systems specially conceived as TUIs, interaction has most often not only employed radial rotation, but also translational repositioning on and off of augmenting surfaces, in association with a variety of inferred computational semantics. Tagged handles offered interchangeable, tracked knob-like elements with haptic feedback [44], and have often been used in audio contexts [37, 51]. Where tagged handles were "labeled" with radial arrays of shapes and textures, the wheels of Strata/ICC [66] and tangible query interfaces [64] labeled tokens with static text and visuals, and applied these to parametric navigation of diverse datasets. [44, 66, 64] structured knob interaction around fixed mechanical constraints, while Sensetable and ReacTable allowed tangibles to be sensed and graphically mediated through continuous manipulation across interactive tabletops [37, 51]. More recently, SLAP widgets [72] and FacetStreams [35] have evolved the visual, domain application, and implementational strategies. In other variations, the smart tokens of [21] employed new commodity platforms toward realizing active knob-like tokens with dynamically updatable faces.

Posters

The tradition of writings on walls dates back at least 5,000-12,000 years [74, 49, 29]. The modern paper poster was invented in France, in the mid-19th century. The medium was first recognized as an artistic expression by Jules Cheret, "the father of the poster," for which he received the Legion of Honor. Posters spread throughout Europe within a decade [45]. Today, posters are commonly used in classrooms and by many research communities.

In academic conferences, presenters typically stand near their posters for a specified period of time, and present the content to interested visitors. During the remaining time, posters are mostly unattended. In the medical community, posters are often presented consecutively; each person has a short period of time to present the poster. [28].

Others have explored computationally-mediated platforms for poster presentations at conferences [30, 28, 56, 50]. De Simone et al. [28] investigated such a platform in which images could be zoomed during presentations. The MediaPoster [56] explored the combination of linked documents and images with a system that replaced paper posters with interactive LCD displays. To illustrate a conference employing similar platforms, the Society for Neuroscience has experimented with interactive posters in their annual meetings since 2013. In 2015, the conference in total hosted more than 12.000 posters, of which a small fraction were dynamic posters [50].

Commercial solutions have also emerged. With Multieposter [11], authors submit digital content using an online portal, and an specialized team generates the digital poster. Das Terminal [5] provides an online management tool in which authors themselves create the digital posters. Das Terminal also provides the hardware (stands and large displays) to present the posters. Similar to one of our approaches, presenters use tablets to interact with the content. In the classroom, Cook et al. [27] had undergraduate students create HTML-based digital posters with interactive content using Google Sites [6]. For the same purpose, a number of websites exist that generate digital posters [7, 8, 1, 4]. Many target young poster creators and have several pre-defined templates that can accelerate the creation of the posters.

Virtual worlds have also been explored in the context of learning activities, posters sessions and conferences [31, 43, 69]. Without real world constraints, poster sessions can occupy tall buildings [43], or spread along many streets [31], with poster viewers instantly teleporting to engage desired posters.

Regarding the design of posters, recently Pedwell et al. [52] applied multimedia learning theories to define a framework for best practices in poster design. This framework is especially relevant for computationally-mediated posters. We are unaware of poster-related platforms that combine forms of multi-touch and tangible interaction.

MIXING MULTI-TOUCH AND TANGIBLE INTERACTION

A key aspect of our cyberphysical interface (CPI) approach is support for interaction with and without physical tangibles, and with and without virtual/"soft" interaction elements. Several examples are illustrative. For text entry with contemporary tablet computers and smartphones, an ubiquitous feature is support for both virtual keyboards, and physical keyboards. We understand neither is in all respects "better." Physical keyboards allow eyes-free operation, liberated screen real estate, and (supported by tactility) generally greater speed; while virtual keyboards can lessen a mobile user's "baggage" [25].

We see a similar prospect, extended to many aspects of previously "pure-tangible" interfaces, as holding potential for greatly increasing their use and deployment. Perhaps the strongest example of which we are aware is the ReacTable [37] and ReacTable Mobile [12, 14, 13] family of music interfaces. The ReacTable is one of the best-known tangible interfaces of the last decade, while ReacTable Mobile is a purely virtual version. The two variations are marked by tradeoffs between screen and physical real estate, eyes-busy and kinesthetic performance, mobility, and cost. In a similar spirit, our hybrid poster-related interfaces are designed with the capacity to receive physical/"hard" input (e.g., with physical, dial-like tangibles), and the capacity to receive input from on-screen elements (e.g., via button press or virtual/"soft" tangible interaction), with the choice of interaction modality varying by user, time, and context. In the presence of good design [53], such systems could leverage the complementary benefits of physical and virtual interaction modalities, and allow flexibility to accommodate contextual and preferential differences (including varying availability of enabling hardware).

Before presenting the grounding prototypes we and our collaborating poster creators have developed, we first introduce our concept of "soft" (virtual) tangibles.

SOFT TANGIBLES

Initially, our focus was upon combined interaction of physical dials and "traditional" on-screen multi-touch input elements. Later, we noticed the opportunity for direct finger-touch interaction with on-screen representations of tangibles, without requiring the use of physical/hard tangibles. We refer to these as *soft tangibles* (Figure 2).

Others have considered non-physical elements in tangible interaction. Ullmer et al. [65] focused on physical constraints, but also suggested constraints in dynamic graphical form. Variations blending the use of physical objects and finger-touch have also been explored. Wobbrock et al. [73] and Kammer et al. [39] explored touch gestures for interactions with surfaces. Angelini et al. [19] considered holding an object and touching it as two different components of interaction. Mazalek et al. [46] considered gestural interaction with active tangibles and multitouch elements as a promising approach for exploring Big Data. Morales et al. [47] explored finger-touch to define patterns (by constraining the users' grasp) on capacitive touch-screens, allowing users to interact with on-screen elements.

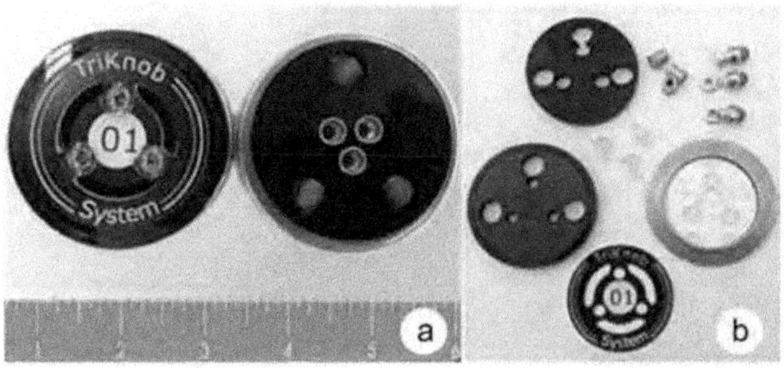

Figure 3. a) detail of the top and bottom of a laser-cut knob; and b) the parts that compose a knob.

Figure 4. a) a dual-extrusion 3D printer fabricating a knob; b) variations on 3D-printed knobs.

We see considerations for soft tangible interaction as likely to be beneficial when combined with "traditional" on-screen elements and physical tangibles. We envision systems employing a dynamically evolving mixture of hard and soft tokens (here, dials) and constraints [65, 61]. Similar to the way contemporary web search engines fuse a mixture of typed and predictive/suggestive text [33], physical dials might be intermingled with soft predictive/suggestive dials.

HARD TANGIBLES

Our systems employ (physical) dial/knob tangibles. We have endeavored to make our knobs general-purpose and with design and engineering efforts invested toward reproducibility. We next present the design and fabrication of tangibles by laser cutting and 3D printing technologies.

Design and fabrication

A number of research [23, 24, 68] and commercial systems [10, 2] have employed partially conductive tangibles on capacitive multi-touch surfaces. Along similar lines, our design of passive capacitive-sensed knobs incorporates constellations of three touch points, sometimes using stylus tips, sometimes flat conductive rubber (in both rigid and pliable forms). The pattern defined allows tangibles to be identified by the capacitive surface. Based on human features studies [54], our knobs diameter is 60 mm. It is comfortable for most teenagers and adults, while also prospectively being suitable for children.

Laser-cut knobs

After earlier experiments with a number of handcrafted designs, our first design was composed entirely of computer-fabricated components constructed using a laser cutter and off-the-shelf hardware components. Most of the body of these knobs were composed of acrylic and/or wooden parts. Figure 3 shows the components of a laser-cut knob. For assembly, three metallic-fiber threaded stylus tips are attached to the perimeter of a metal shim using metallic nuts. The pattern described by these tips is defined by a guide piece that is positioned within the internal circumference of the shim. Two discs are placed on the faces of the guide, and a faceplate is added to the top to support legibility of the knobs.

3D-printed knobs

Additive manufacturing offers another platform for creating knobs (and tangibles in general). We used three different 3D printers in the fabrication of our hard tangibles: the mono-extruder Lulzbot Taz [9], the dual-extruder Makerbot Replicator 2X [3], and a Voxel8 machine [16]. With the Lulzbot and Makerbot we used conductive polylactic acid filament (PLA) for the body of knobs. With the Voxel8, knobs were fabricated with acrylonitrile butadiene styrene thermoplastic (ABS); 3D-printed conductive silver-ink "wires" coupled the user's touch the capacitive display (Figure 4).

In the next sections we present platforms that mix interaction with hard and soft tangibles on capacitive surfaces. First, we present a tightly structured platform; then, a less constrained approach; followed by prototypes created by two separate cohorts of undergraduate students. To explore the concepts we propose, we sought a domain that would engage undergraduate students and the broader public, particularly as relating to science, using platforms that would allow immediate and progressively broadening deployments. We found interaction support for the creation, presentation, and engagement with computationally-mediated research posters to fit well these constraints. These motivated the development of the Entrada and the knob-tray platforms.

ENTRADA PLATFORM

The Entrada platform, depicted in Figure 5, replaces paper posters with screen-based computationally-mediated systems. A full-size poster can be displayed by a vertical screen (in our case, 55-60" diagonal and 3840 X 2160/4k pixels resolution). Microsoft Surface 3 tablets control all aspects of the posters (e.g. selecting content, zooming, manipulating 3D models) with an interface that allows interaction by touch, and by hard and soft tangibles. Our tablet interface, is composed of a 3 by 2 grid, with buttons at the top, and *soft* tangibles for rotational interaction with finger-touch or with *hard* tangibles at the bottom (Figure 5B).

Here, our tablet interface was tightly structured, model-based, and automatically generated, with implementation details managed by system developers (as opposed to poster content creators) [48]. Poster creators define associations between buttons and content for the vertical display. The tablet interface automatically imports these associations, generating the tablet's on-screen elements. The advantage is that poster creators, even without any interface design experience, can implement their posters and rely on the tablet's software to create high-quality interfaces that combine multi-touch with hard and soft tangible interactions. A trade-off is that fewer opportunities for customization are available.

Figure 5. Computationally-mediated poster platform Entrada. *a) Entrada platform; b and c) Students presenting at the NSF REU program.*

KNOB-TRAY PLATFORM

In contrast to the Entrada platform, the knob-tray platform gives poster creators more freedom to create the posters, at the cost of more per-poster software development and less between-poster interaction consistency. Here, our platform provides basic interface building-blocks, without any automatically generated elements constraining the design. Poster creators can choose among several display configurations. Options include a single vertical screen, a single horizontal screen, two screens (one horizontal and one vertical), or pairs of horizontal or vertical screens; all supporting multi-touch and tangible interaction. The basic building-blocks provided for the prototypes developed were:

Soft tangible component: We provided poster creators with a class for the implementation of soft tangible objects. These objects could be easily customized and were capable of identifying our 3D printed or laser cut knobs;

Physical knobs: Eight distinct 3D-printed knobs were provided. Poster creators could also opt to 3D print their own knobs;

Tray component: Poster creators had the option to use standalone soft tangibles or configure a tray with multiple knobs. Trays made it easier for developers to position multiple knobs within their screen layouts (Figure 2); and

Code samples: A set of sample software code was made available to assist poster creators as they began to develop with the knob-tray platform.

Both platforms were developed with the Python [17] Kivy library [67]. Two-way communication is handled by OSC [75] messages exchanged between devices controlling and rendering content. Messages are based on a simplified version of the TUIO protocol [38].

CREATING POSTERS WITH THE PLATFORMS

In June and July of 2016, Louisiana State University (LSU) held the 7th NSF REU (Research Experience for Undergraduates) program [15]. As with many of the ~700 nationally funded REU programs, all participants were required to create paper-posters by the end of the program to show their research accomplishments. During this edition, REU participants were invited to volunteer to create computationally-mediated posters using the Entrada platform, in addition to paper-posters. Twelve students volunteered. Due to our limited ability to support the students, five were selected to participate in ten workshop sessions (A sixth student joined in the final week, without participating in the workshop sessions.) The workshops were designed to help them create content and design the posters, while providing us with feedback. Figures 5c and 5d show students presenting two of the six piloted posters.

Following our experience developing the Entrada platform, during the Spring semester of 2017, 19 undergraduate students, divided into six groups, created six computationally-mediated posters with the knob-tray platform. This time, the creation of the posters was part of the requirements for the Tangible Embedded Interaction (TEI) course offered at Clemson University (CU). The course was mainly attended by senior-year students, and did not require specific programing skills. Each group was asked to select a topic engaging research groups at our university and to create a poster presenting that research. Students were also asked to seek user-experience and usability feedback from the members of the research groups they picked, and from other potential poster viewers. Next, we describe four of the twelve posters created with both platforms.

Poster 1: Additive manufacturing of dial-like tangibles

Figure 5b depicts a poster developed with the Entrada platform being presented by an NSF REU student. This poster displayed information about the fabrication of tangible knobs using 3D printing techniques. Some of the knobs presented were similar to those employed in the operation of other Entrada posters. The student prepared his presentation incorporating knobs, while also explaining how they had been fabricated. The tangibles served as tools to operate the posters, and most importantly, as points of attraction and promoters of engagement. Approximately forty viewers visited the poster and in many cases manipulated the knobs and tried them on the tablets. They often asked questions about both the hardware (the tokens themselves) and the software (running the poster). Soft tangible interactions were also employed, especially when physical knobs were not available (e.g. after handing knobs to viewers).

This poster was awarded one of two awards given to all paper and digital posters, and was invited to represent LSU at the national REU Symposium.

Poster 2: Gravitational waves

Figure 5c depicts the poster developed with the Entrada platform about the detection of gravitational waves in the context of the Laser Interferometer Gravitational Wave Observatory (LIGO) [18]. Here, the student chose not to emphasize the

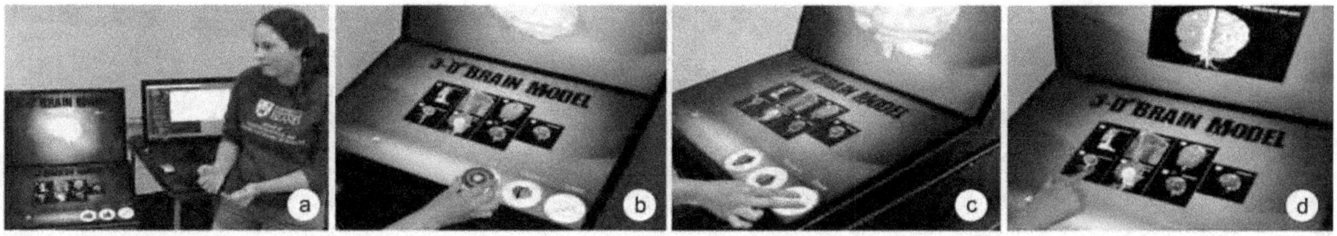

Figure 6. Brain-model poster. *a) Student giving a classroom presentation of her poster; b) Student rotates the 3D model with a knob; c) Student controls zoom and rotation of the 3D model with soft tangibles; and d) Student touches the tiles to select a video.*

use of knobs, instead focusing on implementation of content and text for different target groups. Most of the interaction occurred either via button-press or rotation of soft dials with fingers. Although not emphasizing tangibles, this poster gathered substantial attention from viewers. About forty users experienced this poster. It employed a variety of animations and short clips to explain the subject, a concept that would most likely be challenging to present with a (static) paper-poster. Buttons were usually employed to change discrete parameters (e.g. selecting slides), while soft-tangibles were used for controlling continuous parameters, such as zoom.

Poster 3: 3D brain-model

The 3D brain-model poster was created with the knob-tray platform (Figure 6). The poster was based on the work of a research group from CU on 3D printing brain models replicated from human MRI scans. In contrast to the REU posters, this poster was designed to be a stand-alone system, without the presence of a stand-by presenter.

The development process adopted a user-centered iterative approach. The project began with pencil and digital storyboards, which were used as a visual basis for coding the program. Soft and hard tangibles were arranged on a knob tray. The first major project milestone was a rigid, but functioning, version. Once realized, the development team sought feedback by showing demos to five respondents and had them complete a questionnaire.

By the end of March, a new version of the program was developed, and soon after, poster creators sought more extensive feedback. Five poster viewers (three members of the research group and two external undergraduate students) from CU were asked to interact with the poster's interface without guided instruction. Poster creators observed and recorded the interactions. Viewers were interviewed about the program and asked to complete a written follow-up survey. The final version ran on two paired Microsoft Surface Studio machines; one used in vertical orientation, and the other used in horizontal. The interface mixed pure finger-touch with hard and soft tangible interactions. The horizontal display worked as a control panel, featuring seven buttons, each bound to a specific video. 3D rotation of the brain could be controlled directly by touch on the vertical screen, and indirectly through the hard and soft dials on the horizontal screen.

Poster 4: Vertebrate biomechanics

Figure 7 depicts a vertebrate biomechanics poster. This poster was inspired by CU's Creative Inquiry "Comparative Vertebrate Musculoskeletal Biomechanics" project. The poster displays information related to the movement of turtles and fish in their habitats. The interface consists of a single multi-touch vertical screen for content selection and display.

The tangibles envisioned for this project were 3D printed turtle and fish tokens, and a rotational parameter-control knob. For interaction, besides parameter-controls, students explored a variation on the "Pick-and-Drop" concept [55], in which poster viewers can pick up an object (i.e., the turtle token) and "drop" it onto the screen to display or manipulate content (at which point the virtual turtle could "swim free" from the physical token). During lectures, we emphasized the goal of allowing all actions to be performed in multiple ways (e.g. with tangibles and by touch). In practice, students did not always achieve this. Some actions strictly required the use of tangibles, such as selecting content by placing tokens on hot-spots. Other actions, such as video-playback functions, could be performed with hard tangibles, by finger-touch, or with soft tangibles.

During development, students sought feedback from four participants in two separate sessions of informal evaluation (two per session). The final poster was visually appealing and viewers found the interaction to be exciting and enjoyable.

The implementation of each poster taught us lessons regarding how to combine multiple interaction modalities (e.g. multi-touch, hard and soft tangible interaction), how to create and implement computationally-mediated scientific posters, and how poster creators and viewers interact with them. In the next section we briefly analyze how viewers and poster creators chose the interaction modality.

INTERACTION MODALITY CHOICE

With our platforms supporting hard and soft tangibles, as well as multi-touch elements, how do users choose among these modes of interaction? Interaction researchers in the multimodal interfaces field have long noted the criticality of context – e.g., user role, physical locale, parallel primary or secondary tasks, system properties – to modality selection [57, 71, 70]. We considered modality choice with our prototypes observing user role and physical locale.

User role: we regard users as in three classes: poster creators, presenters, and viewers,

Physical locale: Two locales have been identified: controlled environment and public setting.

With the Entrada platform, we observed poster creators (as they interacted with the systems creating and presenting the posters) and viewers during the NSF REU poster session.

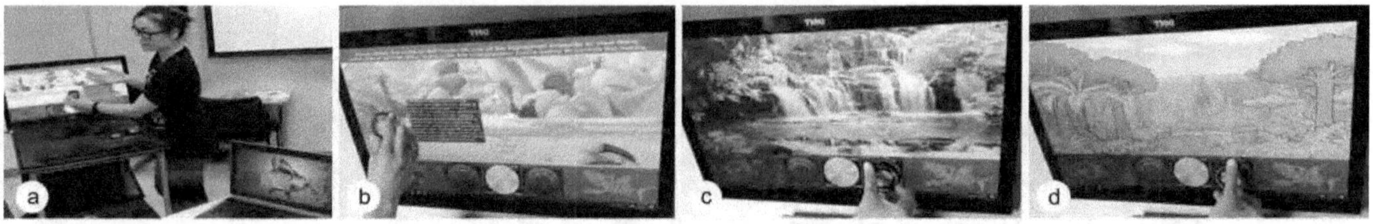

Figure 7. Vertebrate biomechanics poster. *Student demonstrating her poster during a classroom presentation; b) User "drops" the knob onto one of the hot-spots to display textual information; c and d) User rotates a knob to chose among several habitats for the turtle.*

Following the final poster presentation, six poster creators responded to 11-question Likert-scale questionnaires regarding usability factors of the Entrada platform and the effectiveness of their presentations. Poster creators were also asked to comment on their overall impressions. Most (four out of six) poster creators strongly agreed that they felt the interactive content attracted more attention of delegates when compared to regular posters, and five of them agreed that the interactive posters were an effective medium of knowledge transfer. Two of the poster developers expressed their desire to create other posters using the platform, as they perceived it to have a positive impact in exposing their research. With the knob-tray platform, poster creators were observed during seven one-hour long development sessions, and three project presentations that occurred within the course. By the end of the course, they were required to produce a written report including questionnaires applied during the development process of the prototypes. Next, we summarize our observations.

Entrada platform lessons

The uniformity of the tablet control-interfaces generated by the Entrada platform meant that poster creators adopted similar interaction strategies and modality-choices across the posters, and viewers could also leverage this familiarity.

Poster creators tended to use buttons and soft tangibles while developing the posters. Hard tangibles were mainly used for testing purposes during short periods of time, independently of the activity performed (e.g. selecting content or zooming an image). Early in the development stage not many knobs were available, and poster creators had to share them. We suspected that the small number of available knobs was one cause for their low adoption. As research prototypes, the physical knobs had some performance quirks (e.g., sometimes requiring pressure to operate), which was also likely a factor regarding usage. Later, each poster creator received several knobs (and more, upon request). We noted that the availability of knobs did not change the frequency or duration in which the knobs were used. They still preferred soft tangibles and multi-touch interaction during development.

When presenting the posters in a public setting, most poster creators tended to use all three modes of interaction (hard, soft tangibles and multi-touch interaction,) with choice depending on the activity being performed. For selecting content (e.g. moving from one slide to the next), they tended to use the grid of buttons of the tablet interface. For selecting a function (e.g. zooming, translating), which involved navigating between multiple discrete choices, buttons were still most often used, but poster creators also chose hard and soft tangibles to perform this task, frequently using the physical knobs. For performing an action involving a continuous variable (e.g. zooming), hard and soft tangibles were used, with a tendency toward directly manipulating the soft tangibles.

The apparent contrasting behavior toward tangibles we observed between poster creators while developing posters in the lab, and while presenting the posters seems to be in agreement with observations by others. Tangibles tend to be chosen more often when multiple users are collaborating, and not as often when working individually [26, 59].

Besides the student who created poster 1, two other poster creators were particularly enthusiastic about employing tangibles in their presentations. Some design choices appear to have contributed to their enthusiasm. Both opted to have two to three tokens, in addition to a token for controlling the poster, each linking to specific content. During presentation time, the tokens would be used to summon the content to be displayed. One student used the tokens as an integral part of his presentation, while the other used the tokens to display additional content only upon necessity, depending on the audience. In both cases, viewers and presenters seemed to enjoy the role of tokens as content containers, with the tokens embodying various facets of the topic presented.

Viewers of the Entrada posters had the opportunity to navigate them by themselves. In this situation, viewers tended to emulate the interaction patterns of poster creators. Upon learning that the use of hard+soft tangibles and multi-touch was supported for all functions, some viewers tried different variations. Many seemed curious about the tangibles and tried to use them even when they were not the expected choice (e.g. to select slides), indicating that some choices were driven by curiosity, not necessarily convenience or ease of use.

Knob-tray platform lessons

The knob-tray platform supports more diverse designs. Consequently, distinct interaction patterns were implemented by each group. Nevertheless, many similarities were observed between the prototypes created with both platforms.

With the 3D Brain Model project, presenters and viewers preferred direct finger-touch (on the brain model or on the soft tangibles) to rotate the model on the 3D space. For zooming, they would sometimes pinch-and-zoom, and sometimes use the soft tangibles; few used the hard tangibles.

With the turtle project, the use of hard tangibles was required to select content. With a well executed, relatively intuitive design, presenters and viewers seemed to feel comfortable using the hard tangibles. For navigating video playback, the use of the hard tangibles did not feel as natural, with soft tangibles being the preferred mode of interaction.

Similar to the Entrada platform, poster creators tended to use buttons and soft tangibles instead of hard tangibles while developing posters. While presenting to the public, they tended to use all three modes of interaction, if available.

Viewers generally seemed more confused by the variety of possibilities and diverse designs of the knob-tray interfaces. The more tightly-structured format of the tablet interface of the Entrada platform seemed more intuitive to viewers, although more limiting for poster creators.

LESSONS LEARNED

With poster 1, we observed that tangible knobs can enhance poster presentations by promoting viewer engagement, and that multi-touch, hard and soft interaction can be effectively combined into a single experience. Viewers were curious and eager to touch and operate the interface with the tangibles, while the presenter fluidly chose between the interaction modalities available. With posters 4 and 5, we learned that tangibles can have a down side, sometimes distracting users and leading them to focus more on the tangibles themselves rather than the poster's main topic.

We also observed that tangibles seemed to enhance poster presentations only when the presentation was carefully designed to employ them and leverage their characteristics. Otherwise, users tended to ignore the hard tangibles and use touch (either to operate buttons or the soft tangibles). Without explicitly integrating tangibles or dynamic content into the presentation, we felt their presence did not intrinsically enhance the experience or attract the attention of viewers. In most cases we observed (and had iteratively helped to facilitate), employing tangibles clearly added to the poster presentation experience, attracting and engaging viewers. Nonetheless, the adoption of soft and hard tangibles by developers and users was not as high as we first anticipated.

Reflecting upon the adoption of soft and hard tangibles, we noted two important challenges. First, in general, poster developers were familiar with multi-touch interfaces, and unfamiliar with (soft or hard) tangibles. We did not provide preexisting posters to avoid unduly biasing content; but this initially left developers unclear how to integrate and allow users to interact with soft and hard tangibles. Also, between the Knob-tray and the Entrada platforms, the latter more closely engaged Shneiderman's information visualization mantra:

> Overview first, zoom and filter, then details-on-demand [62]

All Entrada posters began with an overview of the content. A sidebar to the left of the screen provided access to specific sections. None of the Knob-tray posters followed this structure. This may have contributed to more limited interface designs and, consequently, poor adoption of tangibles with the knob-tray platform.

Second, our prototypes do not yet realize our envisionment of predictive, deeply integrated functional and visual interaction between soft and hard tangibles with "traditional" on-screen elements. The simple nature of our current interactions may contribute to relatively modest use of hard and soft tangibles when compared to the (usual) multi-touch actions.

CONCLUSION AND FUTURE WORK

We have introduced our approach mixing multi-touch with "hard" and "soft" tangible interactors. We illustrated this with two groups of prototypes that support the creation, presentation, and engagement with computationally-mediated scientific posters, as created by undergraduate students. Within these systems, we and our content creator collaborations have begun to explore combinations of multi-touch and tangible interactions with dial-like (hard and soft) tangibles.

Neither our templated nor freeform approaches were inherently "better" than the other. The templated approach facilitated focus on content development, increased consistency, and raised the lower-bound bar on interaction quality and consistency. The second, more freeform approach allowed greater creativity and flexibility, sometimes facilitating standout results, while also allowing more marginal variations and sometimes distracting from content creation.

As with other multi-device digital poster systems such as [5], our addition of horizontal interactive surfaces extends the per-"station" footprint of ours versus traditional paper posters. Cost, weight, and logistics considerations are also present. With these tradeoffs comes the potential for greater interactivity, and (again as per [5]) the prospect for interacting with many different posters at a given station. By analogy, web page interactions also have different physical "space requirements" and functional potentials than do paper pages. Similarly, we see CPIs and paper posters as holding both similarities and differences, with neither direct replacing the other.

In future studies, we plan to explore more complex interactions, including the ability to compellingly inhabit different expanses of screen real estate across a number of displays. Also, similar to the way contemporary web search engines fuse a mixture of typed and predictive/suggestive text, hard tokens might be intermingled with predictive/suggestive soft tokens. Future work will also focus on the design of interfaces that involve active tokens (incorporating active electronics), including those with embedded displays. We hope this work helps point to a future where tangible interfaces are not intrinsically segregated, but intimately integrated in hybrid ecologies with other families of interaction paradigms.

ACKNOWLEDGEMENTS

This research was partially supported by the NSF under award CNS-1126739 and NIH under award INBRE 5 P20 GM103424-15 with additional support from LSU, CU, and the Coordination for the Improvement of Higher Education Personnel (CAPES). We thank Drs. Wischusen, Carmichael, Moreno, Butler, and Allison from LSU who provided insight and opportunities that supported this research. We thank the undergraduate students Eli Berkowitz, Grey Patterson, Dwayne Hinton, Bianca Hilderbrad, Sarah Thompson, Tracy Nguyen and Logan Bartell for their work and dedication developing the prototypes discussed in this paper.

REFERENCES

1. Annotate images and videos thinglink. http://www.thinglink.com/. (Accessed on 07/19/2017).
2. Appmates. http://www.appmatestoys.com/. (Accessed on 07/20/2017).
3. Connected 3d printing solutions — makerbot. https://www.makerbot.com/. (Accessed on 07/21/2017).
4. Create easy infographics, reports, presentations — piktochart. https://piktochart.com/. (Accessed on 07/19/2017).
5. Das terminal. https://www.dasterminal.com/. (Accessed on 07/19/2017).
6. Google sites. https://sites.google.com/new?usp=jotspot_si. (Accessed on 07/19/2017).
7. How to use glogster - web / desktop. http://webuse.glogster.com/. (Accessed on 07/19/2017).
8. Interactive posters - web tools for kids. https://sites.google.com/site/webtoolsbox/interactive-posters. (Accessed on 07/19/2017).
9. Lulzbot — 3d printer, parts, and filament. https://www.lulzbot.com/. (Accessed on 07/21/2017).
10. Mattel brings powerhouse brands to the ipad with apptivity play — mattel inc. https://goo.gl/cx6o8K. (Accessed on 07/20/2017).
11. Multieposter - state-of-the-art eposter solution & services. http://www.multieposter.com/. (Accessed on 07/19/2017).
12. Reactable mobile - android apps on google play. https://play.google.com/store/apps/details?id=com.reactable&hl=en. (Accessed on 07/20/2017).
13. Reactable mobile - youtube. https://www.youtube.com/watch?v=Tbo2Wk5PgVQ. (Accessed on 07/20/2017).
14. Reactable mobile on the app store. https://itunes.apple.com/us/app/reactable-mobile/id381127666?mt=8. (Accessed on 07/20/2017).
15. Research experiences for undergraduates - wikipedia. https://en.wikipedia.org/wiki/Research_Experiences_for_Undergraduates. (Accessed on 07/27/2017).
16. Voxel8. http://www.voxel8.com/. (Accessed on 07/21/2017).
17. Welcome to python.org. https://www.python.org/. (Accessed on 07/26/2017).
18. Abbott, B. P., Abbott, R., Abbott, T., Abernathy, M., Acernese, F., Ackley, K., Adams, C., Adams, T., Addesso, P., Adhikari, R., et al. Observation of gravitational waves from a binary black hole merger. *Physical review letters 116*, 6 (2016), 061102.
19. Angelini, L., Lalanne, D., Hoven, E. v. d., Khaled, O. A., and Mugellini, E. Move, hold and touch: a framework for tangible gesture interactive systems. *Machines 3*, 3 (2015), 173–207.
20. Antle, A. N., and Wang, S. Comparing motor-cognitive strategies for spatial problem solving with tangible and multi-touch interfaces. In *Proc. of TEI'13*, ACM (2013), 65–72.
21. Arif, A. S., Manshaei, R., Delong, S., East, B., Kyan, M., and Mazalek, A. Sparse tangibles: Collaborative exploration of gene networks using active tangibles and interactive tabletops. In *Proc. of TEI'16*, ACM (2016), 287–295.
22. Astrahan, M., Housman, B., Jacobs, J., Mayer, R., and Thomas, W. Logical design of the digital computer for the sage system. *IBM Journal of Research and Development 1*, 1 (1957), 76–83.
23. Blagojevic, R., Chen, X., Tan, R., Sheehan, R., and Plimmer, B. Using tangible drawing tools on a capacitive multi-touch display. In *Proc. of the 26th Annual BCS Interaction Specialist Group Conference on People and Computers*, British Computer Society (2012), 315–320.
24. Chan, L., Müller, S., Roudaut, A., and Baudisch, P. Capstones and zebrawidgets: sensing stacks of building blocks, dials and sliders on capacitive touch screens. In *Proc. CHI'12*, ACM (2012), 2189–2192.
25. Chaparro, B. S., Phan, M. H., Siu, C., and Jardina, J. R. User performance and satisfaction of tablet physical keyboards. *Journal of Usability Studies 9*, 2 (2014), 70–80.
26. Cohen, J., Withgott, M., and Piernot, P. Logjam: a tangible multi-person interface for video logging. In *Proc. of CHI'99* (1999), 128–135.
27. Cook, R., and Fenn, P. Dynamic digital posters: Making the most of collaborative learning spaces. In *Proc. of 30th ascilite Conference," Electric Dreams"*, ascilite (2013), 195–200.
28. De Simone, R., Rodrian, J., Osswald, B., Sack, F.-U., De Simone, E., and Hagl, S. Initial experience with a new communication tool: the 'digital interactive poster presentation'. *European Journal of Cardio-thoracic Surgery 19*, 6 (2001), 953–955.
29. Dubois, P. Reading the writing on the wall. *Classical Philology 102*, 1 (2007), 45–56.
30. DAngelo, L. From posters to e-posters: The evolution of a genre. *LANGUAGE 4* (2012), 46–54.
31. Erickson, T., Shami, N. S., Kellogg, W. A., and Levine, D. W. Synchronous interaction among hundreds: an evaluation of a conference in an avatar-based virtual environment. In *Proc. of CHI'11*, ACM (2011), 503–512.

32. Goldstine, H. H., and Goldstine, A. The electronic numerical integrator and computer (eniac). *Mathematical Tables and Other Aids to Computation 2*, 15 (1946), 97–110.

33. Hood, S., Rabbat, R., Shah, M., Durfee, A., Gourlay, A., Anick, P., Kasperski, R., Bayley, O. T., Hall, A. W., Kapur, S., et al. Speculative search result based on a not-yet-submitted search query, Mar. 2 2010. US Patent 7,672,932.

34. Ishii, H., and Ullmer, B. Tangible Bits: towards seamless interfaces between people, bits and atoms. In *Proc. of CHI'97*, ACM (1997), 234–241.

35. Jetter, H.-C., Gerken, J., Zöllner, M., Reiterer, H., and Milic-Frayling, N. Materializing the query with facet-streams: a hybrid surface for collaborative search on tabletops. In *Prof. of CHI'11*, ACM (2011), 3013–3022.

36. Johnson, J., Roberts, T., Verplank, W., Smith, D., Irby, C., Beard, M., and Mackey, K. The Xerox Star: a retrospective. *Computer 22*, 9 (Sep. 1989), 11 –26.

37. Jordà, S., Geiger, G., Alonso, M., and Kaltenbrunner, M. The reacTable: exploring the synergy between live music performance and tabletop tangible interfaces. In *Proc. of TEI'07*, ACM (2007), 139–146.

38. Kaltenbrunner, M., Bovermann, T., Bencina, R., and Costanza, E. Tuio: A protocol for table-top tangible user interfaces. In *Proc. of the The 6th Intl Workshop on Gesture in Human-Computer Interaction and Simulation* (2005), 1–5.

39. Kammer, D., Wojdziak, J., Keck, M., Groh, R., and Taranko, S. Towards a formalization of multi-touch gestures. In *Proc. of ITS'10*, ACM (2010), 49–58.

40. Krishna, P. V. *Challenges, Opportunities, and Dimensions of Cyber-Physical Systems*. IGI Global, 2014.

41. Lee, E. Cyber physical systems: Design challenges. In *Proc. of ISORC'08* (2008), 363–369.

42. Lee, J., Bagheri, B., and Kao, H.-A. A cyber-physical systems architecture for industry 4.0-based manufacturing systems. *Manufacturing Letters 3* (2015), 18–23.

43. Lee, S. J., Fox, E. A., Marchionini, G., Velacso, J., Antunes, G., and Borbinha, J. Virtual DL poster sessions in Second Life. In *Proc. of Digital Libraries'09*, ACM (2009), 473–474.

44. MacLean, K. E., Snibbe, S. S., and Levin, G. Tagged handles: merging discrete and continuous manual control. In *Proc. of CHI '00*, ACM (2010), 225–232.

45. Marx, R. *Masters of the Poster, 1896-1900*. Academy Publications, 1977. p. 7.

46. Mazalek, A., Shaer, O., Ullmer, B., Konkel, M. K., et al. Tangible meets gestural: Gesture based interaction with active tokens. In *Proc. of CHI'14*, ACM (2014).

47. Morales González, R., Appert, C., Bailly, G., and Pietriga, E. Touchtokens: Guiding touch patterns with passive tokens. In *Proc. of CHI'16*, ACM (2016), 4189–4202.

48. Myers, B., Hudson, S. E., and Pausch, R. Past, present, and future of user interface software tools. *TOCHI'00 7*, 1 (2000), 3–28.

49. Neundorf, H. Turkish archaeologists discover the world's oldest known writings. `https://news.artnet.com/art-world/turkey-worlds-oldest-writing-pictograph-319107`. (Accessed on 07/18/2017).

50. Neuroscience. Neuroscience 2015 annual conference poster abstracts. `https://www.sfn.org/Annual-Meeting/Neuroscience-2015/Sessions-and-Events/Program/Abstract-PDFs-2015`. (Accessed on 07/10/2017).

51. Patten, J., Ishii, H., Hines, J., and Pangaro, G. Sensetable: a wireless object tracking platform for tangible user interfaces. In *Proc. of CHI'01*, ACM (2001), 253–260.

52. Pedwell, R. K., Hardy, J. A., and Rowland, S. L. Effective visual design and communication practices for research posters: Exemplars based on the theory and practice of multimedia learning and rhetoric. *Biochemistry and Molecular Biology Education 45*, 3 (2017), 249–261.

53. Petre, M. Why looking isn't always seeing: Readership skills and graphical programming. *Communications of the ACM 38* (June 1995), 33–44.

54. Poston, A. Human engineering design data digest: human factors standardization systems. *Human Factors Standardization SubTAG* (2000).

55. Rekimoto, J. Pick-and-drop: a direct manipulation technique for multiple computer environments. In *Proc. of UIST'97*, ACM (1997), 31–39.

56. Rowe, N., and Ilic, D. What impact do posters have on academic knowledge transfer? a pilot survey on author attitudes and experiences. *BMC medical education 9*, 1 (2009), 1.

57. Schmidt, A. *Ubiquitous computing-computing in context*. PhD thesis, Lancaster University, 2003.

58. Schneider, B., Jermann, P., Zufferey, G., and Dillenbourg, P. Benefits of a tangible interface for collaborative learning and interaction. *IEEE Transactions on Learning Technologies 4*, 3 (2011), 222–232.

59. Schneider, B., Jermann, P., Zufferey, G., and Dillenbourg, P. Benefits of a tangible interface for collaborative learning and interaction. *IEEE Transactions on Learning Technologies 4*, 3 (2011), 222–232.

60. Shaer, O., and Hornecker, E. Tangible User Interfaces: past, present, and future directions. *Found. Trends Hum.-Comput. Interact. 3*, 1–2 (Jan. 2010), 1–137.

61. Shaer, O., Leland, N., Calvillo-Gamez, E. H., and Jacob, R. J. K. The TAC paradigm: specifying tangible user interfaces. *Personal and Ubiquitous Computing 8*, 5 (2004), 359–369.

62. Shneiderman, B. The eyes have it: A task by data type taxonomy for information visualizations. In *Visual Languages, 1996. Proceedings., IEEE Symposium on*, IEEE (1996), 336–343.

63. Sutherland, I. E. Sketch pad a man-machine graphical communication system. In *Proc. of SHARE design automation workshop*, ACM (1964), 6–329.

64. Ullmer, B., Ishii, H., and Jacob, R. Tangible query interfaces: physically constrained tokens for manipulating database queries. In *Proc. of INTERACT'03* (2003), 279–286.

65. Ullmer, B., Ishii, H., and Jacob, R. Token+constraint systems for tangible interaction with digital information. *TOCHI'05 12*, 1 (2005), 81–118.

66. Ullmer, B., Kim, E., Kilian, A., Gray, S., and Ishii, H. Strata/icc: physical models as computational interfaces. In *Proc. of CHI'01*, ACM (2001), 373–374.

67. Virbel, M., Hansen, T. E., and Lobunets, O. Kivy-a framework for rapid creation of innovative user interfaces. In *Proc. of Mensch & Computer Workshopband* (2011), 69–73.

68. Voelker, S., Nakajima, K., Thoresen, C., Itoh, Y., Øvergård, K. I., and Borchers, J. Pucs: Detecting transparent, passive untouched capacitive widgets on unmodified multi-touch displays. In *Proc. of ITS'13*, ACM (2013), 101–104.

69. Vrellis, I., Avouris, N., and Mikropoulos, T. A. Learning outcome, presence and satisfaction from a science activity in second life. *Australasian Journal of Educational Technology 32*, 1 (2016).

70. Wechsung, I., Engelbrecht, K.-P., Naumann, A., Möller, S., Schaffer, S., and Schleicher, R. Investigating modality selection strategies. In *Proc. of SLT'10*, IEEE (2010), 31–36.

71. Wechsung, I., Schleicher, R., and Möller, S. How context determines perceived quality and modality choice. secondary task paradigm applied to the evaluation of multimodal interfaces. In *Proc. of Paralinguistic Information and its Integration in Spoken Dialogue Systems Workshop*, Springer (2011), 327–340.

72. Weiss, M., Jennings, R., Khoshabeh, R., Borchers, J., Wagner, J., Jansen, Y., and Hollan, J. D. Slap widgets: bridging the gap between virtual and physical controls on tabletops. In *Proc. of CHI'09*, ACM (2009), 3229–3234.

73. Wobbrock, J. O., Morris, M. R., and Wilson, A. D. User-defined gestures for surface computing. In *Proc. of CHI'09*, ACM (2009), 1083–1092.

74. Woods, C. Visible language: the earliest writing systems. *Visible Language: Inventions of Writing in the Ancient Middle East and Beyond. The Oriental Institute of the University of Chicago, Chicago* (2010), 15–25.

75. Wright, M. Open sound control: an enabling technology for musical networking. *Organised Sound 10*, 03 (2005), 193–200.

76. Xie, L., Antle, A. N., and Motamedi, N. Are tangibles more fun?: comparing children's enjoyment and engagement using physical, graphical and tangible user interfaces. In *Proc. of TEI'08*, ACM (2008), 191–198.

Opto-Phono-Kinesia (OPK): Designing Motion-Based Interaction for Expert Performers

Dr. Steve Gibson
Associate Professor
School of Design
Northumbria University
Newcastle upon Tyne,
NE1 8ST, UK
stephen.gibson@northumbria.ac.uk

TEI '18, March 18–21, 2018, Stockholm, Sweden

ACM ISBN 978-1-4503-5568-1/18/03.
https://doi.org/10.1145/3173225.3173295

Abstract

Opto-Phono-Kinesia (*OPK*) is an audio-visual performance piece in which all media elements are controlled by the body movements of a single performer. The title is a play on a possible synesthetic state involving connections between vision, sound and body motion. Theoretically, for a person who experiences this state, a specific colour could trigger both a sound and a body action. This synesthetic intersection is simulated in *OPK* by simultaneity of body movement, and audio-visual result.

Using the Gesture and Media System 3.0 motion-tracking system, the performer can dynamically manipulate an immersive environment using two small infrared trackers. The project employs a multipart interface design based on a formal model of increasing complexity in visual-sound-body mapping, and is therefore best performed by an expert performer with strong spatial memory and advanced musical ability. *OPK* utilizes the "body as experience, instrument and interface" [1] for control of a large-scale environment.

Author Keywords

Immersive environments; motion-tracking; live audio-visuals; synesthesia; ephemeral interfaces; multi-modal experiences; interaction design; media art.

Figure 1 – Steve Gibson wears the two infrared trackers used in *OPK.* The position of the trackers is triangulated by four 100fps infrared cameras situated in the corners of a room (usually placed at height on a light grid). The trackers have different flash patterns so that they can be easily identified. The trackers are small and unobtrusive, and are fitted with Velcro straps that can be adjusted to be attached to different parts of the body (hands, feet, shoulders, etc.). The trackers can be programmed as spatial controllers using the FlashTrack software. This GUI-based PC application allows the user to program different media layers in 3D space and save these as 'Maps.' The different planes (x, y, and z) can be layered with media triggers and controls, therefore enabling the simultaneous manipulation of audio, video and lights via performer movement with the trackers. Photo by Liam Hardy, ©2017. Used by permission.

Conference Themes

OPK responds to the following conference themes:

- Body as experience, instrument and interface
- Ephemeral interfaces
- Haptic and multi-modal experiences
- Aesthetic experience through tangible or full body interactions

Introduction

OPK is an audio-visual performance to be performed solo by an expert, trained performer. *OPK* consists of several shorter pieces that explore the relation of particular 3D planes to media control. Each piece takes a different approach to 3D motion and media control, thus relying on performer memory.

In contrast to most media art and interactive environments, *OPK* is not intended for interaction by the general public, but instead is a live performance that requires a trained body-based performer to execute it in real-time. *OPK* has embedded within it the possibility of musical timing errors, and contains complex spatial access points for media control, thus making it only suitable for an expert performer. *OPK* continues my 20-year project to design an interface strategy for body-based performance, in which all media aspects are controlled by a single user. *OPK* is body-based and immersive, but also employs a formal design strategy of multi-modal mapping via a simulation of the condition of synesthesia.

The Gesture and Media System 3.0 (GAMS)

OPK makes use of the Gesture and Media System 3.0 (GAMS) motion tracking system, and the FlashTrack 3D mapping software. With GAMS four infrared cameras are used to detect user position and velocity in 3D space. Up to four infrared trackers can be used simultaneously. Media can be mapped in different spatial zones using FlashTrack, and dynamic relationships can be established between user motion and common audio-visual parameters. Audio and video parameters are controlled by MIDI (for control of sound and video), and lights are controlled by DMX (the standard protocol for light control). Remote controls can be used to load new 'Maps' containing different media configurations. The software can also use other motion-based data – e.g. velocity of the trackers, proximity of the different trackers to each other - to change media parameters. Figure 1 shows the trackers and explains in detail about their functionality and use.

Synesthesia

Synesthesia is a condition is which a person experiences sensations from one sense in a second different sense. "How does it feel to hear music in color, or to see someone's name in color? These are examples of synesthesia, a neurological phenomenon that occurs when a stimulus in one sense modality immediately evokes a sensation in another sense modality. Literally, 'synesthesia' means to perceive (*esthesia*) together (*syn*)." [2]

Note	Colour
C	red (intense)
C#	violet or purple
D	yellow
D#	flesh (glint of steel)
E	sky blue (moonshine or frost)
F	deep red
F#	bright blue or violet
G	orange
G#	violet or lilac
A	green
A#	rose or steel
B	blue or pearly plue

Figure 2 - Scriabin's colour scheme for the 'chromola' used in *Prometheus: Poem of Fire.* The chromola was a keyboard instrument that was capable of changing two coloured lights simultaneously.

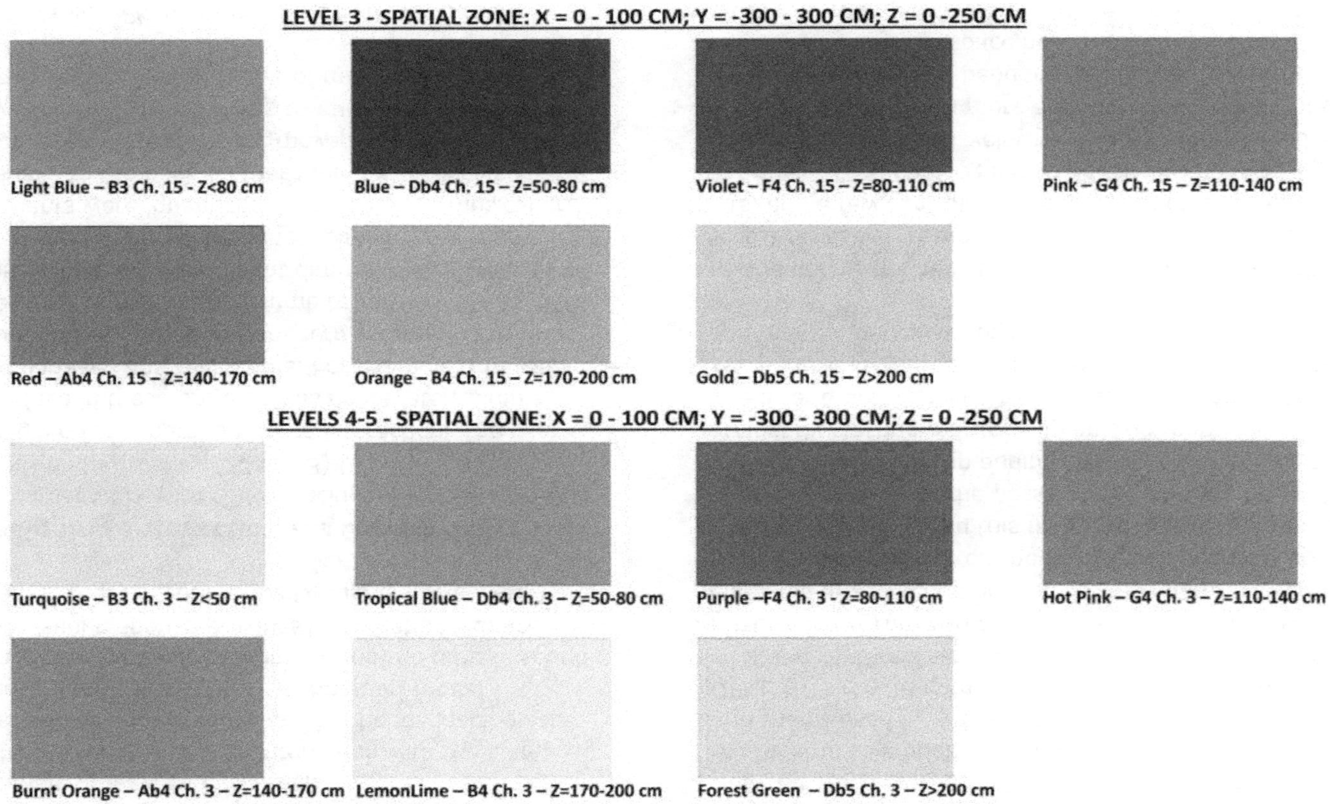

Figure 3 - Synesthesia map for two specific (related) melodies in *OPK*. The videos and light colours are matched to specific notes at specific spatial coordinates. Image by Steve Gibson, 2017.

Various devices have been created over the past 150 years to simulate the effects of synesthesia for non-synesthetes. "The British inventor Alexander Wallace Rimington (1854-1918), a professor of arts in London was the first to use the phrase 'Colour Organ,' in his patent application of 1893." [3] The Colour Organ played lighted coloured lamps by means of an organ-type keyboard. In the succeeding years following the invention of Rimington's Light Organ, other devices were created in order to play visuals simultaneously with music. The most well-known of these is Scriabin's 'chromola' used in his *Prometheus: Poem of Fire* from 1912 (see Figure 2). What these and other similar devices share in common is the ability to mimic the

Figure 4 - Steve Gibson uses two motion-trackers to perform *OPK*. The first tracker controls drums, and the second controls bass, melodies and samples. Audio events can be programmed to be triggered anywhere in 3D space. Similarly, robotic lights can be used as follow-spots, with the light parameters matched to the changes in sound parameters (i.e. sound volume could be matched to light dimmer). Simple geometric videos are also triggered in synch with each note of the melodies, and are matched to the robot light colours. The formal matching is based on a simulation of the effects of synesthesia. Photo by Liam Hardy, ©2017. Used by permission.

effect of audio-visual synesthesia through a single control technology. In *OPK* the audio-visual synesthetic simulation uses motion control instead of a keyboard or other musical device, extending the synesthetic experience into a third medium, that of the spatial - not precisely 'dance', but close (see Figure 3 for an example of a synesthesia map from *OPK*). Although the ephemeral nature of the interaction with the GAMS system does not produce any haptic feedback on the trackers themselves, in *OPK* the multi-modal connection between movement and the precise sound and visual response provides kinesthetic feedback through proprioception (joint/muscle senses, etc.).

Designing Interaction for Expert Users

My earlier work with GAMS, including *Virtual DJ* (2002-2005) and *Virtual VJ* (2011-13) [4], was primarily designed for general audience interaction. The user interface in these projects was deliberately simple, standardised and repeatable. For example, in *Virtual DJ* drums always faded in from zero volume in the back of the room to maximum volume towards the front. This was accompanied by a light dimmer that increased in intensity in a parallel manner. Similarly, all musical elements were 'quantized' to a very wide musical grid (usually to the bar), so that timing was always on the beat, even if the audience movements were slightly off rhythmically. The goal was to make the audience enjoy the experience without fear of making errors.

In contrast *OPK* is designed explicitly for a more rehearsed expert performer, in this case myself. I have over 20-years of experience in working with the GAMS system, and therefore almost certainly have a more developed spatial sense than the general population. In addition, I have a PhD in Music Composition and Theory and therefore my musical ability is likely higher than most of the general population.

My intention was to push myself as a performer so that an effort was needed to both keep the performance in synch, and to retain a level of musical coherence. This was partly achieved by setting the input quantization in the Ableton Live audio software to a much finer musical grid than I used in *Virtual DJ* (usually 1/8th notes for *OPK*), thus requiring me to pay very close attention to all of the rhythmic elements in order to keep them in relative time. This also enabled me to bring in musical elements in a syncopated fashion, thus getting away from an over-reliance on the 4/4 (time signature) grid. Another effect of using this finer grid was the possibility of errors, or at least the possibility of bringing in musical elements in an audibly 'wrong' manner - i.e. accidently starting a drum loop an 1/8th note early or late after a breakdown. The possibility of errors was key here: it increased the intensity of the performance and made it demonstrably more 'live.'

In addition to the above, the structure of *OPK* is such that it starts very simply, with a bass note, a few drum hits, and a few controls applied to each of these objects and their accompanying lights/videos via changing coordinates or tracker velocity. As *OPK* progresses the 3D space is filled with more and more sound, light and visual layers until the penultimate section, in which every part of the 3D space has an audio-visual layer, often with multiple layers on different parts of the z plane (floor-to-ceiling) in the same bounding x/y coordinates. Simultaneously the degree of dynamic control is increased as the piece progresses. Table 1 shows all of the MIDI controls that are sent via the GAMS system to Ableton Live.

OPK MIDI controls

MIDI continuous controllers (CC) are used to send MIDI data dynamically so that musical parameters can be changed smoothly in real-time. This list shows some common continuous controls used in *OPK*.

Filters – CCs 99 and 100
Filter Resonance – CC 101
Tremolo – CC 102
Beat Repeat – CC 103
Reverb Mix – CC 104
Delay Mix 1 – CC 105
Delay Mix 2 – CC 106
Delay Feedback – CC 107
Distortion – CC 108
Pre-Distortion – CC 109
Distortion Filter – CC 110
Beat Repeat Grid – CC 113
Auto Pan amount – CC 114
Vocoder balance – CC 115
Volcano Mix – CC 116
Synth 1 volume – CC 117
Synth 2 volume – CC 118
Resonator Mix – CC 119
Tempo – CC 120

Table 1: A list of MIDI continuous controls sent from GAMS to control audio parameters in Ableton Live. See Figure 5 for an example of how a MIDI control is mapped in FlashTrack.

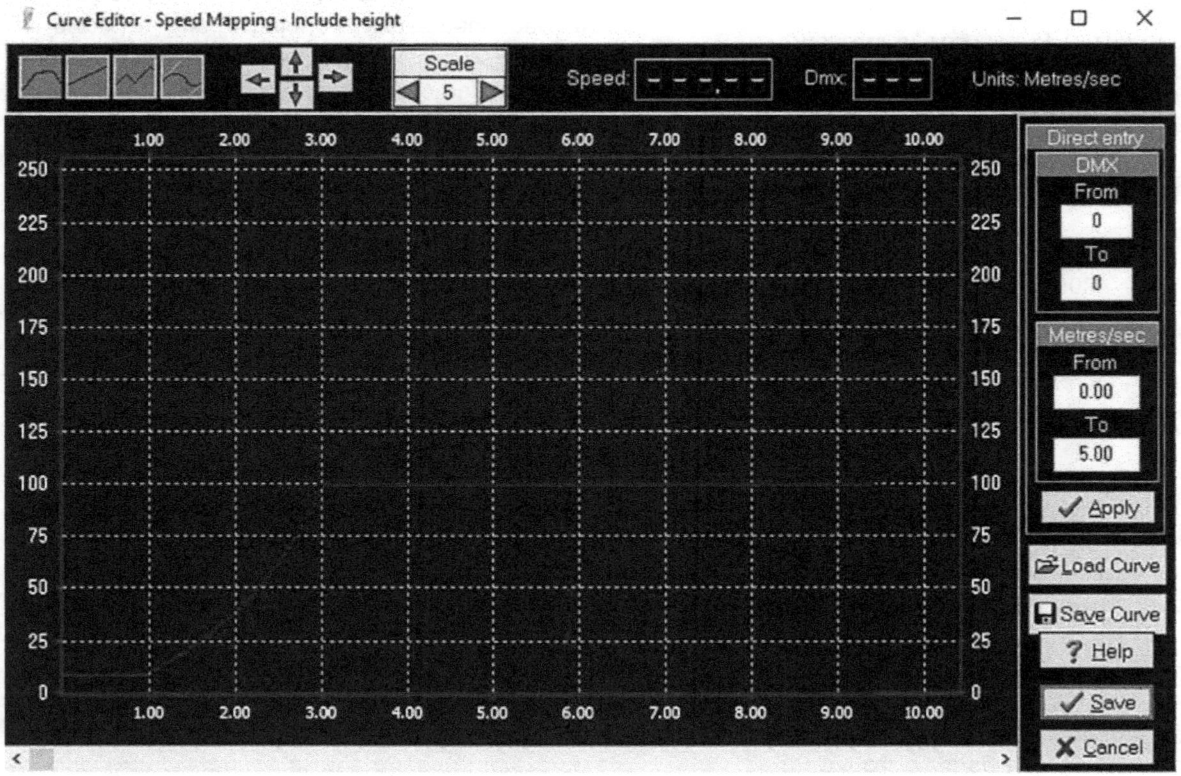

Figure 5 - This screen shows how dynamic controls are mapped in FlashTrack. In this case tracker velocity is used to change the amount of delay applied to the drums. When I move between 0-1 metre per second there is a small amount of delay. The delay amount increases from 10-100 when I move between 1-3 metres per second, and tops out at 100 when I move 3 metres per second or faster.

As a performer, I have to be continuously aware of these controls. It takes a mental, musical and visual effort to recall the planes to which these controls are attached, and which controls may be active at any time. This includes many instances in which controls are being applied on multiple sound channels and different lights simultaneously.

The use of multi-modal mapping between the sound, light and video elements, using a synesthetic strategy, assists in bringing coherence to the performance, both for the performer and the audience. For example, at the start of *OPK* a very soft bass note is triggered in the back of the room. As I move forward (on the y plane) the bass filter is opened, and the dimmer on the light

Audio-Light pairing in OPK
This shows how one audio track is paired to a light, with the MIDI and DMX mapped to the same tracker data.

FlashTrack Layer 1
Audio - Synth Filter CC99 (y)
Light - Dimmer (y)

- minimum at -250 y, and values change smoothly to maximum at +100 y

FlashTrack Layer 2
Audio - Beat Repeat CC113 (point)
Light – Rotating Prism (point) (Defined Point – x = 0 cm; y = +100 cm; z = +100 cm)

- minimum >200 cm from point, and values change smoothly to maximum <50 cm from point

FlashTrack Layer 3
Audio - Reverb Mix CC104 (z)
Light - Focus (z)

- minimum <130 z and values change smoothly to maximum at 200 z

Table 2: A list of Audio and Light parameters controlled by specific tracker movements, attached to one Bass sound at the start of *OPK.*

becomes brighter. As I near a specific point at the front of the room the bass note is repeated and bent (Beat Repeat), which simultaneously causes the light prism to rotate. As I lift my hand up beyond 130 cm (on the z plane) reverb is applied increasingly to the bass, and the light becomes increasingly unfocused. Table 2 shows how the audio and light controls are mapped to specific 3D movements, as described in the example above.

These synchronized actions between the audio-visual domains are what provides the formal coherence in *OPK,* and they are also what gives the performer feedback on how his movements are affecting the audio-visual elements. Only through logical and careful mapping of motion to audio-visual parameters does this control become instinctive and intuitive for the performer.

Finally, much of *OPK* requires considerably physical exertion to achieve an effect. For example, some control changes are spread out of over longish distances (5-6m), therefore requiring me to make a physical effort to change the audio-visual parameters with a degree of coherence.

Conclusion
The different factors described above promote the 'liveness' of *OPK*, and are an effort to humanise both immersive interactive media and audio-visual performance. The technique of synesthetic mapping between audio, visual and movement domains allows for the intricate performance of an immersive environment by one individual performer. While we might instinctively presume that controlling two mediums with a third (movement) might be more difficult than controlling one, with thoughtful and careful mapping of movement to sound and visual result, the multi-modal performance is actually simpler for the performer and more rewarding for the audience. Similarly, the audience perception that the piece is open to performer variation, error and physical exhaustion re-humanizes digital audio-visual performance, creating a more genuinely live experience via the displacement of the body in 3D space.

Acknowledgements
Special thanks to: Liam Hardy for the camera on the *OPK* shoot; David Leonard for the loan of the Black Magic Camera for the *OPK* shoot; Moment Research and Limbic Media for GAMS 3.0; Northumbria University and Gilbert Cockton for GAMS 3.0 funding; Conroy Badger for FlashTrack fixes.

Documentation
Video documentation of *OPK* can be viewed at https://vimeo.com/228634638. A full performance of one piece from *OPK* can be viewed at https://vimeo.com/228541508

References
1. ACM. TEI Arts Track website. 2018. Retrieved October 10, 2017 from https://tei.acm.org/2018/arts-track/
2. Cretien van Campen. 2007. *The Hidden Sense: Synesthesia in Art and Science*. Massachusetts Institute of Technology (MIT), Cambridge, MA, 1.
3. Cretien van Campen. 2007. *The Hidden Sense: Synesthesia in Art and Science.* Massachusetts Institute of Technology (MIT), Cambridge, MA, 49.
4. Steve Gibson, Virtual DJ website. 2006. Retrieved October 11, 2017 from http://www.telebody.ws/VirtualDJ

PainByte: Chronic Pain And BioMedical Engineering Through The Lens Of Classical Ballet & Virtual Reality

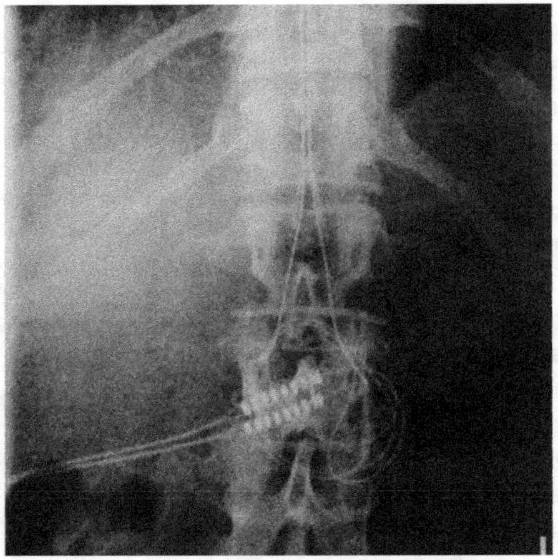

Figure 1: Fluoroscope of first author's spinal implant. The image shows the electrodes Image © G. Smith-Nunes

Genevieve Smith-Nunes
ReadySaltedCode
Brighton, United Kingdom
genevieve@readysaltedcode.org

Alex Shaw
GlastonBridge Software
Edinburgh, Uniited Kingdom
Alex.shaw@glastonbridge.com

Camilla Neale
Worcester University
Worcester, United Kingdom
C.Neale@worcs.ac.uk

TEI '18, March 18–21, 2018, Stockholm, Sweden

ACM ISBN 978-1-4503-5568-1/18/03.
https://doi.org/10.1145/3173225.3173296

Abstract

[pain]Byte is looks at the world of chronic pain. The invisible disability of spinal chronic pain which is manifested and represented through data driven dance (classical ballet) and virtual reality (VR). Enabling the non sufferer audience to 'see' the hidden nature and challenges of chronic pain linked to the benefits of biomedical engineering and implanted technology. The body as analogue represented through the digital of the wearables and the virtual in the VR experience. Humanising implanted technology and exposing the invisible nature of chronic pain for audiences. In our exhibit, people can watch the VR, interact with the biometric sensors and our single Kinect motion capture. A recording of the ballet will be projected.

Author Keywords

Chronic pain; pain systems; invisible disability; virtual reality (VR); ballet; data visualisation

ACM Classification Keywords

Applied computing → Performing arts.
Human-centered computing → Displays and imagers

Figure 2: In this series of images, the dancers are representing different pain types from top to bottom: Inflammatory, Nociceptive and Neuropathic. Image © G. Smith-Nunes

Inflammatory: relating to or causing inflammation of a part of the body.

Nociceptive: relating to or denoting pain arising from the stimulation of nerve cell.

Neuropathic: a chronic condition which leads to persistent pain symptoms. Arising from damage or disease in the nerves themselves.

Introduction

[pain]Byte tells a story is about chronic pain and biomedical engineering, in particular the use of implanted technology as a form of drug-free pain relief known as - neuromodulation. It can be describe as technology that acts directly upon nerves. (Al-Kaisey et al). In order to enhance ballet audiences experience, we developed a stand alone but complimentary VR experience. The ballet is a representation of a single day. From the unseen, hidden pain when out in the real world with surrounding nature of neuropathic pain. Through pain flare ups and the relief of the bio-tech. This 'Breaking the Pain' that can come with this type of treatment. [pain]Byte is the third ballet which is part of the ongoing project Data Driven Dance.

How chronic pain and the invisible world of that pain is seen from the sufferers perspective. Hiding the pain to the outside worlds to seeing that same pain as a system. For the audiences it is about what it means to be in pain everyday in an unforgiving world. How technology (biomedical engineering and VR) can bring a drug-free relief option to sufferers.

[pain]Byte: VR storytelling. An experience to bring the hidden and invisible to light. The story is a personal representation of the first authors forty years of being in chronic pain and the challenges that chronic pain present. The decision to use VR came from the research into chronic pain

"Gate theory of attention postulates that VR reduces the perception of pain by absorbing and diverting attention away from the pain." (Jones, Moore & Choo 2016)

With the ever faster changes in technology in all aspects of our lives these tend to have fear associated with them. Through the presentations of the VR storytelling experience, video and hands ons delegates.

The creation of VR gaming as a treatment for chronic pain sufferers.

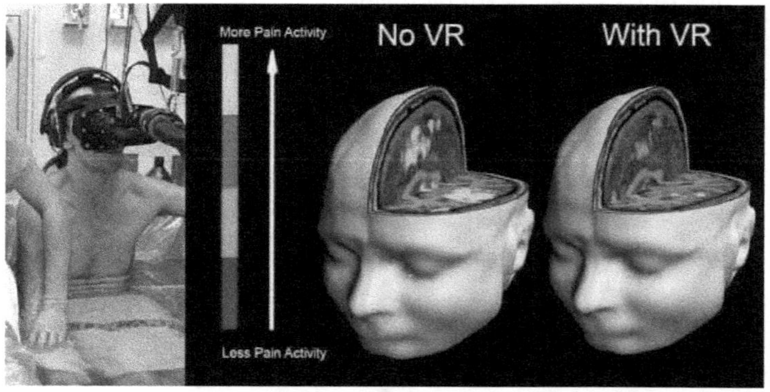

Figure 3: Image of MRI showing the pain centres of the brain when using VR or not. Image by Duff Hendrickson, U.W., Copyright Hunter Hoffman, U.W.

Choreography to Computing

The analogue nature of classical ballet mixed with the digital of the virtual. The precise attributes of classical ballet, with set structures, routines, rules and terminology, can be married with that of social network theory, programming and computational thinking. It is because of association that classical ballet was selected as the dance medium over other forms of dance. An alternative dance form was initially researched, Contemporary but this is less codified and the movements are more stylised than classical ballet.

Figure 3: Arabesque Image © G. Smith-Nunes

Figure 4: Posé Image © G. Smith-Nunes

Recreating, in ballet, the different pain pathway patterns and associated theories and concepts. It is about making ballet a visual medium for the audience as well as for the aesthetics of the piece. The dancers and choreography used both the network and pain pathway illustrations as the basis for their individual movements and motifs. The movement across the stage makes use of a node map to show motif change and pathway for each dancer. The dancers prior understanding of the development process from the previous ballet [data]Storm (Smith-Nunes et al 2016) enabled the dancers the master the choreography of the Neuropathic section quickly and effortlessly. Using reference diagrams and visualisations of the pain gateway control to ensure choreography reflects the theory.

Coding through ballet

The choreography shows the development of the invisible pain signal by using smooth, delicate arm lines, flowing footwork and group formations. This combination gave way for the transmission of the pain signal to seem simple and elegant. Thus creating the illusion of not being in pain. The deliberate shadowing and pattern formation of the pain signals dancers is to visualises the invisible nature chronic pain. In selecting specific steps such as Posé, Faille and Chaînés to represent pain types and signals. See figures 3 & 4

Choreography for VR

The choreography for the VR comes from the middle section of the live performance. From the dancer perspective, learning sections out of order does not pose any problems. It had to completed in this order to enable motion capture and data smoothing to take place. The VR experience for [pain]Byte has been developed for Google's DayDream headset. The design of the VR experience echoes some of the visuals from the live ballet performance. It has been designed to be an independent piece. As the world of VR is very much like theatre or stage we decided to take unmodified choreography for use in the VR world. The impact on the choreography was that it had to be design for a 360 audience. The use of the same choreography altered the timing of the project to ensure that is was complete first.

VR Development

We developed a Kinect server to output the data to JSON and OBJ. These are common file formats for data visualisation experts and 3D modellers. Designed for non technical artists to be able to use and develop their own works. Taking our analogue body as a system and turning into a digital resources. The digital ubiquitous world where rejection of the digital is not always possible therefore an augmentation of our world view is needed. The live ballet performance only exists in the presents for audience. A video of that same performance is a snapshot of that performance. Does that lessen the experience for the viewer? Questions for further development.

The motion capture was completed with a marker less system as the dancers are aged 14-17 years old. We tested a few different systems that would work within a non studio/theatre setting and were within the budget of the project. The VR used a variety of data sets and captured methods. For motion capture during rehearsals we use several set-ups including: a JSON data capture with a single Kinect. Two Kinect2 sensor and motion capture software, 6 PS eye cameras and accelerometer data from wearable sensors and Arduino boards. The reason for predominately using marker less motion tracking systems is for the dancers' safety but also for the ability to use any output as a virtual dancer within the VR or live performance.

Figure 5: Screen shot from the VR experience mid way through. Inside the "dome of pain". The graphics are darker, angular. Representing the wholeness of pain within the body for non pain suffers. Image © G. Smith-Nunes

While the term "post-digital" can mean media that may or may not be created or consumed digitally. The creation of that said piece could be derived from digitisation, culture and proceed can affect their final output (Wizinsky & Brier 2016). The content of seeing the hidden world of pain through the virtual lens of VR and the real world lens of the LEDs on the 'heart beat' triggered interactive display. All lead to the bringing the abstract world of 'pain' to the concrete via visual and physical interaction.

The Exhibition

This art work will be exhibited using distinct but linked elements. The VR experience, Projection of the Kinect server live, Biometric LED installation and a video recording of the ballet. The VR experience in full which is 4 minutes in duration. Linked to this will the human interaction via the single Kinect to show how the human body translates into the digital. These live images will be project or displayed to the visitors to see themselves and others. This will be mixed with video of the ballet performance that was used for the VR experience. Bio metric sensors connected to an interactive Led display showing the (for example) heart beat of the VR viewers. We will help the audience learn and play with some of the life-changing technological concepts we present through [pain]byte

Gaining feedback from a different audience will be invaluable to the further development of this and further projects. The audiences from the live ballet and VR experience are very diverse, general public audiences. Having discussion and being able to ask the delegates of the conference will enhance and benefit iterations and future works.

Conclusion

The goal of this work has two strands that can be used together or independently. Firstly the invisible disability and how society views chronic pains suffers. Secondly the the humanising of computing/ technology as the subject for story telling. Further development in the field of Computing Education research is another key area for this project. The use of Ballet, wearables and VR all aim to make the hidden visible. Demystify what it is to be in pain and what implanted technology really is. The Cyborg self is not dystopian but mistrust of what we do not understand can make us afraid of treatments with a cybernetic components. Creative expression, combining personal experience and scientific discovery, can help us recognise the humanity beyond the digital.

DataDrivenDance is the ongoing project that [pain]byte is part of which aims to break the social barriers between traditional performance and tech. Democratising new technology through creativity and open-source. Motion capture as human expression injected into the virtual space.

Acknowledgements

We would like to the thank the student dancers from Battle Abbey School, United Kingdom. The Ballet was funded with a Arts Council England, Grants for the Arts Award.

Video:

http://www.datadrivendance.org/painbyte/vr.html

References

1. Buyten, V., Al-Kaisy, A., Smet, I., Palmisani, S. and Smith, T., 2013. High-frequency spinal cord stimulation for the treatment of chronic back pain patients: Results of a prospective multicenter
2. Melzack, R. and Wall, P.D., 1967. Pain mechanisms: a new theory. Survey of Anesthesiology, 11(2), pp. 89-90.
3. Hoffman, H.G., Richards, T.L., Bills, A.R., Van Oostrom, T., Magula, J., Seibel, E.J. and Sharar, S.R. (2006). Using FMRI to study the neural correlates of virtual reality analgesia. CNS Spectrums, 11(1), 45-51
4. Sih, A., Hanser, S.F. & McHugh, K.A. Behav Ecol Sociobiol (2009) 63: 975. doi:10.1007/s00265-009-0725-6. http://link.springer.com/article/10.1007/s00265-009-0725-6
5. Kemler MA, Barendse GA, Van Kleef et al. Spinal cord stimulation in patients with chronic reflex sympathetic dystrophy. N Engl J Med. 2000; 343 (9):618-624
6. Anna Cavender, Shari Trewin, Vicki Hanson. 2014. Accessible Writing Guide. Retrieved August 22, 2014 from http://www.sigaccess.org/welcome-to-sigaccess/resources/accessible-writing-guide/
7. Smith-Nunes, G., Cook, P ., Neale, C. and Golz, P ., 2016, July. Data network simulator with classical ballet. In Proceedings of the conference on Electronic Visualisation and the Arts (pp. 70-75). British Computer Society.
8. Cramer, F. ,2014. What is 'Post-digital'? | a peer-reviewed journal about_. [online] Available at: http://www.aprja.net/what-is-post-digital.
9. Wizinsky, M. and Brier, J., 2016. History Moves: Mobilizing Public Histories in Post-Digital Space. Scholarly and Research Communication, 7(2/3).

Figures

Figures 1, 2, 4, 5 by Author taken during rehearsal, live performance and post production. Smith-Nunes 2016 Copyright G Smith-Nunes, ReadySaltedCode CIC.

Figure 3: Image by Duff Hendrickson, U.W., Copyright Hunter Hoffman, U.W.

The Cloakroom: Documentary Narratives in Embodied Installation

Ella Dagan
University of California, Santa Cruz
Santa Cruz, CA 95064, USA
ella@ucsc.edu

TEI '18, March 18–21, 2018, Stockholm, Sweden

ACM ISBN 978-1-4503-5568-1/18/03.
https://doi.org/10.1145/3173225.3173297.

Abstract
This paper presents the concept and instances of implementation of a documentary embodied art installation named 'The Cloakroom'. The Cloakroom is an interactive aesthetic experience which is made out of multiple interpersonal relationship stories and their connection to objects. People are invited to embody a relationship by literally donning a jacket and going through the motions of finding things in its pockets. The objects they find are then used as triggers to play pre-recorded stories, bringing analog artifacts to meet the digital content. The use of pockets highlights the physical intersection between tangibles and wearables.

Author Keywords
tangible user interface; objects; interactive documentary; storytelling; embodied interaction; interpersonal relationships; embedded computing.

Figure 1. An overview illustration of The Cloakroom installation setup and embodied interaction.

Introduction

Sherry Turkle wrote, "We think with the objects we love; we love the objects we think with" [19]. Throughout our lives we encounter and interact with countless objects. Sometimes those objects become mementos. When objects are physical — we touch, see, smell and hear them — in a sense, by experiencing objects, we also insert pieces of ourselves into their being. To communicate memories to others sometimes would mean to pass on some of those sensorial references. The activities of the mind are deeply rooted in the ways bodies interact with the world [21].

Jackets can be viewed as a kind of temporary shell people don. Jackets are worn as the outer layer of the body, they are positioned between ourselves and the world. The jackets people choose to wear could externally communicate to others about who they are, and internally make them feel protected and warm. Simultaneously, jackets create an intimate space around people's bodies. Many times jackets have pockets which are used to store things on our bodies as we move through space. Pockets are a private place we wear in public.

The design of The Cloakroom experience began with asking, how could we share personal memories with strangers? Could we find new ways to share those memories without feeling too exposed? What could make us feel the interconnectedness we all share? Could ubiquitous objects tell our stories? I engaged unknowingly with an "autobiographical design" approach [10], initially serving my own need by designing a sharing method for my own personal stories of relations, as means for catharsis. As The Cloakroom developed it was inspired by popular projects such as Humans of New York [7] and StoryCorps [14]. Both projects compile diverse documentary personal stories and share them with the public. Similarly, the goal of The Cloakroom is to create a collection of diverse people's personal relationship stories.

The physical design of the installation is hoping to achieve Mark Weiser's early ubiquitous computing ideas. Embedding the technology in the environments and thus making it disappear [20]. The purpose of this installation is that the main focus of attention will be the aesthetic experience and not the computing device. Objects and clothing come with their histories, they are the design fabric of our environments. This project could remind HCI researchers and practitioners of the interwoven history tangible design affords and is aligned with the longstanding HCI approach to ubiquitous computing.

The Cloakroom is an embodied interaction of enriched emotional and sensory exploration. You learn about someone else's memories by wearing a jacket, rummaging through its pockets and listening to recorded stories playing in headphones. This creates a kinesthetically intimate and cozy experience. Links are embedded in tangible objects which are placed inside jacket pockets. The use of objects to trigger narratives to play sets a nonlinear structure for the exploration.

Related Aesthetic Work

The Cloakroom has much in common with The Reading Glove [15, 16] in terms of the tangible User Interface (TUI) for interactive storytelling as well as in the underlying technology and the attention to ubiquitous objects as story triggers. Drawing attention to the objects we hold in our pockets and their stories was also explored in the Portable Effects exhibit at the Exploratorium in San Francisco. There, the exhibit creators experimented with asking people to expose what they carried in their pockets and reflect on these objects, using input stations. The creators found that "Many visitors welcomed an opportunity to introspect" [13]. In the work Pockets Full of Memories, visitors of the Centre Pompidou digitally scanned and described objects they carried in their pockets [12]. Both Object Stories [11], an ongoing project of Portland Art Museum, and Museum of Broken Relationships [2] collect objects from the public and showcase people's stories along with their objects.

StoryCorps's organization facilitates and shares recordings of people's introspection stories and makes animations to accompany them in support of their mission to "preserve and share humanity's stories in order to build connections between people and create a more just and compassionate world" [14]. Janet Cardiff's audio tour "Her Long Black Hair" [3] leads people through New York City's Central Park and manages to augment the situated experience by creating an alternate intimate soundscape, immersing the participants within the narrator's fragmented storytelling, similar to a stream of consciousness. The stories are triggered by a collection of old photographs which the artist found in a flea market, and are overlaid on the environment. Although the photographs are viewed through a smartphone device, these are reminiscent of physical objects. The effect of using intimate voice recording for telling personal stories was carried into The Cloakroom as part of the aesthetic experience.

The Cloakroom Experience

Tangible Narrative Navigation

The Cloakroom is an aesthetic experience of full body interaction with analog artefacts, which mask digital technology. The artefacts are used as analog triggers to play and navigate the recorded stories (digital content). The installation is made out of a collection of jackets and a whole array of small objects which are placed inside the pockets of the jackets, see Figures 1 and 2 for installation illustration. See project video link in references [4].

Visitors to the installation experience stories of personal relationships by donning jackets from the installation, searching their pockets, finding objects and listening to the pre-recorded stories which relate to these objects and to the relationship, all pre-linked to the objects using disguised near field communication (NFC) tags, forming embedded hypermedia.

Figure 2. Installation interaction illustration: The basket is embedded with a smartphone. The cloth is masking it to create an environment that feels mostly analog.

Many researchers have examined and demonstrated the value of using objects as tangible interfaces, and specifically for allowing interactive digital content storytelling [e.g., 1, 6, 9, 15, 16]. This project relates to previous work done in the field and corresponds with preliminary outlined framework for narrative characteristics of storytelling systems which use interactive tangible objects formed by [5].

Embodied Interaction

The Cloakroom installation is a collection of suspended jackets locked onto hangers, each representing a real relationship and serving as a documentary representation of that relationship. On a nearby wall hangs a key holder with numbered keys and a set of Bluetooth headphones. A basket is placed on top of a pedestal near the suspended jackets.

As a visitor of the installation you would choose a key at random from the key holder installed on a wall (see

Figure 3. A key older with numbered keys, each trigger an introduction story for a particular jacket.

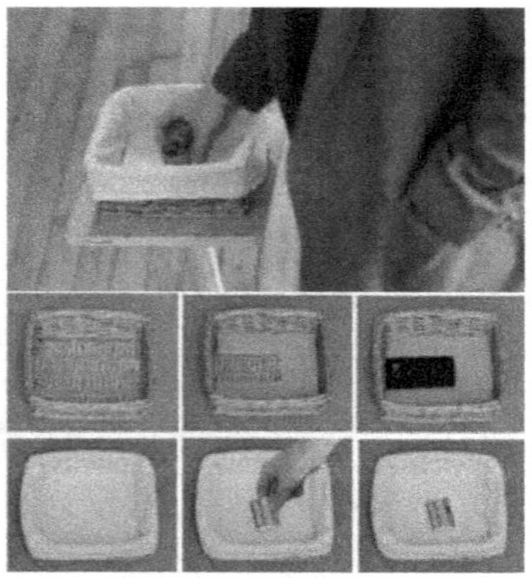

Figure 5. A demonstration of how the smartphone is triggered with an object, and how it is embedded inside the basket with a cloth.

Figure 3). The number key you chose will direct you to the jacket with the matching numbered lock. That is the jacket you will don after releasing it from its hanger. You put on the Bluetooth headphones and place the first object you have in your hand, which is the key. The key is linked to an introduction story about the jacket you have on, which will start playing in your headphones. Then you will rummage through the jacket's pockets to find objects and unveil the rest of its stories. When you place each object in the basket its story will begin to play. In each of the jackets there are between four and six pocket-size-fitting common analog objects (e.g., bag of seeds, ping pong ball, bone, knitting needle, piece of bark etc., see Figure 4), which are placed inside the pockets and are not noticeable just by glancing at the jacket collection. All these objects are embedded with NFC tags and are pre-linked to trigger the particular story.

For example, if you had reached into the left inside pocket of the jacket that represents Brad, you would have found the orange juice box and which would play this story narrated by the person who knew him: "I dream about him sometimes though, one dream which was so real and tangible, I told him that I loved him. And he was lying in bed looking at me and I was in the bed that I was actually in, in that moment. I feel like I couldn't really believe it, or I was half lucid dreaming and so I asked him what type of orange juice he liked, because, I don't know, for some reason he really liked pulpy orange juice, I also really like pulpy orange juice. I think I asked him that in the dream to confirm for myself that it was really him". This story particularly highlights the way we associate things in the world and people.

Figure 4. Some of the objects used as tangible triggers for the digital recorded documentary stories.

A smartphone installed with the Apps Tasker [17] and Trigger [18] is used as the central computing device for launching and playing the audio links of the documentary stories. The basket is embedding the smartphone, its purpose is to keep the interaction feeling mostly analog, see Figure 5. When an object is placed in the basket the story related to the object will start to play in the Bluetooth headphone set.

Project Development

As an early proof of concept, I developed and installed three jackets based on my own recorded stories of relationships at the ITP Winter Show [8]. This was the first opportunity for public user testing and it drew people's attention and curiosity. There I recognized the impactful instance of experiencing one's stories being shared, without actually telling those stories directly to people. I watched as the stories were shared over and over again and felt an unexpected cathartic relief. As a result of realizing the opportunity for such catharsis, I wanted to extend and grow The Cloakroom, to create an environment where more people could introspect, share their personal stories and listen to others' stories.

Next I invited people to contribute their stories to the installation. An open call for participation was sent to peers and I met with the ones who responded. The meetings were held as private recording sessions lasting about one hour each. Before the session the participants chose a relationship to reflect upon. When I met them we had a conversation and the responses to open questions were recorded. They were asked to record an introduction story. This story is linked to the key/lock which connects the jacket to the hanger. The participants were also asked to answer a few specific questions and describe the jacket the person they were reflecting upon would wear. The jacket they described served as a reference for sourcing in thrift stores the jacket used in the installation. The participants answered questions like: Who are you thinking about?; When was the last time you have seen them?; How long do/did you know them?. Then they were asked to think about objects which could relate to the chosen person or to their relationship with that person. Some people found this exercise easier than others. Some could not think about the objects and just wanted to tell stories about their relationship propless. So at times the objects served as triggers for story recollection and when no objects were associated, participants attributed the objects to their stories in retrospect. Eventually together with the participants, all the small objects were selected. After finishing the recorded sessions, I edited with a sound engineer the recordings into approx. 30 seconds to one and half minutes long stories. These edited stories were sent back to the participants to be approved for use before they were incorporated into the installation.

The Cloakroom was installed again during NYU's xStory exhibition [22], this time representing seven stories of relationships with a total of five different storytellers. While I have not conducted a formal analysis, people reacted to the installation. Surprise and excitement were common reactions in the moment when people found out the interaction involved putting on a jacket. One visitor reported it felt strangely intimate to listen to stories while wearing someone else's jacket. Another wanted to find more objects in hope of hearing more stories. A few people were flooded with emotions and became a bit tearful. Someone told me the stories he heard reminded him of his own relationship with his father. A recurring question was about the origin of the jackets; people were curious if the jacket was the actual jacket of the person they heard about.

Conclusion

I see The Cloakroom as an aesthetically successful project. The use of pockets was especially meaningful in this project. The pockets intimately held objects that triggered intimate stories. Also, the interaction with the objects happens kinesthetically before visually seeing the object, and before listening to the recorded story. This allows time for the person experiencing a jacket to project their own thoughts and memories on the object, and makes the interaction with each object and each story deeper. The Cloakroom project resonated with many of those who experienced it. It creates an opportunity for catharsis. The goal for this project is to grow the jackets collection by continuing to document a variety of interpersonal relationships. The project invites people to reflect on objects and memory creation, intimacy between strangers and their own personal relationships.

Acknowledgements

Thanks to the Interactive Telecommunications Program (ITP) of Tisch School of The Arts at New York University and its community at large for supporting this project. Thanks to those who contributed their personal stories to create the content of the current installation version. Thanks to all those who advised, tested and supported the creation of the project and its document-tation.

References

1. Andrea Bellucci, Paloma Diaz, and Ignacio Aedo. 2014. Digitally Augmented Narratives for Physical Artifacts. *Proceedings of the 2014 International Working Conference on Advanced Visual Interfaces*, ACM, 229–232.
2. Brokenships. *Brokenships*. Retrieved November 1, 2017 from https://brokenships.com/.
3. Public Art Fund: Janet Cardiff. Retrieved October 24, 2017 from https://phiffer.org/hlbh/.
4. The Cloakroom. *Vimeo*. Retrieved October 27, 2017 from https://vimeo.com/216112391.
5. Daniel Harley, Jean Ho Chu, Jamie Kwan, and Ali Mazalek. 2016. Towards a Framework for Tangible Narratives. *Proceedings of the TEI '16: Tenth International Conference on Tangible, Embedded, and Embodied Interaction*, ACM, 62–69.
6. Jean Ho Chu. 2015. Designing Tangible Interfaces to Support Expression and Sensemaking in Interactive Narratives. *Proceedings of the Ninth International Conference on Tangible, Embedded, and Embodied Interaction*, ACM, 457–460.
7. Humans of New York. *Humans of New York*. Retrieved October 22, 2017 from http://www.humansofnewyork.com/.
8. Show | ITP Winter Show 2016. Retrieved October 22, 2017 from https://itp.nyu.edu/shows/winter2016/show/.
9. Mark T. Marshall, Nick Dulake, Luigina Ciolfi, Daniele Duranti, Hub Kockelkorn, and Daniela Petrelli. 2016. Using Tangible Smart Replicas As Controls for an Interactive Museum Exhibition. *Proceedings of the TEI '16: Tenth International Conference on Tangible, Embedded, and Embodied Interaction*, ACM, 159–167.
10. Carman Neustaedter and Phoebe Sengers. 2012. Autobiographical Design in HCI Research: Designing and Learning Through Use-it-yourself. *Proceedings of the Designing Interactive Systems Conference*, ACM, 514–523.
11. Object Stories. *Portland Art Museum*. Retrieved October 24, 2017 from https://portlandartmuseum.org/objectstories/.
12. Pockets Full of Memories. Retrieved November 1, 2017 from https://www.mat.ucsb.edu/g.legrady/glWeb/Projects/pfom/Pfom.html.
13. portable effects: synopsis. Retrieved October 24, 2017 from http://www.portablefx.com/synopsis/PFXTR1998-003.html.
14. StoryCorps. *StoryCorps*. Retrieved October 22, 2017 from https://storycorps.org.
15. Joshua Tanenbaum, Karen Tanenbaum, and Alissa Antle. 2010. The Reading Glove: Designing Interactions for Object-based Tangible Storytelling. *Proceedings of the 1st Augmented Human International Conference*, ACM, 19:1–19:9.
16. Karen Tanenbaum, Joshua Tanenbaum, Alissa N. Antle, Jim Bizzocchi, Magy Seif el-Nasr, and Marek Hatala. 2011. Experiencing the Reading Glove. *Proceedings of the Fifth International Conference on Tangible, Embedded, and Embodied Interaction*, ACM, 137–144.
17. Crafty Apps EU. 2017. *Tasker*. Crafty Apps EU.
18. Coleridge Apps LLC. 2017. *Trigger - Task Launcher*. Coleridge Apps LLC.
19. Sherry Turkle, ed. 2011. *Evocative Objects: Things We Think With*. The MIT Press, Cambridge, Mass. London, England.

20. Mark Weiser. 1999. The Computer for the 21st Century. *SIGMOBILE Mob. Comput. Commun. Rev.* 3, 3: 3–11.
21. Margaret Wilson. 2002. Six Views of Embodied Cognition. Psychonomic bulletin & review 9, 4, 625 - 36.
22. xStory Showcase 2017. Retrieved October 22, 2017 from https://itp.nyu.edu/xstory/xstory/xstory-showcase-2017/.

Nettle: An Exploration of Communication Interface Design for Older Adults

Audrey M. Fox
Parsons School of Design
New York, NY, 10011 USA
fox@thenewschool.edu

TEI 2018, March 18–21, 2018, Stockholm, Sweden.
ACM ISBN 978-1-4503-5568-1/18/03.
https://doi.org/10.1145/3173225.3173298

Abstract

Telecommunication with family and friends is often offered as a solution for aging adults facing social isolation. While strengthening existing ties is important, it fails to address the importance of spontaneous community interactions. This paper presents Nettle, a system that is designed to build casual human connection into one's daily routine. Nettle is based on the artist's alternate vision of smart home design where interfaces are playful, based on familiar household forms and warmly inviting. The audience will observe a performance where Nettle fosters a spontaneous spoken conversation alongside the process of making a pot of tea.

Author Keywords

Older Adults; Internet of Things; Communication

ACM Classification Keywords

• Human-centered computing~Interaction design theory, concepts and paradigms • Social and professional topics~Seniors • Applied computing~Arts and humanities • Applied computing~Telecommunications

Introduction

Social dynamics in the twenty-first century are different than in past generations. Older adults today tend to live further from family, choose single occupant housing, and have less connection to traditional organizations.[1] While it may be natural to have one's social circle constrict with age as friends pass away or move, traditionally, lost connections have been offset by participation in religious organizations, clubs, and active community outreach. In order to mitigate negative health effects[2] and provide a better quality of life to aging people, this rising tide of social isolation must be addressed. The artist wanted to create a novel concept which highlighted how technology might encourage the building and maintenance of intergenerational relationships at a local community level.

Concept

Everyday artifacts appeal to human nature. Domestic tools have been honed over the course of human history to be usable and to feel good in the hand. Shape and handles suggest how each tool can be held. Features, such as a broom's bristles, communicate function in an obvious manner. Common item can be nearly universal. If a person has used one broom, one watering can, one chair, all future types they encounter are essentially known. These artifacts also fade seamlessly into the background when not in use. Contextualizing interaction through existing cultural models can afford more accessibility for older adults without diminishing their dignity.[3] Considering these qualities, the artist believes that specialized smart home objects which appropriate domestic forms may pose less friction in adoption than black box, (or cylinder) options. With Nettle, the artist has applied the beloved form of a tea set to an Internet of Things (IoT) device. If one can make tea, they know how to use Nettle.

Figure 1. Fabrication process

Related Work

A handful of projects have a similar focus on mitigating isolation for older adults. A student project called inSight, from the National University of Singapore, uses a form of augmented teleconferencing to connect two locations with a fogged window style of interaction.[4] This fogging is an attempt to maintain privacy while allowing for impromptu communications. Both sides need to wipe a digitally clouded layer from the screen to create a clear view between the two locations.

A future of isolated single person households was explored in a project by Umeå Institute of Design student Madyana Torres. She created a speculative screenless system which uses a series of token artifacts. These objects would embody one remote friend or family member, transmitting their activity and wellness state as well as passing asynchronous messages from one home to another. The physicality of the artifacts at hand provides an intriguing step towards shared experience through tangible interfaces.[5]

The Messaging Kettle, an Australian project headed by Margot Brereton from the Queensland University of Technology, connects communication technology to a useful item.[6] Similar to this project, the Messaging Kettle ties an interface into the act of tea making. Unlike Nettle, Brereton focus on bridging communication between adult children and their parents through notes and doodles exchanged via tablet interface.

Technical Description

Nettle connects users through a novel application of internet networking, cellular communication, and interface design. A sensor in the base of the teapot registers the act of pouring in boiling water as an indicator of availability. When an internal cellular system pings the Twilio API, the first available contact is pulled from the server and sent back to Nettle.

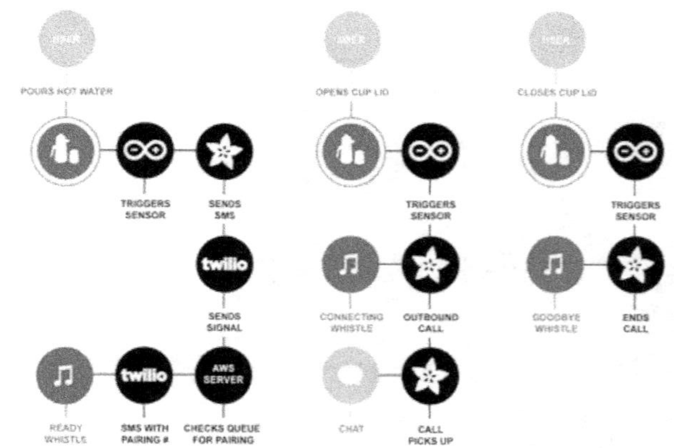

Figure 2. Technical Map

Sound indicates a connection has been found. Placing the mug's lid into its recessed place on the base triggers the call connection between users and removing the lid from the base to close the mug cuts off the call. A microphone and speaker leave hands free during conversations.

Aesthetics

Although documented changes in perception, cognition, and physical mobility affect how an older user is able to interact with and learn new technology,[7] these changes do not affect aesthetic sensibilities. Senior focused technology is often pandering, with giant childlike buttons and encased in ugly plastic. This is unfortunate considering the important role that everyday objects play in our sensory lives. Deliberate touches of materiality enrich our relationships with objects in the home. Smart home objects are not exempt from this type of sensory relationship. The artist considered her grandmother who would have wanted a system made from appealing natural materials with sleek finishing. Nettle is constructed from cast ceramic components and polished wood. All electronic components are housed in the base. There is a fine line between creating an object with integrated aesthetics and one in which the form is merely decorative. With Nettle, the artist balanced interface touch points with a minimalist design.

Figure 3: Nettle in its finished state

Presentation

Nettle will be presented at a table with one chair, staged with minimal domestic props for context. The performance will entail making a pot of tea and engaging in spontaneous conversation through Nettle's interface. Apart from the performance, some elements of Nettle will be displayed on the table and available for people to touch. The video supporting Nettle will loop when the performance is not actively happening.

Conclusion

Services and products can only help older adults maintain a high quality of life and mitigate loneliness if they are used. Additionally, redesigning interaction means little without addressing the broader social issues such as affordability or privacy which impact technology adoption. However, Nettle is not intended to be a practical solution but the beginning of a conversation. Instead it offers up a vision of an alternative IoT paradigm. The artist believes that when smart home interfaces are as intuitive as any other domestic object they can be put to use for older adults, for everyone.

Acknowledgements

This project was completed at Parsons School of Design under the guidance of the artist's thesis advisors, Aneta Genova, Andrew Zornoza, Anezka Sebek, and Ethan Silverman. Gareth Price was an invaluable help coding and consulting. Advice and feedback were provided by Adriel Tong, Andrew McCandlish, and Gyungju Chyon.

References

1. Robert D. Putnam. 2000. Bowling Alone: The Collapse and Revival of American Community. Simon & Schuster, New York.
2. Andrew Steptoe, Aparna Shankar, Panayotes Demakakos, and Jane Wardle. 2013. Social isolation, loneliness, and all-cause mortality in older men and women. *Proceedings of the National Academy of Sciences of the United States of America*, vol. 110 no. 15, 5797–5801
3. C.B.Rébola and B. Jones. 2013. Sympathetic Devices: Designing Technologies for Older Adults. *SIG DOC'13: ACM* International Conference on Design of Communication, 151-156.
4. Zhide Loh, Edmund Zhang, and Zhi Ying Lim. 2015. InSight: Kick-Starting Communications for Elderlies Ageing in Place. *CHI EA*, (April 2015), 25-30.
5. Maddy Torres. 2015. The Home Network. Retrieved from https://www.madytorres.com/the-home-network/
6. Margot Brereton, Alessandro Soro, Kate Vaisutis, Paul Roe. 2015. The Messaging Kettle: Prototyping Connection over a Distance between Adult Children and Older Parents. *ACM 33* Conference on Human Factors in Computing Systems, 713-716.
7. Arthur D. Fisk. 2004. Designing for Older Adults: Principles and Creative Human Factors Approaches. CRC Press, Boca Raton, FL.

The Shared Individual

Asreen Rostami
Department of Computer and Systems Sciences, Stockholm University, Sweden
asreen@dsv.su.se

Emma Bexell
Bombina Bombast
Malmö, Sweden
Emma Bexell
emma@bombinabombast.se

Stefan Stanisic
Bombina Bombast
Malmö, Sweden
stefan@bombinabombast.se

Abstract
The Shared Individual is a live collaborative Mixed-Reality Performance in which a group of audience members can observe themselves from an individual's point of view. In this performance, a performer shares her view with audience members by wearing a head-mounted camera and steaming live video. By wearing a head-mounted display audience members can see themselves and follow performer's instruction to "occupy" her body and become her. This instruction, in the form of performance, is designed to help the audience to sync with the performer in three different stages: visual synchronization, physical synchronization and emotional synchronization.

Author Keywords
Video streaming; first person view; immersive performance; telepresence; mixed-reality performance.

ACM Classification Keywords
• Human-centered computing~Human computer interaction (HCI) • Human-centered computing~Mixed / augmented reality • Human-centered computing~Virtual reality • *Human-centered computing~Collaborative interaction* • Applied computing~Performing arts • *Applied computing~Media arts*

TEI '18, March 18–21, 2018, Stockholm, Sweden

ACM ISBN 978-1-4503-5568-1/18/03.
https://doi.org/10.1145/3173225.3173299

Introduction

The Shared Individual is a Mixed-Reality Performance (MRP), designed and performed by the Swedish artists group Bombina Bombast in collaboration with Danish film studio Makropol.

While interactive performance uses digital technologies to create an interactive experience, MRP combines such interactivities with live performance in order to create a real or virtual experience, for the audience member (sometimes described as a participant) [4]. In this regard, *The Shared Individual* combines live performance with Virtual Reality (VR) experience and live streaming video to explore the possibility of telepresence in a collective audience experiment. This out-of-body [8] experience is designed by the artists to detach the audience members from their physical body, and challenge their visual perception by giving up the control over their bodies in VR. This, perhaps uncomfortable experience [5], becomes instrumental for the artists to challenge the notion of perception with and without physical engagement of the audience in the performance, or through visually mediated telepresence.

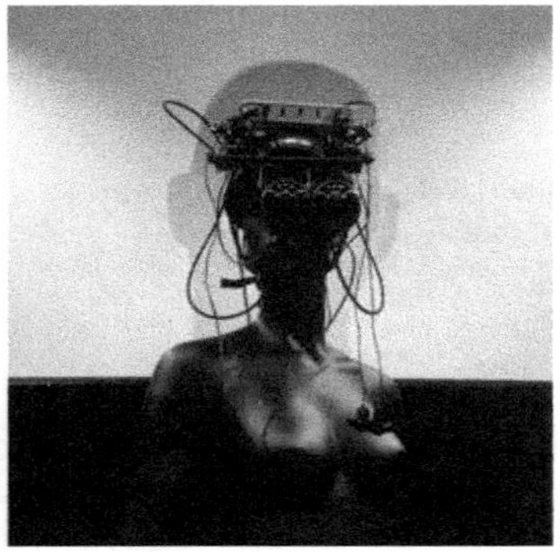

Figure 2: The Shared Individual

Figure 3: Becoming The Shared Individual

The Shared Individual

The Shared Individual was designed to explore the possibilities and limitations of interweaving novel technologies (in this case VR) in artistic practices. At first glance, *The Shared Individual* follows the traditional form of performing on stage in which actor-performer, acts on stage in front of audience. Consequently, audience is located only in front of the stage, also known as "in the house" (Figure 1). However, the design of *The Shared Individual* changes this organisation as the audience becomes the performer in the performance. In this new set up, "house" becomes the stage while audience-performer observes own performance through the eyes of the performer on stage. The performance is about 30 minutes, and it consists of three different phases:

Figure 1: Stage orientation and organization

The visual synchronization

At the beginning of the performance, two performers introduce *The Shared Individual* to the audience, which is a mannequin wearing a custom built helmet (Figure 2). This helmet broadcasts the live video to VR headset. Each audience member has access to a VR-headset, which is required during the performance.

After a brief introduction, one of the performers becomes *The Shared Individual* by wearing the helmet (Figure 3). At this point audience members are asked to wear their VR headset and follow *The Shared Individual*'s guideline. From now on, the audience can

Figure 4: *The Shared Individual* performs the physical synchronization

Figure 5: Physical synchronization between the audience and *The Shared Individual*

Figure 6: Touching *The Shared Individual*'s hand to stablishing an emotional synchronization

see through the eyes and listen through the ears (embedded cameras and microphones in the helmet) of *The Shared Individual* (Figure 3).

At this moment, asks the audience to locate themselves among the crowd, so that they can better understand the occurred telepresence. At this part the visual synchronization between the audience and *The Shared Individual* is stablished.

The physical synchronization
Next, performer asks everyone to look at their hands (The Shared Individual's hands) and mirror the same movements with their own (physical) hands (Figure 4,5). This connects the audience's body to *The Shared Individual*'s body and completes the physical and visual telepresence.

The emotional synchronization
For the last step of becoming *The Shared Individual*, the performer blocks the audiences' view by placing a black screen in front of *The Shared Individual.* As a result, the audience can only see the second performer through the eyes of *The Shared Individual*. Aiming for an intimate and emotional connection, the performer asks to hold audiences' hand through a face-to-face conversation with *The Shared Individual*. The performer then, touches *The Shared Individual*'s hand in order to create an emotional connection (Figure 6).

When this part is performed, the performer announces the successful transformation of *all* becoming *one* individual. The performer then removes the black screen so that the audience once again can see the full house though *The Shared Individual*'s eyes. However, what the audience sees is an empty room and seats, as

Figure 7: Stablishing the emotional synchronization by virtually touching the audience's hand

their physical body is now disappeared and they all became *The Shared Individual*. To better demonstrate this absence, the performer starts walking on (now empty) seats to prove that audiences' body don't exist anymore. In this void *The Shared Individual* performs a song and when it is finished the audience reappears in their seats again.

The performer then explains that *The Shared Individual* is a simulation and the audience members are collectively inhabiting this simulation. The first one to take off the headsets will terminate the simulation, and will see *The Shared Individual* standing on stage, alone and in the spotlight. Removing the headset, breaks the synchronization between *The Shared Individual* and everyone else, and ends the performance.

Technical Description
The Shared Individual consists of two GoPro cameras mounted on the helmet with an interpupillary

Figure 9: Due to technical limitations of VR performances "behind the scene" became part of the performance

Figure 10: Due to technical limitations of VR performances production crew became part of the performance

distance (IPD) of 6.5 to capture omnidirectional video. These videos are transmitted to a computer, using Blackmagic video grabber. Then, these videos are stitched together using Resolume VJ software. Through embedded binaural microphones in the helmet, the sound is also streamed to be merged with the video in another computer. The enhanced video is streamed over the network through Wirecast and Wowza Streaming Engine which is connected to a dedicated router.

On the audience side, each head-mounted display (Gear VR) is equipped with a smart phone. Each of these smart phones uses a dedicated app (developed for this performance) to receive the live stream and play it simultaneously for everyone. Due to network capacity, there is a 30 seconds latency in streaming.

Considering the network capacity (and router), the performance can host 25 audiences in each run.

Performance History

Bombina Bombast and Makropol have premiered *The Shared Individual* at International Documentary Film Festival Amsterdam (IDFA) 2016, and toured internationally in different festivals and performance houses such as: Flatpack - Birmingham (6 runs), The Swedish Embassy in Beijing (10 runs), Det Kongelige - Copenhagen (2 runs), Malmöfestivalen - Malmö (4 runs), and Festival du nouveau cinéma 2017 – Montréal (4 runs).

The Shared Individual has received an award for the best presentation of a VR project in development from Festival du nouveau cinéma 2017 [20] and has

Figure 8: The absence of audience after becoming *The Shared Individual*

received coverage from local and international [2,19] media publications.

Interweaving Technology with Mixed-Reality Performance

There has been a growing interest in the use of technologies (i.e. mobile phones [13], sensors [10], pulse and movement [15] and etc.) in different artistic and cultural domains such as entertainment, music or theatre. These practices – sometimes in the form of performing art – provide a new forms of experience for different involved individuals. It also creates different research interests; from design [9,16,17] for the designer, to communication [3,12] between the artists and audience, to perhaps the most intriguing topic among both artists and researcher which is audience engagement with the art piece [1,6,7,11,14,18].

The performance presented here is being explored in connection to the growing interest in studying MRPs with VR within the field of Human-Computer Interaction (HCI). One overarching goal of the future research in relation to this performance is be to better understand how creative teams and artists can incorporate novel interactive technologies into MRPs. Furthermore, how these technologies and interactions with them can reflect on the role of the audience participation and audience perception of the performance. And how does immersion emerge from interleaving VR into Mixed-Reality Performances?

Acknowledgements

We are grateful to Makropol, Mads Damsbo and Johan Knattrup Jensen. The Shared Individual is developed with Inter Arts Centre and supported by Danish Arts Council, KulturBryggan and The Nordic Culture Fund.

Photo credits: Bombina Bombast, Makropol, Nichon Glerum and International Documentary Film Festival Amsterdam 2016.

References

1. Adam Alston. 2013. Audience Participation and Neoliberal Value: Risk, agency and responsibility in immersive theatre. *Performance Research* 18, 2: 128–138. https://doi.org/10.1080/13528165.2013.807177
2. Bor Beekman. 2016. Met zijn allen in het hoofd van Emma - Film - Voor nieuws, achtergronden en columns. *De Volkskrant*. Retrieved November 8, 2017 from https://www.volkskrant.nl/film/met-zijn-allen-in-het-hoofd-van-emma~a4418249/
3. Steve Benford, Martin Flintham, Adam Drozd, Rob Anastasi, Duncan Rowland, Nick Tandavanitj, Matt Adams, Ju Row-Farr, Amanda Oldroyd, and Jon Sutton. 2004. Uncle Roy All Around You: Implicating the city in a location-based performance. *Proc. Advances in Computer Entertainment (ACE 2004)* 21: 47.
4. Steve Benford and Gabriella Giannachi. 2011. *Performing Mixed Reality*. The MIT Press, Cambridge, Mass.
5. Steve Benford, Chris Greenhalgh, Gabriella Giannachi, Brendan Walker, Joe Marshall, and Tom Rodden. 2013. Uncomfortable User Experience. *Commun. ACM* 56, 9: 66–73. https://doi.org/10.1145/2500468.2500889
6. Steve Benford, Irma Lindt, Andy Crabtree, Martin Flintham, Chris Greenhalgh, Boriana Koleva, Matt Adams, Nick Tandavanitj, Ju Row Farr, and Gabriella Giannachi. 2011. Creating the spectacle: Designing interactional trajectories through spectator interfaces. *ACM Transactions on Computer-Human Interaction* 18, 3: 1–28. https://doi.org/10.1145/1993060.1993061
7. Teresa Cerratto-Pargman, Chiara Rossitto, and Louise Barkhuus. 2014. Understanding audience participation in an interactive theater performance. 608–617. https://doi.org/10.1145/2639189.2641213
8. Shunichi Kasahara and Jun Rekimoto. 2014. JackIn: Integrating First-person View with Out-of-body Vision Generation for Human-human Augmentation. In *Proceedings of the 5th Augmented Human International Conference* (AH '14), 46:1–46:8. https://doi.org/10.1145/2582051.2582097
9. Boriana Koleva, Ian Taylor, Steve Benford, Mike Fraser, Chris Greenhalgh, Holger Schnädelbach, Dirk vom Lehn, Christian Heath, Ju Row-Farr, and Matt Adams. 2001. Orchestrating a mixed reality performance. In *Proceedings of the SIGCHI Conference on Human Factors in Computing Systems*, 38–45.

10. Martin Ouwerkerk, Pierre Dandine, Dennis Bolio, Rafal Kocielnik, Johanna Mercurio, Henk Huijgen, and Joyce Westerink. 2013. Wireless Multi Sensor Bracelet with Discreet Feedback. In *Proceedings of the 4th Conference on Wireless Health* (WH '13), 6:1–6:8. https://doi.org/10.1145/2534088.2534104
11. Stuart Reeves. 2011. *Designing Interfaces in Public Settings*. Springer London, London. Retrieved August 8, 2016 from http://link.springer.com/10.1007/978-0-85729-265-0
12. Chiara Rossitto and Louise Barkhuus. 2013. Maryam: Blending Drama into Cityscape. In *Women in Science*. Styxförlag, Stockholm, 71–78.
13. Chiara Rossitto, Louise Barkhuus, and Arvid Engström. 2016. Interweaving Place and Story in a Location-based Audio Drama. *Personal Ubiquitous Comput.* 20, 2: 245–260. https://doi.org/10.1007/s00779-016-0908-x
14. Asreen Rostami, Donald McMillan, Elena Márquez Segura, Chiara Rossitto, and Louise Barkhuus. 2017. Bio-Sensed and Embodied Participation in Interactive Performance. In *Proceedings of the TEI '17: Tenth International Conference on Tangible, Embedded, and Embodied Interaction* (TEI '17). https://doi.org/10.1145/3024969.3024998
15. Vygandas Simbelis and Kristina Höök. 2013. Metaphone: An Artistic Exploration of Biofeedback and Machine Aesthetics. In *CHI '13 Extended Abstracts on Human Factors in Computing Systems* (CHI EA '13), 2995–2998. https://doi.org/10.1145/2468356.2479593
16. Jocelyn Spence. 2016. Introducing Performative Experience Design. In *Performative Experience Design*. Springer International Publishing, 1–23. Retrieved August 15, 2016 from http://link.springer.com/chapter/10.1007/978-3-319-28395-1_1
17. Robyn Taylor, Guy Schofield, John Shearer, Jayne Wallace, Peter Wright, Pierre Boulanger, and Patrick Olivier. 2011. Designing from Within: Humanaquarium. In *Proceedings of the SIGCHI Conference on Human Factors in Computing Systems* (CHI '11), 1855–1864. https://doi.org/10.1145/1978942.1979211
18. Annika Waern. 2016. The Ethics of Unaware Participation in Public Interventions. In *Proceedings of the 2016 CHI Conference on Human Factors in Computing Systems* (CHI '16), 803–814. https://doi.org/10.1145/2858036.2858188
19. Damon Wise and Damon Wise. 2016. IDFA DocLab's Caspar Sonnen: "We"re Losing the Internet That We Fell in Love With'. *Variety*. Retrieved November 8, 2017 from http://variety.com/2016/film/festivals/caspar-sonnen-idfa-doclab-talks-2016-edition-1201923198/
20. PRIZES AND AWARDS - 46TH EDITION. *Festival du nouveau cinéma*. Retrieved November 8, 2017 from http://www.nouveaucinema.ca/en/news/news/prizes-and-awards-46th-edition

Au Clair de la Lune on Gramophone —For Édouard-Léon Scott and László Moholy-Nagy— (1860 / 1923 / 2015)

Kazuhiro Jo
Faculty of Design
Kyushu University
Fukuoka, JAPAN
YCAM
Yamaguchi, JAPAN
jo@jp.org

TEI '18, March 18–21, 2018, Stockholm, Sweden

ACM ISBN 978-1-4503-5568-1/18/03.
https://doi.org/10.1145/3173225.3173300

Abstract
"Au Clair de la Lune on Gramophone - For Édouard-Léon Scott and László Moholy-Nagy - (1860/1923/2015)" is a work that realizes the provocative idea of Moholy-Nagy, "a record without prior acoustic information" (1923), with the help of mature vinyl audio recording technology and current personal fabrication tools. In this paper, I explain the body, background, and characteristics of the work.

Author Keywords
Gramophone; personal fabrication; media archeology

ACM Classification Keywords
Human-centered computing~Human computer interaction (HCI); Applied computing~Media arts

Description of the Work

"I have suggested to change the gramophone from a reproductive instrument to a productive one, so that on a record without prior acoustic information, the acoustic information, the acoustic phenomenon itself originates by engraving the necessary Ritchriftreihen (etched grooves)." [10]

In 1923, Bauhaus master László Moholy-Nagy made the above proposal to produce a record without inputting acoustic information. At the time, it was simply a provocative idea. Nine decades later, the idea of "a record without prior acoustic information" can be realized on several materials, including paper, wood, and acrylic, owing to mature vinyl audio recording technology and current personal fabrication tools [5][6].

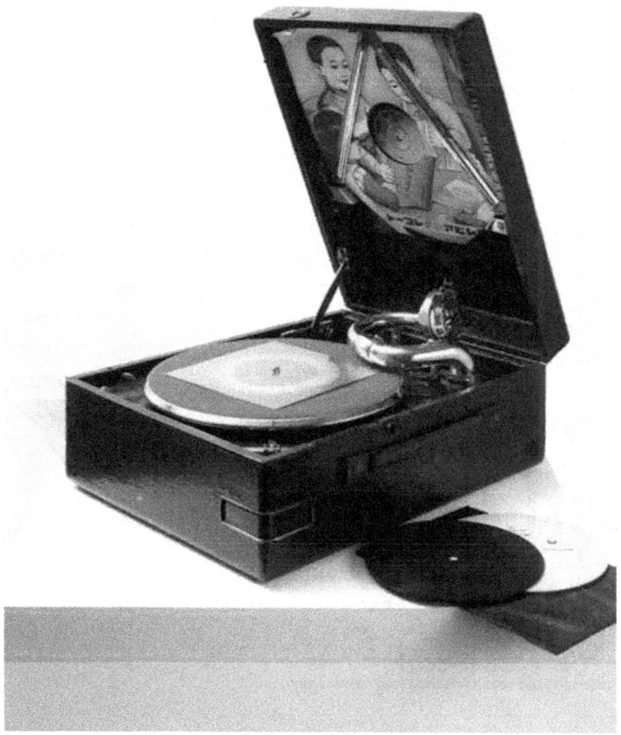

Figure 1: Kazuhiro Jo, "Au Clair de la Lune on Gramophone - For Édouard-Léon Scott and László Moholy-Nagy - (1860/1923/2015)" (photo by Takeru Koroda).

"Au Clair de la Lune on Gramophone - For Édouard-Léon Scott and László Moholy-Nagy - (1860/1923/2015)" is one such realization. In this work, I reproduced a French folk song, the oldest recorded music by Léon Scott [1], "Au Clair de la Lune," with the form of a record for a gramophone, shown in Figure 1. Instead of using a recording of the music, I computationally drew a waveform with a conventional vector graphics application, namely, Adobe Illustrator, by calculating the frequency of every note of the music. After a thorough examination of the materials aimed at overcoming the weight of the soundbox of a gramophone, I used a lacquered anodized aluminum plate horizontally engraved by a laser cutter. The outcome could be played on conventional analog record players in 78 rpm, including a traditional gramophone, shown in Figure 2.

Figure 2: Playing a lacquered anodized aluminum plate (i.e., a record without prior acoustic information) on a gramophone soundbox.

The work was premiered at Materializing Exhibition III - Between Information and Materiality in May–June 2015 at Kyoto City University of Arts Art Gallery, Kyoto, Japan, and also exhibited as a part of the Re-inventing the Wheel project at Open Space 2015, NTT InterCommunication Center, Tokyo, Japan.

Re-inventing the Wheel Project

"Au Clair de la Lune on Gramophone - For Édouard-Léon Scott and László Moholy-Nagy - (1860/1923/2015)" is a part of the Re-inventing the Wheel project, which I co-organized with colleagues and students at the Institute of Advanced Media Arts and Sciences (IAMAS) from 2013 to 2016. The project aimed to embody "the possible presents" instead of the preferable futures [2] by re-reading the history of media technologies. By utilizing the literature of media archeology [4] as our foothold, we firstly deepened our understanding of the role and function of various media, especially in the audio and visual fields, before their establishment in the history of humankind. Then, we applied each acquired notion as a technique for diverse aesthetic practices in the era of personal fabrication [3]. Instead of depicting the future or excavating the past, we attempted to redefine the reality of our circumstances by producing its alternatives.

Lack of Original Sounds

A characteristic of my work is the lack of original sounds (the outcome is not a literal record). It is reminiscent of the 1930s practices of Rudolf Pfenninger and Oskar Fischinger [9], who produced sounds, such as sine and square waves, without recordings. Of course, my technique differs from theirs in my use of computational vector lines instead of optical patterns.

Nonetheless, I could produce a sine wave from a smooth zigzag pattern, as shown in Figure 3.

Figure 3: Sine waves as a computational vector waveform of a record without prior acoustic information.

For calculating desired frequencies, the following function can be used:

Frequency [Hz] = Number of zigzags × (360/degrees) × (rpm/60)

For example, a frequency of 75 Hz would result from 100 zigzags in one revolution of the disc at 45 rpm; and 440 Hz would result from 50 zigzags × 22.5° at 33 rpm. While playing the result on a traditional gramophone by hand, typical electronic sounds (i.e., a sine wave) could be produced even without electricity.

Spreading the Technique

As expansion of my practice, I have conducted a number of workshops. I have held workshops mainly with undergraduate-level students who have little knowledge or experience with vinyl records because of the generation gap. For the workshops, I prepare step-by-step instructions, which I have made available online [7], and provide a selection of paper materials, vinyl cutters, and record players for students' use. Within this setting, each participant can produce and play her/his outcomes within a few hours. For most of them, it is their first experience of playing/making (what was formerly known as) a record. We have released some of the results in the form of (data) compilations [8].

Acknowledgements

I appreciate all of the members of the Re-inventing the Wheel project and colleagues at IAMAS, as well as the organizers of Materializing Exhibition III and the staff of NTT InterCommunication Center. The work was supported by JSPS KAKENHI Grant Numbers JP17H04772, JP15K12842.

References

1. Ron Cowen. 2012. Archaeologist of Sound. *Science* 335, 6066: 278-280.
2. Anthony Dunne and Fiona Raby. 2013. *Speculative everything: design, fiction, and social dreaming*. MIT Press, Cambridge, MA.
3. Neil Gershenfeld. 2005. *Fab: The Coming Revolution on Your Desktop--from Personal Computers to Personal Fabrication*. Basic Books, New York, NY.
4. Erkki Huhtamo, ed. 2011. *Media archeology: Approaches, applications, and implications*. University of California Press, Berkeley CA.
5. Kazuhiro Jo and Mitsuhito Ando. 2013. Cutting record--a record without (or with) prior acoustic information. In *Proceedings of NIME*, 283-286.
6. Kazuhiro Jo. 2014. The role of mechanical reproduction in (what was formerly known as) the record in the age of personal fabrication. *Leonardo Music Journal* 24: 65–67.
7. Kazuhiro Jo (jojporg). 2013. How to Make a Record without Prior Acoustic Information. Retrieved January 1st, 2018 from http://www.instructables.com/id/How-to-make-a-record-without-prior-acoustic-inform/
8. Kazuhiro Jo (jojporg). 2013. Cutting records .0---records without prior acoustic information. Retrieved January 1st, 2018 from http://www.thingiverse.com/thing:51923
9. Thomas Y. Levin. 2003. "Tones from out of Nowhere": Rudolph Pfenninger and the Archaeology of Synthetic Sound. *Grey Room* 12 (Summer 2003): 32-79.
10. László Moholy-Nagy. 1923/1989. New Plasticism in Music. Possibilities of the Gramophone. In *Broken Music: Artists' Recordworks*, Ursula Block and Michael Glasmeier (Eds.). Berliner Kunstlerprogramm des Daad and gelbe Musik, Berlin, Germany, 53-58.

Objektivisering: Text Physicalization and Self-introspective Post-digital Objecthood.

Marinos Koutsomichalis
Norwegian University of Science and Technology
Trondheim 7034, Norway
marinos@marinoskoutsomichalis.com

TEI '18, March 18–21, 2018, Stockholm, Sweden
ACM 978-1-4503-5568-1/18/03.
https://doi.org/10.1145/3173225.3173301

Abstract

Objektivisering is an experimental system for the computational modeling of generative 3D-printable models. The system pivots on Natural Language Understanding technologies and big 3D data. It processes arbitrary text input, eventually generating an array of words and phrases that summarise its meaning. These are then used as queries to retrieve 3D data from Thingiverse. Finally, the resulting bag of models is concatenated, in this way producing original 3D-printable designs in a computational fashion. Albeit being concretely physical, the resulting artefacts also incorporate the cybernetic encodings of their own making. They celebrate a certain kind of objecthood which is hybrid, post-digital, and self-introspective at a structural level, in this way concretely accelerating materialist aesthetics.

Author Keywords

Natural Language Processing; postdigital objecthood; 3D printing; generative solid modelling; new materialisms.

Introduction

Data physicalization is relevant to miscellaneous artistic, functional, and scientific milieus. It comprises a wide array of practices [10, 1] ranging from straightforward, InfoVIS-inspired, ones that prioritise readability and the dissemination of information [24], to ones revolving around more liberal, and abstract, mappings that rather promote per-

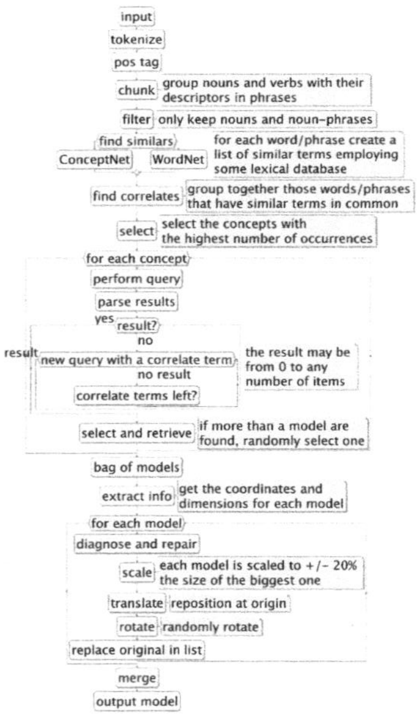

Figure 1: The complete algorithm.

sonalised readings and self-reflection [11, 23], to ones that emphasise participation and community-specific interaction [18]. With a few exceptional cases [22, 13], however, relevant endeavors tend to largely concern numerical kinds of data.

Objectivisering concerns the computational production of 3D-printable objects—such as the ones illustrated in figure 2. The endeavor employs bespoke software that processes arbitrary text input, collapsing it into a series of key words, or phrases, that are, then, used as queries in order to retrieve 3D data from Thingiverse—an online repository containing a few millions 3D models[1]. These models are, then, concatenated to produce new, original, models to be digitally fabricated. *Objectivisering* is intended as a hands-on material interrogation zeroing in on non-numerical kinds of data and, to boot, the technologies we rely upon to retrieve, process, and instantiate them. In particular, it zooms in natural language, big 3D data, lexical databases, and networks for semantic analysis. In line with an explicit materialist approach, the resulting artifacts are meant as posing, looking into, and fumbling about the technological affordancies of their own making.

Technical affairs

The entire algorithm is given in compact form in figure 1. It can be thought of as comprising three stages:

Natural Language Understanding the input is parsed and processed, resulting in a bag of nouns and noun-phrases; co-reference chains are resolved (by means of semantic analysis) to produce nested lists of associated words/phrases and similar terms; then, the lists associated with the 'concepts' occurring more often are passed to the next stage.

[1] https://www.thingiverse.com Accessed October 27, 2017

Figure 2: Examples of generated artifacts.

Mine 3D data 3D data are queried and retrieved from Thingiverse.

Synthesis downloaded models are scaled, rotated, translated and, eventually, synthesised into new digital artefacts.

The system is implemented in Python, employing the Natural Language Toolkit (NLTK) [5] and relying on either ConceptNet [20], or WordNet [15], for semantic analysis and the resolution of co-reference chains. The first stages in the pipeline comprise a module for Natural Language Understanding (NLU) designed taking into account relevant research [3, 17, 4, 6, 14] and, most importantly, heuristics brought forth while interacting with Thingiverse, and, secondarily, ConceptNet and WordNet. The latter tend to 'disregard', to a greater or lesser extend, the intended, human-specific, situated and contextualised, semantics of a concept, rather responding according to schemata laid out by the available 3D data and inherent technological quirks.

Thingiverse typically responds with 3D data that are too

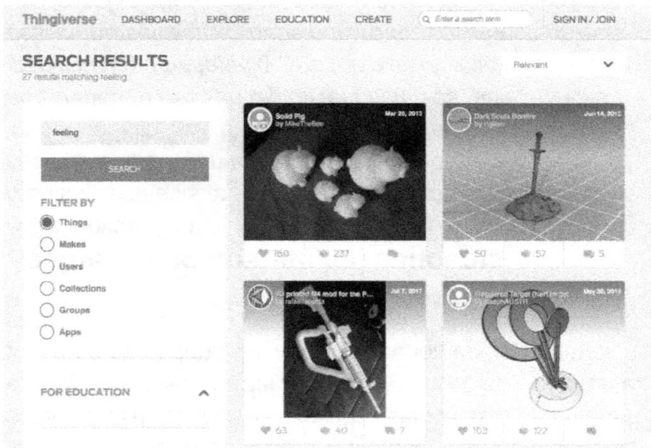

Figure 3: Thingiverse's responses tend to be too implicit.

broadly, or too implicitly, related with the connotations of the original query—see, for instance, figure 3. Peers do not have to adhere to any code of conduct regarding what kinds of objects they should upload, or how should they name and annotate them. Accordingly, content and associated meta-data are constantly forged with respect to trending popular culture, maker ideologies and thematic inclinations, fashion, and all sorts of other topical cultural veins. Then, both ConceptNet and WordNet, often respond with concepts that are too broad, too implicit, too context-dependent, or simply relevant to a non-intended reading of the original narrative. It is exactly due to such technological, and maybe cultural, shortcomings, that a materialist introspection of the production process becomes possible. Neither the extracted words/phrases, nor their resulting bag of models, *represent* or *describe* the original narrative. They rather exemplify how it is *interpreted* by virtue of an intelligent system that adheres to own congenital peculiarities and, more importantly, that draws on emergent,

Figure 4: Individuals reflecting upon the generated artefacts.

decentralised, and dynamically ever-changing patterns (big 3D data and their associated meta-data).

Conceptually, and aesthetically, this venture claims artistic legitimacy on top of contextual ambiguities, and technical shortcomings, of the sort. However, too abstract, or entirely random, behaviour is not desired. The bag of models retrieved from Thingiverse must be surprising enough to allow for a materialist technological introspection, they should, nonetheless, remain coherent and loosely related to their associated queries. Heuristics seem to testify what is required in order to arrive at useful results, in a nutshell: fewer verbs, more nouns, less abstract queries. The software has been implemented along these lines.

Results

Figure 5 illustrates examples of synthesised models. A series of fabricated 3D printed artefacts are illustrated in figures 6–9. Arguably, such artefacts are original, surprising, and indicative of a generative process. A mixed group of individuals has been asked—in a largely informal context as shown in figure 4—to reflect upon such objects, to write

Figure 6: Input text is an excerpt from Asimov's novel *The End Of Eternity*, referring to the operation of a time-travel machine [2, p. 7]. Largest dimension: $27cm$

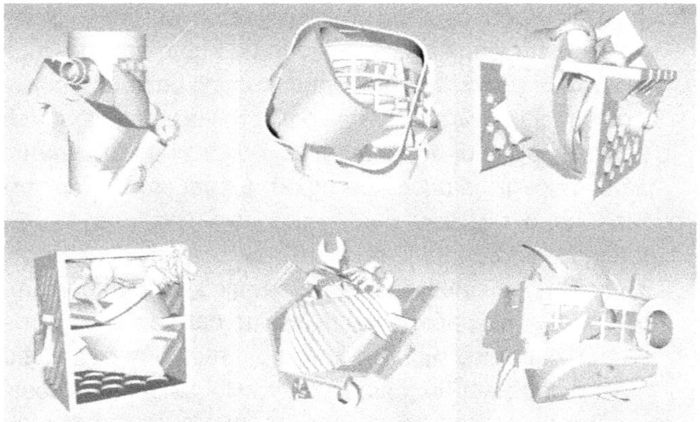

Figure 5: Examples of generated models.

down the words, thoughts and images that sprung in their minds, and to attempt to match them with their originating texts. Their responses seem to suggest that, up to a certain extent, those artefacts still reverberate aspects of their generating narrative. Further research is necessary, of course, to better understand the kinds of phenomenological processes at play.

Aesthetic and post-digital concerns

Albeit physical, in the most literal sense of the word, the resulting artefacts are embedded with the cybernetic encodings of their own making. They celebrate a cybernetic 'neomateriality', which captures "*an objecthood that incorporates networked digital technologies*" and "*reveals its own coded materiality and the way in which digital processes perceive and shape our world*" [19]. Such objects *are* digital information that can be archived, retrieved and re-produced at will, in the very same fashion that digital images [9], or digital audio does [12]. To boot, they are physically *present* in all possible ways: they are situated, tan-

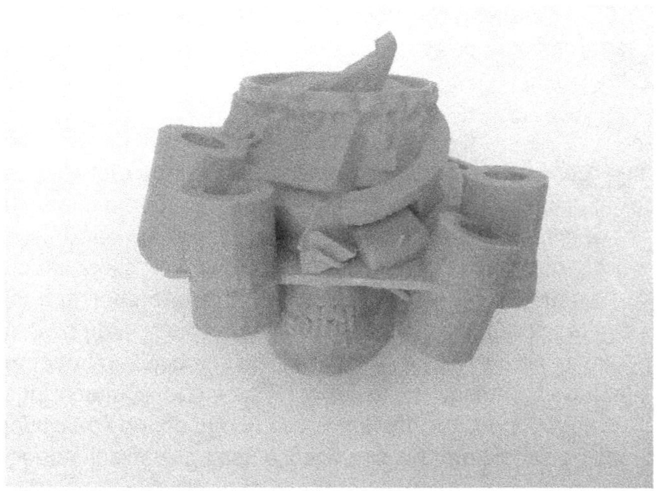

Figure 7: The input text is a several paragraphs long excerpt from Greg Egan's sci-fi novel *Diaspora*, describing the process of "*Orphanogenesis*"—that is, the birth of new software-based form of life from a previously unused "*seed*" [8, p. 3]. Largest dimension: $20cm$.

Figure 8: Input text: *"The mass of men lead lives of quiet desperation. What is called resignation is confirmed desperation. [. . .] A stereotyped but unconscious despair is concealed even under what are called the games and amusements of mankind"* [25, p. 12]. Largest dimension: $25cm$

Figure 9: Input text is an excerpt discussing contemporary representations of finance [21]. Largest dimension: $6cm$

gible, having mass, producing sound when hit—they even smell in very characteristic ways and depending, of course, on the kind of filament use. Still they can be, re-produced and re-instantiated in-situ with respect to localised technologies for digital fabrication. Such objects are physical *not despite* being digital but, instead, *because of, and in addition to*, it.

In light of such a hybrid objecthood, the technicalities discussed in the previous section are understood as requisite conditions bringing forth a materialist introspection at a structural level. It is exactly because the retrieved bag of models mostly comprises arbitrary, ambiguous, and 'nerdy' kinds of models, that the generated artefacts eventually succeed in surprising us, and, more importantly, that they do foreground their own cybernetic encodings. Their very structure is self-introspective, in that it points back to the technologies and databases—that is, the material basis—responsible for their own making, as well as to all those broader cultural veins associated with them. Moreover, it introduces a wide array of ideological and micro-political affairs associated with the technological layers at play. 3D-printed objects are not 'ordinary' objects; they are implicit, or explicit, calls to either DIY micro-fabrication, p2p sharing, political activism, 'start-up' entrepreneurship, or socially-empowered hacking [7, 16, 26]. In this sense, the resulting artefacts can be said to aestheticise both their own making, as well as the politics of their own making.

Indeed, both the produced artefacts, and the underlying algorithm, pivot on technologies that accelerate openness, participation, and open-sourcing. Potential audiences do not simply involve passive viewers in a gallery setting, but, additionally, all sorts of experts that are interested in extending, or building upon, it to design own systems for generative modelling of objects, 'users', that dynamically interact with the system to spawn new models, and 'makers', that are interested in fabricating designs others have generated (which, of course, they appreciate as worth having). This situation evidently disrupts the traditional Romantic view of the artist as the unique keeper of some special know-how, exhibiting their work to an audience unaware of the technicalities involved. This case is much more ambiguous and much more complex: the know-how is largely distributed or open-sourced, and audiences are not simply potentially knowledgeable, but also implicitly challenged to *use*, or build upon, the system. Accordingly, the traditional gap between poetics and aesthetics is significantly blurred, and the technological specifics of the work become an intrinsic part of the artistic dimension of the work, and, additionally, of any first-person phenomenological experiences of it.

Furthermore, and aesthetic-wise, it is hard not to notice that both the artefacts under scrutiny, and their underlying algorithmic logic, disregard clarity and functionality altogether. Instead, they resonate crudeness of design, hardware glitches, hacking, retro-styling, and abstractness. Indeed, dysfunctional, problematic, and 'hackish' transliterations between textual narratives and 3D data are both accelerated and foregrounded here. To some extent, artistic legitimacy is claimed by virtue of such a 'crude' materialist approach, which is only possible by means of an uncanny discourse between algorithms, data, and humans that mutually 'misinterpret' each other. This opens up the question of ambiguity as a requisite of the system. Here, creativity is established on top of an eclectic 'bag of models', which is neither easy, nor straightforward, to ascribe concrete, or definite, meaning. Accordingly, the algorithm should guarantee that such 'bags' would always be coherent enough—either allowing for 'misinterpretations' of the original narrative, or spawning new narratives altogether—but, at the same time, ever-eclectic, ambiguous, and surprising—so that the resulting objects' structural specifics do point back to the very technologies that brought such ambiguities forth.

Acknowledgements

I would like to thank Prof. Björn Gambäck, both for his valuable feedback, and for granting me the opportunity to work on this project in the first place. I would also like to thank *Commons Lab Heraklion*, where the very first experiments have been 3D-printed.

REFERENCES

1. Jason Alexander, Yvonne Jansen, Kasper Hornbæk, Johan Kildal, and Abhijit Karnik. 2015. Exploring the Challenges of Making Data Physical. In *Proceedings of the 33rd Annual ACM Conference Extended Abstracts on Human Factors in Computing Systems (CHI EA '15)*. ACM, New York, NY, USA, 2417–2420. DOI: http://dx.doi.org/10.1145/2702613.2702659
2. I. Asimov. 2010. *The End of Eternity: A Novel.* Tom Doherty Associates, New York, NY.
3. Regina Barzilay and Michael Elhadad. 1999. Using lexical chains for text summarization. In *Advances in automatic text summarization*, Inderjeet Mani and Mark T. Maybury (Eds.). MIT Press, Cambridge, MA, 111–121.
4. Sabine Bergler, René Witte, Michelle Khalife, Zhuoyan Li, and Frank Rudzicz. 2003. Using knowledge-poor coreference resolution for text summarization. In *Proceedings of Document Understanding Conference*, Vol. 3. Retrieved December 18, 2017 from http://duc.nist.gov/pubs/2003final.papers/concordia.final.pdf.
5. Steven Bird, Ewan Klein, and Edward Loper. 2009. *Natural language processing with Python: analyzing text with the natural language toolkit.* O'Reilly Media, Inc, Sebastopol, CA.
6. Meru Brunn, Yllias Chali, and Christopher J Pinchak. 2001. Text summarization using lexical chains. In *Proceedings of Document Understanding Conference.* Retrieved December 18, 2017 from http://www-nlpir.nist.gov/projects/duc/pubs/2001papers/lethbridge.pdf.
7. Deven R Desai and Gerard N Magliocca. 2013. Patents, meet Napster: 3D printing and the digitization of things. *Geo. LJ* 102 (2013), 1691.
8. G. Egan. 2015. *Diaspora: A Novel.* Skyhorse Publishing Company, New York, NY.
9. Boris Groys. 2008. From Image to Image-File–and Back: Art in the Age of Digitalization. In *Art Power*, Boris Groys (Ed.). MIT Press, Cambridge, MA, 83–91.
10. Yvonne Jansen, Pierre Dragicevic, Petra Isenberg, Jason Alexander, Abhijit Karnik, Johan Kildal, Sriram Subramanian, and Kasper Hornbæk. 2015. Opportunities and Challenges for Data Physicalization. In *Proceedings of the 33rd Annual ACM Conference on Human Factors in Computing Systems (CHI '15).* ACM, New York, NY, USA, 3227–3236. DOI: http://dx.doi.org/10.1145/2702123.2702180
11. Rohit Ashok Khot, Larissa Hjorth, and Florian 'Floyd' Mueller. 2014. Understanding Physical Activity Through 3D Printed Material Artifacts. In *Proceedings of the SIGCHI Conference on Human Factors in Computing Systems (CHI '14).* ACM, New York, NY, USA, 3835–3844. DOI: http://dx.doi.org/10.1145/2556288.2557144

12. Marinos Koutsomichalis. 2016. From music to big music: Listening in the age of big data. *Leonardo Music Journal* 26 (2016), 24–27. DOI: http://dx.doi.org/10.1162/LMJ_a_00962
13. Taekyeom Lee. 2017. New Typographic Experience in the Post-digital Age with 3D Printing and Ceramics. In *International Conference on Applied Human Factors and Ergonomics*. Springer, New York, NY, 161–170. DOI: http://dx.doi.org/10.1007/978-3-319-60495-4_17
14. Hans Peter Luhn. 1958. The automatic creation of literature abstracts. *IBM Journal of research and development* 2, 2 (1958), 159–165. DOI: http://dx.doi.org/10.1147/rd.22.0159
15. George A Miller, Richard Beckwith, Christiane Fellbaum, Derek Gross, and Katherine J Miller. 1990. Introduction to WordNet: An on-line lexical database. *International journal of lexicography* 3, 4 (1990), 235–244. DOI: http://dx.doi.org/10.1093/ijl/3.4.235
16. Jarkko Moilanen, Angela Daly, Ramon Lobato, and Darcy WE Allen. 2015. Cultures of sharing in 3D printing: What can we learn from the licence choices of Thingiverse users? *Journal of Peer Production* 6 (2015). Retrieved December 18, 2017 from https://papers.ssrn.com/sol3/papers.cfm?abstract_id=2440027.
17. Jane Morris and Graeme Hirst. 1991. Lexical Cohesion Computed by Thesaural Relations As an Indicator of the Structure of Text. *Comput. Linguist.* 17, 1 (March 1991), 21–48.
18. Bettina Nissen and John Bowers. 2015. Data-Things: Digital Fabrication Situated Within Participatory Data Translation Activities. In *Proceedings of the 33rd Annual ACM Conference on Human Factors in Computing Systems (CHI '15)*. ACM, New York, NY, USA, 2467–2476. DOI: http://dx.doi.org/10.1145/2702123.2702245
19. Christiane Paul. 2015. From Immateriality to Neomateriality: Art and the Conditions of Digital Materiality. In *Proceedings of the 21st International Symposium on Electronic Art*. Retrieved December 18, 2017 from http://isea2015.org/proceeding/submissions/ISEA2015_submission_154.pdf.
20. Robert Speer and Catherine Havasi. 2013. ConceptNet 5: A large semantic network for relational knowledge. In *The People's Web Meets NLP*. Springer, New York, NY, 161–176. DOI: http://dx.doi.org/10.1007/978-3-642-35085-6_6
21. Nick Srnicek and Alex Williams. 2014. On cunning automata: Financial acceleration and the limits of the dromological. *Collapse: Philosophical Research and Development* 8 (2014), 463–506.
22. Janos Stone. 2010. Systems and methods for transforming and/or generating a tangible physical structure based on user input information. (Aug. 24 2010). US Patent App. 12/862,190.
23. S. Stusak, A. Tabard, F. Sauka, R. A. Khot, and A. Butz. 2014. Activity Sculptures: Exploring the Impact of Physical Visualizations on Running Activity. *IEEE Transactions on Visualization and Computer Graphics* 20, 12 (Dec 2014), 2201–2210. DOI: http://dx.doi.org/10.1109/TVCG.2014.2352953

24. Faisal Taher, John Hardy, Abhijit Karnik, Christian Weichel, Yvonne Jansen, Kasper Hornbæk, and Jason Alexander. 2015. Exploring Interactions with Physically Dynamic Bar Charts. In *Proceedings of the 33rd Annual ACM Conference on Human Factors in Computing Systems (CHI '15)*. ACM, New York, NY, USA, 3237–3246. DOI: http://dx.doi.org/10.1145/2702123.2702604

25. H.D. Thoreau. 2010. *Walden*. Pan Macmillan, Longon, UK.

26. Amanda Williams, Alicia Gibb, and David Weekly. 2012. Research with a Hacker Ethos: What DIY Means for Tangible Interaction Research. *interactions* 19, 2 (March 2012), 14–19. DOI: http://dx.doi.org/10.1145/2090150.2090156

DeepWear: a Case Study of Collaborative Design between Human and Artificial Intelligence

Natsumi Kato*
University of Tsukuba
Hiroyuki Osone*
University of Tsukuba
Daitetsu Sato
University of Tsukuba

Naoya Muramatsu
University of Tsukuba
Yoichi Ochiai
University of Tsukuba

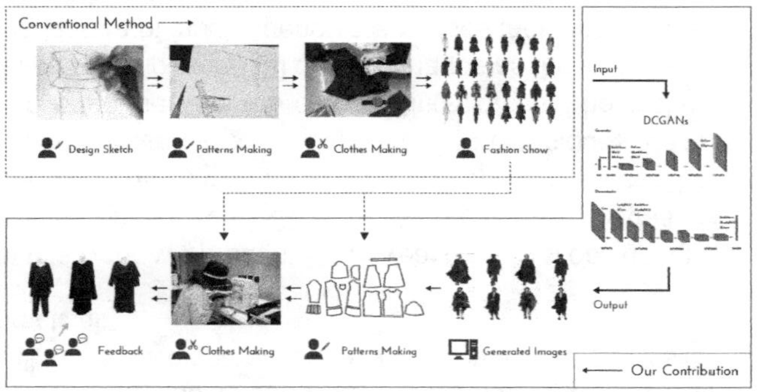

Figure 1: Our system's workflow. Conventional fashion design is a feedback loop. First, designers make their clothes design. Next, patterners draw patterns from the design and designers instrucion. The We use DCGANs to make new feedback loop. Fashion design process In this process, making design inspiration easier for designers.

*Kato and Osone are equally contributed to this paper.

TEI '18, March 18–21, 2018, Stockholm, Sweden
ACM 978-1-4503-5568-1/18/03.
https://doi.org/10.1145/3173225.3173302

Abstract
Deep neural networks (DNNs) applications are now increasingly pervasive and powerful. However, fashion designers are lagging behind in leveraging this increasingly common technology. DNNs are not yet a standard part of fashion de sign practice, either clothes patterns or prototyping tools. In this paper, we present DeepWear, a method using deep convolutional generative adversarial networks for clothes design. The DNNs learn the feature of specific brand clothes and generate images then patterns instructed from the images are made, and an author creates clothes based on that. We evaluated this system by evaluating the credibility of the actual sold clothes on market with our clothes. As the result, we found it is possible to make clothes look like actual products from the generated images. Our findings have implications for collaborative design between machine and human intelligence.

Author Keywords
Fashion; Creativity support; DCGANs.

Introduction
Recent advances in computational fabrication have afforded the opportunity to use automated tools and machines to support fashion design. However, obtaining inspiration of fashion design is still a difficult task. To address this challenge, there are projects to improve the process by incorpo-

rating DNNs into fashion design, such as Project Muze[1] or Amazon's AI [14]. Project Muze use DNNs to learn the trend and design clothes. Amazon's DNNs are GANs based architecture. To internalize properties of a particular style simply by looking at many examples and apply that style to existing clothing. However, there are articles [22, 25] which doubt as to whether the styles created by Project Muze are actually that people can wear. Also, since Amazon's AI is still in the development stage, these projects are not still practical.

In this work, we present DeepWear, practical designing clothes system use DCGANs [23] to generate images and designers make clothes by receiving instruction from those images. State-of-the-art deep learning techniques are first applied to the workflow of designing clothes. The system takes specific brand [2] clothes images as the input, learns the feature of inputs, generates images that looks close to the clothes, then patterns instructed from the images are made, and an author creates clothes based on that.

In the evaluation, we conduct a content analysis about the theme related to our system practicality by comparing the actually sold clothes with our clothes and other brand clothes by questioning which are the actually sold the specific brand clothes. The results show that our system is possible to make clothes look like actual products from the generated images. This paper shows the implications for collaborative design between machine and human intelligence.

Related Works

Image Generation

Recently, the deep generation model has attracted a lot of attention and the ability to learn large (unlabeled) data potential and vitality [3, 24]. In [7], the deep belief net (DBN) using a contrast divergence algorithm was initially proposed to efficiently training. denoising autoencoder (DAE) learns data distribution with supervised learning method [3]. Both DBN and DAE learn the low dimensional representation (encoding) of each data instance and generate from the decode network. In recent years, Variational AutoEncoder (VAE) combine deep learning and statistical inference for represent data instances in a latent [13] hidden space while utilizing a deep neural network for nonlinear mapping is used. All of these generation models are trained by maximizing the possibility of training data i.e. generative adversarial networks (GANs) [6] are generative model which are minimax game between generator model and discriminator model. This framework avoids the difficulty of maximum likelihood learning and has remarkable success in natural image generation [4].

GANs show impressive results in image generation [4], image transfer [11, 30], super resolution [15] and many other generation tasks. DCGANs utilize deep convolutional networks architecture and batch normalization [10] to extract the feature [23], and show significantly great output. Therefore, in this study, we used DCGANs architecture for image generation network.

Machine Intelligence Creativity Support

In other than fashion design, there are researches to support human creative activities by incorporating machine intelligence. AutoDraw is a new kind of drawing tool that combines machine learning and drawing of an artist so that anyone can create something visual quickly [9]. User experience designers integrate machine learning services in new apps, devices, and systems [5, 28]. Many studies have been issued for the purpose of supporting the creation of cartoons and animation. There are systems that inputs black-and-white line drawing manga images and automatically outputs colored images [29]. In order to support character design, there is research to automatically generate facial images using GANs [12]. The method to identify structural lines from pattern-rich cartoons without being conscious of patterns is developed [18]. Extracting structural lines from pattern-rich manga is an important step for transferring legacy manga to the digital domain.

Machine Intelligence & Fashion Design
There are several works trying to support or recommend everyday life fashion design [26]. Especially, there are many recommendation[19, 20] or classification systems [21, 27]. Heterogeneous graphs to link fashion items, make up stylish costumes, and link items to their attributes are used [16]. In [8], a tensor decomposition approach is proposed to recommend a set of fashion items. Rather than learning item features based on sets, use discrete item attributes or low-level image features. In [17], implemented a representation learning framework for fashion items that includes latent styles in which learned expressions are shared by items in the style set.

Research AI fashion design. Project Muze [1] is based on Google's open source TensorFlow[1]. It is developed as a predictive design engine. It consists of two parts: neural networks and a set of aesthetic parameters. The neural network learn the color, texture and style preferences of over 600 fashion experts. Over time, it learned to connect those preferences to other people with similar interests. Then a set of aesthetic parameters from the Google Fashion Trends Report and Zalando's[2] deep knowledge of fashion trends is used to refine the designs and make sure they're fashion forward. However, there are articles doubt whether the styles created by Project Muze are actually the structures that people actually can wear [22, 25]. Amazon's Project use GANs based DNNs architecture [14] internalize properties of a particular style simply by looking at many examples and apply that style to existing clothing. Amazon's AI is still in the development stage, and these projects are not yet practical.

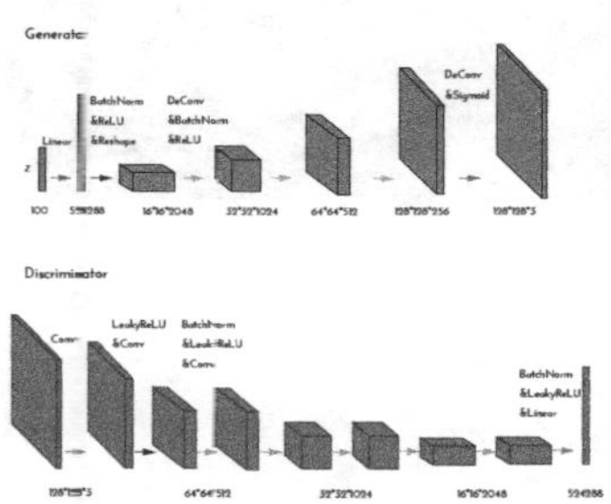

Figure 2: Our Networks

[1]https://github.com/tensorflow/tensorflow (last accessed January 9, 2018)

[2]https://www.zalando.co.uk (last accessed January 9, 2018)

In summary, our approach is distinct from the above in that we aim to make practically usable clothes from a specific brand clothes dataset. Our approach captures fashion semantics on the style space, which can be effectively utilized by fashion design systems. We asked patterners to write a pattern based on the generated image, and investigated whether we could actually make clothes. Finally, we implemented clothes based on that pattern and user-studied the quality.

Deep Convolutional Generative Adversarial Networks

Deep Convolutional Generative Adversarial Networks (DCGANs) is a neural networks that has been popular in recent years. This lets the network learn to generate data with the same internal structure as other data (Figure 2). One of the most common applications is image generation. The Generative adversarial network consists of a generator network *G* and a discriminator network *D*. Given training data *x*, *G* will take input from random noise *z* and try to generate data with distribution similar to *x*. The discriminator network *D* receives inputs from both *x* and the generated from *G* and estimate the probability that the sample came from the training data, not *G*. *G* and *D* are trained at the same time: Adjust the parameters of *D* to maximize the probability of assigning the correct label to both the training example and the *G* sample, and adjust the parameters of *G* to minimize $\log(1-D(G(z))$. In other words, *D* and *G* play the following two player min-max game with value function $V(G,D)$ (1).

$$\min_G \max_D V(D,G) = E_{x \sim p_{data}(x)}\big[\log D(x)\big] + E_{z \sim p_z(z)}\big[\log(1 - D(G(z)))\big] \quad (1)$$

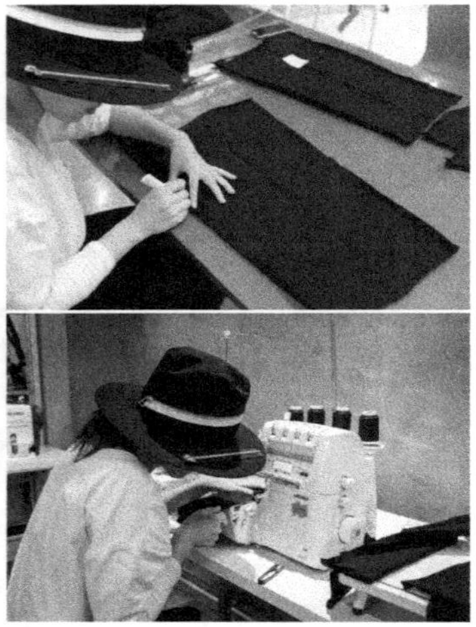

Figure 3: Making clothes from patterns.

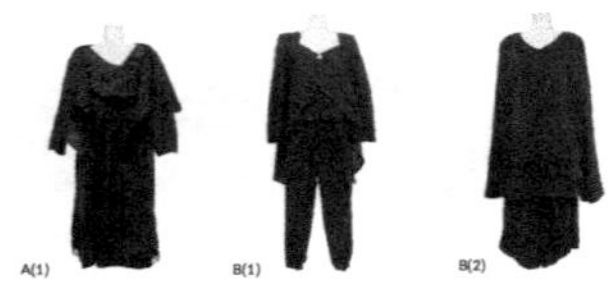

Figure 4: Our system's output clothes.

data collection
We collected images of a specific brand announced between 2014 and 2017. We used web scraping Python code to create the training dataset. Scraping consists of three steps. In the first step, follow the link from the top page of the target website. Second, we list all HTML pages with the URL structure as directory structures. Then, we acquire all the image URLs specified by *src* of the *img* tag in the HTML pages detected in the second step. In the third step, we downloaded all image URLs. In order to prevent overloading the server, we restricted the request to 10 times / 1 s. For pages that restricted crawler behavior by robots.txt, we followed that restriction. As the result, over 1.1K images were collected. Several steps were performed to learn the feature of the images. We paint the background white so that only people and clothes are cut out, and processed it into full color image of 128 px x 128 px (resized dataset is here.[3] (last accessed January 9, 2018)).

Training
We implemented our network with Chainer[4], a deep learning framework. We followed implementation and training procedure recent work by Radford et al. [23]. Our network architecture is shown in Figure 2, where training was done with a batch size of 7, using Adam with hyperparameters (α=0.0002, $\beta_1 = 0.5$, $\beta_2 = 0.999$, $\epsilon = 1e-08$), and run on an NVIDIA Titan X GPU for 1000 epochs. We stopped running around 43000 iteration (about 270 peoch), because the loss has become quite small and generated images looks good. At the 43,000 iteration, G loss is 16.1374, D loss is 1.39158.

Clothing implementation

Draw Patterns
Seven participants(6 females and 1 male) aged between 21 and 23 years partcipated. They experienced fashion design patterners and had clothing experience of 1 year and a half to 5 years (Patterners are people who draw patterns of clothes based on instructions from designers). We ask them to draw patterns based on images generated by DCGANs. This work were done under the presence of an author or by online calls. We set time limit 70 minutes for all subjects. The pattern created for the first was the image in Figure 5 A, the second pattern was asked to draw the pattern based on the image selected by each subject (shown in Figure 5 B). Subjects were asked to use writing tools such as rulers and pencils are usually used when drawing patterns. Actually, they made a pattern of size within the required time, not full size sufficient to make clothes. The patterns that the patterner drew based on the image we specified are the Figure 5 A, and drew based on the images selected by each are the Figure 5 B. The numbers (1) - (7) are the numbers of the subjects. Based on the generated image, the patterners drew patterns with each idea. In A, 4 out of 7 of the subjects drew a pattern of a combination of a one-piece dress and outer. Two subjects drew a one-piece dress pattern. One person drew a pattern of tops, skirts, and outer combinations. Six subjects drew one-piece dress patterns.

Make Clothes from the Patterns
Based on the pattern that the patterner handwritten, tracing with Illustrator, converting it to data, making it the size of the

[3]https://drive.google.com/open?id=0BywMLxsmMEnROGNKZzAtVkR3aFE

[4]https://github.com/chainer/chainer https://drive.google.com/open?id=0BywMLxsmMEnROGNKZzAtVkR3aFE (last accessed January 9, 2018)

Figure 5: Patterns made from the patterners. A patterns are drawn from same image by each patterners, B patterns are drawn from what patterners selected.

full size that can be worn as clothes. Then, using two kinds of black cloth, an author made three kinds of clothes from drawn pattern by two subjects. The working time was about 50 hours.

We found that the silhouette considerably. Figure 4 shows images of clothes. A (1) and B (1) are produced based on the pattern made by subject 1 pattern and B (2) are based on subject 2 pattern.

A (1), B (1) are clothes made using black cotton sheeting, B (2) has a shiny feeling and is made from a heavy black cloth. Sheeting is a cloth generally used for prototypes, the density of weaving is low, breathable fabric and thin. B (2) was made with a heavy, shiny, soft-touching and thick cloth. The concept of the brand used as data set of the generated image is to break the stereotype of gender by incorporating the style of male clothes into women's clothes. One of its characteristics is that clothes are oversize. Looking at the output clothes, the B (2) made of a heavy black cloth dropped down the silhouette of the entire clothing than the A (1) and A (2) made of the sheeting. Therefore, we think that making clothes with a heavy black cloth was able to capture the characteristics of the original data brand.

Qualification & User Reaction

We conducted an experiment to evaluate whether the image generated from DNNs can be instruction sources for creating a new clothes. The experiment is evaluating the quality of the actually sold clothes on market with our clothes and the other brand clothes.

Participants
Thirty two people who didn't experience clothes design (14 females, 18 males) aged between 19 and 61 years (M = 24.3, SD = 8.96) answered this questionnaire.

				Ave
Other	80 (1)	78 (5)	97 (7)	85
DeepWear	121 (3)	87 (6)	107 (8)	105(+23.5%)
Source brand	131 (2)	120 (4)	115 (9)	122(+43.5%)

Table 1: The result of the questionnaire that to distinguish the source brand clothes.

Experimental Design
We prepared images of the source brand and output of our method and clothes images of other brands[5][6][7], respectively three. To the subjects, six clothes of the source brand were first exemplified. After that, we asked clothing images one by one in random order and evaluated whether or not the displayed image can be seen closer to the product of the source brand in 7 stages of 1 (looks different) to 7 (looks learning source brand).

Result & Discussion
An weighted averages of these results are shown in the Table 1. For the costumes designed based on our system, they are understood that the subjects were more impressed by the learning source brand and ours than the other brand costumes. In addition, we have shown that our output is close enough to the learning source brand, as the output costumes are significantly closer to the learning source brand than other brand costumes. Looking at the answers of the subjects, the clothes that were judged to be most similar to the clothes of the original brand were the output of our system (Table 1: (3)) and the clothes of the actual learning source brand.

[5]https://page.auctions.yahoo.co.jp/jp/auction/v499221070
[6]https://page.auctions.yahoo.co.jp/jp/auction/260446858
[7]https://page.auctions.yahoo.co.jp/jp/auction/m218550387 (last accessed January 9, 2018)

Figure 6: Wearing DeepWear.

The concept of the brand is to emphasize genderless design, however for image 6, we think that the chest race was emphasized as a feminine design, so it doesn't look like the brand. It is difficult for a patterner to judge detailed details from the generated image, and we thought that the difference has come out by the intention of the patterner entering the design. From the above, since the silhouette of the clothing is greatly different depending on the cloth used as the material, we consider important to choose which cloth to use in order to make clothes similar to genuine brand clothes. In addition, many of the clothing of the learning source brand are black in color and simple design, so texture of the cloth is more emphasized. Also, garments made entirely with large silhouettes tended to resemble real ones.

Patterners Feedback to Experiment
We took a questionnaire on how the patterner sees the answer to this experiment.

Some of a kind are quite simple clothes, but if they are not similar, looking at the whole and putting effort into detail such as frills are attached to the front neck.

(Patterner 1: Male, 21, design experience 1 and half years)

I think that the judgment criteria of similarity or dissimilarity are mainly the length and the whole image. I thought that it was judged by those with a center of gravity on the upper body were not judged to be similar, the lower body had a center of gravity, and those with a long sense of resemblance were similar. Also, I think that it was difficult to judge that many cases of the brand have the similarities like oversize, straight line, and big silhouette image because the waistline of other companies' brand products is narrow.

(Patterner 2: Female, 22, design experience 3 years)

I think that the feature of the specific brand's design is silhouette that is comfortable between the body and clothes, so I think that such a silhouette design was chosen as the brand. I felt that the thing judged not to be similar was judged that detail or material are not like the brand. I thought that the brand does not have much design of material like organza decorated with neck tuck.

(Patterner 3: Female, 22, design experience 5 years)

Conclusion

DNNs are now a fairly established technology, and fashion designers have begun to integrate DNNs application into the things that they design. This paper presents a system conducted with application DCGANs to design clothes in practice. When asked the patterner to write a pattern based on the generated image, a pattern which can actually make clothes was created after obtaining a good response from the patterner to the work. Finally, we implemented clothes based on that pattern and we conducted a user study on that quality, and found that the clothes made by DeepWear are high quality clothes. Our findings show that our system enable collaborative design between machine and human intelligence. We expand on these findings to present a series of challenges for DNNs and fashion design research.

Video link (https://youtu.be/pVlLwvRVdb8)

REFERENCES

1. 2016. PROJECT MUZE. (2016). Retrieved September 15, 2017 from `https://projectmuze.squarespace.com`.
2. 2017. FASHION PRESS. (2017). Retrieved September 15, 2017 from `https://megalodon.jp/2018-0108-0109-31/https://www.fashion-press.net:443/collections/brand/42`.

3. Yoshua Bengio, Li Yao, Guillaume Alain, and Pascal Vincent. 2013. Generalized denoising auto-encoders as generative models. In *Advances in Neural Information Processing Systems*. 899–907.
4. Emily L Denton, Soumith Chintala, Rob Fergus, and others. 2015. Deep Generative Image Models using a Laplacian Pyramid of Adversarial Networks. In *Advances in neural information processing systems*. 1486–1494.
5. Graham Dove, Kim Halskov, Jodi Forlizzi, and John Zimmerman. 2017. UX Design Innovation: Challenges for Working with Machine Learning as a Design Material. In *Proceedings of the 2017 CHI Conference on Human Factors in Computing Systems*. ACM, 278–288.
6. Ian Goodfellow, Jean Pouget-Abadie, Mehdi Mirza, Bing Xu, David Warde-Farley, Sherjil Ozair, Aaron Courville, and Yoshua Bengio. 2014. Generative adversarial nets. In *Advances in neural information processing systems*. 2672–2680.
7. Geoffrey E Hinton, Simon Osindero, and Yee-Whye Teh. 2006. A fast learning algorithm for deep belief nets. *Neural computation* 18, 7 (2006), 1527–1554.
8. Yang Hu, Xi Yi, and Larry S Davis. 2015. Collaborative fashion recommendation: A functional tensor factorization approach. In *Proceedings of the 23rd ACM international conference on Multimedia*. ACM, 129–138.
9. Google Inc. 2017. AutoDraw. (2017). Retrieved September 18, 2017 from `https://www.autodraw.com`.
10. Sergey Ioffe and Christian Szegedy. 2015. Batch normalization: Accelerating deep network training by reducing internal covariate shift. In *International Conference on Machine Learning*. 448–456.
11. Phillip Isola, Jun-Yan Zhu, Tinghui Zhou, and Alexei A Efros. 2016. Image-to-image translation with conditional adversarial networks. *arXiv preprint arXiv:1611.07004* (2016).
12. Yanghua Jin, Jiakai Zhang, Minjun Li, Yingtao Tian, Huachun Zhu, and Zhihao Fang. 2017. Towards the Automatic Anime Characters Creation with Generative Adversarial Networks. *arXiv preprint arXiv:1708.05509* (2017).
13. Diederik Kingma and Jimmy Ba. 2014. Adam: A method for stochastic optimization. *arXiv preprint arXiv:1412.6980* (2014).
14. Will Knight. 2017. Amazon Has Developed an AI Fashion Designer. (24 August 2017). Retrieved September 15, 2017 from `https://www.technologyreview.com/s/608668/amazon-has-developed-an-ai-fashion-designer/`.
15. Christian Ledig, Lucas Theis, Ferenc Huszár, Jose Caballero, Andrew Cunningham, Alejandro Acosta, Andrew Aitken, Alykhan Tejani, Johannes Totz, Zehan Wang, and others. 2016. Photo-realistic single image super-resolution using a generative adversarial network. *arXiv preprint arXiv:1609.04802* (2016).
16. Hanbit Lee and Sang-goo Lee. 2015. Style Recommendation for Fashion Items using Heterogeneous Information Network.. In *RecSys Posters*.
17. Hanbit Lee, Jinseok Seol, and Sang-goo Lee. 2017. Style2Vec: Representation Learning for Fashion Items from Style Sets. *arXiv preprint arXiv:1708.04014* (2017).

18. Chengze Li, Xueting Liu, and Tien-Tsin Wong. 2017. Deep extraction of manga structural lines. *ACM Transactions on Graphics (TOG)* 36, 4 (2017), 117.

19. Zequn Li, Honglei Li, and Ling Shao. 2016. Improving Online Customer Shopping Experience with Computer Vision and Machine Learning Methods. In *International Conference on HCI in Business, Government and Organizations*. Springer, 427–436.

20. Qiang Liu, Shu Wu, and Liang Wang. 2017. DeepStyle: Learning User Preferences for Visual Recommendation. In *Proceedings of the 40th International ACM SIGIR Conference on Research and Development in Information Retrieval*. ACM, 841–844.

21. Ziwei Liu, Ping Luo, Shi Qiu, Xiaogang Wang, and Xiaoou Tang. 2016. Deepfashion: Powering robust clothes recognition and retrieval with rich annotations. In *Proceedings of the IEEE Conference on Computer Vision and Pattern Recognition*. 1096–1104.

22. Sarah Perez. 2016. Google's new Project Muze proves machines aren't that great at fashion design. (2 September 2016). Retrieved September 18, 2017 from `https://projectmuze.squarespace.com`.

23. Alec Radford, Luke Metz, and Soumith Chintala. 2015. Unsupervised representation learning with deep convolutional generative adversarial networks. *arXiv preprint arXiv:1511.06434* (2015).

24. Ruslan Salakhutdinov. 2009. *Learning deep generative models*. University of Toronto.

25. Brittany Vincent. 2016. Google's Project Muze creates unwearable fashion pieces. (2 September 2016). Retrieved September 18, 2017 from `https://www.engadget.com:443/2016/09/02/googles-project-muze-creates-unwearable-fashion-pieces/`.

26. Haosha Wang and Khaled Rasheed. 2014. Artificial intelligence in clothing fashion. In *Proceedings on the International Conference on Artificial Intelligence (ICAI)*. The Steering Committee of The World Congress in Computer Science, Computer Engineering and Applied Computing (WorldComp), 1.

27. Lixuan Yang, Helena Rodriguez, Michel Crucianu, and Marin Ferecatu. 2017. Fully Convolutional Network with Superpixel Parsing for Fashion Web Image Segmentation. In *International Conference on Multimedia Modeling*. Springer, 139–151.

28. Qian Yang. 2017. The Role of Design in Creating Machine-Learning-Enhanced User Experience. (2017).

29. Taizan Yonetsuji. 2017. PaintsChainer. (2017). Retrieved September 18, 2017 from `https://paintschainer.preferred.tech/index_en.html`.

30. Jun-Yan Zhu, Taesung Park, Phillip Isola, and Alexei A Efros. 2017. Unpaired image-to-image translation using cycle-consistent adversarial networks. *arXiv preprint arXiv:1703.10593* (2017).

Op 1254: Music for Neutrons, Networks and Solenoids using a Restored Organ in a Nuclear Reactor

Leif Handberg
KTH Royal Institute of Technology
Stockholm, Sweden
leifh@kth.se
Ludvig Elblaus
KTH Royal Institute of Technology
Stockholm, Sweden
elblaus@kth.se
Chris Chafe
Center for Computer Research in Music and Acoustics (CCRMA)
Stanford University, USA
cc@ccrma.stanford.edu
Elliot Kermit Canfield-Dafilou
Center for Computer Research in Music and Acoustics (CCRMA)
Stanford University, USA
kermit@ccrma.stanford.edu

TEI 2018, March 18–21, 2018, Stockholm, Sweden.
ACM ISBN 978-1-4503-5568-1/18/03.
http://dx.doi.org/10.1145/3173225.3173304

Abstract

In this paper, an installation is presented that connects Stanford and Stockholm through a one-of-a-kind combination of instrument and venue: the Skandia Wurlitzer theatre organ (Wurlitzer serial no. 1254) situated in the KTH R1 Experimental Performance Space, a disused nuclear reactor. A continuous stream of musical data, audio, and video between the two places explored the capabilities of the digital to play with the concepts of presence and embodiment, virtuality and the physical.

In the installation, a series of performances presented new pieces written especially for this setting. The pieces were performed by musicians in Stanford, mediated in real-time, allowing them to play together with the theatre organ in Stockholm, temporarily fusing the two venues to create one ensemble, one audience, in one space.

Author Keywords

Presence; Musical Instrument; Theatre Organ; Algorithmic Composition; Musification; Mediated Musicianship

Introduction

A century ago, the Mighty Wurlitzer went into production and into thousands of cinemas accompanying silent movies, however it was far from a silent experience. Its sound-producing technology was made from wood and metal,

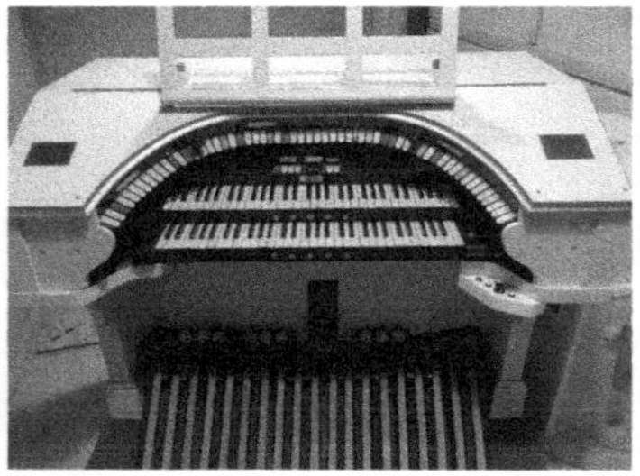

Figure 1: The consol of the Skandia Wurlitzer with registration stops and manuals.

Figure 2: The innards of the Skandia Wurlitzer, showing some of the pipes.

solenoids and pipes. Based on the flute principle, an electric motor was attached to a blower and hundreds of pneumatic valves were operated by an electrically-connected keyboard (flute sound is created by forcing air across a mouthpiece and into a pipe which resonates at a pitch determined by its length). The Wurlitzer Theatre Organ is a descendant of millenia-old instruments massing groups of pipes of different pitches and opening or closing an air supply by way of a manual control (literally, the "manual", see Fig 1).

The Mighty Wurlitzer's earliest predecessor was the *Hydraulis*. Steady air pressure to the pipes was created by dunking an air-filled bladder into water. The music of the Hydraulis and how to play it are obscure, but what we do know is that these instruments were among the most complex mechanisms for their time. This characteristic has put all organs in league with tools for big science. Their operation required devoted practices and skills, technically, artistically, and even ritualistically given historical roles in church music.

Organs evolved to put more and more capability in the hands of a single musician. From Baroque organs to digital synthesizers, the push has been for more pitches, more timbres and more opportunity for solo music to reach the realm of the symphonic orchestration. For cinema accompaniment, the Wurlitzer gained a large percussion section and "foley" sound effects (door bell, horn, etc.).

A set of musical pieces for the Wurlitzer was created for an event which engaged the TEI '18 conference themes to "bring analogue to meet the digital" and foreground "vintage materials and craftsmanship." Elblaus and Chafe wrote music and gathered other musicians for the concert and Handberg curated the special multi-media aspect of the events in KTH R1 subterranean nuclear reactor space.

Handberg and Chafe have collaborated on previous network-based co-located concert co-productions. Using low-latency software for audio and video transmission over research internets (Geant, Internet2), musicians in the KTH R1 performed with musicians in California. Audiences were able to experience shared presence through carefully calibrated camera and video display in which seating arrangements spanned the remote venues [4]. This effect was so seamless that the conjoined audiences spontaneously performed a (transcontinental) "wave." In contrast to this illusory presence, digital technology has also been successfully used to stage the eerie qualities of the removed, the uncanny [3]. Artistically, the installation and concerts explored this continuum, discarding the idea that digital technology is inherently prone to connecting or dividing and acknowledging instead its potentials for exploratory play in the domain of presence.

Two important technical components for the realization of this work are *Jacktrip* and *UltraGrid*. Jacktrip is an open source low-latency uncompressed bi-directional streaming system, with multiple audio channels [2, 1]. UltraGrid is an open source high-definition streaming project intended for concert use and research-grade networks [5].

The venue

The KTH R1 Experimental Performance Space was originally the location for Sweden's first nuclear reactor, the research reactor R1, which was operational between 1954 and 1970, dismounted in 1982 and the space decommissioned in 1993. The space is a research cultural heritage and a manifestation of Sweden's entry into the nuclear age. The researchers called the space "The Cathedral of Science," and it is only fitting that a cathedral is equipped with an organ.

Figure 3: The old relay-based control system.

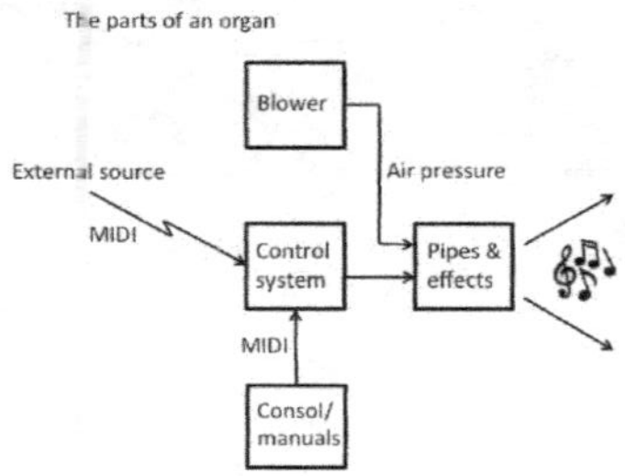

Figure 4: A schematic view of the Skandia Wurlitzer.

In 1998, the R1 Reactor Hall got a new life following a call from Sweden's higher education authority about getting funding to universities for collaboration with artists. The concept of using it as an experimental performance space and creative meeting space has proven successful. Over the years many performances, courses and installations have taken place, quite often as collaborations between the Royal Institute of Technology and the University Colleges of Arts in Stockholm, acknowledging the university motto: "Science and Arts".

Restoring the Organ

The organ has always been an exquisite piece of craftsmanship and engineering. After being dismantled, forgotten, rediscovered, renovated and brought into contact with the digital world, this is even more true.

The Skandia Theatre organ was originally ordered from the Wurlitzer company in 1926 and installed in the Skandia Cinema Theatre, one of the most prominent in Stockholm, in 1927. For some years it was used to accompany silent movies, but after audio films were introduced, the Wurlitzer soon became obsolete and was sporadically used for concerts. When the wider Cinemascope format came there was no room for the Wurlitzer anymore. At the same time the large organ in the Stockholm City Hall needed a renovation, and for some years in the 1960's the Skandia Wurlitzer was used as an instrument for ceremonies. After the renovation, the parts to the Skandia Wurlitzer were stored in the attic above the Blue Hall, where they would be lying for 40 years.

In 2005, a group gathered to investigate the possibilities of restoring the Skandia Wurlitzer, a project that was considered feasible. The City of Stockholm donated the parts. The restoration process started in the workshops of some enthusiasts, and later in the Reactor Hall where the new organ housing was built. An important decision in the restoration was to modernize the control system and change the old telephone exchange-like relay based system (see Fig. 3) to a modern computer-controlled system based on MIDI (see Fig 4). This retrofit, together with network access and the cathedral-like resonances of the hall itself (cinema venues are quite dry by comparison), affords new possibilities to interact with the instrument which is the basis for this entry. In October 2015 the Skandia Wurlitzer was fully restored in the Reactor Hall and re-inauguration concerts were held.

Embodying a tension between the immense electro-mechanical pneumatic physicality and the precise digital control, the organ now allows for particular and situated action to be explored remotely. The thundering body of the organ can be haunted by specters on another continent.

The Installation and Concerts

For the conference, we invited the audience to explore a special installation in the Reactor Hall and experience the linking of Stanford and Stockholm through the vintage pneumatic and electro-mechanical machine: the Skandia Wurlitzer. For the duration of one evening (in Stockholm), the installation was present simultaneously in both places. A generative piece by Elblaus was performed where a real time data stream controlled the organ, and the resulting sounds in the Reactor Hall were picked up and transmitted back to Stanford. A visual link between the two spaces was established so that visitors in one could see what is going on in the other place (using custom minimal delay, high-definition video streaming).

In addition to the continuous streams, a series of performances took place in the installation. During these performances, the control of the organ was relinquished to Stan-

Figure 5: Elblaus performing in the Reactor Hall at the 2010 event "Hackoustics." Photo by Axel Hammarbäck.

ford, where musicians also performed live, using both the organ as well as other means of sound production.

Chafe's musical contribution employed "musification" of nuclear science-related data from the old days of the reactor. His interest alligns with another TEI '18 conference theme to "focus on how computing can bridge atoms and bits into cohesive interactive systems," in this case literally how atoms can become the Wurlitzer's notes (performing the organ using archival data). The concept for the work treated the organ as the reactor's core. As neutron (notes) impinged, the music got hotter and a critical stage was passed. The team made a successful test-run of algorithmic control of the MIDI system in May 2017 using the organ to perform environmental data (CO2 and temperature for the past 1100 years)[1].

Elblaus' piece focused on the physicality of the space in which the organ is situated, acknowledging the fact that anything written for such a particular instrument in such a unique setting must be considered site-specific. This opens up an interesting design space regarding the staging at CCRMA of the physical and embodied experience of the Wurlitzer in the Reactor Hall. Exploring the outer limits of the Wurlitzer's contemporary digital control system combined a technical inquiry with an artistic one: what non-linearities and chaotic behaviors emerge when the digital is physically manifest, both in the mechanical innards of the Mighty Wurlitzer and in the resonant space of the Reactor Hall.

In addition to the authors' pieces, other composers from both Stanford and Stockholm were invited to compose works that explored complementary themes to the pieces composed by Chafe and Elblaus.

While informed by previous artistic work and research, the performances and installation were exploratory. Rather than a final presentation of a compositional process, the space and its visitors became a part of an investigation about presence, embodiment, tangibility, virtuality, and the inherent tension between the infinite reach and multiplicity of digital technologies and the unique singular physical presence of a one-of-a-kind instrument housed in a one-of-a-kind space.

Summary

This report details an installation and performances that explored themes of presence and absence, connectivity and distance. Contrasting the vintage, physically embodied, unique acoustic experience of the organ in the R1 Reactor Hall, with state of the art digital control systems, an aesthetic space was opened up that probed the tension in the anachronisms of the theatre organ. Once cutting edge technology, a precursor to the modern synthesizer, it is now a vintage marvel, reborn through a digital control system, yet owing its power to its physical presence. Metal, wood, skin, and bellows anchor the believable yet somewhat incomprehensible fact that real-time presence over enormous distances is now possible. Together with the attendees at TEI '18 and invited musicians and composers, the authors explored how the virtual can become tangible and embodied.

REFERENCES

1. Juan-Pablo Cáceres and Chris Chafe. 2010a. JackTrip: Under the hood of an engine for network audio. *Journal of New Music Research* 39, 3 (2010), 183–187.

[1] A sound clip of this test can be found at https://ccrma.stanford.edu/~cc/vox/wurlTest.wav

2. Juan-Pablo Cáceres and Chris Chafe. 2010b. Jacktrip/Soundwire meets server farm. *Computer Music Journal* 34, 3 (2010), 29–34.

3. Ludvig Elblaus, Åsa Unander-Scharin, and Carl Unander-Scharin. 2017. Uncanny Materialities: Digital Strategies for Staging Supernatural Themes Drawn from Medieval Ballads. *Leonardo Music Journal* (2017).

4. Leif Handberg, Alex Jonsson, and Knudsen Claus. 2005. Community building through cultural exchange in mediated performance events: A conference 2005. In *The Virtual - a room without borders?* School of Communication, Technology and Design Södertörn College University.

5. Petr Holub, Jiří Matela, Martin Pulec, and Martin Šrom. 2012. UltraGrid: Low-latency high-quality video transmissions on commodity hardware. In *Proceedings of the 20th ACM international conference on Multimedia*. ACM, 1457–1460.

Embodisuit: A Wearable Platform for Embodied Knowledge

Sophia Brueckner
University of Michigan
Ann Arbor, MI, USA
sbrueckn@umich.edu

Rachel Freire
Rachel Freire Studio
London, UK
rachel@rachelfreire.com

Figure 1: Video still of the Embodisuit. Video by Oliver David.

TEI 2018, March 18–21, 2018, Stockholm, Sweden.
ACM ISBN 978-1-4503-5568-1/18/03.
https://doi.org/10.1145/3173225.3173305

Abstract
The Embodisuit allows its wearer to map signals onto different places on their body. Informed by embodied cognition, the suit receives signals from an IoT platform, and each signal controls a different haptic actuator on the body. Knowledge is experienced ambiently without necessitating the interpretation of symbols by the conscious mind. The suit empowers wearers to reconfigure the boundaries of their selves strengthening their connection to the people, places, and things that are meaningful to them. It both critiques and offers an alternative to current trends in wearable technology. Most wearables harvest data from their users to be sent and processed elsewhere. The Embodisuit flips this paradigm such that data is taken in through the body instead. Furthermore, we believe that by changing the way people live with data, it will change the type of data that people create.

Author Keywords
Embodied cognition; wearable electronics; haptic I/O; internet of things; prototyping; electronic textiles.

Introduction
Technology is not neutral. We're inside of what we make, and it's inside of us. We're living in a world of connections —and it matters which ones get made and unmade.

—Donna Haraway [3]

The Embodisuit allows its wearer to map personally chosen signals from an IoT platform to physical sensations on their body. The wearer customizes the garment with haptic modules attached with snaps. In addition to showcasing novel e-textile innovations, the Embodisuit demonstrates the potential of the application of embodied cognition to the design of wearable technologies. Knowledge can be experienced ambiently without interpretation of symbols by the conscious mind [1, 5]. The suit empowers the wearer to reconfigure the boundaries of their self tying them to the people, places, and things that are important to them. It both critiques and offers an alternative to current trends in wearable technology. Challenging the assumptions of the Quantified Self, the Embodisuit is a garment of resistance. Instead of harvesting data from the wearer to be sent elsewhere, it allows the wearer to take data in through the skin.

Embodied Cognition

In *Philosophy in the Flesh*, George Lakoff and Mark Johnson consider how embodied cognition, which very simply put states that the body influences the mind, challenges fundamental aspects of Western philosophy and our understanding of human reason. In particular, embodied cognition teaches us that most of our thoughts operate beneath the level of cognitive awareness and are inaccessible to our conscious minds. Lakoff and Johnson write, “It is the rule of thumb among cognitive scientists that unconscious thought is 95 percent of all thought. . . Moreover, the 95 percent below the surface of conscious awareness shapes and structures all conscious thought. If the cognitive unconscious were not there doing this shaping, there could be no conscious thought,” [5].

Figure 2: The Embodisuit.

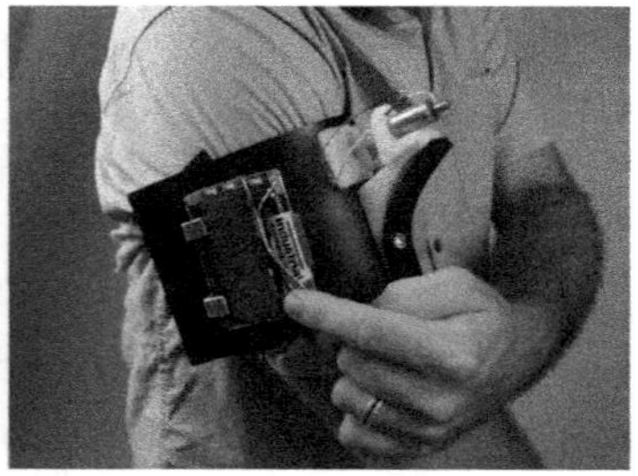

Figure 3: I. E. D (Improvised Empathy Device). Image courtesy of Matt Kenyon.

Figure 4: Empathy Amulet.

This suggests that haptic, ambient interfaces that can be experienced unconsciously are underutilized in the development of new wearable technologies, which frequently focus on measurement through wearable sensors or alarm-like notifications.

Quantified Self

In recent years, the Quantified Self movement has rapidly gained popularity. Its proponents use technology, most often wearable devices paired with smartphone and web applications, for self-tracking. The Fitbit is one of the most well-known examples, and other technologies exist to track all aspects of life including fitness, diet, mood, relationships, and more. The goal is self-knowledge and self-improvement through data collection and analysis. However, this approach is misguided for many reasons. These technologies track naive, easily measured metrics and then confront the user with data, graphs, and distracting notifications. They also raise significant concerns about surveillance and the collection of personal information for the targeting of ads. The Embodisuit does not farm people for data.

Related Work

FeelSpace Belt
The feelSpace belt was developed by team of cognitive scientists from the University of Osnabrück to give its wearer an unconscious sense of direction. The belt projects the direction north onto the wearer's waist using thirty vibrating actuators. Because the brain is plastic, the researchers believe that exposing the brain to a novel set of sensorimotor contingencies will engender a new perceptual experience and thus result in a new modality [6].

Empathy Amulet
Sophia Brueckner's Empathy Amulet is a socially networked wearable that cultivates a sense of connectedness with strangers through asynchronously shared warmth on the body. Across cultures, people use warm/cold metaphors to communicate the concepts of social connection and affection [1, 5].

I.E.D (Improvised Empathetic Device)
I.E.D by Matt Kenyon and Doug Easterly is a wearable device that injects the wearer with a needle to cause pain whenever an American soldier dies in the Middle East [4].

The Embodisuit is a modular platform that can be used to recreate the types of interactions listed above, but it also allows for many other types and combinations of embodied experiences.

Interaction

The Embodisuit allows its wearer to map personally chosen signals from an IoT platform to combinations of physical sensations on their body. The wearer customizes the garment with haptic modules attached with snaps to create sensations of heat, cold, vibration, and more. These sensations can be constant or infrequent, subtle or jarring, singular or grouped, and they are entirely configurable by the wearer for both practical and poetic purposes. A few examples:

- Inspired by "feeling the weather in your bones", you feel a gentle buzz on your wrist 20 minutes before it rains.
- The sun shines in your favorite place. The modules across your back gently warm your neck and shoulders.
- A hummingbird flies under your window at home. You feel a ripple down your spine.

The Embodisuit is meant to be worn underneath your clothing like lingerie and is designed for everyday wear. The

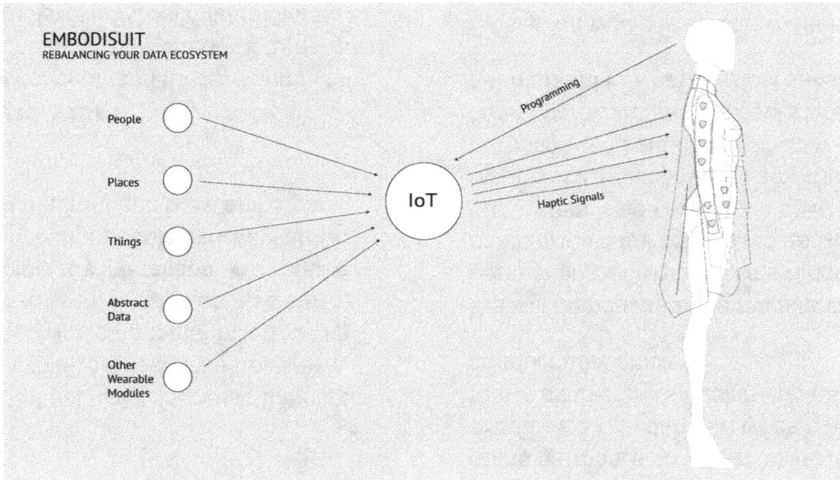

Figure 5: Flow of information in the Embodisuit.

haptic sensations are felt by you alone and not seen by others.

Implementation

The construction of the Embodisuit builds on Rachel Freire's materials investigations in Second Skin, an ongoing project that explores the body as a canvas for technology combining traditional electronics housing with e-textile stretch circuits and sportswear technology [2]. The Embodisuit is made of two layers of stretchy, breathable technical fabric with ultraflexible silicone wire flowing freely in between. Earlier prototypes used conductive fabric traces, but they did not work reliably over longer distances.

The design of the Embodisuit is modular with custom PCBs that snap into the garment. The snaps close the circuits between the traces in the suit and the traces on the modules. Each module has a haptic actuator on the bottom. We made modules with vibrotactile motors, heaters (Peltiers and flexible Kapton), and coolers (Peltiers), but the suit can easily accommodate new types of modules for different haptic sensations as long as the snaps are in the same configuration.

The modules are laid out in a simple serial bus, and each addressable module can be turned on and off through an Adafruit Feather Bluefruit tethered to an Android phone. An Android application allows the garment to receive signals from an IoT platform.

Exhibition Information

We will show the garment on a full-size, clear plastic mannequin. When exhibited, we communicate that the garment is meant to be worn under your clothes by showing the suit

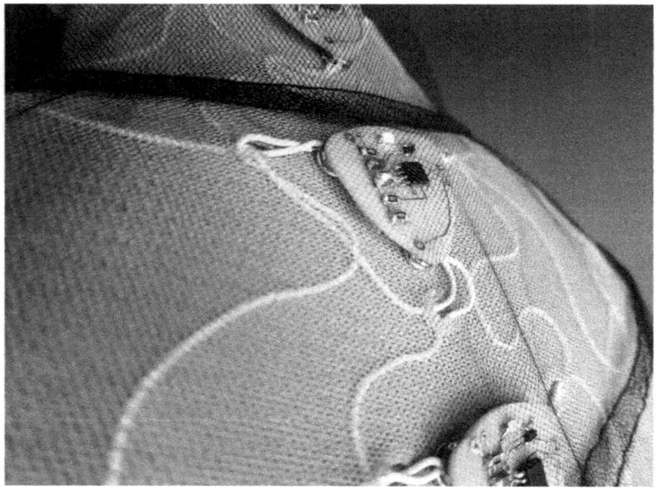

Figure 6: Haptic modules on the Embodisuit.

underneath a see-through "ghost" shirt. Because the haptic sensations are invisible to exhibition-goers, we use small white LEDs on the modules to indicate that they are being activated. We would prefer to show a video on a screen near the mannequin to explain the interaction. We require power and enough room such that people can walk around the mannequin to see both the front and back of the garment.

Limitations and Future Work

The Embodisuit is proof of concept, and its development is ongoing. Rigid PCBs are cheap and have a quick turnaround time, but we plan to explore flexible PCBs in future iterations. In addition, we also will continue to push the limits of conductive fabric traces, especially in smaller garments and with the more forgiving vibrotactile motors. Some haptic actuators like Peltiers and flexible Kapton heaters require more power and a bulkier battery. This can be mitigated by not activating these types of modules often. However, we will experiment with incorporating larger LiPo batteries in ways that are still comfortable. We will create new types of haptic modules as well as leverage the research of haptics experts to improve the effectiveness of existing modules. In addition, because people can experience physical sensations like temperature so differently, the intensity of the sensations must be easily customizable.

Designing a software user interface that allows the wearer to intuitively program the garment is also necessary and will be improved in a future iteration.

In this version of the Embodisuit, we focused on pushing materials exploration and the conceptual and aesthetic qualities of the project. As a result, the complexity and cost of the garment's construction limited us from evaluating the experience with different types of users. A future iteration that is simpler in its design and easier to fit will be used to conduct user studies.

We will demonstrate the modularity of our system by experimenting with other forms ranging from something as complex as a full bodysuit to as simple as a collar. Because our system is so flexible, we believe it could be leveraged by other HCI researchers, designers, and artists for different purposes. Without having to do much coding or customization of hardware, people could focus simply on what signals get mapped to what physical sensations on a wearable.

Finally, we would like to draw attention to a potential risk within these types of systems. Designing technologies that work with both our conscious and unconscious minds is a way to interface with our complete selves. It is more natural as well as more efficient. However, allowing ourselves to

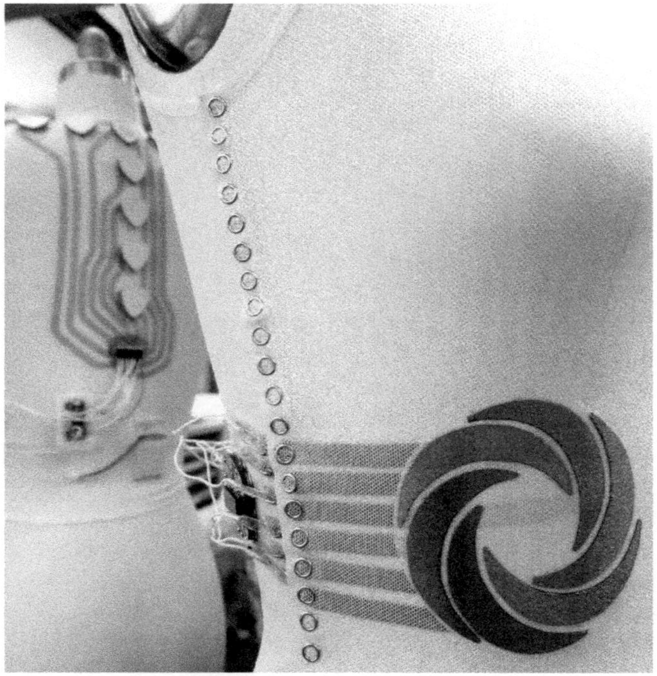

Figure 7: Embodisuit prototypes with conductive fabric.

be manipulated through our unconscious mind is extremely dangerous, and we must be very cautious to whom or what we give that sort of power. When interfaces influence the unconscious mind, we may discover too late (maybe never) that we are being controlled, abused, or changed in ways we don't like. The Embodisuit gives as much control as possible to the wearer, but this must not be forgotten.

Acknowledgements
We thank Autodesk Pier 9 and University of Michigan's Stamps School of Art & Design for making this project possible.

Conclusions
In addition to showcasing novel e-textile innovations, the Embodisuit demonstrates the potential of the application of embodied cognition to the design of wearable technologies. Experiencing information through the body is more natural and efficient but also affords opportunities for greater imagination and meaning-making. The Embodisuit is a highly flexible, modular platform that can be reconfigured into other wearable forms as well as utilized by other artists and researchers. We hope to inspire people to design and consume technology and data more mindfully, with greater awareness of embodied cognition and issues of power. Challenging the assumptions of the Quantified Self, the Embodisuit is a garment of resistance allowing the wearer to experience data through the body instead of harvesting data from the body to be sent elsewhere. We envision the Embodisuit as a way to rebalance our data ecosystems, taking back control of the configuration of our boundaries and the direction of our cyborg evolution. Furthermore, we hypothesize that by changing the way people live with data, it will change the type of data that people create.

Video Figure
https://vimeo.com/219233767/3652d7ee4b

REFERENCES

1. Sophia Brueckner. 2014. *Out of Network*. Master's thesis. Massachusetts Institute of Technology, Cambridge, MA.
2. Rachel Freire, Cedric Honnet, and Paul Strohmeier. 2017. Second Skin: An Exploration of eTextile Stretch

Circuits on the Body. In *Proceedings of the Tenth International Conference on Tangible, Embedded, and Embodied Interaction - TEI 17*. ACM Press, Yokohama, JP, 2–17.

3. Donna Haraway. 1990. *Simians, Cyborgs, and Women: The Reinvention of Nature*. Routledge, New York, NY, USA.
4. Matt Kenyon and Doug Easterly. 2009. I.E.D (Improvised Empathetic Device). (2009). `http://www.swamp.nu/projects/ied`
5. George Lakoff and Mark Johnson. 1999. *Philosophy in the Flesh*. Basic Books, New York.
6. Saskia K Nagel, Christine Carl, Tobias Kringe, Robert Märtin, and Peter König. 2005. Beyond sensory substitution–learning the sixth sense. *Journal of Neural Engineering* 2, 4 (2005), R13 – R26. DOI: `http://dx.doi.org/10.1088/1741-2560/2/4/R02`

The Bronze Key: Performing Data Encryption

Susan Kozel
Malmö University
205 06 Malmö, Sweden
susan.kozel@mah.se

Ruth Gibson
Gibson/Martelli, and
Coventry University
Coventry, UK
ruth@gibsonmartelli.com

Bruno Martelli
Gibson/Martelli
London, UK
www.gibsonmartelli.com
bruno@gibsonmartelli.com

TEI '18, March 18–21, 2018, Stockholm, Sweden

ACM ISBN 978-1-4503-5568-1/18/03.
https://doi.org/10.1145/3173225.3173306

Abstract
The Bronze Key art installation is the result of performative re-materializations of bodily data. This collaborative experiment in data encryption expands research into practices of archiving and critical discourses around open data. It integrates bodily movement, motion capture and Virtual Reality (VR) with a critical awareness of data trails and data protection. A symmetric cryptosystem was enacted producing a post-digital cipher system, along with archival artefacts of the encryption process. Material components for inclusion in the TEI Arts Track include: an audio file of text to speech of the raw motion capture data from the original movement sequence on cassette tape (*The Plaintext*), a 3D printed bronze shape produced from a motion captured gesture (*The Encryption Key*), and a printed book containing the scrambled motion capture data (*The Ciphertext*).

Author Keywords
Materiality, performativity, embodied interaction, encryption, motion capture, data

ACM Classification
Human Centered Computing - Interaction design theory, concepts and paradigms, - Virtual Reality; Security & Privacy - Cryptography

Introduction
The Bronze Key is the result of a collaboration between designers and artists within the rubric of a major

Jacob Applebaum

"Over the last forty years, a revolution has swept the planet. It happened quietly and those who noticed were ridiculed at best. It is a revolution where nearly all of our data is devoured in an automated fashion – machine to machine, person to person, voice, text. Communications, movements, all of life is consumed, quantified, searched, and catalogued." [Applebaum 2016, 55]

research project at Malmö University (Sweden) called Living Archives.[1] It points to one of the most urgent issues around archiving in the contemporary climate: we archive but we are archived. If we realize that our data – in particular our bodily data – are archived often without our awareness or consent, then encryption becomes a necessity that filters down to everyday usage. Jacob Appelbaum provides a succinct description of the cultural context. (See sidebar quote).

General attitudes towards encryption are that it is complex, mathematical or only used to mask illegal activities. An aesthetic approach to encryption explores the potential for new performances of encryption, removing it from the domain of the paranoid, criminal or hacker elite [13]. Obfuscation practices can be performative, playful and daily, as simple as switching off a device [4]. The design materials for *The Bronze Key* experiment are: movement sequences revealing an affective bodily state; the digital data they produce; motion capture (Perception Neuron system); VR (Oculus Rift's Quill); animation software for visualisation (Motion Builder) and various material extractions from the encryption process. The installation for TEI's Art Track will focus on three non-digital artifacts (audio, bronze, print) embodying the combination of digital and physical practices that produced them. As this is an on-going research process the objects will be produced in early 2018.[2]

[1] http://livingarchives.mah.se/

[2] http://gibsonmartelli.com/SpacePlace/2017/10/12/performing-encryption/

The goal is for performative material translations to foster an awareness of the need for encryption and to spark a range of ideas around what shape encryption might take: whether or not these processes are functional is less pressing than generate ideas for how control over bodily data traces.

The Design Context: Embodied, Somatic and Political

The Bronze Key is located at the junction where Embodied Interaction opens onto an interdisciplinary domain, taking in politics, performance, data security and legal issues around media privacy [2], [4], [6], [8]. The work is post-digital by playing across the ways human physical interactions are digitally captured and then re-materialized once again in the physical world. This process of material translations reveal how digital materials and digital culture are not peeled away, like the unwanted skin of an orange, but remain within the newly designed object.

A somatic dimension is implied, because gestures and bodily motion cannot be disconnected from deeper affective and somatic states. Practices of somatic attention (in other words inner-sensing) that subsequently radiate into designed prototypes and design thinking are increasingly influential in the interaction design community [9], [16], as are performative approaches to engagement with designed systems [5], [11]. However, this project adopts an approach to somatics (and by extension somaesthetics) that expands outwards from these respected perspectives in the design community, in an attempt both to capture a frightening aspect of the human condition in digital culture and to operate with a definition of performativity that is based on

Laura Poitras:

"The sound of blood moving in my brain wouldn't stop. I need to decide what to carry today. Very strange – I'm less worried about crossing borders in Europe than in the U.S. But still I need to consider the danger of taking a computer. This is all total madness – this level of feeling watched And feeling I could be causing harm to others." [Poitras 2016, 94]

transformation [7] and emergence [12]. The feeling of surveillance, and powerlessness in the face of it, produces strong affective and emotional states. Laura Poitras is the film maker who worked with Edward Snowden in 2013 to release the NSA documents revealing the extent to which the personal daily communications of citizens of the US and UK are intercepted, analyzed, recorded, and archived without consent. She kept a journal from that time. In it she combines strategies for data and personal security with poignant phenomenological descriptions of her somatic state. (See sidebar quote.)

Two design takeaways emerge: 1) that the embodied/somatic/affective is rarely far removed from the digital in our culture of pervasive computing, and 2) given that our data is manipulated constantly, all of us very soon will have to decide what data we carry with us and whether to find our own ways to encrypt. Or as danah boyd says: "we need to reconsider what security looks like in a data driven world." [3]

Developing new encryption practices can begin with aesthetic, metaphoric and digital experimentation.

Cryptography

Cryptography refers quite broadly to the history and science of keeping information or communication secret. Encryption is a stage within this process, made up of a set of practices that render confidential communication unintelligible, or intelligible only to those with whom we desire to communicate [14]. This standard definition of encryption can be refined for performance and affective exchanges. The performance of encryption is not based on creating impermeable barriers or permanent containment, rather it emphasizes a re-patterning or a distortion of a flow of communication. Ambiguity and translation of bodily movement into other material forms are foregrounded, making translation and interpretation essential to the process [12], [13].

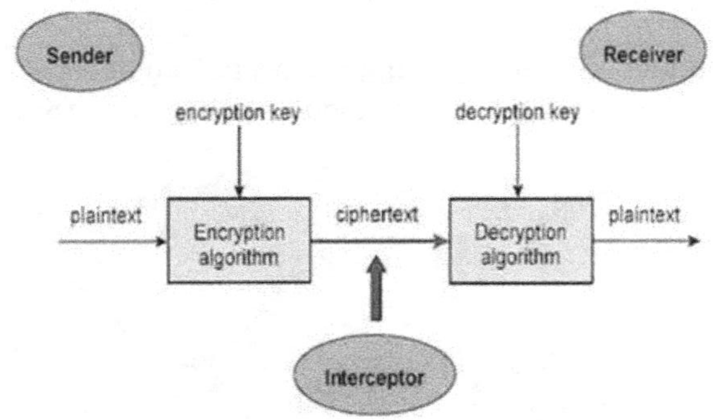

Figure 1: Basic cipher system (Piper & Murphy 2002, 8)

A basic symmetrical cipher system (Figure 1) has the following stages: A *plaintext* (readable message) is encrypted by means of an encryption algorithm embedded in a *key*. This is used to translate the plaintext into an incomprehensible *ciphertext (*or *cryptogram)*. The ciphertext is decrypted by a recipient who already possesses, or is able to guess, the key. After decryption, the plaintext is revealed once more. Classic encryption systems are symmetrical, meaning the sender and the receiver know each other and use the same key. They are also dynamic, meaning the passage of material information through time and space is usually implied. In a symmetric system the encryption and decryption algorithms are the same. It is worth noting that the contemporary encryption system securing all confidential internet transactions – such as banking -- is asymmetrical [14].

The Bronze Key

For *The Bronze Key* experiment we performed the basic cipher system and produced various materializations of each stage. The proposal for the Arts Track exhibition will consist in materializations of the first 3 steps: *The Plaintext*, *The Key*, and *The Ciphertext*.

Figure 4: Key capture using Oculus Rift

Figure 5: Key capture using Oculus Rift

[Hips]				
1	-4034.899902	951.2000122	6003	-1.341766
2	-4034.582275	951.2000122	6002.58252	-
3	-4034.399902	951.2333984	6002.263184	-
4	-4034.399902	951.3062134	6001.943848	-
5	-4034.399902	951.2999878	6001.729004	-
6	-4034.405762	951.1943359	6001.599609	-
7	-4034.299805	951.2999878	6001.599609	-
8	-4034.187988	951.2062988	6001.5	-1.257140
9	-4034.070313	951.2999878	6001.400391	-
10	-4033.950195	951.2999878	6001.350098	-
11	-4033.82959	951.2999878	6001.196289	-
12	-4033.69873	951.2999878	6001.105469	-
13	-4033.800049	951.2999878	6000.900391	-
14	-4033.905029	951.2999878	6000.693848	-
15	-4033.996338	951.4074097	6000.603516	-

Figure 2: *The Plaintext* mocap data in .htr format

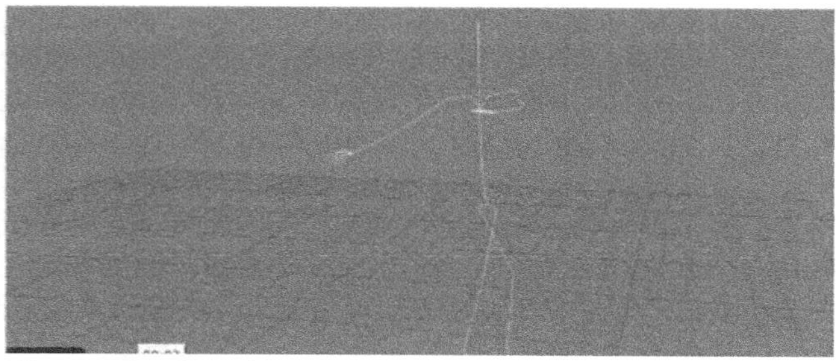

Figure 3: *The Plaintext* in mocap animation. For video see https://vimeo.com/238730550

The Plaintext was a full body movement sequence (30 seconds) capturing a general state of being of one person as a message to be sent to another person. It was captured by the Perception Neuron motion capture system producing approximately 57,000 lines of numerical data representing the spatial and rotational information of each limb. (See Figures 2 & 3). *Materialization: text to speech of the numerical data recorded on magnetic audio tape and played on a cassette player.*

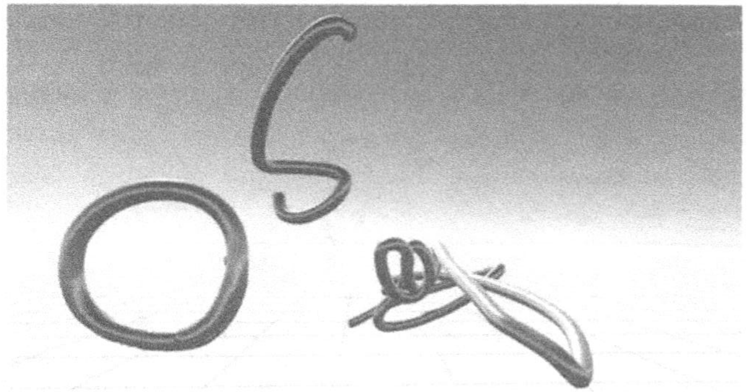

Figure 6: Three sample keys in VR using Quill, 3D package for the Oculus Rift in 3D .fbx file format

The Key was an arm and hand gesture (1 second) intended to unlock the movement sequence (Figures 4 & 5). It was captured using the Quill program in Oculus Rift (Figure 6). *Materialization: the 3D path of the gesture captured in VR space (looking like a squiggle) and cast as a bronze object.*

The Encryption Algorithm was a mathematical process whereby the mocap data was scrambled by applying the data from the key: each line of movement data was subject to modification by a rolling series of mathematical functions (basic addition and subtraction) of the data from the key.

Figure 7: *The Ciphertext* in mocap animation. For video see https://vimeo.com/238730451

Figure 8: Alternate *Ciphertext*, on multiple bodies in Motion Builder

The Ciphertext or *Cryptogram* was the scrambled mocap data. When fed into an animation program such as Motion Builder the movement it generated was an obfuscation of the original sequence, making the affective and movement qualities unintelligible (Figures 7 & 8). *Materialization: a book containing the raw scrambled numerical data.*

Decryption, or "guessing the key," was a sort of game by which the recipient of the message wore the Oculus Rift running neural network gesture recognition software. By repeatedly attempting to perform the gesture represented by the bronze shape of The Key, the recipient would eventually hit the right gesture that the originator of the message provided. Once the gesture was recognized the scrambled data could – in theory – be decrypted and returned to plain text of coherent motion data, fed into Motion Builder again to produce an animation of the original sequence.

Conclusion

The Bronze Key art installation is the result of performative re-materializations of bodily data pointing to a complex or layered notion of the post-digital. The premise is that bodily gestures and motions are fundamentally personal and act as identifiers in the wider domain of data analytics and forensic data analysis. Retaining power over whether to be seen or not is important. It is a design issue of increasing importance.

Acknowledgements

Thanks to Christian Skovbjerg Jensen of the Inter Arts Centre in Malmö (Sweden), the Swedish National Research Council for support of the Living Archives Research Project at Malmö University, and the AHRC funded Error Network (UK) for early research.

References

1. Jacob Applebaum. 2016. Letter to a Young Selector. In Astro Noise, Laura Poitras, (Ed.). Whitney Museum of America, New York, distributed by Yale University Press, New Haven and London, 154-159
2. Rocco Bellanova. 2014. Data protection, with love. In International Political Sociology, 8:1, 112–15.
3. danah boyd. 2017. Your data is being manipulated. Retrieved 31 October 2017 from https://points.datasociety.net/your-data-is-being-manipulated-a7e31a83577b
4. Finn Brunton and Helen Nissenbaum. 2016. Obfuscation: A User's Guide for Privacy and Protest. The MIT Press, Cambridge MA and London.
5. Peter Dalsgaard and Lone Koefoed Hansen. 2008. Performing perception—staging aesthetics of interaction. ACM Trans. Comput.-Hum. Interact. 15, 3, Article 13 (December 2008), 33 pages. DOI=http://dx.doi.org/10.1145/1453152.1453156
6. Marieke de Goede. 2017. Chain of Security. In Review of International Studies, 1-19. doi:10.1017/S0260210517000353
7. Erika Fischer-Lichte. 2008. The Transformative Power of Performance. Routledge, London, UK.
8. Matthew Fuller and Andrew Goffey. 2012. Evil Media. The MIT Press, Cambridge MA.
9. Kristina Höök, Anna Ståhl, Martin Jonsson, Johanna Mercurio, Anna Karlsson, and Eva-Carin Banka Johnson. 2015. COVER STORY: Somaesthetic design. interactions 22, 4 (June 2015), 26-33. DOI: https://doi.org/10.1145/2770888
10. Giulio Jacucci and Ina Wagner. 2007. Performative roles of materiality for collective creativity. In Proceedings of the 6th ACM SIGCHI conference on Creativity & cognition (C&C '07). ACM, New York, NY, USA, 73-82. DOI: https://doi.org/10.1145/1254960.1254971
11. Susan Kozel. 2012. AffeXity: Performing Affect with Augmented Reality. In Fibreculture Journel, Issue 21: Exploring Affective Interactions, Jonas Fritsh and Thomas Markussen (Eds.), FCJ-150, 72-97.
12. Susan Kozel. 2016. From Openness to Encryption. In Openenss: Politics, Practices, Poetics. Retrieved 30 October, 2017 from http://livingarchives.mah.se
13. Susan Kozel. 2017. Performing Encryption. In Performing the Digital, Martina Leeker, Imanuel Shipper and Timo Beyes, (Eds.). Transcript Verlag, Bielefeld, Germany, 117-134.
14. Fred Piper and Sean Murphy. 2002. Cryptography: A Very Short Introduction. Oxford University Press, Oxford, UK.
15. Laura Poitras. 2016. Berlin Journal. In Astro Noise, Laura Poitras, (Ed.). Whitney Museum of America, New York, distributed by Yale University Press, New Haven and London, 80-101.
16. Thecla Schiphorst. 2007. Really, really small: the palpability of the invisible. In Proceedings of the 6th ACM SIGCHI conference on Creativity & cognition (C&C '07). ACM, New York, NY, USA, 7-16. DOI: https://doi.org/10.1145/1254960.1254962.

Tracking, Animating, and 3D Printing Elements of the Fine Arts Freehand Drawing Process

Piyum Fernando
Arizona State University
Tempe, AZ, USA
piyum.fernando@asu.edu

Stacey Kuznetsov
Arizona State University
Tempe, AZ, USA
kstace@asu.edu

Jennifer Weiler
Arizona State University
Tempe, AZ, USA
jjweiler@asu.edu

Pavan Turaga
Arizona State University
Tempe, AZ, USA
pturaga@asu.edu

TEI '18, March 18—21, 2018, Stockholm, Sweden

ACM ISBN 978-1-4503-5568-1/18/03.
https://doi.org/10.1145/3173225.3173307

Abstract
Dynamic elements of traditional drawing processes such as the order of compilation, and speed, length, and pressure of strokes can be as important as the final art piece because they can reveal the technique, process, and emotions of the artist. In this paper, we present an interactive system that unobtrusively tracks the freehand drawing process (movement and pressure of artist's pencil) on a regular easel. The system outputs captured information using 2D video renderings and 3D-printed sculptures. We also present a summery of findings from a user study with 6 experienced artists who created multiple pencil drawings using our system. The resulting digital and physical outputs from our system revealed vast differences in drawing speeds, styles, and techniques. At TEI arts track, the attendees will likely engage in lively discussion around the analog, digital, and tangible aspects of our exhibit. We believe that such a discussion will be critical not only in shaping the future of our work, but also in understanding novel research directions at the intersection of art and computation.

Author Keywords
Interactive drawing; Digital visualizaion; Movement tracking

Introduction
Drawing is one of the oldest forms of human creative expression and is highly regarded as the foundation of human

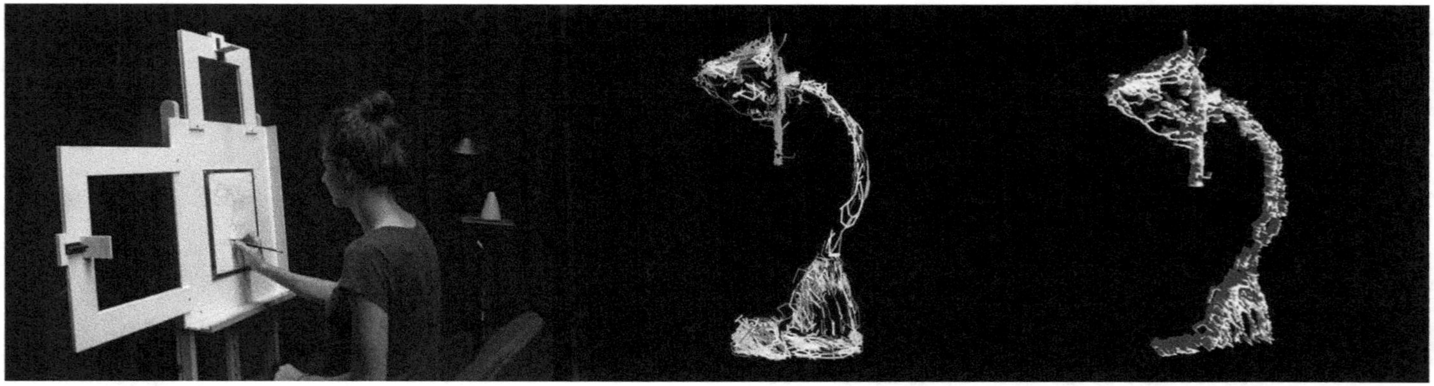

Figure 1: Our interactive drawing setup(left), 2D visualization(middle) and 3D bas-relief model(right) generated by our system

artistic practices. Over the years, the TEI community has shown a great interest in exploring novel ways of blending human creativity with digital technologies [2, 5, 8]. The creation process of a drawing can be as fascinating and valuable as the final static end-product because it represents the moment of time in which it was created [11]. Dynamic elements of the drawing process such as the order of compilation, lengths of strokes, speed of the movement, and the pressure applied to the drawing surface reveal unique aspects of the drawing process, including the artists' skill, technique, artistic apprehension, and mood [1]. Although the final art piece can reflect these elements, more dynamic visualizations such as video recordings, animations, or tangible mediums such as 3D printed sculptures can vividly represent the nuances of the drawing process to create richer experiences of art making and art appreciation.

Within prior HCI research, the intersection of art and computation has been broadly examined through interactive drawing interfaces [6, 4], digital-physical hybrid fabrication tools [13], and interactive art installations [7, 9]. However, the work presented here follows a different trajectory by tracking dynamic elements of drawing processes such as speed of hand movements and pressure exerted on the drawing surface. The key goal of our work is to explore a novel way of creating a digitally mediated art making and viewing experience by visualizing dynamic elements of drawing processes. To this end, we developed a system that unobtrusively tracks the freehand drawing process on a regular easel and then visualizes the output. Using cameras and acoustic sensing, the easel tracks pencil movements and the pressure exerted on the drawing surface without disrupting traditional freehand drawing practice. The captured information is shown using 2D video renderings and 3D printed sculptures, which represent sequential order of stroke compilation, pencil speed, and pressure at each point of the drawing process (Figure 1). Unlike existing digital drawing applications for tablets [6] our system supports traditional pencil and paper based drawing process and allows us to study traditional fine arts practice.

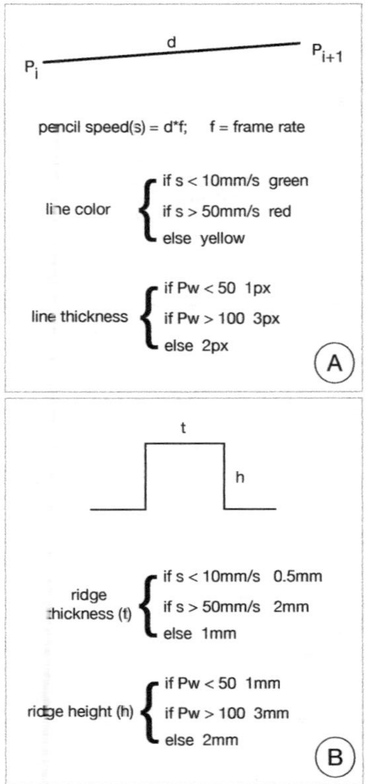

Figure 2: Representation of pencil movement and pressure in (A)2D video renderings and (B) 3D bas-relief models

We conducted a user study with six experienced artists whereby they created multiple pencil drawings using our setup. Afterwards, they reflected on the digitally synthesized outputs of their drawings during a group discussion of all six artists. Our study provided the opportunity for constructive discussions between artists and researchers. Hence, in this paper we describe—1) our interactive drawing system, and 2) a summary of insights gained by working with experienced artists. By presenting our system at the TEI arts track, we hope to engage a wide audience—from processional artists to anyone who can make a simple sketch with a pencil—to use our system and reflect on the broader implications for TEI in the realm of fine art and computation.

System

Our interactive system is comprised of a regular drawing easel, which is augmented with two independently functioning subsystems — the pencil tracking system and the pencil pressure sensing system.

Pencil Tracking

In order to track the drawing pencil, our system uses two cameras, which are mounted on the top and left sides of the easel. Images captured at 20 fps from these cameras are processed by a custom implemented image processing program in order to determine the vertical and horizontal positions of the drawing pencil. To increase the accuracy of the tracking mechanism, we use drawing pencils, which are fully covered with a layer of blue ink, except for the graphite tip. In addition, we mounted two green colored background strips along the bottom and right edges each facing the camera mounted on the opposite side (Please refer to Figure 1(left)) The horizontal and vertical locations of the drawing pencil is determined by locating the blue color blob created by the pencil against the green background. In order to map the pencil's pixel locations to the physical coordinates of the drawing surface, the system was calibrated by placing a grid marked in millimeters on drawing surface. Please refer supplementary materials for more details. Since the cameras were permanently fixed to the easel, this calibration process was only required once.

Pressure Sensing

Our pencil pressure sensing system is based on an acoustic sensing mechanism [3]. We experimentally observed that the intensity of the sound wave created by friction between the drawing surface and the tip of the pencil can be used as a close approximation for pencil pressure . Even though this relationship is not reliable enough to measure the subtle variations of pressure accurately, we found it is sufficient for detecting the major changes. In implementing this system, we designed an acoustic sensing module which contains a Teensy 3.2 microcontroller and an Adafruit electret microphone module with built-in amplifier. We placed 12 of these modules in a 3 X 4 grid on the back side of the easel. Each of these modules were programmed to read the digital output of the microphones 20 times per second in sync with the two cameras of the pencil tracking system. Weighted averages *(Pw)* of the three sensors closest to the pencil (based on the pencil position determined by the tracking system and microphone) are used as the approximation of pencil pressure exerted on the drawing surface at each frame.

Data Visualization

In order to visually represent the pencil location and pressure data captured from our system, we implemented a Processing 3.0 based application. This application renders the pencil speed and the pressure exerted on the drawing surface as an animation. Figure 3 shows multiple frames of the animations of a single art piece, while Figure 4 shows

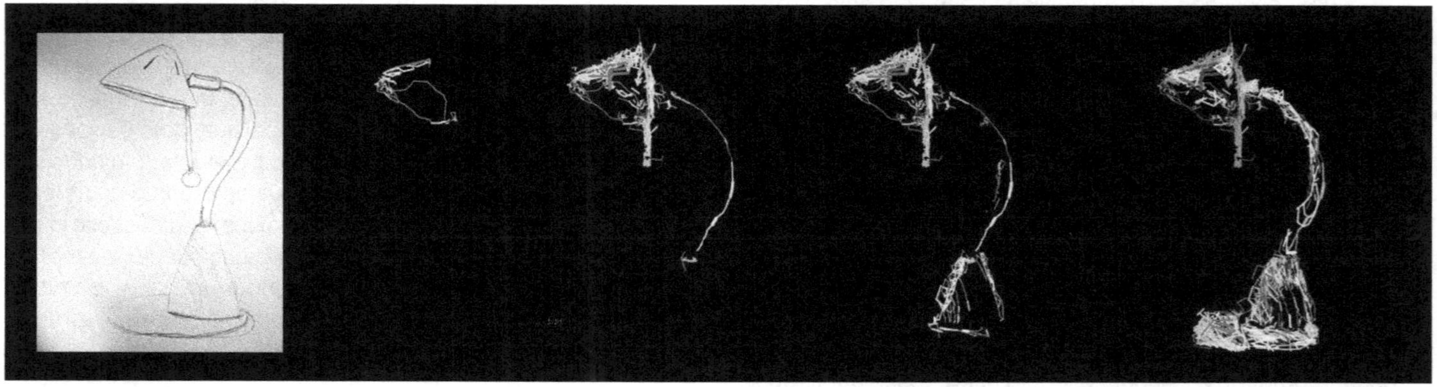

Figure 3: Pencil drawing of the table lamp by a study participant (on left) and 4 stages of the drawing progression as seen in the digital visualization (on right).

the final renderings of drawings by multiple artists. Please refer the supplementary video to see full 2D renderings. Here the pencil speed is determined by calculating the cartesian distance *(d)* between two adjacent data points. The pencil strokes which were drawn in slow (< 10mm/s), medium (>= 10mm/s and <50mm/s), or high (>= 50mm/s) speeds are represented distinctly in the visualization using green, yellow, and red colors respectively. By analysing the pencil pressure data collected from our study, we observed the practical range of *Pw* as 0 -170 (audio signal ranged from 0 to 2.5Vrms with 50x gain). Therefore the different pressure levels are depicted using different line thicknesses (Low 1px, Medium 2px and High 3px) based on the Pw value as shown in Figure 2(A).

Additionally, we implemented another Processing 3.0 programe to generate 3D bas-relief models displaying the drawing data of each artist. The model takes the form of a slate with raised ridges where lines were drawn. Figure 1(right) shows an example of one of the printed 3D models. Here the thickness *(t)* of the ridges is based on the speed of the drawing , while the height *(h)* of the ridges is based on the pressure of the drawing stroke. Please refer Figure 2(B). The height of the ridge can be compounded if several lines are drawn over the same area.

User Study with Artists

To explore the potential applications and limitations of our system and gain insights from experienced art practitioners, we conducted a study with six local artists—two female MFA students, two male cartoonists, one female primary school art teacher, and a female independent fine artist. Each artist was invited to a drawing session during which they created three sketches. For the first two sketches, we requested that all participants draw specific objects located in the room (a table lamp and a flower pot). For the third sketch, participants were invited to draw whatever they wanted, including non-representational or imaginary

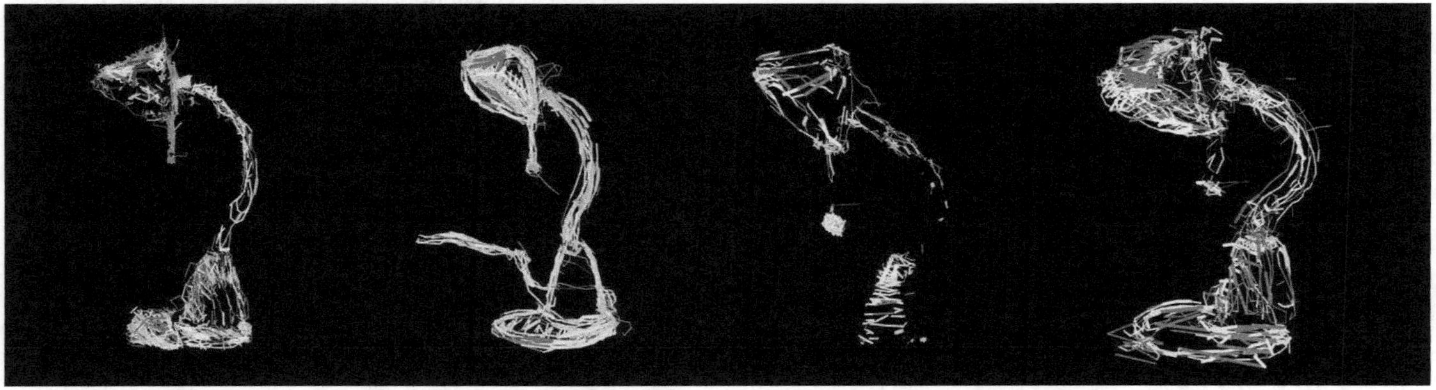

Figure 4: Corresponding 2D renderings of pencil drawings by 4 different artists

scenes. In between creating the sketches, the artists were shown the 2D video rendering and the 3D bas-relief rendering of the sketch they had just completed. In addition, between the drawings and at the end of each artist's session, we used semi-structured interviews to gather feedback about the artists' opinion of the process. Furthermore, they discussed potential application areas of our system especially in the domain of art education. Participants were compensated $15 per hour for their time spent participating in the drawing session and workshop.

Summary of Findings

All artists who took part in our study were able to complete the drawing tasks and considered our tracking system to be unobtrusive. From the onset, all artists were very interested in being able to see an animation of their pencil movements. Most of them mentioned that the digital output of their drawings enabled them to re-live the experience of performing the drawing and compared the 2D video rendering to *"seeing the muscle memory on the screen"*. Moreover the 2D video renderings revealed unique characteristics among the drawing styles of participants. For example, they clearly showed that some participants, particularly the cartoonists, tend to use thicker lines in their drawings when compared to the others. In addition, the participants discussed the different drawing approaches that each artist used, such as starting with lighter, quicker lines to sketch in broad shapes before adding finer details. Some of our participants remarked on the potential of our system to be used as a learning tool. As studying the techniques of experienced artists and trying to mimic their styles (known as *"learning through art reproduction"*) is widely used in classical and contemporary art pedagogies, artists discussed the potential of using 2D video rendering of trained artists to help beginners grasp new approaches. In addition, some of them mentioned that our system may be used as a tool to study the evolution of a particular artist's style or track the improvements of art students' drawing techniques.

The participants also reflected on the potential of enhancing engagement with art audiences through the digital outputs of our system. They pointed out that the sequential order of strokes and the pressure variations at each point, when shown in combination with the original drawing, enable audiences to understand unique traits of the artist's technical process. This in turn allows the audience to be more aware of the subtle differences each pencil stroke has made in the final piece. The artists also noted that the 3D prints offered an interesting physical representation of their work. In the realm of TEI, this suggests future systems that materialize aspects of 2D drawings in order to provide multi-sensory art viewing experiences.

Presentation

Our system creatively visualizes aspects of the freehand drawing process, and we propose to demonstrate it at TEI for two reasons. First, TEI is increasingly interested in supporting and intersecting with practices with the fine arts [10, 12]. Second, our system is engaging for a wide audience, including anyone who likes to sketch design ideas, or simply "doodle" for fun, which will make our technology a valuable contribution to TEI arts track.

The art exhibit will consist of the interactive drawing easel and the digital and physical artifacts (original pencil drawings, 2D video renderings, and 3D printed bas-relief models) from our study with artists. The 2D video renderings will be displayed in digital photo frames. Viewers will have the opportunity to create quick pencil drawings using our interactive drawing setup and see the resulting digital renderings. Our visualization will reveal unique aspects of each person's drawing process, and attendees will likely engage in lively discussion around drawing techniques and the broader implications of applying TEI research in the domain of fine arts. Our goal is that the analog, digital, and tangible aspects of our exhibit will be a catalyst for broader discussion on digitally mediated art making and art viewing within the TEI community. We believe that the outcome of such a discussion will be critical not only in shaping the future of our work, but also in understanding novel research directions at the intersection of art and computation.

REFERENCES

1. Jo Davies and Leo Duff. 2005. *Drawing the process.* Intellect Books.

2. Hisakazu Hada, Daisuke Tozuka, Sho Kamei, Tatsumi Hasegawa, Fuhito Morita, Shuntaro Ootsuki, and Akito Nakano. 2015. Sootoid: Generative Art Drawing by Flame of Candle. In *Proceedings of the Ninth International Conference on Tangible, Embedded, and Embodied Interaction (TEI '15)*. ACM, New York, NY, USA, 401–402. DOI: http://dx.doi.org/10.1145/2677199.2690869

3. Chris Harrison, Julia Schwarz, and Scott E. Hudson. 2011. TapSense: Enhancing Finger Interaction on Touch Surfaces. In *Proceedings of the 24th Annual ACM Symposium on User Interface Software and Technology (UIST '11)*. ACM, New York, NY, USA, 627–636. DOI: http://dx.doi.org/10.1145/2047196.2047279

4. Emmanuel Iarussi, Adrien Bousseau, and Theophanis Tsandilas. 2013. The Drawing Assistant: Automated Drawing Guidance and Feedback from Photographs. In *Proceedings of the 26th Annual ACM Symposium on User Interface Software and Technology (UIST '13)*. ACM, New York, NY, USA, 183–192. DOI: http://dx.doi.org/10.1145/2501988.2501997

5. Kazuhiro Jo. 2008. DrawSound: A Drawing Instrument for Sound Performance. In *Proceedings of the 2Nd International Conference on Tangible and Embedded*

Interaction (TEI '08). ACM, New York, NY, USA, 59–62. DOI:http://dx.doi.org/10.1145/1347390.1347405

6. Rubaiat Habib Kazi, Fanny Chevalier, Tovi Grossman, Shengdong Zhao, and George Fitzmaurice. 2014. Draco: Bringing Life to Illustrations with Kinetic Textures. In *Proceedings of the SIGCHI Conference on Human Factors in Computing Systems (CHI '14)*. ACM, New York, NY, USA, 351–360. DOI: http://dx.doi.org/10.1145/2556288.2556987

7. Younghui Kim, Geri Gay, Lindsay Reynolds, and Hyuns Hong. 2015. Mood.Cloud: Data As Art. In *Proceedings of the 33rd Annual ACM Conference Extended Abstracts on Human Factors in Computing Systems (CHI EA '15)*. ACM, New York, NY, USA, 347–350. DOI:http://dx.doi.org/10.1145/2702613.2744699

8. Sang-won Leigh, Harshit Agrawal, and Pattie Maes. 2016. A Flying Pantograph: Interleaving Expressivity of Human and Machine. In *Proceedings of the TEI '16: Tenth International Conference on Tangible, Embedded, and Embodied Interaction (TEI '16)*. ACM, New York, NY, USA, 653–657. DOI: http://dx.doi.org/10.1145/2839462.2856347

9. Sang-won Leigh, Asta Roseway, Ann Paradiso, and Pattie Maes. 2015. Remnance of Form: Interactive Narratives Through Unexpected Behaviors of a Shadow. In *Proceedings of the 33rd Annual ACM Conference Extended Abstracts on Human Factors in Computing Systems (CHI EA '15)*. ACM, New York, NY, USA, 387–390. DOI: http://dx.doi.org/10.1145/2702613.2725434

10. Deborah Turnbull Tillman, Mari Velonaki, and Petra Gemeinboeck. 2015. Authenticating Experience: Curating Digital Interactive Art. In *Proceedings of the Ninth International Conference on Tangible, Embedded, and Embodied Interaction (TEI '15)*. ACM, New York, NY, USA, 429–432. DOI: http://dx.doi.org/10.1145/2677199.2691602

11. Barbara Tversky. 2011. Visualizing Thought. *Topics in Cognitive Science* 3, 3 (2011), 499–535. DOI:http://dx.doi.org/10.1111/j.1756-8765.2010.01113.x

12. Shahar Zaks. 2012. Drawing Tool. In *Proceedings of the Sixth International Conference on Tangible, Embedded and Embodied Interaction (TEI '12)*. ACM, New York, NY, USA, 337–338. DOI: http://dx.doi.org/10.1145/2148131.2148210

13. Amit Zoran and Joseph A. Paradiso. 2013. FreeD: A Freehand Digital Sculpting Tool. In *Proceedings of the SIGCHI Conference on Human Factors in Computing Systems (CHI '13)*. ACM, New York, NY, USA, 2613–2616. DOI: http://dx.doi.org/10.1145/2470654.2481361

The Screaming Sun: Choreographing Synesthesia

Mithru Vigneshwara
New York University
(Interactive Telecommunications Program)
721 Broadway 4th Floor
New York NY 10003

TEI '18, March 18–21, 2018, Stockholm, Sweden

ACM ISBN 978-1-4503-5568-1/18/03.
https://doi.org/10.1145/3173225.3173308

Abstract
Digital devices usually contain pre-programmed constraints and behaviours. These behaviours are programmed by the architect of these devices. Analogue devices, on the other hand, are bound by the properties of the components connected to them. Controlling these components and external physical properties will in-turn lead to controlling the output of these devices. Many devices are built to perceive physical phenomena and react to certain stimuli. The Screaming Sun is an analogue noise-making instrument that experiments with light as a stimulus. It is a solar-powered interactive artifact that is meant to be played with and explored. The instrument, much like a living being, thrives on light. The performer plays the instrument by actually influencing the physical properties of light that shines on the instrument, and not by pushing buttons or turning knobs.

Author Keywords
Noise generation; synesthesia; interactive instrument; solar power;

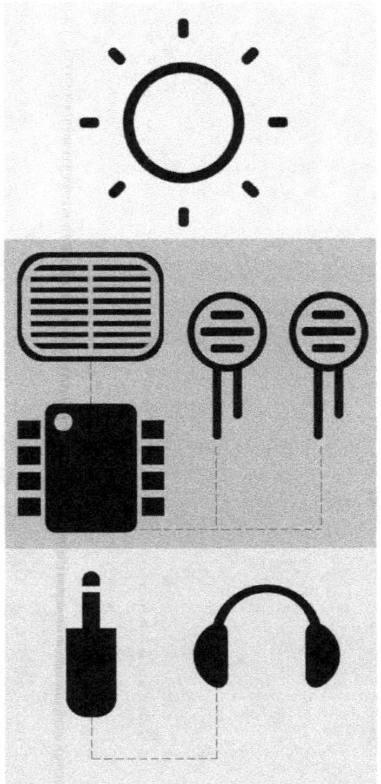

Figure 1 -
In th s image, the light source is the yellow section. It can be the sun or any powerful artificial light.
The process is the blue section. The solar panel (top-left in blue section) powers the electronics.
The sound output is the green section.

Introduction

The Screaming Sun is an interactive noise-making analogue instrument that runs completely off light. It is powered by light and also gets signal from light. The instrument consists of an analogue timer chip, which is powered by a solar panel. When powered, the timer sends out a frequency to headphones. The output frequency of the timer is based on two factors: firstly, the relative amount of light hitting two light-dependent resistors (LDRs) and secondly, the brightness and colour of the light received by the solar panel. To play the instrument, the performer either casts shadows or controls the colour or brightness of lights. A custom-designed laser-cut cardboard container forms the shell of the artifact.

Being an analogue system, there is no code required. At its most basic version, the system works with just sunlight, as depicted in Figure 1.However, attaching digital lights enables additional interesting interactions and sounds. In the current iteration, I've explored using a controllable LED bulb and mobile phone as the light sources.

The light from the LED bulb is sufficient to power the analogue circuit. The performer affects frequency that the circuit produces by placing their hand between the bulb and the solar panel. Moving the bulb or their hand, relative to the solar panel, affects the amount of light energy converted by the panel. This in-turn affects the frequency of sound produced. In this iteration, the LED bulb is controllable using an app.

Interface

A custom-built laser-cut cardboard case holds all the parts. The solar panel snuggly fits on the top of the case. The electronic components are placed inside the case. In the front, lies an audio slot for a pair of headphones or speakers. Above the audio slot, there is a pocket to place a phone. Inside the pocket, the light dependent resistors are placed such that they pick up light from two different sections on the phone's screen. The entire setup is shown in Figure 2.

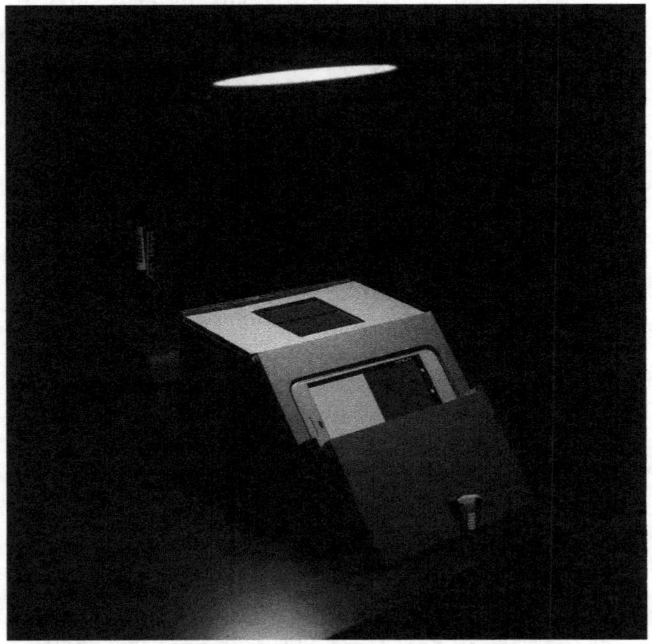

Figure 2 – A custom-built laser-cut cardboard container encases the components.

As long as the light shines on the panel, a sound is produced. The performer may block the light completely, which would stop all sounds, or partially block it by casting shadows. Choreographing the shadows cast will change the frequency of sound produced. Making gestures similar to pinching or chopping the path of light produces interesting results.

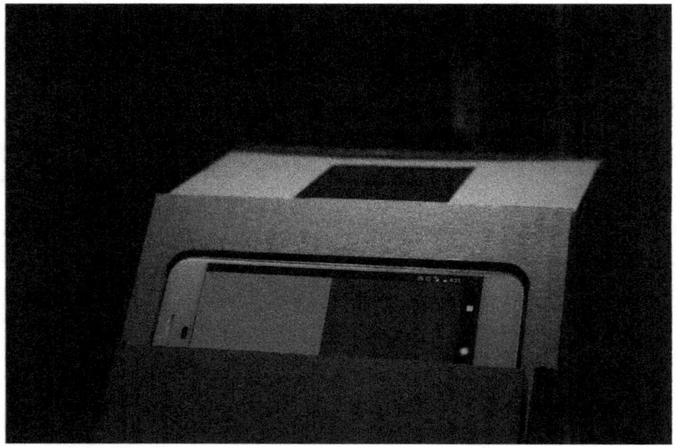

Figure 3 – The phone's screen is divided into two sections. Each section is a gray-scale block. The amount of gray can be changed from black to white by sliding across that section with a finger.

The light from the LED bulb also tends to leak onto the LDRs, which also affects the frequency produced. The LDRs are positioned within the custom-built cardboard case to be positioned flat on to a phone's screen. The relative light on the areas of the phone where the LDRs are positioned also affects the frequency. It is important to note that the phone is not digitally connected to the system in any way, but is merely a light source. In theory, any graphic on the phone's screen should affect the frequency. However, through tests and experiments, I have found that having a controllable gray-scale graphic between the two sections work the best (Figure 3). The performer can change the amount of gray by swiping horizontally across that section. The relative amount of gray between the two sections, in turn reflect the resistance produced by the light dependent resistors. This relative resistance controls the frequency produced.

The light source used in this setup is a LIFX smart LED bulb. It can be controlled using an app. The colour and brightness of the LED can be set. The app also has presets effects like strobe and random colour cycles, each of which produce noteworthy sounds.

Implementation

The system uses a 555 timer chip. The timer chip has multiple ways in which it can be configured, one of which produces a pulse[1]. The frequency of this pulse is defined by the relative resistance across particular pins on the chip. When a speaker is connected to the chip, it vibrates at that frequency and produces sound. The resistors used for this artifact are light dependent resistors (LDRs).

A small 5V solar panel is used to power the chip. The solar panel reacts to sunlight as well as relatively strong indoor lights. In my setup, I use a LIFX smart bulb, which can be controlled via an app. The amount of light absorbed by the panel with different colours varies. As a result, the energy produced by the solar panel for different colours and brightness values of the light is not the same.As this changes, the voltage coming out of the solar panel and into the timer chip affects the frequency that the chip produces. Casting shadows on the panel by partially blocking the amount of light that hits the panel also affects the power the timer gets and as a result the frequency of sound produced.

The electronic components are encased within a laser-cut cardboard shell. The shell has the provision to hold a phone against the LDRs. The light coming out of thephone affects the resistance on each LDR, which in turn affects the frequency.

Figure 4 – Affecting the light on both the solar panel (left hand) and the light dependent resistors that look at the phone (right hand)

Presentation

The current setup requires a relatively dark space. The smart LED bulb and artifact are placed on a table. The LED bulb requires power from a wall socket. A phone is placed inside the pocket of the cardboard case. The phone accesses a locally stored webpage that displays the gray-scale blocks. The smart bulb is connected to and controlled by another phone via an app over WiFi. The performer, using the app, can control colour, brightness and strobe effects.

Conclusion

The Screaming Sun is intended to be an experimental artifact that invites performers to play with it and produce interesting sounds by affecting light. Solar-based analogue theremins are not uncommon in the DIY electronics community. The Screaming Sun differentiates itself in that it is about the playful acts of choreographing hand movements to control the light sources through digital interfaces. This synesthetic choreography involves understanding the various parts in the analogue system. In the current iteration digital components are used to externally affect the light.That is an important distinction - the digital components only exist as light sources that influence the system. There is no digital processing that is used to produce the sound directly. In my future experiments, I will replace the smart bulb with a normal light bulb. The colours from the smart LED can be simulated on the normal bulb by using colour filters. The phone can be replaced entirely by redesigning the case to expose the light dependent resistors to the bulb. These changes make the factors that influence the light into analogue factors, effectively making every entity in the project analogue.

Figure 5: A young performer explores and plays with the artifact at an event; the colour of the light, the light from the phone and the shadows he casts on the panel affect the sound produced. In this setup, external speakers are connected instead of headphones.

Acknowledgements

I thank Jeff Feddersen for his guidance and support during his Energy class in Spring 2017, which was where this project started. I also thank everyone at NYU's Interactive Telecommunications Program who helped with their feedback, advice, documentation and play-test help along the way.

References

1. Texas Instruments. LM555 Timer Datasheet. Retrieved from http://www.ti.com/lit/ds/symlink/lm555.pdf
2. Andreas Schlegel. sound. light. study. Retrieved from https://vimeo.com/113691940
3. Jacky Boen, Benjamin Low, Mui Rui Yi, Zac Ong, Mithru Vigneshwara Synesthete's Music Box. Retrieved from http://mithru.com/works/the-synesthetes-music-box-2014/

Figure 1a: Twinkles lead people's way back home.

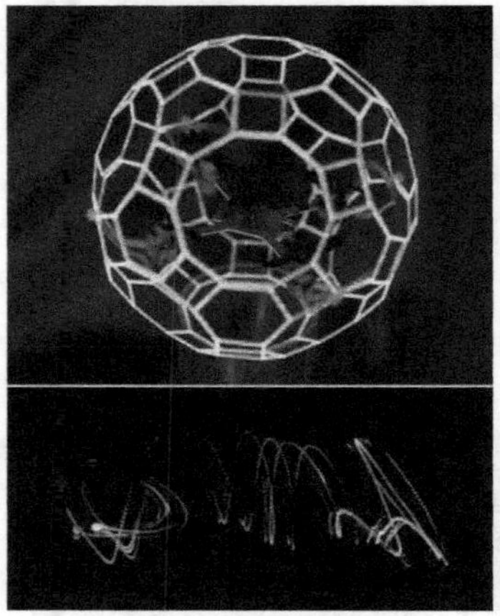

Figure 1b: The "puppy" twinkle prototype and its flying trajectory.

Twinkle: A Flying Lighting Companion for Urban Safety

Honghao Deng*
Harvard University
48 Quincy St.
Cambridge, MA 02138 USA
hdeng@gsd.harvard.edu

Jiabao Li*
Harvard University
48 Quincy St.
Cambridge, MA 02138 USA
jli@gsd.harvard.edu

* These authors contributed equally to this work

Allen Sayegh
Harvard University
48 Quincy St.
Cambridge, MA 02138 USA
asayegh@gsd.harvard.edu

Sebastian Birolini
University of Bergamo
19 Via Salvecchio.
Bergamo, BG 24129 Italy
sebastian.birolini@unibg.it

Stefano Andreani
Harvard University
48 Quincy St.
Cambridge, MA 02138 USA
andreani@gsd.harvard.edu

TEI '18, March 18–21, 2018, Stockholm, Sweden

ACM ISBN 978-1-4503-5568-1/18/03.
https://doi.org/10.1145/3173225.3173309

Abstract

The current city lighting system that leaves many areas uncovered induces unsafe perceptions and instigates crimes. The addition of ubiquitous surveillance is an intrusion on privacy and does not take real-time actions. The cold, lifeless light shines in the darkness, trapping people in the solitude of silence. These absences motivated us to create Twinkle - a luminous transformative creature inhabits on light posts. They are curious aerial animals attracted by human activities. During daytime, they rest on urban light posts, expanding their solar panels for charging. At night, they interact with individuals walking on the street in their own way based on their distinct personalities. Twinkles are indirect solutions for improving urban safety without surveillance. We envisage a future that appliance goes beyond machine and becomes a companion with us.

Author Keywords
Affective computing; UAV; Urban Lighting; Autonomous Aircraft; Interactive; Play.

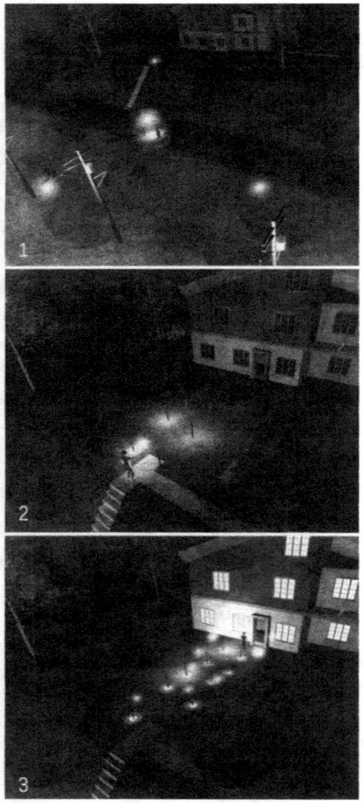

Figure 2: 1. Twinkle escorts the girl's way back home; 2. As the girl enters the yard, street Twinkle communicates with yard Twinkles to light up, and then flies back to its original light post; 3. As the girl enters her room, yard Twinkles turn on the lights in the room.

Introduction

Imagine a city with flying light: as night fell and darkness creeps in, all of a sudden there's a bright sparkle, and another – one by one lighting up the city street. Soon the sullen city comes alive, orchestrated with a natural rhythm of "Twinkle".

Lighting, as one major part of urban infrastructure providing areas with an abundance of potential witnesses, contributes significantly to feelings of safety [1, 2]. Farrington et al. suggested that crime can be prevented by environmental measures that directly affect offenders' perceptions of increased risks and decreased rewards [3]. However, the current city lighting system leaves many areas uncovered. Especially in remote regions with few populations, the sparse and dim streetlights cause unsafe feelings and instigate criminal activities. An additional way of environmental improvement is closed-circuit television (CCTV) cameras, but these surveillance systems creepily invade people's privacy. Moreover, they cannot make real-time actions, as most of them become evidences and clues to chase back the already happened crimes.

These absences motivated us to create Twinkle – a dynamic lighting companion that can light up areas on demand, and make pre-crime preventions (fig 1). Twinkles are luminous transformative creatures inhabit on light posts. They are aerial animals like fireflies that are curious, playful and are attracted by human activities. During daytime, they rest on urban light posts, expanding their solar panels for charging, which becomes shading for pedestrians. At night, they fly over to each individual walking on the street to offer abundant lighting for their way ahead. Twinkles are indirect solutions for improving urban safety without surveillance. Twinkles' behavior and habit help everyone walking nearby to have a better observation of the surroundings. At the same time, this indifferent act exposes the individuals who attempt to conduct misbehaviors to dazzling light to prevent crime ahead of time.

Personality

Twinkles are living creatures sharing the same space with human. Like human, they possess various emotions and personalities.

Within the many different parameters of each drone, we selected speed, reaction time, altitude, power and consistency as the key factors toward their characteristics (fig. 4). These physical properties result in the drones' distinct behaviors and hence lead to their unique personalities (fig. 5).

From friendly to annoying, from inactive to active, these flying creatures interact with people in their own way (fig. 3): "Puppy", with trusting and affectionate characteristic, is interested in playing with children. It feels comfortable when getting close to people. It flies around an intermediate altitude up and down without a consistent focus point and predictable path. It's naughty and curious, turning the night into a playground. "Big Boss", being confident and disciplined, stands at a high altitude to be aware of the surroundings within its territory. During emergency, it reacts fast to direct people's way by showing evacuation directions with its light skin. The powerful light has high visibility even in smoky and foggy areas. It can turn into alarms or light up dark areas for smoother evacuation. It's consistent, fast, and strong.

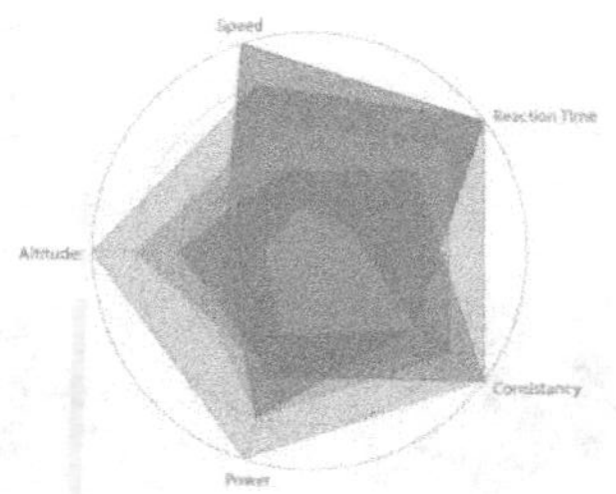

Figure 4. Speed, reaction time, altitude, power and consistency as the key factors towards Twinkle's characteristics.

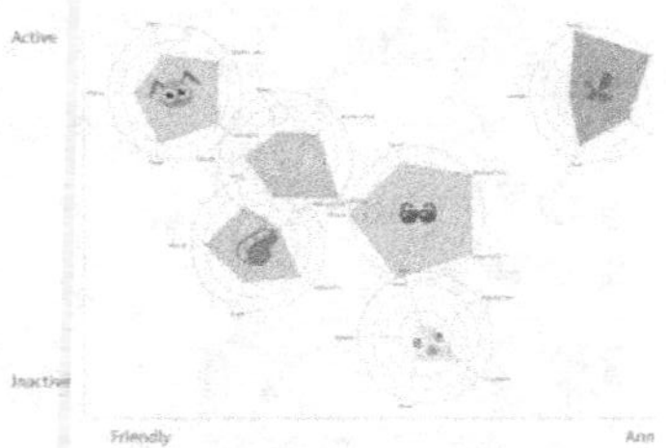

Figure 5. Physical properties of Twinkles result in their distinct behaviors and hence lead to their unique personalities.

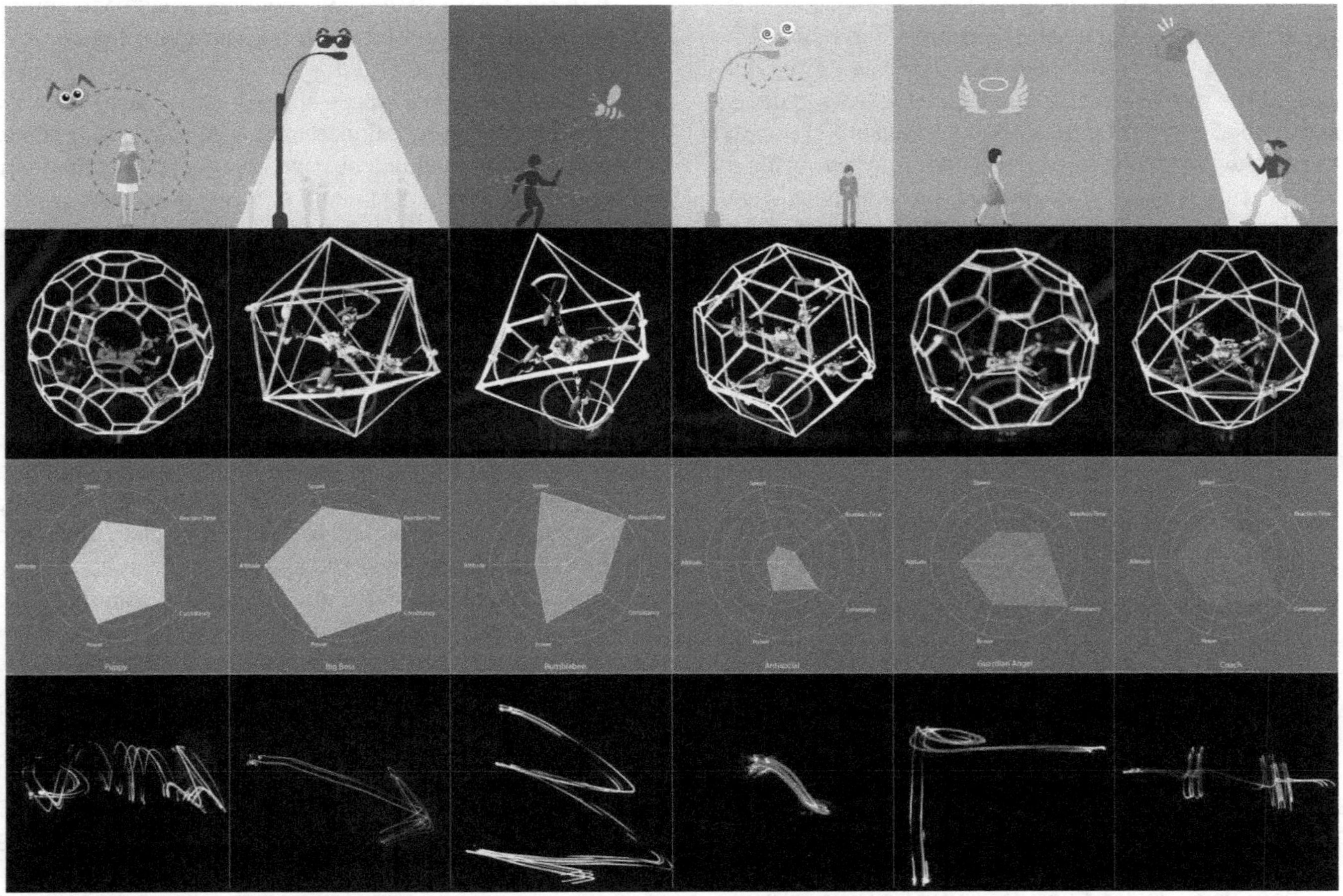

Figure 3. Twinkles family: from left to right are "Puppy", "Big Boss", "Bumblebee", "Anti-social Guy", "Guardian Angel", and "Coach". From top to bottom are each personality's application scenarios, appearances, flying parameters, and

"Bumblebee" is very sensitive to suspected behaviors and acts fast accordingly. Being suspicious and nervous, it looks around for danger all the time. Once detected, it attacks the criminal with dazzling light in full speed. By putting the potential criminal under exposure, it performs pre-crime preventions. "Anti-social Guy" is not interested in anything happening around. It's reserved, insensitive, burying in its own world. When a person comes into its view, it wobbles a little (may bumps into things) and then flies back to its original position, always keeping a distance to people. Sporadic light appears indistinctly depending on its

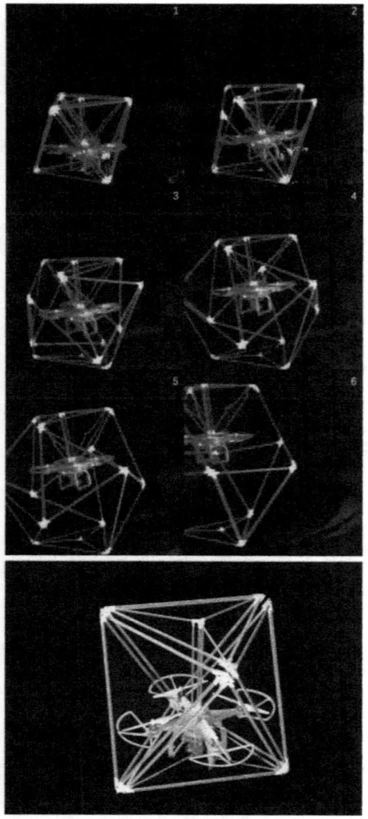

Figure 6. Twinkle's skeleton transformation based on the octahedron- cuboctahedron jitterbug structure. During nighttime, the triangle frames are compressed into smaller octahedron profile. During daytime, the actuator pushes the bottom and top triangle frames to trigger the symmetry rotation of each triangle frame on the rotation nodes.

mood. "Coach" guides people's sports training and helps optimizing training route. All along the outdoor workout, it keeps a constant distance ahead of the person, and illuminates the road underneath. It cheers trainees up when they are tired and leads the pace to the best benefit of trainees' health.

Skin

The outer polyhedron skeleton is Twinkle's skin, which mainly plays three roles: convey Twinkle's emotion, prevent direct contact to propellers, and change Twinkle's shape and function. When Twinkle expresses a different emotional state, the LED lights in the node will display different colors, frequencies, and rhythms correspondingly. The light will travel through the optical fiber to the entire skin. When there is a dramatic change in Twinkle's mood, the linear actuator will be enabled. The actuator's elongation and shortening drive each group of skeletons to synchronically rotate around the joint, which achieve the expansion and contraction effect of the entire skin structure to dramatically convey Twinkle's emotion.

Light

The light connects to the quadcopter body via a three-axis gimbal to achieve maximum degrees of freedom (fig. 7). Equipped with the 100w LED omnidirectional flood light, each Twinkle has the competence of a wide range light intensity with directional control. Together with the Glimmer on Twinkle's skin, the two systems make it possible for Twinkles' different personalities and versatile applications. For example, the bumblebees blink cautionary yellow on their skins in a rapid manner when there are suspicious people approaching them. The frequency gradually ramps up when the suspect gets closer. When triggered by certain behaviors such as screaming, the flood light will be fiercely bumped up to maximum brightness without any buffering time. Unlike other Twinkles focusing their light cone on people's way ahead, the bumblebees shed their intensive light directly on people. When the suspect gets closer, the light beam will steadily focus on the suspect's face through parabolic reflectors that come with an unpleasant flash. These lighting features make people tend to run away from them, which resemble the same reaction when people encounter real-life bees. On the other hand, the anti-social guy's Glimmer blinks in sleepy rhythm, like he is always groggy. He is hardly triggered by any kind of activities around. Even being triggered, he increases the intensity so slowly that he starts to dim down even before reaching full brightness, because he loses interest.

Transformative Elytron

Twinkle's skeleton transformation is based on the octahedron-cuboctahedron jitterbug transformation (fig. 6). During nighttime, the triangle frames are compressed into smaller octahedron profile to minimize the impact on aerodynamics of the center quadcopter. During daytime, the actuator pushes the bottom and top triangle frames to trigger the symmetry rotation of each triangle frame on the rotation nods. This transformation gradually reveals the thin-film solar cell folded in quadrangle gap between the isosceles triangle structures. When the actuator extends the structural height to twice as the original, the skin is fully expanded to a cuboctahedron skeleton covered with 6 square solar panels. This design creates solar absorbance coverage as big as the original octahedron surface area and provides shading on the pedestrian

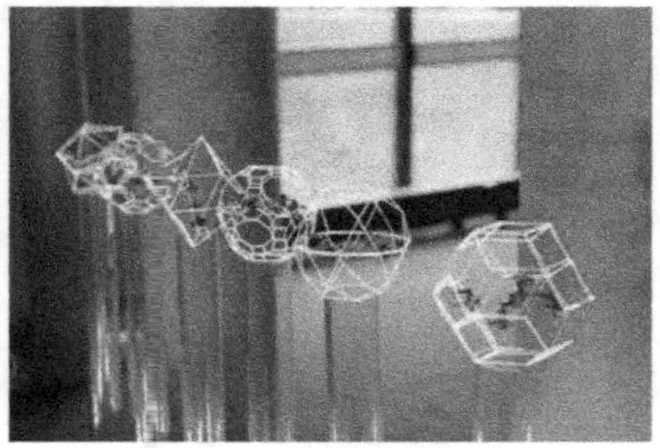

Figure 8. Prototypes of Twinkles using 3D-printed UV reflective resin as skeleton and UV LED as light source.

Figure 9: Twinkles' stations analyze people's behavior and position and send the data to twinkles.

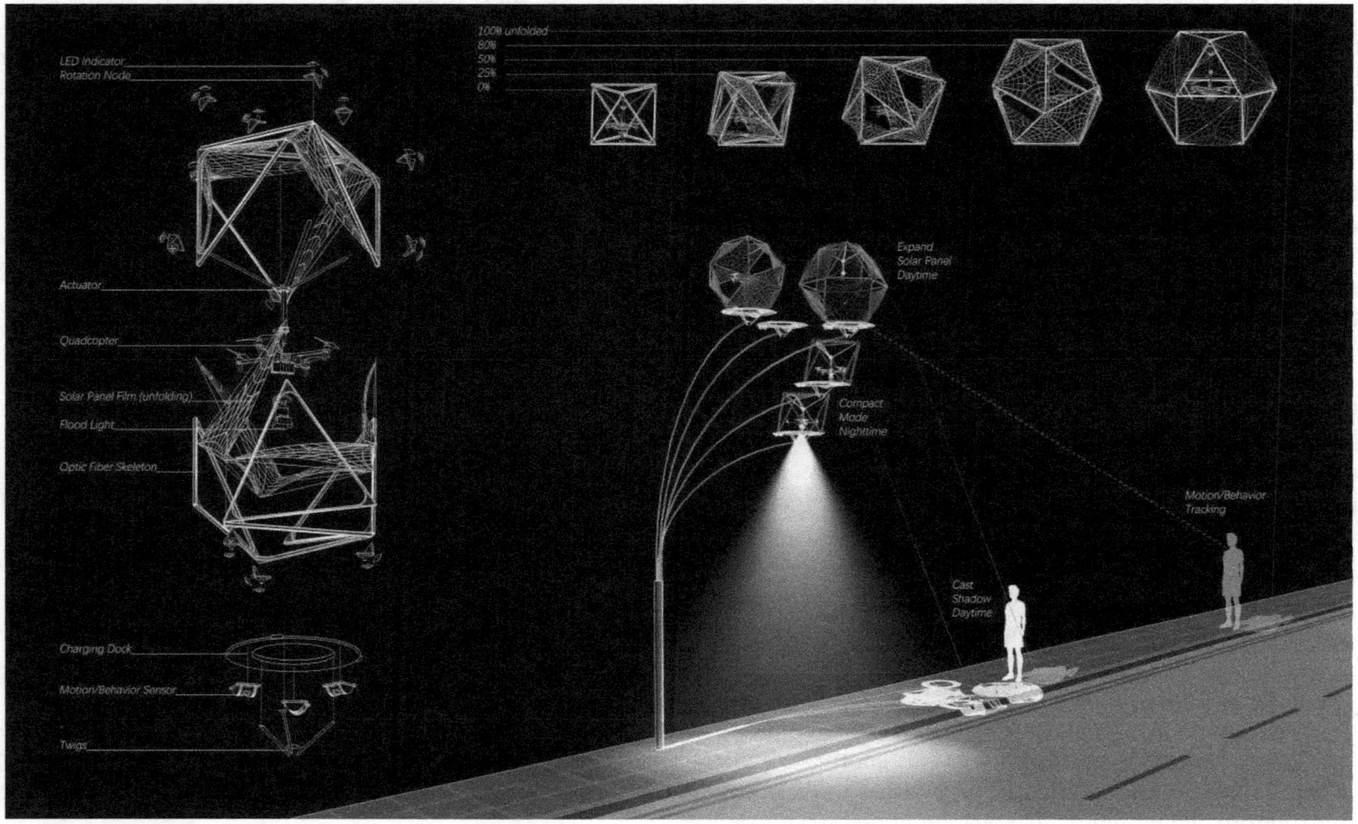

Figure 7. Anatomy of Twinkles: transformative Twinkle composed of optical fiber skeleton, flood light, solar panel film, quadcopter, actuator, and LEDs (top left); Twinkle's nest consists charging dock and behavior sensor (bottom left); Twinkle unfolds solar film from 0% to 100% to absorb sunlight and create shadow during daytime (top right), and folds back to compact mode during nighttime (bottom right).

during daytime. The structure is wrapped back to octahedron to improve mobility and prevent the solar cells from blocking lighting after sunset.

NEST

A base station can have multiple twigs to host more than one Twinkle. During daytime, when Twinkle expands its solar sail for charging, the nest stores excessive electricity. In the case of insufficient sunlight, it transmits power to Twinkle through the wireless charging dock. At night, it is the data hub of signal collection and analysis. When someone enters the responsive range, it captures and analyzes the location information of people to guide Twinkle's flight path.

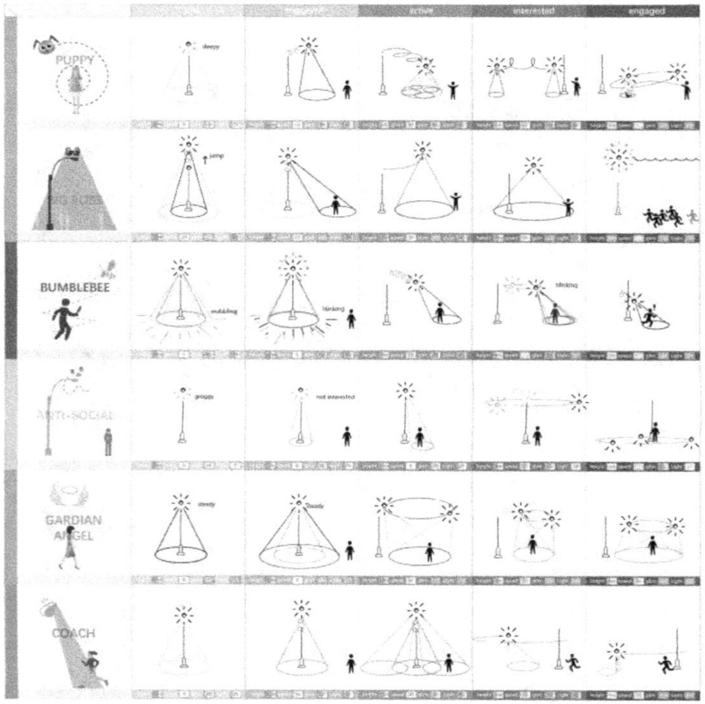

Figure 10. Twinkles embody different traits and habits in various surroundings according to their own personalities. These different behaviors are quantified into parameters including height, speed, glim, and light. From left to right as their distance to human increases there are five states: idle, triggered, active, interested, and engaged.

Impact on human lives

For everyone's daily life, the urban lighting is no longer a cold, immutable infrastructure but a new form of companionship with personalities and responses. Community wise, Twinkle's habitual nature exerts a subtle influence on improvement of public security and city's environment. The flying along habit with anyone passing by indirectly obstructs crime, reshaping the neighborhood from dangerous to safe. The companionship reduces not only crimes but also people's misbehaviors like public graffiti and littering. Furthermore, as a result of Twinkles' personality, the unsafe neighborhood will attract more bumblebees and guardian angels. In the long run, Twinkle's ethnic groups will migrate in accordance with the city's development and change, forming an autonomous dynamic lighting distribution. The communities will also be slowly reshaped respectively for Twinkles to bring in new vitality to people's activities at night.

REFERENCES

1. J. R. R. Naik N, Philipoom and C. Hidalgo. Streetscore: Predicting the perceived safety of one million streetscapes. CVPR Workshop on Web-scale Vision and Social Media., 2014.
2. C. Alm, E. Lindberg, Perceived Risk, Feelings of Safety and Worry Associated with Different Travel Modes, KFB, Stockholm, 2000.
3. David P. Farrington & Brandon C. Welsh (2002) Improved street lighting and crime prevention, Justice Quarterly, 19:2, 313-342, DOI: 10.1080/07418820200095261
4. J. Cauchard, K. Zhai, M. Spadafora, J. Landay, "Emotion Encoding in Human-Drone Interaction", *The Eleventh ACM/IEEE International Conference on Human Robot Interaction*, pp. 263-270.

5. Cirque du Soleil, ETH Zürich, and Verity Studios, SPARKED: A Live Interaction Between Humans and Quadcopters, SIGGRAPH, Computer Animation Festival, 2015.
6. Sky Magic. 2016. Sky Magic Live at Mt.Fuji : Drone Ballet Show by MicroAd, Inc. Video. Retrieved July 15, 2017 from https://vimeo.com/163266757
7. Intel. 2016. Intel's 500 Drone Light Show. Retrieved July 15, 2017 from https://www.intel.com/content/www/us/en/technology-innovation/aerial-technology-light-show.html
8. B. Kim, HY. Kim, J. Kim, Getting Home Safely with Drone, UBICOMP/ISWC, 2016. http://dx.doi.org/10.1145/2968219.2971426
9. F. Mueller, M. Muirhead. 2015. Jogging with a Quadcopter. In Proc. CHI '15, ACM Press, Seoul, Korea. DOI: 10.1145/2702123.2702472
10. H. Agrawal. S. Leigh, P. Maes. *L'evolved*: Autonomous and Ubiquitous Utilities as Smart Agents. *Proceedings of the 2015 ACM International Joint Conference on Pervasive and Ubiquitous Computing, 2015*, pp. 487-491.
11. M. Kljun, K. C. Pucihar, M. lochrie, P. Egglestone, StreetGamez: a Moving Projector Platform for Projected Street Games, CHI PLAY 2015. DOI: http://dx.doi.org/10.1145/2793107.2810305
12. J. Lindley, P. Coulton, Game of Drones, CHI PLAY 2015, DOI:

    http://dx.doi.org/10.1145/2793107.2810300
13. S. Leigh, H. Agrawal, P. Maes, A Flying Pantograph: Interleaving Expressivity of Human and Machine, TEI 2016 Art Exhibition, DOI: http://dx.doi.org/10.1145/2839462.2856347
14. M. Matrosov, O. Volkova, D. Tsetserukou, LightAir: a Novel System for Tangible Communication with Quadcopters using Foot Gestures and Projected Image, SIGGRAPH '16 Emerging Technologies, DOI: http://dx.doi.org/10.1145/2929464.2932429
15. R. Mustadin, J. Wehner, W. Sattler, K. Gohlke, T.F.O. – Tangible Flying Objects, TEI 2012
16. Stratus 100W LED Modules, Stratus Productions, Retrieved July 23, 2017 from https://www.stratusleds.com/module/
17. Light Levels and Uniformity, City & County of San Francisco, Retrieved July 23, 2017 from http://www.sfbetterstreets.org/find-project-types/streetscape-elements/street-lighting/#codes_docs
18. H. Verheyen. (1989) The complete set of Jitterbug transformers and the analysis of their motion. Computers & Mathematics with Applications, vol.17 (Issues 1–3), pp.203-250, DOI: https://doi.org/10.1016/0898-1221(89)90160-0
19. R. Stuart, Polyhedral and Mosaic Transformations, Student Publications of the School of Design, Univ. of North Carolina, vol. 12, 1963, No. 1.
20. CoDrone, Robolink, 2017, Retrieved July 23, 2017 from http://www.robolink.com/codrone/
21. C. Breazeal, "Emotion and sociable humanoid robots", International Journal of Human-Computer Studies, 1st–2nd ed., vol. 59, 2003, pp.119–155.

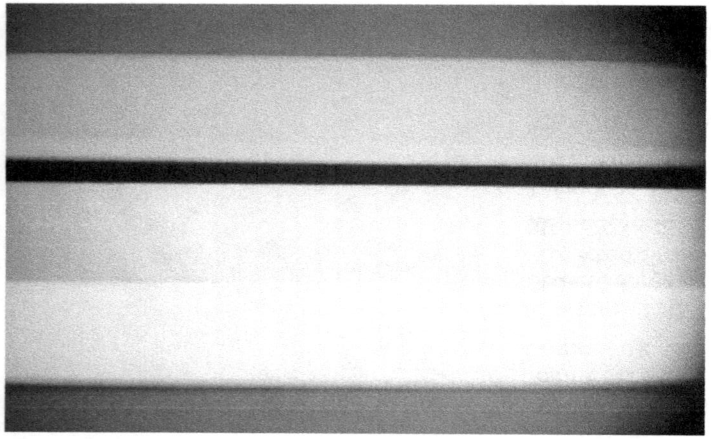

Synesthetic Experience in S T R A T I C

Vygandas "Vegas" Šimbelis
KTH Royal Institute of Technology
Stockholm, Sweden
Vygandas@kth.se

Anders Lundström
KTH Royal Institute of Technology
Stockholm, Sweden
Andelund@kth.se

 ACM ISBN 978-1-4503-5568-1/18/03.
https://doi.org/10.1145/3173225.3173310

Abstract

How do we humanize digital interactive technology? One way is through our experience with technology. With S T R A T I C we present several post-digital concepts to discuss the relationship of the digital in regard to our human lives. We emphasize the *synesthetic experience* along with other aesthetic experiences and materiality issues with manifestations of the digital in the physical world, tangible approaches to sonic performances, or exposure of internal logics of technological processes.

In this paper, we propose both exhibiting our work as an art installation and via a live performance. We regard it as being highly relevant to the topic of the TEI Arts Track exhibition: post-digital materiality at the intersection of the analog and the digital, and to its tangible aspects.

Author keywords

Synesthetic experience; post digital; post-digital aesthetics; interactive art; interaction design; audio-visual performance; sampling rate.

Figure 1. Three still images from the S T R A T I C visuals.

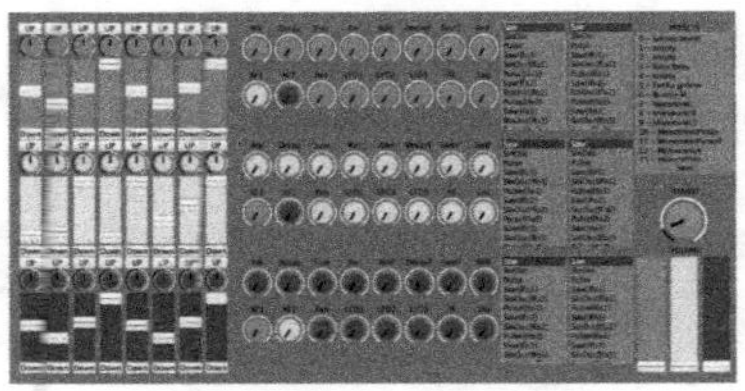

Figure 2. Audio control panel, digital interface.

Introduction

Art-driven research is becoming increasingly important in interaction design and human-computer interaction (HCI) and research that is not problem-driven is finding new ways of conducting research, for instance, by focusing instead on artistic rethinking, reimagining and reinterpreting in comparison to established methods derived from cognitive psychology and computer science. Examples of other approaches are concepts such as ambiguity [15], defamiliarization [3], alienation and uncomfortable interactions [4], aesthetic experience [11], and interaction criticism [2]. In such research the HCI field has borrowed concepts and practices from art theory, philosophy of aesthetics, and critical theory in order to address problems arising as interactive technologies enter into every walk of life. The so-called third wave in HCI is heading towards experiential qualities and shifts from the workplace to more broader and intermixed contexts such as the home, everyday life and culture. It "addresses the topics of multiplicity, context, boundaries, experience and participation" [7].

Recently, audio-visual performances have been receiving more attention and interest in academia (e.g. [13,28]), particularly in the fields of interaction design and HCI that focus more on artistic expression [16,18,24]. Artists exhibit interactive art installations more often and designers demo their prototypes with a focus on aesthetic qualities in conferences such as TEI, ACE, NIME, CHI and ISEA.

The intention of this project is to serve artistic audiences and those interested in aesthetic pursuits and the logics of perception. Thus, the experiential qualities have been strongly expressed. The aesthetic experience with an emphasis on synesthetic experience is discussed below in relation to the post digital.

We want to expand the ongoing discussion about the post digital [6,20] in the arts and materiality research connecting the old and new [9,17], the digital and the physical in HCI [12]. In this domain, art practices and interaction design, as well as theories related to art, technology and science, have been taken into account.

S T R A T I C project

The S T R A T I C project[1] explores the interplay of the sensory actuation in interactive media expression, and the aesthetic properties of analog/digital transformations engendered by the limitations and qualities of various forms of sensing apparatus. The result takes the form of noisy and hypnotic soundscapes linked to an abstract animation (examples in Figure 1). The abstract animation is directly generated from the sound.

This S T R A T I C project is based on the phenomenon that occurs when filming a pulsating light – lines appear on the screen. This phenomenon is produced without any additional computational processes incorporated as the phenomenon happens inside the camera between the pulsation of RGB LED light and the use of the shutter speed and frame rate of a camera. In other words, the sound generates the visuals in real time. The sound is generated digitally and controlled through the digital interface in processing software (see Figure 2) and then sent to a circuit board.

[1] http://stratic.net

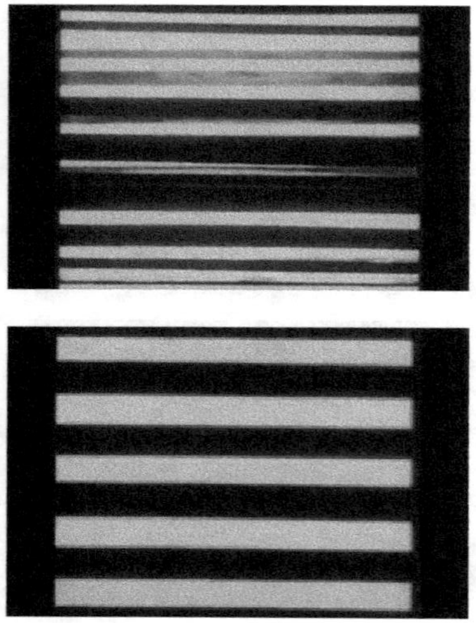

Figure 3. Opus IV by Ruttmann.

Thus, the thickness and movement of these lines are directly related to the frequency of the sound and of the pulsation of the light in relation to the sampling rate [23,27] of the camera. In this project we explore the interactive potential and the space for aesthetic expression by synthesizing the audio and the visuals.

Project Background

The project is grounded in a form of aesthetics referred to in the art tradition as "avant-garde cinema". *Visual-music* genre originated in the beginning of XX century with silent films in which sound was directly translated into a related visual presentation. In particular, abstract films with their avant-garde experiments, such as Walter Ruttmann's "Opus" series (1921–1925) in which he uses the film medium to expand formalist artistic expression, see Figure 3. In Opus, Ruttmann uses analog film materials to express the dynamics of abstract graphic elements, which are accompanied by music, creating a synchronized audio-visual journey. In Opus IV (1925), it bears a resemblance to the STRATIC of its horizontal moving lines.

This project also relates to the futurist art movement of noise music promoting aesthetics that draw directly on machines and their processes. This, in turn, relates to the glitch as an artistic resource and might be perceived in relation to the separation of glitches into *fault aesthetics* and *glitch aesthetics* [25]. This is connected to how Italian futurist composer Luigi Russolo (1883–1947) embraced the aesthetics of noises created by machines and used them for artistic expression by tuning the noises into a polyphony of an "*intoxicating orchestra of noises*".[21] His definition of noise is broad and ever growing as new machines continuously give rise to new forms of noise.

We find interesting parallels between the Modernist tradition and digital culture and its relationship to the post digital [1]. On the one hand, the importance to the whole post-digital condition with references between the old and new [9,17] though, on the other hand, important steps towards the historical foundation of the glitch with the futurist noise approach. The glitch is directly derived from the early art experiments, for example, Magnet TV (1965) by Nam June Paik video artwork, or examples of early avant-garde film editing techniques such as the Soviet Montage Theory of Sergei Eisenstein through formalist and futurist approaches. However, in this work, of course, we align with the digital glitch, which manifests via digital means and is being introduced as a resource for post-digital expression [8].

Mapping concepts of the project

By examining the post-digital qualities of the S T R A T I C project, we employed important concepts, material inquiries, aesthetic decisions and experiences.

Abstraction

In this project, a particular focus has been put on researching the concept of *abstraction* and how abstraction takes place in HCI and the arts field. However, we also see the importance of abstraction in redirecting focus from a displayed content and storytelling to more visual, minimalistic and formalistic presentations, in which more extreme and sensual experiences may arise by examining the ways perception affects our experience.

One example is op (optical) art. Op art employs perception at its best as it explores the visual field of abstract images and creates illusory and imaginary

Figure 4. The process scheme of the system.

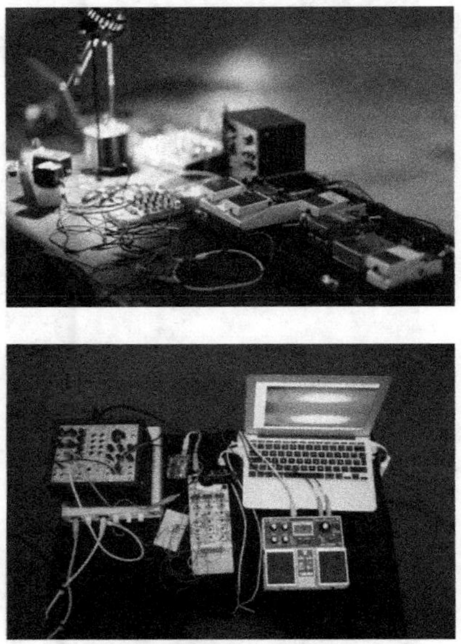

Figure 5. Exposure of internal processes of the system.

spheres in which the viewer's vision becomes confused and new visual narratives are created.

The general notion of abstraction relates to the rejection of the representation of realistic and visual references in the world. This notion shifts the focus from the content of the message to the sensual experience and explores the logic of the formal and minimalistic constructs using highly synchronized audio and visuals. This consolidated minimalistic appearance relates to the *synesthetic experience*, in which cross-modal associations create an involuntary physical experience.

Synesthetic experience with audio and video
In the S T R A T I C performances the audience reflected on a highly perceivable synchronization between the visuals and the sound. Such performances affect how the viewers hear the visuals and see the audio as, technically, both these modalities get generated directly from each other. In our project two modalities correlate, however, it is not a limit: "...the stimulation of one sensory modality reliably causes a perception in one or more different senses".[10] The HCI researcher Ilias Bergström also discusses the effects of audio-visual stimuli on the audience in connection with more than one modality and relates visual music and synesthesia with audio-visual perception: "Most relevant to the present discussion is the experience of sound as animated colors and/or shapes".[5]

The experienced synesthesia is a bodily and sensory perception of sound and imagery, in which sound and visuals merge into a single whole and the overlap creates a multi-modal experience. The interconnection between the audio-visual formats is shown through engaging the audience through bodily engagement. In the S T R A T I C installation, sound is perceived through sight while also following the visuals through hearing.

Post-digital bodily experience of sound
Another no less important quality was raised regarding audio when using powerful professional sound systems supporting low frequencies (deep bass) for the performances. This is one of the post-digital qualities discussed by Rasmus Fleischer, 2009, in which digital sound is amplified using a powerful analog system and is perceived through the full-body experience [14]. Following this, the S T R A T I C project embodies the digital dimension by using powerful sound systems, so the whole body physically and bodily perceives digital sound through deep bass frequencies.

Exposure of internal processes
By explicitly escaping the formal laptop performance notion, we should consider Andrews' [1] advice and his discussion on laptop performances through the exposure of processes and the incorporation of physical clues. In this regard, we tried to bring the internal production processes of the S T R A T I C system to be exposed. The devices and processes are made transparent through the *machine aesthetics* approach [22,24] and what is happening on the table is perceivable by the audience. The circuit board with pulsating LED, the process of capturing a pulsating light with a camera is revealed to the audience, and is also shown in Figures 4 and 5.

The notion of the digital and networks is key to understand the post-digital. We may look beyond the

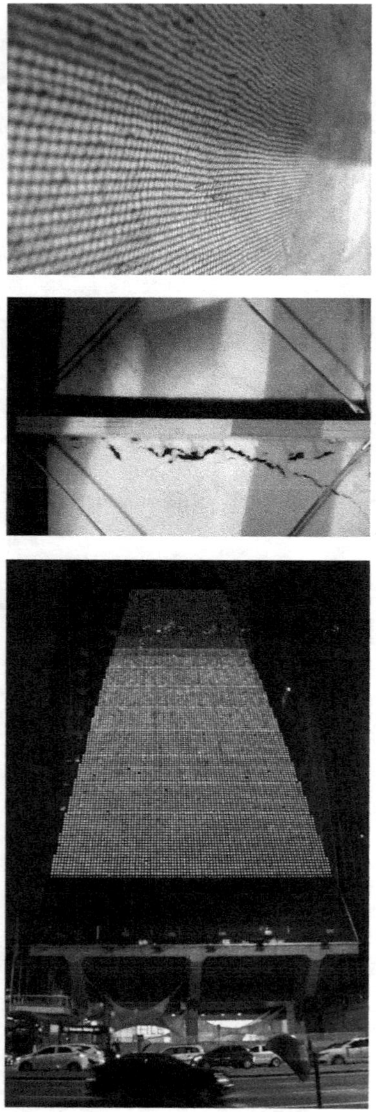

Figure 6. "Digital paintings": top, installation at DKTUS; middle, snow projection; bottom, building screen at FILE festival.

digital through the exposure of its inner machinic processes and behaviors or "an objecthood that incorporates networked digital technologies".[19] This brings us to re-examine the logics of what is going on the production and generative side of the project.

Glitch aesthetics

Returning to the emphasized post-digital quality of technological malfunctioning and its manifestation in artistic works [8], in the S T R A T I C the glitch appears directly from the electrical leaps, through which glitch appearances break the smooth flow of visual lines. This accidental glitch is derived from the electrical charges and appears out of nowhere. Such "glitch approach" refers to *fault aesthetics* [25] principles. However, it is hard to notice a glitch in sonic appearances such as this, as the whole soundscape comprises drone-like music and incorporates many glitch-like sounds.

Manifestations of the video in physicality

Experiments with various screen surfaces caused us to add another layer in our performance and exhibit "digital paintings" [23,27]. The different surfaces examine the notion of manifesting the digital and the glitch in other materialities. Many aspects become evident. For instance, the shape and size of the screen, the materials onto which the projection is beamed, the reflections emerging from the reflective surfaces, and the texture and materials of the screen. All these aspects cause both the digital and the analog to manifest in physicality. The post-digital attribute of the materialization of the digital manifests in the context of projecting the visuals onto various physical surfaces, as well as through hybridization of various formats and forms.

Exhibitions in various contexts

Earlier explorations of the S T R A T I C project have been exhibited at various events and in different contexts from art exhibitions and digital art festivals to conferences. The "digital paintings" (Figure 6) were displayed on various physical surfaces: the rough surface of the wall transformed the projection into a vibrant and wavy movement of colorful lines at the DKTUS art project space in Stockholm. The glass dome building was illuminated from inside by projecting the visuals onto the snow's surface (Dome of Visions, Stockholm). The mega projection of the project was exhibited on a façade of a skyscraper at FILE - Electronic Language International Festival - Fiesp Cultural Center, São Paulo, Brazil, 2016.

Discussion through the post digital

Despite various insights into materiality and discussions of the interrelated concepts, we argue that one of the major implications and take-aways of the project is the *aesthetic synesthetic experience*. Such experience brings a bodily and sensory perception of the sounds and imagery, in which sound and visuals converge into a single coherent whole and create intrinsic multi-modal experiences. The sound is seen and the visuals are heard. Through this process, other modalities of full-body sound experience and exposure of the internal processes are taken into account. The convergence of the digital and analog, the manifestations of the digital in the physical world become part of the same aesthetic experience. We argue that its main relevance is to the fields of both post digital and HCI.

From the start, the S T R A T I C project concerned itself with the limits of human senses at those edges where the boundaries between various formats and

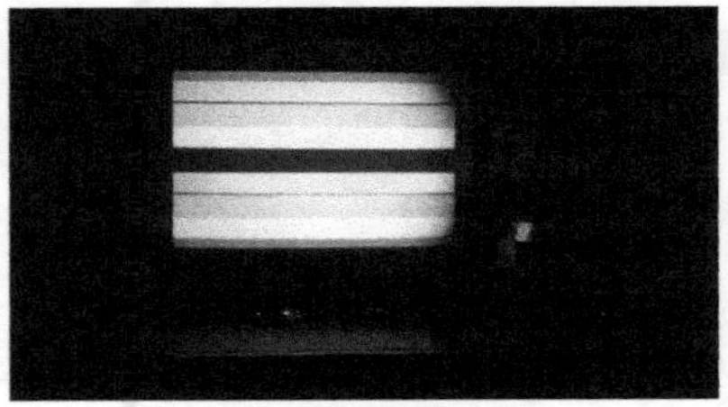

Figure 7. Live performances: top image. Reactor Hall R1, Stockholm; bottom, ACE 2016 conference.

Figure 8. Installation at Open Fields exhibition and conference RIXC 2016, Riga, Latvia.

forms dissolve and new modalities and experiences arise. In the audio-visual performance and art installation, both the audio and the visual work together – to create evocative and extreme experiences. The project seeks to overcome the separation of the audio and the visual. It also draws on convergences of practices and attitudes in order to evoke various sensations.

With this project looking through a post-digital lens we have aimed for the humanization of interactive technology. One way of humanizing digital technologies is through encompassing and relating to our complex and rich cultural capacities. The other way is through the deeper involvement and engagement of our bodies, emotions and experiences with the technologies with which we interact. With this project we have aimed for creating evocative experiences that are at the limits of our human perception.

With such evocative experiences, which manifest through listening to the visuals and seeing the sounds, i.e. perceiving synesthesia, we can relate and inspect the life-logging movement with its "cold" understanding of *numerical aesthetics* and also compare it with other more humane approaches towards quality of life. In this case, our work complements the notion of the post digital with a concept of *qualified-self* by bringing evocative experiences and supporting the notion with more humane qualities and values in our interactions, such as: to cope with the mass of information we generate without the information losing its sentimental value – a form of *qualified-self* instead of the more recognized quantified-self movement.[26]

TEI 2018 The Arts Track proposals

For the TEI Arts Track, we propose an art installation and a live performance. Both could be conducted on their own or in combination.

In the live audio-visual performance (Figure 7) we will use a more complex tool to control the light in order to create more evocative and extreme experiences and compose a show. The performance could take place on a stage, in an art gallery, or in an open space.

In the installation (example in Figure 8), the film of the phenomenon will be screened to share the core of the project – the synesthetic experience – and will function on its own, without the presence of the artist.

Artist

Vygandas "Vegas" Šimbelis is an artist and researcher who combines various approaches in his artistic practice and research. His work is founded on visual, conceptual and media art paradigms, which recently became strongly focused on the technological aspect of new media through the notion of the post digital.

Anders Lundström is a researcher and musician. Combining design and technology is key to his work and he has particular interests in the interaction with abstract data, visual and sonic feedback, meaning-making, and aspects of interactional coupling with technology.

References

1. Ian Andrews. Post-digital aesthetics and the return to modernism.
2. Jeffrey Bardzell. 2011. Interaction criticism: An introduction to the practice. *Interacting with Computers* 23, 6: 604–621.
3. Genevieve Bell, Mark Blythe, and Phoebe Sengers. 2005. Making by Making Strange: Defamiliarization and the Design of Domestic Technologies. *ACM Transactions on Computer-Human Interaction* 12, 2: 149–173.
4. Steve Benford, Chris Greenhalgh, Gabriella Giannachi, Brendan Walker, Joe Marshall, and Tom Rodden. 2012. Uncomfortable interactions. *In Proc. CHI'12*, ACM Press.
5. Ilias Bergström. 2011. Soma: live performance where congruent musical, visual, and proprioceptive stimuli fuse to form a combined aesthetic narrative.
6. David Berry and Michael Dieter. 2015. *Post-digital Aesthetics. Art, Computation and Design*. Palgrave Macmillan.
7. Susanne Bødker. 2006. When second wave HCI meets third wave challenges. *Proceedings of the 4th Nordic conference on Human-computer interaction*, ACM.
8. Kim Cascone. 2000. The Aesthetics of Failure - Post Digital Tendencies in Contemporary Computer Music. *Computer Music Journal* 24, 4: 12–18.
9. Florian Cramer. 2015. What is "Post-digital"? In *Post-digital Aesthetics. Art, Computation and Design.* Palgrave Macmillan, 12–26.
10. Richard E. Cytowic. 1995. Synesthesia: Phenomenology and neuropsychology. *Psyche* 2.10.
11. John Dewey. 2005. *Art as Experience*. Penguin.
12. Paul Dourish. 2017. *The Stuff of Bits: An Essay on the Materialities of Information.* MIT Press.
13. Ludvig Elblaus, Kjetil Hansen, and Roberto Bresin. 2014. NIME Design and Contemporary Music Practice: Benefits and Challenges. NIME.
14. Rasmus Fleischer. 2009. The Postdigital Manifesto. How music takes place.
15. William W. Gaver, Jacob Beaver, and Steve Benford. 2003. Ambiguity as a resource for design. *In Proc. CHI'03*, ACM Press, 233–240.
16. Kristina Höök, Phoebe Sengers, and Gerd Andersson. 2003. Sense and Sensibility: Evaluation and Interactive Art. 5: 241–248.
17. Holger Lund. 2015. Make It Real & Get Dirty! *Post-digital Culture*.
18. John McCarthy and Peter Wright. 2004. *Technology as experience*. The MIT Press.
19. Christiane Paul. 2015. From Immateriality to Neomateriality: Art and the Conditions of Digital Materiality. *Proceedings of the 21st International Symposium on Electronic Art.*
20. Christiane Paul. 2016. *A Companion to Digital Art*. John Wiley & Sons.
21. Lawrence Rainey, Christine Poggi, and Wittman Laura. 2009. *Futurism: an anthology*. Yale University Press.
22. Vygandas Simbelis. 2013. Metaphone: An Artistic Exploration of Biofeedback and Machine Aesthetics. *Ext. Abstracts CHI'13*: 2995–2998.
23. Vygandas Šimbelis and Anders Lundström. 2015. S T R A T I C: Performing the Sampling Rate. *In Proc. ACE'15*, ACM.
24. Vygandas Šimbelis, Anders Lundström, Kristina Höök, Jordi Solsona, and Vincent Lewandowski. 2014. Metaphone: Machine Aesthetics Meets Interaction Design. *In Proc. CHI'14*, ACM Press: 1–10.
25. Vygandas Vegas Simbelis. 2017. Time and Space in Broken Panorama. *Proceedings of the 2017 Conference on Designing Interactive Systems*, ACM.
26. Vygandas "Vegas" Šimbelis, Pedro Ferreira, Elsa Vaara, Jarmo Laaksolahti, and Kristina Höök. 2016. Repurposing Bits and Pieces of the Digital. *CHI´16*, ACM Press.
27. Vygandas "Vegas" Šimbelis and Anders Lundström. 2016. Synthesis in the Audiovisual. *CHI'16*, ACM Press.
28. Carl Unander-Scharin, Kristina Höök, and Ludvig Elblaus. 2013. The throat III. *SIGCHI Conference on Human Factors in Computing Systems*, ACM Press.

Thou and I: Exploring Expressive Digital Interaction with Interactive Characteristic Wigs

Young Suk Lee
Indiana University, South Bend
South Bend, IN 46615, USA
artdesignys@gmail.com

Figure1. Don't Talk To me
Motion Interactive wig

TEI 2018, March 18–21, 2018, Stockholm, Sweden.
ACM ISBN 978-1-4503-5568-1/18/03.
https://doi.org/10.1145/3173225.3173311

Abstract
My project involves the construction of a series of experimental wearable digital technologies as expressive wigs. These wigs are designed to explore the interactions of the wearers and the spectators as the wig moves in elaborate ways to highlight the realms of aesthetic value and sensory experience. The participants are provoked, they are engaged, they are compelled into a state of awareness and curiosity while the digital object constitutes novel experiences that coincide with anthropomorphic interactivity.
Furthermore, the expressive value of a digital object is turned inwards as it becomes an extension of the self and a source of multi-sensory communication.
Ultimately, the digital object seeks to open a social dialogue on the aesthetic purpose of technology by encouraging people to extend their imagination through bodily interaction. Here the digital object enables the wearers to create engaging narratives and provocative expressions.

Author Keywords
Art; Experimental Wearable Technologies; Aesthetic Interaction; Expressive Digital Interaction

ACM Classification Keywords
• General and reference~Design • Human-centered computing~HCI theory, concepts and models

Figure2. Thou and I
Touch Interactive wig

Introduction
Towards Expressive and Provocative Technology Experience

Today people use wearable technology for informative purposes. Some of wearable devices are designed to generate data about some activity that people undertake, whether it is consumption, activity or internal biological functions (i.e. counting calories, measuring steps, heart rates). These modern digital consumer products are passive in their execution, even if they produce a specific correlation between personal perceptions via numerical data (acknowledgement of activity or value of engagement). There is some inherent limitation in people's ability to express themselves through the wearable device while being measured by it.

My work, on the other hand, seeks to explore technology's capacity to affect people's idea in a creative manner. As Anthony Dunne claimed, "The electronic object does not have to fulfill our expectations; it can surprise and provoke." [1]. In a similar vein, I open an innovative space for people to formulate new ideas of using wearable digital object towards more expressive way by introducing a series of interactive wigs. By taking a holistic design approach in the construction of the intriguing narratives through the characteristic wigs, both the wearer and the spectator are encouraged to explore the aesthetic use of technology while connecting their emotion and intention to the interactivities. Ultimately, The multi-sensory interactivities are designed to fertilize expressive and provocative technology experience concurring with people's sensual and ethereal engagement. These wigs address dual perspectives aiming to bridge the possible connections through Human-to-Human-Interaction and Human-and-Digital-Interaction.

Creating Imaginative Digital Interaction

Five different characteristic wigs were created using embedded multi-sensory for exploring Human-to-Human-Interaction; *"Thou and I", "I Smile at You", "So Do I", "Greeting"*, and *"Don't Talk to Me"*. All the wigs explore how the wearers are engaged with people around them while the digital object constitutes novel experiences that coincide with anthropomorphic interactivity. The digitally enhanced wigs construct non-verbal communication through their lifelike movement by encouraging wearer's imagination. Just as Stead et al. emphasized the aesthetic purpose of technology in the social contents through computer-aided, human-human communication while examining the affectiveness of wearable interactivity [2], my wigs aim to bridge the dynamic relationship between the wearer and society by embedding our everyday life's story-telling in an imaginative way.

"Thou and I" [Figure2] is an interactive wig that reacts to the spectator rubbing the wearer's shoulder while sitting side by side. Ideally, wearers reserve their expression or action. It is the wig that generates the interactive conversation. Activated by the spectator's touch and turning in the direction of either left or right, depending on which shoulder has been touched, the wig's kinetic motion is engaging and the hairs rub and reach for the other person's head and face slowly and softly. When the spectator moves away from the wearer, then all the hair go back to their resting position. The interaction symbolizes or embodies ethereal human emotional relationships. At the same time the wig's interactivity aims to mediate the complex nuances of personal interaction with the tangible expressions which people sometimes feel unease to externalize themselves. Metaphorically, *"Thou and I"* speaks to the emotional intimacy and connection between people, but the relationship is fragile, and breaks apart at the moment the two physically disengage. This video demonstrates how the real time interaction works between the wig ("Thou and I") and a spectator.
http://www.youngsuklee.com/ThouandI.html

Figure5. Greeting
Motion Interactive wig

The wig, "I smile at you" [Figure 3], explores the ambiguous space in social contents between how one adorns and expresses self, and how the spectator perceives and interprets the wearer's expression. It creates a wave-dancing motion, most often interpreted as representing excitement by welcoming the visitor who comes towards the wearer. However, the movements of the wig can also stimulate different feelings such as surprise, or even alarm. The wave dancing hair motion could be displayed as an intimate life form, like the hair of Medusa, even if the wearers had not intended to express themselves that way. The interaction could lead to another perspective for the spectator, that the wearers are angry or offended by their approach. This ambiguous interpretation of the digital interactions creates the unexpected experience and it evokes dynamic feelings between people. This demands the participants investigate and ignites one's imagination as a result of the encounter. This video demonstrates how the real-time interaction works; http://www.youngsuklee.com/Ismileatyou.html

Figure 4. Greeting
Motion Interactive wig

The wig, *"So do I"*, gently caresses the spectator with a small hairy hand, but only when the spectator caresses the wearer of the wig. *"Greeting"* [Figure 4,5] has two mechanical joint components like a pair of shoulders and elbows as two interactive hairy arms. Each part sequentially rises up and 'hugs' the spectator who is in front of the wig-wearer mimicking how a person opens his or her arms out wide and hugs. This video demonstrates how the bodily interaction works between the wearer and the spectator through the interactive wig, *"Greeting"*.
http://www.youngsuklee.com/Greeting.html

Figure 3. I Smile at You
Motion Interactive wig

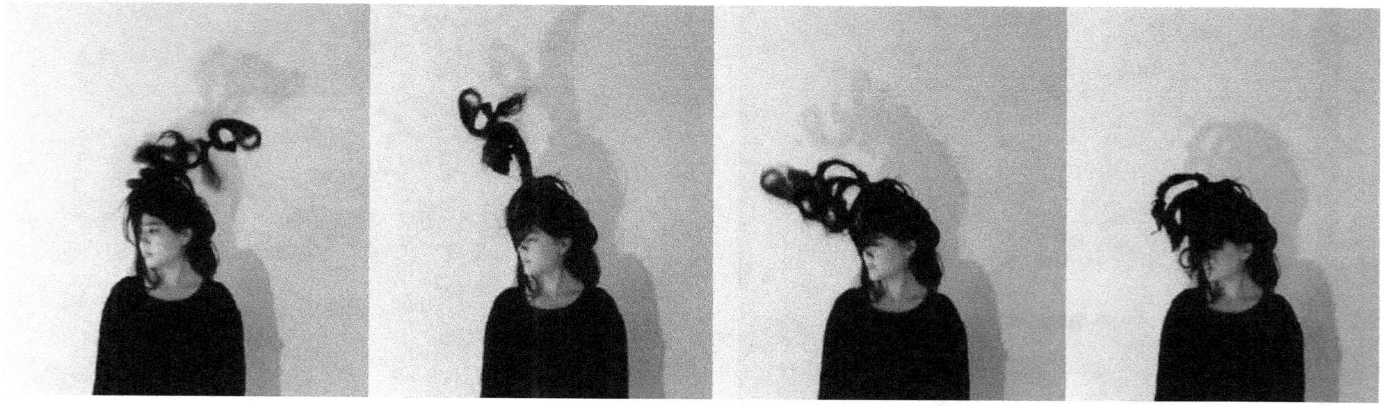

Figure 6. Don't Talk To Me

Motion Interactive Wig

While these two wigs explore warm and intimate interactions, the last wig, *"Don't talk to me"*, is designed to ostracize people rather than show affection or be submissive. When the spectator is approached, the wig turns in the opposite direction. Furthermore, the hairs bend over against the approach, and all hairs are completely curled up inwards, eventually, the hairs are covering the wearer's face. In this way, the wig communicates that it doesn't want to interact with spectator. This digital interaction physically embodies the anthropomorphic character of alienation. This video demonstrates how the real-time interaction works. http://www.youngsuklee.com/Dontalktome.html

Adorning with Expressive Digital Objects

I create expressive digital wearable designs as extensions of oneself for exploring the connection between the Human-and-Digital-Interaction. I sought to constitute a creative dialogue with the interactive characteristic wigs that make them become a sensitive vehicle for the wearers. The expressive embodiment produced through the various anthropomorphic qualities of the wig is my attempt to open the meaning making interaction for both the wearers and the digital object, and wearers and spectator. These interactive wigs not only offer an opportunity to adorn our appearance with a new hairstyle, but the interactions aim to create theatrical encounters in which the digital wigs enable the wearers to reveal personal emotion or conceal their identity dramatically. In this way, the wearers can be more blatantly expressive themselves through bodily interaction.

Stead et al. also examine how the wearable technology could be an expressive and reflective medium that creates a personalized vision of identity and a "poetic use of technology" with the emotional wardrobe project. [2] However, my design does not focus on the visual information generated from the internal simulation because the wearers are not given any options to control the digital object. The display of garment's texture or shape that responds to the people's emotions becomes reflective, but this interaction could create a vulnerable position for the wearers, in which their internal emotions are visually

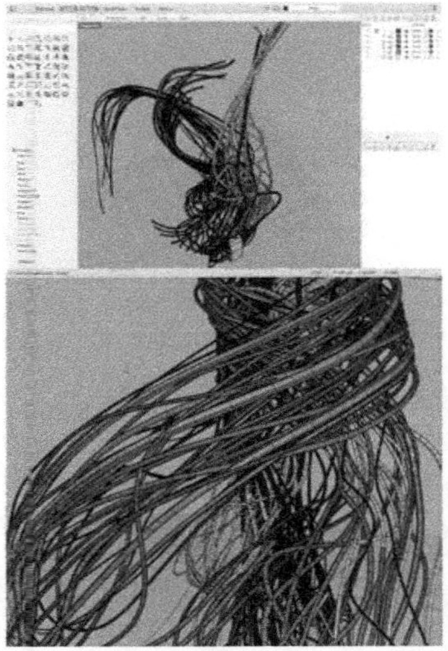

Figure7. 3D modeling & 3D printing process

Figure8. Crafting materials

plastic, flexible and hard resin, hair, fabric, leather, sensor, servo motors, Arduino, etc.

and tactically revealed to others regardless of their willingness to be exposed.

In order to advocate people's proactive engagement, I introduced the different personalities or dispositions of the wigs by letting the wearers voluntarily choose a certain wig depending on how they want to visually and tactically express themselves and conceptually communicate to others. The wigs are like choosing any clothing or accessories. It's an active process to wear the aesthetic object and involves understanding the individual wigs characters and being willing to create a narrative of interactivity as an extended self. In this way, the wearers connect to the expressive adorning experiences by the digital object that enables people to reflect themselves, reserve or exaggerate personal expression through the wig's performance.

Making process

The multisensory interactive wigs are created by a combination of 3D digital printing, hand-crafting, and digital mechanical implications. First, the wig is carefully modeled using 3D software and printed these pieces to create the organic form of bodily structures and the fragile hair 'architecture' [Figure7]. These are then embellished with hairs. Though delicate, these intricate 3D printed elements are at the same time solid enough to support the kinetic hair motions that are operated by servo motors. The numerous digital print segments necessary for a single wig are fabricated by using various 3D printing materials of hard, flexible resin and PLA plastics. All of digitally printed pieces is elaborated by a sophisticated mixed media crafting process involving sewing leather, fabric and hair. Last, the digital mechanisms, such as the servo motors and the sound, motion, and force sensors, are embedded into the wigs [Figure8, 9]

Figure8. Crafting process

Acknowledgement

This project is partially funded by a Faculty Research Grant 2017 of Indiana University, South Bend.

Some of the projects were developed at the Center for HCI, University Salzburg, Austria during subnet AIR artist residency, 2017.

References

1. Anthony Dunne, Hertzian Tales: Electronic Products, Aesthetic Experience, and Critical Design, The MIT Press, 2006
2. Lisa Stead, Petar Goulev, Caroline Evans, Ebrahim Mamdani, The Emotional Wardrobe, Personal and Ubiquitous Computing, v.8 n.3-4, p.282-290, July 2004 [doi>10.1007/s00779-004-0289-4]

Beacon: Exploring Physicality in Digital Performance

Anna Weisling
Georgia Institute of Technology
North Ave NW, Atlanta, GA
30332, USA
aweisling3@gatech.edu

Anna Xambó
Queen Mary University of London
Mile End Road, London E1 4NS, UK
a.xambo@qmul.ac.uk

TEI '18, March 18–21, 2018, Stockholm, Sweden
ACM 978-1-4503-5568-1/18/03.
https://doi.org/10.1145/3173225.3173312

Abstract
Live performances which involve digital technology often strive toward clear correspondences between distinct media modes, particularly those works which combine audio and video. Often, the process of creating and executing such performances involves mapping schemes which are encased within the digital system, producing content which is tightly synchronized but with relationships which can feel rigid and unexpressive. Within this paper we present a collaborative process between visualist and musician, which builds toward a method for promoting co-creativity in multimedia performance and prioritizes the performer's physical presence and interaction with digital content. Through the development of two autonomous systems, a novel physical interface and an interactive music system, we summarize our creative process of co-exploration of system capabilities, and extended periods of experimentation and exploration. From this experience, we offer an early-stage framework for approaching engaging digital audiovisual relationships in live performance settings.

Author Keywords
Digital performance; co-creativity; tangible user interfaces.

CCS Concepts
•Hardware → Tactile and hand-based interfaces; •Applied computing → *Sound and music computing;*

Introduction

The physical and the digital share a performance space with increasing frequency. We attach sensors to dancers (e.g., [1]), we mount cameras in the rafters (e.g., [8]). We map our media onto our bodies, our screens, and our speakers, we utilize computer technology to extend technique, build novel relationships with media and technology, and produce richer performances [4]. But the physical-digital contract is too often considered a system with which to send information from one media or discipline to another, rather than a framework within which we can collaborate in new ways.

One of the byproducts of this development is that the computer, as it extends our capabilities, at the same time runs the risk of removing expressivity from our hands [6]. Technology is commonly used in ways which allow any spectator to experience a piece as a polished, safe production, with little regard for what expressive or collaborative capabilities might have been sacrificed in the interest of ease or security. Often culminating in one-to-one mapping, this synchronous input-output relationship is digital mickey-mousing, a way for a secondary source of content to be driven by the primary element of performance. The visual content becomes a music video to accompany musicians, or music becomes the soundtrack for a dancer. This approach abandons the rich potential for experimental performances before it even begins. Though this condition can be observed in nearly all facets of performance, audiovisual pieces are a prime example of both the potential for engaging new work as well as the pitfalls of poor or misguided design.

In *Beacon*, aural and visual content is considered as expressive material which evolves together over time, shaped by both the digital system's properties as well as the agency of the human performers. Several guiding principals have been employed in order to explore the possible performance dynamics in this work, including exploring physical and digital system capabilities, identifying and experimenting with audiovisual relationships, developing compositional form, and building toward an audiovisual performance framework. In the following sections, we will discuss these techniques and the resulting consequences for composition, instrument design, and performance.

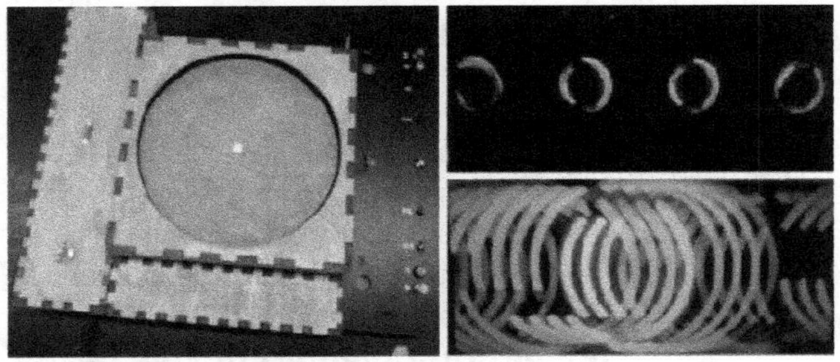

Figure 1: Distaff, a visual instrument.

Beacon

Beacon is an audiovisual performance for electronic musician and live visualist. The audiovisual paradigm presented in the work is decidedly musical, though each agent acts with autonomy, and the resulting dynamics embody a reconsideration of both visual music and soundtracks. The visualist and musician are linked through more than their dynamics; the visual system itself is amplified, contributing to the shape and dynamics of the sonic material.

Beacon has been performed twice to date, in very different spaces. The first performance was tailored to an 8-channel sound system at the 2017 Root Signals Festival (Georgia

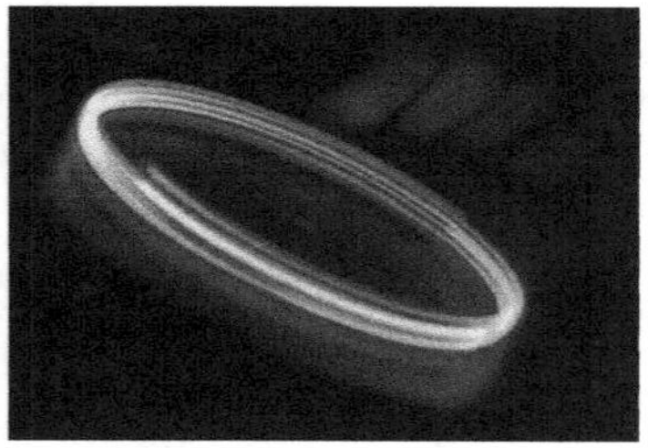

Figure 2: Fingertip pressing on the Distaff. Photo: NIME 2017 / Stengade.

Figure 3: Operating the Distaff. Photo: NIME 2017 / Stengade.

Southern University, Statesboro, Georgia, United States), and the second performance was held at the NIME 2017 conference (Stengade, Copenhagen, Denmark).

All of the visual content for the piece is produced live on a specialized visual instrument, the Distaff [14], which requires the performer to focus on gesture, feedback, and physicality within the collaborative space (see Figure 1). With core mechanics pulled from a Technics turntable, the visualist must control the instrument's rate of rotation through power and pressure, allowing the object to effectively "push back" against the fingertips (see Figures 2 and 3). With physiological phenomena such as reverse-rotation (the "wagon-wheel effect") and persistence of vision considered, the output of the instrument ranges from fluid textural movements to stuttered, strobing lights; both ends of the spectrum geared toward immersing the viewer in an unfiltered physical experience of the senses.

The audio engine is a prototype built on the audio programming language SuperCollider [9]. An example of code is shown in Figure 4. The prototype aims at working with the sound material that comes in as audio generated from a performer, in the tradition of Schaeffer's *musique concrète* [12]. This prototype is built within an overall system, MIRLC, that explores the use of Music Information Retrieval (MIR) in live coding (https://github.com/axambo/MIRLC). The sound of the fingers interacting with the instrument as well as the inner mechanical sound produced by the device are captured with a lavalier microphone mounted inside the Distaff system. This input signal controls the sound at different levels: from no modification of the audio signal, to the use of the audio signal to control parameters of digital audio filters or other audio signals. In this prototype, we explore unidirectional control (i.e., from one audio signal input to one audio signal output). In the future, we are interested

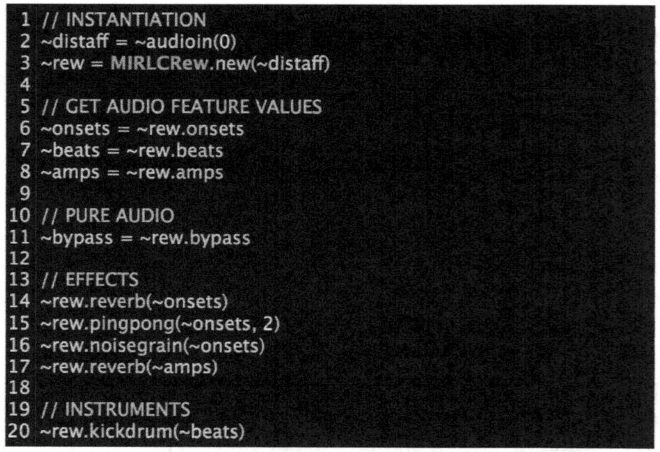

Figure 4: An example of code of MIRLC, the audio engine.

in exploring mutual interaction. This refers to bidirectional control, and therefore the use of feedback is welcome. The challenge here is to frame how to modify a visual instrument that is not designed to generate sound.

Physicality in Digital Performance

In order to move away from pure data mapping and toward a more human-centered approach to multimedia performance, a strong focus on the performer was embraced. Laptop performance [3] diverges from more traditional performance practices in that it is less physical in terms of content actuation, and the mechanics of the system are often opaque to audience members. Particularly within the traditions of acoustic musical practices such as chamber ensembles, the ability to "read" one another throughout the course of a piece is highly dependent on visible physical cueing, which can be lost if too much attention is required by a glowing screen. The field of new music increasingly turns its focus toward this issue, producing New Interfaces for Musical Expression (NIME, see http://nime.org), which facilitate corporeal involvement in computer music. In more recent years, this notion has been explored in terms of "embodiment," or "embodied cognition," [5] wherein participants and spectators perceive music through multiple senses, and the relationship between bodily movement and conceptual meaning are closely tied through the act of gesturing [11, 13].

The concept that the body serves as a bridge between the physical world (external) and perception (internal) places gesture, physicality, and expression in a reciprocal meaning-making process which can become complex, detailed, and layered with the proper tools and training. Gestures carry with them cultural and social meaning in their physicality [7, 10]. Not only do these movements convey meaningful information to other performers and the audience, they also represent the connective tissue between the performer and instrument, and illustrate the functioning relationship between the two [2, 13]. The visual nature of these actions is a crucial element of traditional musical performance, as ensemble members read each other throughout the course of a work and the audience interprets the emotions, efforts, and other non-verbal communications of the performer. It is therefore important to us that physical instruments are employed in order to bridge the human and digital systems, both to provide tangible means for digital production as well as convey meaningful gestural information to the audience.

Utilizing Space

One of the advantages of computer-aided art is the seemingly endless array of creative capabilities, both in terms of content generation and manipulation. The compositional space in new media works is often limited only by the desires and choices of the composer, who strives to create a believable and immersive experience through the curation of the material with which they are working. In *Beacon*, the aural and visual components are required to share a physical and conceptual space, one in which they can evolve separately while still influencing each other and existing in an experience which feels authentic. In order to ground the experience temporally and spatially, natural sounds are exploited within the performance space. By amplifying the sounds of the visual instrument, purposeful and incidental content is integrated into the sonic palette available to the musician, and can be included or disregarded as deemed appropriate. The visualist can intentionally contribute to the musical aspects of the piece by employing her fingertips or nails on the spinning wooden platter, or tapping rhythms on the enclosure. However, the inherent sounds produced by the motor and the actuation of the instrument are continually available to influence the direction of the piece, meaning that mistakes, accidents, and errors are an uncontrolled contributor to the work. The physical affordances of the system enable expression, but also introduce a level of analog risk into an otherwise stable digital system.

The sonic exploration of the physical properties of the visual engine can be explicitly combined with the sonic properties of the performance venue. Spatial audio is a relevant approach in live performance that brings materiality to the space and can range from a standard stereo panning to a multichannel spatialization. This approach brings the opportunity to create meaningful mappings for both the performers and the audience. At the same time, aesthetic and practical reasons determine the shape of the compositional decisions.

Evoking Themes Through Material System Properties

The content for *Beacon* is driven by structured improvisation and experimentation with the instruments at hand. We argue that, in the same way that a cellist learns the curves and textures of his instrument, intimacy with certain digital systems is crucial in the facilitation of compelling computational art. The capabilities and limits of the aural and visual systems inform the structure of the work, guiding the compositional process over time. At each rehearsal during development, new findings are presented and discussed, with new audiovisual correspondences and divergences discovered. In the end, no part of the work is without its partner, and even the improvisational aspects of *Beacon* are executed within a conceptual space which has been explored together. Exploring materiality, both visual and aural, through improvisation within the rehearsal space, helps the performers to elicit new ways of thinking about the audiovisual piece, which in turn shapes the compositional form.

Emerging Framework

By embracing the physicality of the digital performer, utilizing and reinforcing shared temporal and spatial elements of the performance, and allowing the possibilities of distinct sonic and visual systems to guide aesthetic themes and compositional form, a new framework for audiovisual composition begins to emerge. Through the experience of composing and performing *Beacon*, we have encouraged certain elements of collaboration and creativity which we believe to be beneficial to those of us working across media:

- **Expressivity**: Prioritizing human agency and expression in computational practice.
- **Collaboration**: Co-creation of multimedia content from the ground-up.
- **Physicality**: Embracing material limitations as design guidelines.
- **Autonomy**: Freedom to make independent artistic decisions within a tightly-coupled multimodal dynamic.
- **Aesthetics**: A unified trajectory between distinct media which mutually shape an experience.

The next steps include reflecting on this emerging framework by (1) nurturing each section with nitty-gritty examples, and (2) refining the categories so that it can be used by other performers interested in exploring potential relationships between the physical and digital in live audiovisual performance.

Reflections and Future Work

As a piece, *Beacon* is the product of extended experimentation with sonic and visual systems as distinct but related media modes. The work is shaped by the physicality of the human performers and their bodily connections to digital systems, and strives to reinforce and support expressive capabilities of collaborators and harness the physical affordances of either analog or digital interfacing devices. Sharing our explorations in a live performance at TEI will inform our future work toward that end.

These early investigations into a more human-centered way of digital composition raise questions of the role of human and computer in technologically-driven performances, and how the physical manipulation of digital content might shift new media production away from automation and mapping toward a more organic and intimate dynamic. The authors believe the emerging framework to be a valuable tool for individuals collaborating across media, especially visual and audio, as a way to reconsider the activities of the composer, performer, and digital system in a space of co-creation. It is our hope that further collaborations can be undertaken with increasing emphasis on the emergent features of co-creative audiovisual composition, including the development of new physical instruments, increased emphasis on expressivity and physicality, and an eye toward a unified and robust multi-modal aesthetic.

REFERENCES

1. Johannes Birringer. 2008. After Choreography. *Performance Research* 13, 1 (2008), 118–122.
2. Antonio Camurri, Gualtiero Volpe, Giovanni De Poli, and Marc Leman. 2005. Communicating Expressiveness and Affect in Multimodal Interactive Systems. *IEEE Multimedia* 12, 1 (2005), 43–53.
3. Nick Collins, Alex McLean, Julian Rohrhuber, and Adrian Ward. 2003. Live Coding in Laptop Performance. *Organised Sound* 8, 3 (2003), 321–330.
4. Steve Dixon. 2007. *Digital Performance: A History of New Media in Theater, Dance, Performance Art, and Installation.* MIT press.
5. Rolf Inge Godøy and Marc Leman. 2010. *Musical Gestures: Sound, Movement, and Meaning.* Routledge, New York.
6. Michael Gurevich and Jeffrey Treviño. 2007. Expression and its Discontents: Toward an Ecology of Musical Creation. In *Proceedings of the 7th International Conference on New Interfaces for Musical Expression.* ACM, 106–111.
7. Tomie Hahn. 1996. *Sensational Knowledge: Transmitting Japanese Dance and Music.* Ph.D. Dissertation. Wesleyan University.
8. Alexander Refsum Jensenius, Rolf Inge Godøy, and Marcelo M Wanderley. 2005. Developing Tools for Studying Musical Gestures within the Max/MSP/Jitter Environment. In *Proceedings of the International Computer Music Conference.* 282–285.
9. James McCartney. 2002. Rethinking the Computer Music Language: SuperCollider. *Computer Music Journal* 26, 4 (2002), 61–68.
10. Carrie Noland. 2010. *Agency and Embodiment.* Harvard University Press.
11. John Rink, Neta Spiro, and Nicolas Gold. 2011. Motive, Gesture, and the Analysis of Performance. *New Perspectives on Music and Gesture* (2011), 267–292.
12. Pierre Schaeffer. 2016. *Traité des Objets Musicaux.* Le Seuil.
13. Federico Visi, Rodrigo Schramm, and Eduardo Miranda. 2014. Gesture in Performance with Traditional Musical Instruments and Electronics: Use of Embodied Music Cognition and Multimodal Motion Capture to Design Gestural Mapping Strategies. In *Proceedings of the 2014 International Workshop on Movement and Computing.* ACM, 100:100–100:105.
14. Anna Weisling. 2017. The Distaff: A Physical Interface to Facilitate Interdisciplinary Collaborative Performance. In *Proceedings of the 2017 Conference on Designing Interactive Systems.* ACM, 1365–1368.

Marching Cubes Made Tangible

Jesse Colin Jackson
University of California, Irvine
Irvine, CA 92697, USA
j.c.jackson@uci.edu

TEI '18, March 18–21, 2018, Stockholm, Sweden

ACM ISBN 978-1-4503-5568-1/18/03.
https://doi.org/10.1145/3173225.3173313

Abstract
Drawing inspiration from a computer algorithm of the same name, *Marching Cubes Made Tangible* leverages 3D printing to make the virtual world physical. In the 1980s, researchers devised an algorithm for generating computer graphics from medical scan data that featured an underlying language of faceted cubes. *Marching Cubes Made Tangible* translates this virtual procedure into interactive installations, which are assembled from a modular set of 3D printed components. By enacting the algorithm in the real world, this project generates dialogue about the ways in which information technologies create the building blocks of contemporary culture.

Author Keywords
Tangibility; Materiality; Embodied interaction; Critical design; Additive manufacturing

ACM Classification Keywords
• Applied computing~Performing arts • Applied computing~Media arts

Introduction
Marching Cubes is an algorithm that constructs a continuous three-dimensional surface from a collection of points in space. First presented in 1986 and later refined for the purpose of generating high-resolution

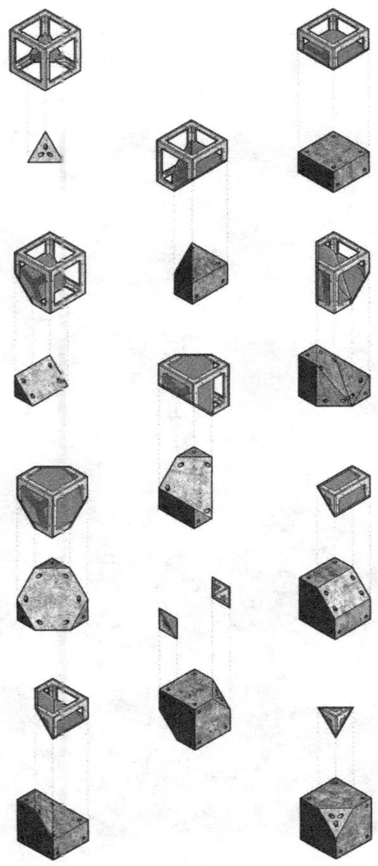

Figure 1: The first physical interpretation of the Marching Cubes algorithm: *Automatic/Revisited* (2009) plywood forms and their reciprocal concrete block results.

renderings of medical scan data, Marching Cubes and its descendants have become some of the most widely adopted graphics algorithms ever created. Vestiges of this algorithm's geometric signature remain present in screen-based representations of three-dimensional information: it is part of the visual language that defines our virtual environments.

Marching Cubes Made Tangible is an interactive installation comprised of plastic construction units that permit participants to, through playful interaction enabled by media technology, directly experience the algorithm and the visual language it represents. This project is the culmination of a ten years research, experimentation, and artwork focused on deploying this language in the sculptural realm, by interpreting the algorithm as a tool for provocative form making at a variety of scales.

Precedent Projects

The Marching Cubes algorithm provides a first order refinement of a voxel grid approximation of a volume. A voxel grid is a cubic subdivision of space, and can be understood as the three-dimensional analogue of a pixel grid. Voxels grids have been of long-standing interest to interactive media artists. For example, in the work of David Rokeby, beginning with *Very Nervous System* (1986) and continuing in contemporary projects such as *Dark Matter* (2010), the voxel grid is an invisible instrument for which the artist provides a navigable structure, which he describes as "an articulation of a space, either real, virtual, or conceptual." Taking up Rokeby's challenge, *Marching Cubes Made Tangible* provides a navigable structure for algorithmic space by articulating it both literally—as a virtual space made real, physical, and tactile—as well as conceptually, by mapping a computational procedure onto the agency of human interaction.

Several precedents within my own practice also inform this project. *Automatic/Revisited* (2009/2013), produced in collaboration with architect Luke Stern, precipitated my first encounter with the Marching Cubes algorithm. Inspired by principles developed by Frank Lloyd Wright, this interpretation consists of a set of plywood forms that, when used as casting apparatus, generate a reciprocal set of lightweight concrete block units (Figure 1). These units can be flexibly assembled at an architectural scale while consistently retaining the aesthetic imprint of their algorithmic origin. Pursued as both a novel contribution to architectural knowledge and as a meditation on sculptural modularity, these installations (Figure 2) made Marching Cubes physical for the first time.

Figure 2: Exhibition of the first physical interpretation: *Automatic/Revisited* (2009) installation view.

Figure 3: The source of inspiration for a new interpretation: playful 3D printed powder/binder prototypes.

Inspired by the playful qualities recognized in 3D printed powder/binder prototypes created for the *Automatic/Revisited* project (Figure 3), in 2013 I completed *Marching Cubes Units #4* (Figure 4), a new interpretation made from 3D printed plastic.

Figure 4: A new physical interpretation made from 3D printed plastic: *Marching Cubes Units #4* (2013).

Later iterations of this prototype incorporated an improved connection mechanism that makes use of a rotating spherical neodymium magnet.

Marching Cubes, Made Tangible

Grants from the Hellman Foundation and the Canada Council for the Arts permitted the promise of these prototypes to come to full fruition. *Marching Cubes Made Tangible* projects are interactive performances and installations that permit direct physical engagement with the Marching Cubes algorithm. The 3D printed construction units are sized to fit in the hand, and the installations contain enough units to allow participants to freely play, assisted by custom modeling software. This software generates real-time assembly instructions that help participants translate their experimentation into human-scale sculptural assemblies. The units are sufficiently robust to be assembled repeatedly, in near-limitless configurations; the interaction with them is sufficiently intuitive to encourage fluid creativity.

An algorithm is nothing more than a step-by-step procedure. Conceptual artists have a long-standing engagement with step-by-step procedures as generators of form: per Sol Lewitt, the "idea becomes a machine that makes the art." In this case, the "machine" is an algorithm appropriated from one of the most transformative cultural forces in history: information technology. By inverting the normal application of this machine—from a procedure for converting form into computer-digestible units, to a procedure for converting computer-digestible units into form—*Marching Cubes Made Tangible* allows the audience to directly experience, through tangible interaction, the algorithm's procedure and the visual language this procedure embodies. Extended interaction begins to reveal the syntax patterns of this language, and its representational limitations.

Embodying the algorithm in a construction unit—a traditional vehicle for open-ended play and experimentation—places Marching Cubes at our fingertips, extracted from its usual background position within the inner workings of screen-based visualization

Figure 5: *Marching Cubes Assembly #7* (2016), as assembled during a performance at the Experimental Media Performance Lab, Irvine, California.

Figure 6: *Marching Cubes Assembly #7* (2016) assembly performance underway.

technologies. Enabling the algorithm in this way requires physical movement on the part of the user, which, released from the error-correcting mechanisms present in a virtual instantiation, permits them to exploit the potential of "glitches" or other unintended consequences. Put another way: while assembly instructions are provided, they need not be followed.

Phase One: An Interactive Performance

The first phase of *Marching Cubes Made Tangible* took place in the Experimental Media Performance Lab (xMPL) in Irvine, California. The xMPL is a black-box performance space optimized for interdisciplinary, interactive, and experimental new media performance projects. This space provided a unique opportunity to deploy the Marching Cubes construction units as part of an interactive performance.

Approximately 1500 units were located in the xMPL for three days. Volunteers were trained to facilitate public interaction with the construction units. The custom modeling software was used to generate instructions for a series of nine architectonic sculptural assemblies (Figure 5). Participants were given the opportunity to work with the volunteers as a team, acting out the instructions as if they themselves were 3D printers, locating material in space from bottom to top (Figure 6). They were also given the opportunity to ignore the instructions and design assemblies as they saw fit. The hybrid of expert and inexperienced participants deliberately evoked a historic performance previously reenacted in the xMPL: Yvonne Rainer's *Trio A* (1966), in which rhythmic movements, structured like tasks, are enacted without pause or climax. In this case, the regular rhythmic movements of the participants echo those of the algorithm's procedural calculations.

Documentation of the performance through time-lapse photography served to record the performance as well as generate elements required for the next phase.

Phase Two: A Gallery Installation

The second phase of *Marching Cubes Made Tangible* took place at Pari Nadimi Gallery (PNG) in Toronto, Canada. A final evolution of the architectonic sculptural assemblies was installed, along with a complete set of units, and video documentation of the xMPL interactive performances (Figure 7). The documentation was curated so as to provide equal emphasis on the systematic intentions of the algorithmic procedure, as well as the unanticipated results made possible by communication failure or deliberate subterfuge on the part of the participants.

Figure 7: *Marching Cubes Assembly #17* (2016), as installed at Pari Nadimi Gallery, Toronto, Canada.

Subsequent to the PNG exhibition, one further gallery installation has been organized, at the Arts Brookfield Grace Building in New York City, USA (Figure 8), and one further interactive performance has been organized, at the Patkau Project Space in Vancouver, Canada (Figures 9, 10) with collaborator Luke Stern. The latter featured the first sculptural assemblies derived from 3D models of a human figure.

Figure 8: *Marching Cubes Assembly #19* (2017), as installed at Arts Brookfield Grace Building, New York City, USA.

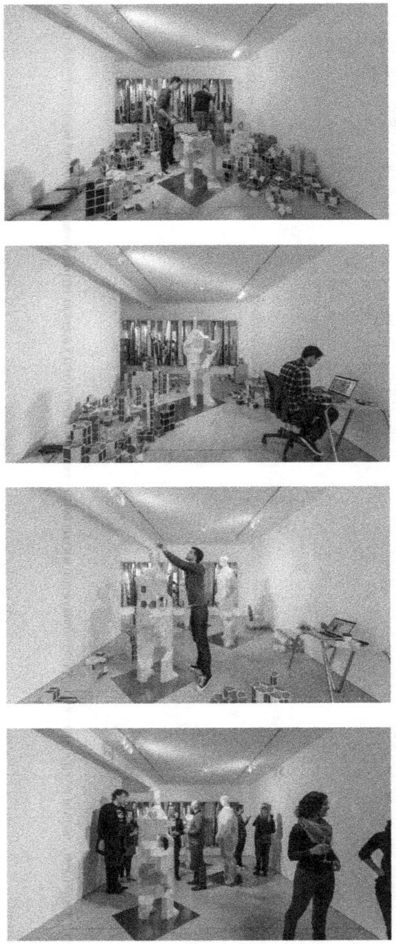

Figure 9: *Marching Cubes: Boris* (2017) assembly performance underway.

One further hybrid performance and installation event has taken place to date, at Platform 28 for Art & Architecture in Tehran, Iran. This opportunity's logistical and financial constraints precipitated the design of a simple continuous volume that, when collapsed, could be transported by plane as a single piece of checked baggage. Also on view was video documentation of the previous Marching Cubes Made Tangible performances and installations.

Figure 10: *Marching Cubes: Boris* (2017), as assembled during a performance at Patkau Project Space, Vancouver, Canada.

Conclusion

The algorithm that drives Marching Cubes Made Tangible is not new. Its applicability to physical form has been established and explored by my previous way. The tangibility of the construction units, enabled by the universally familiar and culturally primal act of play, has rendered the abstract idea of the algorithm accessible. This project provides a way in which one of our foundational computational procedures can be touched and manipulated, generating dialogue about the ways in which information technologies create the building blocks of contemporary culture.

References

1. Huizinga, J. *Homo ludens: a study of the play-element in culture*. Beacon Press, Boston, 1970.
2. Jackson, J.C. and Luke Stern. A Physical Instantiation of the Marching Cubes Algorithm. *Synthetic Digital Ecologies: Proceedings of the 32nd Annual Conference of the Association for Computer Aided Design in Architecture*, (2012), 239–247.
3. Lewitt, S. Paragraphs on Conceptual Art. *Artforum*, (1967), 79–83.
4. Lorensen, W.E. and Cline, H.E. Marching cubes: A high resolution 3D surface construction algorithm. *ACM SIGGRAPH Computer Graphics 21*, 4 (1987), 163–169.
5. Rokeby, D. Transforming Mirrors: Subjectivity and Control in Interactive Media. In S. Penny, ed., *Critical Issues in Electronic Media*. State University of New York Press, Albany, 1995, 133–158.
6. Wyvill, G., Mcpheeters, C., and Wyvill, B. Data structure for soft objects. *The Visual Computer*, 2 (1986), 227–234.

SKIN – Embodied Navigation through WiFi Traffic using Vibro-Tactile Feedback

Bas van den Boogaard
Aalborg University
Aalborg, Denmark
bvande15@student.aau.dk

Vibeke Thorhauge Stephensen
Aalborg University
Aalborg, Denmark
vsteph15@student.aau.dk

Louise Ørsted Jensen
Aalborg University
Aalborg, Denmark
lj15@student.aau.dk

Karina Lindegaard Aae Jensen
Aalborg University
Aalborg, Denmark
klaj15@student.aau.dk

Stefan Engelbrecht Nielsen
Aalborg University
Aalborg, Denmark
stniel15@student.aau.dk

Markus Löchtefeld
Aalborg University
Aalborg, Denmark
mloc@create.aau.dk

TEI 2018, March 18–21, 2018, Stockholm, Sweden.
ACM ISBN 978-1-4503-5568-1/18/03.
http://dx.doi.org/10.1145/3173225.3173314

Abstract
In today's world, radio waves are an integral element of our daily lives but they are mostly hidden to human perception. In this paper we present *SKIN*, a wireless wearable system that creates a new interface between the human and WiFi signals employing sensory augmentation. *SKIN* translates nearby WiFi data transmissions into a vibrotactile experience to alter the perception of the space around the human body. It is designed as a tool for examining how an embodied experience of the invisible waves affects our relation to both the physical environment as well as to the technology emitting the insensible dimension. We present the design and implementation as well as the results of two exhibitions in which *SKIN* was worn by 17 participants that demonstrate how *SKIN* helps to interpret and alters the perception of the built environment.

CCS Concepts
•Human-centered computing → Human computer interaction (HCI); Ubiquitous and mobile computing;

Author Keywords
radio waves; WiFi; wireless; tactile feedback; embodied interaction; wearable computing; sensorial augmentation

Figure 1: A participant exploring the hidden ether of WiFi signals in the build environment using *SKIN*.

Introduction

In today's world, radio waves are an integral element of our daily lives. The benefits they bring to our everyday practices have driven them to surround us in a ubiquitous fashion, and still they are hidden mostly from our bodily perception. The infrastructure that is needed to produce them may be visible as we can spot e.g. WiFi base stations or radio antennas, but the amount of information they are transferring invisibly around our bodies is only perceivable for certain tailored devices (e.g. mobile phones). The only time we are becoming aware of these radio waves is when they are not working as expected, e.g. walls blocking the WiFi signals. Following Mark Weiser's vision these wireless data transmitters have been seamlessly integrated themselves into the fabric of our everyday life [12] and with the current race towards the Internet-of-Things this movement will only increase.

The recent push towards augmenting human capabilities through technology [7] has spurred a variety of sensorial augmentations [8, 6]. These augmentations allow the human body to perceive otherwise non-perceivable phenomena of the environment. So, the question arises how would human behaviour change when we were to become aware of the invisible radio signals. What if we could actually feel and interpret the WiFi transmissions around us? Would it change our relationship to the built environment which heavily dictates the amount of WiFi transmissions around us?

In this paper we present *SKIN*, a wireless wearable system that creates a new interface between the human and its' location employing sensory augmentation. *SKIN* translates nearby WiFi data transmissions into a vibrotactile experience. Humans have always used their senses to navigate in- and gather information about the physical world. As the digital reality proceeds to expand into the physical environment, the human sensory apparatus stays the same. *SKIN* is designed as a tool for examining how an embodied experience of the invisible waves affects our relation to both the physical environment as well as to the technology emitting the insensible dimension.

Related Work

Prior work that focussed on making Radio and WiFi signals perceivable has often been conducted in artistic and more critical manner. Anthony Dunne coined the term "Hertzian Space" with his critical design work exploring the aesthetic aspects of a life in the "electrosphere" [4]. One specific example was the Faraday Chair which supposedly shielded the user of electromagnetic waves emitted by the electric appliances around them. The designed experience forced the participants to lay in a "utilitarian shelter of minimum dimensions" [4]; a claustrophobic glass case. While the experience raised awareness of the radio waves, the Faraday Chair did not allow the participants to physically explore the actual radio waves around them.

With Detektors, Miyazaki presented sonifications of electromagnetic fields and analysed the rhythms of the wireless communications [9]. While mainly pre-created sonifcations have been evaluated, in the experiential mode, the auditory feedback is created in real time. Nevertheless, the focus of this work lied on the rhythm analysis and not on physically experiencing the radio waves. Christina Kubisch followed a similar approach by amplifying electromagnetic fields through amplification in her "electrical walks" [1]. Using coils built-in to headphones participants were able to walk through the city and explore the electromagnetic fields. Between 2004 and 2015, 54 places have been explored using this method. By implementing this kind of new sense,

[1] http://www.christinakubisch.de/en/works/electrical_walks

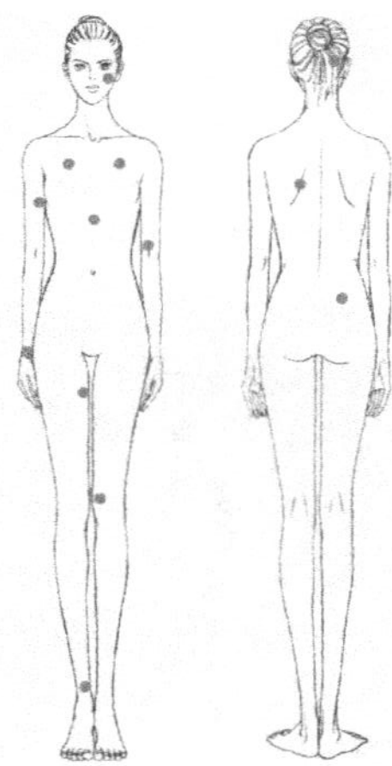

Figure 2: Placement of *SKIN*'s vibrotactile elements.

Kubisch aimed to change the perception of everyday reality and put the participant in a different context. This work rather focussed on estrangement through auditory feedback. Amall et al. presented with the project "Immaterials" a way of visualizing WiFi signal strength [1] using a four meter long rod equipped with an LED strip to visualize the WiFi strength on a given point. Using long exposure photographs and videos the authors could in a post-processing highlight the different exposure to WiFi waves around Oslo. While *SKIN* similar to these projects wants to uncover the hidden radio waves (in our case WiFi) the focus for this paper is to make it directly perceivable and allow the users to react to it immediately.

Human sensorial augmentation has recently seen a strong grow in interest [7] and more technologies are developed that help to overcome the perceptual limitations of the human body. SpiderSense [8] is one of these sensorial augmentations, it is a wearable device that uses tactile feedback on the wearers *SKIN* to make them aware of objects in the near environment and thus creates directional awareness even of objects not visually perceivable. With FeltRadio, Grönvall et al. presented a sensorial augmentation that would allow to visualize and experience radio waves through a LED display and electronic muscle stimulation (EMS) [6]. Using EMS the authors created an embodied sensorial augmentation that allowed the participants to experience WiFi waves. Their exploration demonstrated that using the tactile feedback of EMS "gave a more intensive experience than the visual expression, sometimes leading to quite negative reactions toward the presence of WiFi and radio wave" (p. 9 [6]). This embodiment is very similar to our approach, where a sensorial augmentation is allowing the participants to experience WiFi signals in a tactile fashion. Instead of EMS, *SKIN* is employing vibrotactile feedback from vibration motors. Where FeltRadio by using EMS might have created a bad connotation of WiFi signals, *SKIN* tries to have a neutral stand point.

Vibrotactile feedback present a viable option of creating wearable computing displays [5]. Especially for mobile interactions vibrotactile feedback has been well explored [2]. Especially when it comes to navigational purposes vibrotactile body-worn displays can help [11]. Therefore we chose to employ vibrotactile feedback for *SKIN* to turn WiFi signals into a tangible experience. Closest to *SKIN* is the work of Morrison et al., they designed vibrotactile patterns for a wearable vest to invoke different sensations (e.g. calming or activating) [10]. Their work highlights the possibilities of large-scale vibrotactile feedback in a wearable device. The design of *SKIN* in terms of placement of actuators and vibrational patterns is based on their work.

Design

The goal of *SKIN* is to challenge the habitual way in which we perceive our surroundings. The presence and use of wireless networked devices increasingly manifests itself in the social and physical environment. In the interaction with modern digital technology the primary senses for receiving information are vision and hearing which are limited to be mainly mentally processed. The tactile sense on the other hand is connected to the largest organ, the skin. We chose vibrotactile feedback for communication because it holds the capacity for activating the entire body's surface and thereby embodied experiences [3]. To contrast normal experiences we designed *SKIN* to extend the human sense through vibration to enable a communication about the otherwise insensible dimension of the local environment. It gives the wearer the ability to navigate through the surroundings inspired by the WiFi traffic surrounding them.

In the development process we conducted a survey to examine how vibrations are perceived at different locations on the body. Our findings resembled that of other studies into vibrotactile feedback [10] in that no experience is completely generic. The survey and literature review informed the decision to place the vibration motors at 13 different locations spanning from the ankle to the chin (a detailed overview can be seen in Figure 2). The 13 locations chosen were experienced as both pleasant, neutral and unpleasant which supported the intention of not assigning connotations of either a pro or contra attitude towards WiFi signals.

The design aimed at a universal fit as we wanted as many people as possible to be able to try *SKIN*. The main criteria was a close fit to the body to ensure that the output from the vibrating motors would be well perceivable but also to give the feeling and look of real *SKIN* being the continuation of the wearer's body. *SKIN* contains two layers. The inner *SKIN* has a base of a stretchy morphsuit where fabric tubes direct and secure the wires to the small pockets where the vibration motors are sown in. For the outer layer we decided to employ an imaginative, organic and mysterious expression. We created the outer *SKIN* of tightly knitted wool which made it stretchy. The slow and time consuming construction of knitting stands in contrast to the mechanical efficiency of modern digital technology. To keep *SKIN* wireless we needed a more voluminous part for the electronics. We created a collar foam vest covered with egg-like bubbles felted with carded wool. To play with the imagination and the performative qualities we decided to cover the entire body including the head but left the hand and feet free for practical reasons. The covering of the head attenuates the vision of the wearer. It was the aim that *SKIN* would facilitate an experience of embodied incubation in the warm mix of old techniques and new technology that could enhance the experience of a new sensory information input.

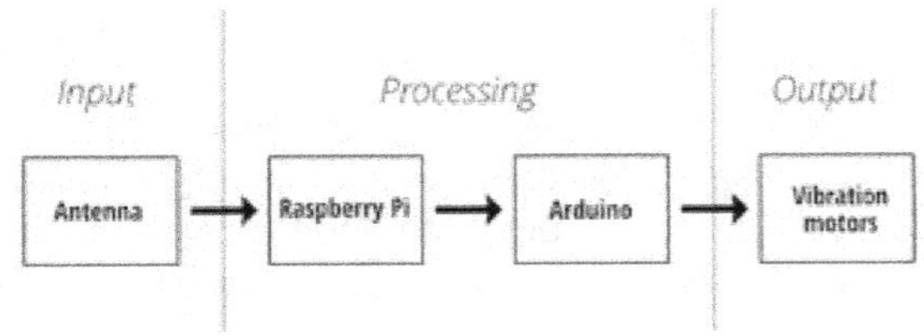

Figure 3: Overview of *SKIN*'s hardware.

Implementation

The hardware side of *SKIN* is composed of four parts; a USB WiFi dongle, a Raspberry Pi 3, an Arduino UNO and the circuit for the vibration motors (see Figure 3). As the Raspberry Pi 3's onboard WiFi adapter is not capable of monitor mode we used a TP-LINK TL-WN722N WiFi dongle connected to the Raspberry Pi. Upon startup, the Raspberry Pi runs a Python sketch that controls the data collection process and the communication with the Arduino. The sketch will first activate tshark[2], a software tool analyse network traffic. The amount of packets captured and their average length is then send to the Arduino microcontroller via a serial connection.

The Arduino will use the number of data packets in order to categorise the intensity of the WiFi data signals. With a low intensity, it will compose a vibration pattern that is concentrated at the body's peripherals and in which two vibration motors are only occasionally on at the same time. Higher intensities will result in a vibration pattern that will span the entire body as well as having multiple vibration motors on

[2]https://www.wireshark.org/docs/man-pages/tshark.html

simultaneously. Upon entering an environment with a high intensity of wireless communication the wearer of *SKIN* gets an experience of being completely enveloped and frequently stimulated by signals. The Arduino uses the average length of the data packets to determine how quickly the vibrations move over the body; the longer the average length is the slower they will move over the body. This is done to create a parallel with the physical world. Objects with greater mass have greater inertia, we analogised this by correlating more data with greater inertia. The Arduino also controls the circuit that contains the vibration motors. The circuit is outfitted with four shift registers in order to control the vibration motors with a single microcontroller. Each shift register controls several transistors, that regulate the connection between the vibration motors and the batteries.

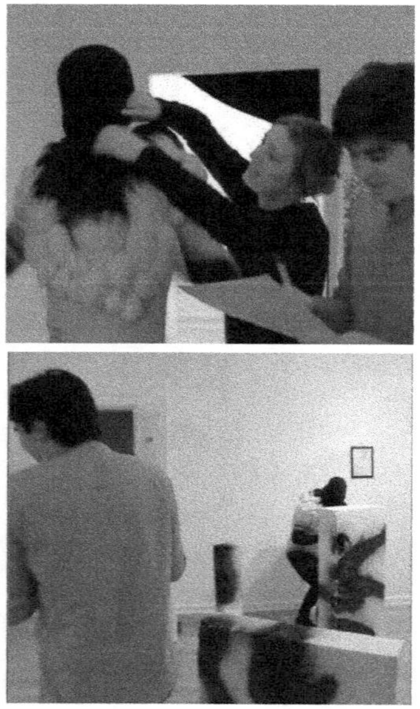

Figure 4: Setting for the User evaluation:The experimenter assisting a participant into *SKIN* suit (top); The participants engaging with the artworks at the local art festival (bottom)

User Evaluation

To explore the effect our sensorial augmentation provides to the user and what insights *SKIN* offers in terms of uncovering the hidden ether of WiFi signals, we conducted two explorative evaluations. The settings for these two evaluations were quite different. The first evaluation took place at an art exhibition in a university building located at the harbour front of (city omitted for blind review). Due to the nature of the building, there was an increased amount of WiFi infrastructure as well as over a hundred people carrying WiFi enabled devices around in the environment. The setting for the second exhibition, which was conducted at a local art festival, was quite different in the sense that it was held in an area with less build environment and less WiFi infrastructure around. The building where the art festival took place was located in a less crowded area next to a graveyard. Still the amount of visitors was relatively high, meaning that there was still a significant amount of WiFi signals available for the users to experience.

Procedure

Before and during the two exhibitions participants were provided with a short introduction to the capabilities and idea behind *SKIN* and could sign up to wear the prototype at a specific time-slot. Once it was the participants time slot they would enter a room where *SKIN* was exhibited with spot lights directed onto the suit. The participants were assisted into the suit (compare Figure 4), and were hereafter free to explore the surroundings for a half an hour. The wearers did not only walk around the small exhibition area but explored the entire buildings as well as the adjacent surrounding areas. Seventeen (ten female) participants have worn and experienced *SKIN* during the two exhibitions; ten (five female) during the exhibition in the university building and seven (five female) during the exhibition at the local art festival (compare Figure 4).

The participants were asked to follow a think-aloud protocol and during their explorations an experimenter would follow them and record the thoughts voiced by the participants as well as additional observations. Following the exploration with *SKIN*, a semi-structured interview was conducted with the participants. We interviewed the participants about their experience and its effect on their perception of their body, surroundings and the influence of technology. The semi-structured interviews were also conducted to understand the potential of the mix of vibrotactile feedback and wireless data as a way of addressing the contemporary technological world. The recordings of the interviews and comments were later transcribed for analysis.

Findings

We analysed the results of the user study by considering the interviews as the primary source for the analysis. The transcribed interviews where analysed using Grounded Theory and axial coding was applied. The analysis and coding was conducted by three of the authors independently and later merged. To understand the experience of *SKIN* and how to improve it we will discuss the main themes that emerged from the analysis here.

Interpretation of WiFi signals
SKIN was successful in enabling the users to grasp the amount and extend of WiFi transmissions in the different environments, *'You understand that it's all around you.'* (P4, male). Our observations confirmed that the users actively tried to engage with the WiFi signals, as some of the participants deliberately walked towards stronger signals while others tried to avoid WiFi signals, *'It is like, it is leading me somewhere.'* (P6, male).

Perception of Environment
In regards to the participants understanding and interpretation of the connection between the felt vibrations and the surroundings some perceived the changes in intensity to be related to amount of people, others to properties of spaces. In both cases the experience seem to have altered the participants perception of their surroundings with the amount of WiFi signals in the environment, as with an increasing amount of people the amount of WiFi enabled devices potentially increase as well, *'In a way, more people, more WiFi'* (P10, female).

Relationship to Technology
One result of the interviews is that the experience made the participants reflect upon technology as either something intimate and natural or as something intrusive and dangerous *'It felt like technology could be a bad thing, because there is no place where there isn't technology or signals it became a negative thing in my eyes'* (P12, female). These two experiences are extremely contrasting, however they both prove an impactful experience affecting and challenging both the bodily and cognitive understanding of technology.

The SKIN *Experience*
Participants express a sense of mystification about the cause and effect of the experience. This can be seen as a disadvantage. However our observations and interviews show that confusion also has the ability to open up for curiosity and serve as a catalyst for new thoughts and discoveries. We were aware of the fact that the appearance of the suit would attract attention and activate a predisposition, due to the culture of the material and known images of full body suits. During the interviews some of the participants expressed a sense of feeling comfortable and safe. Many of the interviewed expressed a sense of losing identity or anonymity while wearing *SKIN* due to the complete coverage of the body, allowing the participants to transform into another character or creature. In connection with this we observed how participants got into a playful, explorative and performative behaviour. Thus *SKIN* allows the users to have the freedom to focus on the vibrotactile experience connected with the invisible transmissions in our surroundings in a public setting.

Conclusion

In this paper we presented *SKIN*, a wireless wearable system that creates a new interface between the human and the normally hidden ether of WiFi signals acting as a sensory augmentation. We conducted two user studies with a total of seventeen participants that whore *SKIN* in two different settings. Through analysis of our observations and interviews we have examined the potentials of the experience that *SKIN* offers. By equipping the body with a new sense, *SKIN* serves as an enriching tool in the investigation and exploration of the relationship between humans and normally hidden radio waves by challenging the users through an embodied experience.

REFERENCES

1. Timo Arnall, Jørn Knutsen, and Einar Sneve Martinussen. 2013. Immaterials: light painting WiFi. *Significance* 10, 4 (2013), 38–39.
2. Stephen Brewster and Lorna M. Brown. 2004. Tactons: Structured Tactile Messages for Non-visual Information Display. In *Proceedings of the Fifth Conference on Australasian User Interface - Volume 28 (AUIC '04)*. Australian Computer Society, Inc., Darlinghurst, Australia, Australia, 15–23. http://dl.acm.org/citation.cfm?id=976310.976313
3. Paul Dourish. 2004. *Where the action is: the foundations of embodied interaction.* MIT press.
4. Anthony Dunne. 2008. Hertzian tales: Electronic products, aesthetic experience, and critical design. (2008).
5. Francine Gemperle, Nathan Ota, and Dan Siewiorek. 2001. Design of a Wearable Tactile Display. In *Proceedings of the 5th IEEE International Symposium on Wearable Computers (ISWC '01)*. IEEE Computer Society, Washington, DC, USA, 5–. http://dl.acm.org/citation.cfm?id=580581.856566
6. Erik Grönvall, Jonas Fritsch, and Anna Vallgårda. 2016. FeltRadio: Sensing and Making Sense of Wireless Traffic. In *Proceedings of the 2016 ACM Conference on Designing Interactive Systems (DIS '16)*. ACM, New York, NY, USA, 829–840. DOI: http://dx.doi.org/10.1145/2901790.2901818
7. Robert V Kenyon and Jason Leigh. 2011. Human augmentics: Augmenting human evolution. In *Engineering in Medicine and Biology Society, EMBC, 2011 Annual International Conference of the IEEE.* IEEE, 6758–6761.
8. Victor Mateevitsi, Brad Haggadone, Jason Leigh, Brian Kunzer, and Robert V. Kenyon. 2013. Sensing the Environment Through SpiderSense. In *Proceedings of the 4th Augmented Human International Conference (AH '13)*. ACM, New York, NY, USA, 51–57. DOI: http://dx.doi.org/10.1145/2459236.2459246
9. Shintaro Miyazaki. 2013. Urban sounds unheard-of: a media archaeology of ubiquitous infospheres. *Continuum* 27, 4 (2013), 514–522.
10. Ann Morrison, Hendrik Knoche, and Cristina Manresa-Yee. 2015. *Designing a Vibrotactile Language for a Wearable Vest.* Springer International Publishing, Cham, 655–666. DOI: http://dx.doi.org/10.1007/978-3-319-20898-5_62
11. Jacob Rosenthal, Nathan Edwards, Daniel Villanueva, Sreekar Krishna, Troy McDaniel, and Sethuraman Panchanathan. 2011. Design, implementation, and case study of a pragmatic vibrotactile belt. *IEEE Transactions on Instrumentation and Measurement* 60, 1 (2011), 114–125.
12. Mark Weiser. 1991. The computer for the 21st century. *Scientific american* 265, 3 (1991), 94–104.

I Want To: Multi-media Installation for Exploring our Desire

Laewoo Kang
Information Science, Cornell University
Ithaca, NY, 14850, USA
lk423@cornell.edu

TEI '18, March 18–21, 2018, Stockholm, Sweden

ACM ISBN 978-1-4503-5568-1/18/03.
https://doi.org/10.1145/3173225.3173315

Abstract
'I Want To' is a multi-media art installation that explores how our desire is presented, negotiated and internalized in contemporary digital media. One hundred custom designed wooden toys, a television screen and speakers comprise the installation. The system extracts live Twitter messages that start with 'I want to.' The expression 'want to' becomes 'have to', and the newly composed sentence is displayed on the television screen while also being vocalized through speakers. With each sentence, the wooden toys respond by marching in unison. This paper explains its background, design approach, and technical detail.

Author Keywords
Multi-media art; desire; social expectation, Twitter

Introduction
When we say that we 'want to do' something, the desire might not be motivated by our minds, but created to satisfy social expectations in everyday social institution such as families and workplaces. As Foucault explains in *Discipline and Punish: The Birth of the Prison* [1], people in society may believe that they are under constant observation through such everyday social mechanisms, and as a result they regulate themselves. Furthermore, such self-discipline may

become internalized and make us think that those disciplines are our actual desires.

Take the following Twitter messages as examples: "I want to get married", "I want to study at Harvard", "I want to get pregnant soon and have a baby", "I want to glorify Jesus". Do these desires present something that they really wish to achieve or something that society makes them believe or present as if they have such desires (or something in-between)?

The project, I Want To, provides a techno-aesthetic space in which the audience can observe our presented desire in digital social media, and to think about such questions through computational, aesthetic and critical ways. One hundred custom-designed wooden toys, a television screen and speakers comprise the installation, which is controlled by public live Twitter messages. The system extracts the most recent Twitter messages starting with the word 'I want to' every 15 seconds, then the expression 'I want to' is replaced to 'I have to.'(e.g. 'I want to get married' becomes 'I have to get married'). The television displays this newly formed sentence while being vocalized through speakers. With each new sentence, all of the wooden toys start to march in unison. Figure 1 shows a picture of the original installation. More pictures and video are accessible on the website: http://www.laewoo.com/iwantto/

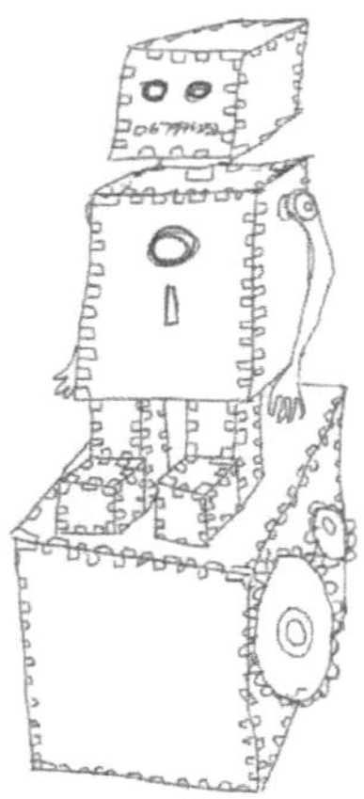

Each wooden toy includes a 5V 100rpm gear motor, a custom-designed circuit board and DC socket that creates a walking motion.

Figure 1. The first version of 'I Want To'

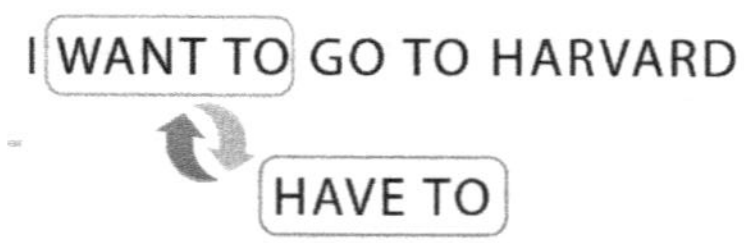

The installation extracts Twitter messages that start with "I want to" and change the "want to" to "have to." This converted message piles up on the screen with the vocalized sound.

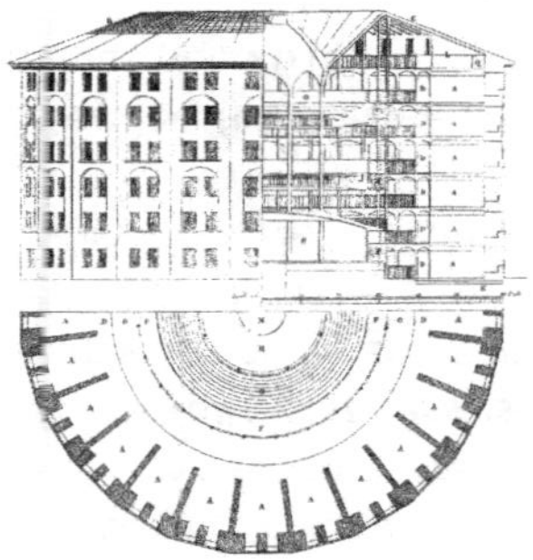

Figure 2: The blueprint of Bentham's Panopticon (drawn by Willey Reveley, 1791)

Figure 3: Listening Post (Hansen & Ben)

Background

The topic of self-discipline, social expectation, and their internalization has been discussed in broad fields of study including philosophy, social science, media art and HCI. For example, Foucault's *Panopticism* [1] examines the social and theoretical mechanisms that control our perception, emotion and behaviors. Foucault employs the theatrical idea and architectural design of the jail called *Panopticon* (Figure 2), which enables a prison guard to observe (-opticon) all (pan-) prisoners without the incarcerated being able to tell whether they are being surveilled. Foucault likens our everyday social environments such as schools, workspaces, and families to this prison system, which require that our bodies must be individuated according to tasks, as well as for training, observation, and control. Foucault explains that such processes necessarily regulate themselves, and such self-discipline becomes "internalized" making individuals believe that those disciplines are their own desires.

Similarly, Erving Goffman's *Dramaturgy* [2] likens our world to the performing stage and explains that we protagonists (must) perform given roles or scripts to satisfy cultural value and social expectations. Goffman conceptualizes people's everyday behaviors as ritual exchanges, or "performances" in the "front stage", and explains that most of our social interactions are "conventionalized", which leave humans few options for patterns of verbal (language) and non-verbal (gestures) that they can adopt in a specific situation.

However, different from the Panopticon (which presumably may watch performer all the time), Goffman additionally suggests a more personal, unwatched, and reflective space called "backstage" where performers are present without audience, so "the performer can relax; he can drop his front, forgo speaking his lines, and step out of character (280)". Goffman argues that individual identity is not stable, but continuously re-defined and reconstructed by multiple roles that he/she plays in both front- and backstage. In other words, one's true identity might exist in the place where diverse identities projected in different stages are intertwined and influenced by each other.

Recent studies in the field of communication and HCI have started to explore how users present, reflect and negotiate their identity and desire in various digital and social media services (see, inter alia, [3,6–8]). For example, Marshall & Shipman's study [4] based on Mechanical Turk survey of Twitter users explores how users deploy Twitter as a window onto their current social attitudes and beliefs. Zhao et al. [9] explains an implicit negotiation between users and the Facebook system in the terms of how personal data on social media platform should be "exhibited [3]"

In media art, Listening post (figure 3) by Hansen & Rubin involves dynamic collage of live conversation drawn from online sources in a room-sized installation that feature 232 text displays generating sound and voice [5]. Another piece by the author, Mirror in the Backstage (2014), provides a two-way mirror where users can observe their old Twitter messages while looking into the mirror.

"I think the toys visualize me, my friends, and furthermore, all of us in the society. Basically, I wanted to design it to represent the life that I have experienced, just following social norms and expectations. The toys make repetitive movements and march in unison with each desire shown on the TV screen, which intends to asks the question: *Aren't we just following desires to satisfy social expectations rather than trying to achieve our own dreams?"*

Interview from 'Make: magazine', 2012

Figure 4: Alternative version of 'I Want To' that uses a beam projector, Tjaden Gallery, Ithaca, NY, 201

Design Approach

The purpose of the installation 'I Want To' is to invite audiences to this discourse and ask them to consider whether our desires come from our internal mind or external social mechanisms. For this, we set the design approach as follows: First, the system observes our "presented" desires in social media. Second, the desires are viewed as "regulated" desire to help people to reconsider the possibility that they are not created by their minds. Third, numerous wooden toys visualize the controlled crowd and provide visual stimulus to the audience.

In order to watch our presented desires, the system monitors live Twitter messages. This system extracts Twitter messages that start with "I want to" and changes the "want to" to "have to." In other words, the installation intentionally converts the message from

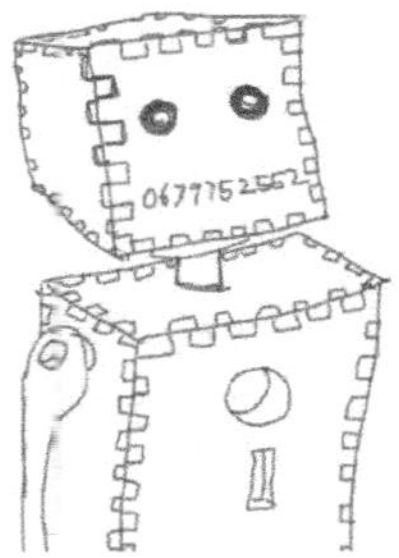

Laewoo (Leo) Kang is a Ph.D. candidate in the information science department at Cornell University as well as a multimedia artist. His work explores art-research integration in the fields of human-computer-interaction (HCI), design, and media art. More information: http://www.laewoo.com

(presented) desire to self-regulation in order to make audience confused whether it is his or her real desire or self-regulation. This conversion emphasizes the cadence and the rhythm of the before and after sentences. In other words, the meaning changes, but the sentence structure remains the same.

In addition to displaying these converted sentences to the audience, numerous automata wooden toys visualize controlled people. The toys make repetitive walking movements in place like an army and a prisoner, which are representative of a controlled institution. In addition, the toys mimic a walking-motion, but do not actually go forward. This also expresses the idea that we often think we are moving towards our dream when in fact we are only marching in place within the dreams that the boundary of our society will allow.

The project, I Want To, currently involves three different versions of design. In the original version, 100 toys are placed on a 80″ x 60″ custom-designed stage with the tube TV screen. The size of each toy is 3 inch(W) x 3.5 inch(D) x 8.5 inch(H). Each toy is placed with a 1 inch to 3-inch difference to the other toy. The second version involves a bigger exhibition space (figure 3). A beam projector has been used instead of the tube screen for this version. The third version involves three different tangible interfaces (crank, button, sound) where users can individually and collectively enable wooden toy's marching and visualization of Twitter message in the mini LED screen (figure 5).

Figure 5: Third version of I Want To and its tangible interfaces.

Technical Details and Floor Setting

Arduino, DC gear motor, TV signal converter (TellyMate) and NPN transistor are utilized in the installation. The software is implemented by Processing, a Java-based open source platform with Twitter API and Java Text Voice Synthesizer. In version 3, Raspberry PI 3 and Amazon Text Voice Synthesizer have been used.

Conclusion and Future works

How do we present, reflect and negotiate our desire especially through digital communication and human-computer-interaction? The project, I Want To, explores this research inquiry through the form of multi-media artwork. This artwork suggests a heuristic space where the audience can think and engage this topic through computational, aesthetic and critical means. This artwork also intends to open up the broader discussion regarding how the field of HCI and design can employ such techno-aesthetic objects and installations for alternative forms of knowledge representation through which core research questions can be explored in more playful, critical, and speculative ways.

References

1. Michel Foucault. 2012. *Discipline and punish: The birth of the prison*. Vintage.
2. Erving Goffman. 1959. The Presentation of Self in. *Butler, Bodies that Matter*.
3. Bernie Hogan. 2010. The presentation of self in the age of social media: Distinguishing performances and exhibitions online. *Bulletin of Science, Technology & Society* 30, 6: 377–386.
4. Catherine C Marshall and Frank M Shipman. 2011. Social media ownership: using twitter as a window onto current attitudes and beliefs. In *Proceedings of the SIGCHI Conference on Human Factors in Computing Systems*, 1081–1090.
5. Wes Modes. 2013. Revisiting the technical achievements of listening post ten years on. The Journal of New Media & Culture, 9(1).
6. Laura Robinson. 2007. The cyberself: the self-ing project goes online, symbolic interaction in the digital age. *New Media & Society* 9, 1: 93–110.
7. Victoria Schwanda Sosik, Xuan Zhao, and Dan Cosley. 2012. See friendship, sort of: How conversation and digital traces might support reflection on friendships. In *Proceedings of the ACM 2012 conference on Computer Supported Cooperative Work*, 1145–1154.
8. Zeynep Tufekci. 2008. Grooming, gossip, Facebook and MySpace: What can we learn about these sites from those who won't assimilate? *Information, Communication & Society* 11, 4: 544–564.
9. Xuan Zhao, Niloufar Salehi, Sasha Naranjit, Sara Alwaalan, Stephen Voida, and Dan Cosley. 2013. The many faces of Facebook: Experiencing social media as performance, exhibition, and personal archive. In *Proceedings of the SIGCHI Conference on Human Factors in Computing Systems*, 1–10.

Rewilding Wearables: Sympoeitic Interfaces for Empathic Experience of Other-than-human Entities

First Author
Patricia Flanagan
University of New South Wales
Australia
Patricia.flanagan@unsw.edu.au

Second Author
Raune Frankjaer
Aarhus University
Denmark
frankjaer@cc.au.dk

TEI '18, March 18–21, 2018, Stockholm, Sweden

ACM ISBN 978-1-4503-5568-1/18/03.
https://doi.org/10.1145/3173225.3173316

Abstract
This project involves a series of walks in rewilded environments mediated by a wearable interface that enables the interlocutor to perceive the environment from an alien perspective. The aim is to foster empathy for other-than-human entities and promulgate holistic and biodiverse ecologies. Technocrafting the prosthetic device from organic and electronic materials by blending traditional with digital techniques, create devices that the authors term 'cyborganic'. The focus of this paper is a device that sits as if grafted around the human head, and appears to come to life embodied with its own sense of 'agency'. This paper describes the 1st and 2nd generation prototype of this device and its current configuration as an aid for empathetic experience of insects in rewilded spaces. To conclude we describe a testing methodology developed in Aarhus based on a series of walks with users where they engage in semi-structured interviews post-walk to evaluate their experience.

Author Keywords
Cyborganic; sympoeitic interfaces; wearables; rewilding; empathy; interactive media; post-humanism, human-machine interaction; agency; technocrafting.

ACM Classification Keywords
- Human-centered computing~Haptic devices

Introduction

There is no beauty without things, and there are no things without technology, and there is no technology without politics, so we might as well start working out a politics of beauty [1]

The authors have been experimenting with technocrafting to explore its potential to understand the post-human condition [3]. The 1st generation of the device described in this paper began its existence as a twin: Bamboo Whisper. A pair of sympoeitic devices [7] that communicate through translation of voice to vibration picked up by sound sensors incorporated in the collars of vests and transmitted between wearers. Each hat responds to the other, engaging the wearers in an immersive, interactive, haptic, audio-visual experience. The hats vibrate causing the brim sticks to chatter like a whisper or wind in the trees. The movement produces sounds reminiscent of communication employed primarily by smaller non-vocal creatures such as amphibians and insects [2]. The 2nd generation device evolved from the insect like qualities of the first. This time the Cyborganic is imagined as "a fantasy, a design fiction, living in a world where technology is not cold, hard, and dead, but warm, soft and alive. A human-machine-nature hybrid of organic augmentation. A temporal assemblage, where old wisdom and future vision can meet. Human and nonhuman" [4].

The internal physiology of the Cyborganic

The device detects rewilded locations with high interspecies populations, particularly insects, through a GPS module and continuously checks the time of year and day, and the local weather conditions through an online service and decides if the conditions are

Figure 1: Still image from video documentation of interaction Bamboo Whisper 2013.

agreeable to insect-life. Locally a photo-sensor detects rapidly changing conditions, such as sudden cloud cover or moving to an inside environment. Fulfilling all requirements: close proximity to an insect-friendly space, correct time of year and day, agreeable weather conditions and correct light-levels, triggers a DC motor, connected to the protruding reeds, causing an insect-like vibration and rattle of the bonnet [4].

Rewilding Wearables

Biodiverse environments are key to sustainable ecosystems. Through guided walks in Stockholm, as part of TEI Arts Track and in Sydney as part of the Sydney Design Festival, participants wearing the prosthetic device will experience the environment from an alternative mind-set, emulating an insect and experiencing the city from a non-anthropocentric view, thereby becoming aware of the city as a, not purely human, space. They will enter a rewilded urban environment which largely goes unnoticed to us humans, "a city of crevices, borrows, cracks and places

Figure 2: Video still from *Cyborganic*

of weeds and rotting wood. It is the wild, feral city. Its citizens, a heterogeneous crowd of unregistered little creatures. For a long-time they were unwelcomed, hunted, displaced, exterminated" [4].

	EPI overall score	EPI rank	10-year trend out of 100%
Sweden	90.43	3	+1.81
Denmark	89.21	4	+1.38
Australia	87.22	13	0

	Bio diversity score	Bio diversity rank
Denmark	97.60	17
Sweden	88.76	57
Australia	87.18	68

Table 1 and 2: Environmental Performance Index (EPI) 2016

Case Study: Rewilding walk Aarhus

In Aarhus the Natural History Museum, the city council and private citizens are working to diversify the species inhabiting the city, to promote connection to landscape and dialogue about long term sustainable land management practices. Initiatives range from letting wild grasses and flowers grow on the roadsides, to building structures like insect-hotels and greening facades, even fountains. As an experiential, sympoetic link, living in the shadowy borderland of them and us, the Cyborganic responds to environmental factors in a similar manner to insects, and connects us to this feral city topology. The parameters that controlled the hats behaviour in Aarhus, Denmark were as follows:

- dry weather, i.e. less than 2mm precipitation within the last hour
- no strong wind, i.e. less than 7 m/s
- temperatures above 12º Celsius in spring and autumn, 18º Celsius in summer

Figure 3: Arial photo of Aarhus green spaces. Source: Google maps

Two Cyborganic pioneers walked 2.1 km from Vesterbro Torv to Frederik Nielsens Vej in central Aarhus, encountering five biodiverse sites on their journey. After the walk, they spoke about their experiences:

...like getting used to having a different shaped head...

... the perception of the city and also the perception of the body, like giving it a different shape...

"oh it's like a cricket" or something like that, insect...

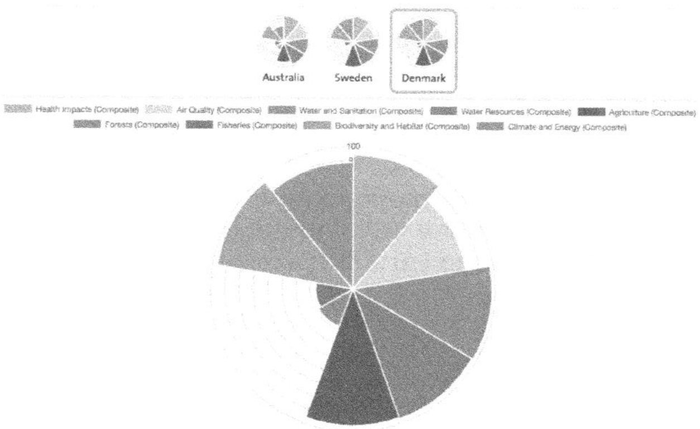

Figure 4:Data source, EPI report 2016, http://epi.yale.edu/

Rewilding Walks Stockholm and Sydney

In terms of The Environmental Performance Index (EPI) Sweden ranked 3rd on the global index in 2016 with a score of 90.43. Finland 90.86 and Iceland 90.51 took 1st and 2nd place respectively and Australia came 13th with a score of 87.22. The environmental Performance Index is a project run jointly by Yale University and the World Economic Forum. Sweden has only reached about half of what the government proposed they would do by 2020. In the last 10-years it's score has improved by only 1.81 percent. Sweden's overall EPI score was higher than Denmark, but in terms of the biodiversity metric Denmark ranked better, so it will be interesting to see what the Rewilding Walks will

Figure 5. Arial photo of Stockholm showing green space. Source: Google maps

discover in Stockholm, the capital of Sweden and the host for Tangible Embedded Interaction 2018. Australia is running well behind Sweden and Denmark in the EPI ranking. Yet there are many active groups such as the rewilding Australia network whose aims are: "To improve the trajectory for Australia's wildlife.

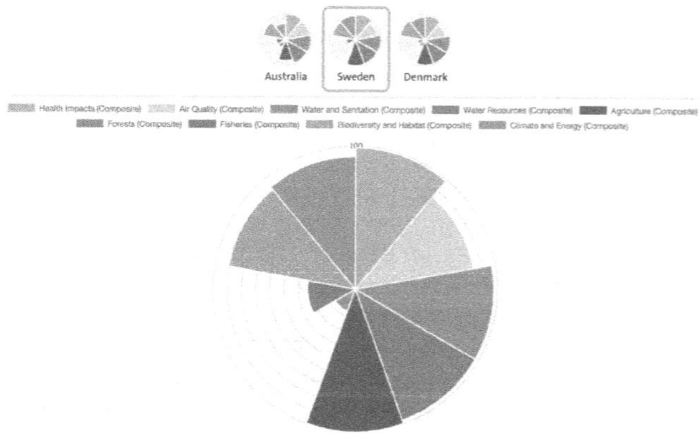

Figure 6: Data source, EPI report 2016, http://epi.yale.edu/

To restore lost ecosystem function and species interactions. To increase ecosystem resilience to future threats" w.rewildingaustralia.org.au. As part of the 2018 Sydney Design Festival in March 2018 we plan to guide walks to the botanical gardens, centennial park and la peruse with event visitors. The walk will be followed by a semi structured interview about their experience of the Cyborganic prosthetic and the environment.

Figure 7: Arial photo of Sydney showing green spaces. Source: Google maps

Discussion

Cyborganic as symbiotic prosthetic:

The cyborganic prosthetic, has a varied relationship with the body, parasitic and symbiotic. It enables us to access invisible worlds, whilst it is our legs that take it walking. Organic materials are grafted around the head, obscuring vision and muffling external sound, while enhancing the experience of the vibrations and chattering sticks of the bamboo brim. The affect of this blend of bio and electronic data leverages human biophilia. The 'love of life or living systems' is how Erich Fromm [5] first described the term biophila, an innate attraction that we possess, to forms of life or living systems. The term 'biophila' was promulgated in Edward O. Wilsons [9] 1984 publication of the same name where he makes a poignant statement that is critical today. "The one process now going on that will take millions of years to correct is the loss of genetic and species diversity by the destruction of natural habitats. This is the folly our descendants are least likely to forgive us".

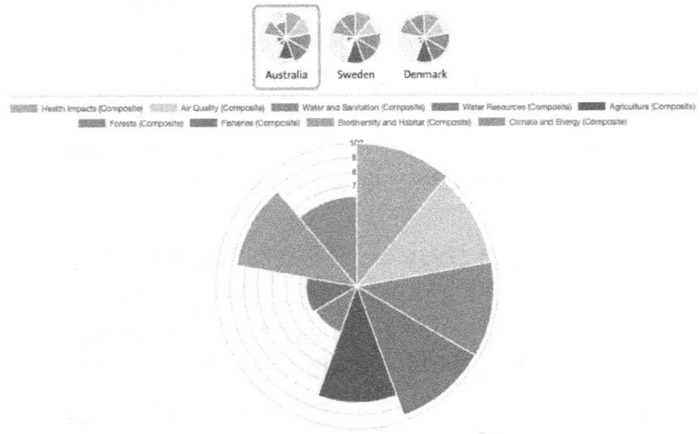

Figure 8: Data source, EPI report 2016, http://epi.yale.edu/

Developing empathy with insects:

Influenced by Alfred Gell's theory of art viewed as instrumental action, the Cyborganic prosthetic cannot be understood without consideration of both its animacy and its agency. The complexities of its behaviour are dependent on technologies. From crafting to coding, through the making of things, we can influence the behaviour of others. Wearing the prosthetic alters human perception to consider our environment from an insect's perspective. When the hat remains silent, this indicates a hostile place for insect populations. Through an iterative practice-led research process the prosthetic interface is evolving in accordance with feedback from participant wearers who we interview about their relationship to the Cyborganic and how it mediates their relationship to the environment. The authors acknowledge the agency of materials as collaborative elements in the design of artefacts and work with an expanded notion of interactive media that is not limited to interaction between humans and computers but also the interaction between the physical world and computers [8]. In this case the wearable interface device is woven from bamboo, sea grass, and electronics and seems to develop its own agency through reactions to unique sense parameters, some of which are invisible to human perception. Some of these behaviours, that were initially thought of as failure or lack of control, began to be understood as an emerging character of the artefact.

Conclusion and future directions

In this paper, we have presented a sympoetic wearable, which we define as a Cyborganic. We have described the function of the device and its relation to the nonhuman environment. We have described and analysed a pilot study as well as proposed further studies, one of which will take place at the TEI18 in Stockholm. The importance of bio diversity for environmental sustainability is clear. This research project aims to foster discussion about ways to better manage our ecosystem and provoke awareness of the environment from other than a human centric perspective. The data collected at the TEI18 will inform future iterations of the wearable interface and a video created to document the project will share our findings.

Acknowledgements

Thank you to: Lars Brøndum from Natural History Museum: Human Futures Research Group at Aarhus University, Denmark for financial support. The Interactive Media Lab at the Creative Robotics Lab UNSW for infrastructure funding; and Poul Madsen for videography. Author's ORCID numbers: Patricia Flanagan 0000-0003-2605-7630. Raune Frankjaer 0000-0002-4349-1263

References

1. J. Brouwer, A. Mulder, and L. Spuybroek. 2012. "Vital beauty: reclaiming aesthetics in the tangle of technology and nature," Rotterdam: V2 Publishing: NAI. 9.
2. Patricia Flanagan. 2013. Haptic Interface Aesthetics – Feedback loops, live coding and how to harness the potential of embodied estrangement in artistic practices and aesthetic theories within interface culture. IN: Marcus, Aaron (Ed.); Design, User Experience, and Usability - Design Philosophy, Methods, and Tools. Springer Berlin Heidelberg, 58-67.
3. Raune Frankjaer and Patricia Flanagan. Forthcoming. "The Technocrafted Posthuman: Introducing Cyborganics". Open Fields, Acoustic Space Journal, RIXC Center for New Media Culture.
4. Frankjaer, Raune. 2017. Cyborganics. Retrieved November 07, 2017 from http://frankjaer.de/cyborganics/
5. Erich Fromm. 1964. "The Heart of Man". Harper & Row.
6. Alfred Gell. 1998. "Art and agency: an anthropological theory," Oxford: Clarendon.
7. Donna Haraway. 2016. Staying with the trouble: Making kin in the Chthulucene. Duke University Press
8. Jun Rekimoto. 2008. "Organic Interaction Technologies: From Stone to Skin," Association for Computing Machinery. Communications of the ACM, vol. 51, no. 6, 38.
9. Edward O. Wilson. 1984. "Biophilia", Cambridge: Harvard University Press. 121.

Code{strata} Sonifying Software Complexity

Denez Thomas
University of Rennes 2
Rennes, 35000, France
denezthomas@gmail.com

Bruno Bossis
University of Rennes 2
Rennes, 35000, France
bruno.bossis@univ-rennes2.fr

Nicolas Harrand
INRIA
Rennes, 35000, France
nicolas.harrand@inria.fr

Benoit Baudry
KTH, Royal Institute of Technology
Stockholm, Sweden
baudry@kth.se

TEI '18, March 18–21, 2018, Stockholm, Sweden

ACM ISBN 978-1-4503-5568-1/18/03.
https://doi.org/10.1145/3173225.3173317

Abstract
Code{strata} is an interdisciplinary collaboration between art studies researchers (Rennes 2) and computer scientists (INRIA, KTH). It is a sound installation: a computer system unit made of concrete that sits on a wooden desk. The purpose of this project is to question the opacity and simplicity of high-level interfaces used in daily gestures. It takes the form of a 3-D sonification of a full software trace that is collected when performing a copy and paste command in a simple text editor. The user may hear, through headphones, a poetic interpretation of what happens in a computer, behind the of graphical interfaces. The sentence "Copy and paste" is played back in as many pieces as there are nested functions called during the execution of the command.

Author Keywords
Copy and paste; Instrumentation; Java; Sonification; spatialization; Cycling 74 Max 7.

ACM Classification Keywords
Operational Analysis, Auditory Feedback, Media Arts.

Introduction
Software is, by nature, invisible, yet it is omnipresent in our lives. This pervasiveness of software is the result of organic and decentralized processes. A growing number

Code{strata}

Materials: The installation itself is made of concrete, and sits on a wooden board and trestles. The audio is diffused through Beyerdynamic headphones (DT-770 Pro, 80Ohm or higher), with a Raspberry Pi 3 model B and a I2S sound card (IQAudio Pi-DAC+). 5V (2A min.) USB power supply.

Preparation: The whole device must be positioned as shown in Figure 1. The concrete computer sits on the left of the desk, headphones on its right. If shipping appears to be too complicated, a new piece of concrete can be poured in situ. This installation can be exhibited either in light or dark place. In the latter case, it might be slightly illuminated with a warm white.

of companies and individuals have contributed to the development and aggregation of millions of software pieces. The assembly and coordination between all these pieces relies on a flexible hierarchical organization of software and a stratified organization of the code. Inspired by the natural wonders of structure and complexity, we want to restore a more tangible relation between users and the software world through artistic representations. We choose to focus first on the strata of *ctrl-c ctrl-v*, an iconic action that symbolizes the major impact of software on all sectors of our societies. We deconstruct all the code that has been stacked to provide this action in almost any software tool. We choose an open source text editor to pursue this deconstruction of code strata. The choice of open source code is essential for us since it provides an access to all strata, but also to the origin of these strata.

The idea behind this project is not to frighten by showing how complex software is, but to reveal the beauty of those great networks of organized data and computation. The first example that we were looking at, when we started working on the project, was a work by William Bradford Paley, entitled *CodeProfiles* [4]. To illustrate the complexity of a running software, he chose to show the lines of code. He was actually able to show an exhaustive visualization of the code, because the entire program was written in order to display itself. That is what makes our approach at opposite ends of Bradford Paley's. As we didn't want to come to a simple data visualization, we chose to build a static installation, made of wood and concrete. This paper describes the creation process and gets into the ins and outs of the installation.

A sound installation

Representing a computer system unit with a concrete block was a way for us to illustrate the opacity and the simplicity of high-level interfaces. A very strong contrast is made between what we may see, namely a fully closed and compact block, and what we can actually hear.

Figure 1: Full installation front view.

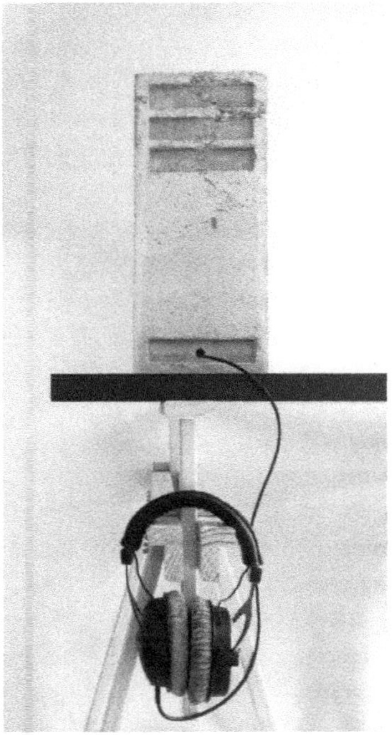

Figure 2: Closer view of the concrete computer.

The audio spatialization is meant to virtually place the listener in the center of a very wide room. The symbolic act of listening through headphones to what is happening inside the computer gives the installation all its meaning. This is why the diffusion is only possible through headphones. As if we were using a stethoscope, we can hear each individual detail in all of the complex activity. The user cannot interact with the complete loop (about 15 minutes). What we can hear may be considered as kind of sound landscape [7], in which the beginning and the end are of little relevance.

During the first exhibition of the project, a few visitors told us it was reminding them of the sound of a multitude of insects. More generally, the idea of nature has been raised a lot. The analogy with nature, and more precisely with geology has been part and parcel of the project's early stages. Imperfections that are inherent to concrete (see Figure 2) are giving the device an almost archeological aspect. It seems necessary to remember that all the functions called by the program we analyzed were someday written by humans, hence the construction materials. Wood and concrete are somewhat reminiscent of this nature-culture duality. Resting on a wooden table and trestles, the concrete block has visible foundations which are not without pointing out the concept of strata.

An audio interpretation of software data

One could consider this project as a zoom or a slow motion of what happens when a 'copy and paste' action is performed. Nevertheless, it is important to understand that this is not a realistic or exhaustive interpretation of data. Because as soon as there is interpretation, there are choices to be made. This project intends to convey a positive and tangible image of computing complexity. In that sense, this project aims at letting human users reclaim software complexity, as a genuine postdigital artistic installation [1]. Actually, an exhaustive exploration is impossible. For instance, we cannot measure the exact time elapsed between two instructions. In fact, time is subject to exogenous variations, starting with all the instrumentation methods that have been implemented into the source code, which are drastically slowing down the whole process. Another issue that needs to be taken into account is the high concentration of activity in the mid-range levels. The first stratum we work with is the application and libraries calls (JavaFX, the software library for the graphical interface). The code and the dataset are open source[1].

In Figure 3, columns represent the strata of code execution, when rectangles are the functions (blue for the application itself and green for the JavaFX library). White lines represent the way each function is calling sub functions. If we read linearly through the whole data set, we must consider the fact that the sound, which will be created in Cycling 74's Max, will be looping a long time around the same levels. As the average visitor only listens to the sound for a few tens of seconds, the experience may be different for each one of them. Sometimes, some will hear only little or no variations during their listening, such moment should not be perceived as less relevant than another.

[1] https://github.com/DIVERSIFY-project/code-strata

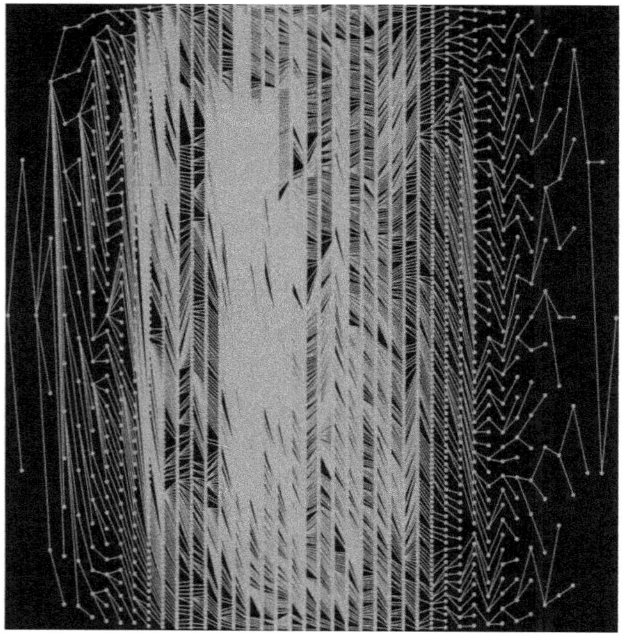

Figure 3: Application and library calls.

The use of Cycling 74's Max programming environment [4] is particularly appropriate when dealing with interpreting data. In fact, the results of the source code instrumentation in a JSON text file can later be loaded into Max for it to be usable. Max can read through the entire data and use all elements as parameters for manipulating sounds. For now, each JSON object represents a method that has been instrumentalized, and contains a few elements describing it. The data structure must be considered as a tree, where each method necessarily has a parent, and possibly brothers and children. The first element of an object is its maximum depth, followed by its number of brothers, children, the method's name, the weight and current absolute level. By scaling/mapping the output of each element, the values are adjusted to fit the parameters we want to modify in the audio synthesis or processing. Inspired by the work of composers like Gérard Grisey in *Les Chants de l'amour* [2], or Jonathan Harvey in *Mortuos Plango, Vivos Voco* [3], we worked on the ambiguity between human voice and computer processing.

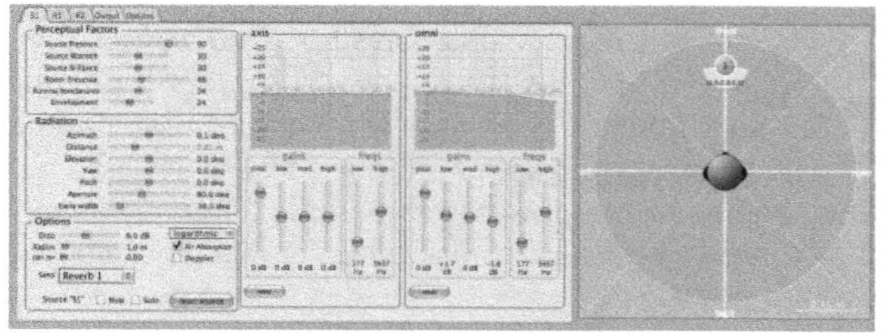

Figure 4: IRCAM Spat Operator (Graphical User Interface).

We took a sample of human voice, whispering the sentence 'copy and paste'. The whole sound is played back in as many fragments as there are nested functions called during the execution of the command. The length of each grain is indexed to the maximum depth of the function. If a method is called by many other methods, then we may hear a long grain ("cop", "pa", "and"). If it is called by a few other methods, then we shall hear very short grains ("t", "k", "p"). The position of the sample's reading head is directly linked to the reading of the tree. In our case the copy and paste takes almost fifteen minutes to be fully heard. Using human voice as raw material for the sonification of the software reminds us of all the work that has been indirectly made by so many for us to be able to perform even such simple operations. We also spatialize the sound with a binaural encoding by IRCAM's Spat [6].

The virtual distance between the audio source and the listener depends on the function's calling level. We are placed in the middle of the 45 levels, the first one being behind our head, the last one being in front of us.

References

1. David M. Berry. 2014. Post-digital humanities: Computation and cultural critique in the arts and humanities. *Educause*, *49*(3): 22-26.
2. Bruno Bossis. 2004. Les Chants de l'amour de Gérard Grisey, entre rigueur formelle et jubilation humaniste. In Danielle Cohen-Lévinas, *Le temps de l'écoute, Gérard Grisey ou la beauté des ombres sonores*. Paris, L'Harmattan, p. 229-270.
3. Bruno Bossis. 2004. *Mortuos Plango, Vivos Voco* de Jonathan Harvey ou le miroir de la spiritualité. *Musurgia*, *XI (1-2)*: 119-144.
4. William Bradford Paley. Whitney ArtPort. Retrieved November 4, 2017, from http://artport.whitney.org/commissions/codedoc/paley.shtml
5. Cycling'74. About Max. Retrieved November 4, 2017, from https://cycling74.com/products/max
6. IRCAM. Spat. Retrieved November 4, 2017, from http://forumnet.ircam.fr/product/spat-en/
7. Raymond Murray Schafer. 1993. *The Soundscape: Our Sonic Environment and the Tuning of theWorld*. Rochester, Inner Traditions Bear and Company, VT.

'Let's *F*ake News'

Dr. Léon McCarthy
University of Limerick
Limerick, Co. Limerick, Ireland
leon.mccarthy@ul.ie

Abstract
'Let's *F*ake News' is an interactive media art installation that forces participants to realize that anyone can create fake news and may even find joy in doing so. The artwork addresses the conference themes as an interactive installation that challenges ideas around 'post-truth', creating an experience that engages with digital representations of the discursive interactions.

Author Keywords
Fake News; Natural Language Processing; Data Visualisation; Real-time Audio-Visuals

ACM Classification Keywords
• Collaborative and social computing • Visualization • Applied computing • Media arts • Natural Language Processing

TEI '18, March 18–21, 2018, Stockholm, Sweden

ACM ISBN 978-1-4503-5568-1/18/03.
https://doi.org/10.1145/3173225.3173318

Introduction
'Let's Fake News' is an interactive media installation that brings participants together in questioning how well they can create fake news. Visitors congregate around an intelligent screen that, in a nod to the past is called 'HAL'. HAL invites visitors to use their phones to spontaneously create the script for a 'fake news' report, pushing the group of participants to make it as fantastical and unbelievable as possible. The phone-based nature of their interactions gives them free reign to exercise their imagination, whether they are amongst groups of strangers or friends. It is not long before they are competing to out do each other in terms of believability!

When they are finished, HAL takes a moment to process it's thoughts and then renders back a fake news report replete with audio, graphics and video that compliments their script. The result may shock, surprise or simply leave the group in fits of laughter. Notwithstanding, the participants are left to ponder the impact of their actions - they leave HAL behind considering how they could have been duped into enjoying the act of creating their own fake news story?

Context
It is generally accepted that we live in a post-truth era in which news stories that are misleading, fake or openly outlandish compete for our attention [6]. Perhaps this started when advertisers realized that

'shock and awe' tactics are more effective at grabbing ones attention than presenting more complicated, honest and considered content. Videos that 'go viral' can be shared and clicked on by the millions and so meet the demands of companies seeking to reach the eyeballs of the masses. This has led to the present in which importance is placed on 'ad-clicks' and 'page-views', often at the expense of content, truth and quality. Along with the rise in popularity of social-media platforms, this has led society to a place in which the user is the message, with self-promotion often taking precedence. Society has spawned what the author likes to call the '*make it, snap it, share it'* generation.

Recently, this has led to some rather unseemly developments: it now seems clear that the medium of Twitter facilitated the manipulation of the most recent US election, with this New York Times article outlining the basis for such claims [5]. Meanwhile, Facebook's live video streaming facility has led to the streaming of illegal activities – a development that can safely be labelled an appalling use of technology [1]. There is then of course the challenge we all now face in determining the validity of the news we consume as the loss of many respected news publications has been countered by the emergence of websites and social-media-channels that restrict our wider view of the world outside their narrow 'filter-bubble'.

Treatment

Many artists see their role as a form of social 'agent provocateur'. This can be traced from the works of Shakespeare through to Brecht. More specifically, many artworks critique the impact that technological developments have had on the society of their time.

Real-time video has been a medium through which artists have striven to re-negotiate our awareness for how we consume mass media: in the late 1990's artists such EBN were creating scratch-video backdrops for U2's Zoo-TV tour that brought then contemporary issues to the site of mass entertainment [7]. In 1999, artist/entrepreneur Josh Harris initiated the mass human experiment he called "Quiet: We Live in Public" to see what would happen when a group of humans are given free reign to indulge themselves with abandon. It influenced the emergence of the TV sensation 'Big Brother' and foresaw the social interactions that now occur on social-media platforms; the human tendency to celebrate the self as the reason for online communication.

Artists began to address such 'virtual' human interactions when they first emerged via Internet chat-rooms [2]. Our ability to do interact virtually became far more refined when platforms such as Facebook came online. When APIs were attached to the 'back-end' of social-media platforms, developers could tap into the large sets of data being shared, and so artists used sentiment analysis techniques to visualise such interactions in new ways; the resulting artworks explored the connections and meanings behind our online personas.

We have now developed AI technology to the extent that we are seeing the rise of the 'bot'; the medium-term looks set to see 'bots' become ubiquitous as our unseen speaking assistants. Developments in NLP now see voice-assistants in the home as well as the car; subtle information extraction algorithms enable such bots to understand and then respond to verbal commands.

It is at this juncture that the proposed artwork 'Let's Fake News' posits itself: the creation of an experience in which technology encourages humans to master the art of fake news making, only to then 'slap-them-in-the-face' with the visual reality of doing so. Thematically, it is perceived that the proposed installation addresses three of the conference themes, namely:

- An installation engaging with this 'post-truth' era by forcing participants to create fake-news
- A discursive design that engages with how our conversations can get represented digitally
- A 'wizard-of-oz' experience that deliberately undermines participants' opinion of their 'real' self by having them create 'unreal' scenarios

The installation can be seen as an 'imaginarium'; a liminal space where 'mock-the-week' meets 'trump-on-twitter. It creates a communal experience around the act of creating fake-news together. However, on leaving the installation visitors will be left wondering as to the validity of the experience they have just had. Was it an experience they care to repeat? If so, then does that say there is more worth in their own momentary-engagement than lasting truth and validity?

Figure 1 L. McCarthy: Live Discursive Cinema, 'Pigtown Performance, Limerick (photo: G. Stack)

Technology

The author's research expertise is in creating real-time platforms for audience engagement, often as a means for him to interact with his own audiences in real-time during performance. A series of his recent performances established a form of 'live cinema' in which the audience and performer collaborated & conversed through the 2nd-screen, leading to an emergent audio-visual narrative; an aesthetic well suited to discursive contexts [3]. Technically, these performances required the author to develop a bespoke 2nd-screening communication platform sometimes hosted on his own local intranet but at other times hosted as an Internet-based web-service.[4]

The author's more recent research questions the validity of a performer's on-stage presence by task-sharing with a 'bot': the bot's role is to extract meaning from the audience's conversations and then run automated web-content searches in response. Technically, so as to facilitate the audience's phone-based conversations, such performances continue to use his bespoke 2nd-screening platform but add background python-based scripts that mine their conversations and then run web searches to fetch related content. The result is an audio-visual backdrop generated in real-time as a complement to the live discussions taking place.

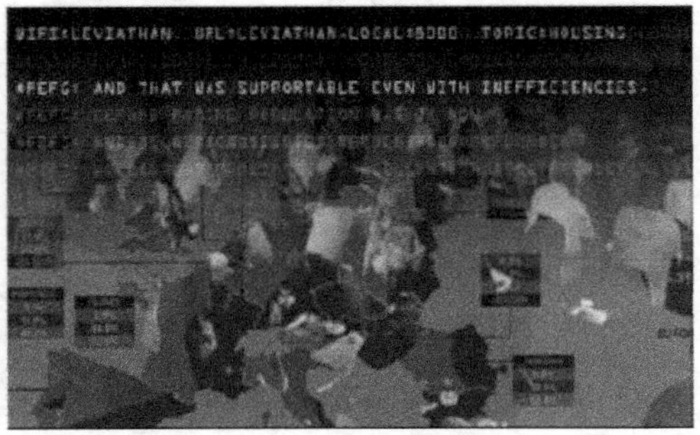

Figure 2 L.McCarthy: Realtime Visualisation of Conversation, 'Mindfield Performance', Electric Picnic (photo: E. Horgan)

For the proposed installation, the author will run a similar platform as above. Visitors will first approach a large screen and then scan a QR code that redirects them to the web-based 2nd-screening platform. Mediated by HAL, they will cooperate in spontaneously creating the script for a fake-news story. For every phrase they submit, HAL will be extracting key 'meaning-terms' via python-scripts based on Natural Language Processing (NLP) algorithms. When the fake-news story is finished, HAL will then use these extracted meaning-terms as Internet search-terms. The content that is returned is then used to create a visual composite that, along with the motion-graphics of the submitted text, render the fictional narrative as a convincing and compelling fake-news media report.

Figure 3 L.McCarthy: Composite of a rendered 'Fake News' Story (graphic: L. McCarthy)

References

[1] Dreyfuss, E. Facebook Streams a Murder, and Must Now Face Itself. *Wired*, 2017. https://www.wired.com/2017/04/facebook-live-murder-steve-stephens/.

[2] Freyer, C., Noel, S., Antonelli, P., and Rucki, E. *Digital by Design*. 2011.

[3] McCarthy, L. Steering Audience Engagement During Audio-Visual Performance L. McCarthy PhD 2016. (2016), 1–184.

[4] McCarthy, L. Dance Limerick Performance - "Pigtown Scratchings" Series. https://vimeo.com/127505360.

[5] Shane, S. and Wakabayashi, D. Twitter, With Accounts Linked to Russia, to Face Congress Over Role in Election. *New York Times*, 2017. https://www.nytimes.com/2017/09/27/technology/twitter-russia-election.html.

[6] Twitter, With Accounts Linked to Russia, to Face Congress Over Role in Election. (2017), 1–6.

[7] Emergency Broadcast Network - Wikipedia, the free encyclopedia. https://en.wikipedia.org/wiki/Emergency_Broadcast_Network.

Evaluating Learning with Tangible and Virtual Representations of Archaeological Artifacts

Christina Pollalis[1], Elizabeth Joanna Minor[1], Lauren Westendorf[1], Whitney Fahnbulleh[1], Isabella Virgilio[1], Andrew L. Kun[2], Orit Shaer[1]

[1]Wellesley College
Wellesley, MA, USA
{cpollali, eminor, lwestend, wfahnbul, ivirgilio}@wellesley.edu

[2]University of New Hampshire
Durham, NH, USA
andrew.kun@unh.edu

ABSTRACT

Technological advances offer new methods of representing physical objects in tangible and virtual forms. This study compares learning outcomes from 61 students as they interact with ancient Egyptian sculptures using three increasingly popular educational technologies: HoloLens AR headset, 3D model viewing website (SketchFab), and plastic extrusion 3D prints. We explored how differences in interaction styles affect the learning process, quantitative and qualitative learning outcomes, and critical analysis.

Author Keywords

Augmented Reality; 3D Models; 3D Printing; Archaeology; Object-based learning

INTRODUCTION

Emerging technologies, such as virtual and augmented reality (AR), wearable computing, and digital fabrication, have improved the engagement and experiences of learners in a wide range of content domains [3, 22, 31]. In particular, these technologies pose unique opportunities for enhancing object-based learning. Object-based learning places interaction with physical artifacts in a central position in the learning process [55].

Disciplines that use physical artifacts for their base of analysis include anthropology, archaeology, art history, classics, and museum studies. Traditional learning paths in these disciplines do not often afford students the opportunity to engage directly with authentic objects until they have reached advanced stages of instruction. First, access to authentic artifacts is limited by the availability of museums and cultural institutions in the region of instruction. Furthermore, most museum visits do not offer opportunities for students to interact directly with artifacts, engaging with objects on a deeper level.

TEI '18, March 18–21, 2018, Stockholm, Sweden

ACM ISBN 978-1-4503-5568-1/18/03…$15.00
https://doi.org/10.1145/3173225.3173260

AR technology allows for virtual objects or superimposed information to appear as if they coexist with the real world [2]. As such, it enables educators to bring digital representations of artifacts into the classroom, and allows students to explore these objects while present in the class and in conversation with peers and instructors. However, current AR applications utilize tablets and phones, providing only limited interactions through on-screen touch gestures. The increasing availability of wearable AR devices, such as the Microsoft HoloLens headset [35], provides opportunities to develop AR experiences in which users can see and interact with digital representations of artifacts without holding an additional mediating device.

Advances in 3D scanning and fabrication technologies allow educators to engage students in exploring virtual or tangible replicas of original artifacts. Several museums, including the British Museum and the Smithsonian Museum, released 3D models of important artifacts, making them available freely for educators and the public. These digital replicas could be explored using direct manipulation interfaces (e.g. SketchFab). Alternatively, models could be 3D printed so that users can explore physical replicas of the original artifacts using tangible interaction.

However, when considering the use of such emergent technologies for fostering object-based learning, important questions include: How do differences in interaction styles affect learning process and outcomes? How does close examination of virtual vs. tangible replicas support learning? We are interested in three interaction styles along the tangible-virtual continuum: physical interaction with tangible representations (3D prints), direct manipulation interaction with virtual representations (SketchFab), and gesture-based interaction with virtual replicas (HoloLens application). We selected to study these particular interaction styles because of their increasing availability for higher education [22].

To address these questions, we conducted a comprehensive user study with 61 adult learners, which integrates quantitative measures and qualitative indicators to explore whether and how the above three interaction styles augment object-based learning. Our findings indicate that interaction style has significant impact on various aspects of object-based learning with digital replicas. In particular, we found that the gesture-based interaction with virtual replicas (implemented on the HoloLens AR headset) was superior in terms of the learning process - demonstrating higher levels of enjoyment and reported strengths. The AR headset also showed positive effects on learning outcomes that were comparable to the on-screen interaction (SketchFab), but superior to the 3D prints. The paper continues with background and related work followed by experimental design, methods, and findings.

BACKGROUND AND RELATED WORK

Object-Based Learning

Object-based learning is a pedagogy that views direct interaction with physical objects as central for learning. The immediate goals of object-based learning are for students to practice close observation, determine what set of information to collect for research, and to build critical thinking skills for comparing and contrasting examples [55]. Learning begins with a base of direct observation and leads to higher-level interpretation. Students are expected to build their observational skills to produce comprehensive and detailed descriptions of objects, which can then be used to interpret social, political, and/or historical trends. These skills are developed by interacting with a set of artifacts. The goals of object-based learning are also related to active and experiential learning. These pedagogies view hands-on engagement with artifacts as central to constructing meaning and internalizing new concepts [55].

A large body of research in cognitive sciences and museum studies demonstrates that the manipulation of physical objects promotes understanding and learning, and even benefits mental and physical health. By manipulating an object, a student builds a mental conception through testing and observing its characteristics and relationships with other concepts [26, 27]. Object handling has traditionally been used for young students and public engagement, but pedagogical research suggests that creatively expanding its use in higher education has positive results [18]. As viewers interact with objects they make emotional associations with remembered experiences, which has been found to have positive effects on mental and physical health, both in tangible [11, 12] and virtual [34] forms.

In this study, the experience of interacting with a set of artifacts was emulated using three different, increasingly available, digital means of artifact reproduction: 3D printed physical objects, on-screen 3D models, and head-worn AR display visualization. Each modality offers different potential benefits to achieving learning outcomes: physical 3D prints provide multi-sensory input allowing students to touch and manually manipulate objects in literal hands-on learning, on-screen 3D models offer a high degree of realism as well as the ability to zoom and spin visual representations without physical constraints and with familiar control features, and head-worn AR devices provide a fully visually immersive environment that replicates the scale and presence of the object. To our knowledge, this is the first study to compare the learning outcomes achieved with these three technologies.

Learning with Physical Models

Much research indicates that tangible user interfaces can enhance learning and problem solving [1, 32, 43]. However, in this study, we focus on tangible interaction with fabricated physical models that are not augmented computationally. Research has shown that scientists often employ external artifacts to support their reasoning while tackling complex problems [40, 41, 46]. A known example is the model of DNA built by Watson and Crick, which enabled them to form and test hypotheses about the double helix structure. Research has shown that physical models can augment cognitive processes by facilitating both conceptual and material manipulation [4].

Several studies compare the use of fabricated physical objects to on-screen or paper-based interaction, demonstrating that physical objects provide cognitive support and improve information retrieval [21], as well as positively impact memorability [13, 24]. However, other studies did not find clear differences between physical and digital modalities [29, 33, 54, 58]. Additional research is needed to better understand the impact of physical educational materials on learning.

In addition, as makerspaces and 3D printing become more accessible and common in educational settings, students and teachers are able to not only use physical learning materials but also to easily produce their own physical artifacts. However, the majority of the literature that addresses the pedagogical use of 3D printing focuses on the design and production process rather than the end use [6, 10, 15-17, 19, 30, 42, 47, 48].

In this study, we evaluate the potentials of using 3D prints in the classroom, which can reflect on the *end use* of digital fabrication. Additionally, we chose to contrast the learning goals achieved through tangible models with virtual modalities that could offer their own pedagogical benefits.

Learning with AR

Recent studies comparing the use of AR and traditional content within the classroom found that AR positively affected learning outcomes. In one case, students responded positively and preferred to use AR platforms over traditional PC-based interfaces [23]. Additionally, using AR to provide the opportunity to manipulate objects that were otherwise difficult to visualize was found to significantly improve learning outcomes [14]. Comparative studies have found that AR platforms promote group collaboration over traditional media [36]. As the rapidly-expanding body of literature on pedagogical use of AR suggests a variety of benefits, there is a need for further research to discern how specific qualities of AR support cognitive, collaborative, and situated learning [9].

On a logistical level, AR holds many advantages in an educational setting, such as flexible access for otherwise limited lab hours and spaces and allowing for collaboration between remote groups [8]. Teachers and students are also able to create experiences that would be otherwise physically impossible, such as moving celestial bodies [14], building complex interactive artwork [9], or effortlessly manipulating massive sculpture as in the study we present in this paper. As AR connects virtual content with real world spaces, it offers an additive synergy that goes beyond the potentials of using either alone [8]. The "infusion" of digital content bridges between virtual and authentic experiences, potentially affording the maximum benefit of each [9]. In courses in the Humanities and Social Sciences, dialogue about different perspectives and interpretations is often as important as absorbing content. AR technology maintains interactivity with instructors and peers while viewing virtual objects, versus the completely immersive VR headset experience.

This study is motivated by these larger discussions on how visualization, connection, and engagement promote object-based learning outcomes. We explore this promise by investigating the differences in experience and in learning outcomes between physical interaction with 3D prints, direct manipulation of on-screen 3D models, and gestural interaction with virtual objects using an AR headset. Each modality offers different strengths in tangibility, flexibility of manipulation, and immersion, respectively.

Emerging Technologies for Cultural Heritage

Technological advances offer opportunities for enhancing museum visitors' interaction with cultural heritage [44, 51]. However, these opportunities also pose new challenges for curators and educators as hand-held screens and digital kiosks often distract visitors from viewing the artifacts [44].

Emerging interactive technologies also provide curators and educators with new ways to engage learners with cultural heritage artifacts outside of the museum environment. 3D scanning and 3D printing are increasingly used in archaeology and anthropology to capture representations of authentic artifacts [50]. Prominent institutions including the British Museum (used in this study), the Smithsonian Museum, and the Google Cultural Institute made scans of important cultural heritage pieces available to educators and to the public [28, 38]. There are many advantages to using 3D scanning in the museology and archaeology fields, including capturing details, preservation, replication, and broadening access. However, 3D printed replicas, in plastic or other materials, might lose the authenticity of the original object. This concern is echoed by curators in regards to digital replicas [44]. This study provides new insights into the strengths and weaknesses of digital vs. physical 3D printed replicas.

STUDY

Goals and Research Questions

The goal of this study is to investigate whether and how different interaction styles with physical and virtual replicas augment object-based learning. In particular, we explored the following questions: 1) How do differences in interaction styles affect the learning process (time on task, perceived workload, spatial presence, and attention allocation)? 2) How do differences in interaction style affect quantitative and qualitative learning outcomes? 3) How does close examination of virtual vs. tangible replicas support visual and critical analysis?

Experimental Task

The study task was adapted from an archaeology class, where it was applied to help students develop their visual observational skills and to hone their critical analysis. The task involves selecting two artifacts from an available inventory with six artifacts, exploring them, and completing the respective object questionnaire. For each object, participants were asked to state the first detail they noticed, all the details they noticed, and what seemed to be unique or similar about the object compared to the rest in the set.

Experimental Design

We used a between-subjects design across three conditions. We chose to compare interaction styles along the tangible-virtual continuum: physical interaction with tangible replicas (3D prints), direct manipulation interaction with virtual replicas (SketchFab), and gestural interaction with holographic replicas (HoloLens application). These interaction styles were selected because of the increasing availability of their underlying technologies for educational settings [22]. We chose a between-subjects design in order to balance a meaningful object-based learning activity with a reasonable (less than 1 hour) session duration. Participants were randomly assigned to one of the following conditions:

Figure 1. 3D Prints artifact inventory (left) and participant exploring and reading about the selected 3D print (right).

3D prints

This condition presented participants with 3D printed replicas of six artifacts, produced using scans provided by the British Museum of 42k – 1.1M faces and 23.9k – 529k vertices and printed through the MakerBot Replicator 2X and Afinia H800. All models were printed using either PLA or ABS Natural filament. The 3D models were printed at the highest resolution and largest size possible, while retaining correct between-model scale. We chose to use 3D printers that are currently available in many educational spaces. Descriptions of the artifacts were presented using printed cards set next to each artifact (Figure 1). Participants could pick up an object and explore it tactilely.

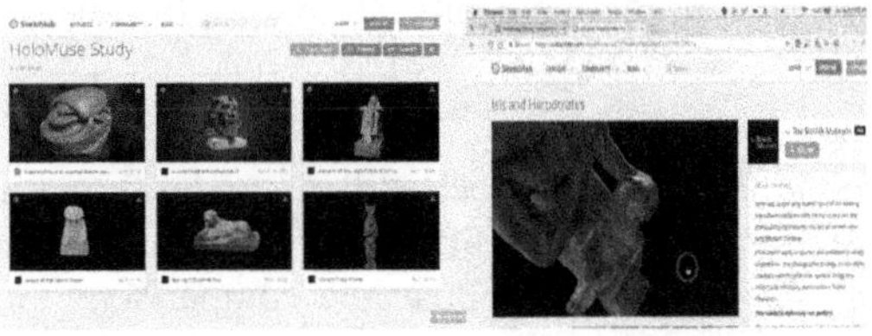

Figure 2. SketchFab artifact inventory (left) and artifact selected and being explored in SketchFab condition (right).

SketchFab

This condition presented participants with an inventory comprising of 3D scans of six artifacts through the online 3D modeling desktop platform, SketchFab (Figure 2). Participants could select an artifact and explore it using the mouse and a direct manipulation interface. The platform also presented a description for each artifact.

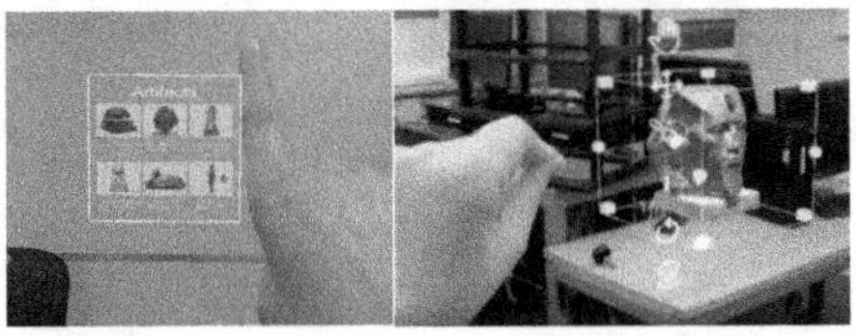

Figure 3. Holographic artifact inventory (left) and participant rotating the selected holographic artifact (right).

HoloMuse

In this condition, participants used HoloMuse [45], a Microsoft HoloLens AR application developed using Unity and C#, which presents users with an inventory comprising of six holographic artifacts (Figure 3). Participants could select an artifact and explore it by moving, rotating, and scaling the artifact using in-air gestures. Participants could also show or hide the artifact's material to see its surface, and display additional information about the object.

Throughout all conditions, the artifact inventory, artifact order, artifact descriptions, and settings were consistent.

Procedure

Participants signed a consent form and then filled a pre-task questionnaire, providing demographic information, specifying their prior experience with visual analysis (e.g. art history class), and reporting prior experience with AR, VR, and 3D modeling software. Participants were then shown an artifact inventory of six models and given training on how to select an artifact and manipulate it.

Following this training, each participant was given the task of exploring two objects of their choice and completing an object questionnaire for each using a laptop we provided. Following the completion of the task, each participant completed a post-task questionnaire with 15 Likert-type questions, each rated on a 5-point scale from "Strongly Disagree" to "Strongly Agree" (Table 4); a NASA TLX questionnaire [19, 39]; and four open-ended questions about the platform. Participants in the HoloLens condition were also asked whether they experienced a headache or discomfort while wearing the device. Throughout each section of the study, participants were not limited in time. We collected data through questionnaires, application logs, and video recording of the session.

Measures and Indicators

In order to evaluate the following measures and indicators, we collected both quantitative and qualitative data which were assessed through standardized enjoyment and workload metrics, as well as content-specific coding developed in consultation with a domain expert:

Time on task

We explored the effect of interaction style on total time on task as well as on the time spent exploring selected objects. In this study, time on task was not used to deduce efficiency, but rather to deduce meaningful engagement.

Enjoyment

We also asked participants to rate their level of enjoyment using the interface. We used a Likert scale of 1 to 10 from low enjoyment to high enjoyment.

Perceived task workload

We measured users' perceived task workload with the NASA TLX questionnaire [18]. We interpret the results of the unweighted, raw NASA TLX data, grouped by category (i.e. frustration, effort, mental demand, physical demand).

Spatial presence

We measured users' perceived spatial presence with a series of questions loosely based on the MEC-SPQ standardized questionnaire [56], which consists of eight dimensions. Table 4 shows question content and results by condition.

Learning outcomes

The qualitative assessment of learning outcomes was based on insight-based evaluation methodology [48], and was developed in consultation with a domain expert, who drew on their 15 years of experience in teaching and assessing learning outcomes in related content at the university level. We analyzed the open response questions about the viewed artifacts, such that for each response, we derived the number of words, number and type of concepts referred to, and the level of analysis. The concept codes used were selected to demonstrate desired progression from observation to interpretation. Participants were expected to produce comprehensive and detailed descriptions of objects, which can then be used to interpret social, political, and/or historical trends. The content codes were developed in consultation with the domain expert, and after an initial round of coding were condensed into more general categories. We used the following codes: *Visual inspection* - shape, color, and texture; *Complex visual observation* - damage, detail, and facial feature; *Inferences* - material, size and weight; and *Interpretation* - aesthetic, analysis, and context. In addition, the domain expert co-author assigned the open responses from each participant a score between 1-5 based on complexity and on cognitive engagement with the artifacts. We used the following classification, which is based on Bloom's taxonomy [7]: Score 1 - Response was brief and included a single descriptive observation; 2 - Response was brief and included several descriptive observations; 3 - Response was short to medium length and included several descriptive observations, and at least one critical or comparative assessment of the object; 4 - Response was medium length and included more critical or comparative assessment than descriptive observation; and 5 - Response was medium to long and was primarily critical or comparative assessment.

Post-task

Finally, we asked participants about the *strengths and weaknesses* of viewing and learning about an object using the interface they interacted with.

Data Analysis

Quantitative data was analyzed using IBM SPSS Statistics, Version 24. Mean comparison was conducted using ANOVA. Post hoc differences between conditions were analyzed with Tukey tests. Responses to open questions were analyzed using content analysis methods. First level codes were developed from preliminary review of the data by the content domain expert. Two independent coders were trained to code the data, and thematic categories were identified and analyzed (see table 3). After an initial coding of 10% of the data, the coders discussed inconsistencies in their codes and calibrated. The final inter-coder reliability based on all the data was excellent with agreement >95%.

Participants

We recruited 61 participants, all students and recent graduates (42 female, 16 male, 3 not specified; age M=20.9 SD=2.5). Each participant was randomly assigned to a condition; however, we did balance for gender. We found no significant differences based on self-reported experience with visual analysis or 3D interaction (AR or VR). All participants completed the study, and were compensated with a $10 gift card.

RESULTS

	3D Prints	SketchFab	HoloLens
N	20	20	21
Female	14	14	14
Male	5	5	6
Not specified	1	1	1
Minutes on task	20:05 (4:32)	23:51 (7:34)	32:30 (6:40)
Minutes on objects	10:48 (3:04)	13:52 (5:41)	12:35 (4:34)
Enjoyment	6.05 (2.14)	6.70 (1.42)	7.52 (2.16)

Table 1. Gender distribution, and mean and standard deviation for time spent on the entire task, time spent investigating the objects, and enjoyment, by condition.

Time on Task

Time spent investigating objects, and total time spent in each condition can be found in Table 1. There was a significant effect of condition on total time spent on the task [F(2,58)=20.397, p<.001]. Post hoc comparisons indicated that the average time spent in the HoloLens condition was significantly different than the time spent in the other two conditions. However, there was no significant effect of condition on time spent investigating the two selected objects [F(2,58)=2.555, p=.086].

Enjoyment

Enjoyment scores for each condition can be found in Table 1. There was a significant effect of condition on enjoyment [F(2,58)=2.974, p= .047]. Post hoc comparisons indicate a significant difference in enjoyment between the HoloLens and 3D prints conditions.

Perceived Task Workload

There was a significant difference in the perceived physical workload between conditions [F(2,58)=6.103, p=.004]. Post hoc comparisons indicated that the mean score for the HoloLens condition (M=4.76, SD=2.45) was significantly different than the 3D prints (M=2.40, SD=1.87) and SketchFab conditions (M=3.05, SD=2.35). There were no other significant differences. Figure 4 shows NASA TLX dimensions per condition.

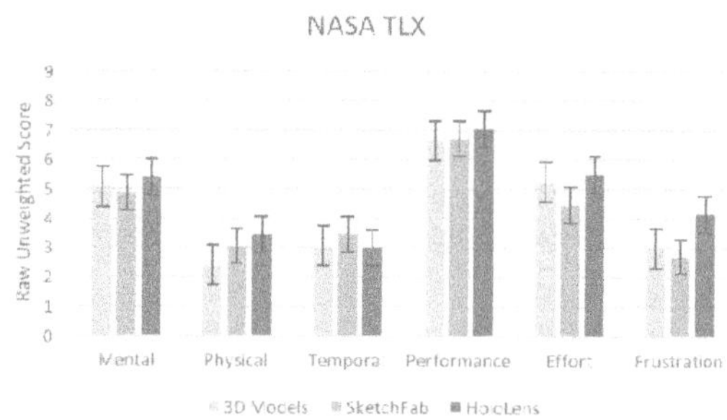

Figure 4. Average unweighted NASA TLX scores and standard error bars by condition.

Learning Outcomes

We evaluated learning outcomes in terms of number of words of the open responses, number and content of thematic codes, and a complexity score assigned by a domain expert. Table 2 includes the word count, number of themes mentioned, and complexity scores for task questions. There was no significant difference in the combined complexity score across conditions.

However, for the question asking participants to list all details noticed about an object (see Table 2), the number of thematic codes appeared in the responses was significantly higher in the HoloLens and SketchFab conditions as compared to the 3D prints condition.

Looking at the frequency of specific thematic codes (see Table 3), we found the following significant differences. Material was mentioned significantly more in the SketchFab and HoloLens conditions, as compared to the 3D prints condition. Facial features were mentioned significantly more in the 3D prints condition as compared to the HoloLens condition. Color was mentioned significantly more in the HoloLens condition, as compared to the 3D prints condition. Lastly, context was mentioned significantly more in the SketchFab and HoloLens conditions, as compared to the 3D prints condition. There was also a significant difference in the number of users who mentioned size in response to the question about selecting a favorite object and explaining why, between the Sketchfab (0/20) and HoloLens (7/21) conditions and the 3D prints (5/20) and SketchFab, but not between the HoloLens and 3D prints conditions.

There was no significant difference found in the number of codes used, word count, or complexity score for self-reported "Experts" and "Non-Experts" in visual analysis.

Thematic code	3D Prints (N=20)	SketchFab (N=20)	HoloLens (N=21)	F	*p*
texture	7	12	11	1.308	.278
material	7	16	16	6.287	**.003**
detail	19	20	20	.488	.616
facial feature	19	14	10	6.422	**.003**
color	6	13	14	3.741	**.030**
damage	9	10	15	1.657	.200
size	12	8	14	1.591	.213
analysis	11	15	16	1.327	.273
weight	1	1	1	.001	.999
context	5	16	16	10.236	**<.001**

Table 3. Frequency of thematic codes and one-way ANOVA results.

Spatial Presence

Question content and scores by condition for the spatial presence questionnaire can be found in Table 4. Participants in the SketchFab and HoloLens conditions reported feeling that the artifact was present in their environment significantly more than the 3D prints condition participants.

Participants in the SketchFab and HoloLens conditions responded that they still maintained a concrete mental image of the artifact during the post-task at higher levels than those in the 3D prints condition. Finally, participants in the SketchFab condition reported significantly higher levels of consideration of the usage of the objects than participants in the 3D prints condition.

Object Distribution and Favorite Objects

Participants were allowed to select which objects they viewed, and later were asked to describe their favorite object. Table 5 lists the objects in the order they arranged in the inventory for participants, as well as participants' choices. In general, participants chose objects they were drawn to. When statues of animals were chosen and viewed, they had the highest frequency of becoming the participant's favorite object for the session. Viewers seem to have preferentially chosen the Right Prudhoe Lion and the statue of Isis and Harpocrates. There were no apparent differences across conditions.

Platform Strengths and Weaknesses

In the post-task questionnaire, participants mentioned significantly more strengths in the HoloLens condition compared to SketchFab. Participants also mentioned significantly more weaknesses in the 3D prints condition compared to the other two conditions.

In the 3D prints, most mentioned strengths were tactility (15/20), manipulation (7/20), and angles (7/20). As one participant stated: "You get to feel the details, see the object up close, it is easier to rotate it and look at it from all angles." Notable weaknesses were details (11/20) and colors (10/20). One participant said: "Much of the detail of the objects is taken away when you are just viewing a basic, white-colored 3-D printed replica. It's impossible to imagine the colors or the medium of the actual object." A higher 3D print resolution could change user perception of damage and details; however, since the models were printed at the highest resolution possible, these observations remain relevant.

In the SketchFab condition, the most common strength mentioned was angles (11/20). As one participant noted: "I think it was great to see all angles of the objects in views that I would not have been able to in a museum." The most common themes for weaknesses were lack of interaction (9/20) and size (9/20). In the words of one participant: "The weaknesses of exploring an object in this way is that some viewers may not feel as if they are interacting with the object." Another participant mentioned: "It is still not physically in your view and some picturing must be done in order to understand the dimensions of an object."

Finally, in the HoloLens condition, the most reported strengths include manipulation (6/21), size (6/21), scaling (4/21), and kinetic movement (4/21). In the words of one participant: "I found myself engaging with the objects in a way that I likely wouldn't have in a museum or certainly image format. The ability to manipulate the objects yourself, change their sizes and perspective, and truly interact has a certain draw." Another participant noted: "I loved being able to walk around an object in its entirety and have it to myself." Most prevalent weaknesses were: hard to use (7/21), and size (5/21). As one participant noted: "I did struggle with gauging size/scale of the objects and would have valued from some type of scale indicator. I also found that if I tried to move the objects they jumped closer to me in my range of vision and that made it more difficult for me to see and manipulate the objects." Additionally, 52% of participants (11/21) reported headache or eyestrain while wearing the device. This is a critical limitation of this device; future studies will determine to what extent the discomfort is associated with the current version of the HoloLens device.

DISCUSSION

Here we discuss our main findings from comparing learning process and outcomes across the three different conditions:

Assessing Quantitative Learning Results

Across all three conditions, there were no significant differences in the combined complexity score of participants' task responses to open questions about the artifacts they viewed. However, there were significant differences in the frequency of particular thematic codes: codes for color, material and context were notably rarely mentioned while participants viewed the 3D prints. This suggests that educators have the flexibility to select a platform that offers strengths specific to the tasks or concepts they wish to highlight in their lesson, without sacrificing an overall quality of student learning.

When asked to list all the details about an object, the word counts of the participant responses were significantly lowest when using the HoloLens. This brevity is perhaps due to the headset slightly impairing users' ability to see the computer screen and keyboard. As the overall complexity of responses did not differ, this suggests that students are still able to achieve expected learning goals despite the condensed nature of their answers.

Assessing Qualitative Learning Results

Each platform offers different means of visualizing digital replicas of artifacts, which in turn directs viewers' attention to different attributes. Overall, SketchFab and HoloLens results were comparable, while 3D prints underperformed in several areas, including the lowest instances of mentions of color and material. As the prints do not have surface details, participants were not able to infer the material of the originals. Mentions of context (time and place) were also the lowest for 3D prints. The lack of visual cues about the material of the object seems to have impaired the overall perception of the "authentic" aspect of the object.

HoloLens responses had a significantly lower mention of facial features over the other two platforms. The reason for this difference is not immediately forthcoming, but may be due to participants' unfamiliarity with the interaction style, which perhaps impaired their ability to zoom in on faces.

Workload Measurement and Enjoyment

Participants' perceived physical demand using the HoloLens was significantly higher. HoloLens use involved standing, moving arms, and in-air gestures that can be physically demanding as well as create accessibility issues. Viewing 3D models on SketchFab and 3D prints can be done while sitting and involve less arm and hand movement. The tactile nature of 3D prints also makes them more accessible to students with visual disabilities [34]. In addition, more than half of participants in the AR condition reported headache or eyestrain while wearing the device.

Of the three conditions, the HoloLens is most novel to participants. Despite the unfamiliarity of the gesture-based interface, we did not find a significantly higher level of frustration while using this AR headset. The HoloLens ranked the highest in enjoyment, followed by SketchFab, and although the 3D prints ranked the lowest they were still perceived as enjoyable overall. The enjoyment ranking results are further supported by the detailed responses about the strengths and weaknesses of each platform. However, longitudinal studies are needed to determine to what extent the novelty of the HoloLens impacted user enjoyment.

Attention Allocation

When asked if the "ancient artifact captured [their] senses," (see Table 4) the participants ranked the 3D prints as trending significantly lower than the HoloLens, although the prints are the only platform to include a sense of touch. Haptic interaction cannot be achieved through traditional museum display, with artifacts behind glass due to preservation concerns. Although the 3D prints offered this novel form of contact with museum objects, participants did not respond as strongly to their perceived level of interaction, as the models were a single color and therefore lacked visual cures such as texture. The importance of haptic interaction for participants with visual impairments should be considered, however, to ensure that educational resources are accessible [25, 53]. Future study design should address the issue of physical model with higher fidelity in terms of color as well as of combining visual information with additional senses.

Spatial Situational Models and Presence

Interestingly, when asked if they still had "a concrete mental image of the ancient artifact," participants ranked the 3D prints the lowest, although they were the only condition that had physically concrete examples in the study. The virtual 3D models allowed the participants to view more physical aspects of the artifacts, such as color and texture, which led to a stronger mental image with lasting impression. The participants confirmed the immersive nature of AR by ranking it the highest when asked if they "felt as though the original ancient artifact was physically present in [their] environment". Once again, although the 3D prints were the only objects to be physically present in the real world, participants ranked them the lowest in this evaluation.

Implications for Design

Each of the three interaction styles employed in this study provides educators with important tools for engaging students. Here, we discuss implications for designers of interactive experiences for object-based learning:

Context

The essential goal of object-based learning is to investigate an artifact in its temporal, physical, and cultural context. The results suggest that participants rely on color and texture to infer the material of the object, and that those visual cues are more important to envisioning context than shapes or volumetric details. As discussed above, the 3D prints had the significantly lowest mentions of color, texture, and material. In order to achieve the learning goals of object-based learning, methods such as computational hydrographic printing [59] or projection mapping [49] could be used to enhance 3D prints. However, such methods still need to become accessible to educators and students through novel and easy-to-use tools.

Perception of size and authenticity

Results regarding the mention of size in participant responses were mixed. This suggests that the three platforms tested in this study do not appear to have inherent qualities that represent a sense of scale. This poses an opportunity for interaction designers to enhance the communication of size and scale through design interventions. Solutions could involve projecting measurements, for example, or providing reference frames and measurement instruments.

Augmented Reality as a classroom tool

The results of this study demonstrate that AR headsets offer a promise for effective use in the classroom. Despite the novelty of the platform and its significant challenges, including the physical effort and the discomfort that ~50% of users experienced, object-based learning goals were achieved in comparable levels to SketchFab. Also, the enjoyment level and reported strengths were highest for the HoloLens despite the discomfort of using the system, though these measures could be impacted by a novelty effect. As educators seek out methods to integrate active learning into their classrooms, the immersive nature of AR headsets uniquely offers a simulated "hands-on" experience while maintaining awareness of activities in the classroom. Although the AR interaction is with virtual artifacts, the physical, kinetic, and gesture-based interactions with virtual objects result in higher perceived presence and sensory interaction than with physical replicas. Interaction designers could further enhance learning by integrating tactile feedback with virtual objects, leveraging emerging technologies (e.g. [5]).

Access and accessibility

Participants achieved object-based learning goals while using freely-accessible content. On-screen direct manipulation is a viable solution in the face of budgetary and logistical constraints, although it was not as enjoyable or physically active as with the HoloLens AR. The potential for 3D prints to make content accessible to people with visual impairment should also be considered. Most importantly, as cultural heritage is captured digitally by researchers, ethical protections for culturally sensitive or endangered material must be taken into account. Increased free access can result in better public understanding of the importance of preserving cultural resources and appreciation for global diversity.

Limitations and Future Work

This study has several limitations that point towards future work. First, we studied one-time use in a between-subjects experiment conducted in laboratory settings. Future work could utilize within-subjects design where participants try more than one interaction style. We also intend to conduct studies of longitudinal use in classroom settings in order to understand to what extent our findings are affected by novelty. Second, our measurement of learning outcomes in this study is limited and does not assess the ability to apply learning to other contexts. We plan to use additional assessment instruments to further measure learning outcomes. Third, the results of this study demonstrate that participants had a strong reliance on visual information for their understanding of artifacts and their contexts. Future studies should incorporate improved methods of 3D printing (e.g. [57]) to test if participants can accept fabricated physical replicas in place of authentic artifacts. Finally, wider application of these technologies in classroom settings should include provisions to be inclusive of different abilities and learning styles.

CONCLUSION

We presented findings from a study, which compares object-based learning outcomes from students as they interact with representations of ancient Egyptian sculptures using three different educational technologies: HoloLens AR headset, 3D model viewing website (SketchFab), and 3D prints. We explored how differences in interaction styles affect the learning process, quantitative and qualitative learning outcomes, and critical analysis. Our findings indicate that both tangible and virtual representations of artifacts can be used to achieve object-based learning goals such as building observation skills, and critically synthesizing information for comparisons. However, differences in interaction styles have significant impacts on various aspects of object-based learning including the learning process, quantitative and qualitative learning outcomes, and critical analysis.

The AR headset, despite its current challenges, which include a high number of participants reporting discomfort, headaches, and physical effort, allowed participants to accomplish object-based learning goals in comparable levels to SketchFab. We believe that most of the discomfort will be resolved in future versions of the AR headset, which could result in even higher learning gains, to be evaluated in future studies. In addition, participants who used the AR system reported higher levels of enjoyment and identified a higher number of strengths for that technology than participants who used the Sketchfab or the 3D prints. The absence of some visual information (color and texture) in the 3D prints hindered students' critical interpretation and contextualization, highlighting a need for making more advanced 3D printing techniques available for educators. While a longitudinal study is needed for further understanding how these technologies facilitate object-based learning, this study demonstrates the feasibility and value of applying interaction with virtual and tangible representations to enhance object-based learning.

ACKNOWLEDGMENTS

We thank Jordan Tynes and the Wellesley Library and Technology Service, and the British Museum for releasing 3D models of objects in their collection under Creative Commons Attribution Non-Commercial license.

REFERENCES

1. Alissa N Antle and Alyssa F Wise. 2013. Getting down to details: Using theories of cognition and

learning to inform tangible user interface design. *Interacting with Computers*. 25, 1 (January 2013), 1-20. https://doi.org/10.1093/iwc/iws007

2. Ronald Azuma, Yohan Baillot, Reinhold Behringer, Steven Feiner, Simon Julier and Blair MacIntyre. 2001. *Recent Advances in Augmented Reality*. 2, 6 (November/December 2001), 34-47. https://doi.org/10.1109/38.963459
3. Jorge Bacca, Silvia Baldiris, Ramon Fabregat and Sabine Graf. 2014. Augmented reality trends in education: a systematic review of research and applications. *Journal of Educational Technology & Society*. 17, 4 (October 2014), 133-149.
4. Davis Baird. 2004. *Thing knowledge: A philosophy of scientific instruments*. Univ of California Press.
5. Hrvoje Benko, Christian Holz, Mike Sinclair and Eyal Ofek. 2016. Normaltouch and texturetouch: High-fidelity 3d haptic shape rendering on handheld virtual reality controllers. In *Proceedings of the 29th Annual Symposium on User Interface Software and Technology* (UIST '16), 717-728. http://doi.acm.org/10.1145/2984511.2984526
6. Alexander Berman, Brittany Garcia, Beth Nam, Sharon Chu and Francis Quek. 2016. Toward a Making Community of Practice: The Social Aspects of Elementary Classroom-Based Making. In *Proceedings of the 6th Annual Conference on Creativity and Fabrication in Education* (FabLearn '16), 9-16. http://doi.acm.org/10.1145/3003397/303399
7. Benjamin S Bloom, Max D Engelhart, Edward J Furst, Walker H Hill and David R Krathwohl. 1956. Taxonomy of educational objectives, handbook I: The cognitive domain. New York: David McKay Co Inc.
8. A Mejías Borrero and JM Andújar Márquez. 2012. A pilot study of the effectiveness of augmented reality to enhance the use of remote labs in electrical engineering education. *Journal of science education and technology*. 21, 5 (October 2012), 540-557. https://doi.org/10.1007/s10956-011-9345-9
9. Matt Bower, Cathie Howe, Nerida McCredie, Austin Robinson and David Grover. 2014. Augmented Reality in education–cases, places and potentials. *Educational Media International*. 51, 1 (March 2014), 1-15. https://doi.org/10.1080/09523987.2014.889400
10. Gabriela Celani. 2012. Digital Fabrication Laboratories: Pedagogy and Impacts on Architectural Education. *Digital Fabrication*. 469-482. https://doi.org/10.1007/978-3-0348-0582-7_6
11. Helen J. Chatterjee. 2008. Staying essential: Articulating the value of object based learning. *University Museums and Collections Journal*. 1 (2008), 1-6.
12. Helen J. Chatterjee. 2011. Object-based learning in higher education: The pedagogical power of museums. *International Committee for University Museums and Collections (UMAC) Proceedings*. 3 (February 2011).
13. Andy Cockburn and Bruce McKenzie. 2002. Evaluating the effectiveness of spatial memory in 2D and 3D physical and virtual environments. In *Proceedings of the SIGCHI conference on Human factors in computing systems* (CHI '02), 203-210. http://doi.acm.org/10.1145/503376.503413
14. Stéphanie Fleck and Gilles Simon. 2013. An Augmented Reality Environment for Astronomy Learning in Elementary Grades: An Exploratory Study. In *Proceedings of the 25th Conference on l'Interaction Homme-Machine* (IHM '13), 14. http://doi.acm.org/10.1145/2534903.2534907
15. Ricardo Dutra Goncalves and Sonali Ojha. 2016. Designing Learning Environments for Social Dreaming: From Inquiry to Insight, and Action. In *Proceedings of the 6th Annual Conference on Creativity and Fabrication in Education* (FabLearn '16), 34-40. http://doi.acm.org/10.1145/3003397.3003402
16. Rich Halstead-Nussloch and William Carpenter. 2002. Teaching and learning ubiquitous CHI (UCHI) design: suggestions from the Bauhaus Model. In *CHI'02 Extended Abstracts on Human Factors in Computing Systems* (CHI EA '02), 660-661. http://doi.acm.org/10.1145/506443.506533
17. Foad Hamidi, Thomas S Young, Josh Sideris, Ramtin Ardeshiri, Jacob Leung, Pouya Rezai and Barbara Whitmer. 2017. Using Robotics and 3D Printing to Introduce Youth to Computer Science and Electromechanical Engineering. In *Proceedings of the 2017 CHI Conference Extended Abstracts on Human Factors in Computing Systems* (CHI EA '17), 942-950. http://doi.acm.org/10.1145/3027063.3053346
18. Leonie Hannan, H. Chatterjee, and R. Duhs. 2016. Object Based Learning: A powerful pedagogy for higher education. *Museums and Higher Education Working Together: Challenges and Opportunities*. ed./Anne Boddington (April 2016), 159-168.
19. Sandra G Hart and Lowell E Staveland. 1988. Development of NASA-TLX (Task Load Index): Results of empirical and theoretical research. *Advances in psychology*. 52 (December 1988), 139-183. https://doi.org/10.1016/S0166-4115(08)62386-9

20. Mikkel Hjorth, Rachel Charlotte Smith, Daria Loi, Ole Sejer Iversen and Kasper Skov Christensen. 2016. Educating the Reflective Educator: Design Processes and Digital Fabrication for the Classroom. In *Proceedings of the 6th Annual Conference on Creativity and Fabrication in Education* (FabLearn '16), 26-33. http://doi.acm.org/10.1145/3003397.3003401

21. Yvonne Jansen, Pierre Dragicevic and Jean-Daniel Fekete. 2013. Evaluating the efficiency of physical visualizations. In *Proceedings of the SIGCHI Conference on Human Factors in Computing Systems* (CHI '13), 2593-2602. http://doi.acm.org/10.1145/2470654.2481359

22. L Johnson, S Adams, M Cummins, V Estrada, A Freeman and C Hall. 2016. *NMC horizon report: 2016 higher education edition.*

23. M Carmen Juan, David Furió, Ignacio Seguí, Noemi Rando Aiju and Juan Cano. 2011. Lessons learnt from an experience with an augmented reality iPhone learning game. In *Proceedings of the 8th International Conference on Advances in Computer Entertainment Technology* (ACE '11), 52. http://doi.acm.org/10.1145/2071423.2071488

24. Jonathan W Kelly, Marios N Avraamides and Nicholas A Giudice. 2011. Haptic experiences influence visually acquired memories: Reference frames during multimodal spatial learning. *Psychonomic bulletin & review.* 18, 6 (December 2011), 1119-1125. https://doi.org/10.3758/s13423-011-0162-1

25. Jeeeun Kim and Tom Yeh. 2015. Toward 3d-printed movable tactile pictures for children with visual impairments. In *Proceedings of the 33rd Annual ACM Conference on Human Factors in Computing Systems* (CHI '15), 2815-2824. http://doi.acm.org/10.1145/2702123.2702144

26. David Kirsh. 1995. Complementary strategies: Why we use our hands when we think. In *Proceedings of the seventeenth annual conference of the cognitive science society* (CogSci '95), 212-217.

27. David Kirsh and Paul Maglio. 1994. On Distinguishing Epistemic from Pragmatic Action. *Cognitive Science.* 18, 4 (October 1994), 513-549. https://doi.org/10.1207/s15516709cog1804_1

28. Frederic Lardinois. 2015. Google's Online Art Museum Adds 3D Scans, Tech Crunch. Retrieved August 2, 2017 from https://techcrunch.com/2015/04/09/googles-online-art-museum-adds-3d-scans/

29. Anna Loparev, Lauren Westendorf, Margaret Flemings, Jennifer Cho, Romie Littrell, Anja Scholze and Orit Shaer. 2017. BacPack: Exploring the Role of Tangibles in a Museum Exhibit for Bio-Design. In *Proceedings of the 11th International Conference on Tangible and Embedded Interaction* (TEI '17), 111-120. http://doi.acm.org/10.1145/3024969.3025000

30. Covadonga Lorenzo. 2017. Digital Fabrication as a Tool for Teaching High-School Students STEM at the University. In *Proceedings of the 2017 Conference on Interaction Design and Children* (IDC '17), 549-554. http://doi.acm.org/10.1145/3078072.3084323

31. Jennifer Loy. 2014. eLearning and eMaking: 3D Printing Blurring the Digital and the Physical. *Education Sciences.* 4, 1 (February 2014), 108-121. https://doi.org/10.3390/educsci4010108

32. Paul Marshall. 2007. Do tangible interfaces enhance learning? In *Proceedings of the 1st international conference on Tangible and embedded interaction* (TEI '07), 163-170. http://doi.acm.org/10.1145/1226969.1227004

33. Paul Marshall, Peter C-H Cheng and Rosemary Luckin. 2010. Tangibles in the balance: a discovery learning task with physical or graphical materials. In *Proceedings of the fourth international conference on Tangible, embedded, and embodied interaction* (TEI '10), 153-160. http://doi.acm.org/10.1145/1709886.1709914

34. Camillia Matuk. 2016. The Learning Affordances of Augmented Reality for Museum Exhibits on Human Health. *Museums & Social Issues.* 11, 1 (May 2016), 73-87. http://doi.org/10.1080/15596893.2016.1142815

35. Rebecca McGinnis. 2014. Islands of Stimulation. The Multisensory Museum: Cross-Disciplinary Perspectives on Touch, Sound, Smell, Memory, and Space. 319.

36. Microsoft. 2017. Microsoft HoloLens.

37. Ann Morrison, Antti Oulasvirta, Peter Peltonen, Saija Lemmela, Giulio Jacucci, Gerhard Reitmayr, Jaana Näsänen and Antti Juustila. 2009. Like bees around the hive: a comparative study of a mobile augmented reality map. In *Proceedings of the SIGCHI Conference on Human Factors in Computing Systems* (CHI '09), 1889-1898. http://doi.acm.org/10.1145/1518701.1518991

38. The British Museum. 2017. The British Museum on Sketchfab, Sketchfab. Retrieved August 2, 2017 from https://sketchfab.com/britishmuseum

39. NASA. 2017. NASA TLX: Task Load Index. Retreieved on August 2, 2017 from https://ntrs.nasa.gov/archive/nasa/casi.ntrs.nasa.gov/20000021487.pdf

40. Nancy J Nersessian. 2002. The cognitive basis of model-based reasoning in science. *The cognitive basis of science*. 133-153. http://dx.doi.org/10.1017/CBO9780511613517.008
41. Nancy J Nersessian. 2008. *Creating scientific concepts*. MIT Press.
42. Sean O'Brien, Alexandria K Hansen and Danielle B Harlow. 2016. Educating Teachers for the Maker Movement: Pre-service Teachers' Experiences Facilitating Maker Activities. In *Proceedings of the 6th Annual Conference on Creativity and Fabrication in Education* (FabLearn '16), 99-102. http://doi.acm.org/10.1145/3003397.3003414
43. Claire O'Malley and Danae Stanton Fraser. 2004. Literature Review in Learning with Tangible Technologies. *NESTA Futurelab*. 12 (2004).
44. Daniela Petrelli, Luigina Ciolfi, Dick van Dijk, Eva Hornecker, Elena Not and Albrecht Schmidt. 2013. Integrating material and digital: a new way for cultural heritage. *Magazine Interactions*. 20, 4 (July/August 2013). 58-63. http://doi.acm.org/10.1145/2486227.2486239
45. Christina Pollalis, Whitney Fahnbulleh, Jordan Tynes and Orit Shaer. 2017. HoloMuse: Enhancing Engagement with Archaeological Artifacts through Gesture-Based Interaction with Holograms. In *Proceedings of the Tenth International Conference on Tangible, Embedded, and Embodied Interaction* (TEI '17), 565-570. http://doi.acm.org/10.1145/3024969.3025094
46. Hans-Jorg Rheinberger. 1997. *Toward a history of epistemic things: Synthesizing proteins in the test tube*. Stanford University Press.
47. Jean J Ryoo, Lianna Kali and Bronwyn Bevan. 2016. Equity-Oriented Pedagogical Strategies and Student Learning in After School Making. In *Proceedings of the 6th Annual Conference on Creativity and Fabrication in Education* (FabLearn '16), 49-57. http://doi.acm.org/10.1145/3003397.3003404
48. Saraiya Purvi, Chris North, and Karen Duca. "An insight-based methodology for evaluating bioinformatics visualizations." *IEEE transactions on visualization and computer* graphics. 11, 4 (July-August 2005), 443-456. http://doi.acm.org/10.1109/TVCG.2005.53
49. John T Sherrill. 2016. Teaching Documentation through 3D Printing and Instructables. In *Proceedings of the 34th ACM International Conference on the Design of Communication* (SIGDOC '16), 56. http://doi.acm.org/10.1145/2987592.2987652
50. Christian Siegl, Matteo Colaianni, Lucas Thies, Justus Thies, Michael Zollhöfer, Shahram Izadi, Marc Stamminger and Frank Bauer. 2015. Real-time pixel luminance optimization for dynamic multi-projection mapping. *Journal ACM Transactions on Graphics* (TOG). 34, 6 (November 2015), 237. http://doi.acm.org/10.1145/2816795.2818111
51. Sketchfab. 2017. 3D Museums of the Future. Retrieved December 7, 2017 from https://blog.sketchfab.com/3d-museums-of-the-future/
52. Simon Stusak, Moritz Hobe and Andreas Butz. 2016. If Your Mind Can Grasp It, Your Hands Will Help. In *Proceedings of the TEI '16: Tenth International Conference on Tangible, Embedded, and Embodied Interaction* (TEI '16), 92-99. http://doi.acm.org/10.1145/2839462.2839476
53. Saiganesh Swaminathan, Thijs Roumen, Robert Kovacs, David Stangl, Stefanie Mueller and Patrick Baudisch. 2016. Linespace: A sensemaking platform for the blind. In *Proceedings of the 2016 CHI Conference on Human Factors in Computing Systems* (CHI '16), 2175-2185. http://doi.acm.org/10.1145/2852036.2858245
54. Lara M Triona and David Klahr. 2003. Point and click or grab and heft: Comparing the influence of physical and virtual instructional materials on elementary school students' ability to design experiments. *Cognition and Instruction*. 21, 2 (June 2003). 149-173. https://doi.org/10.1207/S1532690XCI2102_02
55. UCL. 2017. Research, Teaching & OBL across UCL Culture, UCL. Retrieved August 2, 2017 from https://www.ucl.ac.uk/culture/schools/teaching-object-based-learning
56. Peter Vorderer, Werner Wirth, Feliz Ribeiro Gouveia, Frank Biocca, Timo Saari, Lutz Jäncke, Saskia Böcking, Holger Schramm, Andre Gysbers and Tilo Hartmann. 2004. MEC Spatial Presence Questionnaire (MEC-SPQ): Short documentation and instructions for application. *Report to the European Community Project Presence*. 3 (June 2004).
57. Jennifer Weiler and Stacey Kuznetsov. 2017. Crafting Colorful Objects: a DIY Method for Adding Surface Detail to 3D Prints. In *Proceedings of the 2017 CHI Conference Extended Abstracts on Human Factors in Computing Systems* (CHI EA '17), 2217-2223. http://doi.acm.org/10.1145/3027063.3053144

58. Zacharias C Zacharia and Georgios Olympiou. 2011. Physical versus virtual manipulative experimentation in physics learning. *Learning and Instruction*. 21, 3 (June 2011). 317-331. https://doi.org/10.1016/j.learninstruc.2010.03.001

59. Yizhong Zhang, Chunji Yin, Changxi Zheng and Kun Zhou. 2015. Computational hydrographic printing. *Journal Transactions on Graphics* (TOG). 34, 4 (August 2015), 131. http://doi.acm.org/10.1145/2766932

The Impact of Tangible Props on Gaming Performance and Experience in Gestural Interaction

Daniel Reinhardt
Julius-Maximilians-Universität
Würzburg, Germany
daniel.reinhardt@uni-wuerzburg.de

Jörn Hurtienne
Julius-Maximilians-Universität
Würzburg, Germany
hurtienne@acm.org

ABSTRACT

There is a widely-held belief in the TEI and games communities that using tangible props enhances the player performance and gaming experience. Building on prior research in gaming, we studied people playing a video game using a gestural interface without props, with an incomplete or a complete tangible prop. The interaction with the tangibles was judged to be more natural, led to higher flow experience and was preferred, but there were no differences regarding performance, enjoyment, autonomy, presence and mental effort. There was a tendency that especially the incomplete tangible prop was judged as less intuitive and people felt less competent in gameplay. In contrast to prior research, the results show that tangible interaction is not always more beneficial than gestural interaction and that, especially for incomplete tangibles, any beneficial effects may be domain-dependent.

Author Keywords

Tangible Interface; Natural Mapping; Tangible Interaction; Gameplay; Player experience.

ACM Classification Keywords

Human-centered computing~Empirical studies in HCI

INTRODUCTION

TEI research and practice are fuelled by the idea that tangible interaction amplifies our rich experiences with handling objects in the real world to also make interaction with digital information natural and easy [16,21,30]. As much as this assumption underlies many TEI publications, not many studies are actually devoted to empirically test this assumption [21]. Although results are often in favour of tangible interfaces, most of the research has been mainly informal. Users tend to like tangible interfaces [25] and find them easy to use. However, empirical studies also show that GUIs and TUIs are roughly equivalent regarding user performance [20,21,30] and sometimes TUIs are faster than GUIs and foster easier understanding, collaboration and cognition [1,12,14,18,26]. But how do tangible interfaces compare to other forms of natural interaction like speech, touch and gesture? Here the benefits of higher bandwidth and more direct interaction are also given and the use of tangible props may seem even cumbersome or unnecessary. Imagine playing a game of virtual tennis with the Microsoft Xbox Kinect. The Kinect allows for whole-body interaction. No controller is needed; the game is ready to play. From a TEI perspective, however, the game should be even more enticing if using tangible props like a tennis racket that, although not adding functionality, could provide the right affordances to enhance the game experience. Sometimes even incomplete tangibility might be of benefit. In a study about sketching in Virtual Reality, Israel employed either a physical pen, a virtual pen or a hybrid pen, the latter consisting of a physical handle and a virtual top [17]. It turned out that the hybrid pen was most beneficial for the task in terms of user confidence, perceived control and user experience in terms of the hedonic and pragmatic qualities of the tool. Transferred to the game scenario this could mean that holding just the (sawn-off) handle of a tennis racket might be enough to give the illusion of holding the whole racket. To find out about the benefits and drawbacks of using additional tangibles in a Kinect gaming scenario we conducted a study that looked at the effects of different forms of tangible props on player performance and experience.

TEI '18, March 18–21, 2018, Stockholm, Sweden

ACM ISBN 978-1-4503-5568-1/18/03…$15.00
https://doi.org/10.1145/3173225.3173258

Prior Work: Tangibility in Game Controller Interfaces

Skalski et al. [32] introduce a continuum to describe the degree of natural mapping of video game controllers. Their natural mappings draw on physical and cultural analogies to increase the level of correspondence between the physical control interface and the virtual effects in the game world. The most basic form of natural mapping is that of *directional correspondence* that can be found in more traditional game controllers or the arrow keys of a standard PC keyboard. Directional correspondence happens when there is a directional concordance between physical control and virtual output, such as when an analogue stick makes a player character move in the same direction in the virtual world as the position of the stick on the physical device indicates. The next type of mapping is *kinesic natural mapping*. Kinesic natural mapping takes place when natural body movements are captured and translated into equivalent actions in the virtual world without a tangible component (e.g., camera-based devices like Microsoft Kinect). The next stage is *incomplete tangible mapping*. Incomplete tangible natural mapping occurs when the player is provided with a tangible to manipulate, which partially simulates' the form and function of the equivalent virtual object, such as with using a Wii remote as a tennis racket. But the pinnacle of natural mapping, according to [32], is the *realistic tangible natural mapping*. Realistic tangible natural mapping happens when the tangible object looks, feels and is manipulated like the real world tool being simulated in the game, as with a spring-loaded leather-bound steering wheel controller used in a car racing game [24]. The specific advantage of realistic tangible mappings is that they enhance the mental accessibility of the original game, and therefore game play appears more realistic and engaging.

The higher on the continuum a controller can be classified, the higher its perceived naturalness, feeling of spatial presence, and video game enjoyment [23,32]. To confirm their hypothesis, Skalski et al. [32] tested multiple controllers using either a directional natural mapping or an incomplete tangible natural mapping for both a racing and a golf game. While the relationship with enjoyment could not be confirmed, the tangible mapping enhanced spatial presence in the game and the perceived naturalness of the controller. Other researchers provided further validation of the continuum [5,24,28,31], with Cairns et al. [5] examining the effects of the extent of natural mapping on immersion in mobile games. However, relatively few studies have compared more than two types from the continuum, few have investigated the impact of player characteristics (e.g., gender, age, previous gaming experience) and have included broader measures of game experience [21,22,23].

To obtain a richer understanding of how natural controllers influence the player experience, McEwan et al. investigated the effects of three natural controller types on a broader range of player experience variables [23]. In a racing game, they used the traditional gamepad controller of the Microsoft Xbox 360 (directional mapping), the u-shape accelerometer-based Wireless Speed Wheel for Microsoft Xbox 360 (incomplete tangible mapping) and the Xbox 360 Wireless Racing Wheel (realistic tangible mapping). Overall, controllers with mappings higher on the Skalski et al. continuum facilitated a more positive player experience in terms of Flow, Autonomy and Presence [23]. However, controller familiarity and game performance were lower for these devices. In order to validate these results, McEwan conducted another study in a tennis video game setting, with a new set of controllers: Microsoft Kinect (kinesic mapping), Sony Move (incomplete tangible mapping) and Sony Move in a tennis racket shell (realistic tangible mapping). Again, mappings higher on the continuum facilitated a more positive player experience in terms of Flow, Presence, Competence and Enjoyment/Satisfaction. This time game performance and controller familiarity were higher the higher the controller was located in the continuum [22]. However, in contrast to their first study, the game consoles and motion sensors differed between conditions (Xbox Kinect V1 versus Playstation Move) Therefore, the different mean latencies (Kinect V1: 142 ms [19]; Playstation Move: 68 ms [27]) and sampling frequency of the platforms (Kinect V1: 30 Hz [19]; Playstation Move: 87 Hz [27]) could have led to different results. In contrast to the PlayStation Move, the Kinect skeleton tracking suffers from occlusion, self-occlusion and unconventional body postures which reduce the tracking accuracy [11]. Accordingly, it is difficult to compare classical motion controllers with motion capture systems like Kinect in terms of performance, and consequently, experience. The more detrimental effects of the Kinesic mapping in [22] could have been due to technical inaccuracies and not to a generally inferior interaction style that just does not involve tangibles.

To resolve these issues of prior studies and to test the general effectiveness of tangible props we present a replication of [22], ensuring this time that all controller types are used on the same game console. Participants played the tennis videogame Microsoft Kinect Sports Rivals on a Xbox One S using a Kinect V2 system, where the player's physical gestures and body movements are tracked and translated into in-game actions without the need for a controller. Due to the fact that the fuzzy skeletal tracking algorithm of the Kinect V2 allows to track only four skeletal joints [33] per hand (i.e., wrist, handtip, hand, thump), it should not make a difference whether participants interact with bare hands or holding a tangible in addition with a consisting sampling frequency of 30 Hz and mean latency of 60 ms for all interactions [8,33]. We tested several sizes of the tangibles in a pilot study (N = 4) to test this assumption and also to check if occlusion, self-occlusion and unconventional body postures were an issue.

The final setup included three controller types: the participant's hand for the kinesic mapping, the sawn-off handle of a tennis racket for the incomplete tangible mapping and a complete tennis racket for the realistic tangible mapping (see Figure 1). If the Skalski et al. continuum [32] is correct, we expect a more positive player experience and higher performance when increasing the natural mapping of the controllers from kinesic to incomplete tangible to complete tangible mappings.

METHODOLOGY

Participants

Sample sizes were estimated based on the effects obtained in the previous study of McEwan et al. [22,23]. An a-priori power analysis with $1-\beta = .85$, $\alpha = .05$, and a small effect ($\eta_p^2 = .057$) resulted in a required sample size of 93 participants. Thus, a convenience sample of 93 participants (64 female, 29 male) were recruited from a German university campus. Most were students of human-computer interaction and media communication. The age of the participants ranged from 18 to 27 years (M = 21.33, SD = 2.10). Participants were reimbursed for their time in form of partial course credit. All participants were naive to the subject of investigation.

Procedure

The experiment was conducted with participants individually in our lab and took about an hour to complete. Each participant used all three controller types in randomised order (within-subjects design to eliminate problems based on individual differences, following [22]) when playing the tennis videogame Microsoft Kinect Sports Rivals. Upon arrival, the participants were given a short standardised verbal overview. Then they completed a questionnaire, delivered on a tablet, to capture demographic data, their familiarity with the tennis video game and the control devices used during the study.

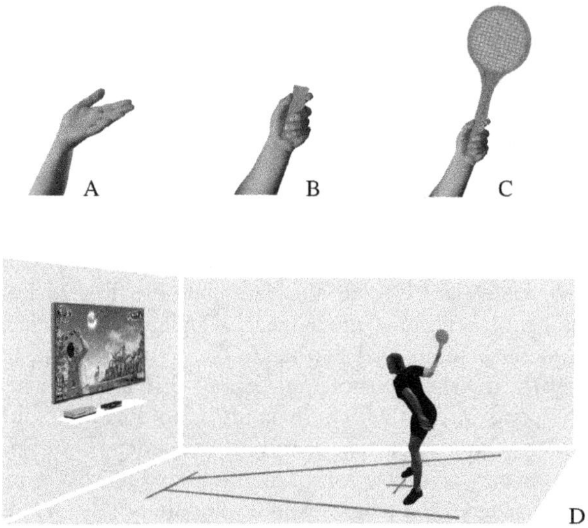

Figure 1. Controllers tested: (A) Kinesic (hand), (B) Incomplete Tangible (sawn-off racket handle) and (C) Complete Tangible (tennis racket).The test environment for the study: (D) A participant performs a serve using the tennis racket.

Subsequently, participants were randomly assigned to the first control condition. At the start of each experimental condition, the test facilitator gave a brief overview of the play session including a basic demonstration of how to use the control and instructed the participants to play until they or their opponents have won one game. The participants were also asked to perform as well as they could while still having fun. In order to play the game, the participants were instructed to go to the starting mark in the centre of the play area, located about two metres in front of a 48-inch TV connected to a Microsoft Xbox One S and a Kinect 2 (see Figure 2). The play area was approximately 2.5 metres wide and 1.5 metres from front to rear, confined by lines of gaffa tape on the floor. The space dimensions were set according to the play environment recommendations given by Microsoft and the descriptions of [22] for play with Kinect. Participants were instructed to stay within the play area during the game in order to remain within the range of the Kinect sensors. Once participants confirmed that they understood the instructions and stood ready on the starting position, the test facilitator un-paused the game and started the recording of the screen. During the play session, the researcher sat out of the player´s sight monitoring the study´s execution. After either six minutes of play time or after a play of tennis was won, whichever fell earlier, the game was remotely paused, the recording saved and the participants were asked to complete an online player experience questionnaire based on their experience with the assigned control device. A semi-structured interview followed that captured participants' positive and negative impressions of the control device. Then the participants were assigned the second control interface and were instructed to play the game again. The above procedure was repeated for the second and third control conditions. After completing the third controller-centred interview, another semi-structured interview sampled overall controller preferences and general feedback before the session was completed. Finally, participants were debriefed and thanked for their participation.

Dependent Measures

The following instruments were selected to measure player experience very broadly, focusing on components that have proven sustainable or are frequently measured factors in the literature [22,23]. The questionnaires measuring Flow, Perceived Naturalness of Control Action Mapping, PENS, Enjoyment/Satisfaction and Mental Effort, were presented in a randomised sequence to counterbalance effects of fatigue.

Previous Gaming Experience, Age and Gender

Due to the fact that recent research has shown that player characteristics like previous gaming experience, age or gender can play an important role on performance and player experience [22,23,32], we captured these attributes as control variables. Previous gaming experience with other video games was sampled as well as experience with real life tennis games [see 22]. Experience with video games was measured using a seven-point Likert scale ranging from '1 (not all experienced)' to '7 (very experienced)'. Real-life tennis experience was measured with two items (playing tennis in real life, spectating tennis) using the same seven-point Likert scale.

Flow

Flow describes a deep focus on and involvement with a task, where the balance between challenge and skill is finely tuned [6]. For measuring Flow we used the 33-item core module of the Game Experience Questionnaire (GEQ) [15]. Although the whole core module was administered to participants, all items except the Flow items (five items related to concentration, transportation and occupation with the game) were excluded from the analysis due to major similarities to other measures used. The GEQ implementation asked participants to rate how they felt during playing the game with the control interface they just used. Example items for Flow include 'I forgot everything around me' and 'I was deeply concentrated in the game' that were rated on a five-point Likert scale between '0 (not at all)' and '4 (extremely)'. The order of all GEQ items was randomised when presented to the participants and the score of Flow was calculated as the average of its five items. The higher this score, the greater the perceived level of Flow.

Perceived Naturalness of Control Action Mapping (PNCAM)
Player experience was also measured via the Perceived Naturalness of Control Action Mapping (PNCAM) between physical and virtual controls for the main control actions [see 22]. The main control actions in the tennis game were hitting the ball, moving the racket, serving and moving on the court. Participants rated the level of naturalness of the main control actions for the used control interface on a seven-point Likert scale between '1 (not natural at all)' and '7 (completely natural)'. The item scores were then averaged to create an overall Perceived Naturalness of Control Action Mapping (PNCAM) score. Sampling perceived controller naturalness is important in Tangible Interaction research, since it reveals whether the providing of tangibles differ significantly in terms of the perception of the characteristics that determined their controller type [see 30].

Player Experience of Need Satisfaction (PENS)
As a third measure of user experience, the 18-item version of the Player Experience of Need Satisfaction (PENS) instrument [29] was used, which measures in-game satisfaction of psychological needs. The PENS is based on Cognitive Evaluation Theory, a branch of Self-Determination Theory, which suggests that a person's feeling of *autonomy*, *competence* and *relatedness* derived from an activity support its intrinsic appeal [22,23]. Autonomy is high when the player's freedom of choice is perceived to be voluntary and unrestrained. Competence is high when the player perceives their skills/abilities are being challenged and successfully shown [29]. Relatedness is high when the player has an intrinsic desire to connect with others in a way that feels supportive and authentic [29]. However, this component was not used in our study, because it lacks relevance in the tested single-player version of the game [see 22]. Ryan et al. added two more major sub components to the PENS questionnaire that they believe are integral to any sort of sustained enjoyment from video games, *presence* and *intuitive controls* [29]. Presence is high when the mediating technologies disappear and the players perceives themselves to be in the game world. Intuitive Controls is high when the controls make sense and do not interfere with playing the game [29]. The implementation of the PENS asked participants to think about the just experienced gameplay with the assigned control interfaces and to rate their agreement to different statements on a seven-point Likert scale ranging from '1 (do not agree)' to '7 (strongly agree)'. The order of the items was randomized upon presentation to the participants and the scores of the different components were calculated by averaging the corresponding items. The higher the score of a component, the greater the satisfaction with the related PENS component.

Enjoyment/Satisfaction
To measure Enjoyment/Satisfaction, a customised measure from [22,23] was adapted. This instrument asked participants to think about playing the game with the assigned control interface and rate their agreement with three statements on a seven-point Likert scale between '1 (strongly disagree)' and '7 (strongly agree)'. The three statements to be assessed were 'it was fun', 'it was enjoyable' and 'it was satisfying'. In accordance with [22,23], it was decided to use this custom approach instead of extrapolating Enjoyment/Satisfaction from other constructs (e.g., presence) [see 2].

Mental Effort and Performance
In the area of game research, in-game performance has been established as an important aspect of the player experience [4]. Two measures were used to operationalize and assess in-game performance: Perceived mental workload (i.e. mental efficiency) was measured with the SEA scale [7]. Game effectiveness was measured as successful hits during the tennis game expressed as a percentage. The SEA scale is the German translation of the 'subjective mental effort questionnaire (SMEQ)' [34] where participants mark on a vertical scale between 0 and 220 the amount of mental workload experienced when executing the previous task. The successful hits were measured as a percentage of all racket swings coded using Techsmith Morae. Successful hits were coded as all hits (including serves) where the player was able to return the ball over the net and landing the ball inside the tennis court's boundary. Unsuccessful hits were all hits (including serves) where the player either missed the ball completely or the ball bounced off their racket, because there was not enough force in their swing for the ball to travel over the net. The number of successful hits was converted into a percentage of the total number of hit opportunities (sum of successful and unsuccessful hits) for this analysis. This coding procedure was adapted from [22] with minor changes.

RESULTS

A series of repeated measures analyses of variance (RM ANOVAs) were conducted using 'controller type' (Kinesic, Incomplete Tangible, Realistic Tangible) as the within-subjects factor. Fisher's LSD test was used for all multiple pairwise comparisons. An alpha level of $p < .05$ was used. Descriptive statistics (mean and standard deviations) can be found in detail in Table 1. When calculating the effectiveness measure the videos of only 54 participants could be considered because of the limited local storage on the Xbox and subsequent problems with cloud synchronization due to a poor WLAN connection. We, however, expect no systematic bias through this loss of data as this problem only occurred in the beginning of the study and participants were not assigned to time slots because of certain other characteristics. For all other measures the whole sample could be analysed.

	Kinesic		Incomplete Tangible		Realistic Tangible	
Measure	*M*	*SD*	*M*	*SD*	*M*	*SD*
Flow*	2.85	.85	2.95	.81	3.00	.78
Naturalness*	3.58	1.21	4.17	1.46	4.12	1.42
Autonomy	3.62	1.24	3.49	1.29	3.78	1.40
Competence*	4.00	1.59	3.59	1.51	4.22	1.43
Intuitive Controls*	5.28	1.43	4.71	1.48	5.49	1.21
Presence	3.22	1.12	3.24	1.00	3.28	1.16
Enjoyment/ Satisfaction	4.57	1.46	4.61	1.61	4.69	1.52
Mental Workload	77.29	43.29	70.94	38.44	69.25	40.49
Performance	82.30	9.98	82.87	19.73	80.00	13.81

Table 1. Descriptive statistics for the study. * indicates significant differences between controller types

As the sample showed a non equal gender distribution, independent *t*-tests were performed to check for differences in age, previous videogame experience and real life tennis experience. With regard to video games experience, women reported significantly lower experience (M = 3.44, SD = 1.34) than men (M = 5.59, SD = 1.43), $t(91) = 7.01, p < .01$, d = 1.57. Age and tennis experience did not differ ($p >$ .05). In order to test the effect of the sampled control variables ANCOVAs were performed, provided that the potential covariate correlated with the appropriate measure [see 3,9].

Flow (GEQ)

A one-way ANOVA revealed no significant differences between the three control interfaces regarding Flow, $F(2,184) = 2.71$, $p = .069.$, $\eta_p^2 = .029$. Due to the fact that gender showed a significant positive correlation (i.e., men experienced more flow) with the reported Flow, an ANCOVA with gender as covariate was performed. The covariate, gender, was significantly related to the participant's flow, $F(1,91) = 4.30$, $p = .04$, $\eta_p^2 = .045$. There was also a significant main effect of the Control Device on Flow, $F(2,182) = 3.69$, $p = .027$, $\eta_p^2 = .039$. The interaction between Control Device and gender was non-significant, $F(2,182) = 2.78$, $p = .064$, $\eta_p^2 = .030$. Subsequent pairwise comparisons using Fisher's LSD method showed that participants reported lower Flow for the Kinesic than for the Realistic Tangible ($p < .05$). Other comparisons were non-significant ($p > .05$).

Perceived Naturalness

A one-way ANOVA revealed a significant main effect of the controller type on Perceived Naturalness of the Control-Action Mappings, $F(2,184) = 6.49$, $p < .05$, $\eta_p^2 = .066$. Subsequent pairwise comparisons using Fisher's LSD method showed that participants reported lower Perceived Naturalness for the Kinesic control condition than for the Incomplete Tangible ($p < .01$) or the Realistic Tangible ($p <$ .05) control conditions. Other comparisons were non-significant ($p > .05$). Because age, gender, and previous gaming experience (either virtual or in real life) showed no significant correlations with the Perceived Naturalness (all $p > .05$), a corresponding ANCOVA was not performed.

Autonomy (PENS):

A one-way ANOVA revealed no significant differences between the three control interfaces regarding Autonomy, $F(2,184) = 2.62$, $p = .075.$, $\eta_p^2 = .028$. Because all collected control variables showed no significant correlations with the reported Autonomy of the participants for all three control devices (all $p > .05$), an ANCOVA was not performed.

Competence (PENS):

A one-way ANOVA revealed a significant main effect of the controller type on Competence, $F(2,184) = 7.22$, $p <$ .01, $\eta_p^2 = .073$. Subsequent pairwise comparisons using Fisher's LSD method showed that participants reported lower Competence for Incomplete Tangible than for the Kinesic ($p < .05$) and for the Realistic Tangible ($p < .01$). Other comparisons were non-significant ($p > .05$). As the collected control variables may have had an influence on participants' competence, we checked for correlations with these variables, but with no significant differences (all $p <$ .05). On this account, an ANCOVA was not performed.

Intuitive Controls (PENS):

Mauchly's Test indicated that the assumption of sphericity had been violated for Intuitive Controls and so a Greenhouse-Geisser adjustment ($\varepsilon = .91$) was used for the within-subjects analysis. A one-way ANOVA revealed a significant main effect of the used control interface on Intuitive Controls, $F(1.82,167.12) = 18.22$, $p < .001$, $\eta_p^2 =$ .165. Subsequent pairwise comparisons using Fisher's LSD method showed that participants reported lower Intuitive Controls for the Incomplete Tangible than for the Kinesic ($p < .001$) and the Realistic Tangible ($p < .001$). Other comparisons were non-significant ($p > .05$). As the collected control variables age, gender and previous gaming experience (either in real life or on the console) may have had an influence on participants' intuitive controls, we checked for correlations with these variables, but only gender showed a significant positive correlation with the intuitive controls (i.e., men experienced controls as more intuitive). A subsequent ANCOVA showed that the covariate, gender, was significantly related to the participant's intuitive controls, $F(1,91) = 4.00$, $p = .049$, η_p^2 = .042. There was also a significant effect of the Control Device on intuitive controls after controlling for the effect of participant's gender, $F(1.82,165.58) = 3.58$, $p = .034$, $\eta_p^2 = .038$. Pairwise comparisons remain significant as reported above.

Presence (PENS):

Mauchly's Test indicated that the assumption of sphericity had been violated for the SEA scale and so a Greenhouse-Geisser adjustment (ε = .88) was used for the within-subjects analysis. A one-way ANOVA revealed no significant differences between the three control interfaces regarding Mental Workload, $F(1.76,161.63) = 2.36$, $p = .613.$, $\eta_p^2 = .005$. As the collected control variables may have had an influence on participants' presence, we checked for correlations with these variables, but only gender and general game experience showed a significant correlation with presence. Gender correlated significantly with participants' presence (i.e., men experienced more presence). A subsequent ANCOVA showed that the covariate, gender, was significantly related to the participant's presence, $F(1,91) = 15.21$, $p = .000$, $\eta_p^2 = .143$. However, a main effect or interaction effect of the control device and gender on presence could not be detected ($p > .05$). General game experience also correlated significantly with participants' presence. Another ANCOVA showed that the covariate, general game experience, was significantly related to the participants' presence, $F(1,91) = 6.8$, $p = .011$, $\eta_p^2 = .069$. However, a main effect or interaction effect of the control device and general game experience on presence could not be detected ($p > .05$).

Enjoyment/Satisfaction

A one-way ANOVA reveals no significant differences between the three control interfaces regarding Enjoyment/Satisfaction, $F(2,184) = .18$, $p = .84.$, $\eta_p^2 = .002$. As the collected control variables may have had an influence on participants' enjoyment/satisfaction, we checked for correlations with these variables, but no significant differences were found (all $p < .05$). On this account, an ANCOVA was not performed.

Mental Workload (SEA)

Mauchly's Test indicated that the assumption of sphericity had been violated for the SEA scale and so a Greenhouse-Geisser adjustment (ε = .92) was used for the within-subjects analysis. A one-way ANOVA revealed no significant differences between the three control interfaces regarding Mental Workload, $F(1.84,169.19) = 2.36$, $p = .102.$, $\eta_p^2 = .025$. As the collected control variables may have had an influence on participants' mental workload, we checked for correlations with these variables. Gender, general game experience and experience in real life tennis showed significant correlations. Gender correlated significantly with participant's mental workload (i.e., men experienced less mental workload). A subsequent ANCOVA showed that gender was significantly related to the participant's mental workload, $F(1,91) = 8.98$, $p = .004$, $\eta_p^2 = .090$. However, a main effect or interaction effect of the control device and gender on mental workload could not be detected ($p > .05$). General game experience correlated significantly with participant's mental workload. A subsequent ANCOVA showed that the covariate, general game experience, was significantly related to the participant's mental workload, $F(1,91) = 5.63$, $p = .020$, $\eta_p^2 = .058$. However, a main effect or interaction effect of the control device and general game experience on mental workload could not be detected ($p > .05$). Experience in real life tennis also correlated significantly with participant's mental workload. A subsequent ANCOVA showed that the covariate, experience in real life tennis, was not significantly related to the participant's mental workload, $F(1,91) = 1.85$, $p = .178$, $\eta_p^2 = .020$. However, there was a significant effect of Control Device on mental workload after controlling for the effect of participant's real life tennis experience, $F(1.86,169.30) = 3.20$, $p = .047$, $\eta_p^2 = .034$. But pairwise comparisons remain non-significant ($p > .05$).

Performance (Successful Hits in %)

Mauchly's Test indicated that the assumption of sphericity had been violated for Intuitive Controls and so a Greenhouse-Geisser adjustment (ε = .77) was used for the within-subjects analysis. A one-way ANOVA revealed no significant differences between the three control interfaces regarding Performance, $F(1.53,81.05) =.90$, $p = .386$, $\eta_p^2 = .017$. To ensure the reliability of the video analysis, we let an independent coder rate a random subset of the videos. He received the videos of 16 participants and coded them in accordance with the coding procedure as described above. Using Cohen's kappa, the inter-rater reliability between performance ratings was $\kappa = .68$, suggesting a substantial agreement beyond chance [9]. Due to the fact that all collected control variables showed no significant correlations with the participant's performance (all $p > .05$), a corresponding ANCOVA was not performed.

Player Preferences for the Control Interfaces:

Descriptive analysis on player preferences for their favourite control interface was undertaken for the overall sample. The Racket was the most preferred control device for playing the tennis game, with 71.13% (N=93) of all participants selecting it as their favourite interface. The Handle was the second most preferred control device, with 19.59% (N=93) of the sample selecting it, while the player´s hand was the favourite control interface for only 9.28% (N=93) of all participants.

DISCUSSION

Are tangible control interfaces better than natural interfaces without tangible controllers and do the data support the predictions of the continuum of Skalski et al.? While previous studies tend to confirm the Skalski et al. continuum [5,22,23,24,28,31], this study, using all controller types on the same platform, reveals mixed evidence. Participants found both tangible mappings to be more natural for the task of playing tennis than using no tangible controller. This corresponds roughly to what the TEI literature expects – a general effect of tangibility. Two other variables followed the predictions of the Skalski et al. [32] continuum. Flow and controller preference seem to follow the continuum with the kinesic natural mapping at one end, the complete tangible mapping at the other end and the incomplete tangible mapping in between. The measures of Competence and Intuitive Controls did not follow the predicted patterns: the incomplete tangible controller scored worse than either the kinesic or the complete tangible. Varying the controller type had no effects on Enjoyment, Autonomy, Presence, Mental Workload and Performance (in terms of effectiveness).

The Cogntive Evaluation Theory, what is the basis of the PENS measures (e.g., autonomy, competence, presence), describes the factors that are responsible for intrinsic motivation of the player. Here, presence in games is normally fostered by competence and autonomy experienced while playing and is also related to the flow concept, which can be seen as the highest state of presence [6]. According to [22,32] the perceived controller naturalness has a determinant effect on presence as well. Our results suggest that the inherent naturalness of the tangible alone may be suffice for inducing a state of flow, even when players did not experience competence and autonomy in the game (for which to develop the gameplay may have been too easy).

What do these results tell us? First, in comparison to McEwan's earlier tennis study it turns out that it is important to conduct experiments using the same platform in all conditions. In [22] the kinesic controller condition ran on a Microsoft Xbox Kinect and both tangible mapping conditions ran on a much more accurate PlayStation Move. McEwan's results were in line with the Skalski et al. continuum. Our results show that when making a more adequate comparison between conditions on the same platform, the kinesic interface is not at a disadvantage anymore. Or said in another way: the tangible condition is not always better than pure gestures if the technical compatibility of examined controllers is granted. If such comparisons would be possible for other games, we would expect our findings to replicate.

Second, it is interesting to speculate what a tangible prop actually means to the participants. What is the essence of the tangible in the tennis game context? McEwan [22] has already noted that the Skalski et al. continuum conflates at least three dimensions: (1) prop fidelity [10], i.e. the realism of the physical control interface in terms of the extent to which it looks and feels like the equivalent real-life prop; (2) interaction fidelity [10], i.e. the coupling between input mechanism and effects in the digital world in terms of how sensed movements of the controlling input are translated into digital behaviours; and (3) naturalness, i.e. the extent to which the physical and virtual control actions correspond with those that would be required when engaging in the equivalent real-life activity. Of these three dimensions our study manipulated prop fidelity. Higher prop fidelity increased the naturalness of the interaction and the preference, but except on flow, had little other effects on game experience or performance. Note that this seems to parallel the results of [10] in a table-tennis game who also found that high prop fidelity is preferred when interaction fidelity is high, but there were no effects on performance. So, one effect of using tangible props seems to be to enhance the similarity to the real world, but tangibility per se does not increase player experience. Otherwise the incomplete tangible would have fared better than it did.

Third, the differences between the racket handle and the full racket indicate that just holding a tangible without further affordances or meaning (the handle) is not necessarily equal or even better than having a full realistic tangible (the racket). In this our results are in contrast with the findings of [17] where a hybrid tool with a tangible handle and a virtual top was the best option. This contrast between [17] and our study reminds us that there may be no uniform effects of tangibles across different contexts. When comparing our findings with those of [17], the effects of incomplete versus complete versus no tangibles depend on whether these are studied in a domain with high precision requirements and with a high overlap in perception and action space [17] or in a domain with low precision requirements and a low overlap in perception and action space (our study).

CONCLUSIONS AND OUTLOOK

Our study contributes empirical findings to illuminate the benefits and drawbacks of using tangible props – a concern that has been at the heart of the TEI community from the beginning. In particular, we looked at tangibility in a video games interface and compared their usefulness to pure gesture control as another form of natural interaction. Altogether and in this context, tangibility seems to have a slight advantage over non-tangibility. Our study allows to differentiate between different types of tangibility on the underlying dimension of prop fidelity. Comparing the findings to earlier results [17] we propose the effects of prop fidelity on performance, preference and user experience of the tangible interface may be highly context-dependent. Our study also shows that other forms of natural user interfaces that do not employ tangibles might be as good regarding the performance and user experience as interfaces employing tangibles. Thus, there is no universal advantage of tangible interaction over other forms of natural interfaces.

Our results reveal opportunities for developing further studies. First, the differences between incomplete and complete tangibles are not fully understood. How important is the prop fidelity of an incomplete tangible? In other words, would it make a difference if we replaced the sawn-off handle of the tennis racket for a neutral-looking stick? The lower prop fidelity of the stick could make it a worse user experience. However, as the sawn-off handle actually looks like a damaged tennis racket, the stick may also turn out to be more beneficial. Second, it might be very fruitful to disentangle the three dimensions suggested by [22] and what they contribute to the performance and user experience of tangible interfaces. Third, there also might be interactions with expectations: high prop fidelity may evoke higher expectations of naturalness [10,13]. If the system does not deliver on these expectations, this may lead to the failure of the TUI. That is, the effects are not explained by varying levels of prop fidelity alone, but rather by the (mis)match or interaction between the actual fidelity of the prop and the actual naturalness of the interaction (i.e. what can be done with the prop in the game).

ACKNOWLEDGEMENTS

We would like to thank Michael Roth for his help with data gathering and Clara Hüsch for creating the figures.

REFERENCES

1. Lonni Besançon, Paul Issartel, Mehdi Ammi, and Tobias Isenberg. 2017. Mouse, tactile, and tangible input for 3D manipulation. In *Proceedings of the 2017 CHI Conference on Human Factors in Computing Systems* (CHI '17). ACM, New York, NY, USA, 4727-4740.
2. Max Birk and Regan L. Mandryk. 2013. Control your game-self: effects of controller type on enjoyment, motivation, and personality in game. In *Proceedings of the SIGCHI Conference on Human Factors in Computing Systems* (CHI '13). ACM, New York, NY, USA, 685-694.
3. Jürgen Bortz. 2006. *Statistik: Für Human- und Sozialwissenschaftler*. Heidelberg: Springer-Verlag.
4. Michael Brown, Aidan Kehoe, Jurek Kirakowski, and Ian Pitt. 2015. Beyond the gamepad: HCI and game controller design and evaluation. In *Game User Experience Evaluation*. Springer, Heidelberg, Germany, 263–285.
5. Paul Cairns, Jing Li, Wendy Wang, and A. Imran Nordin. 2014. The influence of controllers on immersion in mobile games. In *Proceedings of the SIGCHI Conference on Human Factors in Computing Systems* (CHI '14). ACM, New York, NY, USA, 371-380.
6. Mihaly Csikszentmihalyi. 1996. *Flow and the psychology of discovery and invention*. New York: Harper Collins.
7. Karin Eilers, Friedhelm Nachreiner, and Kerstin Hänecke. 1986. Entwicklung und Überprüfung einer Skala zur Erfassung subjektiv erlebter Anstrengung. *Zeitschrift für Arbeitswissenschaft* 40, 4: 215-224.
8. Péter Fankhauser, Michael Bloesch, Diego Rodriguez, Ralf Kaestner, Marco Hutter, and Roland Siegwart. 2015. Kinect v2 for mobile robot navigation: Evaluation and modeling. In *Proceedings of the International Conference on Advanced Robotics (ICAR)*, 388-394.
9. Andy Field. 2013. *Discovering statistics using IBM SPSS statistics*. London: Sage publications.
10. Dustin Freeman, Otmar Hilliges, Abigail Sellen, Kenton O'Hara, Shahram Izadi, and Kenneth Wood. 2012. The role of physical controllers in motion video gaming. In *Proceedings of the Designing Interactive Systems Conference* (DIS '12). ACM, New York, NY, USA, 701-710.
11. Hossein M. Hondori and Maryam Khademi. 2014. A review on technical and clinical impact of microsoft kinect on physical therapy and rehabilitation. *Journal of Medical Engineering, 2014*, 1-16.
12. Eva Hornecker and Jacob Buur. 2006. Getting a grip on tangible interaction: A framework on physical space and social interaction. In *Proceedings of the SIGCHI Conference on Human Factors in Computing Systems* (CHI '06), Rebecca Grinter, Thomas Rodden, Paul Aoki, Ed Cutrell, Robin Jeffries, and Gary Olson (Eds.). ACM, New York, NY, USA, 437-446.
13. Eva Hornecker and Andreas Dünser. 2008. Of pages and paddles: Children's expectations and mistaken interactions with physical–digital tools. *Interacting with Computers* 21, 1-2: 95–107.
14. Michael S. Horn, Erin Treacy Solovey, R. Jordan Crouser, and Robert J. K. Jacob. 2009. Comparing the use of tangible and graphical programming languages for informal science education. In *Proceedings of the SIGCHI Conference on Human Factors in Computing Systems* (CHI '09). ACM, New York, NY, USA, 975-984.
15. Wijnand IJsselsteijn, Yvonne De Kort, Karolien Poels, Audrius Jurgelionis, and France Bellotti. 2007. Characterising and measuring user experiences in digital games. In *International conference on advances in computer entertainment technology* 2, 27.
16. Hiroshi Ishii and Brygg Ullmer. 1997. Tangible bits: towards seamless interfaces between people, bits and atoms. In *Proceedings of the ACM SIGCHI Conference on Human factors in computing systems* (CHI '97). ACM, New York, NY, USA, 234-241.
17. Johann H. Israel. 2010. Hybride Interaktionstechniken des immersiven Skizzierens in frühen Phasen der Produktentwicklung. Ph.D Dissertation. TU Berlin, Berlin, Germany.
18. Mi J. Kim and Mary L. Maher. 2008. The impact of tangible user interfaces on spatial cognition during collaborative design. *Design Studies* 29. 3: 222–253.
19. Mark A. Livingston, Jay Sebastian, Zhuming Ai, and Jonathan W. Decker. 2012. Performance measurements for the Microsoft Kinect skeleton. In *Proceedings of the International Conference of the Virtual Reality (VRW)*, 119-120.
20. Paul Marshall. 2007. Do tangible interfaces enhance learning?. In *Proceedings of the 1st international conference on Tangible and embedded interaction* (TEI '07). ACM, New York, NY, USA, 163-170.
21. Paul Marshall, Yvonne Rogers, and Eva Hornecker. 2007. Are tangible interfaces really any better than other kinds of interfaces? Retrieved August 1, 2017

from http://oro.open.ac.uk/19535/1/TUIworkshop-Marshall.pdf

22. Mitchell W. McEwan. 2017. *The influence of naturally mapped control interfaces for video games on the player experience and intuitive interaction.* Ph.D Dissertation. Queensland University of Technology, Queensland, Australia.
23. Mitchell W. McEwan, Alethea L. Blackler, Daniel M. Johnson, and Peta A. Wyeth. 2014. Natural mapping and intuitive interaction in videogames. In *Proceedings of the first ACM SIGCHI annual symposium on Computer-human interaction in play* (CHI PLAY '14). ACM, New York, NY, USA, 191-200.
24. Mitchell W. McEwan, Daniel M. Johnson, Peta A. Wyeth, and Alethea L. Blackler. 2012. Videogame control device impact on the play experience. In *Proceedings of The 8th Australasian Conference on Interactive Entertainment: Playing the System* (IE '12). ACM, New York, NY, USA, , Article 18 , 3 pages.
25. Edward F. Melcer, Victoria Hollis, and Katherine Isbister. 2017. Tangibles vs. Mouse in Educational Programming Games: Influences on Enjoyment and Self-Beliefs. In *Proceedings of the 2016 CHI Conference Extended Abstracts on Human Factors in Computing Systems* (CHI EA '17). ACM, New York, NY, USA, 1901-1908.
26. James Patten and Hiroshi Ishii. 2000. A comparison of spatial organization strategies in graphical and tangible user interfaces. In *Proceedings of DARE 2000 on Designing augmented reality environments* (DARE '00). ACM, New York, NY, USA, 41-50.
27. Thomas Perl. 2012. Cross-platform tracking of a 6dof motion controller. *Using Computer Vision and Sensor Fusion, Austria.*
28. Ryan Rogers, Nicholas D. Bowman, and Mary B. Oliver. 2015. It's not the model that doesn't fit, it's the controller! The role of cognitive skills in understanding the links between natural mapping, performance, and enjoyment of console video games. *Computers in Human Behavior* 49, 588–596.
29. Richard M. Ryan, C. Scott Rigby, and Andrew Przybylski. 2006. The motivational pull of video games: A self-determination theory approach. *Motivation and Emotion* 30, 4: 344–360.
30. Orit Shaer and Eva Hornecker. 2010. Tangible user interfaces: past, present, and future directions. *Foundations and Trends in Human-Computer Interaction* 3, 1–2: 1–137.
31. Daniel M. Shafer, Corey P. Carbonara, and Lucy Popova. 2014. Controller required? The impact of natural mapping on interactivity, realism, presence, and enjoyment in motion-based video games. *Presence* 23, 3: 267–286.
32. Paul Skalski, Ron Tamborini, Ashleigh Shelton, Michael Buncher, and Pete Lindmark. 2011. Mapping the road to fun: Natural video game controllers, presence, and game enjoyment. *New Media & Society* 13, 2: 224–242.
33. Qifei Wang, Gregorij Kurillo, Ferda Ofli, and Ruzena Bajcsy. 2015. Evaluation of pose tracking accuracy in the first and second generations of microsoft kinect. In *Proceedings of the International Conference on Healthcare Informatics (ICHI),* 380-389.
34. Fred R. H. Zijlstra. 1993. *Efficiency in work behaviour: A design approach for modern tools.* Ph.D Dissertation. Delft University of Technology, Delft, The Netherlands.

Multimodal Effects of Color and Haptics on Intuitive Interaction with Tangible User Interfaces

Diana Löffler
University of Würzburg
Würzburg, Germany
diana.loeffler@uni-wuerzburg.de

Robert Tscharn
University of Würzburg
Würzburg, Germany
robert.tscharn@uni-wuerzburg.de

Jörn Hurtienne
University of Würzburg
Würzburg, Germany
joern.hurtienne@uni-wuerzburg.de

ABSTRACT
Tangible User Interfaces (TUIs) allow users to sense and manipulate digital information through physical objects. Although haptic properties are emphasized, TUIs are presented in and perceived through multiple modalities. Especially visual properties like color shape the users' expectations about the relation between tangibles and the abstract data they represent and control. Viewing TUIs as multisensory percepts, we present an empirical study that quantifies benefits of an explicit design for color for intuitive interaction. In a cross-cultural experiment, 75 participants (Germans and Japanese) matched tangible objects of different colors, sizes, weights or temperatures with abstract words. The results indicate that multimodal representations increase the efficiency, effectiveness and user satisfaction, but only if colors and haptic properties evoke congruent associations. Incongruently designed tangibles led to a 17% increase in response speed, -28% lower accuracy and -61% lower preference ratings compared to congruently designed tangibles.

CCS CONCEPTS
• **Human-centered computing → Human computer interaction (HCI)** → Empirical studies in HCI

Author Keywords
Colors; embodied cognition; conceptual metaphor theory; image schemas; tangible user interfaces; intuitive interaction; design guidelines; multimodal interaction; cross-modal interaction.

INTRODUCTION
Humans perceive and interact with their environment through several modalities (e.g., visual, auditive, haptic). Over the past decades, digitalization has narrowed down the diversity of modalities necessary for interacting with the increasingly digital environment. To reverse this trend, TUIs incorporate physical objects in human-computer interaction (HCI) [23]. Tangible systems distinguish and identify physical objects, their location, orientation and other aspects of their physical state and link them with digital content [7]. As tangibles are in the physical world, they offer opportunities for using multiple modalities (i.e., at least haptic and visual) with the goal of optimally drawing upon our skills to physically interact with the world [40]. Since we perceive and interact with our physical world in a multimodal way, TUIs promise to exploit this human potential of already available and multimodal information channels also in the realm of the digital world.

In general, multimodality is regarded as facilitating HCI in several ways [7,38,39]. For example, multimodal systems can offer redundant input and output channels, allowing users with different available modalities to interact with the same system and to counterbalance chronically or temporarily dysfunctional sensing channels (e.g., visually impaired or distracted people). Moreover, information provided by one source can be used to resolve ambiguities in another, thereby reducing errors on the side of human (e.g., when interpreting information provided by a computer) and computer (e.g., when interpreting user input), resulting in better user experience [14] and better learning opportunities [13].

In the context of TUIs, benefits of multimodality have been investigated both for input and output technologies. Especially multimodal feedback that enriches tangible objects with active feedback capabilities in several modalities has been subject to research [11,24,41,52]. As tangible objects almost always provide the user with some sort of visual and haptic information, they impact the interaction as a perceptual whole, even though some channels might not have been explicitly designed. For example, darker objects are expected to be heavier, regardless of their actual weight [31]. We argue that this mutual influence of different sensory properties affects the intuitive use of TUIs. Intuitive interaction is hereby defined as the extent to which the subconscious application of prior knowledge leads to an effective, efficient and satisfying interaction [36].

TEI '18, March 18–21, 2018, Stockholm, Sweden

ACM ISBN 978-1-4503-5568-1/18/03...$15.00
https://doi.org/10.1145/3173225.3173257

In this paper, we aim to quantify benefits of an explicit multimodal design of tangibles for intuitive interaction. Exemplified on the example of color, consequences of multimodal perception when one or two sensing channels (visual and haptic) communicate congruent or opposing information are investigated. The expected decrease of intuitive use when sensory information is not in line between different modalities is measured in a user study. The results of this study demonstrate that the interplay of visual and haptic information should be actively addressed in TUIs.

MULTISENSORY INTEGRATION OF VISION AND TOUCH

Beside efforts to combine multimodal interaction with tangible systems and enriching tangibles with multimodal feedback, TUIs are also perceived through multiple modalities and impact the users' interaction as a perceptual whole. This is because our brain integrates corresponding sensory input into mental representations of objects, which guide our interaction with them. Components of these representations are for example color, graspability, function or material [28]. The overall advantage of the process of multisensory integration of a correlated input from an object (object-based perception) or event is to increase accuracy and speed of the sensory estimate based on information from redundant sources, resulting in a rich coherent percept [10,12,20,29,50,53].

Vision dominates other senses in multisensory integration to a degree that their input can be distorted in favor of vision [16,46,47]. For example, in their classic experiment, Rock and Victor asked participants to look at and touch an object. They created a conflict between vision and touch by distorting the visual perceived shape from the actual shape perceived by touch. As a result, the participants reported that the object felt the way it looked, suggesting that the conflict between vision and touch was completely resolved in favor of vision, and participants were unaware of the conflict [42]. Although both visual and tactual information make object identification easiest and support memory retrieval best [44,45], vision has the advantage that it is perceived very fast and over distance and thus dominates touch in assessing materials. Without looking at materials, we are often unable to identify them correctly by touch [54]. Therefore, vision, as an active sense that probes information, is our primary source of objective data from the environment [15].

Color, in turn, is an important visual component that plays a fundamental role in the construction of coherent percepts as well as the organization of memory [8]. As a surface cue, color provides important information about an object's identity [5] and facilitates object recognition. In its function as an indicator of material properties, color shapes the interaction with objects and the environment and is an important dimension to be considered in the design of tangibles. Thus, intuitive interaction with TUIs can benefit when colors evoke expectations that are consistent with the relation between tangibles and the abstract data they represent. When perceiving tangibles and interpreting their meaning, people rely on implicit knowledge about cross-modal correspondences [34], for example between color and haptic properties.

Cross-modal correspondences are 'acquired, malleable, relative, and transitive pairings between sensory dimensions' [9] and are shared by a large number of people [48]. Three factors are presumed to facilitate cross-modal binding: extensive spatial and temporal coincidence as well as semantic congruency [12,48]. Semantic congruency describes a match of objects or events across sensory modalities, even when they are not co-experienced on a regular basis [55]. In this case, the congruency arises from a structural or semantic overlap on conceptual dimensions like activity, evaluation and potency [37]. Consider the examples of perceiving fire and holding a hot coffee in a blue cup. In both cases, spatiotemporal congruency of color and tactile temperature cues is given and temperature awareness is conveyed through multiple complementary modalities [2]. However, fire as a 'naturally' colored object produces a correlated sensory stream of information in which the input from different modalities correspond, e.g., the colors red/yellow and the heat of fire. Long wavelength colors are associated with warm and red/yellow as well as warm have a high factor loading on the dimension of potency [37]. On the contrary, an arbitrarily colored man-made object like the blue cup filled with hot coffee may produce a sensory mismatch between different modalities. While the blue of the cup is perceived prior to the heat, expectations are based on the visual information (blue is associated with cold), which will be disconfirmed by consecutively perceiving physical heat. In this example, the appearance of the cup generates a direct expectation of how it will feel through learned associations, cultural conventions or lawful relationships [32,33].

However, color and tactile temperature cue neither match on an experiential basis (short wavelength colors naturally correlate with cold, reinforced through cultural habits [30]), nor on any structural dimension. This conflict or sensory incongruence is costly in terms of cognitive performance [6] and results in different emotional reactions like surprise, amusement, interest, confusion or disappointment [32,33] as well as a decrease in intuitive interaction [30]. Thus, depending on the degree of the incongruence (specific type of blue and apparent physical warmth) the conflicting color of the cup might alter temperature perception in a contrary way compared to the tactile feedback and might cause cognitive dissonance which can hamper intuitive interaction.

CROSS-MODAL CORRESPONDENCES INCLUDED IN THIS STUDY

To study potential benefits of aligning colors with haptic properties for intuitive interaction with TUIs, cross-modal correspondences between colors and haptics have to be identified. Cross-modal correspondences that are identified through so-called conceptual metaphors are very likely to be independent of culture (for a review see [30]) and are thus suitable for a 'universal' multimodal design of TUIs. Conceptual metaphors represent a mapping between a source and target domain which is expressed in language [26]. For example, linguistic expressions like "cold blue" and "loud pink" link color attributes to haptic properties. Expressions such as "cold logic" and "heavy sadness", in turn, provide hints to underlying associations between physical attributes and more abstract content (see [30,31] for detailed descriptions of this method). Based on these, cross-modal correspondences between colors, haptics and abstract ideas can be derived.

Table 1 depicts candidates of four selected haptic domains (size, weight, strength and temperature), associated color properties and examples of abstract content the cross-modal correspondence can stand for. To quantify each modality's contribution to how intuitive the abstract content can be matched, a cross-cultural user study was conducted that required participants to interact with tangible objects with varying haptic and visual properties using one or two of their senses.

Haptic property	Color property	Abstract content
big	high background contrast	importance, power
small	low background contrast	insignificance, ignorance
heavy	low relative brightness, high saturation	sadness, difficulty
light	high relative brightness, low saturation	innocence, happiness
strong	long wavelength hues, black, low brightness	competence, intensity
weak	high brightness	incompetence, femininity
warm	long wavelength hues	emotionality, activeness
cold	short wavelength hues	distance, sadness

Table 1. Cross-modal correspondences between color and haptic properties and associated abstract content.

METHOD

Participants

In total, 28 German students from a German university campus, and 47 Japanese volunteers from a Japanese university campus, were recruited and participated for course credit or 11 Euro. The participants' ages ranged from 19 to 55 years (M = 22.3, SD = 5.33). All German participants were German native speakers and all Japanese subjects had Japanese as their mother tongue. All participants had no reported defective color vision and passed at least three out of the four plates 1, 7, 8 and 17 of the Ishihara Color Test [22] that tested for the most common red-green color impairment.

Procedure

Before starting with the main experiment, participants completed a demographic questionnaire. After that, they were instructed that in each experimental trial they will be presented with two objects and an adjective describing an abstract concept (e.g., powerful). Their task was to inspect the objects and select the object that best matched the given adjective. Depending on condition, participants inspected the objects either through looking at them while lifting them with both hands (conditions 1-4), or through lifting them with both hands while being blindfolded (condition 5), or by only visual inspection (condition 6). The details of each condition are described in the 'Design and Material' section. The adjective was printed in black letters on white paper and placed together with two objects on a wooden tray in front of the participants. In the condition in which the participants were blindfolded, the adjective was read out loud by the experimenter.

No time limit was imposed on the participants, but the time participants needed to give their answers was recorded (*efficiency*). The recording started when subjects had both objects in their hands and stopped when the chosen object was placed on the table. Note that in the experimental condition in which the participants were not allowed to touch the objects (condition 6), time recording started when the objects were placed on the table and stopped when the participants pointed to one object. To avoid sequence effects, the objects and adjectives were presented in random order. After finishing all trials, the participants were asked to fill out a questionnaire indicating which design was the most preferable and suitable to represent a specific metaphor on a 5-point Likert scale from (-- = very ill-suited to ++ very well suited) (*satisfaction/preference*).

The whole experiment lasted about 45 minutes, with no considerable variance between the participants. The Japanese subjects participated in the experiment in July 2014, whereas the German subjects took part in the experiment using the same stimulus material in August 2014. The laboratories in which the experiment took place had covered windows and were equipped with daylight lamps (about 220 Lux).

Condition	Object Pair	Inter-action	Size	Weight	Strength	Temperature
(1) Unimodal haptic (UH)	A	look and grasp	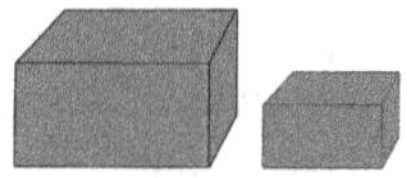 big small	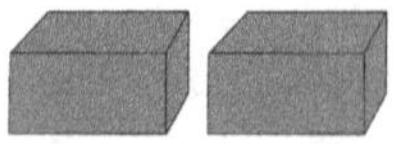 heavy light	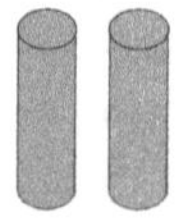 strong weak	 warm cold
(2) Unimodal visual (UV)	B	look and grasp	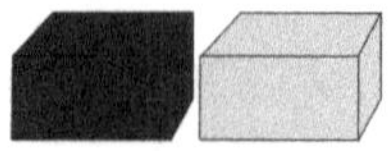 same size	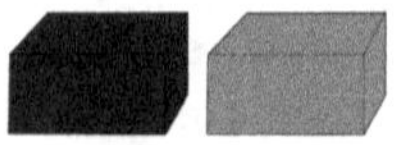 same weight	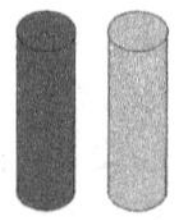 same strength	 same temperature
(3) Multimodal congruent (MC)	C	look and grasp	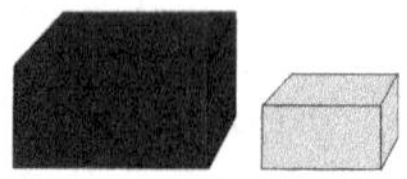 big small	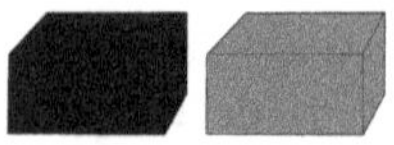 heavy light	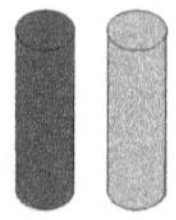 strong weak	 warm cold
(4) Multimodal incongruent (MI)	D	look and grasp	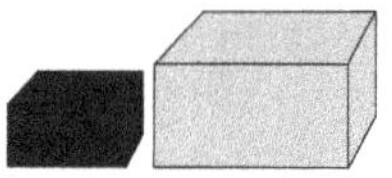 small big	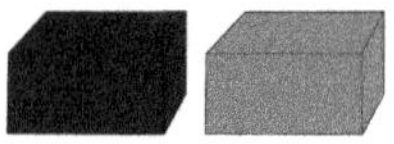 light heavy	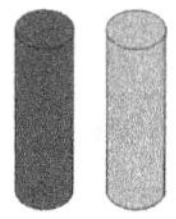 weak strong	 cold warm
(5) Unimodal haptic (blindfolded) (UHh)	A	grasp	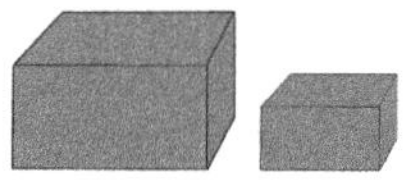 big small	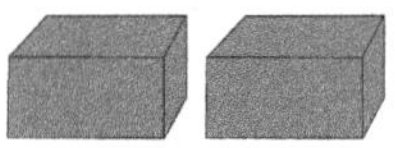 heavy light	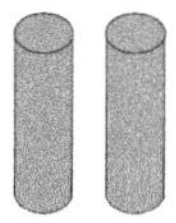 strong weak	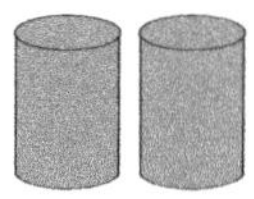 warm cold
(6) Unimodal visual (only looking) (UVv)	B	look	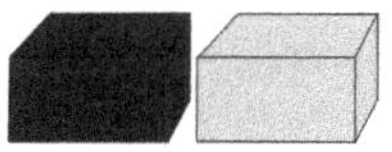 same size	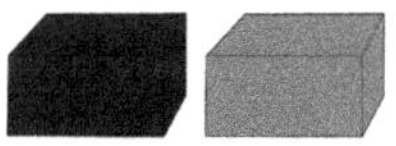 same weight	 same strength	 same temperature

Table 2. Overview of the six experimental conditions, four object pairs and interaction modalities for size, weight, strength and temperature.

Design and Material

Four suitable pairs of objects were created for each of the four haptic dimensions size, weight, strength and temperature based on the literature [31] and the summary depicted in Table 1, making a total of 16 object pairs (see Table 2, first four rows). Pair A instantiated the dimension in a haptic way while keeping color constant at neutral gray. Pair B instantiated the dimension in a color variant without haptic differences. Pair C instantiated the dimension both haptically and via color cues in a congruent way, while pair D combined the color cues in an incongruent way compared to the haptic cues. The chromatic colors were chosen to resemble the four haptic dimensions and were based on the literature [30,31] and the summary depicted in Table 1. While color-temperature associations were mainly influenced by hue, the main drivers for size-, strength- and weight-associations are saturation and brightness. Therefore, the hues in the size-, strength- and weight-conditions were kept constant. The object color was achieved by covering the objects in colored cardboard paper.

In detail, the objects had the following properties (HSB values in parentheses):

• size:

A. differently sized cardboard boxes in neutral gray (n.d.,0,50): 2.5x5.1x 5.1cm (big), 1.25x2.5x2.5cm (small)
B. same sized cardboard boxes (1.87x3.75x3.75cm): dark red (0,100,25) (big), pink (0,25,100) (small)
C. differently sized cardboard boxes: 2.5x5.1x5.1cm in dark red (0,100,25) (big), 1.25x2.5x2.5cm in pink (0,25,100) (small)
D. differently sized cardboard boxes: 2.5x5.1x5.1cm in pink (0,25,100) (big), 1.25x2.5x2.5cm in dark red (0,100,25) (small)

• weight:

A. same sized cardboard boxes with different weights in neutral gray (n.d.,0,50): 200g (heavy), 14g (light)
B. same sized cardboard boxes with same weight (100g): dark violet (282,100,25) (heavy), violet (282,75,100) (light)
C. same sized cardboard boxes with different weights: 200g in dark violet (282,100,25) (heavy), 14g in violet (282,75,100) (light)
D. same sized cardboard boxes with different weights: 200g in violet (282,75,100) (heavy), 14g in dark violet (282,100,25) (light)

• strength:

A. same sized magnets in neutral gray (n.d.,0,50): 4000g/39.2N (strong), 408g/4N (weak)
B. same sized magnets with same strength 2200g/21.6N: brown (37,100,50) (strong), bright brown (37,25,75) (weak)
C. same sized magnets: 4000g/39.2N in brown (37,100,50) (strong), 408g/4N in bright brown (37,25,75) (weak)
D. same sized magnets: 4000g/39.2N in bright brown (37,25,75) (strong), 408g/4N in brown (37,100,50) (weak)

• temperature:

A. two identical glass jars in neutral gray (n.d.,0,50) filled with water: 50.0°C (warm), 5.0°C (cold)
B. two identical glass jars filled with water at room temperature: orange (50,100,100) (warm), blue (250,75,100) (cold)
C. two identical glass jars filled with water: 50.0°C in orange (50,100,100) (warm), 5.0°C in blue (250,75,100) (cold)
D. two identical glass jars filled with water: 50.0°C in blue (250,75,100) (warm), 5.0°C in orange (50,100,100) (cold)

Six experimental conditions were created for each haptic dimension, all of which are depicted in Table 2. In the first condition, the object pairs described under A., only differing in a haptic property but not in color, were inspected by the participants both visually and haptically (this condition is referred to as *unimodal haptic* condition UH). The different sized boxes of the size dimension are an exception, since size is perceived visually as well as haptically. For the second condition (referred to as *unimodal visual* condition UV) the objects described under B., differing in color but not in the haptic property, were visually and haptically inspected. In the third condition, called *multimodal congruent* condition MC, participants visually and haptically inspected the metaphorically congruent object pairs described under C. and in the fourth condition, consisting of the metaphorically incongruent pair D., visual and haptic inspection was encouraged as well (*multimodal incongruent* condition MI).

In condition five (*unimodal haptic (blindfolded)* UHh), the object pairs described under A. were used, and the participants were blindfolded, being only able to inspect the items haptically. Finally, in condition six (*unimodal visual (only looking)* UVv), the objects described under B. were used, but participants were only allowed to have a look at the objects without touching or lifting them.

Adjectives were chosen to represent abstract content that is likely associated with the dimensions size, weight, strength and temperature and shown to the participants. The adjectives were taken from linguistic literature on conceptual metaphor:

- big-small: important-unimportant [25], significant-insignificant [26], powerful-powerless [3], more-less [3], knowing-unknowing [51]
- heavy-light: important-unimportant [3], sad-happy [49], more-less [25], difficult-easy [18], guilty-innocent [3]
- strong-weak: more-less [3], powerful-powerless [3], intense-less intense [30], competent-incompetent [3], male-female [30]
- warm-cold: emotional-unemotional [3], active-inactive [43], intimate-distant [1], problematic-unproblematic [3], happy-sad [49]

Two lists of adjectives were prepared. On list 1, one word from each of the 20 adjective pairs was placed (e.g. knowing), and its opposite was placed on list 2 (e.g. unknowing). The lists were balanced regarding the number of positive and negative words they contained. Half of the participants were presented with list 1, the other half with list 2. Therefore, each participant matched 20 adjectives (metaphors across all four haptic dimensions) to all object pairs in the six conditions, resulting in 120 trials per session.

Hypotheses

We had four clusters of hypotheses related to a) cultural influence, b) efficiency, c) effectiveness and d) satisfaction as components of intuitive use.

a) We expected that both subjects of German and Japanese cultural background perform similar in measures of effectiveness, efficiency and satisfaction [30].

b) The reaction time of matching the objects to the adjectives is longer for haptics compared to vision, as these modalities have different inherent interaction times [17]. Multimodal representations are identified faster than unimodal and congruent are identified faster than incongruent representations [19].

c) The effectiveness of the matching process is higher for congruent than for incongruent representations, higher for redundant multimodal representations than for unimodal [4], and higher when subjects base their decisions on less ambiguous haptic properties compared to visual (color) [30].

d) Congruent representations are preferred over incongruent, multimodal over unimodal and haptic over visual representations.

RESULTS AND DISCUSSION

The results are shown in Table 3. The columns show the percentage of answers that were consistent with the predicted cross-modal association (effectiveness), mean reaction times (efficiency) and preference ratings (satisfaction) across all six experimental conditions with varying presentation and interaction styles. The results are grouped per hypotheses cluster a-d). Note that instead of applying Bonferroni-corrections to account for alpha-error accumulation, exact p-values and effect sizes are reported [35]. The reported degrees of freedom may differ between different conditions because of missing data due to technical problems while recording reaction times. The level of significance was set at 0.05.

a) To answer if German and Japanese subjects performed differently, their overall responses (metaphor consistency in answers, reaction times, preference ratings if applicable) were compared using an independent measures ANOVA. The agreement with the cross-modal correspondence and preference data did not differ between both cultural groups, $F(1,72) = .002$, $p = .965$ and $F(1,71) = 0.282$, $p = .597$, respectively. However, Japanese subjects needed significantly more time before they subjected their answers in all conditions, $F(1,62) = 13.347$, $p = .001$. Speculating, a reason for this slower decision making process might be inherent to the Japanese society, characterized by strict hierarchy, high uncertainty and risk avoidance as well as decision making by consensus [21]. Nevertheless, the response time pattern was the same for Japanese and German subjects for all six conditions. Because of this it is concluded that the perception and interpretation of the studied object sets is quite robust against cultural variation, and therefore the data of German and Japanese participants were averaged for hypotheses b-d) and addressed with multiple dependent-samples *t*-tests.

b) Reaction times were longer when subjects inspected the objects only with their hands (UHh) compared to visual inspection (UVv), $t(63) = 19.140$, $p < .001$. The congruent multimodal representation (MC) was matched faster than the object sets in which only the visual modality carried relevant information (UV), $t(63) = 8.008$, $p = .469$, but there was no difference in the reaction times between multimodal and unimodal haptic (UH) display, $t < 1$. The congruent multimodal object set (MC) was matched faster than the incongruent set (MI), $t(63) = 3.104$, $p = .003$.

c) The effectiveness of the matching process was higher for congruent (MC) than for incongruent representations (MI), $t(71) = 10.706$, $p < .001$. There was no difference in matching performance between the unimodal haptic display (UH) and the multimodal congruent representation (MC), $t(71) = 1.895$, $p = .062$, but the participants achieved more correct matches in the congruent multimodal (MC) condition compared to the unimodal visual (UV), $t(71) = 5.064$, $p < .001$ and more matches in the unimodal haptic (UH) compared to the unimodal visual presentation (UV), $t(71) = 2.777$, $p = .007$.

d) Congruent representations (MC) were preferred over incongruent (MI), $t(72) = 10.730$, $p < .001$, multimodal (MC) over unimodal (UH, UV), $t(72) = 7.292$, $p < .001$ and $t(72) = 11.303$, $p < .001$, respectively, and haptic (UH) over visual representations (UV), $t(72) = 4.530$, $p < .001$.

The results suggest that when the efficiency of the interaction is emphasized, the best results can be achieved by indicating concepts visually without requiring the user to feel any haptic properties (41% increase in response speed compared to multimodal assessment involving touch). If the interaction is multimodal (visual, haptic), a representation that carries relevant information on more than one modality increases the speed of the interaction by 13%, but only if the information appears to be congruent. An incongruent design decreases response speed by 17%.

The greatest accuracy and highest preference ratings can be obtained when concepts are represented in a multimodal and congruent fashion, probably because this presentation style resolves perceptual ambiguities best [27]. Incongruently designed tangibles, e.g., colors that are counterintuitively applied to haptic properties, received the overall lowest accuracy (-28%) and preference ratings (-61%) compared to the congruent condition.

These findings can be summarized into the following five design guidelines that help informing the multimodal design of TUIs:

1. To facilitate intuitive interaction, the different modalities involved in a TUI should cross-modally correspond to each other. For example, heavy tangibles should be designed in darker colors.
2. Culture-independent cross-modal correspondences can be derived from conceptual metaphors, which are expressed in language. For example, *heavy red* makes the association between physical weight and a color with low relative brightness and high saturation explicit (i.e., a dark saturated red). Similar examples can usually be found in different languages.
3. For short reaction times with TUIs, a visual indication of physical properties is important. For example, haptic properties can be indicated through cross-modally matching colors (e.g., heaviness – dark colors).
4. For avoiding errors when interacting with TUIs, haptic interaction is important. Errors are further reduced when physical properties are also congruently expressed in other modalities, so the advantages of redundant multimodal coding can be harnessed.
5. For achieving high user satisfaction, tangibles should be explicitly designed in a multimodal fashion, e.g. appropriately colored according to their physical properties.

Condition	Size			Weight			Strength			Temperature		
	%	t	p	%	t	p	%	t	p	%	t	p
UH	85	2.31	0.81	94	2.45	0.77	91	2.91	0.79	88	2.79	0.51
UV	86	2.44	0.15	84	2.96	0.25	86	3.32	0.07	88	2.95	0.17
MC	89	2.33	1.04	96	2.43	1.51	92	2.91	1.19	89	2.73	1.54
MI	65	2.53	0.35	70	2.85	-0.51	74	3.31	0.06	67	3.39	-0.42
UHh	85	2.72	n/a	91	3.26	n/a	84	4.42	n/a	86	3.35	n/a
UVv	80	1.63	n/a	84	1.54	n/a	88	1.62	n/a	83	1.56	n/a

Table 3. % agreement with the cross-modal correspondence, mean reaction times (t) in seconds and preference ratings (p) from -2 to +2 across four presentation styles in six conditions (German and Japanese subjects). Values in the column "incongruent" represent choices in favor of the haptic property.

CONCLUSION AND OUTLOOK

We have shown that explicitly designing for multiple sensory channels can enhance intuitive interaction with TUIs. The introduced experimental split modality approach allowed investigating each modality's contribution to the overall performance [44]. Demonstrated on the examples of color and the haptic attributes size, weight, magnetic strength and temperature, multimodal representations increase efficiency, effectiveness and user satisfaction, but only if the information between haptics and color appears to be congruent. Cultural differences in performance between German and Japanese subjects were negligible. Following the results gathered in the empirical study, it is recommended that colors are aligned with haptic properties to make use of the benefits of redundant multimodal coding [4,19]. The greatest pitfall of such an explicit multimodal design lies in the correct choice of colors, since the greatest decrease in effectiveness, efficiency and user satisfaction could be observed between congruent and incongruent designs (-28% accuracy, +17% more response time, -61% preference). This decrease in measures of intuitive use was consistent over all haptic dimensions. The large congruity effect obtained between congruent and incongruent designs implies that the participants were very sensitive to the congruence or incongruence of the perceptual whole, stressing the importance of considering this factor in the design of TUIs.

For the effectiveness and satisfaction data, a 'haptic premium' effect could be observed: when concepts were represented in a haptic way or explored haptically, accuracy and preference ratings increased. It is therefore concluded that the haptic properties size, weight, strength and temperature are better suited to represent abstract concepts compared to the visual property color. However, color can also be used as a substitute of sometimes difficult to implement or expensive haptic system output, which will increase efficiency if no haptic interaction is required, but also slightly decrease effectiveness and user satisfaction. It is therefore argued that when a dynamic change in a physical property like temperature, size, strength or weight is hard to implement in a user interface, color-for-haptic-substitution could be a viable approach.

Future studies are needed that test other cross-modal relationships between haptics and other physical domains, and that investigate these in more applied contexts than this initial study could provide. The here applied experimental paradigm of two-alternative force choice tasks also has some drawbacks, like a general overestimation of the obtained effects. Moreover, the choices participants made were explicit. It therefore remains an open question if similar results for intuitive use can be obtained when conceptual choices are made more subconsciously.

REFERENCES

1. Fabienne Baider and Sara Gesuato. 2002. Burning with desire in English and French: cross-linguistic lexical restrictions on the LOVE IS FIRE metaphor. In *8th International Pragmatics Conference*.
2. Carrie Anne Balcer. 2014. Visual Cues Effects on Temperature Perception. Northern Michigan University.
3. Christa Baldauf. 1997. *Metapher und Kognition. Grundlagen einer neuen Theorie der Alltagsmetapher*. Peter Lang Verlag.
4. Paul Bertelson and De Gelder. 2004. The psychology of multimodal perception. In *Crossmodal space and crossmodal attention*. 141–177.
5. Jonathan S. Cant, Mary Ellen Large, Lindsay McCall, and Melvyn A. Goodale. 2008. Independent processing of form, colour, and texture in object perception. *Perception* 37, 1: 57–78.
6. David B Centerbar, Simone Schnall, Gerald L Clore, and Erika D Garvin. 2008. Affective incoherence: when affective concepts and embodied reactions clash. *Journal of personality and social psychology* 94, 4: 560–578.

7. Philip R. Cohen and David R. McGee. 2004. Tangible multimodal interfaces for safety-critical applications. *Communications of the ACM* 47, 1: 41. https://doi.org/10.1145/962081.962103
8. Jules B. Davidoff. 1991. *Cognition through color*. Mit Press Cambridge, MA.
9. Ophelia Deroy and Charles Spence. 2013. Why we are not all synesthetes (not even weakly so). *Psychonomic bulletin & review* 20, 4: 643–64.
10. Marc O Ernst and Martin S Banks. 2002. Humans integrate visual and haptic information in a statistically optimal fashion. *Nature* 415, 6870: 429–433.
11. JBF van Erp, CJAM Willemse, JB Janssen, and A Toet. 2014. Sensators: Active multisensory tangible user interfaces.
12. Karla K Evans and Anne Treisman. 2010. Natural cross-modal mappings between visual and auditory features. *Journal of Vision* 10, 6.
13. Min Fan and Alissa N. Antle. 2015. Tactile Letters. In *Proceedings of the Ninth International Conference on Tangible, Embedded, and Embodied Interaction - TEI '14*, 673–678. https://doi.org/10.1145/2677199.2688806
14. Feng Feng and Tony Stockman. 2017. An investigation of dynamic crossmodal instantiation in TUIs. In *Proceedings of the 19th ACM International Conference on Multimodal Interaction - ICMI 2017*, 82–90. https://doi.org/10.1145/3136755.3136782
15. Anna Fenko, Jacco J. Otten, and Hendrik N J Schifferstein. 2010. Describing product experience in different languages: The role of sensory modalities. *Journal of Pragmatics* 42, 12: 3314–3327.
16. Anna Fenko, Hendrik N J Schifferstein, and Paul Hekkert. 2009. Which senses dominate at different stages of product experience? In *Undisciplined! Design Research Society Conference 2008*, 289/1-289/12.
17. Nina Gaißert, Christian Wallraven, and Heinrich H. Bülthoff. 2010. Visual and haptic perceptual spaces show high similarity in humans. *Journal of Vision* 10, 11: 2–2. https://doi.org/10.1167/10.11.2
18. Raymond W. Gibbs, Paula Lenz Costa Lima, and Edson Francozo. 2004. Metaphor is grounded in embodied experience. *Journal of Pragmatics* 36, 7: 1189–1210.
19. David Hecht, Miriam Reiner, and Avi Karni. 2008. Multisensory enhancement: gains in choice and in simple response times. *Experimental Brain Research* 189, 2: 133–143. https://doi.org/10.1007/s00221-008-1410-0
20. Hsin-Ni Ho, Daisuke Iwai, Yuki Yoshikawa, Junji Watanabe, and Shinya Nishida. 2014. Combining colour and temperature: A blue object is more likely to be judged as warm than a red object. *Scientific reports* 4: 5527.
21. Geert Hofstede. 2001. *Culture's consequences: comparing values, behavior, institutions and organizations across nations*. Sage Publications, Inc.
22. Shinobu Ishihara. 1917. *Tests for Colour Blindness*. Handaya Hongo Harukich, Tokyo.
23. Hiroshi Ishii. 2008. Tangible bits: beyond pixels. In *Proceedings of the 2nd international conference on Tangible and Embedded Intreaction*, xv–xxv.
24. L Kim, H Cho, S Park, and M Han. 2007. A tangible user interface with multimodal feedback. *conference on human-computer interaction*.
25. George Lakoff. 1994. *Master Metaphor List*. University of California.
26. George Lakoff and Mark Johnson. 1997. Metaphors We Live By. *The production of reality: essays and reading on social interaction*: 124–134. https://doi.org/10.1016/0024-3841(82)90031-6
27. Christophe Lalanne and Jean Lorenceau. 2004. Crossmodal integration for perception and action. *Journal of Physiology Paris* 98, 1: 265–279.
28. Sophie Lebrecht. 2012. "Micro-valences": Affective valence in "neutral" everyday objects. Brown University.
29. Susan J. Lederman, Georgie Thorne, and Bill Jones. 1986. Perception of texture by vision and touch: multidimensionality and intersensory integration. *Journal of Experimental Psychology. Human Perception and Performance* 12, 2: 169–180.
30. Diana Löffler. 2017. Color, Metaphor and Culture. PhD dissertation. University of Würzburg. Retrieved from https://d-nb.info/1141054450
31. Diana Löffler, L. Arlt, T. Toriizuka, Robert Tscharn, and J Hurtienne. 2016. Substituting Color for Haptic Attributes in Conceptual Metaphors for Tangible Interaction Design. In *TEI'16: Tenth International Conference on Tangible, Embedded, and Embodied Interaction*, 118–125.
32. Geke Ludden, Hendrik Schifferstein, and Paul Hekkert. 2009. Visual-Tactual Incongruities in Products as Sources of Surprise. *Empirical Studies of the Arts* 27, 1: 61–87.
33. Geke Ludden, Hendrik Schifferstein, and Paul Hekkert. 2012. Beyond surprise: A longitudinal study on the experience of visual-tactual incongruities in products. *International Journal of Design* 6, 1: 1–10.
34. Lawrence E Marks. 1990. Synaesthesia: Perception and Metaphor. In *Aesthetic Illusion: Theoretical and*

Historical Approaches. Walter de Gruyter, 28–40.

35. Shinichi Nakagawa. 2004. A farewell to Bonferroni: the problem of low statistical power and publication bias. *Behavioral Ecology* 15, 6: 1044–1045.

36. Anja Naumann, Jörn Hurtienne, Johann Habakuk Israel, Carsten Mohs, Martin Christof Kindsmüller, Herbert A. Meyer, Steffi Hußlein, and IUUI Research Group. 2007. Intuitive use of user interfaces: Defining a vague concept. In *Engineering Psychology and Cognitive Ergonomics*, 128–136.

37. Charles E Osgood, William H May, and M S Miron. 1975. *Cross-Cultural Universals of Affective Meaning*. University of Illinois Press, Urbana.

38. Sharon Oviatt and Philip Cohen. 2000. Perceptual user interfaces: multimodal interfaces that process what comes naturally. *Communications of the ACM* 43, 3: 45–53. https://doi.org/10.1145/330534.330538

39. Sharon Oviatt and Sharon. 1999. Ten myths of multimodal interaction. *Communications of the ACM* 42, 11: 74–81. https://doi.org/10.1145/319382.319398

40. Sara Price and Carey Jewitt. 2013. A multimodal approach to examining "embodiment" in tangible learning environments. In *Proceedings of the 7th International Conference on Tangible, Embedded and Embodied Interaction - TEI '13*, 43. https://doi.org/10.1145/2460625.2460632

41. Eckard Riedenklau, Thomas Hermann, and Helge Ritter. 2012. An integrated multi-modal actuated tangible user interface for distributed collaborative planning. In *Proceedings of the Sixth International Conference on Tangible, Embedded and Embodied Interaction - TEI '12*, 169. https://doi.org/10.1145/2148131.2148167

42. Irvin Rock and Jack Victor. 1964. Vision and touch: An experimentally created conflict between the two senses. *Science* 143, 3606: 594–596.

43. Paul Sambre. 2000. Metaphor and Metonymy at the Crossroads: A Cognitive Perspective. *Pragmatics* 10, 3: 344–345.

44. Hendrik Schifferstein. 2006. The perceived importance of sensory modalities in product usage: A study of self-reports. *Acta Psychologica* 121, 1: 41–64.

45. Hendrik Schifferstein and Marc P.H.D. Cleiren. 2005. Capturing Product Experience - A split modality approach. *Acta Psychologica* 118, 3: 293–318.

46. Hendrik Schifferstein, Anna Fenko, Pieter M A Desmet, David Labbe, and Nathalie Martin. 2013. Influence of package design on the dynamics of multisensory and emotional food experience. *Food Quality and Preference* 27, 1: 18–25.

47. Hendrik Schifferstein, Jacco J. Otten, Fien Thoolen, and Paul Hekkert. 2010. The experimental assessment of sensory dominance in a product development context. *Journal of Design Research* 8, 2: 119–144.

48. Charles Spence. 2011. Crossmodal correspondences: A tutorial review. *Attention, Perception, & Psychophysics* 73, 4: 971–995.

49. Anatol Stefanowitsch. 2006. Words and their metaphors: A corpus-based approach. *Trends in Linguistics Studies and Monographs* 171, 63.

50. Barry Stein and Alex Meredith. 1993. *The Merging of the Sense*. Mit Press Cambridge, MA.

51. Jon Tolaas. 1991. Notes on the Origin of Some Spatialization Metaphors. *Metaphor and Symbolic Activity* 6, 3: 203–218.

52. W Valk, J Rypkema, and JBF van Erp. 2014. Facilitating planning: Tangible objects with multimodal feedback mitigate cognitive workload. *Auvray, M. Duriez, C., 9th.*

53. Laura Walker, Peter Walker, and Brian Francis. 2012. A common scheme for cross-sensory correspondences across stimulus domains. *Perception* 41, 10: 1186–1192.

54. Lisa Wastiels, Hendrik N J Schifferstein, Ine Wouters, and Ann Heylighen. 2013. Touching materials visually: About the dominance of vision in building material assessment. *International Journal of Design* 7, 2: 31–41.

55. Andy T. Woods, Charles Spence, Natalie Butcher, and Ophelia Deroy. 2013. Fast lemons and sour boulders: Testing crossmodal correspondences using an internet-based testing methodology. *i-Perception* 4, 6: 365–379.

Being in the Sky: Framing Tangible and Embodied Interaction for Future Airliner Cockpits

Catherine Letondal [1], Jean-Luc Vinot [1], Sylvain Pauchet [1,5], Caroline Boussiron [2], Stéphanie Rey [1,3], Valentin Becquet [1], Claire Lavenir [4]

[1] University of Toulouse - ENAC Toulouse, France, <first name>.<last name>@enac.fr
[2] Ingenuity i/o, Ramonville Saint-Agne, France, boussiron@ingenuity.io
[3] Berger-Levrault, Toulouse, France, stephanie.rey@berger-levrault.com
[4] Intactile Design, Montpellier, France, lavenir.c@intactile.com
[5] Astrolab, Toulouse, France, s.pauchet@astrolab.net

ABSTRACT

In order to contribute to a design for future airline cockpits that can address the limitations of touch-based interfaces, we analyze tangible dimensions of cockpit activity based on observations and pilot interviews. Working from these data, using TEI theory and concepts of phenomenology, we discuss the implications for tangible design of our findings. We found that the status of sensation in perception, the required level of control in actions, the safety issues using physical objects and the restricted mode of externalization, raise challenges for tangible design. Accordingly, we discuss key concepts for the design of the future cockpit, such as the use of a protected space where interaction may involve compressed externalization, rhythmic structures and customized context-aware adaptations.

Author Keywords

Tangible interaction; physical skills; time-based interaction; design; ethnography; phenomenology; aeronautics.

ACM Classification Keywords

• **Human-centered computing~Human computer interaction (HCI)** • Human-centered computing~HCI design and evaluation methods • Human-centered computing~Field studies

INTRODUCTION

Touch technologies are replacing current electronic displays in airline pilot system interfaces. However, while safety and performance require interactive instruments to maximize the perception, action and collaboration spaces offered to pilots, the literature highlights the limits of touch interaction for these aspects [1,5,9,24,30]. Tangible, Embedded and Embodied Interaction (TEI) frameworks and themes [28,42,48,62,70] appeared to be a promising means to address these limitations and might help frame useful directions [68], while also raising certain issues. Firstly, TEI focuses on the materiality of the interface, the physical embodiment of data, and physical objects as representation and control for digital information. It may also involve whole-body interaction, or the embedding of the interface and user interaction with physical objects in real spaces. The first type of issue concerning these themes and concepts is only technical: there are safety constraints that prevent the use of physical objects, and bodily movements are restricted. Additionally, this raises the question whether technically "adding" physicality is the sole valid design approach.

Another approach [13,14,15,58,65], is to take a broader stance on tangible and embodied interaction as described by Dourish that emphasizes the primacy of practical interaction as a meaningful experience in the world [15]. Exploring this more theoretical standpoint, grounded in phenomenological concepts, helped us to frame an application of TEI themes to the aeronautical field, where a specific experience of body, time and space for pilots involves somewhat modified perception habits.

In this paper, working from our observations and interviews, and using tangible interaction theory and its phenomenological conceptual apparatus [15,63,64,49,26,17], we try to understand what interaction is for pilots, and the implications for design that can be drawn from this understanding. We form hypotheses, based on their utterances, on what it means precisely for pilots to "be in the world" as "lived bodies". We then frame what this implies for the design of the future interactive cockpit. We discuss a set of challenges for tangible design such as the use of haptics, rich representations, physical objects, sensor-based design or space-based externalizations. We propose a set of key concepts, such as compressed externalization, customized context-aware interaction, rhythmic structures and a protected space of interaction.

After describing the context of the study and the methods we applied, we provide key observations on themes that emerged as relevant for the framing of tangible interaction in the airliner cockpit. Then we propose an interpretation of our findings about perception and action using phenomenological concepts. Finally, we discuss tangible design perspectives for the cockpit of the future as informed by our key observations and interpretation.

TEI '18, March 18–21, 2018, Stockholm, Sweden
© 2018 Association for Computing Machinery.
ACM ISBN 978-1-4503-5568-1/18/03…$15.00
https://doi.org/10.1145/3173225.3173229

RELATED WORK

In a context of significant changes in pilot-system interfaces, research on cockpit design addresses human factors issues [59] on complexity (workload and errors involved in concurrent tasks) [45], human-centered or adaptive automation [6,60,36,11,39], and new interaction paradigms. [4,55,38,40,5,8]. Closer to our approach, ethnographic studies describe pilots activity. Hutchins et al. study distributed cognition in the activity [34,32] and how speech and gestures combine to build a coherent interaction, and Nomura et al. analyze the use of paper in the cockpit [52].

In addition to these lines of research, this work also draws on tangible interaction research using phenomenology to frame embodied dimensions of being-in-the world, i.e. where interaction finds its meaning and value in given situations within the physical and social world [15]. It also relates to embodiment as used for the analysis of interactions in collaboration when people are co-located [27,58], where the term "embodied action" is then used to name the publicly available, meaningful actions, such as talking, touching, drawing, or moving around. Studying embodied interaction may also help to establish an understanding of how computing is intertwined with human users and the world [18] and to investigate the active role of the body as a present-at-hand tool [54]. This work finally relies on tangible interaction themes as a design space to be explored, in particular regarding the perceptual-motor-centered concerns, looking more closely at bodily interaction with objects, sensory richness and action potential together with space-centered views discussing the combination and architecture of real space with virtual displays [28].

CONTEXT

Airliner cockpit: a specific workspace

An airliner is typically operated by a crew of two pilots; one, the Pilot-In-Command (PIC), is the captain, while the other is the supporting First Officer (FO). Furthermore, at any time during the flight, the pilots may perform two roles and associated tasks. The Pilot Flying (PF) is the pilot in control of the flight trajectory and the Pilot Monitoring (PM) is responsible for monitoring the current and projected flight path, the energy and the system states of the aircraft. The air crew ensure the security and safety, the smooth running of the flight to the destination airport and the comfort of the passengers. On commercial flights, pilots collaboratively perform five major activities: aircraft piloting (most often with autopilot), navigation (managing and tracking the flight route), aircraft system monitoring, communication with air-traffic controllers and ground support, and accomplishment of the company mission.

Cockpit ergonomics: posture, perception and gestures

To conduct these activities, pilots interact with the aircraft systems through specialized interfaces on the flight deck. The two pilots seat side by side, in front of the dashboard and facing outside. The flight crew seats are electrically and manually adjustable; however, each pilot ultimately remains in a fixed position, strapped on their seat and inserted under the dash. This position enables him/her to lean toward the dash or turn toward another crew member, but ultimately restricts their actions to the attributed controls. The seat height is adjusted to ensure that the operator's eyes are exactly aligned with the standard point of visual fixation, accessing equally the inside and the outside of the aircraft.

Toward the digitalization of pilot-system interfaces

In the 1980s, the Glass Cockpit concept radically changed the flight deck interfaces of commercial aircraft, replacing dozens of analog mechanical instruments by a digital display of the aircraft system information. The data are grouped into functional units and displayed on specialized screens, dedicated to each of the crew's main activities. The crew interacts with these systems and data through physical controllers: knobs, switches, pull buttons or sticks. These finely tuned physical control devices have proven their effectiveness for pilot-system interaction, situational awareness and cooperative work, even in degraded contexts of use, such as poor flight conditions, instability, degraded vision (smoke), pilot fatigue, high cognitive load or stress.

Touch-based cockpit: a new challenge for aeronautics

The increasing complexity of aircraft systems leads to a more integrative approach with an aggregation of cockpit systems. In particular, the continuous increase in data and functions available for pilots requires more flexible information display and interactions, that have been recently proposed using touch screens [71,24,40,5]. Versatile designs may be used in a variety of civil and military avionics platforms, and allow manufacturers to build powerful, flexible and innovative product lines for the cockpit at a lower cost. The new touch-based interfaces have many advantages: direct interaction on data, multitouch gestures, shared access, adaptivity to the flight context and easier maintenance. Nevertheless, tactile interaction results in reduced mutual awareness and has severe limitations in critical contexts. Unlike physical controls, which benefit from the sense of touch and proprioception, such interactive screens are unsuited for eyes-free interaction, do not favor mutual awareness and crew collaboration, and are unreliable in dynamic environments subject to vibrations and acceleration [1,69,5,8,9,68]. Yet, in the context of air safety, life-critical systems demand reliability both in normal and degraded operational situations.

The Airtius project

Funded by the French research agency and an aeronautical industry research consortium, the aim of the Airtius project is to contribute to the evolution of airliner cockpits while guaranteeing air safety. Its technical objective is to explore a mixed interactive approach for safety-critical contexts, based on both touchscreens and physical components (deformable surface, emerging part, physical feedback, connected object) to ensure greater consideration of sensory motor skills and enable more effective crew collaboration. A first step of this project resulted in a structured design space for pilot-system interactions, classifying the design properties of physical interaction depending on relevant usability, safety and industrial requirements [68].

STUDY

The study is based on observations, interviews and participatory workshops organized with 8 airline pilots. Previous project data and observations involving more than 30 pilots were also used as a basis for understanding the activity [10,67,44]. Observations were run either in flight or in airliner simulators. They were all videotaped (5 hours of video), and partially transcribed. Around 20 hours of contextual interviews were conducted, linked to simulator sessions or workshops. They were first transcribed (~ 450 pages) then around 260 quotes were extracted. During 6 workshops, pilots were invited to contribute to reflection, either by providing feedback on preliminary prototypes or design drawings, or by participating in brainstorming and prototyping activities. Quite often, contextual interviews were informally conducted during workshops, letting a pilot report on a recent situation which s/he recalled, triggered by an aspect explored during the session.

As a first analysis step that was aimed at gaining a closer and shared knowledge of the data, the quotes extracted from the transcriptions were classified in a relational database into main topics and subtopics, using an online web application to share data. Topics were selected through an open coding approach, coming either from the activity (safety, cognitive load, monitoring, situational awareness, decision), or from the project focus on tangible interaction (action-perception, shape, space, gestures) or also as emerging topics, such as rhythm, speech or control. Based on this first classification step, we were able to highlight a set of key characteristics that we analyze in the next sections. We also held 10 design meetings where we related key observed characteristics and tangible design questions. Finally, design explorations and tool implementations were made through five 1-month and two 3-months student projects, most of them also involving pilots and performed by students in aeronautics.

KEY OBSERVED CHARACTERISTICS

The insights we have gained from this study[1] are as follows.

I. Status of sensations and body

We observed the characteristics of embodiment in airliner pilot actions and decisions. We distinguish two types of situation: situations where the pilot is in a monitoring role or in a phase of the flight where time is available, which typically occurs during cruise (*I.a,I.d,I.f*); and secondly, situations with a high demand on active piloting and real-time actions (*I.e,I.g*). These two types of situation may be intertwined, and are often distributed among PF and PM.

I.a) Indirect instrumented perceptions. The airliner pilots highlight the air safety requirement to always rely on indirect perception through instruments (this is in contrast to VFR pilots). Proprioception or visual perception looking out from the window is potentially illusory [21], and, as one pilot explained: *"You mustn't believe your sensations, you may experience an illusion, believe your instrument."* (1). Pilots are even more confident in exact, digital information abstractly provided on their displays, such as a numerical value, rather than a synthetic visual representation. One pilot said that *"a representation of relief is an improvement but you still need to check your security altitudes."* (2). The only sense that pilots seem to trust is the tactile sense, that enables them to differentiate controls or buttons through their form (Figure 1), as one of them commented: *"you know that the button with larger notches is the speed"* (3).

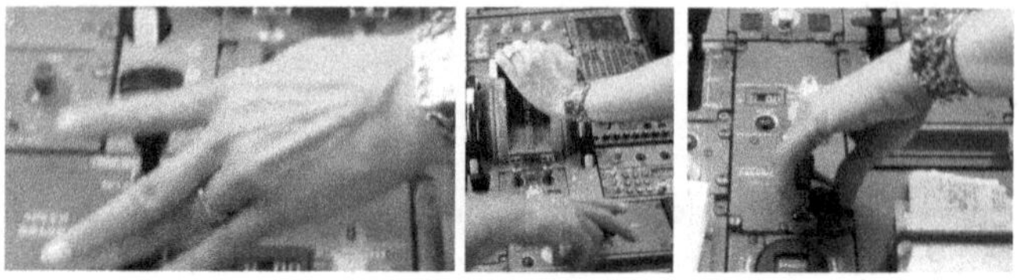

Figure 1. Using the form properties of the physical controls: a) flap; b) throttle; c) parking break.

I.b) Body considered as technical. Pilots may describe their body in a technical way, for instance explaining that it is not provided with sensors, as in this description of landing: *"Landing is still a kinesthetic phase. We don't have sensors that give us the sensations of the plane, our sensors are ourselves. So, how are we going to feel this plane?"* (4). In another example, a pilot uses the metaphor of a sensor that would inform of the other pilot's nervousness with their hand on the stick: *"As we don't have an instrument to tell us about 'the other pilot's stick activity', you have to look"* (5).

I.c) Reluctance towards body-based interaction. During participatory design workshops, we noted that pilots were reticent towards ideas involving interaction through their own body, such as palm-based interaction [23]. One of them explained that when in a degraded context, for instance under stress, you cannot anticipate how the body would react, explaining for instance that palm-based interaction would be impossible if the pilot clenched his hands.

I.d) Gestures for perception. Perception of information is described by a pilot through actions and gestures to reach and catch the data, sometimes within a rhythmic cycle of fast operations, as illustrated by this quote: *"In fact when we say that we 'are looking'... we know what we are looking for [...] you go and take the information you need, you put it in your head, you come back to your instruments."* (6), where the pilot explained that they capture the information, rather than look at it, illustrating their explanation with a repeated grasping gesture. About scanning the instruments a pilot said: *"muscular with the eyes, it won't be enough"*. They need to touch the displays and controls: *"we'll go like this; we'll touch the panel, there, there, that's like that"* (7).

I.e) Sensations needed for piloting actions. In contrast with abstract perception, concrete sensations are put forward in actions involving intense control, where pilots need to feel their movements and their body. In such situations, as one pilot described, they need to *"be one with the plane"* (8), to *"feel"* it

[1] Quotes are referred to by an ID, their full text (original and translated) is available as an auxiliary file.

(4). One pilot described such a situation: *"We had a real sensation of control* [grasping gesture with the left hand]*, all the senses were ... adapted ...* [hands clasped] *to the plane... what was going on outside was represented by the action on the stick* [activating the stick]*... and there's a correlation between what you see* [points] *what you feel* [right hand fingers tight on his leg] *and what you act on* [right hand indicates left hand]*"* (9). This pilot explains: *"when you say sensation: it is an effort on the stick, it is muscular"* (10). It has to be noted that this highlighting of sensation occurs in control loops where the pilot suffers the situation and follows the plane, where actions are not entirely voluntary. Landing is the phase with the least control: *"the last second before impact... before touchdown [...] you can't control it any more... you can feel whether it'll go well or not."* (11). The embodied nature of this situation is underlined as a lack of an objective technical sensor: *"there is no instrument that could give us that information at that moment – it's what you experience – the speed of the runway rising* [hits the back of his hand on his palm]*"* (11).

I.f) Sensations optional for voluntary actions. In contrast, actions involving switches or rotary buttons are not considered as requiring sensations, since they are fully controlled: *"it's an objective you give yourself, we'll display something", "it's that we have gone and displayed something on purpose* [makes a gesture towards the instrument with tightened fingers] *it is not something that is done in ... how could you say that, in the form of sensations"* (12).

I.g) Role of the eyes. Eyes play a role in physical situation of control: *"'Being one with the plane' as an image means: this plane, you put it where your eyes lead you. [...]If you decide to land it in a certain place, well, you just have to target the place [...] you just have to act, and the plane will go where you placed your eyes."* (13). As explained by Gibson [22], sight targeting a runway in a landing glide builds an optical array that is invariable at the aiming point, and this invariance, created by sight, is similar to the artificial horizon symmetry indicator of the PFD that the pilot has to keep aligned (they call it *"keep the ball centered"*). Here again the body has a technical role similar to that of an instrument.

II. Externalization and speech

Oral communication in pilot activity is primordial and has been already widely studied (e.g [50, 33], to cite a few). We are only interested here in properties of oral communication between pilots that we feel are relevant for tangible design. Almost all interaction involving collaborative decisions or collaboration design (mutual and situational awareness, etc.) is based on verbal communication, as a formalized (and recorded) yet flexible tool. Speech has also a significant connection with temporal structures, as we describe later.

II.a) Oral communication as externalization. During interviews, pilots repeatedly use verbs denoting speech: they explain that they "say", "tell", "report" something. For instance, instead of simply describing actions while tuning a parameter (such as speed), they state: *"He **says** 'speed'. The other pilot **replies**: 'I'm correcting that.'"* (14). This highlights how pilots need to bring their representations into a shared and perceptible space, externalizing their thoughts in a way quite similar to Air Traffic Controllers using paper strips to collaborate [46]. Speech has a display role, in the absence of a central shared area in current cockpits, as illustrated by the comment from a pilot: *"you cannot trust the other pilot, who **says** he has got the proper folder hierarchy"* (15), although speech may miss important aspects *"we are each on our own side, we each have an EFB and when the other pilot, for example, wants to describe a trajectory we lack some visual elements"* (16). This display role is enforced through the use of narrative forms. Indeed, reporting about the way they collaborate, pilots sometimes almost equate a briefing to a story that is told: *"the briefing during which you **tell** how you see the situation, you **tell** how we have understood everything, and what we are going to do"* (17). As a result of this display role, similar to the one of a screen, oral communication is also a means for cross-checking (as a matter of fact, ATCo do not rely so heavily on oral communication. Except for inter-sector or inter-center communications they might not need to, since they know each other very well, as opposed to pilots).

II.b) Utterances as control actions, while independent from the system. Oral communication has a primary active role during the flight, but unfolds without any connection to the aircraft systems (at least to a certain extent since it is recorded). Decisions also occur through oral communication, which pilots describe as *"one to one"* communication (18), meaning that it is a task that is disconnected from the systems, yet a structured one. In briefings, an action plan is turned into an oral encoding that stands for itself and should not be interrupted. Doubtful aspects should be dealt with beforehand. *"When you're ready for the briefing, you are ready and it's all set. [...] and you are not going to say stop, because at the end of the day, a briefing is something that's almost held sacred, as it's our action plan."* (19). Switching the roles from PF to PM and the reverse merely involves an utterance, such as: *"my control, your ATC"* and utterances have a role in procedures, e.g : *"The fact of saying 'flaps' in the checklist 'after start' triggers a change in the items of 'before take-off' checklist"* (20). Oral communication also has a validation role, too, with statements such as *"gear down"* (21), as a valid display of the state of the system.

III. Embodied temporal and rhythmic structures

As demonstrated by Gibson [22], there is nothing such as abstract time, but rather the perception of a succession of events, moves or changes. Therefore time is perceived through its effects starting with, in the case of a flight, continuous changes in location. Obviously, activity is shaped by the duration and phases of the flight and by concerns related to time, while expressed in various units: this is the case for fuel, distance and speed. Finally, many pilot tasks are constrained by synchronization and real-time events.

III.a) Rhythms as an embodied resource. A prominent temporal aspect that we were able to note was that pilot activity is structured through rhythms. This is not only through temporal patterns repeated over time, as in many collaborative and time dependent activities [57], but also as an embodied resource and capacity, through speech or gestures. This helps to support various tasks, such as visual scanning to check instruments through a predetermined path. The repetition of *"we touch"* in the following quote, underlined with bodily touch gestures says something about these embodied rhythms: *"In fact, we touch when we go on the throttle [...] we go and to touch... we go like this, like this... we go and touch... it's like this, like this... we touch... you see it's* ***like a sort of music"*** (7). Together with this rhythmic sequence the pilot underlined the embodied nature of the task, explaining that scanning is not only visual, but also tactile, tactile being more muscular than the use of the eyes only. The sequence is also compared to music, i.e. something that you learn by heart, ensuring some physical automation to obtain a safe and exhaustive check. We indeed noticed several associations of *rhythms* and *monitoring* tasks, illustrating that rhythms, as embodied routines, are a resource to support pilot work. Highlighting its rhythmic structure, a pilot also compared the briefing to a *"chronology"*, i.e. a temporal structure where elements are arranged in the order of time and with a given pace: *"well we build that chronology as we go through the charts"* (22). A rhythmic structure is also observable, using repetitions and associated with speech (*"you talk"*), in this description using a spatial metaphor comparing the arrival sequence to a physical thread: *"it's as if we unwound a thread from where we are to where we're going... so we talk about the descent, we talk about the approach, we talk about the final..."* (23).

III.b) Collaborative synchronization patterns. Rhythms and temporal structures also help in synchronizing collaboration [51,57]. Pilots have an embodied knowledge of task durations, and as the tasks are organized in a linear way, they know when they will be able to cross-check and resynchronize each other: *"You've got your flight path, the runway in use is that long, so I have to take-off with so much thrust and such a flap setting. So it all goes together in fact, therefore you can imagine that in any case we will have to cross-check the other pilot's task."* (24). Pilots first need to perform independent parallel individual tasks, afterwards, they are able to share, synchronize, and cross-check, because "[they] *have to remain independent,* [they] *cannot rely on the other pilot only."* (15).

IV. Embodied anticipation of lacks of time

IV.a) Externalization for anticipation. Spatialization helps to anticipate any lack of time in preparing ready to use action plans. These plans take the form of " control structures " to be instantiated later. In some companies such as Air France, pilots even have control structures at hand, called " FORDEC " for Fact, Options, Decisions, Execution, Control. There are times for preparation actions, too: *"So now it's time for me to tell my copilot that if* [...] *we'll* [...]*"* (25). However, spatial and temporal resources are also subject to a trade-off: when no time is left, spatialization is no longer possible, resulting in a compressed style of externalization that involves mostly language or gestures.

IV.b) Gestures for anticipation. Anticipation continuously occurs in gestures that may simultaneously perform a task, such as monitoring the throttle (Boeing) and be ready for other ones, such as deictic ones for checks (Figure 2.b).

V. Embodied use of the cockpit space

With training, pilots know precisely the cockpit shape and dimensions, the position of each panel; they are able to automatically locate controls without using their eyes (Figure 2.a): *"These are gestures that are done so often... the amplitude, the position...* [the hands] *fall automatically in the right place."* (26), even more so when commands are grouped logically in subsystems, or when their distance is consistent with the standard position of the pilot's body: *"You know when you are piloting and you look outside, your hand will fall on the weather radar, and you'll be able to set the tilt* [antenna angle] *without looking."* (27).

Figure 2. a) Bodily use of the internal physical space of the cockpit; b) anticipation in gestures.

FRAMING QUESTIONS TOWARDS EMBODIMENT

Prior to drawing implications for designing tangible interactions for airliner cockpits, we need to reflect on how to account for our key observed characteristics, in particular regarding: 1. the status of sensation and body in both perception and action and 2. the level of awareness and control involved in pilots' actions. For this purpose, we attempt in this section to build an interpretation of our findings using theoretical work, to help us rephrase what embodied interaction may mean for airline pilots.

Phenomenological account of perception and action.

During our study, we became aware that pilots experience a dual embodied space, which has a deep impact on perception and action in the cockpit.

The proximal embodied space

The first element is formed by the surrounding internal space of the cockpit. This protected living space can be considered as a bubble, where natural laws apply. Elements such as walls, openings, fittings, instruments, but also pilots or embedded objects, all are part of a continuous, consistent and stable space. Inside this proximal space, perceptual and physical access is direct. It is encoded in the pilot's body by the thorough knowledge of their place of work and by the skills resulting from constantly repeated procedures, postures and gestures: the pilot's hand that automatically falls on the appropriate control, the gesture-gaze coordination that crosses the flight deck or the body-based collaborative work between the air crew members. In this internal space, pilots trust and make full use of their sensations and physical capacities, they can even get up or move if needed. This part of the space where pilots interact shows the usual features and properties of the human physical space, even for degraded contexts where visual or physical access is made difficult by e.g, instability or fire.

The outer strange space

The second part of this dual embodied and perceptive space is the outer of the cockpit. Strapped into their seat at the flight controls, the pilots become an extension of the aircraft itself, like a centaur, projected at high speed through the sky, a "non-human" space. In this unstable egocentric world, landmarks are weaker, less numerous, moving, inaccurate (cf. cloud masses) and without measure. In this outer space, only visual access is available to pilots, at a distance, and, as they experience spatial disorientation very often, pilots tend to distrust their perception.

From abstract perception to extended body

Our analysis of the different status of sensations according to the control situation (*I.a, I.e*) is consistent with this concept of a dual space. Merleau-Ponty's theory of perception [49], as applied for instance in Svanæs work [63,64], may also provide a coherent account of our findings. This view considers perception as active, based on the whole body and intentional. In particular, it provides a concept of the body as not only able to adapt to technical artefacts, but as extending itself through devices. This view is in line with the way airline pilots distance their perceptions. They do not "trust their eyes" to get critical information because they are in fact "blind" when flying at over 600 mph in poor visibility conditions. As a consequence, they perform an active scanning of their instruments, in a manner analogous to ocular movements. Therefore we can refine our analysis: perception is not exactly "indirect" or "abstract" (*I.a*). The PFD being an extension of his sensory apparatus for the airline pilot, perception is adapted rather than indirect, or more exactly *transferred* to instruments.

A distributed bodily space

We also need to account for a contrasting need for "feeling" during real-time piloting phases (*I.f-g*). Taking our reflection one step further and viewing the instruments as an extension of the pilots, could *the plane itself* be considered as *an extension of the pilot's body, as an object modifying their bodily space* [63]? In these phases, being "one with the plane", the pilot needs strong physical feedback with their proprioceptive senses that are tightly coupled with the machine. At the same time, pilots distrust their own perception and give an account of their body in technical terms (*I.b*), so that their "real" body [2] tends to fade (see [54]). This distributed and highly coupled body may also explain why, while research demonstrates that moving one's body increases one's cognitive abilities [61], pilots may be reluctant to the idea of not staying seated, preferring to stay in contact with the equipment.

Maintaining an envelope

The issue of control is constantly present in pilots' work, as shown in many of the characteristics described above. However, it remains difficult to define exactly what control is. Another approach is to look at what control is not, to understand what is removed when things are not under control. It turns out that "not controlling" may result in situations where an envelope [47] of standard, expected or predictable behavior is lost, leading to a situation subject to dispersion or explosion. For pilots the core objective is indeed to maintain the plane in a safe envelope and trajectory to carry passengers safely to a location on the ground. Distance from bodily sensations (*I.a*), visibility of actions and reflections through oral utterances (*II.a*) and physical control in piloting actions (*I.g*) all contribute to this control: they both keep pilots in the loop and provide the tools required for anticipating and taking appropriate decisions.

Level of awareness and intention in actions

We believe that phenomenology again provides an interesting way to account for the manner pilots manage the problem of control, combining two concepts. The first one is the distinction by Heidegger [26] of *ready-at-hand* and *present-at-hand*, as already used in HCI [15,54,64]. The second one is the duality of *abstract / concrete* actions from Merleau-Ponty [49], has used by Svanæs (as an equivalent to *foreground / background* duality [63,54]) to account for context aware systems [63]. These two pairs of concepts are relevant for the issue of control, but *foreground/background* is more related to intention, while *ready-at-hand/present-at-hand* is more related to awareness. Given the constant need to maintain this envelope, the control actions and even perception actions performed by pilots show a high degree of awareness. In particular, anticipation tasks involve a present-at-hand mode, and rely on various externalizations through speech, maps, and notes [52].

At the same time, these highly controlled actions are based on many ready-at-hand skills. Automated actions are, however, considered both as critical resources and a potential threat by pilots: *"Doing actions like a robot can lead to errors"* (20). Automation (Flight Director, Auto-Pilot) is also considered by pilots as a ready-at-hand resource that they are happy to collaborate with when required (low visibility, fatigue). However, automation is also a concern: they have to monitor and adapt to it, which involves a significant cognitive load: *"So you have to adapt to the automatisms. And we see all sorts of things in the cockpit. And we can say that the automatism has been badly thought out, that is doesn't cover all cases."* (28). As described by Dourish [15], there is in fact a "*constant interplay between both levels, a variable coupling* [that] *is so crucial that the effective use of tools inherently involves a continual process of engagement, separation, and re-engagements*". Such interplay is also supported through rhythms (*III.a*) that help stay in the loop, and synchronize and switch between action and control.

Foreground vs background actions refer to intended and abstract actions vs indirect but also concrete actions [49,63]. What is considered as foreground according to Merleau Ponty indeed depends on our focus of attention and our intention and not on the physical action itself. Pilots not only show a significant level of awareness in their actions. They also describe them as voluntary, such as taking information from the instruments (*I.a, I.d, I.f*), except for actions that are suffered, such as landing (*I.e*).

In the next section, one of the issues that we discuss is to what extent ready-at-hand and background control modes raise a challenge for tangible interaction design.

IMPLICATIONS FOR DESIGN

Transposing embodied interaction in the sky context.

As a result of these reflections, we can see that, for pilots, meaningful interaction [15] translates to safe, comfortable, efficient and possibly cost efficient flying in a much adapted environment. The voluntary transposition of the body and perception is adapted to piloting and monitoring needs in the proximal and outer spaces, and to the transition back and forth between the two. Consequently, "being in the sky", pilots have to consider their "distributed bodily space" as a controlled tool or subsystem [54]. Flying therefore involves a specific design for embodiment and interaction, where transferring a significant part of the "being in the world" abilities (perception, body) into artefacts is challenging. Translating Merleau-Ponty's statement that "*The body is our general medium for having a world.*" [49, p 146] to being-in-the-sky would thus results in the coupled entity composed of pilot skills and plane subsystems being able to control what has to happen in that world.

Anticipating TEI design for airliner cockpits involves several discussions: 1) pilots expect large improvements from touch-based displays, while knowing their limitations, and " physicalizing " displays raises important *safety issues* [68]; 2) the values of tangible and embodied interaction " in-the-sky ", as described in the previous section, *challenge* the values of TEI " in-the-world "; 3) which are the *key design concepts* that could bring meaningful interaction in the sky context. In the following, we first briefly present the pilot viewpoint on touch-based applications. We then discuss TEI directions informed by our analyses, addressing both design challenges and key concepts.

The pilot viewpoint on touch-based tools

In our study, pilots discussed the trade-offs using touch-based applications against old fashion specialized displays. They believe in their advantages for taking context and system state into account dynamically. They are eager to use electronic checklists appearing at the appropriate time and place, *"checklist that comes up on the ECAM"* (29), rather than having over 50 paper-based and hard to memorize checklists (*"On Boeing we've got an enormous manual."*). Touch-based applications could also prevent paper scattering, as explained by a pilot showing how he would *"hold"* an electronic checklist in place with his hand (30). The same applies for maps, where a single zoomable document would be preferred: *"Because here today at Orly, we have 8 or 9 ground maps, in the end, the very best thing would be just a single large map on which we could zoom in an out."* (32). Globally speaking, touch-based applications tend to be preferred for long-term strategic management actions. In contrast, a "fully digitalized" MCDU (Multifunction Control and Display Unit), or any other short-term tactical controller, would result in a less-integrated tool [3], where no link (causal, mechanical) can be made to what is going to happen: *"We could say for all short term management, for example everything on the MCDU which is in front ... in my opinion .. it's not acceptable that this is digital [. . .] when you touch [a physical button], if you get the wrong button and you're flying at the same time, you say to yourself: 'something is not right'. We'll make the connection. "* (3).

Challenges and key concepts for embodied interaction in the future cockpit

In the following, we draw implications for design based on our analyses of transferred perception, awareness levels in control, compressed externalization in speech, disconnected and free interactions in speech and gestures, and embodiment through rhythmic temporal structures.

1. Sensory-rich interactions

The distance maintained by the pilots toward their own bodily perception, while understandable as transferred perception, raises challenges for TEI design. First, designs involving haptics may be explored with caution: pilots value enhanced perception [43], rather than enhanced reality. Pilots are suspicious towards expressive representations [29], even for abstract tasks [12,7] which advises against using physical representations of digital data [66], in line with studies that highlight the potential safety outcome of synthetic vision systems [4, 55]. Using reality-based interaction [37] would consist in applying naïve physics, which is debatable for the highly trained engineers that pilots also are. Above all, it would be probably irrelevant for the modified and abstract awareness of their body and environment. Finally, pilots are quite suspicious towards direct interaction using the body, be it only the arms [25] or the palms [23]. A pilot indeed criticized a palm-based prototype for selecting frequencies: *"How the other pilot can check if it's been done properly, under stress if he is uptight, how he's going to tense his muscles, this can cause problems."* (31). Relying on eyes-free, proprioceptive and kinesthetic control of physical shapes, as explored for instance through dynamic shape-changing interfaces [56,68], seems however a promising key concept (*I.a*, Figure 1).

2. Control, sensor-based interaction

TEI discusses control in several ways: 1) in standard models [35], the physical object is said to serve as representation and *control* for a digital one; 2) graspability is a founding theme [20]: to grasp is a physical gesture to hold an object, with a precise control thanks to the shape of fingers; 3) shared visibility and multiple access points [27,28] provide distributed control. Control is also discussed as an issue in TEI when using context-aware systems [16,63]. The background mode of control involved in such systems actually challenges the need for pilots to interact in foreground mode, especially when using instruments. As one of them said about interaction with such instruments: *"There are no involuntary actions"* (12). As a result, we explore context-aware features, such as gesture-based or gaze-based interactions, as long as they can be controlled and customized by pilots [16, 63], and provide a reasonable level of system state awareness.

3. Externalization, spatial-based design

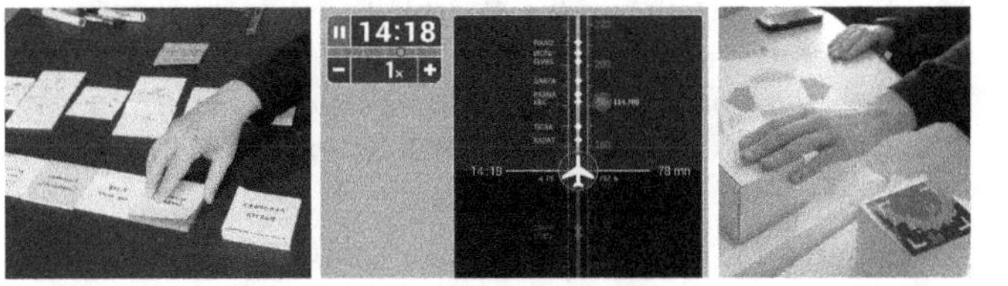

Figure 3. a) Prototyping a tangible briefing; b) a timeline; c) tangible cubes for data management and crew collaboration.

Distributed cognition in the cockpit has been studied [52], showing how pilots use paper and physical cues to support activity. A pilot who had a demonstration a tangible augmented system for ATC [31] told us how Boeing pilots sometimes use a dust-cloth as a constraint [53] to prevent them from wrongly changing the current frequency on the radio panel. We are interested in supporting distributed cognition, possibly using properties of oral communication as a major means of externalization. We indeed observed that speech is a lightweight, *compressed* and efficient way of externalizing cognitive concerns, which challenges spatial-based interaction, especially when using physical objects. During a workshop, we explored the idea of a tangible tool to run briefing (Figure 3.a), but the pilot was highly reserved towards the idea. *"In such conditions, over 4 flight legs, … well I mean, it's a bit of a marathon. It's not that you have no time, but you have to manage your effort. And you are not going to lose … you can't consider every case. For such a briefing, you just need to highlight what is important. We prefer a strategy where you say, ok, something has changed. You do a holding pattern, you take the time to do everything properly to make sure it's all as it should be."* (33). With this key concept of compressed and lightweight externalization for short-term physical tasks in mind, we explored ideas involving spatial interaction for long-term tasks. Spatialization of time has been studied through a timeline in a student project, involving two pilots in design sessions. A first pilot participated in a brainstorm to generate ideas and detailed scenarios about the features of the timeline. The second was invited for a design walkthrough of the developed prototype (Fig. 3.b), and emphasized the usefulness of these tool for collaboration, mutual awareness and sharing of the flight data. The idea of a physical cube aimed at reducing data complexity and supporting collaboration was explored with another pilot (Fig. 3.c). He confirmed their relevance as customizable tools to interact with aircraft systems for long-term strategic tasks. Relevant properties of these cubes include leveraging pilots spatial inferencing skills [33,41] while avoiding spatial cluttering.

4. Protected space of interaction

Another important property of speech is that it is "disconnected" from the system (*II.b*). This property is all the more true for gestures, which are currently an essential resource for control, monitoring and collaboration, and are not recorded at all. This refers to a potential need for a protected interaction space, where interactions could be modulated into various types, from free annotation to speech, involving tasks that already include flexibility, individual preferences and practices towards procedures, for a pilot *"has their own favorite habits."* (34). In such a protected space, levels of user control can also be flexible, letting pilots decide freely to be sensored or not [63]. Pilots mention the value of having tools separated from the aircraft systems. Speaking about the physical QRH (Quick Reference Handbook), that you can hold in your hands, a pilot valued it in case of degraded contexts, when there is no longer control available *"And in some way, it's a physical thing that is independent from the plane. Something which comes onto the screen, you may say, 'ok, it is still linked to the plane'. Here it's something serious, but it's dematerialized from the aircraft and physically I am holding it in my hands."* (35). This concept of proximal and protected interaction space, while not completely "offline" [19], seems to be the right place for tangible design.

5. Embodied temporal and rhythmic structures.

We analyzed the observed rhythms in the activity as an important embodied resource. We see in the properties of rhythmic structures a potential to help the pilots go back and forth from automatic, background or ready-at-hand interactions to present-at-hand and voluntary actions. We have started to explore how to translate these properties into our design space, using principles related to homogeneous repetitive physical structures providing a spatial equivalent of a duration. This type of structures, which are the objective of on-going work, could provide the pilots with a meaningful frame for interaction and collaboration.

CONCLUSION

In this paper, we seek to understand pilots' activity in order to inform TEI in the future cockpit. A first level of analysis is provided through key findings, based on interviews where pilots describe their activity in their own words. At a second level of analysis, we build an interpretation of elements related to perception and control using concepts drawn from the phenomenology of perception and technical actions. In particular, we suggest the idea of a distributed bodily space articulated into two separated environments and involving two levels of perception and action. Based on these key findings and interpretation, we discuss design challenges and concepts for "in-the-sky" embodied interaction. Challenges lie in the emphasis on rich sensations and representations, and in the use of physical objects to support externalization or sensors to build a connected space. Key concepts include kinesthetic control of graspable shapes, compressed externalization, customized context-aware interaction, protected interaction space and the use of rhythmic structures.

ACKNOWLEDGMENTS

Special thanks to the pilots who contributed greatly to this research work, and to the French National Research Agency (ANR) and the FRAE who funded the AIRTIUS project.

REFERENCES

1. Alapetite, A., Fogh, R., Zammit-Mangion, D. et al. Direct Tactile Manipulation of the Flight Plan in a Modern Aircraft Cockpit. *In* Proc. of HCI Aero 2012.

2. Allucquere R. S.. 1991. Will the real body please stand up?: boundary stories about virtual cultures. In *Cyberspace*, Michael Benedikt (Ed.). MIT Press, Cambridge, MA, USA 81-118.
3. Angelini, L., Lalanne, D., van den Hoven, E., Abou Khaled, O. and Mugellini, E. Move, hold and touch: a framework for tangible gesture interactive systems. Machines, 2015, vol. 3, no 3, p. 173-207.
4. Bailey, R. E., Parrish, R. V., Kramer, L. J., Harrah, S.D., & Arthur III, J. J. 2002. Technical challenges in the development of a NASA synthetic vision system concept.
5. Barbé J., Mollard, R. and Wolff, M. 2014. Ergonomic approaches to integrate touch screen in future aircraft cockpits. JESA volume 48 11/2014.
6. Billings, C.E. 1997. Aviation Automation. The Search for a Human-Centered Approach. Lawrence Erlbaum Associates : Mahwah, NJ.
7. Clifton, P. 2014. Designing embodied interfaces to support spatial ability. In *Proceedings of the 8th International Conference on Tangible, Embedded and Embodied Interaction* (TEI '14). ACM, New York, NY, USA, 309-312.
8. Cockburn, A., Gutwin, C., Palanque, P., Deleris, Y., Trask, C., Coveney, A., Yung, M. and MacLean, K. 2017. Turbulent Touch: Touchscreen Input for Cockpit Flight Displays. In *Proceedings of the 2017 CHI Conference on Human Factors in Computing Systems* (CHI '17). ACM, New York, NY, USA, 6742-6753.
9. Cohen, P.R., and McGee, D.R. 2004. Tangible Multimodal Interfaces for Safety-Critical Applications. Communications of the ACM 47.
10. Conversy, S., Chatty, S., Gaspard-Boulinc, H. and Vinot, J.L. 2014. The accident of flight AF447 Rio-Paris: a case study for HCI research. In *Proceedings of the 26th Conference on l'Interaction Homme-Machine* (IHM '14). ACM, New York, NY, USA, 60-69.
11. Crow, J., Javaux and D., Rushby, J. 2000. Models and Mechanized Methods that Integrate Human Factors into Automation Design. In *Proceedings of the International Conference on Human-Computer Interaction in Aeronautics*: HCI-Aero 2000.
12. van Dijk, D., Moussette, C., Kuenen, S. and Hummels, C. 2013. Radical clashes: what tangible interaction is made of. In Proc. of the 7th International Conference on Tangible, Embedded and Embodied Interaction (TEI '13). ACM, New York, NY, USA, 323-326.
13. van Dijk, J., van der Lugt, R., and Hummels, C. 2014. Beyond distributed representation: embodied cognition design supporting socio-sensorimotor couplings. In *Proceedings of the 8th International Conference on Tangible, Embedded and Embodied Interaction* (TEI '14). ACM, New York, NY, USA, 181-188.
14. van Dijk, J. and Hummels, C. 2017. Designing for Embodied Being-in-the-World: Two Cases, Seven Principles and One Framework. In *Proceedings of the Eleventh International Conference on Tangible, Embedded, and Embodied Interaction* (TEI '17). ACM, New York, NY, USA, 47-56.
15. Dourish, P. (2001): Where the Action Is. The Foundations of Embodied Interaction. MIT Press.
16. Dourish, P. 2004. What we talk about when we talk about context. Personal Ubiquitous Comput. 8, 1 (February 2004), 19-30.
17. Dreyfus, H. L. 1991. Being-in-the-World: A Commentary on Heidegger's Being and Time, Division I. The MIT Press, Cambridge, MA.
18. Fallman, D. 2003. Enabling physical collaboration in industrial settings by designing for embodied interaction. In *Proceedings of the Latin American conference on Human-computer interaction* (CLIHC '03). ACM, New York, NY, USA, 41-51.
19. Fernaeus, Y. and Tholander, J. 2006. "Finding design qualities in a tangible programming space," in Proceedings of CHI06, pp. 447–456, NY: ACM, 2006.
20. Fitzmaurice, G., Ishii, H., Buxton, W. Bricks: laying the foundations for graspable user interfaces. In Proc. of CHI'95.
21. Gibb R, Ercoline B, Scharff L . Spatial disorientation: decades of pilot fatalities . Aviat Space Environ Med 2011 ; 82 : 717 – 24 .
22. Gibson, J. J. (1979), The Ecological Approach to Visual Perception, Boston, MA: Houghton-Mifihin.
23. Gustafson, S., Rabe B., Baudisch, P., Understanding palm-based imaginary interfaces: the role of visual and tactile cues when browsing. In Proc. of CHI '13.
24. Hamon, A., Palanque, P., Andrea, R., Barboni, E., Cronel, M. and Navarre, D. MultiTouch interactions for control and display in interactive cockpits: issues and a proposal. Proceedings of the International Conference on Human Computer Interaction in Aerospace, ACM, Santa Clara, California, 2014, 1-10.
25. Harrison, C., Tan, D. and Morris, D. 2010. Skinput: appropriating the body as an input surface. In *Proceedings of the SIGCHI Conference on Human Factors in Computing Systems* (CHI '10). ACM, New York, NY, USA, 453-462.
26. Heidegger, M. 1927. Being and Time. SUNY Press, Albany, NY. Republished 1996.
27. Hornecker, E. 2005. A design theme for tangible interaction: embodied facilitation. In *Proceedings of the ninth conference on European Conference on Computer Supported Cooperative Work* (ECSCW'05), Hans Gellersen, Kjeld Schmidt, Michel Beaudouin-

Lafon, and Wendy Mackay (Eds.). Springer-Verlag New York, Inc., New York, NY, USA, 23-43.

28. Hornecker, E., Buur, J., Getting a grip on tangible interaction: a framework on physical space and social interaction. In Proc. of CHI '06. ACM.

29. Hornecker, E. 2012. Beyond affordance: tangibles' hybrid nature. In *Proceedings of the Sixth International Conference on Tangible, Embedded and Embodied Interaction* (TEI '12), Stephen N. Spencer (Ed.). ACM, New York, NY, USA, 175-182.

30. Hourlier, S., Guérard, S., Barou, J.L and Servantie, X., 2015. Testing Touch Screens in Realistic Aeronautic Turbulent Conditions (Light to Severe). SAE International Journal of Aerospace 8.

31. Hurter, C., Lesbordes, R., Letondal, C., Vinot, J.L and Conversy, S. 2012. Strip'TIC: exploring augmented paper strips for air traffic controllers. In Proceedings of the International Working Conference on Advanced Visual Interfaces (AVI '12), Genny Tortora, Stefano Levialdi, and Maurizio Tucci (Eds.). ACM, New York, NY, USA, 225-232.

32. Hutchins E. (1995). How A Cockpit Remembers its Speeds. Cognitive Science, 19, 265-288.

33. Hutchins, E. and Palen, L. 1997. Constructing Meaning from Space, Gesture, and Speech. In Discourse, Tools and Reasoning, Resnick L. B. et al. (eds). NATO ASI Series (160), pp 23-40.

34. Hutchins, E. and Klausen, T. 1998: Distributed Cognition in an Airline Cockpit. In Engeström, Middleton (eds.) Cognition and Communication at Work. Cambridge Univ. Press. pp. 15-34.

35. Ishii, H. (2008) Tangible bits: Beyond pixels. In: *Proc. of TEI'08*, Feb 18-20, pp. XV-XXV. New York: ACM.

36. Javaux, D. 1998. Explaining Sarter and Woods classical results. the cognitive complexity of pilot-autopilot interaction on the Boeing 737-EIS," in Procs of Human Error, Safety, and System Development (HESSD98). Seattle, Washington, April 1-2 1998.

37. Jacob, R.J.K, Girouard, A., Hirshfield, L.M, Horn, M.S, Shaer, O., Solovey, E.T. and Zigelbaum, J. Reality-based interaction: a framework for post-WIMP interfaces. In Proc. of CHI '08. ACM.

38. Johnson, N., Wiegmann, D., Wickens, C. 2006. Effects of Advanced Cockpit Displays on General Aviation Pilots' Decisions to Continue Visual Flight Rules Flight into Instrument Meteorological Conditions. In Procs of the Human Factors and Ergonomics Society Annual Meeting. Vol 50, Issue 1, pp. 30 - 34

39. Kaber, D. B., Riley, J. M., Tan, K. W., & Endsley, M. R. 2001. On the design of adaptive automation for complex systems. *International Journal of Cognitive Ergonomics*, *5*(1), 37-57.

40. Kaminani, S. 2011. Human computer interaction issues with touch screen interfaces in the flight deck. in Digital Avionics Systems Conference (DASC), 2011. IEEE/AIAA 30th, (2011), 6B4-1-6B4-7.

41. Kirsh, D. (1995) The intelligent use of space. Artificial Intelligence.

42. Klemmer, S.R., Hartmann, B. and Takayama, L. How bodies matter: five themes for interaction design. DIS '06.

43. Laine, F., Louise, P., Giuliano, S., Chauveau, N. and Deroo, M.. Dispositif d'affichage d'un horizon artificiel. Patent FR3017704 (A1). https://worldwide.espacenet.com/publicationDetails/biblio?II=0&adjacent=true&locale=en_EP&CC=FR&NR=3017704#> (accessed on 26.04.2017)

44. Letondal, C., Zimmerman, C., Vinot J. L., and Conversy, S. 3D visualization to mitigate weather hazards in the flight deck: Findings from a user study. In 2015 IEEE Symposium on 3D User Interfaces (3DUI), Arles, 2015, pp. 27-30.

45. Loukopoulos, L.D., Dismukes, R.K., Barshi, I., 2001. Cockpit interruptions and distractions: a line observation study. In: 11th International Symposium on Aviation Psychology. Columbus, Ohio.

46. Mackay, W.E., Is paper safer? The role of paper flight strips in air traffic control. *ACM Trans. Comput.-Hum. Interact.* 6, 4 (December 1999), 311-340.

47. Maturana, H. R., & Varela, F. J. (1992). The tree of knowledge: The biological roots of human understanding (Rev. ed.). Boston: Shambhala.

48. Mazalek, A. and Van den hoven, E. 2009. Framing tangible interaction frameworks. Artif. Intell. Eng. Des. Anal. Manuf. 23, 3 (August 2009), 225-235.

49. Merleau-Ponty, M. 1962. Phenomenology of Perception. Routledge & Kegan Paul, London, UK.

50. Nevile, M. 2001. Beyond the Black Box: Talk-in-Interaction in the Airline Cockpit. PhD dissertation, Department of Linguistics, Australian National University.

51. Nevile, M. 2007. Action in time: Ensuring timeliness for collaborative work in the airline cockpit. Language in Society.

52. Nomura, S., Hutchins, E. and Holder, B.E. 2006. The uses of paper in commercial airline flight operations. In Proc. of CSCW '06.

53. Norman, D. 1999. Affordance, Conventions, and Design. Interactions, vol. 6, no. 3, pp. 38–43, 1999.

54. Nunez-Pacheco, C. and Loke, L. 2014. Crafting the body-tool: a body-centred perspective on wearable technology. In Proceedings of the 2014 conference on Designing interactive systems (DIS '14). ACM, New York, NY, USA, 553-566.

55. Prinzel III, L. J., Hughes, M. F., Arthur III, J. J., Kramer, L. J., Glaab, L. J., Bailey, R. E. & Uenking, M. D. 2003. Synthetic vision CFIT experiments for GA and commercial aircraft:"A picture is worth a thousand lives". In *Procs of the Human Factors and Ergonomics Society Annual Meeting* (Vol. 47, No. 1, pp. 164-168). Sage CA: Los Angeles, CA: SAGE Publications.

56. Rasmussen, M.K., Pedersen, E.W., Petersen, M.G. Hornbæk, K. Shape-changing interfaces: a review of the design space and open research questions. CHI '12.

57. Reddy, M., and Dourish, P. (2002). A finger on the pulse: Temporal rhythms and information seeking in medical work. In Proceedings of the ACM Conference on Computer Supported Cooperative Work (pp. 344-353).

58. Robertson, T. (1997). Cooperative Work and Lived Cognition: A Taxonomy of Embodied Actions. In Proceedings of the Fifth European Conference on Computer-Supported Cooperative Work (CSCW'97), Lancaster, UK, September 7-11, 1997. Kluwer Academic Publishers, Dordrecht, The Netherlands, pp. 205-220.

59. Salas, E. Jentsch, F. Maurino, D. (eds). 2010. Human Factors in Aviation. Academic Press, Technology & Engineering - 744 pages.

60. Sarter, N. B., & Woods, D. D. (1992). Pilot interaction with cockpit automation: Operational experiences with the flight management system. *The International Journal of Aviation Psychology*, *2*(4), 303-321.

61. Schraefel, m. c. 2014. Burn the chair, we're wired to move: exploring the brain/body connexion for HCI creativity & cognition. In *Proceedings of HCI Korea* (HCIK '15). Hanbit Media, Inc., , South Korea, 153-161.

62. Shaer, O. and Hornecker, E. 2010. Tangible User Interfaces: Past, Present, and Future Directions. *Found. Trends Hum.-Comput. Interact.* 3, 1–2 (January 2010), 1-137.

63. Svanæs, D. 2001. Context-aware technology: a phenomenological perspective. Hum.-Comput. Interact. 16, 2 (December 2001), 379-400.

64. Svanæs, D. 2013. Interaction design for and with *the lived body*: Some implications of Merleau-Ponty's phenomenology. *ACM Trans. Comput.-Hum. Interact.* 20, 1, Article 8 (April 2013), 30 pages.

65. Twenebowa Larssen, A. Robertson, T. and Edwards,J. 2007. The feel dimension of technology interaction: exploring tangibles through movement and touch. In *Proceedings of the 1st international conference on Tangible and embedded interaction* (TEI '07). ACM, New York, NY, USA, 271-278.

66. Ullmer, B. and Ishii, H. 2001. Emerging Frameworks for Tangible User Interfaces. In HCI in the New Millenium, John M. Carroll, Ed. pp. 579–601.

67. Vinot, J.L. Athenes, S. 2012. Legible, are you sure?: an experimentation-based typographical design in safety-critical context. In Proceedings of the SIGCHI Conference on Human Factors in Computing Systems (CHI '12). ACM, New York, NY, USA, pp. 2287–2296.

68. Vinot, J.L, Letondal C.L., Pauchet, S. and Chatty, S. Could tangibility improve the safety of touch-based Interaction? Exploring a new Physical Design Space for Pilot-System Interfaces. In Procs. of HCI Aero 2016.

69. Voelker, S., Øvergård, K.I., Wacharamanotham, C. and Borchers, J. 2015. Knobology Revisited: A Comparison of User Performance between Tangible and Virtual Rotary Knobs. In Proc. Of ITS'15.

70. Wu, A., Jog,J. Mendenhall, D. and Mazalek, A. 2011. A framework interweaving tangible objects, surfaces and spaces. In Proceedings of the 14th international conference on Human-computer interaction: interaction techniques and environments - Volume Part II (HCII'11), Julie A. Jacko (Ed.), Vol. Part II. Springer-Verlag, Berlin, Heidelberg, 148-157.

71. Zammit-Mangion, D., Becouarn, L., Aymeric, B., Fabbri, M. and Bader, J. 2011. A Single Interactive Display Concept for Commercial and Business Jet Cockpits. in 11th AIAA Aviation Technology, Integration, and Operations (ATIO) Conference, American Institute of Aeronautics and Astronautics, 2011.

Cohousing IoT: Design Prototyping for Community Life

Tom Jenkins
Georgia Institute of Technology
Atlanta, GA, USA
tom.jenkins@gatech.edu

ABSTRACT
Cohousing IoT uses research through design to both probe alternative modes of living and prototype speculative domestic Internet of Things devices. These prototype technologies are informed by a public design process that works in two ways. First, it imagines alternatives to existing arrangements of things and devices in the home; and second, it produces prototypes that argue for new roles for internet-connected things that both support and sustain the social life of a cohousing community.

Author Keywords
Cohousing; prototyping; material speculation; Internet of Things; IoT

INTRODUCTION
Cohousing IoT is a research through design project that prototypes social Internet of Things devices for cohousing communities. Cohousing provides a rich context for exploring an Internet of Things—commonly abbreviated IoT—that is designed to support social values in ways that are currently excluded from contemporary technology conversations. Existing home IoT platforms promise seamless interconnectivity, where devices do their part to make human homes and lives simpler, and more efficient. In general, "smart home" technology is designed for what are considered "traditional" homes: free-standing, single-family residences. This narrow definition backs a design philosophy that excludes a great deal of people and their homes that are configured in non-traditional ways.

This paper describes the prototyping goals and material outcomes of designing IoT technologies explicitly for cohousing that postulate community-based alternatives to the contemporary smart home. Cohousing is a type of intentional community that is designed to operate like a village. Residents are active in the community as neighbors, live independently in their own homes, and share ownership of a larger "common house" as well as the community's land. Cohousing is governed via consensus and has shared meals once or twice weekly. In short, cohousing is designed to support strong social connections among and between houses. An environment like this offers a new setting to consider what a domestic Internet of Things could be like. This Internet of Things operates across multiple residences, but only one home. From an organizational standpoint, cohousing is a social covenant grafted on top of a standard condominium agreement. This project asks, "How might a design approach to developing technologies that are structured in a similar, socially-oriented way influence what a domestic Internet of Things might be or could become?"

TEI '18, March 18–21, 2018, Stockholm, Sweden

ACM ISBN 978-1-4503-5568-1/18/03...$15.00
https://doi.org/10.1145/3173225.3173244

COHOUSING
Cohousing offers a way of life that is meant to alleviate the sense of and alienation that is engendered by free-standing single-family homes [18]. It creates connection among neighbors through the arrangement of private and common space, instituting and maintaining strong social norms, and a consensus-based process for community decision-making. Residents own their individual houses while sharing ownership of common spaces. These common spaces include open outside areas and storage facilities as well as a large "common house" used for community events, entertaining, and shared meals. cohousing communities are committed to social values like sharing resources, participating in community life, care, sustainability, and diversity. Weekly meetings for various committees—as well as frequent community-wide meetings—emphasize and reaffirm these values in practice. Together, residents work to maintain the community. Adults are each expected to provide a small amount of their time each month to assist with landscaping, cooking, cleaning, and so on.

Within HCI, efforts at understanding the home have mostly taken place within the boundaries of a dwelling, leaving alternative spatial arrangements and configurations out of the picture. Shifting patterns of contemporary living, influenced by economic, geographic, and demographic factors, have led to new models for habitation becoming more popular. This paper argues that alternative models of living offer a broader understanding of what "home" can be, and help to generate a fresh perspective on how and where domesticity occurs. Further, the Internet of Things provides a testbed for how ideas of social domestic life can be constructed and embedded into technical prototypes.

Figure 1: Germantown Cohousing in Nashville, Tennessee, USA. Individual homes (left), and the common house (right).

Cohousing as a venue for design

As a socially-oriented project that demands architectural, legal, and planning consideration, cohousing communities are designed to support broader community values. Many of these design decisions serve to facilitate a sense of shared community life: Cars stay on the periphery of the property, leaving space between and among the homes to become play areas for children or community social life in general. Common houses are often in the center of the property or near commonly-accessed parts of the plot to facilitate equitable access. Homes face pathways, and front windows in residences are large enough to let neighbors see whether a resident is home to facilitate visiting [10]. Cohousing communities are neighborhoods designed expressly for social interaction [26]. These communities become homes beyond a set of single houses. The common house, for example, is both common space and an extension of an individual residents' home. Cohousing stretches how homes operate in ways that provide provocative and interesting inspiration for IoT design [14].

Designing IoT for cohousing

Through its design, cohousing problematizes the idea of the "smart home." Most visions of the domestic IoT extend from Weiser's vision of the computer for the 21st Century [25] or Tolmie's notion of "unremarkable computing" [22]. To this point, descriptions of what future life might be like in IoT-enabled smart homes offer standalone residences with garages and pools as being representative of "typical" domestic life. From this perspective, much of domestic technology design has focused on the homeowner's ability to control their premises, either for security reasons (with devices like IP cameras, or for efficiency and awareness (using devices like the Nest Thermostat). Cohousing offers a different understanding of what a smart home might be. Here, there are three different kinds of life in the community: public life in a city at large, public/private life within the cohousing community, and the private life of the individual family home. Discrete houses in a community couple with shared space. Cohousing features like the common house exemplify this variety of semi-permeability. Considering how these three layers interact serves as a model for how designing alternative IoT for extreme users might eventually support more broadly-applicable domestic technologies in communities [5,17].

One way to design IoT technologies for cohousing is to consider the role that the things themselves are taking on. What might it mean to create objects that actively participate in constructing and perpetuating intentional community? Cohousing consists of a public that is driven by certain values, and is invested in particular issues and matters of concern [24]. Designing for and supporting these matters of concern means that the objects themselves must represent and address these social concerns in relevant, material ways. From this perspective, IoT designed for cohousing communities can participates in the public life of community itself [15].

A cohousing perspective also serves to complicate smart homes by emphasizing the connection among and between residences, rather than simply taking houses as having an "inside" and an "outside." Many current services and platforms operate through the fringes of the home and make the home permeable. Contemporary smart home technologies like Amazon's Alexa or Dash buttons provide access to massive industrial infrastructure for purchasing and shipping. The social values of cohousing provide an alternative ways to approach this infrastructure [12]. The home's relationship to water, electricity, internet, gas, mail, and so on might be productively reframed by considering social settings and how services could be designed to support broader community life. Here, designers should approach "smart homes" as providing more than access to product or service infrastructure, but instead as offering endpoints to social or civic infrastructure [14].

How things play a role in the IoT

Designing for the IoT provides a means to examine how the computational relationships between things operate to produce social effects in domestic settings. The IoT relies on and generates infrastructure, but in a nascent product space, it is *proto-infrastructure*. Among others, Star notes that "infrastructure" has characteristics of transparency, standardization, being built from an installed base, and that it only becomes visible on breakdown [20]. In an environment where domestic IoT is currently contested and partial as multiple companies develop their own proprietary hub and spoke systems, the IoT is gesturing towards becoming infrastructure. It is assembling complex mixtures of standards (Wi-Fi, Bluetooth, electrical power), and practices (APIs, use cases, consumer demand, and investor responsibility). Presently, we can see multiple aspects that construct the contemporary IoT: it is simultaneously a site for contestation regarding what "home" can and should mean, a corporate battleground for future influence, and a *design thing* [2], that is being performed by residents, enthusiasts, and designers. More and more often, the Internet of things is creating the design thing as *proto-infrastructure* [12]. From a design research perspective, prototyping speculative devices for the Internet of Things serves to reveal the edges of the present IoT. By articulating the IoT's component parts and their assumptions as representing assumptions about future infrastructure, it becomes possible to examine their implicit social relations and value propositions before they become invisible.

PROCESS

As a research through design project [27,28], *Cohousing IoT* intends to understand how people live together and speculate about the role that computing technology can play in that living together. This work uses multiple ways to engage with cohousing communities to understand how cohousing operates in practice. This combination of methods informs prototyping, as bits and pieces of these approaches are integrated into the ongoing design process.

The first approach to understand cohousing was through examining USA-based cohousing community web pages. Communities across the country describe their goals and mission statements, which helped to generate a list of broader "cohousing values." These cohousing values became a starting point to understand how communities on the ground see themselves, and are available in more detail in [14]. Building on these values, this work has used cultural probes [6] and workshops to gain insight as to how residents in these communities understand increasingly-ubiquitous sensing platforms. This probe kit asks residents to create maps of their domestic life, to produce hypothetical sensor concepts for their own home or community, and a photo-elicitation activity provides prompts around what is or might be considered sensor-like in the home (Figure 2). Visiting multiple cohousing communities over the course of two years using a strategy of "diverse engagement" [14] offered a unique look into

Figure 2: A sensor workshop in Atlanta, USA.

what cohousing is and how it operates in practice. Interviews, site tours, and attending common meals provided different perspectives on cohousing. Interviews offer a way to get cohousing residents' experiences in their own words, while attending common meals and going on tours of cohousing sites offer a way to understand through personal experience how shared life is lived and practiced.

PROTOTYPES

Prototyping speculative technological systems creates new configurations of infrastructures and materials. These prototypes generate new contexts for existing products and services as well as new understandings of how they might operate in different social worlds [21]. In this way, technology prototyping instantiates new arrangements of social forces, and not simply objects in themselves [4,11,13]. These prototypes are part of a long line of HCI technologies that are aimed at developing richer social connections in the home. These including using techniques like habituation and ritual to produce connection between geographically distant kettle users[1], tablecloths that leave traces of domestic activity [8], fostering visibility for elderly residents of a housing project [7], and providing a venue for community narratives to be both recorded as well as travel through a deprived community [3].

In a similar vein, this set of three prototypes offers a different cultural imaginary for the Internet of Things in order to explore cohousing's human, social relationships with proto-infrastructures as well as the community-driven domestic life that they are a part of through a process of speculation in materials [23].

Cohousing Radio

Building on themes of connectivity, participation, and collaboration, *Cohousing Radio* (Figure 3) is built to connect residents in cohousing in a new, socio-material way. This prototype system imagines each cohousing

Figure 3: Cohousing Radio.

Figure 4: Physical RSVP.

residence has a small radio placed in the home. Residents can use this device to send audio files to other members of their community. Inside the radio housing is a Wi-Fi-enabled Raspberry Pi Zero driving an amplifier connected to an external speaker. Residents send audio files that they create to an email address. A script then adds the music file attachment to an internet radio station's playlist. The radios are tuned to that station and play what they receive over the air. The prototype can then stream announcements, music, or shows residents create into the homes of other residents in the community.

Like other sound systems designed to produce ambient awareness of energy systems, like Gaver et al's *Energy Babble* [9], or home life, like Petrelli et al's *Family Radio* [19], this prototype builds infrastructure to more richly understand a particular issue—in this case the social life of cohousing. It helps to connect residents together in a new, subtle way that would not otherwise be available before. It generates a creative and collaborative hyperlocal "backchannel" for residents to share bits and pieces of their own lives that might not be possible face to face. For example, at one cohousing community in Atlanta, USA, residents have a monthly "stick-passing ceremony" to discuss issues and experiences, both good and bad, with the broader community. One resident describes this ceremony: "You can share joys, concerns, things going on in your life and anything that's bothering you, or things you're really happy about, and it's just connecting with one another and sharing what's really going on that you might not bring it up in conversation over dinner." The radio provides a community channel for things that are different than lighthearted dinner conversation or the more formal discussions that already have ongoing venues. *Cohousing Radio* offers a way for residents to share personal creative projects like songs or poems, or enthusiasm for old jazz LPs in a casual way that fits into other domestic activities such as preparing morning coffee or doing the dishes. This prototype explicitly seeks to support new relationships between residents of cohousing. Here, making content for or listening to *Cohousing Radio* produces a new social medium inside of the cohousing community. In this way, the prototype radio becomes a material participant in the social life of the community [15].

Physical RSVP

The second prototype builds from ideas around convenience, making social life physical, and the responsibility to the community that cohousing requires. *Physical RSVP* (Figure 4) provides residents of cohousing a way to materially respond to invitations to events within the community. By placing a clay ball in a bowl, a resident registers their intent to attend the event, and that event's organizer can plan for the correct number of people. These balls are embedded with NFC chips that are unique to each resident. By dropping their ball into a bowl, an Arduino-based reader on the underside of the prototype detects the user's string from the NFC card, sends the resident's ID to a webserver, where finally a script updates their attendance for an event on a shared community calendar.

This prototype is meant to be placed in a common area of the cohousing community so that other residents would be able to see who plans to attend an event. This location has led to interesting conversations with cohousing residents about accountability and how neighbors participate in community life. The visibility of the balls in the bowl becomes a way of indicating intention in an unequivocal, public way. The physicality of clay balls unambiguously replaces murky and impenetrable email chains. One resident of cohousing described the confusion around planning over email as "all these different things are going at the same time and sometimes the chains get too long. Sometimes depending on what email platform people are using, how the emails are showing up, they miss out on something that was said before."

Like Durrell Bishop's famous *Marble Answering Machine* [29], *Physical RSVP* makes information material. In this case, that materialized information is not waiting to be processed by a single user or family. Instead, the balls represent the intention to participate in the social life of the community. The balls are meant to be left by residents, and

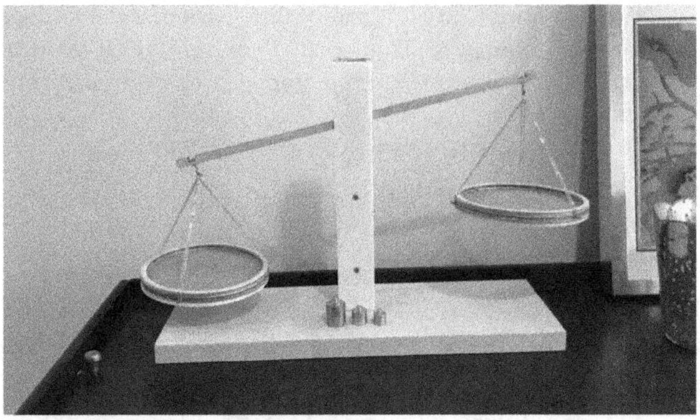

Figure 5: Participation Scales.

be recognizable to other residents as well as event organizers, but the information that they concretize remains accessible through online calendars and phone applications. The relatively simple form of the *Physical RSVP*—a bowl and tray that the bowl sits on—becomes a springboard to reimagining and reconfiguring the device's role in the community. During an interview, one cohousing resident immediately extended the idea of a single bowl to schedule community dinners to an entire row of bowls, each with their own placards that indicate a new, different tally. In his vision, these tallies could take multiple forms for different kinds of events: the bowls could become a means of polling questions to the community (and through that polling, enacting community governance), provide sign-up sheets for cohousing events, and offer a way to commit to doing particular work for the community, as well as being a means of simply letting the community know that you'll be at the common meal on Sunday evening. One interesting implication of this concept is that designers' attempts to simplifying highly bureaucratic processes might quickly be turned back into activities in a complicated community.

Scales

The final *Cohousing IoT* prototype is a set of scales that help a resident reflect on their participation in the community. In many interviews, residents expressed anxiety about their community activity, particularly around the monthly work hours that residents are expected to complete. These work hours can include cleaning the common house, landscaping and yard work, cooking for the group, or managing supplies. Often, the work hours requirement is not met, and residents feel like they should be doing more, afraid of not doing their part.

In the *Participation Scales* prototype (Figure 5), the position of the scales' arms represents an individual household's level of participation in the community. This is measured by attendance at events, work hours, and so on. The arms' position is controlled by a servo motor connected to a Wi-Fi-enabled microcontroller that reads participation data from a server. The left pan is the average level of participation for the community as a whole, and the right pan corresponds to the participation level of a particular home or family. If a resident is not spending enough time for themselves or their household, the left pan will drop. A force sensor on the right pan detects weight placed on it. A resident can place weights on the right pan to balance the scale. Placing a weight becomes a symbolic gesture to take more time for yourself or your household, or, if no weight is needed, to realize that, despite your concerns, your own participation is actually close to the community average.

This scales prototype is not meant to be punitive. Instead, it is intended as a tool for self-care, and making sure that you are not overextending yourself within the larger community. These scales shift current ideas of domestic IoT as monitoring the condition of your home to understanding the conditions of your participation in a community. Alongside this shift comes implications for the social relations in cohousing being mediated through IoT technologies. The scales become a material representation of personal participation in the broader cohousing community, as well as representing and displaying overall participation levels within the community in real time.

CONCLUSION

After DiSalvo et al [4], and building from Latour [16], these prototype objects represent "matters of concern" that are important to cohousing, and together, they articulate a public invested in those concerns [15]. These prototypes are the result of a design process with a public orientation [4]. This orientation means that the prototypes work to support a cohousing public—they provide material scaffolding to support the construction of this public around issues that matter to cohousing residents. This scaffolding supports knowing a condition by experiencing its qualities in a new way, in this case, one built from workshops that provide residents an opportunity to approach the material conditions of computation and sensing rooted in their own lives. The prototypes serve to reframe the constraints and parameters surrounding the issues of cohousing, while proposing new opportunities for community and device collaboration.

This research through design project uses interviews, probes, workshops, and site visits to draw out the themes and practices of cohousing. These are used to produce design work that engages both socially and materially with living situations that are outside of the mainstream. The three prototypes here operate at the edges of the currently-existing smart home, and provide an opportunity to do design work that helps us to understand the social role of technology. This process articulates the components of this network of people and things in a broader, material way, and emphasizes how objects and the relationship between and among them can create and sustain community life.

ACKNOWLEDGEMENTS

Thanks to Carl DiSalvo, Daniela Rosner, Sarah Fox, and James Pierce for collaboration into Public IoT. Thanks especially to residents of cohousing who volunteered their homes, time, and expertise over the course of this project. This research was supported by NSF grant #1523562.

REFERENCES

1. Aloha Hufana Ambe, Margot Brereton, Alessandro Soro, and Paul Roe. 2017. Technology Individuation: The Foibles of Augmented Everyday Objects. In *Proceedings of the 2017 CHI Conference on Human Factors in Computing Systems* (CHI '17), 6632–6644. https://doi.org/10.1145/3025453.3025770
2. Thomas Binder, Giorgio de De Michelis, Pelle Ehn, Giulio Jacucci, Per Linde, and Ina Wagner. 2011. *Design Things*. MIT Press.
3. Clara Crivellaro, Alex Taylor, Vasillis Vlachokyriakos, Rob Comber, Bettina Nissen, and Peter Wright. 2016. Re-Making Places: HCI, "Community Building" and Change. In *Proceedings of the 2016 CHI Conference on Human Factors in Computing Systems* (CHI '16), 2958–2969. https://doi.org/10.1145/2858036.2858332
4. Carl DiSalvo, Jonathan Lukens, Thomas Lodato, Tom Jenkins, and Tanyoung Kim. 2014. Making Public Things: How HCI Design Can Express Matters of Concern. In *Proceedings of the SIGCHI Conference on Human Factors in Computing Systems* (CHI '14). https://doi.org/10.1145/2556288.2557359.
5. J. P. Djajadiningrat, W. W. Gaver, and J. W. Fres. 2000. Interaction Relabelling and Extreme Characters: Methods for Exploring Aesthetic Interactions. In *Proceedings of the 3rd Conference on Designing Interactive Systems: Processes, Practices, Methods, and Techniques* (DIS '00), 66–71. https://doi.org/10.1145/347642.347664
6. Bill Gaver, Tony Dunne, and Elena Pacenti. 1999. Design: Cultural probes. *interactions* 6, 1: 21–29. https://doi.org/10.1145/291224.291235
7. William Gaver and Jacob Beaver. 2006. The Presence Project: Helping Older People Engage with Their Local Communities. In *Networked Neighbourhoods*, Professor Patrick Purcell (ed.). Springer London, 345–371. https://doi.org/10.1007/1-84628-601-8_14
8. William Gaver, John Bowers, Andy Boucher, Andy Law, Sarah Pennington, and Nicholas Villar. 2006. The History Tablecloth: Illuminating Domestic Activity. In *Proceedings of the 6th Conference on Designing Interactive Systems* (DIS '06), 199–208. https://doi.org/10.1145/1142405.1142437
9. William Gaver, Mike Michael, Tobie Kerridge, Alex Wilkie, Andy Boucher, Liliana Ovalle, and Matthew Plummer-Fernandez. 2015. Energy Babble: Mixing Environmentally-Oriented Internet Content to Engage Community Groups. In *Proceedings of the 33rd Annual ACM Conference on Human Factors in Computing Systems* (CHI '15), 1115–1124. https://doi.org/10.1145/2702123.2702546
10. Chris Hanson. 1996. *The Cohousing Handbook: Building a Place for Community*. Hartley & Marks, Point Roberts, WA.
11. Tom Jenkins. 2014. Prototyping Speculative Objects for the Internet of Things. In *Proceedings of the 10th Conference on Designing Interactive Systems* (DIS '14), 163–166. https://doi.org/10.1145/2598784.2598789
12. Tom Jenkins. 2015. The Internet of Things: Designing Proto-Infrastructures. In *Design Antrhopological Futures*.
13. Tom Jenkins. 2015. Designing the "Things" of the IoT. In *Proceedings of the Ninth International Conference on Tangible, Embedded, and Embodied Interaction*, 449–452. https://doi.org/10.1145/2677199.2691608
14. Tom Jenkins. 2017. Living Apart, Together: Cohousing as a Site for ICT Design. In *Proceedings of the 12th Conference on Designing Interactive Systems* (DIS '17). https://doi.org/10.1145/3064663.3064751
15. Tom Jenkins, Christopher A. Le Dantec, Carl DiSalvo, Thomas Lodato, and Mariam Asad. 2016. Object-Oriented Publics. In *Proceedings of the 2016 CHI Conference on Human Factors in Computing Systems* (CHI '16), 827–839. https://doi.org/10.1145/2858036.2858565
16. Bruno Latour. 2004. Why Has Critique Run out of Steam? From Matters of Fact to Matters of Concern. *Critical Inquiry* 30, 2: 225–248. https://doi.org/10.1086/421123
17. Sara Ljungblad and Lars Erik Holmquist. 2007. Transfer Scenarios: Grounding Innovation with Marginal Practices. In *Proceedings of the SIGCHI Conference on Human Factors in Computing Systems* (CHI '07), 737–746. https://doi.org/10.1145/1240624.1240738
18. Kathryn McCamant and Charles Durrett. 2011. *Creating Cohousing: Building Sustainable Communities*. New Society Publishers, Gabriola Island, B.C.
19. Daniela Petrelli, Nicolas Villar, Vaiva Kalnikaite, Lina Dib, and Steve Whittaker. 2010. FM Radio: Family Interplay with Sonic Mementos. In *Proceedings of the SIGCHI Conference on Human Factors in Computing Systems* (CHI '10), 2371–2380. https://doi.org/10.1145/1753326.1753683
20. Susan Leigh Star. 1999. The Ethnography of Infrastructure. *American Behavioral Scientist* 43, 3: 377–391. https://doi.org/10.1177/00027649921955326
21. Anselm Strauss. 1978. A Social World Perspective. *Studies in Symbolic Interaction* 1: 119–128.
22. Peter Tolmie, James Pycock, Tim Diggins, Allan MacLean, and Alain Karsenty. 2002. Unremarkable Computing. In *Proceedings of the SIGCHI Conference on Human Factors in Computing Systems* (CHI '02), 399–406. https://doi.org/10.1145/503376.503448

23. Ron Wakkary, William Odom, Sabrina Hauser, Garnet Hertz, and Henry Lin. 2015. Material Speculation: Actual Artifacts for Critical Inquiry. *Aarhus Series on Human Centered Computing* 1, 1: 12. https://doi.org/10.7146/aahcc.v1i1.21299
24. Peter Weibel and Bruno Latour. 2005. *Making things public: atmospheres of democracy : [exhibition], ZKM, Center for art and media Karlsruhe, 20.03.-03-10.2005.* (Mass.) : MIT press, Cambridge.
25. Mark Weiser. 1999. The Computer for the 21st Century. *SIGMOBILE Mob. Comput. Commun. Rev.* 3, 3: 3–11. https://doi.org/10.1145/329124.329126
26. Jo Williams. 2005. Designing Neighbourhoods for Social Interaction: The Case of Cohousing. *Journal of Urban Design* 10, 2: 195–227. https://doi.org/10.1080/13574800500086998
27. John Zimmerman, Jodi Forlizzi, and Shelley Evenson. 2007. Research through design as a method for interaction design research in HCI. In *Proceedings of the SIGCHI Conference on Human Factors in Computing Systems* (CHI '07), 493–502. https://doi.org/10.1145/1240624.1240704
28. John Zimmerman, Erik Stolterman, and Jodi Forlizzi. 2010. An Analysis and Critique of Research Through Design: Towards a Formalization of a Research Approach. In *Proceedings of the 8th ACM Conference on Designing Interactive Systems* (DIS '10), 310–319. https://doi.org/10.1145/1858171.1858228
29. Durrell Bishop's Marble Answering Machine | List of Physical Visualizations. Retrieved July 31, 2017 from http://dataphys.org/list/durrell-bishops-marble-answering-machine/

Through the Glance Mug: A Familiar Artefact to Support Opportunistic Search in Meetings

Ahmet Börütecene[1], İdil Bostan[1], Ekin Akyürek[3], Alpay Sabuncuoğlu[4], İlker Temuzkuşu[1], Çağlar Genç[1], Tilbe Göksun[2], Oğuzhan Özcan[1]

Koç University, Istanbul, Turkey

{aborutecene13, idbostan, eakyurek13, asabuncuoglu13, itemuzkusu, cgenc14, tgoksun, oozcan@ku.edu.tr}

ABSTRACT

During collocated meetings, the spontaneous need for information, called *opportunistic search*, might arise while conversing. However, using smartphones to look up information might be disruptive, disrespectful or even embarrassing in social contexts. We propose an alternative instrument for this practice: Glance Mug, a touch-sensitive mug prototype that listens to the conversation and displays browsable content-driven results on its inner screen. We organized 15 pairs of one-to-one meetings between students to gather user reflections. The user study revealed that the mug has the potential for supporting instant search and affords sufficient subtlety to conceal user actions. Yet, it provoked some anxiety for the users in maintaining eye contact with their partners. Our main contributions are the context-aware mug concept tested in a real-life setting and the analysis through Hornecker and Buur's Tangible Interaction Framework that discusses its design space, and its impact on the users and social interaction.

Author Keywords

Computer-mediated communication; tangible interaction, smart mug; collocated interaction; subtle interaction; impression management.

INTRODUCTION

Today, everyday objects can incorporate several technological components and become interactive devices while still looking like ordinary artifacts. This offers designers the opportunity to exploit the users' familiarity with the form factor, affordances and cultural aspects of these objects in exploring novel interactions. These aspects make everyday objects resourceful instruments by which we can approach various design challenges regarding our interaction with the information.

[1] Koç University – Arçelik Research Center for Creative Industries (KUAR)

[2] Department of Psychology

[3] Department of Electrical and Electronics Engineering

[4] Department of Computer Engineering

TEI '18, March 18–21, 2018, Stockholm, Sweden

ACM ISBN 978-1-4503-5568-1/18/03...$15.00

https://doi.org/10.1145/3173225.3173236

Figure 1. The Glance Mug prototype and system components

In this paper, we talk about one of these challenges: the need to perform instant search in meetings. During a meeting, we occasionally come across unknown words or subjects and feel the need to look up a piece of information. This phenomenon is called *opportunistic search*. Although previous works addressed design issues related to opportunistic search, they are limited to the use of smartphones and tabletop systems [8,23]. However, in some contexts, especially in one-to-one meetings, reaching one's smartphone or tablet might be perceived as a rude or disruptive act as a certain level of attention, interest and participation is expected for the social interaction [2,22]. Moreover, interlocutors might not want to expose themselves while using their mobile device or doing online search during a conversation. The reason for this can be that of concealing their ignorance or weakness on the subject matter; or their ability to access information, which makes them feel personally empowered [10,23]. As a result, in addition to the need for opportunistic search, a demand for subtle interaction with the artefact also emerges.

In order to address these issues, we propose the Glance Mug, a novel, touch-sensitive mug prototype with an inner display which converts speech to text (Figure 1). Nearly all previous work on augmented mugs addressed well-being issues such as informing the users on their liquid consumption [28,29]. The difference of our research is that we consider the mug as an intelligent companion for social interaction, especially during meetings. The Glance Mug listens to the conversation and, once triggered by touch, it performs an online search based on the actual conversation content. Wikipedia summary and images from Google are displayed as search results on the inner screen of the mug. It allows the users to look up and view information instantly on the artefact itself without using another device.

In order to see the user response to the Glance Mug in a real-life setting, we conducted an exploratory study with the prototype by organizing 15 pairs of one-to-one advising meetings with university students. The users were expected to interact with the mug, in a subtle or open way according to their preference, and subsequently share with us their thoughts on the experience in semi-structured interviews. This study enabled us to gather user reflections on the augmented mug concept, its gestural and visual interface, its support for subtlety, and its influence on opportunistic search and the flow of conversation. On the other hand, we analyzed the Glance Mug by using Hornecker and Buur's Tangible Interaction Framework [19] to reveal its potential for enhancing social interaction and identify, by the help of the user reflections, challenges and opportunities for the design of augmented mugs. This framework has been previously used to explore several tangible experiences in social settings [5,12,24,27], including augmented everyday objects [1]. It is composed of 4 different themes that are related to understanding embodied and social aspects of tangible interfaces: *(a) Tangible Manipulation*; *(b) Spatial Interaction*; *(c) Embodied Facilitation*; and *(d) Expressive Representation*. Each theme is explained separately in the Discussion section.

RELATED WORK

Opportunistic Search

In their theoretical paper Bruijn and Spence [8] introduced the term opportunistic browsing, which refers to "the continuous but largely unconscious monitoring and filtering of information with the potential to trigger more purposeful behavior" (p. 363). They suggested that this kind of browsing is ubiquitous in everyday life and new systems and artifacts supporting this kind of browsing should be studied. In relation to this concept Li and Dillenbourg [23] coined the term opportunistic search and explained it as a phenomenon occurring in meetings where "people may spontaneously seek information for certain terms that they encounter unexpectedly either from meeting conversation or resources (paper documents or other objects in the surroundings) available in the meeting environment".

In their paper, they explored opportunistic search meeting support systems by testing touch-sensitive tabletop designs for brainstorming settings. In place of speech recognition, these designs used Wizard of Oz to transcribe conversations. They found that the search results based on the conversation context showing the related Wikipedia pages and images seemed to be working better as it presented a simple interface for results and offered visual representation of the conversation. Although, the Glance Mug adopts a similar approach to present the search results, our research differs as our aim was to understand what kind of experience a tangible interface could offer for opportunistic search.

Subtle Interaction

Anderson et al. define subtle interaction as "providing input to, or receiving output from, systems without being observed" [2]. The researchers implemented four device prototypes that enabled users to perform some actions during meetings without exposing themselves to the attendees. One of these prototypes was a coffee cup with a flat display placed on the bottom, which enabled users to read messages. In a limited way, the study of Anderson et al. shows that the coffee mug form factor has potential in encouraging subtle interaction. However, the mug was a phone-controlled device. Our Glance Mug differs as it offers both input (touch-sensitive surface) and output (inner display) in a single device, which presents a direct and unified interaction. In this way, we intended to explore the potential of an augmented mug as a tangible interface for subtle interaction.

Augmented Mugs and Tangible Interaction

Although coffee mugs are well-known social artefacts, few studies or products explored the mugs' potential as interactive devices. The earliest effort is The Media Cup developed by Gellersen et al. which is an augmented ceramic coffee mug prototype with diverse sensors placed on the bottom part [4]. It was able to sense its motion, perceive the temperature of the liquid it held and share these data with nearby devices. The researchers' main aim was to design a cup that would be able to connect to a network of devices and to communicate with them. Although they tried to capture human gestures with the cup (drinking and fiddling), they did not explore or discuss its potential to support collocated social interactions.

Interactive mugs designed specifically for social interaction are rare. One of them is the Lover's Cups that allow two people in different places to communicate with each other [9]. The prototype of the device could sense the liquid level, sipping and shaking action, and it used LED illumination as an output method to display information. Although this project considers the cup as a potential interface for interpersonal communication, its focus is on supporting remote social interactions. In this sense, our study differs from others as we examine the role of an augmented mug in a face-to-face social setting. Another noticeable artefact is the Paulig Muki, a coffee mug with a flat e-ink display on its outer surface which was designed for both direct and remote social interaction [30]. This mug allows people to send each other images via its app. These images are shown on the mug display as fresh coffee is poured in the cup. This project is an example of how an ordinary mug can propose novel forms of interaction with/between people by using gestures that are intrinsic to the use of the mug, such as pouring coffee. However, unlike the Glance Mug, it is limited in terms of direct contact as it does not exploit hand gestures performed on/with the mug (drinking, grasping, tilting, revolving), which could introduce novel ways of manipulating the content for social interaction.

Mugshots is another salient project that focuses on both remote and collocated interactions [21]. This work is inspired by Goffman' theory in which he uses the theater metaphor to explain why people act differently in public and private spaces, defined respectively as the front and the backstage [16]. The researchers' aim was to facilitate the switching between public and private performance by proposing a mug interface for communication. In private mode, this mug shows images sent from friends and family in the small, flat LCD display on its outer surface. When the user passes to the public space, the display shows an image preloaded by the user via web/smartphone interface. The researchers also mentioned how these displayed images triggered conversation. Although this project explores how an augmented mug displaying images could affect social interaction, it does not provide any input method on the mug itself like the Glance Mug. Our study also differs from the Mugshots as it addresses the subtle interaction potential of the mug in social encounters.

Coffee Cup Reading Paradigm for Mug Interactions

We previously studied how the cup and saucer were used by fortune-tellers and examined the cup reading phenomenon from an HCI perspective [6] as this centuries-old socio-cultural experience is tightly related to nonverbal interaction and physical manipulation of handheld artefacts. We argued that the cup and saucer could be considered as tangible interfaces to explore interactive handheld systems for enhancing social interaction. In line with this perspective, we also conducted a comprehensive investigation on how fortune-tellers physically engaged with the cup during the sessions. As a result, we derived 11 characteristics that could be a reference for user interactions with handheld cylindrical devices with an inner display [7]. In designing the Glance Mug, we were inspired by this study as it provides a base for exploring the design of augmented mugs in terms of form factor and tangible interaction. Although the Glance Mug differs from the coffee cup mentioned in the study, in terms of purpose and various aspects such as visual content and dimensions, we took into consideration three of these characteristics: *Touching, Contact with the Cup and Interrupting Contact with the Cup.*

Touching referred to the participants' continuous tactile interactions with the outer surface of the coffee cup. These included rubbing or poking, or tapping gestures. In the Glance Mug, we created touch-sensitive areas around the mug that would enable users to perform gestures with fingers. *Contact with the Cup* and *Interrupting Contact with the Cup* referred to the participants' tendency to hold the cup in one hand most of the time during the practice. Inspired by this finding, we arranged the touch-sensitive areas close to the mug handle to make single-hand interaction easier and allow users to still perform communicative gestures with their free hand during a conversation. According to the study, the participants also tended to hold the coffee cup with both hands if they were examining its inner visual content. Keeping this behavior in mind, we employed two touch-sensitive stripes to cover the entire brim of the mug. In this way, the users were able to employ both hands to perform touch-gestures, by positioning them on the sensors around the mug. Our main aim was to propose a simple yet interactive tangible prototype that would enable us to see an augmented mug concept in action and gather initial user reflections on this novel experience. Therefore, at this stage of the research, we limited our study to the mug interactions that were the most feasible for us to prototype with our available resources.

GLANCE MUG

The Glance Mug is a 3D printed augmented mug prototype equipped with a small flat display on its inner wall as well as touch-sensitive areas around its surface (Figure 1). The mug continuously listens to the conversation during meetings, which consequently enables the mug holders to look up information related to the content (e.g., name, concept, location). When needed, they tap on the mug to trigger search. The mug then rewinds 9 seconds backwards [31] and converts the audio recording into text by using Google Speech API [32]. Once it has received the speech-to-text output, the mug processes this textual data as query with an algorithm to search the web. In the end, the screen displays the related title, description and Wikipedia summary received from Google Knowledge Graph Search API [33] and presents the first five image results from Google. The Glance Mug allows users to see and browse these search results instantly on the inner surface of the mug. Users can browse through the results by performing swipe gestures on the outer surface of the mug. Triggering another search updates the display to show new results. At this stage of the research, the mug is not suitable for drinking and cannot contain any liquid as the material we used for 3D printing was not food safe and the electronic components might get damaged. It was also the case in [2] in which the researchers obtained fruitful results in their study on subtle interactions. Likewise, in our study this configuration was sufficient for us to gather user reflections on the mug concept.

Touch-sensitive Interface for Search and Navigation

We placed the touch-sensitive areas as stripes on the outer surface of the mug: two of them are horizontal around the brim and one is vertical on the user side, close to the handle. These are used for swipe gestures. The horizontal stripes are responsible for browsing through images and Wikipedia summary. In addition, tapping/pressing gestures applied on the edge of the stripe that is close to the handle triggers search. The vertical stripe is used to browse different search terms derived from the conversation.

Graphical User Interface

We placed a small and low-resolution flat display on the inner surface of the mug. A simple GUI was designed to minimize the information load, showing only the most essential elements: title (query), description, Wikipedia summary and one image for each frame (Figure 2). The title was shown in the gray stripe while the textual/visual content was displayed below. The interface also shows feedback messages in this gray section when a search is triggered or when there is no result. We used Verdana typeface as it was designed to increase the readability for low-resolution screens. The GUI uses a slide animation to show the transition between one content and the other (e.g., from the Wikipedia description frame to the frame with the coffee cup visual in the Figure 2). This movement-based transition, intended to stimulate also peripheral vision [13], notifies the users whenever there is a change in content on the screen.

Figure 2. Glance Mug GUI. Wikipedia summary on the left and an image from Google on the right.

USER STUDY

As our inspiration was the previous research we conducted on Turkish coffee fortune-telling, a traditional advice-giving practice, we chose an advising setting to test the mug. We designed a study at the university in which two students came together to talk about the experience of going abroad as an exchange student, in 15 minute one-to-one meetings. We issued a call for participants for students who wished to apply for an exchange program (advisee) and for students that had already had such an experience (advisor). We believed this setting would provide a suitable context to look up some information (such as countries, places, universities) to make conversation, answer questions or extend arguments. In this regard, our main aim in conducting this user study was to understand what people would think of the interaction mechanism and opportunities the Glance Mug offered, and whether they could use it while interacting with another person in a social setting.

Although touch-gesture recognition and GUI components of the mug performed well in the pilot sessions, speech recognition results failed most of the time to correspond to the actual content produced during the conversation. However, this did not prevent the participants to have hands-on experience with the augmented mug concept and they were motivated to give feedback. Following these preliminary sessions, we preferred the Wizard of Oz (WoZ) method to solve speech recognition issues. This way, we were able to provide a more stable system and continued with the second series of sessions. The main difference between these two series of sessions was related to the duration and frequency of interaction with the mug. However, as we did not change the mug concept in between the two sessions, and did not aim to measure task performance, we considered the data sufficient for initial user feedback about a novel concept. Therefore, we grouped the user reflections from both series together.

Participants

In total, 30 right-handed participants took part in our study. Fifteen of them were the mug users (4 males, *M*age= 23.33) and 15 were their conversational partners (5 males, *M*age= 21.6).

Experimental Setup

For each session, a mug user and a conversational partner were asked to sit facing each other at a round table in a room. We placed two cameras to frame the face of each participant, their body movements and the Glance Mug. Although we could not put coffee in the Glance Mug for technical and safety reasons, we still provided coffee to the conversational partner to maintain a balance in terms of mug presence on the table. We gave an informed consent form to all participants but we did not present the details of the user study as it might have created a bias. We however provided debriefing right after the sessions. All sessions were conducted by two researchers and were video recorded. As thank-you gifts, we offered vouchers for a coffeehouse on the campus.

Procedure

We wanted the mug users to play and familiarize themselves with the Glance Mug concept for a while before the sessions. Therefore, we invited the mug users to the study room 15 minutes earlier than the others. After giving the informed consent form, we introduced our prototype to the users. We explained what the Glance Mug would do, demonstrated how it worked, and asked them to try to use it during the meeting. We also mentioned that the other participants, the conversational partners, did not know about the Glance Mug, yet we did not guide the mug users to conceal or expose the mug. After this briefing, we let them play with the mug until the partners arrived. Upon arrival, we offered them coffee/tea and asked them to converse for about 15 minutes. During the meetings, there was no researcher in the room. After the sessions each researcher held a semi-structured interview with each of the participants.

FIRST SERIES: PILOT SESSIONS

We conducted these sessions by using the speech recognition system implemented in the Glance Mug. We organized 6 sessions in which 12 students participated. We conducted the first half of these sessions by giving the mug to the advisee students, and the other half by giving the mug to the advisors. This allowed us to observe whether one group tends to use the mug more often. However, we could not find any visible differences. As we based our research on the previous work on Turkish coffee fortune-telling, we proceeded with this traditional advice-giving setting, in which the advisor uses the cup. Therefore, following these preparatory sessions we gave the Glance Mug to the students with an exchange experience as they represented the advisor in these meetings.

SECOND SERIES: WIZARD OF OZ SESSIONS

These sessions were conducted following technical issues with speech recognition results. Eighteen students participated in this series and we organized 9 sessions. The Wizard of Oz (WoZ) is a method to manually operate some features of a system that cannot be implemented at an ideal level, or are currently technologically impossible. By using the WoZ method we imitated the desired speech-to-text output and did the search operation manually for the Glance Mug. These sessions allowed us to create a more stable experience with the mug and thus helped us obtain more reliable user feedback.

USER REFLECTIONS FROM BOTH SESSIONS

In this section, we report the user response gathered from the semi-structured interviews. We took into consideration the interviews conducted with all the mug users in 15 sessions. In 3 sessions, we were informed that the partners were aware that there would be an augmented mug involved in the study, but did not know about the mug's functions or what it was used for. We still involved in our analysis the users of the mug in these sessions as the subtlety the mug provided was not our only interest; we were also interested in its overall user experience.

Interpersonal Communication and Subtle Interaction

An interesting aspect of the Glance Mug was its influence on the language employed by the user. One participant **(P13)** believed the mug changed her style of speech. Instead of using generic nouns such as "city", "home", or "school", she tended to use more proper nouns such as city or university names. She also repeated the words of her partner when she wanted to search for them on the mug. It is inspiring that an augmented mug demonstrated a potential of creating new forms of conversation. One participant **(P14)**, who had shared the contents of the mug with his partner at the beginning of the session, believed that this created a momentary bond among them and acted as an ice-breaker. Interestingly, his partner reported the same feeling when asked about how the conversation went. Adding a sound system to the mug was suggested by four participants so that the mug could play videos and sounds or read the search results out loud. For example, one of the participants **(P7)** who had lived in Australia reported that he would like to play some Australian accent videos for his advisee so that she could get a grasp of what to expect. The same participant also stated that he would not need such a mug as he would use his smartphone to look up information. Yet, he added that the mug would be helpful when there is a need for secrecy. Overall, we see that the mug was considered as an artefact that could contribute to conversations in different ways.

The 3 conversational partners, who knew there would be an augmented mug involved in the study, did not notice an unusual or suspicious activity on the users' side. In the remaining 12 sessions where the partners were oblivious to the mug, only 3 of the users declared to the partners that they were using an augmented mug. Two of the mug users **(P9, P14)** reported that they wanted to be honest and talk about the mug they had. Another participant **(P15)** said that she felt the need to try and involve the mug in the conversation because of its mere presence. One other participant **(P7)** reported that he was planning to share the contents of the mug with his partner, in this case pictures from the city where he studied in Australia, yet the right time never came. The remaining 8 participants kept the mug's function a secret. Although they had the freedom to share the mug's actual content with their advisees, these users chose to keep it to themselves. The reasons for keeping it secret were that they wanted to see whether they would be able to use it secretly, or that there was no need to involve the mug in the conversation.

As a result, secrecy was introduced into the dialogue where one party withheld the information from the other. In these sessions, none of the partners became aware of the mug use during the meeting. However, seven participants reported it was hard to maintain eye contact with the advisees while trying to use the mug covertly and this made them feel uncomfortable. Since they were sitting alone in a room with their advisees with whom they had just met, they did not have much opportunity to direct their gaze elsewhere during the conversation. They found the mug attracted too much of their gaze and attention, and they struggled to focus on the dialogue they were engaged in. In this sense, the mug seems to be more comfortable to use in crowded contexts where the users would be more comfortable with their gaze direction. Yet, a distracting mug might still be helpful in one-to-one encounters. For instance, one participant **(P12)**, who is energetic by nature, started playing with the mug triggering random search to erase her boredom and divert her attention from the conversation that felt stuck at a certain point. This is an example of how the experience presented by the mug could change depending on the personalities.

Opportunistic Search and Use Cases

The majority of the participants appreciated the concept and tried to use the Glance Mug during the conversation. Our mug prototype did not always yield the desired search results during the user studies, nonetheless this did not always result in negative outcomes. In one instance, while trying the Glance Mug for the first time before the session, one of the participants **(P8)** was pleased to see unrelated results as she gained knowledge. Users performed opportunistic search for different reasons. One participant **(P11)** indicated that the mug helped her concretize her thoughts and retrieve her memories during the conversation. Similarly another participant **(P7)** reported that he did not search for things he did not know, but rather for those he already knew and remembered. Two participants **(P7, P10)** mentioned that they did not feel the need to use the mug for facts since they talked about their personal experiences, so searching the net was not a priority for them. One participant **(P14)** said it was not easy to understand which words the mug would pick. He expressed the wish to see on the display all the words for each search so that he could navigate and choose the ones he needed most. Similarly another participant **(P13)** expressed the wish that the mug recorded and displayed all the search results so that she could navigate through that information after the conversation. She said she would put "bookmarks" on the search results she liked in order to come back to them whenever she wanted to. Another participant **(P14)** said he wished the mug could hold liquid which would make him more enthusiastic about it.

By closely examining the use-cases suggested by the participants, we found that they referred to its potential to support interaction in formal encounters: business meetings, seminars, and academic discussions were among the most common suggestions. Users believed the mug could enable them to easily look up small pieces of information they missed in such encounters without creating social discomfort. Another use-case suggestion was presentations, where the mug would be helpful to quickly retrieve needed information, to answer questions from the public, as well as to control the presentation slides via their mug.

Physical Structure and Gestural Interaction

The form of the mug was appreciated by almost all participants. They reported finding the mug's shape, weight and appearance appropriate to its purpose. The most common criticism regarding the form was directed towards the placement of the screen: eight participants reported that it was hard to see the lower end of the screen while the mug was on the table. Participants either had to lean over the mug or tilt it towards themselves to get a better view. To overcome this, participants suggested to incline the screen upwards towards the user's eye level. An interesting comment pointed out the fixed position of the screen; one participant **(P15)** reported that she normally holds mugs with her left hand, thus making the Glance Mug feel reverse to her. She expressed the wish to have the screen on the opposite side of the mug in order to be able to use it with her left hand. Almost all participants found the positioning of the flexible sensors convenient. Most of the participants believed swipe gestures felt natural and comfortable. However, they believed the swipe sensors and touch-sensitive search spot did not provide enough feedback to notify the user that they have been pressed. Five participants reported that they could not understand whether they had pressed on the search spot correctly as there was no physical feedback to communicate whether they had done it correctly. Moreover, four participants suggested that the search spot could be moved to the side facing them or to the top of the handle, where pressing on it would be easier and more seamless.

DISCUSSION

Below we analyze and discuss the current and potential design space of the Glance Mug, and the user reflections through Hornecker and Buur's *Tangible Interaction Framework*. We explain the themes of the framework briefly in the beginning of each section.

Grasping the Opportunity for Search

The first theme of Hornecker and Buur's framework is *Tangible Manipulation.* It refers to the bodily interaction with physical objects equipped with computational resources, that is the users are able to control the computation by directly manipulating objects [19]. The Glance Mug presents the information gathered from the conversation context to the users. The users see the digital representation originated from the ongoing conversation in the space where the coffee is poured. When holding a mug, the users' fingers are in direct contact with the outer surface as well as the handle. The touch-sensitive stripes around the Glance Mug take advantage of this bodily relationship to provide access to the content inside. To trigger a search, or manipulate the textual and visual content represented on the mug's inner display, the users do not need to handle any other device, as they can control these actions from the mug itself. In this way, the Glance Mug couples the intrinsic physical function of the mug (holding liquid) with a new one (holding information). In a similar way, the daily interaction with the mug's surface is transformed into meaningful gestures to instantly search and navigate the digital representations of the conversation content.

We believe that this coupling, together with the concealing form factor of the mug, enables users to perform opportunistic search and engage with the Glance Mug without provoking any doubt in their partner. Even the participants who knew about the mug did not notice the mug user's movements nor did they understand how the mug worked. Although in some sessions the mug did not work in a stable or continuous manner, our user study enabled us to have an understanding of the degree of subtlety the mug could offer. We found the results encouraging as we conducted the study in a real-life setting and did not dedicate much time to polish the 3D printed mug case. Conceived as an everyday object, the Glance Mug should also be considered as a personal object that can be customized and individuated [1]. For instance, with a knitted mug sleeve it can reflect different styles and identities, and could thus be distinguished among others. Although the current prototype does not allow using any liquid, using drinks would add another layer to the tangibility and expressiveness of the Glance Mug. For example, triggering search can be coupled with the drinking gesture and the level of coffee can reveal the representations on the display sip by sip. Similarly, the movement of the liquid inside the mug can be controlled by hand gestures (e.g., fidgeting, revolving, inclining) for navigation or selection purposes [15].

Ambiguity Enables Privacy and Subtlety

Spatial Interaction refers to the fact that tangible interfaces occupy real space in the world and that users interact with them by moving in real space [19]. The Glance Mug is an object that can be moved freely in space. We can talk about two main physical spaces for the Glance Mug. The first one is the surrounding space in which the users handle and move the mug. This mobility allows users to adjust the view of the content inside according to their head and body posture, which helps them reduce the physical effort to follow the textual and visual output presented. Moreover, this handheld object mediates the transition between the private spot (where interaction with the artefact occurs) and the public spot (where interaction with the interlocutor occurs). These two spots can occasionally coincide when users share the content of the mug with others. In this case, the private becomes public and the digital content is enjoyed as a shared element of the conversation. In the Mugshots study, this transition is performed digitally by the users through the mug interface (switching to public/private mode) in separate places [21]. In the Glance Mug case, this transition occurs in the same place and time, and is performed physically by the users through their behavior (showing the mug display to the interlocutor). In this regard, the privacy or disclosure of the Glance Mug depends on the users' bodily interaction as the interlocutors cannot know exactly whether the users are looking at visual information, a blank screen, or simply the coffee. This gives room for users to perform opportunistic search with subtlety. The Glance Mug introduces an ambiguity that allows both sides to maintain the social interaction without feeling interrupted or disruptive. Ambiguity has been discussed extensively in HCI and is considered as a powerful design element. In this case, *ambiguity of context*, originating from the obscuring mug form factor, creates a meaningful space of uncertainty. This proposes an alternative to the activity-exposing smartphone interaction for opportunistic search [14].

The second space, which is also related to the first one, is the inner space of the mug, which is normally used to hold liquid. Because of technological limitations, we currently present the mug's content on only one side of the mug. This prevents the users to freely revolve or tilt the mug, unless they want to expose their activity. With a flexible or embedded screen the entire inner surface of the mug can become a visual space for displaying the content [34]. This would help solve the handedness issue mentioned by one of the participants (**P15**). In such a circular display, the visuals can reposition themselves around the inner surface according to the hand in use so that the content is not exposed to the interlocutors and it can easily be used with the preferred hand.

Privileged Access to the Search Content

Embodied Facilitation refers to the physical and procedural structure of tangible interfaces that influence user actions and behavior, and consequently shape social configurations [19]. We can say that the Glance Mug presents the digital representations in an unconventional way, that is, on the inner surface of the mug. The form factor of the Glance Mug enables people to have privacy in meetings when needed as the interlocutors cannot precisely know whether the user is looking at a piece of information or the liquid inside. As opposed to the use of a smartphone in a meeting, which can be perceived as rude or associated with working on tasks irrelevant to the meeting, handling a coffee mug refers in the first place to the act of drinking [20,22]. When considering this in line with the subtle interfaces framework [2], we can describe the Glance Mug as an artefact that (a) provides functions beyond its appearance (*device visibility: disguised*); (b) enables interactions observable but perceived as normal behaviors (*interaction observability: disguised*); (c) prevents others from noticing the ongoing task (*task transparency: opaque*).

These design and form factor qualities allowed us to explore how users would behave with such an artefact in social interaction. Users are given the opportunity to keep the content for themselves or to reveal and share it with their interlocutors. In this regard, the mug's form factor is marked by a level of privacy and access threshold. The mug users have privileged access to the content for two basic reasons: they own the mug (in case it is a personal artefact) and they are physically the closest person to the mug. While this proximity eases the access for the users, it also limits the access points for the others to the content presented. The movement of the mug in space regulates the privacy and access points as this can manipulate the proximity too. In any case, the Glance Mug has a single and narrow access point by nature as the mugs are not designed to be used by two people at the same time. The access threshold can be lowered only by the user's intention to expose the mug's content. Thus the interlocutors might only know about the content if the users express it verbally or show them the mug display. As it happens in the fortune-telling practice, the mug can be shared between the interlocutors for communication purposes. The users can share the content in order contribute to the conversation (see the account of **P7** on Australian accent videos and city images).

Impressions and Extensions of a Conversation

Expressive Representation refers to how digital functions and data are physically represented in tangible interaction, often implemented by combination of materials and digital elements [19]. The Glance Mug transforms the voice input (physical form) into textual and visual output (digital representation) and offers impressions and extensions of the conversation. These are displayed on a flat screen placed on the inner surface. Topics and concepts produced verbally during conversation might not always stimulate our senses and appear in front of our eyes. Yet, by displaying textual and visual representations of these conversational elements, the mug plays a stimulating role. In this way, the mug provides the user with textual and visual material to learn about an unknown concept, to extend a known one, to share these with the interlocutor, or simply for distraction. As the users can trigger search at any point in the conversation, the Glance Mug opens the way to being stimulated by doing random search for unexpected results. This serendipity adds playfulness to the conversations and might be a trigger for people to talk or learn new things. **(P8, P12)**. User reflections also indicated that the support for opportunistic search does not have to be only limited to displaying information instantly. A suggestion was to keep the log of search results and make them available after meetings as well **(P13)**. Therefore, access to the search history at a later time is expected as opportunistic search results cannot be exploited in a comprehensive manner at the moment of search. In this way, the Glance Mug could extend the momentary impressions beyond the meeting into new spaces of the user, both physical and virtual (e.g., social media, personal archive etc.). In this sense, it is also interrelated with the *Spatial Interaction* theme.

Although most participants preferred to keep the mug's functions and content to themselves, trying to use it for subtle interactions, they had difficulty in maintaining eye contact with the partners while interacting with the mug. As mentioned previously, the distracting visual attraction of the mug is not always a negative aspect as it also has the potential to prevent boredom during the conversation as indicated by **P12**. However, when this is not the intention, communication problems might arise. The most challenging part of an augmented mug for face-to-face interaction is that it divides the user's attention between the visual content (re)presented inside and the conversation in progress. The visual representation on the mug screen is designed to have as little elements as possible to lower the cognitive load during the social interaction. However, the user reflections demonstrated that this was not sufficient to maintain a smooth and flowing conversation. Multisensory Data Representation, that is employing various senses and media for representing data [17], can be a suitable approach. Although, one sensory channel alone might not be sufficient to communicate the desired information (e.g., understanding by taste where a certain building is located in the city), vision can be supported by other senses. In relation to touch gestures, using vibrations or temperature change as haptic feedback might also reduce the attention required to notice whether search and navigation gestures have been triggered.

Ethical considerations

The subtlety and secrecy the Glance Mug offers also raise ethical questions. Some users might consider this device concept as a potentially dishonest instrument **(P9, P14)** as it creates a way for deception, can compromise privacy as well as decrease social engagement by making eye contact difficult. Yet, whenever such an artefact becomes popular, it also has the potential to change people's habits and privacy expectations, as was the case with the first Kodak cameras [18]. Similarly, first-time mobile phone users demonstrated within a few weeks a positive change in behavior towards a technology initially perceived as annoying [25]. Therefore, in the future such adaptation can make us employ IoT devices similar to the Glance Mug as a support for our daily online/offline or context-specific face-work [3,26].

CONCLUSION

We designed the Glance Mug, a 3D printed ordinary-looking mug that listens to conversations. When triggered by touch, it performs an online search based on the conversation content and displays related textual and visual results in its inner screen. Our aim was to explore the potential of the Glance Mug in supporting opportunistic search and subtle interaction during meetings. We conducted an exploratory user study with the mug to gather user reflections about the experience it offers and to identify challenges and opportunities for the design of augmented mugs.

The user study revealed that the participants appreciated the augmented mug concept and the mug allowed the users to subtly perform opportunistic search whenever wanted. Furthermore, we noticed that, although users had not been guided by us to hide the mug's functions, they still tended to keep the mug and its content to themselves. We interpreted this as a result of the mug's form factor which implies secrecy and subtle use because of its concealing physical structure. These outcomes indicate the Glance Mug's potential to be used during meetings without attracting much attention or suspicion. However, the users found it difficult to maintain eye contact in social interaction while performing search and navigating the results. This challenge can be addressed by employing different sensory channels to provide feedback on the users' actions (e.g., triggering search) and to represent search results.

Our two main contributions are (1) designing and prototyping the Glance Mug and testing it in real-life setting; (2) analyzing it through Hornecker and Buur's Tangible Interaction Framework to discuss the current and potential design space of the Glance Mug, and user reflections. The analysis revealed 4 salient traits of our mug prototype: (a) *Grasping the Opportunity to Search*; (b) *Ambiguity Enables Privacy and Subtlety*; (c) *Privileged Access to the Search Content*; (d) *Impressions and Extensions of a Conversation*. These traits indicate the challenges and opportunities that would inform the design of similar augmented mugs for supporting collocated social interaction. In addition, the design directions we shared in the Discussion could also be helpful in reflecting on the behaviors of augmented everyday objects in social contexts.

As a next step, physical mug affordances (e.g., sipping, squeezing the handle etc.) can be further explored to couple them with different input methods for subtlety such as EMG-based motionless gestures [11]. For future work, we plan to deploy the iterated prototype in a group meeting setting with other mobile devices for a comparative study in terms of opportunistic search and subtle interaction experience as well as social acceptance.

REFERENCES

1. Aloha Hufana Ambe, Margot Brereton, Alessandro Soro, and Paul Roe. 2017. Technology Individuation: The Foibles of Augmented Everyday Objects. In *Proceedings of the 2017 CHI Conference on Human Factors in Computing Systems* (CHI '17), 6632–6644. https://doi.org/10.1145/3025453.3025770
2. Fraser Anderson, Tovi Grossman, Daniel Wigdor, and George Fitzmaurice. 2015. Supporting Subtlety with Deceptive Devices and Illusory Interactions. In *Proceedings of the 33rd Annual ACM Conference on Human Factors in Computing Systems* (CHI '15), 1489–1498. https://doi.org/10.1145/2702123.2702336
3. Paul M. Aoki and Allison Woodruff. 2005. Making Space for Stories: Ambiguity in the Design of Personal Communication Systems. In *Proceedings of the SIGCHI Conference on Human Factors in Computing Systems* (CHI '05), 181–190. https://doi.org/10.1145/1054972.1054998
4. Michael Beigl, Hans-W. Gellersen, and Albrecht Schmidt. 2001. Mediacups: experience with design and use of computer-augmented everyday artefacts. *Computer Networks* 35, 4: 401–409. https://doi.org/10.1016/S1389-1286(00)00180-8
5. Tilde Bekker and Janienke Sturm. 2009. Stimulating Physical and Social Activity Through Open-ended Play. In *Proceedings of the 8th International Conference on Interaction Design and Children* (IDC '09), 309–312. https://doi.org/10.1145/1551788.1551869
6. Ahmet Börütecene, İdil Bostan, Tilbe Göksun, and Oğuzhan Özcan. 2016. Informing Design Decisions for Advice Mediating Handheld Devices by Studying Coffee Cup Reading. In *Proceedings of the 9th Nordic Conference on Human-Computer Interaction* (NordiCHI '16), 7:1–7:10. https://doi.org/10.1145/2971485.2971523
7. Ahmet Börütecene, İdil Bostan, Gülben Şanlı, Çağlar Genç, Tilbe Göksun, and Oğuzhan Özcan. 2017. Coffee Cup Reading as an Inspiration for Looking into Augmented Mugs in Social Interaction. In *Design, User Experience, and Usability: Understanding Users and Contexts* (Lecture Notes in Computer Science), 199–218. https://doi.org/10.1007/978-3-319-58640-3_15
8. Oscar de Bruijn and Robert Spence. 2001. Serendipity within a Ubiquitous Computing Environment: A Case for Opportunistic Browsing. In *Ubicomp 2001: Ubiquitous Computing* (Lecture Notes in Computer Science), 362–369. https://doi.org/10.1007/3-540-45427-6_31
9. Hyemin Chung, Chia-Hsun Jackie Lee, and Ted Selker. 2006. Lover's Cups: Drinking Interfaces As New Communication Channels. In *CHI '06 Extended Abstracts on Human Factors in Computing Systems* (CHI EA '06), 375–380. https://doi.org/10.1145/1125451.1125532
10. Karen Church, Antony Cousin, and Nuria Oliver. 2012. I Wanted to Settle a Bet!: Understanding Why and How People Use Mobile Search in Social Settings. In *Proceedings of the 14th International Conference on Human-computer Interaction with Mobile Devices and Services* (MobileHCI '12), 393–402. https://doi.org/10.1145/2371574.2371635
11. Enrico Costanza, Samuel A. Inverso, Rebecca Allen, and Pattie Maes. 2007. Intimate Interfaces in Action: Assessing the Usability and Subtlety of Emg-based Motionless Gestures. In *Proceedings of the SIGCHI Conference on Human Factors in Computing Systems* (CHI '07), 819–828. https://doi.org/10.1145/1240624.1240747
12. Jared Donovan and Robb Mitchell. 2010. Social Contraptions and Embodied Interaction. In *Proceedings of the 12th ACM International Conference Adjunct Papers on Ubiquitous Computing - Adjunct* (UbiComp '10 Adjunct), 403–404. https://doi.org/10.1145/1864431.1864458
13. David Finlay. 1982. Motion Perception in the Peripheral Visual Field. *Perception* 11, 4: 457–462. https://doi.org/10.1068/p110457
14. William W. Gaver, Jacob Beaver, and Steve Benford. 2003. Ambiguity As a Resource for Design. In *Proceedings of the SIGCHI Conference on Human Factors in Computing Systems* (CHI '03), 233–240. https://doi.org/10.1145/642611.642653
15. Luc Geurts and Vero Vanden Abeele. 2012. Splash Controllers: Game Controllers Involving the Uncareful Manipulation of Water. In *Proceedings of the Sixth International Conference on Tangible, Embedded and Embodied Interaction* (TEI '12), 183–186. https://doi.org/10.1145/2148131.2148170
16. Erving Goffman. 1959. *The Presentation of Self in Everyday Life*. Anchor, New York, NY.
17. Trevor Hogan and Eva Hornecker. 2017. Towards a Design Space for Multisensory Data Representation. *Interacting with Computers* 29, 2: 147–167. https://doi.org/10.1093/iwc/iww015
18. Jason Hong. Considering Privacy Issues in the Context of Google Glass. Retrieved December 8, 2017 from https://cacm.acm.org/magazines/2013/11/169041-considering-privacy-issues-in-the-context-of-google-glass/fulltext
19. Eva Hornecker and Jacob Buur. 2006. Getting a Grip on Tangible Interaction: A Framework on Physical Space and Social Interaction. In *Proceedings of the SIGCHI Conference on Human Factors in Computing*

Systems (CHI '06), 437–446. https://doi.org/10.1145/1124772.1124838

20. Shamsi T. Iqbal, Jonathan Grudin, and Eric Horvitz. 2011. Peripheral Computing During Presentations: Perspectives on Costs and Preferences. In *Proceedings of the SIGCHI Conference on Human Factors in Computing Systems* (CHI '11), 891–894. https://doi.org/10.1145/1978942.1979073
21. Hsin-Liu (Cindy) Kao and Chris Schmandt. 2015. MugShots: A Mug Display for Front and Back Stage Social Interaction in the Workplace. In *Proceedings of the Ninth International Conference on Tangible, Embedded, and Embodied Interaction* (TEI '15), 57–60. https://doi.org/10.1145/2677199.2680557
22. Lisa Kleinman. 2007. Physically Present, Mentally Absent: Technology Use in Face-to-face Meetings. In *CHI '07 Extended Abstracts on Human Factors in Computing Systems* (CHI EA '07), 2501–2506. https://doi.org/10.1145/1240866.1241031
23. Nan Li and Pierre Dillenbourg. 2012. Designing Conversation-context Recommendation Display to Support Opportunistic Search in Meetings. In *Proceedings of the 11th International Conference on Mobile and Ubiquitous Multimedia* (MUM '12), 12:1–12:4. https://doi.org/10.1145/2406367.2406382
24. Bruno Nadeau and Amanda Williams. 2009. Tactful Interaction: Exploring Interactive Social Touch Through a Collaborative Tangible Installation. In *Proceedings of the 3rd International Conference on Tangible and Embedded Interaction* (TEI '09), 147–152. https://doi.org/10.1145/1517664.1517700
25. Leysia Palen, Marilyn Salzman, and Ed Youngs. 2000. Going Wireless: Behavior & Practice of New Mobile Phone Users. In *Proceedings of the 2000 ACM Conference on Computer Supported Cooperative Work* (CSCW '00), 201–210. https://doi.org/10.1145/358916.358991
26. Max Van Kleek, Dave Murray-Rust, Amy Guy, Kieron O'Hara, and Nigel Shadbolt. 2016. Computationally Mediated Pro-Social Deception. In *Proceedings of the 2016 CHI Conference on Human Factors in Computing Systems* (CHI '16), 552–563. https://doi.org/10.1145/2858036.2858060
27. Jay Vidyarthi, Alissa N. Antle, and Bernhard E. Riecke. 2011. Sympathetic Guitar: Can a Digitally Augmented Guitar Be a Social Entity? In *CHI '11 Extended Abstracts on Human Factors in Computing Systems* (CHI EA '11), 1819–1824. https://doi.org/10.1145/1979742.1979863
28. Vessyl. Retrieved June 14, 2016 from https://www.myvessyl.com/
29. Yecup: Your Perfect Wireless Smart Mug. Retrieved June 14, 2016 from http://yecup.org/
30. Paulig Muki. Retrieved February 8, 2016 from http://www.pauligmuki.com/index.php?lang=en
31. Cogi - Beyond Notes. Retrieved January 14, 2017 from https://cogi.com/
32. Speech API - Speech Recognition. *Google Cloud Platform*. Retrieved January 16, 2017 from https://cloud.google.com/speech/
33. Google Knowledge Graph Search API | Knowledge Graph Search API. *Google Developers*. Retrieved January 16, 2017 from https://developers.google.com/knowledge-graph/
34. Intel shows off a light-up smart mug, because why not? *Engadget*. Retrieved February 8, 2016 from http://www.engadget.com/2014/01/07/intel-smart-mug-concept/

Focus Framework: Tracking Prototypes' Back-Talk

Markus Lorenz Schilling[1], Ron Wakkary[1,2], William Odom[1]
[1]Simon Fraser University, Surrey, British Columbia, Canada
[2]Eindhoven University of Technology, Eindhoven, Netherlands
{mschilli, rwakkary, wodom}@sfu.ca

ABSTRACT
This paper presents an analytical approach that we call the focus framework. The framework aids the analysis of the intended and unintended design attributes that emerge within a project's design process. The framework helps to reveal how prototypes and decision making interact together to shape the final design features and make visible the trajectory of central design attributes and unexplored alternatives. In this paper, we report on the framework and its development by way of a retrospective analysis of a tangible light installation we designed known as the Urban Data Posts. We see the potential for designers to use the focus framework as a post-mortem tool to retrospectively analyze their own work and thus inform their design practice. The knowledge gained through the analysis can then be applied in future projects more generatively.

Author Keywords
Research through Design; Design; Prototyping; Theory; Annotated Portfolio; Public Display; Installation; Sensing

INTRODUCTION
Prototyping is ubiquitous in nearly all design projects and prototypes are well understood and used, both in interaction design and design research. As a result, various kinds of prototyping tools, methods, and techniques exist [3,4,7,15,23,26]. But is there more to learn about prototypes, especially if we pay closer attention to the interplay between iterative forms, computation, materials and their impact on design decisions? While the TEI community heavily relies on prototypes to develop novel outcomes in tangible and embodied computing, considerably less attention has been paid to the roles of prototypes in this process. There is growing interest in more closely attending to design research processes in the broader interaction design community [19] and there exists an opportunity for conducting more in-depth designerly investigations of the role of prototypes in the tangible computing design process.

TEI '18, March 18–21, 2018, Stockholm, Sweden
© 2018 Association for Computing Machinery.
ACM ISBN 978-1-4503-5568-1/18/03…$15.00
https://doi.org/10.1145/3173225.3173259

Figure 1. One of the three data posts during the installation.

This work reports on the retrospective analysis of the design process behind the Urban Data Posts project. The Urban Data Posts project is a tangible light installation that aims to explore novel and unobtrusive ways of displaying urban renewable energy data in a public setting. It consists of three street bollard like shapes, each reading environmental data and emitting light through thin cracks (see Figure 1) based on the data. In this paper, we examine the series of prototypes we made that led to the final design of the Urban Data Posts. After completing the project, members of the design team wanted to better understand the tacit recognition of a reoccurring unintended design attribute or what we even saw as a "design flaw" and how it transformed into a central design attribute that altered the project's final outcome. The design feature in question are cracks of light (see Figure 1). This feature appeared in earlier prototypes, but, at the time, it was considered as a "design flaw" and was largely neglected. Yet, it re-emerged as the dominant attribute of the final design. This prompted us to critically reflect on our design process and inquire into the design moves and issues that catalyzed the transformation of this feature from unintentional to an intentional and central design feature.

Our retrospective analysis of the Urban Data Posts project evolved into a two-step process. In the first step, we gained a higher level understanding of our design process through the use of annotated portfolios [12], a method proposed by Gaver and Bowers to communicate knowledge developed in research through design. After applying and iterating on our project's annotated portfolio, an analytical framework emerged that we came to call the focus framework. The focus framework consists of 4 "lenses" – *in focus*, *out of focus*, *neglected* and *not present* – each describing the state of a design's attribute over the course of the design process. In the second step of our analysis, the prototypes in our design process were analyzed again, but this time through the lens of the focus framework. Examining the series of prototypes through this lens enabled us to illustrate what Schön [30] describes as a reflective conversation between designer and design object. The focus framework helps to bring to light the "back-talk" of individual prototypes, thus illustrating how a designer responds to (and neglects) the feedback of her prototypes.

The core contribution of this work is the focus framework, which enabled us to better analyze and synthesize the intricacies of our own design process. It revealed to us how our prototypes and decision making shaped the ultimate outcome of the Urban Data Posts project as well as unexplored alternatives. Designers can use the focus framework to retrospectively analyze their own work and thus inform their design practice, as well as better structure the documentation of their own design process to other design researchers and practitioners. The collective knowledge gained through the analysis can then be applied in future projects more generatively. This could be especially useful for the TEI community, which rarely relies on well-established design patterns or social norms, to design novel ways of interaction and interaction technologies.

In what follows, we provide a brief overview of related works and then provide a summary of the Urban Data Post project. We then move to the analysis of our design process to report on the focus framework and how it was developed. Lastly, we discuss the potential of the focus framework to analyze other design projects as a post-mortem tool and in the process inform future design practice.

BACKGROUND AND RELATED WORK

Related work falls into two areas: (i) design as a reflective practice to create tangible and embodied systems, and (ii) prototypes and prototyping in the design process.

Design as a reflective practice

While researchers such as Alexander [1], Simon [33] and many others have articulated definitions of design, Schön's work [30] is most centrally aligned with our approach because of his characterization of design as a reflective practice. In particular, Schön argues that a designer: "*shapes the situation, in accordance with his initial appreciation of it, the situation "talks back", and he [the designer] responds to the situations back-talk.*" [30:79]. Schön and Bennet [31] compare the designer's ability to think about what she is doing to influence further doing to jazz improvisation – players listen to oneself and one-another while still playing and reacting to each other's actions. The same can be said about prototyping. Any act of prototyping prompts the prototype to provide feedback which influences further doing by the designer and so on. The focus framework aims to leverage and extend the notion of back-talk by providing a lens for attending to the complex and, at times, unnoticed or unintended roles that prototypes play across the process of designing tangible and embodied computational systems.

Tangibility and Embodiment TEI

After the introduction of TUIs [17], tangibility and embodiment received growing attention in design and design research. Early contributions provide frameworks and taxonomies to better articulate the field (e.g. [10],[16], and [18]), with more recent work exploring novel interactive artifacts [32] and extending existing physical artifacts and landscapes through interactivity [13]. Prototyping and prototypes play a special role in the field of tangible and embodied systems, simply because of the physical nature of the design artifacts themselves. The TEI community increasingly become concerned with investigating new ways of prototyping [14,24,29,39] and inquiring into materials used when prototyping tangible interfaces [2]. While there is growing interest in attending to the rich and nuanced details of creating radically new forms of interaction and interaction technologies in the broader interaction design community (e.g., [12,19,35]), the role(s) that prototypes play in and across different stages of the tangible interaction design process have retrieved less attention. Our work contributes a framework that can be retrospectively applied to the process of designing tangible systems that aids in better revealing how prototypes shape key design decisions that led to the ultimate design outcome.

Prototypes & prototyping

The understanding of what a prototype is and the various ways it can operate has evolved over the years in the design research community. Researchers have discussed how prototypes can function as tools for design exploration or concept validation [7,20,34], and forms of rhetorical argumentation [11]. Based on a comprehensive review of these works and many others related to prototypes in design, Lim et al. [20] proposes that prototypes are rich resources for manifesting design ideas as well as filtering and exploring specific qualities of emerging concepts. They describe how prototypes operate as externalizations of design ideas that are materialized across three dimensions: material, resolution, and scope. For example, a designer can filter certain parts of a prototype (appearance, data, functionality, interactivity, and spatial structure) to only work on attributes that are currently of importance or that she wants to focus on. This enables the designer to traverse the design space and make decisions without resolving the other attributes. We aim to build on this research by offering a concrete framework that better brings into focus and improves the roles that prototyping and prototypes play across the process of designing tangible and embodied computational systems.

Prototypes within the design process

Dove et. al [9] argue for the importance of design space reflection, concluding that it can be highly beneficial for the designer to retrospectively look at a project's design process. They argue that becoming better attuned to how artifacts and

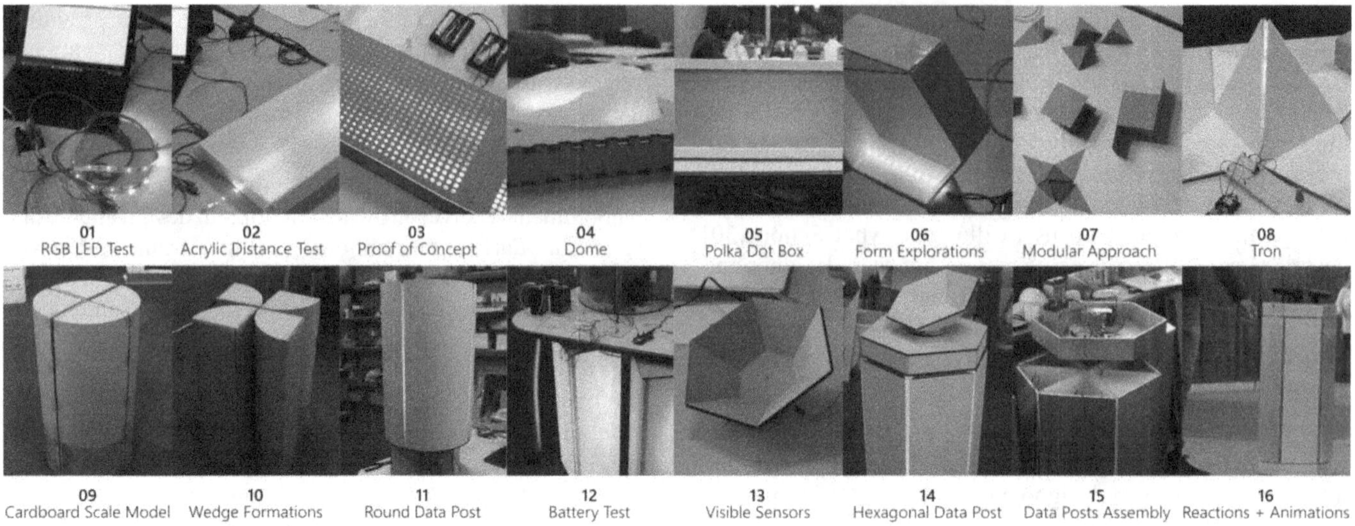

Figure 2. Overview of all prototpyes in the Urban Data Posts project in chronological order.

activities shape the conceptualization of the design space can encourage designers to reconsider valuable alternatives disregarded earlier in the process. Recent research has also emerged that aims to help better capture a project's design process [8,9,22]. For example, Yen et. al [40] explored how reflection can be best combined with the review of feedback during the design process instead of retrospectively. Wakkary et. al [38] reveal the value of reporting on first-hand insights and the lessons learned from building bespoke design artifacts. Boucher [5] unpacks how seemingly trivial design concerns during a design research project are ultimately integral to the nature of research questions manifested by design artifacts themselves. Our work builds on and extends this nascent and growing body of research by contributing the focus framework to better structure first-hand accounts and insights across the process of designing tangibles. The focus framework enables design teams to gain a better understanding of a project's design process and can provide guidance when designing novel tangible objects and interactions.

URBAN DATA POSTS

This section provides a brief overview of the Urban Data Posts project with a focus on its design process. Our aim here is to provide sufficient background information on the project for the reader to follow the analysis of the Urban Data Posts that follows later in the paper.

Overview

The Urban Data Posts project is a tangible light installation deployed in public at Telus World of Science that displays urban renewable energy data. The installation consisted of three street bollard like shapes, called *data posts* (see Figure 1). Each post sensed the energy level of a current (wind and solar) or potential future energy resource (walking) in that urban area. Based on the sensing, the data posts would emit different light animations. The installation was developed over the course of one year and deployed over the course of three weeks. The first author led this entire process, supported by two members of our design studio. While every member brought different abilities to the project (design, woodworking, project management, etc.), all three took part in the concept, design, prototyping, and deployment stages of the Urban Data Posts project.

The goal of the *Urban Data Posts* project is to explore novel and unobtrusive ways of displaying situated data in a public setting, thus aiming to avoid the use of more traditional graphs and charts as well as common displays and screens. Despite the novelty of the display, we wanted the data posts to blend in with the public environment, which required finding a subtle way to display the data. Our intended audience were neighborhood residents and cyclists and pedestrians commuting back and forth to work. Given this, we felt it should take time and multiple interactions for someone to develop a growing understanding and appreciation for our project.

Design Process

The early conceptual work of the design process led to the agreement to develop a tangible light installation with RGB LED strips. The main factors were feasibility and flexibility in designing the final forms of the installation. After that, the design team started to work on one of the main challenges: designing a novel form of display using RGB LED strips.

Various ideas and their respective prototypes looked promising, but were dismissed upon closer investigation due to the lack of visibility, scalability, or visual appearance (see prototypes 2-6 in Figure 2). After a wide variety of prototypes were built the design team tacitly realized the reoccurrence of a "design flaw" in almost all of the prototypes built so far: cracks with light leaking through. These cracks were the result of the tools we used, the time we spent building the prototypes, or our own competencies. However, almost intuitively, this "design flaw", the cracks, were then investigated, iterated and established as a form of display meeting our requirements. While this sounds straightforward, in the midst of the messiness in a design process, the emergence of the cracks as a design feature seemed a surprise and to come out of nowhere. It was unclear to us where exactly this idea emerged from, which is why we refer to this event as a tacit recognition. After more iterations of prototypes, we established the cracks as a form of display. We then improved the design both technically and aesthetically, and professionally manufactured parts for the final installation.

Final Design

The Urban Data Posts project consists of three street hexagonal prisms (i.e. *data posts* – see Figure 1). Each data post consists of three parts: base, wedges, and visible sensor. The base is the short hexagonal prism on the bottom acting as a pedestal. The heart of each artifact are the wedges – six triangular prisms which form a hexagon. Each of the wedge hosts a RGB LED strip which illuminates the space in between the wedges, referred to as cracks. The visible sensor is the top part of each data post. Much like the base, it is a hexagonal prism but with a small model of a sensor attached to it. It also hosts the remaining electronics such as sensors, batteries, circuit and an Arduino Uno.

Deployment and Results

While it is not the aim of this paper to report on the results of the project (forthcoming), we saw it as a success. During our 3 week deployment at Telus World of Science (a science museum situated in a large open urban setting), the data posts fulfilled our goals mentioned previously. They (1) blended in well with their environment due to their similarity with street posts, (2) displayed subtle, yet distinct animations depending on the current readings of renewable energy resources, and (3) evoked curiosity about their nature and playful interactions from many pedestrians during our deployment. This informal evaluation of the project is based on our observations and interactions with pedestrians during the deployment of the three Urban Data Posts, and our own expectations towards a novel display for environmental data.

DEVELOPING THE FOCUS FRAMEWORK: ANNOTATED PORTFOLIO OF THE URBAN DATA POSTS

This section describes our first step in the retrospective analysis of the Urban Data Posts project, during which the focus framework emerged. Our aim here is to give a methodological account for how we approached our analysis from which the framework was developed despite that not being the intention at the outset. It is also important to us to emphasize that the focus framework did not exist *a priori* to the analysis of the project. Rather, it emerged from the analysis of design process. We first used annotated portfolio as an analytical approach. However, it unintentionally resulted in another analytical tool (our focus framework), rather than a satisfactory account of our design process. We do not view this unexpected emergence as problematic. It makes clear the inductive (or 'bottom up') approach to making sense of an ultimate design in which the concrete details and particulars of a design process need to be contended with first. In this way, knowledge is emergent rather than predicted through a top-down theoretical approach. Further, our experience demonstrates the flexibility and strength of annotated portfolios as a means to analyze at the level of design particulars and intermediate theory [21].

Annotated portfolios

After the Urban Data Posts project was complete, members of the design team wanted to understand the various prototypes and their influence in the project's trajectory in the bigger picture. Especially, since a specific design attribute (cracks with light) transitioned from being a "design flaw" in earlier prototypes, to a central idea in the final design. We wanted to understand how the design team came to realize the potential of the cracks in the midst of the design process, how the cracks transitioned from being an unintentional attribute to being an intentional and central feature, and how other design decisions and prototypes may have influenced our ultimate design.

The analysis of the Urban Data Posts project was a group effort. While the first author was in charge of the analysis, the remaining design team members provided frequent feedback and input towards the analysis in form of regular meetings. Decisions affecting the analysis (e.g. choosing criteria, interpretation, etc.) were made through discussions and by mutual consent. The analysis itself was conducted shortly after the project had been deployed, roughly three weeks after the final prototypes were build. The analysis took approximately one week.

To start our analysis, we chose annotated portfolio as a way to dissect our design process and gain a better understanding of how our prototypes and decision making shaped the project's final design. Annotated portfolios was introduced by Gaver and Bower [12] as a way to communicate research through design. An annotated portfolio is a collection of designed artifacts (a portfolio) represented in a suitable medium (images, videos, etc.) and commented with short texts (annotations). A portfolio, as Bowers [6] writes "*can be annotated in several different ways reflecting different purposes and interests.*" (p. 72). Löwgren [21] sees annotated portfolios as a form of intermediate level knowledge. It elicits key ideas, structures and considerations from the actual artifacts it represents, which can then be used in a generative and aspirational way. Thus, annotated portfolios show close resemblance to other forms of intermediate-level knowledge, like strong concepts [15] and design patterns [4].

We chose annotated portfolio as a starting point in our analysis, because it allowed us to take two positions at once: (1) as researchers investigating the design and prototyping process of the Urban Data Posts project and (2) as the designers of that said project and that had access to intimate, first-hand knowledge about it [21]. By utilizing our "first person" account of this research through design project we could draw on our own knowledge and experiences instead of someone else's, in order to gain a more holistic understanding of the prototypes and how they influenced our final design.

Preparation

As a first step in our analysis, all prototypes were identified and chronologically ordered. We also gave every prototype a name to clearly identify them. As a means to represent the single prototypes, we chose to use images because we documented the Urban Data Posts project with roughly 500 images and 40 videos. 2-5 pictures were selected for each prototype that illustrated it from different angles, different stages of completion, and highlighted different features. Printed copies were assembled on a whiteboard, and we began to create categories for our annotated portfolio.

Figure 3. Annotated Portfolio of the Urban Data Posts project.

Guided by our aim to understand the roles of the cracks across the design process and their attendant influence, we created the following points for our annotated portfolio: prototype intention, problems encountered, outcome, time, material and components, tools, and competencies.

Data Collection and Data Wrangling

After the categories were added to the white board, we then started to annotate each prototype. The annotated portfolio then went through several iterations in our attempt to better understand the project's design process. During this back and forth in analysis we deployed several strategies such as: (1) trying to find a correlation between different annotation points (e.g., the tools we used and the outcome of the prototype), (2) gradually adding new annotation points (i.e., conceptual decisions, design insights, design decisions) to elicit more details about the prototype, and (3) clustering annotation points into bigger categories. This process prompted us to rethink our labeling of the cracks of earlier prototypes as "design flaws". We realized they were merely the result of the tools and materials we used, and our own competencies when building the prototypes. Rather than "design flaws", we came to think of them as design attributes, even if unintentional and, at times, unwanted.

Emergence of the Focus Framework

This thinking of "design flaws" as unintentional design attributes helped us to construct the focus framework out or our project annotated portfolio. We realized that in order to better understand the development of the Urban Data Posts, we have to capture both, our intentions building the single prototypes, as well as any unintentional side effects. Furthermore, we cannot look at prototypes in isolation, but need to look at them as part of a bigger process. To help capture our prototypes' intentional and unintentional design aspects over time, we came up with two conceptual lenses, called "in focus" and "out of focus". The idea behind these lenses is to describe a prototypes intention (e.g., why the prototype was built, materials and tools used, etc.), as well as unintentional side effects (e.g., unwanted or unexpected side-effects, problems, etc.). After a few smaller iterations, our work with the project's annotated portfolio yielded what we came to call the *focus framework.* The focus framework is a timeline of prototypes in the design process, which lists each prototype's intention or purpose (*in focus*) and its "back-talk" (*out of focus*). It can be understood as a discrete analytical tool which emerged through the combination of higher level categories created while iterating the on annotated portfolio and attaching elements of it to a timeline.

Although the focus framework emerged through the annotated portfolio of our project, the two are distinct. Annotated portfolios are meant as a way to communicate design research by eliciting key ideas and structures of the final design. The focus framework on the other hand is not concerned with communicating the intent or underlying conceptual thinking of a final design. It is concerned with process, especially how each prototype shaped the designer's decision making that led to the final design. Thus, the focus framework appeared better suited for retrospectively analyzing our design process.

FOCUS FRAMEWORK ANALYSIS

The following section introduces the focus framework and offers an in-depth analysis of the Urban Data Posts project's design process through the framework. Our aim is to describe and demonstrate concisely but concretely the focus framework in a way that is clear and can be seen to be transferable and usable for other design projects.

The focus framework

The focus framework consists of four lenses, called *in focus*, *out of focus*, *neglected* and *not present*. *In focus* and *out of focus* describe a prototypes intentional and unintentional design attributes. They capture a prototypes "back-talk" [30] and help to understand the interplay between designer and her prototypes throughout the design process, bringing to light the underlying decision making. The lenses *neglected* and *not present* are used to round out the framework. After the focus framework had emerged from the annotated portfolio, we moved the framework to a spreadsheet, arranging the prototypes horizontally in chronological order and the 4 lenses vertically. Design attributes were then added with colored boxes and traced through the single prototypes. The spreadsheet was then digitized and brought into an easier to read visualization which shows resemblance to a transit map (see Figure 4).

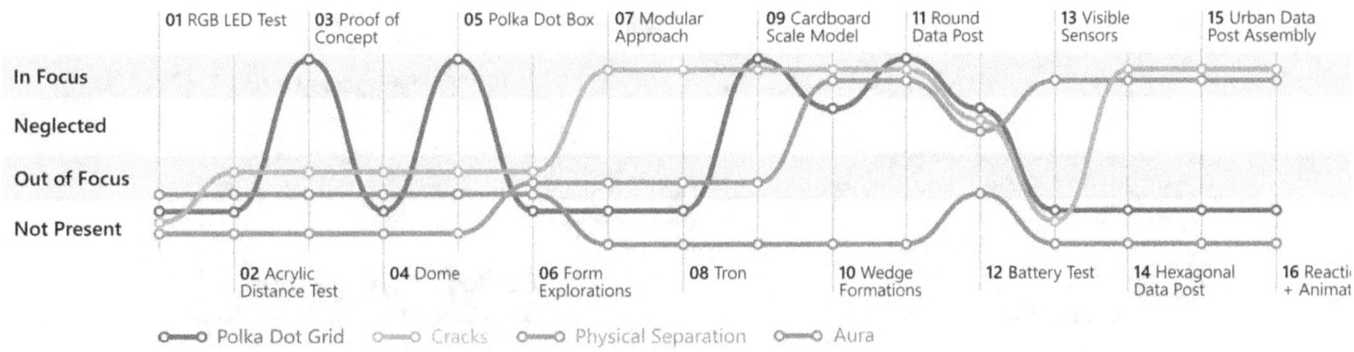

Figure 4. The focus framework showing 4 major threads: Polka Dot Grid (red), Cracks (orange), Physical Separation (green), and Aura (blue).

In focus

In focus describes intentional design attributes in prototypes. Design attributes the designer is *consciously and intentionally* building into the prototype. *In focus* shows resemblance to the filtering dimensions described in the anatomy framework by Lim et al. [20]. Both frameworks describe the intentionality of a designer to build a prototype to explore a specific attribute of her designs. The focus framework uses actual attributes and features of the design. For instance, in our design we were visually separating the data posts, building using a physical model of a sensor which would be needed to read the energy resource this specific data post is representing. The focus was the physical model of a sensor, which we named "Visible Sensor". The design attributes *in focus* obviously differ from project to project, making the focus framework more practice-oriented at the expense of more generalizable theory.

Out of focus

Out of focus describes *unintentional design attributes* in prototypes. Design attributes the designer is *unconsciously and unintentionally* building into the prototype. They are the result of *accidental circumstances* during the build. Before building a prototype, a designer usually visualizes what she wants to build, which can take many forms, such as a mental image, renderings, sketches, and so on. In most cases the actual prototype does not match with the one visualized due to various factors (e.g. materials used, tools, time spent, own competencies, etc.). Any attribute in the actual prototype that differs from the designer's visualization (the intended design), is here referred to as an unintentional design attribute. They are deviations from the 'intended' but are never "big enough" to interfere with a prototype's purpose. Because of that, the designer is unaware of their presence, as her focus is elsewhere. As soon as unintentional design attributes interfere with a prototype's purpose, the designer will likely address them by removing them altogether or altering their appearance.

Neglected and not present

The notions of *neglected* and *not present* help to round out the concept of the focus framework by providing lenses for design attributes that are neither *in focus* nor *out of focus*. *Neglected* are design attributes which are part of a prototype but they aren't *in focus* (because the designer's attention is elsewhere) nor can they be *out of focus* (because the attribute was *in focus* in earlier prototypes). *Not present* simply means a design attribute can't be found in the current prototype. Although these lenses are not fundamental to the framework, they help to keep track of all design attributes during the analysis as we will show when applying the focus framework to analyze the Urban Data Posts project.

Focus Framework Analysis of the Urban Data Posts

Through applying the *focus framework* to examine the prototypes in the Urban Data Posts project's design process, we identified four design attributes that had (or could have had) a major impact on our design. For brevity, only one thread (we refer to the serial occurrences of a design attribute as a *thread)* is described in detail and a quick summary will be given for the remaining three. Figure 4 shows the four different design attributes (colored lines) and their respective status (vertical axis) throughout the design process with its prototypes (horizontal axis).

The Cracks Thread

This thread follows the design attribute called *Cracks*, which are narrow spaces with light leaking through. The idea to work with cracks came from a tacit recognition of their presence in early prototypes (see Figure 5).

Cracks were part of our prototypes as soon as we started to give our prototypes a physical form. Much to our surprise, they appeared in 5 out of the 6 prototypes we built early in the design process. Looking closer at the prototypes, the cracks were the result of the materials and tools we used, how much time we spent building the prototypes and our own competencies. For instance, in one case we had to split our design into two parts, because the laser cutter we were working with couldn't fit the whole piece of our intended design. As a result, we had to "stitch" the two parts together afterwards, resulting in a crack. In another case, we were not able to completely close the lid of our prototype. As a result, some of the finger joints remained open as small cracks, causing light leaking through. However, none of these "issues" interfered with our prototype's purpose and our focus was elsewhere. As a result, the *cracks* in these prototypes were *out of focus*.

02 Acrylic Distance Test | 03 Proof of Concept | 04 Dome | 05 Polka Dot Box | 06 Form Explorations

Figure 5. Cracks appeared in early prototypes but were *out of focus.*

After the cracks reappeared in another prototype (this time due to the material we used), we tacitly realized their potential use for conscious implementation in our design. Our focus shifted and we no longer saw them as a "design flaw" but as an opportunity. We then decided to explore *Cracks* as a form of display and moved them *in focus*.

After we established the *crack's* visibility and utility in the following prototypes, they stayed *in focus* for almost the rest of the design process because they transformed into an integral part of the design. *Cracks* were only once *neglected* and *not present*. While *not present* is rather self-explanatory, they were *neglected* once because we repurposed parts of an earlier prototype in which the *cracks* appeared, but our focus in the prototype was elsewhere (i.e. the circuitry). They couldn't be *out of focus* since we knew about their existence and were working with them. This shows the minor roles *not present* and *neglected* play in the framework and how they help to keep track of all attributes.

Our analysis using the focus framework revealed that the *Cracks* were part of our design process much earlier than we had anticipated. We could now see how the *Cracks* appeared in our prototypes way before we had recognized them in our actual design process. This in turn allowed us to understand *how* they had appeared. Reasons for their appearance include the tools we used, the materials we chose, the time we spent building prototypes, and our own competencies. However, for several prototypes, the *Cracks* were always seen as a "design flaw" and thus *out of focus*. They did not interfere with our prototype's purpose and our attention was elsewhere. This changed when we suddenly became aware of their presence and saw their possible utility. We then started to consciously explore *Cracks* as a form of display and turned them into an integral part of the final design, as the focus framework reveals the *Cracks* stay *in focus*.

Summary of remaining threads

The focus framework also revealed other insights of our design process through the other threads.

The *Polka Dot Grid* is a form of display which uses a polka dot pattern cut into an opaque material to cover an illuminated surface (see Figure 5, prototypes 3 and 5). Following the erratic path of the *Polka Dot Grid* (see Figure 4), one can see how the design attribute appeared and disappeared throughout the design process. This jumping back and forth can be explained by the fact, that we were fond of this design idea and tried to recycle it throughout the design process. However, it never met our requirements, which is why it is not part of the final design.

Physical Separation describes the idea to visually separate the single *data posts* from each other. This design attribute also moved *in focus* after a tacit recognition of their presence and possible utility. After this design attribute had appeared midway through the design process, it moved *in focus* and stayed there (with just one exception) as it became another key attribute in our design. *Physical Separation* follows a very similar, yet delayed, path to the *cracks,* something we were not aware before our analysis.

Aura is a design attribute which was recognized during our analysis. It describes the appearance of a very subtle halo around an artifact, without a noticeable light source. As can be seen in the overview (see Figure 4), it appeared almost at the same time as *Physical Separation*, yet never moved *in focus*. Aura is a very interesting design attribute, as it represents a missed and unexplored design opportunity which was discovered through the framework.

Summary of the focus framework

As seen in the Urban Data Posts project, unintentional design attributes can have a major impact on the design process, but it is up to the designer to capitalize on them. She needs to engage in a reflective conversation with her prototypes and closely listen to their "back-talk" [30]. The focus framework allows one to better understand the reflective conversation between design and her prototypes, as it captures each prototypes intentional and unintentional design attributes. Although simplified, the focus framework shows the reality of prototyping from a designer's perspective – constantly gauging which design attributes she wants to explore, while at the same time looking for new opportunities, combining ideas and making decisions for the final design.

DISCUSSION

The goal of this research is to motivate and develop the focus framework as a post mortem analytical tool to better understand and articulate the process of designing tangible and embodied computational artifacts.

The *focus framework* helped us to bring clarity to our design process in the Urban Data Posts project. Specifically, it enabled us to better articulate and critically reflect on when and why *Cracks* appeared in our prototypes, and how they ultimately influenced the final design. It also enabled us to better identify other design attributes that dramatically shaped our design (Polka Dot Grid and Physical Separation). While *Physical Separation* explains the distinct visual appearance of each *data post*, the *Polka Dot Grid* is an example of a failed attempt to shape the design in a certain way. Conversely, *Aura* represents a missed opportunity in our design process. In this way, the focus framework provided a structure that we could productively scaffold to better understand how our final design came to be, and how competing influences of different prototypes and their attributes shaped the trajectory of our design process. This is valuable knowledge to the designer, in order to better understand her own process to advance her practice. In our case, prior to our retrospective analysis, the design process, particularly the appearance and influence of the *Cracks*, was described as a tacit recognition that was largely mysterious. The insights distilled through the focus framework, enabled us to acutely see that the *Cracks* were actually part of our design for quite some time. We, as designers, were just not sensitive enough to their existence, utility, and generative potential. Or as Schön [30] would put it, we were not receptive enough to the prototype's "back-talk" because it was obscured by so many other design elements and attribute form the various prototypes we created.

After establishing the focus framework, its application to the design processes of other projects in our design research studio became apparent. We could see how in several cases design attributes transitioned from being unintentional (*out of focus*) to being intentional (*in focus*). For example, in case of the *table-non-table* [25,27,36,37]—a material speculation investigation into ideas of unselfconscious interaction [37] and unawareness [25]—we could better see and understand how *sound* transitioned from *out of focus* to *in focus*. The table-non-table is a stack of paper supported by a motorized aluminum chassis that infrequently moves. At first, it was very important to us that the table-non-table was as quiet as possible. We therefore looked into different ways of building the table-non-table, and specifically how we could soundproof the casing for the actuators. However, as the project progressed we came to realize that sound is very important to the experience of the table-non-table, as it is one of the key attributes that gives away the object's otherwise barely visible movement. We then focused on refining and integrating sound as a key design feature.

This application of the focus framework outside the Urban Data Posts project, is a promising sign that the framework has value as a post mortem analytical tool to better understand the development of a tangible design artifacts. It can help to unpack how a final design came to be and where specific design attributes originated and trace their influence. This helps a designer to grow her understanding of a design process, and develop a sensibility and repertoire for designing novel tangible objects in future projects.

The focus framework could also be used in a generative way. The design attributes distilled through the focus framework in one project, might be useful in other projects. For instance, the design attribute *Aura*, which we discovered in the Urban Data Posts project, might be applicable in future design situations. In this way, the focus framework thus could act as an archive of design attributes and can be used to gain inspiration for other projects.

LIMITATIONS

There are two main limitations to this research. One, the findings of this research are based on a single design case. We can see the framework's utility after informally applying it to the design process of other projects that came out of our studio, but future research is needed to verify and refine the focus framework. Second, the Urban Data Posts project was conducted in an academic research context – and not in a professional design context. There are clear differences between the two when it comes to the execution of a design project [28]. Projects in a professional design context tend to have different constraints than projects in an academic setting. Projects in an academic research setting also tend to be paced differently and have more flexible timeframes.

FUTURE RESEARCH OPPORTUNITIES

Based on one of the limitations, future research opportunities include the application of the focus framework to other projects, both in academia and in industry. In the practice of interaction design, it would be interesting to see the framework applied to projects in software design or projects with faceless interaction (e.g., gestural or audio-based interfaces). We see the focus framework to be specifically useful within a field such as TEI. There is an opportunity to leverage the focus framework in future work in the TEI community to better communicate the design processes of novel tangible objects and, in doing so, to extend the framework itself further.

CONCLUSION

This work introduced the *focus framework,* which was used to retrospectively examine the prototypes in the design process of the Urban Data Posts project. The focus framework allowed us to gain a better understanding of the emergence and transformation of important design attributes in our project. We propose the focus framework as a post mortem analytical tool for designers in the TEI community to better articulate their own design projects and inquiries into creating novel tangible objects and systems. Better capturing and communicating this knowledge will increase our collective understanding of the intricacies in the process of designing novel tangible objects and systems, and will enable designers in our community to grow and mature as it influences their future decision making.

REFERENCES

1. Christopher Alexander. 1964. *Notes on the synthesis of form*. Harvard University Press, Cambridge.
2. Alissa N. Antle. 2008. Inquiring materials for tangible prototyping. In *Proceedings of the 2nd international conference on Tangible and embedded interaction*, 139–140. Retrieved July 24, 2017 from http://dl.acm.org/citation.cfm?id=1347420
3. Laurens Boer and Jared Donovan. 2012. Provotypes for participatory innovation. In *Proceedings of the designing interactive systems conference*, 388–397. Retrieved November 10, 2016 from http://dl.acm.org/citation.cfm?id=2318014
4. Jan Borchers. 2000. A Pattern Approach to Interaction Design. In *Proceedings of the Designing Interactive Systems Conference*, 369–378.
5. Andy Boucher. 2016. The Form Design of the Datacatcher: A Research Prototype. In *Proceedings of the 2016 ACM Conference on Designing Interactive Systems*, 595–606. https://doi.org/10.1145/2901790.2901907
6. John Bowers. 2012. The logic of annotated portfolios: communicating the value of'research through design'. In *Proceedings of the Designing Interactive Systems Conference*, 68–77. Retrieved October 6, 2016 from http://dl.acm.org/citation.cfm?id=2317968
7. Marion Buchenau and Jane Fulton Suri. 2000. Experience prototyping. In *Proceedings of the 3rd conference on Designing interactive systems: processes, practices, methods, and techniques*, 424–433. Retrieved November 10, 2016 from http://dl.acm.org/citation.cfm?id=347802
8. Peter Dalsgaard and Kim Halskov. 2012. Reflective design documentation. In *Proceedings of the Designing Interactive Systems Conference*, 428–437. Retrieved July 30, 2017 from http://dl.acm.org/citation.cfm?id=2318020
9. Graham Dove, Nicolai Brodersen Hansen, and Kim Halskov. 2016. An Argument For Design Space Reflection. In *Proceedings of the 9th Nordic Conference on Human-Computer Interaction*, 1–10. https://doi.org/10.1145/2971485.2971528
10. KennethP. Fishkin. 2004. A taxonomy for and analysis of tangible interfaces. *Personal and Ubiquitous Computing* 8, 5. https://doi.org/10.1007/s00779-004-0297-4
11. A. Galey and S. Ruecker. 2010. How a prototype argues. *Literary and Linguistic Computing* 25, 4: 405–424. https://doi.org/10.1093/llc/fqq021
12. Bill Gaver and John Bowers. 2012. Annotated Portfolios. *interactions* 19, 4: 40–49. https://doi.org/10.1145/2212877.2212889
13. Jonna Häkkilä, Olli Koskenranta, Maaret Posti, and Yun He. 2013. City landmark as an interactive installation: experiences with stone, water and public space. In *Proceedings of the 8th International Conference on Tangible, Embedded and Embodied Interaction*, 221–224. https://doi.org/10.1145/2540930.2540980
14. Thorsten Hochreuter. 2013. LemonGrasp: a tool for touch-interaction prototyping. In *Proceedings of the 8th International Conference on Tangible, Embedded and Embodied Interaction*, 317–320. https://doi.org/10.1145/2540930.2558130
15. Kristina Höök and Jonas Löwgren. 2012. Strong concepts: Intermediate-level knowledge in interaction design research. *ACM Transactions on Computer-Human Interaction* 19, 3: 1–18. https://doi.org/10.1145/2362364.2362371
16. Eva Hornecker and Jacob Buur. 2006. Getting a grip on tangible interaction: a framework on physical space and social interaction. In *Proceedings of the SIGCHI conference on Human Factors in computing systems*, 437–446. Retrieved July 25, 2017 from http://dl.acm.org/citation.cfm?id=1124838
17. Hiroshi Ishii and Brygg Ullmer. 1997. Tangible bits: towards seamless interfaces between people, bits and atoms. In *Proceedings of the ACM SIGCHI Conference on Human factors in computing systems*, 234–241. Retrieved July 24, 2017 from http://dl.acm.org/citation.cfm?id=258715
18. Robert JK Jacob, Audrey Girouard, Leanne M. Hirshfield, Michael S. Horn, Orit Shaer, Erin Treacy Solovey, and Jamie Zigelbaum. 2008. Reality-based interaction: a framework for post-WIMP interfaces. In *Proceedings of the SIGCHI conference on Human factors in computing systems*, 201–210. Retrieved July 25, 2017 from http://dl.acm.org/citation.cfm?id=1357089
19. Nadine Jarvis, David Cameron, and Andy Boucher. 2012. Attention to detail: annotations of a design process. In *Proceedings of the 7th Nordic Conference on Human-Computer Interaction: Making Sense Through Design*, 11–20. Retrieved August 9, 2017 from http://dl.acm.org/citation.cfm?id=2399019
20. Youn-Kyung Lim, Erik Stolterman, and Josh Tenenberg. 2008. The anatomy of prototypes: Prototypes as filters, prototypes as manifestations of design ideas. *ACM Transactions on Computer-Human Interaction* 15, 2: 1–27. https://doi.org/10.1145/1375761.1375762
21. Jonas Löwgren. 2013. Annotated portfolios and other forms of intermediate-level knowledge. *Interactions* 20, 1: 30–34.
22. Allan MacLean, Richard M. Young, Victoria ME Bellotti, and Thomas P. Moran. 1991. Questions, options, and criteria: Elements of design space analysis. *Human–computer interaction* 6, 3–4: 201–250.
23. Michael McCurdy, Christopher Connors, Guy Pyrzak, Bob Kanefsky, and Alonso Vera. 2006. Breaking the fidelity barrier: an examination of our current characterization of prototypes and an example

of a mixed-fidelity success. In *Proceedings of the SIGCHI conference on Human Factors in computing systems*, 1233–1242. Retrieved October 6, 2016 from http://dl.acm.org/citation.cfm?id=1124959

24. Satoshi Nakamaru, Jakob Bak, and Dhruv Saxena. 2016. Tangible Modeling Methods for Faster Rapid Prototyping. In *Proceedings of the TEI '16: Tenth International Conference on Tangible, Embedded, and Embodied Interaction*, 518–523. https://doi.org/10.1145/2839462.2856530
25. William Odom and Ron Wakkary. 2015. Intersecting with Unaware Objects. In *Proceedings of the 2015 ACM SIGCHI Conference on Creativity and Cognition,* 33–42. https://doi.org/10.1145/2757226.2757240
26. William Odom, Ron Wakkary, Youn-kyung Lim, Audrey Desjardins, Bart Hengeveld, and Richard Banks. 2016. From Research Prototype to Research Product. In *Proceedings of the 2016 CHI Conference on Human Factors in Computing Systems,* 2549–2561. https://doi.org/10.1145/2858036.2858447
27. Doenja Oogjes and Ron Wakkary. 2017. Videos of Things: speculating on, anticipating and synthesizing technological mediations. In *Proceedings of the 35th Annual ACM Conference on Human Factors in Computing Systems.* (CHI'17).
28. David J. Roedl and Erik Stolterman. 2013. Design research at CHI and its applicability to design practice. In *Proceedings of the SIGCHI Conference on Human Factors in Computing Systems,* 1951-1954. https://doi.org/10.1145/2470654.2466257
29. Joel Sadler, Kevin Durfee, Lauren Shluzas, and Paulo Blikstein. 2015. Bloctopus: A Novice Modular Sensor System for Playful Prototyping. In *Proceedings of the Ninth International Conference on Tangible, Embedded, and Embodied Interaction,* 347–354. https://doi.org/10.1145/2677199.2680581
30. Donald A. Schön. 2000. *Reflective practitioner: how professionals think in action.* BasicBooks, New York.
31. Donald Schön and John Bennett. 1996. Reflective Conversation with Materials. In *Bringing Design to Software*, Terry Winograd (ed.). ACM, New York, NY, USA, 171–189. Retrieved November 11, 2016 from http://doi.acm.org/10.1145/229868.230044
32. Susanne Seitinger, Daniel M. Taub, and Alex S. Taylor. 2010. Light bodies: exploring interactions with responsive lights. In *Proceedings of the fourth international conference on Tangible, embedded, and embodied interaction*, 113–120. Retrieved July 24, 2017 from http://dl.acm.org/citation.cfm?id=1709908
33. Herbert A. (Herbert Alexander) Simon. 1981. *The sciences of the artificial.* MIT Press, Cambridge, Mass.
34. Pieter Jan Stappers. 2013. Prototypes as Central Vein for Knowledge Development. In *Prototype: design and craft in the 21st century*, Louise Valentine (ed.). Bloomsbury, London, 85–98.
35. Erik Stolterman and Mikael Wiberg. 2010. Concept-Driven Interaction Design Research. *Human-Computer Interaction* 25, 2: 95–118. https://doi.org/10.1080/07370020903586696
36. Ron Wakkary. 2016. Designing to know: chairs, bowls and other everyday technological things. Retrieved from https://pure.tue.nl/ws/files/41066084/Wakkary_2016.pdf
37. Ron Wakkary, Audrey Desjardins, and Sabrina Hauser. 2016. Unselfconscious Interaction: A Conceptual Construct. *Interacting with Computers* 28, 4: 501–520. https://doi.org/10.1093/iwc/iwv018
38. Ron Wakkary, Henry Lin, Shannon Mortimer, Lauren Low, Audrey Desjardins, Keith Doyle, and Philip Robbins. 2016. Productive Frictions: Moving from Digital to Material Prototyping and Low-Volume Production for Design Research. In *Proceedings of the 2016 ACM Conference on Designing Interactive Systems*, 1258–1269. https://doi.org/10.1145/2901790.2901880
39. Alexander Wiethoff, Hanna Schneider, Michael Rohs, Andreas Butz, and Saul Greenberg. 2012. Sketch-a-TUI: low cost prototyping of tangible interactions using cardboard and conductive ink. In *Proceedings of the Sixth International Conference on Tangible, Embedded and Embodied Interaction*, 309–312. Retrieved July 24, 2017 from http://dl.acm.org/citation.cfm?id=2148196
40. Yu-Chun Grace Yen, Steven P. Dow, Elizabeth Gerber, and Brian P. Bailey. 2017. Listen to Others, Listen to Yourself: Combining Feedback Review and Reflection to Improve Iterative Design. In *Proceedings of the 2017 ACM SIGCHI Conference on Creativity and Cognition*, 158–170. https://doi.org/10.1145/3059454.3059468

Understanding Transformations through Design: Can Resilience Thinking Help?

Rosa van der Veen
RISE Interactive and Eindhoven University of Technology
rosa.v.d.veen@ri.se

Viola Hakkarainen
Stockholm Resilience Centre
Stockholm, Sweden
viola.hakkarainen@gmail.com

Jeroen Peeters
RISE Interactive
Umeå, Sweden
jeroen.peeters@ri.se

Ambra Trotto
RISE Interactive and Umeå School of Architecture
ambra.trotto@ri.se

ABSTRACT
The interaction design community increasingly addresses how digital technologies may contribute to societal transformations. This paper aims at understanding transformation ignited by a particular constructive design research project. This transformation will be discussed and analysed using resilience thinking, an established approach within sustainability science. By creating a common language between these two disciplines, we start to identify what kind of transformation took place, what factors played a role in the transformation, and which transformative qualities played a role in creating these factors. Our intention is to set out how the notion of resilience might provide a new perspective to understand how constructive design research may produce results that have a sustainable social impact. The findings point towards ways in which these two different perspectives on transformation – the analytical perspective of resilience thinking and the generative perspective of constructive design research - may become complementary in both igniting and understanding transformations.

Author Keywords
transformation; embodied interaction; constructive design research; resilience thinking; transformative qualities

INTRODUCTION
The interaction design research community is concerned, among other matters, with the production of knowledge regarding the use of digital technologies by people. Increasingly, the interaction design community responds to its responsibility by directly addressing big challenges that societies face today. Topics addressed in such work range widely, and amongst others, address how digital technologies may support ecological sustainability [4] or civic engagement [3, 6] to name just a few laudable examples.

TEI '18, March 18–21, 2018, Stockholm, Sweden

ACM ISBN 978-1-4503-5568-1/18/03…$15.00
https://doi.org/10.1145/3173225.3173261

Proposing visions for the role digital technologies in society, whether through theoretical papers or designed artefacts, inherently proposes new values [20]. This means that to design new ways for people to interact with technologies, is to propose ways in which our world, shaped by such technologies in it, may become better [21]. It follows that a transformation is part of every interaction design research project, may it be addressed either explicitly or implicitly. In this paper, we will start to sketch an approach that we believe can aid the wider research community to better understand how such a transformation may be understood.

Our design and design research work, draws inspiration from the body and its acting in the world, as a key notion to achieve such transformation. We draw upon phenomenology and embodied cognition to support this work, by arguing that we make sense of the world in a way that is fundamentally physical and social [5, 12, 20]. Or, to be more specific: our understanding of the world emerges in dialogue with that world, as we act in it. The dynamic relationships between our brain, body and the social and physical environment around us, together shape how we make sense of the world [9]. These dynamic relationships are complex and ephemeral, yet from the perspective of transformation, they become important dimensions along which to understand the impact of a designed artefact.

Our focus, as design researchers tends to be on the designed artefact: the qualities it possesses and the experience these qualities elicit for people using the design. Such qualities have a transformational power, which means that, through the aesthetics that they express, they may elicit long-term transitions of the ways people using it, relate, use and think about the topic that the design addresses. Designs that embed such transformational qualities, will produce a change in the contexts and the practices that the designs deal with and will therefore have an ethical repercussion on people's lives [10]. It is however difficult to understand the farther reaching and less direct societal transformations that a designed artefact has. Furthermore, design researchers rarely follow their work to reach a phase in which they are adopted by the public and the market. So how do we assess the transformation and transformative qualities? What other disciplines can support us in this endeavour?

This paper uses a design case, where embodied interaction is key, as a starting point for bridging two disciplines in an attempt to understand the transformation that was ignited by the design. The transformation will be discussed and analysed using resilience thinking, an established approach within sustainability science, as well as constructive design research. Resilience research is a field that focuses on the transformative capacities of social-ecological systems, and might provide a useful, different perspective for providing insights on the transformations elicited by artefacts created through constructive design research. By creating a common language between the two disciplines, we attempt to identify what kind of transformation took place, what factors played a role in the transformation, and which transformative qualities created these factors. Our intention is to set out how the notion of resilience might provide a new perspective to understand how constructive design research may achieve and produce results that have a sustainable social impact.

To set a context for the analysis, we first position our approach based on constructive design research. Second, we introduce the concept of resilience thinking in the context of transformations. Following this, we attempt to bridge the two different disciplines by sculpting a common language. Here, key factors for a transformation identified in resilience literature become a starting point for understanding the landscape of transformations in the context of design. With these key factors, we (1) identify the type of transformation that took place after the design project was implemented (2) describe the landscape that made the transformation happen (3) find the transformative qualities within the design case that allowed the landscape to form. Lastly, we conclude with more general reflections on the opportunities we see for resilience thinking and constructive design research to be mutually informative in terms of transformations.

DESIGN RESEARCH, EMBODIMENT AND TRANSFORMATION

Our approach is based on Constructive Design Research, a particular form of design research where the design and production of an artefact takes centre stage in the process of knowledge production [13]. The core of this design research approach is thus the artefact created by design. Koskinen et al. go on to present a topology of three different ways in which this artefact can be leveraged to generate knowledge: The *Lab*, the *Showroom* and the *Field* [13]. In this last context, the artefact is deployed in real-life settings and observed in use. We consider the design case presented further on in this paper to fall under the *Field* context, as its explicit aim was to be used by the public in the real world. Furthermore, the constructive design research project presented in this paper builds on the notion of embodiment as a fundamental component. This stance is rooted in theories of ecological psychology [8], phenomenology [15], post-phenomenology [11], American pragmatism [2] and embodied cognition [1]. This background places the idea of Merleau-Ponty's *body-in-action* as a central part of how design can contribute to attribute specific qualities to the designed (personal) experiences [15]. The body-in-action approach opposes the Cartesian mind-body division, in which the mind is able to fully develop, without interference of the physicality of our existence. The body-in-action implies that we perceive the world with what we can do with it, how we can transform it, and by physically interacting with it, we access and express this meaning [14, 19]. We thus need our body, and the social, physical, cultural environment surrounding it, to give meaning to situations around us. It is relevant to bring this notion of embodiment forward, because it tells us something of the how a meaningful experience unfolds and we, as design researchers, can have an impact on people's behaviour. Embodiment asserts for example, after Klemmer [12], that learning and reasoning are dependent on physical action, and that being present in a space together, using our bodies to interact with artefacts, impacts how we collaborate, cooperate and interact with one another. The artefacts that are produced are therefore means for sense-making and, within the scope of our research practice, we focus on designing what might lead to long-term, short-term, individual or community change, where the change has a transformational nature. The change is considered to be transformational when "the ethics of a person, group or society has long-lastingly changed, and has been embodied in the way the person or people (inter)act, perceive, feel and think" [10].

RESILIENCE THINKING

Resilience thinking focuses on natural resource management, and considers human and natural systems as complex and continually changing. We adopt Walker and Salt's definition of resilience [22], i.e., the capacity of a system to absorb disturbances and still retain its basic function and structure. Resilience thus determines persistence, adaptability and transformability of social-ecological systems (SES). The resilience of SES is seen as a key to sustainability (see [22]). Resilient social-ecological systems are able to change while maintaining their functionality. However, social-ecological systems are also able to transform, causing this system to change its functionality. Transformability in SES means the capacity of a system to cross thresholds or tipping points into new development paths [7]. Further, Walker and Salt [22] define transformability as "the capacity to create a fundamentally new system (including new state variables, excluding one or more existing state variables, and usually operating at different scales) when ecological, economic, and/or social conditions make the existing system untenable". Usually, shifts in perceptions and meaning, values and beliefs, social networks configurations, patterns of interactions among actors as well as in associated organisational and institutional arrangements are related to a fundamental transformational change [7, 17]. Further, resilience thinking acknowledges different scales as essentially intertwined:

transformations at small scales can enable larger scale transformations [7].

ANALYSING TRANSFORMATIONS IN RESILIENCE THINKING

We draw our theoretical base in analysing transformations mainly from Olsson et al. [16]. Through analysing several case studies about transitions toward adaptive governance of natural resource, they identified common factors and phases for successful transformations. Due to its practical approach, the use of real time case studies, and the clear conceptualisation of possible causes of transformations, we chose to work with this analytical framework. Olsson et al., [16] divide a transformation into three phases: (1) preparing the system for transformation, (2) navigating the transition and (3) building resilience after the transformation. In the two former phases (1,2), they describe key factors that are necessary to create the possibility to shift and navigate a system through a transformation. We consider these factors forming a landscape for change. The key factors entail: (i) the emergence of networks, (ii) building knowledge (iii) the emergence of leadership.

Preparation and Navigation

Actions in the preparation phase (1) in relation to natural resource management can be divided into two main groups: "exploring new system configurations and alternative approaches for governance and developing strategies for sorting or annealing alternatives that create conditions for adaptive co-management" [16] Here, named key factors start to play role to push system into the next phase. Learning within social networks and knowledge building is crucial but leadership is needed to i.a. provide vision, connect individuals and trigger collective action (ibid).

The navigation phase (2) is unpredictable and cannot be planned. Therefore, navigation through the phase becomes crucial, and to succeed in this requires preparation. The phase is characterised by emergence of new social structures that link "individuals, organisations, agencies, and institutions at multiple organisational levels" [16]. Also, flexibility and the ability to improvise is important to be able to face the change and maintain system in transition. Here, leadership in addition to diversity in e.g. views, ideas and solutions and right timing play crucial roles (ibid).

Key Factors

The emergence of networks (i) facilitates the generation of new knowledge, sense-making, learning and building up social capital, which in turn can weaken the feedbacks of a negative trajectory [16]. This means that a system is more likely to transform because the current feedback system is weakening. Emergence of networks might happen formally or informally. The informal networks have usually willingness to experiment alternative solutions to existing problems as well as capacity to foster new ideas [16]. Building knowledge (ii) is often enabled by emergent networks that "facilitate information flows, identify knowledge gaps and create nodes of expertise" which can support governance and management of ecosystems in new ways [16]. Furthermore, new knowledge is produced in the networks as they are more experimental, generating new solutions and fostering new ideas (ibid). The emergence of leadership (iii) refers to the role of individual agency in bringing about transformations for sustainability. Leadership facilitates key functions in transformations such as "trust-building, sense-making, managing conflict, linking key individuals and initiating partnerships among actor groups, compiling and generating knowledge, developing and communicating vision, mobilising broad support for change, and gaining and maintaining the momentum needed to navigate the transitions and institutionalise new approaches" [20]. Thus, it plays also a crucial role for the emergence and effectiveness of social networks.

Building Resilience

After the preparation (1) and navigation (2) phase, resilience needs to be built in the new system to stabilise and maintain the new (possibly) more desirable state. This is perceived as the third phase of the transformation. Without, the changes in the system do not necessarily have a long-lasting impact in the system [16]. In other words, as Westley et al. [23] describe, institutionalisation of the change is needed to maintain it. The new system needs to be established and positioned to existing formal and informal institutions such as mental models, management routines, and resource flows.

APPLYING RESILIENCE THINKING TO CONSTRUCTIVE DESIGN RESEARCH

We have outlined the perspective we take on Constructive Design Research, in particular in relation to the role of embodiment as a key notion. We have then introduced the notion of transformation and explained it in the context of resilience thinking. In the following section, we bridge the two perspectives, in in order to create a shared vocabulary.

First, we will use the different phases presented in the previous section: (1) preparation, (2) navigation and (3) building resilience. These three phases have strong commonalities with particular research within Constructive Design. Secondly, key factors, earlier identified in the previous section, are described in relation to constructive design research. These key factors will be used to identify transformative qualities that the design case possesses. In table 1, on the next page, an overview of the relation between the phases, key factors and the corresponding interpretation for both disciplines - design research and resilience thinking - is provided.

Design in relation to phases and key factors

Phases and Design

Preparation phase (1): The preparation phase defined within resilience thinking, finds a parallel in the design activities of a constructive design research approach. This is a stage in which the activities are of three kinds: one is about engaging with the context, experiencing and acquiring data; the second focuses on envisioning, ideating and realising and the third is concerned with analysis of the data, their assessment. By means of these activities, carried out in an iterative way, opportunities are sought for change

Phases	(1) Preparation Phase	(2) Navigation Phase	(3) Building Resilience
Resilience Perspective	Exploring alternative approaches and developing strategies for changes	Characterised by unpredictability. Crucial: flexibility, new social structures, diversity of perspective, timing	Institutionalising the changes in formal and informal domains
Design Research Perspective	Design research & innovation activities	Collaboration and development activities	Phasing in or out

	Key Factors *Emergence of Networks*	*Building Knowledge*	*Emergence of Leadership*
Resilience Perspective	Generation of new knowledge, sense-making, learning and building up social capital, experimenting alternative solutions	Enabled by emergent networks which facilitate information flows, identify knowledge gaps and create nodes of expertise	Supports effectiveness of social networks and knowledge generation and facilitates e.g. trust-building, developing and communicating vision, navigating the transitions and institutionalize new approaches
Design Perspective	Designed artefacts can engage people in actions, practices and discussions	Designed artefacts can engage people in discussions where knowledge is transferred and challenged	Designed artefacts inherently initiate and afford actions from actors that might lead to transformations of any kind.
	Transformative Qualities		

Table 1. Summary of key factors and phases of transformations in relation to resilience thinking and constructive design research. The transformative qualities will be identified throughout this paper and will be presented in Table 2.

and with the aim of triggering the transformative capacity of a system.

Navigation phase (2): To translate this into the constructive design research perspective, the navigation phase overlaps with the activities of a design research process that concern collaboration and development. These activities involve reflection and personal growth within the process, include collaboration and communication and it contributes to educational purposes. It is thus a reflective moment allowing for possible steering and navigating the previously mentioned design activities.

Building resilience (3): Building resilience, thus making sure that the implemented design has long lasting power for transformation, corresponds to the moments of a design research process in which the project is set up at the beginning and phased out to those that will carry it further, defining the terms of involvement of designers after the implementation of the design. Within this stage, decisions have to be made about who is responsible and who will continue with the designed systems, products and services to make it grow into society.

Transformation is hardly linear but an iterative process where different phases can be repeated and reformed in the way towards a fundamental transformation.

Key Factors and Design

Emerging and Mobilising social networks (i): Artefacts can engage people in actions, practices and discussions; this can elicit actions where social networks may be created and mobilised. New ideas can be generated, as well as alternative proposals to tackle current challenges; new partnerships can be formed and informal actions take place. Designed artefacts can, through embodiment, ignite the creation of social networks, or mobilise the already existing structures and networks.

Building knowledge (ii): Designed artefacts can engage people in discussions where knowledge is transferred and challenged. Design can also facilitate the production of new knowledge by bridging values, interests and opinions from different groups. Artefacts, through embodiment, can facilitate opportunities for people to take new perspectives, creating the potential for new insights and evolving the way people normally understand and relate with the contexts in which the design intervention has taken place.

Emergence of leadership (iii): Through embodiment, designed artefacts inherently initiate and afford actions from actors that might lead to transformations of any kind. This might be able to bring different actors together in order to create a momentum in which change happens. This can literally be interpreted as something that 'leads' a transformation from point A to B. However, it might be more interesting to look at the role design researchers have when designing for transformations. The design researcher is operating from a vision, and plays a crucial role in mobilising actors and stakeholders around the created artefact.

Within the following section, the themes and phases will be used to analyse a possible transformation initiated by a design case, *Charged Utopia*. Furthermore, the transformative qualities will be identified and explored in terms of how they are specifically evident in the case.

DESIGN CASE: CHARGED UTOPIA EXHIBITION

Background and Approach

The design case is related to Norrbyskär, a small group of islands in Northern Sweden, known for their rich history. In the year 1895, the islands were bought by a timber magnate, Frans Kempe. He created a community around the large saw-mill that was situated there, once the largest of its kind in Europe. This community was a materialisation of his vision of a just society, modelled on his utopian ideals. Frans Kempe provided the workers that had been selected to work for him with modern homes, gardens, schools and healthcare. However, there was a price to pay. For example, workers were required to abstain from alcohol, live a God-fearing life, and were forbidden to form unions. The good for the community was set above individual wishes or needs. Today, the islands are used as recreation areas and as a place for summer houses. The history is still visible around the island, and is presented in the museum on site.

The *Charged Utopia* exhibition was designed and produced as a physical interactive exhibition situated on the islands themselves. The aim of this exhibition was to engage people with the rich history of the islands, while at the same time using this past as a lens for the present. Visitors to the exhibition were triggered to look at the history of the island and reflect on both parallels and differences with other, perhaps more contemporary societal challenges, in particular the ongoing migration crisis in Europe.

This design case pivots on the notion of embodiment as key element for eliciting active (cognitive) engagement of the public. Interactions with designed artefact are the centre of the experience. From these interactions, meaning is created for each individual visitor, aimed at triggering personal reflections on social coexistence, its paradoxes and challenges [18].

The Exhibition

The exhibition, *Charged Utopia*, was a one-time event in August 2016 on the islands of Norrbyskär. The exhibition was set up as a journey, a metaphor for an imagined migration towards a utopia, and dealt with the risks and costs of searching for an utopian ideal (for further background on the *Charged Utopia*, please refer to [18], or [24] for a brief video registration of the exhibition).

The journey consisted out of different parts: the ferry to the island, receiving a passport, exploring the island through an experiential path and answering questions, handing in a part of one's passport, the exhibition in the museum space and a conclusive discussion. The trip on the ferry towards the islands already prepared the visitors of what they could expect. Poems hanging on the ferry indicated and suggested the notion of identity and the migration towards an unknown land.

Once on the islands, visitors were handed a passport, made from wood and with this passport they continued to the experiential path. The experiential path guided the visitors to and through the woods of the island. Throughout the path, visitors were confronted with 7 different, large, wooden interactive installations. Visitors were required to physically engage with the stations and co-operate within their group to reveal questions that represented issues concerned with choices to be made when shaping one's personal utopia. The questions were ambiguous and open-ended, opening possibilities for discussion and reflection. The path ended in the museum space (the former machinery room of the saw-mill), where interactive installations, this time involving audio and video projections, communicated different stories and perspectives, slowly composing the history of the island. However, before entering the exhibition, visitors were obliged to give away half of their passport. The passports had been used to visualise the answers given at each interactive installation in the woods, each colour indicating a different answer. The visitors were thus required to choose which side they gave away. After visiting the exhibition in the machinery room, the experience was concluded by a debate. The debate was organised to project the event itself within a wider frame of reference: first of all, content wise, i.e., how did participants experience this exhibition and what parallels were found in today's situations? Furthermore, the discussion also revolved around the role of design in exposing and discussing such situations.

In the following analysis, we will address the three topics introduced in the introduction. We will try to: (1) identify the type of transformation that took place after the design project was implemented, (2) describe the landscape that made the transformation happen and (3) find the transformative qualities within the design case that allowed the landscape to form, using the formulated relationship between resilience thinking and constructive design research.

Figure 1: Museum Space, Machinery Room

ANALYSIS OF THE DESIGN CASE *CHARGED UTOPIA*

Type of Transformation

The exhibition had impact on two different levels. There was a noticeable short term impact that was observed through the behaviour of the visitors. There were vibrant discussions, the tone of the debate was strong, opinions and personal experiences were shared. Next to this, the experience also triggered doubts and reflections. People were wandering around, silent and thoughtful, carried away by the issues raised by the installations.

The long-term impact are concerned with stakeholders, who, because of *Charged Utopia*, have developed or are now developing several larger projects concerning the islands (Please also see [18]):

- The formation of a consortium between partners in the *Charged Utopia* project, and several partners based in a neighbouring municipality. The aim of this consortium is to develop a project for a two-year design research project with the intention of deploying permanent interactive interventions that support the communication of cultural heritage.
- The formation of a partnership between the museum on the island and the Umeå School of Architecture: an obligatory component of the second-year curriculum is now centred around the island and its social and cultural layers in order to propose ideas for new architectural landscapes to revitalise the place, while dealing responsibly with its industrial heritage.
- Residents of the island, some of whom have lived there in independent communes started during the 60's, have become revitalised in their concern for the island. They have reached out actively to the partners of this project, in order to tell their stories. Moreover, some have become involved in the ongoing development of design and architecture projects on the island, as well as proposing new ones on their own.

In addition, the board of the Museum has seen, through the exhibition *Charged Utopia*, the potential valorisation process that the island and the Museum can be subjects of. Where before the board of the Museum was almost forced to close the museum, due to a financially challenging situation, the exhibition *Charged Utopia* showed the latent potential of the Museum, leading to the decision of keeping the Museum operative.

Charged Utopia was a one-time event. However, the exhibition facilitated and founded a way to bring parties together that are all continuously affecting the island. The compulsory course for second year students within an Architecture School, dealing with the landscape on the islands, is a stable factor that was a direct result of the exhibition. As are the formation of a consortium for a separate design research project, and the revitalised and continuous active engagement of citizens on the island within a series of different, smaller initiatives. Due to the social networks and relations that were established during the exhibition, the one-time event opened up possibilities for more projects on and around the island. Other design opportunities emerged and were realised: a mobile app navigating visitors through the island using GPS locations to discover stories and poems about the island was developed. Just as a Virtual Reality (VR) experience, in which the history of the island could be explored and could connect the present and a possible future with stories from the past.

The long-term effect of the *Charged Utopia* exhibition is thus visible through all these different new projects. Municipalities see more possibilities in developing the islands, and a growing interest in the island's cultural heritage can be observed, insuring the continuity of the museum after the exhibition. Considering these short term, individual, transformations and the long term, systemic transformation, we can say that a transformation happened.

To answer the question what was transformed and what type of transformation this design case ignited, we can draw from the examples of the effects of *Charged Utopia* above. Firstly, shifts in individual perceptions took place through participation indicating a small-scale transformation on individual level, and on a small community level on the islands itself, towards a revitalised connection with the island and its history. Secondly, the impact of exhibition reached out from just being a one-time event to new institutional collaborations, which indicates a meso-level transitions in the use of the island as well as how it is valued by the larger public. It is important to recognise the relation between this small-scale transformation and the meso-level transformation, since these two can reinforce each other in the long term. The following sections will formulate how these transformations were set in place.

Landscape Allowing the Transformation

The small and meso-scale transformation that took place after the exhibition happened due to a specific landscape that was created, allowing for transformations to happen.

Following, we conceptualise this through the key factors and phases, as described in the section *Applying Resilience Thinking to Constructive Design Research* and in table 1.
The first factor, *Emerging Networks (1)*, stresses the importance of shifts of perspectives, the creation of new social networks and the connection of institutions where new experiments can lead to alternative solutions and new ideas. Looking at the long-term effects of the exhibition, we see a strong connection here: connecting an Architecture School with the museum, the formed consortium between a neighbouring municipality and partners in *Charged Utopia*, and the connection to the residents of the island formed informal and formal networks that actively engaged and are still engaging in the revitalisation of the island. The exhibition formed a physical, shared space in which these partners engaged with one another.

The second factor, *Building knowledge (2)*, articulates the importance of the above described networks in order to "facilitate information flows, identify knowledge gaps and create nodes of expertise" [16], but also the creation of new knowledge, since the described networks are often open for more experimental things to foster new ideas [16]. Within the exhibition, where different people were brought together through the installations and the debate, different perspectives were shared. However, it is important to recognise the artefact within this section as well. Not only the emerged networks were the drivers of this knowledge transfer and production. The exhibition, the artefact, created a platform in which the newly formed networks could communicate, discuss and propose new ideas. The interaction with the artefact, together with the formed networks were the drivers of knowledge transfer and production.

The third factor, *Leadership (3)*, is in this case, strongly connected to the previous theme where we stress the importance of the artefact for the creation of networks and the facilitation of knowledge transfer and knowledge production. The resilience perspective is describing leadership as a form of mediation, able to navigate, steer, compile and manage conflict through a transformation when necessary. Within *Charged Utopia*, the choices of the designers lead the process of a possible transformation. The designed artefacts led the visitors into a direction in which they could explore, reflect and connect with each other and with the content of the exhibition. The artefacts provided the platform for a *possible* change, but was not used to push the visitors in one direction. The artefact was created in such a way that interpretation was key, so that personal experiences and subjectivity became important in discussions and reflections. Leadership in terms of this project thus facilitates, but does not necessarily steer into a specific direction and outcome.

As the relation between the key factors and the phases (see table 1) suggests, the key factors are central in inciting the first and second phase of a transformation. Hence, we can conclude that a transformation was at least starting to take place relating to the phases 1 and 2 (preparation and navigation). The system was prepared to change through alternative visions for the island and experimental ways to implement these: before the exhibition took place, connections between different institutions were created and different views on the future of island were brought into the table.

The exhibition itself and further connections triggered by the design case, can be considered as a part of the navigation phase. However, here it is important to acknowledge the possibly overlapping and iterative nature of these phases and challenges of making a clear division between them in relation to the design case.

When it comes to the third phase of a transformation, described in design terms as the *phasing in or out* of the design process, the design provided a moment in which participants of the exhibition were able to share thought, make new relations and establish their own view about the content. This last part of the exhibition was intended to create an opportunity for others to 'take over' and for the designers to take a step back. A result of this is the continuing relation between the museum on the island and the local architecture school, as well as the growing interest of municipalities in the islands, which can be seen to build resilience for gained changes on the island in the future.

Transformative Qualities within Design; Forming the Transformative Landscape

By taking a close look at the design case, we identify transformative qualities enabling the emergence of the key factors. In the table 2, these qualities are presented and linked to specific parts of the exhibition (see section *The Exhibition)*. The presented transformative qualities within the design case are: *storytelling, tangibility, ownership, physical interaction, teamwork, use of local elements and materials, allowing for making choice, open approach and ambiguity.* The way these are implement in the design case, have a strong embodied nature. This points into the direction that embodiment is an important aspect when defining the transformational power of this specific design case.

DISCUSSION

The above analysis describes the effects of a design case, created through a constructive design research approach, using perspectives on transformation from resilience thinking and constructive design research. What design researchers often imply with their design is the intention of eliciting a change: a transformation on a short-term or long-term base. This was also the case with *Charged Utopia.*

Within this paper, we have addressed the fact that there is a difference in approach in constructive design research and resilience thinking when identifying transformations. Nevertheless, within the analysis of *Charged Utopia,* it becomes very evident that the key factors from the resilience perspective played a role in the transformational aspects of the studied design case. This might indicate the value of bridging those two disciplines in order to understand transformations and explore how the two modes of inquiry can empower and influence each other. We suggest that resilience thinking might be able to provide a wider frame of reference for addressing and identifying transformative qualities in other design cases. In this particular case, we found that transformative qualities included a strong notion of embodiment, which might be a valuable insight for future research on transformations. We do not imply that the identified transformative qualities within this paper are the only key to design for transformations. However, we do believe that these transformative qualities are valuable for designing for transformations, and see an opportunity for further research.

Exhibition Stage	Elements & Actions	Transformative Qualities
Ferry	- Poems - Audio - Evoking the experience of immigrating	- Strong storytelling approach - Immersiveness - Identifying onself
Passport (1)	- Ownership of tangible passport, used for answering questions	- Tangibility - Ownership
Experiential path	- Interactive installation - Ambiguous questions - Voyage and travel through island	- Tangible & Physical Interaction - Ambiguity - Teamwork - Use of local elements/ materials
Passport (2)	- Choose what part of the passport to be exhibited, making room for choice for participants	- Tangibility - Ownership - Allowing/forcing into making choices
Museum Space	- Video & audio about history & stories of the island with an ambiguous way of storytelling - Interactivity with local materials to make own choices about exhibition	- Poetic Storytelling
Debate	- Relate to current societal situation - Exchange of perspectives & allow for reflections	- Experiential starting point - Open approach - Space for input - No right or wrong

Table 2. Transformative Qualities of the Design Case

CONCLUSION

Within this paper, we have looked at the transformative powers of the design case, the exhibition *Charged Utopia*. Our intention was to set out how the notion of resilience might provide a new understanding of how constructive design research may achieve and produce results that have a sustainable social impact. We bridged the disciplines to create a common language on transformation with a focus on key factors and phases in the process. In other words, we have connected the two vocabularies and played with the respective notions. By this, we were able to do the following: (1) identify the type of transformation that took place after the design project was implemented (2) describe of the landscape that made the transformation happen (3) find the transformative qualities within the design case that allowed the landscape to form. Our analysis suggests that transformative changes took place at individual, local and meso levels. These include shifts in individual perceptions, how the island is used as well as it relation to larger institutional domain. The landscape of the transformation that was set in place was formed by the emergence of the necessary key factors (emerging networks, building knowledge and leadership) identified within the resilience perspective. Furthermore, we gained insights on the phases of transformation through which the process took place, understanding that transformation was prepared and navigated throughout the design process. The last phase (building resilience) was also identified in the design case: the design created an opportunity for others to 'take over' and where the transformation could thus grow into a stabilised state. Next, we identified the following transformative qualities: *storytelling, tangibility, ownership, physical interaction, teamwork, use of local elements and materials, allowing for making choice, open approach and ambiguity.* The way these were implemented in the design case, suggested a strong embodied nature. This points into the direction that embodiment is an important aspect when defining the transformational power of this specific design case.

By adopting this novel approach to study a transformation through a design case from perspectives of two disciplines, we suggest that resilience thinking might be able to provide a wider frame of reference for addressing and identifying transformative qualities in other design cases. Thus, we see a strong value in bridging the disciplines of constructive design research and resilience thinking. Therefore, we hope to have provided an opening for a dialogue in which both vocabularies can help in the realisation of a transformations tackling current and future societal challenges.

REFERENCES

1. Clark, A. (1997). Being there: Putting brain, body and world together again. Cambridge, MA: MIT Press
2. Dewey, J. (1934). Art as Experience. New York, NY: Perigree
3. DiSalvo, C., Lukens, J., Lodato T., Jenkins T., and Kim, T. (2014). Making public things: how HCI design

can express matters of concern. In Proceedings of the SIGCHI Conference on Human Factors in Computing Systems (CHI '14). ACM, New York, NY, USA, 2397-2406. DOI: https://doi.org/10.1145/2556288.2557359

4. DiSalvo, C., Sengers P., and Brynjarsdóttir, H. (2010). Mapping the landscape of sustainable HCI. In Proceedings of the SIGCHI Conference on Human Factors in Computing Systems (CHI '10). ACM, New York, NY, USA, 1975-1984. DOI: https://doi.org/10.1145/1753326.1753625
5. Dourish, P. (2001). Where the action is. Cambridge: MIT press.
6. Erete, S and Burrell, S, O. (2017). Empowered Participation: How Citizens Use Technology in Local Governance. In Proceedings of the 2017 CHI Conference on Human Factors in Computing Systems (CHI '17). ACM, New York, NY, USA, 2307-2319. DOI: https://doi-org.proxy.ub.umu.se/10.1145/3025453.3025996
7. Folke, C., Carpenter, S., Walker, B., Scheffer, M., Chapin, T., & Rockström, J. (2010). Resilience thinking: integrating resilience, adaptability and transformability. Ecology and society, 15(4), 20.
8. Gibson, J.J. (1979). The Ecological Approach to Human Perception. Boston, MA; Houghton Mifflin.
9. Hummels, C. & van Dijk, J. (2015). Seven Principles to Design for Embodied Sensemaking.
10. Hummels et al. (2018). DRIving Transformative Qualities. International Journal of a Design. Forthcoming.
11. Ihde, D. (1973). Postphenomenology: Essays in the Postmodern Context, Northwestern.
12. Klemmer, S. R., Hartmann, B. and Takayama L. (2006). How bodies matter: five themes for interaction design. DIS '06 Proceedings of the 6th conference on Designing Interactive systems. New York, USA: ACM, 140-149.
13. Koskinen, I., Zimmerman, J., Binder, T., Redstrom, J., & Wensveen, S. (2011). Design research through practice: From the lab, field, and showroom. Elsevier.
14. Matthews, E. (2006). Merleau Ponty. A guide for the perplexed , Continuum: London, UK.
15. Merleau-Ponty, M. (1962) Phenomenology of Perception , trans. Colin Smith. New York: Humanities Press.
16. Olsson, P., Gunderson, L., Carpenter, S., Ryan, P., Lebel, L., Folke, C., & Holling, C. S. (2006). Shooting the rapids: navigating transitions to adaptive governance of social-ecological systems. Ecology and society, 11(1):18.
17. Olsson, P., Galaz, V., and Boonstra, W. (2014). Sustainability transformations: a resilience perspective. Ecology and Society, 19(4):1
18. Peeters, J., Papworth, N., Glaser, P., Collevecchio, C. Betancour, A., Trotto, A. (2017) No Man is an Island. Situated Design Research and Wicked Impact, The Design Journal, 20:sup1, S3354-S3367, DOI: 10.1080/14606925.2017.1352840
19. Trotto, A., Hummels, C. and Levy, P. (2012). Developing a Kansei design approach to cater for ethics. Proceedings of Kansai Engineering and Emotion Research (KEER) 2012 Conference, May 22 - 25, 2012, Penghu.
20. Van Dijk, J., Moussette, C., Kuenen, C.D. & Hummels, C.C.M. (2013). Radical Clashes: What Tangible Interaction is Made of. In Proceedings of the 7th Int. TEI'13 Conference. New York, USA: ACM, 323-326.
21. Verbeek, P.P. (2006). Materializing Morality – design ethics and technological mediation', in: Science, Technology and Human Values, Vol. 31 no. 3. ISSN 0162. 2439, 361-380.
22. Walker, B. H. and D. Salt (2006). Resilience Thinking: Sustaining Ecosystems and People in a Changing World. Island Press. Washington, U.S.A.
23. Westley, F. R., O. Tjornbo, L. Schultz, P. Olsson, C. Folke, B. Crona, and Ö. Bodin. (2013). A theory of transformative agency in linked social-ecological systems. Ecology and Society 18(3): 27. http://dx.doi.org/10.5751/ES-05072-180327
24. Video of the exhibition: https://vimeo.com/181787781

Exploring the Potential of Data Physicalization for STEM Learning

Sarah Hayes
Human-Data Interaction Group
Cork Institute of Technology
Cork, Ireland
sarah.hayes@mycit.ie

ABSTRACT
This paper presents an overview of the research that I have conducted as part of my PhD studies. The aim of this research is to explore the potential of data physicalization to enhance and improve STEM learning. Specifically, this research is focused on exploring the ways in which physical data representations can be used to clarify dense scientific, technological, engineering or mathematical concepts, and support novel interactions to increase user engagement and learning. My aim is to achieve this through the design, deployment and evaluation of a series of data physicalizations representing STEM concepts and data sets.

Author Keywords
Data physicalization; experience; materials

RESEARCH SITUATION
I am a full-time PhD student based in Cork Institute of Technology, Ireland, under the supervision of Dr. Trevor Hogan and Dr. Kieran Delaney and I am currently nearing the end of the first year of a four-year program of study. My work is situated at the intersection of fields such as Data Physicalization, Tangible Interaction and Human-Computer Interaction. My research is based on the idea that data physicalization and tangible user interfaces (TUIs) can be utilized to increase user engagement and learning of STEM subjects, both in formal and informal educational contexts. To date, I have completed a number of exploratory research and design activities. In particular, I have designed and conducted a study exploring people's experiences of the most common TUI materials [9]. This study involved a large-scale literature review of the TUI design space over the past decade, which was followed by a series of empirical studies that utilised data collection techniques such as the Repertory Grid (RepGrid) to elicit individuals' reported experiences of the twelve most common of these materials. The results of this study was presented in a paper submitted to TEI'18.

Figure 1: Participants taking part in my TUI materials RepGrid study

Additionally, I have taken steps towards designing data representation artefacts for a STEM-learning environment by gathering user experience data. Working with partners from within my institute, I aided in the development a 'makerspace' environment for teenagers (aged 14-16) as part of a week-long summer camp. As well as taking on the role of a facilitator at this camp, I collected data, in the form of a reflective journal, from the other facilitators on their experience of delivering the lessons. These revealed interesting insights on how facilitators felt the introduced concepts were adopted by the learners. By taking on the role as a facilitator of STEM, I have been able to form a stronger personal understanding of how data physicalization can integrate with the learning process.

BACKGROUND, CONTEXT AND MOTIVATION
The importance of STEM education is recognised globally as being vital, both from a social and economic perspective [17, 8, 2]. It is acknowledged that some of the most critical social issues affecting today's world, including climate change, disease research and food shortages, are realistically going to be solved through research occurring within STEM fields [14]. Outside of education, public engagement and awareness of information relating to these issues is seen as critical to ensure the informed and ongoing support required to combat them [1]. It can therefore be argued that STEM-related data should be communicated in an engaging and inviting manner.

TEI '18, March 18–21, 2018, Stockholm, Sweden

ACM ISBN 978-1-4503-5568-1/18/03.
https://doi.org/10.1145/3173225.3173338

Due to the huge advancements in Information and Communications Technology (ICT) we have seen over the past two decades, it has become increasingly possible for non-traditional representational modalities (e.g. haptics, audio) to be used to encode data in new ways [12, 18]. In particular, the notion of representing data through physical forms has recently received increased attention (cf. 13, 11, 15]). My PhD research aims to contribute to this emerging field by exploring how data physicalization artefacts can be used to support a specific task, in my case: improving learning and engagement with STEM topics. My motivation for conducting this research is based on the belief that data physicalizations, in terms of novel interaction styles and improved understanding, are suited to the often inaccessible and complex data sets that accompany STEM topics.

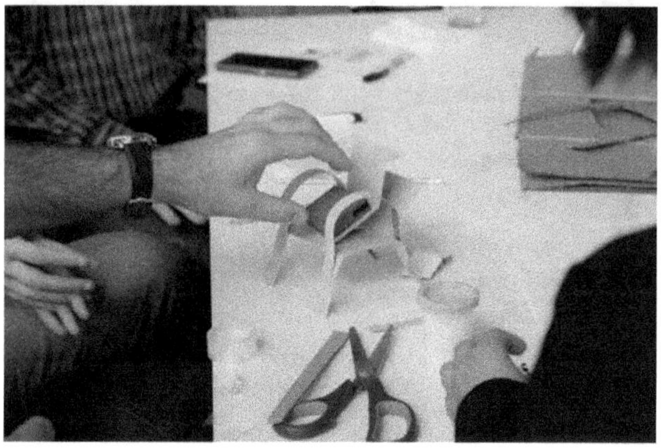

Figure 2: Participants modelling a posture-monitoring chair as part of prototyping camp

The use of physical tools to support STEM learning is not a novel concept [16]. Researchers have suggested that TUIs have the potential to provide learning engagement and support for children [6, 20], in both formal and informal situations. Given that a primary focus of Tangible Interaction is the design of interactions that are intuitive, natural and embodied [7, 3], TUIs are highly suited to supporting children's learning. It has been shown that physical interfaces are easier to use, support learning and development and can facilitate collaboration [4, 9, 19, 20]. It is therefore apparent that Tangible Computing has strong potential to revive and progress the way children interact with learning materials. The prospective impact this body of research has on enhancing educational activities is readily apparent. My research seeks to build upon this potential to further expand and develop the relationship between learners and STEM content through the adoption of a Data Physicalization approach.

THESIS STATEMENT AND RESEARCH GOALS

The goal of this research is to examine how the concept of physicalizing data can be of use for increasing learners' ability to engage with and understand STEM subjects. One of my key objectives is to encode data into physical dynamic forms and then empirically evaluate the effects these have on user engagement and learning. Following several iterations of this process, my research goal is to reveal how STEM data can be made more accessible to learners.

RESEARCH APPROACH

As my research is concerned with understanding how people engage with physicalizations at an experiential level, I have adopted a phenomenological approach that employs methods such as the RepGrid and Semantic Differential surveys to collect rich qualitative data surrounding individuals' experiences. As the project extends to the design evaluation phase, this experience-centred approach will be utilised to determine if users' experience with the learning of STEM topics can be altered for the better through the use of my designs.

DISSERTATION STATUS

At TEI'18, I will be half way through the second year of my research. By that stage, my aim is to have completed the first in a series of studies in which a designed data physicalization tool is deployed and evaluated in a public space. It is envisioned that this study will provide useful insights into both the design process behind representing STEM data physically, and the way in which people in a public setting choose to interact with it.

In addition to this, I aim to form a deeper understanding of how learners experience and engage with STEM-related data. This will be achieved through the introduction of data physicalization objects into 'makerspace' sessions with novice students learning prototyping techniques. Concurrently, I plan to engage in a series of exploratory sessions with college-level design students in which they are challenged to physically represent STEM concepts during a 5-week design project, with the aim of revealing useful insights into how people approach the idea of giving scientific or mathematical data a physical form.

EXPECTED CONTRIBUTION

In an age where so many critical societal problems are presented as charts and graphs, there is a need to rethink how designers expect people to interact and engage with this vital information. It is my proposal that data physicalization has the potential to provide a solution to this issue in a number of refreshing and highly novel ways. My research aims to work towards filling an existing gap in this field of study by developing and evaluating a series of informative, accessible tools for use in a number of learning environments to lower the threshold for learner engagement with complex STEM data.

ACKNOWLEDGMENTS

I would like to thank the participants of my studies for kindly giving their time and my supervisors for all their help.

REFERENCES

1. Massimo Amadio (2015). STEM Education and the Curriculum: Issues, Tensions and Challenges. Kuala Lumpur, Malaysia: UNESCO International Bureau of Education. Accessed 21 Sept. 2017.

2. Robert D. Atkinson and Merrilea Mayo (2010). "Refueling the U.S. Innovation Economy: Fresh Approaches to STEM Education." Itif.org. Accessed 21 Sept. 2017.
3. Ester Baauw and Panos Markopoulous (2004). A Comparison of Think-Aloud and Post-Task Interview for Usability Testing with Children. In Proceedings of the 2004 conference on Interaction Design and Children: building a community. 115-116.
4. Saskia Bakker, Alissa N. Antle and Elise Van Den Hoven (2012). Embodied metaphors in tangible interaction design. Personal Ubiquitous Computing. 16, 4, 433-449.
5. Paulo Blikstein (2010). A New Age in Digital Tangible Interfaces for Learning. Learning in the Disciplines: In Proceedings of International Conference of the Learning Sciences 2010 (ISLS).
6. Kira J. Carbonneau, Scott C. Marley and James C. Selg (2013). A meta-analysis of the efficacy of teaching mathematics with concrete manipulatives. Journal of Educational Psychology. Vol 105 (2) pp. 380-400.
7. Paul Dourish (2001). Where the action is: The foundations of embodied interaction. MIT Press, Cambridge, UK.
8. Francis Eberle (2010). "Workforce Development: Why STEM Education Is Important - ISA." Isa.org. Accessed 21 Sept. 2017.
9. Sarah Hayes, Trevor Hogan and Kieran Delaney (2017). Exploring the Materials of TUIs: A Multi-Method Approach. In Proceedings of the 2017 ACM Conference Companion Publication on Designing Interactive Systems (DIS'17). ACM. 55-60.
10. Bart Hengeveld, Caroline Hummels, Kees Overbeeke, Riny Voort, Hans van Balkom, and Jan de Moor (2008). Let me actuate you. In Proceedings of the 2nd international conference on Tangible and embedded interaction (TEI '08) (p. 159). New York, New York, USA: ACM Press.
11. Trevor Hogan, Eva Hornecker, Simon Stusak, Yvonne Jansen, Jason Alexander, Andrew Vande Moere, Uta Hinrichs and Kieran Nolan (2016). Tangible Data, Explorations in Data Physicalization. In Proceedings of the TEI '16: Tenth International Conference on Tangible, Embedded, and Embodied Interaction - TEI '16 (pp. 753–756). New York, New York, USA: ACM Press.
12. Hiroshi Ishii (2008). Tangible Bits: Beyond Pixels. In Proceedings of the 2nd international conference on Tangible and Embedded Interaction (TEI '08) (p. xv). New York, New York, USA: ACM Press.
13. Yvonne Jansen, Pierre Dragicevic, Petra Isenberg, Jason Alexander, Abhijit Karnik, Johan Kildal, Sriram Subramanian and Kasper Hornbæk (2015). Opportunities and Challenges for Data Physicalization. Proceedings of the ACM CHI'15 Conference on Human Factors in Computing Systems, 1, 3227–3236.
14. Alex Katsomitros (2013) "The Global Race for STEM Skills." Obhe.ac.uk. Accessed 21 Sept. 2017.
15. Andrew Manches and Sara Price (2011). Designing learning representations around physical manipulation. In Proceedings of the 10th International Conference on Interaction Design and Children - IDC '11 (pp. 81–89). New York, New York, USA: ACM Press.
16. Patricia Moyer. (2001). Are we having fun yet? How teachers use manipulatives to teach mathematics. Educational Studies in Mathematics 47: 175-197. Netherlands: Kluwer.
17. Silicon Republic (2017) "It's Time to Get Serious About STEM Education in Ireland, Siliconrepublic.com - Ireland's Technology News Service." Accessed 21 Sept. 2017.
18. Tangible Media Group (2006). Tangibles at play. In ACM SIGGRAPH 2006. Emerging technologies (SIGGRAPH '06). ACM, New York, NY, USA. Article 32.
19. Lesley Xie, Alissa N. Antle and Nima Motamedi (2008). Are Tangibles More Fun?: Comparing Children's Enjoyment and Engagement using Physical, Graphical and Tangible User Interfaces. In Proceedings of the 2nd international conference on Tangible and embedded interaction. 191-198.
20. Bieke Zaman, Vero Vanden Abeele, Panos Markopoulos, and Paul Marshall (2012). Editorial: the evolving field of tangible interaction for children: the challenge of empirical validation. Personal Ubiquitous Computing. 16, 4 (April 2012), 367-378.

Designing for Instructed Physical Training

Laia Turmo Vidal
Uppsala University
Uppsala, Sweden
laia.turmo@im.uu.se

ABSTRACT

The use of technology to assist in instructed physical training in collocated, social settings remains underexplored. In this short paper, I present an overview of my PhD research, which focuses on designing for supporting these activities and opening up their design space by taking into consideration the spatial, physical and social contexts in which they unravel. Following a Research Through Design approach, I conduct a series of design explorations to investigate how to ecologically design technological support for in-the-moment instructed physical training.

Author Keywords

Instructed Physical Training; Sports; Fitness Training; Collocated Social Settings; Embodied Interaction.

CONTEXT AND MOTIVATION

Following the growing interest in movement-based interaction, physical training as a domain fit for technology inclusion has been gaining traction during the past recent years in HCI, both in industry (e.g. a proliferation of a performance-focused quantified self-movement in industry [4]) and research (e.g. Special Interest Groups for sports [15], workshops [14], and an array of research prototypes [20]), in a wide array of application domains, e.g. sports [9], game-based applications [22], individual training [20], rehabilitation [12]). Despite the broad application domain, both industry advances and HCI research have echoed physical training literature's traditional focus on motivation, and designs have focused on motivating people to achieve certain goals (e.g. lose weight) by making the activity easier, funnier, or more socially rewarding [20].

However, the potential use of technology to support the physical training activities through a deep engagement with the details of their execution remains underexplored [20].

In addition to this focus on motivation, both physical training literature and HCI research have traditionally resorted to positivistic perspectives to understand, articulate, theorize [2] and (the latter) design for training activities [20]. More than a decade ago, a now ever-growing group of physical training scholars started to argue for the need of re-conceptualizing training as complex, contextual practices that are shaped by their physical and social realities [2]; grounding this understanding on thorough empirical studies [2]. Despite this reconceptualization, the HCI counterpart of designing for such training activities has been, and is still, prominently permeated by said positivistic models and approaches [20]. As in other bodily-based application domains, design solutions have not yet fully explored the physical, spatial and social context where the activity unfolds as key design resources [11,13]. Therefore, in my PhD research, I draw from the aforementioned physical training literature to obtain an understanding of embodied action in instructed physical training activities. I argue that possibilities for design in the domain are underexplored, and that this opens up the space for developing a good design-oriented understanding and array of design exemplars of how interactive technologies can support these practices. I focus on co-located, social training activities, and on technology to support the in-the-moment performance.

TEI '18, March 18–21, 2018, Stockholm, Sweden

ACM ISBN 978-1-4503-5568-1/18/03.
https://doi.org/10.1145/3173225.3173339

RESEARCH OBJECTIVES AND QUESTIONS

The overall topic of the thesis revolves around understanding and opening up the design space of instructed physical training activities in co-located, social settings, through designing activities and interactive support tools in a way that foregrounds and supports physical and social engagement. I frame this perspective through an open and explorative overarching research question: *How can we design for co-located, social and instructed physical training, foregrounding the social and physical engagement in the training activity?*

Three perspectives are in focus in my thesis work, articulated as three sub-research questions. The first one is: *What aspects of the physical and social engagement with an instructed physical training activity can be supported by an activity-centric design approach?* This first sub question relates to theoretical concerns (what can be designed), and involves a design-oriented exploration of training activities, in order to identify salient aspects of the activities that can be addressed by design.

What can be designed to foreground the social and physical engagement with the instructed physical training activity? This second sub question relates to theoretical concerns too.

I aim at identifying actual design possibilities and important design considerations within the domain. The question of '*what* can be designed' should be taken very literally, as the answer may not be limited to technological installations but can include training practices and even spatial components.

How can we take into account, and foreground, the social and physical engagement with the training activity throughout the design? This third sub question allows me to explore different methodological considerations at different stages of the design process, relating to methods and processes employed.

THEORETICAL UNDERPINNINGS

I situate my research in the domain of *Embodied Interaction* within HCI [19]. Given the focus of my research on social and physical engagement with an activity, this perspective is in consonance with it, and offers a suitable basis for further developing the theoretical underpinnings of my thesis. Drawing from this perspective (e.g. [19]), in my thesis I turn to phenomenological accounts. First, Merleau-Ponty's phenomenology of perception, for a theoretical conceptualization of the body and its role in perception and action; which has been used to understand bodily interactions with technology [19], offering a series of theoretical concepts and lenses. Secondly, to underpin the nature of interaction between designed artefacts and humans, and their role in engagement with an activity, I turn to Post-phenomenology [6], which makes technology a foreground phenomenon and offers a way to "*probe and analyze the role of technologies in social, personal and cultural life (...) by concrete empirical studies of technologies*" ([6] pg.23). Post-phenomenological concepts, such as the intentionality analysis of human relations with and through technology [6], might offer both a theoretical base for, and an array of concepts worth exploring in, design. Finally, I turn to phenomenological conceptualizations of social actors to underpin the complexity of the social texture (i.e. [16]). This relates to methodological considerations of my PhD research: I make use of ethnomethodologically derived methods to understand social coordination of action.

RESEARCH APPROACH AND METHODS

In my PhD research, I adopt a Research through Design (RtD) approach, a methodology that understands the creation of design artefacts as a way of gaining knowledge about a design situation [3]. However, my approach maintains an activity-centric design perspective [21], which advocates for looking at activities in itself rather than 'artifacts' as the ultimate particulars [18] of IxD research. In this approach, designed technology supports rather than sustains the activity [13], becoming one of the multiple design resources at hand (e.g. artefacts, technology, spatial layouts, social arrangements, people involved [13]). In addition, I draw from Participatory Design traditions [17], with the aim to better understand for whom and for what we are designing, mapping out the practice, identifying design opportunities and problems, taking into consideration the experiences of the people involved [17]. In my research, the people involved are the different trainees and instructors of the different practices.

Methods

In order to explore the design space, I use an approach inspired in the *technology probes* method [1,5], which makes use of low-fi prototypes to understand and track how people engage with, and respond, to the probes, in order to open up new design possibilities [1]. I make use of wearable Arduino-based platforms [23], which allow for attachment and mobility. Secondly, in order to engage participants in the design process, I use and intend to further advance embodied ideation methods, on which I have been previously working in close-related domains (see [10,11]). Finally, in order to understand the social structure of the lived experience of an activity [8], analytically I draw from ethnomethodologically informed approaches such as Interaction Analysis [7], focusing on the sequential organization of the interaction between the people involved, and the resources and procedures through which they engage and make sense of an activity [7].

PRELIMINARY RESULTS

I have taken part of a series of explorations of novel embodied ideation methods (Embodied Sketching practices) that aim at fostering physical and social engagement with the activity, and allow to access the experience of, and spur creativity when, designing for movement-based interaction in co-located, social settings. These practices have been articulated in [10,11]. I have also been involved in a series of explorations of non-technologically mediated instructed training activities. I have conducted interviews in, and observations and video-analysis of, three activities: Pilates, AntiGravity Fitness, and Circus training. Through these observations, several design opportunities and design considerations have been articulated, that relate to the importance of capitalizing on the different social actors and the different strategies and tools that they use in their practice.

FUTURE PLANNED ACTIVITIES

The next step in my research is to investigate these opportunities for design through practical explorative design workshops. In the first workshops, I intend to focus on activities that I have already explored, and make use of the aforementioned embodied ideation methods to engage with participants in refining what, and how, technological inclusions could support the aforementioned opportunities. I intend to explore how wearable solutions, working in conjunction with the social and spatial design of the activity, can be designed. In addition, I also intend to explore in future workshops how theoretical concepts that form the base of my PhD could be used practically in design, e.g. generatively or analytically.

REFERENCES

1. Kirsten Boehner, Janet Vertesi, Phoebe Sengers, and Paul Dourish. 2007. How HCI Interprets the Probes. In *Proceedings of the SIGCHI Conference on Human Factors in Computing Systems* (CHI '07), 1077–1086.
2. Bryn Evans. 2017. Sports coaching as action-in-context: using ethnomethodological conversation analysis to understand the coaching process. *Qualitative Research in Sport, Exercise and Health* 9, 1: 111–132.
3. William Gaver. 2012. What Should We Expect from Research Through Design? In *Proceedings of the SIGCHI Conference on Human Factors in Computing Systems* (CHI '12), 937–946.
4. Dize Hilviu and Amon Rapp. 2015. Narrating the Quantified Self. In *Adjunct Proceedings of the 2015 ACM International Joint Conference on Pervasive and Ubiquitous Computing and Proceedings of the 2015 ACM International Symposium on Wearable Computers* (UbiComp/ISWC'15 Adjunct), 1051–1056.
5. Hilary Hutchinson, Wendy Mackay, Bo Westerlund, Benjamin B. Bederson, Allison Druin, Catherine Plaisant, Michel Beaudouin-Lafon, Stéphane Conversy, Helen Evans, Heiko Hansen, Nicolas Roussel, and Björn Eiderbäck. 2003. Technology Probes: Inspiring Design for and with Families. In *Proceedings of the SIGCHI Conference on Human Factors in Computing Systems* (CHI '03), 17–24.
6. Don Ihde. 2009. *Postphenomenology and Technoscience: The Peking University Lectures*. State University of New York Press, Albany.
7. Brigitte Jordan and Austin Henderson. 1995. Interaction Analysis: Foundations and Practice. *The Journal of the Learning Sciences* 4, 1: 39–103.
8. Anthony J. Liddicoat. 2007. *An Introduction to Conversation Analysis*. A&C Black.
9. Martin Ludvigsen, Maiken Hillerup Fogtmann, and Kaj Grønb\a ek. 2010. TacTowers: An Interactive Training Equipment for Elite Athletes. In *Proceedings of the 8th ACM Conference on Designing Interactive Systems* (DIS '10), 412–415.
10. Elena Márquez Segura, Laia Turmo Vidal, and Asreen Rostami. 2016. Bodystorming for movement-based interaction design. *Human Technology: An Interdisciplinary Journal on Humans in ICT Environments*.http://humantechnology.jyu.fi/archive/vol-12/issue-2/bodystorming-for-movement-based-interaction-design
11. Elena Márquez Segura, Laia Turmo Vidal, Asreen Rostami, and Annika Waern. 2016. Embodied Sketching. In *Proceedings of the 2016 CHI Conference on Human Factors in Computing Systems* (CHI '16),
12. Elena Márquez Segura, Annika Waern, Luis Márquez Segura, and David López Recio. 2016. Playification: The PhySeEar Case. In *Proceedings of the 2016 Annual Symposium on Computer-Human Interaction in Play* (CHI PLAY '16), 376–388.
13. Elena Márquez Segura, Annika Waern, Jin Moen, and Carolina Johansson. 2013. The Design Space of Body Games: Technological, Physical, and Social Design. In *Proceedings of the SIGCHI Conference on Human Factors in Computing Systems* (CHI '13), 3365–3374.
14. Christine F. Martindale, Markus Wirth, Stefan Schneegass, Markus Zrenner, Benjamin H. Groh, Peter Blank, Dominik Schuldhaus, Thomas Kautz, and Bjoern M. Eskofier. 2016. Workshop on Wearables for Sports. In *Proceedings of the 2016 ACM International Joint Conference on Pervasive and Ubiquitous Computing: Adjunct* (UbiComp '16), 877–880.
15. Florian Floyd Mueller, Joe Marshall, Rohit Ashok Khot, Stina Nylander, and Jakob Tholander. 2015. Understanding Sports-HCI by Going Jogging at CHI. In *Proceedings of the 33rd Annual ACM Conference Extended Abstracts on Human Factors in Computing Systems* (CHI EA '15), 869–872.
16. Lucia Ruggerone. 2013. Science and Life-World: Husserl, Schutz, Garfinkel. *Human Studies* 36, 2: 179–197. https://doi.org/10.1007/s10746-012-9249-6
17. Jesper Simonsen and Toni Robertson (eds.). 2013. *Routledge International Handbook of Participatory Design*. Routledge, New York.
18. Erik Stolterman. 2008. The Nature of Design Practice and Implications for Interaction Design Research. *International Journal of Design; Taipei* 2, 1. Retrieved October 23, 2017 from https://search.proquest.com/docview/921472711/abstract/C4CAC95A44D54330PQ/1
19. Dag Svanæs. 2013. Interaction Design for and with the Lived Body: Some Implications of Merleau-Ponty's Phenomenology. *ACM Trans. Comput.-Hum. Interact.* 20, 1: 8:1–8:30.
20. Jakob Tholander and Stina Nylander. 2015. Snot, Sweat, Pain, Mud, and Snow: Performance and Experience in the Use of Sports Watches. In *Proceedings of the 33rd Annual ACM Conference on Human Factors in Computing Systems* (CHI '15), 2913–2922. https://doi.org/10.1145/2702123.2702482
21. Annika Waern and Jon Back. 2017. Activity As the Ultimate Particular of Interaction Design. In *Proceedings of the 2017 CHI Conference on Human Factors in Computing Systems* (CHI '17), 3390–3402. https://doi.org/10.1145/3025453.3025990
22. Wii Sports for Wii - Nintendo Game Details. Retrieved April 26, 2017 from http://www.nintendo.com/games/detail/1OTtO06SP7M52gi5m8pD6CnahbW8CzxE
23. Adafruit Industries, Unique & fun DIY electronics and kits. Retrieved March 3, 2017 from https://www.adafruit.com/

Understanding and Designing Embodied Experiences Through Mid-air Tactile Stimulation

Dario Pittera
Sussex House, BN19RH
Brighton, UK
d.pittera@sussex.ac.uk

ABSTRACT
Current attempts to render touch in multimedia technology still represents a challenge. Touch is indeed a complex system and there are many aspects to take into account when trying to rendering it (e.g. the compliance of an object, its weight, orientation, geometric properties and forces on the skin). This is especially true for VR, where touch is an important factor to achieve the embodiment in virtual environments. Recently, new tactile technology has been developed: the mid-air devices, capable of delivering tactile feedback without entering in contact with the skin. One of the contributions of the doctoral research described in this paper is to overcome design challenges and create immersive experiences by applying psychological principles and paradigms, exploiting the advantages of the mid-air technology. We designed possible embodied interaction scenarios in mid-air and physical touch. Findings from these research point to opportunities for designing new immersive experiences. Future work will involve different parts of the body and different tactile properties (e.g. thermal stimulation).

Author Keywords
Touch; Mid-air; Embodiment; Virtual reality; VR; Haptics; User Experiences; Multisensory design.

CONTENT AND MOTIVATION
Touch is a complex sense that conveys information about pressure, pain, proprioception, movement, temperature, and pleasure (through the C-tactile fibers) [9, 1]. Designing for tactile experiences has become of primary interest in the field of HCI and the design of new technologies; e.g. the Disney AIREAL exploring mid-air touch through vortexes by Sodhi et al. [17], the laser approach to create tactile feedback by Lee et al. [12], the Ultrahaptics device, employing ultrasounds by Carter et al. [7] or the fingertip tactile device by Schorr and Okamura [15]. Interactive technologies are increasingly exploiting touch and implementing tactile feedback to provide

TEI '18, March 18–21, 2018, Stockholm, Sweden

ACM ISBN 978-1-4503-5568-1/18/03.
https://doi.org/10.1145/3173225.3173340

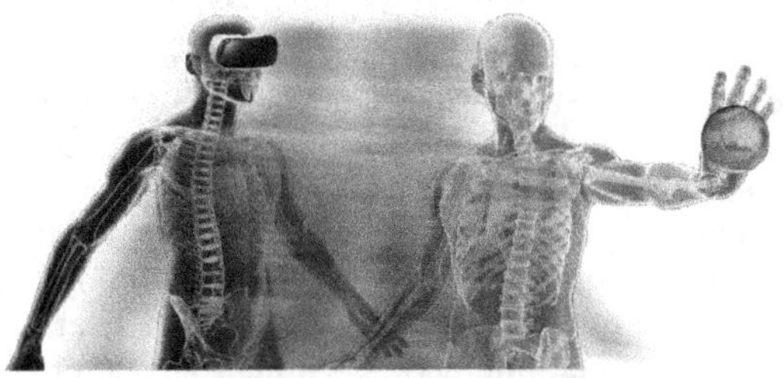

Figure 1. Designing embodied experiences in VR.

the user with an additional information channel in the interaction with devices, products, and services (e.g. Oculus and HTC Touch Controllers, Apple Touch). Most recently, mid-air haptics technology (i.e., devices that enable the creation of contactless tactile feedback in mid-air) represents an exciting new approach to convey tactile feedback to users.

While various mid-air devices are becoming available on the consumer market, the ones that employ focalized ultrasounds to deliver a tactile feedback on the users' bare hands, are the most promising. The ultrasound technology has a greater temporal and spatial resolution (1cm [13]) compared to vortex based and compressed air systems, it allows to design complex patterns (static and dynamic) [13], and it is also safer than, for instance, laser-based approaches. Advantages of mid-air technology compared to other touch interfaces is that they allow users to interact without any physical attachment to the body and they can provide fast changing tactile patterns. In the realm of HCI and interaction design, we can exploit these advantages to create new scenarios, especially relevant in the design of VR experiences. The current challenge in VR is to make experiences and interactions more realistic and immersive. However, current efforts to go beyond audio-visual stimulation, involving the sense of touch, are limited due to the challenge of rendering tactile sensations in a compelling way.

The ambition of this Ph.D. project is to contribute to the challenge of creating convincing and immersive embodied experiences through tactile stimulation. We are particularly interested in the systematic investigation of mid-air tactile stimulation to created embodied experiences. Defining the embodiment is not straightforward as one would hope [8, 14]. Carruthers [6] defines the sense of embodiment as an offline representation of the body; what we usually think of as our body, opposed to what our body looks like moment by moment.

The sense of embodiment mainly consists of two components: 1) the feeling of being distinct from other objects and people [5]; 2) the fact that everyone experiences the world in the first-person perspective. A human being is a fusion between the mind and the body, and this is located in an environment, that is also social and with whom it acts and interacts [4]. The embodiment is telling us what is to be considered self-related and what it is the external world. In essence, the sense of embodiment can be defined as the system that makes us distinguish ourselves from the rest (the world, the other people); it is the perception of our physical boundaries.

RESEARCH OBJECTIVES AND QUESTIONS

Mid-air devices are relatively new and an unexploited design space. There are still various unanswered questions and challenges on how mid-air stimulation can be used to create new experiences. This Ph.D. aims to contribute to this emerging field and understanding of mid-air technology in HCI through increasing the understanding of such technology for experience design especially in the context of a users' sense of embodiment when interacting within a virtual environment. The main objectives are:

1. Explore the users' body sensitivity to ultrasound stimulation. *Where can people perceive mid-air stimulation?*
2. Apply psychological paradigms to test the occurrence of bodily illusions in real and virtual environments. *How well does mid-air touch work in relation to physical touch creating embodied experiences?*
3. Design specific application scenarios integrating tactile stimulation with other sensory stimuli (vision and sound) to create interactive embodied experiences, especially in VR. *How will the brain integrate different sensory stimuli?*

METHOD AND PRELIMINARY RESULTS

In order to address the above research challenges and objectives, we draw upon well-established principles and paradigms in psychology such as the rubber hand illusion [3], the body transfer illusion [16], or the out of body experiences [2]. These paradigms are being studied by means of physical touch and it is not clear if mid-air technology is capable of delivering the same percept. Therefore, we think that exploiting specific psychological paradigms in combination with mid-air touch in comparison to physical touch could provide novel insights and advancement for designing immersive and embodied interaction experiences in HCI.

More specifically, to address objective 1 we use principles of psychophysics methodology. The psychophysics studies the minimum quantity of stimulus needed for a human to recognize, feel, the stimulus. The main techniques are the method of constant stimuli, the staircase procedure and the method of limits [11]. The most indicative measurements in psychophysics are usually the detection thresholds and the just noticeable difference JND [10]. The first measure provides researchers with the minimum stimulus intensity a human (or animal) can detect, the second one, is the smallest change in a stimulus which a person can detect 50% of the time. These thresholds are known to vary depending on the area of stimulation [18]. Therefore, knowing these psychophysical parameters allows us to design optimal systems in tune with our perception ability. *Preliminary results*: not the entire surface of the body skin is sensitive to mid-air stimulation. We believe that the main explanation dwells in the lacking of Pacinian corpuscles. We explore the body starting from the arm and the hand. The main results are illustrated in Figure 2.

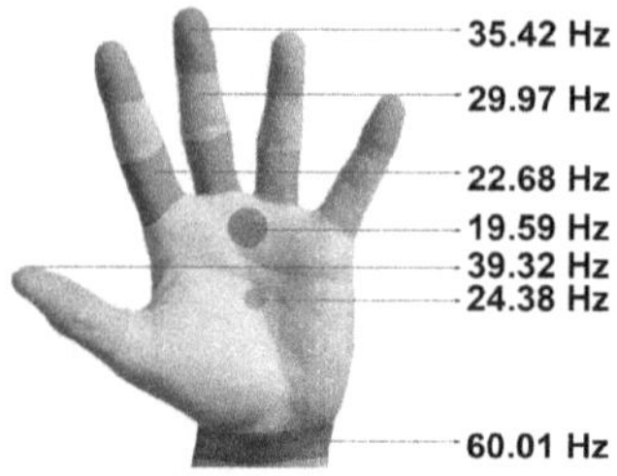

Figure 2. Psychophysics results for mid-air stimulation.

Moreover, to address objective 2 we employed a typical paradigm used for the study of embodiment and to demonstrate the plasticity of our body schema: the rubber hand illusion (RHI) [3]. The subject sits with the real hand covered and out of the sight, while a rubber hand is located in front of him/her. By stroking the fake hand synchronized with the real one, it is possible to induce the illusion that the fake hand is actually the real one. *Preliminary results*: we replicated the RHI paradigm in VR employing mid-air touch. Classically the experiment consists of two conditions: one synchronous stimulation and one asynchronous stimulation where the illusion is broken. We added another condition: incongruent but with multiple stimuli to investigate if the same illusion could be achieved. We illustrated that it is possible to create the illusion mediated by mid-air touch and that the illusion can be reached even in an incongruent condition.

Finally, to address objective 3, we investigated the visual-tactile integration in a virtual environment. In the realm of psychology's constructs, tactile illusions appear to be another tool we can potentially use in our research. Hence, we exploited the apparent tactile movement illusion. Two actuators are activated and the stimulus-onset asynchrony (SOA) is modulated so that the user will perceive a feeling of movement between the two sites of stimulation. Only when the SOA is optimal the two vibrations appear as a continuous movement. *Preliminary results*: We explored the tactile illusion of movement between the two hands. We calculated the optimal onset time between the two actuators. We then observed the different time perception when tactile and visual cues are integrated.

PLANNED ACTIVITIES

I will deepen the illusion of movement in mid-air and I will implement thermal stimuli in my future studies.

We believe that the outcomes of our research could be useful for scientists and designers who want to create new embodied experiences to an always more demanding public.

REFERENCES

1. Wouter M Bergmann Tiest and Astrid M.L. Kappers. 2006. Analysis of haptic perception of materials by

multidimensional scaling and physical measurements of roughness and compressibility. *Acta Psychologica* 121, 1 (2006), 1–20. DOI: http://dx.doi.org/10.1016/j.actpsy.2005.04.005

2. Olaf Blanke, Theodor Landis, Laurent Spinelli, and Margitta Seeck. 2004. OutâĂŘofâĂŘbody experience and autoscopy of neurological origin. *Brain* 127, 2 (2 2004), 243–258. DOI: http://dx.doi.org/10.1093/brain/awh040
3. M. Botvinick and J. Cohen. 1998. Rubber hands 'feel' touch that eyes see. *Nature* 391, 6669 (1998), 756. DOI: http://dx.doi.org/10.1038/35784
4. Peter Brugger and Bigna Lenggenhager. 2014. The bodily self and its disorders. *Current Opinion in Neurology* 27, 6 (2014), 644–652. DOI: http://dx.doi.org/10.1097/WCO.0000000000000151
5. Glenn Carruthers. 2007. A model of the synchronic self. *Consciousness and Cognition* 16, 2 (2007), 533–550. DOI:http://dx.doi.org/10.1016/j.concog.2006.06.002
6. Glenn Carruthers. 2008. Types of body representation and the sense of embodiment. *Consciousness and Cognition* 17, 4 (2008), 1302–1316. DOI: http://dx.doi.org/10.1016/j.concog.2008.02.001
7. Tom Carter, Sue Ann Seah, Benjamin Long, Bruce Drinkwater, and Sriram Subramanian. 2013. UltraHaptics. *Proceedings of the 26th annual ACM symposium on User interface software and technology - UIST '13* (2013), 505–514. DOI: http://dx.doi.org/10.1145/2501988.2502018
8. Arthur M. Glenberg. 2010. Embodiment as a unifying perspective for psychology. *Wiley Interdisciplinary Reviews: Cognitive Science* (2010), n/a–n/a. DOI: http://dx.doi.org/10.1002/wcs.55
9. David Katz and Lester E. Krueger. *World of touch*. 260 pages.
10. Frederick A. A. Kingdom and Nicolaas Prins. 2010. *Psychophysics : a practical introduction*. Elsevier/Academic Press. 279 pages.
11. Frederick a a Prins Kingdom. 2010. *Psychophysics: a pratical introduction*. 297 pages.
12. Hojin Lee, Ji-sun Kim, Seungmoon Choi, Jae-hoon Jun, A-hee Kim, Han-byeol Oh, Jong-rak Park, Hyung-sik Kim, and Soon-cheol Chung. 2015. Mid-Air Tactile Rendering Using Laser-Induced Thermoelastic Effects : The First Study for Indirect Radiation. (2015).
13. Benjamin Long, Sue Ann Seah, Tom Carter, and Sriram Subramanian. 2014. Rendering volumetric haptic shapes in mid-air using ultrasound. *ACM Transactions on Graphics* 33, 6 (2014), 1–10. DOI: http://dx.doi.org/10.1145/2661229.2661257
14. Matthew R. Longo, Friederike Schüür, Marjolein P.M. Kammers, Manos Tsakiris, and Patrick Haggard. 2008. What is embodiment? A psychometric approach. *Cognition* 107, 3 (2008), 978–998. DOI: http://dx.doi.org/10.1016/j.cognition.2007.12.004
15. Samuel B Schorr and Allison M Okamura. 2017. Fingertip Tactile Devices for Virtual Object Manipulation and Exploration. In *Proceedings of the 2017 CHI Conference on Human Factors in Computing Systems - CHI '17*. 3115–3119. DOI: http://dx.doi.org/10.1145/3025453.3025744
16. Mel Slater, Bernhard Spanlang, Maria V. Sanchez-Vives, and Olaf Blanke. 2010. First person experience of body transfer in virtual reality. *PLoS ONE* 5, 5 (2010), 1–9. DOI:http://dx.doi.org/10.1371/journal.pone.0010564
17. R Sodhi, Poupyrev, M Glisson, and a Israr. 2013. AIREAL: interactive tactile experiences in free air. *ACM Transactions on Graphics* 32, 4 (2013), 134. DOI: http://dx.doi.org/10.1145/2461912.2462007
18. S. Weinstein. 1968. Intensive and Extensive Aspects of Tactile Sensitivity as a Function of Body Part, Sex and Laterality. In *Proc. 1st Int. Symp. on the Skin Senses*.

The Interactive Carpet - Smart Textile Interface for Children on Autism Spectrum Disorder

Yulia Zhiglova
Tallinn University
Tallinn, Estonia
yzhigl@tlu.ee

ABSTRACT
This paper discusses the socializing potential of the smart textile based interface and presents the design and future study method of the Interactive Carpet prototype, designed in cooperation with Autism Spectrum Disorder (ASD) specialists. The future exploratory study will shed a light on the potential effect on social skills of children with ASD and how its physical properties and multi-sensory feedback could promote interaction between caregiver and a child with ASD.

Author Keywords
Autism; Tangible Interactions; Smart Textiles;

INTRODUCTION
Autism Spectrum Disorder (ASD) is a lifelong neurodevelopmental disorder (NDD) characterized by repetitive behaviors and impairment in verbal communication [1, 2]. This paper proposes to investigate tangible properties of smart textiles and incorporate them in building the prototype to help children on low - functioning autism in enhancing social skills and attention.

LITERATURE REVIEW
There is a number of studies on how the technology may assist with intervention practices of kids with NDD, including ASD. A prevailing number of studies investigate various digital applications [6, 8, 12, 13] and how these solutions may help kids on ASD with recognizing emotions, organizing daily routines, and developing empathy. Another body of research investigates how robotic toys may enhance social skills of kids with autism [9]. Other studies are concerned with research of the natural-user interfaces (NUI) and how the whole-body interaction systems may augment sensory-integration therapies and creativity [11]. More so, integrating Tangible User Interfaces (TUIs) into occupational therapies has proven its efficacy in children with ASD [7, 10, 14, 15]. Overall research on integrating TUIs into ASD occupational therapies has shown positive effects for stimulating attention, shortening duration of solitary activities, lowering arousal. That said, to our best of knowledge, there was no thorough study done on the soft interfaces incorporating smart textile technology for autistic children and how the interaction with soft physical objects with multi-sensory feedback may stimulate attention and enhance socializing of children on low-functioning ASD.

TEI '18, March 18–21, 2018, Stockholm, Sweden

ACM ISBN 978-1-4503-5568-1/18/03.
https://doi.org/10.1145/3173225.3173341

GOALS AND OBJECTIVES
This paper proposes to explore different properties of the interactive, textile based prototype and how they may stimulate attention and enhance social skills and promote better child-care giver interaction. Considering the plethora of research on TUIs and sensory integration therapy, we hypothesize, that soft properties of the interface with various sensory feedback and physical soft objects should promote attention and enhance socializing [2, 7, 9, 10].

THE DESIGN OF THE PROTOTYPE
A user centered design method has been used to design and construct first iteration of the prototype (Image 1). First, literature review has been conducted to understand current state of the art concerning integration of TUI's into occupational practices with children on autism. Then, there was a close cooperation with a special educators, and a pediatric neuropsychologist, who 1) were interviewed about needs and requirements for therapeutic practices 2) demonstrated tools and practice and gave overview of typical reactions of children on ASD to specific tools and games, 3) consulted on including specific properties to the prototype and viability of the proposed interactions. In addition, the intervention techniques developed by the Autism Diagnostic Observation Schedule (ADOS – 2) were taken in consideration. Based on the ADOS-2, the prototype will be most appropriate for the age group of 5 – 10 years old children on low-functioning spectrum [3]. The prototype is meant for a caregiver and one child to play at a time.

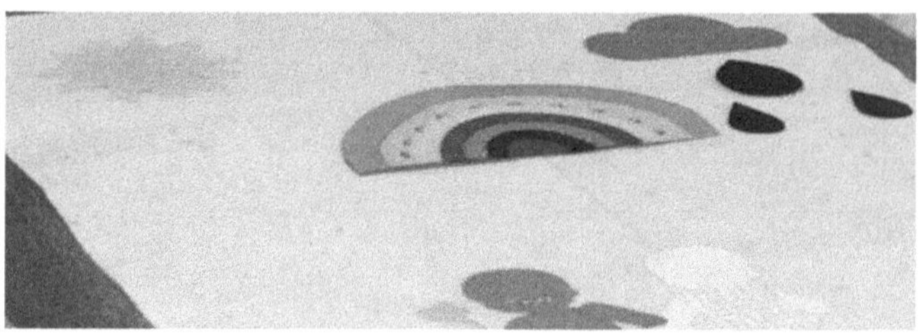

Image 1. Partial view of the Interactive Carpet prototype.

Materials Used
The Interactive Carpet prototype is constructed of various soft materials, using existing smart textile technologies and practices. The carpet is constructed using conductive thread, conductive textiles, soft buttons, soft pressure sensors, stroke sensors, and regular textiles of various colors and textures. In addition to various soft surfaces, the vibration motors, LEDs and audio has been embedded seamlessly. The logic of the game was implemented with Lilypad Arduino microprocessor. The soft textile based interface provides a broader range of interactions to a child and allows squeeze, stroke, folding and other manipulations. Tangibles provide a safety net for encouraging social interaction as they allow for a broad range of interaction styles [4].

Mix and Match Concept
All physical elements of the game that construct various interactions are detachable. This allows an additional creativity and ability to add new elements to the game. Thus, at the start of the game a child and a caregiver will have a woolen carpet and a box with various elements. On the surface of the carpet there will be signifiers (stitched by thread), outlining the borders of the shapes of the elements which have to be matched by the physical elements provided. The rationale behind this is based on the research and interviews with therapists who identified as one of the favorite activities of kids with autism is to match objects to patterns and colors [2, 3].

Storytelling Interactions
The first iteration of the prototype represents six main interactions. The interactive elements are meant to provoke interaction between caregiver and a child based on the storytelling, associative and cause-effect play. Different elements of the game will require different inputs (touch, pressure, placing objects onto a matching pattern, stroke) and will produce different outputs (light, vibration, sound).

Elements
Family. This element represents a family of three soft dolls which can demonstrate a "happy" emotional state. For instance, if a player attaches a flower to a hand of a doll, its face will show a smile (the smile will light up with LEDs). This element demonstrates a cause – effect interaction.

Rainbow. This is a collaborative element. Two players should place on a carpet the physical object of a sun and of a cloud simultaneously in order to get a rainbow (the embedded LEDs will start blinking).

Fish. This element requires placing an object of a fish onto a signifier and after a gentle pressure onto a fish object a player will receive a vibration feedback under his/her palm.

Grass. This element will require a player to stroke the surface of the soft textile grass. The embedded soft stroke sensor will provide light (via embedded LEDs) feedback upon stroking.

Color Mixing Flower. This element shows different colors and engages into a collaborative play. When two flower petals of different colors are squeezed simultaneously, a new color will be in the center of the flower.

Rain drops and a bird. By placing an element on the momentary pressure switch a sound will start accordingly. If a rain drop is attached to the matching signifier, the sound of the rain will start playing. This element provides an auditory stimulation and a cause-effect play scenario.

The elements are a medium for storytelling and meant to stimulate attention through multi-sensory feedback, and enhance socializing through storytelling and stimulated touch senses of children. The rational of this assumption is based on the previous research which demonstrates that sensory integration techniques, such as pressure-touch can facilitate attention and awareness, and reduce overall arousal [1, 2]. Moreover, there is an abundant evidence that storytelling plays an important role in educational practices for children with NDD [1, 2, 3].

FUTURE EXPLORATORY STUDY
The next phase of the research will be an exploratory study and iterative prototyping to investigate the effect of the Interactive Carpet on social skills and attention of the children with low-functioning ASD in a day care center. The prototype will be given to a caregiver and one child at a time to play for about 30 minutes. Each child will have three sessions of play. The target audience of the prototype are children with low-functioning autism of 5 – 10 years old.

Each play will be videotaped and analyzed against the degree of socializing and attention during the playtime. The degree of socializing will be measured using the variables adopted from the ADOS – 2. Specifically, frequency of the following variables will be coded: eye gaze, joint attention, pointing, and verbal expressions [3]. The attention will be measured through duration of the concentration on each of the six interactions of the prototype. Before testing the prototype with children, the level of cognitive development and autism spectrum of each child should be identified. The pre and post study interviews with the caregivers about each child's behavioral habits will be conducted as well. The results of this type of study cannot be generalized on the bigger population but may suggest useful applications of soft interactive interfaces for ASD occupational purposes, and suggest a need for a bigger study.

CONCLUSION
The Interactive Carpet prototype has been designed in cooperation with ASD specialists and is grounded on the previous research on use of TUIs in ASD therapies [2, 4]. Still, the potential impact of integrating the Interactive Carpet in regular occupational sessions for enhancing socializing and stimulating attention of children with low-functioning ASD has yet to be tested in an empirical study.

REFERENCES
1. American Psychiatric Association. 2013. In *Diagnostic and Statistical Manual of Mental Disorders*. DSM

Library. doi:10.5555/appi.books.9780890425596.x00pre.

2. American Journal of Occupational Therapy, September/October 1999, Vol. 53, 489-497. doi:10.5014/ajot.53.5.489
3. Catherine Lord, PhD, Michael Rutter, MD, et al. 2012. Autism Diagnostic Observation Schedule, Second Edition (ADOS®-2)
4. Rowland, C. M., & Schweigert, P. D. (2009). Object lessons: How children with autism spectrum disorders use objects to interact with the physical and social environments. *Research in Autism Spectrum Disorders*, *3*(2), 517-527. DOI: 10.1016/j.rasd.2008.10.005
5. Laura Benton, Hilary Johnson, Mark Brosnan, Emma Ashwin, and Beate Grawemeyer. 2011. IDEAS: an interface design experience for the autistic spectrum. In CHI '11 Extended Abstracts on Human Factors in Computing Systems (CHI EA '11). ACM, New York, NY, USA, 1759-1764. DOI=http://dx.doi.org.ezproxy.tlu.ee/10.1145/1979742.1979841
6. Cong Chen, Ajay Chander, Kanji Uchino, and Kimiko Ryokai. 2016. Guided Play: Automatic Stereotypical Behavior Analysis and Intervention during Play. In Proceedings of the 2016 Annual Symposium on Computer-Human Interaction in Play Companion Extended Abstracts (CHI PLAY Companion '16). ACM, New York, NY, USA, 109-115. DOI: https://doi-org.ezproxy.tlu.ee/10.1145/2968120.2987727
7. William Farr, Nicola Yuill, Eric Harris, and Steve Hinske. 2010. In my own words: configuration of tangibles, object interaction and children with autism. In *Proceedings of the 9th International Conference on Interaction Design and Children* (IDC '10). ACM, New York, NY, USA, 30-38. DOI=http://dx.doi.org.ezproxy.tlu.ee/10.1145/1810543.1810548
8. Franca Garzotto, Mirko Gelsomini, Daniele Occhiuto, Vito Matarazzo, and Nicolò Messina. 2017. Wearable Immersive Virtual Reality for Children with Disability: a Case Study. In *Proceedings of the 2017 Conference on Interaction Design and Children* (IDC '17). ACM, New York, NY, USA, 478-483. DOI: https://doi-org.ezproxy.tlu.ee/10.1145/3078072.3084312
9. Mirko Gelsomini, Giulia Leonardi, Marzia Degiorgi, Franca Garzotto, Simone Penati, Jacopo Silvestri, Noëlie Ramuzat, and Francesco Clasadonte. 2017. Puffy - an Inflatable Mobile Interactive Companion for Children with Neurodevelopmental Disorders. In *Proceedings of the 2017 CHI Conference Extended Abstracts on Human Factors in Computing Systems* (CHI EA '17). ACM, New York, NY, USA, 2599-2606. DOI: https://doi-org.ezproxy.tlu.ee/10.1145/3027063.3053245
10. Eva Hornecker and Jacob Buur. 2006. Getting a grip on tangible interaction: a framework on physical space and social interaction. In *Proceedings of the SIGCHI Conference on Human Factors in Computing Systems* (CHI '06), Rebecca Grinter, Thomas Rodden, Paul Aoki, Ed Cutrell, Robin Jeffries, and Gary Olson (Eds.). ACM, New York, NY, USA, 437-446. DOI=http://dx.doi.org.ezproxy.tlu.ee/10.1145/1124772.1124838
11. Kathryn E. Ringland, Rodrigo Zalapa, Megan Neal, Lizbeth Escobedo, Monica E. Tentori, and Gillian R. Hayes. 2014. SensoryPaint: a natural user interface supporting sensory integration in children with neurodevelopmental disorders. In CHI '14 Extended Abstracts on Human Factors in Computing Systems (CHI EA '14). ACM, New York, NY, USA, 1681-1686. DOI=http://dx.doi.org.ezproxy.tlu.ee/10.1145/2559206.2581249
12. Harini Sampath, Ravi Agarwal, and Bipin Indurkhya. 2013. Assistive technology for children with autism - lessons for interaction design. In Proceedings of the 11th Asia Pacific Conference on Computer Human Interaction (APCHI '13). ACM, New York, NY, USA, 325-333. DOI=http://dx.doi.org.ezproxy.tlu.ee/10.1145/2525194.2525300
13. Will Simm, Maria Angela Ferrario, Adrian Gradinar, and Jon Whittle. 2014. Prototyping 'clasp': implications for designing digital technology for and with adults with autism. In *Proceedings of the 2014 conference on Designing interactive systems* (DIS '14). ACM, New York, NY, USA, 345-354. DOI: https://doi-org.ezproxy.tlu.ee/10.1145/2598510.2600880
14. Karanya Sitdhisanguan, Nopporn Chotikakamthorn, Ajchara Dechaboon, and Patcharaporn Out. 2012. Using tangible user interfaces in computer-based training systems for low-functioning autistic children. *Personal Ubiquitous Comput.* 16, 2 (February 2012), 143-155. DOI=http://dx.doi.org.ezproxy.tlu.ee/10.1007/s00779-011-0382-4
15. Lilia Villafuerte, Milena Markova, and Sergi Jorda. 2012. Acquisition of social abilities through musical tangible user interface: children with autism spectrum condition and the reactable. In CHI '12 Extended Abstracts on Human Factors in Computing Systems (CHI EA '12). ACM, New York, NY, USA, 745-760. DOI: http://dx.doi.org.ezproxy.tlu.ee/10.1145/2212776.2212847

Choreographic Computational Composites: Investigating Small-Size Shape-Change Architecture through Performative Arts

Alice Rzezonka
University of Wuppertal
Wuppertal, Germany
rzezonka@uni-wuppertal.de

ABSTRACT
Dynamically changing the form or surface of objects enables new and rich ways of communicating through (memorized) movement. Previous work has addressed the social perception of and interaction with shape-changing objects in a laboratory setting or everyday surrounding. But, the complex link between human movement, shape-change, and material memory has not yet explicitly been addressed. In this doctoral research project, it is assumed that designing in cooperation with dancers reveals insights into these interrelations. Therefore, this project aims at documentating the design process of and performance with a shape-change architecture. Since dancers are specialists in memorizing movement and communicating through movement, I expect to reveal insights that are of relevance for future design projects and, at the same, explore the work with dancers as a method of Embodied Design Ideation (EDI).

Author Keywords
Shape-change; dance; choreography; material memory; embodied design ideation (EDI); performative arts;

ACM Classification Keywords
• *Human-centered computing~Empirical studies in HCI*
• Human-centered computing~HCI theory, concepts and models

INTRODUCTION
Dynamically changing the form or surface of objects has emerged as a topic in the research areas of Human-Computer Interaction (HCI) and architecture [5, 10, 13]. While HCI researchers focus mainly on small, hand-held devices [1, 16], some researchers have explored furniture-size change of shape [5, 10]. The concept behind the latter is to situate interactivity into our physical environment. This approach poses new questions of an experience-based, embodied interaction with architectural elements. Previous research in this area has not yet addressed how this technique explicitly relates to the link between the moving human body, material memory, and communication through movement.

In this research project, this link is explored through an Embodied Design Ideation (EDI) [17] approach combining the overlapping research fields of dance, architecture, and digital technology. To do so, a collective of dancers is incorporated into the development process of a small-size, shape-changing architecture, while the cooperative process is documented and analyzed. This approach is considered as doing Research through Design (RtD) [18] with the aim of not only outputting a choreographic computational composite [6, 15], but at the same time extracting insights into the embodied human interaction with it.

DANCE, TECHNOLOGY, AND AN EMBODIED PERSPECTIVE ON CHANGE OF SHAPE
Performative artists have cultivated various aspects of interactive media, electronic arts, and new technological developments. For example, projection mapping [2], robotic arms [7], or motion tracking [12] have been integrated by artists into choreographic assembles. This cross-fertilization of ideas not only challenges technical development but is also regarded as a "knowledge-producing" collaboration [11].

One technical development that has not yet been actively explored by performative artists is the concept of change of shape. Thus far, researchers who explore this field have focused on social perception, creation of, and interaction with shape change either in a laboratory setting or everyday surroundings such as private households or semi-public shopping malls [3, 10, 14]. However, this emerging field of research raises further questions: How does shape change relate to the moving human body, material memory, and communication through movement?

When looking at this from the perspective of performative arts, dancers are specialized in movement, memory of movement, and communication through movement. Therefore, the cross-pollination between the two fields promises to not only challenge technical development but also gaining insights into how dancers think with their bodies in relation to objects and communication through movement.

TEI '18, March 18–21, 2018, Stockholm, Sweden

ACM ISBN 978-1-4503-5568-1/18/03.
https://doi.org/10.1145/3173225.3173342

Figure 1. Visualization of possible interactions between shape-change architecture and dancers *(photomontage by the author)*

CHANGE OF SHAPE TRHOUGH DANCE

The dissertation project pursues a twofold objective. The first step is to realize a performance in public space with a collective of dancers. The performance title chosen by the collective is »parasympathetic«. In this performance, the dancers will act as half-asleep bodies. The small-size, shape-change architecture to be developed for this performance will serve as a choreographic computational composite. It will have the ability to change its shape dynamically and store and restore past shapes in interaction with the dancers.

In this first step, the research is focused on how the material structure can enable communication between the dancers. The theme of the performance plays an important part, since it implicates slow, dream-like movements that need to be translated into the quality and the memory of movement of the shape-change architecture. To further develop this approach as a method of Embodied Design Ideation (EDI) the framework serves as a lens that refracts the various aspects of the concept.

The second step is a reflection on the process and the retransition into the field of HCI research and related disciplines. As I am actively involved in the development process as a designer, the method of participant observation is regarded as a key element to reflect on the cooperation process. In addition, I regard the shape-change architecture itself as a communication medium that can stimulate the exchange on the value of this approach with researchers and practitioners from related areas.

Framework: Embodied Design Ideation (EDI)

EDI is an emerging approach in HCI [17]. The common aim of differing methods in this field is to incorporate embodied experience in the design ideation process. Wilde et al. have proposed EDI as a framework to help compare different embodied approaches and at the same time verbalize the experience-based perspective for the research community. Wilde et al. formulate four questions that serve as a starting point for comparing EDI methods: What is *disrupted*? What is *destabilized*? What *emerges* from the destabilization? And what is overall *embodied*?

Concept: Movement, Memory, and Communication

The planned shape-change architecture to be realized focuses on three aspects of the complex field of possible choreographic computational composites.

First, movement is crucial for continuous change. Complex movements are a challenge on the technical, aesthetic, and qualitative level. Second, when interacting with shape-change elements, memory becomes relevant: Will the movement always repeat identically? What does material memory mean in this context? Third, if the changing of a shape is not considered from a mere technical perspective, then communication is a key mean of shape change: How does movement and the memory of movement communicate different states?

Through the lens of EDI, it is anticipated that the performance in public space *disrupts* the expectation how dancers move and interact with technology. By *destabilizing* the idea of material and body memory, unforeseeable outcomes are expected to *emerge*. Overall, the communication though movement and memory are *embodied*.

Methods of Reflection: Participant Observation

Being actively involved as both a designer and a researcher at the same time is considered a crucial part of the proposed research project. Therefore, the chosen method of participant observation is rooted in ethnology and anthropology and has been adapted to HCI research [5, 8].

Additionally, interviews will be conducted with practitioners and researchers from the field of HCI and related disciplines. The interviewees will be questioned on how they perceive the performance and approach as value for their discipline. The aim of these two methods is to verbalize the experiential insights and to return knowledge into the field of HCI.

OUTLOOK

The doctoral research project aims to combine technological development with experience-based, embodied artistic practice. While the project is still in an explorative state, the performance is planned to be realized in mid-2018.

In the project, I consider conceptualizing, technologically realizing, and documenting an artistic performance as an important advance into the complex topic of human body-material-technology relationship. It is expected that the wide variety of data and experiences collected during the project will present a challenge for a concise analysis, but taking this risk is worthwhile given the expected depth of insight.

REFERENCES

1. Bau, O., Petrevski, U., and Mackay, W. 2009. BubbleWrap. In CHI '09 Extended Abstracts on Human Factors in Computing Systems. ACM Digital Library. ACM, New York,USA, 3607. http://dx.doi.org/10.1145/1520340.1520542
2. Beira, J., Carvalho, R., and Kox, S. Mixed Reality Immersive Design. In the 2013 ACM international workshop, 45–50. http://dx.doi.org/10.1145/2512142.2512147
3. Bergström, J., Clark, B., Frigo, A., Mazé, R., Redström, J., and Vallgårda, A. 2010. Becoming Materials. Material forms and forms of practice. Digital Creativity 21, 3, 155–172.
4. Dewalt, K., Dewalt, B., and Wayland, C. 2000. Participant Observation. In Handbook of methods in cultural anthropology, H. R. Bernard, Ed. AltaMira Press, Walnut Creek, 259–300.
5. Follmer, S., Leithinger, D., Olwal, A., Hogge, A., and Ishii, H. 2013. inFORM. In UIST'13. Proceedings of the 26th Annual ACM Symposium and Symposium Adjunct on User Interface Software and Technology; October 8 - 11, 2013, St. Andrews, UK. ACM, New York, USA, 417–426. http://dx.doi.org/10.1145/2501988.2502032
6. Forsythe, W. Choreographic Objects. Retrieved December 17, 2017 from http://www.william-forsythe.com/essay.html
7. Forsythe, W. 2014. Black Flags. Retrieved December 17, 2017 from http://www.william-forsythe.com/installations.html
8. Grönvall, E., Kinch, S., Petersen, M. G., and Rasmussen, M. K. 2014. Causing Commotion with a Shape-Changing Bench. In Proceedings of the SIGCHI Conference on Human Factors in Computing Systems. ACM, New York, USA, 2559–2568. http://dx.doi.org/10.1145/2556288.2557360
9. Gunn, W., Otto, T., and Smith, R. C., Eds. 2016. *Design anthropology. Theory and practice.* Bloomsbury Academic, an imprint of Bloomsbury Publishing Plc, London.
10. Holman, D. and Vertegaal, R. 2008. Organic User Interfaces. Commun. ACM 51, 6-48.
11. Leach, J. 2013. Choreographic Objects. Journal of Cultural Economy 7, 4, 458–475.
12. Leach, J. and deLahunta, S. 2017. Dance Becoming Knowledge. Designing a Digital "Body". Leonardo 50, 5, 461–467.
13. Nabil, S., Plötz, T., and Kirk, D. S. Interactive Architecture. In the Tenth International Conference, 89–100. http://dx.doi.org/10.1145//3024969.3024981
14. Sturdee, M., Hardy, J., Dunn, N., and Alexander, J. 2015. A Public Ideation of Shape-Changing Applications. In ITS'15. Proceedings of the 2015 ACM International Conference on Interactive Tabletops & Surfaces: November 15-18, 2015, Madeira, Portugal. ACM, New York, 219–228. http://dx.doi.org/10.1145/2817721.2817734
15. Vallgårda, A. and Redström, J. 2007. Computational Composites. In Proceedings of the SIGCHI Conference on Human Factors in Computing Systems. ACM, New York, USA, 513–522. http://dx.doi.org/10.1145/1240624.1240706
16. Wald, I., Orlev, Y., Grishko, A., and Zuckerman, O. 2017. Animating Matter. In Proceedings of the 2016 ACM Conference Companion Publication on Designing Interactive Systems - DIS '17 Companion. ACM Press, New York, USA, 84–89. http://dx.doi.org/10.1145/3064857.3079124
17. Wilde, D., Vallgårda, A., and Tomico, O. 2017. Embodied Design Ideation Methods. In CHI'17. Proceedings of the 2017 ACM SIGCHI Conference on Human Factors in Computing Systems, May 6-11, 2017, Denver, CO, USA. ACM, New York, NY, New York, USA, 5158–5170. http://dx.doi.org/10.1145/3025453.3025873
18. Zimmerman, J., Stolterman, E., Forlizzi, J. 2010. An Analysis and Critique of Research through Design: towards a formalization of a research approach. In Proceedings of the 2010 ACM Conference Companion Publication on Designing Interactive Systems - DIS '10 Companion. ACM Press, New York, USA, 310–319.

Creating and Staging Interactive Costumes

Michaela Honauer
Bauhaus-Universität Weimar, HCI Group
Weimar, Germany
michaela.honauer@uni-weimar.de

ABSTRACT

A growing part of HCI is research on wearables, e-textiles and performances with technology. However, conventional theatre productions underlie traditionally grown structures and have predefined production process that do not allow for in-house creations of interactive costumes. This research project addresses this issue and tries to figure out how this cultural sector and traditional costume design could engage with contemporary e-textile and wearable technologies.

Author Keywords

E-Textiles, Performing Arts, Theatre Production, Crafting.

INTRODUCTION AND BACKGROUND

For ages, costumes are the working garments of actors, dancers, and singers. Contemporary e-textile and wearable technologies enable us to create innovative costumes that can enhance performances, and extend the performer's expressivity [1]. However, there is a gap between traditional costume design and interactive costume design [2]. The latter is in most cases an individually organized interdisciplinary process with early user involvement, often carried out over a longer period of time. A lot of free performance groups and individual artists demonstrate their results onstage [e.g. 1, 2, 8, 10]. In contrast, traditional productions usually take place within a fixed time frame (six to eight weeks), and technical and design competencies are separated until a few days before premiere when performers rehearse the very first time with the costumes [3]. This different creation approach might be the main reason why traditional houses rarely stage interactive costumes. Nevertheless, a few examples show how interactive costumes can enrich more traditional productions – for instance the Brooklyn Ballet's interpretation of *The Nutcracker* (vimeo.com/109596734).

The HCI literature provides lots of e-textile or wearable examples, and likewise general readings on performances and interactive technologies have relevance for my research [6, 7]. Recent works engage with design processes and interaction qualities [6, 9], and crafting wearable costumes [2, 8]. However, there is a lack of HCI research in closing the gap between the interactive costume design process and traditional theatre production processes.

TEI '18, March 18–21, 2018, Stockholm, Sweden

ACM ISBN 978-1-4503-5568-1/18/03.
https://doi.org/10.1145/3173225.3173343

RESEARCH OBJECTIVES

My investigations aim at deeply understanding how e-textiles and wearables for the performing arts are crafted and staged. I am interested in how design thinking, engineering knowledge, and crafting skills influence each other. Compared with traditional costume design, I want to figure out the differentiations, and in best case, traditional productions benefit from being enabled to stage interactive costumes within their given infrastructures. My major research question is (1) how can interactive costumes be appropriately integrated into traditional theatre productions? Subordinated to this are the following questions: (2) What is to be considered when creating and staging interactive costumes? (3) What is characteristic for interactive costume design processes? (4) How do users and stakeholders adapt to working with interactive costumes?

Expected Outcome

As a major contribution, I expect to reveal further theoretical knowledge about creating and staging interactive costumes. The creation process includes practices on costume and interaction design, technical implementations, and crafting procedures. The staging process is related to the costumes' usage by primary (the wearer), secondary (e.g. chorographer) or tertiary (e.g. theatre dresser) stakeholders, including rehearsals as well as public performances. In detail, I want to achieve the following:

- A *process framework* for interactive costume design, to suggest how traditional theatre productions can integrate interactive costume design into their given structures.
- A list of *design principles* for creating interactive costumes that help to design and craft onstage wearables and e-textiles.
- Provide *techniques and tools for costume designers* to design and craft interactive costumes.
- Provide *methods and techniques for involving users and stakeholders* of interactive costumes into the creation process from early-on, and to allow for their feedback.

METHODOLOGICAL APPROACH

My research is qualitative and practice-led. I use different methods, ranging from evaluating users or creators to prototyping costumes. Further, I investigate how traditional theatre processes are described in literature for comparing it to productions that successfully stage interactive costumes.

Case Studies

I initiate and conduct, or participate in case studies on creating and staging interactive costumes (see Figure 2). This approach is often ethnographically-oriented when I am involved as external designer into traditional theatre productions (e.g. Figure 1) [5]. Other projects are within free artist groups, or internally at our university where we create interactive costumes, and test them with performers. Data collection for the seven almost accomplished case studies ranges from (self-) observation over interviews to field notes and supplementary materials.

Study, Year	Classification				Type of Applic.		Role of Researcher					Involvement of User				Method				
	Sen.-on. Act.-on.	Sen.-on. Act.-en.	Sen.-en. Act.-on.	Sen.-en. Act.-en.	Real-world	In-house	Ideation	Design	Develop-ment	Super-vision	Other	Who?*	Design	Develop-ment	Evalu-ation	Interview	Obser-vation	Diary	Question-naire	Other
CucumaDanceSensation, 2011				x	x		x	x	x			Da, T	x	x	x	(x)	x	x		(x)
Expl. Interact. Theatre Costumes, 2014	x					x				x		Di, Ac	(x)		x	x	x			x
Theater-Haus Jena, 2014	x				x		(x)	x	x			CD, T, Ac, Di	(x)	x	(x)		(x)	x		x
CucuMagic, 2014				x	x		x	x	x			Da, T	x	x	x	(x)	x	x		(x)
Expl. Interactive Theatre, 2014/2015		x		x	(x)	x				x	x	Di, Ac, Au	(x)	x	x	x	x			
Dance Costumes & DIY-Sensors, 2016	x	x				x				x		Ch, Da	(x)		x	x	x			(x)
The Little Mermaid, 2016/2017	x				x		(x)	(x)	x	x		Ch, Da, CD, Au	x	x	x	x	x	x	x	

Acting Theatre Dance Theatre

*Abbreviations: Ac - Actor, Au - Audience, Ch - Choreographer, CD - Costume Designer, Da - Dancer, Di - Director, T - Technician, WM - Wardrobe Mistress

Figure 2. Overview of case studies.

Expert Interviews

Further, I have conducted 13 semi-structured interviews with designers, engineers, choreographers, and researchers from all over the world. They are professionals that have been involved in creating and staging interactive costumes. This helps to deeper understand processes behind.

PRELIMINARY RESULTS

I recently started analyzing the expert interviews according to qualitative content analysis. For this I develop coding categories based on my research objectives and existing background literature. Furthermore, the case studies are to be compared on the basis of similar categories (cp. Fig. 2).

Costume Requirements

An initial stage of expert interviews and case studies, plus in-depth literature review resulted in developing design requirements for traditional theatre costumes [4]: *safety, robustness, easy cleaning, respect to aesthetics of the overall show, role support, changeability over time, enabling quick (un)dressing*, and *perceptibility for the whole audience*. Moreover, I posed additional requirements

Figure 1. Example of deploying interactive costumes in traditional productions. Image courtesy of Sabina Sabovic ©.

for interactive costumes. These are: *interdisciplinary team work, early rehearsals with prototypes, reliable functionality*, and *easy technical maintenance*. These underlie the planned design principles and will further inform the intended process framework.

Classification of Interactive Costumes

After reflecting on case studies and other examples from the literature, I sorted existing costume examples according to applied technologies. Fig. 3 shows a classification model based on actuators and sensors, either situated on-body or in the environment. Fig. 4 shows a hybrid concept out of it. To support the planned process framework, this model will be improved by adding creation and staging processes, assigned competencies, and performance purposes.

FURTHER WORK

Next to the final analysis of expert interviews, the evaluation of all case studies is to be finished. Based on the results, I develop the process framework and design principles. In case of remaining questions, further case studies targeting them are to be conducted. Further, I consider discussing my results with experts in the field, and conducting workshops with costume designers for reviewing my proposals on best practice integration of interactive costumes in traditional productions.

CONCLUSION

My research explores how interactive costumes can be created and staged for professional, but traditionally determined, theater stages. The studies are to contribute best practice knowledge on interactive costume design, and to suggest how traditional houses can integrate it into their given structures and production cycles. Above, it might also have relevance for other application areas, e.g. interactive fashion design, or teaching in e-textiles and wearables.

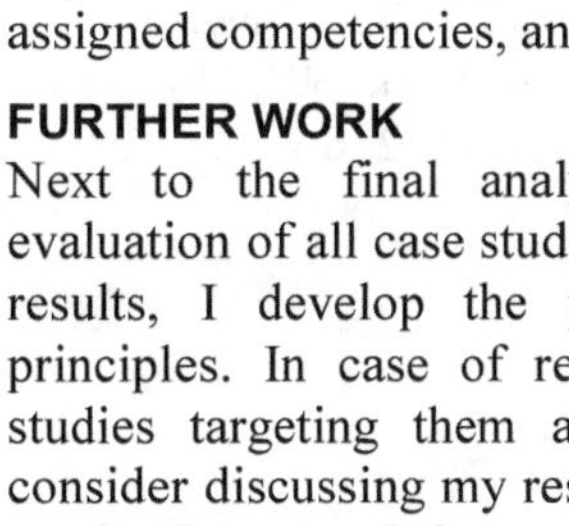

Fig. 4. Classification based on in/output technologies.

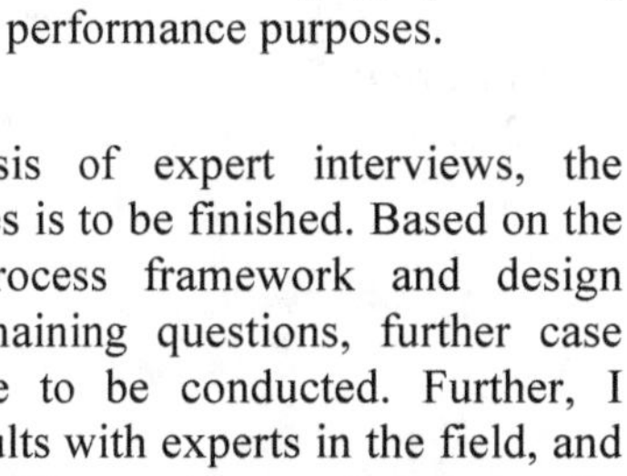

Fig. 3. Hybrid concept.

REFERENCES

1. Johannes Birringer and Michèle Danjoux. 2009. Wearable Performance. Digital Creativity 20, No. 1-2, 95-113. DOI: https://doi.org/10.1080/14626260902868095
2. Yu-I Ha and Yi-Kyung Kim. 2014. The design process of wearable computers for extending the performer's expression. In *HCI International 2014 - Posters' Extended Abstracts. Communications in Computer and Information Science*, Stephanidis, C. (Ed.). Vol. 434, Springer International Publishing, Cham, Switzerland, 421–426. DOI: https://doi.org/10.1007/978-3-319-07857-1_74
3. Michael Holt. 1993. *A Phaidon Theatre Manual - Costume and Make-up*. Phaidon Press, London.
4. Michaela Honauer. 2017. Designing (Inter)Active Costumes for Professional Stages. In Smart Textiles – Fundamentals, Design, and Interaction, Stefan Schneegass and Oliver Amft (eds.). Springer International Publishing, Cham, Switzerland, 279-302. DOI: https://doi.org/10.1007/978-3-319-50124-6_13
5. Michaela Honauer and Eva Hornecker. 2015. Challenges for Creating and Staging Interactive Costumes for the Theatre Stage. In *Proceedings of the 2015 ACM SIGCHI Conference on Creativity and Cognition* (C&C '15). ACM, New York, NY, USA, 13-22. DOI: https://doi.org/10.1145/2757226.2757242
6. Celine Latulipe, David Wilson, Sybil Huskey, Berto Gonzalez, and Melissa Word. 2011. Temporal integration of interactive technology in dance: creative process impacts. In *Proceedings of the 8th ACM conference on Creativity and cognition* (C&C '11). ACM, New York, NY, USA, 107-116. DOI: https://doi.org/10.1145/2069618.2069639
7. Chris Salter. 2010. *Entangled: Technology and the Transformation of Performance*. The MIT Press. DOI: https://doi.org/10.7551/mitpress/9780262195881.001.0001
8. Kate Sicchio. 2016. Wearable Costumes. In *Crafting Wearables*, Sibel D. Guler (ed.). Apress, Berkeley, CA, USA, 175-182. DOI: http://dx.doi.org/10.1007/978-1-4842-1808-2
9. Oscar Tomico and Danielle Wilde. 2016. Soft, embodied, situated & connected: enriching interactions with soft wearables. *mUX: The Journal of Mobile User Experience* 5, 1 (2016). DOI: https://doi.org/10.1186/s13678-016-0006-z
10. Clint Zeagler, Scott Gilliland, Katherine Fisher, Shimmy Boyle, and Laura Levy. 2017. Le Monstré: an interactive participatory performance costume. In *Proceedings of the 2017 ACM International Symposium on Wearable Computers* (ISWC '17). ACM, NY, USA, 260-264. DOI: https://doi.org/10.1145/3123021.3123070

Unfolding an Industrial Design Approach to Physical Computing

Clement Zheng
ATLAS Institute
University of Colorado, Boulder
clement.zheng@colorado.edu

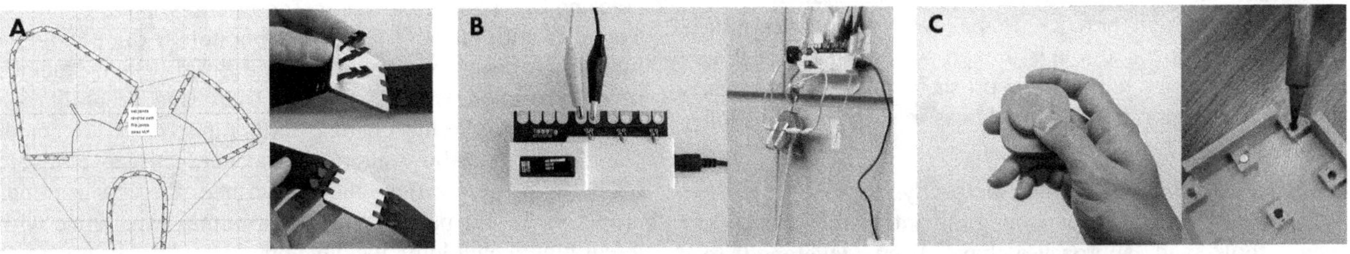

Figure 1. A) Joinery interface and loop insert joint profile. B) Press.kit microcontroller and hacking a therapy object. C) Mechamagnet interface and inserting a magnet into a 3D printed part.

ABSTRACT
Industrial designers working to develop tangible interactive systems require new skills to integrate technology into their prototypes. My research investigates how to facilitate physical computing for industrial design students in a manner that is in line with the practices and values of the profession. Different toolkits have been developed through this research to scaffold industrial designers as they make tangible interactive artifacts. Through investigating this toolkits in the wild, I aim to develop an approach to inform educators as they structure industrial design programs to support students in design tangible interactive systems.

Author Keywords
Industrial Design; Physical Computing; Making.

INTRODUCTION
As a field rooted in investigating and producing physical products, industrial design seems poised to tackle the challenges posed by three-dimensional interfaces and physical materials [14]. However, for industrial designers to contribute to the development of tangible interactive systems, they would need to pick up new skills for technology integration. These skills will help them create functioning prototypes that reflect the actual interaction experience [5,12]. However, technology integration is complex and requires significant skills and effort—even for experts [6]. This could lead to a "bracketed" process of technology integration; separating it from the human-centered design process [13]. *Physical computing* is often used to collective describe the skills and processes for integrating technology into tangible interactive systems [7]. I am motivated to facilitate industrial design students as they explore and develop their skills in this area. Furthermore, as a profession entrenched in the design and development of tangible, user-facing objects, industrial design institutions provide a rich curriculum covering skills such as human factors, materials and fabrication; such skills are typically integrated in studios set up to resemble professional design scenarios. Thus, for new skills such as physical computing, the challenge is not simply about communicating the relevant concepts; rather, industrial design educators also need to address how such new skills can be synthesized with existing practice.

TEI '18, March 18–21, 2018, Stockholm, Sweden

ACM ISBN 978-1-4503-5568-1/18/03.
https://doi.org/10.1145/3173225.3173344

RESEARCH OBJECTIVES
To guide this research, I am pursuing two parallel lines of investigation. Firstly, I want to understand how physical computing can be introduced to industrial design students in a manner that is integrative to the profession's values and processes. Secondly, artifacts embody a designer's concepts and skills in addressing an external design space; simultaneously, these external representations are a source of professional knowledge [2]. Given this, I want to explore how artifacts and artifact-making can facilitate the acquisition and integration of new and existing skills.

BACKGROUND
This research is primarily informed by literature in tangible interaction design, design process as well as material culture. Following the two lines of research, the related literature can be organized into two themes.

Facilitating Designing & Learning-through-designing
Schön describes the professional design process as an iterative process of action and reflection [11]; designers

create and evaluate models to probe and gain more insight about an external design space. This bears a strong resemblance to the constructionist approach to learning described by Papert [8]; in fact, another label for this learning paradigm is "learning through designing" [10]. While the professional design process focuses on uncovering knowledge about an extrinsic problem space, learning through designing focuses on using the design process to gain knowledge from the learner's experiences. As industrial design institutions prepare students for professional design practice, it makes sense that learning new skills happens through the process of designing as well. Scaffolds and tools to support such situated learning is therefore an important area to address in such an education paradigm for industrial design [1,4].

Artifact Making for Tangible Interactive Systems

With regard to prototyping tangible interactive systems, many tools and approaches have been developed to facilitate physical computing. Among these, I am particularly inspired by the *kit-of-no-parts* approach proposed by Perner-wilson et al. [9]. Rather than use standardized electronic parts, they facilitated crafters in making tangible interactive systems from processes and materials native to the craft. Their approach resulted in functional prototypes which were not only more personalized; their inner workings were also more transparent to the maker. Similarly—as a profession with a deep tradition in shaping and assembling materials into functional forms—I believe that a more fundamental material-centered approach to physical computing will facilitate industrial designers to develop their own "language" in designing *with* and *for* technology.

APPROACH & CURRENT WORK

My approach can be described as a *research through design, for design* [3]. Throughout my research, I have developed tools and processes which I believe can facilitate industrial designers in developing tangible interactive systems. These toolkits are evaluated in an iterative manner, starting with: (1) a personal investigation exploring the different applications and limitations of the toolkit, followed by (2) pilot testing in the lab with other researchers and design educators to refine the usability of the toolkit, and finally (3) running workshops with actual industrial design students to understand how the toolkits affect their design process. Here are a few toolkits I developed following this approach:

Joinery: Parametric Joints for Laser Cut Assemblies

Laser cutting is widely used as a fabrication process for prototyping tangible objects as it is able to rapidly and precisely cut a wide variety of sheet materials. The flat parts produced by the laser cutter can thereafter be put together into three-dimensional assemblies; for instance, a wearable e-textile platform, or an enclosure for electronics. Joint design is a tedious and error-prone task when creating such laser cut assemblies. With this challenge in mind, I developed *Joinery* (Figure 1A), a web application that generates parametric joints on a user's pattern design [15]. *Joinery* offers a variety of joint profiles that cater to different materials, such as finger joints for soft wood, or tab inserts for paper stock. This tool was deployed in a physical computing class in an industrial design institution, and students used it as part of their development of tangible interactive artifacts.

Press.kit: Hacking Everyday Objects into Tangible Interfaces

Together with other research collaborators, I ran a tangible interaction design workshop for industrial design students in collaboration with a senior activity and rehabilitation center. Due to the high patient-to-therapist ratio, the center wants to explore how interactive technology can motivate patients in performing the prescribed therapy routines properly. As our participants had minimal experience with integrating technology, we developed a toolkit (*Press.kit*) to scaffold students as they engage in physical computing. *Press.kit* consists of a microcontroller with a custom firmware and printed circuit board (Figure 1B), as well as a sensor building curriculum employing simple materials like magnets, copper tape and conductive thread. Via *Press.kit*, our participants were able to hack and build on top of existing therapy objects to create six different functional prototypes for therapists to evaluate.

Mechamagnets: Tactile Mechanisms with Magnets and Digital Fabrication

While advances in digital fabrication have enabled industrial designers to rapidly prototype physical parts, integrating functional mechanisms into these parts is still a complex process. *Mechamagnets* explores how magnets can be embedded into 3D printed parts to create tangible interfaces that provide tactile feedback (Figure 1C). Through simply reconfiguring the arrangement of a magnetic unit, I demonstrate how different tactile mechanisms can be efficiently fabricated. In addition, *Mechamagnet* interfaces can be easily instrumented through simple materials like copper tape, or sensors like a magnetometer.

FUTURE WORK

Each of the toolkits introduced offers a small contribution in facilitating industrial designers as they design tangible interactive systems. However, the tools and processes for design is always evolving, and my aim is certainly not to define an exhaustive list of physical computing toolkits for industrial designers. Rather, by understanding the impact of my existing collection of toolkits, I aim to abstract an industrial design approach to physical computing—an approach which I hope will support other educators as they structure industrial design programs to support their students in design tangible interactive systems.

REFERENCES

1. John Seely Brown, Allan Collins, and Paul Duguid. 1989. Situated cognition and the culture of learning. *Educational researcher* 18, 1: 32–42.
2. Charles Eastman. 2001. New directions in design cognition: studies of representation and recall. *Design knowing and learning: Cognition in design education* 1: 147–198.
3. Christopher Frayling. 1993. Research in art and design.
4. Cindy E. Hmelo and Mark Guzdial. 1996. Of Black and Glass Boxes: Scaffolding for Doing and Learning. In *Proceedings of the 1996 International Conference on Learning Sciences* (ICLS '96), 128–134. Retrieved from http://dl.acm.org/citation.cfm?id=1161135.1161153
5. Stephanie Houde and Charles Hill. 1997. What do prototypes prototype. *Handbook of human-computer interaction* 2: 367–381.
6. Johnny C. Lee, Daniel Avrahami, Scott E. Hudson, Jodi Forlizzi, Paul H. Dietz, and Darren Leigh. 2004. The Calder Toolkit: Wired and Wireless Components for Rapidly Prototyping Interactive Devices. In *Proceedings of the 5th Conference on Designing Interactive Systems: Processes, Practices, Methods, and Techniques* (DIS '04), 167–175. https://doi.org/10.1145/1013115.1013139
7. Dan O'Sullivan and Tom Igoe. 2004. *Physical Computing: Sensing and Controlling the Physical World with Computers*. Course Technology Press, Boston, MA, United States.
8. Seymour Papert. 1993. *Mindstorms: children, computers, and powerful ideas*. Basic Books, New York.
9. Hannah Perner-Wilson, Leah Buechley, and Mika Satomi. 2011. Handcrafting textile interfaces from a kit-of-no-parts. In *Proceedings of the fifth international conference on Tangible, embedded, and embodied interaction*, 61. https://doi.org/10.1145/1935701.1935715
10. Mitchel Resnick and Brian Silverman. 2005. Some Reflections on Designing Construction Kits for Kids. In *Proceedings of the 2005 Conference on Interaction Design and Children* (IDC '05), 117–122. https://doi.org/10.1145/1109540.1109556
11. D. A. Schön. 1992. Designing as reflective conversation with the materials of a design situation. *Knowledge-Based Systems* 5, 1: 3–14. https://doi.org/http://dx.doi.org/10.1016/0950-7051(92)90020-G
12. Pieter Jan Stappers. 2013. Prototypes as central vein for knowledge development. *Prototype: Design and Craft in the 21st Century. Bloomsbury Academic.*
13. Petra Sundström, Alex Taylor, Katja Grufberg, Niklas Wirström, Jordi Solsona Belenguer, and Marcus Lundén. 2011. Inspirational Bits: Towards a Shared Understanding of the Digital Material. In *Proceedings of the SIGCHI Conference on Human Factors in Computing Systems* (CHI '11), 1561–1570. https://doi.org/10.1145/1978942.1979170
14. Roel Vertegaal. 2011. The (Re)Usability of Everyday Computational Things: Why Industrial Design Will Be the New Interaction Design. *interactions* 18, 1: 38–41. https://doi.org/10.1145/1897239.1897251
15. Clement Zheng, Ellen Yi-Luen Do, and Jim Budd. 2017. Joinery: Parametric Joint Generation for Laser Cut Assemblies. In *Proceedings of the 2017 ACM SIGCHI Conference on Creativity and Cognition* (C&C '17), 63–74. https://doi.org/10.1145/3059454.3059459

Sociomateriality: Infrastructuring and Appropriation of Artifacts

Tom Jenkins
Digital Media Program
Georgia Institute of Technology
Atlanta, GA, USA
tom.jenkins@gatech.edu

Karey Helms
Vasiliki Tsaknaki
Ludvig Elblaus
Royal Institute of Technology
Stockholm, Sweden
karey@kth.se
tsaknaki@kth.se
elblaus@kth.se

Nicolai Brodersen Hansen
Department of Industrial Design
Eindhoven University of Technology
Eindhoven, Netherlands
n.b.hansen@tue.nl

TEI '18, March 18-21, 2018, Stockholm, Sweden

ACM 978-1-4503-5568-1/18/03.
https://doi.org/10.1145/3173225.3173330

Abstract

This Studio offers researchers and designers an opportunity to investigate and discuss prototypes and in-process projects from a perspective that expands beyond material aspects, to also cover social and cultural ones. Participants will bring a project, device, or platform, which will be discussed as *sociomaterials* that actively participate across multiple social and cultural contexts. This perspective, as well as the prototypes and projects brought by the participants, forms the core of the Studio, where conversation will emerge over several phases: from the demonstration of the individual projects as things, to the generation of speculative fictions as to the role and use of these artifacts in the world. Finally, we end with a discussion of infrastructuring and appropriation of the artefacts and their social roles. The themes that will be examined in this Studio are agency, emerging behaviors, embeddedness and design strategies from a sociomaterial perspective of artifacts.

Author Keywords

Materiality; design; prototypes; research through design; design things; sociomaterials; infrastructuring.

Introduction

From the physical to the digital, materiality is central to TEI. The post-digital theme of TEI 2018 continues to address materiality, yet emphasizes a paradigm shift as digital materials transition from novel and virtuous to ubiquitous and distrustful, and physical materials to celebrate craft, nostalgia, and nature. Fundamental to this shift are the dynamic social meanings embedded within the material of artifacts, objects, and systems. How then are we to design for these material meanings? One way to consider how devices serve to frame the world and possible relations within it is through the idea of *infrastructuring* [2]. Infrastructuring reflects the social role of an object or system in relation to its context and use, and reflects a collaboration over time and among stakeholders and between contexts [14]. Understanding the role of designed objects as being socially active substances that operate inside of infrastructural concerns to support broader values and practices opens a way to discuss how designs might be put to use [12].

The social implications of these materials are not often discussed at venues like TEI. The core argument of this workshop is that a sociomaterial perspective might become a theoretical lens to discuss tangible, embodied, and embedded interactions at TEI beyond demo contexts or research studios, into social structures and organizations. We believe that making space for conversations among designers about both social and material issues of computational artifacts is essential for design research.

Being a community highly focused on tangible interaction, a central theme of TEI and HCI has been materiality [6,13], reflecting the availability of a new and diverse materials as well as competing views of materiality reflecting TUIs, material computation and crafting [8]. These contributions emphasize how computation is both material and post-digital, and as such has challenged existing perspectives in HCI [9,16,17]. One way that TEI can contribute to the broader field of HCI is by drawing on the strong tradition of the community in exemplifying and developing material research agendas, but also by bringing them into dialogue with ongoing discussions regarding their social and cultural implications. The material turn is also reflected in contemporary discourses in design research. To designers, the substance has long been an essential part of understanding how or whether a design "works." A key idea we want explore is that the objects that are produced as part of practice-based research are *design things* [1]. Design things enact multiple roles in the context of the process of design; they are messy, and support the negotiation and alignment of different values and viewpoints [5]. In HCI, design things can take the form of design notebooks [3,7], strong conceptual insights into design processes [11], and reflection on provocative hardware prototypes, e.g. [4,10,15]. These design things produce, constitute, and perform knowledge about social relations via their dissemination and use. As such, it is important to attend to the context and intended role of these prototypes as well as the material and scholarly documentation produced after the fact—to consider the role of the device, what it is infrastructuring, and how it might be appropriated by future users.

Studio Proposal

In the interaction design/HCI community, and in the TEI community in particular, materiality is a highly important and strong topic. This studio contributes to this research space by examining and elaborating on how the design of interactive things expands beyond the material aspects, to also cover social and cultural ones. In particular, we want to explore how things and materials affect social structures and practices. In this Studio we intend to study, discuss and explore the fidelity of the prototype as design things. This involves moving the conversation beyond novel or technically robust prototypes that will be operated in a demonstrative context to also consider the possible social implications of the things we design. In particular, we are interested in how the three core concepts of TEI, namely *embeddedness*, *embodiment* and *tangibility,* can be re-addressed and revisited in a post-digital era. We use the idea of sociomaterials—devices and objects that actively play a role in social worlds—as a lens to this discussion, as it addresses the material and social arrangements of technological prototypes together, and bridges the demonstration, workshop, or research lab with the "real" world.

Studio Topics

This Studio will closely investigate computational design things that are brought by the participants. Having tangible things and prototypes at the core of the Studio activities, the format is meant to be conversational and generative around issues relating to design prototypes and the material and social roles that they infrastructure. These include to:

- Agency: How do materials participate? In design? In use? In context?
- Emerging Behaviors: How can computational capabilities embedded in materials shift how the materials participate?
- Embeddedness: How do devices embedded in cultures perform cultural values?
- Design Strategies: How can design researchers produce technologies that are deeply embedded in social or cultural contexts?

Studio Learning Goals/Discussion Objectives

Participants of this Studio will have the chance to critically examine and discuss one another's prototypes, artifacts or demos from both social and material perspectives, as well as how these perspectives interweave. This means that a strong focus will be put on how materiality—in its many facets—is both socially and culturally embedded and prototypes and devices participate in these discourses. The material form and the presentation of the objects themselves will be used to ground the discussion of the role that these devices play in social worlds. This will include the device's materiality, the goals and intentions of the designer, and how design decisions can be translated to how a device will leave its life outside a workshop or a research space to perform social and cultural roles.

Acknowledgements

Helms' is funded via the Smart Implicit Interactions project by Strategic Research Foundation (SSF) in Sweden. Hansen's is funded by the research programme 'STEC: Smart Technologies, Empowered Citizens' with project number 652.001.005 which is (partly) financed by the Netherlands Organization for Scientific Research (NWO).

References

1. Thomas Binder, Giorgio de De Michelis, Pelle Ehn, Giulio Jacucci, Per Linde, and Ina Wagner. 2011. *Design Things*. MIT Press.

2. Erling Björgvinsson, Pelle Ehn, and Per-Anders Hillgren. 2010. Participatory design and "democratizing innovation." *Proceedings of the 11th Biennial Participatory Design Conference*, ACM, 41–50.
3. John Bowers. 2012. The Logic of Annotated Portfolios: Communicating the Value of "Research Through Design." *Proceedings of the Designing Interactive Systems Conference*, ACM, 68–77.
4. Carl DiSalvo and Tom Jenkins. 2017. Fruit Are Heavy: A Prototype Public IoT System to Support Urban Foraging. *Proceedings of the 2017 Conference on Designing Interactive Systems*, ACM, 541–553.
5. Pelle Ehn. 2008. Participation in design things. *Proceedings of the Tenth Anniversary Conference on Participatory Design 2008*, Indiana University, 92–101.
6. Ylva Fernaeus and Petra Sundström. 2012. The Material Move How Materials Matter in Interaction Design Research. *Proceedings of the Designing Interactive Systems Conference*, ACM, 486–495.
7. William Gaver. 2011. Making Spaces: How Design Workbooks Work. *Proceedings of the SIGCHI Conference on Human Factors in Computing Systems*, ACM, 1551–1560.
8. Shad Gross, Jeffrey Bardzell, and Shaowen Bardzell. 2014. Structures, forms, and stuff: the materiality and medium of interaction. *Personal and Ubiquitous Computing* 18, 3: 637–649.
9. Nicolai Brodersen Hansen, Rikke Toft Nørgård, and Kim Halskov. 2014. Crafting Code at the Demo-scene. *Proceedings of the 2014 Conference on Designing Interactive Systems*, ACM, 35–38.
10. Karey Helms. 2017. Leaky Objects: Implicit Information, Unintentional Communication. *Proceedings of the 2017 ACM Conference Companion Publication on Designing Interactive Systems*, ACM, 182–186.
11. Kristina Höök and Jonas Löwgren. 2012. Strong Concepts: Intermediate-level Knowledge in Interaction Design Research. *ACM Trans. Comput.-Hum. Interact.* 19, 3: 23:1–23:18.
12. Le Dantec, Christopher A. *Designing Publics*. 1st ed. The MIT Press, 2016.
13. Erica Robles and Mikael Wiberg. 2010. Texturing the "Material Turn" in Interaction Design. *Proceedings of the Fourth International Conference on Tangible, Embedded, and Embodied Interaction*, ACM, 137–144.
14. Star, Susan Leigh, and Karen Ruhleder. "Steps Towards an Ecology of Infrastructure: Complex Problems in Design and Access for Large-Scale Collaborative Systems." In *Proceedings of the 1994 ACM Conference on Computer Supported Cooperative Work*, ACM 253–264ACM, 1994.
15. Vasiliki Tsaknaki and Ylva Fernaeus. 2016. Expanding on Wabi-Sabi As a Design Resource in HCI. *Proceedings of the 2016 CHI Conference on Human Factors in Computing Systems*, ACM, 5970–5983.
16. Anna Vallgårda, Laurens Boer, Vasiliki Tsaknaki, and Dag Svanaes. 2016. Material Programming: A New Interaction Design Practice. *Proceedings of the 2016 ACM Conference Companion Publication on Designing Interactive Systems*, ACM, 149–152.
17. Anna Vallgårda and Johan Redström. 2007. Computational Composites. *Proceedings of the SIGCHI Conference on Human Factors in Computing Systems*, ACM, 513–522.

Designing eTextiles for the Body: Shape, Volume & Motion

Rachel Freire
Rachel Freire Studio
London, United Kingdom
rachel@rachelfreire.com

Paul Strohmeier
Human Centred Computing
University of Copenhagen
Copenhagen, Denmark
p.strohmeier@di.ku.dk

Cedric Honnet
Sorbonne Universities
UPMC, CNRS, ISIR
Paris, France
cedric@honnet.eu

Jarrod Knibbe
Human Centred Computing
University of Copenhagen
Copenhagen, Denmark
jarrod@di.ku.dk

Sophia Brueckner
Stamps School of Art & Design,
University of Michigan,
Ann Arbor, MI, USA
sbrueckn@umich.edu

TEI '18, March 18-21, 2018, Stockholm, Sweden
ACM ISBN 978-1-4503-5568-1/18/03.
https://doi.org/10.1145/3173225.3173331

Abstract
In this studio, we will improve our tailoring skills in order to better integrate technology into clothing. Leveraging the volumetric nature of clothing, we will create eTextile interfaces that fit the shape of the body and are designed around how bodies move. This studio will consist of a short masterclass led by an expert fashion designer followed by materials experimentation and working on individual projects. We will introduce and demo a variety of ways to design and implement 3-dimensional eTextiles as well as how to integrate them with interactive systems.

Author Keywords
eTextile, tailoring, fabric, sewing, craft, wearables

ACM Classification Keywords
Human-centered computing~Human computer interaction (HCI) • Hardware~Sensors and actuators

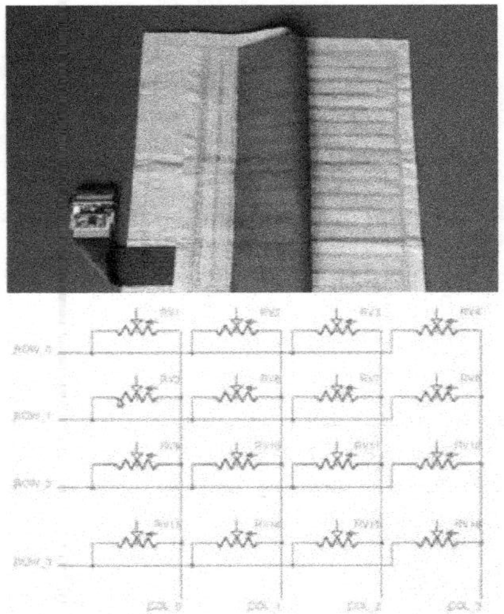

Figure 1 – Pressure-Matrix Sensor by Donneaud et al. [2] and corresponding schematic.

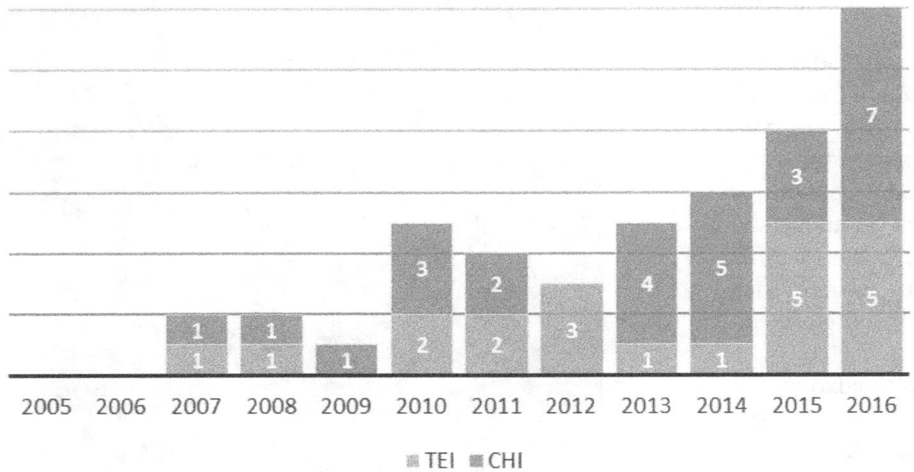

Figure 2 - Number of papers at CHI that refer to 'eTextiles', 'e-textiles' or 'electronic textiles' in their text (orange) and number of papers at TEI that refer to textiles or fabric in their abstract (blue).

(Tool for full-text search of the CHI proceedings is still under development and not yet published. CHI data for 2017 not yet available. TEI data based on manual search. Graph makes no claim to completeness).

Introduction

The academic interest in textiles as a design material is gradually increasing. This can be seen from the number of publications at TEI and less specialized venues, such as CHI (Figure 1). With some exceptions (e.g.: [1, 3]) this work appears driven by computer-scientists and designers who have little experience or training in working with textiles. The result are designs such as the popular multiplexed sensor matrix (e.g.: [2, 4, 5]). This is an obvious design from a computer-science perspective, but rather counter-intuitive from a fashion or tailoring perspective: individual textile elements of garments have complex shapes which are rarely square.

Such a sensor and its corresponding schematic can be seen in Figure 2. The organization of the schematic and the organization of the textile are almost identical. This is not required by the technology and, looking at patterns used for creating garments (see figure 4), possibly not desirable.

We believe that technology should adapt to the shape of the body and that compelling wearable technology is not a plastic gadget attached to clothing, but clothing which *is* technology. To achieve this, we suggest that considerations regarding the body's shape and movements must be made much earlier in the design process than is current practice.

We are hosting this studio to improve our own understanding of how to design fashionable and functional eTextile garments. While we share the workflows and methods which we have developed for ourselves, we hope to learn from the diverse background of the other participants of the studio.

While the workshop will be focused on fabrication skills, we will discuss potential applications for the near future as well as speculate on the long-term future of clothing and wearable technology.

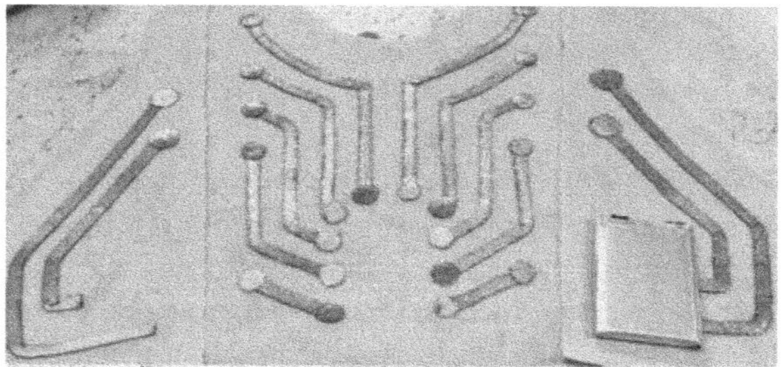

Figure 3 – Traces are added to fabric by layering heat bonding method

Figure 4 – Fabric cut into pattern and laid out flat. Note the complexity of the shape

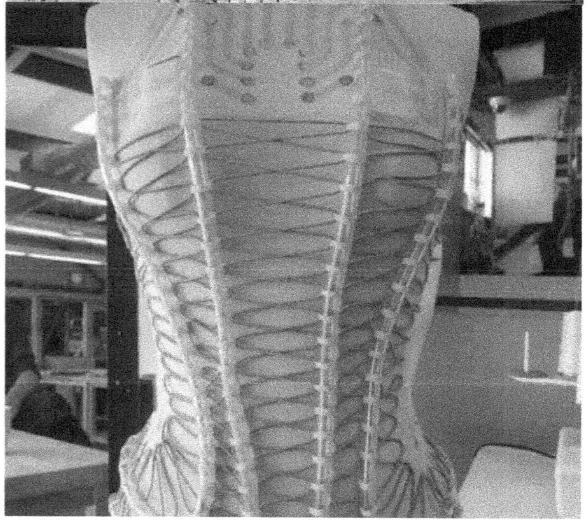

Figure 5 – Pattern assembled to volumetric garment, conforming to the wearer's body

Studio Proposal

This studio has a two-part structure, a masterclass designed by us and a collaborative prototyping session in which the studio hosts and the participants together apply the methods demonstrated in the masterclass.

Masterclass

We will start out with a master-class-crash-course on fashion-design and functional materials lead by Rachel Freire. Rachel will introduce the group to her method of using heat-bonding to integrate conductive fabric traces in her designs (Figure 3). She will discuss and share her approach to creating patterns (Figure 4) which eventually transform from two dimensional layouts into three dimensional garments (Figure 5 & 6).

Collaborative Prototyping

After the masterclass, the studio will split into smaller interests groups. These groups will use the rest of the day to explore ideas through physical prototyping.

All studio hosts have extensive experience in working with textiles. They each contribute unique perspectives and will share their experience with embedded development, sensor design, Sci-Fi prototyping, EMS-stimulation, haptic feedback and connected devices in the context of eTextiles. We hope that participants will diversify this further. Together, hosts and participants will create subgroups and spend an afternoon prototyping wearable concepts.

We will provide a selection of fabrics, mannequins and tailoring tools as well as basic electronics to facilitate the prototyping of novel eTextile technologies.

Figure 6 - Dynamic tulle sensor cape: pattern cutting can also be used to create dynamic garments with contrasting shapes. This can add functionality as well as compliment and augment the silhouette

Participant Profile

To start prototyping as fast as possible, we expect all participants to have prepared some concepts or ideas that they would like to explore. We will also only bring very basic electronic prototyping supplies and assume all participants will bring their prototyping platform of choice and any more advanced tools, materials or devices they might want to use.

We are looking for participants with an interest in eTextiles and basic electronic hardware or software prototyping skills. We assume that participants will have basic electronic prototyping skills. We do not expect participants to have prior experience or skills working with fabric, though if they do that is a plus.

Studio Topics to be Covered

We will discuss methods for designing eTextiles that both conform and contrast to the shape and motion of the body (see Figure 5 & 6). We will introduce participants to functional and non-functional materials which are used for designing eTextiles. We will present basic methods for designing patterns as well as measuring and fitting garments. We will discuss approaches for sensing in eTextiles and demonstrate manufacturing techniques based on heat-bonding as a quick and accessible way to prototype and iterate.

Studio Goals

We pursue goals on different levels with this studio. First off, we hope to help people expand their knowledge of eTextile design. In doing so we hope to also improve our own understanding of the domain.

Through prototyping we plan to achieve a tangible outcome consisting of a series of eTextile garments. Our intent is for such a tangible outcome to support future collaboration between participants. The workshop will foster ideation on current and near future applications of eTextiles as well as their future role in transhumanism and our cyborg evolution.

Acknowledgements

This work was supported by the European Research Council, grant no. 648785, by Labex SMART (ANR-11-LABX-65) and by French state funds under reference ANR-11-IDEX-0004-02. The authors would like to thank Maurin Donneaud from DataPaulette.

References

[1] Berzowska, J. 2005. Memory rich clothing: second skins that communicate physical memory. *Proceedings of the 5th conference on Creativity and Cognition.*

[2] Donneaud, M. et al. 2017. Designing a Multi-Touch eTextile for Music Performances. *Proceedings of the International Conference on New Interfaces for Musical Expression - NIME '17*

[3] Freire, R. et al. 2017. Second Skin: An Exploration of eTextile Stretch Circuits on the Body. *Proceedings of the Tenth International Conference on Tangible, Embedded, and Embodied Interaction - TEI '17.*

[4] Schneegass, S. and Voit, A. 2016. GestureSleeve: using touch sensitive fabrics for gestural input on the forearm for controlling smartwatches. *Proceedings of the 2016 ACM International Symposium on Wearable Computers - ISWC '16.*

[5] Zhou, B. et al. 2014. From smart clothing to smart table cloth: Design and implementation of a large scale, textile pressure matrix sensor. *Lecture Notes in Computer Science*, 159–170.

Deformable Controllers: Fabrication and Design to Promote Novel Hand Gestural Interaction Mechanisms

Victor Cheung
Carleton University
Ottawa, Canada
victor.cheung@carleton.ca

Alexander Keith Eady
Carleton University
Ottawa, Canada
alex.eady@carleton.ca

Audrey Girouard
Carleton University
Ottawa, Canada
audrey.girouard@carleton.ca

TEI '18, March 18–21, 2018, Stockholm, Sweden

ACM ISBN 978-1-4503-5568-1/18/03.
https://doi.org/10.1145/3173225.3173332

Abstract
When compared to mainstream touch/button-centric devices, deformable devices enable a more organic and tangible way for human-computer interaction. This studio provides participants an opportunity to have hands-on experience in fabricating controllers that use various deformation inputs (e.g., bending, stretching), and promote novel interaction mechanisms using hand gestures. Participants will learn different types of deformation inputs and create their own sensors. They will work in groups to design deformable controllers using both the sensors they make in-session and/or pre-built ones, to afford novel hand gestural inputs beyond conventional touches and clicks. The main objectives of this studio are to facilitate exchange of experience in fabricating deformable sensors/materials, and to foster creativity in using such controllers as inputs with hand gestures.

Author Keywords
Deformation; input devices; fabrication; prototyping; hand gestural inputs; tangible interaction.

Introduction
Recent advancements in sensing technologies have enabled user input modalities beyond touches and

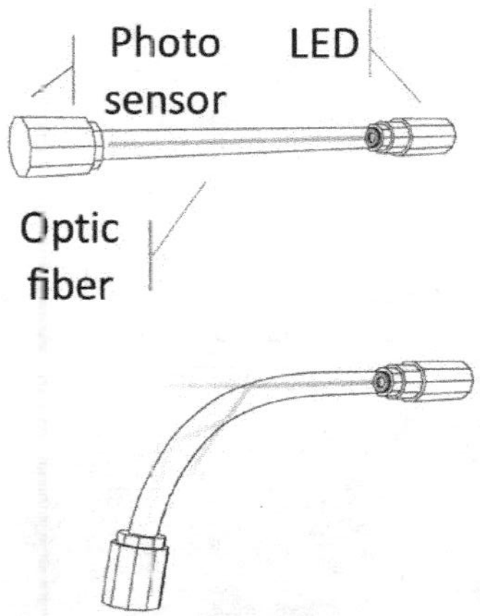

Figure 1. Illustration of an optical-based bend sensor. When bent, some of the light emitted from the LED escape, thus reducing the intensity of light reaching the photo sensor end.

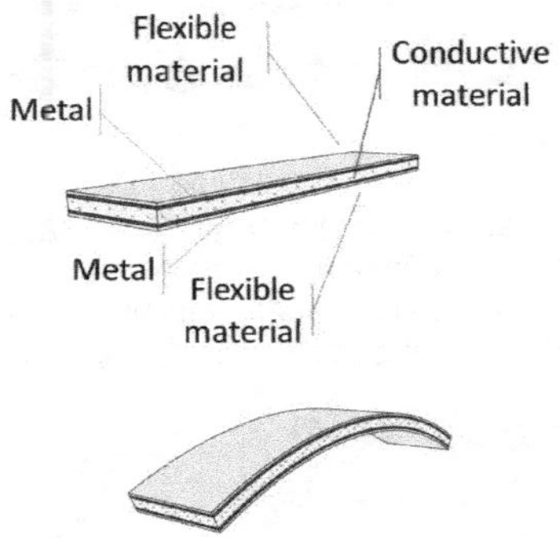

Figure 2. Illustration of a resistance-based bend/pressure sensor. When bent, the conductive material in the middle is compressed, thus reducing its resistance.

button-clicks on rigid surfaces, thereby creating opportunities for more articulate interactions. One such modality is deformation, involving user-driven changes of an object's shape, such as bend, squeeze, and stretch (e.g., [5,7]), as an input language. This form of input often leads to more naturalistic input mappings [11,12], especially due to its tangibility and intrinsic tactile feedback, and is useful in various contexts (e.g., games [10,11], interface navigation [2] and content creation [1,3]).

The increased availability of deformation sensors both commercially and in the DIY community [17], and their customizability in shape [13], have allowed researchers and designers to focus on how these deformable devices can better mediate human-computer interaction through hand gestures. Yet, as a relatively new interaction paradigm, there is still little knowledge in how they can impact our current ways of interacting, such as grip patterns and interaction metaphors.

Studio Proposal

We propose a studio that hosts 15-20 participants exploring the impact and potential brought forth by this new form of tangible interaction. We have designed the studio to educate our participants on deformable interactions, and encourage them to experiment with this new paradigm to create input mechanisms.

Participants are expected to be comfortable with crafting and have a basic knowledge of using Arduino (e.g., programming, circuit board wiring), and should bring a laptop with the Arduino IDE installed.

Studio Topics to be Covered

We intend to cover a variety of deformation sensors, and provide hands-on experience to build two of them.

Making Deformation Sensors
We present a brief history and basic working principles of deformation sensors, followed by a crafting session where participants make their own sensors. We selected two types of sensors that require no special equipment and use electronic components that are easily available, to complement previous work and workshops discussing printed circuitry or conductive ink [9,13,16]. Figures 1 & 2 show the basic working principle of these sensors that participants will be making at the studio.

Optical-based Bend Sensors – by measuring changes in the intensity of light passing through an optical fiber, one can determine the degree of bend (Figure 3). This method is inexpensive and robust [6], and is used in several prior projects [1,4].

Resistance-based Bend/Pressure Sensors – by measuring changes in resistance of a conductive layer, one can determine the degree of bend as well as amount of pressure (Figure 4). This method is a popular choice within the DIY community [18] due to the availability of the composing materials and ease of making (e.g., plastic sheets, copper tape, velostat).

Assembling Deformable Controllers
We demonstrate how multiple deformable sensors can be assembled into a controller, using prototyping tools such as foam boards, 3D printing, and silicone molding. By assembling sensors in specific ways, it is possible to detect complex deformations such as directional bends

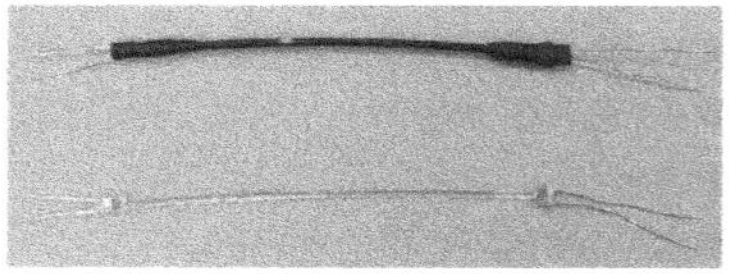

Figure 3. Optical-based bend senor. (Top) Finished sensor wrapped to prevent light leakage. (Bottom) Internal components: LED, optic fiber, photosensor

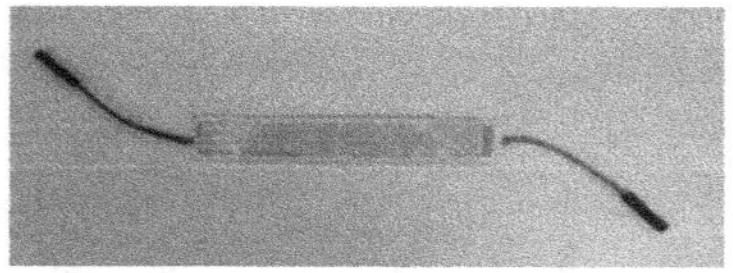

Figure 4. Resistance-based bend/pressure senor.

Figure 5. Placement of two bi-directional sensors in a cross pattern to detect bends and twists.

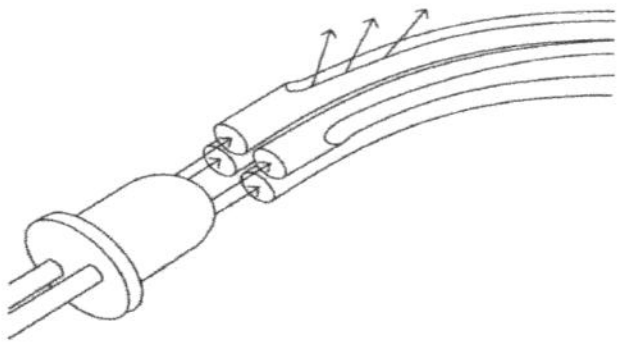

Figure 6. Placement of four optical-bend sensors along the stylus shaft to detect bend orientation [1].

and twist. For example, Bendtroller [11] puts two bi-directional bend sensors in a cross pattern to detect up-/downward bends and twists (Figure 5), FlexStylus [1] puts four optical bend sensors along the pen's shaft to detect bend orientation (Figure 6).

Designing for Novel Hand-Gestural Inputs
Sensing deformation allows novel interaction when the interactive device affords novel inputs. We will lead a design exercise that guides participants to create interactive controllers for various applications that use deformation as novel gestural interactions.

We will use games as a warm-up exercise and lead participants to first design gestural inputs using one or both hands, and/or wrist and arm movements inspired by in-game actions. For instance, what is a one-handed gesture that embodies the action of jumping? Next, participants will design hand-held devices with form-factors and affordances that support these interactions. Participant are then free to continue using the provided games, or other applications of their choosing.

Finally, we will have a demo session where the participants present their designs to each other. Presenters will have the chance to receive feedback from each other, and further improve their designs. We also invite participants to propose relevant discussion topics based on their own experience with deformable devices. If possible, the demos can also be presented to the conference attendees during the demo session.

Studio Learning Goals/Discussion Objectives

The first objective of the studio is to provide participants a platform to share resources and exchange experience in deformable sensor/material fabrication. Researchers have proposed novel ways to fabricate devices that detect various deformation types [4,9,13,14,15], and it is important to examine the strengths and weaknesses of these methods, such as ease and cost of fabrication, accuracy, and durability.

The second objective is to foster creativity in using deformable devices as input controllers harnessing the wide range of hand gestures. Besides fabrication techniques, researchers have also elicited interaction languages and metaphors with deformable devices [8], and explored their applicability in various context [1,2,3,10,11]. They have found that these novel input mechanisms lead to enjoyment and expressiveness not found in standard touch/click inputs, mostly due to better support for natural hand gestures [10,11]. Having a session to design controllers to promote hand gestural interaction will help advancing research and development of deformable interactions.

Finally, the third objective is to better understand how designers approach the creation of deformable interactions and controllers, in moving beyond recreating touch/click inputs in deformable devices. We aim to observe how researchers embody action and metaphor in the conceptualization of an interaction or a device. Our end goal will be to run this workshop with different participants and report our observations as design guidelines for such devices.

The experience shared and the ideas formed in the studio are directly relevant to Tangible Embedded and Embodied Interfaces, as evidenced by much related work in the conference proceedings (e.g., [10,12,13]).

Acknowledgements

This work was supported and funded by the Natural Sciences and Engineering Research Council of Canada (NSERC) through a Discovery grant (2017-06300), a Create grant (465639-2015), and by the Ministry of Ontario through an Early Researcher Award (ER15-11-101). The views expressed in the publication are the views of the Institution and do not necessarily reflect those of the Province.

References

1. Fellion, N., Eady, A.K., and Girouard, A. FlexStylus: A deformable stylus for digital art. *Proc. CHI EA*, ACM Press (2016), 2482–2489.
2. Girouard, A., Lo, J., Riyadh, M., Daliri, F., Eady, A.K., and Pasquero, J. One-Handed Bend Interactions with Deformable Smartphones. *Proc. CHI*, ACM (2015), 1509–1518.
3. Gomes, A., Priyadarshana, L., Carrascal, J.P., and Vertegaal, R. WhammyPhone: Exploring Tangible Audio Manipulation Using Bend Input on a Flexible Smartphone. *Proc. UIST Adjunct*, ACM (2016), 159–161.
4. Herkenrath, G., Karrer, T., and Borchers, J. Twend: Twisting and Bending as new Interaction Gesture in Mobile Devices. *Proc. CHI EA*, ACM (2008), 3819–3824.
5. Kildal, J., Paasovaara, S., and Aaltonen, V. Kinetic device: Designing Interactions with a Deformable Mobile Interface. *CHI EA*, ACM (2012), 1871.
6. Kuang, K.S.C., Cantwell, W.J., and Scully, P.J. An evaluation of a novel plastic optical fibre sensor for axial strain and bend measurements. *Meas. Sci. Technol. 13*, 10 (2002), 1523–1534.
7. Lahey, B., Girouard, A., Burleson, W., and Vertegaal, R. PaperPhone: Understanding the use of bend gestures in mobile devices with flexible electronic paper displays. *Proc. CHI*, ACM (2011), 1303–1312.
8. Lee, S.-S., Kim, S., Jin, B., et al. How users manipulate deformable displays as input devices. *Proc. CHI*, ACM (2010), 1647–1656.
9. Lo, J. and Girouard, A. Fabricating Bendy: Design and Development of Deformable Prototypes. *IEEE Pervasive Comput. Spec. Issue Fabr. Print. 13*, 3 (2014), 40–46.
10. Lo, J. and Girouard, A. Bendy: An exploration into gaming with mobile flexible devices. *Proc. TEI*, ACM (2017), 163–172.
11. Shorey, P. and Girouard, A. Bendtroller: An exploration of in-game action mappings with a deformable game controller. *Proc. CHI*, ACM (2017), 1447–1458.
12. Strohmeier, P., Burstyn, J., Carrascal, J.P., Levesque, V., and Vertegaal, R. ReFlex: A Flexible Smartphone with Active Haptic Feedback for Bend Input. *Proc. TEI*, (2016), 185–192.
13. Vadgama, N. and Steimle, J. Flexy: Shape-Customizable, Single-Layer, Inkjet Printable Patterns for 1D and 2D Flex Sensing. *Proc. TEI*, ACM (2017), 153–162.
14. Vanderloock, K., Vanden Abeele, V., Suykens, J.A.K., and Geurts, L. The skweezee system: enabling the design and the programming of squeeze interactions. *Proc. UIST*, ACM (2013), 521–530.
15. Wessely, M., Tsandilas, T., and Mackay, W.E. Stretchis : Fabricating Highly Stretchable User Interfaces. *Proc. UIST*, ACM (2016), 697–704.
16. Withana, A. and Steimle, J. Tutorial: Personalized interactive surfaces with printed electronics. *Proc. ISS*, ACM (2017).
17. Flex Sensors Instructables. http://www.instructables.com/howto/flex+sensor/.
18. Neoprene Bend Sensor. http://www.kobakant.at/DIY/?p=20.

Kinetic Body Extensions for Social Interactions

Kate Hartman
OCAD University
Toronto, ON M5T 1W1, Canada
khartman@faculty.ocadu.ca

Boris Kourtoukov
Oslo School of Architecture and Design
Maridalsveien 29, 0175 Oslo
boris@kourtoukov.com

Erin Lewis
University of Borås
Borås, 501 90, Sweden
erin.lewis@hb.se

TEI '18, March 18–21, 2018, Stockholm, Sweden

ACM ISBN 978-1-4503-5568-1/18/03.
https://doi.org/10.1145/3173225.3173333

Abstract
This studio invites participants to explore ways of extending physical expressivity through a combined use of wearable electronics and structural textile design. Participants are introduced to an electronics and material prototyping method developed by Social Body Lab for constructing kinetic textile body extensions intended for use in social interactions.

Participants will learn to use a servo motor in combination with folded and pleated paper, textiles, and structural materials to create a kinetic wearable module that can expand and contract in form. These kinetic modules can vary in size, form, complexity, and placement on the body, depending on the intended application. Pressure, flexion, ambient light, and electromyography (EMG) are sensors that will be explored as possible triggers for these modules using body movements and gestures. Through prototyping, testing, wearing, and group discussion, participants will explore ways in which their kinetic body extensions can amplify, extend, or subvert existing body language.

Author Keywords
wearables; body language; kinetic textiles; electromyography sensors; body augmentation

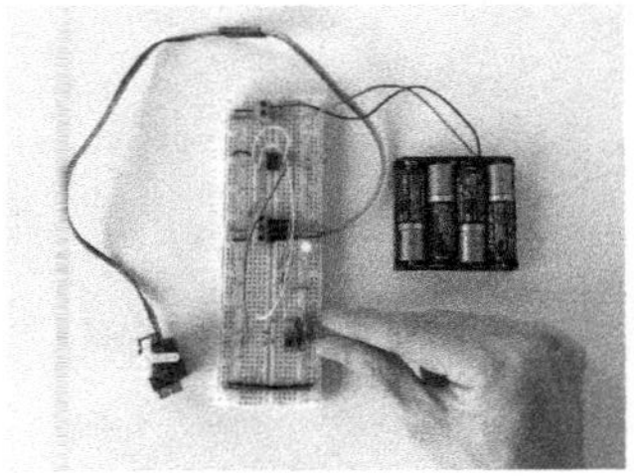

Figure 1: Breadboard prototype of 555 timer servo control circuit.

Studio Proposal

As our engagement with computational devices continues to expand, we are offered more extensive and diverse ways to connect with each other digitally. However, it is our view that few of the wearable computational devices on the consumer market focus on enhancing or augmenting how we as humans connect through our in person, "real life", physical interactions. We see body language as an innate and powerful form of communication.

With this in mind, this studio creates an opportunity to explore the following question: *"How can kinetic body extensions augment social interaction through the amplification, extension, or subversion of body language?"*

The first section of this studio will provide both context and a theoretical framework with which to take a critical look at the concept of body extensions. An overview will be provided of works that seek to physically expand upon the human form, with references stemming from contemporary art and design practice, interaction design, human computer interaction, sociology, trans-humanism, fashion, textile design, architecture, sculpture, and performance art. Participants will also be asked to source and present their own examples.

The second section of the studio will provide a technical framework in which participants will be introduced to electronic circuit building as well as sheet material manipulation through folding and pleating. This framework was developed by Social Body Lab as part of the Monarch project [5]. The electronic circuit will trigger a position-sensing servo motor which, in turn, will actuate a sculptural folded-paper form designed and prototyped by the participants.

Rather than using a microcontroller, the servo motor will be controlled using a 555 timer circuit (Figure 1). Using this

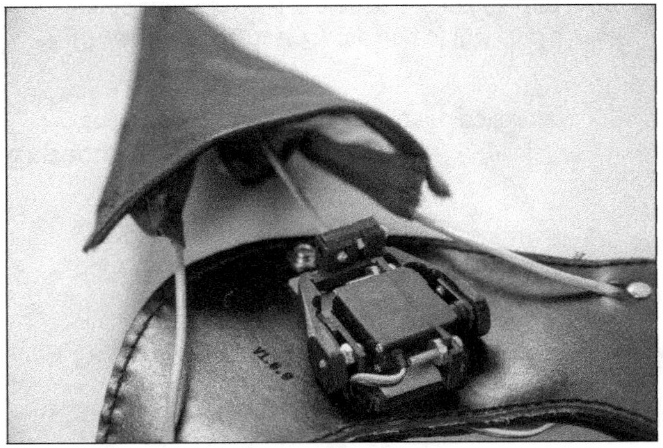

Figure 2: Servo motor, mount, and attachment with rod to control textile form.

simple pulse generator chip allows for motor control without the need for programming [2]. Circuits will be constructed with soldered prototyping board to allow for secure, sturdy connections. There exists a rich history of using electronic textiles in the construction of wearable circuits [1, 3, 4]. However, in this case we choose to employ more traditional circuit building methods as the focus of this studio is the expressiveness of the kinetic modules rather than the construction of the circuit itself.

Participants will be provided with 3D printed mounts and attachments that are custom fit to the supplied servo motors (Figure 2). The servo mount allows the motors to be attached to straps or other bases which can then be attached to the body. This enables the motor to remain in a stable position when activated. The servo attachment extends the mechanical possibilities of the servos movement. When outfitted with a rod, its movement can be used to open and

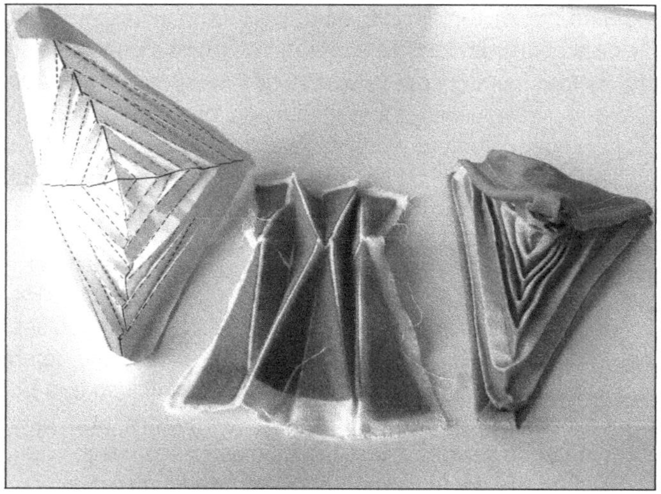

Figure 3: Folding and pleating tests.

close a pleated or folded form. The design of these forms will be inspired by examples from the worlds of paper folding [6] and fabric pleating [7]. Forms that emphasize motion and volume will be prioritized (Figure 3).

Once an initial prototype is assembled, participants will be asked to play with the expressivity of their functional kinetic body extension prototype. Ideas for potential applications and methods for wearing will be discussed.

The third section of the studio will provide time for participants to further customize and contextualize their designs based on their intended application. They will explore a range of body-based sensors such as pressure, flex, ambient light, and electromyography (EMG), that can trigger the kinetic body extension. Participants will further iterate on their structural form using either textiles or paper, in addition to learning strategies for making wearable electronics and mechanical systems more wearable.

Finally, participants will have an opportunity to document their creations as well as their intended use. A simple video shoot setup will be provided so that a series of video portraits of these kinetic body extensions can be created as one of the outcomes of the studio.

Previous knowledge of electronics prototyping is helpful but not required.

Studio Topics To Be Covered
This studio will cover:

- Folding techniques for creating form-changing structures
- Methods of designing for movement and the body
- Sensors and kinetic actuators
- Physical strategies for making wearable electronic circuits and mechanical systems
- Body extensions and body augmentation as a means of expanding body language

Expected Outcomes
The expected outcomes of this studio are as follows:

- Physical Prototypes: By the end of this studio each participant will have prototyped, personalized, worn, and iterated upon a new kinetic body extension that they can then bring back to their own communities.

- Video portraits: The design and functionality of these prototypes will be captured in a compiled set of video portraits to be made publicly accessible after the completion of the studio.
- Shared Ideas and Learning: It is our hope that through exploring their own creativity as well as that of their peers that participants will leave this studio with awareness of the potential impact, challenges, and opportunities for incorporating body-extending technologies into our in-person social interactions.

Studio Supporting Web Documents

The following supporting web documents are available for this studio:

- Documentation of previous related Social Body project "Prosthetic Technologies of Being": https://www2.ocadu.ca/research/socialbody/project/prosthetic-technologies-of-being
- Documentation of previous related Social Body project "Monarch V2": https://www2.ocadu.ca/research/socialbody/project/monarch-v2
- An illustrated, do-it-yourself tutorial for how to how to construct Kinetic Body Extensions for Social Interactions: http://socialbodylab.com/kinetic-body-extensions-for-social-interactions/

References

[1] Joanna Berzowska. 2005. Electronic Textiles: Wearable Computers, Reactive Fashion, and Soft Computation. *Textile* 3, 1 (2005), 2–19.

[2] Jonathan Best. 2012. Control a Servo Motor Without Programming. (Dec 2012). Retrieved January 13, 2018 from https://makezine.com/projects/control-a-servo-motor-without-programming/

[3] Leah Buechley, Mike Eisenberg, Jaime Catchen, and Ali Crockett. 2008. The LilyPad Arduino: Using Computational Textiles to Investigate Engagement, Aesthetics, and Diversity in Computer Science Education. In *Proceedings of the SIGCHI Conference on Human Factors in Computing Systems (CHI '08)*. ACM, New York, NY, USA, 423–432. DOI: http://dx.doi.org/10.1145/1357054.1357123

[4] Leah Buechley and Benjamin Mako Hill. 2010. LilyPad in the Wild: How Hardware's Long Tail is Supporting New Engineering and Design Communities. In *Proceedings of the 8th ACM Conference on Designing Interactive Systems (DIS '10)*. ACM, New York, NY, USA, 199–207. DOI: http://dx.doi.org/10.1145/1858171.1858206

[5] Kate Hartman, Jackson McConnell, Boris Kourtoukov, Hillary Predko, and Izzie Colpitts-Campbell. 2015. Monarch: Self-Expression Through Wearable Kinetic Textiles. In *Proceedings of the Ninth International Conference on Tangible, Embedded, and Embodied Interaction (TEI '15)*. ACM, New York, NY, USA, 413–414. DOI: http://dx.doi.org/10.1145/2677199.2690875

[6] Paul Jackson. 2011. *Folding Techniques for Designers: From Sheet to Form*. Lawrence King Publishing, London, United Kingdom.

[7] Colette Wolff. 1996. *The Art of Manipulating Fabric*. Krause Publications, Iola, WI, USA.

Internet of Tangibles: Exploring the Interaction-Attention Continuum

Leonardo Angelini
Elena Mugellini
Omar Abou Khaled
HumanTech Institute
University of Applied Sciences and Arts Western Switzerland
1700, Fribourg, Switzerland
leonardo.angelini@hes-so.ch
elena.mugellini@hes-so.ch
omar.aboukhaled@hes-so.ch

Nadine Couture
ESTIA LaBRI, UMR 5800
64210 Bidart, France
nadine.couture@u-bordeaux.fr

Elise van den Hoven
University of Technology Sydney, Australia
University of Technology Eindhoven, the Netherlands
University of Dundee, the United Kingdom
ARC Centre of Excellence on Cognition and its Disorders, Australia
elise.vandenhoven@uts.edu.au

Saskia Bakker
Industrial Design Department
Eindhoven University of Technology
The Netherlands
s.bakker@tue.nl

ACM ISBN 978-1-4503-5568-1/18/03.
https://doi.org/10.1145/3173225.3173334

Abstract
There is an increasing interest in the HCI research community to design richer user interactions with the Internet of Things (IoT). This studio will allow exploring the design of tangible interaction with the IoT, what we call Internet of Tangibles. In particular, we aim at investigating the full interaction-attention continuum, with the purpose of designing IoT tangible interfaces that can switch between peripheral interactions that do not disrupt everyday routines, and focused interactions that support user's reflections. This investigation will be conducted through hands-on activities where participants will prototype tangible IoT objects, starting by a paper prototyping phase, supported by design cards, and followed by an Arduino prototype phase. The purpose of the studio is also establishing a community of researchers and practitioners, from both academy and industry, interested in the field of tangible interaction with the Internet of Things.

Author Keywords
Internet of Things; Tangible Interaction properties; Interaction-Attention Continuum; Peripheral Interaction; Focused Interaction.

Introduction
The Internet of Things [4] is entering our daily routines through the increasing number of commercially

available connected objects and devices. Such connected objects are able to collect an enormous quantity of information about our life and to offer us useful services. Most of such services are accessible at a tap of one finger through intuitive smartphone or web apps [10], thus poorly exploiting users' manipulative and cognitive skills. Within this context, a question arises: "can we design richer interaction experiences with IoT objects, exploiting the affordances of the physical world, instead of constraining users in the digital bubbles created by smartphones?". Recently, some researchers [1, 2] are arguing that tangible interaction properties can be beneficial to supporting richer and long-lasting interactions with IoT objects. Angelini et al. adopted the term Internet of Tangible Things (IoTT) for promoting a paradigm switch to the interaction design with IoT [2, 3]. In particular, we believe that the hybrid nature of tangible interaction [8] can be exploited to improve the user experience with IoT, enabling either immediate interactions that happen in the periphery of users' attention or more focused interactions that stimulate users' reflections. These two interaction types were classified by Bakker and Niemantsverdriet on a continuum, i.e., the interaction-attention continuum [5], which spans from implicit interaction, requiring no user attention, to focused interaction. In this workshop, we build on this recent concept to frame the design space of tangible interaction with IoT.

Studio Proposal

The studio aims at gathering practitioners and researchers (10 to 18 participants) from both academy and industry, interested in the design of the interaction with the IoT. We aim at gathering people with different backgrounds (e.g., social sciences, computer science, psychology, design, future studies, etc.), creating groups of 3-4 people with heterogeneous skills, in order to encourage ideas and knowledge sharing from different perspectives. No particular skills are required for the studio: we will take care that each group will have at least one participant with technical skills. The studio will allow participants to explore the design space of tangible interaction with IoT objects, focusing in particular on the design of interactions for the full interaction-attention continuum. The studio will also allocate time for plenary discussions, allowing participants to know each other better and to get mutual knowledge of ongoing research, for networking purposes.

The hands-on activities will be carried out in different phases, following a methodology already tested in a workshop conducted during the 3rd European Tangible Interaction Studio [3]. The workshop will be split in two parts. During the first part, participants will develop an idea of a tangible IoT object through storyboarding and paper prototyping. During this phase, design cards will be used to support a structured reflection on how to exploit the full interaction-attention continuum for the interaction with tangible IoT objects. The card set used in this workshop will be derived from the card set already used in the previous workshop [3] and will include tangible interaction properties that span across the full interaction attention continuum (cf. [2] for a complete list) and IoT properties that can be embodied in the tangible interface. During the second part, through Arduino prototyping, the participants will develop one or more tangible IoT objects. By implementing the idea generated during the first part of the workshop, they will eventually reuse, improve and adapt the paper prototype previously created. A various range of sensors and actuators to be connected to the Arduino will be provided to the participants, together with implementation examples for each tangible interaction property. Each example will include the necessary hardware material, the assembling instructions and the sample code. At the end of each phase, each group will present the results of the idea generation, how they tried to explore the full interaction-attention continuum and which benefits this could bring for the end-user of the designed IoT object(s). In particular, we will ask to the participants to depict where the designed interactions and the corresponding tangible interaction properties situate in the full interaction-attention continuum.

Studio Topics to be Covered

Topics to be covered in this workshop are related to tangible interaction with the Internet of Things. A list of tangible interaction properties for IoT has been elicited in [2]. Among others, the following tangible interaction properties will be explored, ordered in the interaction-attention continuum from the less to the most attention demanding:

- *Peripheral interaction:* Peripheral interaction [6] is a relatively new field of research in HCI that try to promote interactions that happen in the periphery of the user's attention. In this manner, digital interaction with IoT objects could be effectuated during daily routines, without disrupting the attention from primary tasks.
- *Intuitiveness and immediacy*: Tangible interaction is often considered as a natural interaction means thanks to the easiness to learn and thanks to the intuitive affordances provided by physical objects and users' knowledge of basic physics principles [9]. This could be particularly useful to simplify the understanding of the complex behavior of some IoT objects.
- *Reflection and memories*: Particular IoT objects can stimulate reflection, boasting unexpected behaviors that would catch the attention of the user. Object physicality can also help for memory recollection [12], especially if IoT capabilities are associated to souvenirs or personal items.
- *Long-lasting interactions and emotional bonding*: Some IoT objects can benefit of life-like behaviors [11] to create an emotional bonding with the user and ensure long-lasting interactions thank, overcoming technological obsolescence and waste [7].

Studio Learning Goals/Discussion Objectives

The activities carried out during the workshop are focused on the exploration of the design space of tangible interaction with the Internet of Things, with a particular focus on the exploration of the full interaction-attention continuum. The purpose of the workshop is promoting the discussion in small groups, reasoning on a practical case during the different phases of the IoT object design, from the idea generation of the IoT object, to the physical paper embodiment and hardware implementation. Through the hands-on activity, we strive to promote a learning-by-doing process. Results of this process will be discussed at the end of the studio, to individuate common ideas that can be applied to the design of different IoT objects. In particular, we want to focus participants' reflections on how would be possible the design of tangible interactions that can span across different levels of the users' attention. Moreover, through this workshop, we aim at gathering and establishing a community of researchers and practitioners with different backgrounds, interested in discussing the theoretical opportunities and challenges of tangible interaction applied to IoT and possible practical applications of tangible interfaces for IoT. At the beginning of the workshop, participants will briefly present themselves and their research, in order to facilitate connection and exchanges between workshop participants and support future connections and collaborations.

Studio Supporting Web Documents

A dedicated website will provide all the relevant information to the participants and will host materials (such as tutorials and Arduino code samples) for the studio participants. The website will be a point of reference for the community and will publicize other future events on the topic of tangible interaction with the IoT.

References

1. Aloha Hufana Ambe, Margot Brereton, Alessandro Soro and Paul Roe. 2017. Technology individuation: The foibles of augmented everyday objects. in *Proceedings of CHI'17*, ACM, 6632-6644.
2. Leonardo Angelini, Nadine Couture, Omar Abou Khaled and Elena Mugellini. Submitted. Internet of Tangible Things (IoTT): Challenges and Opportunities for Tangible Interaction with IoT. *MDPI Informatics* (Special Issue "Tangible and Embodied Interaction"). 1-28.
3. Leonardo Angelini, Nadine Couture, Omar Abou Khaled and Elena Mugellini. 2017. Interaction with the Internet of Tangible Things (IoTT). in *CEUR Workshop Proceedings of the Third European Tangible Interaction Studio (ETIS)*.
4. Luigi Atzori, Antonio Iera and Giacomo Morabito. 2010. The internet of things: A survey. *Computer networks*, 54 (15). 2787-2805.
5. Saskia Bakker and Karin Niemantsverdriet. 2016. The interaction-attention continuum: considering various levels of human attention in interaction design. *International Journal of Design*, 10 (2).
6. Saskia Bakker, Elise van den Hoven and Berry Eggen. 2015. Peripheral interaction: characteristics and considerations. *Personal and Ubiquitous Computing*, 19 (1). 239-254.
7. Jonathan Chapman. 2015. *Emotionally durable design: objects, experiences and empathy*. Routledge.
8. Eva Hornecker. 2012. Beyond affordance: tangibles' hybrid nature. in *Proceedings of the TEI'12*, ACM, 175-182.
9. Robert JK Jacob, Audrey Girouard, Leanne M Hirshfield, Michael S Horn, Orit Shaer, Erin Treacy Solovey and Jamie Zigelbaum. 2008. Reality-based interaction: a framework for post-WIMP interfaces. in *Proceedings of CHI'08*, ACM, 201-210.
10. Treffyn Lynch Koreshoff, Toni Robertson and Tuck Wah Leong. 2013. Internet of things: a review of literature and products. in *Proceedings of OzCHI'13*, ACM, 335-344.
11. Michael Schmitz. 2011. Concepts for life-like interactive objects. in *Proceedings of TEI'11*, ACM, 157-164.
12. Elise Van Den Hoven and Berry Eggen. 2004. Tangible computing in everyday life: Extending current frameworks for tangible user interfaces with personal objects. in *Ambient Intelligence*, Springer, 230-242.

Tracking Well-Being – Design Explorations Through Object Theatre

Figure 1: Exploring objects with hands and body.

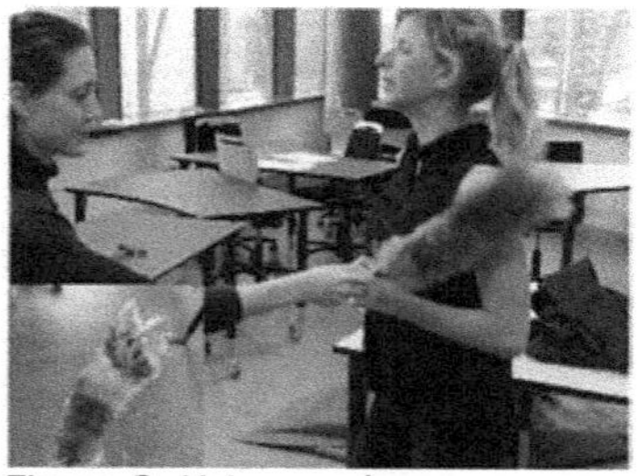

Figure 2. Using analogue methods to track well-being

Andreas A. Heiberg Skouby
University of Southern Denmark
Universitetsparken 1
6000 Kolding, DK
heiberg@sdu.dk

Merja Ryöppy
University of Southern Denmark
Universitetsparken 1
6000 Kolding, DK
merja@sdu.dk

Robb Mitchell
University of Southern Denmark
Universitetsparken 1
6000 Kolding, DK
robb@sdu.dk

TEI '18, March 18–21, 2018, Stockholm, Sweden

ACM ISBN 978-1-4503-5568-1/18/03.
https://doi.org/10.1145/3173225.3173335

Abstract
We introduce Object Theatre for Design as a hands-on approach to enable healthcare tracking to move beyond numbers and empower patients to monitor and convey their subjective well-being. A transformed perspective on relating to artifacts will drive tangible and bodily explorations in order to collaboratively create mockups for logging and expressing emotions and perceptions in novel tangible forms.

Author Keywords
Subjective well-being; tracking; object theatre

Introduction
Healthcare providers are increasingly tracking users in their daily routines at home; this can provide rich information to support accurate and cheaper treatment [8] or help to self-report pain and emotions [5,13]. In pre-digital times, data to support healthcare was logged through analogue methods, such as keeping a diary or a logbook, putting coins in a jar or cutting a spike from a comb. More recently digital devices such as mobile phones, apps, cameras, audio recorders, smart watches and activity trackers has made it possible to collect data real-time without conscious actions from the user (Figure 3), and present and share it in multiple forms (visuals, audio, video, graphs). However the existing trackers do not enable rich

manipulation with hands or body, and lack opportunities for logging and presenting data in a subjective way.

Wearable activity trackers (Figure 3) collect quantitative data based on movement, pulse or GPS coordinates, and use algorithms to transform it to graphs displayed on a screen (Figure 4). However there is very little attention given to "tracking" the patient's feelings or their *perception* of well-being in tangible form. What can design do to support this function and help convey changes in well-being?

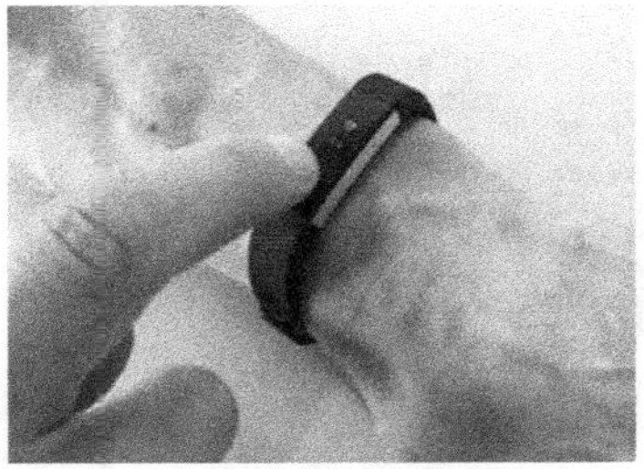
Figure 3. A digital activity tracker from user's perspective

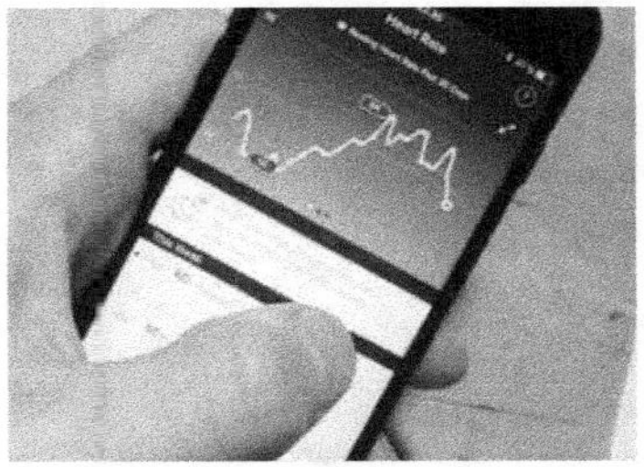
Figure 4. Collected data displayed on smartphone.

Are you feeling well today?
According to Desmet & Pohlmeyer *"Subjective well-being represents a person's personal perceptions or value judgments of her quality of life."* [4:10]. In the healthcare domain, only patients themself can feel, experience, sense and make sense of their perception of well-being in everyday life. We approach subjective well-being through Mead's theory of the social self [10] and Stacey's responsive processes of relating [15], where well-being can be understood as relational and emergent in interaction with other people, as constantly changing perception of oneself. For example, if you feel slightly under the weather, but then talk with a terminally ill friend, you might then not feel sick at all.

Existing research shows how frequent observations of a single precursor symptom may support the treatment of illness [8]. Researchers have proposed novel interfaces to self-report symptoms e.g. sensations of pain. Larsen et al. [8] present how the instrumentation of a wearable one-button tracker can result to deeper investigative dialogue about personal sensations based on the data. Rodríguez et al. [13] suggest self-monitoring through wearable interfaces to collect real-time information from chronic-pain patients. On the same note, researchers have been studying subjective self-reporting of emotions through digital interfaces, and found a potential for tangible user interfaces [5]. Physicalized data instead, presents the personal activity data in a tangible form [7,9,16]. The tangibility of data opens up for new conversations about user's personal insights. We add to this development with a novel approach, exploring how techniques from object theatre and theatre improvisation contributes to designing for tracking subjective well-being in tangible forms.

Object Theatre For Design
In the workshop we will use techniques from Object Theatre to speculate with existing tracking practices, to relate to a role of an object (medium), to create novel tracking ideas with objects and to produce mock-ups to share your insights in tangible ways. Object Theatre is a form of theatre where performers use readymade objects, such as bottles, toys, household objects, sand or trash, to tell a story [12] (Figure 5). *"In object theatre often the use(fulnesss) of the object is brought into question, altered, and made quite different."* [12:1]. Improvising with multiple, transformational objects eventually bring different interaction qualities to the surface (Figure 1).

Inspired by object theatre, and methods applied in interaction design, such as tangible tools [3], interaction relabeling, scenario-acting with props and puppets [1,2,6], our humble aim is to take the theatre methods further from concentrating on single user's perspective to exploring multiple stakeholder perspectives, as well as taking the object perspective (Figure 5). We find Object Theatre For Design beneficial

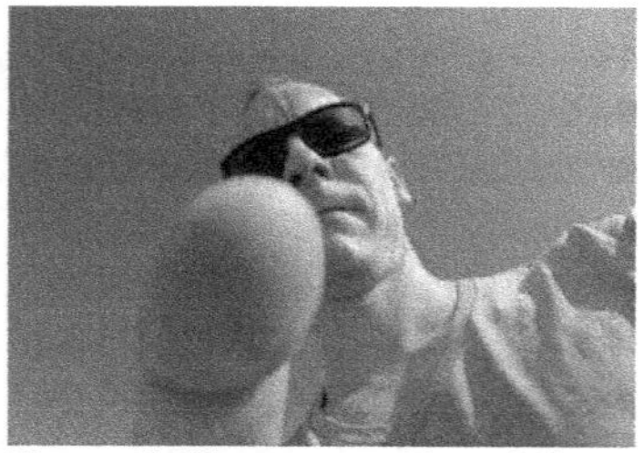

Figure 5. The perspective of the activity tracker to its user.

Figure 6. Sean Myatt performing 'Conflict in paper' with paper.

Figure 7. Arranging tracking objects.

as it suggests diverse ways of relating to everyday objects (animated, symbolic, props), and to switch freely between those. It prompts designers to move out from 'normal' way of relating to objects and people as separate entities, for instance by encouraging to approach an in-animate object as a living being, or to perform the object from within [2,14]. Different relating to objects is reached gradually through object theatre techniques applied in an exploratory design workshop. This might include emphasizing with an in-animate object by speaking and acting as the object, by playing multiple stakeholder perspectives to the object, or by interacting with it in a new and unforeseen way [2,14]. Through Object Theatre, designers can explore how to become the medium and embody object functionalities to develop personal understanding of object interactions and eventually re-design new products.

Invitation to change perspective

In the studio we want to be able to understand subjective well-being and how can we log and convey this to other people through explorations with Object Theatre For Design. We ask, how to imagine what can be tracked or logged in relation to your well-being? This raises a challenge to tracking/logging currently being driven by quantitative methods and a series of questions on how to record personal perception. The participants are invited to investigate this question in a novel way by applying theatre methods into a field often relying on algorithms and use of digital tracking devices. Studio participants will try out wearable tracking device and work in small design teams to take different perspectives.

User, Relative/Friend, Object and Designer.
The design process builds upon participant own tracking experiences as well as specific user cases. The participants will try out enacting design scenarios and taking perspectives different from their own, such as an activity tracker or a friend/relative. They will be guided through a process of improvising with objects in a bodily and collaborative series of exercises, exploring the material properties, senses and social connections with objects. Finally turning their fresh insights into product mock-ups to log and convey perceptions of well-being. Each team will produce at least one mock-up of their new idea.

We will provide simple tracking devices to capture activity data. We will also bring a set of selected objects and building materials to support the deisgn explorations. Materials such as cardboard, sticks, toys and household objects are brought to the session to facilitate the work. We will strive to attract researchers and practitioners from a range of disciplines who are open towards collaborative experimentation.

Acknowledgements

We are grateful for the support at SDU Design Research, and want to thank all the researchers, practitioners and students for their contributions. This project was co-financed by PROMETHEUS with funds from INTERREG 5A the European Regional Development Fund. Also collaborating with the Nordic network of Participatory Theatre in the Design of Public Services funded by NOS-HS.

References

1. Thomas Binder. 1999. Setting the stage for improvised video scenarios. In *CHI '99 Extended Abstracts*, 230–231.
2. Jacob Buur and Preben Friis. 2015. Object Theatre in Design Education. In *NORDES'15*.
3. Jacob Buur and Robb Mitchell. 2011. The business modeling lab. In *Proceedings of Participatory Innovation Conference*. 368–373.
4. Pieter M. A. Desmet and Anna E. Pohlmeyer. 2013. Positive design: An introduction to design for subjective well-being. In *International Journal of Design* 7, 3: 5–19.
5. Carolina Fuentes, Carmen Gerea, Valeria Herskovic, Maíra Marques, Iyubanit Rodríguez and Pedro O. Rossel. 2015. User interfaces for self-reporting emotions: a systematic literature review. In *UCAmI*, 321–333.
6. Giulio Iacucci, Carlo Iacucci and Kari Kuutti. 2002. Imagining and experiencing in design, the role of performances. In *NordiCHI'02* 167–176
7. Rohit A. Khot, Deepti Aggarwal, Ryan Pennings, Larissa Hjorth and Florian "Floyd" Mueller. 2017. EdiPulse: Investigating a Playful Approach to Self-monitoring through 3D Printed Chocolate Treats. *CHI'17* 6593–6607.
8. Jakob Eg Larsen, Kasper Eskelund, and Thomas Blomseth Christiansen. 2017. Active Self-Tracking of Subjective Experience with a One-Button Wearable: A Case Study in Military PTSD. In *2nd Symp Computing & Mental Health*
9. Deborah Lupton. 2015. Fabricated data bodies: Reflections on 3D printed digital body objects in medical and health domains. *Social Theory & Health* 13, 2: 99–115.
10. George H. Mead. 1934. *Mind, self, and society*. University of Chicago Press.
11. Robb Mitchell and Pirkko Raudaskoski. 2013. Whose Line Is It Anyway? Collaborative Turn-Making. In *Participatory Innovation Conference* 2013, 103–11
12. Sean Myatt and Daniel Watt. 2012. From Frozen Sponges to Plastic Bags: Object Theatre - A Developing Network. In *Puppet Notebook 22*, 19–22.
13. Iyubanit Rodríguez, Gabriela Cajamarca, Valeria Herskovic, Carolina Fuentes and Mauricio Campos. 2017. Helping Elderly Users Report Pain Levels: A Study of User Experience with Mobile and Wearable Interfaces. In *Mobile Information Systems* 2017.
14. Merja Ryöppy and Andreas H. Skouby. 2015. Object theatre-a playful understanding of design. In *Proceedings of the Participatory Innovation Conference 2015*, 47–50.
15. Ralph D Stacey. 2003. *Complexity and group processes: a radically social understanding of individuals*. Routledge New York
16. Simon Stusak, Aurelien Tabard, Franziska Sauka, Rohit Ashok Khot and Andreas Butz. 2014. Activity Sculptures: Exploring the Impact of Physical Visualizations on Running Activity. *IEEE TVCG* 20, 12: 2201–2210.

Author Index

Abou Khaled, Omar 299, 740
Achberger, Alexander 329
Akyürek, Ekin 674
An, Pengcheng 357
Anderson, Zann 221
Andreani, Stefano 567
Angelini, Leonardo 299, 740
Aoyama, Shuhei 115
Arnold, Peter 398
Asplund, Simon 470
Bakker, Saskia 205, 357, 740
Barrett, Cassandra 211
Barthet, Mathieu 80
Baudry, Benoit 617
Becquet, Valentin 656
Bennett, Peter 49
Bers, Marina 101
Bexell, Emma 511
Birolini, Sebastian 567
Bock, Wilfried 245
Boll, Susanne 177
Bonani, Andrea 65
Bontje, Mathijs 237
Boring, Sebastian 188
Börütecene, Ahmet 674
Bossis, Bruno 617
Bostan, İdil 674
Boussiron, Caroline 656
Bozzo, Lucas 386
Branton, Chris 476
Brons, Annette 349
Brown, Shannon 337
Brueckner, Sophia 542, 728
Byrne, Virginia 320
Cafaro, Francesco 313
Caltenco, Héctor A. 245
Campbell, Joey 279
Campos, Pedro 260
Canfield-Dafilou, Elliot Kermit . 537
Cao, Yuanzhi 419
Carvalho, Alberto 271
Chafe, Chris 537
Cheung, Victor 108, 732
Clegg, Tamara 320
Colley, Ashley 266
Cook, Margaret 131
Correia, Catarina 271
Costanza, Enrico 1
Cottrell, Peter 42
Couture, Nadine 140, 299, 740
Dagan, Ella 498
Daniel, Maxime 140
de Rooij, Alwin 73, 237
de Schipper, Antoine 349
de Siqueira, Alexandre G. 476
Del Fatto, Vincenzo 65
Delarosa, Mark 476
Deng, Honghao 567
Denton, Timothy 11
Dev, Siona 337
Dierk, Christine 148
Do, Ellen Yi-Luen 57
Du, Jiachun 166
Eady, Alexander Keith 732
Eggen, Berry 357
Ehrenberg, Nils 260
Elblaus, Ludvig 537, 724
Fahnbulleh, Whitney 626
Fernando, Piyum 211, 555
Fikar, Peter 35, 451
Fitzpatrick, Geraldine 158
Flanagan, Patricia 611
Flemings, Margaret 343
Forsman, Meri-Tuulia 266
Fox, Audrey M. 506
Frankjaer, Raune 611
Fraser, Mike 279
Freire, Rachel 542, 728
Froehlich, Jon E. 320
Fujii, Juri 199
Funk, Markus 329
Ganhör, Roman 35, 451
Garcia, Trisha 337
Gardner, Paula 286
Geiger, Shachar 307
Genç, Çağlar 674
Gennari, Rosella 65, 368
Gibson, Ruth 549
Gibson, Steve 487
Girouard, Audrey 108, 732
Gjøæter, Tor 123
Glenn, Terrell 419
Göksun, Tilbe 674
Gong, Ting 166
Grah, Thomas 253
Grow, April 42
Güldenpfennig,
Florian 35, 231, 451
Guribye, Frode 123
Hakkerainen, Viola 694
Häkkilä, Jonna 266
Handberg, Leif 537
Hansen, Nicolai Brodersen 724
Harley, Daniel 386
Harrand, Nicolas 617
Hartman, Kate 736
Hashimoto, Yuki 115
Hayes, Sarah 703
Helms, Karey 724
Hendricks, Sarah 443
Hermen, Johannes 94
Hernandez, Lucie 136
Hogan, Trevor 279
Honauer, Michaela 718
Honnet, Cedric 728
Hornbæk, Kasper 188
Huo, Ke 419
Hurtienne, Jörn 638, 647
Hwang, Jemin 435
Ikegawa, Koshi 115
Isbister, Katherine 42
Itzhak, Kinneret 307
Iurgel, Ido 88
Jackson, Jesse Colin 592
Jenkins, Tom 667, 724
Jo, Kazuhiro 517
Johnson, Magnus 11
Jones, Lee 286
Jones, Michael 221
Jonsson, Martin 470
Kakehi, Yasuaki 199
Kaltenbrunner, Martin 429
Kang, Laewoo 605
Kang, Seokbin 320
Kantek, Kamila 307
Kato, Natsumi 529
Kazmi, Shanzay 343
Khot, Rohit Ashok 398

Kirk, David 1
Kleinberger, Rebecca 27
Knibbe, Jarrod 188, 728
Knierim, Pascal 329
Koelle, Marion 177
Koleva, Boriana 376
Konkel, Miriam K. 476
Kosch, Thomas 329
Kourtoukov, Boris 736
Koutsomichalis, Marinos 521
Kozel, Susan 549
Kröse, Ben 349
Kun, Andrew L. 626
Kuznetsov, Stacey 211, 555
Kytö, Mikko 245
Lavenir, Claire 656
Lee, Young Suk 581
Lei, Kehua 19
Leigh, Sang-won 11
Leinonen, Aki 266
Letondal, Catherine 656
Levi, Dafna 307
Lewis, Erin 736
Li, Jiabao 567
Li, Zhichun 19
Lindegaard Aae Jensen, Karina ... 598
Lochrie, Mark 49
Löchtefeld, Markus 598
Löffler, Diana 647
Lundström, Anders 574
Maes, Pattie 11
Magnusson, Charlotte 245
Maquil, Valérie 94
Markopoulos, Panos 166
Martelli, Bruno 549
Matsunobu, Takuya 199
Mazalek, Ali 386
McCarthy, Léon 622
McCoy, Joshua 443
McGookin, David 245
McNamara, Daniel 460
Melonio, Alessandra 368
Metcalfe, Tom 49
Mi, Haipeng 19
Michel, Anna 88
Mills, John 49
Minor, Elizabeth Joanna 626
Mironcika, Svetlana 349
Mishra, Swati 313
Mitchell, Robb 744
Moll, Christian 94
Momeni, Ali 460
Mueller, Florian 'Floyd' 398
Mugellini, Elena 299, 740
Müller, Wolfgang 88
Muramatsu, Naoya 529
Murer, Martin 253
Nakamura, Takuto 115
Neale, Camilla 493
Ng, Ashley 386
Ng, Gary 409
Nicholas, Molly Jane Pearce 148
Nielsen, Stefan Engelbrecht 598
Nir, Shoval 307
Norooz, Leyla 320
Nowacka, Diana 1
Nunes, Francisco 271
Ochiai, Yoichi 529
Odom, William 684
Ordanovski, Sara 357
Ørsted Jensen, Louise 598
Osone, Hiroyuki 529
Özcan, Oğuzhan 674
Pak, Rachel 343
Panjwani, Alisha 27
Parekh, Kush 11
Park, Jeonghyeok 435
Patel, Roma 376
Pauchet, Sylvain 656
Paulos, Eric 148
Peebles, William 11
Peeters, Jeroen 292, 694
Pine, Michelle 131
Pittera, Dario 709
Plopski, Alexander 409
Pollalis, Christina 626
Posch, Irene 158
Puckett, Nick 286
Ramani, Karthik 419
Reinhardt, Daniel 638
Ressel, Christian 88
Rey, Stéphanie 656
Ribeiro, Pedro 88
Rinott, Michal 307
Ritter, Emily 211
Rivière, Guillaume 140
Rizvi, Mehdi 368
Rohr, Marissa 211
Rostami, Asreen 511
Ruhl, Antal 73
Ryöppy, Merja 744
Rzezonka, Alice 715
Saakes, Daniel 409
Sabuncuoğlu, Alpay 674
Sandor, Christian 409
Sato, Daitetsu 529
Sayegh, Allen 567
Schilling, Markus Lorenz 684
Schnädelbach, Holger 376
Schouten, Ben 349
Schraffenberger, Hanna 237
Schwartz, Lou 94
Seo, Jinsil Hwaryoung 131
Seol, Soonuk 435
Seppi, Kevin 221
Shaer, Orit 101, 343, 626
Shaw, Alex 493
Shin, Joon Gi 409
Shin, Yejin 435
Shizuki, Buntarou 115
Silva, José Luís 260
Šimbelis, Vygandas "Vegas" 574
Skach, Sophie 80
Skouby, Andreas A. Heiberg 744
Smit, Dorothé 253
Smith-Nunes, Genevieve 493
Stanisic, Stefan 511
Stephensen, Vibeke Thorhauge ..598
Sterman, Sarah 148
Stewart, Rebecca 80
Stolfi, Ariane 80
Strawhacker, Amanda 101
Strohmeier, Paul 188, 728
Sullivan, Anne 443
Sungkajun, Annie 131
Sylla, Cristina 88
Taconis, Ruurd 357
Temuzkuşu, İlker 674
Thomas, Denez 617
Toeters, Marina 166
Toussaint, Huub 349
Trotto, Ambra 292, 694
Tsaknaki, Vasiliki 724
Tscharn, Robert 647

[illegible], Manfred 253
[illegible]suchikiri, Shogo 115
Turaga, Pavan 555
Turchet, Luca 80
Turmo Vidal, Laia 706
Ullmer, Brygg 476
van Dartel, Michel 73
van den Boogaard, Bas 598
van den Hoven, Elise 740
van der Veen, Rosa 292, 694
van Rheden, Vincent 253
van Rooij, Tom 205
Vasconcelos, Ana 271
Verish, Clarissa 101
Verni, Alexander 386
Vetter, Jens 429
Vigneshwara, Mithru 562
Vinot, Jean-Luc 656
Virgilio, Isabella 626
Wakkary, Ron 684
Wang, Meng 19
Wang, Qi 166
Weiler, Jennifer 211, 555
Weisling, Anna 586
Westendorf, Lauren 626
Williams, Brittany 443
Willis, Mackenzie 386
Wolf, Katrin 1, 177
Xambó, Anna 80, 586
Xu, Yingqing 19
Xu, Zhuangying 419
Zheng, Clement 57, 721
Zhiglova, Yulia 712

www.ingramcontent.com/pod-product-compliance
Lightning Source LLC
LaVergne TN
LVHW080107011026
849160LV00013B/1046